The Cambridge Handbook of Personality Psychology

Personality psychology is a rapidly maturing science making important advances on both conceptual and methodological fronts. *The Cambridge Handbook of Personality Psychology* offers a one-stop source for the most up-to-date scientific personality psychology. It provides a summary of cutting-edge personality research in all its forms, from DNA to political influences on its development, expression, pathology and applications. The chapters are informative, lively, stimulating and, sometimes, controversial and the team of international authors, led by two esteemed editors, ensures a truly wide range of theoretical perspectives. Each research area is discussed in terms of scientific foundations, main theories and findings, and future directions for research. With useful descriptions of technological approaches (for example, molecular genetics and functional neuroimaging) the *Handbook* is an invaluable aid to understanding the central role played by personality in psychology and will appeal to students of occupational, health, clinical, cognitive and forensic psychology.

PHILIP J. CORR is Professor of Psychology at the University of East Anglia.

GERALD MATTHEWS is Professor of Psychology at the University of Cincinnati.

The Cambridge Handbook of Personality Psychology

Edited by
Philip J. Corr
and
Gerald Matthews

CAMBRIDGE
UNIVERSITY PRESS

CAMBRIDGE UNIVERSITY PRESS
Cambridge, New York, Melbourne, Madrid, Cape Town, Singapore, São Paulo, Delhi

Cambridge University Press
The Edinburgh Building, Cambridge CB2 8RU, UK

Published in the United States of America by Cambridge University Press, New York

www.cambridge.org
Information on this title: www.cambridge.org/9780521680516

First published 2009

Printed in the United Kingdom at the University Press, Cambridge

A catalogue record for this publication is available from the British Library

Library of Congress Cataloguing in Publication data
The Cambridge handbook of personality psychology / edited by Philip J. Corr and Gerald Matthews.
   p.   cm.
ISBN 978-0-521-86218-9 (hdbk : alk. paper) – ISBN 978-0-521-68051-6 (pbk : alk. paper)
1. Personality.   I. Corr, Philip J.   II. Matthews, Gerald.   III. Title.
BF698.C155   2009
155.2–dc22

2009019281

ISBN 978-0-521-86218-9 hardback
ISBN 978-0-521-68051-6 paperback

Contents

Figures

Tables

Contributors

PHILLIP L. ACKERMAN, Georgia Institute of Technology

NEIL ANDERSON, University of Amsterdam

JENS B. ASENDORPF, Humboldt-Universität Berlin

R. MICHAEL BAGBY, University of Toronto

MICHAEL HARRIS BOND, Chinese University of Hong Kong

GREGORY J. BOYLE, Bond University

ANDREA L. BRIGGS, DePaul University

GILES ST J. BURCH, University of Auckland

TURHAN CANLI, Stony Brook University

DAVID CANTER, University of Liverpool

GIANVITTORIO CAPRARA, University of Rome

CHARLES S. CARVER, University of Miami

DOUGLAS F. CELLAR, DePaul University

GORDON CLARIDGE, University of Oxford

SUSAN CLONINGER, The Sage Colleges

ELISABETH D. CONRADT, University of Oregon

PHILIP J. CORR, University of East Anglia

SHARON DAWE, Griffith University

IAN J. DEARY, University of Edinburgh

BOELE DE RAAD, University of Groningen

EDWARD L. DECI, University of Rochester

COLIN G. DEYOUNG, Yale University

M. BRENT DONNELLAN, Michigan State University

JURIS G. DRAGUNS, Pennsylvania State University

MARKO ELOVAINIO, University of Helsinki

AURELIO JOSÉ FIGUEREDO, University of Arizona

DAVID C. FUNDER, University of California, Riverside

PAUL GLADDEN, University of Arizona

RAPSON GOMEZ, University of Tasmania

SAMUEL D. GOSLING, University of Texas at Austin

JEREMY R. GRAY, Yale University

ROBERT D. HARE, University of British Columbia and Darkstone Research Group

B. AUSTIN HARLEY, University of Texas at Austin

EDWARD HELMES, James Cook University

ROBERT HOGAN, Hogan Assessment System

LAURI A. JENSEN-CAMPBELL, University of Texas at Arlington

DANIEL NELSON JONES, University of Arizona

MIKA KIVIMÄKI, University of Helsinki

JENNIFER M. KNACK, University of Texas at Arlington

JAMES T. LAMIELL, Georgetown University

NATALIE J. LOXTON, University of Queensland

GEOFF MACDONALD, University of Toronto

GERALD MATTHEWS, University of Cincinnati

ROBERT R. MCCRAE, National Institute on Aging

MARIO MIKULINCER, Bar-Ilan University

STEPHANIE N. MULLINS-SWEATT, University of Kentucky

MARCUS R. MUNAFÒ, University of Bristol

VICKIE NAM, University of California, Santa Cruz

CRAIG S. NEWMANN, University of North Texas

RAINER REISENZEIN, University of Greifswald

MADELINE REX-LEAR, University of Texas at Arlington

RICHARD W. ROBINS, University of California, Davis

MICHAEL D. ROBINSON, North Dakota State University

MARY K. ROTHBART, University of Oregon

RICHARD M. RYAN, University of Rochester

GERARD SAUCIER, University of Oregon

MICHAEL F. SCHEIER, Carnegie Mellon University

CONSTANTINE SEDIKIDES, University of Southampton

PHILLIP R. SHAVER, University of California, Davis

BRAD E. SHEESE, University of Oregon

YUICHI SHODA, University of Washington

RONALD E. SMITH, University of Washington

ALICE F. STUHLMACHER, DePaul University

RHONDA SWICKERT, College of Charleston

AVRIL THORNE, University of California, Santa Cruz

DAVID D. VACHON, University of Toronto

GENEVA VÁSQUEZ, University of Arizona

MICHELE VECCHIONE, University of Rome

SETH A. WAGERMAN, University of California, Riverside

FIONA WARREN, University of Surrey

HANNELORE WEBER, University of Greifswald

THOMAS A. WIDIGER, University of Kentucky

PEDRO SOFIO ABRIL WOLF, University of Arizona

DONNA YOUNGS, University of Liverpool

MOSHE ZEIDNER, University of Haifa

Abbreviations

A	Agreeableness
ACC	anterior cingulate cortex
ADHD	attention deficit hyperactive disorder
APA	American Psychiatric Association
APD	antisocial personality disorder
APIM	actor-partner independence model
APSD	Antisocial Process Screening Device
ARAS	ascending reticular activating system
BAS	behavioural approach system
BED	binge eating disorder
BFI	Big Five Inventory
BIS	behavioural inhibition system
BPI	Basic Personality Inventory
C	Conscientiousness
CAPS	cognitive-affective processing system
CAQ-sort	California Adult Q-sort
CAQ	Clinical Analysis Questionnaire
CBT	cognitive-behavioural therapy
CD	conduct disorder
CFA	confirmatory factor analysis
cns	conceptual nervous system
CNS	central nervous system
CPAI	Chinese Personality Assessment Inventory
CPS	Child Psychopathy Scale
CR	conditioned response
CS	conditioned stimulus
DAPP	Dimensional Assessment of Personality Pathology
DBT	dialectical behaviour therapy
DIF	differential item functioning
DTC	democratic therapeutic community
E	Extraversion
ECR	Experiences in Close Relationships
EFA	exploratory factor analysis
EI	emotional intelligence
FFM	Five-Factor Model
FFFS	fight-flight-freeze system
FFS	fight-flight system
FHID	factored homogeneous item dimension

fMRI	functional magnetic resonance imaging
FUPC	first unrotated principal component
GAS	general adaptation syndrome
HPI	Hogan Personality Inventory
HRM	human resource management
IAPS	International Affective Picture Series
IAS	Interpersonal Adjective Scale
ICD	International Classification of Diseases
IO	industrial/organizational
IRT	item response theory
LGM	latent growth model
LPFC	lateral prefrontal cortex
MBT	mentalization-based treatment
MDS	multidimensional scaling
MedPFC	medial prefrontal cortex
MMPI	Minnesota Multiphasic Personality Inventory
MPQ	Multidimensional Personality Questionnaire
N	Neuroticism
NA	negative affectivity
NEO-FFI	NEO Five-Factor Inventory
NEO-PI-R	Revised NEO Personality Inventory
O	Openness to Experience
OCD	obsessive-compulsive disorder
ODD	oppositional defiant disorder
O-LIFE	Oxford-Liverpool Inventory of Feelings and Experiences
P	Psychoticism
PA	positive affectivity
PAI	Personality Assessment Inventory
PANAS	Positive and Negative Affect Scale
PCL	Psychopathy Checklist
PCL–R	Psychopathy Checklist–Revised
PD	personality disorder
PDNOS	personality disorder not otherwise specified
PFC	prefrontal cortex
PPI	Psychopathy Personality Inventory
QTL	quantitative trait loci
ROI	regions of interest
ROV	regions of variance
RST	Reinforcement Sensitivity Theory
16PF	Sixteen Personality Factor Questionnaire
SDT	self-determination theory
SEL	social and emotional learning
SEM	structural equation modelling
SIT	sustained information transfer
SNAP	Schedule for Nonadaptive and Adaptive Personality
SPQ	Schizotypal Personality Questionnaire
SRL	self-regulated learning

SRM	social relations model
SRP	Self-Report Psychopathy
SSSM	standard social science model
STM	short-term memory
SWB	subjective wellbeing
TCI	Temperament and Character Inventory
TIE	typical intellectual engagement
TMI	transmarginal inhibition
UCR	unconditioned response
UCS	unconditioned stimulus
YPI	Youth Psychopathic Traits Inventory

Preface

The study of personality requires an unusual feat of mental vision. Those of us who work in this field must focus narrowly on one or more specialized research topics, while simultaneously maintaining a wide-angle view of personality in a broader sense. The day-to-day demands of doing research can make it hard to preserve the broader focus, especially when immediate research projects are progressing well. The aim of this Handbook is to assist researchers, practitioners and students to regard the larger picture of personality research. Recent years have seen a resurgence of interest in personality, directed along lines of research that sometimes converge and sometimes seem to diverge. Our motivation in compiling this Handbook was to provide a general overview of the many areas of study that together define this branch of psychological science – that many of us consider to be becoming increasingly relevant and important in psychology more generally.

The contributors to this Handbook rose to their task admirably, producing relatively brief summaries of their respective areas of expertise in an accessible style that are intended to inform and stimulate, and at times provoke. We instructed contributors to present their material in a way that they thought most appropriate: our concern was to ensure that chapters were presented in the way that best suited the topics – as a result, some chapters are longer than others, and some topics are divided over several chapters. We offer a collective 'thank you' to all contributors not only for producing such high-quality chapters but also for their forbearance in the production process which, as a result of the number of chapters, was slower than anticipated. We can only hope that contributors are pleased by the finished Handbook.

We are very grateful to Cambridge University Press for agreeing to publish this work; especially to Sarah Caro, Commissioning Editor, for her constant encouragement and advice, and then, after Sarah's departure, to Andrew Peart and Carrie Cheek for their patience and skill in bringing this project to fruition. Gerald Matthews wishes to thank the University of Cincinnati for allowing a period of sabbatical leave, and the Japan Society for the Promotion for Science for supporting a study visit to the University of Kyushu, which assisted him in his editorial role.

Philip J. Corr
Gerald Matthews

Editors' general introduction

Philip J. Corr and Gerald Matthews

Personality psychology has never been in better health than at the present time. The idea that we can describe and measure meaningful stable traits, such as extraversion and emotionality, is no longer very controversial (though see James T. Lamiell, Chapter 5). The study of traits has been boosted by, at least, a partial consensus among researchers on the nature of the major traits, by advances in genetics and neuroscience, and by increasing integration with various fields of mainstream psychology (Matthews, Deary and Whiteman 2003). Other perspectives on personality have also flourished, stimulated by advances in social-cognitive theory (Cervone 2008; Ronald E. Smith and Yuichi Shoda, Chapter 27), by the rediscovery of the unconscious and implicit personality processes (Bargh and Williams 2006), and by increasing interest in the relationship between emotion and personality (Rainer Reisenzein and Hannelore Weber, Chapter 4). The growing prominence of personality as an arena for an integrated understanding of psychology (Susan Cloninger, Chapter 1) has motivated the present Handbook. In this introductory chapter, we provide a brief overview of the main issues, themes and research topics that are addressed in more depth by the contributors to this volume.

Despite contemporary optimism, the study of personality has often been contentious and riven by fundamental disputes among researchers. A persistent issue is the nature of personality itself: what issues are central to investigating personality, and which properly belong to other sub-disciplines of psychology? At times, it has seemed as though different schools of 'personality' research have been addressing entirely different topics. Until quite recently, there was little communication between biologically and socially oriented researchers, for example. Debates in the field tended to devolve into rigid dichotomies, forcing researchers into one camp or another:

- Is personality a 'nomothetic' quality, described by general principles applying to all individuals? Or should personality be studied 'idiographically', focusing on the uniqueness of each individual?
- Does behaviour primarily depend on personality, or is it more powerfully shaped by situation and context?
- Is personality infused into conscious experience, so that people can explicitly describe their own traits? Or, as Freud argued, is much of personality unconscious, so that people lack insight into their own natures?

- Is personality primarily a consequence of individual differences in brain functioning, or of social learning and culture?
- Is personality mainly determined by the individual's DNA, or by environmental factors? (note that this dichotomy is not the same as the preceding one: environment affects brain development)
- Is personality fixed and stable throughout adulthood, or does the person generally change over time, and perhaps grow into maturity and wisdom?

The increasing wisdom of the field is suggested by progress in finding satisfying syntheses to these various dialectics, including a recognition of the importance of person-situation interaction in shaping behaviour, and the intertwining of genes and environment (and brain and culture) in personality development (Matthews, Deary and Whiteman 2003). Nonetheless, important and sometimes fundamental differences in perspective remain (Caprara and Cervone 2000). Many contributors to the present Handbook approach personality via the resurgent notion of stable personality traits that exert a wide-ranging influence on many areas of psychological functioning. The editors' own work aligns with this perspective. However, it is important to present a historical perspective on the controversies within the field, to examine critically the core assumptions of trait theory, and to expose some of the fissures that remain within different versions of this theory. Part I of this Handbook briefly introduces some of the basic conceptual issues that have shaped inquiries into personality.

The historical arc that has seen trait psychology go into and out of favour may (most simply) reflect the changing dialectic between scientific and humanistic approaches noted by Susan Cloninger (Chapter 1). One can do personality research as a 'hard' or natural science without subscribing to universal traits, as demonstrated by work on 'behavioural signatures' (the *individual*'s consistencies in behaviour across different environments: e.g., Shoda 1999). However, trait theories have had a lasting appeal through their aspirations towards a universal measurement framework (akin to Cartesian mapping of the Earth or the periodic table), and their relevance to all branches of personality theory. Nonetheless, trait theory does not satisfy those seeking to understand the individual person, or the intimacy of the person-situation relationship, or the humanists that want to help humankind. Contributors to Part I of this Handbook address some of the central issues that define a struggle for the soul of personality theory. We especially highlight (1) the psychological meaning of measures of personality, (2) the role of personality in predicting behaviour, and (3) the holistic coherence of personality.

There are some points of agreement that are close to universal, at least among scientifically-oriented researchers. As further explored in Part II of this Handbook, personality researchers have a special concern with the meaning of measurements of personality (whatever the particular scale or instrument). Numerical measurements must be anchored by some process of external validation to reach theoretical understanding. For example, a theory that specifies multiple brain systems allows us to link the numbers we get from personality scales to parameters of those systems (Philip J. Corr, Chapter 21), and to make predictions about how trait measurements relate to objective measurements of brain functioning (e.g., from functional magnetic resonance imaging, fMRI). We are right to be wary of the factor analysis of questionnaires interpreted without such theoretical and external referents.

Another basic concern is the prediction of behaviour (whether at individual or group level). We are all interactionists now, in accepting the importance of both person and situation factors, but the simple acknowledgement of interaction does not take us very far (see Seth A. Wagerman and David C. Funder, Chapter 2; Jens B. Asendorpf, Chapter 3). At the least, we need both a fine-grained understanding of how personality factors bias the dynamic interaction between the individual and the environment in some given social encounter, as well as a longer-focus understanding on how personality and situations interact developmentally over periods of years, or even decades (see M. Brent Donnellan and Richard W. Robins, Chapter 12).

A focus on the general functioning of the person, emerging from many individual components or modules, is a further common theme. There is a tension between the idea of a coherent self and several features of biological science, including the division of the brain into many functionally distinct areas (neuroscience), the determination of brain structure by multiple genes (molecular genetics), and the evolution of the brain to support multiple adaptive modules (evolutionary psychology). Contrasting with these fissile tendencies, if there is one issue on which most personality psychologists agree, it is that the whole is more than the sum of the parts. Comparable difficulties in finding personality coherence also arise in social-cognitive approaches which discriminate multiple cognitive, affective and motivational processes underlying personality (Caprara and Cervone 2000). Should we see personality as a fundamental causal attribute of the brain that, in Jeffrey Gray's (1981) phrase, becomes a great flowering tree as it guides the development of many seemingly disparate psychological functions? Or does personality coherence reside in the idiosyncratic schemas that lend unique meanings to the lives of individuals (Caprara and Cervone 2000)? Or is personality coherence functional rather than structural in nature, reflecting the person's core goals and strategies for adaptation to the major challenges of life (Matthews 2008a)? Defining personality in some holistic sense, as opposed to a collection of functional biases in independent modules, may be informed by integration of personality and emotion research. As discussed by Rainer Reisenzein and Hannelore Weber (Chapter 4), the study of emotion has similar integrative aims.

Trait researchers pursue 'normal science' (Kuhn 1962), in that they share common core assumptions about the nature of personality. There is a reasonable degree of consensus on dimensional models, the importance of both biology and social factors, and person x situation interaction. Some alternative perspectives on personality, such as those grounded in social constructivism, are clearly outside the paradigm. Social-cognitive perspectives appear to be in the process of negotiating their stance towards trait models. Some aspects of social-cognitive research use normative trait-like measures (e.g., self-esteem), and might be integrated with the trait paradigm (Michael D. Robinson and Constantine Sedikides, Chapter 26). Other aspects that take an idiographic view of personality coherence (Caprara and Cervone 2000) may represent an alternative paradigm.

This volume primarily covers the various expressions and applications of trait theory as the dominant paradigm in personality, while recognizing the important contributions of social-cognitive models (Ronald E. Smith and Yuichi Shoda, Chapter 27) and the idiographic (Auril Thorne and Vickie Nam, Chapter 28) and humanistic (Edward L. Deci and Richard M. Ryan, Chapter 25) traditions of the field. The remainder of this introductory chapter briefly highlights key issues relating to the focal issues reflected in the section structure of the book: measurement issues, theoretical stances (biological, cognitive and social), personality development, the role of culture, and applications.

Measurement of personality

Measurement issues may be broken down into a series of interlinked questions. First, should quantitative measurements be at the center of personality research at all? Answers in the negative would come from psychodynamic theorists, and from social constructivists (cf., Avril Thorne and Vickie Nam, Chapter 28). There are also those who challenge the basic assumptions of psychometric methods used in personality assessment (James T. Lamiell, Chapter 5), or even the validity of any psychological measurement (Barrett 2003). For the most part, however, personality researchers share the assumption that scientific tests of personality theory require quantitative assessments of personality. Typically, it is dimensional traits such as extraversion, anxiety and sensation-seeking which are assessed, but personality characteristics unique to the individual may also be quantified (Ronald E. Smith and Yuichi Shoda, Chapter 27).

Assuming that measurement is desirable, the next question is what do we measure? As Ian J. Deary (Chapter 6) points out, Gordon Allport raised a question that still awaits an answer: what is the basic unit of personality? In practice, various sources of trait data have been used, following Raymond Cattell's classification (see Gregory J. Boyle and Edward Helmes, Chapter 7), that distinguishes self-reports (which need not be accepted at face value), objective behaviours and life-record data. Questionnaire assessments of traits are familiar, and need no introduction. The major structural models of personality such as the Five-Factor Model (FFM) (Robert R. McCrae, Chapter 9) are largely based on questionnaire scales, although they gain authority from evidence on the convergence of self-report with other measurement media, such as the reports of others on the personality of the individual (Goldberg 1992). Assessment may also be reconfigured by the resurgence of interest in the unconscious. Implicit personality dimensions distinct from self-report dimensions assessed via behavioural techniques based on speed of response to trait-relevant stimuli are promising, although psychometric challenges remain (Schnabel, Banse and Asendorpf 2006).

Having chosen a data source, the next issue for trait researchers is what specific analytic techniques should be used to identify and discriminate multiple dimensions of personality (Gregory J. Boyle and Edward Helmes, Chapter 7). The traditional tool here (Cattell 1973) is exploratory factor analysis (EFA), which assigns the reliable variance in responses (e.g., on a questionnaire) to a reduced set of underlying factors or dimensions. For example, factor analysis of the various English-language verbal descriptors of personality suggests that most of the variation in response can be attributed to just five underlying factors that provide a comprehensive description of personality in this medium (Goldberg 1990). EFA, however, is subject to various limitations, including the existence of an infinite number of mathematically-equivalent factor solutions (alternate 'rotations'), different principles for factor extraction, and the lack of any definitive method for deciding on the key question of how many factors to extract (Haig 2005). These difficulties have been known from the beginning of research using factor analysis, and most theorists have advocated using factor analysis only in conjunction with other approaches that may provide converging evidence, such as discriminating clinical groups and performing experimental investigations (Eysenck 1967).

As Gregory J. Boyle and Edward Helmes (Chapter 7) discuss, interest is growing in 'modern' methods for scale construction that contrast with classical test theory; these methods include item response theory and Rasch scaling. Multivariate methods that complement or replace traditional EFA have also become increasingly sophisticated. The single most important advance may be the development of confirmatory techniques, which are used to test whether or not a factor model specified in advance fits a given data set. Testing goodness of fit provides some protection against making too much of the serendipitous factor solutions that may emerge from EFA. Confirmatory factor analysis is itself one instance of a larger family of structural equation modelling techniques that allow detailed causal models to be tested against data (Bentler 1995).

The final set of questions concerns the nature of the measurement models that emerge from the application of multivariate statistical methods. For many years, debate over the structure of personality revolved around disputes over the optimal number of factors for personality description. Famously, Cattell advocated sixteen (or more) factors, whereas Eysenck preferred a more economical three. The Five-Factor Model represents the most popular resolution of the debate (Robert R. McCrae, Chapter 9), although there remain significant dissenting voices (e.g., Boyle 2008). In addition, disputes can to some extent be resolved within hierarchical, multilevel models that differentiate broad superfactors such as the 'Big Five', along with more numerous and narrowly defined 'primary' factors (Boele De Raad, Chapter 8).

A more subtle issue is how to discriminate dimensions of personality from other domains of individual differences, especially intelligence (Phillip L. Ackerman, Chapter 10). The term 'personality' is sometimes used in a wider sense to refer to the full spectrum of personal characteristics, including abilities. Careful psycho-metric modelling can help to resolve the boundaries of different domains within this broader sphere of individual differences. The new construct of 'emotional intelligence' is an example of the problems that may arise. Different versions of the construct have been proposed that seem variously to belong in either the ability or personality domain, or some no man's land in between (Matthews, Zeidner and Roberts 2007).

Developmental processes

Given that we can assess personality descriptively, one of the next fundamental issues to consider is personality development. How do our person-alities originate? How do they change over time? What psychological processes support development? Broadly, two rather different perspectives have been adop-ted historically. An essentialist position (see Haslam, Bastian and Bissett 2004) supposes that individuals have a rather stable nature, evident early in childhood, which is perpetuated, with minor changes, throughout the lifespan. This position is compatible with a strong hereditary component to personality and a view that biology is destiny. Conversely, in the spirit of J. B. Watson, we may see person-ality as accumulating over time through significant learning experiences. Theories as various as psychoanalysis, traditional learning theory and modern social-cognitive theory have all seen learning as central to personality. Such approaches tend to suggest a more malleable view of personality.

Understanding development breaks down into a number of discrete research issues, including measurement models for the lifespan, identifying qualitative differences between child and adult personality, modelling the processes that contribute to development, and linking personality development to the person's broader experience of life and wellbeing. Contributors to this volume address some of the key issues involved.

Assessment and continuity of personality in the early years are often attacked via studies of temperament. The general idea is that even infants may show rudimentary qualities such as emotionality and activity. These basic 'tempera-ments' may persist into adulthood, for example as positive and negative emotion-ality, and also provide a platform for development of more sophisticated personality attributes. It is sometimes assumed that temperament is closer to biological substrates than adult personality, which is more strongly influenced by social-cultural factors (Strelau 2001). Just as with adult personality, we can investigate the dimensional structure of temperament, although, with young children, the primary data source must be observations of the child's behaviour rather than self-report.

One of the most parsimonious and also most influential models of temperament is that proposed by Rothbart and Bates (1998; Mary K. Rothbart *et al.*, Chapter 11). Its major dimensions include Surgency/Extraversion (including activity and sociability), negative affectivity and effortful control, all of which may be identified through observational methods. A key question is the extent to which childhood temperament shows continuity with adolescent and adult personality. Do active children become extraverted adults? Do 'whiny' infants become emotionally unstable in later life? The consensus on such issues is that temperament does indeed predict adult personality, although personality may be somewhat unstable during the childhood years. An important line of research constitutes longitudinal studies that track temperament, personality and real-life behaviours of periods of years. For example, the Dunedin study in New Zealand has tracked around one thousand infants into adulthood, and demonstrated that childhood temperament is modestly but reliably predictive of adult personality and further criteria including criminal behaviour and mental disorder (e.g., Caspi, Harrington, Milne *et al.* 2003).

As M. Brent Donnellan and Richard W. Robins (Chapter 12) discuss, the FFM has proved a useful framework for investigating both stability and change in personality over the lifespan. Factor analytic studies confirm the convergence of personality and temperament dimensions (Strelau 2001). We should note that factorial convergence does not preclude qualitative changes in the nature of the dimension over time.

Coupled with statistical modelling of personality change over the lifespan is a concern with the underlying processes driving change and stability. We prefigure our later discussion of personality theory by indicating several avenues towards understanding development. The grounding of temperament in biology points towards the role of neuroscience. There are good correspondences between the fundamental dimensions of temperament and some of the key constructs of biological theories of personality (Mary K. Rothbart *et al.*, Chapter 11). Importantly, brain development depends on both genes and environmental influences, and, as genes may become active at different ages, genetic influences may incorporate personality change. Cognitive and social processes are also critical for personality development. Traits such as Extraversion and Neuroticism are associated with biases in cognitive functioning that confer, for example, an aptitude for acquiring social skills in extraverts, and heightened awareness of threat in high neurotic persons (Matthews 2008a). Self-regulative theories (Charles S. Carver and Michael F. Scheier, Chapter 24; Michael D. Robinson and Constantine Sedikides, Chapter 26) have addressed how cognitive representations of the self mediate the individual's attempts to satisfy personal goals in a changing external environment. Furthermore, cognitive development takes place within a social context (Bandura 1997) that may powerfully affect personality, for example, in relation to exposure to role models, internalization of cultural norms and educational experiences (Moshe Zeidner, Chapters 41, 42).

Most researchers accept that neural, cognitive and social processes interact in the course of personality development, although building and validating detailed models of the developmental process is difficult. Two examples will suffice. There is a growing appreciation that research on personality and health should be placed in the context of the lifespan (Marko Elovainio and Mika Kivimäki, Chapter 13).

Activities such as smoking and exercise exert their effects over long intervals. Whiteman, Deary and Fowkes (2000) suggested that a full understanding of personality requires the integration of two models, a structural weakness model that focuses on internal vulnerabilities (e.g., genetic predispositions to illness), and a psychosocial vulnerability model that focuses on external factors such as life/work stress. Cognitive factors such as choosing health-promoting coping strategies may play a mediating role.

Similarly, development of emotional competence depends on the interaction between biologically-based elements of temperament that confer emotionality on the child, and social learning processes, such as modelling of emotional response. Individual differences in brain systems for handling reward and punishment stimuli (Philip J. Corr, Chapter 21) may govern whether children develop cheerful or distress-prone temperaments, respectively. However, the distress-prone child may still grow up to be well-adapted if he or she learns effective strategies from parents and peers for coping with vulnerability to negative emotion. Cognitions are also critical in that language capabilities influence the child's capacity to understand and express emotion. Traits such as emotional intelligence emerge from this complex and enigmatic interactional process (Zeidner, Matthews, Roberts and McCann 2003).

Finally, in this section, we note the resurgence of one of the grand theories of personality, John Bowlby's attachment theory, reviewed in this volume in two chapters authored by Phillip R. Shaver and Mario Mikulincer (Chapters 14, 15). Bowlby's insight was that the child's pattern of relationships with its primary care-giver affected adult personality; secure attachment to the care-giver promoted healthy adjustment in later life. The theory references many of the key themes of this review of personality. Attachment style may be measured by observation or questionnaire; a common distinction is between secure, anxious and avoidant styles (Ainsworth, Blehar, Waters and Wall 1978). It also corresponds to standard traits; for example, secure attachment correlates with Extraversion and Agreeableness (Carver 1997). Attachment likely possesses biological aspects (evident in ethological studies of primates), social aspects (evident in data on adult relationships), and cognitive aspects (evident in studies of the mental representations supporting attachment style) (Phillip R. Shaver and Mario Mikulincer, Chapter 14). As with other personality theories, a major challenge is developing a model that integrates these different facets of the attachment construct.

Theories of personality

Allport (1937) saw personality traits as possessing causal force. Traits correspond to 'generalized neuropsychic structures' that modulate the individual's understanding of stimuli and choice of adaptive behaviours. Thus, traits represent more than some running average of behaviour. For example, we could see trait anxiety as simply the integral of a plot of state anxiety over time, but this perspective tells us nothing about the underlying roots of vulnerability to anxiety.

A theory of the trait is required to understand the causal basis for stability in individual differences, and the processes that incline the person to view stimuli as threatening, and to engage in defensive and self-protective behaviours.

One of the hallmarks of personality theory is the diversity of explanatory concepts it invokes (Susan Cloninger, Chapter 1). We could variously attribute trait anxiety to sensitivity of brain systems controlling response to threat, to cognitive processes that direct attention to environmental threat, or to culture-bound socialization to see oneself as threat-vulnerable. Three sections of this Handbook address three major perspectives that mould contrasting theories. According to biological perspectives, personality is a window on the brain. Hans Eysenck and Jeffrey Gray articulated the influential view that individual differences in simple but critical brain parameters, such as arousability and sensitivity to reinforcing stimuli, can drive far-reaching personality changes, expressed in traits such as Extraversion and Neuroticism. These theories emphasized the role of individual differences in genes for brain development (polymorphisms) in generating personality variation (in conjunction with environmental factors). As a broad research project, biological theory thus emphasizes studies of behaviour and molecular genetics, psychophysiology, and the linkage between neuroscience and real-world behavioural functioning, including clinical disorder.

Cognitive and social-psychological theories bring different issues into the foreground of research. The essence of cognitive theories is that personality is supported by differing representations of the world, and the person's place within it, coupled with individual differences in information-processing. For example, Aaron Beck (Beck, Emery and Greenberg 2005) attributed depression to the negative content of self-schema, such as beliefs in personal worthlessness. Emotional pathology also relates to biases in attention, memory and strategies for coping. A major feature of cognitive approaches is the use of the experimental methods of cognitive psychology to link traits to specific components of information-processing. These approaches typically link cognition to real-life behaviour and adaptation through self-regulative models that seek to specify stable individual differences in the processing supporting goal attainment (Charles S. Carver and Michael F. Scheier, Chapter 24).

Social psychological accounts focus on the interplay between personality and social relationships (Lauri A. Jensen-Campbell *et al.*, Chapter 29), and several interlocking issues. These include the extent to which personality characteristics (including traits) arise out of social interaction, the reciprocal influence of personality on social interaction, and the role of culture in modulating these relationships. Biological and cognitive theories typically conform to a natural sciences model, but at least some variants of social psychological theory owe more to the idiographic and humanistic traditions of the field discussed by Susan Cloninger (Chapter 1). A vigorous research programme that looks back to the social learning theories of Walter Mischel and Albert Bandura combines elements of both cognitive and social psychology within an idiographic framework (Caprara and Cervone 2000; Ronald E. Smith and Yuichi Shoda, Chapter 27).

In a sense, each research tradition may stand alone. Each has its own distinct research agenda and methods supporting a self-contained domain of scientific discourse. However, each perspective on theory faces contemporary challenges that are a product of previous progress. We will review these shortly. The more general point to emphasize is that there is increasing convergence between different approaches. Cognitive and social neuroscience approaches are increasingly infusing personality research, and it is also clear that core social-psychological constructs, such as the self-concept, overlap with trait-based constructs (Matthews, Deary and Whiteman 2003). There are still unresolved issues regarding the extent to which, for example, cognitive and social accounts of personality may be reduced to neuroscience (Matthews 2008b; Corr and McNaughton 2008). It can be agreed, though, that there has never been a greater need for proponents of different research traditions to talk to one another in the service of theoretical integration.

Next, we reflect briefly on some of the main challenges for each theoretical perspective, which are taken up by contributors to this volume.

Neuroscience

The neuroscience of personality has advanced considerably from Hans Eysenck's (1981) pioneering efforts to advance biological models as a new Kuhnian paradigm for the field. Genetic studies, psychophysiology and 'the neuroscience of real life' have all made major advances. The leading biological theories, such as Reinforcement Sensitivity Theory (Philip J. Corr, Chapter 21), aim to integrate various strands of evidence in delineating the neuroscience of personality.

The case of heritability of personality was originally based on behaviour genetics, and the finding that the similarity between related individuals, such as siblings, related to their degree of genetic similarity (Johnson, Vernon and Mackie 2008). The attribution of around 50 per cent of the variance in major personality traits to heritability is uncontroversial. The field has also tackled such important issues as non-additive effects of genes and gene-environment interaction. Studies of personality variation within a given population are not, however, informative about the mechanisms through which genes build the individual brains that differ in the familiar personality traits.

There is currently some excitement about the prospects for molecular genetics, i.e., identifying polymorphisms (different variants of the same gene) that may produce individual differences in neural functioning and ultimately observed personality. Approaches focusing on genes for neurotransmitter function have had some success in linking personality to DNA (Marcus R. Munafò, Chapter 18). The search is on for 'endophenotypes' – highly specific traits that are shaped by the genes and influence broader personality traits and vulnerability to mental illness. At the same time, the likely complexity of mappings between genes, brain systems and behaviour may present a barrier to future progress (Turkheimer 2000).

There is also growing interest in the evolutionary basis for human neural functioning. Initially, evolutionary psychology was more concerned with personality in the sense of 'how all people are the same', rather than with individual differences.

Recently, however, researchers (e.g., Penke, Dennisen and Miller 2007) have begun to explore how evolutionary genetic mechanisms may produce variation in traits across individuals. Aurelio José Figueredo *et al.* (Chapter 16) point out that variability in strategies for managing social relationships, including sexual relationships, may be critical for human personality. Furthermore, the evolutionary perspective aligns with growing evidence for continuity between animal and human personality (or temperament), as Samuel D. Gosling and B. Austin Harley (Chapter 17) discuss.

Research methodology has also advanced since the heydays of Hans Eysenck and Jeffrey Gray. The traditional indices of central and autonomic arousal remain important, but contemporary brain-imaging methods offer the prospect of transforming personality neuroscience. Two chapters in this volume (Turhan Canli, Chapter 19; Colin G. DeYoung and Jeremy R. Gray, Chapter 20) review how methods such as functional magnetic resonance imaging (fMRI) establish associations between personality traits and specific brain areas. Excitement about such research has justification. At the same time, much remains to be done to go beyond establishing correlations between traits and neurology, to develop causal models that explain the correlations. It also remains to be seen whether the psychometric models based on questionnaire data will prove adequate to capture personality variation seen at the neural level (Ian J. Deary, Chapter 6).

Cognitive science of personality

For forty years or so, cognitive-psychological research on personality has traded quite successfully on the insights and methods of the 'cognitive revolution' of the 1960s. As previously indicated, major themes include the importance of stable self-knowledge, studies of information-processing using objective performance indices, and the concept of self-regulation as an approach to handling dynamic interaction between the person and the outside world. The use of language in the assessment of personality also raises important issues regarding the role of cognitive representations and semantics (Gerard Saucier, Chapter 22). Theoretical landmarks include schema theories of emotional pathology (Beck, Emery and Greenberg 2005), information-processing accounts of anxiety and impulsivity (Eysenck, Derakshan, Santos and Calvo 2007; Revelle 1993) and the cybernetics of self-regulation (Carver and Scheier 1998).

As in other realms of personality, these well-established theories face new challenges. We will briefly highlight three of these here: the scope of cognitive models, the relevance of social psychology, and the development of causal models of person-situation interaction. The first issue is whether cognitive personality theories can really explain the full range of personality phenomena. It is something of a cliché to say that cognitive models suggest a dehumanized, robot-like perspective on human functioning (although, arguably, one based on a misunderstanding of cognitive science: Matthews, Zeidner and Roberts 2002). By contrast, investigations of the emotional basis of personality have been a staple of the field, addressed from multiple perspectives (Rainer Reisenzein and Hannelore Weber, Chapter 4). Recent work on emotional intelligence (Mayer, Salovey and Caruso

2000) suggests that there may be affective elements of personality that are not easily reduced to cognitive processes. Positive psychology emphasizes the generative role of emotions in signalling peak experiences and personal fulfilment (cf., Edward L. Deci and Richard M. Ryan, Chapter 25).

It is also unclear whether cognitive theories can accommodate renewed interest in unconscious processes. Although the classical psychodynamic theories have their defenders, most cognitive psychologists see only weak parallels, at most, between the Freudian unconscious and the unconscious information-processing revealed by experiments on information-processing (Kihlstrom 1999). Of more interest is that stable traits can be revealed through implicit behavioural measures, whose place in some over-arching dimensional model of personality remains to be explored (Schnabel, Banse and Asendorpf 2006).

A second challenge comes from social psychological approaches that situate both cognition and personality within social interaction. The self-schema may be attributed to generalized self-knowledge relevant to all individuals (Michael D. Robinson and Constantine Sedikides, Chapter 26; Wells and Matthews 1994). We can assess self-esteem, for example, using standard instruments – and relate the measurements to traits such as neuroticism. The contrasting social-psychological perspective is that self-related constructs can only be understood in the context of social relationships and the cultural milieu (Caprara and Cervone 2000). Not only is the self shaped through social interaction, but it is negotiated via discourse with others; so that it resides 'between' rather than 'within' people (Hampson 1988). A potentially important compromise between social constructivism of this kind and conventional cognitive theory was advanced by Mischel and Shoda (1995). Social learning may lead to the development of organized networks of cognitive-affective processing units that support the individual's unique patterns of interaction with the social world (Ronald E. Smith and Yuichi Shoda, Chapter 27).

The third issue here is the causal role of individual differences in cognition in generating personality differences. Information-processing models typically establish correlations between traits and multifarious processing components (Gerald Matthews, Chapter 23), but it remains unclear whether processing causes personality or vice versa. Recent work on anxiety (Wilson, MacLeod, Mathews and Rutherford 2006) establishes a causal role for processing: training participants to respond to threat stimuli appears to increase anxiety (stress vulnerability). At the same time, trait anxiety relates to processing biases and strategic preferences that influence cognitions of threat. Self-regulative theories may be usefully extended by specifying reciprocal relationships between personality traits and specific processing functions that support adaptation to external social environments (Matthews 2008a).

Social psychology and personality

Traditional social psychological approaches to personality face the converse issue to cognitive theories; that is, much of what has been seen as uniquely social about personality may, in fact, be understood in terms of trait constructs and the individual's mental representations. As previously discussed, many of the core attributes of the self such as self-esteem and self-efficacy may be represented as generalized self-knowledge (Matthews, Schwean, Campbell *et al.* 2000; Michael D. Robinson and Constantine Sedikides, Chapter 26). This perspective supports empirical work on the interplay between personality and social relationships (Lauri A. Jensen-Campbell *et al.*, Chapter 29) that shows how various social processes are biased by traits. For example, highly agreeable individuals broadly view others more positively, express higher empathy, and adopt more helpful and constructive interaction strategies. An understanding of traits may similarly inform research on social support (Rhonda Swickert, Chapter 30) and social emotions such as the hurt of rejection (Geoff MacDonald, Chapter 31). As Lauri A. Jensen-Campbell *et al.* (Chapter 29) also discuss, effects of personality on social functioning must be understood in the broader context of reciprocal interaction between personality and social relations across the lifespan.

Social-psychological research is also increasingly exploring the wider cultural context of personality. The traditional argument is that culture shapes the social interactions which, in turn, shape the self and personality. This view continues to inform cross-cultural studies (see Juris G. Draguns, Chapter 32; Matsumoto 2007) that explore how contrasting social values such as individualism and collectivism are expressed in personality in cultures such as the United States and East Asia. At the same time, the cultural relativism traditionally promoted by anthropology has been challenged by the new awareness of universal human nature supported by evolutionary psychology and empirical evidence for the generality of personality structure. Research is needed on the extent to which 'universal personality' constrains cultural variability in personality (Robert Hogan and Michael Harris Bond, Chapter 33).

At the time of writing, the United States is in the midst of a presidential primary season that appears highly driven by (perceptions of) the personalities of the candidates. The obsession of contemporary Western culture with celebrities is also widely acknowledged. Another frontier for social personality research is to investigate the role of such personality perceptions in the public arena. This new focus on personality builds on earlier research on the influence of personality on political attitudes, such as Adorno's classic work on authoritarian personality. As Gianvittorio Caprara and Michele Vecchione (Chapter 34) discuss, effects of personality transcend simple right-left divisions, and must be understood within a cultural context.

Psychopathology and abnormality

Abnormal personality and its role in mental illness has been a major focus of inquiry since Freud's initial studies of 'hysteria' (Eysenck and Eysenck 1985). As with other areas of personality research, research centres on issues of conceptualization, measurement and theoretical understanding. In addition, the applied goal of improving clinical treatments is never far away. The conventional model accepted by psychiatrists is called the diathesis-stressor model. The 'diathesis' refers to an underlying vulnerability to disorder, which is triggered by an external stressful event. For example, neurotic personality seems to constitute a diathesis for various emotional disorders (David D. Vachon and R. Michael Bagby, Chapter 35). The highly neurotic individual may be especially prone to develop depression following a personal loss, such as the death of a loved one. Understanding the role of personality in mental illness requires both assessment of elements of personality that confer vulnerability, and detailed investigation of how the various traits of interest play into the processes that generate pathology.

In regard to assessment, one of the most important developments of recent years has been the growing acceptance of dimensional models of abnormal personality (Stephanie N. Mullins-Sweatt and Thomas A. Widiger, Chapter 37; Widiger and Trull 2007). As with normal personality, it can be shown that abnormal traits, such as schizotypy and antisocial personality, exist on a continuum in the general population; that is, there is no sharp categorical distinction, between, for example, people with and without antisocial personality. Application of the normal psychometric methods has developed multidimensional models of abnormality that correspond well to the variation seen in clinical populations (Livesley 2007). This work calls into question the traditional assumption of clinical psychology that mental disorders exist in all-or-nothing fashion. If a person meets a sufficient number of diagnostic criteria for generalized anxiety, they have a disorder; if they meet some but not enough criteria, they are deemed mentally healthy. The dimensional approach indicates that there are people for whom anxiety may be problematic but who are not 'mentally ill' in the formal sense, and that people who meet diagnostic criteria will differ in the severity of illness.

One of the traditional debates in abnormal psychology was the extent to which it was something qualitatively distinct from normal variation. Cattell (1973), for example, proposed a separate abnormal sphere, whereas Eysenck (Eysenck and Eysenck 1985) viewed neurotic and psychotic disorders as the extremes of the normal dimensions of neuroticism and psychoticism. For the most part, psychometric studies have supported the Eysenckian view that abnormality lies at the extremes of dimensions evident in the general population, although we note recent interest in 'taxometric' procedures that may identify typologically distinct categories of disorder (Beauchaine 2007). Although the symptoms of schizophrenia seem bizarre and unrelated to normal personality, Gordon Claridge (Chapter 36) points to the quotidian nature of perceptual distortions, unusual and creative thinking, and spiritual experiences. As David D. Vachon and R. Michael Bagby (Chapter 35) discuss, abnormal and normal personality dimensions may be integrated within common dimensional models. Of course, instruments specialized for clinical practice, such as the Minnesota Multiphasic Personality Inventory (MMPI), may be especially useful in context, but the overlap of normal and abnormal personality cannot be ignored. It is also common to break down broad dimensions, such as psychopathy, into correlated sub-dimensions referring to interpersonal, affective, lifestyle and antisocial symptoms (Robert D. Hare and Craig S. Newmann, Chapter 38).

Theories of psychopathology also recapitulate the theoretical issues previously described. Gordon Claridge (Chapter 36) argues that, like other disorders, understanding schizophrenia requires investigating interactions between biological predispositions, long-term social influences and immediate environmental triggers. We may add that related issues attach to the personality change effected by successful psychotherapy, change which is typically substantial enough to affect the person's scores on personality scales (Barnett and Gotlib 1988). Nevertheless, treated patients remain vulnerable to further episodes of clinical illness, and probably multiple processes contribute to that continuing vulnerability.

Research on abnormal personality is also driven by social and cultural concerns. For example, as Natalie J. Loxton and Sharon Dawe (Chapter 39) discuss, eating disorders such as anorexia and bulimia are almost unknown in some cultures, but have become increasingly prevalent among Western women. Although a biologically-based vulnerability linked to neuroticism may be identified, its expression as pathology of eating behaviours is powerfully shaped by cultural factors. Similarly, concerns about the educational attainments of children have encouraged research on ADHD (Rapson Gomez, Chapter 40) and feed into wider issues for educational practice (Moshe Zeidner, Chapters 41, 42).

Applications

On the basis that 'nothing is as practical as a good theory' we should anticipate that the progressing science of personality should feed into increasing practical application. The two major traditional applications to clinical and organizational psychology have both proved somewhat controversial. The use of clinical personality questionnaires, such as the MMPI, as an aid to diagnosis is well-established. Nevertheless, clinicians may feel that their own insights into the case override quantitative personality data. In addition, projective tests of dubious validity, such as the Rorschach inkblots, have also been popular. The second application is the use of personality scales in occupational selection, again accompanied, at times, by pseudo-scientific procedures, such as graphology. At different times, several influential reviews (e.g., Barrick and Mount 1991; Barrick, Mount and Judge 2001; Guion and Gottier 1965) have called into question the practical utility of personality assessments, on the basis of the small effect sizes for correlations between personality and occupational performance.

At the present time, there is renewed optimism in the practical value of personality assessment. Several factors contribute to optimism. First, the popularity of the Five-Factor Model provides a standard framework that may be used to organize research in a variety of domains (Giles St J. Burch and Neil Anderson, Chapter 43; Robert R. McCrae, Chapter 9; Stephanie N. Mullins-Sweatt and Thomas A. Widiger, Chapter 37), although not all practitioners advocate its use

(Hogan and Holland 2003). Secondly, evidence has been accumulating in favour of the 'consequential validity' of traits; that is, traits predict meaningful real-world outcomes. A recent review (Ozer and Benet-Martinez 2006) identifies a variety of domains where the Big Five traits are of demonstrable relevance, including physical and mental health, quality of social relationships, occupational choice, satisfaction and performance, and pro- and antisocial behaviours in the community. Thirdly, in many cases, applied research has moved on from purely exploratory research to theory-driven insights; for example, social-cognitive theories of personality provide constructs such as self-concept, self-efficacy and goal-setting that are directly relevant to educational interventions (Moshe Zeidner, Chapters 41, 42). Fourthly, although the typical dependence of assessments on self-report rightly gives practitioners cause for concern, empirical studies suggest that the problem of response bias may not be so great as sometimes supposed (Hogan, Barrett and Hogan 2007).

Encouraging progress is also being made in each of the various domains of assessment of personality assessment. As already mentioned, the organizational utility of personality scales was challenged by data showing only weak relationships between traits and job performance measures. The problem with some of the reviews of the field was that they averaged together good and bad studies, relevant and irrelevant personality traits, and even positive and negative correlations obtained under different contexts. Other reviews (Hogan and Holland 2003; Tett and Christiansen 2007) have shown that where organizational studies are designed using theory and insight (choosing traits that are relevant to the job of interest), associations between traits and performance are moderate but practically useful. Traits also predict a host of work-related behaviours in addition to performance, including vocational interests, career progression, job satisfaction, integrity and counter-productive behaviours such as stealing and using drugs (Ones, Viswesvaran and Dilchert 2005; Tokar, Ficher and Subich 1998). There is also growing understanding of the processes that mediate effects of personality traits (Giles St J. Burch and Neil Anderson, Chapter 43), a development that is likely further to enhance practical utility. Laboratory research has long implicated personality in risk-taking (Zuckerman 2007); there is extensive evidence that traits predict risk-taking and accident involvement in industrial settings (Alice F. Stuhlmacher, Andrea L. Briggs and Douglas F. Cellar, Chapter 44).

We have already described how understanding personality is essential in clinical psychology for understanding the etiology and classification of mental disorders. Expertise in abnormal personality also helps the clinician in the practical business of diagnosis and treatment, in conjunction with the idiographic case conceptualization. The growing depth of knowledge in the field (e.g., Gordon Claridge, Chapter 36; David D. Vachon and R. Michael Bagby, Chapter 35) is such that identification of abnormal traits provides a wealth of information on the biological, cognitive and social processes that may underpin pathology in the individual, suggesting avenues for therapy. The Five-Factor Model, through its accommodation of abnormal traits, provides a comprehensive aid to diagnosis;

Stephanie N. Mullins-Sweatt and Thomas A. Widiger (Chapter 37) set out a systematic diagnostic procedure on this basis. Diagnosis may be followed by treatment recommendations that match the client's personality. The diversity of personality processes supports a diversity of therapeutic options (Fiona Warren, Chapter 46). Understanding of the client's personality also helps the clinician gauge the likely progress of therapy and the client's compliance with instructions (Harkness and Lilienfeld 1997) – beware the unconscientious patient!

The third major arena for personality assessment is educational psychology (Moshe Zeidner, Chapters 41, 42). The intelligent use of personality assessment supports full-spectrum assessment of the strengths and weaknesses of the student and the matching of the educational environment to student personality (Matthews, Zeidner and Roberts 2006). As in clinical psychology, understanding personality helps school psychologists to address students with internalizing and externalizing problems (Moshe Zeidner, Chapter 41). Growing research literatures are adding to understanding of common conditions and disorders, including test anxiety, ADHD and antisocial behaviour (see Matthews, Zeidner and Roberts 2007). In line with the aims of the positive psychology movement, personality may also require attention in promoting engagement with learning, prosocial behaviour and personal development.

Finally, personality research finds increasing application beyond the organizational, clinical and educational domains. David Canter and Donna Youngs (Chapter 45) evaluate the role of personality in criminal behaviour; by contrast with other contributors, they focus more on the narrative meaning of the crime for the individual than on trait assessments. Personality is also important for diverse fields, including road safety (Matthews 2002; Alice F. Stuhlmacher *et al.*, Chapter 44), military psychology (Bartram 1995), health psychology (Whiteman, Deary and Fowkes 2000) and substance abuse (Ball 2004). There are few, if any, real-life domains where personality does not play some part in shaping behaviour.

Conclusion

This chapter has aimed to convey the vigour and diversity of current personality research, expressed in its conceptual, methodological, theoretical and applied aspects. The scope of the field is such that a single chapter can do no more than highlight some of the major research issues – the contributors to the Handbook perform the harder work of setting out the various research programmes in detail. We hope that the organization of the book will demonstrate the growing coherence of personality psychology around a number of major themes. We have emphasized work on personality traits as a focus for an integrated approach to assessment, theory and practice, but alternative approaches, such as social-cognitive theory, may also make a strong case to be viable paradigms for research. A persistent theme in this introduction has been the multilayered nature of personality, expressed in individual differences in neural functioning, in cognition and information-processing, and in social relationships. Abnormal personality too is expressed at multiple levels. Despite the inevitable difficulties, a major task for future research is to develop models of personality that integrate these different processes. We believe that the chapters in this Handbook point the way towards the objective of adopting a 'synthetic' approach to integrating different levels of analysis.

References

Ainsworth, M. D. S., Blehar, M. C., Waters, E. and Wall, S. 1978. *Patterns of attachment: a psychological study of the strange situation*. Hillsdale, NJ: Lawrence Erlbaum

Allport, G. W. 1937. *Personality: a psychological interpretation*. New York: Holt

Ball, S. A. 2004. Personality traits, disorders, and substance abuse, in R. Stelmack (ed.), *On the psychobiology of personality: essays in honor of Marvin Zuckerman*, pp. 203–22. Amsterdam: Elsevier Science

Bandura, A. 1997. *Self-efficacy: the exercise of control*. New York: W. H. Freeman and Co.

Bargh, J. A. and Williams, L. 2006. The automaticity of social life, *Current Directions in Psychological Science* 15: 1–4

Barnett, P. A. and Gotlib, H. 1988. Psychosocial functioning and depression: distinguishing among antecedents, concomitants, and consequences, *Psychological Bulletin* 104: 97–126

Barrett, P. 2003. Beyond psychometrics: measurement, non-quantitative structure, and applied numerics, *Journal of Managerial Psychology* 18: 421–39

Barrick, M. R. and Mount, M. K. 1991. The Big Five personality dimensions and job performance: a meta-analysis, *Personnel Psychology* 44: 1–26

Barrick, M. R., Mount, M. K. and Judge, T. A. 2001. Personality and job performance at the beginning of the new millenium: what do we know and where do we go next?, *International Journal of Selection and Assessment* 9: 9–30

Bartram, D. 1995. The predictive validity of the EPI and 16PF for military training, *Journal of Occupational and Organizational Psychology* 68: 219

Beauchaine, T. P. 2007. A brief taxometrics primer, *Journal of Clinical Child and Adolescent Psychology* 36: 654–76

Beck, A. T., Emery, G. and Greenberg, R. L. 2005. *Anxiety disorders and phobias: a cognitive perspective*. New York: Basic Books

Bentler, P. M. 1995. *EQS structural equations program manual*. Encino, CA: Multivariate Software

Boyle, G. J. 2008. Critique of the five-factor model of personality, in G. J. Boyle, G. Matthews and D. H. Saklofske (eds.), *Handbook of personality theory and assessment*, vol. I, *Personality theories and models*, pp. 295–312. Thousand Oaks, CA: Sage

Caprara, G. V. and Cervone, D. 2000. *Personality: determinants, dynamics, and potentials*. Cambridge University Press

Carver, C. S. 1997. Adult attachment and personality: converging evidence and a new measure, *Personality and Social Psychology Bulletin* 23: 865–83

Carver, C. S. and Scheier, M. F. 1998. *On the self-regulation of behaviour*. New York: Cambridge University Press

Caspi, A., Harrington, H., Milne, B., Amell, J. W., Theodore, R. F. and Moffitt, T. E. 2003. Children's behavioural styles at age 3 are linked to their adult personality traits at age 26, *Journal of Personality* 71: 495–513

Cattell, R. B. 1973. *Personality and mood by questionnaire*. New York: Jossey Bass

Cervone, D. 2008. Explanatory models of personality: social-cognitive approaches, in G. J. Boyle, G. Matthews and D. H. Saklofske (eds.), *Handbook of personality theory and assessment,* vol. I, *Personality theories and models*, pp. 80–100. Thousand Oaks, CA: Sage

Corr, P. J. and McNaughton, N. 2008. Reinforcement Sensitivity Theory and personality, in P. J. Corr (ed.), *The Reinforcement Sensitivity Theory of personality*, pp. 155–87. Cambridge University Press

Eysenck, H. J. 1967. *The biological basis of personality.* Springfield, IL: Thomas
1981. General features of the model, in H. J. Eysenck (ed.), *A model for personality*, pp. 1–37. Berlin: Springer

Eysenck, H. J. and Eysenck, M. W. 1985. *Personality and individual differences: a natural science approach.* New York: Plenum

Eysenck, M. W., Derakshan, N., Santos, R. and Calvo, M. G. 2007. Anxiety and cognitive performance: attentional control theory, *Emotion* 7: 336–53

Goldberg, L. R. 1990. An alternative 'description of personality': the Big-Five factor structure, *Journal of Personality and Social Psychology* 59: 1216–29
1992. The development of markers for the Big-Five factor structure, *Psychological Assessment* 4: 26–42

Gray, J. A. 1981. A critique of Eysenck's theory of personality, in H. J. Eysenck (ed.) *A model for personality*, pp. 246–76. Berlin: Springer

Guion, R. M. and Gottier, R. F. 1965. Validity of personality measures in personnel selection, *Personnel Psychology* 18: 135–64

Haig, B. D. 2005. Exploratory factor analysis, theory generation, and scientific method, *Multivariate Behavioural Research* 40: 303–29

Hampson, S. E. 1988. *The construction of personality*, 2nd edn. London: Routledge

Harkness, A. R. and Lilienfeld, S. O. 1997. Individual differences science for treatment planning: personality traits, *Psychological Assessment* 9: 349–60

Haslam, N., Bastian, B. and Bissett, M. 2004. Essentialist beliefs about personality and their implications, *Personality and Social Psychology Bulletin* 30: 1661–73

Hogan, J., Barrett, P. and Hogan, R. 2007. Personality measurement, faking, and employment selection, *Journal of Applied Psychology* 92: 1270–85

Hogan, J. and Holland, B. 2003. Using theory to evaluate personality and job performance relations, *Journal of Applied Psychology* 88: 100–12

Johnson, A. M., Vernon, P. A. and Feiler, A. R. 2008. Behavioral genetic studies of personality: an introduction and review of 50+ years of research, in G. J. Boyle, G. Matthews and D. H. Saklofske (eds.), *Handbook of personality theory and assessment,* vol. I, *Personality theories and models*, pp. 145–73. Thousand Oaks, CA: Sage

Kihlstrom, J. F. 1999. The psychological unconscious, in L. A. Pervin and O. P. John (eds.), *Handbook of personality: theory and research*, 2nd edn, pp. 424–42. New York: Guilford Press

Kuhn, T. S. 1962. *The structure of scientific revolutions*. University of Chicago Press

Livesley, W. J. 2007. A framework for integrating dimensional and categorical classifications of personality disorder, *Journal of Personality Disorders* 21: 199–224

Matsumoto, D. 2007. Culture, context, and behaviour, *Journal of Personality* 75: 1285–320

Matthews, G. 2002. Towards a transactional ergonomics for driver stress and fatigue, *Theoretical Issues in Ergonomics Science* 3: 195–211

  2008a. Personality and information processing: a cognitive-adaptive theory, in G. J. Boyle, G. Matthews and D. H. Saklofske (eds.), *Handbook of personality theory and assessment,* vol. I, *Personality theories and models,* pp. 56–79. Thousand Oaks, CA: Sage

  2008b. Reinforcement Sensitivity Theory: a critique from cognitive science, in P. J. Corr (ed.), *The Reinforcement Sensitivity Theory of personality,* pp. 482–507. Cambridge University Press

Matthews, G., Deary, I. J. and Whiteman, M. C. 2003. *Personality traits,* 2nd edn. Cambridge University Press

Matthews, G., Schwean, V. L., Campbell, S. E., Saklofske, D. H. and Mohamed, A. A. R. 2000. Personality, self-regulation and adaptation: a cognitive-social framework, in M. Boekarts, P. R. Pintrich and M. Zeidner (eds.), *Handbook of self-regulation,* pp. 171–207. New York: Academic

Matthews, G., Zeidner, M. and Roberts, R. D. 2002. *Emotional intelligence: science and myth.* Cambridge, MA: MIT Press

  2006. Models of personality and affect for education: a review and synthesis, in P. Winne and P. Alexander (eds.), *Handbook of educational psychology,* 2nd edn, pp. 163–86. Mahwah, NJ: Lawrence Erlbaum

  2007. Emotional intelligence: consensus, controversies, and questions, in G. Matthews, M. Zeidner and R. D. Roberts (eds.), *Science of emotional intelligence: knowns and unknowns,* pp. 3–46. Cambridge, MA: Oxford University Press

Mayer, J. D., Salovey, P. and Caruso, D. R. 2000. Competing models of emotional intelligence, in R. J. Sternberg (ed.), *Handbook of human intelligence,* 2nd edn, pp. 396–420. New York: Cambridge University Press

Mischel, W. and Shoda, Y. 1995. A cognitive-affective system theory of personality: reconceptualizing situations, dispositions, dynamics, and invariance in personality structure, *Psychological Review* 102: 246–68

Ones, D. S., Viswesvaran, C. and Dilchert, S. 2005. Personality at work: raising awareness and correcting misconceptions, *Human Performance* 18: 389–404

Ozer, D. J. and Benet-Martinez, V. 2006. Personality and the prediction of consequential outcomes, *Annual Review of Psychology* 57: 401–21

Penke, L., Dennissen, J. J. A. and Miller, G. F. 2007. The evolutionary genetics of personality, *European Journal of Personality* 21: 549–87

Revelle, W. 1993. Individual differences in personality and motivation: 'noncognitive' determinants of cognitive performance, in A. Baddeley and L. Weiskrantz (eds.), *Attention: selection, awareness and control,* pp. 346–73. Oxford University Press

Rothbart, M. K. and Bates, J. E. 1998. Temperament, in N. Eisenberg (ed.), *Handbook of child psychology,* vol. III. *Social, emotional and personality development,* 5th edn, pp. 105–76. New York: Wiley

Schnabel, K., Banse, R. and Asendorpf, J. 2006. Employing automatic approach and avoidance tendencies for the assessment of implicit personality self-concept: the Implicit Association Procedure (IAP), *Experimental Psychology* 53: 69–76

Shoda, Y. 1999. Behavioural expressions of a personality system: generation and perception of behavioural signatures, in D. Cervone and Y. Shoda (eds.), *The coherence of personality: social-cognitive bases of consistency, variability, and organization*, pp. 155–81. New York: Guilford

Strelau, J. 2001. The concept and status of trait in research on temperament, *European Journal of Personality* 15: 311–25

Tett, R. P. and Christiansen, D. 2007. Personality tests at the crossroads: a response to Morgeson, Campion, Dipboye, Hollenbeck, Murphy, and Schmitt, *Personnel Psychology* 60: 967–93

Tokar, D. M., Fischer, A. R. and Subich, L. M. 1998. Personality and vocational behavior: a selective review of the literature, 1993–1997, *Journal of Vocational Behavior* 53: 115–53

Turkheimer, E. 2000. Three laws of behaviour genetics and what they mean, *Current Directions in Psychological Science* 9: 160–4

Wells, A. and Matthews, G. 1994. *Attention and emotion: a clinical perspective*. Hove: Lawrence Erlbaum

Whiteman, M. C., Deary, I. J. and Fowkes, F. G. R. 2000. Personality and health: cardiovascular disease, in S. E. Hampson (ed.), *Advances in personality psychology*, vol. I, pp. 157–98. London: Routledge

Widiger, T. A. and Trull, J. 2007. Plate tectonics in the classification of personality disorder: shifting to a dimensional model, *American Psychologist* 62: 71–83

Wilson, E. J., MacLeod, C., Mathews, A. and Rutherford, E. M. 2006. The causal role of interpretive bias in anxiety reactivity, *Journal of Abnormal Psychology* 115: 103–11

Zeidner, M., Matthews, G., Roberts, R. D. and McCann, C. 2003. Development of emotional intelligence: towards a multi-level investment model, *Human Development* 46: 69–96

Zuckerman, M. 2007. *Sensation seeking and risky behaviour*. Washington, DC: American Psychological Association

Editors' introduction to Parts I to VIII

Part I. Foundation Issues

Personality psychology covers a multitude of conceptual approaches, research methodologies and theoretical constructs. Any overview of the field must first address the tension between the diversity of research in the area, and the need to present a coherent account of personality. The first part of this Handbook presents foundation issues in defining and conceptualizing personality. Major themes include finding paths towards integrating diverse approaches, specifying the interaction between personality and situational factors, and exploring emotional bases for personality. The majority of contributions to this Handbook assume the validity of the trait approach, but it is also worth examining challenges to this leading paradigm.

Cloninger notes the continuing fragmentation of the personality field, whether expressed in the multiplicity of stand-alone 'grand theories' traditional in the area, or in the topical organizations which have become more prominent in recent surveys. She also delineates some of the fault-lines contributing to fragmentation, of which perhaps the most basic is that between science and humanism. Despite fundamental differences in orientation, there is some agreement on the issues pivotal to the study of personality, including the nature of the self, biological versus social-cultural influences, personality development and wellbeing. Cloninger ends on an optistimic note: personality is the area of psychology best placed to integrate different levels of explanation, including neuroscience and culture.

Wagerman and Funder begin by noting that, although both personality and situational influences on behaviour are important, assessment of situational factors has lagged behind development of trait measures. Situational variables have proved hard to define and conceptualize. They review their own research using the Riverside Situational Q-sort, which aims to discriminate features of the situation that are independent of the individual's perceptions of the situation. They believe that such measures will open up many doors for future research, including the promotion of a new symbiosis between personality and social psychology.

Asendorpf also explores the relationship between trait and situational factors in personality psychology. Picking up on themes from the preceding chapter, he discusses the aggregation of data across multiple occasions as an important method for demonstrating the impact of trait factors, and highlights the danger

of confounding situational measures with the personality of the individual evaluating the situation. The chapter discusses different tactics for separating person
and situation effects, and the limits on what can be learned from the different
approaches.

Reisenzein and Weber begin by viewing emotion as a sub-system of personality. The emotion system monitors the importance of events and communicates
these evaluations to other personality sub-systems. Empirical studies confirm that
traits are infused with emotion. It is well known that extraversion and neuroticism
tend to predispose the person to positive and negative affects, respectively, but
recent research shows further, more subtle links between additional traits and
emotion. Personality may also play an important part in emotion-regulation.

Lamiell's chapter provides a perspective at variance with the current orthodoxy
on personality traits. He challenges the prevailing methodology of studying the
person through quantification of individual differences, and normative measurement of individual persons. Instead, it is more meaningful to use an 'interactive
measurement' approach based on Allport's personology, in which personality is
quantified in relation to what an individual might potentially be like, as opposed to
making comparisons with other individuals. The approach is underpinned by a
rationalist rather than an empiricist philosophy of science.

Part II. Personality Description and Measurement

The second part of this Handbook focuses on the measurement issues
raised by trait models, which the editors see as the dominant paradigm in contemporary research. Researchers share the basic assumption that we can assess
multiple stable traits on a normative bias, typically via questionnaire. It is decep-
tively easy to obtain numeric values for various personality traits, but validating
the numbers as psychologically-meaningful constructs is harder. Various controversies in assessment remain, including fundamental questions such as the nature
of the basic units for personality research, and technical/statistical issues such as
the preferred method for generating and testing structural models of personality
dimensions. There also remain important issues regarding the content of psychometric models, including the nature of major personality dimensions, and overlap
between personality and other domains, such as ability.

Deary evaluates the status of personality trait theory in the light of the issues
originally raised by Allport and Cattell. Despite the successes of trait theory, the
nature of traits remains elusive. Allport's question – what is the essential unit of
personality? – awaits an answer. Despite the empirical accomplishments of the
field, future research may provide some surprises regarding the origins of traits.

Boyle and Helmes emphasize the importance of understanding the methods by
which popular personality measures are constructed. They review some of the main
techniques used, including factor analysis and construct-oriented methods, and their
limitations. They also discuss problems attaching to the use of the self-report

measures that dominate the field; attention to item characteristics can mitigate these difficulties.

Moving on from general conceptual and psychometric issues, de Raad surveys the structural personality models revealed by empirical research. Such models are typically remarkably parsimonious, given the complexity of human performance. De Raad discusses salient developments, including Eysenck's differentiation of extraversion and neuroticism, the Five-Factor Model, and alternative structures that would add further dimensions to the 'Big Five'. Hierarchical models provide multiple levels of personality differentiation.

A more detailed evaluation of the Five-Factor Model is provided by McCrae, which he states is the dominant paradigm in personality research. In favour of the model, McCrae adduces evidence for the discriminant validity, heritability and developmental course of the traits concerned, as well as their support from cross-cultural research. He also discusses evidence on the completeness of coverage of the personality domain offered by the Big Five.

Intelligence is traditionally considered a domain of individual differences that is quite separate from personality. Ackerman differentiates the two domains on the basis of 'maximal' as opposed to 'typical' behaviour, respectively. However, various overlaps and linkages between ability and personality have been established. Work on trait constructs, such as openness and typical intellectual engagement, has been especially productive.

Part III. Development, Health and Personality Change

This part of the Handbook addresses the development of personality. From its beginnings, personality research has recognized the importance of childhood in shaping adult personality. Research on 'temperament' has demonstrated robust individual differences in behaviour and emotionality in the early years that show continuity with later personality. However, developmental research is increasingly taking a lifespan approach that investigates personality change and growth in the adult years, and explores the long-term interactions between personality, wellbeing and health. It is important to develop strong psychometric models both for temperament in childhood, and for stability and change throughout the lifespan. Dynamic models of person-situation interaction are needed to interrelate the mutual influences of personality and health. Theory in this area requires multiple facets to integrate the influences of neural and cognitive development and changing social environments and relationships on personality. John Bowlby's attachment theory, and its application to individual differences, provides an influential vehicle for interrelating these different perspectives.

Rothbart et al. begin by defining temperament as constitutionally based individual differences in emotional, motor and attentional reactivity and self-regulation, showing some consistency across situations and time. They review methods for assessment of temperament, including those suitable for children. These methods support structural models, including dimensions such as surgency (extraversion), negative affectivity and effortful control. Understanding the development of temperament, and its relationship with adult personality, requires attention to the interplay between neural development and the changing social environment.

Donnelan and Robins use the Five-Factor Model as a framework for examining personality development from childhood to adulthood. Both stability and change in personality development result from the dynamic interplay between individuals and their environment. Different aspects of stability are differentiated. Stability in the sense of the rank ordering of individuals increases throughout the lifespan, but even children show some stable individual differences. It is also instructive to look at absolute changes in personality traits, which reflect increasing psychological maturity with age.

Elovainio and Kivimäki examine the relationship between personality and health, focusing especially on models of the dynamic and multidirectional associations between personality and health. Personality differences may intensify physiological reactions directly or through indirect pathways, but health outcomes feed back to influence personality. These transactional models may be placed within a developmental context that specifies the interaction between personality and health throughout the lifespan. Maladaptive transactional cycles may lead to poor social outcomes, health-related personality traits (hostility, Type A personality), and health problems that are mutually interdependent.

One of the major theoretical perspectives on personality and development is attachment theory. Adult personality may be shaped by the nature of the child's attachment to care-givers. In two linked chapters, Shaver and Mikulincer examine the far-reaching impact of the theory. In the first, the authors examine the personality constructs that arise from attachment theory. Individual differences in attachment may be understood in relation to dimensions of attachment anxiety and avoidance. Personality structure may derive from working models in memory of interactions with attachment figures. In the second chapter, Mikulincer and Shaver explore the developmental and psychodynamic processes related to attachment. The cognitive representations that support attachment style are updated dynamically by successive transactions between the person and the environment across the lifespan. Development of a sense of attachment security provides the basis for optimal personality functioning referenced by humanistic psychology and positive psychology.

Part IV. Biological Perspectives

This part of the Handbook is the first of three that survey three major theoretical perspectives on personality: biological, cognitive and social. Trait theorists have inclined to biological explanations from the early days of the field. Biological accounts of personality have received new impetus from the emergence of evolutionary psychology as an over-arching theory, and from methodological advances in molecular genetics and neuroscience (especially fMRI). In addition to developing the insights of pioneers such as Hans Eysenck and Jeffrey Gray, the modern neuroscience of personality faces new challenges. These include establishing continuities between animal and human traits, integrating molecular genetics with studies of specific neural systems and mechanisms, and using fMRI to understand the psychology as well as the brain physiology of personality.

Figueredo et al. begin their account of evolutionary psychological approaches by noting that personality theory tends to neglect ultimate causes; i.e., why the mechanisms governing personality operate as they do. They discuss how evolution by natural and sexual selection may have shaped various adaptive mechanisms that have led to the differentiation of personality traits among individuals. Variation in adaptive strategies for handling social and sexual relationships may be especially important for personality.

The growing sophistication of biological models includes renewed interest in the continuities between animal and human personalities suggested by evolutionary theory. Gosling and Harley begin by making the case that animal personality traits exist, and can be measured using techniques including coding the animal's behaviour and making subjective ratings of traits. Correspondences between human and animal personality can then be seen as special cases of a wider effort at cross-species comparisons. Although making comparisons is challenging, this work is stimulating a new interdisciplinary understanding of personality.

The inheritance of personality traits is no longer controversial but the mechanisms that link DNA to individual differences in behaviour remain to be elucidated. Munafo advocates two complementary approaches to realizing the potential of the behavioural genetics of personality. The first is to apply molecular genetic approaches to study gene x environment interactions; the second is to dissect in detail the neurobiological mechanisms that mediate genetic effects. Caution is necessary but there are good prospects for a comprehensive neurobiology of personality.

Canli reviews research on the increasingly important topic of neuroimaging of personality. He focuses especially on studies of brain emotion-processing which may contribute to understanding 'emotionality' traits, such as neuroticism and extraversion. These studies link traits to the functioning of key brain structures for emotion, e.g., amygdala and anterior cingulate cortex. Recent research has opened up new approaches, including analyses of functional connectivity and temporal dynamics; the range of traits investigated is also widening.

DeYoung and Gray discuss the vibrant personality neuroscience that is emerging from new techniques, including brain imaging and molecular genetics. Neuroscience may now have developed to the point where explanatory models of the sources of traits may be advanced. They review what is known about each of the 'Big Five' traits, in terms of neural circuitry, biochemistry and other elements of psychophysiology. Biological models may also elucidate the hierarchical nature of traits.

Corr reviews Reinforcement Sensitivity Theory, a broad neuroscience theory based on the groundbreaking work of Jeffrey Gray, aimed at bringing order to the broad array of data available (e.g., behavioural and pharmacological). It seeks to relate the major personality traits, and related clinical disorders, to three fundamental brain systems for emotion and motivation, relating to behavioural approach, behavioural avoidance and behavioural inhibition. Corr explores various lines of evidence from animal and human research which support the model and its application to understanding psychopathology.

Part V. Cognitive Perspectives

Cognitive models provide a counterpoint to neuroscience in understanding personality, in relating traits to a 'virtual' architecture for information-processing. Traits may be understood in relation to constructs such as attention and memory, as well as representations of self-beliefs (or 'schemas'). Cognitive theories referring to information-processing and self-regulation are well established. However, such theories face challenges in relation to their scope and whether they converge or conflict with alternative perspectives. Current research is tackling whether cognitive models of personality are compatible with social-psychological theories and with theories of needs and motives based in the humanistic tradition. As with other perspectives, theory has yet fully to accommodate the various forms of person-situation interaction and their representation in cognitive structures.

As Saucier points out, the science of personality builds on the extent to which personality concepts are embedded in language and semantics. Understanding the linguistic aspects of personality is important for conceptualizing the personal attributes that define traits (and the dimensional structures that emerge from them). Language-based representations also support the beliefs, values and goals that mediate cultural influences on personality.

Matthews discusses how cognitive models of personality may be developed from performance data. Traits such as extraversion and neuroticism correlate with a variety of information-processing functions, including attention and memory. Various stable biases in information-processing may work together to support adaptations characteristic of the trait; for example, cognitive attributes of extraversion facilitate social skill acquisition and adaptation to demanding social environments.

Carver and Scheier review the self-regulative processes that govern the expression of personality in behaviour. Their well-established theory describes the feedback processes that control goal-directed behaviours, generating positive or negative affect according to the rate of progress over time. They identify priority management as a core issue in self-regulation, such that affect is intimately related to shifts in goal prioritization.

Deci and Ryan have advanced another prominent cognitive theory that relates personality to motivation: self-determination theory. Personality interacts with interpersonal environments to influence satisfaction or thwarting of three basic needs: competence, autonomy and relatedness. Understanding these needs provides the basis for organizing research on different types of motivation and goals in relation to social contexts. The chapter reviews various applications of this broad theory of personality.

Robinson and Sedikides discuss the growing integration of trait and social cognitive perspectives on the self. Understanding traits contributes to theories of the self, in that constructs such as self-esteem and approach/avoidance motives relate to stable personality characteristics. Conversely, the traits revealed by self-report may themselves reflect memory structures that perpetuate stable self-knowledge.

Smith and Shoda provide a perspective on stability and variability in behaviour that owes more to social learning theory than to the trait concept. A key concept is the behavioural signature: the individual's idiosyncratic pattern of stabilities in behaviour in specific situations. Their theory also specifies the dynamic cognitive-affective processing system (CAPS) that creates a stable personality structure capable of producing situation-bound regularities in behaviour. The chapter also serves as a bridge between this section, and the social-psychological section that follows.

Part VI. Social and Cultural Processes

This section covers social-psychological perspectives on personality. Traditionally, social psychologists have adopted an idiographic perspective, focusing on the social context for the individual's sense of self. Contemporary research on personal narratives continues this tradition. However, social psychology increasingly benefits from the introduction of trait constructs, in understanding individual differences in social relationships, in social support, and in social emotions. It is fairly straightforward to demonstrate that traits correlate with a variety of social outcome and process variables; the more difficult issue is to preserve the insights of both trait and social researchers in developing integrated theories. Social psychology has also done much to support cross-cultural research. Studies of cross-cultural differences and similarities in personality structure must also find new ways to integrate the idea of a universal human nature with culture-bound influences on beliefs, motivations and values. A further application of social psychology is to the political domain, and understanding the public's perceptions of our political and cultural leaders.

Thorne and Nam review studies of understanding personality through narrative research. One of the ways in which people connect with each other is through telling personal stories. The process of storytelling, for example from mothers to children, may contribute to personality development and the shaping of the self. A separate line of research is concerned with the content and structure of the stories themselves. The study of life stories may make important contributions to understanding the coherence of personality across the lifespan.

Jensen-Campbell, Knack and Rex-Lear discuss the influence of personality on social relations. Personality and interpersonal relationships are reciprocally related. Personality influences social relations throughout the lifespan – but social relations also can shape personality. The broader cultural context may also influence this interactive process; for example, cultures may value different traits. The authors conclude by discussing new statistical methodologies for uncovering the unique role of personality in social relations.

An important form of social relations is concerned with the seeking and providing of social support in adverse circumstances. Swickert reviews the relationship between personality and social support. Traits including extraversion and neuroticism have been related to two types of social support. Functional support refers to perceived and actual support available from others, whereas structural support is defined as the embeddedness of the individual within a social network of significant others. Swickert proposes that the field needs to move on from establishing bivariate personality-support associations to develop more sophisticated models.

MacDonald reviews the impact of personality on vulnerability to 'hurt feelings' or social pain – feelings that should be construed as genuinely painful and discrete from other emotions. Various sources of social pain may be distinguished, including social exclusion and devaluing of important relationships. Reactions to hurt feelings may be understood as conflicting approach and avoidance action tendencies. Thus, individual differences in approach and avoidance tendencies may shape the individual's sensitivity to social pain.

Draguns places personality in a cross-cultural perspective. He points out that traditional cultural anthropology underestimated the extent to which personality possesses features that are universal across cultures. Considerable progress has been made both in the search for personality universals and, concurrently, in identifying dimensions such as individualism-collectivism that differentiate cultures rather than individuals. There are considerable challenges arising from efforts at interrelating cultural and personality dimensions; multiple research strategies are needed to investigate how personality and culture interact.

Hogan and Bond focus on the role of social interactions in linking personality and culture. The authors propose that there is a universal core to human nature defined by needs for social acceptance, status and meaning. Cultures differ in their rules for the social interactions that support attainments of these needs. They argue that social status will influence personality similarly across different cultures. Hogan and Bond also assert that increasing globalization requires an applied agenda for investigating and enhancing intercultural adaptability and resourcefulness.

Caprara and Vecchione begin their account of personality and politics by pointing out that contemporary politics is increasingly personalized. Research has illuminated how personality may underpin ideological orientations such as conservatism and liberalism, and influence political choices. Individual differences in personal goals and standards may play a key role. Caprara and Vecchione also describe various subtleties surrounding cleavages between the political left and right, including different cultural and political contexts.

Part VII. Psychopathology

The final parts of this Handbook shift the focus from personality theory to applications. In making this transition, there is a special place for abnormal personality and clinical psychology. Historically, the need to explain and treat abnormality in personality functioning has been a major driver for advances in the field, across perspectives ranging from the psychodynamic to the biological. The chapters in this part of the Handbook survey modern understanding of abnormal personality, as a necessary precursor to therapeutic perspectives. Two developments have been especially influential in recent years. The first is the widespread acceptance of dimensional models of abnormality, in place of rigidly categorical systems. The second is appreciation of abnormality as the extremes of normal personality. Thus, neuroticism grades into mood and anxiety disorders, psychoticism and schizotypy into actual psychosis, and lack of conscientiousness and agreeableness into antisocial personality and psychopathy. As well as these central foci of abnormal psychology, research is also increasingly exploring the role of personality in specialized disorders, including eating disorders and attention deficit hyperactive disorder (ADHD). Contributors to this part of the Handbook explore issues of both psychometrics and structural modelling, as well as theory and etiology of disorders.

Vachon and Bagby seek to provide an overview of the relationship between personality traits and mood and anxiety disorders, within the framework of models that specify a joint structure for normal and abnormal personality. The authors review hierarchical models of mental disorder that seek to relate each diagnosis in the DSM system to general vulnerability factors, such as negative affectivity (neuroticism), combined with more specific risk factors. A major task for future research is to articulate causal models that describe the observed relationships between personality factors and psychopathology.

Claridge takes up the challenge of considering how serious mental disorders (e.g., schizophrenia) relate to normal personality. The constructs that provide the bridge between personality and psychosis are dimensional traits for abnormal personality. Traits such as schizotypy and psychoticism may act as vulnerability factors for clinical psychosis. 'Input dysfunction' – difficulties in controlling stimulus processing – may play a key mediating role. Claridge concludes by addressing the intriguing question of whether abnormal traits may convey some benefits to the person, countering elevated risk of psychosis.

Psychopathy is another important abnormal trait that may be measured as a continuous dimension, using questionnaires. Hare and Neumann review research on psychopathy and its measurement. Four correlated dimensions, referring to interpersonal, affective, lifestyle and antisocial elements of psychopathy, may be distinguished. This structural model is supported by various psychometric techniques, including confirmatory factor analysis and multidimensional scaling. Longitudinal studies are addressing the development of psychopathy and its relationship with antisocial behaviours.

Eating disorders have become increasingly prominent in Western cultures in recent years. Loxton and Dawe review the role of personality in disorders such as anorexia and bulimia. Although cultural factors are important, various traits related to both anxiety and impulsivity may operate as risk factors. The individual's vulnerability to eating disorders may be understood in terms of their approach and avoidance tendencies, as specified within neuroscience models of personality.

Another disorder that increasingly vexes the general public is ADHD, which may severely limit students' educational attainments. Gomez describes how ADHD is systematically related to major temperament and personality dimensions. The condition appears to relate to emotional reactivity expressed in traits such as neuroticism. ADHD is also associated with an inhibition deficit associated with low conscientiousness and constraint. Like other contributors to this part of the Handbook, Gomez points to the need for longitudinal studies to establish causal relationships between personality and psychopathology.

Part VIII. Applied Personality Psychology

Proof of the value of personality psychology comes from its various real-world applications. For many years, personality scales have been applied in various domains in which assessment and evaluation of the individual are critical. These include diagnosing mental disorders, identifying exceptional or troubled children, and hiring people for jobs that may fit their personality. Contributors to this part of the Handbook cover the major applications of personality to assessment in the educational, occupational and clinical domains, including criminology. Beyond selection of individuals for therapy or employment, understanding of personality may also support and inform interventions, including choosing appropriate treatments for clinical patients, supporting the rehabilitation of criminals and creating supportive learning environments for individual students in schools and universities. These more 'active' applications require a more detailed, theory-driven understanding of personality. For example, the clinician needs to know what an individual's personality profile means in relation to their neurological, cognitive and social functioning. Best practice in all of the areas surveyed requires integration of psychometrically rigorous assessment with theory-based understanding.

In two linked chapters, Zeidner reviews educational applications of personality. The first chapter addresses school psychology, which is concerned with fostering students' emotional and intellectual adjustment, often in relation to abnormality. By contrast, educational psychologists focus primarily on issues of student learning and achievement. School psychologists have become especially focused on the emotional health needs of students. Students may benefit from various psychological interventions directed toward problems, including limited social skills, test anxiety and traumatic reactions. Zeidner's second chapter, on educational psychology, considers how personality influences such key educational outcomes as academic performance, social interactions with teachers and other children, and motivation and classroom conduct. Educational psychologists may usefully seek to influence the social-cognitive factors that may mediate the impact of personality on the educational experience, including academic self-concept, self-efficacy, attributions and goal-setting. Educational interventions may thus be founded on the social-cognitive theory described in previous chapters of this Handbook.

The workplace is also a major arena for the application of personality psychology. In the first of two chapters on industrial-organizational applications, Burch and Anderson review personality at work. Improved psychometric models of personality, coupled with advances in understanding of personality processes, have lead to a resurgence of this field. The Five-Factor Model provides a useful framework for organizing evidence that personality traits relate to both job performance and additional work-related behaviours, such as organizational citizenship, leadership, career path and counter-productive behaviours.

Stuhlmacher, Briggs and Cellar review workplace safety and personality. Various personality traits have been linked to measures of indices in safety in domains such as hazardous industries (e.g., mining, construction) and vehicle driving. High neuroticism, low agreeableness and low conscientiousness have all been linked to higher accident involvement in occupational settings, although effect sizes are often modest. The authors recommend a greater focus on narrow rather than broad traits in future research; for example, sensation-seeking may be more predictive in comparison with the broader trait of extraversion.

Canter and Young consider the relationship between personality and crime. Two major themes are interpersonal characteristics of crime, which may differentiate criminals, and the emotional benefits the offender derives from criminality. Although criminality may be linked to traits such as extraversion and neuroticism, it may be more useful to explore the narrative meaning of the crime for the offender. The role of personality in the performance of criminal actions must be understood within the social and cultural context of those actions.

Mullins-Sweatt and Widiger adopt the Five-Factor Model (FFM) as a framework for discussing diagnosis and assessment of personality disorders. Dimensional models of personality have advantages for diagnosis over traditional categorical schemes, exemplified by the DSM-IV-TR. They conclude by recommending a four-step diagnostic procedure that assesses the 'Big Five' traits, identifies concurrent social impairments, evaluates whether impairments are clinically significant and matches the individual's personality profile to prototypic profiles of important diagnostic constructs. However, they argue that the optimal description is provided by the person's actual FFM profile.

The treatment of personality disorders is discussed by Warren. She begins by discussing the difficulties of diagnosing personality disordered clients and engaging them in treatment. The treatments themselves may be divided into three main strands, related to the medical model (e.g., pharmacological treatments), psychodynamic theory and cognitive-behavioural theory. However, therapy often involves an eclectic approach that borrows elements from several different theories, pointing the way towards a more integrative understanding of personality disorder.

PART I

Foundation Issues

1   Conceptual issues in personality theory

Susan Cloninger

The scientific field of personality is generally traced back to the year 1937, when Gordon Allport published *Personality: a psychological interpretation*, Ross Stagner published *Psychology of personality*, and Henry Murray's 1938 book *Explorations in personality* was rising on the horizon. These American developments built upon earlier philosophical and psychiatric, as well as psychological, work in the United States (e.g., William James) and in Europe (e.g., Sigmund Freud, Pierre Janet, Kurt Lewin, and many others) (Lombardo and Foschi 2002).

As it developed, the field of personality changed its conceptualizations. Some themes endured, while others faded. Diverse perspectives have always coexisted, and changes that pleased some were mourned by others. Besides this internal dialogue among personality psychologists themselves, psychologists in other specialties and the public at large influenced and reacted to these developments. As part of a larger intellectual dialogue, the worldviews of various theorists (Freud's pessimistic emphasis on repression and sexual conflict, Maslow's optimism about human potential, Skinner's emphasis on environmental determinism and the possibility of a Utopian community, to name a few), capture diverse worldviews that contribute to their acceptance or rejection, based on their compatibility and perceived usefulness for individual lives (cf. Koltko-Rivera 2004).

A diversity of personality theories

Throughout the history of scientific psychology, diverse approaches to the field have competed. Among the perspectives that each have a distinct history are the psychodynamic perspective, the trait perspective, the learning perspective, the humanistic perspective, the cognitive perspective, and the biological perspective. (See Table 1.1.) Each approach has developed over time with contributions from major theorists and researchers, and while the perspectives have sometimes influenced one another, they have taken different tactics toward a global theory of personality and in guiding the observations that researchers make and the interventions that practitioners implement.

Definitions of personality highlight the distinct concerns of each perspective. Raymond Cattell used traits to predict behaviour, defining personality as 'that which permits a prediction of what a person will do in a given situation' (Cattell 1950, p. 2), and later defining a personality trait as that 'which defines what a

Table 1.1 *Major perspectives in personality.*

Perspective	Major concepts	Contributors
Biological	temperament, evolution, adaptation, altruism, sexual jealousy, heredity, neurotransmitter pathways, cerebral hemisphere function	D. Buss, Eysenck, J. A. Gray, C. R. Cloninger, Kagan
Cognitive	expectancy, self-efficacy, outcome expectation, schema, cognitive person variable, personal construct, reciprocal determinism, modelling, constructive alternativism, life narrative	Mischel, Bandura, Kelly, Beck
Humanistic	self-actualization, creativity, flow, spirituality, personal responsibility, freedom, choice, openness to experience, unconditional positive regard, acceptance, empathy, real self, hierarchy of needs, peak experience, positive psychology	Maslow, Rogers, Seligman, Csikszentmihalyi
Learning	reinforcement, punishment, stimulus, response, conditioning, extinction, shaping, discrimination learning, generalization, situation, act frequency, basic behavioural repertoire, labelling, gradients of approach and avoidance	Skinner, Staats, Dollard and Miller
Psychodynamic	libido, conflict, id, ego, superego, defence mechanisms, Oedipal conflict, fixation, repression, attachment, object-relations	Freud, Jung, Adler, Erikson, Horney, Klein, Sullivan, Chodorow, Westen, Kohut, Kernberg
Trait	trait, type, facet, factors, Neuroticism/ Emotional Stability, Extraversion	Allport, Cattell, McCrae and Costa

person will do when faced with a defined situation' (Cattell 1979, p. 14). Behavioural definitions are typically more sparse, focusing on behaviour itself, and the behavioural habits formed by experience. In its early radical form, behaviourism avoided positing concepts that were not observable (Skinner 1950), but later cognitive behavioural approaches include expectations and other cognitions as component parts of personality, theorized to determine an individual's behaviour (Bandura 1986).

Some definitions emphasize integration of personality, specifying what must be integrated. From his personological trait approach (an approach that asserts the importance of traits, but also the integration of the whole person), Gordon Allport (1937) defined personality as 'the dynamic organization within the individual of those psychophysical systems that determine his unique adjustments to the environment' (Allport 1937, p. 48). A definition that gives a modern twist to this personological integration is offered by McAdams and Pals (2006), who define personality as 'an individual's unique variation on the general evolutionary design for human nature, expressed as a developing pattern of dispositional traits, characteristic adaptations, and integrative life stories complexly and differentially situated in culture' (McAdams and Pals 2006, p. 212). The emphasis on dynamics and development in these two personological definitions reminds us that some theories emphasize function and change, in contrast to the typically more static trait emphasis on description. If commonality is to be found among these diverse definitions, it may be a frequently shared assumption that an individual's personality begins with biologically innate components, both those shared with others and those that are distinct because of heredity or other influences; that over the life course, these innate tendencies are channelled by the influence of many factors, including family experience, culture and other experience; and that the resulting pattern of habitual behaviours, cognitions, emotional patterns, and so on constitutes personality.

The detailed history of the exploration of the various personality perspectives would be exciting and informative, but the task of this chapter is to stand back and look at a broader picture in order to take stock of where we have been and what might guide future explorations in personality.

The grand theorist approach

Historically, personality theory was taught from a 'grand theorist' approach in which selected theories proposed by individuals were presented separately. Many of these theorists (Sigmund Freud, Alfred Adler, Gordon Allport, Carl Rogers, to name a few) have become well known and are cited in most introductory psychology texts. (See Table 1.2.) This telling of our discipline's history has the advantage of presenting comprehensive theories that have an internal logic, but the disadvantage of omitting or understating more recent advances that seldom fit this model. The classical grand theories often reflected the professional and life experience of their originators (Monte 1977), and their fundamental assumptions (Skinner's belief in environmental determination; Maslow's optimism; Freud's assumption of conflict) are not universally shared. This particularity fosters fragmentation in the discipline of personality. Followers of each grand theorist adopted, applied and revised the competing theories in relative isolation, only occasionally reaching across their separate schools of thought to find a common language. As the history of personality theory is generally told, diverse theoretical paradigms as they were described by philosopher of science, Thomas Kuhn (1970) have coexisted, and the field – like the early physical sciences that Kuhn described – has not agreed upon a shared paradigm that would foster cooperation and steady incremental scientific growth. Instead, it is divided by conflict among paradigms. Others describe the competition but doubt that the combatants have

Table 1.2 *Milestones in the history of personality.*

1890	William James publishes *Principles of psychology* (with sections on the self and other personality-related issues)
1900	Sigmund Freud publishes *The interpretation of dreams*
1907	Alfred Adler publishes A study of organic inferiority and its psychical compensation
1908	Mary Calkins describes the self (in several papers)
1910	Carl Jung publishes The association method (research on complexes)
1923	Sigmund Freud publishes *The ego and the id* (structures of personality)
1927	Gordon Allport publishes Concepts of trait and personality
1935	Henry Murray publishes the Thematic Apperception Test (TAT)
1936	Anna Freud publishes *The ego and the mechanisms of defence*
1937	Gordon Allport publishes *Personality: a psychological interpretation*
1937	Karen Horney publishes *The neurotic personality of our time*
1938	B. F. Skinner publishes *The behaviour of the organisms*
1938	Henry Murray publishes *Explorations in personality*
1939	John Dollard and Neal Miller publish *Frustration and aggression*
1943	Abraham Maslow publishes A theory of human motivation
1950	Erik Erikson publishes *Childhood and society*
1951	Carl Rogers publishes *Client-centered therapy*
1952	Hans Eysenck publishes *The structure of human personality*
1954	Abraham Maslow publishes *Motivation and personality*
1955	Lee Cronbach and Paul Meehl publish Construct validity in psychological tests
1955	George Kelly publishes *The psychology of personal constructs*
1957	Lee Cronbach publishes The two disciplines of scientific psychology
1961	The *Journal of Humanistic Psychology* begins
1961	Albert Bandura and collaborators describe learning of aggression through modelling (Bobo doll study)
1962	Founding of the Association for Humanistic Psychology
1967	Hans Eysenck publishes *The biological basis of personality*
1968	Abraham Maslow publishes *Toward a psychology of being*
1968	Walter Mischel challenges the trait model in *Personality and assessment*
1971	B. F. Skinner publishes *Beyond freedom and dignity*
1973	Albert Bandura publishes *Aggression: a social learning analysis*
1976	Richard Dawkins publishes *The selfish gene*
1978	Mary Ainsworth describes attachment in young children
1987	McCrae and Costa present data on the Five-Factor trait Model
1987	Daniel Schachter describes implicit memory (alternative view of unconscious cognition)
1989	David Buss describes cross-cultural universals in the evolution of mating behaviour
2000	Martin Seligman and Mihaly Csikszentmihalyi publish Positive psychology: an introduction

matured sufficiently to be labelled paradigms in the Kuhnian sense. In either case, personality is a fragmented discipline.

The conceptual breadth of each of the grand theories and their implications for practice and research contributed to their historical importance. Additionally, social factors elevated their influence, including many theorists' professorships at prestigious institutions, such as Harvard University, where they influenced the next generation of personality psychologists. Hall and Lindzey's (1957) influential personality textbook gave enduring recognition to many of these theorists (including Freud and Jung), adding others with new editions (e.g., Eysenck, Bandura and Kelly in the 1978 third edition). Even its fourth edition (Hall, Lindzey and Campbell 1998) continues the 'grand theorist' organizational structure, which has been adopted by many others (e.g., Ewen 2003; Feist and Feist 2001; Schultz and Schultz 2005). To be sure, these 'grand theorists' are grouped to show shared perspectives (e.g., psychoanalytic, humanistic, behavioural or learning, and so on), and the underlying assumptions of the theories (such as Rogers' assumption that people have, at core, a tendency toward self-actualization) can be elaborately compared across theories (Maddi 1996, 2006). Sometimes the great names are omitted from all or at least some chapter titles to call attention to the underlying theoretical perspectives or to acknowledge the difficulty of selecting a single seminal founder of a particular perspective (Carver and Scheier 2008; Cloninger 2008; Magnavita 2002). Explicit discussion of future trends that build on, but go beyond, these grand theories may be added briefly as a final chapter (Ryckman 2004). This provides some sense of theoretical progress over time, both within these perspectives, and in the historical waxing and waning of the various perspectives. Nonetheless, both the grand theorist approach and the competing perspectives organization of this approach portray the field of personality as fragmented.

Another approach is to focus on the content areas in which personality research is conducted – a *topical organization* of the field (Cervone and Pervin 2008; Larsen and Buss 2008). Connections with historical grand theories remain (as is to be expected) in some areas, but the focus shifts to particular areas of research and limited domain theories, instead of the broad comprehensive theories of the past. This strategy avoids undue preoccupation with affirming or challenging the fundamental assumptions of a theory, and avoids defending or attacking the theorist or accusing revisionists of disloyalty or personal pathology – a non-professional sort of discourse that has made its way even into scholarly journals. The topical approach facilitates research progress in particular content areas, though it lacks the integrative vision of a comprehensive theory.

Could the prevailing fragmentation of personality theory be overcome? The effort has been made to portray an integrated field of personality, combining contributions from various theorists (Lester 1995), but in general, consensus is missing in describing the theoretical connections among the fragments in sufficient detail to guide researchers and practitioners. Personality remains split.

Psychology's two disciplines

Throughout the history of psychology, observers have noted a dichotomy between those who emphasize rigorous scientific methods, on the one hand, and those who are more open to subjective experience and a holistic study of the person: what William James (1902) called the 'tough-minded' and the 'tender-minded'. This dichotomy has been variously called the 'two disciplines of scientific psychology', experimental and correlational (Cronbach 1957) and the 'two cultures', scientific and humanistic (Kimble 1984). It reflects a broader intellectual rift between science and humanism, impacting both the content and methods of personality theory and research. As James indicated, the two poles arguably reflect the personalities of those on each side of the dichotomy (Conway 1992; Feist 2006).

The founder of American psychology, William James (1890), included 'tender-minded' topics such as consciousness and religion from a viewpoint that embraced both psychology and philosophy. Gordon Allport, often credited with the founding of personality as a separate field, himself 'found a way to exploit the value in each [of these] perspective[s]', the science and the art of psychology (Gifford 2004). The 'tough-minded' pole, well represented in experimental laboratories modelled after that of Wilhelm Wundt, found its influence in personality through behaviourism, with the work of John B. Watson and, later, B. F. Skinner. The other pole, the tender-minded or humanistic, persisted as well. For example, during the 1950s, Gardner Murphy took a more integrative stance, and a humanistic psychology movement grew, marking its entry by the establishment of the Association for Humanistic Psychology in 1962, with Abraham Maslow, Carl Rogers and Rollo May among the founding members. Today, we feel the tension between those who would emphasize the physical basis of personality and those who tend toward thoughts and consciousness. Bridges are being forged, however, as theorists and researchers try to apply rigorous empirical methods to the 'big picture' issues like consciousness, religion and free will that early psychology left to the tender-minded (e.g., Greenberg, Koole and Pyszczynski 2004; Rychlak 1997).

Major issues in personality theory

What questions should personality theory address? What data should be collected, using what methods?

First person or third person: the experience of the self or observers

Some of the grand theorists, we know, drew on their own subjective life experience in developing their formal theories. Should a theory be a formalized version of personal insights that come from one's own experience, or does science require greater distance? Should personal experiences of research participants be data for theory validation? We know that, whether conceptualized as a defence mechanism or a cognitive deficit, people's self-understanding is error-prone (McKay, Langdon and Coltheart 2005), and so those reports should not necessarily be taken at face value. Nonetheless, people's first person experiences have proved a useful concept throughout the history of psychology and personality theory. Approaches that emphasize people's subjective experience and the stories of their lives have a personal, lively appeal that cannot be matched by more abstract theories or comprehensive organizing schemes (cf., Loevinger 1996). Aside from their value for psychologists, such ideas also appeal to popular audiences.

The introspectionist methods of early scientific psychology, at the beginning of the twentieth century, studied the mind by subjective observation, relying on subjects' verbal reports for data. The historical descriptions of introspectionism are often exaggerated and the usual version of a subsequent behavioural revolution and then a cognitive revolution in psychology is overly simplified (Costall 2006). Subjective experience, especially experience of ourselves, not of external stimuli, has been an important theme throughout the history of personality theories. Over a century ago, William James (1890) wrote thoughtfully on the self, retaining the idea of a 'spiritual me' from the era when scientific constraints had not yet strengthened their veto voice over such a soul-like idea, supplementing the spiritual self with a variety of selves (material, social, and so on) more appealing to a secular audience. Historians note that James' descriptions of the self resemble an earlier French publication by Paul Janet (Lombardo and Foschi 2003). With the rise of scientific psychology laboratories, the self received less attention, until its re-emergence with the personological emphases of Gordon Allport, Henry Murray, and others in the late 1930s (Coon 2000). Among therapists, Carl Rogers (1961) claimed that progress in psychotherapy requires attending to a person's experience of self. In this tradition, Bohart (2006) interprets diverse findings from psychotherapy research as evidence that it is the clients themselves, not their therapists, who are the most important change agents in psychotherapy.

Self-reflection is an implicit basis for using self-report questionnaires to measure personality. It is explicit in some theoretical formulations, such as those popular in recent decades that describe life stories or narratives as important aspects of identity and functioning (e.g., McAdams 1996), and those that emphasize self-concept and identity (Loevinger and Knoll 1983). In terror management theory, self-esteem provides a buffer against the anxiety caused by awareness of mortality (Greenberg, Pyszczynski and Solomon 1986; Pyszczynski, Greenberg, Solomon et al. 2004). The theoretical concept of possible selves demonstrates the power of self-reflective cognition to change behaviour, at least when the social context provides needed support and opportunity (Oyserman, Bybee and Terry 2006). Self-referent cognitions are obviously developed with experience, and so these concepts provide a place for theorists to link the influence of family and culture on personality.

Social and cultural factors

Since personality is presumably learned in a familial and societal context, theory should elaborate on these processes. So far, progress is slow. The historical theories have proposed influences of the family (Freud, Adler), of gender (Horney), and of social class (Dollard and Miller), but all of these in a Euro-American context, and assuming the values and expectations of an individualistic society. More recently, cross-cultural investigations of personality measures report similarities in the factor structure of personality tests across cultures, but there are differences too, and much theoretical and empirical work remains (Cahan and White 1992; Fung and Ng 2006; Norenzayan and Heine 2005; Rothbaum, Weisz, Pott *et al.* 2000; Sedikides, Gaertner and Vevea 2005).

Studying the individual or comparing people: idiographic and nomothetic approaches

Should we emphasize intensive study of individuals, or comparisons between people? On the one hand, understanding a personality suggests knowing the details of the individual: his or her history, actions in various settings, thoughts and emotions, and so on. Personality from this point of view is a scientific version of a biography or autobiography, a life story. On the other hand, a compelling argument can be made for emphasizing comparisons among individuals, which we do in everyday life (Who is more assertive? Who is more responsible?) and which is useful for such practical purposes as deciding whom to hire for a particular job.

Idiographic approaches study individuals, while *nomothetic* approaches seek generalizations and make comparisons based on the study of many people. This distinction, proposed by the German philosopher Wilhelm Windelband in 1892, was discussed by American personality psychologist Gordon Allport (1937), who argued that idiographic traits that resided within individuals were the 'real' causes within personality. Windelband's idiographic approach was what he called a 'historical science' in that it emphasized the history of one person (Maher and Gottesman 2005). This approach requires considerable investigation of one person and so is suitable to psychohistorical investigation and to clinical applications.

European psychiatrists in the nineteenth century, whose work influenced later American personality psychology, reported individual case studies. Therapy traditions such as that begun by Freud (Bornstein 2005) use idiographic approaches. Early publications in the American *Journal of Abnormal Psychology* also featured a majority of idiographic reports until its transformation to become the *Journal of Abnormal and Social Psychology* under the American Psychological Association, when nomothetic methods prevailed; and from the 1920s to the 1930s, other publications reflected a rise in nomothetic trait research (Lombardo and Foschi 2003).

Idiographic approaches produce understanding and offer intervention insights for particular individuals, whether through psychotherapy or behaviour modification. They are particularly useful for studying personality dynamics, that is, how motivated processes occur over time in an individual. Without additional evidence from other people, though, we cannot assume that what is found in one individual will also apply to others. Freud's claim that the Oedipus conflict that he found in himself and a few patients was universal to all men, without nomothetic research validation, went beyond his observations. Nomothetic approaches, such as the Five-Factor Model, provide evidence for generality of concepts across the populations studied and are suited for studying individual differences, that is, identifying how one person compares with others. Nomothetic research is more often quantitative, expressed in mathematical measures, but some idiographic research (including behaviour modification reports and Cattell's P-technique) goes beyond qualitative descriptions to include quantitative counts of behaviour. The two approaches complement one another, and the study of personality needs both.

Individual differences

Personality theory has been persistently concerned with the description of individual differences. In principle, if there are naturally existing categories, we may speak of *types*, of natural categories. Though the word 'type' has been used to refer to types of temperament (Kagan 1994), and attachment (Ainsworth *et al.* 1978), for example, the underlying determinants (such as anxiety) that produce these categories are continuous. However convenient for descriptive and even analytical purposes, these are not types in the sense of discrete, natural categories; nor are the popular Jungian types, measured by the Myers-Briggs Type Indicator. Continuous dimensions (traits and factors) are far easier to find.

Allport (1937) argued that traits are a central concept in personality, building on European research and theory (Matthews and Deary 1998). The question 'What units shall we employ?' had no easy answer when Allport (1958) asked it, and the choices have become even more bewildering since then (Ozer 1996). Researchers have measured a variety of specific traits, such as field dependence, sensation-seeking and achievement motivation, predicting specific behaviours from domain-specific personality tests. The trait concept suffered a setback when Walter Mischel (1968) pointed out that situations were more influential than traits in predicting behaviour. This *situational challenge* to the trait paradigm came with the rise of social psychology and decline of personality psychology, as sub-fields in psychology. But the issue itself was oversimplified. The impact of personality on behaviour requires more sophisticated theory and analysis than a simple correlation (Epstein 1980, 2007). Mischel himself later offered a conceptually more sophisticated, interactionist version of trait theory in which the effect of a person's trait depends upon the situational context of behaviour (Mischel and Shoda 1995).

Along with this advance in trait theory, Mischel and other cognitive behaviourists (Bandura 1986) emphasized a person's cognitions as refined trait concepts: no longer defined in terms of the observable behaviour alone, but the person's thoughts or beliefs about the situation, his capabilities, her probable outcomes, and so on. The proliferation of measures of self-efficacy expectations in many domains of behaviour attests to the impact of this cognitive reconceptualization of trait concepts.

In addition to cognitive traits, factor analytic and biological trait models are popular today. Comprehensive trait models assess several traits derived from factor analysis of self-report items, intended to represent the major variations in the human population and thought to originate from biological variations. These include the Five-Factor Model, consisting of extraversion, neuroticism, openness, conscientiousness and agreeableness (Goldberg 1993; McCrae 1991); Eysenck's (1967) three-factor model consisting of extraversion, neuroticism and psychoticism; J. A. Gray's (1970) model of behavioural activation and behavioural inhibition; and others. Two reoccurring dimensions across diverse models are extraversion-introversion and emotional stability-instability (neuroticism). Biological investigations and recent cross-cultural investigations generally support that these are largely universal, biologically-based dimensions of individual differences.

An alternative descriptive strategy is to select units based on their function within personality. Freud's id, ego and superego are such functional structures, as are the three functions of motivation, emotion and cognition (Mayer 2003). Behavioural approaches call for measurement of a person's behaviours, such as the early learned habits that constitute a basic behavioural repertoire in Arthur Staats' (1996) model. Although trait and factor models prevail as descriptors of individual differences, then, there are theoretical alternatives.

Development: continuity and change over time

Personality theories address development in various ways. Does the progress of time simply reveal the innate personality as it unfolds (as biological and many trait approaches imply), or provide opportunities for change (as learning theories suggest)? Do people develop in a gradual, continuous way, or through discontinuous stages (as Erikson's psychosocial theory outlines)? Are there critical or sensitive stages, when experience has a particularly strong influence (as psychoanalytic and attachment theories describe)?

Longitudinal research, which is needed to address questions of change or continuity, is challenging, but fortunately some major longitudinal studies enlighten us about personality continuity and change, including ego-control (Block and Block 2006), and emotionality and self-regulation (Kubzansky, Martin and Buka 2004). Stability from childhood to adulthood, while significant in many cases, is low enough to suggest that significant change occurs, especially before adulthood (Caspi, Roberts and Shiner 2005; Hampson and Goldberg 2006).

Biology and nature

The idea that biology influences personality is nothing new. It was a familiar concept to the ancient Greeks, and an assumption behind the eugenics movement in the late nineteenth and first half of the twentieth centuries. Many personality theorists over the years have assumed the influence of biology, even before scientific data were available to inform these assertions. Some models describe biology in terms of a reservoir of energy or drive – Freud's libido or Cattell's ergs – common to all, but that each person channels in a distinct way. Currently popular evolutionary approaches describe a common ancestral basis of personality, but one that is adaptive by having individual differences in the population in the distribution of personality traits – empathy to some, dominance to others, and so on, with many of these traits distributed differently for males and females (Buss 1999; Silverman, Choi and Peters 2007). The idea that an inherited personality predisposition, *temperament*, produces enduring individual differences across the lifespan has been a pervasive assumption in the field (Kagan 1994).

Today, an explosion in neuroscience knowledge permits modern personality theorists to describe detailed biological mechanisms that underlie individual differences in personality. Neurotransmitter explanations are offered by Eysenck (1967), Gray (1970), and others. Modern theories describe biology and experience (e.g., reward and punishment) interacting to shape personality, in contrast to antiquated 'either-or' conceptualization of the nature-nurture question.

Based on the assumption that the psychological mind is grounded in the biological brain and body, emerging neuroscience evidence of the brain as modular suggests a model of personality that is also built of components. Pleasure, pain and other emotions have different neural pathways, helping theorists understand why people differ in their reaction to the same events. Defence mechanisms, described since Freud's time and part of the established language of psychoanalytically inspired theory, are being recast in terms of brain processes and learning, instead of flow of libido (Kandel 2006; Northoff, Bermpohl, Schoeneich and Boeker 2007). Neuroscientists collaborating with experienced Buddhist meditators report that the mind can influence the brain, as well as the reverse (Davidson 2001).

Adjustment and wellbeing

Personality psychologists investigate 'normal' personality, but many concepts relate to adjustment, and the boundary between the personality and the clinical psychology areas is fuzzy. Clinical psychology, despite its close connections with medicine (e.g., using the same *Diagnostic and statistical manual of mental disorders*), has had important influences on personality theory. Many of the classic personality theories were devised in a therapy context, either by physicians (e.g., Sigmund Freud, Alfred Adler, Karen Horney) or by psychologists (e.g., Carl Rogers). The psychology clinic at Harvard University, from the 1920s onward, provided a place for psychologists to conduct research on personality from a more holistic view of the person, influenced strongly by the psychoanalytic ideas of Henry Murray (1938). This approach lent itself to the idiographic study of individual persons. Murray applied the psychoanalytic model to interpret the personality of Adolf Hitler during the Second World War and to predict his future behaviour, in a report commissioned by the United States government to assist the Allies in defeating him (Langer 1972).

Although adjustment and pathology have been reoccurring themes throughout the history of personality theory, the proper conceptualization of these themes is controversial. Some theorists (Allport and Freud, for example) describe conflict or fragmentation within personality as a sign of maladjustment, and unity as evidence of health. Borrowing from medicine, the medical model of disease had some appeal, such as its non-judgmental implications. However, it has been criticized as overemphasizing the biological causes of personality maladjustment and neglecting social and cultural aspects (Szasz 1960). Behavioural interpretations emphasize maladaptive learning.

Empirically, some researchers describe pathology from a trait perspective as extreme scores on various traits (e.g., Eysenck 1994; Markon, Krueger and Watson 2005; O'Connor 2002). An obvious example is extremely high neuroticism, predisposing a person to high anxiety. Purely descriptive trait measures, of course, beg the question of whether the developmental origins and dynamic implications of those measured traits are comparable in the normal and abnormal populations.

Humanists, including Abraham Maslow (1976), advocated studying the healthy personality, not only those who are disturbed. Recent trends mark a fulfilment of this mandate. The popular movement called *positive psychology* continues the theme from humanistic psychology, focusing on healthy and creative human potentials (Gable and Haidt 2005; Seligman and Csikszentmihalyi 2000). The approach strives to understand and promote such individual strengths as happiness and creativity, and desirable societal conditions such as peace. Even brief interventions are reported to increase happiness (Seligman, Steen, Park and Peterson 2005).

These reoccurring issues in the study of personality are addressed from various theoretical perspectives.

Theories in science

Knowing something about scientific theories and how they are tested can help to understand the past and enhance the future of personality psychology. The classical view of theory describes a level of theoretical terms, which are abstract, and a level of observations, which can be empirically observed (Carnap 1956). The two levels are associated by correspondence rules. At the abstract level, a theory includes concepts (or theoretical constructs, as described below) and statements about how they are related (propositions). At this abstract level, a theory offers a framework for organizing knowledge. When the theory is translated into a format that can be tested, by means of correspondence rules, it can be accepted or modified, and scientific progress can occur. (See Figure 1.1.)

Theoretical constructs

Personality psychology has many concepts that cannot, themselves, be directly observed. Called *hypothetical constructs* in a classic theoretical description by

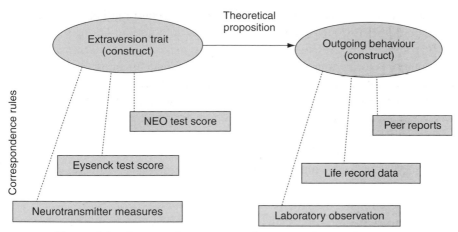

Figure 1.1. *Theoretical constructs and correspondence rules.*

MacCorquodale and Meehl (1948), these theoretical terms can be inferred indirectly but are not themselves directly observable. Personality psychologists use terms like 'adjustment' and 'extraversion' and 'self-esteem' but cannot observe any of them directly, only indirectly through observations and measurements that are imperfect. The constructs are inferred by a network of correlations with various observations. Converging evidence affirms the reality, or at least the usefulness, of a construct. Consider 'extraversion': if the same people are found to be extraverted when measured by self-report, by peer-report, and by behavioural measures, then the construct of 'extraversion' is supported. If not, the construct may be invalid, or perhaps there is a problem with the measurement. Thus theorists propose a *nomological net* of associations among constructs and observables that can guide research (Cronbach and Meehl 1955).

The idea of construct validity stimulated theoretical advances and efforts to measure the elusive units of theory, not only in the clinical psychology area where Paul Meehl first proposed them, but also in the broader personality area of trait psychology (Peterson 2006). The extreme radical behaviourism of B. F. Skinner, in contrast, focused solely on observables, excluding theoretical constructs, and thus limiting its explanatory power (cf., Botterill and Carruthers 1999), until cognitive behaviourism expanded its scope.

Measuring constructs: correspondence rules

Science requires systematic, controlled observation. Since constructs themselves are not directly observable, they must be translated into a form that can be observed, in order for empirical testing to be possible. This is implemented through *correspondence rules*, which specify observable phenomena that are manifestations of a construct. Personality assessment provides diverse ways to measure the amount of a theoretical construct that a person has. Since no measure corresponds perfectly to the theorized construct, it is helpful to use a variety of measures, each with different imperfections, to make an assessment: self-report questionnaires, behaviour ratings, peer nomination, responses to laboratory tasks, and so on. Strong evidence for a construct exists if these various measures of a particular trait correlate highly with one another. Lower correlations are expected with other traits, even if they are both measured in the same way (e.g., self-esteem and achievement motivation both measured by self-report should not be highly correlated). These considerations inspired advances in personality assessment by using what is called a 'multi-trait, multi-method matrix' (Campbell and Fiske 1959) to demonstrate that abstract theoretical constructs, not measurement techniques, explain high correlations among observations.

When clearly defined and stated in advance of observation, these correspondence rules distinguish science from pseudo-science (Klee 1997). They serve as checks on perception of verification that is based on expectation and hope instead of on objective prediction. If an expectation is incorrect, well formulated correspondence rules contribute to discovering the error. While this rigorous practice is necessary for testing the validity of a theory, some argue that an approach more open to intuition is needed for the earlier phase of developing theory – for proposing the constructs and their relationships to other constructs in the first place. Ignoring the importance of this intuitive, theory-generation phase can lead to a rigorous but sterile science.

Measuring a proposed construct by multiple methods (self-report questionnaire, behavioural observation, and so forth) and finding similar results supports the *construct validity* of the proposed construct. If predicted results are not confirmed, then the theory may need revision (Smith 2005). For example, if one method finds one result, and another method disagrees (as is the case when achievement motivation is measured by self-report and by projective test (McClelland, Koestner and Weinberger 1989; Winter, John, Stewart *et al.* 1998)), that undermines the claim of construct validity. It might be that one of the measures accurately measures the proposed construct, but they do not both do so, or they would agree. In the case of achievement motivation, the correlation between the two measures is about zero, and one of them (the projective measure), but not the other (the self-report measure) predicts achievement behaviour. This finding is a reminder that self-report measures of personality should not be taken at face value; empirical evidence of their construct validity, from their ability to predict a criterion measure, is needed.

The availability of new measurement techniques can stimulate theoretical advances by providing additional ways to observe and test theoretical constructs. Advancement in biomedical technology has made it possible to measure the physical aspects of personality (brain function, biochemical profiles, and so on) with unprecedented detail. With that has come a dizzying parade of advancement in theories that relate personality constructs to the body. Another sort of new measure, this time of the mind, has come with the availability of well-trained meditators from Buddhist culture collaborating with Richard Davidson (2001), leading to research showing the power of the mind (meditation) over the brain (measured by brain imaging techniques). Mind and brain are separate measures in these studies, but the associations challenge our theoretical constructs. Is a physical construct causing a change in the mental? Is a mental construct causing a change in the physical? In either of these two cases, the brain and mind relationship would be represented by a theoretical proposition, in which one construct causes the other to change. Or are the mental and the physical simply two manifestations of a single theoretical mind-body construct? In that case, there would be no need for a theoretical proposition in the form of 'brain influences mind' or 'mind influences brain'. Instead, a single brain-mind construct would be tapped by correspondence rules for each. As measurement advances, it stimulates theory as well as confirming or disconfirming it, and theorists are devoting great attention to understanding the body-mind connection in human consciousness.

Criteria of a good theory

Theories that are consistent with known observations, and that encourage new observations, keep science moving forward. To maintain vitality, a perspective within personality must rejuvenate itself through continually checking its theory. Robert Bornstein (2005) explains what he terms the marginalization of psycho-analysis, which is often criticized for scientific failure, this way (p. 325):

> the diminished influence of contemporary psychoanalysis is largely a product of theory mismanagement: Rather than looking forward (to the evolving demands of science and practice) and outward (to ideas and findings in other areas of psychology and medicine), many psychoanalysts have chosen to look backward (at the seminal but dated contributions of early psychoanalytic practitioners) and inward (at their like-minded colleagues' own analytic writings).

Theories evolve. Criteria for judging the worth of theories offer directions for their growth, not static rules for accepting or rejecting them once and for all.

Prediction and validation

A good theory should make accurate predictions about observations. This is not to say that a person's every thought and action can be anticipated. There are too many influences, and too much imperfection in measuring even those determinants that have been identified, to expect perfect prediction. Even under the best of circumstances, theories can be expected to make only imperfect predictions about particular events. Theories offer idealized descriptions of natural events (Worrall 2000). So we settle for approximate prediction, for prediction that is statistically significant when aggregated over several cases. After all, predicting ahead of time is a stringent criterion. Like historians, personality psychologists may be able to make sense of almost any observation after the fact. Advance prediction is more difficult, but of course more convincing of theoretical validity.

Another kind of prediction is reported in some studies, in which outcomes of psychotherapy are predicted in two ways to see which is more accurate: by a mental health professional who has case material available, and by a statistical method in which data are used to make predictions, based on past research findings. A meta-analysis of such studies reports that the statistical method offers more accurate prediction (Aegisdottir, White, Spengler *et al.* 2006), and such results have been interpreted to forcefully argue for the superiority of science over clinical judgement (Dawes 1994). Statistical prediction is quite impressive and can be of practical value in making clinical decisions, but it is not the same as prediction from a theory. The statistical equations used to make prediction are not determined by a theory, but by empirical exploration (though theory may suggest where to look). So this sort of statistical prediction should not be confused with prediction that validates theory.

Simplicity and comprehensiveness

In addition, scientists prefer theories that are as *simple* as possible, predicting with as few variables as possible without sacrificing the accuracy of the prediction. While there is no guarantee that the universe is simple, *parsimony* gives theories an edge. Why would astronomers accept a convoluted set of planetary orbits around the earth to explain celestial observations, when simpler elliptical orbits around the sun explained the same observations, unless for non-scientific reasons, to maintain the worldview of an Earth-centred universe? In personality (more controversially), why add an elaborate psychoanalytic model of personality structures and defence mechanisms to explain forgetting of childhood memories, if well-supported, simple cognitive mechanisms can account for the same phenomena (Hassin, Uleman and Bargh 2005; Kihlstrom 1987)? There may be reasons for selecting a less parsimonious explanation; it may account for other phenomena, for example. But the traditional advice of *Ockham's razor* dictates choosing the simpler of two competing explanations, other things being equal.

Another criterion for selecting one theory over another is the breadth of phenomena that it can explain. Those theories that are more *comprehensive*, explaining more observations, are preferred. Comprehensiveness should not come at the expense of precision, however. A scientist would be unlikely to accept 'the will of God' as an adequate scientific explanation of all that happens, from triumphs to catastrophes, because of the imprecision of prediction. Within personality, consider the comprehensive application of evolutionary explanation for a wide range of behaviour: parent-child interactions, sex differences in sexual fidelity and spatial ability, aggression and war, empathy, deception, and more. Scientific acceptance of these explanations is diminished, though, to the extent that the theory fails to account for the precise circumstances when the phenomena will occur.

Scientific evaluation of psychoanalytic theory

Psychoanalytic theory has often been criticized for failure to use the scientific method, preferring clinical observation and induction to empirical testing and falsification. Psychoanalysts' rejection of the scientific process of objective empirical verification leaves them isolated from the rest of the academic community and has been manifested in heated professional and sometimes personal criticisms. Not all therapists have objected to this call for scientific scrutiny. Outside of psychoanalytic theory, Carl Rogers pioneered the empirical testing of person-centred therapy techniques, and the research that he began has, cumulatively, supported most of his therapy suggestions (Kirschenbaum and Jourdan 2005; Rogers and Dymond 1954).

Can psychoanalysis be reconciled with scientific methods? There are hopeful signs. Some psychoanalytically informed researchers are using methods in the scientific tradition of hypothesis testing to put psychoanalytic hypotheses to the test, challenging others to do the same in order to prevent the demise of psychoanalytic theory and to facilitate its reconnection with the mainstream (Bornstein 2001, 2005). Many concepts in personality theory today, including implicit memory, retrieval error, cognitive avoidance, person schema, and a central executive, to name a few, offer other language for phenomena observed earlier by psychoanalysis, according to Bornstein (2005). For example, the self-control depletion interpretation of how cognition is impaired after thoughts of death (Gailliot, Schmeichel and Baumeister 2006) is reminiscent of Freud's energy hypothesis in which the ego has limited resources, though the new theoretical framework lends itself more readily to laboratory research.

Beyond falsification? Questioning the traditional philosophy of science

Standard psychology textbooks, at least in American universities, emphasize hypothesis testing as central to the scientific method, instead of describing it as a late stage in a longer process (Proctor and Capaldi 2001b). (Europeans, according to Proctor and Capaldi, are less short-sighted.) This view of research is not limited to students, but is also prevalent among mainstream researchers, for whom a significant statistical test of a hypothesis has disproportionate value in the larger scheme of scientific progress. Some psychologists hold contrary views, criticizing this focus on hypothesis testing and urging more attention to interpretation and to appreciating that the particular methods of research are, themselves, in need of a more critical evaluation (Proctor and Capaldi 2001a).

Psychology's emphasis on disproving the null hypothesis as a research basic, is an assumption that reflects the impact of the philosophy of science espoused by Karl Popper. His influential 1934 book, *Logik der Forschung*, translated into English in 1959 as *The logic of scientific discovery* (Watkins 2000), challenged the earlier role of induction in science and elevated the alternative of deducting predictions from theory and conducting research to falsify these deductions, thus permitting errors to be uncovered and rejected.

This traditional philosophy of science was not devised for social science. Rychlak (1968) proposes that the content of our field requires a more dialectical science, more open to discovery of human nature, to supplement traditional science's emphasis on validation. In their effort to be scientific, many psychologists excluded teleological responses (such as self-directed goals and growth principles), looking for mechanistic cause-effect relationships instead. Rychlak (1997, 2000) proposes an alternative Logical Learning Theory that emphasizes intention and choice as central personality concepts. Rychlak (2000) and others contend that a theory that includes constructs like choice and free will does not contradict the scientific method of validation. To think that it does so is to erroneously equate the content of a theory with the method for its validation. More sophistication about philosophy of science may preclude this oversimplification, as well as other misunderstandings stemming from an exaggerated portrayal of paradigm conflict, based on Kuhn's (1970) theory, to foster a portrayal of scientific progress (Driver-Linn 2003; Green 2004; Klee 1997). A greater role for induction in creating theoretical ideas would be possible by using the approach of *grounded theory*, which gathers qualitative data and involves considerably more back and forth interaction between the researcher and the participant, thus differing from the quantitative, objective methods favoured by most researchers. It is more often used in counselling and psychotherapy (Ponterotto 2005; Rennie 2002) than in academic personality research.

Although textbooks generally teach that experiments function to test theory and are essentially independent of the theory, thus giving an objective, independent test, this idealizes the actual process by which sciences make progress. According to Gooding (2000), trial and error occurs in the laboratory as researchers attempt to find procedures that more or less match theoretical predictions, refining their measuring instruments, manipulations, and so forth. This unacknowledged shaping of experiments so that they work and can be portrayed as tests of theory, makes the findings of experiments less 'universal and timeless', more 'particular and local' (Gooding 2000, p. 124) than they appear to be. If this is so in the presumably more objective physical sciences, which Gooding (2000) describes, then how much more it can be in the psychological realm. Personality psychologists may be cautioned, therefore, to be particularly cautious about generalizing results from research settings to other places and times. The meanings of our theoretical constructs should not be assumed to be universal, unless considerable observation in diverse contexts provides an empirical basis for such an assumption.

Closing remarks

The field of personality is in a promising position for integrating its own diverse themes with knowledge from neuroscience and other disciplines in the family of biological and social sciences. Personality, among all the areas of psychology, is best suited to bridge the levels of explanation, to balance the competing intellectual appeals of neuroscience and of culture. It has always had a concern with the whole functioning person, though sometimes up close, like a mosaic, the pieces were more conspicuous than the overall picture. Those who argue for a holistic, integrative approach coexist with others who strive for rigorous methodology. That neither has prevailed has created a healthy tension that can stimulate theoretical development and exciting research.

References

Aegisdottir, S., White, M. J., Spengler, P. M., Maugherman, A. S., Anderson, L. A., Cook, R. S., Nichols, C. N., Lampropoulos, G. K., Walker, B. S., Cohen, G. and Rush, J. D. 2006. The meta-analysis of clinical judgment project: fifty-six years of accumulated research on clinical versus statistical prediction, *Counseling Psychologist* 34: 341–82

Ainsworth, M. D. S., Blehar, M. C., Waters, E. and Wall, S. 1978. *Patterns of attachment: a psychological study of the strange situation*. Hillsdale, NJ: Erlbaum

Allport, G. W. 1937. *Personality: a psychological interpretation*. New York: Holt
    1958. What units shall we employ?, in G. Lindzey (ed.), *Assessment of human motives*, pp. 239–60. New York: Rinehart

Bandura, A. 1986. *Social foundations of thought and action: a social cognitive theory*. Englewood Cliffs, NJ: Prentice-Hall

Block, J. and Block, J. H. 2006. Venturing a 30-year longitudinal study, *American Psychologist* 61: 315–27

Bohart, A. C. 2006. The client as active self-healer, in G. Stricker and J. Gold (eds.), *A casebook of psychotherapy integration*, pp. 241–51. Washington, DC: American Psychological Association

Bornstein, R. F. 2001. The impending death of psychoanalysis, *Psychoanalytic Psychology* 18: 3–20
    2005. Reconnecting psychoanalysis to mainstream psychology: challenges and opportunities, *Psychoanalytic Psychology* 22: 323–40

Botterill, G. and Carruthers, P. 1999. *The philosophy of psychology*. Cambridge University Press

Buss, D. M. 1999. Human nature and individual differences: the evolution of personality, in L. A. Pervin and O. P. John (eds.), *Handbook of personality: theory and research*, 2nd edn, pp. 31–56. New York: Guilford

Cahan, E. D. and White, S. H. 1992. Proposals for a second psychology, *American Psychologist* 47: 224–35

Campbell, D. and Fiske, D. 1959. Convergent and discriminant validation by the multitrait-multimethod matrix, *Psychological Bulletin* 56: 81–105

Carnap, R. 1956. The methodological character of theoretical concepts, in H. Feigel and M. Sciven (eds.), *Minnesota studies in the philosophy of science*, vol. I, *The foundations of science and the concepts of psychology and psychoanalysis*. Minneapolis: University of Minnesota Press

Carver, C. S. and Scheier, M. F. 2008. *Perspectives on personality*, 6th edn. Boston: Pearson/Allyn and Bacon

Caspi, A., Roberts, B. W. and Shiner, R. L. 2005. Personality development: stability and change, *Annual Review of Psychology* 56: 453–84

Cattell, R. B. 1950. *Personality: a systematic theoretical and factual study.* New York: McGraw-Hill

1979. *Personality and learning theory,* vol. I, *The structure of personality in its environment.* New York: Springer-Verlag

Cervone, D. and Pervin, L. A. 2008. *Personality: theory and research,* (10th edn. Hoboken, NJ: Wiley

Cloninger, S. C. 2008. *Theories of personality: understanding persons,* 5th edn. Upper Saddle River, NJ: Pearson Prentice Hall

Conway, J. 1992. A world of differences among psychologists, *Canadian Psychology* 33: 1–24

Coon, D. J. 2000. Salvaging the self in a world without a soul: William James's *The Principles of Psychology, History of Psychology* 3: 83–103

Costall, A. 2006. 'Introspection' and the mythical origins of scientific psychology, *Consciousness and Cognition* 15: 634–54

Cronbach, L. J. 1957. The two disciplines of scientific psychology, *American Psychologist* 12: 671–84

Cronbach, L. J. and Meehl, P. E. 1955. Construct validity in psychological tests, *Psychological Bulletin* 52: 281–302

Davidson, R. J. 2001. Toward a biology of positive affect and compassion, in R. J. Davidson and A. Harrington (eds.), *Visions of compassion: Western scientists and Tibetan Buddhists examine human nature,* pp. 107–30. Cary, NC: Oxford University Press

Dawes, R. M. 1994. *House of cards: psychology and psychotherapy built on myth.* New York: Free Press

Driver-Linn, E. 2003. Where is psychology going? Structural fault lines revealed by psychologists' use of Kuhn, *American Psychologist* 58: 269–78

Epstein, S. 1980. The self-concept: a review and the proposal of an integrated theory of personality, in E. Staub (ed.), *Personality: basic issues and current research,* pp. 82–131. Englewood Cliffs, NJ: Prentice-Hall

2007. Problems with McAdams and Pals's (2006) proposal of a framework for an integrative theory of personality, *American Psychologist* 62: 59–60

Ewen, R. B. 2003. *An introduction to theories of personality,* 6th edn. Mahwah, NJ: Erlbaum

Eysenck, H. J. 1967. *The biological basis of personality.* Springfield, IL: Thomas

1994. Normality-abnormality and the three-factor model of personality, in S. Strack and M. Lorr (eds.), *Differentiating normal and abnormal personality,* pp. 3–25. New York: Springer

Feist, G. J. 2006. How development and personality influence scientific thought, interest, and achievement, *Review of General Psychology* 10: 163–82

Feist, J. and Feist, G. J. 2001. *Theories of personality,* 5th edn. Boston: McGraw-Hill

Fung, H. H. and Ng, S. K. 2006. Age differences in the sixth personality factor: age differences in interpersonal relatedness among Canadians and Hong Kong Chinese, *Psychology and Aging* 21: 810–14

Gable, S. L. and Haidt, J. 2005. What (and why) is positive psychology?, *Review of General Psychology* 9: 103–10

Gailliot, M. T., Schmeichel, B. J. and Baumeister, R. F. 2006. Self-regulatory processes defend against the threat of death: effects of self-control depletion and trait self-control on thoughts and fears of dying, *Journal of Personality and Social Psychology* 91: 49–62

Gifford, R. 2004. Review of the book *Inventing personality: Gordon Allport and the science of selfhood*, *Canadian Psychology* 45: 187–8

Goldberg, L. R. 1993. The structure of phenotypic personality traits, *American Psychologist* 48: 26–34

Gooding, D. C. 2000. Experimentation, in W. Newton-Smith (ed.), *A Companion to the Philosophy of Science*, pp. 117–26. Malden, MA: Blackwell

Gray, J. A. 1970. The psychophysiological basis of introversion-extraversion, *Behaviour Research and Therapy* 8: 249–66

Green, C. 2004. Where is Kuhn going?, *American Psychologist* 59: 271–2

Greenberg, J., Koole, S. L. and Pyszczynski T. A. 2004. *Handbook of experimental existential psychology*. New York: Guilford Press

Greenberg, J., Pyszczynski, T. and Solomon, S. 1986. The causes and consequences of a need for self-esteem: a terror management theory, in R. F. Baumeister (ed.), *Public self and private self*, pp. 189–212. New York: Springer-Verlag

Hall, C. S. and Lindzey, G. 1957. *Theories of personality*. New York: Wiley

Hall, C. S., Lindzey, G. and Campbell, J. B. 1998. *Theories of personality*. New York: J. Wiley and Sons

Hampson, S. E. and Goldberg, L. R. 2006. A first large cohort study of personality stability over the 40 years between elementary school and midlife, *Journal of Personality and Social Psychology* 91: 763–79

Hassin, R. R., Uleman, J. S. and Bargh, J. A. 2005. *The new unconscious*. New York: Oxford University Press

James, W. 1890. *The principles of psychology*. New York: Holt
 1902. *The varieties of religious experience; a study in human nature; being the Gifford lectures on natural religion delivered at Edinburgh in 1901–1902*. New York: Modern Library

Kagan, J. 1994. *Galen's prophecy: temperament in human nature*. New York: Westview Press

Kandel, E. R. 2006. *In search of memory: the emergence of a new science of mind*. New York: Norton

Kihlstrom, J. F. 1987. The cognitive unconscious, *Science* 237: 1445–52

Kimble, G. A. 1984. Psychology's two cultures, *American Psychologist* 39: 833–9

Kirschenbaum, H. and Jourdan, A. 2005. The current status of Carl Rogers and the person-centered approach, *Psychotherapy: Theory, Research, Practice, Training* 42: 37–51

Klee, R. 1997. *Introduction to the philosophy of science: cutting nature at its seams*. New York: Oxford University Press

Koltko-Rivera, M. E. 2004. The psychology of worldviews, *Review of General Psychology* 8: 3–58

Kubzansky, L. D., Martin, L. T. and Buka, S. L. 2004. Early manifestations of personality and adult emotional functioning, *Emotion* 4: 364–77

Kuhn, T. S. 1970. *The structure of scientific revolutions*, 2nd edn. University of Chicago Press

Langer, W. 1972. *The mind of Adolph Hitler: the secret wartime report*. New York: Basic Books

Larsen, R. J. and Buss, D. M. 2008. *Personality psychology: domains of knowledge about human nature*, 3rd edn. Boston: McGraw Hill

Lester, D. 1995. *Theories of personality: a systems approach*. Washington, DC: Taylor and Francis

Loevinger, J. 1996. In defense of the individuality of personality theories, *Psychological Inquiry* 7: 344–6

Loevinger, J. and Knoll, E. 1983. Personality: stages, traits, and the self, *Annual Review of Psychology* 34: 195–222

Lombardo, G. P. and Foschi, R. 2002. The European origins of 'personality psychology', *European Psychologist* 7: 134–45

  2003. The concept of personality in 19th-century French and 20th-century America, *History of Psychology* 6: 123–42

MacCorquodale, K. and Meehl, P. E. 1948. On a distinction between hypothetical constructs and intervening variables, *Psychological Review* 55: 95–107

Maddi, S. 1996. *Personality theories: a comparative analysis*, 6th edn. Prospect Heights, IL: Waveland Press

  2006. Taking the theorizing in personality theories seriously, *American Psychologist* 61: 330–1

Magnavita, J. J. 2002. *Theories of personality: contemporary approaches to the science of personality*. New York: J. Wiley and Sons

Maher, B. A. and Gottesman, I. I. 2005. Deconstructing, reconstructing, preserving Paul E. Meehl's legacy of construct validity, *Psychological Assessment* 17: 415–22

Markon, K. E., Krueger, R. F. and Watson, D. 2005. Delineating the structure of normal and abnormal personality: an integrative hierarchical approach, *Journal of Personality and Social Psychology* 88: 139–57

Maslow, A. H. 1976. *The farther reaches of human nature*, 2nd edn. New York: Viking

Matthews, G. and Deary, I. J. 1998. *Personality traits*. Cambridge University Press

Mayer, J. D. 2003. Structural divisions of personality and the classification of traits, *Review of General Psychology* 7: 381–401

McAdams, D. P. 1996. Personality, modernity, and the storied self: a contemporary framework for studying persons, *Psychological Inquiry* 7: 295–321

McAdams, D. P. and Pals, J. L. 2006. A new Big Five: fundamental principles for an integrative science of personality, *American Psychologist* 61: 204–17

McClelland, D. C., Koestner, R. and Weinberger, J. 1989. How do self-attributed and implicit motives differ?, *Psychological Review* 96: 690–702

McCrae, R. R. 1991. The five-factor model and its assessment in clinical settings, *Journal of Personality Assessment* 57: 399–414

McKay, R., Langdon, R. and Coltheart, M. 2005. 'Sleights of mind': delusions, defences, and self-deception, *Cognitive Neuropsychiatry* 10: 305–26

Mischel, W. 1968. *Personality and assessment*. New York: Wiley

Mischel, W. and Shoda, Y. 1995. A cognitive-affective system theory of personality: reconceptualizing situations, dispositions, dynamics, and invariance in personality structure, *Psychological Review* 102: 246–68

Monte, C. 1977. *Beneath the mask: an introduction to theories of personality*. New York: Praeger

Murray, H. A. 1938. *Explorations in personality: a clinical and experimental study of fifty men of college age*. New York: Oxford University Press

Norenzayan A. and Heine, S. J. 2005. Psychological universals: what are they and how can we know?, *Psychological Bulletin* 131: 763–84

Northoff, G., Bermpohl, F., Schoeneich, F. and Boeker, H. 2007. How does our brain constitute defense mechanisms? First-person neuroscience and psychoanalysis, *Psychotherapy and Psychosomatics* 76: 141–53

O'Connor, B. P. 2002. The search for dimensional structure differences between normality and abnormality: a statistical review of published data on personality and psychopathology, *Journal of Personality and Social Psychology* 83: 962–82

Oyserman, D., Bybee, D. and Terry, K. 2006. Possible selves and academic outcomes: how and when possible selves impel action, *Journal of Personality and Social Psychology* 91: 188–204

Ozer, D. J. 1996. The units we should employ, *Psychological Inquiry* 7: 360–3

Peterson, D. R. 2006. Paul E. Meehl's contributions to personality assessment, *Journal of Abnormal Psychology* 115: 201–4

Ponterotto, J. G. 2005. Qualitative research in counseling psychology: a primer on research paradigms and philosophy of science, *Journal of Counseling Psychology* 52: 126–36

Popper, K. 1959. *The logic of scientific discovery.* New York: Basic Books (original work published 1934)

Proctor, R. W., and Capaldi, E. J. 2001a. Evaluation and justification of methodologies in psychological science, *Psychological Bulletin* 127: 759–72

2001b. Improving the science education of psychology students: better teaching of methodology, *Teaching of Psychology* 28: 173–81

Pyszczynski, T., Greenberg, J., Solomon, S., Arndt, J. and Schimel, J. 2004. Why do people need self-esteem? A theoretical and empirical review, *Psychological Bulletin* 130: 435–68

Rennie, D. L. 2002. Experiencing psychotherapy: grounded theory studies, in D. J. Cain and J. Seeman (eds.), *Humanistic psychotherapies: Handbook of research and practice*, pp. 117–44. Washington, DC: American Psychological Association

Rogers, C. R. 1961. *On becoming a person: a therapist's view of psychotherapy.* Boston: Houghton-Mifflin

Rogers, C. R. and Dymond, R. (eds.) 1954. *Psychotherapy and personality change.* Chicago University Press.

Rothbaum, F., Weisz, J., Pott, M., Miyake, K. and Morelli, G. 2000. Attachment and culture: security in the United States and Japan, *American Psychologist* 55: 1093–104

Rychlak, J. F. 1968. *A philosophy of science for personality theory.* Boston, MA: Houghton Mifflin

1997. *In defense of human consciousness.* Washington, DC: American Psychological Association

2000. A psychotherapist's lessons from the philosophy of science, *American Psychologist* 55: 1126–32

Ryckman, R. M. 2004. *Theories of personality*, 8th edn. Belmont, CA: Thomson/ Wadsworth

Schultz, D. P. and Schultz, S. E. 2005. *Theories of personality*, 8th edn. Australia: Thomson/Wadsworth

Sedikides, C., Gaertner, L. and Vevea, J. L. 2005. Pancultural self-enhancement reloaded: a meta-analytic reply to Heine (2005), *Journal of Personality and Social Psychology* 89: 539–51

Seligman, M. E. P. and Csikszentmihalyi, M. 2000. Positive psychology: an introduction, *American Psychologist* 55: 5–14

Seligman, M. E. P., Steen, T. A., Park, N. and Peterson, C. 2005. Positive psychology progress: empirical validation of interventions, *American Psychologist* 60: 410–21

Silverman, I., Choi, J. and Peters, M. 2007. The hunter-gatherer theory of sex differences in spatial abilities: data from 40 countries, *Archives of Sexual Behaviour* 36: 261–8

Skinner, B. F. 1950. Are theories of learning necessary?, *Psychological Review* 57: 193–216

Smith, G. T. 2005. On construct validity: issues of method and measurement, *Psychological Assessment* 17: 396–408

Staats, A. W. 1996. *Behavior and personality: psychological behaviorism.* New York: Springer

Stagner, R. 1937. *Psychology of personality.* New York: McGraw-Hill

Szasz, T. 1960. The myth of mental illness, *American Psychologist* 15: 113–18

Watkins, J. 2000. Popper, in W. Newton-Smith (ed.), *A companion to the philosophy of science*, pp. 343–8. Malden, MA: Blackwell

Winter, D. G., John, O. P., Stewart, A. J., Klohnen, E. C. and Duncan, L. E. 1998. Traits and motives: toward an integration of two traditions in personality research, *Psychological Review* 105: 230–50

Worrall, J. 2000. Pragmatic factors in theory acceptance, in W. Newton-Smith (ed.), *A companion to the philosophy of science*, pp. 349–57. Malden, MA: Blackwell

2 Personality psychology of situations

Seth A. Wagerman and David C. Funder

What people do depends, to an important extent, on the situation they are in. But while this fact has been discussed and sometimes disputed for the past several decades, situations rarely receive the focused examination they deserve. What *is* known about the psychological properties of situations?

In this chapter, we pose a number of questions about situations and attempt to provide answers to some of them. Are persons, situations and behaviours so hopelessly entangled that they can never be teased apart? How can a situation be defined, and what are its properties? How have past researchers gone about studying situations? What remains to be done?

Why study situations?

The key question of psychology is: what causes people to behave the way they do? The stakes were high, therefore, when protagonists of the 'person-situation debate' argued about whether behaviour is mainly determined by the characteristic personality of the individual, or his or her immediate situation (Mischel 1968; Kenrick and Funder 1988; Swann and Seyle 2005). Among other implications, the debate seemed to pit two major sub-fields of psychology against each other: personality psychology, which generally emphasizes the influence of the person, and social psychology, which emphasizes the situation (Funder and Ozer 1983; Ross and Nisbett 1991). Yet despite the vehemence of the person-situation debate, its deep roots, its wide implications, and its persistence into the twenty-first century, the underlying dichotomy is arguably false (Funder 2006; Roberts and Pomerantz 2004). While it is possible to identify and to compare statistical main effects of personal and situational variables, it is not true that one gains power only at the expense of the other. Strong effects of situations *and* strong effects of persons can and often do coexist in the very same data, and the degree to which a given behaviour is affected by one of these variables may be unrelated to the degree to which it is affected by the other (in one study, the empirical correlation between individual consistency and situational change, across behaviours, was $r = -.01$; Funder and Colvin 1991).

Preparation of this chapter was supported, in part, by National Science Foundation grant BCS-0642243 and a Visiting Research Fellowship from the Max Planck Institute for Human Development (Berlin) to the second author.

Modern psychology still has not fully accommodated this realization, but it has a long history. Kurt Lewin (1936) expressed it in terms of his classic formula, $B = f(P, S)$ (behaviour is a function of an interaction between the person and the situation).[1] This implies that if a researcher knew everything there was to know about a person, psychologically, and also knew everything there was to know about the psychological aspects of the situation he or she was in, the ability to predict the individual's behaviour should follow as a matter of course. More recent writings have suggested that the three elements of Lewin's formula – behaviour, person and situation – form a 'personality triad' in the sense that if any two were completely understood, the third should in principle be derivable (Funder 2001, 2006; see also Bandura 1978), which suggests two additional formulae. One is $P = f(S,B)$ (i.e., to know everything about a person entails knowledge of what he or she would do in any situation). This notion resembles Mischel's (1999) '*if ... then*' conception in which an individual's personality is represented in terms of his or her characteristic pattern of behaviour across situations (see Shoda, Mischel and Wright 1994). The other formula is $S = f(P,B)$ (complete understanding of a situation entails knowing what any person would do in it), reminiscent of Bem and Funder's (1978) 'template matching' conception which described situations in terms of the people who would behave in specified ways within them.

The translation of this abstract theoretical structure into empirical research requires specific variables and methods for describing and assessing persons, behaviours and situations. However, the methodological foundations of the elements of the personality triad are seriously unbalanced. Methods for measuring aspects of *persons* are readily available, including countless personality inventories and the 100 comprehensive items of the California Adult Q-sort (CAQ-sort) (Block 1961/1978; Bem and Funder 1978).[2] Many means for measuring *behaviours* are also available, ranging from reaction time to measures of attitude change, obedience and altruism. A general tool, the Riverside Behavioural Q-sort (RBQ) (Funder, Furr and Colvin 2000) is in increasingly wide use, has been translated into German and Dutch (Spinath and Spinath 2004; De Corte and Buysse n.d.), and a revision that expands its range of application has recently been completed.

However, even though the past half-decade of social psychological literature has granted the lion's share of explanatory power to situational forces, still missing is any real technology for defining, for characterizing, or measuring them. This lack has been noted repeatedly: Swann and Seyle (2005) argue that certain current avenues of research (such as Mischel and Shoda's (1999) CAPS model) will not recognize their full potential until 'the development of a comprehensive taxonomy of situations' (Swann and Seyle 2005, p. 162). Mischel himself once suggested

---

[1] Contemporary interactionists often interpret Lewin's dictum statistically, as a regression formula of sorts: $B = f(P + S + (P \times S))$, but this is not what Lewin intended. His use of a comma as the operator between the two constructs was instead meant to convey his belief that the person and situation formed a 'mutually dependent' unit, the 'life space' (Lewin 1936, p. 240).

[2] Terminological note: the term Q-*set* is often used to refer to the list of items which, when rated, become a complete Q-*sort*, but for simplicity the present chapter will use the term Q-*sort* throughout.

that describing differences in situations might be more productive than describing the behaviours of people in them (Mischel and Peake 1983). Hogan and Roberts (2000) lament that that in ninety years of research, social psychology still has yet to offer a reasonable taxonomy of situations, and Endler (1993, p. 258) rates our knowledge of situations as being in 'the dark ages' in comparison to our knowledge of individual differences. Funder (2000, p. 211) points out that 'little is empirically known or even theorized about how situations influence behaviour, or what the basic kinds of situations are (or, alternatively, what variables are useful for comparing one situation with another)'. Kenny, Mohr and Levesque (2001, p. 129) note that we lack 'major competing schemes' let alone a 'universally-accepted scheme for understanding what is meant by situation'. Gelfand (2007) has gone so far as to accuse scientists of making the fundamental attribution error in regards to their taxonomical priorities. Clearly, the need to study situations is not in question. The question is: how might we go about doing so?

Defining situations

As Jens B. Asendorpf (Chapter 3) correctly observes, the very definition of a situation is 'a tricky question'. One problem concerns where to set the boundaries. For example, one might very simply describe a situation in terms of place or locality, in which case 'in the Czech Republic' is as valid a situation as 'in the grocery store'. But at best, this sort of description provides little more than a label. The psychologically-relevant attributes of the setting remain to be characterized and explored. Therefore, one might attempt to define situations on a very molecular level: a snapshot of the exact and complex arrangement of all things physical, psychological and social at a particular moment in time. But because every moment is always different from the next, this approach makes it difficult to state where one situation ends and the next begins. 'Eating lunch in the cafeteria' might be segmented into (literally) a number of bite-sized situations. While there may or may not be something psychologically different between the first mouthful of Salisbury steak and the last, a definition of situations that tries to take into account minute-by-minute[3] variances in the physical and/or social environment quickly becomes unwieldy.

A second definitional problem involves perspective. The short airplane flight from Los Angeles, CA to Las Vegas, NV would be described very differently indeed from the eyes of a severe aviophobe than it would be from the eyes of a frequent flier or from the eyes of the pilot (one hopes). A high school dance might be described as 'demoralizing' or 'lame' by a certain teen, but as 'romantic' and 'memorable' by another, and 'precious' or perhaps 'tiresome' by the chaperones. Does a situation have independent properties of its own *outside of the perceptions of the people in it*?

---

[3] Indeed, why stop there? On a truly molecular level, each nanosecond sees a subtly altered individual interacting with a subtly altered environment.

Both of these definitional questions raise difficult philosophical puzzles and a final resolution to either one is not in sight. However, that does not mean that further conceptualization and research must remain immobilized. For purposes of our own current research, summarized briefly later in this chapter, we have developed provisional answers to each. The first of these questions, concerning boundaries, can be provisionally finessed by asking people to use their common sense when answering the question, what situation are you in right now? Either a participant or observer, we believe, is likely to immediately identify the psychologically pertinent limits to the situation he or she is in, or is observing, and will be able to describe it as 'studying for finals', 'arguing with my room-mate', and so on. Whether situations so defined can be further characterized in psychologically interesting and useful ways, is an empirical question. The second definitional question, we believe, requires at least a provisional answer of 'yes', for any effort to characterize situations to proceed. Without denying that a given situation may have different meanings for every individual in it, the analysis of any situation surely must begin with an attempt to specify the attributes of it that are psychologically relevant to people in general.

Conceptualizing situations

One of the earliest and most notable conceptions of situations comes from Henry Murray (1938), whose theories illuminate the question of whether or not situations and persons are separable. Specifically, he was interested in the role that the environment played in a person's ability to express his or her psychogenic needs[4] and dubbed the forces exerted on behaviour by an environment its *press*. He distinguished between the forces that are intrinsically present in situations (which he called *alpha press*) and the forces that come about from an individual's idiosyncratic reaction to objective properties of the situation (which he called *beta press*). This distinction is useful in that it intimates that situations do exist in some form outside of people's individual perceptions of them. A very crude example is that of getting stuck in a walk-in freezer: the freezer, with no one in it, still has the intrinsic property of being quite cold. Once someone accidentally is stuck in it, the situation may be seen as terrifying and perilous, ironically amusing or annoyingly inconvenient – but this depends to some degree upon the person. Thus it is reasonable to imagine examining situations from either one of these perspectives, or both.

A number of researchers (notably, Magnusson (1981), Block (1981), Saucier, Bel-Bahar and Fernandez (2007), and recently Gelfand (2007)) are in agreement that situations may be addressed from different conceptual levels. Block calls these levels physico-biological, canonical and subjective; Saucier *et al.* call them

---

[4] Murray posited twenty-seven basic needs, the best known of which are the need for power, achievement and affiliation.

environmental, consensual and functional; Gelfand simply calls them macro, meso and micro – but all these authors seem to be referring to the same or very similar three levels of analysis.

Level 1: macro/physico-biological/environmental. Early definitions of situation were behavioural and based on learning theory: fragmenting the physical environment into discrete, quantifiable stimuli examining the satisfying and bothersome effects of environments. At this level, the broadest of the three, a situation is simply the raw sensory information available to us, unfiltered by perception. According to Saucier, this would include, for example, temperature, location and number of people in the room; for Block, this might also include physiological arousal. Gelfand describes this level as including ecological, historical and socio-political factors. This level corresponds to alpha press in its most rudimentary form, having removed all aspects of the social and psychological world from consideration.

Level 2: meso/canonical/consensual. This level of description refers to properties of the situation that are consensual in a social, cultural and sociological way. Situations at this level are described objectively (e.g., 'funeral', 'argument') and are selected and 'structured to exclude certain [behavioural] possibilities and to emphasize others' (Block 1981, p. 87). Although this will vary from social group to social group, region to region, and culture to culture, it provides possibly the most useful level at which to conceptualize alpha press, being both objective and sufficiently encompassing of socio-cultural properties.

Level 3: micro/subjective/functional. The micro/subjective/functional level describes the psychological demand-properties of the situation as it registers on the individual. This, then, is the level of situation that individuals subjectively experience and react to and can be quite idiosyncratic. It is most closely relatable to Murray's notion of beta press.

Past attempts at studying situations

As mentioned earlier, one of the first things notable about the past literature on situational assessment is its paucity relative to the intrinsic importance of the topic. Only a few systematic efforts have been made to understand or classify situations. Prior efforts have taken several approaches, which may be organized into a loose conceptual grouping of methodologies. The *lexical approach*, based on the hypothesis that sufficiently important dimensions will have been represented in language (e.g., Goldberg 1981), has occasionally been used as a starting point for exploration into the structure of situations. More frequently, an *empirical approach* is used, in which either (a) participants describe their probable feelings and behaviours in response to a list of hypothetical situations; (b) participants generate their own such lists, which are then categorized by factor or cluster analysis; or (c) researchers observe participants directly in terms of certain behaviours or their physical locations and then use these variables to group situations. Finally, researchers have occasionally followed a *theoretical approach*, building on some prior framework for understanding persons, situations or behaviours.

Lexical approach. One of the earliest examples of the lexical approach to the study of situations was a study by Van Heck (1984), in which he combed the dictionary for words that could be used to fill in the blank, 'being confronted with a ... situation'. The resulting 263 terms were then rated and reduced to ten factors that included 'interpersonal conflict', 'joint working' and 'recreation'. Edwards and Templeton (2005) used a dictionary and a separate database to find 1,039 words that could complete the sentences 'that situation was ...' or 'that was a ... situation'. This list of words was reduced through factor analysis to four factors called positivity, negativity, productivity and 'ease of negotiation'. Finally, a particularly interesting study by Yang, Read and Miller (2006) applied the lexical approach to both Chinese idioms and their English translations. Chinese idioms were chosen for their generally uniform length (roughly four characters) and the surprisingly large number of them which refer to situational properties. Examples of idioms used are 'too late for regrets' and 'catching up from behind', both of which can be seen to capture interesting psychological properties of situations in an abstract manner. Native speakers of English and Chinese both sorted the situation-idioms in their native languages. Yang *et al.* reduced the resulting data cluster analysis, finding good agreement between both Chinese and American participants on twenty clusters of situations, all seeming to pertain in some way or another to the means of attaining goals.

Empirical approach. A number of early attempts at this approach resulted in what might be termed 'restricted-domain taxonomies', that is to say, taxonomies focused on particular responses or settings rather than being widely applicable. For example, Endler, Hunt and Rosenstein (1962) used 'stimulus-response' questionnaires to ask participants, 'how anxious would you be if ...?'. Using this method, they discovered what they felt were three kinds of situations that caused anxiety: interpersonal situations, situations of inanimate danger (e.g., hurtling car, earthquake), and ambiguous situations. However, if one is interested in situations for which anxiety is not the most salient characteristic, this taxonomy becomes less helpful. Similarly, Fredericksen, Jensen and Beaton (1972) analysed executives' responses to a weekend in-basket exercise, resulting in a taxonomy of executive business situations with categories including evaluation of procedures, routine problems, interorganizational problems, personnel problems, policy issues and time conflicts. Along similar lines, Magnusson (1971) asked students to list all the situations they had encountered during academic study, and then had all possible pairs rated for similarity. The resulting taxonomy spanned five dimensions: positive and negative academic situations, passive and active academic situations, and social academic situations.

Upon rare occasions, empirically-based studies of situations have taken the form of researchers focusing on the first level of study (macro/physico-biological/ environmental). By visiting psychiatric wards, student residences and classrooms,

Moos (1973) was able to develop scales to measure what he called 'perceived climate' based upon psychosocial features. He found three broad dimensions he labelled 'relationships' (e.g., social support), 'personal development' (e.g., academic achievement) and 'system maintenance/change' (e.g., order and organization). Price and Bouffard (1974) used student diaries but focused on physical location by categorizing situations based upon what they called 'constraint' – the number and kinds of behaviours that were considered appropriate within them. Among the results was the finding that burping and fighting were inappropriate in almost any location, whereas laughing was appropriate in almost all places; and that only a small repertoire of behaviours were available to someone at church, while almost anything went in someone's own bedroom. The resulting taxonomy, unfortunately, resulted in five difficult-to-interpret clusters labelled 'park/ sidewalk/football game', 'date/family dinner/movie', 'bar/elevator/job interview/ restroom' 'class/church/bus' and 'dorm lounge/own room'. Perhaps it is apparent why structuring a taxonomy of situations by location is somewhat difficult.[5]

Researchers have sometimes asked participants to describe their hypothetical feelings or behaviours in response to hypothetical situations: Forgas and Van Heck (1992) used questionnaires to measure behavioural reactions in a series of situations (e.g., 'you are going to meet a new date') and were then able to allocate the variance in responses to persons, situations and interactions. Vansteelandt and Van Mechelen (1998) asked people about their reactions (mostly hostile) to situations classified as 'high frustrating', 'moderately frustrating' and 'low frustrating' (p. 761). Ten Berge and De Raad (2001) posit that situations are only useful in that they render the understanding of traits less ambiguous, and thus asked students to write sentences explicating how traits might be expressed in certain situations. They then grouped these sentences by meaning and structured them according to the likeliness of trait-related behaviour in them. For example, 'Situations of adversity' arose from Neuroticism, 'situations of enjoyment' arose from Extraversion, and 'situations of positioning' arose from Conscientiousness.

Rather than asking participants to rate hypothetical situations, some investigators have asked them instead to generate their own; such as Forgas (1976), who asked housewives and students to provide two descriptions each for every interaction they had experienced in the previous twenty-four hours. He found a two-dimensional episode structure for housewives (intimacy/involvement and self-confidence) and a three-dimensional structure for students (involvement, pleasantness and knowing how to behave). Pervin (1976) used the free-response descriptions of his participants of situations they had experienced over the past year to create a taxonomy of daily situations. Using factor analyses of the feelings and behaviours associated with these situations, he found groups, including home-family, friends-peers, relaxation-play, work-school, and alone.

---

[5] Football game/sidewalk/park can be seen as a cluster of situations in which one might 'lounge,' 'chatter', or 'recreate'; it is difficult and possibly unwise to speculate upon what behaviours are equally appropriate in a restroom/job interview/bar.

Very rarely in this line of research are participants directly observed in actual situations. A recent exception is Furr and Funder (2004), who asked participants to rate the degree to which two experimental situations they had previously experienced seemed similar – a measurement of what might be called beta press. In a second study, they assessed the relative similarity of six experimental situations in objective terms (based upon the similarity of the task and participants involved), tapping alpha press. Actual behaviour, using the Riverside Behavioural Q-sort, was coded from videotapes of the participants in each experimental situation. The first study found that participants who saw the two experimental situations as more similar tended to be more consistent in their behaviour across them. The second study found that participants were more consistent in their behaviour across pairs of situations that were more objectively similar. These results demonstrate the importance of both alpha and beta press by showing that behaviour is more consistent across situations to the degree they are similar in either sense.

Theoretical approach. Krause (1970) drew on sociological theory in an attempt to categorize situations on theoretical grounds. Based upon the way in which he posited that cultures assimilate novel situations into traditional, generic situations, Krause suggested seven classes, including joint working, fighting and playing, among others (a classification that guided the recovery of similar factors in the study by Van Heck (1984) cited above.) In a major project based around interdependence theory, an 'Atlas' of interpersonal situations has recently been created. The Atlas is organized around a set of twenty-one 2×2 contingency tables akin to Prisoner's Dilemma contexts (e.g., outcome is good for A but bad for B, good for B but bad for A, good for both, or bad for both) (Kelly, Holmes, Kerr *et al.* 2003). The objective is to capture the ways in which the structure of interpersonal interactions determines individual's outcomes.

Riverside Situational Q-Sort

It is clear that research on situations is far from complete. To begin with, very little consensus has been reached as to what the basic dimensions of situations are, or how properties of situations might reasonably be described, or what counts as a situation in the first place. Further, the comprehensiveness of prior studies is quite uneven: many were limited to hypothetical situations rather than ones actually experienced, or to specific *types* of situations rather than situations in general. Finally, the three pieces of the 'triad' are hardly ever addressed in relation to each other: while a very few studies have examined situations and behaviour, they are usually limited to what participants think they *might* do *if* … rather than what was actually done; likewise, only a rare study has examined individual differences in the perception of and reaction to situations.

This led to our current work with the Riverside Situational Q-Sort (RSQ) (Wagerman and Funder 2006), an assessment tool built around the following assumptions regarding the two main questions that have been posed in this chapter.

(1) *Can situations ever be viewed independently from people's perception of them (or from the behaviours engaged in them, for that matter)?* The answer, we believe, must be a resounding 'yes'. Indeed, interactions between people, situations and behaviour may *only* be studied successfully if they are kept independent at the level of conceptualization and measurement (Reis 2007). Some might argue for a subjective or constructivist approach: that persons and situations are fundamentally inseparable, thus rendering study of any one of them difficult or impossible (Lewin 1936; Johnson 1999). However, such arguments, while philosophically interesting, risk analytic and empirical paralysis. As Jens B. Asendorpf (Chapter 3) notes, 'subjective situations are confounded with personality traits *by definition of the situation*' (emphasis in the original). If examination of the triad begins with two or even all three of its threads already woven together, it will be impossible to use any measure thus created as a situational predictor independent of the person or behaviour. In fact, conceptualizing situations in terms of individual differences (e.g., an extravert sees situation 'X' in a particular way, while a shy person sees the same situation in a completely different manner), effectively absorbs the study of situations into the domain of personality psychology. In order to be equal partners with personality variables in the prediction of behaviour, situational variables need to be distinguished from rather than merely mashed into them. There must be something about the situation that is influential across both the shy and extraverted person, or else social psychologists, and psychological experimentalists in general, have been wrong all along.

(2) *At what level should situations be examined?* Level 1 (the macro/physico-biological/environmental level) might have the advantage of being easily clustered, but while such variables undoubtedly have their effect on behaviour, location clusters like those found by Price and Bouffard (1974), as discussed earlier, seem behaviourally uninformative and unpsychological; the situation as it affects human behaviour must be more than its location or raw physical facts. Studying situations at Level 3 (the micro/subjective/functional level) has all the problems contested above regarding the necessity of separating persons from situations, and in behavioural analysis runs the risk of circularity.[6] A large literature in cognitive psychology, however, suggests that among possible levels of abstraction the most easily communicated and generally useful is the middle or 'basic' one (Rosch 1973; Cantor and Mischel 1977). Accordingly, it might be best to aim research on the properties of situations at Level 2 (the meso/canonical/consensual level of description), which is analogous to personality description: while the traits of any given person are of psychological interest, data is often aggregated across individuals in order to understand people in general. In much the same way, any one subjective perception of a situation, while psychologically interesting, can be forsaken by aggregating across many such perceptions to arrive at some consensual and objective description of what that situation's properties

---

[6] For example, an individual's hostile behaviour might be 'explained' on the basis of his or her idiosyncratic perception of the situation as hostility-inducing.

are. While this approach still has some limits (for example, as Jens B. Asendorpf (Chapter 3) notes, it may not be useful in the study of intimate relationships), we still expect that it may prove to have a wide range of applicability.

With these considerations in mind, we chose to develop a situationally descriptive Q-sort tool (Funder 2006; Wagerman and Funder 2006). In a Q-sort, raters sort descriptive items into a forced distribution, ranging in this case across nine steps from 'highly uncharacteristic' of the situation being described (category 1) to 'highly characteristic' (category 9). For our instrument, dubbed the Riverside Situational Q-sort (RSQ), the prescribed distribution of the eighty-one items (of the most recent version) across the nine categories is 3-6-10-14-15-14-10-6-3. This peaked, quasi-normal distribution, commonly used in Q-technique (Block 1961/1978) has three implications. First, all items are judged against each other on the basis of how well (or poorly) they capture the situation in question, rather than being rated on absolute scales. This aspect has numerous advantages, including forcing raters to make careful comparisons between items that otherwise might be quickly and superficially deemed to be equally descriptive, and lessening the influence of certain response sets, such as extremity. Secondly, almost exactly half of the items are placed in the middle three categories (4, 5 and 6), which encourages raters to give relatively neutral ratings to terms that are not clearly descriptive. Thirdly, because of the small numbers of items allowed in the extreme categories, rating an item as 1 or 2, or 8 or 9, amounts to a strong – and carefully considered – statement about the relevance of that item for the situation in question. A long history of theoretical development and empirical application of Q-technique shows that these are important advantages, particular in cases where the ratings are difficult or the object of the rating is complex (Block 1961/1978).

Turning to item content, we drew upon a particular prior Q-Sort (the California Adult Q-Sort (CAQ)) that has a good reputation as a widely-validated measure of personality, and which we have used previously as the basis of behavioural Q-sort items, to provide a solid backbone for this endeavour. Each of the 100 CAQ items was examined and converted into phraseology that described characteristics of situations that afforded the opportunity for expression of each of the corresponding personality characteristics. For example, the CAQ item, 'is critical, sceptical, not easily impressed' yielded the RSQ item, 'someone is trying to impress someone or convince someone of something', the assumption here being that in a situation that is accurately described by this property, a sceptical and critical person has an excellent opportunity to act accordingly, whereas the opposite sort of person may instead reveal a penchant for gullibility.[7] Raters sort the RSQ items into a nine-step, forced distribution ranging from 'highly uncharacteristic' of the situation being described (category 1) to 'highly characteristic' (category 9).

---

[7] See www.rap.ucr.edu for the complete text of the current, eighty-one item incarnation of the RSQ, as well as other relevant information, and a freely-available computer program to facilitate Q-sorting.

Preliminary studies have shown promising results. In a pilot study, eighty-one undergraduates told us about a situation they had been in the previous day at a randomly assigned time both qualitatively and using the RSQ. They also told us what they had been feeling during this situation by way of the Positive and Negative Affect Schedule (PANAS) (Watson, Clark and Tellegen 1988) and what they had been doing during the situation using a modified version of the RBQ that had been converted into a Likert-type rating scale. We also gathered personality data using the Big Five Inventory (BFI) (John, Donahue and Kentle 1991). Thus armed with information about persons, situations, emotions and behaviour, we have been able to examine some interesting interactions among these variables. For example, when participants described the RSQ item 'P(arti-cipant) is being insulted' as particularly characteristic of the situation they had been in, they described themselves as having fantasized in response ($r = 0.25$; about revenge, perhaps?), having been sarcastic ($r = 0.25$), and having blamed others ($r = 0.24$). Many other patterns, interesting in this way, can be found in our preliminary data. Other analyses examined the situational properties associated with the experience of positive and negative affect, for example, positive affect was found to be associated with (among others) the potential for being complimented or praised ($r = 0.41$), presence of members of the opposite sex ($r = 0.25$), and a lack of potential anxiety ($r = -0.27$) or a need to restrain one's impulses ($r = 0.25$).

Further analyses of our preliminary data illustrated other enticing aspects of situations. For example, male participants viewed the item 'context includes stimuli that may be construed sexually' as significantly more descriptive of whatever situations they had been in than females did (whether this is a commentary on the types of situations that males and females seek or simply an indication that males are more likely to ascribe sexual connotations to situational cues than are females – or a combination of both! – is still up for interpretation). Our Latino participants perceived whatever situations they had been in as significantly more affording of an opportunity to be talkative than did our Asian participants; Caucasian participants described their situations as significantly more enjoyable than did African-American participants.

The analyses of the associations between the situational variables, behaviour and personality using the RSQ (of which the ones summarized above are just a tiny sample) encouraged us to conclude that aspects of real-life situations can be reliably and meaningfully described with such an instrument, and that the properties it captures are related to behaviour, emotional experience and personality, and perhaps even gender and cultural background. Research is continuing.

Future directions

A developing technology for situational assessment has the potential to open many research doors. While studies so far have mostly focused on mundane, everyday situations recently experienced by our participants, extreme situations (e.g., emergencies, crises), even if rare, can be consequential and revealing of personality, and deserve to be considered in future work. Future research should also include direct observations of behaviour in experimental situations designed to accentuate selected situational dimensions. More broadly, perhaps the wide range of experimental situations studied by social psychology could be conceptualized in terms of standard descriptive variables such as those offered by the RSQ, allowing their effects on behaviour (to the extent they have the same or related dependent variables) to be systematized across the literature, for the first time. This move towards systemization could help promote a new symbiosis between personality and social psychology (Swann and Seyle 2005), by permitting 'the effect of the situation' long studied by social psychologists to be analysed in terms of the same kinds of general variables long used within personality psychology to conceptualize the effects of persons (Funder and Ozer 1983). Another important purpose for situational variables could be to examine *within*-person variability in behaviour as a function of situational variation, thus simultaneously addressing behavioural change as well as consistency (Fleeson 2004).

In applied contexts, a technology for situational assessment offers possibilities for predicting the specific situations under which people, or certain kinds of people, or even people with certain genotypes, are likely to lose their temper, engage in criminal behaviour, perform jobs well or live longer (cf., Caspi, McClay, Moffitt *et al.* 2002; Moffitt 2005). Different people thrive and suffer in different situations, a fact that could make a developed science of situational assessment useful for enhancing the individualized selection and design of workplace, educational and general life contexts to promote mental and physical health and the attainment of important individual goals.

References

Allport, G. W. and Odbert, H. S. 1936. Trait-names: a psycho-lexical study, *Psychological Monographs: General and Applied* 47: 171–200 (1, Whole No. 211)

Argyle, M. and Little, B. R. 1972. Do personality traits apply to social behaviour?, *Journal for the Theory of Social Behaviour* 2: 1–35

Bandura, A. 1978. The self system in reciprocal determinism, *American Psychologist* 33: 344–58

Bem, D. J. and Funder, D. C. 1978. Predicting more of the people more of the time: assessing the personality of situations, *Psychological Review* 85: 485–501

Block, J. 1961/1978. *The Q-Sort method in personality assessment and psychiatric research.* Palo Alto, CA: Consulting Psychologist Press. Originally published 1961

  1981. Studying situational dimensions: a grand perspective and some limited empiricism, in D. Magnusson (ed.), *Toward a Psychology of situations: an interactional perspective*, pp. 85–102. Hillside, NJ: Erlbaum

Block, J. and Block, J. H. 1981. Studying situational dimensions: a grand perspective and some limited empiricism, in D. M. Magnusson (ed.), *Toward a psychology of situations: an interactional perspective*, pp. 85–103. Hillsdale, N.J.: Lawrence Erlbaum Associates

Bowers, K. S. 1973. Situationism in psychology: an analysis and critique, *Psychological Review* 80: 307–36

Campbell, D. T. and Fiske, D. W. 1959. Convergent and discriminant validation by the multi-trait multi-method matrix, *Psychological Bulletin* 56: 81–105

Cantor, N. and Mischel, W. 1977. Traits as prototypes: effects on recognition memory, *Journal of Personality and Social Psychology* 35: 38–48

Caspi, A., McClay, J., Moffitt, T. E., Mill, J., Martin, J., Craig, I., Taylor, A. and Poulton, R. 2002. Role of genotype in the cycle of violence in maltreated children, *Science* 297: 851–4

De Corte, C.K. and Buysse, A. (n.d.). *The Riverside Behavioral Q-sort*. Dutch translation, http://rap.ucr.edu/qsorter/dutch RBQ.htm

Eaton, L. G. and Funder, D. C. 2001. Emotion in daily life: valence, variability, and rate of change, *Emotion* 1: 413–21

Edwards, J. A. and Templeton, A. 2005. The structure of perceived qualities of situations. *European Journal of Social Psychology* 35: 705–23

Ekman, P. 1999. basic emotions, in T. Dalgleish and T. Power (eds.), *The Handbook of Cognition and Emotion*, pp. 45–60. Chichester: John Wiley and Sons Ltd

Endler, N.S. 1993. Personality: an international perspective, in J. Hetterna and I.J. Deary (eds.), *Foundations of personality*, pp. 251–68. Dordrecht: Kluwer

Endler, N. S., Hunt, J. McV. and Rosenstein, A. J. 1962: An S-R inventory of anxiousness, *Psychological Monographs* 76: 1–33 (17, Whole No. 536)

Feldman-Barrett, L. and Russell, J. A. 1998. Independence and bipolarity in the structure of current affect, *Journal of Personality and Social Psychology* 74: 967–84.

Fleeson, W. 2004. Moving personality beyond the person-situation debate: the challenge and the opportunity of within-person variability, *Current Directions in Psychological Science* 13: 83–7

Forgas, J. P. 1976. The perception of social episodes: categorical and dimensional representations in two different social milieus, *Journal of Personality and Social Psychology* 34: 199–209

Forgas, J. P. and Van Heck, G. L. 1992. The psychology of situations, in G. V. Caprara and G. L. Van Heck (eds.), *Modern personality psychology: critical reviews and new directions*, pp. 418–55. New York: Harvester Wheatsheaf

Frederiksen N., Jensen O. and Beaton A. 1972. *Prediction of organizational behaviour.* New York: Pergammon

Funder, D. C. 2001. Personality, *Annual Review of Psychology* 52: 197–221
    2006. Towards a resolution of the personality triad: persons, situations and behaviours, *Journal of Research in Personality* 40: 21–34

Funder, D. C. and Colvin, C. R. 1991. Explorations in behavioural consistency: properties of persons, situations, and behaviours, *Journal of Personality and Social Psychology* 60: 773–94

Funder, D. C., Furr, R. M. and Colvin, C. R. 2000. The Riverside Behavioural Q-sort: a tool for the description of social behaviour, *Journal of Personality* 68: 450–89

Funder, D. C. and Ozer, D. J. 1983. Behaviour as a function of the situation, *Journal of Personality and Social Psychology* 44: 107–12

Furr, R. M. and Funder, D. C. 2004. Situational similarity and behavioural consistency: subjective, objective, variable-centered and person-centered approaches, *Journal of Research in Personality* 38: 421–47

Gelfand, M. J. 2007. Situated culture: a multilevel analysis of situational constraint across 35 nations. Colloquium delivered at the University of California, Berkeley, 7 March 2007

Goldberg, L. R. 1981. Language and individual differences: the search for universals in personality lexicons, in L. Wheeler (ed.), *Review of personality and social psychology*, vol. 2, pp. 141–65. Beverly Hills, CA: Sage

1990. An alternative 'description of personality': the big-five factor structure, *Journal of Personality and Social Psychology* 59: 1216–29

Hogan, R. and Roberts, B. W. 2000. A socioanalytic perspective on person-environment interaction, in W. B. Walsh, K. H. Craik and R. H. Price (eds.), *Person-environment psychology: new directions and perspectives*, 2nd edn, pp. 1–23. Mahwah, NJ: Lawrence Erlbaum Associates

John, O., Donahue, E. and Kentle, R. 1991. *The 'Big Five'*, Technical Report, Institute of Personality Assessment and Research. Berkeley, CA: University of California.

Johnson, J. A. 1999. Some hypotheses concerning attempts to separate situations from personality dispositions. Paper presented at the sixth European Congress of Psychology, Rome, July 1999. Available at www.personal.psu.edu/~j5j/papers/rome.html

Kelly, H. H., Holmes, J. G., Kerr, N. L., Reis, H. T., Rusbult, C. E. and Van Lange, P. A. 2003. *An atlas of interpersonal situations*. New York: Cambridge University Press

Kenny, D. A., Mohr, C. D. and Levesque, M. J. 2001. A social relations variance partitioning of dyadic behavior, *Psychological Bulletin* 127: 128–41

Kenrick, D. T. and Funder, D. C. 1988. Profiting from controversy: lessons from the person-situation debate, *American Psychologist* 43: 23–34

Krause, M. S. 1970. Use of social situations for research purposes, *American Psychologist* 25: 748–53

Letzring, T. D., Block, J. and Funder, D. C. 2005. Ego-control and ego-resiliency: generalization of self-report scales based on personality descriptions from acquaintances, clinicians, and the self, *Journal of Research in Personality* 39: 395–422

Lewin, K. 1936. *Principles of topographical psychology*. New York, NY: McGraw Hill

Magnusson, D. 1971. An analysis of situational dimensions, *Perceptual and Motor Skills* 32: 851–67

1981. *Toward a psychology of situations: an interactional perspective*. Hillsdale, NJ: Erlbaum

Markey, P. M., Funder, D. C. and Ozer, D. J. 2003. Complementarity of interpersonal behaviours in dyadic interactions, *Personality and Social Psychology Bulletin* 29: 1082–90

McCrae, R. R. and Costa, P. T. 1987. Validation of the five-factor model of personality across instruments and observers, *Journal of Personality and Social Psychology* 52: 307–17

McCrae, R. R., Costa, P. T. and Busch, C. M. 1986. Evaluating comprehensiveness in personality systems: the California Q-set and the five-factor model, *Journal of Personality* 54: 430–46

Mischel, W. 1968. *Personality and assessment.* New York, NY: Wiley

    1999. Personality coherence and dispositions in a cognitive-affective personality system (CAPS) approach, in D. Cervone and Y. Shoda (eds.), *The coherence of personality: social-cognitive bases of consistency, variability and organization*, pp. 37–60. New York: Guilford Press

Mischel, W. and Peake, P. K. 1983. Some facets of consistency: replies to Epstein, Funder, and Bem, *Psychological Review* 90: 394–402

Mischel, W. and Shoda, Y. 1999. *Integrating dispositions and processing dynamics within a unified theory of personality: the cognitive-affective personality system.* New York, NY: Guilford Press

Moffitt, T.E. 2005. The new look of behavioral genetics in developmental psychopathology: gene–environment interplay in artisocial behaviors, *Psychological Bulletin* 131: 533–54

Moos, R. H. 1973. Conceptualizations of human environments, *American Psychologist* 28: 652–65

Murray, H. A. 1938. *Explorations in personality.* New York: Oxford University Press

Norman, W. T. 1963. Toward an adequate taxonomy of personality attributes: replicated factor structure in peer nomination personality ratings, *Journal of Abnormal and Social Psychology* 66: 574–83

Pervin, L. A. 1976. A free-response approach to the analysis of person-situation interaction, *Journal of Personality and Social Psychology* 34: 465–74

Price, R. H. and Bouffard, D. L. 1974. Behavioural appropriateness and situational constraint as dimensions of social behaviour, *Journal of Personality and Social Psychology* 30: 579–86

Reis, H. 2007. Being social and why it matters: reinvigorating the concept of situation in social psychology. Presidential Address, Society for Social and Personality Psychology, Memphis, February 2007

Roberts, B. W. and Pomerantz, E. M. 2004. On traits, situations, and their integration: a developmental perspective, *Personality and Social Psychology Review* 8: 402–16

Rosch, E. H. 1973. Natural categories, *Cognitive Psychology* 4: 328–50

Ross, L. and Nisbett, R.E. 1991. *The person and the situation: perspectives of social psychology.* New York: McGraw-Hill

Saucier, G., Bel-Bahar, T. and Fernandez, C. 2005. What modifies the expression of personality tendencies? Defining basic domains of situation variables, *Journal of Personality* 75: 479–504

Shoda, Y., Mischel, W. and Wright, J. C. 1994. Intraindividual stability in the organization and patterning of behaviour: incorporating psychological situations into the idiographic analysis of personality, *Journal of Personality and Social Psychology* 67: 674–87

Spain, J. S., Eaton, L. G. and Funder, D. C. 2000. Perspectives on personality: the relative accuracy of self versus others for the prediction of emotion and behaviour, *Journal of Personality* 68: 837–67

Spinath, B. and Spinath, F. M. 2004. Behaviour observation in dyadic interaction situations: the German form of the Riverside Behaviour Q-Sort (RBQ-D), *Journal of Differential Diagnostic Psychology* 25: 105–15

Swann, W. B. and Seyle, C. 2005, Personality psychology's comeback and its emerging symbiosis with social psychology, *Personality and Social Psychology Bulletin* 31: 155–65

Ten Berge, M. A. and De Raad, B. 2001. Construction of a joint taxonomy of traits and situations, *European Journal of Personality* 15: 253–76

Tupes, E. C. and Christal, R. E. 1961. *Recurrent personality factors based on trait ratings* (ASD-TR-61-97). Lackland Air Force Base, TX: Aeronautical Systems Division, Personnel Laboratory

Van Heck, G.L. 1984. The construction of a general taxonomy of situations, in H. Bonarivs, G.L. Van Heck and N. Smid (eds.), *Personality psychology in Europe: theoretical and empirical developments*, pp. 149–64. Lisse: Swets and Zeitlinger

Vansteelandt, K. and Van Mechelen, I. 1998. Individual differences in situation-behaviour profiles: a triple typology model, *Journal of Personality and Social Psychology* 75: 751–65

Vazire, S. and Funder, D. C. 2006. Impulsivity and the self-defeating behaviour of narcissists, *Personality and Social Psychology Review* 10: 154–65

Wagerman, S. A. and Funder, D. C. 2006. The Riverside Situational Q-Sort: a tool for understanding the psychological properties of situations. Poster presented at the annual meeting of the Society for Personality and Social Psychology, Palm Springs, CA, January 2006

Wagerman, S. A., Greve, L. A. and Funder, D. C. 2006. You did what where? Behavioural correlates of situational affordances. Poster presented at the annual meeting of the Western Psychological Association, Palm Springs, CA, April 2006

Watson, D., Clark, L. A. and Tellegen, A. 1988. Development and validation of brief measures of positive and negative affect: the PANAS scales, *Journal of Personality and Social Psychology* 54: 1063–70

Yang, Y., Read, S. J. and Miller, L. C. 2006. A taxonomy of situations from Chinese idioms, *Journal of Research in Personality* 40: 750–78

3 Personality: traits and situations

Jens B. Asendorpf

According to a famous, albeit sexist, quotation, 'Every man is in certain respects (a) like all other men, (b) like some other men, (c) like no other man' (Kluckhohn and Murray 1953, p. 53). General psychology is concerned with (a), and personality psychology with (b) and (c) (Allport 1937, who owed most of his ideas to Stern 1911). Personality psychology attempts to describe, predict and explain those recurrent behaviours that set an individual apart from some or all other agemates. In other words, personality psychology is concerned with those temporally stable tendencies of behaviour in which persons of a similar age differ from one another.

Temporally stable tendencies of behaviour are called *dispositions* in psychology but also other sciences such as medicine, biology and physics. Dispositions that characterize the personality of an individual are called personality dispositions, or personality *traits* (Allport 1937; Funder 1991).

In this chapter I provide an overview of empirical personality research on traits, with a particular focus on the relations between traits and situations. First, I discuss the most simple case of one trait of one individual in one situation. Secondly, I expand this analysis from a variable-centred perspective to inter-individual differences in one trait in one situation. Thirdly, I further expand this perspective to inter-individual differences in one trait across multiple situations, including the important case where the situation is defined by another person. Fourthly, I deal with the tricky question of how one should define a situation in personality research. Finally, I conclude with a discussion of possible mechanisms that relate traits to situations.

One individual, one situation

Did Einstein spend a lot of time sailing on Berlin's lakes? Yes, he did, at least between 1929 and 1932. During this time, Einstein showed a stable tendency to sail. Before then and later in life, he did not exhibit this trait as much. This is a borderline case of a trait because it is 'narrow' in terms of behaviour and situations (hence sometimes called a 'habit' rather than a 'trait') and because the behavioural tendency was stable only for a certain phase of Einstein's life. Nevertheless, traits do change over longer time periods (see M. Brent Donnellan and Richard W. Robins, Chapter 12), and the distinction between habits and traits is a fuzzy one.

43

More prototypic for a trait are constructs such as neuroticism (temperamental), intelligence (cognitive), or the achievement motive (motivational) that comprise many characteristic behaviours in many situations (they are 'broader') and that are stable over many years for most adults. But, as we shall see shortly, that broad traits exist is an assumption that often conflicts with reality to some extent when we do not rely on people's beliefs about their own traits or the traits of others, but instead on observed behaviour.

Therefore, let us start with considering a trait that is defined by a recurrent tendency to show a particular observable behaviour in a particular type of situation: aggression toward same-sex peers. In order to measure the trait of aggressiveness to same-sex peers for a particular individual, it is necessary to observe this one person in many social interactions with same-sex peers. Even strong aggression is not an indication of high aggressiveness if only one situation is observed; observing aggressiveness requires observation of many situations. The occurrence of aggression within these situations can be standardized with regard to time (e.g., rate of aggression per interaction), and after having observed the individual in, say, fifty interactions with same-sex peers we may arrive at an aggressiveness score of, say, 10 per cent aggressive interactions. In order to make sure that we have measured a disposition, we have to repeat the same procedure for a similar number of interactions, and to check whether the rate of interaction is similarly high. If it is similarly high, we can conclude that we have captured a disposition of the individual. If not, we have only captured a fluctuating *state* of the individual; we still might arrive at a disposition if we observe the individual for a longer time, but this is by no means guaranteed.

If we find a stable disposition, e.g., 10 per cent aggressive interactions, we cannot be sure that this disposition is a personality trait. It might be characteristic of every age-mate (pathological exceptions granted); in this case, it would be a universal disposition but not something that sets the observed individual apart from some or all other age-mates. The important lesson at this point is that a single case study alone ('idiographic approach'; see Lamiell 2003) is insufficient for describing personality (something often ignored by advocates of idiographic approaches to individuality).

Many individuals, one situation

Instead, we have to compare many individuals to be sure that we really capture a personality trait ('nomothetic approach'; see Lamiell 2003). Thus, we have to observe, say, fifty individuals, each in fifty interactions, and to repeat this procedure, in order to reliably determine the distribution of the aggression rates. In this case, the retest correlation for the aggressiveness scores tells us whether we have observed stable inter-individual differences. Traditionally, a retest correlation of .80 and above would be considered as good evidence that we have captured stable inter-individual differences, and therefore a personality trait *for*

Table 3.1 *Stability, agreement and coherence of observed and judged dominance in pre-school children.*

		Agreement[a] and coherence[b]		
		1 teacher	2 teachers	4 teachers
Observation	Stability[c]	.68	.81	.91
1 week	.34	.33	.36	.38
4 weeks	.67	.46	.51	.54
8 weeks	.76	.51	.56	.59

$N = 56$ four-year-old children.
[a] Correlations between single teachers, between mean of 2 teachers, and Cronbach's *alpha* for 4 teachers.
[b] Correlation between teacher judgement and observation.
[c] Correlations between single weeks, between mean of 4 weeks, and Cronbach's *alpha* for 8 weeks.

most persons. Note, however, that such a high retest correlation is compatible with unstable aggression in *some* individuals because the retest correlation character-izes a sample of individuals, not each single person. As Stern (1911) put it, a retest correlation is a measure of the *probability* that we have found a personality trait for each single person. This statement is certainly not perfectly correct from a statistical point of view but it well describes the fact that inferences from correla-tional findings at the sample level to the individual level are only possible with some probability (except for the unrealistic case of a correlation of 1 or −1).

Observing fifty individuals each in fifty interactions is a laborious procedure, and therefore most personality psychologists try to circumvent observation by asking knowledgeable informants about the trait in question, including the target individuals themselves. Obviously, this is a risky strategy because the informants' perception of the trait may be more stable than the trait really is, and may be biased in numerous ways, including social desirability biases. For example, same-sex friends may overlook aggressive acts of the target person toward other same-sex age-mates, or downplay their friend's aggressiveness in their reports. These biases can be minimized by (a) asking informants that have no close relationship with the target person, and (b) averaging the reports of multiple informants. In this case, informants' reports can show a pretty good coherence with behavioural observations.

For example, Moskowitz and Schwarz (1982) observed pre-school children's dominance in their peer group daily for eight weeks and compared the dominance scores with the dominance judgements of four teachers who knew the children well (see Table 3.1). The stability of the observed inter-individual differences in domi-nance increased from .34 between weekly observations to .76 (estimated stability between two eight-week intervals); thus, it was necessary to observe the children daily for at least eight weeks in order to arrive at sufficiently stable dominance scores. The coherence between these stable dominance scores and the average dominance judgement of four teachers was .59, attesting to a good validity of the aggregated teacher judgement. However, Table 3.1 also shows that the validity of only one teacher was only moderate.

Many individuals, many situations

The study by Moskowitz and Schwarz (1982) also provides good evidence that traits are consistent across highly similar but non-identical situations, because the children were observed always in the same room of the same school in the same peer group, and aggregation across days cancelled out some of the day-to-day fluctuations of the situation, but not all of these fluctuations. Therefore, on the one hand, high stability guarantees cross-situational consistency between highly similar situations simply because one cannot observe the same person at different times in an identical situation. On the other hand, no one would expect that traits generalize across *all* possible situations. For example, dominance cannot occur when people are alone, so dominance may generalize from interactions with peers to interactions with parents, but not to non-social situations. Therefore, the question of this section is to which extent traits generalize across *moderately similar* situations. Is a dominant child in the familiar pre-school group also a dominant child in interactions with unfamiliar peers in the playground, with similar-aged siblings at home, with a clearly older sibling at home? Most people would assume that, but empirical personality research over the past eighty years has questioned such popular beliefs.

The first large study along these lines was conducted by Hartshorne and May (1928) who designed eight tests and observational settings in order to observe inter-individual differences in honest behaviour among more than 800 school children. The cross-situational consistency between two such situations was only .19 which was much lower than the retest stability within situations. This problem was debated for some time but remained unresolved and nearly forgotten until Mischel (1968) revived this *consistency debate* by more empirical evidence, proposing a 'magic limit' of .30 for what he called the 'cross-situational consistency of behaviour'. His conclusion was that traits exist only in the eye of the observers but have no reality, because behaviour is so much situation-dependent.

Although many opposed this obviously incorrect conclusion (Mischel 1968 confused behaviour with inter-individual differences in behaviour), it took twenty years until the consistency debate resulted in a more balanced, consensual view (Kenrick and Funder 1988; Funder 1991). According to this view, the obvious cross-situational variation of the behaviour of *one individual* does not imply that the *inter-individual differences* in the same behaviour across the same situations are inconsistent (the cross-situational correlation is 1 if the cross-situational variation of the behaviour is shared by all individuals; see Figure 3.1). Furthermore, the

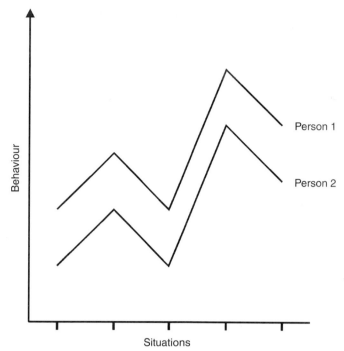

Figure 3.1. *Perfect cross-situational consistency of inter-individual differences despite strong situational effects on behaviour.*

consistency is often higher than .30 if it is corrected for the unreliability of the measurement within situations (e.g., .37 in the classic study by Hartshorne and May 1928), and it depends, of course, on the similarity of the situations: more similar situations lead to higher cross-situational consistency. Also, when situations are grouped into different domains, such as home versus school, or home versus work, aggregation of situations within domains often once more increases the consistency between domains because of further reductions of measurement error.

Finally, and most importantly, a low cross-situational consistency despite high temporal stability within situations does not violate the assumption of a stable personality as long as the inter-individual differences in the cross-situational differences are stable: such stable *individual situation profiles* are an indication of a stable personality. Best evidence for the stability of individual situational profiles comes from a study by Shoda, Mischel and Wright (1994). These authors trained staff of a summer camp to closely observe fifty-three children aged 7–13 years over the full six-week period of the camp. Each child was observed for 167 hours on average, a huge database. Analyses of children's verbal aggression in five different types of situations revealed individual aggression profiles as illustrated in Figure 3.2. The temporal stability of these profiles varied considerably, with an average of .47. Thus, many children showed stable situation profiles for verbal aggression.

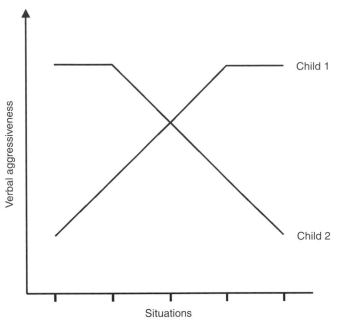

Figure 3.2. *Situational profile of two children in verbal aggressiveness across five situations.*

Such stable situational profiles are used, for example, in clinical assessment in order to determine critical situations that evoke a particular problem. For example, Wolpe and Lang (1964) developed a Fear Survey Schedule to assess the degree to which situations such as spiders, crossing a street, blood extraction, social evaluation, and so forth, evoke fear. The resulting situation profile tells the therapist what the critical situations are. Should the profiles be unstable, there would be no stable specific fear problems and no basis for a situation-specific intervention.

If psychologists trained in experimental psychology look at Figure 3.2, they may make the mistake of interpreting the two profiles in Figure 3.2 as an indication of a situation by trait interaction. Note that Figure 3.2 does not show a situation by trait interaction. Instead, it depicts a situation by person interaction. Actually, the two cases were designed such that the trait of verbal aggressiveness, estimated by the average aggression score across all situations, is identical for both children. If each person's score depends upon only a few observations for each situation, a large portion of the situation by person interaction will very likely be due to measurement error. Only if the situational differences within persons are reliable (as in the study by Shoda, Mischel and Wright 1994) does it make sense to interpret the person by situation interaction at all.

In the early days of the so-called *interactionism* in personality research, researchers tried to identify generalizable estimates of the proportion of variance that can be attributed to persons, situations and person by situation interaction (e.g., Endler and Hunt 1966). Such attempts are in vain because empirical studies which controlled measurement error by aggregating behaviour over time or across similar situations have found that the size of person-situation interaction varies greatly between different traits. For example, Diener and Larsen (1984) found that the interaction component was virtually zero for subjective wellbeing but maximum (equivalent to zero cross-situational consistency) for sociability at work versus in recreational situations. Furthermore, the size of the interaction also varies greatly according to the similarity of the selected situations: the more similar the situations, the smaller the interaction components. Theoretically, this problem could be solved by studying representative samples of trait-relevant situations but it is still an unresolved issue how one should determine the population of trait-relevant situations in the first place (Ten Berge and De Raad 1999). We need a serious study of the 'ecology of traits' to solve this problem.

One particularly relevant source of person-situation interaction has been surprisingly often ignored in discussions of cross-situational consistency within personality psychology: variation of dyadic social interaction in terms of who the interaction partners are. This question has been discussed much more by social psychologists but is obviously of great importance for personality psychology, because many of our daily situations are dyadic interactions. In this case, person-situation interactions are by and large person-person interactions because the interaction partner largely defines the situation. Because persons cannot interact with themselves and because persons and situations are not statistically independent factors (e.g., friendliness correlates positively between the two members of a dyad across different dyads), traditional ANOVA or correlational methods are not valid in this case.

Kenny and colleagues developed the *social relations model* (SRM) that distinguishes *actor effects*, *target effects* and *relationship effects*. Consider again a study of aggressiveness. In SRM, the actor parameter corresponds to the trait of aggressiveness: to what extent do I react aggressively to others? The target parameter (sometimes also called partner parameter) is a different trait, often ignored in studies of aggression: to what extent do I make *others* aggressive? From the perspective of the actor, this is a situational parameter: I will be more likely to behave aggressively if I meet someone with a high target parameter. Actor and target parameters can correlate positively or negatively; in the case of aggressiveness, a positive correlation is expected (aggressive persons tend to make others aggressive). Finally, the relationship parameter describes the extent to which the amount of an actor's aggression in a particular dyad cannot be predicted additively from the actor and the target parameter of the two people involved in the dyad. For example, I may have experienced a special history of aggressive exchanges with someone who is generally not particularly aggressive, and neither am I; in this case, we entertain a particularly aggressive relationship due to our interaction history that cannot be predicted from our broad traits alone. SRM analyses are increasingly used in person perception, dyadic relationship and family research (e.g., Cook 2000; Kenny, Mohr and Levesque 2001).

How should we define situations in personality research?

Up to this point I have avoided defining what a situation is. For good reasons, because this is a tricky question (Vansteenlandt and Van Mechelen 1998). A useful distinction is made in ecological psychology between a *setting* of a person that is defined completely by an observer (e.g., 'Fritz is together with his mother'), and a *subjective situation* that is partly defined by the person (e.g., 'Fritz is together with his friend Hans') (Barker 1968). Whether Hans is a friend of Fritz can ultimately be decided not by observers but only by Fritz himself. This person-dependency of the situational definition opens the door for personality influences *on the very definition of a situation.*

It can happen that Fritz considers Hans as his friend but Franz does not consider Hans as *his* friend although, from the perspective of any observer (including Hans) Fritz and Franz have the same relationship with Hans. The reason for the fact that Fritz, but not Franz, considers Hans as a friend could be, for example, that Fritz is a joyful extravert who considers most people as friends even if the relationship is superficial, whereas Franz is a critical introvert who is more restrictive in his usage of the term 'friend'. If we conduct a diary study on social interaction where the participants classify their interaction partner according to relationship types, including 'friends', Fritz and other extraverts will report more friends than Franz and other introverts. This correlation between extraversion (a trait measure) and amount of interaction with self-reported friends (a situational measure) is probably higher than the similar correlation between extraversion and amount of interaction with observer-reported friends, because extraversion biases the definition of what a friend is. The bottom line is that subjective situations are confounded with personality traits *by definition of the situation*, and therefore personality effects are often confounded with situational effects on behaviour, an unfortunate state of affairs that many personality researchers tend to ignore.

For example, Sarason, Shearin, Pierce and Sarason (1987) studied the correlation between self-reported loneliness and self-reported quantity and quality of social relationships. Loneliness correlated $-.28$ with the number of relationships, $-.53$ with the number of supportive relationships, and $-.63$ with satisfaction with the support of others. The more subjective the definition of the relationship quality, the higher the negative correlation with loneliness. Even the correlation of $-.28$ with the number of relationships is confounded with an effect of loneliness on the definition of what a relationship is.

Researchers can disentangle personality effects from situational effects in two main ways. First, they can restrict their analyses to settings that are completely defined by observers. In this case, the definition of the situation is independent from the personality of the actor in the situation. Although this seems to be a good solution at the first glance, a second look shows that it leads to an extreme reduction of information on personality antecedents, concomitants and effects. Studies that have stuck to a setting approach have resulted in rather trivial findings, for instance, that sociable people spend more time in social interaction outside work (Diener and Larsen 1984), or that the bedrooms and offices of conscientious people look more orderly than those of unconscientious people (Gosling, Ko, Mannarelli and Morris 2002). We would also like to know how sociable or highly conscientious people make friends and deal with friends, but a strict setting approach cannot answer such questions.

Alternatively, researchers can define a situation by aggregating the subjective situation perception across all actors in the situation. This approach underlies the SRM model used by Kenny and colleagues. It requires that each situation is judged by many actors such that the influence of each judge's personality is minimized. There are obvious limits to this approach, e.g., when one is interested in intimate relationships.

Some mechanisms linking traits and situations

In addition to the rather subtle influences of traits on situations by the situational definition itself, there are four main ways in which traits can correlate with situations (Buss 1987; Plomin, DeFries and Loehlin 1977). First, people tend to actively *select* (approach or avoid) situations according to their personality. In the pre-pdf era, intelligent people visited libraries more often than less intelligent people; shy people tend to avoid social interactions where they are the centre of others' attention, and so on. Secondly, people passively *evoke* situations by their personality. A physically attractive woman entering a room of strangers immediately creates (sometimes against her will) a different situation than a less attractive woman, who will be initially ignored by most of the people in the room. Thirdly, people *manipulate* (actively change or even create) situations by their personality. Socially competent people can settle an interpersonal conflict between others in a group better than less competent people, and they are more able to create a cooperative team of co-workers from a bunch of stubborn individualists.

Last but not least, situational exposure can affect personality traits over the long run. This is at least the assumption of traditional socialization research, with its one-sided look on personality as a consequence of situational exposure in the family. Although we know today that things are much more complex due to personality effects on the environment (see e.g., Asendorpf and Wilpers 1998; Lytton 1990), there is clear evidence that long-term situational exposure can change traits (e.g., effects of parenting or of the intellectual climate in the family on children's social-emotional and intellectual development even when indirect genetic influences on both the situational exposure and children's personality are controlled because only adoptive children or only within-family differences are studied; see Rutter 2006 for an overview). It should be noted, however, that these are situational effects on a different timescale than the personality effects on situations that were described before. Effects of exposure to just one situation on personality traits are rare and concern only extremely critical life events with long-lasting effects, such as natural disasters, sudden death of a beloved spouse or child, and other traumatic events.

Conclusion

To what extent situations present a problem for personality research very much depends on the specificity of the traits in terms of behaviour and situations. Everything else being equal, the more narrowly a trait is defined, the more likely are person-situation interactions and a low cross-situational consistency of the inter-individual differences in the trait-descriptive behaviours. Many of the resulting problems can be resolved by aggregating across more and more heterogeneous behaviours and situations. This leads, however, to the new problem that we will increasingly lose our hold of what the aggregate means. To illustrate this problem with a last example, Lasky, Hover, Smith *et al.* (1956) predicted the relapse rate of psychiatric patients by four different methods: psychiatric diagnosis, judgement by the non-academic staff members, judgement by other patients on the same ward, and the size of the patient's file (measured in inches). Best predictor was the size of the file, simply because it optimally capitalizes on aggregation across situations and behaviours. One may consider the file size as a measure of the trait of risking relapse, but beyond that, the file size alone does not tell us anything more about the patient. If we wish to learn more, we have to open the file and begin to study the complexities of person-situation interaction that were described in this chapter.

References

Allport, G. W. 1937. *Personality: a psychological interpretation*. New York: Holt

Asendorpf, J. B. and Wilpers, S. 1998. Personality effects on social relationships, *Journal of Personality and Social Psychology* 74: 1531–44

Barker, R. G. 1968. *Ecological psychology: concepts and methods for studying the environment of human behaviour*. Stanford University Press

Buss, D. M. 1987. Selection, evocation, and manipulation, *Journal of Personality and Social Psychology* 53: 1214–21

Cook, W. L. 2000. Understanding attachment security in family context, *Journal of Personality and Social Psychology* 78: 285–94

Diener, E. and Larsen, R. J. 1984. Temporal stability and cross-situational consistency of affective, behavioural, and cognitive responses, *Journal of Personality and Social Psychology* 47: 871–83

Endler, N. S. and Hunt, J. McV. 1966. Sources of behavioural variance as measured by the S-R inventory of anxiousness, *Psychological Bulletin* 65: 336–46

Funder, D. C. 1991. Global traits: a neo-Allportian approach to personality, *Psychological Science* 2: 31–9

Gosling, S. D., Ko, S. J., Mannarelli, T. and Morris, M. E. 2002. A room with a cue: personality judgments based on offices and bedrooms, *Journal of Personality and Social Psychology* 82: 379–98

Hartshorne, H. and May, M. A. 1928. *Studies in the nature of character,* vol. 1, *Studies in deceit.* New York: MacMillan

Kenny, D. A., Mohr, C. D. and Levesque, M. J. 2001. A social relations variance partitioning of dyadic behaviour, *Psychological Bulletin* 127: 128–41

Kenrick, D. T. and Funder, D. C. 1988. Profiting from controversy: lessons from the person-situation debate, *American Psychologist* 43: 23–34

Kluckhohn, C. and Murray, H. A. 1953. Personality formation: the determinants, in C. Kluckhohn, H. A. Murray and D. M. Schneider, *Personality in nature, society, and culture,* 2nd edn. Oxford: Knopf

Lamiell, J. T. 2003. *Beyond individual and group differences: human individuality, scientific psychology, and William Stern's critical personalism.* Thousand Oaks, CA: Sage

Lasky, J. J., Hover, G. L., Smith, P. A., Duffendack, S. C. and Nord, C. L. 1956. Post-hospital adjustment as predicted by psychiatric patients and their staff, *Journal of Consulting Psychology* 23: 213–18

Lytton, H. 1990. Child and parent effects in boys' conduct disorder: a reinterpretation, *Developmental Psychology* 26: 683–97

Mischel, W. 1968. *Personality and assessment.* New York: Wiley

Moskowitz, D. S. and Schwarz, J. C. 1982. Validity comparison of behaviour counts and ratings by knowledgeable informants, *Journal of Personality and Social Psychology* 42: 518–28

Plomin, R., DeFries, J. C. and Loehlin, J. C. 1977. Genotype-environment interaction and correlation in the analysis of human behaviour, *Psychological Bulletin* 84: 309–22

Rutter, M. 2006. *Genes and behaviour: nature-nurture interplay explained.* London: Blackwell

Sarason, B. R., Shearin, E. N., Pierce, G. R. and Sarason, I. G. 1987. Interrelations of social support measures: theoretical and practical implications, *Journal of Personality and Social Psychology* 52: 813–32

Shoda, Y., Mischel, W. and Wright, J. C. 1994. Intraindividual stability in the organization and patterning of behaviour: incorporating psychological situations into the idiographic analysis of personality, *Journal of Personality and Social Psychology* 67: 674–87

Stern, W. 1911. *Die Differentielle Psychologie in ihren methodischen Grundlagen [Methodological foundations of differential psychology].* Leipzig: Johann Ambrosius Barth

Ten Berge M. A. and De Raad, B. 1999. Taxonomies of situations from a trait psychological perspective: a review, *European Journal of Personality* 13: 337–60

Vansteenlandt, K. and Van Mechelen, I. 1998. Individual differences in situation-behaviour profiles: a triple typology model, *Journal of Personality and Social Psychology* 75: 751–65

Wolpe, J. and Lang, P. J. 1964. A Fear Survey Schedule for use in behaviour therapy, *Behaviour Research and Therapy* 2: 27–30

4 Personality and emotion

Rainer Reisenzein and Hannelore Weber

Since its beginnings as a sub-discipline of psychology (e.g., Allport 1937; Shand 1914), personality psychology has aimed at two different though related goals (see e.g., Cervone 2005; Mischel and Shoda 1998). The first goal is to construct a *general theory of the person*, understood as the integrated whole of the several sub-systems of the mind. The second goal is to describe and explain the interesting *psychological differences between individuals*, that is, the relatively stable psychological attributes that allow us uniquely to characterize individuals and to distinguish them from each other. If one accepts that the emotion system is an important sub-system of personality, and that inter-individual differences traceable to this system are important for describing individuals, it follows immediately that, to attain its goals, personality psychology must consider the emotions.

In accordance with this conclusion, most classical personality theorists proposed an affective (or affective-motivational) system as a core system of the mind; and most taxonomic systems of personality descriptors include a sub-set that refer directly or indirectly to emotions. Nonetheless, the in-depth investigation of emotions from a personality perspective has only begun fairly recently, in the wake of an upsurge of interest in the emotions that arose in the 1980s and continues to this day. Since that time, the two historically largely separate fields of personality psychology and emotion psychology (the latter being the sub-discipline of psychology that deals with the emotions) have become increasingly integrated, to the benefit of both fields.

In keeping with the two tasks of personality psychology, we will in this chapter first outline a model of the emotion system as a sub-system of personality (see also, Reisenzein and Horstmann 2006). As the basis of this model, we will then address emotion-related personality differences.

The emotion system as a sub-system of personality

On the definition of emotion

Although there is as yet no generally accepted theoretical definition of emotion, there is widespread agreement among emotion researchers that the objects of their

The authors thank Lars Penke and Uli Schimmack for their helpful comments on a previous version of the manuscript.

inquiry are, centrally, the transitory states of persons denoted by ordinary language words such as 'happiness', 'sadness', 'fear', 'anger', 'pity', 'pride', 'guilt', and so forth. There is also agreement that emotion episodes normally occur as reactions to the perception or imagination of 'objects' (typically events or states of affairs), and that they have both subjective and objective (intersubjectively observable) manifestations. Subjectively, emotions manifest themselves as pleasant or unpleasant feelings that seem to be directed at the eliciting objects (e.g., one feels happy about the arrival of a friend, see Reisenzein 1994; Russell 2003). Objectively, emotions manifest themselves, at least at times, in particular actions (e.g., flight or avoidance in the case of fear), expressive reactions (e.g., smiling in the case of joy), and physiological changes (e.g., a blood pressure increase in anger). Most classical and many contemporary emotion theorists, following common-sense psychology, *identify* emotions with the mentioned subjective experiences. However, some theorists (e.g., Lazarus 1991; Scherer 1984) define emotions more broadly as *response syndromes* that include not only mental but also bodily components, such as facial expressions and physiological arousal. This definition of emotions is problematic, however, because the correlations between the mental and bodily components of emotion syndromes are typically low (Reisenzein 2007). For this reason, and to keep in touch with common sense, we will use the general term 'emotion', as well as terms for specific emotions (e.g., 'fear', 'anger'), to refer to subjective experiences.

How emotions are generated

Today, the dominant theory of emotion generation is the *cognitive* or *appraisal theory* of emotion (e.g., Lazarus 1991; Ortony, Clore and Collins 1988; Scherer 2001; see Scherer, Schorr and Johnstone 2001, for an overview). Appraisal theory assumes that emotions arise if an event is *appraised in a motive-relevant manner*, that is, as representing an actual or potential fulfilment or frustration of a motive (= desire, wish). For example, Liz feels happy that Schmidt was elected chancellor if she (a) comes to believe that Schmidt was, indeed, elected and (b) evaluates this event positively, meaning that she takes it to be congruent with her motives. Analogously, Oscar is unhappy that Schmidt was elected chancellor if he comes to believe that this event happened and evaluates it negatively (as motive-incongruent). Hence, apart from cognitions in the narrow sense (i.e., beliefs), emotions also presuppose motives (Lazarus 1991; Roseman 1979; see Reisenzein 2006, for further discussion).

The appraisal of an event determines not only *whether or not* this event elicits an emotion, but also *which* emotion it elicits. Hedonically positive (i.e., experientially pleasant) emotions occur if an event is evaluated as motive-congruent, whereas hedonically negative (experientially unpleasant) emotions occur if an event is evaluated as motive-incongruent. The further distinctions between emotions depend, first, on the *kind of evaluation* made, for example, on whether an event is evaluated as just personally undesirable or as morally wrong (Ortony,

Clore and Collins 1988). Secondly, they depend on particular *factual* (*non-evaluative*) *appraisals*, including the appraisal of the event's probability, unexpectedness, controllability, and the appraisal of one's own or other people's responsibility for bringing it about (see Ellsworth and Scherer 2003). The relations between appraisals and specific emotions have been spelled out in several structural appraisal models (e.g., Lazarus 1991; Ortony, Clore and Collins 1988; Roseman, Antoniou and Jose 1996; Scherer 2001). In addition, attempts have been made to develop information-processing models of appraisal and emotion (for overviews, see e.g., Power and Dalgleish 1997; Scherer, Schorr and Johnstone 2001; Teasdale 1999). An important assumption shared by most of these information-processing models is that appraisal processes can occur in different *modes*. Of particular importance is the distinction between *non-automatic* and *automatic* modes of appraisal and, hence, of emotion generation. Whereas non-automatic appraisal processes are conscious inference strategies, automatic appraisals are unconscious and are 'triggered' fairly directly by the perception of eliciting events. Like other mental processes, initially non-automatic, conscious appraisals can become automatized as a result of their repeated execution (e.g., Reisenzein 2001; Siemer and Reisenzein 2007). Automatic appraisals can explain why emotions frequently follow eliciting events rapidly. They may also explain *moods*, that is, emotional experiences which seem to lack concrete objects (for further discussion of moods, see Schwarz and Clore 2007; Siemer 2005).

Functional effects of emotions

Both common-sense and scientific psychology assume that emotions can have strong effects on thought and action. Indeed, this is a main reason why emotions interest both lay people and psychologists. Traditionally, psychologists have tended to emphasize the negative, maladaptive effects of emotions. However, during the past twenty-five years, the view has increasingly gained acceptance that, notwithstanding their occasional negative consequences, emotions are *overall* adaptive. The adaptive effects of emotions are their (evolutionary) *functions*: the reasons why the emotion system came into existence in the first place. The two main, over-arching functions of emotions are widely thought to be the motivational and the informational functions of emotions (e.g., Frijda 1994).

The *motivational function* of emotions consists in their adaptive effects on motivation (the action goals of the person) and, thereby, on action itself. Two main routes from emotion to motivation have been proposed (Reisenzein 1996). According to the first route, emotions influence motivation by becoming goals of action – states one seeks to regulate by one's actions. This path from emotion to motivation is central in hedonistic theories of emotion (e.g., Bentham 1789/1970; Cox and Klinger 2004). These theories assume that one ultimate goal or basic motive of humans, if not their only basic motive, is the desire to maximize pleasure and to minimize pain (displeasure). The hedonistic desire can be activated by both actual and anticipated emotions: Negative feelings generate a desire to reduce them (if present) or to avoid them (if anticipated); positive feelings generate a desire to maintain them (if present) or to bring them about (if an opportunity arises). Note that these hedonistic desires can also influence cognitive processes, including appraisals. For example, the unpleasant feeling of fear elicited by a threatening event may motivate the person to avoid thinking about the event, or to try to actively reappraise it in more benign terms (Lazarus 1991; Gross 1998).

There can be little doubt that emotions influence motivation partly through the hedonistic route (see e.g., Baumeister, Vohs, DeWall and Zhang 2007). However, many emotion theorists believe that this is neither the only nor even the most important route from emotion to action (e.g., Frijda 1986; McDougall 1928; Lazarus 1991; Weiner 1995). Rather, according to these theorists, at least some emotions (e.g., fear) evoke adaptive action tendencies (e.g., to flee or to avoid) *directly*, that is, without the mediation of hedonistic desires (see Reisenzein 1996). This non-hedonistic theory of the emotion-action link seems better able than the hedonistic theory to account for the motivational effects of some emotions, such as the effect of pity on helping and of anger on aggression (Rudolph, Roesch, Greitemeyer and Weiner 2004).

The *informational function* of emotions consists in their making adaptively useful information available and/or salient to other sub-systems of personality (e.g., Forgas 2003; Schwarz and Clore 2007; Slovic, Peters, Finucane and MacGregor 2005). To illustrate, nervousness experienced when meeting a stranger can inform the decision-making system about the subconscious appraisal of the encounter as threatening. Similarly, a pleasant feeling experienced when reflecting on a possible course of action may signal the subconscious approval of the action. In addition, emotions can increase the salience or apparent plausibility of 'emotion-congruent' interpretations of ambiguous events. For example, when angry, people are more ready to interpret ambiguous negative events in an anger-typical way (e.g., to blame them on others; Siemer 2001; Lerner and Tiedens 2006). Although the resulting 'emotion-tinged' event interpretations may appear biased and even irrational, it can be argued that this biasing effect of emotions on cognitions is adaptive in many evolutionarily significant situations. Both the information provided by feelings and their effect on event interpretations can, indirectly, again influence action.

The emotion system as a component of personality

To sum up the preceding discussion, the emotion system seems to consist at its core of a mechanism that (1) *monitors* the relevance of cognized events for the person's desires or motives, and (2) *communicates* detected motive-relevant changes to other personality sub-systems and simultaneously proposes particular action goals (Frijda 1994; Reisenzein 2009).

It needs to be emphasized, however, that the described effects of emotion on thought and action are by no means inevitable. Rather, the person can to a considerable degree decide to heed versus ignore the 'suggestions' made by her emotions, as well as control or regulate the emotions themselves. As Frijda (1986, p. 401) put it, 'people not only *have* emotions, they also *handle* them' (emphasis added). Even radical hedonist theorists usually do not claim that humans are slaves to their *momentary* emotions but instead emphasize, for example, that people can decide to tolerate a current unpleasant feeling if they believe that this will spare them greater pain in the future (e.g., Bentham 1789/1970). And if, as most contemporary motivation theorists believe, people are also motivated by other than hedonistic concerns (e.g., Reiss 2000), possible reasons for emotion regulation multiply (see also, Parrott 1993; Tamir, Chiu and Gross 2007). To understand emotions and the role they play in personality, it is therefore also important to consider how people 'handle' their emotions (e.g., Gross 1998).

Emotion and personality: inter-individual differences

Having sketched the emotion system as a sub-system of personality, we turn to the second traditional task of personality psychology: to describe and explain the interesting, psychological differences between individuals. In the present context, interest is of course on inter-individual differences related to emotions. We consider this topic from two perspectives, a descriptive and an explanatory one (see also, Krohne 2003; Pekrun 2000): (a) emotional dispositions as descriptive dimensions of personality, and (b) personality determinants of emotions, with a focus on general motives and beliefs and on habitual styles of emotion regulation.

Emotional dispositions as descriptive dimensions of personality

So far, the bulk of the research on emotion-related individual differences has had a descriptive focus; that is, the main aim has been to identify the relatively stable *emotional dispositions* (i.e., propensities to experience emotions) in which people differ from each other, and to clarify their relations to each other and to established personality traits such as neuroticism or extraversion. One reason why research has concentrated on these questions is probably that they can be addressed without making many assumptions about the structure of the emotion system (as described earlier), or that of personality in general. About all that needs to be done is to measure emotional dispositions reliably, and to analyze the patterns of statistical co-variation among them and to other personality traits.

The ideal method of measuring emotional dispositions would be to confront people with a wide variety of carefully crafted realistic emotion-evoking events and to record their emotional reactions. However, this is in general unfeasible for ethical or practical reasons. As an alternative, emotional dispositions have been estimated from repeated self-reports of emotional experiences in daily life (e.g., Diener, Smith and Fujita 1995; Schimmack 2003), from reports of emotional reactions to hypothetical scenarios (e.g., Schimmack 1997), from retrospective self-ratings of habitually experienced emotions (e.g., Watson and Clark 1992; Izard, Libero, Putnam and Haynes 1993), and from direct self-ratings of perceived emotional propensities (e.g., Spielberger 1999; Wolpe and Lang 1964). Although each of these methods has its drawbacks, their results were broadly consistent, and can be summarized as follows.

Structure of emotional dispositions

Regarding the structure of emotional dispositions, three main conclusions can be made. First, at least moderately stable, reliable inter-individual differences in the propensities to experience emotions seem to exist for all commonly distinguished emotions (anger, fear, etc.) as well as for sub-types of these emotions directed at particular classes of objects (e.g., fear of dogs, fear of exams). Secondly, dispositions for hedonically positive emotions correlate with each other, and dispositions for hedonically negative emotions do so as well. For example, people who are prone to sadness also tend to be prone to fear, anger and guilt (note that this does not necessarily mean that the corresponding emotional states are experienced *at the same time*). Thirdly, the two superordinate dispositions to experience pleasant and unpleasant emotions seem to be largely independent (e.g., Diener, Smith and Fujita 1995; Schimmack, Oishi and Diener 2002). Hence, for example, people who get easily angry are about as likely as people who do not get easily angry to get quickly euphoric. In sum, emotional propensities seem to be structured in the form of two largely independent (or slightly negatively correlated) hierarchies of correlated dispositions, one for pleasant and the other for unpleasant emotions. This structure is compatible with appraisal theory.

Emotional dispositions and the Five-Factor Model of personality

Emotional dispositions, at least those that are stable and general, are a species of personality traits. How are they related to the personality dispositions typically featured in trait theories of personality? As already noted in the introduction, nearly all proposed taxonomies of personality descriptors contain terms that refer directly or indirectly to emotions. In fact, closer inspection suggests that emotional dispositions lie at the core of these taxonomies. To document this claim, let us look at the currently most popular trait model of personality, the Five-Factor Model. The Five-Factor Model of personality posits five main, relatively independent, broad personality dimensions: neuroticism, extraversion, agreeableness, conscientiousness, and openness to experience (see e.g., John and Srivastava 1999; McCrae and Costa 1999). Of these traits, four (neuroticism, extraversion, agreeableness and openness) are related to emotional dispositions. This is suggested by an examination of the theoretical definitions of these factors, by content analyses of the questionnaires used to measure them (Pytlik Zillig, Hemenover and Dienstbier 2002), and by their correlations to explicit measures of emotional dispositions, such as the trait form of the Positive and Negative Affect Schedule (PANAS) (a frequently used instrument for the assessment of pleasant and unpleasant affect; Watson, Clark and Tellegen 1988).

The strongest and most obvious link between the Big Five and emotional dispositions exists for *neuroticism*. As a matter of fact, neuroticism *is* primarily an emotional disposition: the propensity to experience negative emotions, in particular fear, anger and depression. No wonder, then, that strong correlations have been obtained between standard measures of neuroticism and measures of dispositional negative affect, such as the trait form of the Negative Affect sub-scale of the PANAS. The robustness of this finding led Tellegen (1985) to argue that neuroticism be renamed 'negative emotionality', which is indeed offered as an alternative label for neuroticism in a more recent chapter on the Five-Factor Model (John and Srivastava 1999).

Tellegen (1985) also proposed to rename *extraversion* 'positive emotionality' because of its conceptual and empirical relations to the propensity to experience positive affect (measured, for example, with the Positive Affect sub-scale of the PANAS), which he considered to be the core of extraversion. However, although positive emotionality may be its core, extraversion also subsumes other dispositions, in particular sociability (the tendency to be outgoing and sociable versus withdrawn and reserved) (see Costa and McCrae 1992; John and Srivastava 1999). Empirically, too, the correlations between extraversion and positive emotionality are not strong enough to warrant the identification of these dispositions (Lucas and Fujita 2000).

Agreeableness is usually defined as a behavioural disposition that contrasts a prosocial, communal orientation towards others with an antagonistic attitude. However, some of the best markers of agreeableness refer to emotional dispositions towards other people (e.g., 'affectionate', 'soft-hearted' versus 'cold'; John and Srivastava 1999); and empirically, agreeableness has been found to correlate negatively with trait anger (agreeable people are less anger-prone; e.g., Kuppens 2005) and positively with the tendency to experience empathic emotions (i.e., emotional reactions to the fate of others; Del Barrio, Aluja and García 2004). In addition, agreeable persons seem to try harder than non-agreeable persons to control the expression of negative emotions (Geisler, Wiedig-Allison and Weber in press; Tobin, Graziano, Vanman and Tassinary 2000).

Finally, individuals who score highly on *openness to experience* seem to be more emotionally sensitive to art and beauty, and to experience a wider range of feelings and emotions than people low on this trait (McCrae 2007; Terracciano, McCrae, Hagemann and Costa 2003).

In sum, of the five major dimensions of personality postulated by the Five-Factor Model, neuroticism is essentially a broad emotional disposition (to experience negative emotions); extraversion and agreeableness comprise emotional dispositions (toward positive affect and interpersonally relevant emotions, respectively) as central sub-components; and openness to experience is related to a specific emotional disposition (the capacity to experience aesthetic feelings) as well as to emotional differentiation.

As mentioned before, it is widely accepted today that emotions have adaptive effects, which were the reason why the emotion system (at least its core) emerged in evolution. This raises the question of whether *individual differences in emotionality* (e.g., fearfulness or irascibility) are likewise, at least in part, the product of natural selection. Although there is now strong evidence for the partial heritability of the Big Five (e.g., Bouchard 2004), and hence for the heritability of basic inter-individual differences in emotionality, this does not imply that these heritable inter-individual differences are adaptive. On the contrary, it has been argued that the very existence of heritable variation in a trait signals a *lack* of adaptive significance (Tooby and Cosmides 1990). Applied to emotional dispositions, Tooby and Cosmides' argument is that, if differences in emotionality (e.g., low versus high fearfulness) had been subject to selection pressure, they would not have prevailed over evolutionary times but would have converged to an optimal level of emotionality (e.g., medium fearfulness). However, as noted by Penke, Denissen and Miller (2007), inter-individual differences in emotionality could have evolved if, as seems plausible, a generally optimal level of fearfulness, irascibility, etc. did not exist in our evolutionary past, but different levels of emotionality were most adaptive in different environments or social niches.

Personality determinants of emotions

One strength of the appraisal theory of emotion is that it can readily explain how inter-individual differences in emotional reactions to the same event arise at the psychological level (Roseman and Smith 2001). For example, in answer to the question why Liz is happy that Schmidt was elected chancellor whereas Oscar is unhappy about this event, appraisal theory proposes the following two-step explan-ation: (a) Liz appraised Schmidt's election as desirable, whereas Oscar appraised it as undesirable; (b) these differences in appraisal, in turn, are due to inter-individual differences in the cognitive and motivational structures (e.g., memory schemas) that underlie appraisal processes. At least some of these structures are sufficiently stable to be regarded as components of personality. These are, in particular, relatively stable and general *desires*, and relatively stable and general *beliefs* about the world and the self (Lazarus 1991; Pekrun 1988; Smith and Kirby 2001). For example, Oscar's and Liz's opposing appraisals of Schmidt's election as chancellor may be traceable to their different, long-standing political preferences: Oscar is a conserva-tive, whereas Liz is left-wing. Viewed from an information-processing perspective, these personality determinants of appraisal concern the *content* of the cognitive and motivational structures that underlie the appraisal of concrete events (Reisenzein 2001). The information-processing perspective suggests that the personality deter-minants of appraisal may comprise, in addition, inter-individual differences in the *chronic accessibility* of appraisal-relevant cognitive and motivational structures (e.g., memory schemas; for support see e.g., Higgins, Bond, Klein and Strauman 1986) as well as differences in the *procedures* habitually used for processing appraisal-relevant information (e.g., Cacioppo, Petty and Feinstein 1996).

Although clarifying the personality determinants of appraisals, and thereby those of emotions, was already declared a main task of emotion psychology by

Lazarus, Averill and Opton (1970), so far only limited systematic research has been devoted to this issue. Nearly all of this research has been concerned with the effects of stable, general desires and beliefs on emotional states.

General desires as personality determinants of emotions

Appraisal theory postulates that emotions arise if an event is appraised as motive-congruent or motive-incongruent, and that the intensity of the resulting emotions depends on the strength of the motive, or the subjective importance of the goal (i.e., the content of the desire) at stake. Motive and goal theorists commonly assume that the goals that a person has in a specific situation (e.g., a student's goal to pass a particular examination) are derived from more fundamental goals for which the specific goals are viewed as means to ends (e.g., Brunstein, Schultheiss and Grässmann 1998; Reiss 2000). At the top of the motive hierarchy are presumably a set of basic desires which constitute the ultimate sources of human motivation (e.g., Reiss 2000). These assumptions entail that the emotional reaction to a concrete event should be influenced by the degree to which superordinate desires are affected by this event, as well as the strength of these desires.

A number of tests of this assumption have been made. For example, Sheldon, Elliot, Kim and Kasser (2001) asked participants to recall the single most satisfying event experienced during the last month and to rate the extent to which this event satisfied each of ten candidate basic desires (e.g., the desire for competence, security, relatedness, popularity and personal autonomy). For nine of the ten desires, the satisfaction scores correlated significantly positively with ratings of positive affect experienced during the event. Other research has focused on an intermediate level of the motive hierarchy, where the top-level desires (e.g., the achievement motive) are concretized to more specific desires that represent what the person wants to attain in her current life situation (e.g., getting good grades; see Brunstein, Schultheiss and Grässmann 1998). For example, Emmons (1986) related these intermediate-level desires, called *personal strivings*, to emotions using an experiencing-sampling method. He obtained evidence that successful versus unsuccessful pursuit of personal strivings constitutes a major source of positive versus negative affect in everyday life (for additional information, see Emmons 1996; Brunstein, Schultheiss and Maier 1999).

Beyond relating positive and negative emotions to desire fulfilment and desire frustration, respectively, appraisal theorists have linked particular emotions to particular *kinds* of desires (e.g., Lazarus 1991; Ortony, Clore and Collins 1988; Roseman 1979). An important distinction in this context is that between *wanting* versus *diswanting* a state of affairs (Roseman 1979), or between having an *approach goal* versus an *avoidance goal*. It has been proposed that qualitatively different positive and negative emotions are experienced if an approach versus an avoidance goal, respectively, is attained or non-attained. To illustrate, assume Oscar has informed Liz that he intends to visit her. If Liz *wants* Oscar to visit (approach goal) she will be happy if he comes and disappointed if he does not; whereas if Liz *diswants* Oscar to visit (avoidance goal), she will be dismayed if he comes and relieved if he does not (e.g., Ortony, Clore and Collins 1988; Roseman 1979). Several theorists (e.g., Gray 1994; see Carver 2006 for a review) proposed (a) that the pursuit of approach versus avoidance goals activates one of two different, basic motivational systems, a behavioural approach system (BAS) or a behavioural inhibition (BIS) system; and (b) that people differ in central parameters of these systems, specifically in the relative strength of their general approach and avoidance motivation. If so, these inter-individual differences should be related to the intensity of the emotions connected to the attainment or non-attainment of approach and avoidance goals. Supporting this assumption, Carver (2004) found that a measure of inter-individual differences in general approach motivation (BAS sensitivity) predicted the intensity of sadness and anger in response to frustration (the non-occurrence of an expected positive event).

General beliefs as personality determinants of emotions

There is also evidence that appraisal-related, general beliefs influence emotional reactions to events. The two general beliefs that have been most extensively researched in this regard are (a) optimism (versus pessimism), defined as a generalized expectancy for positive (versus negative) outcomes (Scheier, Carver and Bridges 2001); and (b) general self-efficacy, defined as a person's generalized belief in her ability to reach her goals and to master difficult or stressful situations (Bandura 1997; Schwarzer and Jerusalem 1995).

Optimism has been found, for example, to correlate negatively with depressive symptoms and negative habitual mood, but positively with positive habitual mood (e.g., Scheier, Carver and Bridges 2001; Symister and Friend 2003). *General self-efficacy* has been found, for example, to be associated with lower state anxiety during a stressful cognitive task (Endler, Speer, Johnson and Flett 2001) and lower levels of depression and anxiety in medical patients (e.g., Luszczynska, Gutiérrez-Doña and Schwarzer 2005). These findings are consistent with the hypothesis that optimism and general self-efficacy affect emotional states at least partly by influencing the appraisals of events; it should be noted, however, that direct evidence for this mediating path is so far scarce (e.g., Kaiser, Major and McCoy 2004; Schwarzer and Jerusalem 1999). Furthermore, this is most likely not the only causal path through which optimism and general self-efficacy influence emotions. For example, compared to pessimists, optimists also use more active coping strategies aimed at eliminating or reducing problems and negative emotions (Solberg Nes and Segerstrom 2006).

Other general beliefs that have been found to predict the emotional reactions to events include interpersonal trust, hostility and sensitivity to injustice. *General interpersonal trust* was found to moderate the effects of a violation of the social norm of equality on negative emotions (Stouten, De Cremer and van Dijk 2006). *Hostility*, defined as a disposition whose core is the general belief that other people are unworthy and likely to be sources of frustration and aggression, was found to predict state anger caused by negative interpersonal events (see Aquino, Douglas and Martinko 2004; Smith 1992). *Sensitivity to injustice*, a disposition character-ized among others by the belief that one is frequently the victim of unfairness, was found to predict state anger caused by a concrete unfair treatment (Mohiyeddini and Schmitt 1997; Schmitt 1996).

Personality determinants of emotion regulation and coping

As mentioned, people are not slaves to their emotions and in fact often try to control their emotions and their effects on thought and action. This consideration suggests that the personality determinants of emotions may also comprise habitual strategies, or 'styles' of regulating emotions and of coping with emotional events, a suggestion that has been explored in numerous studies (e.g., Carver, Scheier and Weintraub 1989; Lazarus and Folkman 1984). Emotion regulation and coping styles have been investigated for emotion in general, for groups of emotions (in particular stress-related emotions), and for specific emotions, notably anger, anxiety and depression.

Research on habitual tendencies of 'handling' anger initially distinguished two coping styles: *anger-out* (showing overt, aggressive reactions) and *anger-in* (suppressing the overt expression of anger; Spielberger 1999). Neither of these strategies is very effective in reducing anger, however (Deffenbacher, Oetting, Thwaites *et al.* 1996). More recent research has taken a broader range of anger regulation strategies into view (Linden, Hogan, Rutledge *et al.* 2003), including effective anger-reduction strategies such as non-hostile feedback and humour (e.g., Geisler, Wiedig-Allison and Weber in press; Weber and Wiedig-Allison 2007). Theory and research on *anxiety regulation* focused traditionally on the dichotomy of avoiding versus approaching anxiety-related information (e.g., Byrne 1964; Krohne 2003). For example, Krohne (2003) distinguished between *cognitive avoidance* and *vigilance* as the two fundamental forms of anxiety regulation and proposed that avoidance is motivated by the short-term hedonistic desire to reduce the feeling of fear, whereas vigilance is motivated by the epistemic desire to gain information about the threatening event. According to Krohne, these two coping strategies are uncorrelated at the dispositional level, that is, individuals may score either low or high on both dimensions. Finally, in research on depression, a ruminative coping style, defined as thoughts and actions that focus attention on symptoms and their possible causes and consequences, has been extensively studied (Nolen-Hoeksema 1991). Rumination has been found to increase negative feelings and to impair cognitive and social functioning, in particular when compared with distraction (Lyubomirsky and Tkach 2004; Thomsen 2006).

A general taxonomy of emotion regulation methods that subsumes the described strategies was proposed by Gross (1998; John and Gross 2007). This taxonomy distinguishes five classes of emotion regulation strategies: situation selection, situation modification, attentional deployment (e.g., vigilance versus avoidance), reappraisal and response modulation.

In 1990, Salovey and Meyer proposed that the capacity to regulate one's emotions in situationally appropriate ways should be viewed as but one facet of a broader capacity termed *emotional intelligence*, which they defined as: the ability to recognize one's own and other's emotions, to use the information contained in emotional experience to guide judgement and action, and to manage the experience and expression of emotions (Salovey and Mayer 1990; see also, Mayer, Salovey and Caruso 2004). Since then, the concept of emotional intelligence has become enormously popular, and numerous studies have been conducted that related individual differences in emotional intelligence, measured through various tests (some of which are, however, based on competing concepts of emotional intelligence, e.g., Bar-On 1997) to a variety of outcome measures. These studies found that emotional intelligence has a small to moderate positive correlation to performance (Van Rooy and Viswesvaran 2004) and to mental and physical health (Schutte, Malouff, Thorsteinsson *et al.* 2007). Although measures of emotional intelligence also correlate substantially with measures of more traditional personality dispositions, including coping style (e.g., Day, Therrien and Carroll 2005; Van Rooy and Viswesvaran 2004), they appear to retain some predictive validity even when these correlations to traditional measures are taken into account.

References

Allport, G. W. 1937. *Personality: a psychological interpretation*. New York: Holt

Aquino, K., Douglas, S. and Martinko, M. J. 2004. Overt anger in response to victimization: attributional style and organizational norms as moderators, *Journal of Occupational Health Psychology* 9: 152–64

Bandura, A. 1997. *Self-efficacy: the exercise of control*. New York: Freeman

Bar-On, R. 1997. *Emotional Quotient Inventory: technical manual*. Toronto: Multi-Health Systems

Baumeister, R. F., Vohs, K. D., DeWall, C. N. and Zhang, L. 2007. How emotion shapes behaviour: feedback, anticipation, and reflection, rather than direct causation, *Personality and Social Psychology Review* 11: 167–203

Bentham, J. 1789/1970. *An introduction to the principles of morals and legislation*. London: Athlone Press

Bouchard, T. J. Jr. 2004. Genetic influence on human psychological traits, *Current Directions in Psychological Science* 13: 148–51

Brunstein, J. C., Schultheiss, O. C. and Grässmann, R. 1998. Personal goals and emotional well-being: the moderating role of motive dispositions, *Journal of Personality and Social Psychology* 75: 494–508

Brunstein, J. C., Schultheiss, O. C. and Maier, G. W. 1999. The pursuit of personal goals: a motivational approach to well-being and life adjustment, in J. Brandtstädter and R. M. Lerner (eds.), *Action and self-development: theory and research through the life span*, pp. 169–96. New York: Sage

Byrne, D. 1964. Repression-sensitization as a dimension of personality, in B. A. Maher (ed.), *Progress in experimental personality research*, vol. I, pp. 169–220. New York: Academic Press

Cacioppo, J. T., Petty, R. E. and Feinstein, J. 1996. Dispositional differences in cognitive motivation: the life and times of individuals varying in need for cognition, *Psychological Bulletin* 119: 197–253

Carver, C. S. 2004. Negative affects deriving from the behavioural approach system, *Emotion* 4: 3–22

    2006. Approach, avoidance, and the self-regulation of affect and action, *Motivation and Emotion* 30: 105–10

Carver, C. S., Scheier, M. F. and Weintraub, J. G. 1989. Assessing coping strategies: a theoretically based approach, *Journal of Personality and Social Psychology* 56: 267–83

Cervone, D. 2005. Personality architecture: within-person structures and processes, *Annual Review of Psychology* 56: 423–52

Costa, P. T. and McCrae, R. R. 1992. *NEO PI-R Professional manual*. Odessa, FL: Psychological Assessment Resources

Cox, W. M. and Klinger, E. 2004. *Handbook of motivational counseling*. Chichester: Wiley

Day, A. L., Therrien, D. L. and Carroll, S. A. 2005. Predicting psychological health: assessing the incremental validity of emotional intelligence beyond personality, type A behaviour, and daily hassles, *European Journal of Personality* 19: 519–36

Deffenbacher, J. L., Oetting, E. R., Thwaites, G. A., Lynch, R. S., Baker, D. A., Stark, R. S., Thacker, S. and Eiswerth-Cox, L. 1996. State-trait anger theory and the utility of the trait anger scale, *Journal of Counseling Psychology* 43: 131–48

Del Barrio, V., Aluja, A. and García, L. F. 2004. Relationship between empathy and the Big Five of personality traits in a sample of Spanish adolescents, *Social Behaviour and Personality* 32: 677–82

Diener, E., Smith, H. and Fujita, F. 1995. The personality structure of affect, *Journal of Personality and Social Psychology* 69: 130–41

Ellsworth, P. C. and Scherer, K. R. 2003. Appraisal processes in emotion, in R. J. Davidson, K. R. Scherer and H. H. Goldsmith (eds.), *Handbook of affective sciences*, pp. 572–95. Oxford University Press

Emmons, R. A. 1986. Personal strivings: an approach to personality and subjective well-being, *Journal of Personality and Social Psychology* 51: 1058–68

    1996. Striving and feeling: personal goals and subjective well-being, in P. M. Gollwitzer and J. A. Bargh (eds.), *The psychology of action: linking cognition and motivation to behaviour*, pp. 313–37. New York: Guilford Press

Endler, N. S., Speer, R. L., Johnson, J. M. and Flett, G. L. 2001. General self-efficacy and control in relation to anxiety and cognitive performance, *Current Psychology: Developmental, Learning, Personality, Social* 20: 36–52

Forgas, J. P. 2003. Affective influences on attitudes and judgments, in R. J. Davidson, K. R. Scherer, and H. H. Goldsmith (eds.), *Handbook of affective sciences*, pp. 596–618. Oxford University Press

Frijda, N. H. 1986. *The emotions*. Cambridge University Press

    1994. Emotions are functional, most of the time, in P. Ekman and R. J. Davidson (eds.), *The nature of emotion*, pp. 112–36. Oxford University Press

Geisler, F. C. M., Wiedig-Allison, M. and Weber, H. in press. What coping tells about personality, *European Journal of Personality*

Gray, J. A. 1994. *Three fundamental emotion systems*, in P. Ekman and R. J. Davidson (eds.), *The nature of emotion*, pp. 243–8. Oxford University Press

Gross, J. J. 1998. The emerging field of emotion regulation: an integrative review, *Review of General Psychology* 2: 271–99

Higgins, E. T. Bond, R. N., Klein, R. and Strauman, T. 1986. Self-discrepancies and emotional vulnerability: how magnitude, accessibility, and type of discrepancy influence affect, *Journal of Personality and Social Psychology* 51: 5–15

Izard, C. E., Libero, D. Z., Putnam, P. and Haynes, O. M. 1993. Stability of emotional experiences and their relations to traits of personality, *Journal of Personality and Social Psychology* 64: 847–60

John, O. P. and Gross, J. J. 2007. Individual differences in emotion regulation, in J. J. Gross (ed.), *Handbook of emotion regulation*, pp. 351–72. New York: Guilford Press

John, O. P. and Srivastava, S. 1999. The Big Five trait taxonomy: history, measurement, and theoretical perspectives, in L. A. Pervin and O. P. John (eds.), *Handbook of personality: theory and research*, 2nd edn, pp. 102–38. New York: Guilford Press

Kaiser, C. R., Major, B. and McCoy, S. K. 2004. Expectations about the future and the emotional consequences of perceiving prejudice, *Personality and Social Psychology Bulletin* 30: 173–84

Krohne, H. W. 2003. Individual differences in emotional reactions and coping, in R. J. Davidson, K. R. Scherer and H. H. Goldsmith (eds.), *Handbook of affective science*, pp. 698–725. New York: Oxford University Press

Kuppens, P. 2005. Interpersonal determinants of trait anger: low agreeableness, perceived low social esteem, and the amplifying role of the importance attached to social relationships, *Personality and Individual Differences* 38: 13–23

Lazarus, R. S. 1991. *Emotion and adaptation*. New York: Oxford University Press

Lazarus, R. S., Averill, J. R. and Opton, E. M. Jr. 1970. Toward a cognitive theory of emotion, in M. B. Arnold (ed.), *Feelings and emotions*, pp. 207–32. New York: Academic Press

Lazarus, R. S. and Folkman, S. 1984. *Stress, appraisal, and coping*. New York: Springer

Lerner, J. S. and Tiedens, L. Z. 2006. Portrait of the angry decision maker: how appraisal tendencies shape anger's influence on cognition, *Journal of Behavioural Decision Making* 19: 115–37

Linden, W., Hogan, B. E., Rutledge, T., Chawla, A., Lenz, J. W. and Leung, D. 2003. There is more to anger coping than 'in' or 'out', *Emotion* 3: 12–29

Lucas, R. E. and Fujita, F. 2000. Factors influencing the relation between extraversion and pleasant affect, *Journal of Personality and Social Psychology* 79: 1039–56

Luszczynska, A., Gutiérrez-Doña, B. and Schwarzer, R. 2005. General self-efficacy in various domains of human functioning: evidence from five countries, *International Journal of Psychology* 40: 80–9

Lyubomirsky, S. and Tkach, C. 2004. The consequences of dysphoric rumination, in C. Papageorgiou and A. Wells (eds.), *Depressive rumination: nature, theory and treatment*, pp. 21–42. Chichester: Wiley

Mayer, J. D., Salovey, P. and Caruso, D. R. 2004. Emotional intelligence: theory, findings, and implications, *Psychological Inquiry* 15: 197–215

McCrae, R. R. 2007. Aesthetic chills as a universal marker of openness to experience, *Motivation and Emotion* 31: 5–11

McCrae, R. R. and Costa, P. T., Jr 1999. A five-factor theory of personality, in L. A. Pervin and O.P. John (eds.), *Handbook of personality: theory and research*, 2nd edn, pp. 139–53. New York: Guilford Press

McDougall, W. 1928. *An outline of psychology*, 4th ed. London: Methuen

Mischel, W. and Shoda, Y. 1998. Reconciling processing dynamics and personality dispositions, *Annual Review of Psychology* 49: 229–58

Mohiyeddini, C. and Schmitt, M. J. 1997. Sensitivity to befallen injustice and reactions to unfair treatment in a laboratory situation, *Social Justice Research* 10: 333–53

Nolen-Hoeksema, S. 1991. Responses to depression and their effects on the duration of depressive episodes, *Journal of Abnormal Psychology* 100: 569–82

Ortony, A., Clore, G. L. and Collins, A. 1988. *The cognitive structure of emotions*. New York: Cambridge University Press

Parrott, W. G. 1993. Beyond hedonism: motives for inhibiting good moods and for maintaining bad moods, in D. M. Wegner and J. W. Pennebaker (eds.), *Handbook of mental control*, pp. 278–305. Englewood Cliffs, NJ: Prentice-Hall

Pekrun, R. 1988. *Emotion, Motivation und Persönlichkeit* [*Emotion, motivation and personality*]. Munich: Psychologie Verlags Union

  2000. Persönlichkeit und Emotion [Personality and emotion], in J. H. Otto and H. A. Euler (eds.), *Emotionspsychologie: Ein Handbuch*, pp. 334–48. Munich: Psychologie Verlags Union

Penke, L., Denissen, J. J. A. and Miller, G. F. 2007. The evolutionary genetics of personality, *European Journal of Personality* 21: 549–87

Power, M. and Dalgleish, T. 1997. *Cognition and emotion: from order to disorder*. Hove: Psychology Press

Pytlik Zillig, L. M., Hemenover, S. H. and Dienstbier, R. A. 2002. What do we assess when we assess a 'Big Five' trait?: a content analysis of the affective, behavioural, and cognitive (ABC) processes represented in Big Five personality inventories, *Personality and Social Psychology Bulletin* 28: 847–58

Reisenzein, R. 1994. Pleasure-arousal theory and the intensity of emotions, *Journal of Personality and Social Psychology* 67: 525–39

  1996. Emotional action generation, in W. Battmann and S. Dutke (eds.), *Processes of the molar regulation of behaviour*, pp. 151–65. Lengerich: Pabst Science Publishers

  2001. Appraisal processes conceptualized from a schema-theoretic perspective: contributions to a process analysis of emotions, in K. R. Scherer, A. Schorr and T. Johnstone (eds.), *Appraisal processes in emotion: theory, methods, research*, pp. 187–201. Oxford University Press

  2006. Arnold's theory of emotion in historical perspective, *Cognition and Emotion* 20: 920–51

  2007. What is a definition of emotion? And are emotions mental-behavioural processes?, *Social Science Information* 46: 424–8

  2009. Emotions as metarepresentational states of mind: naturalizing the belief-desire theory of emotion, *Cognitive Systems Research* 10: 6–20

Reisenzein, R. and Horstmann, G. 2006. Emotion, in H. Spada (ed.), *Lehrbuch Allgemeine Psychologie*, vol. III, pp. 435–500. Bern: Huber

Reiss, S. 2000. *Who am I: the 16 basic desires that motivate our actions and define our personality*. New York: Tarcher Putnam

Roseman, I. J. 1979. Cognitive aspects of emotions and emotional behaviour. Paper presented at the 87th Annual Convention of the APA, New York City, September 1979

Roseman, I. J., Antoniou, A. A. and Jose, P. E. 1996. Appraisal determinants of emotions: constructing a more accurate and comprehensive theory, *Cognition and Emotion* 10: 241–77

Roseman, I. J. and Smith, C. A. 2001. Appraisal theory: overview, assumptions, varieties, controversies, in K. R. Scherer, A. Schorr, and T. Johnstone (eds.), *Appraisal processes in emotion: theory, methods, research*, pp. 3–19. Oxford University Press

Rudolph, U., Roesch, S., Greitemeyer, T. and Weiner, B. 2004. A meta-analytic review of help giving and aggression from an attributional perspective: contributions to a general theory of motivation, *Cognition and Emotion* 18: 815–48

Russell, J. A. 2003. Core affect and the psychological construction of emotion, *Psychological Review* 110: 145–72

Salovey, P. and Mayer, J. D. 1990. Emotional intelligence, *Imagination, Cognition and Personality* 9: 185–211

Scheier, M. F., Carver, C. S. and Bridges, M. W. 2001. Optimism, pessimism, and psychological well-being, in E. C. Chang (ed.), *Optimism and pessimism: implications for theory, research, and practice*, pp. 189–216. Washington, DC: American Psychological Association

Scherer, K. R. 1984. On the nature and function of emotion: a component process approach, in K. R. Scherer and P. Ekman (eds.), *Approaches to emotion*, pp. 293–317. Hillsdale, NJ: Erlbaum

  2001. Appraisal considered as a process of multilevel sequential checking, in K. R. Scherer, A. Schorr and T. Johnstone (eds.), *Appraisal processes in emotion: theory, methods, research*, pp. 92–120. Oxford University Press

Scherer, K. R., Schorr, A. and Johnstone, T. 2001. *Appraisal processes in emotion: theory, methods, research*. Oxford University Press

Schimmack, U. 1997. Affect intensity: separating intensity and frequency in repeatedly measured affect, *Journal of Personality and Social Psychology* 73: 1313–29

  2003. Affect measurement in experience sampling research, *Journal of Happiness Studies* 4: 79–106

Schimmack, U, Oishi, S. and Diener, E. 2002. Cultural influences on the relation between pleasant emotions and unpleasant emotions: Asian dialectic philosophies or individualism-collectivism?, *Cognition and Emotion* 16: 705–19

Schmitt, M. 1996. Individual differences in sensitivity to befallen injustice, *Personality and Individual Differences* 21: 3–20

Schutte, N., Malouff, J., Thorsteinsson, E., Bhullar, N. and Rooke, S. 2007. A meta-analytic investigation of the relationship between emotional intelligence and health, *Personality and Individual Differences* 42: 921–33

Schwarz, N. and Clore, G. L. 2007. Feelings and phenomenal experiences, in A. W. Kruglanski and E. T. Higgins (eds.), *Social psychology: Handbook of basic principles*, 2nd edn, pp. 385–407. New York: Guilford Press

Schwarzer, R. and Jerusalem, M. 1995. Generalized Self-Efficacy Scale, in J. Weinman, S. Wright and M. Johnston (eds.), *Measures in health psychology: a user's portfolio. Causal and control beliefs*, pp. 35–7. Windsor: NFER-Nelson

  1999. *Skalen zur Erfassung von Lehrer- und Schülermerkmalen* [Scales for the assessment of teacher and student characteristics]. Berlin: Freie Universität Berlin

Shand, A. F. 1914. *The foundations of character*. London: Macmillan

Sheldon, K. M., Elliot, A. J., Kim, Y. and Kasser, T. 2001. What is satisfying about satisfying events? Testing 10 candidate psychological needs, *Journal of Personality and Social Psychology* 80: 325–39

Siemer, M. 2001. Mood-specific effects on appraisal and emotion judgments, *Cognition and Emotion* 15: 453–85

    2005. Moods as multiple-object directed and as objectless affective states: an examination of the dispositional theory of moods, *Cognition and Emotion* 19: 815–45

Siemer, M. and Reisenzein, R. 2007. The process of emotion inference, *Emotion* 7: 1–20

Slovic, P., Peters, E., Finucane, M. L. and MacGregor, D. G. 2005. Affect, risk, and decision making, *Health Psychology* 24: 35–40

Smith, C. A. and Kirby, L. D. 2001. Toward delivering on the promise of appraisal theory, in K. R. Scherer A. Schorr, and T. Johnstone (eds.), *Appraisal processes in emotion: theory, methods, research*, pp. 121–38. New York: Oxford University Press

Smith, T. W. 1992. Hostility and health: status of a psychosomatic hypothesis, *Health Psychology* 11: 139–50

Solberg Nes, L. and Segerstrom, S. C. 2006. Dispositional optimism and coping: a meta-analytic review, *Personality and Social Psychology Review* 10: 235–51

Spielberger, C. D. 1999. *Manual for the State-Trait Anger Expression Inventory-2*. Odessa, FL: Psychological Assessment Resources

Stouten, J., De Cremer, D. and van Dijk, E. 2006. Violating equality in social dilemmas: emotional and retributive reactions as a function of trust, attribution, and honesty, *Personality and Social Psychology Bulletin* 32: 894–906

Symister, P. and Friend, R. 2003. The influence of social support and problematic support on optimism and depression in chronic illness: a prospective study evaluating self-esteem as a mediator, *Health Psychology* 4: 249–88

Tamir, M., Chiu, C.-Y. and Gross, J. E. 2007. Business or pleasure? Utilitarian versus hedonic considerations in emotion regulation, *Emotion* 7: 546–54

Teasdale, J. D. 1999. Multi-level theories of cognition-emotion relations, in T. Dalgleish and M. Power (eds.), *Handbook of cognition and emotion*, pp. 665–81. Chicester: Wiley

Tellegen, A. 1985. Structures of mood and personality and their relevance to assessing anxiety, with an emphasis on self-report, in A. H. Tuma and J. D. Maser (eds.), *Anxiety and the anxiety disorders*, pp. 681–706. Hillsdale, NJ: Erlbaum

Terracciano, A., McCrae, R. R., Hagemann, D. and Costa, P. T. Jr. 2003. Individual difference variables, affective differentiation, and the structures of affect, *Journal of Personality* 71: 669–703

Thomsen, D. K. 2006. The association between rumination and negative affect: a review, *Cognition and Emotion* 20: 1216–35

Tobin, R. M., Graziano, W. G., Vanman, E. J. and Tassinary, L. G. 2000. Personality, emotional experience, and efforts to control emotions, *Journal of Personality and Social Psychology* 79: 656–69

Tooby, J. and Cosmides, L. 1990. On the universality of human nature and the uniqueness of the individual: the role of genetics and adaptation, *Journal of Personality* 58: 17–67

Van Rooy, D. L. and Viswesvaran, C. 2004. Emotional intelligence: a meta-analytic investigation of predictive validity and nomological net, *Journal of Vocational Behaviour* 65: 71–95

Watson, D. and Clark, L. A. 1992. On traits and temperament: general and specific factors of emotional experience and their relation to the five factor model, *Journal of Personality* 60: 441–76

Watson, D., Clark, L. A. and Tellegen, A. 1988. Development and validation of brief measures of positive and negative affect: the PANAS scales, *Journal of Personality and Social Psychology* 54: 1063–70

Weber, H. and Wiedig-Allison, M. 2007. Sex differences in anger-related behaviour: comparing expectancies to actual behaviour, *Cognition and Emotion* 21: 1669–98

Weiner, B. 1995. *Judgments of responsibility: a foundation for a theory of social conduct.* New York: Guilford

Wolpe, J. and Lang, P. J. 1964. A fear survey schedule for use in behaviour therapy, *Behaviour Research and Therapy* 2: 27–30

5   The characterization of persons: some fundamental conceptual issues

James T. Lamiell

Since early in the twentieth century, mainstream empirical research in the psychology of personality has revolved around the assessment and study of individual differences. The essential tasks of the field have been understood as those of (a) identifying a set of basic dimensions in terms of which all individuals can be differentially characterized within a common overall framework; (b) investigating the sources ('causes') of individual differences along the identified dimensions in terms of nature and nurture, and (c) determining the manifestations ('effects') of these differences in various domains of human behaviour such as school, work, interpersonal relations, etc. As I have noted in other works, this investigative agenda can be schematized as in Figure 5.1 (Lamiell 2000, 2003).

Unfortunately, this entire enterprise has been predicated on the notion that our scientific understanding of the behaviour/psychological functioning of *individuals* can be advanced through the systematic investigation of *variables* representing *individual differences* (Lamiell 1987, 1997, 2003). Though mainstream thinkers still stubbornly refuse to acknowledge the mistakenness of this notion (see e.g., recent articles by McAdams and Pals 2006; and by McAdams 2007; also Hofstee 2007), signs of its recognition are appearing with increasing regularity around the discipline's periphery (see e.g., Cervone 2005, 2006; Harré 1998; Molenaar 2004; Molenaar, Huizenga and Nesselroade 2002; Valsiner 1986, 2005), and the paradigmatic shift which these signs harbinger now seems likely.

The advent of this development – in the eyes of some as long overdue as it is welcome (see e.g., Harré 2005; Valsiner 2005) – gives occasion for re-examining many long unquestioned assumptions, including those pertaining to the fundamental nature of that basic process I shall refer to here as *person characterization*. The central question is: what, exactly, do statements about the personality characteristics of an individual entail? Put otherwise: what is the nature of the considerations grounding assertions of the general sort, Smith is 'highly' extraverted (conscientious, agreeable, etc.)? It is this basic question to which the present contribution is addressed.

Reflecting the long-prevalent view within the mainstream on this question, Epstein (1983) summarily dismissed as meaningless any attempt to characterize an individual apart from statistically-based comparisons of that individual with others (see Epstein 1983, p. 381). If this is true, then all attempts to prosecute a

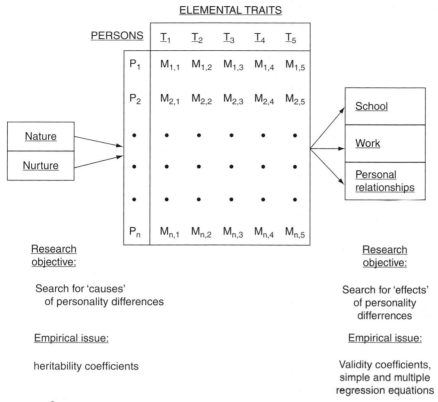

Figure 5.1. *Schematic representation of the traditional framework for scientific personality research.*

scientific psychology outside of the traditional individual differences framework will fail, and the paradigm shift forecast above will in fact never happen. Alternatively, if the view espoused by Epstein (and many others throughout the history of the discipline; see below) can be shown to be invalid, then prospects for the realization of that paradigm shift are greatly enhanced. Evidently, then, much of conceptual significance hinges on our understanding of the nature of person characterization.

Some instructive historical considerations

As part of his famous but ill-fated attempt to free the thinking of personality investigators from the grip of what he called the *common trait* approach to personality studies,[1] Allport (1937) argued that person characterization

---

[1] It is this framework that Allport so ill-advisedly branded 'nomothetic' (cf., Lamiell 1986, 1998, 2003).

must somehow be possible outside of that framework. After all, he reasoned, psychologists working in non-research settings, e.g., as counsellors or clinicians, face daily the challenge of characterizing their clients in ways often peculiar to each one of them individually, and hence not necessarily on the basis of considerations about how that client compares with others along some pre-specified dimension(s) presumed applicable to all ('common traits').

Within the mainstream, Allport's arguments along this line were widely (and sometimes harshly) dismissed on the grounds that person characterizations grounded in what he had called 'clinical' considerations were either (a) implicitly grounded in statistically-guided considerations of individual-differences after all, or (b) simply non-sensical. For example, in one commentary on Allport's views, Lundberg (1941, p. 383) argued as follows (where, as I suggest, the terms 'prediction' and 'predictor' can be replaced with the terms 'characterization' and 'characterizer' with no alteration in the essential point being asserted):

> Study, if you will, a given individual as thoroughly as can be imagined … What possible basis for prediction [characterization] could the most intimate knowledge of a case provide … unless the predicter *[sic]* [characterizer] can interpret this knowledge in terms of knowledge of other cases and how they behaved? … To the degree that [clinical] methods achieve reliable prediction [characterizations], analysis of the procedures involved will show that they are of the same basic character as those employed by the statistician. (emphasis in original)

In a very similar vein, Sarbin (1944, p. 214) argued (with terminological substitutions parallel to those made above also indicated here):

> The operations of those who reject the statistical method of prediction [characterization] and substitute for it a 'dynamic' clinical or individual prediction [characterization], may be described in one of two ways: Either they are making statistical predictions [characterizations] in an informal, subjective, and uncontrolled way, or else they are performing purely verbal manipulations which are unverifiable and akin to magic.

In the light of these forceful claims, it is perhaps not surprising that later commentaries on the matter were often equally dogmatic. Epstein's (1983) emphatic pronouncement in this regard has already been noted. Quite in line with this received view was the claim by Kleinmuntz (1967), made within the context of a discussion of personality measurement (which is, in essence, a highly formalized process of person characterization; see below) that 'all meaning for a given score of a person derives from comparing his [her] score with those of other persons' (Kleinmuntz 1967, p. 45). In yet another and more recent affirmation of this same basic point, Cloninger (1996, p. 5) stated flatly that 'any description of a person (for example, "Mary is outgoing") implies comparison with other people, even if this comparison is only in the memory of the one doing the analysis'.

In what follows, a challenge to this long-dominant conviction will be mounted on the basis of both conceptual and empirical considerations.

Trait Measurement As a Formal Exercise in Person Characterization

A quite serviceable pathway into the issues of relevance here is open to us by virtue of the fact that the procedures commonly employed by investigators to measure personality traits 'objectively' constitute a formal exercise in person characterization. By examining the rudiments of those procedures, then, it is possible to articulate the relevant conceptual issues in fairly precise terms.

Trait measurements are grounded in information about behaviour. On occasion, this information might be acquired through direct, *in vivo* observations of a person's behaviours, but much more commonly the information consists of statements about a person's behaviour expressed through the items on some sort of an assessment instrument such as a questionnaire (Goldfried and Kent 1972). In any case, the psychometrician's objective is to represent behavioural information in terms of numerical values that can in turn be used to derive quantitative assessments of the target person with respect to the trait variable(s) of interest. Equation [1] expresses the typical nature of this assessment operation:

$$A_{pd} = \sum_{i=1}^{m} (B_{pi})(W_{id}) \qquad [1]$$

where

A_{pd} represents the 'raw' assessment of person p with respect to some underlying trait represented by dimension d,

(B_{pi}) represents the i-th member of a set of m observations conveying information about the behaviour of person p,

(W_{id}) represents the weight or importance attached by the assessor to the i-th item of behavioural information as an empirical indicator of the trait represented by dimension d, and

$\sum_{i=1}^{m}$ represents the operation through which the assessor sums the m weighted items of behavioural information about person p in deriving an overall assessment of that person with respect to dimension d.

To illustrate, let us consider the NEO Personality Inventory (Costa and McCrae 1992), an instrument currently in wide use for purposes of measuring the so-called 'Big Five' personality traits of neuroticism, extraversion, openness, agreeableness and conscientiousness. This instrument is comprised of 240 items, for each of which the respondent indicates his/her level of agreement with the content of the item as a characterization of him/herself.[2] For each item, the response alternatives are strongly disagree, disagree, neither agree nor disagree, agree, and strongly agree.

In scoring a respondent's protocol, the response alternatives are assigned the numerical values 0, 1, 2, 3 and 4, respectively, with the direction of the scoring

---

[2] In an alternative version of the inventory, the respondent indicates his/her level of agreement with each item as a characterization of someone else.

Table 5.1 *Illustrative assessments, population norms and standard scores.*

Dimension	Raw scores	Means, (sd-s)	Z-scores
Neuroticism	90	79.1 (21.2)	+.51
Extraversion	128	109.4 (18.4)	+1.01
Openness	110	110.6 (17.3)	−.03
Agreeableness	100	124.3 (15.8)	−1.54
Conscient'ness	92	123.1 (17.6)	−1.77

depending upon the wording of the item. These numerical values define the (B) component of Equation [1].

In the 240 item NEO Inventory, forty-eight items are designated as relevant to each of the 'Big Five' dimensions, and the sum of scores for the forty-eight items designated as relevant to a particular trait dimension defines the respondent's 'raw' assessment, A, for that dimension. In the execution of this additive operation the (W) component of Equation [1] is being defined implicitly: each item designated as relevant to a given dimension is, in effect, weighted one (1), while each of the remaining 192 items is, in effect, weighted zero (0). Proceeding in accordance with Equation [1] in this fashion, then, the result is a set of five assessments for each respondent. Assessments illustrative of this obtained by means of the NEO Personality Inventory are given in the left-most data column of Table 5.1.

From assessments to measures via the traditional normative model

Consider now assessment 90 in Table 5.1. The question is: what does this number reveal about the standing of the target person along the dimension of 'neuroticism'? The answer, of course, is that we do not yet know, and the reason we do not yet know is that the assessment lacks *context*. In *normative* measurement, which is the formal procedure for person characterization proper to the study of individual differences, the context needed to lend meaning to 'raw' assessments is specified statistically by estimates of the means and standard deviations of those assessments within relevant populations. The middle data column in Table 5.1 displays numbers illustrating these statistics in the form of data drawn from published NEO Inventory population norms (Costa and McCrae 1992). On the basis of these values, each of the 'raw' *assessments* can be transformed into an interpretable *measure* in accordance with Equation [2]:

$$Z_{pd} = (A_{pd} - M_{.d})/sd._d$$

[2]

where

Z_{pd} represents a normative measure of person p along dimension d,
A_{pd} is defined by Equation [1],

M.$_d$ represents the arithmetic mean computed for an aggregate of individuals by summing across those individuals their respective 'raw' assessments for dimension d and then dividing that sum by the number of individuals in the aggregate, and, finally,

sd.$_d$ represents the standard deviation within the aggregate of the set of assessments just named.

Measures of the sort represented by the Z-scores displayed in Table 5.1 are thus taken to provide a meaningful answer to the question posed above, in that each such score serves to express the target's position along some dimension of measurement as some number of standard deviation units above or below the mean. That a modicum of ambiguity remains even after the derivation of such measures is revealed by the fact that it would be impossible to express these measures graphically, e.g., in the form of the sort of personality profile that is often the culmination of a personality measurement exercise, absent some definition of the endpoints of the scales used to physically represent the measurement dimensions. This is conceptually problematic because the standard (Z-) scores that constitute the derived measures are defined on a scale that, theoretically speaking, has no endpoints. The conceptual importance of this point will be discussed further below. For the moment, we will simply focus our attention on the fact that the practical solution to this problem is typically achieved by the transformation of Z-scores into T-scores[3] via Equation [3]:

$$T_{pd} = 10(Z_{pd}) + 50 \hspace{3cm} [3]$$

where

T_{pd} represents the T-score for person p along dimension d, and
Z_{pd} is defined by Equation [2].

By convention, the T-scale ranges from zero (0) to one hundred (100), which means that $Z = -5.00$ is taken to define the bottom of the scale while $Z = +5.00$ defines the top. Applying this equation to the Z-scores displayed in Table 5.1, the reader can verify that the resulting T-scores in this example (rounded to nearest unit) are, respectively, 55, 60, 50, 35 and 32.

Interactive measurement as an alternative to the traditional normative model

It has been noted above that, within the mainstream of twentieth century personality psychology, thinking about person characterization has been and continues to be thoroughly dominated by the conviction that in order for the characterizations

---

[3] The expression 'T-score' was invented by William A. McCall (1939) to honour two historically prominent proponents of this approach to psychological measurement: E. L. Thorndike (1874–1949) and Lewis Terman (1877–1956).

to be meaningful, the process *must* entail the comparison of individuals with one another. Notwithstanding the widespread consensus on this point, the present author suggested in a 1981 *American Psychologist* article (Lamiell 1981) that an alternative to traditional thinking could be formulated in terms of Equation [4], which is one formal expression of an approach to psychological measurement that Cattell (1944) called 'interactive':

$$I_{pd} = (A_{pd} - A'_{pd\ min})/|A'_{pd\ max} - A'_{pd\ min}|$$

where
[4]

I_{pd}	represents an interactive measure of person p with respect to dimension d,
A_{pd}	is defined by Equation [1], and
$A'_{pd\ max}$ and $A'_{pd\ min}$	represent, respectively, the lowest and highest values that any A_{pd} could *possibly* assume on a given dimension of measurement, given the constraints imposed by the assessment operation itself.[4]

This can be illustrated in terms of the example begun above. As already noted, the NEO Inventory includes forty-eight items for assessing each of the 'Big Five' dimensions, with each item being scored on a numerical scale ranging from zero (0) to four (4). This means that the lowest possible assessment, A'_{min}, on each dimension is zero (0), a value that would be obtained by a respondent whose answers were scored zero for all forty-eight of the items used to assess persons along that dimension. The highest possible assessment, A'_{max}, on each dimension is 192, a value that would be obtained by a respondent whose answers were scored four (4) for all forty-eight items relevant to the dimension in question. Using these A'_{min} and A'_{max} values to contextualize the 'raw' assessments displayed in Table 5.1, Equation [4] yields the interactive measures that, after multiplication by 100 to express them as values numerically comparable to the T-scores derived previously, are, respectively for neuroticism, extraversion, openness, agreeableness and conscientiousness, 47, 67, 57, 52 and 48. Figure 5.2 displays these measures graphically in juxtaposition with the previously-derived T-scores.

Clearly, the 'portrait' of an individual that emerges from a set of 'raw' assessments can differ depending upon the way in which those assessments are contextualized. In traditional normative measurement, assertions about what any one individual is like are formulated within a context defined by considerations about *what other individuals are like*, as operationalized in terms of statistical estimates of assessment means and standard deviations in populations. In interactive measurement, however, assertions about what any one individual is like are formulated

---

[4] In his recent review of my 2003 book, Hofstee (2007, p. 253) characterizes interactive measurement as 'absolute measurement'. However, I do not myself employ this characterization and in fact I reject it. *All* measurement is *relative* measurement. The question is: *relative to what?* Normative measurement entails an answer to this question that is quite different from that entailed by interactive measurement. *This does not make the latter 'absolute' measurement.*

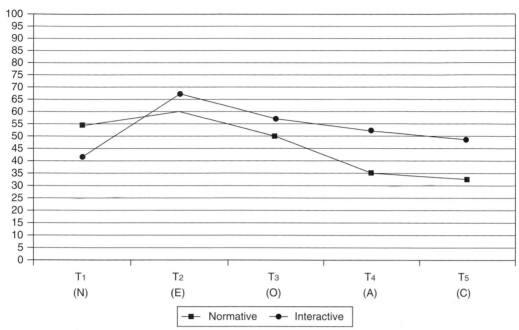

Figure 5.2. *Illustrative 'Big Five' personality profile based on interactive measurements, juxtaposed with previously-derived normative profile.*

within a context defined by considerations about *what that same individual is not but might otherwise be like*, as operationalized in terms of the maximum and minimum possible assessments that could *possibly* have been made of him/her under the constraints imposed by the assessment procedure itself.

Revisiting Allport's discredited conjecture

It should be clear from the foregoing that under the terms of interactive measurement it is not necessary to assume that the dimensions in terms of which some one individual is characterized are applicable to all (or even any) other individuals.[5] This suggests, in turn, that Allport's conjectures on this topic (see above) might well merit the serious consideration they never received in his lifetime. The findings of several investigations carried out by the present author in collaboration with various colleagues offer substantial empirical support for this view (Lamiell and Durbeck 1987; Lamiell, Foss, Larsen and Hempel 1983; Lamiell, Foss, Trierweiler and Leffel 1983).

Although differing in various procedural details, all of those studies were designed to shed light on the question of which of the two approaches to 'objective'

---

[5] Of course, the dimensions of interest *could* be applicable to other individuals, but in interactive measurement this *need not* be so whereas in normative measurement it *must* be so.

person characterization just described, normative or interactive, better models the judgement process through which lay persons subjectively characterize themselves and one another.

In one of these studies, Lamiell and Durbeck (1987) asked each of sixty-seven participants to rate forty target peers on each of three attribute dimensions. Each target peer was described in terms of the extent to which s/he engaged in each of sixteen different activities proper to college student life. The extent of engagement in these activities (e.g., studying or reading intellectual material, engaging in artistic or creative activities, engaging in athletic/physical activities, working at a part time job, etc.) was defined on a ten-point continuum ranging from 'very little or no' time or effort (0) to 'very much time or effort' (9), and for purposes of formally assessing the targets on the three attribute dimensions, these numerical values were used to define the [B] component of Equation [1]. The forty target profiles defined in terms of these values were identical for all sixty-seven subjects. The [W] component of Equation [1], on the other hand, was defined for each subject individually, so as to reflect that particular subject's sense of the weight or importance of information about each behavioural variable to judgements of the targets on each of the three designated dimensions.

With the [B] and [W] components of Equation [1] thus defined, it was possible to formally derive 'raw' assessments of the forty targets on each of the three attribute dimensions for each subject individually. The central question of the study could then be put as follows: Which of the two measurement models discussed above, normative or interactive, would, when applied to the 'raw' assessments of the targets rated by a given subject, yield trait profiles of those targets that better matched the profiles of those same targets defined by the subject's direct subjective ratings of them?

To answer this question, two Cronbach-Gleser profile dissimilarity indices were computed for each of the forty targets rated by a given subject (Cronbach and Gleser 1953). These two indices (which are essentially Euclidean distances) measured the degree of dissimilarity between the subjective rating profile for a given target and, respectively, the normative and interactive profiles defined for that same target by applying, in turn, Equation [2] and Equation [3] to the 'raw' assessments derived for the target as described above. The measurement model more predictive of the subject's ratings of a given target was the one resulting in the smaller profile dissimilarity index. A comparison of the average dissimilarity values obtained for each of the two models, computed across targets for each subject individually, provided a basis for determining whether one or the other model could be said to be superior for that individual subject.

Of the sixty-seven individuals investigated by Lamiell and Durbeck (1987) in this fashion, the interactive model proved superior to the normative model in fifty-seven cases. There were ten inconclusive cases in which neither model consistently outperformed the other. Strikingly, there was no subject – *not one* – for whom the normative model proved superior to the interactive model. These results corresponded closely with results that had previously been reported by Lamiell,

Foss, Larsen and Hempel (1983) and by Lamiell, Foss, Trierweiler and Leffel (1983), and, considered together, this body of evidence strongly suggests that lay persons both *can*, and with great regularity *do*, formulate and express subjective judgements of themselves and others on the basis of considerations that *do not* entail between-person (target) comparisons.

Still further evidence consistent with this view has been reported by Weigert (2000). Her research posed the question: In application to standard NEO Personality Inventory protocols, which method for deriving trait measures, normative or interactive, would yield 'Big Five' profiles matching more closely those obtained when subjects simply rated themselves and a well-known other on the relevant dimensions, given only a 'thumbnail' description of each?[6]

Weigert's subjects were thirty-six husband-wife couples whose respective marriages had lasted for a minimum of ten years. In one set of analyses carried out on Form S of the revised NEO Inventory (Costa and McCrae 1992), on which each subject's responses refer to himself/herself, Weigert (2000) found in sixty-two of seventy-two cases that an interactive scoring of a given subject's NEO protocol (following the method described above) yielded a 'Big Five' profile that better matched the profile defined by that subject's direct self-ratings than did the profile constructed from a normative scoring of his/her NEO protocol. When the profile to be matched was defined by the direct ratings a given subject made of his/her spouse, the interactive profile constructed from the spouse's NEO Form S protocol outperformed the normative profile constructed from the same NEO protocol in sixty-four of the seventy-two cases.

When the profile defined by a given subject's direct self-ratings was to be matched by the responses of his/her partner on Form R of the NEO (where the items are worded in the third person and the respondent is describing that third person), interactive profiles matched the self-rating profiles better than did the normative profiles in sixty-three of seventy-one cases.[7] Finally, when these same alternative sets of measures were investigated for their match to the profiles defined by partners' direct ratings of their respective spouses, the interactive model outperformed the normative model in sixty-eight of the seventy-one cases.

Of carts and horses

Considered together, the research findings reviewed above point emphatically in favour of interactive measurement over normative measurement as a formal model of the judgement process through which lay persons characterize themselves and others. That is, the subjective ratings seem to be expressing

---

[6] For example, in the case of 'extraversion,' the 'thumbnail' description read: 'A person *high* on this factor would be well-described by such terms as *sociable, fun-loving*, and *affectionate*, while a person *low* on this factor would be well-described by such terms as *retiring, sober*, and *reserved*.'

[7] One of the seventy-two subjects who participated in Weigert's study was unable to complete Form R of the NEO Inventory.

considerations about who the target *is* in contrast with considerations about who that *same* target *is not* but might otherwise be, rather than in contrast with considerations about who *other* targets *are*. The suggestion that this is the case is often rejoined with the claim that considerations about 'who one is not but might otherwise be' must themselves be grounded ultimately in considerations about who others are, and so the process must ultimately be regarded as a normative one after all. As intuitively plausible as this argument might seem at first blush, it is found wanting on close inspection.

Suppose, for example, that a man named Smith is to be characterized in terms of a dimension representing introversion at one extreme and extraversion at the other. As noted earlier, Epstein (1983) has claimed (consistent with a long-standing and widely shared view among personality investigators) that it would be *meaningless* to try to characterize Smith in any way at all with respect to this dimension without comparing him with others. To claim this, however, is to claim that prior to comparing Smith with others he has no standing at all along the dimension. This, however, is tantamount to saying that with respect to the dimension in question Smith *does not exist*, and if this is so, then of course no comparison of Smith with others could ever be carried out. On the traditional view, it turns out, person characterization is impossible!

In order for an individual to be 'higher than' or 'lower than' or 'equal to' some other(s) with respect to some dimension of characterization, that individual must be *somewhere* along that dimension *prior* to any and all such between-person comparisons. This means that there must be some meaningful rationale for characterizing individuals that does not appeal to between-person comparisons and that, indeed, constitutes an epistemic precondition for such comparisons. Interactive measurement is just such a rationale.

Certainly, it is mechanically possible, by exercising the arithmetic of normative measurement, to suspend any substantive characterization of an individual with respect to some dimension until it has been determined that his/her 'raw' assessment on some instrument intended to measure that dimension places him/her, say, two standard deviations above the group mean. But this purely arithmetic manoeuvre would leave begging the substantive question of whether a standard score of $Z = +2.00$ marks an individual as relatively introverted or relatively extraverted! In order to answer this question, it would be necessary to know whether 'extraversion' is reflected by relatively high assessments (hence positive Z-scores) or by relatively low assessments (hence negative Z-scores), and this is hardly a question that can be answered by examining more data, or statistics compiled of them, or indeed anything empirical at all.

The question is answered by a rational consideration of the alternative possibilities that have been built into the assessment instrument, for only in this way could it ever be determined that a Z-score of $+2.00$ not only places an individual two standard deviations above the group mean, but also (to continue with the above example) *toward that end of the scale representing extreme extraversion* (or, should it be the case, extreme introversion). Note that this is precisely the sort of consideration – 'what are the alternative possibilities here?' – to which inter-active measurement appeals from the start.

The lesson here is that considerations of an essentially interactive sort must inevitably be invoked in person characterization *even where one's ultimate objective is to derive normative characterizations*. The converse of this is not true: characterizations grounded in considerations of an interactive nature can be formulated meaningfully wholly apart from considerations of a normative nature. Stated otherwise: instead of interactive considerations being dependent on normative knowledge, the exact opposite is the case: normative characterizations cannot be achieved wholly apart from considerations, however implicit, that are ultimately interactive in nature.[8] This is why Cattell (1944, p. 299) was correct in his claim that 'true normative measurements are bound to be founded on inter-active measurement', not vice versa, and this is also why the long-accepted truism that *all* meaning of an assessment of a person with respect to some dimension of characterization derives from the comparison of that assessment with the assess-ments made of others (Kleinmuntz 1967, see above) could not possibly be valid.

Concluding observations

The research agenda sketched at the outset of this chapter and schema-tized in Figure 5.1 found its first home within the framework of what William Stern (1871–1938) called *differential* psychology (Stern 1900, 1911, esp. p. 18; cf., Lamiell 2003). Significantly, however, Stern did *not* regard the assessment and study of individual differences as suitable for advancing our understanding of *personalities* (or what he termed 'individualities'). On the contrary, he saw (correctly) that studies of individual *differences* generate knowledge of *person variables*, and that what is needed in any psychology of personality worthy of the name is knowledge of *persons*. Unfortunately, but for reasons I have thoroughly discussed elsewhere (see esp. Lamiell 2003, ch. 5), this distinction was all but obliterated by developments within the field during the first three decades of the twentieth century – against Stern's strenuous and repeatedly-voiced objections (see Lamiell 2006). This most unfortunate historical development is a major source of current conceptual difficulties within the field.

It is also of more than passing interest to note that when Stern turned his attention to the topic of 'principles of personality measurement', as he did in chapter VI of his 1918 book, *Die menschliche Persönlichkeit* [*The human person-ality*] (Stern 1918), he explicitly distanced himself from the logic of normative measurement, arguing that 'the comparison of many personalities' to one another

---

[8] In the afore-mentioned review of my 2003 book by Hofstee (2007), he claims that I dismiss normative ('relative') measurement as 'meaningless' (Hofstee 2007, p. 253). However, nowhere in my published work have I ever made such a claim. The claim is that the meaningfulness of normative measures hinges on their grounding in considerations of a fundamentally non-normative (in the statistical sense) nature.

would be beside the point, 'since the problem at hand pertains specifically to the relationship between the person and his/her world' (Stern 1918, pp. 186–7). The language here is remarkably similar in its spirit to that used by Cattell (1944, p. 293) nearly three decades later in describing interactive measurement as an approach to person characterization that:

> recognizes the oneness of the organism-environment, and pays tribute to the oft-forgotten fact that a trait is never resident only in the organism, but is a relation between the organism and the environment.[9]

Despite Cattell's high regard for interactive measurement from a conceptual standpoint (he even referred to it as 'the queen' of psychological measurement, Cattell 1944 p. 299), his thoroughly empiricist sensibilities forbade him from embracing the approach in practice.[10] In normative measurement, only assessments that actually obtain empirically may be included in the computation of the population norms that serve as the context for transforming 'raw' assessments into interpretable measures. In interactive measurement, on the other hand, context is established by reference to extreme scores, A'_{min} and A'_{max}, that need not and typically would not ever obtain empirically.[11] For this reason, empiricism as a philosophy of science is decidedly inhospitable to the core idea underlying interactive measurement, the latter being much more compatible with a rationalist philosophy of science (see Lamiell 1987, pp. 188–9 for an elaboration of this point). To the extent, therefore, that rationalist thinking succeeds in supplanting the 'cult of empiricism' (Toulmin and Leary 1985) that came to dominate twentieth century thinking in psychology generally and in personality psychology in particular, ideas more compatible with the thinking of Stern (among others), and with the alternative perspective on person characterization developed in this chapter, will, in the twenty-first century, receive broader consideration for their theoretical and empirical potential than has heretofore been the case.

References

Allport, G. W. 1937. *Personality: a psychological interpretation.* New York: Holt, Rinehart and Winston

Cattell, R. B. 1944. Psychological measurement: normative, ipsative, interactive, *Psychological Review* 51: 292–303

---

[9] I do not mean to suggest here that Cattell was knowingly following Stern in this matter. Indeed, I know of no evidence that Cattell was familiar at all with Stern's work.

[10] Cattell (1944) maintained that in an investigative domain where the data are grounded in 'dimensions of consciousness', which would surely include the domain of personality studies, true interactive measurement is 'impossible in the absence of E.S.P.' (Cattell 1944, p. 294).

[11] Hence Cattell's (1944) allegation (see note 7) that an investigator would need 'E. S. P.' in order to divine the reference points used by a given individual to contextualize his/her subjective judgements of self and others.

Cervone, D. 2005. Personality architecture: within-person structures and processes, *Annual Review of Psychology* 56: 423–52

    2006. Systèmes de personnalité au niveau de l'individu: vers une évaluation socio-cognitive de l'architecture de la personnalité [Personality systems at the level of the individual: assessing social-cognitive personality architecture], *Psychologie Français* 51: 357–76

Cloninger, S. C. 1996. *Personality: description, dynamics and development.* New York: Freeman

Costa, P. T. and McCrae, R. R. 1992. *Revised NEO Personality Inventory (NEO-PI-R) and NEO Five-Factor Inventory (NEO-FFI) professional manual.* Odessa, FL: Psychological Assessment Resources

Cronbach, L. J. and Gleser, G. 1953. Assessing similarity between profiles, *Psychological Bulletin* 50: 456–73

Epstein, S. 1983. Aggregation and beyond: some basic issues in the prediction of behaviour, *Journal of Personality* 51: 360–92

Goldfried, M. R. and Kent, R. N. 1972. Traditional versus behavioural personality assessment: a comparison of methodological and theoretical assumptions, *Psychological Bulletin* 77: 409–20

Harré, R. 1998. *The singular self: an introduction to the psychology of personhood.* London: Sage

    2005. *Key thinkers in psychology.* London: Sage

Hofstee, W. K. B. 2007. *Unbehagen* in individual differences: a review, *Journal of Individual Differences* 28: 252–3

Kleinmuntz, B. 1967. *Personality measurement: an introduction.* Homewood, IL: Dorsey Press

Lamiell, J. T. 1981. Toward an idiothetic psychology of personality, *American Psychologist* 36: 276–89

    1986. What is nomothetic about 'nomothetic' personality research?, *Journal of Theoretical and Philosophical Psychology* 6: 97–107

    1987. *The psychology of personality: an epistemological inquiry.* New York: Columbia University Press

    1997. Individuals and the differences between them, in R. Hogan, J. Johnson and S. Briggs (eds.), *Handbook of personality psychology*, pp. 117–41. New York: Academic Press

    1998. 'Nomothetic' and 'idiographic': contrasting Windelband's understanding with contemporary usage, *Theory and Psychology* 10: 715–30

    2000. A periodic table of personality elements? The 'Big Five' and trait 'psychology' in critical perspective, *Journal of Theoretical and Philosophical Psychology* 20: 1–24

    2003. *Beyond individual and group differences: human individuality, scientific psychology, and William Stern's critical personalism.* Thousand Oaks, CA: Sage Publications

    2006. William Stern (1871–1938) und der 'Ursprungsmythos' der Differentiellen Psychologie, *Journal für Psychologie* 14: 253–73

Lamiell, J. T. and Durbeck, P. 1987. Whence cognitive prototypes in impression formation? Some empirical evidence for dialectical reasoning as a generative process, *Journal of Mind and Behaviour* 8: 223–44

Lamiell, J. T., Foss, M. A., Larsen, R. J. and Hempel, A. 1983. Studies in intuitive person-ology from an idiothetic point of view: implications for personality theory, *Journal of Personality* 51: 438–67

Lamiell, J. T., Foss, M. A., Trierweiler, S. J. and Leffel, G. M. 1983. Toward a further understanding of the intuitive personologist: some preliminary evidence for the dialectical quality of subjective personality impressions, *Journal of Personality* 53: 213–35

Lundberg, G. A. 1941. Case-studies vs. statistical methods: an issue based on misunder-standing, *Sociometry* 4: 379–83

McAdams, D. P. 2007. On grandiosity in personality psychology, *American Psychologist* 62: 60–1 (comment)

McAdams, D. P. and Pals, J. L. 2006. A new Big Five: fundamental principles for an integrative science of personality, *American Psychologist* 61: 204–17

McCall, W. A. 1939. *Measurement*. New York: Macmillan

Molenaar, P. C. M. 2004. A manifesto on psychology as idiographic science: bringing the person back into scientific psychology, this time forever, *Measurement* 2: 201–18

Molenaar, P. C. M., Huizenga, H. M. and Nesselroade, J. R. 2002. The relationship between the structure of inter-individual and intraindividual variability: a theo-retical and empirical vindication of developmental systems theory, in U. M. Staudinger and U. Lindenberger (eds.), *Understanding human develop-ment*, pp. 339–60. Dordrecht: Kluwer

Sarbin, T. R. 1944. The logic of prediction in psychology, *Psychological Review* 51: 210–28

Stern, W. 1900. *Über Psychologie der individuellen Differenzen (Ideen zu einer 'differ-entiellen Psychologie')*. Leipzig: Barth

1911. *Die Differentielle Psychologie in ihren methodischen Grundlagen*. Leipzig: Barth

1918. *Person und Sache: System der philosophischen Weltanschauung. Zweiter Band: Die menschliche Persönlichkeit*. Leipzig: Barth

Toulmin, S. and Leary, D. E. 1985. The cult of empiricism in psychology, and beyond, in S. Koch and D. E. Leary (eds.), *A century of psychology as science*, pp. 594–617. New York: McGraw-Hill

Valsiner, J. 1986. Between groups and individuals: psychologists' and laypersons' inter-pretations of correlational findings, in J. Valsiner (ed.), *The individual subject and scientific psychology*, pp. 113–51. New York: Plenum Press

2005. Towards a new science of the person: the potentials of the critical personology of William Stern, *Theory and Psychology* 15: 401–13

Weigert, S. C. 2000. The predictive accuracy of normative and interactive frameworks for personality measurement (unpublished doctoral dissertation, Georgetown University, Washington, DC)

PART II

Personality Description and Measurement

6 The trait approach to personality

Ian J. Deary

Nothwithstanding the successes of the trait approach to personality in the last century-plus (which are undeniable as one of psychology's major achievements, and this will be outlined first), problems persist. There are still issues about how psychologists know whether traits, and any given model of traits, are the right way to construe human personality differences, and their nature is still largely mysterious. These questions concern whether we have summary or causal views of traits (Allport 1937), and whether we have identified surface or source traits (Cattell 1945).

Personality traits are alive and well

There are many good reasons to keep repeating this message: that humans cottoned on to the idea of traits in classical times, and that the scientific approach has simply cleaned up their number, provided reliable measures, and validated them. Theophrastus (371–287 BCE) enumerated various typical human 'characters' that the translator also reckoned could be called traits (Rusten 1993). Our language has many thousands of words used to describe people's typical ways of behaving (Allport and Odbert 1936). We talk and write, at least, as if there were traits, and as if these traits were a part of our constitution and influenced our behaviours. The humoral theory of bodily health, illness and personal wellbeing that can be traced to Hippocrates and Galen (Stelmack and Stalikas 1991), and which held sway for about 1,500 years, described four temperaments, or personality types, which map rather well on to the quadrants provided by the two orthogonal dimensions of Neuroticism and Extraversion: melancholic, choleric, sanguine and phlegmatic.

Just because the ideas have always been around, and have got into the language as well as some archaic medical theories, does not mean that there are such entities as traits. Key developments in turning a popular into a scientific, market-leading approach to personality included: the suggestion that using language terms might be useful in studying human personality (Galton 1884); the collection of empirical data on trait-like terms (Heymans and Wiersma 1906–1909; Webb 1915); the development of trait theory more fully (e.g., Allport 1937); the development of multiple factor analysis (Thurstone 1947); and the combination of developing trait scales and the application of multivariate statistical analyses to them (e.g., Cattell

Thanks to David Lubinski for advising on the literature on classic articles on traits. Ian Deary is the recipient of a Royal Society-Wolfson Research Merit Award.

1945; Eysenck 1947). These developments resulted in a number of different personality models and instruments which, although based on different numbers of, and often differently-named, traits had more in common than was superficially obvious. For example, the overlaps in coverage of Cattell's, Eysenck's, various Five Factor Models' (De Raad 2000; Digman and Takemoto-Chock 1981; Goldberg 1981, 1993; McCrae and Costa 1985, 2003), and Cloninger's (Cloninger, Svrakic and Przybeck 1993) traits are substantial (e.g., Aluja, Garcia and Garcia 2002). The history of, and convergence around the currently dominant Five-Factor Model of personality traits has been described by Digman (1996), who recounted how the prior research that retrospectively supported a Five-Factor Model was better appreciated after a key seminar by Goldberg (1983) and the development of the first five factor inventory and its comparison with other models (Costa and McCrae 1985). Some recent research questions emphasize its successes.

The completeness of the Five-Factor Model has been questioned, regarding whether it captures the major sources of human personality variation. For example, from Paunonen's (2002) 'supernumerary personality inventory', Ashton and Lee (e.g., Ashton and Lee 2005; Lee and Ashton 2006) provided evidence for Honesty-Humility's being an additional important and relatively separate trait from the five. Going in the other direction, DeYoung (2006) has emphasized that the Big Five are not orthogonal, and that higher-order traits (named Stability and Plasticity) – though not based on especially strong correlations – could be important when it comes to biological theories of personality. For the most part, though, the suggested revisions to the model are not large. Remarkably, the Five-Factor Model (or, at least, four of its factors, with openness as a partial exception) does a fair job in accounting for variation in abnormal as well as normal personality (Markon, Krueger and Watson 2005).

The applicability of the Five-Factor Model to other cultures and language groups has been questioned, and the model has largely done well in this sphere too. The NEO Personality Inventory-Revised has been translated into many different languages. In a study of twenty-six cultures, many non-Western, McCrae (2001) reported that factor analyses retrieved very similar structures of personality description. A later report, in which almost 12,000 students in fifty cultures rated another person's traits, found good agreement with regard to the American self-report structure (McCrae and 79 others 2005). This study found similar sex and age differences across cultures. Eysenck's personality questionnaires perform well on this type of cross-cultural comparison too (e.g., Eysenck and Eysenck 1982). This type of research is known as the 'etic' approach, in which a personality questionnaire developed in one culture (usually Western) is translated and applied to others. The other type of research is 'emic', which starts with the culture's own lexicon and asks if a similar personality structure is found in each. Peabody and De Raad's (2002) summary of emic research was that the 'effort to achieve Big Five universality has been overextended'. They found the best generality across cultures for Conscientiousness, Extraversion and Agreeableness but also that, 'emotional stability and intellect frequently do not appear as cohesive factors'. There is especially good agreement across some languages.

For example, English and German have very similar five factor structures in the lexicons (Saucier and Ostendorf 1999). On the other hand, whereas the Greek lexicon did afford a five factor solution, there were also possible one, two, six and seven factor solutions (Saucier, Georgiades, Tsaousis and Goldberg 2005).

The consensual validation of personality trait ratings has been questioned. As McCrae, Costa, Martin *et al.* (2004) argue, consensual validation can answer objections to rated traits such as response sets and cognitive schemata; consensual validation can help to suggest that traits are objective psychological attributes. They conducted a review of nineteen studies of cross-observer agreement and concluded that, in disparate cultures, people 'include trait information in their self-reports and observer ratings'. In the self versus spouse ratings (highest of those reported), consensual validity coefficients were: Neuroticism = .44; Extraversion = .57; Openness = .51; Agreeableness = .50; and Conscientiousness = .42. A more stringent test of consensual validity was conducted in the German Observational Study of Adult Twins (Borkenau, Mauer, Riemann *et al.* 2004). Subjects performed fifteen short acts that were video-recorded, such as introducing oneself, telling a story from pictures, singing a song, and so forth. Judges rated the videos using the NEO-Personality Inventory-Revised, which was also completed by the persons who had been rated. The consensual validity coefficients were: Neuroticism = .19; Extraversion = .30; Openness = .31; Agreeableness = .22; and Conscientiousness = .08. Cross-judge agreement was very good, with a mean coefficient of .69, and these modest, positive associations between ratings done by strangers and people's self-reports are impressive (note the unreliability of the outcome variables), especially for Openness and Extraversion.

The stability of personality trait ratings has been questioned. A review of over 152 longitudinal studies with over 3,000 correlation coefficients found that trait stability increased from childhood to adulthood, rising from about 0.3 to over 0.7 (Roberts and DelVecchio 2000). This supported earlier research with traits from the Five Factor Model (Costa and McCrae 1994) and Eysenck's factors (Sanderman and Ranchor 1994), which had found stability coefficients of well above 0.6, rising to above 0.8, for periods of between six and thirty years. The stability of individual differences among children can be high, given an appropriate measurement instrument. Using the Berkeley Puppet Inventory, in which identical puppets make opposite statements, and the children choose which applies better to them, the stability coefficients between age six and seven years were often well above 0.5, and considerably higher when corrected for period-free unreliability (Measelle, John, Ablow *et al.* 2005). Traits are stable aspects of people's (including children's) make-up.

There is also the well-supported heritability of traits including those of the Five Factor Model (Bouchard and Loehlin 2001). However, in ten years of molecular genetic studies of personality, there are still no solid associations between genetic variations and personality traits (Ebstein 2006). There is evidence that other species, including primates (Weiss, King and Perkins 2006) and others (Gosling 2001), have something like a Five-Factor Model of personality. There is the predictive validity of personality traits: Neuroticism and Extraversion relate to mood and its disorders (Ivkovic, Vitart, Rudan *et al.* 2007; Stewart, Ebmeier and Deary 2005); and Conscientiousness relates to survival (Friedman, Tucker, Schwartz *et al.* 1995; Weiss and Costa 2005).

Few psychological constructs could muster such a rich nomological network. Problems in the field, therefore, can be addressed with the knowledge of this background strength.

Problem with the trait approach to personality

There are several evaluative accounts of the emerging consensus concerning there being about five broad personality factors in humans. One good example is by John and Robins (1993). An especially useful aspect of their overview is the description of how the descriptive scheme emerged and then started to be called a 'theory' and a 'theoretical structure'. But the worrying explanatory gap appears as they state (p. 224): 'The Big Five structure was derived through purely empirical and purposely atheoretical procedures; theoretical considerations, such as questions about the existence and explanatory status of traits, were deemed unimportant.' After that, as others have done, they pull a rabbit out of the five factor hat. That is, the descriptive – Big Five – scheme, which is atheoretical, undergoes a Clark Kent-to-Superman transformation, by being renamed (by others) the Five-Factor Model. What has changed? The Five-Factor Model is the Big Five with some other stuff that we know about it, added to it: the factors have facets, the factors have stability and a genetic basis, and they are founded on (unknown) biological mechanisms. Of course, this could be contrasted with those who might seek explanations of trait differences in cognitive or social mechanisms, so perhaps it is a model. John and Robins (1993) go on to discuss the difference between two views. First, there are those who hold to traits as merely descriptive: the summary view. On the other hand, there are those who hold the causal view. The causal view seems irresistible, if only to try to test it and to think how. When discussing the causal view one gets various reiterations of what this means to people: 'unknown neuropsychiatric structures', 'entities that exist "in our skins"', 'underlying causal mechanisms', 'some neurophysiological or hormonal basis for personality', and 'causal and dynamic principles' (John and Robins 1993, pp. 227–8). Most of this is hand-waving, signalling an explanatory chasm in personality trait research.

John and Robins (1993) wriggled out of this limitation by stating, understandably, that classification often comes before explanation in science, and that one can get on and do a lot of useful work with traits without actually losing sleep about their foundations. But the issue is not just one of the descriptive versus explanatory status of traits. It is a basic issue of what sorts of entities we have found, and whether we have got the right ones, and what that means. And these things had been a worry since the dawn of modern personality research. The contemporary work on this takes its lead from Galton (1884). He reckoned that aspects of character other than cognitive ability might be measurable. Observations of similarity in conduct between parents and their children, in feeling between pairs of twins, and of his own apparent free will convinced him (p. 181):

> that the character which shapes our conduct has a definite and durable 'something', and therefore that it is reasonable to attempt to measure it.

Galton stated the problem of choosing the entities that are to mark our personality traits (1884, p. 181):

> We must guard ourselves against supposing that the moral faculties which we distinguish by different names, as courage, sociability, niggardness, are separate entities.

Galton headed for the store of human trait terms to which others, in what was to become known as the lexical approach, would follow (p. 181):

> I tried to gain an idea of the number of the more conspicuous aspects of the character by counting in an appropriate dictionary the words used to express them. Roget's *Thesaurus* was selected for the purpose … and [I] estimated that it contained fully one thousand words expressive of character, each of which has a separate shade of meaning, while each shares a large part of its meaning with some of the rest.

Galton (1884) reckoned that individual differences in character might be tested before the phenomena of character themselves were fully charted (p. 182): 'Definite acts in response to definite emergencies have alone to be noted. No accurate map of character is required to start from.' His pithy phrase for what he was proposing was to get at people's 'statistics of conduct in a limited number of well-defined small trials' (p. 182). One of the most obvious areas of difference, he thought, was in man's 'emotional temperament' (p. 182); also, 'Some men are easily provoked, others remain cheerful even when affairs go very contrary to their liking' (p. 184). Galton ended his piece by stating that (p. 185): 'It is the statistics of each man's conduct in small every-day affairs, that will probably be found to give the simplest and most precise measure of his character.'

Much of Galton's 130-years-old sketchy agenda is recognizable: that character traits might in part be heritable; that trait terms may be sought in the lexicon; that the entities are not clear, because words are mongrels of underlying traits; that character had not been mapped out; that perhaps we should bash on and measure traits using a number of short trials; and that emotional, anger responses were notable aspects of personality. Much of what Galton suggested has successfully been realized in subsequent research. But the issue of *which traits we have* and the *nature of traits* have been persistent problems, revisited by many influential thinkers in the field.

Nature of traits

The issue of the conceptual nature of traits was often uppermost in G. W. Allport's thinking about personality. He worried that researchers 'give only an occasional glance at problems of terminology and theory', and that 'disingenuous investigators have made it appear that quantitative distinctions can outrun qualitative, and that adjectival distinctions can outrun substantive' (Allport 1927, p. 284). The latter comment is especially applicable today, where the quantitative aspect of traits has been so successful and where there has still not been an answer to Allport's (1927, p. 285) problem of 'what constitutes the essential unit of personality'. Even in Allport's eighty-year-old piece there were dawnings of the well-established findings that broad traits such as Extraversion-Introversion comprised correlated narrower traits (Freyd 1924), and there was discussion of a hierarchy in which traits sat above narrower entities such as habits and responses, a scheme that was to be found in Eysenck's (e.g., 1947, p. 29; 1953, p. 13) descriptions of traits. Whether or not it was conditioned reflexes or habits that formed the underlying units of traits, Allport (1927, p. 289) emphasized that traits were 'noncontingent higher units ... they lead an existence *sui generis* ... a definite new entity of its own, different from its components and from everything else ... a trait is functionally independent of its origins'. Thus, emerged his famous phrase that 'A trait is known not by its cause, but by what it causes; not by its roots but by its fruits' (p. 289). This is a pity; de-emphasizing the founding units of traits casts the superficial phenotype free from them, and can lead to our leaving unaddressed the crucial issue of isomorphism between trait patterns and bodily make-up. Indeed, it might strongly be argued that the problem of what traits we have will be settled only when we know more about the nature of traits; we might never know the correct outlines until we have understood the foundations. Whether consciously or not, much of more recent research has taken this aspect of Allport too seriously, providing the fruits of traits while our knowledge about the roots (founding units) is much less. However, by the next paragraph Allport was back on the reductionistic agenda (p. 290): 'The definition of the unit of personality is one problem pressing for solution.'

Allport (1931) put forward his classic doctrine of traits:

(1) A trait has more than nominal existence.
(2) A trait is more than a generalized habit.
(3) A trait is dynamic, or at least determinative.
(4) The existence of a trait may be established empirically or at least statistically.
(5) Traits are only relatively independent of each other.
(6) A trait of personality, psychologically considered, is not the same as a moral quality.
(7) Acts, and even habits, that are inconsistent with a trait are not proof of the non-existence of the trait.
(8) A trait may be viewed either in the light of the personality which contains it, or in the light of its distribution in the population at large.

This is still a useful manifesto, in parts. In fact Allport (1931, p. 368) started with a plea to common sense that we should recognize the 'more generalized habits'. As Eysenck would emphasize later (1947, 1953), the identification of traits went past the regularities of habits that we can recognize easily; statistical techniques of data reduction (and perhaps even genetic co-variance) are required (Allport 1931, p. 369):

> If the habit of dominating a tradesman can be shown, statistically or genetically, to be related to the habit of bluffing one's way past guards, there is the presumption that a common trait of personality exists which includes these two habits.

Under point 3, Allport emphasized that it was the trait and not the stimulus that was the driving force behind behaviour that expresses personality. This idea was recast by Matthews, Deary and Whiteman (2003) when they articulated the key assumptions of the 'inner locus' and 'causal precedence' of personality traits. Allport suggested the definitions 'derived drives' or 'derived motives' for traits and summed up that (1931, p. 369):

> Whatever they are called they may be regarded as playing a motivating role in each act, thus endowing the separate adjustments of the individual to specific stimuli with that *adverbial* quality that is the very essence of personality.

Today's trait researchers are keener on adjectives than adverbs. Under point 4 Allport made the point about requiring 'evidence of repeated reactions which, though not necessarily constant in type, seem none the less to be consistently a function of the same underlying determinant'. Taken more seriously, this could have prevented the futile detour of the situationist debate. Under points 4 and 5, Allport saw that evidence of traits would come from factor analytic-type techniques, and he then mused on how separate these traits would be, and at what level of generality one would begin to accept separable traits. Under point 7, Allport helpfully points out that traits are dispositions, not deterministic (1931, p. 371): 'Even the characteristically neat person may become careless in his haste to catch a train.' Under point 6 Allport's discussion is broader than its title might suggest. He worried that traits might be loaded with the conventional meanings of the words allocated to them and that 'It would be ideal if we could ... find our traits first and then name them' (p. 371). Of course he also stated that the words might actually represent the true traits but, on the other hand, the 'conventional meanings ... [might lead us] away from the precise integration as it exists in the given individual' (p. 371). Allport wanted to have his lexical cake and eat it here, and also begs the most profound question. He explicitly seems to recognize that our likeliest road into traits is from language terms. However, he hints at but does not directly address how one might craft a research programme to get at 'the precise integration as it exists in the given individual'. However one opts to interpret that vague phrase, it is at the heart of the chronic and current problem of personality trait research: traits look good from the outside, but we have little idea about their bodily foundations and the trait-underlying system isomorphism. The surprise at the end of Allport's (1931) doctrine is his guess that there might be a few hundred nomothetic traits in a population, and that each person might have a thousand or so identifiable traits. That would give the innocent question – 'what's she like?' – quite a long reply.

Allport's was not a lone voice in the inter-war years' thinking about the conceptual nature of traits. Carr and Kingsbury (1938) recognized that there were trait names in everyday life, that we knew what we meant by them in practical terms, and that they had been introduced to psychology. However, the worry was that 'we may be unable to give any analytical and systematic definition of the concept' (Carr and Kingsbury 1938 p. 497). They opened up by attempting a definition (p. 497): 'A trait is a conceptual attribute or definition of the reactive nature of the individual. The nature of the individual is defined on the basis of certain observable behaviour characteristics.' These characteristics, lexically, were nicely described: how an adverbial description of a response (acting persistently), can become a characteristic adjective if it is observed consistently (a persistent person), and how these can become abstracted from people as trait nouns (persistence). They summarized three aspects of traits, on the surface, that would draw agreement: trait attributions come from observed behaviours; they are to do with how people react to situations; and trait attributions allow some better-than-chance prediction about people's future behaviour. But, relevant to the main theme of this section, their essential nature lies beyond this (Carr and Kingsbury 1938, p. 498):

> The observed modes of conduct [traits] are judged to be functions of the constitutional nature of the individual, and the nature and locus of these organic conditions will presumably vary with the trait. Since the nature and locus of these conditions for any trait are unknown ...

Many dense pages later, Carr and Kingsbury (1938, p. 510) return to the issue of the conceptual nature of traits. If we knew the 'organic conditions' underlying traits we should probably define traits in those terms; but we don't, so we use 'behavioural correlates'. Despite the psychologists' ignorance about the fundamentals of traits (p. 510):

> trait terms are not mere words. They are applied to the individual in virtue of his possession of these organic conditions, and they are thus symbols that indirectly denote those conditions. Traits are conceptual realities that are highly similar to such concepts as engrams, nerve traces, neural modifications, etc.

Unfortunately dated comparisons, perhaps, for those of us looking forward to the discovery of the biological foundation of traits. They immediately follow that with two astute comments. First, they eschew naïve isomorphism in the biology of traits (p. 510): 'we must inhibit the naïve tendency to conceive of their [traits'] organic conditions as simple and unitary in character and occupying a distinctive location within the organism'. And they eschew mystification of traits just on the basis that their bases are unobservable (p. 510): 'Any tendency to reify these trait concepts in terms of an unsubstantial or immaterial content must be inhibited ... Any such tendency leads directly to an ontological dualism.' They understood that some trait terms were universal, nomothetic. They saw that people could be located on a dimension made up from antagonistic trait names. They saw similarities in groups of trait words that would allow for groups of similar trait names.

Towards the end of Carr and Kingsbury's (1938) piece is a stark reminder of what was at stake for personality traits at that time. They enumerated various possibilities regarding whether or not traits should be included in 'general and systematic psychology' (p. 523). To the current trait theorist, who views traits as basic aspects of individual differences, the idea that traits might not be of use as concepts that help us understand people in general comes as a shock. And a further irony comes from their last item regarding this issue (p. 523): 'that abnormal and clinical psychology have evinced no interest in popular traits, but have developed a set of new traits that are supposed to possess a distinctive value for their purposes'. Surprisingly, among these purely clinical and abnormal traits, they included Introversion and Extraversion, and emotional stability, the very rocks on which the systematic psychology of traits in the normal person has been founded.[1] And they might not be far from having made a still-relevant comment when they wrote about traits that 'psychology is at present groping somewhat blindly about because of the absence of any definite and accepted principles of orientation in reference to the concept' (p. 524). We still lack such anchors for traits.

Allport (1966) revisited the trait field, and his doctrinal list specifically, thirty-six years later. The field was a battlefield, with trait workers not only trying to pursue their own research agendas, but having to defend against the situationist 'gunfire' (Allport 1966, p. 2) abroad at the time. Ten years after that Epstein (1979, p. 649) agreed that personality research had 'slipped into the dark ages … method has become more important than substance'. His targets were largely the situationist critics of the time, and their inability to appreciate the unreliability of single observations of behaviour. By the 1960s, Allport had the benefit of mature multiple factor analysis methods, and emerging results about the main traits and their hierarchical arrangement. Whereas he recognized the efforts of Eysenck, Cattell, Thurstone and Guilford in classifying traits, and he makes it clear that he has doubts as to whether factor analytically-derived traits are the sorts of things his personality ideas wanted, Allport asserted that (Allport 1966, p. 3): 'Traits are cortical, subcortical, or postural dispositions having the capacity to gate or guide specific phasic reactions. It is only the phasic aspect that is visible; the tonic is carried somehow in the still mysterious realm of neurodynamic structure.' It was this serious lack of grounding traits somewhere in the brain and body that had always exercised Eysenck (1967), whose book on the biological bases of traits would appear a year later. Eysenck's (1957) general ideas about Extraversion's basis in individual differences in cortical arousability were already stated ten years before, and had an acknowledged basis in McDougall's (1929) ideas that were contemporaneous with Allport's own earliest writings. McDougall and Eysenck might not have been right (there is hardly a single replicable discovery concerning

---

[1] In fact, prior to their article there were many writers developing trait scales of 'neurotic tendencies' and 'Introversion-Extraversion' that were obviously intended to be applied to normal personality differences (e.g., Thurstone and Thurstone 1930; Bernreuter 1933; Guilford and Guilford 1934, 1936). Some items from these early scales were used in the various personality questionnaires devised later by Eysenck.

the biological basis of personality that has arisen from these pioneering ideas), but their scientific instincts were correct: that traits were unsatisfying fare unless one attacked the problem from both the outside and the inside at the same time. Allport (1966, p. 3) wondered whether factor-analytically-derived traits and biological research would meet in the middle or whether statistically derived traits, 'through item selection, correlation, axis manipulation, homogenization, and alphabetical labelling … impose an artefact of method upon the personal neural network as it exists in nature'.

Even this late in his writings Allport (1966) stuck to his plea to reasonableness about traits, urging 'heuristic realism' which 'holds that the person who confronts us possesses inside his skin generalized action tendencies (or traits) and that it is our job scientifically to discover what they are' (p. 3). He knew that that involved 'cleavage' of human behaviour, and that such cleaving might need revising. He warned against the 'positivistic gamesmanship' of those who denied the existence of traits, and the 'galloping empiricism' (p. 3) of those whose only criteria were mathematical. He returned to the latter fault at the end of the article where he spoke his mind as follows (p. 8): 'We find ourselves confused by our intemperate empiricism which often yields un-namable factors, arbitrary codes, unintelligible interaction effects, and sheer flatulence from our computers.' One wonders what he would say if, nowadays, he saw the profusion of factor analyses, often ungrounded in a theory of the biological origins of traits. Near the end, one can extract from Allort (1966, p. 8) a shorter and defensible agenda for trait research:

> persons are real beings … each has a real neuropsychic organization, and … our job is to comprehend this organization as well as we can … To do so requires that we be guided by theory in selecting our trait slices for study, that we employ rationally relevant methods, and be strictly bound by empirical verification.

That makes it sound as if the science of traits had progressed little in the forty years or so that Allport had been working, and the forty years again between his early writings and those of Galton before him. However, just before Allport's (1966) valedictory there was a remarkable report about the regularity of human trait structure that derived from Allport's early work, and also still stands fairly well today as the Five Factor Model of personality. Tupes and Christal (1961, reprinted 1991), despite acknowledging the work of Eysenck and Cattell and some others, stated that little work had been done on trait ratings from the 1920s to the time of their writing, and that there was little agreement about which traits were agreed from different studies; though they did reckon that there was evidence by then for Extraversion-Introversion and Emotionality-Stability. Their focus was on the usefulness of ratings, in order to provide predictive validity for real-life outcomes, and for validating paper and pencil tests. Their short introduction concentrates solely on the rating aspect of traits and its factor structure; there is no mention of the essential nature of traits.

The starting point for Tupes and Christal (1961) was the thirty-five trait variables developed by Cattell (1947), whose work in turn derived from the identification of dictionary trait terms by Allport and Odbert (1936). Their analyses of eight studies seemed ideally set up not to find regularities in trait ratings: the raters knew their ratees for different lengths of time, the relationships were of different kinds, the subject types were different across the studies, and the raters across the studies ranged from naïve lay people to clinical psychologists and psychiatrists. The result (Tupes and Christal 1961, p. 232): from their eight heterogeneous studies 'five fairly strong rotated factors emerged': Surgency (Extraversion), Agreeableness, Dependability (Conscientiousness), Emotional Stability (opposite of Neuroticism) and Culture. This was a breakthrough in dispelling some uncertainty about the structure of personality trait ratings, at least with these chosen traits and in these settings (p. 244):

> The results of these analyses clearly indicate that differences in samples, situations, raters, and lengths and kinds of acquaintanceship have little effect on the factor structure underlying ratings of personality traits. Statistical tests are not needed to indicate the similarity of corresponding factors from one analysis to another. There can be no doubt that the five factors found throughout all eight analyses are recurrent.

There was some discussion over the rotational position, and some about the number of factors that should be extracted, but not about whether one had got real phenomena that could be translated into brain system functioning. There was modesty in acknowledging that their factors were not new; they had appeared before in others' analyses, though in different combinations and called by different names. Three comments toward the end of the discussion attract attention (all on p. 247):

> One interpretation is that there are only five fundamental concepts running through the 35 trait names used in these studies ... It is unlikely that the five factors identified are the *only* fundamental personality factors ... it is likely that other fundamental factors may be identified in future studies.

The use of 'fundamental' is moot. The five traits identified from the ratings were recurrent, but in what sense were they fundamental? Certainly not with respect to their origins, or their known bodily foundations.

At about the same time, citing the same empirical history and with a similar aim, Norman (1963) found similar results. The focus was on clarifying the observational language of personality, arguing that research into personality 'will be facilitated by having available an extensive and well-organised vocabulary by means of which to denote the phenotypic attributes of persons' (Norman 1963, p. 574). There was no simple assumption that such taxonomic efforts would actually provide traits as such (p. 574): 'It is explicitly *not* assumed that complete theories of personality will simply emerge automatically from such taxonomic efforts. In the opinion of this writer, there is a good deal more to theory construction and refinement than the development of an observational language – even a good one.' That is the key issue, stated about as clearly as it can be; that even if one achieves a well-ordered structure for personality trait terms from the language, that does not comprise a personality theory, and nor does it necessarily identify the traits as such, or inform about their bases. Norman acknowledged the difference in results between Cattell's (1947) and Tupes and Christal's (1961) findings, despite the fact that they had used the same stimuli. Norman used the four best marker scales for each of the five factors from the Tupes and Christal (1961) work. A total of 622 subjects in four samples (all males) was used to make personality ratings. Five clear factors emerged in the analyses from all four samples; those we know in the Five Factor Model. Although the factors were clear, there were sizeable correlations among them. Among the ten possible correlations for the five factors, one of the samples had four correlations above 0.4 and one had three. In both samples, for example, there were positive correlations of around 0.6 between Conscientiousness and Culture. There were positive correlations of between .44 and .55 between Agreeableness and Conscientiousness and Emotional Stability. One of Norman's (1963) conclusions was that researchers should go back to the pool of trait items to search for traits beyond the five.

By this stage, one can discern three processes (there might be more) going on in the trait approach to personality. First, there was good progress in identifying traits for measurement and predictive validity. Secondly, there was the process of defending the trait approach from whatever was the zeitgeist in psychology (Freudiansim, behaviourism, situationism, etc.). Thirdly, there was the process of thinking about and studying what traits actually were, beyond scores from an inventory or rating scales. And so, forty years on from Allport and Cattell, who were forty years on from Galton, Meehl (1986) addressed the third issue by going back to Cattell's (e.g. 1945) surface traits and source traits distinction. He gave a good account of how, in everyday language we make trait attributions, and how these generalize from narrow to broader traits. These are from observed behaviours, and they are surface traits. Narrow traits that go to make up broader traits are 'related by a) empirical covariation and b) content similarity' (p. 317). And Meehl was good in bringing together very disparate-seeming psychologists and showing how they essentially recognize something like traits (Meehl 1986, p. 329):

> what is shared methodologically by Skinner, Freud, Allport, Murray, and Thurstone? ... The answer, of course, is that they all take as the rock bottom basis for their views the *fact of covariation*.

Getting beyond surface traits, what causes the co-variation? One possibility Meehl considered was Cattell's idea of the environmental mould. Trait correlation could occur because something like social class brought about certain correlated (but not otherwise causally linked) preferences in lifestyle. However, there were other possibilities (pp. 323–4):

> The problem of understanding surface trait correlations that seem to lack content similarity gives rise to the postulation of various causal sources that are, in some of several senses, *latent*. Some of these latent causal sources are traits (more or less stable dispositions, manifesting sizeable individual differences).

The trait entity is rather sneaked in here. Meehl goes on to discuss four possible sources of apparent traits. The first three are to do with learning processes, with mentions both of Skinnerian and Freudian ideas. The last of the four (what Meehl calls 'postulated internal entities') are Freudian concepts. Thus, the choice about true as opposed to apparent traits is between learning theory and Freudian psychoanalytic ideas. What the differential psychologist means by traits was discussed after that (Meehl 1986, p. 326):

> When psychometrician Cattell introduced the phrase 'source traits', what he had in mind was *factors*, those strange mathematical entities alleged to be discovered (some would say invented) by the statistical methods of Spearman, Kelly [sic], Thurstone and Co. … If one conceives factors merely as parameters parsimoniously representing the cross-sectional correlations among surface traits, the operant behaviourist should have no problem accepting them. But if one conducts factor analytic studies with a theoretical interest, aiming to discover source traits that are explanatory, *causal* entities, the interpretative problem is muddy. Having worried about the reality status of factors for some 45 years (meanwhile using it sparingly in my research with a fairly clear conscience) I will not be so foolish as to engage *that* terrible problem here.

Meehl's discussion was clearly meant to be emollient to behaviourists, but is still telling, in the admission that he admits and wrangles with the possibility of psychometrically-derived traits being valid mental entities. A little later on he states that (p. 326):

> It seems rather obvious that no mathematical reduction of cross-sectional trait correlations could warrant giving *causal* meaning to a factor in the interpretative text. I am not saying that psychometric factors never represent a kind of physical reality. Sometimes they do, for example, the heritable component of g must correspond to some quasi-fungible properties of brain microstructure or, if you prefer entities we know more about, the set of polygenes involved.

There is a strong assertion there: that the statistical entity g is given the breath of construct-validity life by having heritability; and the remark about polygenes is in line with current thinking and findings on g. Perhaps personality traits now deserve that recognition too. But perhaps not. The term 'quasi-fungible' is a clear admission that the nature of g (and personality traits) was still mysterious; it adds nothing beyond stating that g emerges as a statistical entity and we know nothing about what aspects of the brain contribute to the individual differences it represents. But Meehl does end with a strong statement about the ultimate causal underpinnings of personality variation (p. 330):

> A mathematical expression of the functional relations holding among behavioural variables always contains parameters. These parameters exhibit individual differences over organisms. Such individual differences have a heritable component … The genes provide what the logicians call *dispositions*, of varying orders; and the dispositions of any order exist in varying *amounts*.

That is a reasonable account of where we still are, and does not tell us how the parameters map to the underlying dispositions. Ultimately this piece, delivered to a potentially antagonistic audience, is an appeal to keep open the possibility that surface co-variation in behavioural aspects might be caused by what the differential psychologist calls traits.

A useful basis for more up-to-date thinking about traits may be had from Tellegen (1991). He assesses Cattell as having been too ready to accept factor-analytically-derived factors as actual traits, and characterizes Meehl as a believer in traits as entities with 'biological underpinnings' (Tellegen 1991, p. 10). Tellegen carpet-bombed seven anti-trait ideas, by giving a useful summary of Kenrick and Funder's (1988) answer to those who see traits, even at the phenotypic level, as fictions. Kenrick and Funder also described the conditions under which traits show best predictive power. The attacks on traits that were dismissed by Kenrick and Funder, and the lessons they declared having learned from the consideration of anti-trait ideas, were important achievements in establishing that traits as phenotypes should be taken seriously. But the by-now-old problem remains (Tellegen 1991, p. 12):

> Remarkably, from the perspective taken in the present article, the trait debate did not deal directly with one core issue; the nature of personality traits, that is, the nature and viability of a strong, rather than straw-man, trait position.

Tellegen (p. 13) attempted a definition of traits that predated the inner locus and causal primacy ideas of Matthews and Deary (1998):

> We can begin by defining traits as an inferred relatively enduring organismic (psychological, psychobiological) *structure* underlying an extended family of behavioural dispositions. In the case of personality traits it is expected that the manifestations of these dispositions can substantially affect a person's life.

Tellegen argued that, if we merely proceed by observing behaviour, inferring a trait and then successfully predicting another behaviour, we have got to co-variation but not explanation. Even if we induce a broader construct of a trait cluster and use that successfully to predict behaviour, we still have the limitation that 'from an explanatory viewpoint the construct is vacuous', and nothing but a 'tautological statement', and 'no causal explanations are provided' (1991, p. 14). Other accounts of traits did have 'explanatory content', 'surplus meaning' and 'causal accounts' and were able to go from surface to source traits. One example he gives is Gray's (1982) linking of the trait of positive emotionality to the behavioural activation system. He offers other biological accounts, besides. Tellegen seemed not to be accepting such accounts, but indicating that this was a possible route to getting at the nature of source traits. He reiterated that phenotypic traits might not be isomorphic with source traits (1991, p. 15): 'A trait dimension is clearly not in itself an individual organismic structure.' He also warned that factor analysis might not (probably would not) reveal a structure of traits that was isomorphic with underlying traits (p. 16):

What is more, the study of personality and personality disorders cannot simply be reduced to an analysis of how lay persons or even experts process information about people. To psychologize to that degree is to turn serious inquiry into trivial pursuits. Nineteenth-century astronomers formulated and developed the 'personal equation' to capture and correct for observers' systematic errors in timing stellar transits ... These developments did not reduce stellar events to mere perceptual-judgmental phenomena or turn astronomy into a branch of experimental psychology. Likewise, awareness and investigation of prototypes is no reason for viewing the structure of traits and disorders of personality as merely person-perceptual and labeling phenomena, or for turning all of personality assessment and psychodiagnostics over to social-cognition theorists.

Or leaving it all to psychometricians. Tellegen was clear, too, that the 'psychological nature' (1991, p. 30) of the Big Five traits had yet to be clarified.

One of the leading lights of current-day personality research described the 'celebrated achievement' of the growing consensus on the 'Five-Factor Model (FFM) as a reasonably comprehensive taxonomy of personality traits' (McCrae 2004, p. 4). When he asserted that 'traits are not cognitive fictions, but real psychological structures' (p. 4) the supporting evidence included consensual validation, prediction of life outcomes, longitudinal stability and heritability. Almost as a provocative challenge McCrae suggests that personality traits are unaffected by the environment, and totally caused by biological factors. The idea was that biologically-founded traits influence characteristic adaptations (like attitudes, goals, etc.). But these 'do not include personality traits, which FFT depicts as deeper structures, basic tendencies that are grounded in biology' (2004, p. 5). McCrae's very strong commitment to the biological underpinnings of traits is argued on the basis of substantial heritability, virtually zero contribution from shared environment, and the fact that even the residual in the 'non-shared' environment probably contains variance that is actually attributable to genetic and other biological variance, 'such as intrauterine environment, disease, and aging' (p. 6). The stability of personality traits over the lifespan is also cited as evidence of the strong claims made for 'Five-Factor Theory' as illustrated in Figure 6.1.

McCrae argues further that, because personality traits are 'shaped solely by biology, which is the common heritage of the human species ... their characteristic properties ought to be universal' (1991, p. 7). The universalities tested and

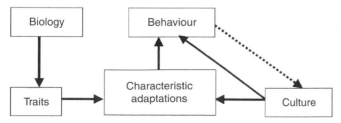

Figure 6.1. *A simplified representation of components of the personality system and their interrelations, according to Five-Factor Theory.*

confirmed to date include: universality of Five-Factor Model structure, though this means the factor structure of the NEO personality instrument (McCrae and Allik 2002); universality of the age-related declines in Neuroticism, Extraversion and Openness, and the increases in Agreeableness and Conscientiousness (McCrae and Costa 2003); universality of women scoring higher in Neuroticism and Agreeableness (Costa, Terracciano and McCrae 2001); and universality of cross-observer agreement (McCrae, Costa, Martin *et al.* 2004). These are impressive empirical achievements, and some were adumbrated above, but they still do not pull the last (or even the last goodness-knows-how-many) veils off to reveal what traits look like under the skin.

Conclusion

According to others, Allport might have agreed with the reservations entertained above about the current state of personality theory. John and Robbins (1993) remind us that 'the FFM is not based on idiographic methods, nor does it explicate the neuropsychiatric structures Allport believed to underlie personality'. There are two extreme conclusions possible about current work in personality traits.

The first would be to extract defeat from the jaws of partial victory. The consensus around the approximate number of broad personality traits, and their reliability, predictive validity, consensual validity, heritability, and so forth, are an empirical achievement that is worth defending and pursuing further. To abandon or overcriticize traits, therefore, would be violence to one of the better-attested constructs in psychology.

The second would be to declare victory and withdraw prematurely: that is, to announce that we have valid personality traits already. To mistake the findings collected already as better than they are, and to fudge the issue about the nature of traits would be a disservice to the steady empirical gains. The psychometric structure of traits and their usefulness have been progress to celebrate. However, it is not enough to say that, if it looks, walks and quacks like a duck, then it is a duck. Understanding the origins of traits – apart from the sure knowledge that they are partly heritable – has hardly got off the ground. Until that does happen, we cannot be sure that the pattern of phenotypes that most of us are looking at just now will not make a massive shift.

A way forward for the provisional quantitative personality traits that we already have is likely to be a steady revising of the phenotype, through more psychometric work, including lexical and questionnaire studies, across cultures and time, and more predictive validity work. This should be done while recognizing that even our notion of the correct trait outlines could be altered after we know more about the foundations of traits. As more knowledge is gained about the foundations of quantitative psychological traits, there is likely to be an iterative revising of which surface traits it is most useful to recognize and measure. It is a good time for quantitative traits. Genome-wide scans are revealing some of the genetic loci that contribute to variance in them, and this knowledge will be followed up to give some clues as to the biological mechanisms of the variation. For example, susceptibility loci have been found in relation to coronary artery disease, types 1 and 2 diabetes and bipolar mood disorder (Wellcome Trust Case Consortium 2007). Perhaps because it comes closer to medical problems, like anxiety and depression, it is likely that Neuroticism will feature in the efforts to find genetic susceptibility loci (Fullerton 2006), with some linkages already suggested (Kuo, Neale, Piley *et al.* 2007). Exciting-looking individual associations have not replicated, leading some to urge that there should be more recognition of the shared personality traits between humans and other animals and that discoveries in rodents should guide human work (Willis-Owen and Flint 2007). Ebstein (2006) has urged that two ways forward to the foundations of traits are studies that include genetics and brain imaging (e.g., Eisenberger, Lieberman and Satpute 2005), and studies of gene-environment interactions, the latter of which is well-exemplified in the work of Caspi and Moffitt (2006).

It is hoped, from the point of view of a believer in personality traits' existence and importance, that this emphasis on their limitations does not underplay their achievements. In past times, the attacks on traits were strong and much of the work was defensive. Traits are now so well established that more self-critical work can be done to get at two long-standing, highly-related issues: the correct descriptions of traits and their foundations.

References

Allport, G. W. 1927. Concepts of trait and personality, *Psychological Bulletin* 24: 284–93

  1931. What is a trait of personality?, *Journal of Abnormal and Social Psychology* 25: 368–72

  1937. *Personality: a psychological interpretation*. New York: Holt

  1966. Traits revisited, *American Psychologist* 21: 1–10

Allport, G. W. and Odbert, H. S. 1936. Trait-names: a psycho-lexical study, *Psychological Monographs* 47: No. 211

Aluja, A., Garcia, O. and Garcia, L. F. 2002. A comparative study of Zuckerman's three structural models for personality through the NEO-PI-R, ZKPQ-III-R, EPQ-RS and Goldberg's 50-bipolar adjectives, *Personality and Individual Differences* 33: 713–25

Ashton, M. C. and Lee, K. 2005. Honesty-humility, the Big Five, and the Five Factor Model, *Journal of Personality* 73: 1321–53

Bernreuter, R. G. 1933. The theory and construction of the personality inventory, *Journal of Social Psychology* 4: 387–405

Borkenau, P., Mauer, N., Riemann, R., Spinath, F. M. and Angleitner, A. 2004. Thin slices of behaviour as cues of personality and intelligence, *Journal of Personality and Social Psychology* 86: 599–614

Bouchard, T. J. and Loehlin, J. C. 2001. Genes, evolution, and personality, *Behaviour Genetics* 31: 243–73

Carr, H. A. and Kingsbury, F. A. 1938. The concept of traits, *Psychological Review* 45: 497–524

Caspi, A. and Moffitt, T. 2006. Gene-environment interactions in psychiatry: joining forces with neuroscience, *Nature Reviews Neuroscience* 7: 583–90

Cattell, R. B. 1945. The principal trait clusters for describing personality, *Psychological Bulletin* 42: 129–61

1947. Confirmation and clarification of primary personality factors, *Psychometrika* 12: 197–220

Cloninger, C. R., Svrakic, D. M. and Przybeck, T. R. 1993. A psychobiological model of temperament and character, *Archives of General Psychiatry* 50: 975–90

Costa, P. T. and McCrae, R. R. 1985. *The NEO Personality Inventory Manual*. Odessa, FL: Psychological Assessment Resources

1994. Set like plaster? Evidence for the stability of adult personality, in T. Heatherton and J. Weinberger (eds.), *Can personality change?*, pp. 21–40. Washington, DC: American Psychological Association

Costa, P. T., Terracciano, A. and McCrae, R. R. 2001. Gender differences in personality traits across cultures: robust and surprising findings, *Journal of Personality and Social Psychology* 81: 322–31

De Raad, B. 2000. The big five personality factors: the psycholexical approach to personality. Seattle, WA: Hogrefe and Huber

De Young, C. G. 2006. Higher-order factors of the big five in a multi-informant sample, *Journal of Personality and Social Psychology* 91: 1138–51

Digman, J. M. 1996. The curious history of the five factor model, in J. S. Wiggins (ed.), *The five factor model of personality: theoretical perspectives*, pp. 1–20. New York: Guilford

Digman, J. M. and Takemoto-Chock, N. K. 1981. Factors in the natural language of personality: re-analysis, comparison and interpretation of six major studies, *Multivariate Behavioural Research* 16: 149–70

Ebstein, R. P. 2006. The molecular genetic architecture of human personality: beyond self-report questionnaires, *Molecular Psychiatry* 11: 427–45

Eisenberger, N. I., Lieberman, M. D. and Satpute, A. B. 2005. Personality from a controlled processing perspective: an fMRI study of neuroticism, extraversion, and self-consciousness, *Cognitive, Affective, and Behavioural Neuroscience* 5: 169–81

Epstein, S. 1979. Explorations in personality today and tomorrow: a tribute to Henry Murray, *American Psychologist* 34: 649–53

Eysenck, H. J. 1947. *Dimensions of personality*. London: Kegan Paul

1953. *The structure of human personality*. London: Methuen

1957. *The dynamics of anxiety and hysteria*. London: Routledge and Kegan Paul

1967. *The biological basis of personality*. Springfield, IL: Thomas

Eysenck, H. J. and Eysenck, S. B. G. 1982. Recent advances in the cross-cultural study of personality, in C. D. Spielberger and J. N. Butcher (eds.), *Advances in personality assessment*, pp. 41–69. Hillsdale, NJ: Erlbaum

Freyd, M. 1924. The personalities of the socially and mechanically inclined, *Psychological Monographs* 33: No. 151

Friedman, H. S., Tucker, J. S., Schwartz, J. E., Tomlinson-Keasey, C., Martin, L. R., Wingard, D. L. and Criqui, M. H. 1995. Psychosocial and behavioural predictors of longevity: the aging and death of the 'Termites', *American Psychologist* 50: 69–78

Fullerton, J. 2006. New approaches to the genetic analysis of neuroticism and anxiety, *Behaviour Genetics* 36: 147–61

Galton, F. 1884. Measurement of character, *Fortnightly Review* 36: 179–85

Goldberg, L. R. 1981. Language and individual differences: the search for universals in personality lexicons, in L. Wheeler (ed.), *Review of Personality and Social Psychology*, vol. II, pp. 141–65. Beverly Hills, CA: Sage

1983. The magical number five, plus or minus two: some considerations on the dimensionality of personality descriptors. Paper presented at a research seminar, Gerontology Research Center, NIA/NIH, Baltimore, MD

1993. The structure of phenotypic personality traits, *American Psychologist* 48: 26–34

Gosling, S. D. 2001. From mice to men: what can we learn about personality from animal research?, *Psychological Bulletin* 127: 45–86

Gray, J. A. 1982. *The neuropsychology of anxiety: an inquiry into the function of the septo-hippocampal system*. Oxford University Press

Guilford, J. P. and Guilford, R. B. 1934. An analysis of the factors in a typical test of introversion-extroversion, *Journal of Abnormal and Social Psychology* 28: 377–99

1936. Personality factors S, E, and M, and their measurement, *Journal of Psychology* 2: 109–27

Heymans, G. and Wiersma, E. 1909. Beitrage zur apeziellen Psychologie auf Grund einer massenuntersuchung [Contributions to differential psychology based on a large scale investigation], *Zeitschrift fur Psychologic* 51: 1–72

Ivkovic, V., Vitart, V., Rudan, I., Janicijevic, B., Smolej-Narancic, N., Skaric-Juric, T., Barbalic, M., Polasek, O., Kolcic, I., Biloglav, Z., Visscher, P. M., Hayward, C., Hastie, N. D., Anderson, N., Campbell, H., Wright, A. F., Rudan, P. and Deary, I. J. 2007. The Eysenck personality factors: psychometric structure, reliability, heritability and phenotypic and genetic correlations with psychological distress in an isolated Croatian population, *Personality and Individual Differences* 42: 123–33

John, O. P. and Robbins, R. W. 1993. Gordon Allport: father and critic of the five-factor model, in K. H. Craik, R. Hogan and R. N. Wolfe (eds.), *Fifty years of personality psychology*, pp. 215–36. New York: Plenum

Kenrick, D. T. and Funder, D. C. 1988. Profiting from controversy: lessons from the person-situation debate, *American Psychologist* 43: 23–34

Kuo, P. H., Neale, M. C., Piley, B. P., Patterson, D. G., Walsh, D., Prescott, C. A. and Kendler, K. S. 2007. A genome-wide linkage analysis for the personality trait neuroticism in the Irish affected sib-pair study of alcohol dependence, *American Journal of Medical Genetics B: Neuropsychiatric Genetics* 144: 463–8

Lee, K. and Ashton, M. C. 2006. Further assessment of the HEXACO Personality Inventory: two new facet scales and an observer report form, *Psychological Assessment* 18: 182–91

Markon, K. E., Krueger, R. F. and Watson, D. 2005. Delineating the structure of normal and abnormal personality: an integrative hierarchical approach, *Journal of Personality and Social Psychology* 88: 139–57

Matthews, G. and Deary, I. J. 1998. *Personality traits*. Cambridge University Press

Matthews, G., Deary, I. J. and Whiteman, M. C. 2003. *Personality traits*, 2nd edn. Cambridge University Press

McCrae, R. R. 2001. Trait psychology and culture: exploring intercultural comparison, *Journal of Personality* 69: 819–46

   2004. Human nature and culture: a trait perspective, *Journal of Research in Personality* 38: 3–14

McCrae, R. R. and Allik, J. (eds.) 2002. *The Five-Factor Model of personality across cultures*. New York: Kluwer Academic/Plenum

McCrae, R. R. and Costa, P. T. 1985. Updating Norman's 'adequate taxonomy': intelligence and personality dimensions in natural language and in questionnaires, *Journal of Personality and Social Psychology* 49: 710–21

   2003. *Personality in adulthood: a Five-Factor Theory perspective*, 2nd edn. New York: Guilford

McCrae, R. R., Costa, P. T., Martin, T. A., Oryol, V. E., Rukavnishnikov, A. A., Senin, I. G., Hrebickova, M. and Urbanek, T. 2004. Consensual validation of personality traits across cultures, *Journal of Research in Personality* 38: 179–201

McCrae, R. R. and 79 others 2005. Universal features of personality traits from the observer's perspective: data from 50 cultures, *Journal of Personality and Social Psychology* 88: 547–61

McDougall, W. 1929. The chemical theory of temperament applied to Introversion and Extroversion, *Journal of Abnormal and Social Psychology* 24: 293–309

Measelle, J. R., John, O. P., Ablow, J. C., Cowan, P. A. and Cowan, C. P. 2005. Can children provide coherent, stable, and valid self-reports on the Big Five dimensions? A longitudinal study from ages 5 to 7, *Journal of Personality and Social Psychology* 89: 90–106

Meehl, P. E. 1986. Trait language and behaviourese, in T. Thompson and M. Zeiler (eds.), *Analysis and integration of behavioural units*, pp. 315–34. Hillsdale, NJ: Lawrence Erlbaum Associates

Norman, W. T. 1963. Toward an adequate taxonomy of personality attributes, *Journal of Abnormal and Social Psychology* 66: 574–83

Paunonen, S. V. 2002. *Design and construction of the Supernumerary Personality Inventory*, Research Bulletin 763. London, ON: University of Western Ontario

Peanbody, D. and De Raad, B. 2002. The substantive nature of psycholexical personality factors: a comparison across languages, *Journal of Personality and Social Psychology* 83: 983–97

Roberts, B. W. and DelVecchio, W. F. 2000. The rank-order consistency of personality from childhood to old age: a quantitative review of longitudinal studies, *Psychological Bulletin* 126: 3–25

Rusten, J. (ed.) 1993. *3astus: Characters*. Cambridge, MA: Harvard University Press

Sanderman, R. and Ranchor, A. V. 1994. Stability of personality traits and psychological distress over six years, *Perceptual and Motor Skills* 78: 89–90

Saucier, G., Georgiades, S., Tsaousis, I. and Goldberg, L. R. 2005. The factor structure of Greek personality adjectives, *Journal of Personality and Social Psychology* 88: 856–75

Saucier, G. and Ostendorf, F. 1999. Hierarchical subcomponents of the Big Five personality factors: a cross-language replication, *Journal of Personality and Social Psychology* 76: 613–27

Stelmack, R. M. and Stalikas, A. 1991. Galen and the humour theory of temperament, *Personality and Individual Differences* 12: 255–63

Stewart, M. E., Ebmeier, K. P. and Deary I. J. 2005. Personality correlates of happiness and sadness: EPQ-R and TPQ compared, *Personality and Individual Differences* 38: 1085–96

Tellegen, A. 1991. Personality traits: issues of definition, evidence, and assessment, in W. Grove and D. Ciccetti (eds.), *Thinking clearly about psychology*, pp. 10–35. Minneapolis: University of Minnesota Press

Thurstone, L. L. and Thurstone, T. G. 1930. A neurotic inventory, *Journal of Social Psychology* 1: 3–30

Tupes, E. C. and Christal, R. E. 1961. ASD Technical Report (reprinted in 1991 as Recurrent personality factors based on trait ratings), *Journal of Personality* 60: 225–51

Webb, E. 1915. Character and intelligence, *British Journal of Psychology Monographs* 7: 1–99

Weiss, A. and Costa, P. T. 2005. Domain and facet personality predictors of all-cause mortality among medicare patients aged 65 to 100, *Psychosomatic Medicine* 67: 724–33

Weiss, A., King, J. E. and Perkins, L. 2006. Personality and subjective well-being in orangutans, *Journal of Personality and Social Psychology* 90: 501–11

Wellcome Trust Case Consortium 2007. Genome-wide association study of 14,000 cases of seven common diseases and 3,000 shared controls, *Nature* 447: 661–78

Willis-Owen, A. A. G. and Flint, J. 2007. Identifying the genetic determinants of emotionality in humans: insights from rodents, *Neuroscience and Biobehavioural Reviews* 31: 115–24

7 Methods of personality assessment

Gregory J. Boyle and Edward Helmes

This chapter cannot provide an exhaustive review of the many approaches to personality assessment that are in common use because of the size of the area. With entire books devoted to individual tests, a chapter such as this is necessarily limited in its scope. In particular, the chapter will not address methods of projective personality assessment. Those interested in an introduction to such methods can consult the relevant chapters in Groth-Marnat (2003), and by Weiner (1997) and the following commentaries in the *Journal of Personality Assessment* for the use of the Rorschach. For a more critical perspective, readers can consult Hunsley, Lee and Wood (2003). The approach being taken is in part a focus on contrasting the multidimensional personality assessment instruments constructed using factor analysis by Raymond B. Cattell and his colleagues and those multidimensional scales developed using other approaches to assessing people, notably the construct-oriented methods advocated by Douglas Jackson. Despite its known limitations, the self-report questionnaire has become the dominant method for assessing personality. Even though other approaches to assessment remain in use, self-report instruments, whether administered on a computer screen and scored online (e.g., Drasgow and Olson-Buchanan 1999) or through a traditional answer sheet and question booklet or combined question and answer sheet, remain the dominant form of assessment. Their economy, apparent ease of use and interpretation, and freedom of the need for trained interviewers (or even third parties in some cases) provide advantages that often outweigh benefits of other approaches to assessment. Such other methods will be mentioned briefly, but the bulk of this chapter will be on self-report techniques.

For many users of personality assessment instruments, the methods by which a measure is constructed are irrelevant or of little interest. The methods used do, however, directly relate to the content of measures and influence how the measures should be interpreted. The assumptions made by the test developer and the choice of procedures used during the process of refining and selecting items very much determine the final product. For example, concerns for reading level can influence item phrasing and the complexity of ideas being expressed, while assumptions about gender differences will influence whether scales will have gender-based norms or not, thus determining the nature of inferences about clients that can be drawn. The work of Cattell is notable for its use of the method of factor analysis with items that were felt to reflect personality as it is expressed and structured in the English language. His work was pioneering psychometric research into the structure and measurement of human personality (see Boyle 2006). In contrast, Jackson's work in personality assessment derived from a different direction, starting in clinical psychology and being influenced by Gardner Murphy and by the seminal papers of Cronbach and Meehl (1955), Campbell and Fiske (1959), Loevinger (1957) and Jackson (2000). His interest in multivariate assessment and factor analytic methods rivalled Cattell's, but his approach to test development relied upon there being substantive theory in place that guided the processes of item writing and item analysis. He also valued the multitrait-multimethod approach to construct validity and this technique formed part of the development process for many of his instruments. While both these test developers used factor analysis, their emphasis on it differed. Cattell argued that when properly used, the method provided insights into the natural structure of personality and he used it as the primary method to form scales from sets of items. Cattell (1973; Burdsal and Vaughn 1974) argued against the use of individual items in factor analyzing items and for the use of homogeneous groups of items (parcels). Later Comrey (1988) also argued for the use of sets of items, which he termed factored homogeneous item dimensions (FHIDs) (Comrey 1967, 1984), and not individual items as the input to factor analysis. In contrast, Jackson used factor analysis more as a method of confirming structures that had been developed on theoretical grounds, but he often relied more upon basic correlational analyses of item pools than upon item factor analyses.

Briggs and Cheek (1986) provide an overview of the relevant issues that need to be considered in using factor analysis for scale construction and give examples of where factor analysis can help refine a scale intended to measure a single construct and where it can obscure matters. They note the increasingly important distinction between *exploratory* methods, in which the goal in item factor analysis is to identify any structure underlying a set of test items, and *confirmatory* methods in which the goal is to verify if a theoretical or predetermined structure is indeed supported in the set of items. Item factor analysis involves several complex issues and there are now several alternative computational methods for analyzing personality questionnaire items (see Wirth and Edwards 2007 for a review of current methods).

Exploratory factor analysis (EFA) methodology has progressed since the publication of Cattell's 1978 treatise (for a detailed discussion of EFA methodological requirements, see Boyle, Stankov and Cattell 1995; Gorsuch 1983, 1988). With the development of more powerful and cheaper computers, newer techniques including confirmatory factor analysis or CFA (Mulaik 1988), as one application of structural equation modelling (SEM) implemented via, for example, LISREL or other similar computer programs have become commonplace (Bentler 1988). Over the past three decades, issues related to EFA have continued to simmer without a clear consensus upon several major issues that involve the commonly used methods. Historically, Cattell (1978, 1988) favoured the traditional factor analytic model for developing measures and evaluating them. By contrast, component analysis, which uses a different underlying mathematical model, became in practice the most commonly used procedure. The various issues on this topic were reviewed by Velicer and Jackson (1990) and an extensive series of comments and rebuttals followed in that issue of *Multivariate Behavioural Research* that suggested that no clear consensus among experts was evident on several basic matters. One unfortunate aspect of the differing perspectives on the best form of analysis is that the various methods that can be used in EFA are frequently used without a full understanding of their limitations, as are the exploratory applications of SEM procedures. When properly applied, the various CFA procedures that are in common use can be quite powerful and informative, but they also have their shortcomings, particularly when they are used for exploratory analyses. Cuttance (1987, p. 243) comments on such applications with one example of the pitfalls in using structural equation models for exploratory ends:

> MacCallum (1985) investigated the process of the exploratory fitting of models in simulated data ... for which the true model was known. He found that only about half of the exploratory searches located the true model ... He obtained this limited rate of success ... in samples of 300 observations ... and his success rate in smaller samples (N= 100) was zero ... An exploratory analysis of data thus entails the risk of inducing an interpretation founded on the idiosyncracies of individual samples.

Wirth and Edwards (2007) also note that most SEM programs both require substantial sample sizes and cannot handle the number of parameters required if large multiscale personality measures are analyzed at the item level. Most item response theory (IRT) programs can deal with the number of items, but may encounter difficulties if the assumption of homogeneous scales is violated, which is likely to happen with many personality constructs.

In order to enable comprehensive assessment and to undertake multidimensional measurement of personality traits, it is generally considered desirable to use a variety of measurement media, including subjective questionnaires, structured interviews and objective test instruments (Cattell 1986a, 1986b; Smith 1988). Cattell argued cogently that personality traits should be identified through multiple measurement media, including subjective ratings or life-record data (L-Data), subjective self-report questionnaire data (Q-data), and objective test data (T-data). The choice of specific media of measurement has critically important implications in terms of susceptibility to response distortion, as well as for psychometric properties such as reliability and validity (Cattell 1986a, 1986c, 1986d). These issues of response distortion were also addressed in more depth by other workers, including those who addressed the specific question of response styles, such as social desirability and acquiescence in the Minnesota Multiphasic Personality Inventory (MMPI) and other self-report instruments, beginning with Alan Edwards (1957) and finalized (in some eyes at least) by Jack Block (1965). The importance of social desirability as an alternative explanation for certain results or as a confounding variable has faded somewhat in visibility in personality assessment since the major debates on the topic of the 1960s and 1970s. At the same time, there is widespread recognition of the nature of social desirability as a measurement confound and as an important personality variable in itself (Helmes 2000). The latter position is illustrated by the work of Paulhus (1984, 1986) and the development of his measures of self-deception and impression management as the major dimensions of social desirability (Paulhus 1998).

The types of information referred to by Cattell as L-data are more commonly known as *biodata*, and include such biographical information as education, work experience and volunteer activities. Biodata have been used in various applications (Stokes, Mumford and Owens 1994), but are most widely used in personnel selection in industry and the military. Some research suggests that biographical data appear to account for additional variance over self-report personality measures and general mental ability (Mount, Witt and Barrick 2000), which supports Cattell's argument that this form of self-report data can provide valuable information beyond that obtained with conventional personality measures.

Based on the assumption that personality characteristics are represented linguistically, a major Q-data instrument, the Sixteen Personality Factor Questionnaire (16PF) was constructed factor analytically by Cattell and his colleagues (e.g., Cattell, Eber and Tatsuoka 1970; Cattell 1994; Cattell and Krug 1986; Krug 1981). The 16PF was based on exploratory factor analyses of several clusters of personality traits that had been derived from a comprehensive search of over 4,000 trait-descriptive terms relating to personality in the English language compiled by Allport and Odbert (1936). This work represented a significant development in both its scope and its reliance upon factor analysis.

Psychological measures can, of course, be developed by other methods than the use of factor analysis. Burisch (1984) classed factor analytic methods as *inductive*, in contrast to external methods such as the criterion groups method used for the original development of the MMPI (Butcher, Dahlstrom, Graham *et al.* 1989). Burisch classes Jackson's construct-oriented approach as *deductive*, along with other methods that can be described as rational, intuitive or theoretical. Burisch's (1984) review of the relevant literature concluded that there were no demonstrable differences in validity correlations among scales constructed using different approaches to test development. Later research suggested that some methods do lead to higher validity coefficients than others. For example, a more recent study using the traits of Extraversion and Dominance contrasted the Personality Research Form (PRF) and 16PF fourth edition (16PF4) in predicting job performance of a group of 487 managers and did find some differences (Goffin, Rothstein and Johnston 2000). They concluded that the construct-based PRF had 'distinct predictive advantages' (p. 261) over the 16PF4 in that context, but also noted that there was still very little relevant literature on such comparisons. Hough and Paullin (1994) also concluded that there were some benefits of the construct-based method of scale development, as did Burisch (1986) in his later comparison of methods of scale construction. What limited evidence exists thus suggests that the method of test construction may well have implications for the validity of personality measures.

The development of multiscale measurement instruments has become a multi-stage process, and it is likely significant that nearly all the major instruments in use today were developed decades ago. The actual procedures used go beyond the simple classifications used to compare strategies that were used by Burisch (1984, 1986) and others. The methods used can be illustrated by the procedures outlined by Jackson (1970), who advocated a sequential process that stressed the importance of convergent and divergent validity and the suppression of confounding response styles. Factor analysis could be used at different stages in the process, but it was always secondary to substantive considerations. These procedures were used in his measures of normal personality, the Personality Research Form (Jackson 1984) and Jackson Personality Inventory (Jackson 1994). Interestingly, the latest (fifth) edition of the 16PF (Cattell, Cattell and Cattell 1994) adopted item analytic approaches similar to those used by Jackson in order to promote convergent properties among the items of given scales.

One important issue in evaluating personality assessment instruments involves the actual items and how they are phrased. Emphasis on this aspect of instruments has been more evident in the area of public opinion and attitude measurement (Sudman and Bradburn 1982; Schwarz and Sudman 1996), but has also been an issue with personality measures (e.g., Nicholls, Licht and Pearl 1982) and with life history (L-data) in the form of symptoms (Schwarz 1999). Care on these matters is important for defining both how a particular scale measures what it is designed to measure (Angleitner, John and Lohr 1986) and what it is not intended to measure, which are aspects of convergent and discriminant validity. Angleitner *et al.* rated various item characteristics and noted that ostensibly parallel forms had some scales with different item properties across forms, and that item complexity frequently affected the ability to immediately understand the item. They noted that all but two 16PF A and B scales had more than 50 per cent of the items with poor understandability or high ambiguity. This illustrates how sequential test construction strategies that incorporate structured analysis of item properties in the early stages can lead to better quality items for final testing. Such strategies can also build in analyses to foster convergent and discriminant properties in the scales. Rudinger and Dommel (1986) provide an analysis of a multitrait-multimethod analysis of the German translation of Jackson's PRF that illustrates both how such analyses can be performed, but also the properties of the instrument itself.

Within the normal personality trait domain, potentially controversial items pertaining to religion, sex and politics are often excluded from questionnaires. The presence of such items was one factor leading to the revision of the MMPI (Butcher, Dahlstrom, Graham *et al.* 1989). Likewise, items relating to social desirability and other response sets typically are kept at a minimum during the developmental stages for large, multiscale measures. This may not be the case for shorter, more narrowly focused measures of single or a few attributes where extensive developmental research on a measure may not have been completed before an instrument appeared in the research literature. Of course, users of such instruments should always investigate the methods by which a scale was developed and the reported psychometric properties of personality measures before using them, but detailed information on the development of scales may not be widely available.

One issue that test developers must address is the question of gender differences. The recent tendency towards production of neutral ('unisex') personality inventories (by removing items that exhibit significant sex differences) makes it well nigh impossible to obtain complete and accurate personality profiles that distinguish between males and females. One example of such an instrument is Morey's (1991) Personality Assessment Inventory (PAI), for which a decision was made to minimize gender differences and not only remove items that showed a gender difference, but also not to report gender-based norms. One justification for the decision derives from the nature of the PAI as a measure of psychopathology where a stronger argument can be made for less emphasis upon the direct assessment of gender differences. Measures of normal personality must address the matter of there being notable gender differences in psychological functioning resulting from differences in genes, brain anatomy and sex hormone levels, in addition to significant differences in acculturation and social conditioning in some way. The most common method is the provision of separate norms for males and females. Other scales, such as those of Comrey, include scales that reflect behavioural and attitudinal differences between males and females.

Issues such as gender differences become interwoven with issues such as the prevalence of forms of psychopathology when we consider that domain of content. Several measures that assess psychopathology use the word 'personality' in their title in order to reduce the negative reaction among respondents. But at the same time, similar contrasts within the domain of psychopathology between the approaches to the development of measures can be seen as with measures of normal personality. The Clinical Analysis Questionnaire (CAQ) (Krug 1980) was constructed to provide a questionnaire (Q-data) measure of abnormal personality traits. Part 1 of the CAQ measures the traditional 16PF normal personality trait factors, while Part 2 measures twelve abnormal personality trait dimensions. Part 2 of the CAQ was constructed from an extensive series of factor analyses that included the entire MMPI item pool, together with many additional items pertaining to depression and other aspects of psychopathology to measure more fundamental, underlying source trait factors (Boyle 1990, 2006; Boyle and Comer 1990; Smith 1988). Note again the emphasis upon the use of factor analysis to derive scales to reflect areas of content that are presumed to be present in the initial pool of items. Recently the CAQ has been upgraded to the 325-item *PsychEval Personality Questionnaire* (PEPQ) produced by the Institute for Personality and Ability Testing. Factor analysis was also prominent in constructing the Basic Personality Inventory (BPI) (Jackson 1989). In its case, content dimensions were identified through a factor analysis of the scales of the MMPI and Jackson's Differential Personality Inventory (DPI) (Jackson and Messick 1971), which was based upon considerations of symptoms that reflect established domains of psychopathology. This preliminary analysis, that was intended to define the domains common to the two measures, led to the identification of psychopathological constructs for which a new item pool could be written, with the use of sequential item analytic strategies to finalize the scales.

While the MMPI remains the most widely used measure of psychopathology, indeed of personality in general (Piotrowski and Keller 1989), the 1989 revision failed to correct significant weaknesses (Helmes and Reddon 1993). Some of those weaknesses derive directly from the contrasted groups method used to select items for the MMPI scales. Such problems are not as striking with either the CAQ or the DPI and BPI. However, the methods of scale construction used with these measures clearly do influence the contents. For example, the CAQ has scales for Boredom and withdrawal, Guilt and resentment, Low energy depression, Anxious depression and Suicidal depression. The BPI merges into a single Depression scale the fine distinctions based upon severity and associated symptoms that are made by the factor analytic method used in the development of the CAQ. The two instruments converge on scales for the constructs of hypochondriasis, paranoia/ideas of persecution, anxiety, and thinking disturbance/schizophrenia. The CAQ has additional scales for Agitation, Psychopathic deviation, Psychasthenia and Psychological inadequacy, scales with clear links to the parent MMPI item pool and its associated psychiatric syndromes, some of which are no longer used diagnostically. In contrast, the BPI has scales that diverge to assess a wider range of other forms of psychopathology: Interpersonal Problems, Alienation, Impulse Expression, Social Introversion and Self Depreciation.

Both the 16PF and the PRF have withstood the test of critical scrutiny over many years, both in the *Test Critiques* series of psychological test reviews, and in the *Buros Mental Measurements Yearbooks*. Unlike the fifth edition of the 16PF (16PF5) (see Conn and Rieke 1994), the fourth edition with its multiple parallel forms (A, B, C, D, E) has the decided advantage of being able to attain virtually any desired level of reliability through the administration of more items. It is important to note that Cattell had always recommended that at least two forms of the 16PF (Forms A + B or C + D) should be administered together, in order to ensure high reliabilities for each of the 16PF sub-scales. In contrast, while parallel forms for the PRF are available for both shorter (A + B), and longer versions (AA + BB), the current version (PRF-E) is only available in one form. Differences with the 16PF are evident in other ways, with all PRF forms having readability evaluated during the item selection stage, while the 16PF uses different forms for different educational levels: Forms A and B are suitable for use with most adults whereas Forms C and D are less demanding of vocabulary and administration time, while Forms E and F are intended for individuals with low literacy levels. While the longer PRF scales tend to be more reliable because of their increased length, all forms in themselves are sufficiently reliable for most uses.

Both the PRF and the original forms of the 16PF were developed before the popularity of the Big Five or Five Factor Model, which emphasizes five supraordinate dimensions of Neuroticism, Extraversion, Openness to experience, Agreeableness and Conscientiousness, became widely accepted (see Goldberg 1990; Costa and McCrae 1992; McCrae and Costa 1987). Interestingly, both

Cattell (1995; Cattell, Boyle and Chant 2002) and Jackson (Jackson, Ashton and Tomes 1996) are among those who have argued for additional dimensions, in addition to those who have criticized the Five-Factor Model on other grounds (e.g., Block 1995). An additional point in debates over the utility of the Five-Factor Model is that fewer relevant predictors necessarily account for less variance than does prediction based on a larger set of primary factors (Mershon and Gorsuch 1988).

When the consequences of personality assessment might be negative (e.g., admission to a mental institution; incarceration in a prison), or positive (e.g., job selection; approval from the therapist; or release from a mental institution) there may be strong motivation (either conscious or unconscious) to distort responses to personality questionnaire items. In order to control for motivational/response distortion, many instruments incorporate various validity and correction scales, ranging from simple 'lie scales' such as in the Eysenck Personality Questionnaire (EPQ-R) (Eysenck and Eysenck 1975) or the correction scales of the MMPI/ MMPI-2, social desirability measures, scales for detecting random responses, and scales that identify other response sets. Measures of psychopathology such as the MMPI/MMPI-2 (Butcher, Dahlstrom, Graham *et al.* 1989) frequently have multiple measures to assess the validity of the responses (see Bagby, Marshall, Bury *et al.* 2006 and Helmes 2008 for reviews of the MMPI-2 validity measures and related issues). The issue of response distortion is complex, with trait view corrections (Cattell and Krug 1971) suggesting that there are various distinct 'desirability response tendencies' which differentially distort responses on Q-data instruments, which can be distorted all too easily because of their transparency.

A recent development in the assessment of people where distortion of self-reports or minimization of reporting problems is likely to be present is based upon conditional reasoning, a process in which response alternatives are designed to elicit responses based upon self-serving cognitive premises (James 1998). This is an indirect or implicit measure of personality, one that may be more resistant to faking than other, more traditional methods (LeBreton, Barksdale, Robin and James 2007), but which uses a conventional self-report format. This approach relies upon knowledge of the forms of self-protective or biased reasoning likely to be used, together with a careful selection of response alternatives. It is thus quite distinct from measures used for the implicit assessment of stereotyped attitudes, such as the Implicit Association Test (Greenwald and Banaji 1995). To date, relatively few applications of conditional reasoning have been published, so it is still unclear how extensive the application of the procedure will be. James, McIntyre, Glisson *et al.* (2005) outline one of the early applications, the measurement of aggression.

While self-report assessments certainly currently dominate personality assessment, other approaches have definite advantages and continue to be used. Ratings based upon previous periods of observation and acquired knowledge of the person being rated have been in use for decades. Such a form of evaluation is particularly useful when there are grounds for believing that self-reports may not be accurate.

In addition, such forms of assessment also provide a different source of information that can be useful to the practitioner to develop a more complete understanding of a client. Psychiatric settings are certainly ones in which there are good reasons for doubting the accuracy of many self-reports and instruments for these purposes have been in existence for some time. One of the first examples of a rating scale for psychiatric problems was that developed by Wittenborn (1951). There is now an extensive literature on psychiatric rating scales that cannot be explored here, but Sajatovic and Ramirez (2003) provide examples of many such scales.

A similar context in which there are solid grounds for doubting the accuracy of self-report is the assessment of young children. This has become one of the major areas in which such rating instruments are used, the evaluation of psychosocial functioning and behaviour problems in children (e.g., Achenbach and McConaughy 2003; Conners 1997; Reynolds and Kamphaus 2004). Hartup and van Lieshout (1995) review many of the issues relevant to the assessment of personality during the course of child development.

The inventory developed by Costa and McCrae (1992) to assess the domains of the Five-Factor Model, the NEO-PI-R, incorporates an unusual form of observer rating. The standard self-report form is converted to third-person format. For example, item 1 on Form S, 'I am not a worrier', is changed on the male version of Form R to 'He is not a worrier' and on the female form to 'She is not a worrier'. The observer-report Forms R are intended to be completed by a spouse, a peer or by an expert who knows the person well. Thus, instead of providing ratings for traits based upon provided definitions, or a series of adjectives, Form R of the NEO-PI-R asks the rater to complete the equivalents of the self-report items. Costa and McCrae (1992) report substantial agreement using intraclass correlations for both the five major domains of the NEO-PI-R, but also for the facet scales across peer/peer, peer/self and spouse/self comparisons. Such results suggest that the reduction in method variance associated with comparisons of other forms of peer rating with self-reports may lead to better reliability and better agreement on personality characteristics between observers, as noted by Kurtz, Lee and Sherker (1999). A series of studies of personality change in people with Alzheimer's disease as rated by spouses and other care-givers has also shown the utility of the observer rating forms of the NEO-PI-R (Siegler, Dawson and Welsh 1994; Strauss, Pasupathi and Chatterjee 1993, Strauss and Pasupathi 1994; Welleford, Harkins and Taylor 1995).

Self-descriptive adjectives have had an extensive history of use in psychological assessment, as much with experimental methods as with use in applied settings. The original compilation by Allport and Odbert (1936) has led to the widespread use of adjectives in various formats and many empirical studies, but with relatively few widely recognized and used standardized versions. One of the best-known such measures based on adjectives is the Multiple Affect Adjective Check List (MAACL) (Zuckerman and Lubin 1965), and its subsequent revisions (MAACL-R) (Zuckerman and Lubin 1985, 1999). A bibliography of research using the MAACL identified over 1,900 articles and dissertations (Lubin, Swearngin and Zuckerman 1997). The original version contained 132 adjectives, of which only 66 were scored for the domains of Anxiety, Depression and Hostility. Ratings of the adjectives could be performed to assess either immediate 'State' responses or longer term 'Trait' attributes through changes in instructions. The revised versions followed new analyses with new samples of respondents, and added two scales for Positive Affect and Sensation Seeking. Of note is that the development of scales for adjective checklists generally relies upon exploratory factor analysis approaches, and so these instruments also become involved in the debates over the most appropriate methodology that are prominent within the domain of personality assessment. The MAACL-R exhibits the advantages of adjective checklists, in that it is very flexible in use and takes little time to complete in comparison to standard multiscale personality inventories.

A more recent development in the use of adjective ratings for personality assessment is based upon theories of interpersonal relationships such as those of Benjamin (1974) and Wiggins (1979). Substantial bodies of theory for both normal personality and psychopathology have now been developed based on interpersonal models (e.g., Kiesler 1996; Horowitz 2004). Such interpersonal models generally involve dimensions of agency (dominance) and communion (warmth) and measures are derived on the basis of two-dimensional factor analytic procedures. Various specialized instruments have been developed to explore particular interpersonal models. One that has been established based entirely upon adjectives is the Interpersonal Adjective Scales (IAS) (Wiggins 1995). The development of the IAS can be traced to the same Allport and Odbert (1936) list of adjectives that had been successively refined by Norman (1967). A total of 567 interpersonal adjectives were classed into 16 categories and successively analyzed and refined to form eight 16-item scales. The 128 items assess the octant domains of Assured-Dominant, Arrogant-Calculating, Cold-hearted, Aloof-Introverted, Unassured-Submissive, Unassuming-Ingenuous, Warm-Agreeable and Gregarious-Extraverted. The influence of interpersonal theories is likely greater in research than in day-to-day psychological assessment practices, but these circumplex models that are used in interpersonal theories are easily understood and appealing to many psychologists. The growing body of research in the area should lead to more applications in professional practice in the future.

There is currently a plethora of 'personality tests' and the number has literally exploded in recent years in both the research literature and from commercial publishers (see the *Buros Mental Measurement Yearbooks* for the latter). Yet, virtually all of these personality instruments are subjective self-rating scales or questionnaires, with a few observer rating scales. Aside from response sets, and (superficial) conscious reporting, a major problem with rating scales is that they depend upon transparent, face valid items unless extensive developmental work has been done to minimize the influence of irrelevant processes and to ensure the items are readily understood by the vast majority of respondents. Otherwise, item transparency may be associated with problematic or invalid responses, or be influenced by motivational distortion. The consequence of insufficient attention to item characteristics is that many current personality assessment instruments may be based on methodology that can be easily criticized and dismissed, with resulting serious questions as to the validity of the measure for many purposes. Correction scales can go only so far (and in some cases, such as that of the MMPI/MMPI-2 K correction scale, the application of such corrections may themselves be problematic). Whereas self-report (Q-data) personality assessment is based on subjective answers to questions, what is needed is increased sensitivity to the characteristics of personality items, increased empirical analysis of items prior to their inclusion in the final version of scales, and the application of the resulting scales across multiple samples of individuals in order to ensure the generalizability of the results. Such considerations should be applied to instruments whether they are traditional or are administered via interactive, computer-based, objective tests of personality. We do know much about how to ask questions of people about both innocuous and sensitive matters. Awareness of this material is often not evident among descriptions of personality measures, but more attention to the constituent items of personality measures and how those instruments were developed will lead to better measures, evidence-based assessment procedures (Hunsley and Mash 2005) and, one hopes, to better practices in personality assessment in general.

References

Achenbach, T. M. and McConaughy, S. H. 2003. The Achenbach System of empirically based assessment, in C. R. Reynolds and R. W. Kamphaus (eds.), *Handbook of psychological and educational assessment of children: personality, behaviour, and context*, pp. 406–30. New York: Guilford Press

Allport, G. W. and Odbert, H. S. 1936. Trait names: a psycho-lexical study, *Psychological Monographs* 47 (No. 211)

Angleitner, A., John, O. P. and Lohr, F.-J. 1986. It's *what* you ask and *how* you ask it: an itemmetric analysis of personality questionnaires, in A. Angleitner and J. S. Wiggins (eds.), *Personality assessment via questionnaires: current issues in theory and measurement*, pp. 61–108. Berlin: Springer-Verlag

Bagby, R. M., Marshall, M. B., Bury, A. S., Bacchiochi, J. R. and Miller, L. S. 2006. Assessing underreporting and overreporting response styles on the MMPI-2, in J. N. Butcher (ed.). *MMPI-2: a practitioner's guide*, pp. 39–69. Washington, DC: American Psychological Association

Benjamin, L. S. 1974. Structural analysis of social behaviour, *Psychological Review* 81: 392–425

Bentler, P. M. 1988. Causal modeling via structural equation systems, in J. R. Nesselroade and R. B. Cattell (eds.), *Handbook of multivariate experimental psychology*, 2nd edn, pp. 317–35. New York: Plenum

Block, J. 1965. *The challenge of response sets: unconfounding meaning, acquiescence, and social desirability in the MMPI*. New York: Appleton-Century-Crofts

1995. A contrarian view of the five-factor approach to personality description, *Psychological Bulletin* 117: 187–215

Boyle, G. J. 1990. A review of the factor structure of the Sixteen Personality Factor Questionnaire and the Clinical Analysis Questionnaire, *Psychological Test Bulletin* 3: 40–5

2006. Scientific analysis of personality and individual differences, D.Sc. Thesis. St. Lucia: University of Queensland

Boyle, G. J. and Comer, P. G. 1990. Personality characteristics of direct-service personnel in community residential units, *Australia and New Zealand Journal of Developmental Disabilities* 16: 125–31

Boyle, G. J., Stankov, L. and Cattell, R. B. 1995. Measurement and statistical models in the study of personality and intelligence, in D. H. Saklofske and M. Zeidner (eds.), *International handbook of personality and intelligence*, pp. 417–46. New York: Plenum

Briggs, S. R. and Cheek, J. M. 1986. The role of factor analysis in the development and evaluation of personality scales, *Journal of Personality* 54: 106–48

Burdsal, C. A. and Vaughn, D. S. 1974. A contrast of the personality structure of college students found in the questionnaire medium by items as compared to parcels, *Journal of Genetic Psychology* 135: 219–24

Burisch, M. 1984. Approaches to personality inventory construction: a comparison of merits, *American Psychologist* 39: 214–27

1986. Methods of personality inventory development: a comparative analysis, in A. Angleitner and J. S. Wiggins (eds.). *Personality assessment via questionnaires: current issues in theory and measurement*, pp. 109–20. Berlin: Springer-Verlag

Butcher, J. N., Dahlstrom, W. G., Graham, J. R., Tellegen, A. and Kaemmer, B. 1989. *Minnesota Multiphasic Personality Inventory-2. Manual for administration and scoring*. Minneapolis, MN: University of Minnesota Press

Campbell, D. T. and Fiske, D. W. 1959. Convergent and discriminant validation by the multitrait-multimethod matrix, *Psychological Bulletin* 56: 81–105

Cattell, R. B. 1973. *Personality and mood by questionnaire*. San Francisco: Jossey-Bass

1978. *The scientific use of factor analysis in behavioural and life sciences*. New York: Plenum

1986a. General principles across the media of assessment, in R. B. Cattell and R. C. Johnson (eds.), *Functional psychological testing: principles and instruments*, pp. 15–32. New York: Brunner/Mazel

1986b. Selecting, administering, scoring, recording, and using tests in assessment, in R. B. Cattell and R. C. Johnson (eds.), *Functional psychological testing: principles and instruments*, pp. 105–26. New York: Brunner/Mazel

1986c. Structured tests and functional diagnoses, in R. B. Cattell and R. C. Johnson (eds.), *Functional psychological testing: principles and instruments*, pp. 3–14. New York: Brunner/Mazel

1986d. The psychometric properties of tests: consistency, validity, and efficiency, in R. B. Cattell and R. C. Johnson (eds.), *Functional psychological testing: principles and instruments*, pp. 54–78. New York: Brunner/Mazel

1988. The meaning and strategic use of factor analysis, in J. R. Nesselroade and R. B. Cattell (eds.), *Handbook of multivariate experimental psychology*, 2nd edn, pp. 131–203. New York: Plenum

1994. A cross-validation of primary personality structure in the 16 P.F. by two parcelled factor analyses, *Multivariate Experimental Clinical Research* 10: 181–90

1995. The fallacy of five factors in the personality sphere, *The Psychologist*, May, 207–8

Cattell, R. B., Boyle, G. J. and Chant, D. 2002. The enriched behavioural prediction equation and its impact on structured learning and the dynamic calculus, *Psychological Review* 109: 202–5

Cattell, R. B., Cattell, A. K. and Cattell, H. E. P. 1994. *The Sixteen Personality Factor Questionnaire*, 5th edn. Champaign, IL: Institute for Personality and Ability Testing

Cattell, R. B., Eber, H. W. and Tatsuoka, M. M. 1970. *Handbook for the Sixteen Personality Factor Questionnaire (16PF)*. Champaign, IL: Institute for Personality and Ability Testing

Cattell, R. B. and Krug, S. E. 1971. A test of the trait-view theory of distortion in measurement of personality questionnaire, *Educational and Psychological Measurement* 31: 721–34

1986. The number of factors in the 16PF: a review of the evidence with special emphasis on methodological problems, *Educational and Psychological Measurement* 46: 509–22

Comrey, A. L. 1967. Tandem criteria for analytic rotation in factor analysis, *Psychometrika* 32: 143–54

1984. Comparison of two methods to identify major personality factors, *Applied Psychological Measurement* 8: 397–408

1988. Factor-analytic methods of scale development in personality and clinical psychology, *Journal of Consulting and Clinical Psychology* 56: 754–61

Conn, S. R. and Rieke, M. L. 1994. *Technical Manual for the 16 P.F.(5th ed.)*. Champaign IL: Institute for Personality and Ability Testing

Conners, C. K. 1997. *Conners' Rating Scales: Revised technical manual*. North Tonawanda, NY: Multi-Health Systems Inc.

Costa, P. T., Jr. and McCrae, R. R. 1992. *Revised NEO Personality Inventory and NEO Five-Factor Inventory: Professional manual*. Odessa, FL: Psychological Assessment Resources

Cronbach, L. and Meehl, P. E. 1955. Construct validity in psychological tests, *Psychological Bulletin* 52: 281–303

Cuttance, P. 1987. Issues and problems in the application of structural equation models, in P. Cuttance and R. Ecob (eds.), *Structural modeling by example: applications in educational, sociological, and behavioural research*, pp. 241–79. Cambridge University Press

Drasgow, F. and Olson-Buchanan, J. B. (eds.) 1999. *Innovations in computerized assessment*. Mahwah, NJ: Lawrence Erlbaum Associates

Edwards, A. L. 1957. *The social desirability variable in personality assessment and research*. New York: Dryden

Eysenck, H. J. and Eysenck, S. B. G. 1975. *Manual of the Eysenck Personality Questionnaire (junior and adult)*. London: Hodder and Stoughton

Goffin, R. D., Rothstein, M. G. and Johnston, N. G. 2000. Predicting job performance using personality constructs: are personality tests created equal?, in R. D. Goffin and E. Helmes (eds.) *Problems and solutions in human assessment: honoring Douglas N. Jackson at seventy*, pp. 249–64. New York: Kluwer Academic

Goldberg, L. R. 1990. An alternative 'description of personality': the Big Five factor structure, *Journal of Personality and Social Psychology* 59: 1216–29

Gorsuch, R. L. 1983. *Factor analysis*, 2nd edn. Hillsdale, NJ: Erlbaum
   1988. Exploratory factor analysis, in J. R. Nesselroade and R. B. Cattell (eds.), *Handbook of multivariate experimental psychology*, 2nd edn, pp. 231–58. New York: Plenum

Greenwald, A. G. and Banaji, M. R. 1995. Implicit social cognition: attitudes, self-esteem, and stereotypes, *Psychological Review* 102: 4–27

Groth-Marnat, G. 2003. *Handbook of psychological assessment*, 4th edn. Hoboken, NJ: Wiley

Hartup, W. W. and van Lieshout, C. F. M. 1995. Personality development in social context, *Annual Review of Psychology* 46: 655–87

Helmes, E. 2000. The role of social desirability in the assessment of personality constructs, in R. D. Goffin and E. Helmes (eds.). *Problems and solutions in human assessment: honoring Douglas N. Jackson at seventy*, pp. 21–40. New York: Kluwer Academic
   2008. Response distortion in applications of the Minnesota Multiphasic Personality Inventory-2 (MMPI-2) in offender rehabilitation, *Journal of Offender Rehabilitation* 47: 101–20

Helmes, E. and Reddon, J. R. 1993. A perspective on developments in assessing psychopathology: a critical review of the MMPI and MMPI-2, *Psychological Bulletin* 113: 453–71

Horowitz, L. M. 2004. *Interpersonal foundations of psychopathology*, Washington, DC: American Psychological Association

Hough, L. and Paullin, C. 1994. Construct-oriented scale construction: the rational approach, in G. S. Stokes, M. D. Mumford and W. A. Owens (eds.). *Biodata handbook: theory, research, and use of biographical information in selection and performance*, pp. 109–45. Palo Alto, CA: Consulting Psychologists Press

Hunsley, J., Lee, C. M. and Wood, J. M. 2003. Controversial and questionable assessment techniques, in S. O. Lilienfeld, Lynn, S. J. and J. M. Lohr (eds.). *Science and pseudoscience in clinical psychology*, pp. 17–38. New York: Guilford

Hunsley, J. and Mash, E. J. 2005. Introduction to the special section on developing guidelines for the evidence-based assessment (EBA) of adult disorders, *Psychological Assessment* 17: 251–5

Jackson, D. N. 1970. A sequential system for personality scale construction, in C. D. Spielberger (ed.), *Current topics in clinical and community psychology*, vol. II, pp. 61–96. New York: Academic Press
   1984. *Personality Research Form manual*. Port Huron, MI: Research Psychologists Press
   1989. *Basic Personality Inventory manual*. Port Huron, MI: Sigma Assessment Systems
   1994. *Jackson Personality Inventory: revised manual*. Port Huron, MI / London, Ontario: Sigma Assessment Systems
   2000. A perspective, in R. D. Goffin and E. Helmes (eds.), *Problems and solutions in human assessment: honoring Douglas N. Jackson at seventy*, pp. 333–44. New York: Kluwer Academic

Jackson, D. N., Ashton, M. C. and Tomes, J. L. 1996. The six-factor model of personality: facets from the big five, *Personality and Individual Differences* 21: 391–402

Jackson, D. N. and Messick, S. 1971. *The Differential Personality Inventory*, London, Ontario: D.N. Jackson and S. Messick

James, L. R. 1998. Measurement of personality via conditional reasoning, *Organizational Research Methods* 1: 131–63

James, L. R., McIntyre, M. D., Glisson, C. A., Green, P. D., Patton, T. W., LeBreton, J. M., Frost, B. C., Russell, S. M., Sablynski, C. J., Mitchell, T. R. and Williams, L. J. 2005. A conditional reasoning measure for aggression, *Organizational Research Methods* 8: 69–99

Kiesler, D. J. 1996. *Contemporary interpersonal theory and research: personality, psychopathology and psychotherapy.* New York: Wiley

Krug, S. E. 1980. *Clinical Analysis Questionnaire manual.* Champaign, IL: Institute for Personality and Ability Testing

 1981. *Interpreting 16PF profile patterns.* Champaign, IL, Institute for Personality and Ability Testing

Kurtz, I. C., Dawson, D. V. and Welsh, K. A. 1994. Caregiver ratings of personality change in Alzheimer's disease patients: a replication, *Psychology and Aging* 9: 464–6

Kurtz, J. E., Lee, P. A. and Sherker, J. L. 1999. Internal and temporal reliability estimates for informant ratings of personality using the NEO-PI-R and IAS, *Assessment* 6: 103–14

LeBreton, J. M., Barksdale, C. D., Robin, J. and James, L. R. 2007. Measurement issues associated with conditional reasoning tests: indirect measurement and test faking, *Journal of Applied Psychology* 92: 1–16

Loevinger, J. 1957. Objective tests as instruments of psychological theory, *Psychological Reports* 3: 635–94

Lubin, B., Swearngin, S. E. and Zuckerman, M. 1997. *Research with the Multiple Affect Adjective Check List (MAACL and the MAACL-R: 1960–1996).* San Diego, CA: Educational and Industrial Testing Service

MacCallum, R. 1985. Some problems in the process of model modification in covariance structure modeling. Paper presented at the European Meeting of the Psychonomic Society, Cambridge

McCrae, R. R. and Costa, P. T. Jr. 1987. Validation of the five-factor model of personality across instruments and observers, *Journal of Personality and Social Psychology* 52: 81–90

Mershon, B. and Gorsuch, R. L. 1988. Number of factors in the personality sphere: does increase in factors increase predictability of real-life criteria?, *Journal of Personality and Social Psychology* 55: 675–80

Morey, L. C. 1991. *Personality Assessment Inventory manual.* Odessa, FL: Psychological Assessment Resources

Mount, M. K., Witt, L. A. and Barrick, M. R. 2000. Incremental validity of empirically keyed biodata scales over GMA and the five factor personality constructs, *Personnel Psychology* 53: 299–323

Mulaik, S. A. 1988. Confirmatory factor analysis, in J. R. Nesselroade and R. B. Cattell (eds.), *Handbook of multivariate experimental psychology*, 2nd edn, pp. 259–88. New York: Plenum

Nicholls, J. G., Licht, B. G. and Pearl, R. A. 1982. Some dangers of using personality questionnaires to study personality, *Psychological Bulletin* 92: 572–80

Norman, W. T. 1967. *2800 personality trait descriptors: normative operating character-istics for a university population*. Ann Arbor: Department of Psychology, University of Michigan

Paulhus, D. L. 1984. Two-component models of socially desirable responding, *Journal of Personality and Social Psychology* 44: 598–609

  1986. Self-deception and impression management in test responses, in A. Angleitner and J. S. Wiggins (eds.). *Personality assessment via questionnaires: current issues in theory and measurement*, pp. 143–65. Berlin: Springer-Verlag

  1998. *Paulhus Deception Scales (PDS): the Balanced Inventory of Desirable Responding-7. User's manual*. Toronto: Multi-Health Systems

Piotrowski, C. and Keller, J. W. 1989. Psychological testing in outpatient mental health facilities: a national study, *Professional Psychology: Research and Practice* 20: 423–5

Reynolds, C. R. and Kamphaus, R. W. 2004. *Behaviour Assessment System for Children, Second Edition manual*. Circles Pines, MN: AGS

Rudinger, G. and Dommel, N. 1986. An example of convergent and discriminant vali-dation of personality questionnaires, in A. Angleitner and J. S. Wiggins (eds.). *Personality assessment via questionnaires: current issues in theory and meas-urement*, pp. 214–24. Berlin: Springer-Verlag

Sajatovic, M. and Ramirez, L. F. 2003. *Rating scales in mental health*, 2nd edn. Hudson, OH: Lexi-Comp

Schwarz, N. 1999. Frequency reports of physical symptoms and health behaviours: how the questionnaire determines the results, in D. C. Park, R. W. Morrell and K. Shifrin (eds.). *Processing of medical information in aging patients: cognitive and human factors perspectives*, pp. 93–108. Mahwah, NJ: Lawrence Erlbaum Associates

Schwarz, N. and Sudman, S. (eds.) 1996. *Answering questions: methodology for determin-ing cognitive and communicative processes in survey research*. San Francisco: Jossey-Bass

Siegler, I. C., Dawson, D. V. and Walsh, K. A. 1994. Caregiver ratings of personality change in Alzheimer's disease patients: a replication, *Psychology and Aging* 9: 464–6

Smith, B. D. 1988. Personality: multivariate systems theory and research, in J. R. Nesselroade and R. B. Cattell (eds.), *Handbook of multivariate experi-mental psychology*, 2nd edn, pp. 687–736. New York: Plenum

Stokes, G. S., Mumford, M. D. and Owens, W. A. 1994. *Biodata handbook: theory, research, and use of biographical information in selection and performance*. Palo Alto, CA: Consulting Psychologists Press

Strauss, M. E. and Pasupathi, M. 1994. Primary caregivers' descriptions of Alzheimer patients' personality traits: temporal stability and sensitivity to change, *Alzheimer Disease and Associated Disorders* 8: 166–76

Strauss, M. E., Pasupathi, M. and Chatterjee, A. 1993. Concordance between observers in descriptions of personality change in Alzheimer's disease, *Psychology and Aging* 8: 475–80

Sudman, S. and Bradburn, N. M. 1982. *Asking questions: a practical guide to question-naire design*. San Francisco: Jossey-Bass

Velicer, W. F. and Jackson, D. N. 1990. Component analysis versus common factor analysis: some issues in selecting an appropriate procedure, *Multivariate Behavioural Research* 25: 1–28

Weiner, I. B. 1997. Current status of the Rorschach inkblot method, *Journal of Personality Assessment* 68: 5–19

Welleford, E. A., Harkins, S. W. and Taylor, J. R. 1995. Personality change in dementia of the Alzheimer's type: relations to caregiver personality and burden, *Experimental Aging Research* 21: 295–314

Wiggins, J. S. 1979. A psychological taxonomy of trait-descriptive terms: the interpersonal domain, *Journal of Personality and Social Psychology* 37: 395–412

    1995. *IAS. Interpersonal Adjective Scales: Professional manual.* Odessa, FL: Professional Assessment Resources

Wirth, R. J. and Edwards, M. C. 2007. Item factor analysis: current approaches and future directions, *Psychological Methods* 12: 58–79

Wittenborn, J. R. 1951. Symptom patterns in a group of mental hospital patients. *Journal of Consulting Psychology* 15: 290–302

Zuckerman, M. and Lubin, B. 1965. *Manual for the Multiple Affect Adjective Check List.* San Diego, CA: Educational and Industrial Testing Service

    1985. *Manual for the Multiple Affect Adjective Check List: Revised.* San Diego, CA: Educational and Industrial Testing Service

    1999. *Manual for the MAACL-R Multiple Affect Adjective Check List. 1999 Edition.* San Diego, CA: Educational and Industrial Testing Service

8 Structural models of personality

Boele De Raad

The large majority of studies on personality models refer to the Big Five structure. Only for that reason, it is important to be explicit about the characteristics and the different forms the Big Five model of personality can take. Yet, the Big Five structure is undoubtedly a restricted view; there are many more interesting topics to discuss pertaining to models, if it was only for the fact that the term 'model' has an ambiguous meaning. Naomi Campbell is a model with a delicate and commanding personality structure. In that case, the term 'model' not only iconizes beauty, it is also the model – Naomi Campbell – who demonstrates the models (cf., Bertels and Nauta 1969). This ambiguity is also found in scientific discourse, for example, where the original Big Five model (cf., Goldberg 1981; Norman 1963) has become a paradigm for research on the structure of personality traits. Similarly, models can sit to be portrayed by painters: they form the originals that may evoke a variety of expressions of a common theme. Thus, a model can be a person, but also a small-scale example, or a schematic representation. Models do not only represent people or objects, but also events, thoughts or theories. There are models of learning, models of rational choice, models of communication, models of political behaviour, etc. (see Lave and March 1975).

Models are most typically simple. A model is a device that can be reproduced, lived after, communicate a concept, and be tested for its adequacy. A model of personality may represent its characteristic traits, its mechanisms, its internal processes, at different levels of abstraction, and from different domains of interest (social, biological, cognitive, etc.). The adjective *structural* in 'structural models' of personality emphasizes the organized character of the various features represented in the model. Of itself, the adjective seems to be tautological because a model is usually recognized by its typical form or its organization. However, while the expression 'structural models of personality' connotes intended features on the one hand, it may, on the other hand, also evoke unintended references. One such unintended reference could be an emphasis on procedures to *test* a model, and on the statistics involved, as in structural equation modelling. In personality research, the standard recipe to arrive at structure typically involves the use of factor analytic techniques. Also, in this chapter factor analysis is used as metonymy for structure, but explicitly not in the sense of panacea. Other procedures to arrive at structure are certainly possible (cf., Panter, Tanaka and Hoyle 1994). In the present chapter, the emphasis is on the uses of the traditional method, factor analysis, in which the focus is on the representation of the contents of dispositional characteristics of persons in an economic way. The focus is also on the organization of those characteristics in the resulting structural model, and on the communicational efficacy of the model. In this case, structural model refers to the model of a structure. The emphasis is on finding a certain order rather than on testing it. We assume such models to be hypothetical by definition.

Three models of personality with a common origin

The model of personality that has drawn most of the attention during the last few decades is possibly the Big Five model of personality traits, which is indeed a model of the organization or the structure of a large number of traits. For that reason we take that model as the referential thematic object of this chapter. The model has obtained the characteristics of an icon, with features that transcend the empirical facts; witness, for example, the exaggerated universality attributed to the model. In the further discussion, the term 'structure' is used to refer to correlations among traits, which should not be equated with structure of personality, and with the term 'model' we refer to economized or simplified representations of such structures. Theoretical notions not only may follow from the formulation of structural models, they may also precede both structures and models, as in, for example, the definition of criteria used for the inclusion or exclusion of trait descriptors in a structuring program.

The Big Five model (De Raad 2000; Goldberg 1981; Norman 1963; Wiggins 1996) is broadly accepted, which is probably a sign of its popularity, but certainly also of its authoritative nature and its adequacy in representing traits. We briefly trace the history of the model, since that history also brought forth the Cattellian model of personality embodied in the sixteen personality factor (16PF) questionnaire. As exclaimed by R. B. Cattell (1965, p. 55), referring to the thousands of traits catalogued by Allport and Odbert (1936), 'the trouble with measuring traits is that there are too many of them'. Cattell pioneered in bringing order in the trait-alphabet by searching for the underlying structure. In his 'lexical' period he was forced to reduce the catalogue of traits ultimately to some tens of trait-variables, because that was the maximum number that could be structured by applying factor-analysis in that early computational era. That number, thirty-five items only, was supposed to represent the full domain of personality traits. It was also that set of items that formed the basis, albeit in different ways, for three different personality models, namely the sixteen primary factor model (16PF) of Cattell, Eber and Tatsuoka (1970), the Big Five model (Goldberg 1981; Norman 1963), and the NEO three factor model (Costa and McCrae 1985).

Cattell's sixteen-factor model

The original set of 35 trait variables was the result of a process of condensing a list of 171 trait descriptive items considered by Cattell (1943) to summarize the complete 'personality sphere'. That condensation took place on the basis of correlations of ratings from 100 subjects. The reduction to thirty-five variables was, in Cattell's (1945, p. 70) words, 'a matter of unhappy necessity', considering the period of time preceding the use of computers.

Cattell (1945) administered the thirty-five items to several small groups of subjects (Totalling to an $N = 208$), obtained correlations based on the ratings and averaged the correlations over these small groups. Factoring those correlations yielded a set of factors of which twelve were obliquely rotated for simple structure (a trial and error procedure covering a six-month period!). These twelve factors, together with four questionnaire-specific scales that Cattell added, constituted the so-called 16PF, the sixteen personality factors questionnaire.

Cattell (1950) distinguished trait-elements (single trait words), surface traits (traits tending to cluster together in a person), and source traits (trait-factors), essentially forming a hierarchy of traits. The concept of hierarchy was extended in Cattell's emphasis on the distinction between primary factors and higher order factors. The results of factoring ratings on trait-elements or on clusters of traits treated as variables were blindly rotated to pursue a simple structure where variables have a substantial loading on only one factor. These primary factors were permitted to be correlated so that factors at a higher level of abstraction would become possible.

In order to understand traits at a higher level of abstraction, global traits of personality or 'secondary order' factors were examined. Cattell (1994), for example, reports on the constancy, over a period of twenty years, of eight secondary factors.

Five secondary factors, not eight

Although research on the secondary factors often gave rise to more than five global factors (e.g., Karson 1961; Krug and Johns 1986), Hofer and Eber (2002) reported strong evidence in support of a five factor structure of the 16PF questionnaire, including Extraversion (e.g., liveliness versus privateness), Tough-mindedness (negatively, e.g., sensitivity and openness to change), Self-control (e.g., perfectionism versus abstractedness), Anxiety (e.g., tension versus emotional stability), and Independence (e.g., dominance).

Costa and McCrae's NEO-PI: three secondary factors, not eight

Costa and McCrae (1976) clustered 16PF scales on the basis of data from three different age groups, resulting into two consistent age-group independent clusters, called Adjustment-Anxiety and Introversion-Extraversion, and a third inconsistent age-group dependent cluster, which was conceptualized as an Experiential Style dimension. The three clusters formed the starting point for the development of the three-factorial NEO-PI (Costa and McCrae 1985).

The Big Five: five primary factors, not twelve

The thirty-five trait variables put forward by Cattell as exhausting the trait sphere and giving rise to the 16PF, also formed the bases for factor analyses in an increasing number of samples of subjects by Fiske (1949), Tupes and Christal (1958, 1961) and Norman (1963). In those analyses, not twelve but five factors were repeatedly considered to best summarize the various correlation matrices. Goldberg (1981) referred to that five-factorial structure as the 'Big Five'.[1]

Three independently developed major structures

Not only Cattell's 16PF model was available to users, but also two other major systems to measure personality, Guilford's model embodied in the Guilford-Zimmerman Temperament Survey (Guilford and Zimmerman 1949), and Eysenck's three-factor model (Eysenck 1952).

Second major structure: the Guilford factors

Although Guilford did not start to design a complete structure of personality, the subsequent studies he performed resulted in an instrument that should enable a comprehensive portrait of someone's personality. Starting with the application of a thirty-six-item questionnaire (Guilford and Guilford 1934, 1936), three clear factors, Introversion-Extraversion, Emotional Sensitivity and Masculinity-Femininity, were found and two less clear factors to summarize the items. In subsequent analyses with additional sets of items, additional factors were isolated, up to a list of thirteen primary factors (Guilford 1975). Sells, Demaree and Will (1970, 1971; cf., Cattell and Gibbons 1968) thoroughly compared the Cattell and Guilford structures, and found major commonalities in only two factors: Emotional Stability and Social Extraversion, and they found fifteen more factors for which one or the other system was primarily responsible. Of the first three or four of these additional fifteen factors, two were related to factors being part of Norman's (1963) Five Factor Model, namely Conscientiousness and Agreeableness versus Hostility.

Third major structure: Eysenck's three factor model

In defining his structural conception of personality, Eysenck (1947) distinguished four levels of behaviour-organization that were hierarchically organized, namely single observable behavioural acts, habitual responses (recurrent acts under specified circumstances), traits (based on intercorrelations of different habitual responses), and types of traits (based on correlations between various traits).

---

[1] Cattell (1995) heavily criticized the Five Factor Model of personality and suggested that the model was the product of incompetence on the part of investigators regarding their knowledge of proper factor-analytic procedures.

Eysenck (1947) originally used a relatively small ($N = 39$) set of items underlying most of his subsequent work. Those items were selected from an 'item-sheet' on which for each patient 'the psychiatrist in charge recorded certain data regarding the patient's family history, personal history, personality, his symptoms, aetiology, diagnosis and treatment, disposal, and various social data'.

On the basis of ratings on this 'intentionally heterogeneous' item list, Eysenck concluded as to two factors, a general 'neuroticism' factor and a factor contrasting 'affective, dysthymic, inhibited' symptoms and traits and 'hysterical and asocial' symptoms and traits. Eysenck suggested this second factor to be related to Jung's Introversion-Extraversion distinction. Further discussions in related literature, especially that of Kretschmer (1948) and Jung (1923), of the distinction between the observed Extraversion-Introversion distinction and the schyzothymia-cyclothymia distinction emphasized by Kretschmer, and further empirical results, led to the emergence of the psychoticism dimension (Eysenck 1952). These three factors or types of traits, Psychoticism, Extraversion and Neuroticism (the PEN-system), continued to play a major role throughout Eysenck's structural modelling of personality.

For the development of his later questionnaires to measure P, E, and N, the Maudsley Personality Inventory (Eysenck 1959) and the Eysenck Personality Inventory (Eysenck 1964), Eysenck made use of items of the Guilford inventories (cf., Guilford 1975).

Eysenck versus Cattell

There are a number of interesting issues regarding the two major structural systems of personality traits, those of the pioneers Cattell and Eysenck. These issues, relating to both common features and distinctions, concern thinking in terms of hierarchies, the reference to syndromes of traits at different levels, the origins of the original item-sets constituting their main trait structures, and their psychometric and theoretical emphases.

Cattell and Eysenck generally agreed about the hierarchical organization of traits. While Cattell's hierarchy conception developed out of presuppositions and observations, and was especially given further form through psychometric considerations and empirical results, Eysenck's hierarchy had a more explicit theoretical format at four levels, from behavioural acts to types of traits, which format was more determined by theoretical and empirical findings than by psychometric considerations. Eysenck's model was derived 'directly from the writings of psychologists like Jung, Kretschmer, and Allport, none of whom can be said to be oriented very positively towards psychometric techniques' (Eysenck 1953, p. 14). Nevertheless, the four-level model 'fits in almost completely with the statistical model elaborated by factor analysis' (p. 14) in which error factors, specific factors, primary factors and second-order factors are distinguished. The levels are supposed to differ only in terms of inclusiveness. Cattell (e.g., 1945, pp. 78–9), on the other hand, let himself be guided by psychometric principles, such as rotation to simple structure, so that results would 'agree with clinical and general psychological syndromes' (p. 79).

Both Cattell and Eysenck made use of the concept of clusters of psychological characteristics. Cattell referred to trait-elements that correlate positively in every possible internal combination as syndromes or surface traits, with very broad surface traits being referred to as types (Cattell 1950, p. 21). Cattell thus essentially referred to primary factors when talking of types. Eysenck used the term type to refer to second-order factors, as organizations of traits based on observed correlations.

At some point in their research history both Cattell and Eysenck made use of a short list of items that ultimately constituted their structural models of personality traits. The Cattell list, consisting of the previously described thirty-five trait-variables, were the result of a thorough process of reduction of the full trait-domain to describe the trait sphere exhaustively. Nevertheless, that thirty-five-variable list later turned out not to be representative of that full trait-domain (John, Angleitner and Ostendorf 1988; Peabody 1987). Eysenck's list, the previously mentioned thirty-nine-item list, was the result of a selection from the 'item-sheet' for patients, a hybrid with items covering the social history, the personality and the symptoms of a patient.

The Big Two: Extraversion and Neuroticism

In his 1968 *Annual Review of Psychology* contribution, Wiggins concluded that if consensus would exist in the realm of temperament structure, it is with respect to the dimensions Extraversion and Anxiety (Neuroticism), dubbed the Big Two by Wiggins. He arrived at that conclusion on the basis of work by Eysenck, Cattell, Guilford (1959) and Gough (1957), among others. Zuckerman, Kuhlman and Camac (1988) asked what is beyond E and N, with which they marked the general contemporary understanding that Extraversion and Neuroticism were beyond dispute.

The new era

Although the Big Five personality structure was hypothesized as an alternative view on summarizing correlations among the thirty-five Cattell scales as early as 1949 by Fiske, firm confirmations of that model, stipulated, among others, by Norman (1967), had to wait half a century. Those confirmations were provided in comprehensive taxonomic studies using trait-descriptive adjectives in three Germanic languages (De Raad, Hendriks and Hofstee 1992; Goldberg 1990; Ostendorf 1990). With that Big Five structure as the major spin-off, undoubtedly a new era had begun in which an all-embracing intention characterized indigenous programmes to catalogue personality traits.

The start of this Big Five era was accompanied with both enthusiasm and critical reactions. Part of the enthusiasm is demonstrated in subsequent psycho-lexical studies in various languages and in utilizing the Big Five model in a large variety of both research fields and applied fields. Critical reactions came from authors of competing systems (e.g., Cattell 1995; Eysenck 1992), and from others who pointed out certain weaknesses of the psycholexical approach (e.g., Block 1995).

A part of the criticism from the authors of the competing systems was about the numbers and contents of trait-factors at the different levels in a hierarchical representation. Cattell (e.g., 1995) suggested that five factors is the wrong number of secondary factors, and Eysenck (e.g., 1991, 1992) suggested that the some of the Big Five factors are primary factors and some are secondaries. There is a certain amount of indeterminateness in that dispute. Where Cattell (1995), for example, refers to the Norman (1963) Big Five, these factors are primary factors derived from the same (35) variables that gave rise to Cattell's twelve primary factors (and the 16PF). Cattell emphasized that there are eight secondary orders of the 16PF. The only competitor of the eight secondary factors of the 16PF is the three-factorial NEO-PI, which questionnaire was indeed based on secondary analyses of the 16PF scales (Costa and McCrae 1976; cf., De Raad 1994). The psychometric issue involved here is mainly about criteria for the extraction of the adequate number of factors.

Eysenck's disagreement was theoretical and empirical; he proposed three factors at the highest level of abstraction, which he conceives of as 'secondary' factors or super-factors. Empirical relations between super-factor Psychoticism and Big Five factors Agreeableness and Conscientiousness (e.g., De Raad and Szirmák 1994; Goldberg and Rosolack 1994; McCrae and Costa 1985), made Eysenck suggest that these latter two factors may be primary order factors constituting partial aspects of the super-order factor Psychoticism.

Three cross-culturally replicable factors, not five

An important issue with the psycholexically derived factors and their indigenous character is their cross-cultural replicability. In pursuit of a cross-lingual trait-structure, Hofstee, Kiers, De Raad et al. (1997), De Raad, Perugini and Szirmák (1997) and De Raad, Perugini, Hrebícková and Szarota (1998) compared several psycholexically derived five factor structures using psychometric criteria. The general conclusion of those studies was that congruence coefficients calculated for corresponding Big Five factors suggested the replicability of the first three factors of the Big Five (Extraversion, Agreeableness and Conscientiousness) and moderate replicability of the fourth factor, Emotional Stability. Such a three-factor solution was also shown to be more stable than others across participant and variable samples in Di Blas and Forzi (1999). Moreover, cross-cultural comparisons based on the substance of Big Five factors from six different psycholexical studies also led to the conclusion that Extraversion, Agreeableness and Conscientiousness are cross-culturally coherent, Emotional Stability and Intellect are not (De Raad and Peabody 2005; Peabody and De Raad 2002).

Exhausting the domain of traits

While the Big Five structure has found large adherence, claims for psycholexically based factors beyond the Big Five have been made, for two reasons mainly. The first reason is that the correlation matrices may not be optimally exhausted, and the second reason is that the trait domain may not be truly exhausted. This second reason comes in two versions, one suggesting that the psycholexical approach has been too restrictive in selecting personality descriptors (Almagor, Tellegen and Waller 1995), and the other suggesting that the psycholexical approach has been restricted to the use of trait-descriptive *adjectives* (cf., De Raad and Hofstee 1993).

Six factors, not five

Ashton and Lee (2001) argued along the lines of exhausting the correlation matrix. They suggested that an additional Honesty-Humility factor, representing such traits as honest, sincere, fair and just, versus dishonest, conceited and boasting, could systematically be extracted. Support for this sixth factor was observed in several languages (Ashton, Lee, Perugini *et al.* 2004), but not, or not clearly, in all languages where this sixth factor was studied, as in American-English (Ashton, Lee and Goldberg 2004), Turkish (Somer and Goldberg 1999) and Croatian (Mlačić and Ostendorf 2005).

Seven factors, not five

Because most psycholexical studies have excluded evaluative, esteem-descriptive terms and state terms used for trait description, Almagor, Tellegen and Waller (1995) and Benet-Martínez and Waller (1997) suggested that the Big Five do not fully capture the personality language domain. Using a so-called 'non-restrictive' approach with respect to selecting personality descriptors, Almagor *et al.* (1995) produced a Big Seven model in Hebrew, that included versions of some of the Big Five factors, and two additional factors, called Negative Valence (e.g., *fabricator*, envious and corrupted, versus honest, sincere and dependable) and Positive Valence (e.g., sophisticated, sharp and original, versus mediocre). Support for one or both of these factors was found in Spanish (Benet-Martínez and Waller 1997), in Filipino (Church, Katigbak and Reyes 1996) and in Greek (Saucier *et al.* 2005).

Eight factors, not five

The Big Five model is based on ratings on trait-descriptive *adjectives*, under the assumption that adjectives are the typical carriers of trait meaning. De Raad and Barelds (2008) argued that on this point the psycholexical approach has not made use of its full potential. In their study they not only used adjectives, but also nouns, verbs, adverbs and some standard expressions as the basis for the formulation of trait-descriptive items. Moreover, trait-descriptive state terms and trait-descriptors with strong evaluative loading were not excluded. Factor analysis of ratings on this truly exhaustive list of 2,331 descriptors yielded eight factors, the Big Five and three new factors called Virtue (trustworthy, good, polite, versus unfair, indecent, annoying), Competence (has vision, solves problems, enterprising, versus gives up, passive, avoids difficulties) and Hedonism (sensation-seeking, fortune-hunter, impulsive, versus impeccable, moderate, home-loving).

The Basic Two: Virtue and Dynamism

Digman (1997) factored fourteen sets of correlations of Big Five personality factors, based on ratings of children, adolescents and adults on instruments with different origins. Two factors were typically evident, provisionally labelled α and β, with α capturing Agreeableness, Conscientiousness and Emotional Stability, and with β capturing Extraversion and Intellect. Central to this basic two-dimensional structure is a distinction between the two metaconcepts *agency* and *communion* (Bakan 1966). These two concepts have been put forward by Wiggins (e.g., 1996) as higher order indicants of the first two factors of the Big Five, Extraversion and Agreeableness, that have been considered as typically comprising the relatively large interpersonal sub-domain of personality traits. From this viewpoint, where Extraversion and Agreeableness are granted conceptual priority, the remaining three factors are seen as facilitating the role of agentic and communal movements in a group, or as interfering with it (Wiggins 1996, p. 134).

Two recent psycholexical studies add to the importance of establishing the Basic Two personality trait-dimensions. Saucier, Georgiades, Tsaousis and Goldberg (2005) distinguished Morality (considerate, humble, responsible, versus bad-tempered, gross, disrespectful) and Dynamism (dynamic, exciting, energetic, versus gutless, hesitant, boring) when extracting only two factors to structure the Greek trait-language. They suggested that these very broad factors have a high degree of cross-cultural generalizability. De Raad and Barelds (2008) similarly distinguished at the two-factor level for the Dutch trait-language between Virtue (good, reliable, polite, versus unfair, indecent, annoying) and Dynamism (enthusiasm, energy, vividness).

The p-factor

In both the previously mentioned studies by Saucier, Georgiades, Tsaousis and Goldberg (2005) and De Raad and Barelds (2008), the first unrotated factor largely captured characteristics of evaluation and morality. It makes sense to identify such a single basic factor, called p-factor by Hofstee (2001) who made a parallel with the structure of intelligence. The p-factor draws its meaning from the positive manifold among the large majority of personality traits (cf., Hofstee and Ten Berge 2004). Arguments for a single general personality factor have previously been given by Webb (1915), who tried to identify a general factor of character next to a general factor of intelligence ('g'), and defined it as the 'sum of all personal qualities which are not distinctly intellectual' (1915, p. 2).

Hierarchy

Throughout the history of developing personality trait structures, hierarchy has played an inherent role. The preceding paragraphs may suggest a basic hierarchy with the *p*-factor at the apex of the hierarchy, representing the most valued psychological characteristics in a person. This possibly concerns the first question one has about a person in a variety of contexts: is this person reliable, trustworthy and decent? At the lower level one would find two basic dispositional orientations, the first being the 'communal' orientation comprising those traits that emphasize the relationship to other individuals or to groups of individuals (captured by Virtue and Morality), and the second being the 'agentic' orientation comprising those traits that emphasize the fulfilment of personal goals (captured by Dynamism). Interestingly, the two Dutch factors Virtue and Dynamism (De Raad and Barelds 2008) turned out to have high correlations (0.90 and 0.85, respectively) with an index of evaluation.

Strict hierarchies

Possibly the most well-known hierarchy of traits is the strict hierarchy hypothesized by Eysenck (1970). Figure 8.1 forms a partial representation of Eysenck's (1970) four-level hierarchy of Extraversion, in which specific responses (e.g., 'telling jokes') are included in one and only one higher level category of habitual responses. The habitual responses ('entertaining strangers' and 'smiling at

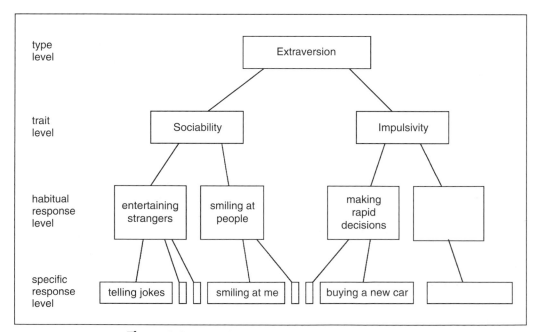

Figure 8.1. *Eysenck's (1970) hierarchical model of Extraversion.*

people') are included in one single higher level category of traits ('sociability'), and the traits (e.g., 'sociability' and 'impulsivity') are finally included in one type level category ('extraversion'). No links are specified between categories at a single level (e.g., between 'sociability' and 'impulsivity'), nor between categories (e.g., 'smiling at people') at one level (e.g., habitual response level) and a different category (e.g., 'impulsivity') at another level (e.g., trait level).

Hierarchy of variables and factors

The methodology used to arrive at some order in the domain of traits produces hierarchy. Principal Components Analysis, for example, produces correlations between trait-variables and the more abstract factors, and after Varimax-rotation the abstract factors are interpreted in terms of clusters of correlating trait-variables within those factors. The result is a hierarchical simple structure model, such as represented in Figure 8.2. In this Dutch five-factor solution (De Raad, Hendriks and Hofstee 1992), after Varimax-rotation, for example, the trait-variable triples beginning with 'spontaneous', 'cheerful', 'energetic', 'vivacious' and 'enthusiastic' each have their highest loadings on the factor Extraversion. Similarly, the

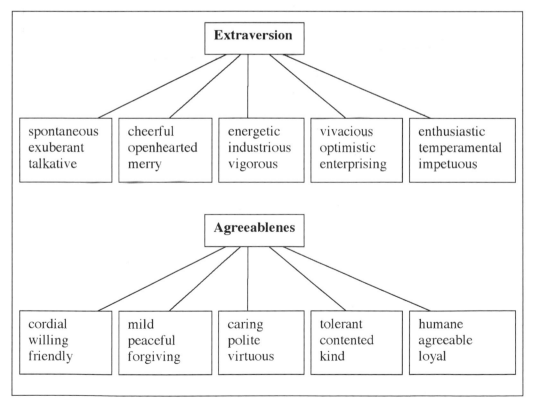

Figure 8.2. *Partial models of Extraversion and Agreeableness of De Raad, Hendriks and Hofstee 1992.*

triples beginning with 'cordial', 'mild', 'caring', 'tolerant', and 'humane' each have their highest loadings on the factor Agreeableness.

In the preceding, simple structure is a relative concept. While Varimax-rotation strives after simple structure, of the trait-variable triples, only those starting with 'spontaneous' and 'mild' actually empirically behave according to the simple structure ideal. Although the trait-variable triples all have their highest (primary) loadings on the indicated factor, for the Extraversion factor, the second up to the fifth trait-variable triples also have substantial positive (secondary) loadings on Agreeableness, Conscientiousness, Emotional Stability and Intellect, respectively. Similarly, the first and the third up to the fifth trait-variable triples for Agreeableness have also secondary loadings on Extraversion, Conscientiousness, Emotional Stability and Intellect, respectively. This feature with primary and secondary loadings is characteristic of the majority of the trait-variables in the Big Five structure. This feature is also indicative of the fuzziness of membership of trait-variables of the categories (e.g., triples) that build the hierarchy.

Hierarchy of factors: successive emergence of factors

An interesting way of looking at hierarchy, which has been applied increasingly over the last decade (e.g., De Raad and Szirmák 1994; Saucier, Georgiades, Tsaousis and Goldberg 2005), is by giving the correlations between factors from different levels of extraction. Figure 8.3 gives a partial representation of the emergence of factors when more factors are extracted and rotated (De Raad and

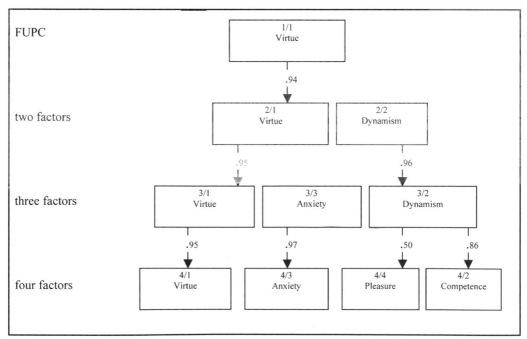

Figure 8.3. *Hierarchical emergence of factors (De Raad and Barelds 2007).*

Barelds 2008). On top is the first unrotated principal component (FUPC, called Virtue). With two factors extracted (labelled Virtue and Dynamism), Virtue appears to correlate 0.94 with FUPC and Dynamism does not correlate substantially with FUPC. With three factors, an additional Anxiety factor emerges with no apparent links to the two factors at the previous level. With four factors, Dynamism seems to split into two sub-factors with dynamic characteristics, Pleasure and Competence.

Testing hierarchies in personality trait domains

Hierarchy is not only brought about psychometrically, through factoring variables or through factoring factors. Hampson, John and Goldberg (1986) explicitly searched for indexes of hierarchy according to principles of Category Breadth and Concept Asymmetry, to enable an empirical test of hierarchy. Category breadth was defined as the number of behaviours subsumed by a trait concept. The broad and narrow trait distinction implied in the Category Breadth principle parallels that between trait-factors and trait-variables, respectively. The Concept Asymmetry principle was operationalized in a technique with the same name, in which subjects had to indicate which of two statements made more sense, the statement 'To be X is a way of being Y' and the statement 'To be Y is a way of being X', X and Y representing trait-terms. If, for example, the second statement was judged to make more sense, Y would represent a narrower trait than X.

Hampson, John and Goldberg (1986) provided supportive empirical evidence for expected two-tiered (e.g., talkative is a way of being social) and three-tiered (e.g., musical is a way of being artistic, and artistic is a way of being talented) hierarchies for different types of descriptors (adjectives, verbs, nouns). Hampson *et al.* suggested that well-differentiated hierarchies are found in certain domains of the Big Five and not in others. For example, when overt occurrence of behaviour is signalled by a trait (e.g., Emotional Instability), differentiated hierarchies are more frequent than when non-occurrence (e.g., being passive, silent, reserved) of behaviour is signalled by a trait (e.g., Introversion).

Circular structures

Enumerating factors in a factor structure, and specifying categories or classes at a certain level in a hierarchy pertains to splitting up the domain of interest into distinct clusters of meaning. In certain models, for example Eysenck's model, those clusters are categorically distinct. The simple structure ideal pursued in Varimax-rotation epitomizes such a 'horizontal' (cf., Goldberg 1993) structuring. From this horizontal perspective, a further differentiation of the trait domain consists of finding additional factors that have scientific and applied relevance. Part of the discussion on a six-factor structure (Ashton, Lee, Perugini *et al.* 2004), a seven-factor model (Almagor, Tallegen and Waller 1995), and the eight-factor structure (De Raad and Barelds 2008), is about how to decide about the next relevant factors beyond the Big Five.

Most of the discussion on factoring the trait-domain thus far has implied fuzzy categories and partially overlapping clusters of trait meaning, as exemplified in Figure 8.2. The figure assumes that most trait-variables correlate with no more than one factor. The study by De Raad, Hendriks and Hofstee (1992) on the so-called Abridged Big Five Circumplex model was based on the finding that the simple structure concept was compromised substantially by the fact that a large number (some 30 per cent) of Big Five trait-variables loaded on two factors. This means that trait-variables can be categorized in terms of pairs of factors with which they correlate, yielding ten two-dimensional planes in which trait-variables are depicted using the pairs of loadings as coordinate values.

With only two factors, as in the case of the two-factor level with Virtue and Dynamism (De Raad and Barelds 2008), the circular arrangement that proceeds from using the pairs of loadings for the variables in a representation is exemplified in Figure 8.4. Figure 8.4 is actually based on data that were ipsatized before

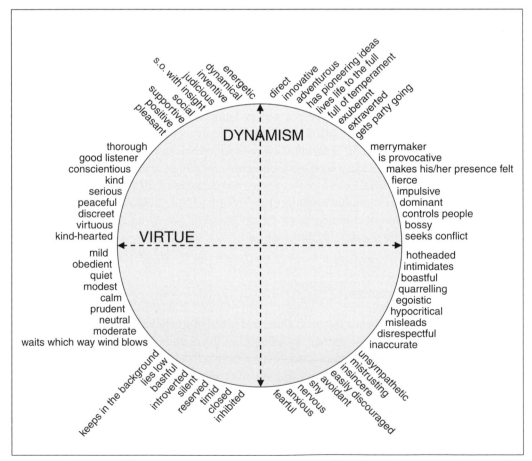

Figure 8.4. *Circumplex representation of two factor solution (De Raad and Barelds 2007).*

factoring them. This ipsatization procedure involved subtracting the mean score (based on pairs of opposites) of an individual from all scores of that individual. The trait-descriptive items along the circumference of the circle form a small selection of a total set of 2,331 variables in the study. The vast majority of those variables did not load high on any of the two variables, and those that are put in Figure 8.4 come closest in representing the varieties in meanings made possible by the two-factor solution. Moreover, the locations of the items along the circle correspond to their actual locations within the circle.

The advantage of using this circumplex representation is that the positions of the trait-variables relative to each other become clear. One could read Figure 8.4 according to simple structure, by focusing on the two sets of opposite clusters of variables. The Virtue set of opposite clusters is pivoted by 'kind-hearted' and 'mild' on the one hand, and 'seeks conflict' and 'hotheaded', on the other hand. The Dynamism set of opposite clusters is pivoted by 'energetic' and 'direct', on the one hand, and by 'inhibited' and 'fearful', on the other hand. In addition, the meanings of adjacent traits on the circle are close to their neighbouring traits and differ in the extent to which they represent the two main dimensions. Considered clockwise, from 'direct' (at twelve o'clock) to 'gets party going' (at seven past twelve) the traits diminish in representing Dynamism features and gain in representing features of the opposite of Virtue. Moreover, each cluster of traits (e.g., from 'direct' to 'gets party going') may be considered as a blend of the two adjacent clusters ('energetic' to 'pleasant' and 'merrymaker' to 'seeks conflict'). Finally, traits or clusters of traits find their semantic and psychological opposites at about 180 degrees further on the circle. Examples are the single traits 'extra-verted' versus 'introverted' and 'unsympathetic' versus 'pleasant', but also the sets of traits 'hotheaded' to 'quarreling' versus 'kind-hearted' to 'peaceful'.

Segmenting the circle

Whether one distinguishes single traits or clusters of traits at the horizontal level depends on the context. Most applied and research contexts follow economic principles and require a segmentation of the circular pie into a level of clustering that has theoretical and applied relevance. The interpersonal circumplex research tradition (cf., Trapnell and Wiggins 1990), for example, distinguishes eight clusters, segments or octants, theoretically defined by a facet theory approach (Foa and Foa 1974). In that circumplex, interpersonal traits are arranged around the underlying coordinates Dominance and Nurturance, dimensions or factors that have respectively been linked to the previously mentioned Agency and Communion concepts by Wiggins and Trapnell (1996). Four of the eight segments capture the interpersonal traits centred around the four poles of Dominance and Nurturance, and the other four segments capture the traits that form the blends of each pair of poles at 90 degrees.

In the Abridged Big Five Circumplex model (De Raad, Hendriks and Hofstee 1992), twelve segments are distinguished. A reason for this finer partitioning is that valid distinctions may be lost when using octants. In Figure 8.4, for example, 'conscientious', 'kind' and 'serious' have a primary loading on I+ (Virtue) and a secondary loading on II+ (Dynamism), whereas 's.o. with insight', 'social' and 'supportive' have a primary loading on II+ and a secondary loading on I+. These sets of traits are distinct from each other and are also distinct from the adjacent factor-pure sets of traits with 'kind-hearted' and 'mild' for Virtue and 'energetic' and 'direct' for Dynamism.

Future directions

According to Lave and March (1975) models should be evaluated on three main characteristics, namely Truth, Beauty and Justice. Restricted to structural models of personality, the Truth-criterion would be about an adequate representation of the trait domain in the model, and its testability. The history of structural models of personality is characterized by a plethora of strong opinions about the proper representation of the trait sphere and the testability of the model, particularly expressed in the works of Cattell (representation) and of Eysenck (theory and testability). In the new era, where the discussion was focused on representation and where testability was restricted to the number five, a certain level of consensus was rapidly obtained with the Big Five model. Yet, part of the consensus is probably due to a form of circular reasoning: pursuing the Big Five while they need to be demonstrated (De Raad and Peabody 2005). More use should be made of sets of markers for expected dimensional structure (see Saucier and Goldberg 1996), of the substantive alternative proposed by Peabody and De Raad (2002), and of psychometric methods of factor comparison (see De Raad, Perugini, Hrébicková and Szarota 1998), in which congruence coefficients are calculated before and after target rotation. A highly interesting technique to find whether a factor or component observed in one set of data or under one particular instruction is also found in another set of data or under a different instruction is a rotation to perfectly congruent weights (Ten Berge 1986; cf., De Raad, Perugini, Hrébicková and Szarota 1988).

The Beauty-criterion suggested by Lave and March (1975) applies to the simplicity of the Big Five model or models with six, seven or eight factors. Part of the attractiveness is in the relatively small number of factors, relative to the enumerable lexically sedimented traits. Part of the attractiveness is also in the inevitable hierarchical or vertical nature of the trait structure. In this respect, historically, the debate consisted of a mixture of psychometric reasoning (Cattell and Guilford) and theoretical consideration (Eysenck). In the new era, with the emergence of the Big Five structure, hierarchy was implied in the relations between trait-variables and the trait-factors, but the emphasis was largely on the 'horizontal' juxtaposition of distinct trait-factors. Subsequently, developments furthered towards circular representations. In the near future, studies on the additional candidates beyond the Big Five factors should be accompanied by psychometric tests. Moreover, both vertical and horizontal differentiations should be an explicit focus in the development of trait-models.

As regards the Justice-criterion, Lave and March (1975) focus on making a better world. Here, the Justice-criterion is embodied in theory development and especially in the development of assessment instruments that enable an adequate tackling of scientific and societal problems. During the last one or two decades, personality questionnaires have been geared towards representing the major trait dimensions as represented in the Big Five model (see De Raad and Perugini 2002). Such instrument-development should gain from establishing the major personality dimensions, but also from the distinctions between the different levels of traits in a hierarchy and the horizontal characteristics demonstrated in the circumplex configuration.

At an international, cross-cultural level, the domain of structural models of personality traits may make an important step forward if consensus is reached over the most fundamental, kernel-structure of personality, both horizontally and vertically, with an emphasis on the basic one, two or three dimensions in the various indigenous psycholexical projects. This should include the assessment of both the p-factor and such Basic Two as conveyed in the generic Communion and Agency concepts.

References

Allport, G. W. and Odbert, H. S. 1936. Trait-names: a psycho-lexical study, *Psychological Monographs* 47 (No. 211)

Almagor, M., Tellegen, A. and Waller, N. 1995. The Big Seven Model: a cross-cultural replication and further exploration of the basic dimensions of natural language of trait descriptions, *Journal of Personality and Social Psychology* 69: 300–7

Ashton, M. C. and Lee, K. 2001. A theoretical basis for the major dimensions of personality, *European Journal of Personality* 15: 327–53

Ashton, M. C., Lee, K. and Goldberg, L. R. 2004. A hierarchical analysis of 1,710 English personality-descriptive adjectives, *Journal of Personality and Social Psychology* 87: 707–21

Ashton, M. C., Lee, K., Perugini, M., Szarota, P., De Vries, R. E., Di Blas, L., Boies, K. and De Raad, B. 2004. A six-factor structure of personality-descriptive adjectives: solutions from psycholexical studies in seven languages, *Journal of Personality and Social Psychology* 86: 356–66

Bakan, D. 1966. *The duality of human existence: isolation and communion in Western man*. Boston: Beacon

Benet-Martínez, V. and Waller, N. G. 1997. Further evidence for the cross-cultural generality of the Big Seven model: indigenous and imported Spanish personality constructs, *Journal of Personality* 65: 567–98

Bertels, K. and Nauta, D. 1969. *Inleiding tot het modelbegrip* [*Introduction to the model concept*]. Amsterdam: Wetenschappelijke Uitgeverij B.V.

Block, J. 1995. A contrarian view of the five-factor approach to personality disorder, *Psychological Bulletin* 117: 187–215

Cattell, R. B. 1943. The description of personality: basic traits resolved into clusters, *Journal of Abnormal and Social Psychology* 38: 476–507

1945. The description of personality: principles and findings in a factor analysis, *American Journal of Psychology* 58: 69–90

1950. *Personality: a systematic theoretical and factual study*, New York: McGraw-Hill

1965. *The scientific analysis of personality*. Chicago: Aldine Publishing Company

1994. Constancy of global, second-order personality factors over a twenty-year-plus period, *Psychological Reports* 75: 3–9

1995. The fallacy of five factors in the personality sphere, *The Psychologist*, May, 207–8

Cattell, R. B., Eber, H. W. and Tatsuoka, M. M. 1970. *The handbook for the sixteen personality factor (16PF) questionnaire*. Champaign, IL: Institute for Personality and Ability Testing

Cattell, R. B. and Gibbons, B. D. 1968. Personality factor structure of the combined Guilford and Cattell personality questionnaires, *Journal of Personality and Social Psychology* 9: 107–20

Church, A. T., Katigbak, M. S. and Reyes, J. A. S. 1996. Toward a taxonomy of trait adjectives in Filipino: comparing personality lexicons across cultures, *European Journal of Personality* 10: 3–24

Costa, P. T., Jr and McCrae, R. R. 1976. Age differences in personality structure: a cluster analytic approach, *Journal of Gerontology* 31: 564–70

1985. *The NEO Personality Inventory manual*. Odessa, FL: Psychological Assessment Resources

De Raad, B. 1994. An expedition in search of a fifth universal factor: key issues in the lexical approach, *European Journal of Personality* 8: 229–50

2000. *The Big Five personality factors*. Seattle: Hogrefe and Huber

De Raad, B. and Barelds, D. P. H. 2008. A new taxonomy of Dutch personality traits based on a comprehensive and unrestricted list of descriptors. *Journal of Personality and Social Psychology* 94: 347–64

De Raad, B., Hendriks, A. A. J. and Hofstee, W. K. B. 1992. Towards a refined structure of personality traits, *European Journal of Personality* 6: 301–19

De Raad, B. and Hofstee, W. K. B. 1993. A circumplex approach to the five factor model: a facet structure of trait adjectives supplemented by trait verbs, *Personality and Individual Differences* 15: 493–505

De Raad, B., Mulder, E., Kloosterman, K. and Hofstee, W. K. B. 1988. Personality-descriptive verbs, *European Journal of Personality* 2: 81–96

De Raad, B. and Peabody, D. 2005. Cross-culturally recurrent personality factors: analyses of three factors, *European Journal of Personality* 19: 451–74

De Raad, B. and Perugini, M. 2002. *Big Five Assessment*. Seattle: Hogrefe and Huber Publishers

De Raad, B., Perugini, M., Hrébicková, M. and Szarota, P. 1998. Lingua franca of personality: taxonomies and structures based on the psycholexical approach, *Journal of Cross-Cultural Psychology* 29: 212–32

De Raad, B., Perugini, M. and Szirmák, Z. 1997. In pursuit of a cross-lingual reference structure of personality traits: comparisons among five languages, *European Journal of Personality* 11: 167–85

De Raad, B. and Szirmák, Z. 1994. The search for the 'Big Five' in a non-Indo-European language: the Hungarian trait structure and its relationship to the *EPQ* and the *PTS, European Review of Applied Psychology* 44: 17–24

Di Blas, L. and Forzi, M. 1999. Refining a descriptive structure of personality attributes in the Italian language: the abridged Big Three circumplex structure, *Journal of Personality and Social Psychology* 76: 451–81

Digman, J. M. 1997. Higher-order factors of the Big Five, *Journal of Personality and Social Psychology* 73: 1246–56

Eysenck, H. J. 1947. *Dimensions of Personality.* London: Kegan Paul

   1952. *The scientific study of personality.* London: Routledge and Kegan Paul

   1953. *The structure of human personality.* London: Methuen and Co.

   1959. *Manual for the Maudsley Personality Inventory.* University of London Press

   1964. *Manual of the Eysenck Personality Inventory.* University of London Press

   1970. *The structure of human personality*, 3rd edn. London: Methuen

   1991. Dimensions of personality: 16-, 5- or 3- criteria for a taxonomic paradigm, *Personality and Individual Differences* 12: 773–90

   1992. Four ways five factors are *not* basic, *Personality and Individual Differences* 13: 667–73

Fiske, D. W. 1949. Consistency of the factorial structures of personality ratings from different sources, *Journal of Abnormal and Social Psychology* 44: 329–44

Foa, U. G. and Foa, E. B. 1974. *Societal structures of the mind.* Springfield, IL: Thomas

Goldberg, L. R. 1981. Language and individual differences: the search for universals in personality lexicons, in L. Wheeler (ed.), *Review of personality and social psychology*, vol. 2, pp. 141–65. Beverley Hills: Sage

   1990. An alternative description of personality: the Big-Five factor structure, *Journal of Personality and Social Psychology* 59: 1216–29

   1993. The structure of personality traits: vertical and horizontal aspects, in D. C. Funder, R. D. Parke, C. Tomlinson-Keasey and K. Widaman (eds.), *Studying lives through time: personality and development*, pp. 169–88. Washington, DC: American Psychological Association

Goldberg, L. R. and Rosolack, T. K. 1994. The Big Five factor structure as an integrative framework: an empirical comparison with Eysenck's P-E-N model, in C. F. Halverson, Jr, G. A. Kohnstamm and R. P. Martin (eds), *The developing structure of temperament and personality from infancy to adulthood*, pp. 7–35. Hillsdale, NJ: Lawrence Erlbaum Associates

Gough, H. G. 1957. *Manual for the California Psychological Inventory.* Palo Alto, CA: Consulting Psychologists Press

Guilford, J. P. 1959. *Personality.* New York: McGraw-Hill

   1975. Factors and factors of personality, *Psychological Bulletin* 82: 802–14

Guilford, J. P. and Guilford, R. B. 1934. An analysis of the factors in a typical test of introversion-extroversion, *Journal of Abnormal and Social Psychology* 28: 377–99

   1936. Personality factors *S*, *E*, and *M*, and their measurement, *Journal of Psychology* 2: 109–27

Guilford, J. P. and Zimmerman, W. S. 1949. *The Guilford-Zimmerman Temperament Survey: manual.* Beverly Hills, CA: Sheridan Supply

Hampson, S. E., John, O. P. and Goldberg, L. R. (1986). Category breadth and hierarchical structure in personality: studies of asymmetries in judgments of trait implications, *Journal of Personality and Social Psychology* 51: 37–54

Hofer, S. M. and Eber, H. W. 2002. Second-order factor structure of the Cattell Sixteen Personality Factor Questionnaire, in B. De Raad and M. Perugini (eds.), *Big Five Assessment*, pp. 397–409. Seattle: Hogrefe and Huber Publishers

Hofstee, W. K. B. 2001. Intelligence and personality: do they mix?, in J. M. Collis and S. Messick (eds.), *Intelligence and personality: bridging the gap in theory and measurement*, pp. 43–60. Mahwah, NJ: Lawrence Erlbaum

Hofstee, W. K. B., Kiers, H. A. L., De Raad, B., Goldberg, L. R. and Ostendorf, F. 1997. A comparison of Big-Five structures of personality traits in Dutch, English, and German, *European Journal of Personality* 11: 15–31

Hofstee, W. K. B. and Ten Berge, J. M. F. 2004. Personality in proportion: a bipolar proportional scale for personality assessments and its consequences for trait structure, *Journal of Personality Assessment* 83: 120–7

John, O. P., Angleitner, A. and Ostendorf, F. 1988. The lexical approach to personality, *European Journal of Personality* 2: 171–205

Jung, C. G. 1923. *Psychological Types*. London: Routledge and Kegan Paul

Karson, S. 1961. Second-order personality factors in positive mental health, *Journal of Clinical Psychology* 17: 14–19

Kretschmer, E. 1948. *Körperbau und Charakter [Constitution and Character]*. Berlin: Springer-Verlag

Krug, S. E. and Johns, E. F. 1986. A large scale cross-validation of second-order personality structure defined by the 16PF, *Psychological Reports* 59: 683–93

Lave, C. A. and March, J. G. 1975. *An Introduction to Models in the Social Sciences*. New York: Harper and Row

McCrae, R. R. and Costa, P. T., Jr 1985. Updating Norman's 'adequate taxonomy': intelligence and personality dimensions in natural language and in questionnaires, *Journal of Personality and Social Psychology* 49: 710–21

Mlačić, B. and Ostendorf, F. 2005. Taxonomy and structure of Croatian personality-descriptive adjectives, *European Journal of Personality* 19: 117–52

Norman, W. T. 1963. Toward an adequate taxonomy of personality attributes: replicated factor structure in peer nomination personality ratings, *Journal of Abnormal and Social Psychology* 66: 574–83

   1967. *2,800 personality trait descriptors: normative operating characteristics for a university population*. Ann Arbor, MI: Department of Psychology, University of Michigan

Ostendorf, F. 1990. *Sprache und Persönlichkeitsstruktur: Zur Validität des Fünf-faktoren modells der Persönlichkeit [Language and personality structure: towards the validity of the five-factor model of personality]*. Regensburg: Roderer-Verlag

Panter, A. T., Tanaka, J. S. and Hoyle, R. H. 1994. Structural models for multimode designs in personality and temperament research, in C. F. Halverson, Jr, G. A. Kohnstamm and R. P. Martin (eds.), *The developing structure of temperament and personality from infancy to adulthood*, pp. 111–38. Hillsdale, NJ: Lawrence Erlbaum Associates

Peabody, D. 1987. Selecting representative trait adjectives, *Journal of Personality and Social Psychology* 52: 59–71

Peabody, D. and De Raad, B. 2002. The substantive nature of psycholexical personality factors: a comparison acrosss languages, *Journal of Personality and Social Psychology* 83: 983–97

Saucier, G., Georgiades, S., Tsaousis, I. and Goldberg, L. R. 2005. The factor structure of Greek personality adjectives, *Journal of Personality and Social Psychology* 88: 856–75

Saucier, G. and Goldberg, L. R. 1996. Evidence for the Big Five in analyses of familiar English personality adjectives, *European Journal of Personality* 10: 61–77

Sells, S. B., Demaree, R. G. and Will, D. P., Jr 1970. Dimensions of personality: I. Conjoint factor structure of Guilford and Cattell trait markers, *Multivariate Behavioural Research* 5: 391–422

    1971. Dimensions of personality: II. Separate factor structures in Guilford and Cattell trait markers, *Multivariate Behavioural Research* 6: 135–85

Somer, O. and Goldberg, L. R. 1999. The structure of Turkish trait-descriptive adjectives, *Journal of Personality and Social Psychology* 76: 431–50

Ten Berge, J. M. F. 1986. Rotation to perfect congruence and the cross-validation of components weights across populations, *Multivariate Behavioural Research* 21: 41–64.

Trapnell, P. D. and Wiggins, J. S. 1990. Extension of interpersonal adjective scales to include the Big Five dimensions of personality, *Journal of Personality and Social Psychology* 59: 781–90

Tupes, E. C. and Christal, R. C. 1958. *Stability of personality trait rating factors obtained under diverse conditions*, USAF ASTIA Doc. No. AD 151 041. Lackland Air Force Base: U.S. Air Force, TX

    1961. *Recurrent personality factors based on trait ratings*, USAF ASD Technical Report, No. 61–97. Lackland Air Force Base: U.S. Air Force, TX.

Webb, E. 1915. *Character and intelligence: an attempt at an exact study of character*. Cambridge University Press

Wiggins, J. S. 1968. Personality structure, *Annual Review of Psychology* 19: 293–350

Wiggins, J. S. (ed.) (1996). *The Five-Factor Model of personality: theoretical perspectives*. New York: Guilford Press

Wiggins, J. S. and Trapnell, P. D. 1996. A dyadic-interactional perspective on the Five-Factor Model, in J. S. Wiggins (ed.), *The Five-Factor Model of personality: theoretical perspectives*, pp. 88–162. New York: Guilford Press

Zuckerman, M., Kuhlman, D. M. and Camac, C. 1988. What lies beyond E and N? Factor analyses of scales believed to measure basic dimensions of personality, *Journal of Personality and Social Psychology* 54: 96–107

9 The Five-Factor Model of personality traits: consensus and controversy

Robert R. McCrae

There is little doubt that the Five-Factor Model (FFM) of personality traits (the 'Big Five') is currently the dominant paradigm in personality research, and one of the most influential models in all of psychology. Digman's 1990 review on the topic has become the most highly cited article in the history of the *Annual Review of Psychology*, with over 1,200 citations. Barrick and Mount's 1991 meta-analysis of job performance and the FFM – itself cited over 900 times – brought personality back into the mainstream of Industrial/Organizational Psychology. The FFM has led to novel and compelling reformulations of the personality disorders that stand a fair chance of reshaping Axis II in the DSM-V (Widiger and Trull 2007). Cross-cultural collaborations have shown the universality of the FFM and demonstrated pervasive fallacies in national character stereotypes (Terracciano, Abdel-Khalak, Ádám *et al*. 2005). Social psychologist Harry Reis (personal communication, 24 April 2006) recently characterized the FFM as 'the most scientifically rigorous taxonomy that behavioural science has', and for his research on the FFM, Paul Costa was selected by the Division of General Psychology of the American Psychological Association to present the 2004 Arthur W. Staats Lecture for Contributions towards Unifying Psychology.

What is it that researchers from so many disciplines have come to appreciate? As Digman and Inouye (1986) put it, 'If a large number of rating scales is used and if the scope of the scales is very broad, the domain of personality descriptors is almost completely accounted for by five robust factors' (p. 116). In other words, these five factors provide a structure in which most personality traits can be classified. This structure arises because traits co-vary. For example, people who are sociable and assertive tend also to be cheerful and energetic; they are high on the Extraversion (E) factor, which is said to be *defined* by sociability, assertiveness, cheerfulness and energy. However, people who are sociable and assertive may or may not be intellectually curious and imaginative. Those traits define a separate factor, Openness to Experience (O). Neuroticism versus Emotional Stability (N), Agreeableness versus Antagonism (A), and Conscientiousness (C) are the remaining factors.

There is a widespread consensus that these five factors are necessary and more-or-less sufficient to account for the co-variation of most personality traits, and it is

Robert R. McCrae receives royalties from the Revised NEO Personality Inventory (NEO-PI-R). This research was supported by the Intramural Research Program, NIH, National Institute on Aging.

this comprehensiveness that chiefly accounts for the utility of the FFM. Researchers who wish to conduct a review of the literature on personality correlates typically find that many different scales and instruments have been used to assess personality. If each is assigned to one of the five factors, their results can be meaningfully combined. Again, the FFM provides a framework for systematic exploratory research. Suppose, for example, one wished to study the effects on personality of growing up in East versus West Germany (Angleitner and Ostendorf 2000). One might hypothesize that East Germans would be, say, higher in C and lower in O, and administer only measures of those two factors. But if the real differences turned out to be in levels of N and A, such a design would not reveal it. By administering measures of the full FFM one can be sure that important traits have not been overlooked.

Origins of the FFM

The origins of the FFM can be traced back to Sir Francis Galton and the beginnings of trait psychology, and the details of its history have been recounted by a number of authors (Digman 1990; John, Angleitner and Ostendorf 1988). Perhaps the most interesting historical question, however, is why the FFM was not widely adopted until the end of the twentieth century. There were a number of contributing causes to this delay.

It was not immediately clear how one could specify the full list of traits in order to determine what structure was needed to organize them. The solution came with the adoption of the lexical hypothesis, which argues that traits are so important in human affairs that common words will have been invented to name them all; an unabridged dictionary ought to provide an exhaustive listing of traits, which could be sorted out into a basic structure. Several generations of researchers pursued this strategy (see John, Angleitner and Ostendorf 1988), and it led to the discovery (Tupes and Christal 1961/1992) and rediscovery (Goldberg 1983) of the FFM.

However, the great majority of personality psychologists did not adopt the lexical hypothesis. They were sceptical that the lay vocabulary could be a proper basis for a scientific account of traits, and they tended to offer and defend their own, competing systems. Eysenck (1947) proposed a highly simplified system with only two factors, E and N; Jungian psychologists assessed four psychological preferences (Myers and McCaulley 1985); Block (1961) created a set of 100 theoretically-eclectic descriptors intended for use in clinical research. Disputes between rival schools continued for decades, but in the 1980s a series of studies showed that all these instruments assessed variations on the FFM. For example, research showed that the Extraversion, Intuition, Feeling and Judging preferences of the Myers-Briggs Type Indicator (Myers and McCaulley 1985) correspond to E, O, A and C, respectively (McCrae and Costa 1989).

The discoverers of the significance of the FFM, Tupes and Christal, were Air Force psychologists who published their work in a Technical Report that was essentially lost to the literature until it was published thirty years later (Tupes and Christal 1961/1992). It had been brought to the attention of psychologists by Norman (1963), but at a time when personality psychology was entering a period of crisis. In 1968 Mischel published a critique of trait psychology that led most psychologists to conclude that traits were cognitive fictions with no predictive value; the FFM was merely an adequate taxonomy of illusions. Slowly, defenders of traits made the case that traits were both real (McCrae 1982; Yamagata, Suzuki, Ando *et al.* 2006) and consequential (Ozer and Benet-Martínez 2006). The revival of trait psychology and the ascendance of the FFM went hand in hand.

Most personality assessment takes the form of self-report inventories, in which respondents are asked to say if, or how well, each of a series of statements describes them. This has proven to be a very useful technique, but it is by no means perfect. People may not understand the questions, or they may not understand themselves. They may be prone to agreeing with almost any assertion, or may choose to endorse only positive statements about themselves. They may be bored by the task and careless in their responses. Sceptics came to believe that self-reports were nothing but a collection of errors and biases.

It was, therefore, an important advance when psychologists showed that there was substantial (though not complete) agreement between descriptions from self-reports and those obtained when the same questions were put to knowledgeable informants – spouses, roommates, friends (Funder 1980; Kurtz and Sherker 2003). In 1987, McCrae and Costa showed that the FFM could be found in analyses of peer ratings as well as self-reports, and that there was substantial agreement across these different methods of measurement on the standing of each individual on all five factors. The FFM was subsequently found using Q-sort methods, in which people sort statements from most to least characteristic (Lanning 1994; McCrae, Costa and Busch 1986), and even in sentence completion tests, in which people describe themselves in response to the question, 'Who am I?' (McCrae and Costa 1988).

Questionnaires, however, remain the most popular and well-validated tools for assessing the FFM. The most widely used is the Revised NEO Personality Inventory (NEO-PI-R) (Costa and McCrae 1992a), whose 240 items assess 30 specific traits (or facets) that define the five factors. A brief version, the NEO Five-Factor Inventory (NEO-FFI) (Costa and McCrae 1992a) assesses only the five factors. The Big Five Inventory (Benet-Martínez and John 1998) is another widely-used measure of the five factors; De Raad and Perugini (2002) have edited an entire volume devoted to alternative measures of the FFM in a variety of languages.

Research discoveries

Armed with a comprehensive model and a variety of validated assessment tools, personality psychologists began to address basic questions about how traits operated. Widely replicated results have yielded a body of knowledge that had proven elusive during most of the twentieth century. Traits had always been assumed to be enduring dispositions; longitudinal research showed that individual differences in all five factors are in fact remarkably stable (Costa and McCrae 1992b; Roberts and DelVecchio 2000). At the same time, there are gradual changes in the average levels of traits. Both cross-sectional and longitudinal studies suggest that between adolescence and old age, individuals generally decline in N and E and increase in A and C. O increases until some time in the twenties, after which it slowly declines.

Research on the FFM has shown consistent patterns in gender differences. These differences are generally small, with substantial overlap between the distribution of traits in men and in women. But in most samples, women score higher in N and A than men. At the level of specific facets, there are sometimes differences within domain. Thus, both Warmth and Assertiveness are facets of E, but women are typically warmer and men more assertive. Again, women are more open to aesthetic experiences, whereas men are more open to ideas.

Over the past twenty years, researchers around the world have begun to translate instruments like the NEO-PI-R (McCrae and Allik 2002) and the Big Five Inventory (BFI) (Schmitt, Allik, McCrae *et al.* 2007), and have administered them to respondents in dozens of countries. Results are easily summarized: personality is much the same everywhere. The FFM structure itself is universal. McCrae and colleagues (McCrae, Terracciano and 78 others 2005) reported an almost perfect replication of the American adult self-report NEO-PI-R structure using 11,985 observer ratings of college-age and adult targets from 50 cultures. The same study replicated the American pattern of age differences (although the age effects for N and A were much smaller in the international sample). As Figure 9.1 shows, that study also replicated gender differences seen in the self-reports of American men and women ($r = .82, p < .001$)

These findings would have astounded psychologists and anthropologists who studied personality and culture in the first half of the twentieth century. They believed that personality was a cultural creation that would probably vary as much across cultures as diets and religious beliefs. As late as 1996, Juni wrote that 'Different cultures and different languages should give rise to other models that have little chance of being five in number nor of having any of the factors resemble those derived from the linguistic/social network of middle-class Americans' (Juni 1996, p. 864). Cross-cultural research on the FFM has created a revolution in thinking on this issue.

There is a plausible explanation for this universality: the FFM is strongly rooted in biology. Each of the five factors is heritable (Riemann, Angleitner and Strelau 1997), and studies of twins (Yamagata, Suzuki, Ando *et al.* 2006) and of family relatives (Pilia, Chen, Scuteri *et al.* 2006) show that the five-factor structure of the observed traits mirrors the structure of their underlying genes. Apparently, Warmth and Assertiveness are both definers of E because they are influenced by some of the same genes. We know that the human race is a single species, so the universality of the FFM is probably a reflection of the fact that variations on the same trait-related genes are found in *Homo sapiens* worldwide.

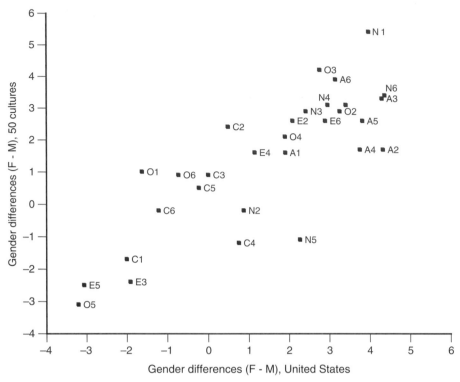

Figure 9.1. *Gender differences, in T-scores, for adults in the United States (self-reports) vs. 50 cultures (observer ratings) on the 30 facets of the NEO-PI-R. See Table 9.1 for facet labels. Women score higher than men on traits in the upper right quadrant, such as N1: Anxiety, O3: Feelings and A6: Altruism. Men score higher than women on traits in the lower left quadrant, such as O5: Ideas, E5: Excitement Seeking and C1: Competence. Data from Costa and McCrae 1992a and from McCrae, Terracciano et al. 2005.*

There is now consensus that the general personality dimension of N is associated with most personality disorders (Widiger and Costa 2002), that E predisposes people to be happy (DeNeve and Cooper 1998), that O predicts social and political liberalism (McCrae 1996), that low A is a risk factor for substance abuse (Ball 2002), that C is associated with good job performance (Barrick and Mount 1991). The utility of the FFM has been securely demonstrated.

Current controversy concerning the FFM

Precisely because it plays such a prominent role in contemporary psychology, the FFM has become the target of numerous critiques. This is healthy; science advances by constantly challenging established views. Sometimes these challenges force a change in thinking, as when Costa and McCrae moved from their three-factor model (Costa and McCrae 1980) to the FFM (McCrae and Costa 1987). Other times, they result in stronger evidence for the challenged ideas. In the end, trait research benefited from Mischel's (1968) critique, because researchers had to design better and more telling studies to demonstrate what they thought they knew about traits.

Objections to the FFM take two different forms. The first is a critique of trait theories themselves from other perspectives in personality psychology. Advocates of a person-centred approach claim that types more faithfully represent the operation of psychological processes than do variable-centred traits (see Asendorpf, Caspi and Hofstee 2002, for a balanced discussion of these issues). Social cognitive theorists (Cervone 2004) have argued that traits merely describe, without explaining, behaviour (see McCrae and Costa 2008a for a rebuttal). Other personality theorists have pointed out that, even if it is a fully adequate model of personality traits, the FFM itself does not constitute a full theory of personality, explaining human development, day-to-day functioning and social interactions in cultural context (McAdams and Pals 2006). This point is well taken, and McCrae and Costa have offered a much broader perspective on personality in the form of Five-Factor Theory (McCrae and Costa 2003, 2008b).

The other class of objections to the FFM, which will be considered in more detail, come from researchers who are committed to trait models and factor analytic methods, but who propose some variation on or refinement of the FFM. The FFM is a hierarchical model of personality traits: each of the five broad factors is defined by more narrow and specific traits or facets. There are currently disagreements among researchers at the level of the five factors; at a level above the five factors; and at the level of the specific facets.

Three and six factor alternatives

The foundation of the FFM and thus of contemporary trait psychology is that five factors are both necessary and sufficient to summarize co-variation among specific personality traits. However, some researchers have argued that more or fewer than five factors are needed. De Raad and Peabody (2005) reported analyses of trait descriptive adjectives in Dutch, Italian, Czech, Hungarian and Polish samples and found more robust support for a three-factor model consisting of E, A and C than for the FFM. Conversely, Ashton and colleagues (Ashton and Lee 2005; Ashton, Lee, Perugini *et al.* 2004) reported lexical studies in a number of languages in which six replicable factors appeared. Ashton's model basically divides FFM A into two factors, the second called Honesty-Humility; in addition, the factors are rotated a bit from their usual positions.

Perhaps the most problematic feature of these studies is that they are, properly speaking, not so much studies of personality traits as of personality trait *language*. The people of two different cultures might have identical traits, but a factor that is richly represented in the vocabulary of the first culture might be missing from the vocabulary of the second. McCrae (1990) noted that there are relatively few English-language adjectives that reflect O. For example, there is no single term that designates sensitivity to aesthetic experience; 'artistic' comes closest, and it refers to the producer rather than the consumer of art. Yet surely English speakers are capable of responding to beauty (McCrae 2007).

Other researchers have argued that entirely new factors are needed. Cheung and her colleagues (Cheung, Cheung, Leung *et al.* 2003; Cheung, Leung, Fan *et al.* 1996) developed an inventory based on indigenous Chinese personality characteristics, which was subsequently translated into English. She argued that the Chinese Personality Assessment Inventory (CPAI) revealed a new factor, originally called Chinese Tradition, but later renamed Interpersonal Relatedness because it was also found in non-Chinese samples. In a joint factor analysis with the NEO-FFI, when six factors were examined, the FFM was supplemented with a factor defined by CPAI Harmony, Relationship Orientation, Thrift, Logical Orientation, Self Orientation, Defensiveness and low Flexibility. However, when only five factors were extracted, the elements of this factor were simply redistributed among A and C factors. It thus appears that the FFM encompasses distinctively Chinese traits.

Spirituality has also been proposed as a sixth factor (Piedmont 1999). The Spiritual Transcendence Scale includes facets assessing Prayer Fulfilment, Universality and Connectedness, and these three defined a separate factor in a joint analysis with the facets of the NEO-PI-R. One might question whether spirituality is in the domain of personality at all, or whether it is better regarded as an attitude or practice. However, in this case another issue is raised. All the items in this version of the Spiritual Transcendence Scale are positively keyed, so their intercorrelation may be inflated by acquiescent responding, the tendency to agree with items regardless of content. (NEO-PI-R facet scales are balanced, with roughly equal numbers of positively- and negatively-keyed items, so acquiescence is not relevant to their structure.)

Some evidence for this hypothesis comes from analyses of a different instrument, the Temperament and Character Inventory (TCI) (Cloninger, Przybeck, Svrakic and Wetzel 1994). The TCI has three scales that define a Self-Transcendence factor, and these scales, too, are susceptible to acquiescent responding, because all the Self-forgetfulness and Transpersonal Identification items and ten of thirteen of the Spiritual Acceptance items are positively keyed. A joint factor analysis of the twenty-five TCI scales with the five NEO-PI-R factors yielded clear N, A and C factors, a factor defined by both E and O, and a separate Self-Transcendence factor (McCrae, Herbst and Costa 2001). However, when acquiescence was assessed and statistically controlled, the full FFM appeared, with the three Self-Transcendence scales loading on the O factor (evidently measuring something like Openness to Spiritual Experience).

A higher-order structure

Digman (1997) proposed that the five factors are not the highest level of personality structure. Across different instruments and samples he showed that the factors were themselves intercorrelated, and that a factor analysis of these correlations revealed two higher-order factors, alpha (defined by A and C versus N) and beta (defined by E and O). Such factors have been reported by a number of other researchers (e.g., DeYoung, Peterson and Higgins 2002), so there is little controversy about their existence. What remains in doubt is their interpretation. Some researchers believe that they are real, if highly abstract, features of the structure of personality, perhaps even with a genetic basis (Jang, Livesley, Ando *et al*. 2006).

Other writers have argued that they are artifacts of evaluative bias (McCrae and Costa in press-a). Such biases come in two forms, called Positive and Negative Valence, and McCrae and Costa (1995) showed that Negative Valence is related to N and low A and C, and thus low alpha, whereas Positive Valence is related to E and O, and thus beta. Biesanz and West (2004) reported that the five factors were correlated when self-reports and observer ratings were examined separately, but were orthogonal across observers; for example, E and O were correlated in self-reports and in observer ratings, but self-reported E was unrelated to observer rated O. DeYoung (2006), however, claimed correlations both within and across raters. It is possible that both substantive and artifactual explanations are correct in part.

Specifying facets

Although scores on the five factors give a general sense of what an individual is like, much more can be learned by assessing the specific traits that define the factors. For example, both cheerfulness and assertiveness are definers of E, because both reflect ways of interacting with others. But some people are cheerful without being assertive, and others are assertive without being cheerful, and knowing which is which is important to clinicians (Singer 2005) and researchers (Paunonen and Ashton 2001). The problem at the facet level is that there is no generally recognized way of sub-dividing the factors into constituent traits. For example, Costa and McCrae (1992a) distinguished between Warmth and Gregariousness facets of E, corresponding to the sub-divisions of the need to belong: 'ongoing mutual caring and concern', and 'a desire for frequent interactions' (Baumeister 2005, p. 112). By contrast, Watson and Clark (1997) thought this distinction was unnecessary, and combined them into a single trait of sociability.

Cattell, Eber and Tatsuoka (1970) argued that there were fifteen primary personality traits (plus intelligence), and an instrument developed by Eysenck and colleagues (Eysenck, Barrett, Wilson and Jackson 1992) assessed twenty-one primary traits. The NEO-PI-R has thirty facet scales, six for each factor. They were chosen to represent the most important constructs in the personality literature, while at the same time being maximally distinct. Items to tap each were written using rational methods, and the best items were selected by item analyses and targeted factor analyses in a series of samples (Costa and McCrae 1995a).

It is instructive to compare the three systems to form an idea of their correspondences. Table 9.1 reports the scales from the 16PF Fifth Edition (16PF) and the Eysenck Personality Profiler (EPP) assigned to the NEO-PI-R facet with which they show the highest correlation. Both the 16PF and EPP have scales representing each of the five factors, and the empirical correspondences of individual scales are all

Table 9.1 *Correspondence of facet-level scales for three inventories.*

NEO-PI-R facet scale	16PF scale	EPP scale
N1: Anxiety	O: Apprehension	Anxious, Hypochondriacal
N2: Angry Hostility	Q4: Tension	
N3: Depression	*C: Emotional Stability*	Unhappy, Dependent
N4: Self-Consciousness		Inferior, Guilty
N5: Impulsiveness		
N6: Vulnerability		
E1: Warmth		
E2: Gregariousness	*Q2: Self-reliance*, A: Warmth	Sociable
E3: Assertiveness	H: Social Boldness, E: Dominance	Assertive
E4: Activity		Active
E5: Excitement Seeking	F: Liveliness	Sensation-seeking
E6: Positive Emotions		
O1: Fantasy	M: Abstractedness	
O2: Aesthetics	I: Sensitivity	*Tough-minded*
O3: Feelings		
O4: Actions	Q1: Openness to Change	
O5: Ideas		*Practical*
O6: Values		*Dogmatic*
A1: Trust	*L: Vigilance, N: Privateness*	
A2: Straightforwardness		*Manipulative*
A3: Altruism		
A4: Compliance		*Aggressive*
A5: Modesty		
A6: Tender-mindedness		
C1: Competence		
C2: Order	Q3: Perfectionism	Obsessive
C3: Dutifulness		*Irresponsible*
C4: Achievement Striving		Ambitious
C5: Self-discipline		
C6: Deliberation	G: Rule-consciousness	*Impulsive, Risk-taking, Expressive*

Note. Each 16PF and EPP scale is assigned to the NEO-PI-R facet with which it is most strongly correlated. Adapted from Conn and Rieke (1994), Table 6.4, $N = 257$; and Costa and McCrae (1995b), Table 1, $N = 229$. Absolute correlations $= .38$ to $.81$, all $p < .001$. Scales given in italics are inversely related to the NEO-PI-R facet. NEO-PI-R = Revised NEO Personality Inventory. 16PF = 16PF Fifth Edition. EPP = Eysenck Personality Profiler.

reasonable: NEO-PI-R N1: Anxiety, for example, is most strongly related to 16PF Apprehension and EPP Anxious; NEO-PI-R C2: Order corresponds to Perfectionism and Obsessive. Some facets, such as N2: Angry Hostility, are represented in the 16PF but not the EPP; other facets, such as N4: Self-Consciousness, are found in the EPP but not the 16PF. Table 9.1 demonstrates that there is in fact considerable consensus at the level of lower-order traits.

Because the NEO-PI-R has thirty facet scales, there are inevitably some facets without corresponding scales in the 16PF and EPP, such as N6: Vulnerability, E6: Positive Emotions, and O3: Feelings. This does not mean that this content is completely absent from the other inventories; every NEO-PI-R facet is significantly correlated with at least one scale from each of the other measures. But the thirty facets of the NEO-PI-R allow one to make distinctions that cannot be made with these other inventories, such as the distinction between Warmth and Gregariousness. An inventory with sixty facet scales could make even more distinctions, but so large a number of subtle distinctions would be difficult to learn and usefully employ.

The facet system of the NEO-PI-R has been criticized as being arbitrary, because 'the key ingredient for a system to provide an adequate lower order structure of the Big Five is some empirical foundation to selecting lower-order traits' in contrast to the 'theoretical insight and intuition' used in developing the NEO-PI-R (Roberts, Walton and Viechtbauer 2006, p. 29). Certainly it would be ideal to identify, solely by empirical means, a set of lower-level traits that consistently emerged across languages, methods of measurement and item pools, as the FFM often does at a higher level (e.g., Markon, Krueger and Watson 2005; McCrae 1989; McCrae, Terracciano and 78 others 2005). So far, however, that has not happened, and an ambitious effort to provide an empirical basis for the facets of C (Roberts, Bogg, Walton, Chernyshenko and Stark 2004; Roberts, Chernyshenko, Stark and Goldberg 2005) illustrates some of the problems (see McCrae and Costa 2008a). The facets of C identified by those researchers in a pool of trait descriptive adjectives bore only limited resemblance to those they found in a selection of personality inventory scales. The eight factors found in adjectives included Punctuality and Formalness facets not found in inventory scales; the six factors found in inventory scales included a Virtue facet not found in adjectives. The empirical strategy does not seem to yield consistent results at the facet level.

In the meantime, the facets of the NEO-PI-R do provide one system that has been successfully used in many applications and in dozens of cultures. Researchers have documented the discriminant validity, heritability and developmental course of all thirty facets, and no obvious gaps in covering the scope of the FFM have been identified. At present, NEO-PI-R facets arguably offer the best available delineation of the FFM at the next-lower level in the trait hierarchy.

References

Angleitner, A. and Ostendorf, F. 2000. The FFM: a comparison of German speaking countries (Austria, Former East and West Germany, and Switzerland). Paper presented at the XXVIIth International Congress of Psychology, Stockholm, Sweden, July 2000

Asendorpf, J. B., Caspi, A. and Hofstee, W. K. B. 2002. The puzzle of personality types [Special Issue], *European Journal of Personality* 16(S1)

Ashton, M. C. and Lee, K. 2005. Honesty-Humility, the Big Five, and the Five-Factor Model, *Journal of Personality* 73: 1321–53

Ashton, M. C., Lee, K., Perugini, M., Szarota, P., De Vries, R. E., Di Blass, L., Boies, K. and De Raad, B. 2004. A six-factor structure of personality descriptive adjectives: solutions from psycholexical studies in seven languages, *Journal of Personality and Social Psychology* 86: 356–66

Ball, S. A. 2002. Big Five, Alternative Five, and seven personality dimensions: validity in substance-dependent patients, in P. T. Costa, Jr and T. A. Widiger (eds.), *Personality disorders and the Five-Factor Model of personality*, 2nd edn, pp. 177–201. Washington, DC: American Psychological Association

Barrick, M. R. and Mount, M. K. 1991. The Big Five personality dimensions and job performance: a meta-analysis, *Personnel Psychology* 44: 1–26

Baumeister, R. F. 2005. *The cultural animal: human nature, meaning, and social life.* New York: Oxford University Press

Benet-Martínez, V. and John, O. P. 1998. *Los cinco Grandes* across cultures and ethnic groups: multitrait multimethod analyses of the Big Five in Spanish and English, *Journal of Personality and Social Psychology* 75: 729–50

Biesanz, J. C. and West, S. G. 2004. Towards understanding assessments of the Big Five: multitrait-multimethod analyses of convergent and discriminant validity across measurement occasion and type of observer, *Journal of Personality* 72: 845–76

Block, J. 1961. *The Q-sort method in personality assessment and psychiatric research*, Springfield, IL: Thomas

Cattell, R. B., Eber, H. W. and Tatsuoka, M. M. 1970. *The handbook for the Sixteen Personality Factor Questionnaire.* Champaign, IL: Institute for Personality and Ability Testing

Cervone, D. 2004. Personality assessment: tapping the social-cognitive architecture of personality, *Behaviour Therapy* 35: 113–29

Cheung, F., Cheung, S. F., Leung, K., Ward, C. and Leong, F. 2003. The English version of the Chinese Personality Assessment Inventory, *Journal of Cross-Cultural Psychology* 34: 433–52

Cheung, F. M., Leung, K., Fan, R. M., Song, W. Z., Zhang, J. X. and Zhang, J. P. 1996. Development of the Chinese Personality Assessment Inventory, *Journal of Cross-Cultural Psychology* 27: 181–99

Cloninger, C. R., Przybeck, T. R., Svrakic, D. M. and Wetzel, R. D. 1994. *The Temperament and Character Inventory (TCI): a guide to its development and use.* St. Louis, MO: C.R. Cloninger *et al.*

Conn, S. R. and Rieke, M. L. (eds.) 1994. *16PF Fifth Edition technical manual.* Champaign, IL: Institute for Personality and Ability Testing

Costa, P. T., Jr and McCrae, R. R. 1980. Still stable after all these years: personality as a key to some issues in adulthood and old age, in P. B. Baltes and O. G. Brim, Jr (eds.), *Life span development and behaviour*, vol. III, pp. 65–102. New York: Academic Press

Costa, P. T., Jr and McCrae, R. R. 1992a. *Revised NEO Personality Inventory (NEO-PI-R) and NEO Five-Factor Inventory (NEO-FFI) professional manual.* Odessa, FL: Psychological Assessment Resources

  1992b. Trait psychology comes of age, in T. B. Sonderegger (ed.), *Nebraska Symposium on motivation: psychology and aging*, pp. 169–204. Lincoln, NE: University of Nebraska Press

1995a. Domains and facets: hierarchical personality assessment using the Revised NEO Personality Inventory, *Journal of Personality Assessment* 64: 21–50

1995b. Primary traits of Eysenck's P-E-N system: three- and five-factor solutions, *Journal of Personality and Social Psychology* 69: 308–17

De Raad, B. and Peabody, D. 2005. Cross-culturally recurrent personality factors: analyses of three factors, *European Journal of Personality* 19: 451–74

De Raad, B. and Perugini, M. (eds.) 2002. *Big Five assessment*. Göttingen: Hogrefe and Huber Publishers

DeNeve, K. M. and Cooper, H. 1998. The happy personality: a meta-analysis of 137 personality traits and subjective well-being, *Psychological Bulletin* 124: 197–229

DeYoung, C. G. 2006. Higher-order factors of the Big Five in a multi-informant sample, *Journal of Personality and Social Psychology* 91: 1138–51

DeYoung, C. G., Peterson, J. B. and Higgins, D. M. 2002. Higher-order factors of the Big Five predict conformity: are there neuroses of health?, *Personality and Individual Differences* 33: 533–52

Digman, J. M. 1990. Personality structure: emergence of the Five-Factor Model, *Annual Review of Psychology* 41: 417–40

1997. Higher-order factors of the Big Five, *Journal of Personality and Social Psychology* 73: 1246–56

Digman, J. M. and Inouye, J. 1986. Further specification of the five robust factors of personality, *Journal of Personality and Social Psychology*, 50: 116–23

Eysenck, H. J. 1947. *Dimensions of personality*. London: Routledge and Kegan Paul

Eysenck, H. J., Barrett, P., Wilson, G. D. and Jackson, C. 1992. Primary trait measurement of the 21 components of the P-E-N system, *European Journal of Personality Assessment* 8: 109–17

Funder, D. C. 1980. On seeing ourselves as others see us: self-other agreement and discrepancy in personality ratings, *Journal of Personality* 48: 473–93

Goldberg, L. R. 1983. The magical number five, plus or minus two: Some considerations on the dimensionality of personality descriptors. Paper presented at a Research Seminar, Gerontology Research Center, Baltimore, MD, June 1983

Jang, K. L., Livesley, W. J., Ando, J., Yamagata, S., Suzuki, A., Angleitner, A., Ostendorf, F., Riemann, R. and Spinath, F. 2006. Behavioural genetics of the higher-order factors of the Big Five, *Personality and Individual Differences* 41: 261–72

John, O. P., Angleitner, A. and Ostendorf, F. 1988. The lexical approach to personality: a historical review of trait taxonomic research, *European Journal of Personality* 2: 171–203

Juni, S. 1996. Review of the Revised NEO Personality Inventory, in J. C. Conoley and J. C. Impara (eds.), *12th Mental Measurements Yearbook*, pp. 863–8. Lincoln: University of Nebraska Press

Kurtz, J. E. and Sherker, J. L. 2003. Relationship quality, trait similarity, and self-other agreement on personality traits in college roommates, *Journal of Personality* 71: 21–48

Lanning, K. 1994. Dimensionality of observer ratings on the California Adult Q-Set, *Journal of Personality and Social Psychology* 67: 151–60

Markon, K. E., Krueger, R. F. and Watson, D. 2005. Delineating the structure of normal and abnormal personality: an integrative hierarchical approach, *Journal of Personality and Social Psychology* 88: 139–57

McAdams, D. P. and Pals, J. L. 2006. A new Big Five: fundamental principles for an integrative science of personality, *American Psychologist* 61: 204–17

McCrae, R. R. 1982. Consensual validation of personality traits: evidence from self-reports and ratings, *Journal of Personality and Social Psychology* 43: 293–303

   1989. Why I advocate the Five-Factor Model: joint analyses of the NEO-PI and other instruments, in D. M. Buss and N. Cantor (eds.), *Personality psychology: recent trends and emerging directions*, pp. 237–45. New York: Springer-Verlag

   1990. Traits and trait names: how well is Openness represented in natural languages?, *European Journal of Personality* 4: 119–29

   1996. Social consequences of experiential Openness, *Psychological Bulletin* 120: 323–37

   2007. Aesthetic chills as a universal marker of Openness to Experience, *Motivation and Emotion* 31: 5–11

McCrae, R. R. and Allik, J. (eds.) 2002. *The Five-Factor Model of personality across cultures*. New York: Kluwer Academic/Plenum Publishers

McCrae, R. R. and Costa, P. T., Jr 1987. Validation of the Five-Factor Model of personality across instruments and observers, *Journal of Personality and Social Psychology* 52: 81–90

   1988. Age, personality, and the spontaneous self-concept, *Journal of Gerontology: Social Sciences* 43: S177–S185

   1989. Reinterpreting the Myers-Briggs Type Indicator from the perspective of the Five-Factor Model of personality, *Journal of Personality* 57: 17–40

   1995. Positive and negative valence within the Five-Factor Model, *Journal of Research in Personality* 29: 443–60

   2003. *Personality in adulthood: a Five-Factor Theory perspective*, 2nd edn. New York: Guilford

   2008a. Empirical and theoretical status of the Five-Factor Model of personality traits, in G. Boyle, G. Matthews and D. H. Saklofske (eds.), *Sage handbook of personality theory and assessment*, vol. I, pp. 273–94. Los Angeles, CA: Sage

   2008b. The Five-Factor Theory of personality, in O. P. John, R. W. Robins and L. A. Pervin (eds.), *Handbook of personality: theory and research*, 3rd edn, pp. 159–81. New York: Guilford Press

McCrae, R. R., Costa, P. T., Jr and Busch, C. M. 1986. Evaluating comprehensiveness in personality systems: the California Q-Set and the Five-Factor Model, *Journal of Personality* 54: 430–46

McCrae, R. R., Herbst, J. H. and Costa, P. T., Jr 2001. Effects of acquiescence on personality factor structures, in R. Riemann, F. Ostendorf and F. Spinath (eds.), *Personality and temperament: genetics, evolution, and structure*, pp. 217–31. Berlin: Pabst Science Publishers

McCrae, R. R., Terracciano, A. and 78 Members of the Personality Profiles of Cultures Project 2005. Universal features of personality traits from the observer's perspective: data from 50 cultures, *Journal of Personality and Social Psychology* 88: 547–61

Mischel, W. 1968. *Personality and assessment*. New York: Wiley

Myers, I. B. and McCaulley, M. H. 1985. *Manual: a guide to the development and use of the Myers-Briggs Type Indicator*. Palo Alto: Consulting Psychologists Press

Norman, W. T. 1963. Toward an adequate taxonomy of personality attributes: replicated factor structure in peer nomination personality ratings, *Journal of Abnormal and Social Psychology* 66: 574–83

Ozer, D. and Benet-Martínez, V. 2006. Personality and the prediction of consequential outcomes, *Annual Review of Psychology* 57: 401–21

Paunonen, S. V. and Ashton, M. C. 2001. Big Five factors and facets and the prediction of behaviour, *Journal of Personality and Social Psychology* 81: 524–39

Piedmont, R. L. 1999. Does spirituality represent the sixth factor of personality? Spiritual transcendence and the Five-Factor Model, *Journal of Personality* 67: 985–1013

Pilia, G., Chen, W.-M., Scuteri, A., Orrú, M., Albai, G., Deo, M. *et al.* 2006. Heritability of cardiovascular and personality traits in 6,148 Sardinians, *PLoS Genetics* 2: 1207–23

Riemann, R., Angleitner, A. and Strelau, J. 1997. Genetic and environmental influences on personality: a study of twins reared together using the self- and peer report NEO-FFI scales, *Journal of Personality* 65: 449–75

Roberts, B. W., Bogg, T., Walton, K. E., Chernyshenko, O. S. and Stark, S. E. 2004. A lexical investigation of the lower-order structure of Conscientiousness, *Journal of Research in Personality* 38: 164–78

Roberts, B. W., Chernyshenko, O. S., Stark, S. E. and Goldberg, L. R. 2005. The structure of Conscientiousness: an empirical investigation based on seven major person-ality questionnaires, *Personnel Psychology* 58: 103–39

Roberts, B. W. and DelVecchio, W. F. 2000. The rank-order consistency of personality traits from childhood to old age: a quantitative review of longitudinal studies, *Psychological Bulletin* 126: 3–25

Roberts, B. W., Walton, K. E. and Viechtbauer, W. 2006. Personality traits change in adult-hood: reply to Costa and McCrae (2006), *Psychological Bulletin* 132: 29–32

Schmitt, D. P., Allik, J., McCrae, R. R., Benet-Martínez, V., Alcalay, L., Ault, L. *et al.* 2007. The geographic distribution of Big Five personality traits: patterns and profiles of human self-description across 56 nations, *Journal of Cross-Cultural Psychology* 38: 173–212

Singer, J. A. 2005. *Personality and psychotherapy: treating the whole person.* New York: Guilford Press

Terracciano, A., Abdel-Khalak, A. M., Ádám, N., Adamovová, L., Ahn, C.-k., Ahn, H.-n. *et al.* 2005. National character does not reflect mean personality trait levels in 49 cultures, *Science* 310: 96–100

Tupes, E. C. and Christal, R. E. 1992. Recurrent personality factors based on trait ratings, *Journal of Personality* 60: 225–51 (original work published 1961)

Watson, D. and Clark, L. A. 1997. Extraversion and its positive emotional core, in R. Hogan, J. Johnson and S. R. Briggs (eds.), *Handbook of personality psychol-ogy*, pp. 767–93. New York: Academic Press

Widiger, T. A. and Costa, P. T., Jr 2002. Five-Factor Model personality disorder research, in P. T. Costa, Jr and T. A. Widiger (eds.), *Personality disorders and the Five-Factor Model of personality*, 2nd edn, pp. 59–87. Washington, DC: American Psychological Association

Widiger, T. A. and Trull, T. J. 2007. Plate tectonics in the classification of personality disorder: shifting to a dimensional model, *American Psychologist* 62: 71–83

Yamagata, S., Suzuki, A., Ando, J., Ono, Y., Kijima, N., Yoshimura, K., Ostendorf, F., Angleitner, A., Riemann, R., Spinath, F., Livesley, W. J. and Jang, K. L. 2006. Is the genetic structure of human personality universal? A cross-cultural twin study from North America, Europe, and Asia, *Journal of Personality and Social Psychology* 90: 987–98

10 Personality and intelligence

Phillip L. Ackerman

Typical behaviours versus maximal performance

In any discussion of personality and intelligence, it must be acknowledged that the traditional conditions for assessment of these two domains are quite different. On the one hand, as Cronbach (1949) noted, personality traits are assessed by asking an individual how he or she 'typically' behaves; that is, to assess a personality trait like Extraversion, the individual might be asked to agree or disagree with a statement like 'I enjoy going to parties'. In other words, the traditional goal of personality assessment is to determine how an individual would behave when there is little or no environmental press on his/her behaviour (i.e., weak situations). Part of the rationale that underlies this approach is that the variability in behaviour across different individuals is expected to be much more restricted when the environmental press or situation is a strong one. For example, if a group of randomly-selected individuals were each offered US $1,000,000 (a strong environmental press) to jump out of an airplane with a parachute (and a spare), one might reasonably predict that a substantial majority of the group would 'jump' at the opportunity. In contrast, if the same group of individuals were simply offered the chance to skydive without any monetary incentive (a weak environmental press), one might reasonably predict that there would be relatively few individuals who agree to jump, and furthermore, that an assessment of personality characteristics such as thrill-seeking might provide a good prediction of which individuals are more or less likely to jump. Therefore, the domain for personality is perhaps best thought of as a tendency to behave in a certain way, especially when there is only a weak environmental press.

Intellectual abilities, on the other hand, are traditionally assessed under 'maximal' performance conditions; that is, the individual being assessed is not asked to complete an ability test as if there were no environmental press. In fact, the key concept to most modern ability assessments is that the individual needs to either internalize or be provided with explicit instructions to treat the test as if performing well was a highly valued goal (Ackerman 1996). In selection contexts (whether for occupational or educational purposes), where the goal is to get the job or to be admitted into a desirable school, the environmental press for maximal performance is very strong – indeed, in some cases, the test situation may lead to anxiety or subjective distress because the press is so strong that it may distract the individual from performing his/her best. Ultimately the goal of ability assessment is not to determine how the individual behaves when there is no environmental press, but rather to determine the limits of the individual's performance if he/she is trying as hard as possible to succeed.

This difference between the traditional approaches to personality and intelligence assessments sets the stage for a mismatch of constructs, in a manner that would be expected to minimize the associations between the two constructs (see e.g., Wittmann and Süß 1999). However, there is no inherent reason why one cannot consider personality in a maximal performance context, such as when one asks whether individuals are capable of public speaking, regardless of whether they might prefer staying home with a cold compress over the eyes to getting up to talk in front of a large group of people (e.g., see Wallace 1966; Willerman, Turner and Peterson 1976). Similarly, intelligence can be considered in a typical behaviour context (see e.g., Ackerman 1994 for a discussion of this issue). In later discussion, a construct of 'typical intellectual engagement' will be discussed in some detail.

Personality disorders and normal personality

Before proceeding in this review, it is important to delineate the domain for the following discussion. Although there is substantial evidence that a wide array of personality disorders are associated with lower levels of assessed intellectual ability (see e.g., Wechsler 1997), the roots of those associations are complex and somewhat controversial. It is not entirely clear, for example, how much the documented impairments in measured intellectual abilities in such clinical populations are a consequence of the individual not being completely capable of understanding the goals of the testing situation or if the individual does not internalize the 'maximal performance' environmental press. Adequate treatment of these issues goes beyond the scope of this chapter. Thus, the focus of the review to follow is with the scope of normal personality, both in terms of the range of particular personality traits, and in terms of eliminating personality traits that are specifically associated with identification of psychopathology, such as clinical measures of affective disorders.

Level of analysis

Intellectual abilities

Another issue that must be addressed when considering the association between personality traits and intellectual abilities is the level of analysis. Modern intellectual ability theories (see e.g., Carroll 1993) represent intelligence in a hierarchical fashion, with a general intellectual ability (the most general construct) at the top of the hierarchy (Strata III), and somewhat narrower ability content as one moves down the hierarchy, as depicted in Figure 10.1. For example, at the second

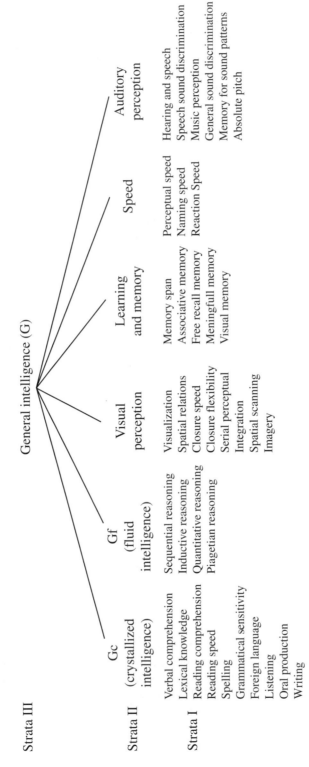

Figure 10.1. *An example of a hierarchical structure of intellectual abilities, derived from information in Carroll 1993. Strata III = third-order ability (general intelligence); Strata II = second-order abilities; Strata I = first-order abilities.*

level (Strata II), one would find crystallized intelligence (which includes verbal abilities), reasoning and visual perception (which includes spatial abilities). Crystallized abilities, in turn, can be further sub-divided into verbal comprehension, reading speed, writing, and so on (Strata I). The key to this structure of intelligence is the concept of 'positive manifold'; that is, all ability measures are positively correlated with one another. Typically, ability measures that have overlapping content (e.g., two different verbal ability tests) have a higher correlation with one another than do measures that do not have overlapping content (e.g., a verbal ability test and a math ability test).

Personality traits

In contrast to intellectual abilities, personality traits do not have the same kind of positive manifold, and as such, there is no equivalent 'general personality trait' that exists in parallel to general intelligence; though there are some personality traits (such as Positive Affect and Negative Affect, see Tellegen and Waller in press) that are more general than others, such as Aggression or Absorption, as illustrated in Figure 10.2. Although some researchers have attempted to reduce the structure of personality traits to a small number of factors, as shown at the top of Figure 10.2 (e.g., Costa and McCrae 1992; Eysenck 1994), the lack of a clear hierarchy of traits with positive manifold means that one must take account of the level of analysis when considering the most likely sources of overlap between personality traits and intellectual abilities. If a narrow personality trait is selected, it may not provide a suitable basis for mapping to a general intellectual ability construct, and if a more general personality trait is selected, it might have only a small relationship with a narrow construct of intellectual ability. Limiting the discussion of personality to a few or five general factors may lead to overlooking sources of potentially important overlap with intellectual abilities traits.

Ultimately, to answer the overarching question of 'what is the degree of association between personality and intelligence?', it will be necessary to consider the generality or specificity of the traits on each side of the equation. The following sections consider the nature of both broad and narrow constructs for personality and intelligence, to address whether there is any substantial association between them.

Most of the basis for explication of the specific associations between personality traits and intellectual abilities is drawn from a meta-analysis of 135 studies containing a total of roughly 2,000 separate correlations, by Ackerman and Heggestad (1997). The correlations from these studies were classified with a nineteen personality trait x ten ability trait framework, adjusted to take into account the reliability of the various instruments, weighted by sample size, and then averaged to provide an estimate of the underlying correlation between each of the unique personality trait × ability trait pairs. The discussion below summarizes some of the key findings from that meta-analysis.

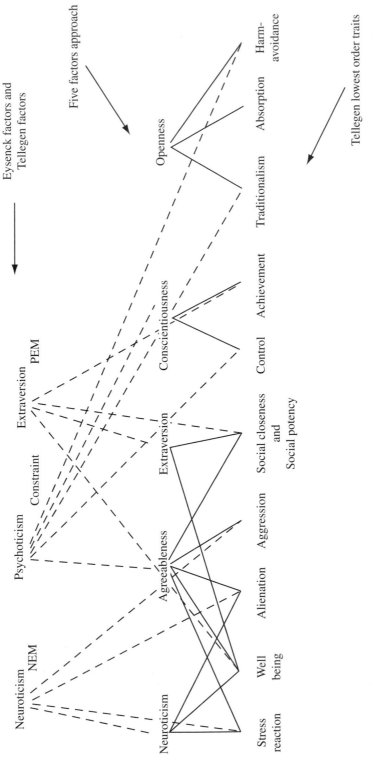

Figure 10.2. *Personality constructs and their relations. Lowest-order constructs (after Tellegen); five factor approach constructs (after Costa and McCrae, Digman, and others); highest-order constructs (after Eysenck, and Tellegen and Waller). Lines indicate both positive and negative correlational (not necessarily causal) relations. Solid lines indicate relations between Tellegen and five factor approach constructs. Dotted lines indicate relations between Tellegen and five factor approach constructs and Eysenck constructs. NEM = Negative Emotionality; PEM = Positive Emotionality.*

Personality traits with construct overlap with intelligence

When trying to address the specific association between personality and intelligence, it is most appropriate to first identify personality traits that share construct overlap with intelligence. One broad personality factor that fits into this framework roughly subsumes a construct variously referred to as Openness to Experience (Costa and McCrae 1992), Culture, Intellectance (e.g., Welsh 1975), and Intellectual Efficiency (Gough 1953). The specific content of assessment instruments for this construct differs across the various measures identified with these different investigators. However, the construct is often broadly framed in terms of a more sensitive orientation, and an interest in culture (e.g., art, theatre, music). Because this class of personality traits is more or less explicitly related to the construct of intelligence (indeed, a few of these personality assessment measures were developed and validated on the basis of intelligence correlations), it should come as no surprise that these measures are positively associated with measures of intellectual abilities, though to varying degrees. The correlations of this broad trait and intellectual abilities is not large, generally ranging from a negligible level (for narrow abilities) to about .30 for estimates of general intelligence.

A measure of typical intellectual engagement (TIE) (Goff and Ackerman 1992) also fits at least partly into this general framework. TIE is defined as the individual's preference toward or away from intellectual activities. Items on the TIE scale include statements such as 'I would enjoy hearing the details about discoveries in any field' and 'I read a great deal' and 'The main reason I studied in school was because it was required of me'. (The last item is reverse scored.) The authors of the TIE hypothesized that scores on the measure would correlate mainly with measures of accumulated knowledge (an ability called 'crystallized intelligence') and less so with measures of fluid intellectual abilities (e.g., deductive reasoning and quantitative reasoning), because the cumulative effects of orienting towards or away from intellectual challenges (e.g., by reading and engaging in discussions of intellectual content) would most likely be revealed in the individual's acquired knowledge about the world in general, and domain knowledge specifically (e.g., literature, arts, humanities, social sciences, etc.). In a series of studies (which were also included in the meta-analysis), the hypothesis of a positive association with crystallized intelligence was largely supported. An estimated correlation of .35 was found for TIE and crystallized intelligence, even though the estimated correlation with fluid intelligence was essentially zero. As with the broad construct of Openness, however, these associations should be considered in light of the fact that the personality measures to a greater or lesser degree were intended to capture some general or specific aspects of an individual's intellectuality.

Another personality trait that is explicitly related to intellectual ability constructs is that of 'Test Anxiety', which is associated with feelings of anxiety reported by individuals when confronted with test situations (both intellectual ability and more typical classroom tests). In an extensive review and meta-analysis of several hundred studies, Hembree (1988) determined that significant negative correlations were found between measures of test anxiety and measures of intelligence ($r = -.23$). However, it is important to note that measures of test anxiety also share a substantial degree of variance with measures of overall anxiety, a much broader personality trait. Hembree estimated the correlation between test anxiety and general anxiety to be $r = .56$.

Broad personality factor overlap

Other broad personality factors were not created with an eye towards their relationship with intelligence, per se. A broad factor of Neuroticism (which usually is considered to include broad Anxiety, Stress Reaction, Negative Affect or Negative Emotionality) shows consistent negative correlations with an array of both general and specific intellectual abilities (e.g., on the order of $r = -.15$ with general intelligence). Correlations between Neuroticism related traits and mathematical abilities are typically larger in magnitude than are correlations between Neuroticism and verbal abilities, though the differences are not large.

The associations between Extraversion and intellectual abilities, and Conscientiousness and intellectual abilities appear to be of a negligible magnitude. Small positive correlations between these traits and abilities are found as often as small negative correlations. In the aggregate, neither of these broad traits tend to have much of an association with either broad or narrow intellectual abilities. However, it is important to keep in mind a central issue with respect to these two personality traits that differs from either the intelligence-related personality constructs or even Neuroticism. That is, what one considers to be 'normal' or optimal is not found at one end of the continuum of the traits, but rather somewhere near the middle. An individual who is near the high end of either the Introvert or Extravert classification might be less well suited to normal everyday functioning than someone at the midpoint of the distribution (i.e., an 'Ambivert'). Similarly, someone who is nearly completely lacking in Conscientiousness may be just as ill-suited to everyday activities as someone who is so focused on structure, rules and perfection (the high end of Conscientiousness) that he or she is unable to complete many tasks.

Theorists who have asserted that individuals who are neither too high nor too low on such traits are optimally adjusted (see e.g., Robinson 1989; though cf., Matthews 1985 for a differing view), have hypothesized that linear correlations are not appropriate measures to assess the relationship between the personality traits and intellectual abilities. Instead, the hypothesized relationship may be an inverted-U shape, with lower abilities associated with the low and high extremes on the personality trait. Under these circumstances, standard meta-analytic techniques are not appropriate for discovering these relationships, partly because they are dependent on simple aggregation of correlations, but more importantly because each different measure of the trait and each different sample of individuals assessed will yield a different function describing the non-linear relationship between the particular personality trait and ability measure. A few individual studies have suggested that there may be some merit in the non-linear association between Extraversion and intellectual ability (see e.g., Wolf and Ackerman 2005 for a review), but there is insufficient cumulative evidence to be able to reach a conclusion about these associations.

Narrow personality factor overlap

The associations between personality trait measures that are narrower in scope than the broad five factors of Neuroticism, Extraversion, Openness, Conscientiousness and Agreeableness typically show modest correlations with measures of intellectual abilities, whether at the general or specific level. Need for Achievement (nAch) probably shows the most robust positive correlations among this group of personality traits, with correlations in the range of $r = .07$ to $.24$. Traits like Alienation, Aggression, Harm-Avoidance and Traditionalism all show small negative correlations with intellectual ability measures, ranging from negligible magnitude to about $r = -.15$.

In general, it can be said that the vast majority of these narrow personality traits do not correlate in a substantial way with traditional measures of intellectual ability. However, it must be kept in mind what was discussed earlier; that is, there is a fundamental mismatch between the context in which personality and intellectual abilities are assessed. Need for Achievement provides a good example for this kind of concern. One might reasonably expect that individuals who are high on nAch would seek out opportunities to excel in many different situations, including those that involve academic or intellectual activities. The strong environmental press of the traditional intelligence test (where everyone is strongly encouraged to do their best, or when there is a desired outcome contingent on test performance), would lead to an inference that individual differences in nAch do not much matter to test performance. One might expect more in the way of cumulative differences between those with high and low nAch, as would be assessed with measures of domain knowledge and skills (see e.g., Ackerman and Heggestad 1997), and the data are suggestive in supporting this proposition. There are, however, too few studies to date examining this particular inference to be able to draw any firm conclusions.

Indirect evidence for personality-intelligence associations

Longitudinal studies

There have been a few studies that have followed the same individuals from birth to adult ages that have examined both personality traits and intellectual growth and change. These older studies (e.g., Bayley 1968; Haan 1963; Kagan, Sontag, Baker and Nelson1958) have all indicated that increases in relative standing on broad measures of intellectual ability during development are associated with positively-oriented personality traits, such as nAch, higher levels of coping, and lower levels of defence mechanisms. In contrast, individuals who show declines in relative intelligence levels tested to be more hostile, negativistic and have higher levels of traditionalism. The samples of these studies were relatively small, and the participants may not be generally representative of the population at large, given their involvement in repeated annual testing over a long period of time. These results do provide support for the notion that positively oriented personality traits (wellbeing, positive affect, low levels of hostility, and the like) are positively associated with intellectual abilities, though the underlying causes of these associations may be quite idiosyncratic.

Personality and information processing task performance

A promising source of evidence for linkages between personality traits and intellectual abilities has been through the examination of information-processing task performance in the context of personality and other factors (e.g., motivation, time-of-day, caffeine, etc.). Information-processing tasks are typically narrower in scope than even the kinds of narrow intellectual abilities discussed earlier. Information-processing tasks usually involve participants comparing objects for similarities or differences, memorizing random digits, watching a computer display for specific signals over an extended period of time, and so on.

Although information-processing tasks are not exactly good indicators for intellectual ability, they are typically associated with abilities to some degree, and some information-processing tasks are components of broader intellectual ability measures. The evidence for personality trait associations with performance on information-processing tasks is much more piecemeal than is the corresponding list of correlations between personality trait measures and intellectual ability measures. The relationships between personality traits such as Impulsivity, Extraversion, Anxiety and nAch, and information-processing task performance also appear to be more complex. For example, Revelle and his colleagues (see e.g., Humphreys and Revelle 1984) have shown that there are interactions between the kinds of information-processing tasks participants are asked to do, the time-of-day in which they are performing the task, and even the amount of caffeine the participants have before the task. At a more general level, one key aspect of this framework is the notion that introverts tend to have a higher basal level of arousal than extraverts, and they tend to perform better early in the morning. When the task, situation or external influences (e.g., consumption of a caffeinated beverage) increase arousal, individuals respond with improved performance or poorer performance, depending on whether the arousal level has increased beyond an optimal level. The optimal level of arousal, according to Revelle and his colleagues, would be different for introverts and extraverts (see also the broader theory of Eysenck 1970). Several studies have provided good support for these hypothesized relationships (see e.g., Revelle 1995 for a review).

The difficulty in generalizing these findings from information-processing tasks to intellectual abilities is that many of the underlying effects are hypothesized to be curvilinear; for example, if introverts do better in the morning and extraverts do better in the afternoon, then assessments of abilities that are given at various times of the day might yield either positive, negative or zero correlations. And, to the degree that abilities are acquired over long periods of time, the expectation is that these various effects would essentially cancel one another out in the long run.

It may be that the ultimate effects of these personality-ability linkages would be found not so much in personality trait-ability correlations, but rather with the interests and orientations of the individuals. Introverts and extraverts, for example, may be more likely to be drawn to school topics or jobs that they are best suited to, and the associations with intellectual abilities would only be an indirect effect of the intellectual demands of the different school topics or jobs. There are, in fact, substantial correlations between some personality traits and vocational interest themes (such as Conscientiousness and conventional vocational interests; Extraversion and social and enterprising vocational interests, and Openness to Experience and artistic vocational interests; see Ackerman and Heggestad 1997).

Concluding remarks

This review of the relationships between personality traits and intellectual abilities indicates that there are many sources of overlap, but the largest associations are found for personality traits that have some theoretical linkage with intellectual abilities and/or the environmental press associated with ability testing (e.g., TIE, Intellectance, Culture, Test Anxiety, etc.). Other personality traits have pervasive, but relatively modest associations. Positive personality traits (e.g., Positive Affect, Absorption) tend to have small positive correlations with both broad and narrow intellectual abilities, while negative personality traits (e.g., Neuroticism, Anxiety, Aggression) tend to have negative correlations with intellectual abilities. Neuroticism and Anxiety in particular tend to have correlations with intellectual abilities that are larger in magnitude than do the positive personality traits. Personality traits where the ideal point is much closer to the middle of the scale (e.g., Introversion-Extraversion) tend to show negligible correlations with intellectual abilities, but these correlations may not be the most appropriate technique for discovering the underlying relationship (which may be non-linear in the sense that having a score at one extreme is just as much a negative indicator for ability as the other extreme).

In general, knowing an individual's standing on various personality traits is not going to inform one a great deal about the individual's standing on various intellectual ability measures, and vice versa. Rather, it is much more likely that because personality traits are tied to a concept of 'typical behaviours', the individual's standing on some personality traits will be much more diagnostic about whether an individual is going to approach or avoid situations with differing levels of intellectual demands. Similarly, an individual's personality traits should be expected to be more highly associated with what level of performance on intellectual tasks is accomplished when there is little or no environmental press for good performance.

One of the final issues to address in terms of the relations between personality traits and intelligence is the direction of causality. Correlational analyses, per se, such as the vast majority of the data reviewed here, do not allow one to pinpoint whether positive aspects of personality have positive influences on intellectual abilities (or negative aspects of personality have negative influences on intellectual abilities), whether high or low intellectual abilities lead to more positive or negative personality patterns, or whether some other variable or variables are responsible for the co-variation of personality traits and intellectual abilities. Some developmental theories (and the few longitudinal studies) provide some theoretical basis for particular patterns of personality (e.g., high levels of Test Anxiety leading to avoidance of situations that might involve evaluation apprehension) leading to lower intellectual abilities over long-term development (see e.g., Sarason 1960).

Other theories of adult intellectual development (e.g., Ackerman 1996) suggest that individuals will gravitate toward acquisition of knowledge and skills in domains that are most consonant with their personality patterns and a set of consistent vocational interests (e.g., individuals high on TIE tending to acquire more general knowledge about the world than individuals low on TIE; or individuals who are high on Extraversion being more likely to avoid academic settings in contrast to those individuals who are high on Introversion). Under this kind of framework, the most likely sources of personality-intelligence relations will be found with domain-specific knowledge (crystallized intelligence) rather than with more abstract reasoning sources of abilities. This theoretical framework is also more concordant with the notion that personality traits are most likely to be expressed in situations with relatively weak environmental press; that is, acquisition of a body of knowledge or skills is only possible with investment of effort over a long period of time. Even in the case of a high environmental press during ability testing, when most individuals are expected to put forth substantial effort, an individual cannot compensate for the lack of a long-term investment in knowledge acquisition. An individual can often improve his/her performance on a basic math test at least to some degree by increasing effort on the task, but if the individual does not know the law of supply and demand, who composed *Symphonie Fantastique*, who wrote *Gulliver's Travels*, or who invented the light bulb, increased effort at testing will have a much more limited effect on performance. Although there are not sufficient data yet to offer a strong assertion of the validity of these claims, early results are supportive of this general proposition (see e.g., Ackerman 2000; Beier and Ackerman 2001).

References

Ackerman, P. L. 1994. Intelligence, attention, and learning: maximal and typical perform-ance, in D. K. Detterman (ed.), *Current topics in human intelligence,* vol. IV, *Theories of intelligence,* pp. 1–27. Norwood, NJ: Ablex

1996. A theory of adult intellectual development: process, personality, interests, and knowledge, *Intelligence* 22: 229–59

2000. Domain-specific knowledge as the 'dark matter' of adult intelligence: gf/gc, personality and interest correlates, *Journal of Gerontology: Psychological Sciences* 55B(2): P69–P84

Ackerman, P. L. and Heggestad, E. D. 1997. Intelligence, personality, and interests: evi-dence for overlapping traits, *Psychological Bulletin* 121: 219–45

Bayley, N. 1968. Behavioural correlates of mental growth: birth to thirty-six years, *American Psychologist* 23: 1–17

Beier, M. E. and Ackerman, P. L. 2001. Current events knowledge in adults: an inves-tigation of age, intelligence and non-ability determinants, *Psychology and Aging* 16: 615–28

Carroll, J. B. 1993. *Human cognitive abilities: a survey of factor-analytic studies.* New York: Cambridge University Press

Costa, P. T., Jr and McCrae, R. R. 1992. Four ways five factors are basic, *Personality and Individual Differences* 13: 653–65

Cronbach, L. J. 1949. *Essentials of psychological testing.* New York: Harper

Eysenck, H. J. 1970. *The structure of human personality,* 3rd edn. London: Methuen

1994. Personality and intelligence: psychometric and experimental approaches, in R. J. Sternberg and P. Ruzgis (eds.). *Personality and intelligence,* pp. 3–31. New York: Cambridge University Press

Goff, M. and Ackerman, P. L. 1992. Personality-intelligence relations: assessing typical intellectual engagement, *Journal of Educational Psychology* 84: 537–52

Gough, H. G. 1953. A nonintellectual intelligence test, *Journal of Consulting Psychology* 17: 242–6

Haan, N. 1963. Proposed model of ego functioning: coping and defense mechanisms in relation to IQ change, *Psychological Monographs* (No. 571)

Hembree, R. 1988. Correlates, causes, effects, and treatment of test anxiety, *Review of Educational Research* 58: 47–77

Humphreys, M. S. and Revelle, W. 1984. Personality, motivation, and performance: a theory of the relationship between individual differences and information pro-cessing, *Psychological Review* 153–84

Kagan, J., Sontag, L. W., Baker, C. T. and Nelson, V. L. 1958. Personality and IQ change, *Journal of Abnormal and Social Psychology* 56: 261–6

Matthews, G. 1985. The effects of extraversion and arousal on intelligence test perform-ance, *British Journal of Psychology* 76: 479–93

Revelle, W. 1995. Personality processes, *Annual Review of Psychology* 46: 295–328

Robinson, D. L. 1989. The neurophysiological bases of high IQ, *International Journal of Neuroscience* 46: 209–34

Sarason, I. G. 1960. Empirical findings and theoretical problems in the use of anxiety scales, *Psychological Bulletin* 57: 403–15

Tellegen, A. T. and Waller, N. G. in press. Exploring personality through test construction: development of the Multidimensional Personality Questionnaire, in S. R. Briggs and J. M. Cheek (eds.), *Personality measures: development and evaluation*, vol. I. Greenwich, CT: JAI Press

Wallace, J. 1966. An abilities conception of personality: some implications for personality measurement, *American Psychologist* 21: 132–8

Wechsler, D. 1997. *WAIS-III/WMS-III technical manual*. San Antonio, TX: Psychological Corporation

Welsh, G. S. 1975. *Creativity and intelligence: a personality approach*. Chapel Hill, NC: Institute for Research in Social Science

Willerman, L., Turner, R. G. and Peterson, M. 1976. A comparison of the predictive validity of typical and maximal personality measures, *Journal of Research in Personality* 10: 482–92

Wittmann, W. W. and Süß, H. M. 1999. Investigating the paths between working memory, intelligence, knowledge, and complex problem-solving performances via Brunswik Symmetry, in P. L. Ackerman, P. C. Kyllonen and R. D. Roberts (eds.), *Learning and individual differences: process, trait, and content determinants*, pp. 77–108. Washington, DC: American Psychological Association

Wolf, M. B. and Ackerman, P. L. 2005. Extraversion and intelligence: a meta-analytic investigation, *Personality and Individual Differences* 39: 531–42

PART III

Development, Health and Personality Change

11 Childhood temperament

Mary K. Rothbart, Brad E. Sheese and
Elisabeth D. Conradt

Temperament in childhood

We have entered a period of rapid advance in understanding how individual differences develop. With flourishing support from temperament, neuroscience, genetics, developmental psychopathology and behavioural research in development, the twenty-first century promises to offer a unique new understanding of the pathways of individual growth. Temperament and personality represent two distinct but interrelated approaches to studying individuality. We have defined temperament as constitutionally based individual differences in emotional, motor and attentional reactivity and self-regulation, showing consistency across situations and relative stability over time (Rothbart and Derryberry 1981). The term 'constitutional' refers to links between temperament and biology. The term 'reactivity' refers to the latency, rise time, intensity and duration of the person's responsiveness to stimulation. The term 'self-regulation' refers to processes that serve to modulate reactivity; these include behavioural approach, withdrawal, inhibition and executive or effortful attention. Rutter (1987) describes personality as the cognitive and social elaborations of temperament as they are expressed in the course of social development. By defining personality and temperament in this way, it is possible to (a) specify the domain of temperamental study, (b) differentiate it from other aspects of personality, and (c) study how temperament and experience together 'grow' personality.

History of temperament

Temperament study has an ancient history: individual differences in temperament were described in the fourfold typology of Greco-Roman physicians, who linked temperamental characteristics to Hippocrates' model of the humoural constitution of the body (Diamond 1974). The term temperament itself derives from the Latin *temperamentum*, meaning a proportionate mixture, denoting the relative preponderance of one or more of the body humours. In Vindician's typology, the melancholic person, quiet and moody, was seen as having a predominance of black bile; the choleric person, touchy, aggressive and active, a predominance of yellow bile; the sanguine person, sociable and easygoing, a predominance of blood, and the phlegmatic person, calm and even-tempered, a predominance of phlegm. Ideas about the fourfold typology of temperament persisted throughout the Middle Ages and the Renaissance, and were found in the writings of Kant.

In modern times separate traditions of research on temperament have developed in Eastern Europe and the West. The Eastern European temperament tradition has its roots in Pavlov's (1951–52) observations of individual differences in his dogs' behaviour in the laboratory. Pavlov linked temperamental differences among the animals (which he argued would generalize to humans) to qualities of the central nervous system, including strength of neural activation. Subsequent work by Nebylitsyn (1972) and others adapted these ideas to the study of individual differences in human adults and, although Eastern European methods changed considerably, contemporary research remains heavily influenced by Pavlov's work (for a discussion see Strelau and Kaczmarek 2004).

In contrast to Eastern European research, early studies of temperament in the West were more focused on identifying regularities in the structure of individual differences through the use of psychometric techniques. For example, in 1908 Heymans and Wiersma asked 3,000 physicians to observe a family (parents and children) and to fill out a temperament/personality questionnaire on each family member. When the more than 2,500 responses were analyzed, three factors were identified: Activity (the tendency to act out what is thought or desired), Emotivity (the tendency to show body symptoms; to be fearful and shy), and Primary versus Secondary process (the tendency to react immediately or to act in a postponed and more organized way).

In Great Britain, factor analytic studies of individual differences in temperament and personality were carried out using adults' self-reports. Early work yielded factors of Introversion-Extraversion, emotional stability-instability (later called Neuroticism by Eysenck) and volition or will (see review by Rothbart 1989). Eysenck related individual differences in temperament to cortical excitation and inhibition and the functioning of the limbic system. Still later, Gray (1991) revised Eysenck's theory by positing individual differences in behavioural activation and inhibition, as well as tendencies to fight and flight. He also related these differences to an underlying neurophysiology. Gray's theory is currently one of the major psychobiological models of temperament, along with models put forward by Panksepp, Cloninger, DePue and Zuckerman (see Canli 2006). Temperament has also featured heavily in personality research in the United States. Allport used temperament in his trait-based theory of personality, and Cattell and Thurstone carried out early factor analytic research on temperament that would later be used in research on the Big Five personality factors in adults (Digman and Inouye 1986).

While temperament has played a central role in personality research over the last few decades, it has not always been a popular topic in developmental research (Rothbart and Bates 2006). Temperament was studied in early research on child development (see Escalona 1968; Shirley 1933), but by the mid-twentieth century, temperament was rarely discussed (see Rothbart 2004). Instead, social learning theories held sway, stressing the influence of reward and punishment in shaping behaviour, and cognitive developmental theories stressed the changes in thinking that occurred with children's development. More recently, however, a resurgence of interest in temperament has stemmed at least in part from the realization that the parent-child influence is bidirectional, not only from parent to child but also from child to parent. Children bring much to interactions with their families (Bell 1968), and a large part of what they bring is related to temperament. Temperament research has also been linked to recent advances in neuroscience, with individual differences in temperament providing links to genes and neural networks, as well as to social interaction.

Methods for assessing temperament

Current research on temperament in childhood makes use of parent report questionnaires, laboratory assessments of children's behavioural response to standardized stimuli, and observations of children's behaviour in the home or school. Measures of temperament have also been related to psychophysiological measures and measures of the developing personality. In temperament research, researchers have often been sceptical about using parents as informants about their children's behaviour (e.g., Kagan and Fox 2006). It has been felt that parental biases or lack of knowledge will yield measures that are invalid, with direct observation seen as a preferable method. However, considerable evidence indicates convergence between parent report and observational measures (Rothbart and Bates 2006). In addition, laboratory observations have their own limitations. For example, it is difficult to collect extensive information about children's emotionality in the laboratory when one emotional experience has carry-over effects that can influence another. Because temperament reflects dynamic interactions between affective and cognitive processes and there are limitations to both questionnaire and observational methods, multitrait multimethod approaches to temperament assessment have been advocated whenever feasible (see Rothbart and Sheese 2006, for a discussion).

Temperament structure

In the United States, contemporary psychometric approaches to describing temperament can be traced back to the research by Thomas and Chess (1977). In their work, parents of infants between the ages of two and six months were interviewed about their children's behaviour across a wide variety of situations. A content analysis of interview information on the first twenty-two infants yielded nine dimensions of temperamental variability: Activity Level, Rhythmicity, Approach-Withdrawal, Adaptability, Threshold, Intensity, Mood, Distractibility and Attention Span-Persistence. The goals of the New York Longitudinal Study (NYLS) were chiefly clinical, and no attempt was made to conceptually distinguish these dimensions from one another. Nevertheless, numerous parent-report questionnaires have been developed based on the NYLS nine dimensions.

As a result of more recent research, however, major revisions to the NYLS list have been proposed (Rothbart and Bates 2006). Both factor analytic research using NYLS items, and research following a more rational approach (e.g., Rothbart 1981), have identified a shorter list of temperament dimensions. In factor analytic studies of parent-reported temperament in childhood, three to four broad factors are frequently found (Rothbart and Bates 1998). The first of these is Surgency or Extraversion, which includes activity level, sociability, impulsivity and enjoyment of high intensity pleasure. The second is Negative Affectivity, including fear, anger/frustration, discomfort and sadness, and the third is Effortful Control, including attentional focusing and shifting, inhibitory control, perceptual sensitivity and low intensity pleasure.

In older children and adults, temperament is often studied through self-reports, allowing analysis of internally experienced feelings as well as behaviour. The self-report method is also frequently used in the study of adult personality. In adult research, highly differentiated scales assessing temperament have been factor analyzed, yielding factors differing slightly but significantly from those found in Big Five or Five-Factor Model research on adult personality (Evans and Rothbart 2007; Rothbart, Ahadi and Evans 2000).

In this research, six factors emerged. Three of these involve affect and are similar to those found in children and in the Big Five personality factors: temperamental Surgency or Extraversion, positively related to personality Extraversion; Fear, related to Neuroticism; and Frustration/Anger related negatively to Agreeableness. Two more attentionally based and self-regulative factors also emerged. Temperamental Effortful Control is related to Conscientiousness. In addition, temperamental Orienting to Low Intensity External and Internal Stimuli is related to personality Openness to Experience; finally, temperamental Affiliativeness is related to personality Agreeableness.

Using a large and demographically diverse group of subjects, Victor, Rothbart and Baker (2007) examined links between temperament and personality in childhood. Parent free-descriptions of their own children and items from existing temperament measures were combined to create a broadband measure of temperament and personality in three- to twelve-year-olds. This measure was refined and the underlying factor structure examined. Results supported a model that differs somewhat from the Big Five personality model and from existing temperament models, but also shows much commonality. Factors similar to previous work included Internalizing Negative Affectivity (related to fear and Neuroticism), Effortful Control, and Openness to Experience. Two factors combining aspects of Extraversion and Agreeableness were also found. These factors were Sociable Extraversion (including aspects such as positive emotionality and sociability) and Unsocialized Stimulation Seeking (including aspects such as anger/hostility, impulsivity and non-compliance/aggression). Activity level is common to both Sociable Extraversion and Unsocialized Stimulation Seeking, suggesting that these two pathways may develop out of Extraversion, one more affected by parental socialization than the other.

Thus, the structures emerging from temperament research (using basic psychological processes of affect, arousal and attention) and from personality research (using a lexical or personality scale analysis) are closely related (Evans and Rothbart 2007). Because temperamental individual differences are based on neural substrates and are present early in life, these findings suggest that early temperamental predispositions form a core or nucleus around which the later developing personality is built.

Development of temperament

Developmental research to date indicates that the reactive systems of emotion and orienting are in place before the development of executive effortful attention (Posner and Rothbart 2007; Rothbart and Bates 2006). In the newborn, individual differences in irritability and orienting can be observed along with variations in alertness, and by two to three months, infants demonstrate clear positive responses to stimulation. Early forms of what will later be called Extraversion or Surgency are present in the smiling and laughter and rapid approach of infants to a novel object by six months, and measures of approach tendencies and smiling and laughter at this early age predict children's extraverted tendencies at seven years (Rothbart, Derryberry and Hershey 2000). Throughout early development, children who are more extraverted also appear to express greater anger and frustration, and are more prone to externalizing disorders (Rothbart and Bates 2006; Rothbart and Posner 2006). Lengua, Wolchik, Sandler and West (2000) found that low positivity and high impulsivity in children, as well as high rejection and inconsistency in parenting, predicted conduct problems. High negative emotionality and low positive emotionality in children and rejection and inconsistency in parenting predicted child depression. Inconsistent discipline had a stronger association with conduct problems and depression for children who were high in impulsivity than children who were lower in impulsivity.

More surgent temperament may also be a protective factor in a highly stressful environment. For instance, children who are more sociable may attract warmth and responsiveness from adults, thereby protecting them from the effects of poor parenting (Werner 1985). Better social skills have also been shown for children whose temperament matched parental expectations and desires, who were more persistent, and whose parents were higher on warmth (Paterson and Sanson 1999).

When infants are four months of age, their distress and body movement to laboratory-presented stimulation predict later fear and behavioural inhibition. Positive affect and body movement, on the other hand, predict later surgency. By six months, it is also possible to predict seven-year-old children's temperamental frustration and anger by their infant anger responses to toys placed out of reach or behind a plastic barrier (Rothbart, Derryberry and Hershey 2000). Infants' behavioural approach tendencies are also measured at six months, and their latency to reach and grasp objects and their smiling and laughter also predict later surgency (Rothbart, Ahadi and Evans 2000).

The onset of fear or behavioural inhibition in the last quarter of the first year of life appears to work in opposition to the infant's approach tendencies, in that some infants who formerly rapidly approached novel objects are now slowed in their response to novel stimuli, and may not approach at all. They may also show distress to threatening objects (Rothbart 1988). As with approach tendencies, individual differences in fearful behavioural inhibition show considerable stability across childhood and even into adolescence (Kagan 1998). Longitudinal research has reported stability of fearful inhibition from two to eight years and from the pre-school period to age eighteen. It has also been related to later development of internalizing disorders such as anxiety (Fox 2004; Kagan, Snidman, Zentner and Peterson 1999). Morris *et al.* (2002) found that mothers' psychological control predicted internalizing behaviour and mothers' hostility predicted externalizing behaviour among children high in irritable distress. Another study found a relation between toddler inhibition with peers and reticence at age four, that was moderated by maternal behaviours. When mothers displayed more intrusive control or made derisive comments, a significant, positive correlation was found between toddler inhibition with peers at age two and social reticence at age four. No significant association was found between inhibition and reticence when mothers were not intrusive or derisive (Rubin, Burgess and Hastings 2002).

Fear-related control of behaviour can be seen in the early development of conscience (Kochanska 1997; Kochanska, Aksan and Joy 2007), with fearful children more likely to show early development of conscience. In addition, fearful children whose mothers use gentle discipline, presumably capitalizing on the child's tendency to experience anxious states, are especially likely to develop internalized conscience. Kochanska *et al.* (2007) have replicated findings by Kochanska (1997) that, among children who were less fearful at twenty-two months, a positive mother-child relationship rather than maternal discipline at twenty-two months predicted a stronger moral self at three years. More fearful infants also later tend to be empathetic and susceptible to guilt reactions in childhood (Rothbart, Ahadi and Hershey 1994). Thus, fear can be seen as a basic control mechanism that is important in socialization, with the pathway toward conscience altered depending on the fearfulness of the child.

Beyond the inhibitory control provided by fear, later developing Effortful Control makes a crucial contribution to socialization. Effortful Control is defined as the ability to inhibit a prepotent response and to activate a non-prepotent response, to detect errors and to engage in planning. As executive attention skills develop in the second or third years of life and beyond, individuals can voluntarily deploy their attention, allowing them to regulate their more reactive tendencies (Posner and Rothbart 2007; Ruff and Rothbart 1996). In situations where immediate approach is not allowed, for example, children can inhibit their actions directly and also limit their attention to the rewarding properties of a stimulus, resisting temptation and delaying gratification. Similarly, when faced with a threatening stimulus, children can control their fear by attending to environmental sources of safety as well as threat. In both of these examples, individual differences in attention allow children to suppress their more reactive tendencies, take in additional sources of information, plan more efficient strategies for coping and enact novel responses to stimulation.

Research indicates some stability of individual differences in effortful control during childhood. For example, the number of seconds delayed by pre-school children while waiting for rewards that are physically present predicts parents' reports of children's attentiveness and ability to concentrate as adolescents (Mischel, Shoda and Peake 1988). A lack of control in pre-school has also been identified as a potential marker for lifecourse persistent antisocial behaviour (Moffitt *et al.* 1996) and the inattentive-disorganized symptoms of ADHD (Nigg 2006).

Effortful Control positively predicts the development of prosocial behaviour and is related to low levels of behaviour problems (Eisenberg and Fabes 2006). In a study by Eisenberg and colleagues of a sample of four and a half to seven-year-olds, children rated as showing higher externalizing or internalizing behaviour displayed lower levels of Effortful Control. Rothbart and colleagues (Rothbart, Ahadi and Hershey 1994) found that mother-reported empathy and Effortful Control at age seven were also positively related. Kochanska (1997) has also found that children rated higher in Effortful Control exhibited more compliance during a clean-up task and identified more prosocial solutions to moral dilemmas, showing greater development of conscience.

Summary

Overall, research on the development of temperament is proceeding along several lines. First, research describing the emergence, structure and stability of temperament across time continues with an emphasis on multimethod designs that integrate questionnaire, observational and psychophysiological methods. Secondly, research has consistently shown links between temperament in infancy and early childhood behaviour, and subsequent psychopathology and social functioning. Thirdly, research is increasingly showing links between temperament and early cognition, including attention and theory of mind (Carlson and Moses 2001).

Biology of temperament

Recent research on the development of temperament has used behavioural genetic and molecular genetic methods to understand how genes and environment influence the individual developmental trajectories described by temperament constructs. We review several recent findings from the molecular genetics area here.

Gene by environment interactions

The relation between temperament and parenting has always been complicated by methodological problems. For instance, temperament and parenting associations may be attributed to genetic similarity between child and parent (Sanson, Hemphill and Smart 2004). In addition, because parenting seems to affect child behaviour very early in life, relations between parenting and temperament at older ages may reflect parenting history.

Recent research has begun to identify specific genetic contributions to temperament. For example, molecular genetic methods, most commonly used for examining how genes are related to adult personality, are now being applied to temperament in infancy and childhood. For example, Ebstein and colleagues (Auerbach, Geller, Letzer *et al.* 1999; Ebstein, Levine, Geller *et al.* 1998) found that DRD4, a gene linked to sensation-seeking in adults, was associated with orientation, range of state, regulation of state and motor organization in newborn infants. In addition, an interaction was found between DRD4 and 5-HTTLPR, a serotonin-related gene that has been linked to fear and distress in adults. 5HTTLPR was related to lower orientation scores, but only for neonates who did not have the long repeat variant of DRD4. For those who did, presence of the 5-HTTLPR short repeat genotype had no effect. In addition, two-month-old infants who shared both short repeat DRD4 alleles and short repeat 5-HTTLPR alleles showed the highest levels of negative emotionality and distress. At four years of age, children with the long DRD4 allele had higher scores on observed disruptive behaviour and parent-reported aggressive and delinquent behaviour (Schmidt and Fox 2002).

The candidate gene approach has also been used to examine how specific genes interact with life experiences to influence development (Caspi, McClay, Moffitt *et al.* 2002; Caspi, Sugden, Moffitt *et al.* 2003). Extending this work to examine genes and their interactions with early environments is an important new direction that will allow us to better understand the basic processes involved and suggest potential methods for intervention (Posner, Rothbart and Sheese 2007). For example, Rueda, Posner and Rothbart (2005) tested a five-day training programme designed to improve aspects of executive attention that have been linked to effortful control. EEG results indicated that the intervention was effective in producing more adult-like patterns of anterior cingulate activation. Combining this kind of targeted intervention with a molecular genetic approach, identifying children who would most likely benefit from it, may allow us to more effectively intervene to adjust the course of early temperament and attention development.

Temperament and neuroscience

Temperamental systems are evolutionarily conserved, and recent research has attempted to apply 'personality' constructs to studies of non-human primates. A review of individual differences identified in studies of twelve non-human species found support for factors of Extraversion, including energy and enthusiasm,

Neuroticism, including negative affectivity and nervousness, Agreeableness, including altruism and affection, and Openness, including originality and open-mindedness (Gosling and John 1999). These are seen in chimpanzee, monkey, hyena, dog and cat. Several species did not give evidence of attentional Openness, however, and evidence for individual differences in Conscientiousness was reported only in chimpanzees.

It seems likely that these studies, although called personality, are getting at the evolutionarily conserved temperamental systems studied in human temperament. In addition, since not all capacities appear to be shared across species, especially conscientiousness (highly related to Effortful Control), this allows us to recognize important phylogenetic *differences* in temperament. For example, the capacity for Effortful Control, when linked with language, provides opportunities for self-regulation of reactive systems in humans that are not present in other species.

Advances in neuroscience imaging technology and our knowledge of brain networks underlying the emotions and attention have yielded important information for students of temperament and development. There is now detailed knowledge of networks subserving fear, Extraversion/surgency, reactive orienting and Effortful Control in adults and adolescents (Posner and Rothbart 2007; Whittle, Allen, Lubman and Yucel 2006). Because imaging studies allow researchers to identify tasks activating these brain networks, it is also possible to adapt the tasks to children of different ages, to study the development of temperamental systems (Posner and Raichle 1994). Marker tasks have been used in the study of the development of Effortful Control, but it is likely that they can also be used to assess more reactive individual differences. In research to date, marker tasks of executive attention in the laboratory are positively related to parents' reports of Effortful Control, that is, children's ability to control attention and emotion (Rothbart and Rueda 2005).

Psychophysiological correlates of temperament have also been studied. Children who are more behaviourally inhibited exhibit elevated cortisol levels, enhanced startle responses, and larger increases in autonomic response to anxiety-provoking situations (Bornstein and Suess 2000; Henderson, Marshall, Fox and Rubin 2004). They also exhibit lower levels of baseline Respiratory Sinus Arrhythmia (RSA), associated with less autonomic flexibility and a decreased ability in physiological self-regulation. Fear is also associated with elevations in cortisol when the child is in less optimal care, but no such association is found when the child's care-giver is sensitive and responsive (Gunnar and Donzella 2002).

It is interesting that surgent children starting pre-school, competent and well-liked by their peers, are the children who show greater elevations of cortisol in the new setting (Gunnar, Trout, de Haan *et al.* 1997). In contrast, children who showed high cortisol reactivity later in the school year were more affectively negative and solitary. Gunnar *et al.* speculated that more fearful children may be more likely to be watching on the sidelines at first rather than jumping in to interact with other children. Thus, it appears that behavioural strategies involving self-regulation, such as behavioural inhibition (an aspect of fear), effortful control and attention, may aid in controlling and guiding temperamental approach.

Future directions

Temperament is a basic integrative construct within psychology, and improvements in temperament concepts and methods will be critical to advances in understanding the development of personality. One goal will be increased understanding of the basic processes of temperament, including components of extraversion, surgency, fear, frustration, affiliation and attention, and how they develop. Many advances will come from areas of affective and cognitive neuroscience, where much progress has been made in understanding the emotions and attention. Progress in the study of brain structure and its relation to molecular genetics will also be of great importance.

We also hope to continue to further develop the theory of temperament and its links to personality. Because temperament encompasses organized systems of emotion and attention, rather than separate traits, studies of relationships among temperament variables allow a much richer view of personality and development. Studies of developmental pathways between early temperament and later personality outcomes will be complex, because childhood and adult individuality unfolds in the context of social relationships, and continuity and change cannot be understood without considering the impact of social experience. To understand developmental pathways, it will be necessary to disentangle complex interactions among early temperament predispositions, socialization processes, relationships and culture, but we are already making progress toward this goal.

An important guiding principle is that temperamentally different children may arrive at similar or equivalent outcomes via different pathways, and pathways of temperamentally different children may converge over development. For example, Kochanska (1997) found that fearful toddlers whose parents used gentle discipline, and fearless toddlers whose parents capitalized on positive motivation in a close relationship, attained conscience following different paths. Van den Boom (1994) found that the links between newborn distress proneness and later secure attachment could be broken when parents were taught to soothe and play with their babies. We expect that these studies will serve as a model for stimulating future work on temperament and development.

References

Auerbach, J., Geller, V., Letzer, S., Shinwell, E., Levine, J., Belmaker, R. H. and Ebstein, R. P. 1999. Dopamine D4 receptor (D4DR) and serotonin transporter promoter (5-HTTLPR) polymorphisms in the determination of temperament in 2-month-old infants, *Molecular Psychiatry* 4: 369–74

Bell, R. Q. 1968. A reinterpretation of the direction of effects in studies of socialization, *Psychological Review* 75: 81–95

Bornstein, M. H. and Suess, P. E. 2000. Physiological self-regulation and information processing in infancy: cardiac vagal tone and habituation, *Child Development* 71: 273–87

Canli, T. (ed.) 2006. *The biology of personality and individual differences*. New York: Guilford Press

Carlson, S. M. and Moses, L. J. 2001. Individual differences in inhibitory control and children's theory of mind, *Child Development* 72: 1032–53

Caspi, A., McClay, J., Moffitt, T. E., Mill, J., Martin, J., Craig, I. W., Taylor, A. and Poulton, R. 2002. Role of genotype in the cycle of violence in maltreated children, *Science* 297: 851–4

Caspi, A., Sugden, K., Moffitt, T. E., Taylor, A., Craig, I. W., Harrington, H., McClay, J., Mill, J., Martin, J., Braithwaite, A. and Poulton, R. 2003. Influence of life stress on depression: moderation by a polymorphism in the 5-HTT gene, *Science* 301: 386–9

Diamond, S. 1974. *The roots of psychology: a sourcebook in the history of ideas*. New York: Basic Books

Digman, J. M. and Inouye, J. 1986. Further specification of the five robust factors of personality, *Journal of Personality and Social Psychology* 50: 116–23

Ebstein, R. P., Levine, J., Geller, V., Auerbach, J., Gritsenko, I. and Belmaker, R. H. 1998. Dopamine D4 receptor and serotonin transporter promoter in the determination of neonatal temperament, *Molecular Psychiatry* 3: 238–46

Eisenberg, N. and Fabes, R. A. 2006. Emotion regulation and children's socioemotional competence, in L. Balter and C. S. Tamis-LeMonda (eds.), *Child psychology: a handbook of contemporary issues*, 2nd edn, pp. 357–81. New York: Psychology Press

Escalona, S. K. 1968. *The roots of individuality: normal patterns of development in infancy*. Chicago: Aldine

Evans, D. and Rothbart, M. K. 2007. Developing a model for adult temperament, *Journal of Research in Personality* 41: 868–8

Fox, N. A. 2004. Temperament and early experience form social behaviour, in S. G. Kaler and O. M. Rennert (eds.), *Understanding and optimizing human development: from cells to patients to populations*, 1st edn, pp. 171–8. New York: New York Academy of Sciences

Gosling, S. D. and John, O. P. 1999. Personality dimensions in nonhuman animals: a cross-species review, *Current Directions in Psychological Science* 8: 69–75

Gray, J. A. 1991. The neuropsychology of temperament, in J. Strelau and A. P. Angleitner (eds.), *Explorations in temperament*, pp. 105–28. New York: Plenum

Gunnar, M. R. and Donzella, B. 2002. Social regulation of the cortisol levels in early human development, *Psychoneuroendocrinology* 27: 199–220

Gunnar, M. R., Trout, K., de Haan, M., Pierce, S. and Stansbury, K. 1997. Temperament, social competence, and adrenocortical activity in preschoolers, *Developmental Psychobiology* 31: 65–85

Henderson, H. A., Marshall, P. J., Fox, N. A. and Rubin, K. H. 2004. Psychophysiological and behavioural evidence for varying forms and functions of nonsocial behaviour in preschoolers, *Child Development* 75: 251–63

Heymans G. and Wiersma, E. D. 1908. Beitrage zur speziellen Psychology auf Grund einer Messenuntersuchungung, *Zeitschrift fur Psychology* 49: 414–39

Kagan, J. 1998. Biology and the child, in W. Damon (Series ed.) and N. Eisenberg (Vol. ed.), *Handbook of child psychology,* vol. III, *Social, emotional and personality development*, 5th edn, pp. 177–235. New York: Wiley

Kagan, J. and Fox, N. A. 2006. Biology, culture, and temperamental biases, in W. Damon and R. Lerner (Series eds.) and N. Eisenberg (Vol. ed.), *Handbook of child psychology,* vol. III, *Social, emotional, and personality development*, 6th edn, pp. 167–225. Hoboken, NJ: Wiley

Kagan, J., Snidman, N., Zentner, M. and Peterson, E. 1999. Infant temperament and anxious symptoms in school age children, *Development and Psychopathology* 11: 209–24

Kochanska, G. 1997. Multiple pathways to conscience for children with different temperaments: from toddlerhood to age 5, *Developmental Psychology* 33: 228–40

Kochanska, G., Aksan, N. and Joy M. E. 2007. Children's fearfulness as a moderator of parenting in early socialization: two longitudinal studies, *Developmental Psychology* 43: 222–37

Lengua, L. J., Wolchik, S. A., Sandler, I. N. and West, S. G. 2000. The additive and interactive effects of parenting and temperament in predicting adjustment problems of children of divorce, *Journal of Clinical Child Psychology* 29: 232–44

Mischel, W., Shoda, Y. and Peake, P. K. 1988. The nature of adolescent competencies predicted by preschool delay of gratification, *Journal of Personality and Social Psychology* 54: 6687–96

Moffitt, T. E., Caspi, A., Dickson, N., Silva, P. and Stanton, W. 1996. Childhood-onset versus adolescent-onset antisocial conduct problems in males: natural history from ages 3 to 18 years, *Development and Psychopathology* 8: 399–424

Morris, A. S., Silk, J. S., Steinberg, L., Sessa, F. M., Avenevoli, S. and Essex, M. J. 2002. Temperamental vulnerability and negative parenting as interacting predictors of child adjustment, *Journal of Marriage and Family* 64: 461–71

Nebylitsyn, V. D. 1972. *Fundamental properties of the human nervous system*. New York: Plenum

Nigg, J. T. 2006. Temperament and developmental psychopathology, *Journal of Child Psychology and Psychiatry* 47: 395–422

Paterson, G. and Sanson, A. 1999. The association of behavioural adjustment to temperament, parenting and family characteristics among 5-year-old children, *Social Development* 8: 293–309

Pavlov, I. P. 1951–52. *Complete works*, 2nd edn. Moscow: SSSR Academy of Sciences

Posner, M. I. and Raichle, M. E. 1994. *Images of mind*. New York: Scientific American Library

Posner, M. I. and Rothbart, M. K. 2007. *Educating the human brain*. Washington, DC: American Psychological Association

Posner, M. I., Rothbart, M. K. and Sheese, B. E. 2007. Attention genes, *Developmental Science* 10: 24–9

Rothbart, M. K. 1981. Measurement of temperament in infancy, *Child Development* 52: 569–78

　　1988. Temperament and the development of inhibited approach, *Child Development* 59: 1241–50

1989. Biological processes of temperament, in G. Kohnstamm, J. Bates and M. K. Rothbart (eds.), *Temperament in childhood*, pp. 77–110. Chichester: Wiley

2004. Temperament and the pursuit of an integrated developmental psychology, *Merrill-Palmer Quarterly* 50: 492–505

Rothbart, M. K., Ahadi, S. A. and Evans, D. E. 2000. Temperament and personality: origins and outcomes, *Journal of Personality and Social Psychology* 78: 122–35

Rothbart, M. K., Ahadi, S. A. and Hershey, K. L. 1994. Temperament and social behaviour in childhood, *Merrill-Palmer Quarterly* 40: 21–39

Rothbart, M. K. and Bates, J. E. 1998. Temperament, in W. Damon (Series ed.) and N. Eisenberg (Vol. ed.), *Handbook of child psychology*, Vol. III, *Social, emotional, and personality development*, 5th edn, pp. 105–76. New York: Wiley

2006. Temperament in children's development, in W. Damon and R. Lerner (Series eds.) and N. Eisenberg (Vol. ed.), *Handbook of child psychology*, vol. III, *Social, emotional, and personality development*, 6th edn, pp. 99–166. Hoboken, NJ: Wiley

Rothbart, M. K. and Derryberry, D. 1981. Development of individual differences in temperament, in M. E. Lamb and A. L. Brown (eds.), *Advances in developmental psychology*, vol. I, pp. 37–86. Hillsdale, NJ: Erlbaum

Rothbart, M. K., Derryberry, D. and Hershey, K. 2000. Stability of temperament in childhood: laboratory infant assessment to parent report at seven years, in V. J. Molfese and D. L. Molfese (eds.), *Temperament and personality development across the life span*, pp. 85–119. Hillsdale, NJ: Erlbaum

Rothbart, M. K. and Posner, M. I. 2006. Temperament, attention, and developmental psychopathology, in D. Cicchetti and D. Cohen eds., *Developmental psychopathology*, vol. II, *Developmental neuroscience*, 2nd edn, pp. 465–501. Hoboken, NJ: Wiley

Rothbart, M. K. and Rueda, M. R. 2005. The development of effortful control, in U. Mayr, E. Awh and S. W. Keele (eds.), *Developing individuality in the human brain: a tribute to Michael I. Posner*, pp. 167–88. Washington, DC: American Psychological Association

Rothbart, M. K. and Sheese, B. E. 2006. Temperament and emotion-regulation, in J. Gross (ed.), *Handbook of emotion-regulation*, pp. 331–50. New York: Guilford Press

Rubin, K. H., Burgess, K. B. and Hastings, P. D. 2002. Stability and social-behavioural consequences of toddlers' inhibited temperament and parenting behaviours, *Child Development* 73: 483–95

Rueda, M. R., Posner, M. I. and Rothbart, M. K. 2005. The development of executive attention: contributions to the emergence of self-regulation, *Developmental Neuropsychology* 28: 573–94

Ruff, H. A. and Rothbart, M. K. 1996. *Attention in early development: themes and variations*. New York: Oxford University Press

Rutter, M. 1987. Continuities and discontinuities from infancy, in J. D. Osofsky (ed.), *Handbook of infant development*, pp. 1150–98. New York: Wiley

Sanson, A., Hemphill, S. A. and Smart, D. 2004. Connections between temperament and social development: a review, *Social Development* 13: 142–70

Schmidt, L. A. and Fox, N. A. 2002. Molecular genetics of temperamental differences in children, in J. Benjamin, R. P. Ebstein and R. H. Belmaker (eds.), *Molecular genetics and the human personality*, pp. 245–55. Washington, DC: American Psychiatric Publishing

Shirley, M. M. 1933. *The first two years: a study of 25 babies*. Minneapolis, MN: University of Minnesota Press

Strelau, J. and Kaczmarek, M. 2004. Warsaw studies on sensation seeking, in R. M. Stelmack (ed.), *On the psychobiology of personality: essays in honor of Marvin Zuckerman*, pp. 29–45. New York: Elsevier

Thomas, A. and Chess, S. 1977. *Temperament and development*. New York: Brunner/ Mazel

Van den Boom, D. C. 1994. The influence of temperament and mothering on attachment and exploration, *Child Development* 65: 1457–77

Victor, J. B., Rothbart, M. K. and Baker, S. R. 2007. *Temperamental components of the developing personality*. Manuscript submitted for publication

Werner, E. E. 1985. Resilient offspring of alcoholics: a longitudinal study from birth to age 18, *Journal of Studies on Alcohol* 47: 34–40

Whittle, S., Allen, N. B., Lubman, D. and Yucel, M. 2006. The neuroanatomical basis of affective temperament: towards a better understanding of psychopathology, *Neuroscience and Biobehavioural Reviews* 30: 511–25

12 The development of personality across the lifespan

M. Brent Donnellan and Richard W. Robins

[E]very personality develops continually from the stage of infancy until death, and throughout this span it persists even though it changes.

Gordon W. Allport

Questions about the development of personality have captured attention and generated controversy for centuries. For example, Aristotle devoted three chapters of Book II of his *Rhetoric* to describing the characteristics of individuals at different phases of the lifespan. Aristotle's student, Theophrastus, created poignant character sketches of thirty personality types (e.g., 'The Surly Man' and 'The Man of Petty Ambition') and noted interesting continuities and discontinuities in these characters over time and across contexts (e.g., at home versus at the public baths). These abiding concerns about the consistency of personality have continued to contemporary times, as vigorous debates rage over the degree to which personality changes over time and whether these changes stem primarily from biological maturation or social experiences (e.g., Costa and McCrae 2006; Roberts, Walton and Viechtbauer 2006). To be sure, the field of personality development is one of the most active, contentious and intellectually vibrant areas of personality psychology.

We focus this chapter on the development of basic traits rather than other important personality constructs such as goals, motives and life stories, given space constraints. We begin by drawing on the well known 'Big Five' personality taxonomy to describe the basic trait domains that can be studied across the lifespan. We then describe the major ways that researchers conceptualize questions about stability and change and summarize what is known about stability and change in the Big Five. Finally, we outline some of the processes that promote personality stability and change across the lifespan.

Using the Big Five to organize the study of personality development

There is consensus that most personality traits can be organized into five broad domains (i.e., the 'Big Five'): Extraversion, Agreeableness,

We thank Richard E. Lucas, Joel T. Nigg and Samuel Putnam for helpful comments on sections of this chapter. Support for the preparation of this article was provided by National Institute on Aging grant 022057 to the second author.

Conscientiousness, Neuroticism and Openness to Experience (e.g., Goldberg 1993; John, Naumann and Soto 2008; but see Ashton and Lee 2007; Block 1995). These trait domains are evident in adolescents (John, Caspi, Robins *et al.* 1994; McCrae, Costa, Terracciano *et al.* 2002) and even in children as young as five years of age (e.g., De Fruyt, Bartels, Van Leeuwen *et al.* 2006; Measelle, John, Ablow *et al.* 2005). There is now growing recognition that the Big Five can provide a coherent framework for organizing the dimensions of temperament studied in very young children (e.g., Caspi and Shiner 2006). For example, the major dimensions of childhood temperament identified by Putnam, Ellis and Rothbart (2001) closely correspond with all of the Big Five except for Openness to Experience. This is not surprising because Openness seems fairly difficult to assess in very young children and it may not become developmentally relevant until middle childhood or even adolescence (see e.g., Caspi and Shiner 2006; John, Caspi, Robins *et al.* 1994).

The degree of correspondence between child temperament and adult personality dimensions is consistent with Allport's (1937) proposal that personality traits are 'neuropsychic entities', and his observation that 'behind all confusion of terms … there are none the less *bona fide* mental structures in each personality that account for the consistency of its behaviour' (1937, p. 289). In keeping with Allport's convictions about the biological basis of traits, there has been considerable interest in identifying the neurobehavioural systems that underlie the basic dimensions of personality (Depue and Lenzenweger 2005; Zuckerman 2005).

Extraversion seems to map onto the biological system governing incentive motivation and approach behaviour (e.g., Depue and Collins 1999; Lucas, Diener, Grob *et al.* 2000; Watson, Wiese, Vaidya and Tellegen 1999). Neuroticism seems to correspond well to the biological system governing withdrawal behaviour, anxiety and the detection of threat (e.g., Gray 1987; Watson, Wiese, Vaidya and Tellegen 1999; but see Smillie, Pickering and Jackson 2006, for an updated treatment of Gray's theory). There is emerging evidence that a separate system governing the enjoyment of social bonds and affection may be linked with aspects of personality captured by Agreeableness (i.e., the affiliative system; see Depue and Morrone-Strupinsky 2005). Finally, aspects of Conscientiousness, and particularly the Effortful Control aspects of this domain, have been linked to systems associated with executive control involving regions of the prefrontal cortex (e.g., Nigg 2000). In contrast to the other four Big Five domains, the biological underpinnings of Openness are not as well understood; however, aspects of Openness related to sensation-seeking and exploratory behaviour might also be related to the approach system.

In sum, there is compelling evidence that the fundamental features of the Big Five are rooted in neurobiological systems that seem to be present in rudimentary forms in young children. This downward extension of the Big Five helps to curb the jangle fallacy (i.e., if two traits have different names then they must be different; see e.g., Block 1995) and focuses attention on a core set of trait domains that are broadly relevant for adapting to the challenges that face individuals throughout the lifespan (see e.g., Ozer and Benet-Martínez 2006; Roberts,

Kuncel, Shiner *et al.* 2007). Consequently, we focus on the Big Five domains for the rest of this chapter. Nonetheless, we emphasize that the potential neurobiological bases of the Big Five in no way precludes the possibility that personality traits are affected by life experiences and change over time.

Defining types of stability and change

How stable is personality? Do shy children become shy adults? Do ill-tempered adolescents become ill-tempered adults? There is no simple answer to these types of questions because there are different ways of conceptualizing and measuring stability and change (e.g., Caspi and Shiner 2006; Roberts and Pomerantz 2004). The broadest distinction is between homotypic and heterotypic stability (or continuity). Homotypic stability refers to the stability of the exact same thoughts, feelings and behaviours across time. In contrast, heterotypic stability refers to the stability of personality traits that are theorized to have different manifestations at different ages. Heterotypic stability can only be understood with reference to a theory that specifies how the same trait 'looks' (i.e., manifests itself) at different ages and it broadly refers to the degree of personality coherence across development. At issue is the fact that many salient indicators of underlying personality traits seem to change with development. For example, superficial behaviours manifested by a highly aggressive toddler bear little resemblance to those manifested by a highly aggressive adult. One bites and throws toys whereas the other uses guns and knives to rob and steal; yet both sets of behaviour are assumed to reflect the same underlying trait.

What is the evidence for heterotypic continuity? Longitudinal studies covering long periods of the lifespan provide important evidence of personality coherence. For example, Caspi, Moffitt, Newman and Silva (1996) found that children who were rated as being irritable and impulsive by clinical examiners at age three were more likely to be dependent on alcohol and to have been convicted of a violent crime by age twenty-one. The fact that there is an association between the impressions that pre-schoolers create on adult examiners and problems with alcohol and violence during early adulthood is impressive evidence for the coherence of traits related to antisocial behaviour. A related example comes from research on delay of gratification (Mischel, Shoda and Peake 1988). Mischel *et al.* found that the amount of time pre-schoolers could delay gratification in a laboratory task predicted academic and social competence ten years later when participants were adolescents. The superficial manifestations of self-control are likely to be quite different in pre-schoolers and adolescents; however, the underlying psychological characteristic of being able to forgo immediate impulses to obtain desired long-term outcomes seems to have an appreciable degree of consistency across development.

In comparison to heterotypic stability, the assessment of homotypic stability is less conceptual and more statistical. Homotypic stability concerns the evaluation of different kinds of change using the exact same measure of personality across time or across age groups. Four types of stability and change are typically examined: (a) absolute stability (i.e., mean-level stability), (b) differential stability (i.e., rank-order consistency), (c) structural stability, and (d) ipsative stability.

Absolute stability refers to consistency in the amount, degree or intensity of a given trait. Absolute stability can be examined longitudinally by following the same sample of individuals across a meaningful interval, such as the transition from adolescence to adulthood, or cross-sectionally by comparing mean levels of traits across different age groups. Assuming that birth cohort differences are not an issue, cross-sectional differences in means can provide insight into the personality characteristics of the so-called 'typical' person at different ages.

Research on age differences in mean-levels are often considered investigations of *normative* personality differences because they tell researchers something about broad developmental trends. The one caveat is that average trends may obscure absolute changes that are evident at the level of the individual, so there is increasing interest in examining how individuals change over time, either by modelling individual change trajectories (e.g., Mroczek 2007) or by identifying the percentage of individuals who conform to or deviate from the sample-level trend (e.g., Robins, Fraley, Roberts and Trzesniewski 2001). To be sure, a small absolute increase in a trait could indicate that the entire population is increasing a little bit, which is the most common interpretation of mean-level changes. However, other patterns of individual change can create a small mean change. For example, a small average increase could occur if some individuals are increasing substantially, some are increasing only slightly, and some are actually decreasing.

Differential stability reflects the degree to which the relative ordering of individuals on a given trait is consistent over time. This type of stability is theoretically and statistically distinct from absolute stability. For example, a population could increase substantially on a trait but the rank ordering of individuals would be maintained if everyone increased by exactly the same amount. Conversely, the rank ordering of individuals could change substantially over time but without any aggregate increases or decreases (e.g., if the number of people who decreased offset the number of people who increased). Changes in rank ordering result from maturational or experiential factors that affect people in relatively unique ways, and from the developmentally less interesting phenomenon of measurement error. Differential stability is typically investigated by calculating the correlation between the same personality measures administered across an interval of a sufficient length to be interesting (e.g., years in adulthood, perhaps months in childhood).

Structural stability refers to similarity over time in patterns of co-variation among traits, or items on a personality scale. For example, one can use structural equation modelling techniques to test whether the intercorrelations among the Big Five domains are the same at the beginning versus the end of college (Robins, Fraley, Roberts and Trzesniewski 2001). Likewise, investigations of structural stability often include the testing of measurement invariance (e.g., Allemand, Zimprich and Hertzog 2007). This process establishes that the same attribute is being measured in the same way on different occasions (e.g., Horn and McArdle 1992) and is considered a prerequisite for making meaningful inferences about absolute stability. The concern is that if measures change psychometric properties over time then comparisons 'may be tantamount to comparing apples and spark plugs' (Vandenberg and Lance 2000, p. 9). Despite the simplicity of this idea, methodologists have yet to determine precisely when slight differences in psychometric properties render comparisons meaningless (Millsap and Meredith 2007).

A final kind of stability, *ipsative* stability, refers to continuity in the patterning of personality characteristics within a person and how well the relative salience (or extremity) of these attributes is preserved over time. For example, a researcher might investigate the degree to which an individual's Big Five profile is stable over time – if an individual's cardinal (i.e., most characteristic) trait in adolescence is Openness to Experience, is this also likely to be true in adulthood? Examinations of these kinds of questions are fairly rare and often use methods that quantify the similarity of personality profiles such as within-person correlation coefficients (e.g., Ozer and Gjerde 1989).

In sum, there are several conceptually and statistically distinct ways of framing and answering questions about stability and change. An examination of all types of stability is necessary to provide a complete understanding of personality development. It is important to be precise about which type of stability is being investigated in any particular study because a great deal of confusion can occur when terms like stability and change are used without further specification. In the next section, we review research on the absolute and differential stability of the Big Five, because these are the most commonly investigated types of stability and change.

Absolute and differential stability of the Big Five across the lifespan

Table 12.1 provides a summary of absolute and differential stability in the Big Five, based on recent studies (Donnellan and Lucas 2008; Terracciano, McCrae, Brant and Costa 2005; Srivastava, John, Gosling and Potter 2003), meta-analytic reviews (Roberts, Walton and Viechtbauer 2006; Roberts and DelVecchio 2000), and narrative reviews (Helson, Kwan, John and Jones 2002; Trzesniewski, Robins, Roberts and Caspi 2004).

Absolute stability. Absolute changes in personality traits can result from maturational processes or from social-contextual factors that influence a population in a similar manner. Roberts, Walton and Viechtbauer (2006) summarized the results of 113 longitudinal samples involving 50,120 participants which covered the period of adolescence through old age (there is very little research examining absolute changes in the Big Five during childhood or the transition from childhood to adolescence). They divided the Extraversion domain into two facets: Social Dominance (traits related to independence and dominance) and Social

Table 12.1 *Summary of stability and change in the Big Five personality domains across the lifespan.*

Trait domain	Absolute stability	Differential stability
Extraversion	Average levels gradually decline across the lifespan; however, the social dominance facet of Extraversion tends to increase to the mid-30s and then plateau whereas the social vitality facet tends to peak during the transition to adulthood, remain stable across mid-life, and then decline after age 55	Retest coefficients increase across the lifespan from about .30 in childhood to a plateau in the.70s in mid-life
Agreeableness	Average levels gradually increase across the lifespan	Same pattern as Extraversion
Conscientiousness	Average levels gradually increase across the lifespan, but may decline in mid-life or old age	Same pattern as Extraversion
Neuroticism	Average levels gradually decline across the lifespan but may increase in old age	Same pattern as Extraversion
Openness to Experience	Average levels increase during adolescence and then gradually decline across the lifespan	Same pattern as Extraversion

Note. Absolute stability findings are based on cross-sectional and longitudinal studies of age differences in mean levels; differential stability findings are based on longitudinal studies of rank-order (i.e., test-retest) stability. Retest coefficients were estimated using a common interval of about seven years (Roberts and DelVecchio 2000).

Vitality (traits related to positive affect, activity level and sociability). Average levels of Social Vitality tended to be fairly stable across the lifespan, although there was a slight spike upward from adolescence to young adulthood followed by a plateau in the average level until the mid-fifties when there was a slight decline. Social Dominance, on the other hand, showed a more pronounced and consistent absolute increase from adolescence to the early thirties where mean-levels remained consistent until the mid-fifties, after which the lack of studies precluded further analyses. Agreeableness and Conscientiousness showed gradual increases in absolute scores across the lifespan whereas Neuroticism showed gradual decreases. Finally, Openness showed a mean-level increase from adolescence to young adulthood and then mean-levels remained constant until the mid-fifties when it started to show a slight decline in average levels.

Similar trends were also found in a very large cross-sectional study conducted via the Internet by Srivastava, John, Gosling and Potter (2003), as well as in both cross-sectional and longitudinal analyses reported by Terracciano, McCrae, Brant and Costa (2005). In broadest terms, average levels of Agreeableness and Conscientiousness increase with age whereas average levels of Extraversion (in the aggregate), Neuroticism and Openness decline. Although many of the absolute changes in the Big Five tend to be small and gradual, these changes are meaningful because they correspond to age-graded changes in social roles and expectations (Helson, Kwan, John and Jones 2002); that is, the general pattern of normative age changes in the Big Five tend to reflect increases in personal qualities that facilitate fulfilment of important adult roles such as worker, romantic partner and parent (Caspi, Roberts and Shiner 2005).

There are two dominant explanations for absolute changes in the Big Five. The *intrinsic maturational position* holds that normative age-related changes in personality are driven by biological processes (e.g., Costa and McCrae 2006) whereas the *life course position* posits that changes stem from involvement in particular social roles and the life experiences that accompany them (e.g., Roberts, Wood and Smith 2005). It is difficult to perform critical tests of these two explanations because true experimental manipulations (i.e., with random assignment) of either biological factors or important social roles are not ethical or feasible. Nonetheless, we believe that the bulk of the existing evidence is broadly consistent with some version of the life course perspective. Although some age-related changes in personality traits are likely to be rooted in biological changes, an invariant maturational unfolding of personality is unlikely to be the only reason that traits change during adulthood.

Indeed, we believe there are compelling findings linking experiences within the important domains of adult life to personality changes. For example, Robins, Caspi and Moffitt (2002) found that individuals who were involved in distressed romantic relationships in their early twenties demonstrated increases in Neuroticism compared to those in relatively satisfying relationships. Likewise, Roberts, Caspi and Moffitt (2003) found that work experiences were tied to a variety of changes in basic personality traits, including the finding that greater autonomy at work was tied to increases in the Social Dominance aspects of Extraversion. Thus, an emerging body of work is demonstrating that life events are tied to changes in personality traits, a pattern which is consistent with the core tenet of life course theory that 'the interplay of social context and the organism [is] the formative process, making people who they are' (Elder and Shanahan 2006, p. 670).

Research on absolute changes in the Big Five challenges the assumption that adolescence is the critical period of maturation in personality (Roberts, Walton and Viechtbauer 2006). Instead, Roberts *et al.* found that most of the action in terms of mean-level changes in personality occurs during young adulthood. Thus, young adulthood is likely to be a particularly important phase of the lifespan for testing hypotheses regarding the association between adult roles and normative personality changes, given that young adulthood is the phase in the lifespan when individuals assume the roles of worker, committed romantic partner and, in many cases, parent and care-giver (Rindfuss 1991). Accordingly, future research on young adult personality development might be particularly important for helping to resolve the debate about the impetus of normative personality development.

Differential stability. Differential stability concerns the degree to which people who are high (vs. low) on a trait at one point in time maintain their relative ordering over time. A meta-analysis involving test-retest correlations from 152 longitudinal studies showed that the Big Five become increasingly stable across the lifespan (Roberts and DelVecchio 2000). In particular, when standardized to a common interval of about seven years, Roberts and DelVecchio found that the test-retest correlations increased from .31 in childhood to .54 in early adulthood and kept gradually increasing until the stability estimates reached a plateau in the .70s between the ages of fifty and seventy. This general pattern held for all of the Big Five domains and for both men and women.

These findings have a few important implications. First, they show that differential stability peaks between the ages of fifty and seventy, which counters William James's claim that personality is 'set like plaster' by the age of thirty. It appears that traits become increasingly stable after age thirty, but never reach the point where change no longer occurs; that is, no matter how old an individual is, it is possible that his/her standing relative to others can fluctuate with the passage of time. Secondly, they counter the claim that personality shows minimal, if any, stability during childhood (e.g., Lewis 2001). Thus, there is accumulating evidence that individual differences in children are not ephemeral qualities but instead show an appreciable degree of stability; however, it also the case that differential stability seems to increase across the lifespan for all of the Big Five traits.

Why does differential stability increase across the lifespan? Lower differential stability is expected when the individual experiences dramatic environmental and/or maturational changes. The transition from childhood to adolescence is a fairly volatile transition that involves rapid maturational changes, shifting societal demands, the exploration of new identities and roles, and the initiation of new relationships with peers and romantic partners. These changes may impact individuals in relatively unique ways, thus shifting their relative ordering on a trait and thereby reducing stability coefficients. However, as individuals make the transition into adulthood, maturational changes are reduced, social roles begin to stabilize, environmental changes are increasingly subject to individual control, and a more stable sense of self is formed. These factors would tend to increase stability coefficients. Thus, changes in differential stability provide insights into the mechanisms underlying personality development and contribute to a richer understanding of the nature of the life course.

Processes responsible for personality stability and change

One central message conveyed by contemporary work in personality development is that stability and change result from complicated transactions between persons and situations. Therefore strong forms of both situationalism (the view that behaviour is determined largely by factors external to the person) and dispositionalism (the view that behaviour is determined largely by factors internal to the person) are difficult to reconcile from a developmental perspective, in which personality characteristics and situations are seen as increasingly interdependent over time. In particular, several potentially interrelated mechanisms of person-situation transaction may promote personality continuity.

First, personality traits 'draw out' or elicit particular responses from the social environment which can promote personality continuity. For instance, individuals who are kinder and friendlier may evoke more pleasant and supportive responses from their peers and this may contribute to more positive social interactions. Such positive interactions may then reinforce the disposition to be friendly.

Secondly, personality traits shape how people construe social situations. The same objective environment, such as a cocktail party, may mean something quite different to an extravert as opposed to an introvert. Moreover, the different expectancies of the extravert and introvert may generate self-fulfilling prophecies. Thus, expectancies coupled with the evocative effects of particular traits may promote personality stability.

Thirdly, individuals play an active role in selecting and manipulating their own social experiences. Given enough agency, it seems that individuals will seek out, modify, or even create environments that are consistent with their individual characteristics. For example, individuals who are outgoing and sociable may choose careers that fit well with these tendencies and shun solitary occupations with limited potential for social interaction.

The upshot of all three of these processes is a matching between personality traits and characteristics of the situation. As a consequence, it seems as if many life experiences accentuate and reinforce the personality characteristics that were partially responsible for the particular environmental elicitations in the first place. This is known as the corresponsive principle of personality development (Caspi, Roberts and Shiner 2005; Roberts, Wood and Caspi 2008) and it summarizes how person-situation transactions facilitate the continuity of personality.

A different set of mechanisms may explain personality changes (Caspi and Roberts 2001; Roberts, Wood and Caspi 2008). First, and perhaps most importantly, individuals are responsive to the rewards and punishments of a given setting and it is possible that long-term exposure to specific contingencies may produce lasting personality changes. In particular, changes in contingencies are one reason why scholars have suggested that behaviour changes are associated with 'turning points' in the life course (e.g., Laub and Sampson 2003). That is, events such as marriage, parenthood or military service launch individuals into more restricted and tightly monitored environments that have new and salient reward and punishment structures. These clear contingencies may produce enduring changes in personality. Secondly, self-reflection may lead to personality changes. Although a fair bit has been written about the difficulty of accurate self-perception (e.g., Dunning 2005; Robins and John 1997), it is possible that lasting personality changes may result from a considerable amount of deliberate attention to the self. Indeed, a belief in the power of self-reflection to promote change is the essence of insight-oriented psychotherapy. Thirdly, observing others might serve as the catalyst for personality changes according to social learning principles. For example, watching a co-worker receive a large raise because of fastidious work habits may promote imitation of those work behaviours to obtain a similar reward.

Finally, perceptions by others or reflected appraisals may create personality changes. According to the looking glass self-model (Cooley 1902; Mead 1934), having important close others such as a romantic partner see an individual as responsible and caring may motivate personality changes in that direction. However, the countervailing force is the pervasive and likely automatic tendency for individuals to process feedback from others in ways that confirm pre-existing self-views (e.g., Swann 1997). Thus, it might be the case that a strong motivation to change is a necessary ingredient for the success of many of these mechanisms of personality change.

Concluding comment

Table 12.2 summarizes the five major take home messages of this chapter based on our reading of the current literature. In closing, we wish to acknowledge that one of the biggest challenges facing the study of personality development is the fact that the field tends to take a 'trait's eye view' of development whereas individuals, not isolated traits, engage in dynamic transactions with social situations over time. Thus, there is an inherent tension between the units of analysis favoured by personality psychologists and the reality of human development. The trick for future studies is to find ways to maintain personality psychology's traditional focus on the person while maintaining its dedication to empirical

Table 12.2 *Summary of core themes in personality development.*

1. The personality traits studied in adults and many of the dimensions of temperament studied in children are conceptually similar and can be integrated. The Big Five framework can facilitate this integration.
2. A complete understanding of personality development requires attention to several conceptually and statistically distinct types of stability and change, including absolute stability (i.e., mean-level stability), differential stability (i.e., rank-order consistency), structural stability and ipsative stability.
3. Absolute changes in personality traits reflect increasing psychological maturity with age (i.e., the changes facilitate the fulfilment of important adult roles). The most concentrated period of absolute change is young adulthood, not adolescence. There is ongoing controversy whether normative changes in personality traits result primarily from intrinsic maturation or the social roles and experiences of adult life.
4. Differential stability increases across the lifespan and peaks at a level below unity. There does not appear to be widespread support for the idea that age 30 is a magic number for personality stability. Contrary to the idea that personality traits are ephemeral in childhood, an appreciable degree of differential stability is also evident during this phase of the lifespan.
5. Personality development (both stability and change) results from the dynamic interplay between individuals and their environments.

rigour. Nonetheless, over the past decade, the field has witnessed a dramatic accumulation of new knowledge about the ways that personality changes across the lifespan, and we believe that there is every reason to be optimistic about the future of the scientific study of personality development.

References

Allemand, M., Zimprich, D. and Hertzog, C. 2007. Cross-sectional age differences and longitudinal age changes of personality in middle adulthood and old age, *Journal of Personality* 75: 323–58

Allport, G. W. 1937. *Personality: a psychological interpretation*. New York: Henry Holt and Company

Ashton, M. C. and Lee, K. 2007. Empirical, theoretical, and practical advantages of the HEXACO model of personality structure, *Personality and Social Psychology Review* 11: 150–66

Block, J. 1995. A contrarian view of the five-factor approach to personality description, *Psychological Bulletin* 117: 187–215

Caspi, A., Moffitt, T. E., Newman, D. L. and Silva, P. A. 1996. Behavioural observations at age 3 years predict adult psychiatric disorders, *Archives of General Psychiatry* 53: 1033–9

Caspi, A. and Roberts, B. W. 2001. Personality development across the life course: the argument for change and continuity, *Psychological Inquiry* 12: 49–66

Caspi, A., Roberts, B. W. and Shiner, R. L. 2005. Personality development: stability and change, *Annual Review of Psychology* 56: 453–84

Caspi, A. and Shiner, R. L. 2006. Personality development, in W. Damon and R. Lerner (Series eds.) and N. Eisenberg (Vol. ed.), *Handbook of child psychology*, vol. III, *Social, emotional, and personality development*, 6th edn, pp. 300–65. Hoboken, NJ: Wiley

Cooley, C. H. 1902. *Human nature and the social order*. New York: Scribner's

Costa, P. T., Jr and McCrae, R. R. 2006. Age changes in personality and their origins: comment on Roberts, Walton, and Viechtbauer (2006), *Psychological Bulletin* 132: 26–8

De Fruyt, F., Bartels, M., Van Leeuwen, K. G., De Clerq, B., Decuyper, M. and Mervielde, I. 2006. Five types of personality continuity in childhood and adolescence, *Journal of Personality and Social Psychology* 91: 538–52

Depue, R. A. and Collins, P. F. 1999. Neurobiology of the structure of personality: dopamine facilitation of incentive motivation and extraversion, *Behavioural and Brain Sciences* 22: 491–569

Depue, R. A. and Lenzenweger, M. F. 2005. A neurobehavioural dimensional model of personality disturbance, in M. F. Lenzenweger and J. F. Clarkin (eds.), *Major theories of personality disorder*, 2nd edn, pp. 391–453. New York: Guilford Press

Depue, R. A. and Morrone-Strupinsky, J. V. 2005. A neurobehavioural model of affiliative bonding: implications for conceptualizing a human trait of affiliation, *Behavioural and Brain Sciences* 28: 313–95

Donnellan, M. B. and Lucas, R. E. 2008. Age differences in the Big Five across the life span: evidence from two nationally representative samples, *Psychology and Aging* 23: 558–66

Dunning, D. 2005. *Self-insight: roadblocks and detours on the path to knowing thyself.* New York: Psychology Press

Elder, G. H., Jr and Shanahan, M. J. 2006. The life course and human development, in W. Damon and R. Lerner (Series eds.), *Handbook of Child Psychology,* vol. I, *Theoretical Models of Human Development,* 6th edn, pp. 665–715. Hoboken, NJ: Wiley

Goldberg, L. R. 1993. The structure of phenotypic traits, *American Psychologist* 48: 26–34

Gray, J. A. 1987. *The psychobiology of fear and stress.* Cambridge University Press

Helson, R., Kwan, V. S. Y., John, O. P. and Jones, C. 2002. The growing evidence for personality change in adulthood: findings from research with personality inventories, *Journal of Research in Personality* 36: 287–306

Horn, J. L. and McArdle, J. J. 1992. A practical and theoretical guide to measurement invariance in aging research, *Experimental Aging Research* 18: 117–44

John, O. P., Caspi, A., Robins, R. W., Moffitt, T. E. and Stouthamer-Loeber, M. 1994. The 'little five': exploring the nomological network of the five-factor model of personality in adolescent boys, *Child Development* 65: 160–78

John, O. P., Naumann, L. P. and Soto, C. J. 2008. Paradigm shift to the integrative Big Five trait taxonomy: history, measurement, and conceptual issues, in O. P. John, R. W. Robins and L. A. Pervin (eds.), *Handbook of personality: theory and research,* 3rd edn, pp. 114–58. New York: Guilford Press

Laub, J. H. and Sampson, R. J. 2003. *Shared beginnings, divergent lives: delinquent boys to age 70.* Cambridge, MA: Harvard University Press

Lewis, M. 2001. Issues in the study of personality development, *Psychological Inquiry* 12: 67–83

Lucas, R. E., Diener, E., Grob, A. Suh, E. M. and Shao, L. 2000. Cross-cultural evidence for the fundamental features of extraversion, *Journal of Personality and Social Psychology* 79: 452–68

McCrae, P. Costa, P. T., Jr, Terracciano, A., Parker, W. D., Mills, C J., De Fruyt, F. *et al.* 2002. Personality trait development from age 12 to age 18: longitudinal, cross-sectional, and cross-cultural analyses, *Journal of Personality and Social Psychology* 83: 1456–68

Mead, G. H. 1934. *Mind, self and society.* University of Chicago Press

Measelle, J. R., John, O. P., Ablow, J. C., Cowan, P. A. and Cowan, C. P. 2005. Can children provide coherent, stable, and valid self-reports on the Big Five dimensions? A longitudinal study from ages 5 to 7, *Journal of Personality and Social Psychology* 89: 90–106

Millsap, R. E. and Meredith, W. 2007. Factorial invariance: historical perspectives and new problems, in R. Cudeck and R. C. MacCallum (eds.), *Factor Analysis at 100: historical developments and future directions,* pp. 131–52. Mahwah, NJ: Lawrence Erlbaum

Mischel, W., Shoda, Y. and Peak, P. K. 1988. The nature of adolescent competencies predicted by preschool delay of gratification, *Journal of Personality and Social Psychology* 54: 687–96

Mroczek, D. K. 2007. The analysis of longitudinal data in personality research, in R. W. Robins, R. C. Fraley and R. Krueger (eds.), *The handbook of research methods in personality psychology,* pp. 543–56. New York: Guilford Press

Nigg, J. T. 2000. On inhibition/disinhibition in developmental psychopathology: views from cognitive and personality psychology and a working inhibition taxonomy, *Psychological Bulletin* 167: 220–46

Ozer, D. J. and Benet-Martínez, V. 2006. Personality and the prediction of consequential outcomes, *Annual Review of Psychology* 57: 401–21

Ozer, D. J. and Gjerde, P. F. 1989. Patterns of personality consistency and change from childhood through adolescence, *Journal of Personality* 57: 483–507

Putnam, S. P., Ellis, L. K. and Rothbart, M. K. 2001. The structure of temperament from infancy through adolescence, in A. Eliasz and A. Angleneiter (eds.), *Advances in research on temperament*, pp. 165–82. Miami, FL: Pabst Science Publishers

Rindfuss, R. R. 1991. The young adult years: diversity, structural change, and fertility, *Demography* 28: 493–512

Roberts, B. W., Caspi, A. and Moffitt, T. E. 2003. Work experiences and personality development in young adulthood, *Journal of Personality and Social Psychology* 84: 582–93

Roberts, B. W. and DelVecchio, W. F. 2000. The rank-order consistency of personality from childhood to old age: a quantitative review of longitudinal studies, *Psychological Bulletin* 126: 3–25

Roberts, B. W., Kuncel, N. R., Shiner, R., Caspi, A. and Goldberg, L. R. 2007. The power of personality: the comparative validity of personality traits, socio-economic status, and cognitive ability for predicting important life outcomes, *Perspective on Psychological Science* 2: 313–45

Roberts, B. W. and Pomerantz, E. M. 2004. On traits, situations, and their integration: a developmental perspective, *Personality and Social Psychology Review* 8: 402–16

Roberts, B.W., Walton, K.E. and Viechtbauer, W. 2006. Patterns of mean-level change in personality traits across the life course: a meta-analysis of longitudinal studies, *Psychological Bulletin* 132: 1–25

Roberts, B. W., Wood, D. and Caspi, A. 2008. The development of personality traits in adulthood, in O. P. John, R. W. Robins and L. A. Pervin (eds.), *Handbook of personality: theory and research*, (3rd edn, pp. 375–98). New York: Guilford Press

Roberts, B. W., Wood, D. and Smith, J. L. 2005. Evaluating the five factor theory and social investment perspective on personality trait development, *Journal of Research in Personality* 39: 166–84

Robins, R. W., Caspi, A. and Moffitt, T. E. 2002. It's not just who you're with, it's who you are: personality and relationship experiences across multiple relationships, *Journal of Personality* 70: 925–64

Robins, R. W., Fraley, R. C., Roberts, B. W. and Trzesniewski, K. H. 2001. A longitudinal study of personality change in young adulthood, *Journal of Personality* 69: 617–40

Robins, R. W. and John, O. P. 1997. The quest for self-insight: theory and research on accuracy and bias in self-perception, in R. Hogan, J. Johnson and S. Briggs (eds.), *Handbook of personality psychology*, pp. 649–79. New York: Academic Press

Smillie, L. D., Pickering, A. D. and Jackson, C. J. 2006. The new reinforcement sensitivity theory: implications for personality measurement, *Personality and Social Psychology Review* 10: 320–35

Srivastava, S., John, O. P., Gosling, S. D. and Potter, J. 2003. Development of personality in early and middle adulthood: set like plaster or persistent change?, *Journal of Personality and Social Psychology* 84: 1041–53

Swann, W. B., Jr 1997. The trouble with change: self-verification and allegiance to the self, *Psychological Science* 8: 177–80

Terracciano, A., McCrae, R. R., Brant, L. J. and Costa, P. T., Jr 2005. Hierarchical linear modeling analyses of the NEO-PI-R scales in the Baltimore Longitudinal Study of Aging, *Psychology and Aging* 20: 493–506

Trzesniewski, K. H., Robins, R. W., Roberts, B. W. and Caspi, A. 2004. Personality and self-esteem development across the life span, in P. T. Costa, Jr and I. C. Siegler (eds), *Recent advances in psychology and aging*, pp. 163–85. Amsterdam: Elsevier

Vandenberg, R. J. and Lance, C. E. 2000. A review and synthesis of the measurement invariance literature: suggestions, practices, and recommendations for organizational research, *Organizational Research Methods* 3: 4–69

Watson, D., Wiese, D., Vaidya, J. and Tellegen, A. 1999. The two general activation systems of affect: structural findings, evolutionary considerations, and psychobiological evidence, *Journal of Personality and Social Psychology* 76: 820–38

Zuckerman, M. 2005. *Psychobiology of personality*, 2nd edn. New York: Cambridge University Press

13 Models of personality and health

Marko Elovainio and Mika Kivimäki

Introduction

The idea that psychological phenomena are associated with ill-health, act as an etiological factor in specific diseases or have a triggering effect on a disease process, is not a new one. In fact, the hypothesis of the crucial role of psychological factors in mortality due to cardiovascular problems was already postulated in the fifteenth century. The early stages of research on the relationship of personality with ill-health, and in particular somatic health problems, may be characterized as black box research. At that time in the 1700s and 1800s, psychological explanations, including personality, were used mainly if there was no evident physiological mechanism found for a somatic disease (for a review see Ravaja 1996)). This kind of reasoning did not necessarily lead to false or unreasonable conclusions. Today, a large body of evidence suggests that psychological factors may have a role in many somatic health problems involving inflammatory and cardiovascular disease processes (Hemingway and Marmot 1999; Miller, Markides, Chiriboga and Ray 1996; Schneiderman 1987; Smith 1992). However, as long as there were no effective scientific methods to link psychological factors to potential pathophysiological mechanisms, the empirical basis of psychosomatic research remained speculative. Not surprisingly, theoretical models at that time were more simplistic than most of the modern theories. The psychological factors were expected to be linked to somatic health without any complicated mechanisms and the psychosomatic diseases were proposed to be caused by specific psychological problems or conflicts, as defined for instance by psychodynamic theories (Lipowski 1984). Later research suggests that this is clearly an oversimplified view.

Along with the development of modern, empirical scientific research methods, such as ambulatory blood pressure assessments, EEG recording, and ultrasound measures of carotid arteries, it has become possible to explicate and test the physiological and biological process underlying the associations between psychological factors and somatic disease processes and morbidity. The expansion of genetic research has shed light on the potentially shared basis of personality development and specific somatic diseases and their interaction. This growth of scientific activity has led, however, to a more and more fragmented picture of the field.

There are multiple factors contributing to this fragmentation. First, although there is a growing consensus about the structure of personality traits at the higher-order level, as defined by the Big Five in adulthood or by temperament theories (Buss, Plomin and Willerman 1973; Cloninger, Svrakic and Przybeck 1993) in childhood, much of the current research about personality and health focuses on single, lower-order traits (e.g., hostility) without examining those traits in relation to other traits. Indeed, it seems that the lower level traits may provide a better prediction of behavioural and health outcomes than higher-order traits (Elovainio, Kivimaki, Puttonen *et al.* 2004; Paunonen and Ashton 2001).

The second problem in the field relates to the lack of a conceptual model of the evidently complex interaction process between personality and health. One challenging part of constructing such models is the lack of a coherent theory of personality development from childhood to adulthood. Much more is also known about assessing adult personality than about measuring personality in childhood and adolescence. Another and no less complex issue concerns the role of personality in the disease processes. Etiological, triggering, prognostic and indirect roles are among the suggested ones.

Thirdly, personality researchers have used a large number of measures and scales to describe individual differences between people in a wide variety of ways. This has contributed to a situation where coherent scientific evidence cumulates extremely slowly compared to the amount of scientific activity in the field. Comparing the results from one study to another is sometimes impossible, because of the differences in conceptualization and operationalization.

Finally, the fragmented picture of the scientific activities in psychosomatic research also reflects its background as a mixture of two different scientific traditions: medicine and behavioural sciences. These traditions have had their own theoretical models and empirical methods. The mixture of hard scientific evidence of medicine and the holistic view of human behaviour of social and psychological sciences has produced new scientific discoveries but also created a dualistic character with integration problems between theoretical and empirical findings in the field. One example is the theoretical construct sense of coherence (Antonovsky 1991) which describes a multidimensional set of psychological resources. Sense of coherence was originally measured with a large number of questions and narrative interviews, but current epidemiological studies of sense of coherence have used only three simple questions which then are correlated with various health outcomes, such as cardiovascular mortality (Lindfors, Lundberg and Lundberg 2005). It should be kept in mind that the status of the psychosocial factors and personality as entities causing health problems is not generally accepted among medical researchers, although the possible biological mechanisms through which personality factors may affect somatic disease or disease processes are relatively widely accepted.

Given the conceptual and methodological challenges described above, there is a risk that the theoretical models on personality and health will become either lists summarizing a variety of separate empirical findings or very general conceptual frameworks with few testable hypotheses. Magnusson and Törestad (1993) stated this in a polemic manner in their article published in *Annual Review of Psychology* by claiming that 'Personality research is characterized by a lack of integration between theory and empirical studies' (p. 447). The reality may not be quite so hopeless, but a need for integration and understanding the fragmented field is always there.

This chapter is aimed at offering an overview of the field of psychosomatic personality research and especially of the models explaining the dynamic and multidirectional associations between personality and health.

Stress as the basic psychosomatic mechanism

The research evidence of the relationships between social, psychological and physiological reactions is hard to understand without the concept of stress. One of the fundamental steps towards exploring the black box between personality and health was taken when the concept of stress was introduced as a biological phenomenon (Selye 1956). Stress is assumed to be a particularly important mediator of personality-health relationships because it is a common and inevitable aspect of life and because its effects can influence a wide range of bodily systems and behaviours. Stress is a kind of conceptual glue that bonds psychological functions to physiological and biological reactions. The term stress was applied to psychology from engineering, where it originally meant pressure in physical structures resulting from outer loads and forces. In psychology and physiology, there remained the idea of stress as an external load or demand on a biological, physiological or psychological system.

Selye (1973) who popularized the use of the term stress, held the view that elevated levels of corticosteroids served as a bodily marker for stress. Selye's general adaptation syndrome (GAS) underscored that any stressor, physiological or psychological, would produce in essence the same physiological stereotyped stress response. The profile of this response varies according to whether the stressor is of short duration (alarm), moderate duration (resistance), or long duration (exhaustion).

Generally, the term stress refers to experiencing events that are perceived as endangering one's physical or psychological wellbeing. Stress reactions typically demonstrate stimulus-response specificity and it is apparent that there is no objective way to predict psychological stress level without taking into account individual capacity (Lazarus 1993). For example, the transactional stress theory by Lazarus (1984) defines stress as a relationship between the person and the environment that is appraised by the person as relevant to his or her own wellbeing and in which the person's resources are taxed. This approach creates also a basis for understanding individual differences in emotions as emergence of emotions is viewed as depending upon an individual's appraised meaning of the event.

In line with this, stress is defined as an imbalance between external forces or loads and individual possibilities to cope with or resist those external forces by many modern theories (Lazarus 1991). Stress is assumed to involve more or less simultaneous activation of psychological and biological systems. Recognition of a threat or challenge is accompanied by immediate systemic arousal produced by the sympathetic nervous system and the hypothalamic-pituitaryadrenocortical axis. At the same time, stress is associated with changes in mood, alertness, attention, memory, problem-solving, task performance and wellbeing.

The paradox of stress lies in the simultaneity of its adaptive nature and its possible role in disease etiology. The effective, orchestrated bodily responses to everyday stressors or daily hassles are crucial for our adaptation and survival, and moderate levels of stress strengthen our resources to cope with similar situations in the future. McEwen (1998; McEwen and Stellar 1993) has described the prevailing conditions where the adaptive functioning may be impaired and the possible health debilitating effects of stress start to emerge. He defines allostasis as the adaptive process for actively maintaining stability through change. Allostatic load can be described as cumulative wear and tear, and it refers to the cost to the body arising from repeated activation or inadequate managing of mediators of allostasis (e.g., adrenal hormones, immuno-cytokines and neurotransmitters).

According to McEwen, there are four basic sources of allostatic load: (1) frequent stress; (2) lack of adaptation to repeated similar stressors; (3) inability to shut off allostatic responses when the stress is terminated; and (4) deficient responses by some allostatic system leading to compensatory increases in other systems (McEwen 1998).

Coping constitutes an important aspect of stress. Coping is directed at minimizing, deflecting or managing distress and sometimes defined as generalized responses to threat or demand and is thought to be selected by individuals because it is well-suited to the stressor or situation (Lazarus and Folkman 1984). Application of particular kinds of coping is also affected by the resources one brings to the situation and by personality variables that influence one's choices or predispositions to act (e.g., Scheier, Carver and Bridges 1994).

The relationship between environmental demands, psychological processes, physiological reactions and health outcomes may be conceptualized by models defining the psychophysiological stress processes. Although the role of personality has been acknowledged early in stress research and it has repeatedly been shown that there are meaningful individual differences in how people react to a challenging or stressful situation, the role of personality in the relationship between external stressors, experienced stress and health outcomes has been under theoretical debate. Next we discuss various ideas of solutions for that debate.

Personality and psychosomatic pathways

A comprehensive review of the progression of the recent personality or personality development theories is beyond the scope of this chapter. Instead, we provide a brief description of the theoretical assumptions behind the main research traditions. However, in most psychosomatic theories, personality and individual differences are quite fundamentally interpreted to develop in a complex adaptive interaction between environment (social and physiological context) and inherited characteristics. The role of personality in health is generally also seen as an interaction/transaction process, with multidirectional causal effects (Krantz and McCeney 2002). This is despite the fact that most of the empirical research in the field attempts to test whether a single personality trait (e.g., hostility) affects some specific disease, part of the disease process or certain risk factors of that disease (Hemingway and Marmot 1999).

The majority of psychosomatic research deals with coronary heart disease (CHD) as the indicator or manifestation of somatic health problems (Miller, Smith, Turner *et al.* 1996). There are at least two reasons for this. First, CHD is a major cause of mortality in industrialized countries, and therefore efforts to prevent the development and progression of coronary risk factors are of great public health relevance. Secondly, psychological entities such as intense emotions and stress seem to be regulated by the same nervous, endocrine and immune systems that are partly responsible for the processes leading to CHD. Recent studies have suggested that similar processes are also responsible for other diseases or health problems, such as depression (Elovainio, Keltikangas-Järvinen, Pulkki-Raback *et al.* 2006).

One way of characterizing differences between various conceptual models of personality and health is to focus on the potential mechanisms through which the psychological or psychosocial factor affects health.

Direct effect models: personality as reactivity pattern, trigger or structural weakness

An important set of theories is based on the idea that personality, as part of the emotional reaction or behaviour pattern, induces direct biological and physiological changes or reactions with potential pathophysiological consequences. Intense emotions are known to involve increases in blood pressure, heart rate and sympathetic arousal and are associated with haematological changes that can contribute directly to heart disease, hypertension or cardiac events (Krantz and Manuck 1984; Schneiderman 1987). Psychological reactions also appear to affect the immune system through a complex array of neural and hormonal pathways (Besedovsky, del Rey, Klusman *et al.* 1991; Besedovsky, Herberman, Temoshok and Sendo 1996; Maier and Watkins 1998). Whether these immune system changes are strong or prolonged enough to enhance vulnerability to infection or illness is not clear, but they have been implicated in the etiology and progression of preclinical atherosclerosis, viral infections, wound healing and even cancer (e.g., Baum and Nesselhof 1988; Baum and Posluszny 1999; Cohen, Tyrrell and Smith 1991; Kiecolt-Glaser and Glaser 1999; Kiecolt-Glaser, Marucha, Malarkey *et al.* 1995). It is also suggested that physiological reactions caused by psychological reactions can act as triggers rather than real etiological causes of disease processes (Strike, Perkins-Porras, Whitehead *et al.* 2006).

According to the reactivity hypothesis, there are significant differences in physiological reactivity that are related to personality factors (Miller, Smith, Turner *et al.*

1996). Individual differences in biobehavioural factors, such as temperament, are suggested to potentiate the effects of various environmental health risk factors on disease through associated responses of the autonomic nervous system. One could even argue that the most fundamental set of models on the relationship between personality and health is closely linked with the reactivity hypothesis, which states that recurrent heightened psychological or physiological stress reactivity can identify individuals with high risk for ill-heath. This basic assumption of the direct effect models suggests that personality factors relate to the development of physiological and behavioural reactions and therefore the relationship between environmental demands or stressors and health effects may be stronger for persons manifesting certain personality factors than for others (Figure 13.1). It is also suggested that personality factors may influence emotional and physiological reactions by modifying the perception of the environment (Figure 13.2). Similarly,

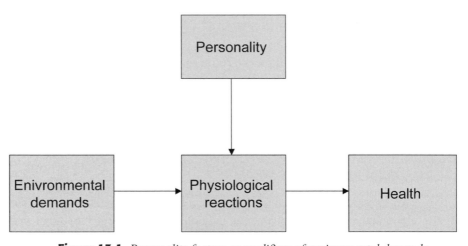

Figure 13.1. *Personality factors as modifiers of environmental demands.*

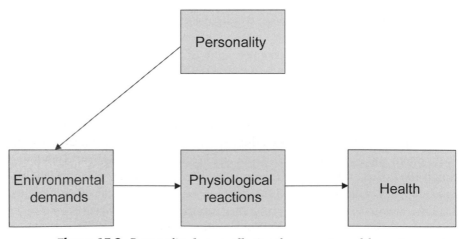

Figure 13.2. *Personality factors affecting the perception of the environment.*

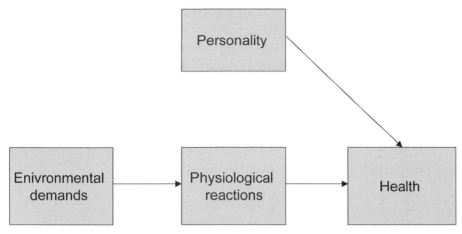

Figure 13.3. *Personality as an independent factor.*

personality may modify psychological and physiological reactions independently from environmental demands (Figure 13.3).

A further model, called the structural weakness hypothesis, is that many of the personality-related features, such as shyness and hostility, share the same genetic or biological background with some physiological problems that are related to or even cause somatic health problems. Indeed, many recent developmental personality theories, such as Cloninger's (Cloninger, Svrakic and Przybeck 1993) temperament theory or the theory of Buss, Plomin and Willerman (1973) propose that personality traits are moderately and specifically genetically determined. It has also been suggested that the differences in autonomic cardiac activity, both during rest and stressful situations, are partially of genetic origin (Carmelli, Chesney, Ward and Rosenman 1985; Miller and Ditto 1991).

Indirect effect models: personality as a determinant of health behaviour or as a selective factor

A second potential mechanism linking personality and health is health-related behaviours, called the health risk behaviour hypothesis (Miller, Smith, Turner *et al.* 1996). Health and disease are influenced by behaviours that convey risks or protect against them. Behaviours may convey health benefits or otherwise protect people from disease. Health risk behaviours are activities that have harmful effects on health. Diet and exercise are often cited as protective behaviours, and tobacco use and alcohol abuse as health-impairing behaviours. Diet and exercise can help minimize the conditions underlying cardiovascular disease and cancer. Tobacco use is associated with biological changes in the lungs, heart and other bodily systems that appear to predispose disease. Similarly, drug use, high-risk sexual activity and other potentially harmful behaviours are important mediators of disease processes. Personality factors have been shown to be associated with many of these health-relevant forms of behaviours.

Less studied and more controversial than those described above is the selection hypothesis proposing that psychological factors, such as personality, may be associated with selection of people to health risk environments or situations (Kivimäki, Virtanen, Elovainio and Vahtera 2006). For example, it has been suggested that some set of traits may increase an individuals' probability of selecting themselves into a high-risk environment likely to produce health problems (Kendler, Kessler, Walters *et al.* 1995). The slightly modified version of the selection model is the transactional model discussed later.

Studies supporting direct and indirect models

Reactivity hypothesis

The significance of the individual differences in reactivity is repeatedly shown (Kivimäki, Virtanen, Elovainio and Vahtera 2006). Numerous experimental studies have indicated that reactions vary significantly depending on the characteristics of the individual. Field studies have also shown that for some persons, psychological and biological reactions in a given situation are strong while for others they are weak. There are various reactivity models and evidence supporting solely one of them over the others is scarce. However, hypotheses related to Type A behaviours and hostility are among the most intensively studied ones.

The model defining personality as a moderator of context perception or physiological and emotional reactivity is supported by well-established literature on Type A behaviour pattern (TABP) first described by Friedman and Rosenman (1959; Friedman and Rosenman 1974). They defined TABP as 'an action-emotion complex that can be observed in any person who is aggressively involved in a chronic, incessant struggle to achieve more and more in less and less time'. TABP individuals were considered to be characterized by extremes in competitive achievement driving and hostility. A large body of evidence supports the association between TABP and increased heart rate and heightened blood pressure and stress-related hormones, such as epinephrine, nonepinephrine and cortisol in stress-provoking situations. Furthermore, TABP persons have been shown to manifest especially greater psychophysiological reactivity in situations characterized as having positive or negative feedback evaluation and socially aversive elements such as verbal criticism (Lyness 1993).

Later, the hostility component was proposed to be the most toxic component of the TABP and many of the recent studies have concentrated on examining the effects of hostility. A number of studies have shown that hostility is associated with greater heart rate, higher blood pressure and cortisol reactivity (Pope and Smith 1991; Smith 1992; Suls and Wan 1993). A recent study of Elovainio and his colleagues (Elovainio, Kivimäki, Keltikangas-Järvinen and Vahtera 2003) suggests that the tendency of hostile persons to make extreme and stereotype-like appraisals of other people and situations and to react negatively when they are not able to apply them, increases their vulnerability to health problems. Hostility has also found to be related to negative affect expressions and unsuccessful coping strategies (Brummett, Babyak, Barefoot *et al.* 1998; Brummett, Maynard, Babyak *et al.* 1998; Kivimäki, Elovainio, Kokko *et al.* 2003; Rosenberg, Ekman and Blumenthal 1998). Negative affectivity has been found to be a non-specific risk factor for poor health outcomes in general, a prognostic factor for cardiac events and cancer (Denollet 1998; Denollet, Vaes and Brutsaert 2000). Hostility has also been associated with increased levels of experienced psychological stress and threat as well as with inadequate coping strategies in stress situations (Blumenthal, Barefoot, Burg and Williams 1987; Kivimäki, Vahtera, Koskenvuo *et al.* 1998a; Smith 1992; Smith and Frohm 1985).

Heart rate reactivity to psychological challenges appears to be an individual characteristic that is stable over time (Cohen, Hamrick, Rodriguez *et al.* 2000; Kamarck, Jennings, Debski *et al.* 1992). Some recent results suggest that personality dispositions, such as hostility and TABP play a significant role in stress-related cardiac reactivity (Heponiemi, Keltikangas-Järvinen, Kettunen *et al.* 2004; Keltikangas-Järvinen and Heponiemi 2004) and may also predispose to the development of elevated risk profile of metabolic syndrome (Keltikangas-Järvinen, Räikkönen and Hautanen 1996) a significant risk for CHD.

Structural weakness hypothesis

Although most of the studies testing the physiological reactivity model are focused on TABP, hostility and related constructs, the more biologically based temperament constructs have recently become increasingly attractive to researchers. One example of those constructs is Gray's (1982, 1991) temperament theory that is strongly based on physiology. It explains the basic temperamental dimensions in terms of biological processes assuming the existence of three fundamental systems with independent neurobiological mechanisms in the mammalian central nervous system: the behavioural inhibition system (BIS), the behavioural approach system (BAS), and the fight-flight system (FFS). Gray has proposed that the individual differences in the functioning of these systems and their interaction underlie differences in human temperament and reactivity.

In terms of emotions, recent evidence supports the connection between the BIS and negative affects, and the BAS and positive affects. Gable, Reis and Elliot (2000) found that BIS sensitive persons reported more negative affects and BAS sensitive persons more positive affects in everyday life when measured with diaries. Furthermore, persons with a sensitive BIS experienced more negative affects after negative life events than persons with less sensitive BIS after similar life events (Heubeck, Wilkinson and Cologon 1998; Jorm, Christensen, Henderson *et al.* 1999). In terms of physiology, significant increases in heart rate have been found among BAS sensitive persons (Arnett and Newman 2000; Tranel, Fisher and Fowles 1982). In addition, a socially relevant stimulus (talking facial image) has been found to elicit greater reactions among high BAS individuals than among low BAS individuals (Ravaja 2004).

Genetic factors have been reported to contribute to a substantial proportion of individual differences in parasympathetic activity during resting situations and tasks (Singh, Larson, O'Donnell and Levy 2001), although the specific genes regulating components of autonomic function are not well known. Some recent studies suggest that inherited serotonin system activity genotypes or genes regulating parasympathetic components of autonomic control may in part underlie the differences in cardiovascular reactivity (McCaffery, Bleil, Pogue-Geile, Ferrell and Manuck 2003).

One research line has been concentrated on the effects of temperament as defined by Cloninger's (Cloninger, Adolfsson and Svrakic 1996; Cloninger, Svrakic and Przybeck 1993) psychobiological reactivity model. According to Cloninger *et al.* (1993), temperament comprises four dimensions: Novelty-Seeking (NS), Harm Avoidance (HA), Reward Dependence (RD) and Persistence (P). Temperament dimensions are assumed to be neurobiologically-based dispositions and the traits NS, HA and RD are thought to be strongly influenced by different neurotransmitter systems, such as the dopaminergic, serotonergic and noradrenergic systems, respectively. Studies on the association between candidate genes of the suggested monoaminergic pathways and the temperament phenotypes have produced somewhat inconsistent results. After the seminal report for an association between NS and dopamine system (DRD4) by Ebstein *et al.* (Ebstein, Novick, Umansky *et al.* 1996), the work on Cloninger's temperaments has been extensive. While several studies have supported the original finding (Ebstein, Nemanov, Klotz *et al.* 1997; Keltikangas-Järvinen, Elovainio, Kivimäki *et al.* 2003) others have reported negative findings (Gebhardt, Leisch, Schussler *et al.* 2000). The genetic association studies with other temperament dimensions of the model have found the most robust association between the 5HTT LPR polymorphism and HA, providing support for the suggested association between HA and central nervous system serotonin activity (Munafo, Clark, Moore *et al.* 2003). Some results suggest that temperamental dispositions play a significant role in stress-related cardiac reactivity (Heponiemi, Keltikangas-Järvinen, Kettunen *et al.* 2004) and may also predispose to the development of elevated risk profile of metabolic syndrome (Keltikangas-Järvinen, Räikkönen and Hautanen 1996). To date, however, no consensus has been reached about the specific genetic factors behind various personality dispositions. The findings have been mixed although significant overlap is assumed.

Health behaviour hypothesis

This hypothesis is far less studied than the reactivity/structural weakness hypotheses. Yet there is a growing body of evidence to support health behaviour and selective processes as correlates of personality. It has been found that impatience and aggressiveness are risk factors for excessive caloric intake and a sedentary lifestyle (Miller, Smith, Turner *et al.* 1996; Pulkki, Kivimäki, Keltikangas-Järvinen, *et al.* 2003; Scherwitz, Perkins, Chesney *et al.* 1992; Yang,

Telama, Keltikangas-Järvinen and Räikkönen 1998; Yang, Telama and Leskinen 2000). These health-related behaviours are associated with general body fat and fat distributed in the abdominal area (Emery, Schmid, Kahn and Filozof 1993; Swinburn, Caterson, Seidell and James 2004), which in turn have been shown to be a risk factor for non-insulin-dependent diabetes mellitus, hypertension, hyper-cholesterolemia, coronary heart disease and cardiovascular mortality, independently of the level of general body fat (Bigaard, Tjonneland, Thomsen *et al.* 2003; Lean, Han and Seidell 1998; Rexrode, Carey, Hennekens *et al.* 1998). Maternally-rated difficult temperament, measured by hyperactivity, unpredictability and low attention span, has been associated with excess weight gain in middle childhood (Carey, Hegvik and McDevitt 1988). A high level of negative emotionality and a lack of energy have been found to correlate with body mass in boys aged nine to fifteen (Ravaja and Keltikangas-Järvinen 1995), and a high level of hostile affect and aggressiveness have been shown to predict increased body mass index in adolescents in a three-year follow-up (Räikkönen, Matthews and Salomon 2003). It has been shown that children with high levels of aggressiveness and impulsivity are likely to engage in risky lifestyles, including smoking and alcohol abuse in adulthood (Caspi, Begg, Dickson *et al.* 1997; Cooper, Wood and Orcutt 2003; Masse and Tremblay 1997; Pulkkinen and Pitkänen 1994). Cynical hostility, or cynical mistrust in adulthood has also been shown to predict behavioural cardiovascular risk factors such as smoking and alcohol use (Pulkki, Kivimäki, Keltikangas-Järvinen *et al.* 2003).

Selection hypothesis

It is shown that exposure to adversities during one's life course is not necessarily random. A genetically influenced set of traits may both increase an individual's probability of selecting themselves into a high-risk environment and increase their vulnerability to health risks or health problems, such as affective disorders (Kendler, Kessler, Walters *et al.* 1995). A typical factor selecting people is education and there are also personality-related differences in academic success and attending to further education (Halsey, Collin and Anderson 1996). Both academic success and educational attainment, in turn, are strongly associated with health (Sweeting and West 1995). For example, personality factors such as shyness, impulsivity and hostility during childhood have been suggested to select people to lower academic careers and greater risk of unstable employment (Keltikangas-Järvinen, Elovainio, Kivimäki *et al.* 2003; Kivimäki *et al.* 2003; Virtanen, Kivimäki, Elovainio and Vahtera 2002) and related higher exposure to stress.

Problems at school and health risk behaviours during adolescence may restrict a person's possibilities of choosing a favourable occupational status, a correlate of health (Sweeting and West 1995). Health-related habits, such as smoking, nutrition and alcohol consumption, tend to be associated with education, which generally has the effect of reducing adverse health behaviours.

In sum, a large number of mechanisms and hypotheses proposed above have gained at least limited support from empirical studies (for a review see *Psychosomatic Medicine*, Reactivity Special Section, 2003: 65(1); Hemingway and Marmot 1999). However, the actual set of mechanisms through which personality may affect health are probably in most cases based on complex, multidirectional interactions of genetic, physiological, behavioural and environmental factors that affect the body's ability to remain or become healthy or to resist or overcome disease. The challenges in testing such complex interactions with multidirectional effects and feedback loops are great but inevitable if we want to understand in depth the associations between psychological and somatic entities.

Transactional and developmental models

The principal conclusion that can be drawn from the reactivity models and indirect models do not suggest that personality factors as such are unhealthy or healthy. The models simply propose that personality differences intensify physiological reactions through direct effects, modified perceptions or health risk behaviours that may lead to health problems in the long run. However, the models have been criticized for ignoring the active role of an individual when trying to adapt to his or her environment and to reach personal goals. A further criticism relates to reliance on a relatively simple stimulus-response paradigm.

As an attempt to overcome some of the criticism, a transactional approach has been developed. The transactional approach involves an understanding of the sequence of interactions between a person and his or her environment. The basic ideas of transactional psychosomatic research are in line with selection hypothesis and in general with the idea of the human being as an active coping subject who affects his or her environment instead of passive adaptation or reaction. Transactional stress models (Lazarus and Folkman 1984; McGrath and Beehr 1990) suggest that the stress process begins when a person evaluates the situation and tries somehow to cope with the demands of this situation. The active coping then may change both the actual situation and the perception of that situation, which in turn may lead to modifications in further coping. Thus, the balance between the person and the environment is actually a continuously changing process or cycle.

Increased stress is also suggested to result from the fact that some individuals or personality types create more frequent and severe contacts with stressors (Smith and Pope 1990). This means that people tend to select themselves, or their personality-related coping recourses /coping styles (Lazarus 1993; Lazarus and Folkman 1984) select them, to risky environments or contexts. In fact, the basic assumption that personality comprises recurring interpersonal situations has been formally represented as the transactional cycle (Gallo and Matthews 2003; Kiesler 1996).

The majority of evidence supporting the selective or transactional health effects of personality is again based on hostility studies showing that hostility predicts breakdown of intimate relationships (Miller, Markides, Chiriboga and Ray 1995), lack of social support, interpersonal conflicts, and thus leads to experienced stress and poor possibilities to related health problems (Appelberg, Romanov, Honkasalo and

Koskenvuo 1991; Houston and Vavak 1991; Kivimaki, Vahtera, Koskenvuo, Uutela and Pentti 1998b; Smith, Allred, Sanders *et al.* 1988). Lack of social support has been shown to be associated with heightened cardiovascular reactivity (Kamarck, Jennings, Debski *et al.* 1992; Kamarck, Peterman and Raynor 1998). Warm and agreeable persons have been suggested to evoke friendliness and support form others and this kind of interpersonal resources protect or buffer from many health risks and enhance positive coping (Smith, Glazer, Ruiz and Gallo 2004).

Although these traditional transactional models are more dynamic than the unidirectional models and are consistent with contemporary social-cognitive views of personality, they miss the aspect of longer-term development of both personality and health (Kivimäki, Virtanen, Elovainio and Vahtera 2006). Considering this, an important expansion to the transaction theories are the current developmental models that emphasize the life course developmental perspective.

Life course approach and suggestions for a new model

The life course perspective on the etiology of various health problems can be divided by their emphases on the importance of early life or adult behaviours (Kuh, Ben-Shloma, Lynch *et al.* 2003). The early origins model (critical period model) suggests that early biological and psychosocial circumstances have long-lasting effects on the structure or function of psychological and physiological development (Lynch, Kaplan and Shema 1997; Power, Matthews and Manor 1998). According to this model, genetic factors or childhood psychosocial environment or both represent a critical basis or developmental period for the interaction between personality and health. The long-lasting or basic personality factors developed during that period have negative or positive consequences that persist to adulthood and later life. Both reactivity hypothesis and structural weakness hypothesis are in line with this idea.

The body of evidence supporting the genetic background of temperament and related health risks or health problems is consistent with the model of early effects. Temperament, which refers to biologically rooted, relatively stable individual differences in emotional self-regulation and reactivity to stimuli (Cloninger, Svrakic and Przybeck 1993; Goldsmith and Lemery 2000; Gray 1991) seem to be associated with health through reactivity or structural weakness mechanisms. This model implies that effects of genes and childhood social circumstances can be relatively independent of adult circumstances. This means that health and later personality features are still seen as unidirectional consequences from high physiological reactivity patterns, inherited psychological and physiological problems or related health risk behaviours.

Recently, models of true developmental ideas have been called for. Temperament, which has been called an inherited part of personality, has also been suggested to be developed in an adaptive interaction between environment (human relationships, child rearing practices, etc.) and inherited reaction patterns.

Recent quantitative genetic studies suggest that there are continuous interaction processes between genes, environment and health. This means that health and coping styles may affect the development of the later personality features and that these effects may became more important or intense in certain phases of life and in certain psychosocial environments than in others. Models underlying these multi-directional effects have been developed in the field studying the dynamic relation-ships between socio-economic status, personality, health risk behaviour and health (Chen, Matthews and Boyce 2002; Gallo, Smith and Cox 2006). One example is the reserve capacity model presented by Gallo and Matthews (2003). It proposes dynamic associations among environments of low socio-economic status, stressful experiences, psychosocial resources (including personality), emotion and cognition, biological factors and behavioural patterns predicting cardiovascular disease and mortality over time. The model is basically still unidirectional, although it includes feedback loops in almost all stages. The testing of such a model is restricted to its implications, such as the association between socio-economic status and emotional experiences (Gallo, Smith and Cox 2006). A corresponding model on the long-term relationship between socio-economic status, psychosocial factors in general and health has been presented by Stansfeld and Marmot (Stansfeld, Fuhrer, Shipley and Marmot 2002).

The transactional developmental model (Gallo and Smith 2006; Smith and Mackenzie 2006) suggests that personality comprises recurring interpersonal situations. Throughout their covert experience and expressive behaviour, individ-uals tend to influence the covert experience and expressive responses of others in their social environments in ways that are consistent with their personality. An individual's style tends to affect restricted classes of responses from others in a dynamic transactional process. If repeated over time and across contexts, devel-opmentally based transactional cycles are assumed to contribute to continuities of personality, relationships, social experiences and other experiences in a reciprocal process and a recurring pattern of transactional cycles would expect to foster a health-relevant trajectory.

Several factors contribute to the evolution of the developmental models of the dynamic relationship between personality and health. First, the development and integration of modern personality theories underlying the long-lasting processes of personality development and change have offered conceptual tools for trans-actional developmental theories. One example is integration of childhood attach-ment theories (Bowlby 1973) and theories of adult relationships and their effects on later personality (Cassidy and Shaver 1999). These theories are in line with the larger framework of the social cognitive view of personality highlighting phe-nomena, such as goals, life tasks, internal representations of self and schemes (Cantor and Kihlström 1989; Mischel and Shoda 1995; Sheldon and Elliot 2000).

Secondly, the expansion of temperament theories emphasizing the long-term effects of early attachment experiences, and especially the physiological basis of human personality, has been influential. The real boost for these theories and empirical research has been given by the development of genetic research techniques and the expansion of research activities on the genetic background of both temperament and of various health problems and health-related physiological mechanisms.

Thirdly, the development of life course epidemiology, an approach that has long been examining health risk factors, especially low socio-economic status, from childhood to health in adulthood at a population level, have offered some theoretical and some methodological tools for testing developmental models.

Fourthly, the long-term prospective databases have made it possible to test the potential life-long effects and processes. Many of the current follow-up studies are based on data collections that were started in the 1980s or even earlier. Such large research projects are Whitehall ll, Cardiovascular Risks in Young Finns Study, the Framingham study and many others.

A personality development theory, which suggests that in the long run negative transactional cycles may lead to unhealthy social context and even health problems, is easily translated to a transactional theory of the core relationship between personality and health. We suggest the theoretical framework shown in Figure 13.4 as the basis for future studies and interpretation of the previous results in the field.

Our model suggests that adverse socio-economic circumstances, a negative family atmosphere, and temperament-related physiological (genetic) and behavioural factors (negative emotions, aggressiveness, impatience and lack of sociability) in childhood may give rise to health risks or health problems later in life through transactional cycles. These transactional cycles may lead to poor educational and occupational achievements, health-related personality traits (hostility, TABP), risky lifestyles and even to metabolic risk factors and health problems. In each developmental stage all factors inevitably interact with the resources (genetic, biological, psychological, social, material) from the previous stages. Two fundamental resources are positive personality features and health. This transactional cycle underlines the developmental feedback effects of poor health or health problems. This means that poor health may affect one's self-esteem and personality especially in early developmental phases and that long-term and short-term developmental cycles and biological, psychological, social and material factors affect both personality and health.

In principle, the transactional theory of the core relationship between personality and health is consistent with all of the basic hypotheses, including selection or pathway and additive effects hypotheses. Selection and pathway hypotheses suggest, for instance, that childhood circumstances represent risks for one's health only if they select one to poor adulthood circumstances (Marmot and Wilkinson 2001). The additive effects hypothesis implies that biological and psychosocial risks during life have an additive effect on one's health (Davey Smith, Hart, Hole *et al.* 1998).

In sum, our model needs to be quite complicated, cover long-term processes and take into account conditional and complementary cycles and wide social contexts and resources.

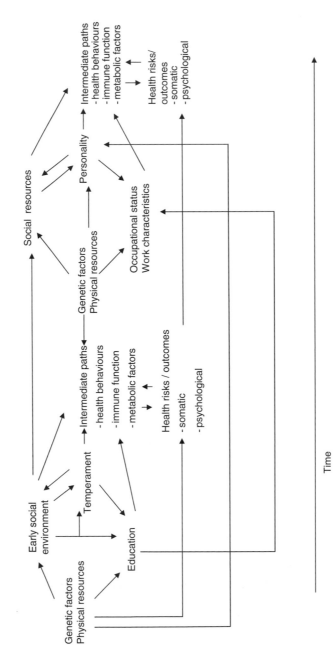

Figure 13.4. *The transactional model of the core relationship between personality and health.*

References

Antonovsky, A. 1991. The structural sources of salutogenic strengths, in C. L. Cooper and R. Payne (eds.), *Personality and stress: individual differences in the stress process*, Wiley series on studies in occupational stress, pp. 67–104. Oxford: John Wiley and Sons

Appelberg, K., Romanov, K., Honkasalo, M. L. and Koskenvuo, M. 1991. Interpersonal conflicts at work and psychosocial characteristics of employees, *Social Science and Medicine* 32: 1051–6

Arnett, P. A. and Newman, J. P. 2000. Gray's three-arousal model: an empirical investigation, *Personality and Individual Differences* 28: 1171–89

Baum, A. and Nesselhof, S. E. 1988. Psychological research and the prevention, etiology, and treatment of AIDS, *American Psychologist* 43: 900–6

Baum, A. and Posluszny, D. M. 1999. Health psychology: mapping biobehavioural contributions to health and illness, *Annual Review of Psychology* 50: 137–63

Besedovsky, H. O., del Rey, A., Klusman, I., Furukawa, H., Monge Arditi, G. and Kabiersch, A. 1991. Cytokines as modulators of the hypothalamus-pituitary-adrenal axis, *Journal of Steroid Biochemistry and Molecular Biology* 40: 613–18

Besedovsky, H. O., Herberman, R. B., Temoshok, L. R. and Sendo, F. 1996. Psychoneuroimmunology and cancer: fifteenth Sapporo Cancer Seminar, *Cancer Research* 56: 4278–81

Bigaard, J., Tjonneland, A., Thomsen, B. L., Overvad, K., Heitmann, B. L. and Sorensen, T. I. A. 2003. Waist circumference, BMI, smoking, and mortality in middle-aged men and women, *Obesity Research* 7: 895–903

Blumenthal, J. A., Barefoot, J. C., Burg, M. M. and Williams, R. B. 1987. Psychological correlates of hostility among patients undergoing coronary angiography, *British Journal of Medical Psychology* 60: 349–55

Bowlby, J. 1973. *Attachment and loss,* vol. II, *Separation: anxiety and anger.* New York: Basic Books

Brummett, B. H., Babyak, M. A., Barefoot, J. C., Bosworth, H. B., Clapp-Channing, N. E., Siegler, I. C. *et al.* 1998. Social support and hostility as predictors of depressive symptoms in cardiac patients one month after hospitalization: a prospective study, *Psychosomatic Medicine* 60: 707–13

Brummett, B. H., Maynard, K. E., Babyak, M. A., Haney, T. L., Siegler, I. C., Helms, M. J. *et al.* 1998. Measures of hostility as predictors of facial affect during social interaction: evidence for construct validity, *Annals of Behavioural Medicine* 20: 168–73

Buss, A. H., Plomin, R. and Willerman, L. 1973. The inheritance of temperaments, *Journal of Personality* 41: 513–24

Cantor, N. and Kihlström, J. F. 1989. *Social intelligence and cognitive assessment of personality.* Hillsdale: LEA

Carey, W. B., Hegvik, R. L. and McDevitt, S. C. 1988. Temperamental factors associated with rapid weight gain and obesity in middle childhood, *Developmental and Behavioural Pediatrics* 9: 197–8

Carmelli, D., Chesney, M. A., Ward, M. M. and Rosenman, R. H. 1985. Twin similarity in cardiovascular stress response, *Health Psychology* 4: 413–23

Caspi, A., Begg, D., Dickson, N., Harrington, H. L., Langley, J., Moffitt, T. E. *et al.* 1997. Personality differences predict health-risk behaviours in young adulthood: evidence from a longitudinal study, *Journal of Personality and Social Psychology* 73: 1052–63

Cassidy, J. and Shaver, P. R. 1999. *Handbook of attachment: theory, research and clinical applications*. New York: Guilford Press

Chen, E., Matthews, K. A. and Boyce, W. T. 2002. Socioeconomic differences in children's health: how and why do these relationships change with age?, *Psychology Bulletin* 128: 295–329

Cloninger, C. R., Adolfsson, R. and Svrakic, N. M. 1996. Mapping genes for human personality, *National Genetics* 12: 3–4

Cloninger, C. R., Svrakic, D. M. and Przybeck, T. R. 1993. A psychobiological model of temperament and character, *Archives of General Psychiatry* 50: 975–90

Cohen, S., Hamrick, N., Rodriguez, M. S., Feldman, P. J., Rabin, B. S. and Manuck, S. B. 2000. The stability of and intercorrelations among cardiovascular, immune, endocrine, and psychological reactivity, *Annals of Behavioural Medicine* 22: 171–9

Cohen, S., Tyrrell, D. A. and Smith, A. P. 1991. Psychological stress and susceptibility to the common cold, *New England Journal of Medicine* 325: 606–12

Cooper, M. L., Wood, P. K. and Orcutt, H. K. 2003. Personality and the predisposition to engage in risky or problem behaviours during adolescence, *Journal of Personality and Social Psychology* 84: 390–410

Davey Smith, G., Hart, C., Hole, D., MacKinnon, P., Gillis, C., Watt, G. *et al.* 1998. Education and occupational social class: which is the more important indicator of mortality risk?, *Journal of Epidemiol Community Health* 52: 153–60

Denollet, J. 1998. Personality and risk of cancer in men with coronary heart disease, *Psychological Medicine* 28: 991–5

Denollet, J., Vaes, J. and Brutsaert, D. L. 2000. Inadequate response to treatment in coronary heart disease: adverse effects of type D personality and younger age on 5-year prognosis and quality of life, *Circulation* 102: 630–5

Ebstein, R. P., Nemanov, L., Klotz, I., Gritsenko, I. and Belmaker, R. H. 1997. Additional evidence for an association between the dopamine D4 receptor (D4DR) exon III repeat polymorphism and the human personality trait of Novelty Seeking, *Molecular Psychiatry* 2: 472–7

Ebstein, R. P., Novick, O., Umansky, R., Priel, B., Osher, Y., Blaine, D. *et al.* 1996. Dopamine D4 receptor (D4DR) exon III polymorphism associated with the human personality trait of Novelty Seeking, *National Genetics* 12: 78–80

Elovainio, M., Keltikangas-Järvinen, L., Pulkki-Raback, L., Kivimäki, M., Puttonen, S., Viikari, L. *et al.* 2006. Depressive symptoms and C-reactive protein: the Cardiovascular Risk in Young Finns Study, *Psychological Medicine* 36: 797–805

Elovainio, M., Kivimäki, M., Keltikangas-Järvinen, L. and Vahtera, J. 2003. Cognitive strategies as a mediator between hostility and health: a longitudinal study on the personal need for structure (PNS). Manuscript submitted for publication

Elovainio, M., Kivimäki, M., Puttonen, S., Heponiemi, T., Pulkki, L. and Keltikangas-Järvinen, L. 2004. Temperament and depressive symptoms: a population-based longitudinal study on Cloninger's psychobiological temperament model, *Journal of Affective Disorders* 83: 227–32

Emery, E. M., Schmid, T. L., Kahn, H. S. and Filozof, P. P. 1993. A review of the association between abdominal fat distribution, health outcome measures and modifiable risk factors, *American Journal of Health Promotion* 7: 342–53

Friedman, M. and Rosenman, R. H. 1959. Association of specific overt behavior pattern with blood and cardiovascular findings, *Journal of American Medical Association* 169: 96–106

  1974. *Type A: your behaviours and your heart.* New York: Knoft

Gable, S. L., Reis, H. T. and Elliot, A. J. 2000. Behavioural activation and inhibition in everyday life, *Journal of Personality and Social Psychology* 78: 1135–49

Gallo, L. C. and Matthews, K. A. 2003. Understanding the association between socioeconomic status and physical health: do negative emotions play a role?, *Psychological Bulletin* 129: 10–51

Gallo, L. C. and Smith, T. W. 2006. Socioeconomic status, psychosocial processes, and perceived health: an interpersonal perspective, *Annals of Behavioural Medicine* 31: 109–19

Gallo, L. C., Smith, T. W. and Cox, C. M. 2006. Socioeconomic status, psychosocial processes, and perceived health: an interpersonal perspective, *Annals of Behavioural Medicine* 31: 109–19

Gebhardt, C., Leisch, F., Schussler, P., Fuchs, K., Stompe, T., Sieghart, W. *et al.* 2000. Non-association of dopamine D4 and D2 receptor genes with personality in healthy individuals, *Psychiatric Genetics* 10: 131–7

Goldsmith, H. H. and Lemery, K. S. 2000. Linking temperamental fearfulness and anxiety symptoms: a behaviour-genetic perspective, *Biological Psychiatry* 48: 1199–1209

Gray, J. A. 1982. *The neuropsychology of anxiety: an enquiry into the functions of the septo-hippocampal system.* New York: Oxford University Press

  1991. The neuropsychology of temperament, in J. Strelau and A. Angleitner (eds.), *Explorations in temperament: international perspectives on theory and measurement. Perspectives on individual differences*, pp. 105–28. New York: Plenum Press

Halsey, C. L., Collin, M. F. and Anderson, C. L. 1996. Extremely low-birth-weight children and their peers: a comparison of school-age outcomes, *Archives of Pediatrics and Adolescent Medicine* 150: 790–4

Hemingway, H. and Marmot, M. 1999. Evidence based cardiology: psychosocial factors in the aetiology and prognosis of coronary heart disease. Systematic review of prospective cohort studies, *British Medical Journal* 318: 1460–7

Heponiemi, T., Keltikangas-Järvinen, L., Kettunen, J., Puttonen, S. and Ravaja, N. 2004. BIS-BAS sensitivity and cardiac autonomic stress profiles, *Psychophysiology* 41: 37–45

Heubeck, B. G., Wilkinson, R. B. and Cologon, J. 1998. A second look at Carver and White's (1994) BIS/BAS scales, *Personality and Individual Differences* 25: 785–800

Houston, B. K. and Vavak, C. R. 1991. Cynical hostility: developmental factors, psychosocial correlates, and health behaviours, *Health Psychology* 10: 9–17

Jorm, A. F., Christensen, H., Henderson, A. S., Jacomb, P. A., Korten, A. E. and Rodgers, B. 1999. Using the BIS/BAS scales to measure behavioural inhibition and behavioural activation: factor structure, validity and norms in a large community sample, *Personality and Individual Differences* 26: 49–58

Kamarck, T. W., Jennings, J. R., Debski, T. T., Glickman-Weiss, E., Johnson, P. S., Eddy, M. J. *et al.* 1992. Reliable measures of behaviourally-evoked cardiovascular reactivity from a PC-based test battery: results from student and community samples, *Psychophysiology* 29: 17–28

Kamarck, T. W., Peterman, A. H. and Raynor, D. A. 1998. The effects of the social environment on stress-related cardiovascular activation: current findings, prospects, and implications, *Annals of Behavioural Medicine* 20: 247–56

Keltikangas-Järvinen, L., Elovainio, M., Kivimäki, M., Ekelund, J. and Peltonen, L. 2003. Novelty seeking as a mediator in relationship between type 4 dopamine receptor gene polymorphism and predisposition to higher education, *Learning and Individual Differences* 14: 23–8

Keltikangas-Järvinen, L., Elovainio, M., Kivimäki, M., Lichtermann, D., Ekelund, J. and Peltonen, L. 2003. Association between the type 4 dopamine receptor gene polymorphism and novelty seeking, *Psychosomatic Medicine* 65: 471–6

Keltikangas-Järvinen, L. and Heponiemi, T. 2004. Vital exhaustion, temperament, and cardiac reactivity in task-induced stress, *Biological Psychology* 65: 121–35

Keltikangas-Järvinen, L., Räikkönen, K. and Hautanen, A. 1996. Type A behaviour and vital exhaustion as related to the metabolic hormonal variables of the hypothalamic-pituitary-adrenal axis, *Behavioural Medicine* 22: 15–22

Kendler, K. S., Kessler, R. C., Walters, E. E., MacLean, C., Neale, M. C., Heath, A. C. *et al.* 1995. Stressful life events, genetic liability, and onset of an episode of major depression in women, *American Journal of Psychiatry* 152: 833–42

Kiecolt-Glaser, J. K. and Glaser, R. 1999. Chronic stress and mortality among older adults, *Jama* 282: 2259–60

Kiecolt-Glaser, J. K., Marucha, P. T., Malarkey, W. B., Mercado, A. M. and Glaser, R. 1995. Slowing of wound healing by psychological stress, *Lancet* 346: 1194–6

Kiesler, D. J. 1996. From communications to interpersonal theory: a personal odyssey, *Journal of Personality Assessment* 66: 267–82

Kivimäki, M., Elovainio, M., Kokko, K., Pulkkinen, L., Kortteinen, M. and Tuomikoski, H. 2003. Hostility, unemployment and health status: testing three theoretical models, *Social Science and Medicine* 56: 2139–52

Kivimäki, M., Vahtera, J., Koskenvuo, M., Uutela, A. and Pentti, J. 1998a. Response of hostile individuals to stressful changes in their working lives: test of a psychosocial vulnerability model, *Psychological Medicine* 28: 903–13

(1998b). Response of hostile individuals to stressful changes in their working lives: test of a psychosocial vulnerability model, *Psychological Medicine* 28: 903–13

Kivimäki, M., Virtanen, M., Elovainio, M. and Vahtera, J. 2006. Personality, work, career and health, in L. Pulkkinen, J. Kaprio and R. J. Rose (eds.), *Socioemotional Development and Health from Adolescence to Adulthood*, pp. 328–42. New York: Cambridge University Press

Krantz, D. S. and Manuck, S. B. 1984. Acute psychophysiologic reactivity and risk of cardiovascular disease: a review and methodologic critique, *Psychological Bulletin* 96: 435–64

Krantz, D. S. and McCeney, M. K. 2002. Effects of psychological and social factors on organic disease: a critical assessment of research on coronary heart disease, *Annual Review of Psychology* 53: 341–69

Kuh, D., Ben-Shlomo, Y., Lynch, J., Hallqvist, J. and Power, C. 2003. Life course epidemiology, *Journal of Epidemiology and Community Health* 57: 778–83

Lazarus, R. S. 1984. On the primacy of cognition, *American Psychologist* 36: 124–9
   1991. Cognition and motivation in emotion, *American Psychologist* 46: 352–67
   1993. From psychological stress to the emotions: a history of changing outlooks, *Annual Review of Psychology* 44: 1–21

Lazarus, R. S. and Folkman, S. 1984. *Stress, appraisal and coping.* New York: Springer

Lean, M. E. J., Han, T. S. and Seidell, J. C. 1998. Impairment of health and quality of life in people with large waist circumference, *Lancet* 351: 853–6

Lindfors, P., Lundberg, O. and Lundberg, U. 2005. Sense of coherence and biomarkers of health in 43-year-old women, *International Journal of Behavioural Medicine* 12: 98–102

Lipowski, Z. J. 1984. What does the word 'psychosomatic' really mean? A historical and semantic inquiry, *Psychosomatic Medicine* 46: 153–71

Lynch, J. W., Kaplan, G. A. and Shema, S. J. 1997. Cumulative impact of sustained economic hardship on physical, cognitive, psychological, and social functioning, *New England Journal of Medicine* 337: 1889–5

Lyness, S. A. 1993. Predictors of differences between Type A and B individuals in heart rate and blood pressure reactivity, *Psychological Bulletin* 114: 266–95

Maier, S. F. and Watkins, L. R. 1998. Cytokines for psychologists: implications of bidirectional immune-to-brain communication for understanding behaviour, mood, and cognition, *Psychological Review* 105: 83–107

Magnusson, D. and Törestad, B. 1993. A holistic view of personality: a model revisited, *Annual Review of Psychology* 44: 427–52

Marmot, M. and Wilkinson, R. G. 2001. Psychosocial and material pathways in the relation between income and health: a response to Lynch *et al.*, *British Medical Journal* 322: 1233–6

Masse, L. C. and Tremblay, R. E. 1997. Behaviour of boys in kindergarten and the onset of substance use during adolescence, *Archives of General Psychiatry* 51: 732–9

McCaffery, J. M., Bleil, M., Pogue-Geile, M. F., Ferrell, R. E. and Manuck, S. B. 2003. Allelic variation in the serotonin transporter gene-linked polymorphic region (5-HTTLPR) and cardiovascular reactivity in young adult male and female twins of European-American descent, *Psychosomatic Medicine* 65: 721–8

McEwen, B. S. 1998. Protective and damaging effects of stress mediators, *New England Journal of Medicine* 338: 171–9

McEwen, B. S. and Stellar, E. 1993. Stress and the individual: mechanisms leading to disease, *Archives of Internal Medicine* 153: 2093–101

McGrath, J. E. and Beehr, T. A. 1990. Time and the stress response, *Stress Medicine* 6: 93–104

Miller, S. B. and Ditto, B. 1991. Exaggerated sympathetic nervous system response to extended psychological stress in offspring of hypertensives, *Psychophysiology* 28: 103–13

Miller, T. Q., Markides, K. S., Chiriboga, D. A. and Ray, L. A. 1995. A test of the psychosocial vulnerability and health behaviour models of hostility: results from an 11-year follow-up study of Mexican Americans, *Psychosometric Medicine* 57: 572–81

Miller, T. Q., Smith, T. W., Turner, C. W., Guijarro, M. L. and Hallet, A. J. 1996. A meta-analytic review of research on hostility and physical health, *Psychological Bulletin* 119: 322–48

Mischel, W. and Shoda, Y. 1995. A cognitive-affective system theory of personality: reconceptualizing situations, dispositions, dynamics, and invariance in personality structure, *Psychological Review* 102: 246–68

Munafo, M. R., Clark, T. G., Moore, L. R., Payne, E., Walton, R. and Flint, J. 2003. Genetic polymorphisms and personality in healthy adults: a systematic review and meta-analysis, *Molecular Psychiatry* 8: 471–84

Paunonen, S. V. and Ashton, M. C. 2001. Big Five factors and facets and the prediction of behaviour, *Journal of Personality and Social Psychology* 81: 524–39

Pope, M. K. and Smith, T. W. 1991. Cortisol excretion in high and low cynically hostile men, *Psychosomatic Medicine* 53: 386–92

Power, C., Matthews, S. and Manor, O. 1998. Inequalities in self-rated health: explanations from different stages of life, *Lancet* 351: 1009–14

Pulkki, L., Kivimäki, M., Keltikangas-Järvinen, L., Elovainio, M., Leino, M. and Viikari, J. 2003. Contribution of adolescent and early adult personality to the inverse association between education and cardiovascular risk behaviours: prospective population-based cohort study, *International Journal of Epidemiology* 32: 968–75

Pulkkinen, L. and Pitkänen, T. 1994. A prospective study of the precursors to problem drinking in young adulthood, *Journal of Studies in Alcoholism* 55: 578–87

Räikkönen, K., Matthews, K. A. and Salomon, K. 2003. Hostility predicts metabolic syndrome risk factors in children and adolescents, *Health Psychology* 22: 279–86

Ravaja, N. 1996. *Psychological antecedents of metabolic syndrome precursors in the young*. Helsinki: Yliopistopaino

    2004. Effects of a small talking facial image on autonomic activity: the moderating influence of dispositional BIS and BAS sensitivities and emotions, *Biological Psychology* 65: 163–83

Ravaja, N. and Keltikangas-Järvinen, L. 1995. Temperament and metabolic syndrome precursors in children: a three-year follow-up, *Preventive Medicine* 24: 518–27

Rexrode, K. M., Carey, V. J., Hennekens, C. H., Walters, E. E., Golditz, G. A., Stampfer, M. J. *et al*. 1998. Abdominal adiposity and coronary heart disease in women, *Journal of the American Medical Association* 280: 1843–8

Rosenberg, E. L., Ekman, P. and Blumenthal, J. A. 1998. Facial expression and the affective component of cynical hostility in male coronary heart disease patients, *Health Psychology* 17: 376–80

Scheier, M. F., Carver, C. S. and Bridges, M. W. 1994. Distinguishing optimism from neuroticism (and trait anxiety, self-mastery, and self-esteem): a reevaluation of the Life Orientation Test, *Journal of Personal Social Psychology* 67: 1063–78

Scherwitz, L. W., Perkins, L. L., Chesney, M. A., Hughes, G. H., Sidney, S. and Manolio, T. A. 1992. Hostility and health behaviours in young adults: the CARDIA study, *American Journal of Epidemiology* 136: 136–45

Schneiderman, M. A. 1987. Mortality experience of employees with occupational exposure to DBCP, *Archives of Environmental Health* 42: 245–7

Schneiderman, N. 1987. Psychophysiologic factors in atherosgenesis and coronary artery disease, *Circulation* 76: 541–7

Selye, H. 1956. What is stress?, *Metabolism* 5: 525

    1973. The evaluation of the stress concept, *American Scientist* 61: 692–9

Sheldon, K. M. and Elliot, A. J. 2000. Personal goals in social roles: divergences and convergences across roles and levels of analysis, *Journal of Personality* 68: 51–84

Singh, J. P., Larson, M. G., O'Donnell, C. J. and Levy, D. 2001. Genetic factors contribute to the variance in frequency domain measures of heart rate variability, *Autonomic Neuroscience-Basic and Clinical* 90: 122–6

Smith, T. W. (1992). Hostility and health: current status of a psychosomatic hypothesis, *Health Psychology* 11: 139–50

Smith, T. W., Allred, K. D., Sanders, J. D., Pope, M. K. and O'Keeffe, J. L. 1988. Cynical hostility at home and work: psychosocial vulnerability across domains, *Journal of Research in Personality* 22: 525–48

Smith, T. W. and Frohm, K. D. 1985. What's so unhealthy about hostility? Construct validity and psychosocial correlates of the Cook and Medley Ho scale, *Health Psychology* 4: 503–20

Smith, T. W., Glazer, K., Ruiz, J. M. and Gallo, L. C. 2004. Hostility, anger, aggressiveness, and coronary heart disease: an interpersonal perspective on personality, emotion, and health, *Journal of Personality* 72: 1217–70

Smith, T. W. and Mackenzie, J. 2006. Personality and risk of physical illness, *Annual Review of Clinical Psychology* 2: 435–67

Smith, T. W. and Pope, M. K. 1990. Cynical hostility as a health risk: current status and future directions, *Journal of Social Behaviour and Personality* 5: 77–88

Stansfeld, S. A., Fuhrer, R., Shipley, M. J. and Marmot, M. G. 2002. Psychological distress as a risk factor for coronary heart disease in the Whitehall II Study, *International Journal of Epidemiology* 31: 248–55

Strike, P. C., Perkins-Porras, L., Whitehead, D. L., McEwan, J. and Steptoe, A. 2006. Triggering of acute coronary syndromes by physical exertion and anger: clinical and sociodemographic characteristics, *Heart* 92: 1035–40

Suls, J. and Wan, C. K. 1993. The relationship between trait hostility and cardiovascular reactivity: a quantitative review and analysis, *Psychophysiology* 30: 615–26

Sweeting, H. and West, P. 1995. Family life and health in adolescence: a role for culture in the health inequalities debate?, *Social Science and Medicine* 40: 163–75

Swinburn, B. A., Caterson, I., Seidell, J. C. and James, W. P. T. 2004. Diet, nutrition and the prevention of excess weight gain and obesity, *Public Health Nutrition* 7: 123–46

Tranel, D. T., Fisher, A. E. and Fowles, D. C. 1982. Magnitude of incentive effects on heart rate, *Psychophysiology* 19: 514–19

Virtanen, M., Kivimäki, M., Elovainio, M. and Vahtera, J. 2002. Selection from fixed term to permanent employment: prospective study on health, job satisfaction, and behavioural risks, *Journal of Epidemiology and Community Health* 56: 693–9

Yang, X., Telama, R., Keltikangas-Järvinen, L. and Räikkönen, K. 1998. Type A behaviour as a determinant of participation in physical activity and sport among adolescents, *European Physical Education Review* 4: 21–33

Yang, X., Telama, R. and Leskinen, E. 2000. Testing a multidisciplinary model of socialization into physical activity: a 6-year follow-up study, *European Journal of Physical Education* 5: 67–87

14 Attachment theory: I. Motivational, individual-differences and structural aspects

Phillip R. Shaver and Mario Mikulincer

Attachment theory, first proposed by British psychoanalyst John Bowlby (1973, 1980, 1982/1969) and then elaborated and empirically tested by Mary Ainsworth and her colleagues (e.g., Ainsworth, Blehar, Waters and Wall 1978), began its intellectual life as a modest attempt on Bowlby's part to understand why separations from mother early in life causes so much psychological difficulty for children, adolescents and adults later in life (e.g., Bowlby 1951, 1958). As Bowlby worked his way deeper and deeper into this problem area, however (Bowlby 1982/1969, p. xxvii)

> it was gradually borne in upon me that the field I had set out to plough so lightheartedly was no less than the one that Freud had started tilling sixty years earlier, and that it contained all those same rocky excrescences and thorny entanglements that he had encountered and grappled with – love and hate, anxiety and defense, attachment and loss.

Bowlby eventually created an alternative to psychoanalytic theory, one much more solidly grounded in primate ethology, cognitive developmental psychology and clinical research. Ainsworth, Blehar, Waters and Wall (1978) added important ideas and assessment procedures, which allowed her and Bowlby's theory to be rigorously tested, revised and expanded for more than thirty years. Today, because of this auspicious theoretical and psychometric foundation, attachment theory has spawned a large and complex literature comprising thousands of empirical studies, a literature that continues to reflect Bowlby's psychoanalytic origins. As a personality theory, attachment theory combines psychoanalytic, evolutionary, developmental, social-cognitive and trait-like constructs in a systematic framework that transcends the usual typologies of personality theories. Still, the subheadings used in textbooks that systematically compare personality theories (e.g., Hall, Lindzey and Campbell 2001) – structure, motivation, dynamics, individual differences, development, and mental health or optimal adjustment – are useful in organizing and explaining attachment theory and its research literature.

In this and the next chapter, we describe attachment theory and research in terms of some of the classic theory-comparison categories, referring to each one as a 'module' of the theory. In the present chapter, we focus on the motivational, individual-difference and structural modules of the theory. In the next chapter, we review its developmental, psychodynamic and 'optimal functioning' components. Our account is based on our recent book, *Attachment in Adulthood* (Mikulincer and Shaver 2007), which comprehensively reviews and integrates the sprawling attachment literature. Because Bowlby's initial efforts were aimed at conceptualizing motivation differently from Freud's drive theory, we begin with attachment theory's motivation module.

Motivation module

In explaining the motivational bases of personality development, Bowlby (1982/1969) rejected Freudian and object relations versions of psychoanalytic theory that conceptualize human motivation in terms of 'drives' and view the mind as powered by 'psychic energy'. Instead, he created a 'behavioural systems' model of motivation, borrowed from ethology and cybernetic control theory, according to which human behaviour is organized and guided by species-universal, innate neural programmes (*behavioural systems*). These attachment, care-giving, exploration and sexual systems facilitate the satisfaction of fundamental human needs and thereby increase the likelihood of survival, adjustment and reproduction. Bowlby (1982/1969) viewed the systems as 'goal directed' and 'goal corrected' (i.e., corrected by changing sub-goals based on feedback about goal non-attainment). Each system was conceptualized as a servomechanism that could be turned on, or 'activated', by certain stimuli or situations and 'deactivated' or 'terminated' by other stimuli and situations (basically, by the attainment of what Bowlby called 'set-goals', which in the case of the attachment system include escape from and avoidance of threats and dangers). Behavioural systems move a person toward set-goals by encouraging him or her to monitor, appraise and evaluate goal-relevant internal and external cues, and to learn new means-end associations and stimulus-response contingencies that increase the likelihood of goal attainment and facilitate need satisfaction.

This new conception of motivation rendered the Freudian notion of general drives (e.g., libido) unnecessary. Goal directed and goal corrected behaviours are activated not by an accumulation of psychic energy or a desire to reduce drive intensity, but by conditions within a person or the person's environment that activated behaviour intended to achieve a certain goal state or to avoid threats and dangers. Behavioural intensity was viewed as a function of the appraised effort needed to attain a targeted set-goal, or of the overriding of one behavioural system by another, either when the set-goal of the overridden system was attained or an alternative behavioural system was activated at a higher intensity level. For example, when an infant encounters environmental threats (e.g., unexpected noises, the appearance of a frightening animal, sudden darkness), he or she terminates whatever activity is in progress (e.g., exploring the environment or playing with a toy) and searches for a care-giver, perhaps calling out to that person or beginning to cry, and, if possible, moving quickly to the person's side and signalling to be picked up and protected. If the care-giver provides adequate comfort, the infant is likely to become interested once again in play or exploration and hence signal to be put down.

In the case of the attachment behavioural system, Bowlby (1982/1969) focused on the fundamental need for care and protection and the innate predisposition to search for and maintain proximity to protective and caring others in times of need. The set-goal of the attachment system is the attainment of actual or perceived protection and security; hence, the system is automatically activated when a potential or actual threat to one's sense of security is noticed. Under these conditions, a person tends automatically to turn for protection and comfort to supportive others (whom Bowlby called *attachment figures*), and to maintain proximity to these 'stronger and wiser' figures until a state of protection and security is attained. Proximity to these figures becomes a source of positive emotions (e.g., joy, gratitude, relief), whereas separation and distance from these figures become sources of anxiety, psychological pain and distress. Although the attachment system is most important early in life, Bowlby (1988) claimed it is active over the entire lifespan and is manifest in thoughts and behaviours related to seeking proximity in times of need. This claim provided the impetus for subsequent theorists and researchers, including ourselves, to conceptualize and study adult attachment.

During infancy, primary care-givers (usually one or both parents but also grandparents, older siblings, daycare workers) are likely to occupy the role of attachment figure. During adolescence and adulthood, other relationship partners often become targets of proximity and support-seeking, including close friends and romantic partners. Teachers and supervisors in academic settings or therapists in clinical settings can also serve as real or potential sources of comfort and support, and therefore can be treated as attachment figures. Moreover, groups, institutions and symbolic personages (e.g., God, the Buddha or the Virgin Mary) can be recruited as attachment figures. They form what Bowlby (1982/1969) called a person's *hierarchy of attachment figures*.

In addition, mental representations of attachment figures and self-sub-routines that develop through the internalization of caring and soothing qualities of attachment figures can serve as symbolic sources of support, comfort and protection (Mikulincer and Shaver 2004). They can also provide models of effective, loving behaviour that influence the way a person regards and treats him- or herself in the temporary absence of an actual attachment figure. Nonetheless, although Bowlby (1982/1969, 1988) assumed that age and psychological development result in an increased ability to gain comfort from attachment-related mental representations, he also assumed that no one of any age is completely free of reliance on actual others when confronting illness, death of loved ones, aging and other natural and human-caused disasters and traumas.

Bowlby's ideas about the predisposition to seek proximity to others for the sake of care and protection have received extensive empirical support. In times of need, infants show a clear preference for their care-giver, engage in intense proximity-seeking, and are soothed by a care-giver's presence and support (e.g., Ainsworth 1991). Conceptually parallel research with adults has shown that people are likely to choose to affiliate with a sympathetic other while awaiting a noxious event (see Shaver and Klinnert 1982, for a review) and to turn to others for support while, or immediately after, encountering stressful events (see Lazarus and Folkman 1984, for a review).

Using contemporary research techniques, we (Mikulincer, Birnbaum and Woddis and Nachmias 2000; Mikulincer, Gillath and Shaver 2002) have found that adults react to even minimal threat cues with activation of proximity-related thoughts and mental representations of security-providing attachment figures. In these studies, subliminal priming with a threat word (e.g., illness, failure) was found to heighten the cognitive accessibility of attachment-related mental representations, indicated by faster lexical-decision times for proximity-related words (e.g., love, closeness) and the names of people nominated as providing protection and security (e.g., the name of a parent, spouse or close friend). Interestingly, these effects were circumscribed to attachment-related representations and were not found for attachment-unrelated words or the names of people other than attachment figures, including family members who were not nominated as security-providing attachment figures. These findings support Bowlby's core claim that the mind turns automatically to attachment figures when threats loom. Moreover, they confirm that attachment figures are not just any relationship partners; they are special people to whom one turns, even unconsciously, when comfort or support is needed.

There is also extensive evidence that separation from and loss of attachment figures are common sources of pain and distress. Ethological observation of infants separated from their mothers (e.g., Heinicke and Westheimer 1966; Robertson and Bowlby 1952) revealed early in the history of attachment research that absence of an attachment figure causes intense distress, anxiety, anger, protest and yearning. In adulthood, bereavement research has also found that loss of a close relationship partner is one of the most painful experiences a person can endure, one that typically elicits extreme sorrow, despair and painful longing for the deceased partner (see Fraley and Shaver 1999, for a review). Similar emotional reactions have also been observed following the break-up of romantic relationships (e.g., Feeney and Noller 1992; Simpson 1990). Milder but still consequential forms of distress arise in reaction to disapproval, criticism or rejection, especially from an attachment figure (Shaver, Mikulincer, Lavy and Cassidy in press).

Researchers have also documented the positive emotional effects of attaining desired proximity to attachment figures. For example, Gump, Polk, Kamarck and Shiffman (2001) recorded blood pressure at least once per hour during study participants' waking hours for a week and found that blood pressure was lower when participants were interacting with their romantic partner than when they were interacting with other people or were alone. Coan, Schaefer and Davidson (2006) scanned the brains (using functional magnetic resonance imaging) of married women who were undergoing a laboratory stressor (threat of electric shock) while holding either their husband's hand, the hand of an otherwise unfamiliar male experimenter, or no hand at all. The findings indicated that spousal hand-holding reduced physiological stress responses, as seen in brain regions associated with distress (e.g., right anterior insula, superior frontal gyrus, and hypothalamus). In another series of studies, Mikulincer, Hirschberger, Nachmias and Gillath (2001) found that a variety of experimentally induced triggers can activate mental representations of internalized attachment figures and cause positive affective reactions similar to those evoked by an actual figure. Specifically, these techniques can cause more positive evaluations of previously neutral stimuli, even under threatening conditions, eliminating the usual negative associations between such situations and negative feelings.

Individual-difference module

As explained thus far, attachment theory provided an alternative psycho-dynamic framework for conceptualizing human motivation and socio-emotional bonds, but it might not have captured the attention of developmental, personality, social and clinical researchers if it had done only that. What captured research psychologists' attention were the patterns or styles of attachment emphasized in Bowlby's (1973, 1980) theory and operationalized in Ainsworth's research on mother-infant dyads (Ainsworth, Blehar, Waters and Wall 1978). Most of the research inspired by the theory focuses on these individual differences.

According to Bowlby (1973), the ability of a behavioural system to achieve its set-goal depends on a person's transactions with the external world. Although behavioural systems are innate intrapsychic mechanisms, which presumably operate mainly at a subcortical level and in an automatic, reflexive manner, they are manifested in actual behaviour, guide people's transactions with the social world, and can be affected or shaped by others' responses. Over time, social encounters mould the parameters of a person's behavioural systems in ways that produce fairly stable individual differences in strategies and behaviours; that is, a person's neural and behavioural capacities become 'programmed' to fit with major close relationship partners, or attachment figures. Bowlby (1973) assumed that the residues of such social encounters are stored as mental representations of person-environment transactions, which he called *working models of self and other*, and that these representations shape the functioning of a person's behavioural system and the way he or she behaves in particular social situations. These models presumably operate mainly at a cortical level and in both unconscious and fairly reflective and intentional ways. Even when they initially operate consciously, however, with repeated use they can become automatic and unconscious, either as most well-formed habits do or by virtue of motivated defensive manoeuvres. These models are an important source of within-person continuity over time and individual differences between persons, so they are properly regarded as important aspects of personality.

In discussing individual differences in the functioning of behavioural systems, Bowlby (1973) rejected psychoanalytic and object relations approaches that placed exclusive emphasis on a person's fantasies, internal conflicts and defences and downplayed a person's actual experiences with relationship partners. Although Bowlby (1980) agreed that behavioural-system functioning is a reflection of intrapsychic processes related to a person's wishes, fears and defences, it is still sensitive to the relational context in general and to a relationship partner's particular responses on a specific occasion. For example, attachment-system functioning involves real or imagined interpersonal interactions with actual or internalized attachment figures and can be altered by these figures' responses to one's bids for proximity and support. In this respect, attachment theory has much in common with interpersonal psychodynamic theories of personality (e.g., Horney 1945; Sullivan 1953) and social-psychological interdependence theories of relationships (e.g., Kelley, Berscheid, Christensen *et al.* 1983; Thibault and Kelley 1959). All of these theories focus on social interactions as the unit of analysis and emphasize the powerful influence that one person's responses exert on a partner's thoughts, feelings and behaviours.

According to Bowlby (1973), individual differences in attachment-system functioning are a result of the availability, responsiveness and supportiveness of attachment figures in times of need. Interactions with attachment figures who are available and responsive facilitate optimal functioning of the attachment system and promote a core sense of *attachment security* – a sense that the world is generally a safe place, that attachment figures are helpful when called upon, and that it is possible to explore the environment curiously and engage effectively with other people without being hurt. During these interactions, a person learns that acknowledgment and display of distress elicit supportive responses from others and that turning to others when threatened is an effective means of coping. These experiences generate positive working models of self and others that increase both self-confidence and confidence in others' goodwill and supportiveness.

When attachment figures are not reliably available and supportive, a sense of security is not attained, negative working models of self and others are formed, and secondary strategies of affect regulation come into play. According to Cassidy and Kobak (1988), these secondary strategies are of two kinds: *hyperactivation* and *deactivation* of the attachment system. Hyperactivation (which Bowlby (1982/1969) called 'protest') is characterized by energetic, insistent attempts to get a relationship partner, viewed as insufficiently available or responsive, to pay more attention and provide better care and support. Hyperactivating strategies include clinging, controlling and coercive responses; cognitive and behavioural efforts to establish physical contact and a sense of 'oneness'; and overdependence on relationship partners as a source of protection (Shaver and Mikulincer 2002). Hyperactivation keeps the attachment system chronically activated and constantly on the alert for threats, separations and betrayals; it therefore unintentionally exacerbates relational conflict, heightens distress associated with attachment-figure unavailability, and reinforces doubts about one's ability ever to attain a sense of security (Mikulincer and Shaver 2003, 2007).

Deactivation refers to inhibition of proximity-seeking inclinations and actions, suppression or discounting of threats that might activate the attachment system, and determination to handle stresses alone (a stance Bowlby (1982/1969), called 'compulsive self-reliance'). These strategies involve maintaining physical and emotional distance from others, being uncomfortable with intimacy and interdependence, ignoring or downplaying threat- and attachment-related cues, and suppressing threat- and attachment-related thoughts (Shaver and Hazan 1993). These tendencies are bolstered by a self-reliant attitude that decreases dependence on others and discourages acknowledgment of personal faults (Mikulincer and Shaver 2007).

In examining individual differences in the functioning of the attachment system in infancy, childhood, adolescence and adulthood, attachment researchers have focused on a person's *attachment style* – the pattern of relational needs, cognitions, emotions and behaviours that results from satisfactory or frustrating interactions with attachment figures. These styles were first described by Ainsworth (1967; Ainsworth, Blehar, Waters and Wall 1978) based on her observations of infants' responses to separations from and reunions with mother in a laboratory 'Strange Situation' assessment procedure. Ainsworth classified infants into one of three style categories: secure, anxious or avoidant. Main and Solomon (1990) later added a fourth category, 'disorganized', characterized by odd, awkward behaviour and unusual alternations or mixtures of anxiety and avoidance.

The responses of infants classified as secure in the Strange Situation are thought to reflect a solid sense of attachment security. Such infants react to separation from mother with overt expressions of distress but then recover quickly when reunited with her and return to exploring the environment with interest and enthusiasm. They greet their mother with joy and affection, initiate contact with her, and respond positively to being held and comforted (Ainsworth, Blehar, Waters and Wall 1978). Avoidant infants, in contrast, seem to possess negative working models and to rely on attachment-system deactivation as a self-regulating defence. They show little overt distress when separated from mother, although their heart rate indicates autonomic arousal, and they actively avoid her upon reunion (Ainsworth *et al.* 1978). Anxious infants also seem to possess negative working models, but tend to rely on attachment-system hyperactivation as a defence. They protest separation loudly and seem conflicted and angry upon reunion (Ainsworth *et al.* 1978).

In the 1980s, researchers from different sub-disciplines (developmental, clinical, personality and social psychology) constructed new measures of attachment style to extend attachment research into adolescence and adulthood. Based on a developmental and clinical approach, for example, Main and her colleagues (George, Kaplan and Main 1985; Main, Kaplan and Cassidy 1985; see Hesse 1999, for a review) devised the Adult Attachment Interview (AAI) to study adolescents' and adults' mental representations of attachment to their parents during childhood. In the AAI, interviewees answer open-ended questions about their childhood relationships with parents and are classified into three, four or five categories parallelling Ainsworth's infant typology, but supplemented with some post-Ainsworth categories: 'secure' (or free and autonomous with respect to attachment); 'dismissing' (of attachment), which is parallel to the infant 'avoidant' category; 'preoccupied' (with attachment), which parallels the 'anxious' category; 'unresolved' (with respect to trauma and losses), which parallels the 'disorganized' category; and 'cannot classify' (because of conflicting indicators within a particular interview; Hesse 1999).

Using the AAI coding system (George, Kaplan and Main 1985), a person is classified as secure if he or she describes parents as available and responsive, and his or her memories of relationships with parents are presented in a clear, convincing and coherent manner. Dismissing persons downplay the importance of attachment relationships and tend to recall few concrete episodes of emotional interactions with parents. Preoccupied individuals are enmeshed in anxious and angry feelings about parents, are hypersensitive to attachment experiences, and can easily retrieve negative memories but cannot discuss them coherently. Unresolved individuals are particularly disorganized mentally when attempting to discuss traumas and losses. Despite the richness of AAI narratives, which are particularly useful in clinical settings, the interview is costly to administer and score, and it deals exclusively with memories of child-parent relationships. It does not directly measure attachment orientations in peer or romantic relationships.

Working from a personality and social psychological perspective, Hazan and Shaver (1987, 1990) developed a self-report measure of adult attachment style suitable for use in experiments and surveys. In its original form, the measure consisted of three brief descriptions of feelings and behaviours in close relationships that were intended to characterize adult romantic analogues of the three infant attachment styles identified by Ainsworth, Blehar, Waters and Wall (1978). Participants were asked to read the descriptions and then place themselves into one of the three attachment categories according to their predominant feelings and behaviour in romantic relationships. The three descriptions were:

> *Secure*: I find it relatively easy to get close to others and am comfortable depending on them and having them depend on me. I don't worry about being abandoned or about someone getting too close to me.
> *Avoidant*: I am somewhat uncomfortable being close to others; I find it difficult to trust them completely, difficult to allow myself to depend on them. I am nervous when anyone gets too close and often, others want me to be more intimate than I feel comfortable being.
> *Anxious*: I find that others are reluctant to get as close as I would like. I often worry that my partner doesn't really love me or won't want to stay with me. I want to get very close to my partner and this sometimes scares people away.

Hazan and Shaver's seminal studies were followed by hundreds of others that used the simple forced-choice self-report measure to examine the interpersonal and intrapersonal correlates of adult attachment style (see reviews by Mikulincer and Shaver 2003, 2007; Shaver and Hazan 1993; Shaver and Mikulincer 2002). Over time, attachment researchers largely agreed that attachment styles are best conceptualized as regions in a two-dimensional (anxiety-by-avoidance) space (e.g., Brennan, Clark and Shaver 1998; Fraley and Waller 1998). These two dimensions are consistently obtained in factor analyses of attachment measures (e.g., Brennan, Clark and Shaver 1998). Moreover, dimensional representations of attachment style are more accurate than categorical representations (Fraley and Waller 1998). The first dimension, attachment-related *avoidance*, is concerned with discomfort with closeness and dependence on relationship partners, preference for emotional distance and self-reliance, and the use of deactivating strategies to deal with insecurity and distress. The second dimension, attachment-related *anxiety*, is concerned with a strong desire for closeness and protection, intense worries about partner availability and one's own value to the partner, and the use of hyperactivating strategies for dealing with insecurity and distress. People who score low on both dimensions are said to be secure or to have a secure attachment style. This region of low anxiety and low avoidance is defined by a chronic sense of attachment security, trust in partners and expectations of partner availability and responsiveness, comfort with closeness and interdependence, and coping with stress in constructive ways.

The two attachment-style dimensions, which are considered to be the two major kinds of attachment insecurity, can be measured with the thirty-six-item Experiences in Close Relationships inventory (ECR) (Brennan, Clark and Shaver 1998), which is reliable in both the internal-consistency and test-retest senses and has high construct, predictive and discriminant validity (Crowell, Fraley and Shaver 1999; Mikulincer and Shaver 2007). Eighteen items tap the avoidance dimension (e.g., 'I try to avoid getting too close to my partner'), and the remaining eighteen items tap the anxiety dimension (e.g., 'I need a lot of reassurance that I am loved by my partner'). The two scales were conceptualized as orthogonal and have been found to be empirically independent in most studies. Moreover, they can be used to assess a person's global attachment orientations in a range of close relationships as well as his or her attachment orientation in a particular relationship or on a particular occasion (Mikulincer and Shaver 2007). Studies using self-report measures of adult attachment style have found them to be coherently related to relationship quality, mental health, social adjustment, ways of coping, emotion regulation, self-esteem, interpersonal behaviour and social cognitions (see Mikulincer and Shaver 2003, 2007, for reviews). Importantly, these attachment-style variations are usually not well explained by less specific, more global personality traits such as Extraversion, Neuroticism or self-esteem (see Mikulincer and Shaver 2007, for a review), although there are predictable and meaningful associations between attachment orientations and personality traits (e.g., Carver 1997; Noftle and Shaver 2006).

There is relatively little research on the heritability of attachment orientations measured with self-report scales, but Crawford, Livesley, Jang *et al.* (2007) reported preliminary evidence for the heritability of attachment anxiety and no evidence for the heritability of avoidant attachment. These results suggest that what is measured by self-report attachment scales is not wholly the same as what is measured by the Strange Situation and the Adult Attachment Interview, which seem to be unrelated to heritable aspects of personality (e.g., O'Connor 2005). Moreover, different studies have suggested different degrees of association between the various adult attachment measures (e.g., Shaver, Belsky and Brennan 2000; Mikulincer and Shaver 2004). Nevertheless, in our review of the broad literature on adult attachment (Mikulincer and Shaver 2007), we noted many cases in which similar results were obtained using the AAI and one of the major self-report measures. For the time being, the differences between measures and associated theoretical conceptions have to be kept in mind when assessing attachment style.

The relational basis of individual differences in attachment style has been strongly supported in infant attachment studies. In the earliest studies of infant attachment, Ainsworth, Blehar, Waters and Wall (1978) identified several maternal behaviours during home observations of mother-child interactions that were associated with an infant's attachment security in the Strange Situation. These behaviours included, for example, being responsive to the infant's crying, timing of feeding, sensitivity to the infant's signals and needs, psychological accessibility when the infant was distressed or signalled a need or desire for support and comfort. In subsequent decades, dozens of studies followed up Ainsworth *et al.*'s (1978) findings and further linked infant attachment security with sensitive maternal behaviour and the quality of paternal care-giving (see Atkinson, Niccols, Paglia *et al.* 2000; De Wolff and van IJzendoorn 1997, for reviews and meta-analyses). Based on this solid evidence, van IJzendoorn and Bakermans-Kranenburg (2004, p. 248) concluded that 'the causal role of maternal sensitivity in the formation of the infant-mother attachment relationship is a strongly corroborated finding. Correlational, experimental, and cross-cultural studies have replicated the association between sensitivity and attachment numerous times, and through different measures and designs'.

With reference to adult attachment, Lavi (2007) recently conducted a prospective longitudinal study of young couples who had been dating for no more than three to four months and followed them up four and eight months later. She found that participants' reports of within-relationship attachment anxiety and avoidance (assessed with a relationship-specific version of the ECR scales) gradually decreased over the eight-month period, implying that a stable premarital relationship contributed to a decline in relationship-specific attachment insecurities. However, these positive changes depended greatly on a partner's sensitivity and supportiveness, as assessed by behavioural observations at the beginning of the study. Partners who were more accurate in decoding facial expressions and non-verbal expressions of negative emotions, and who were coded by judges as more supportive toward participants in a dyadic interaction task, brought about a steeper decline in within-relationship attachment anxiety and avoidance across the eight-month period. In fact, participants showed no significant decrease in within-relationship attachment insecurities if their partners scored relatively low on sensitivity and supportiveness at the beginning of the study.

An analysis of prospectively predicted changes in global attachment orientations in close relationships revealed that whereas a partner's sensitivity and responsiveness predicted a significant decrease in global attachment anxiety over the eight-month study period, there was no such effect on global avoidant attachment, which may be more resistant to change due to partner behaviour because avoidant individuals do not readily engage fully with their partners. Overall, the new research findings support Bowlby's emphasis on real interactions with a sensitive relationship partner as potentially transformative experiences that can move a person toward greater security. The results also suggest some constraints on these positive effects: evidently it is not so easy to induce change in a globally avoidant attachment style, even when an avoidant person is fortunate enough to have a loving and caring partner.

Personality structure

Bowlby (1973, 1988) believed that attachment-style differences can be explained in terms of storing significant interactions or relationships with attachment figures in an associative memory network. This stored knowledge allows a person to predict future interactions with relationship partners and adjust proximity-seeking attempts without having to rethink each one from the ground up. Moreover, with successive recording in memory of attachment-related interactions, these cognitive structures provide increasingly stable knowledge about the self, relationship partners and close relationships, just as increased experience in any domain contributes to the formation of mental schemas related to those domains. As reviewed earlier, Bowlby (1982/1969, 1973) called these cognitive structures *working models* and viewed them as the core of stable attachment-style differences.

From a social cognition standpoint, the concept of working model is similar to such concepts as 'script' and 'social schema'. Like those concepts, working models are viewed as being stored in an associative memory network, as having excitatory and inhibitory connections with other mental representations, and as possessing a certain level of accessibility determined by past experiences and current context (e.g., Collins and Read 1994; Mikulincer and Shaver 2007; Shaver, Collins and Clark 1996). However, as compared with other mental representations, (a) working models also contain or express a person's wishes, fears, conflicts and psychological defences; (b, a related point) working models seem to have a powerful affective component and tend to be shaped by emotion-regulation processes; (c) working models tend to be constructed in relational terms and to organize representations of the social self, interaction partners and social interactions; and (d) attachment working models are broad, rich and complex structures which can include tandem or opposite representations of the same social experiences at episodic, semantic and procedural levels of encoding (Shaver, Collins and Clark 1996). Overall, attachment working models, especially in adulthood, cannot be equated with most other social cognitions, because they evolve not only from simple memories of actual experiences but also from dynamic processes of emotion regulation and psychological defences organized around wishes for proximity and security, and fears of separation and helplessness. As a result, they can distort perceptions of social reality, even though many were originally formed in actual social situations.

Bowlby (1982/1969) argued that interactions with attachment figures are stored in at least two kinds of working models: representations of attachment figures' responses (*working models of others*) and representations of the self's lovability and competence (*working models of self*). He argued that, 'If an individual is to draw up a plan to achieve a set-goal not only does he have to have some sort of working model of his environment, but he must have also some working knowledge of his own behavioural skills and potentialities' (1982/1969, p. 112). Thus the attachment system, once it has been used repeatedly in a given relational setting, includes representations of the availability, responsiveness and sensitivity of a relationship partner, as well as representations of the self's own capabilities for mobilizing the partner's support and one's feelings of being loved and valued by the partner. These representations organize a person's sense of self-esteem and self-efficacy as well as his or her appraisals of relationship partners, with more secure models resulting in more positive appraisals of the self and others.

Adult attachment research has provided extensive evidence concerning the role of attachment working models in a person's appraisals of the self and others. Numerous studies have shown that insecure working models are associated with negative appraisals of other people. Specifically, individuals scoring higher on attachment anxiety or avoidance have been found to hold a more negative view of human nature (Collins and Read 1990), use more negative traits to describe relationship partners (e.g., Feeney and Noller 1991), perceive these partners as less supportive and trustworthy (e.g., Collins and Read 1990; Davis, Morris and Kraus 1998), and believe that their partners do not truly know them (Brennan and Bosson 1998). Both anxiety and avoidance are also associated with negative expectations concerning a partner's behaviour (e.g., Baldwin, Fehr, Keedian *et al.* 1993). Similar attachment-style differences have been found when research participants are asked to explain other people's behaviour. For example, Collins (1996) asked people to explain hypothetical negative behaviours of a romantic partner and found that more anxious and avoidant people were more likely to provide explanations that implied lack of confidence in the partner's love, attribute partner's negative behaviours to stable and global causes, and view these behaviours as negatively motivated.

There is also evidence that insecure working models, particularly along the attachment anxiety dimension, are associated with negative self-appraisals. Compared to secure people, attachment-anxious people report lower self-esteem (e.g., Bartholomew and Horowitz 1991) and hold more negative appraisals of self-competence and more negative expectations of self-efficacy (e.g., Cooper, Shaver and Collins 1998). Mikulincer (1995) also found that people scoring higher on attachment anxiety and avoidance possess a less coherent and integrated network of self-representations and exhibit greater discrepancies between actual self and personal standards. Attachment anxiety and avoidance have also been consistently associated with self-criticism (e.g., Zuroff and Fitzpatrick 1995) and maladaptive perfectionistic forms of goal-setting, such as holding unrealistically high standards, ruminating about mistakes, and feeling pressured by others to be perfect (e.g., Rice, Lopez and Vergara 2005). Studies have also shown that less secure people, particularly those who are attachment-anxious, tend to base their self-appraisals on unstable, conditional sources of self-worth (e.g., others' approval), so that any indications of a partner's disapproval or disinterest can further lower their self-esteem (e.g., Park, Crocker and Mickelson 2004).

Because working models, at least initially, are based on the internalization of specific interactions with a particular attachment figure, a person can hold multiple working models that differ in the outcome of the interaction (success or failure to attain security) and the strategy used to deal with insecurity in that interaction (hyperactivation or deactivation of the attachment system). Like other mental representations, these working models form excitatory and inhibitory associations with each other (e.g., experiencing or thinking about security attainment activates memories of congruent episodes of gaining protection and security), and these associations favour the formation of more abstract and generalized representations of self and others. Thus, models with a specific attachment figure (relationship-specific models) are created, and through excitatory and inhibitory links with models representing interactions with other attachment figures, even more generic working models are formed to summarize or abstract from different relationships. The end result can be conceptualized as a hierarchical associative memory network that includes episodic memories, relationship-specific models, and generic models of the self and others. As a result, with respect to a particular relationship and across different relationships, most people can sometimes think about interpersonal interactions in more secure terms and at other times think about them in less secure terms.

In a recent study, Overall, Fletcher and Friesen (2003) provided evidence for this hierarchical cognitive network of attachment working models. They asked people to complete attachment measures for three specific relationships within each of three domains – family, friendship and romantic – and then examined the structure of these nine relationship descriptions. Confirmatory factor analyses revealed that a hierarchical arrangement of specific and global working models best fit the data, indicating that models of specific relationships (e.g., with a particular family member) are nested within relationship-domain representations (e.g., family members), which in turn are nested within more global models.

The neural network of attachment-related models has all of the usual properties of any cognitive network, e.g., differentiation, integration and coherence among various models (Collins and Read 1994). In addition, each working model within the network differs in cognitive accessibility (the ease with which it is activated and used to guide the functioning of the attachment system in a given social situation). As with other mental representations, the strength or accessibility of each model is determined by the amount of experience on which it is based, the number of times it has been applied in the past, and the density of its connections with other working models (e.g., Collins and Read 1994; Shaver, Collins and

Clark 1996). At a relationship-specific level, the model representing the typical interaction with a particular attachment figure has the highest accessibility in subsequent interactions with that person. At a generic level, the model that represents interactions with major attachment figures (e.g., parents and romantic partners) typically becomes the most chronically accessible attachment-related representation.

Consolidation of a chronically accessible working model is the most important psychological process accounting for the enduring effects on personality functioning of attachment interactions during infancy, childhood and adolescence (Bowlby 1973). Given a fairly consistent pattern of interaction with primary care-givers during infancy and childhood, the most representative or prototypical working models of these interactions become part of a person's implicit procedural knowledge, tend to operate automatically and unconsciously, and are resistant to change. Thus, what began as representations of specific interactions with primary care-givers during childhood become core personality characteristics, tend to be applied in new situations and relationships, and shape one's attachment style in adulthood.

Although activation of a particular working model depends on the history of attachment-related interactions, attachment theory also emphasizes the importance of contextual factors that contribute to this activation (e.g., Collins and Read 1994; Shaver, Collins and Clark 1996). Recent studies have shown that priming thoughts of an available and supportive attachment figure has immediate positive effects on mood, self-views and appraisals of relationship partners, and this happens even if these thoughts are incongruent with a person's chronically accessible insecure models (e.g., Mikulincer, Hirschberger, Nachmias *et al.* 2001; Mikulincer and Shaver 2001; Baccus, Baldwin and Packer 2004; Rowe and Carnelley 2003). In fact, these chronically accessible models coexist with less typical working models in one's memory network, and these non-dominant models can be activated by contextual factors in a given situation or social interaction. This and other issues are discussed in more detail in the next chapter of this book.

Concluding comments

Training as a psychoanalyst at a time when 'object relations' approaches to personality development and psychopathology (i.e., theoretical approaches that emphasized social relations, both real and imagined) were dominant in psychoanalysis, John Bowlby tried to understand why parental treatment is so important to children and adolescents, and why loss of a relationship partner at any age can be devastating. He gradually reconceptualized psychoanalytic theory to align it with the then-contemporary fields of primate ethology, cognitive developmental psychology, and control systems design. He abandoned Freud's drive model of motivation while remaining true to Freud's attempt to ground motivation theory in evolutionary biology. He recast mental representation in terms of cognitive/affective 'working models', which made the theory very compatible with the continuing contemporary cognitive emphasis in psychology generally. He viewed individual differences as a product of secure versus insecure attachment relationships, and he conceptualized them in terms of what we now describe as hyperactivation versus deactivation of the 'attachment behavioural system'. Bowlby viewed other major motives as the purview of other behavioural systems, such as exploration, care-giving and sex.

All of these changes, combined with Mary Ainsworth's creative and powerful methodological innovations, inspired researchers in developmental, personality, social and clinical psychology to test aspects of theory with additional new methods. This has now yielded an empirical literature based on thousands of studies (Mikulincer and Shaver 2007). That literature, interacting with the continually changing fields of psychology and neuroscience, continues to develop new and deeper insights into those 'rocky excrescences and thorny entanglements that [Freud] encountered and grappled with – love and hate, anxiety and defence, attachment and loss' (Bowlby 1982/1969, p. xxvii). The next chapter examines some of these studies, focusing especially on psychodynamics and optimal human development.

References

Ainsworth, M. D. S. 1967. *Infancy in Uganda: infant care and the growth of love.* Baltimore: Johns Hopkins University Press
   1991. Attachment and other affectional bonds across the life cycle, in C. M. Parkes, J. Stevenson-Hinde and P. Marris (eds.), *Attachment across the life cycle*, pp. 33–51. New York: Routledge
Ainsworth, M. D. S., Blehar, M. C., Waters, E. and Wall, S. 1978. *Patterns of attachment: assessed in the Strange Situation and at home.* Hillsdale, NJ: Erlbaum
Atkinson, L., Niccols, A., Paglia, A., Coolbear, J., Parker, K. C. H., Poulton, L., Guger, S. and Sitarenios, G. 2000. A meta-analysis of time between maternal sensitivity and attachment assessments: implications for internal working models in infancy/toddlerhood, *Journal of Social and Personal Relationships* 17: 791–810
Baccus, J. R., Baldwin, M. W. and Packer, D. J. 2004. Increasing implicit self-esteem through classical conditioning, *Psychological Science* 15: 498–502
Baldwin, M. W., Fehr, B., Keedian, E., Seidel, M. and Thompson, D. W. 1993. An exploration of the relational schemata underlying attachment styles: self-report and lexical decision approaches, *Personality and Social Psychology Bulletin* 19: 746–54
Bartholomew, K. and Horowitz, L. M. 1991. Attachment styles among young adults: a test of a four-category model, *Journal of Personality and Social Psychology* 61: 226–44
Bowlby, J. 1951. *Maternal care and mental health.* Geneva: World Health Organization
   1958. The nature of the child's tie to his mother, *International Journal of Psychoanalysis* 39: 350–73
   1973. *Attachment and loss,* vol. II, *Separation: anxiety and anger.* New York: Basic Books

1980. *Attachment and loss,* vol. III, *Sadness and depression.* New York: Basic Books

1982. *Attachment and loss,* vol. I, *Attachment,* 2nd edn. New York: Basic Books (original edn 1969)

1988. *A secure base: clinical applications of attachment theory.* London: Routledge

Brennan, K. A. and Bosson, J. K. 1998. Attachment-style differences in attitudes toward and reactions to feedback from romantic partners: an exploration of the relational bases of self-esteem, *Personality and Social Psychology Bulletin* 24: 699–714

Brennan, K. A., Clark, C. L. and Shaver, P. R. 1998. Self-report measurement of adult romantic attachment: an integrative overview, in J. A. Simpson and W. S. Rholes (eds.), *Attachment theory and close relationships*, pp. 46–76. New York: Guilford Press

Carver, C. S. 1997. Adult attachment and personality: converging evidence and a new measure, *Personality and Social Psychology Bulletin* 23: 865–83

Cassidy, J. and Kobak, R. R. 1988. Avoidance and its relationship with other defensive processes, in J. Belsky and T. Nezworski (eds.), *Clinical implications of attachment*, pp. 300–23. Hillsdale, NJ: Erlbaum

Coan, J. A., Schaefer, H. S. and Davidson, R. J. 2006. Lending a hand: social regulation of the neural response to threat, *Psychological Science* 17: 1032–9

Collins, N. L. 1996. Working models of attachment: implications for explanation, emotion and behaviour, *Journal of Personality and Social Psychology* 71: 810–32

Collins, N. L. and Read, S. J. 1990. Adult attachment, working models, and relationship quality in dating couples, *Journal of Personality and Social Psychology* 58: 644–63

1994. Cognitive representations of attachment: the structure and function of working models, in K. Bartholomew and D. Perlman (eds.), *Advances in personal relationships: attachment processes in adulthood*, vol. V, pp. 53–92. London: Jessica Kingsley

Cooper, M. L., Shaver, P. R. and Collins, N. L. 1998. Attachment styles, emotion regulation, and adjustment in adolescence, *Journal of Personality and Social Psychology* 74: 1380–97

Crawford, T. N., Livesley, W. J., Jang, K. L., Shaver, P. R., Cohen, P. and Ganiban, J. 2007. Insecure attachment and personality disorder: a twin study of adults, *European Journal of Personality* 21: 191–208

Crowell, J. A., Fraley, R. C. and Shaver, P. R. 1999. Measurement of adult attachment, in J. Cassidy and P. R. Shaver (eds.), *Handbook of attachment: theory, research, and clinical applications*, pp. 434–65. New York: Guilford Press

Davis, M. H., Morris, M. M. and Kraus, L. A. 1998. Relationship-specific and global perceptions of social support: associations with well-being and attachment, *Journal of Personality and Social Psychology* 74: 468–81

De Wolff, M. and van IJzendoorn, M. H. 1997. Sensitivity and attachment: a meta-analysis on parental antecedents of infant attachment, *Child Development* 68: 571–91

Feeney, J. A. and Noller, P. 1991. Attachment style and verbal descriptions of romantic partners, *Journal of Social and Personal Relationships* 8: 187–215

1992. Attachment style and romantic love: relationship dissolution, *Australian Journal of Psychology* 44: 69–74

Fraley, R. C. and Shaver, P. R. 1999. Loss and bereavement: attachment theory and recent controversies concerning grief work and the nature of detachment, in J. Cassidy and P. R. Shaver (eds.), *Handbook of attachment: theory, research, and clinical applications*, pp. 735–59. New York: Guilford Press

Fraley, R. C. and Waller, N. G. 1998. Adult attachment patterns: a test of the typological model, in J. A. Simpson and W. S. Rholes (eds.), *Attachment theory and close relationships*, pp. 77–114. New York: Guilford Press

George, C., Kaplan, N. and Main, M. 1985. *The Adult Attachment Interview*. Berkeley, CA: Department of Psychology, University of California, Unpublished protocol

Gump, B. B., Polk, D. E., Kamarck, T. W. and Shiffman, S. M. 2001. Partner interactions are associated with reduced blood pressure in the natural environment: ambulatory monitoring evidence from a healthy, multiethnic adult sample, *Psychosomatic Medicine* 63: 423–33

Hall, C. S., Lindzey, G. and Campbell, J. B. 2001. *Theories of personality*, 4th edn. New York: Wiley

Hazan, C. and Shaver, P. R. 1987. Romantic love conceptualized as an attachment process, *Journal of Personality and Social Psychology* 52: 511–24

1990. Love and work: an attachment-theoretical perspective, *Journal of Personality and Social Psychology* 59: 270–80

Heinicke, C. and Westheimer, I. 1966. *Brief separations*. New York: International Universities Press

Hesse, E. 1999. The Adult Attachment Interview: historical and current perspectives, in J. Cassidy and P. R. Shaver (eds.), *Handbook of attachment: theory, research, and clinical applications*, pp. 395–433. New York: Guilford Press

Horney, K. 1945. *Our inner conflicts*. New York: Norton

Kelley, H. H., Berscheid, E., Christensen, A., Harvey, J. H., Huston, T. L., Levinger, G., McClintock, E., Peplau, L. A. and Peterson, D. R. 1983. *Close relationships*. New York: Freeman

Lavi, N. 2007. *Bolstering attachment security in romantic relationships: the long-term contribution of partner's sensitivity, expressiveness, and supportiveness*. Ramat Gan: Bar-Ilan University. Unpublished doctoral dissertation

Lazarus, R. S. and Folkman, S. 1984. *Stress, appraisal, and coping*. New York: Springer

Main, M., Kaplan, N. and Cassidy, J. 1985. Security in infancy, childhood, and adulthood: a move to the level of representation, *Monographs of the Society for Research in Child Development* 50: 66–104

Main, M. and Solomon, J. 1990. Procedures for identifying infants as disorganized/disoriented during the Ainsworth strange situation, in M. T. Greenberg, D. Cicchetti and M. Cummings (eds.), *Attachment in the preschool years: theory, research, and intervention*, pp. 121–60. University of Chicago Press

Mikulincer, M. 1995. Attachment style and the mental representation of the self, *Journal of Personality and Social Psychology* 69: 1203–15

Mikulincer, M., Birnbaum, G., Woddis, D. and Nachmias, O. 2000. Stress and accessibility of proximity-related thoughts: exploring the normative and intraindividual components of attachment theory, *Journal of Personality and Social Psychology* 78: 509–23

Mikulincer, M., Gillath, O. and Shaver, P. R. 2002. Activation of the attachment system in adulthood: threat-related primes increase the accessibility of mental representations of attachment figures, *Journal of Personality and Social Psychology* 83: 881–95

Mikulincer, M., Hirschberger, G., Nachmias, O. and Gillath, O. 2001. The affective component of the secure base schema: affective priming with representations of attachment security, *Journal of Personality and Social Psychology* 81: 305–21

Mikulincer, M. and Shaver, P. R. 2001. Attachment theory and intergroup bias: evidence that priming the secure base schema attenuates negative reactions to out-groups, *Journal of Personality and Social Psychology* 81: 97–115

2003. The attachment behavioural system in adulthood: activation, psychodynamics, and interpersonal processes, in M. P. Zanna (ed.), *Advances in experimental social psychology*, vol. XXXV, pp. 53–152. New York: Academic Press

2004. Security-based self-representations in adulthood: contents and processes, in W. S. Rholes and J. A. Simpson (eds.), *Adult attachment: theory, research, and clinical implications*, pp. 159–95. New York: Guilford Press

2007. *Attachment in adulthood: structure, dynamics, and change*. New York: Guilford Press

Noftle, E. E. and Shaver, P. R. 2006. Attachment dimensions and the Big Five personality traits: associations and comparative ability to predict relationship quality, *Journal of Research in Personality* 40: 179–208

O'Connor, T. G. 2005. Attachment disturbances associated with early severe deprivation, in C. S. Carter *et al.* (eds.), *Attachment and bonding: a new synthesis*, pp. 257–68. Cambridge, MA: MIT Press

Overall, N. C., Fletcher, G. J. O. and Friesen, M. D. 2003. Mapping the intimate relationship mind: comparisons between three models of attachment representations, *Personality and Social Psychology Bulletin* 29: 1479–93

Park, L. E., Crocker, J. and Mickelson, K. D. 2004. Attachment styles and contingencies of self-worth, *Personality and Social Psychology Bulletin* 30: 1243–54

Rice, K. G., Lopez, F. G. and Vergara, D. 2005. Parental/social influences on perfectionism and adult attachment orientations, *Journal of Social and Clinical Psychology* 24: 580–605

Robertson, J. and Bowlby, J. 1952. Responses of young children to separation from their mothers, *Courier of the International Children's Center, Paris* 2: 131–40

Rowe, A. and Carnelley, K. B. 2003. Attachment style differences in the processing of attachment-relevant information: primed-style effects on recall, interpersonal expectations, and affect, *Personal Relationships* 10: 59–75

Shaver, P. R., Belsky, J. and Brennan, K. A. 2000. The adult attachment interview and self-reports of romantic attachment: associations across domains and methods, *Personal Relationships* 7: 25–43

Shaver, P. R., Collins, N. L. and Clark, C. L. 1996. Attachment styles and internal working models of self and relationship partners, in G. J. O. Fletcher and J. Fitness (eds.), *Knowledge structures in close relationships: a social psychological approach*, pp. 25–61. Mahwah, NJ: Erlbaum

Shaver, P. R. and Hazan, C. 1993. Adult romantic attachment: theory and evidence, in D. Perlman and W. Jones (eds.), *Advances in personal relationships*, vol. IV, pp. 29–70. London: Jessica Kingsley

Shaver, P. R. and Klinnert, M. 1982. Schachter's theories of affiliation and emotions: implications of developmental research, in L. Wheeler (ed.), *Review of Personality and Social Psychology*, vol. III, pp. 37–71. Beverly Hills: Sage

Shaver, P. R. and Mikulincer, M. 2002. Attachment-related psychodynamics, *Attachment and Human Development* 4: 133–61

Shaver, P. R., Mikulincer, M., Lavy, S. and Cassidy, J. in press. Understanding and altering hurt feelings: an attachment-theoretical perspective on the generation and regulation of emotions, in A. Vangelisti (ed.), *Feeling Hurt in Close Relationships*. New York: Cambridge University Press

Simpson, J. A. 1990. Influence of attachment styles on romantic relationships, *Journal of Personality and Social Psychology* 59: 971–80

Sullivan, H. S. 1953. *The interpersonal theory of psychiatry*. New York: Norton

Thibault, J. W. and Kelley, H. H. 1959. *The social psychology of groups*. New York: Wiley

van IJzendoorn, M. H. and Bakermans-Kranenburg, M. J. 2004. Maternal sensitivity and infant temperament in the formation of attachment, in G. Bremner and A. Slater (eds.), *Theories of infant development*, pp. 233–57. Malden, MA: Blackwell Publishing

Zuroff, D. C. and Fitzpatrick, D. K. 1995. Depressive personality styles: implications for adult attachment, *Personality and Individual Differences* 18: 253–365

15 Attachment theory: II. Developmental, psychodynamic and optimal-functioning aspects

Mario Mikulincer and Phillip R. Shaver

In the previous chapter we explained how and why John Bowlby (1982/1969) created attachment theory as an alternative to, or contemporary form of, Freud's psychoanalytic theory. We also explained how Mary Ainsworth (e.g., Ainsworth, Blehar, Waters and Wall 1978) created new methods to study infant-parent interactions, which allowed some of the core propositions of attachment theory to be tested. This contribution inspired subsequent researchers (e.g., Hazan and Shaver 1987; Main, Kaplan and Cassidy 1985) to develop methods for assessing and studying attachment processes and attachment-related personality structures in adolescence and adulthood. In the present chapter we carry the story forward by explaining what has been learned in recent years about developmental and psychodynamic processes related to attachment and what these discoveries imply about adult social life and mental health more generally. We show that attachment theory, despite its grounding in many solid, concrete empirical studies, has strong affinities with broad humanistic and existentialist approaches to human personality.

Development module

As with other psychodynamic theories, one of the pillars of attachment theory is the belief that childhood experiences play an important role in forming what will become a person's adult personality (Bowlby 1973, 1988). According to Bowlby (1982/1969, 1973), individual differences in attachment orientations in adulthood reflect past experiences with relationship partners, especially parents, beginning in infancy. In his view, working models of self and others formed during these early experiences provide a skeleton or foundation for what will continue to be learned over time and across social situations.

This does not mean, however, that attachment theory can simply be equated with psychoanalysis. In fact, attachment theory offers a unique perspective on the development of working models and their interplay with contemporary inter-personal contexts as determinants of adult feelings and relationship outcomes. While contemporary psychoanalysis still views adult mental representations of self and others as mental residues of childhood experiences, Bowlby (1973, 1980) believed that the developmental trajectory of working models is not linear or simple and that these mental representations in adulthood are not exclusively based on early experiences. Rather, they can be updated throughout life and affected by a broad array of contextual factors, such as current interactions with a relationship partner, the partner's attachment style and dynamics, and a person's current life situation, which can moderate or even override the effects of mental residues of past experiences. Thus, attachment theory does not assert that a person's current attachment orientation must mirror or match his or her attachment orientations with parents during childhood. Rather, the current orientation is a complex amalgam of historical and contemporary factors, and it can be changed by updating and reworking mental representations of self and attachment figures.

Borrowing from Waddington's (1957) epigenetic landscape model, Bowlby (1973) emphasized that attachment representations are both 'environmentally stable' and 'environmentally labile'. On one hand, attachment representations need to be somewhat 'environmentally stable' to ensure a degree of continuity over time in a person's understanding of his or her social experiences, despite fluctuations in the social environment. On the other hand, attachment representations need to be somewhat 'environmentally labile' if they are going to allow a person to stay in tune with changes in the social environment, age-related changes in kinds of relationships, and encounters with previously unfamiliar relationship partners. According to Bowlby (1973), the development of adult attachment patterns is constrained by two forces: (a) 'homeothetic forces' (Waddington 1957) that buffer changes in attachment patterns from infancy to adulthood, making it less likely that they will deviate from early working models, and (b) 'destabilizing forces' that encourage deviation from early working models given powerful experiences that demand revision and updating of attachment representations. Hence, adult attachment patterns are rooted in both early interactions with primary care-givers and later attachment experiences that challenge the validity of early working models.

Attachment research has provided evidence for both homeothetic and destabilizing forces. With regard to homeothetic forces, several studies have examined the stability of attachment patterns in infancy (as assessed in the Strange Situation; Ainsworth, Blehar, Waters and Wall 1978) over periods ranging from one month to twenty years. Some of these studies have examined the association between infant attachment patterns in the Strange Situation at twelve months and attachment patterns at three, four or six years of age (using parental Q-sort methods or story completion tests). Fraley (2002) meta-analysed these studies and found moderate levels of stability in attachment classification: a mean correlation of .35 for studies that examined attachment patterns at one and four years and a slightly lower correlation for studies comparing attachment in adolescence with attachment in the Strange Situation years earlier. In the last decade, attachment researchers who administered the Strange Situation to infants in the late 1970s and early 1980s and reassessed the participants as much as eighteen to twenty years later have been able to examine the continuity of attachment patterns all the way to adulthood (see Grossmann, Grossmann and Waters 2005, for reviews). All of these studies used the AAI (Main, Kaplan and Cassidy 1985; Hesse 1999) to assess attachment patterns at age nineteen or twenty. Fraley (2002) meta-analysed these studies and revealed a mean correlation of .27 ($N = 218$) between AAI scores at ages nineteen–twenty and Strange Situation scores, indicating moderate continuity from infancy to young adulthood and replicating findings on continuity of infant attachment during childhood.

Beyond meta-analysing the studies that had examined attachment stability across various time spans in infancy, childhood, adolescence and young adulthood, Fraley (2002) constructed a dynamic mathematical model assuming that a stable prototype of infant attachment is carried through time, but with prototype-discrepant events and relationships tempering the prototype's influence over time, and tested its goodness-of-fit with longitudinal data. He compared this model with the alternative 'revisionist' (continuous change) model, which did not assume the existence of an initial prototype that had a lasting influence. Fraley (2002, p. 135) concluded that 'the prototype model provided the best fit to the data, indicating that a prototype-like process may contribute to attachment stability across the life course ... Furthermore, the prototype model predicts that the continuity between early attachment security and attachment security at any point later in the life course will be equivalent to a correlation of approximately .39'.

Some of the twenty-year longitudinal studies reviewed above provided evidence of lawful discontinuities in attachment patterns between infancy and adulthood (see Grossmann, Grossmann and Waters 2005, for extensive review). Beyond assessing attachment patterns in infancy and twenty years later, these studies also gathered data concerning negative attachment-relevant events (e.g., death of a parent, parental divorce, a parent developing a life-threatening illness, a parent with a psychiatric disorder, physical or sexual abuse by a family member). Overall, these studies showed that attachment-relevant stressful life events occurring during childhood or adolescence produced discontinuities in attachment patterns and increased the likelihood that what were once securely attached infants would be classified as insecure in the AAI.

Carlson, Sroufe and Egeland (2004) re-analysed the data they collected from infancy to young adulthood and found evidence for joint contributions of infant attachment and childhood and adolescent experiences to adult attachment. Specifically, they computed structural equation models of the associations between Strange Situation classifications at twelve months, attachment representations and socio-emotional functioning during early childhood (four and a half years of age), middle childhood (eight years), and early adolescence (twelve years), and AAI classifications at nineteen years. Although Strange Situation classifications were not directly associated with AAI classifications nineteen years later, infant attachment was indirectly related to adult attachment via its effects on attachment representations and socio-emotional functioning throughout childhood and adolescence. That is, infant attachment in the Strange Situation had significant influences on attachment representations and socio-emotional functioning during early childhood, which in turn contributed to later representations and functioning during middle childhood and adolescence. And adolescents' representations and functioning contributed to AAI classifications at age nineteen. A similar multiple-mediation model was found to apply to the association between attachment security at twelve months of age and the affective tone of interpersonal interactions with a romantic partner twenty years later (Simpson, Collins, Tran and Haydon 2007).

According to Carlson, Sroufe and Egeland (2004), these findings suggest that continuity of attachment patterns from infancy to adulthood is a dynamic process resulting from successive transactions between the person and the environment across the lifespan. Infant attachment security or insecurity is carried from one time point to another by attachment representations that are also responsive to socio-emotional functioning in a wide variety of settings (family, school, peer relationships) and current attachment-relevant experiences. Therefore, later attachment representations are always a reflection of the early prototype and the accumulated subsequent experiences. This interpretation fits with Bowlby's (1973) view (based on Waddington 1957) that people travel a specific developmental route early in life and then encounter multiple branch points across childhood and adolescence that can lead to either a similar or a different outcome in adulthood.

Dynamics module

Attachment theory also describes the fears and conflicts that characterize the various forms of attachment insecurity (anxiety, avoidance) as well as the psychological defences that are often activated to manage these conflicts. According to Mikulincer, Shaver and Pereg (2003), the pain caused by the unavailability of attachment figures in times of need can be experienced in different ways and result in different kinds of fears and defences. Mikulincer, Gillath, Sapir-Lavid *et al.* (2003) described two kinds of psychological pain: (a) the distress caused by failing to achieve or maintain proximity to an attachment figure, and (b) the sense of helplessness caused by ineffective co-regulation of distress and the appraisal of oneself as alone and vulnerable. Although these two kinds of painful feelings are related, their relative strength may vary across situations, relationships and individuals. Moreover, each kind of pain predisposes a person to adopt particular kinds of psychological defences.

One state of mind is based on the failure of attachment behaviours to achieve a positive result (closeness, love or protection) and on being punished (with inattention, rejection or hostility) for enacting these behaviours. In such a state, seeking proximity to an attachment figure is likely to become a major source or threat of psychological pain. A person in this predicament tends to appraise closeness and intimacy as aversive states and to fear being in a needy position and involved in close and interdependent relationships that can end in separation or rejection. As a result, such a person is more or less forced to rely on avoidant, deactivating defences. A very different state of mind emerges from emphasizing the failure to co-regulate distress and worrying that one does not have the capacity to deal with threats alone. This state of mind encourages a person to work harder to gain attention, cooperation and protection from an attachment figure, i.e., to hyperactivate the attachment system. Under such conditions, distance from an attachment figure is perceived as threatening and as a source of psychological pain, and one becomes afraid of what will happen if one attempts to cope with the situation and regulate distress alone.

Mikulincer, Gillath, Sapir-Lavid *et al.* (2003) described an array of external and internal factors that contribute to the relative strength of these two different states of mind. Avoidant deactivation seems to be encouraged by (a) consistent inattention, rejection or angry responses from an attachment figure; (b) threats of punishment for proximity-seeking signals and behaviours; (c) violent or abusive behaviour on the part of an attachment figure; and (d) explicit or implicit demands for greater self-reliance and inhibition of expressions of need and vulnerability. Anxious hyperactivation seems to be encouraged by (a) unpredictable or unreliable care-giving experienced as out of synch with one's needs and requests for help; (b) intrusive care-giving that interferes with the acquisition of self-regulation skills and punishes a person for trying to cope autonomously; (c) explicit or implicit messages from an attachment figure that one is stupid, helpless, incompetent or weak; and (d) traumatic or abusive experiences that occur while one is separated from attachment figures. These factors create an ambivalent state in which approaching the attachment figure is sometimes punishing and sometimes rewarding, but avoidance of this figure seems dangerous and painful. According to Mikulincer *et al.* (2003), this state of mind may be exacerbated by temperamental deficits in self-regulation and problems in controlling attention and cognition.

Adult attachment research has provided extensive evidence concerning the fears and psychological defences that characterize avoidant deactivation and anxious hyperactivation of the attachment system. These fears and defences are manifested in the way insecurely attached people construe their interpersonal goals and interactions, organize their appraisals of self and others, and regulate their emotions. At the interpersonal level, anxious hyperactivation forces people to select interpersonal goals that decrease distance from others and the probability of being alone while confronting stress and distress; avoidant deactivation requires that people organize their interactions around desires for optimal distance, self-reliance and control. Whereas attachment-anxious people fear rejection and aloneness, avoidant ones are averse to closeness and interdependence. Indeed, Feeney (1999) and Collins, Guichard, Ford and Feeney (2004) found that, compared with secure young adults, attachment-anxious adults (as assessed with self-report measures, Brennan, Clark and Shaver 1998; Hazan and Shaver 1987) overemphasize the importance of a partner's love and support within couple relationships, and avoidant participants tend to dismiss these closeness-related goals. Similarly, Mikulincer (1998a) found that attachment-anxious individuals trusted others as a means of gaining a partner's love and support, whereas avoidant people viewed expressions of interpersonal trust as manipulations designed to control others' behaviour ('If I trust you, you should trust me and allow me to do what I want').

There is also extensive evidence that avoidant attachment is associated with greater fear of intimacy (e.g., Doi and Thelen 1993). In addition, Rowe and Carnelley (2005) found that people scoring higher on avoidant attachment were more likely to place partners (family members, romantic partners) at a greater distance from their 'core self', and Kaitz, Bar-Haim, Lehrer and Grossman (2004) found that more avoidant people were less tolerant of physical proximity and expressed more discomfort when another person moved into their personal space. Several studies have shown that anxiously attached people, as compared to more secure people, report higher levels of rejection sensitivity – the tendency to anticipate and overreact to rejection (e.g., Downey and Feldman 1996), are quicker to recognize rejection-related words in a lexical decision task, and have difficulty inhibiting rejection-related thoughts (e.g., Baldwin and Kay 2003).

Nevertheless, the attachment-anxious mind is not simply aimed at gaining proximity to a relationship partner or avoiding rejection. Research has shown that attachment-anxious people suffer from a strong, ambivalent conflict between approach and avoidance relational tendencies (e.g., Maio, Fincham and Lycett 2000). On one hand, they place strong emphasis on gaining a partner's attention and love. On the other hand, they suffer from intense fear of rejection and harbour serious doubts about their ability to gain a partner's love. These fears and insecurities can cause anxious individuals to inhibit approach tendencies when they sense the possibility of disapproval or rejection. Being caught in an approach-avoidance conflict, they are likely to ruminate obsessively about how to react in social situations, thereby interfering with adaptive interpersonal regulation. There is evidence that attachment-anxious people make important mistakes, failing to initiate new relationships that might be rewarding (e.g., Bartz and Lydon 2006); effusively expressing their desires to relationship partners (e.g., Mikulincer and Nachshon 1991), which can leave them vulnerable to unwanted sexual experiences, rejection or hurt feelings (e.g., Davis, Shaver and Vernon 2004; Shaver, Mikulincer, Lavy and Cassidy in press); or being unable to end unsatisfactory and abusive relationships (e.g., Davila and Bradbury 2001).

Insecure people's fears and defences also bias the way they appraise themselves and others. With regard to self-appraisals, attachment-anxious people's fears of being rejected and isolated force them to appraise and present themselves in negative and devaluing terms so as to elicit compassion, attention and care. In contrast, avoidant people's fears of being vulnerable and dependent on others' goodwill lead them to defensively inflate their positive self-views so as to convince themselves and others that they strong, independent and self-reliant. In a test of these ideas, Mikulincer (1998b) exposed people to various threatening or neutral situations and then assessed self-appraisals using both self-report scales and subtler cognitive techniques, such as reaction times for trait recognition. Whereas avoidant individuals made more explicit and implicit positive self-appraisals following threatening rather than neutral stimuli, attachment-anxious individuals made more explicit and implicit negative self-appraisals following threatening rather than neutral conditions.

With regard to appraisals of others, attachment-anxious people's fear of being rejected and abandoned cause them to overemphasize self-other similarities so as to maximize cognitive proximity to others. In contrast, avoidant people's fears of closeness and intimacy cause them to overemphasize self-other dissimilarities so as to maximize cognitive distance from others. Indeed, Mikulincer, Orbach and Iavnieli (1998) found that whereas anxious people were more likely than secure ones to perceive others as similar to themselves and to show a false consensus bias in trait and opinion descriptions, avoidant individuals were more likely to perceive others as dissimilar to them and to exhibit a false distinctiveness bias. Mikulincer and Horesh (1999) followed up this line of research and found that insecure people's appraisals of others are defensively organized by projective mechanisms. Avoidant individuals tend to defensively project unwanted, repressed self-traits onto others, which increases self-other differentiation and, by downward social comparison, enhances their sense of self-worth. Attachment-anxious individuals tend to project their self-traits onto others, which increases self-other similarity and increases the sense of solidarity or closeness.

Adult attachment research has also shown that insecure people's fears and defences are evident in the ways in which they regulate emotional experiences and expressions. Attachment-anxious people's fears of being rejected and abandoned cause them to intensify the experience and expression of distress and other negative emotions so as to capture other people's attention and elicit their compassionate and caring responses (Cassidy 1994; Cassidy and Kobak 1988). In contrast, avoidant people's fears of being needy, weak and other-dependent cause them to block or inhibit emotional states that are incongruent with the goal of keeping their attachment system deactivated (Cassidy and Kobak 1988; Mikulincer and Shaver 2003). These inhibitory efforts are directed mainly at fear, anxiety, anger, sadness, shame, guilt and distress, because these emotions are associated with threats and feelings of vulnerability. In addition, anger often implies emotional involvement or investment in a relationship, and such involvement is incongruent with avoidant people's preference for independence and self-reliance (Cassidy 1994). Moreover, fear, anxiety, sadness, shame and guilt can be viewed as signs of personal weakness or vulnerability, all of which contradict the avoidant person's desired sense of personal strength and self-reliance.

There is ample evidence that attachment-anxious people tend to express negative affectivity, report more physical complaints, and have stronger fears of failure, illness and death (see Mikulincer and Shaver 2007, for a review). There is also evidence that more avoidant people are less inclined to disclose personal feelings to others or express emotions (either positive or negative) spontaneously (again, see Mikulincer and Shaver 2007, for a review). These tendencies were also identified in Mikulincer and Orbach's (1995) study of emotional memories. Participants were asked to recall early experiences of anger, sadness, anxiety or happiness, and to rate the intensity of focal and associated emotions in each recalled event. Avoidant people had the poorest access (longest recall latencies) to sad and anxious memories; anxious people had the easiest access to such memories, and secure people fell in between. Moreover, avoidant individuals rated focal emotions (e.g., sadness when retrieving a sad memory) and non-focal emotions (e.g., anger when retrieving a sad memory) as less intense than secure individuals, whereas anxious individuals reported experiencing very intense focal *and* non-focal emotions when asked to remember examples of negative emotions. That is, anxious people exhibited a rapid and extensive spread of activation among negative emotions, whereas avoidant people had trouble accessing negative memories and reported fairly shallow emotions.

Avoidant people's defensive tendency to block the experience of negative emotions was also notable in Fraley and Shaver's (1997) study of thought suppression. Participants wrote continuously about whatever thoughts and feelings they were experiencing while being asked to suppress thoughts about a romantic partner leaving them for someone else. Avoidant attachment was associated with greater ability to suppress separation-related thoughts, as indicated by less frequent thoughts of loss following the suppression task and lower skin conductance during the task. In contrast, attachment anxiety was associated with poorer ability to suppress separation-related thoughts, as indicated by more frequent thoughts of loss following the suppression task and higher skin conductance during the task. A recent fMRI study (Gillath, Bunge, Shaver *et al.* 2005) revealed that these attachment-style differences are also evident in patterns of brain activation and deactivation when people are thinking about break-ups and losses and attempting to suppress such thoughts.

In a recent pair of studies, Mikulincer, Dolev and Shaver (2004) replicated and extended Fraley and Shaver's (1997) findings while assessing, in a Stroop colour-naming task, the cognitive accessibility of previously suppressed thoughts about a painful separation. Avoidant individuals were able to suppress thoughts related to the break-up; for them, such thoughts were relatively inaccessible, and their own positive self-traits became defensively more accessible. However, their ability to maintain this defensive stance was disrupted when a cognitive load (remembering a seven-digit number) was added to the experimental task. Under high cognitive load, avoidant individuals exhibited ready access to thoughts of separation and negative self-traits. That is, the suppressed material resurfaced in experience and behaviour when a high cognitive demand was imposed. Studies showing that avoidant people do sometimes show strong negative emotions and a loss of self-control in response to chronic, uncontrollable and severely distressing events suggest a similar breakdown of defences when such people experience great stress (e.g., Berant, Mikulincer and Florian 2001; Berant, Mikulincer and Shaver 2008).

Adjustment or 'optimal functioning' module

Although attachment theory is similar to Freudian and other psycho-analytic theories in focusing on defences and pathology, it also includes ideas about the path to 'optimal functioning' that have much in common with humanistic and self-actualization theories of personality (e.g., Maslow 1968; Rogers 1961) and today's 'positive psychology' movement (e.g., Seligman 2002). Attachment theory emphasizes not only fears and defences related to attachment insecurities, but also the ways in which good relationships can build psychological resources and broaden perspectives and skills associated with a sense of security. (Following Fredrickson 2001, we call this the 'broaden and build cycle of attachment security'.) Research consistently confirms that the sense of attachment security is associated with positive mental representations of others, a stable sense of self-efficacy and self-esteem, and reliance on constructive ways of coping, which in turn facilitate mental health and psychological functioning even in times of stress (see Mikulincer and Shaver 2003, 2007, for reviews). Moreover, securely attached people tend to feel generally safe and protected, and they can interact with others in a confident and open manner without being driven by defensive social motives and strategies aimed at protecting a fragile or false self-concept (Mikulincer and Shaver 2005).

According to attachment theory, the sense of attachment security is a basic inner strength (Mikulincer and Shaver 2005). There is extensive evidence that securely attached people are more likely than their insecure counterparts to possess personality characteristics emphasized in 'positive psychology', such as resilience, optimism, hope, positive affectivity, curiosity and exploration, healthy autonomy, a capacity for love and forgiveness, feelings of interconnectedness and belongingness, tolerance and kindness (see Lopez and Brennan 2000; Mikulincer and Shaver 2003, 2007; Shaver and Mikulincer 2002). Moreover, there are several similarities between the way attachment security evolves from repeated episodes of attachment-figure availability and ideas discussed by humanistic psychologists about the parenting style that facilitates self-actualization (e.g., Maslow's (1968) concept of B-perception; Rogers' (1961) concept of 'unconditional positive regard'). The common idea that recurs across different 'positive' or humanistic theoretical frameworks is that experiences of being loved, accepted and supported by others constitute the most important form of personal protection and provide a foundation for confronting adversity and maintaining equanimity and effective functioning in times of stress without interrupting natural processes of growth and self-actualization.

Recently, we (Mikulincer and Shaver 2005) reviewed extensive evidence showing that the sense of attachment security attenuates a wide array of defensive motives, such as the need for self-enhancement, needs for consensus and uniqueness, intergroup biases, defence of knowledge structures, and defence of cultural worldviews. Adult attachment studies have consistently shown that a sense of attachment security acts as an inner resource that supersedes defensive needs and renders defensive manoeuvres less necessary. These defensive manoeuvres and the resulting biases in the appraisals of self and others tend to be more characteristic of insecurely attached people. Mikulincer and Shaver (2005) noted that these defensive needs indicate that a person has been forced by social experiences to face the world without adequate mental representations of attachment security and has had to struggle for a sense of self-worth.

The sense of attachment security allows people to devote mental resources that otherwise would be employed in preventive, defensive manoeuvres to more growth-oriented, promotion-focused activities that contribute to the broadening of their perspectives and capacities, and to their attainment of what Rogers (1961) called a fully functioning personality and Maslow (1968) called self-actualization. According to Bowlby (1982/1969), the unavailability of security-providing attachment figures inhibits the activation of other behavioural systems, because a person who feels unprotected in the face of threats tends to be so focused on attachment needs that he or she lacks the attention and resources necessary to engage in other activities. This causes insecure people to be less tolerant of outgroup members (Mikulincer and Shaver 2001), less humane in their values (Mikulincer, Shaver and Pereg 2003) and less compassionate and altruistic (Mikulincer, Shaver, Gillath and Nitzberg 2005). Only when a sense of attachment security is restored can a person devote full attention and energy to other behavioural systems, such as exploration and care-giving.

Research supports the claim that secure individuals are more likely than insecure ones to exhibit all of Rogers' (1961) defining features of the fully functioning person: openness to experience, existential living, organismic trust, experiential freedom and creativity. Secure people are able to experience their thoughts and feelings deeply and openly disclose these feelings to significant others, even if the thoughts and feelings are threatening and painful (e.g., Collins and Read 1990; Mallinckrodt, Porter and Kivlighan 2005; Mikulincer and Orbach 1995). Attachment security also facilitates cognitive openness and adaptive revision of knowledge structures, without arousing much fear of disapproval, criticism or rejection (e.g., Green and Campbell 2000; Mikulincer 1997). Attachment security facilitates the savouring of good times and capitalizing on positive emotions, as evident in diary studies documenting secure people's enjoyment of daily activities and social interactions (e.g., Tidwell, Reis and Shaver 1996), as well as cognitive expansion following inductions of positive affect (e.g., Mikulincer and Sheffi 2000). Moreover, securely attached people are able to engage in creative exploration and participate fully in the wider world while remaining sensitive and responsive to others' needs (e.g., Kunce and Shaver 1994; Mikulincer 1997). They are more likely than their avoidant peers to volunteer in their communities and have humanistic motives for so doing (Gillath, Shaver, Mikulincer et al. 2005).

The qualities of securely attached people correspond to the qualities Allport (1961), in an early humanistic analysis, discussed in terms of 'psychological growth': (a) engagement in activities that are not directly linked to immediate need gratification, ego defences or adjustment pressures; (b) the formation of warm, tolerant and intimate relationships; (c) the consolidation of emotional security, self-acceptance and realistic views of self and social reality; (d) deeply understanding one's own and others' experiences; and (f) authentic exploration of the meaning and purpose of life. Attachment theory and research support Allport's analysis while providing much greater conceptual precision and more solid research evidence.

Concluding comments

Beginning as a psychoanalyst in Second World War I Britain, with eminent colleagues such as Anna Freud, Melanie Klein and Donald Winnicott, John Bowlby gradually created a more empirically oriented psychodynamic theory that could be integrated with the rest of scientific psychology. Ironically, this caused his version of what was then called 'object relations' theory (because Freud had conceptualized attachment figures as 'objects' of 'instincts') eventually to outshine its contemporary competitors, making it today the most completely researched and influential psychodynamic theory. With reference to what Bowlby (1982/1969) wrote in the passage we quoted at the outset of the previous chapter, he eventually conquered the 'rocky excrescences and thorny entanglements that [Freud] had encountered and grappled with – love and hate, anxiety and defense, attachment and loss'. Attachment theory is now the leading theory of love and bereavement; it is a mainstay of both developmental and personality/social psychology, and its major constructs are still being measured and refined through hundreds of studies involving self-report questionnaires, clinical interviews, behavioural observations, social-cognition experiments and neuroimaging techniques. Its insights are being applied clinically with both individuals and couples (e.g., Allen and Fonagy 2006; Holmes 2001; Johnson and Whiffen 2003; Obegi and Berant 2008; Wallin 2007), and it is beginning to be examined in the context of organizations and leadership (e.g., Davidovitz, Mikulincer, Shaver *et al.* 2007). At present, there is no end in sight to the theory's generativity and potential for integration with other theoretical approaches to personality (Mikulincer and Shaver 2007).

References

Ainsworth, M. D. S., Blehar, M. C., Waters, E. and Wall, S. 1978. *Patterns of attachment: assessed in the Strange Situation and at home.* Hillsdale, NJ: Erlbaum

Allen, J. G. and Fonagy, P. (eds.) 2006. *The handbook of mentalization-based treatment.* New York: Wiley

Allport, G. W. 1961. *Pattern and growth in personality.* New York: Holt, Rinehart and Winston

Baldwin, M. W. and Kay, A. C. 2003. Adult attachment and the inhibition of rejection, *Journal of Social and Clinical Psychology* 22: 275–93

Bartz, J. A. and Lydon, J. E. 2006. Navigating the interdependence dilemma: attachment goals and the use of communal norms with potential close others, *Journal of Personality and Social Psychology* 91: 77–96

Berant, E., Mikulincer, M. and Florian, V. 2001. Attachment style and mental health: a 1-year follow-up study of mothers of infants with congenital heart disease, *Personality and Social Psychology Bulletin* 27: 956–68

Berant, E., Mikulincer, M. and Shaver, P. R. 2008. Mothers' attachment style, their mental health, and their children's emotional vulnerabilities: a seven-year study of children with congenital heart disease, *Journal of Personality* 76: 31–66

Bowlby, J. 1973. *Attachment and loss,* vol. II, *Separation: anxiety and anger.* New York: Basic Books

1980. *Attachment and loss,* vol. III, *Sadness and depression.* New York: Basic Books

1982. *Attachment and loss,* vol. I, *Attachment,* 2nd edn. New York: Basic Books (original edn 1969)

1988. *A secure base: clinical applications of attachment theory.* London: Routledge.

Brennan, K. A., Clark, C. L. and Shaver, P. R. 1998. Self-report measurement of adult romantic attachment: an integrative overview, in J. A. Simpson and W. S. Rholes (eds.), *Attachment theory and close relationships,* pp. 46–76. New York: Guilford Press

Carlson, E. A., Sroufe, L. A. and Egeland, B. 2004. The construction of experience: a longitudinal study of representation and behaviour, *Child Development* 75: 66–83

Carver, C. S. 1997. Adult attachment and personality: converging evidence and a new measure, *Personality and Social Psychology Bulletin* 23: 865–83

Cassidy, J. 1994. Emotion regulation: influences of attachment relationships, *Monographs of the Society for Research in Child Development* 59: 228–83

Cassidy, J. and Kobak, R. R. 1988. Avoidance and its relationship with other defensive processes, in J. Belsky and T. Nezworski (eds.), *Clinical implications of attachment,* pp. 300–23. Hillsdale, NJ: Erlbaum

Collins, N. L., Guichard, A. C., Ford, M. B. and Feeney, B. C. 2004. Working models of attachment: new developments and emerging themes, in W. S. Rholes and J. A. Simpson (eds.), *Adult attachment: theory, research, and clinical implications,* pp. 196–239. New York: Guilford Press

Collins, N. L. and Read, S. J. 1990. Adult attachment, working models, and relationship quality in dating couples, *Journal of Personality and Social Psychology* 58: 644–63

Davidovitz, R., Mikulincer, M., Shaver, P. R., Ijzak, R. and Popper, M. 2007. Leaders as attachment figures: their attachment orientations predict leadership-related mental representations and followers' performance and mental health, *Journal of Personality and Social Psychology* 93: 632–50

Davila, J. and Bradbury, T. N. 2001. Attachment insecurity and the distinction between unhappy spouses who do and do not divorce, *Journal of Family Psychology* 15: 371–93

Davis, D., Shaver, P. R. and Vernon, M. L. 2004. Attachment style and subjective motivations for sex, *Personality and Social Psychology Bulletin* 30: 1076–90

Doi, S. C. and Thelen, M. H. 1993. The fear-of-intimacy scale: replication and extension, *Psychological Assessment* 5: 377–83

Downey, G. and Feldman, S. I. 1996. Implications of rejection sensitivity for intimate relationships, *Journal of Personality and Social Psychology* 70: 1327–43

Feeney, J. A. 1999. Issues of closeness and distance in dating relationships: effects of sex and attachment style, *Journal of Social and Personal Relationships* 16: 571–90

Fraley, R. C. 2002. Attachment stability from infancy to adulthood: meta-analysis and dynamic modeling of developmental mechanisms, *Personality and Social Psychology Review* 6: 123–51

Fraley, R. C. and Shaver, P. R. 1997. Adult attachment and the suppression of unwanted thoughts, *Journal of Personality and Social Psychology* 73: 1080–91

Fredrickson, B. L. 2001. The role of positive emotions in positive psychology: the broaden-and-build theory of positive emotions, *American Psychologist* 56: 218–26

Gillath, O., Bunge, S. A., Shaver, P. R., Wendelken, C. and Mikulincer, M. 2005. Attachment-style differences in the ability to suppress negative thoughts: exploring the neural correlates, *NeuroImage* 28: 835–47

Gillath, O., Shaver, P. R., Mikulincer, M., Nitzberg, R. A., Erez, A. and van Ijzendoorn, M. H. 2005. Attachment, caregiving, and volunteering: placing volunteerism in an attachment-theoretical framework, *Personal Relationships* 12: 425–46

Green, J. D. and Campbell, W. 2000. Attachment and exploration in adults: chronic and contextual accessibility, *Personality and Social Psychology Bulletin* 26: 452–61

Grossmann, K. E., Grossmann, K. and Waters, E. (eds.) 2005. *Attachment from infancy to adulthood: the major longitudinal studies*. New York: Guilford Press

Hazan, C. and Shaver, P. R. 1987. Romantic love conceptualized as an attachment process, *Journal of Personality and Social Psychology* 52: 511–24

Hesse, E. 1999. The adult attachment interview: historical and current perspectives, in J. Cassidy and P. R. Shaver (eds.), *Handbook of attachment: theory, research, and clinical applications*, pp. 395–433. New York: Guilford Press

Holmes, J. 2001. *The search for the secure base: attachment theory and psychotherapy*. East Sussex: Brunner-Routledge

Johnson, S. M. and Whiffen, V. E. (eds.) 2003. *Attachment processes in couple and family therapy*. New York: Guilford Press

Kaitz, M., Bar-Haim, Y., Lehrer, M. and Grossman, E. 2004. Adult attachment style and interpersonal distance, *Attachment and Human Development* 6: 285–304

Kunce, L. J. and Shaver, P. R. 1994. An attachment-theoretical approach to caregiving in romantic relationships, in K. Bartholomew and D. Perlman (eds.), *Advances in personal relationships: attachment processes in adulthood*, vol. V, pp. 205–37. London: Jessica Kingsley

Lopez, F. G. and Brennan, K. A. 2000. Dynamic processes underlying adult attachment organization: toward an attachment theoretical perspective on the healthy and effective self: attachment and counseling psychology, *Journal of Counseling Psychology* 47: 283–300

Main, M., Kaplan, N. and Cassidy, J. 1985. Security in infancy, childhood, and adulthood: a move to the level of representation, *Monographs of the Society for Research in Child Development* 50: 66–104

Maio, G. R., Fincham, F. D. and Lycett, E. J. 2000. Attitudinal ambivalence toward parents and attachment style, *Personality and Social Psychology Bulletin* 26: 1451–64

Mallinckrodt, B., Porter, M. J. and Kivlighan, D. M., Jr 2005. Client attachment to therapist, depth of in-session exploration, and object relations in brief psychotherapy, *Psychotherapy* 42: 85–100

Maslow, A. H. 1968. *Toward a psychology of being*, 2nd edn. New York: Van Nostrand

Mikulincer, M. 1997. Adult attachment style and information processing: individual differences in curiosity and cognitive closure, *Journal of Personality and Social Psychology* 72: 1217–30

Mikulincer, M. 1998a. Attachment working models and the sense of trust: an exploration of interaction goals and affect regulation, *Journal of Personality and Social Psychology* 74: 1209–24

   1998b. Adult attachment style and affect regulation: strategic variations in self-appraisals, *Journal of Personality and Social Psychology* 75: 420–35

Mikulincer, M., Dolev, T. and Shaver, P. R. 2004. Attachment-related strategies during thought suppression: ironic rebounds and vulnerable self-representations, *Journal of Personality and Social Psychology* 87: 940–56

Mikulincer, M., Gillath, O., Sapir-Lavid, Y., Yaakobi, E., Arias, K., Tal-Aloni, L. and Bor, G. 2003. Attachment theory and concern for others' welfare: evidence that activation of the sense of secure base promotes endorsement of self-transcendence values, *Basic and Applied Social Psychology* 25: 299–312

Mikulincer, M. and Horesh, N. 1999. Adult attachment style and the perception of others: the role of projective mechanisms, *Journal of Personality and Social Psychology* 76: 1022–34

Mikulincer, M. and Nachshon, O. 1991. Attachment styles and patterns of self-disclosure, *Journal of Personality and Social Psychology* 61: 321–31

Mikulincer, M. and Orbach, I. 1995. Attachment styles and repressive defensiveness: the accessibility and architecture of affective memories, *Journal of Personality and Social Psychology* 68: 917–25

Mikulincer, M., Orbach, I. and Iavnieli, D. 1998. Adult attachment style and affect regulation: strategic variations in subjective self-other similarity, *Journal of Personality and Social Psychology* 75: 436–48

Mikulincer, M. and Shaver, P. R. 2001. Attachment theory and intergroup bias: evidence that priming the secure base schema attenuates negative reactions to out-groups, *Journal of Personality and Social Psychology* 81: 97–115

   2003. The attachment behavioural system in adulthood: activation, psychodynamics, and interpersonal processes, in M. P. Zanna (ed.), *Advances in experimental social psychology*, vol. xxxv, pp. 53–152. New York: Academic Press

   2005. Mental representations of attachment security: theoretical foundation for a positive social psychology, in M. W. Baldwin (ed.), *Interpersonal cognition*, pp. 233–66. New York: Guilford Press

   2007. *Attachment in adulthood: structure, dynamics, and change*. New York: Guilford Press

Mikulincer, M., Shaver, P. R., Gillath, O. and Nitzberg, R. A. 2005. Attachment, care-giving, and altruism: boosting attachment security increases compassion and helping, *Journal of Personality and Social Psychology* 89: 817–39

Mikulincer, M., Shaver, P. R. and Pereg, D. 2003. Attachment theory and affect regulation: the dynamics, development, and cognitive consequences of attachment-related strategies, *Motivation and Emotion* 27: 77–102

Mikulincer, M. and Sheffi, E. 2000. Adult attachment style and cognitive reactions to positive affect: a test of mental categorization and creative problem solving, *Motivation and Emotion* 24: 149–74

Obegi, J. H. and Berant, E. (eds.) 2008. *Clinical applications of adult attachment*. New York: Guilford Press

Rogers, C. R. 1961. *On becoming a person*. Boston, MA: Houghton Mifflin

Rowe, A. C. and Carnelley, K. B. 2005. Preliminary support for the use of a hierarchical mapping technique to examine attachment networks, *Personal Relationships* 12: 499–519

Seligman, M. E. P. 2002. *Authentic happiness: using the new positive psychology to realize your potential for lasting fulfillment*. New York: Free Press

Shaver, P. R. and Mikulincer, M. 2002. Attachment-related psychodynamics, *Attachment and Human Development* 4: 133–61

Shaver, P. R., Mikulincer, M., Lavy, S. and Cassidy, J. in press. Understanding and altering hurt feelings: an attachment-theoretical perspective on the generation and regulation of emotions, in A. Vangelisti (ed.), *Feeling hurt in close relationships*. New York: Cambridge University Press

Simpson, J. A., Collins, A. W., Tran, S. and Haydon, K. C. 2007. Attachment and the experience and expression of emotions in romantic relationships: a developmental perspective, *Journal of Personality and Social Psychology* 92: 355–67

Tidwell, M. C. O., Reis, H. T. and Shaver, P. R. 1996. Attachment, attractiveness, and social interaction: a diary study, *Journal of Personality and Social Psychology* 71: 729–45

Waddington, C. H. 1957. *The strategy of the genes*. London: Allen and Unwin

Wallin, D. J. 2007. *Attachment in psychotherapy*. New York: Guilford Press

PART IV

Biological Perspectives

16 Evolutionary theories of personality

Aurelio José Figueredo, Paul Gladden, Geneva Vásquez, Pedro Sofio Abril Wolf and Daniel Nelson Jones

Integration with evolutionary theory could enhance personality theory by generating original predictions about the mechanisms governing personality. Novel hypotheses about how personality works can be derived from theories about the ultimate function of personality traits. Personality psychology currently describes and explains how personality is structured and how the mechanisms that produce such differences in behavioural patterns work. Personality theorists observe how personality differences develop and explain the proximate ('how it works') causes of these individual differences, but generally do not address ultimate ('why it works') causes. Ultimate explanations address why human personalities are structured in the precise manner that they are, why specific environmental inputs affect individuals in the way that they do, why the specific epigenetic rules that dictate how an individual responds to different environmental input exist and why other rules do not, as well as why personality traits are responsive to the environment at all and what adaptive function personality characteristics may serve. By adopting a framework for answering these questions about evolved function, personality theory would become enriched with novel hypotheses.

Evolutionary psychology views all psychological phenomena through the lens of the theory of evolution, in the hope that by asking why specific psychological mechanisms originally evolved, previously unidentified psychological mechanisms and new aspects of known psychological mechanisms will be illuminated. Evolution by natural and sexual selection is the only coherent framework that can explain why complex, adaptive psychological mechanisms exist and what adaptive problems they are designed to solve (Tooby and Cosmides, 1992). The standard social science model (SSSM) offers no explicit meta-theory to direct the investigation of personality. This leaves personality researchers to follow intuition or trial and error to direct their discovery of new psychological phenomena (Tooby and Cosmides 1992). This may impede significant progress in understanding the mechanisms underlying personality differences and the development of those characteristics.

Although evolutionary psychologists agree that evolution is relevant to all psychological mechanisms, there has been very little research done on personality from an evolutionary perspective. Evolutionary psychologists have generally been interested solely in what Tooby and Cosmides (1992) have termed the *psychic unity of mankind*. Therefore, they have been primarily concerned with human nature rather than individual differences. Consequently, much of evolutionary personality psychology research has focused on universally-shared psychological mechanisms that result in phenotypic plasticity due to varying environmental input without regard to genetic variability or heritable traits.

However, the vast behavioural genetics literature on personality traits indicates strong genetic components for differences in all of the Big Five personality traits (Loehlin, McCrae, Costa and John 1998). The genetic variability of such traits is dismissed or explained by some evolutionary psychologists as selectively neutral or as genetic 'noise' (Tooby and Cosmides 1990). But the argument that personality differences are selectively neutral is unable to account for the fact that our closest living relative, the chimpanzee, exhibits similar versions of the Big Five personality traits (plus Dominance) (King and Figueredo 1997). Evolutionary psychology's focus on the shared genetic endowment of the human species has thus created what is, in our view, an artificial barrier between evolutionary psychology and individual differences psychology (including behavioural genetics), especially as it applies to personality. In our view, ultimate causation ('why') questions can be applied as well to genetically variable traits, such as personality traits, as they can to more species-typical human traits.

Strong ties with evolutionary theories of ultimate function can lead to novel predictions that could facilitate the discovery of new proximate mechanisms governing personality. Theories of evolutionary adaptive significance provide a framework that can inform personality theorists about (a) whether there are adaptive functions for the genetic differences that influence variation in personality characteristics and what those functions are; (b) potential new aspects of mechanisms governing personality structure; (c) what aspects of an individual's developmental environment should be expected to affect that individual; (d) how and to what degree individuals should be affected by different environments; and (e) why personality traits are responsive to environmental modulation.

Evolutionary theory provides an additional way in which to supplement and enrich current personality theory. Data on non-human primate (and other animal) personality structures and the ecological and social conditions associated with the evolutionary development of those personality traits could provide reliable predictions about new aspects of human personality. The current data on animal personalities and the selective pressures responsible for producing those traits is far too sparse to properly contribute to human research. But this information could be important to facilitate the discovery of unforeseen aspects and mechanisms of human personality and this line of inquiry should be pursued vigorously.

A more detailed and specific explanation addressing ultimate questions about evolved function can and is already beginning to inform personality research. We review what we currently know about personality as viewed in the light of evolutionary theory and provide a model for the future study of personality from an evolutionary point of view.

Tooby and Cosmides (1990) have claimed that traits that are heritable and variable, such as the Big Five personality traits that are heritable by a margin of .3 to .5 (MacDonald 1995), cannot be the result of adaptation. Nevertheless, most evolutionary personality psychologists have generally concluded that individual differences in personality traits are adaptive in nature (see Figueredo, Sefcek, Vasquez *et al*. 2005 for a review). Those in the majority include David Buss (e.g. 1991, 1997; Buss and Greiling 1999) whose personality theory suggests that individual differences lead to differences in the effectiveness with which people can adopt different strategies in our complex social groups. Furthermore, Buss has suggested that people are especially aware of personality variation among group members because it is something that must be noticed and contended with in order to be successful in our daily interactions. MacDonald (e.g., 1995, 1998) has taken a similar approach to explaining the adaptive nature of personality differences and expanded it a step further. He proposed that, in addition to needing to manage the personality differences of others and the ability we have to adopt different strategies, personality variation is important because there are a wide variety of continuously graded niches within our social, ecological and physical environments. Personality differences allow different individuals to be suited to particular niches that others would not be suited for. This is adaptive because it leads to decreased competition, due to greater specialization, and renders the various personality characteristics optimal under differing local conditions.

Wilson (1994) and Figueredo (1995) have suggested that the diversification of individual traits to fit different social niches might be ultimately due to frequency-dependent selection. In this view, social competition drives individuals into different social niches and filling these diverse niches offers partial release from competitive pressure from conspecifics. In support of this view, Figueredo (see also Figueredo, Sefcek, Vasquez *et al*. 2005; Figueredo and King 2001) observed that the variation in personality reported in the non-human animal literature appears to be almost exclusively a characteristic of social species; applying concepts from behavioural ecology suggests that intraspecific 'niche-splitting' leads to intraspecific 'character displacement'. Niche-splitting is the fragmentation of the ecological space into more specialized niches, and character displacement is the differentiation of individual traits to adapt to these different niches. According to this model, the cost of deviating from the species-typical optimum is compensated by the benefit of competitive release. The species-typical optimum is the evolved norm of response in any given situation, and competitive release is the relief from intraspecific competition achieved by the displacement of individual behaviour from that modal norm of response. The result is an 'ideal free distribution' of alternative behavioural phenotypes where the balance of costs and benefits are equalized among different individuals. This centrifugal dispersion of individuals will create bell-shaped curves around the modal norm of response along different dimensions of personality (Figueredo, Sefcek, Vasquez *et al*. 2005).

There are essentially three solutions to the problem of adaptation to environments that are variable or heterogeneous in either time or space (including 'ecological space'): (1) developmental plasticity, (2) genetic diversity, and (3) spatial migration. According to Brunswikian Evolutionary Developmental (BED) theory, ecologies that are variable over evolutionary time select for organisms that are phenotypically plastic enough to adapt by means of learning over developmental time (Figueredo, Hammond and McKiernan 2006). However, such behavioural development depends critically on the existence of reliable and valid cues that signal which alternative phenotype is optimal under each set of localized conditions in time, space and ecology; in the absence of such reliable and valid cues, the solution to either environmental temporal variability or spatial heterogeneity is the production of genetically diverse individuals that are dispersed along the expected distribution of locally optimal trait values (West-Eberhard 2003). However, as BED theory elucidates, ecological cues are typically neither completely reliable and valid nor unreliable and invalid; they are instead characterized by some ecological validity coefficient ranging between zero and one. Under those conditions, a hybrid theory would predict that organisms would show a combination of developmental plasticity and genetic diversity to collectively fill the available ecological niche space. Interestingly enough, the partial heritability and partial environmentality of personality variation in humans conforms precisely to the predictions of this synthetic model.

One seemingly paradoxical suggestion derivable from evolutionary psychology is that, while personality differences are likely adaptive, they also constrain individuals' behavioural flexibility. MacDonald (1998) suggested that different personality traits are best suited for the occupation of different social and ecological niches. Viewed differently, this means that individuals may be constrained in their behavioural repertoires based on the particular suite of personality characteristics that they possess, due to heredity and environmental factors. This may, at first, seem extremely maladaptive because it does not allow individuals fully to exploit the range of possibilities inherent in the different situations that they might encounter. In fact, according to some psychologists who favour the situation side of the person-situation debate (e.g., Mischel, Shoda and Smith 2004), the very definition of a personality disorder is unchanging personality in the face of the changing environmental contexts that a person encounters. In contrast, we propose that the biological preparedness for and the developmental plasticity of certain behaviours can and do vary independently of each other (Figueredo, Hammond and McKiernan 2006). In our view, personality traits represent dispositions to respond to environmental contingencies in certain ways, and to seek out environments in which prepared behaviours are suitable, but they do not represent the unalterable necessity to behave in the predisposed manner.

Interestingly, when we consider the actual behaviour of humans, the paradox no longer seems to hold. For example, in keeping with the idea that personality does constrain behaviour, in a naturalistic observation study by Mehl and Pennebaker (2003), which required participants to wear recording devices that recorded examples of conversation and any other aspect of quotidian life that a person might engage in at intervals of approximately twelve minutes, a remarkable amount of temporal and behavioural stability was encountered within subjects. Furthermore, as hypothesized by both MacDonald and Figueredo, they found that individuals possessing different personality types actually did gravitate toward different niches that seemed to suit their personalities best. This indicates that, while human behaviour may be constrained by individual personality traits, the cost of these constraints can be overcome by the benefits entailed in the selection of suitable social niches for the personality traits that each individual possesses. This is also an example of how genetic diversity can work synergistically with migration within ecological niche space to solve the problem of environmental heterogeneity.

To put these evolutionary models of personality into perspective, one must consider the natural history of human evolution. The past 3.5 million years have been a rapidly varying timeframe when it comes to global climate (for a review see Lisieki and Raymo 2005; Zachos, Pagani, Sloan *et al.* 2001). These global fluctuations translated into ecological variability, be it in specific African basins (Wynn 2004) or the waxing and waning of the northern hemisphere's ice sheets. When it comes to human evolution the story starts in Africa and ends with the current worldwide distribution. A complicating factor when considering this timeframe is the onset of the Holocene. During the Holocene, farming and herding were developed, and with it came larger population densities. These larger populations blur the distinction between when, where and why adaptations evolved by increasing the complexity of the problem. These complicating factors, along with others, present difficulties for even the most inclusive evolutionary models.

When considering the paleontological record, evidence suggests that it is likely that organisms which do not adapt to ecological variability by evolving a degree of adaptive plasticity tend to become extinct. Migration to ecologically supportive environments (a form of 'niche picking'), however, can also solve the adaptive problems associated with ecological variability. At the global level, rarely does a specific ecological niche disappear entirely, making it possible for a species to continue existing by merely moving to an appropriate habitat. Examples of the power of migration or niche picking as an adaptive response to the changing world comes from the animals adapted to the glacial environments of the northern hemisphere. Although the last glacial maximum is dated at approximately 15,000 years ago, many species that were adapted to glacial conditions survived well into the warmer climates of the Holocene, with the woolly mammoth surviving in parts of Siberia until approximately 4,000 years ago (Pastor and Moen 2004). Although there are examples of migration successfully working as a solution to variability, this particular example shows that this adaptive tactic does not always work. There are times when other adaptations are necessary if a species is to survive the change or disappearance of an ecosystem. If the change in environment is slow enough, a transition from one set of adapted phenotypes to another is possible. However, depending on the speed of the change, this form of adaptation may not be fast enough and may lead to extinction, as was the case with many large mammals during the late Pleistocene. As mentioned previously, another possible solution to variability is the evolution of versatile phenotypes capable of solving adaptive problems in a diverse array of ecologies. Although measuring behavioural adaptations over evolutionary time is difficult, evidence coming from the study of morphology suggests that whole taxonomic families, including Hominids, evolved more versatile phenotypes in response to increases in variability during both the Pliocene and the Pleistocene (Potts 1998; Wynn 2004).

Geary (2005) has classified the selective pressures on ancestral humans into three basic types: (1) climactic, (2) ecological, and (3) social. After reviewing much of the available evidence, he concludes that the major selective pressures on both recent human ancestors and modern humans have been social in nature. While we agree that social selection provides the most immediate and constant set of adaptive problems needing to be solved by humans, we disagree about the relative lack of importance assigned to the climactic and the ecological forces. Instead, as proposed by Richerson and Boyd (2000) we take the view that changes in social structure were likely an adaptive solution to selective pressures originating with climactic and ecological variability. By solving these adaptive problems through social behaviour, novel adaptive problems arose linked directly to social selection. A more inclusive model would be that climate changes produce ecological changes and these, in turn, exacerbate social competition over resources. For example, migration of some groups out of habitats rendered uninhabitable by climate change into still-habitable habitats ('refugia') already inhabited by other groups set the occasion for conflict both between and within groups over limited resources. Thus, Geary is probably correct in proposing social selection as the most immediate and constant promoter of human evolution, but changes in climate and ecology ultimately heighten social competition.

What all this evolutionary history suggests is that, in accounting for the manifest variation in human personality traits, we should probably observe a strategic mix of adaptive plasticity, genetic diversity, niche picking/migration, and local adaptations to the recently stabilized Holocene climate. This combination of selective pressures accounts for the observed much-debated combination of partial heritability and partial environmentality in human personality traits.

We argue that personality variation is important in guiding the social and sexual relationships of individuals. Personality is an important factor when making friends or finding a romantic partner. What it means to say that someone has a 'great personality' remains unclear, but there is some consensus on what is a desirable personality in a romantic partner (Figueredo, Sefcek and Jones 2006). Variation in personality is likely to drive individuals into different kinds of relationships and to seek and obtain different kinds of friends and lovers. In social and ecological niches that demand particular approaches to relationships, it is likely that different personalities have been selected for and are more likely to enable an organism to survive and reproduce.

Many personality traits seem to predict relationship outcomes across time and across different relationships. Further, research suggests that individual differences in personality are better predictors of relationship outcomes than other factors such as compatibility, similarity and honesty (Eysenck and Wakefield 1981). For example, lower levels of self-esteem (Swann 1996), higher levels of neuroticism (Donnellan, Larsen-Rife and Conger 2005, Eysenck and Wakefield 1981; White, Hendrick and Hendrick 2004;), higher levels of psychoticism (Diener and Seligman 2002; Eysenck and Wakefield 1981), and insecure attachment (see Simms 2002, for review) all predict 'poor' relationship outcomes. If part of the function of personality is to guide our social relationships, one may wonder how such variations in these traits would have been passed on if they were maladaptive.

One explanation deals with the relationship goals of the individual. In highly competitive or harsh environments, it is likely to be adaptive for an individual to be hypervigilant and aggressive. For example, neuroticism is related to increased levels of romantic jealousy in a relationship (Melamed 1991). While jealousy can drive a relationship apart, it can also be a very useful mechanism in keeping a partner from straying in a relationship (Buss 2000). Thus, in environments where hypervigilance or aggressiveness is adaptive, individuals who are neurotic may be more effective in protecting themselves from negative outcomes such as infidelity.

Some individual differences may also interact or co-evolve with other characteristics of individuals to aid in adaptation to a given environment. For example, individuals who are at a competitive disadvantage (e.g., lower intelligence, poor genetic quality) in friendships and reproduction may benefit from having higher levels of mating effort in harsh environments. Such impulsive and sensation-seeking individuals will try harder, and more often, to get romantic partners, and display attributes such as toughness to friends or partners in order to serve short-term interests (Rowe, Vazsonyi and Figueredo 1997). It would also lead the individual to focus on short-term opportunistic encounters, which would be more attainable for someone in a disadvantaged position, rather than long-term meaningful relationships. Further, Brown and Moore (2002) have demonstrated that individuals with higher levels of fluctuating asymmetry report higher levels of dispositional jealousy. Therefore, it seems that individuals who are less attractive have certain traits that lead them to be vigilant against the increased risk of infidelity in a partner.

Individuals also differ in their desire for multiple partners and for sexual contacts (Buss and Schmitt 1993; Figueredo, Sefcek, Vasquez et al. 2005; Simpson and Gangestad 1991; Rowe, Vazsonyi and Figueredo 1997). This, too, leads to a variety of social and romantic relationship outcomes. The demands of the environment and the costs posed by relationships can lead individuals to be careful in choosing which relationships to invest in and how much to invest in them. In harsh and unpredictable environments, where extrinsic mortality is high, it is important for individuals to produce many low-maintenance offspring rather than invest heavily in a smaller number of offspring (Figueredo, Sefcek, Vasquez et al. 2005). As a result, we would expect relationship satisfaction to interfere with such a strategy, since it is likely to impede moving from one sexual partner to another. Research has indeed confirmed that shared traits such as lower levels of mating effort and a generally 'slower' life history strategy significantly predict romantic partner and relationship satisfaction and commitment (Olderbak 2007).

Similarly, those who are altruistic and build long-term, reciprocal friendships may experience higher levels of fitness in environments where it is favourable to do so. However, in harsh and unpredictable environments that favour short-term social relationships, such traits and behaviours may pose severe costs to an individual. Thus, individuals who are less likely to trust others and more willing to exploit others may be best suited in environments where short-term encounters are the norm and immediate extraction of resources is necessary.

In conclusion, we propose that sociality is the major cause of personality variation in humans. Specifically, adaptation to different micro-niches within the overall social ecology of the species is what leads to the differentiation of personality traits among individuals. Climactic and ecological fluctuations during repeated Ice Ages may have historically provided much of the initial impetus by exacerbating social competition, but the larger population densities occasioned by the Neolithic Revolution in human subsistence economies (e.g., farming, herding, industrial and now information-based) have largely taken their place in recent human history. We suggest that this complex combination of selective pressures accounts for the strategic mix of heritability and environmentality observed in human personality development. These selective pressures serve as the ultimate causes of adaptive personality variation and provide some unique predictions regarding these proximate causes of personality. Further, these predictions are not limited to the adaptive aspects of personality. Predictions about by-products and trade-offs that result from pursuing one adaptive personality strategy over another are also derivable. Thus, personality variation retains its adaptive significance even to this day.

References

Brown, W. M. and Moore, C. 2002. Fluctuating asymmetry and romantic jealousy, *Evolution and Human Behaviour* 24: 113–17

Buss, D. M. 1991. Evolutionary personality psychology, *Annual Review of Psychology* 42: 459–91

1997. Evolutionary foundations of personality, in R. Hogan (ed.), *Handbook of personality psychology*, pp. 317–44. London: Academic Press

2000. *The dangerous passion: why jealousy is as necessary as love and sex*. New York: Free Press

Buss, D. M. and Greiling, H. 1999. Adaptive individual differences, *Journal of Personality* 67: 209–43

Buss, D. M. and Schmitt, D. P. 1993. Sexual strategies theory: an evolutionary perspective on human mating, *Psychological Review* 100: 204–32

Diener, E. and Seligman, M. E. P. 2002. Very happy people, *Psychological Science* 13: 81–4

Donnellan, M. B., Larsen-Rife, D. and Conger, R. D. 2005. Personality, family history, and competence in early adult romantic relationships, *Journal of Personality and Social Psychology* 88: 562–76

Eysenck, H. J. and Wakefield, J. A. 1981. Psychological factors as predictors of marital satisfaction, *Advances in Behaviour Research and Therapy* 3: 151–92

Figueredo, A. J. 1995. *The evolution of individual differences*. Paper delivered at Jane Goodall Institute ChimpanZoo Annual Conference, Tucson, Arizona

Figueredo, A. J., Hammond, K. R. and McKiernan, E. C. 2006. A Brunswikian evolutionary developmental theory of preparedness and plasticity, *Intelligence* 34: 211–27

Figueredo, A. J. and King, J. E. 2001. The evolution of individual differences. Paper delivered at Evolution and Individual Differences Symposium, Annual Meeting of the Human Behaviour and Evolution Society, London

Figueredo, A. J., Sefcek, J. and Jones, D. N. 2006. The ideal romantic partner personality, *Personality and Individual Differences* 41: 431–41

Figueredo, A. J., Sefcek, J. A., Vasquez, G., Brumbach, B. H., King, J. E. and Jacobs, W. J. 2005. Evolutionary personality psychology, in D. M. Buss (ed.), *Handbook of evolutionary psychology*, pp. 851–77. Hoboken, NJ: Wiley

Geary, D. C. 2005. *The origin of mind: evolution of brain, cognition, and general intelligence*. Washington, DC: American Psychological Association Press

King, J. E. and Figueredo, A. J. 1997. The five-factor model plus dominance in chimpanzee personality, *Journal of Research in Personality* 31: 257–71

Lisieki, L. E. and Raymo, M. A. 2005. The Pliocene-Pleistocene tack of 57 globally distributed benthic d18O records, *Paleoceanography* 20: 1003

Loehlin, J., McCrae, R., Costa, P. and John, O. 1998. Heritabilities of common and measure-specific components of the Big Five personality factors, *Journal of Research in Personality* 32: 431–53

MacDonald, K. B. 1995. Evolution, the five-factor model, and levels of personality, *Journal of Personality* 63: 525–67

  1998. Evolution, culture, and the five-factor model, *Journal of Cross-Cultural Psychology* 29: 119–49

Mehl, M. R. and Pennebaker, J. W. 2003. The sounds of social life: a psychometric analysis of students' daily social environments and natural conversations, *Journal of Personality and Social Psychology* 84: 857–70

Melamed, T. 1991. Individual differences in romantic jealousy: the moderating effect of relationship characteristics, *European Journal of Social Psychology* 21: 455–61

Mischel, W., Shoda, Y. and Smith, R. E. 2004. *Introduction to personality: toward an integration*, 7th edn. Hoboken, NJ: John Wiley & Sons

Olderbak, S. 2007. Modeling assortative mating, partner satisfaction, and commitment in long-term romantic relationships, *Revista Mexicana de Psicología, Número Especial: XV Congreso Mexicano de Psicología* 364–5

Pastor, J. and Moen R. A. 2004. Ecology of ice-age extinctions, *Nature* 431: 639–40

Potts, R. 1998. Variability selection in hominid evolution, *Evolutionary Anthropology* 7: 81–96

Richerson, P. J. and Boyd, R. 2000. The Pleistocene and the origins of human culture: built for speed, in N. S. Thompson and F. Tonneau (eds.), *Perspectives in ethology: evolution, culture, and behaviour*, vol. XIII, pp. 1–45. New York: Kluwer Academic

Rowe, D. C., Vazsonyi, A. T. and Figueredo, A. J. 1997. Mating effort in adolescence: conditional or alternative strategy?, *Journal of Personality and Individual Differences* 23: 105–15

Simms, L. J. 2002. The application of attachment theory to individual behaviour and functioning in close relationships: theory, research, and practical applications, in J. H. Harvey and A. Wenzel (eds.), *Maintenance and enhancement of close relationships*, vol. II, pp. 63–80. Hillsdale, NJ: Erlbaum

Simpson, J. A. and Gangestad, S. W. 1991. Individual differences in sociosexuality: evidence for convergent and discriminant validity, *Journal of Personality and Social Psychology* 60: 870–83

Swann, W. B. 1996. *Self-traps: the elusive quest for higher self-esteem*. New York: Freeman

Tooby, J. and Cosmides, L. 1990. On the universality of human nature and the uniqueness of the individual: the role of genetics and adaptation, *Journal of Personality, Special Issue: Biological foundations of personality – evolution, behavioural genetics, and psychophysiology* 58: 17–67

    1992. The psychological foundations of culture, in J. Barkow, L. Cosmides and J. Tooby (eds.), *The adapted mind: evolutionary psychology and the generation of culture*, pp. 19–136. New York: Oxford University Press

West-Eberhard, M. J. 2003. *Developmental plasticity and evolution*. New York: Oxford University Press

White, J. K., Hendrick, S. S. and Hendrick, C. 2004. Big five personality variables and relationship constructs, *Personality and Individual Differences* 37: 1519–30

Wilson, D. S. 1994. Adaptive genetic variation and human evolutionary psychology, *Ethology and Sociobiology* 15: 219–35

Wynn, J. G. 2004. Influence of Plio-Pleistocene aridification on human evolution: evidence from paleosols of the Turkana Basin, Kenya, *American Journal of Physical Anthropology* 123: 106–18

Zachos, J., Pagani, M., Sloan, L., Thomas, E. and Billups, K. 2001. Trends, rhythms, and aberrations in global climate 65 Ma to present, *Science* 292: 686–93

17 Animal models of personality and cross-species comparisons

Samuel D. Gosling and B. Austin Harley

Consider two individuals, who we shall call Frank and Fred. Compared with Frank, Fred has consistently proven himself to be more aggressive; that is, he makes more threats than Frank does, he physically pushes others, he even kicks and punches them, and is more reluctant than Frank to retreat from an altercation. Now consider two other individuals, who we shall call Tina and Tracy. Tina is bolder than Tracy; that is, when out and about looking for something to eat Tina is not as bothered as Tracy by venturing into new places to find food or taking unfamiliar routes to eat or even by the presence of threatening characters in the vicinity.

In most contexts, we would not hesitate to explain differences between Frank and Fred and between Tina and Tracy in terms of personality traits like aggression and boldness. However, many researchers might hesitate to use such terms upon learning that Frank and Fred are fruit flies and Tina and Tracy are trout. Yet recent research on behavioural regularities in fruit flies (Edwards, Rollmann, Morgan and Mackay 2006) and trout (Wilson and Stevens 2005) has identified precisely such consistent individual differences in behaviour in these two species. Such studies are pushing psychologists to consider where the boundaries of personality lie; by extending the phylogenetic reach of personality, animal studies are opening a plethora of new research opportunities and raising a host of new questions about the distal origins and proximal bases of personality traits.

In this chapter we review some basic issues in the rapidly growing field of animal personality. We start with the most basic question: does personality exist in animals? We then survey the many different motivations for studying animal personality and review some broad patterns to emerge from the research literature regarding the goals of past research, the methods that have been used, the traits that have been examined, and the species studied. We end by presenting some points to be considered when making cross-species comparisons of personality.

Does personality exist in animals?

To pet owners and many people who work closely with animals it seems self-evident that animals possess consistent individual differences in behaviour; that is, they exhibit patterns of behaviour that in humans would be referred to as 'personality traits'. However, many people, especially those working in sciences, have been reluctant to concede that personality exists in non-human animals. Their concerns range from philosophical arguments regarding the uniqueness of humans to methodological concerns about the perils of anthropomorphism (Gosling 2001).

To address concerns about the existence of personality in animals, Gosling, Lilienfeld and Marino (2003; see also Gosling and Vazire 2002) recently adopted three criteria from the debate concerning the existence of personality in humans (Kenrick and Funder 1988): (1) assessments by independent observers must agree with one another; (2) those assessments must predict behaviours and real-world outcomes; and (3) observer ratings must be shown to reflect genuine attributes of the individuals rated, not just the observers' implicit theories about how personality traits co-vary.

Criterion 1: independent assessments must agree

If individual differences in personality exist and can be detected, then independent observers should agree about the relative standing of individuals on personality traits (Gosling, Kwan and John 2003). Studies of humans rating other humans typically elicit inter-observer agreement correlations in the region of .50 (e.g., Funder, Kolar and Blackman 1995), supporting the idea that humans agree with their ratings of one another and providing a standard by which judgements of animals can be evaluated.

There is now a substantial corpus of research showing that observers agree strongly in their ratings of animals. Gosling (2001) summarized the findings from twenty-one rating studies of animal personality; the mean inter-observer agreement correlation was .52, matching the magnitude of consensus correlations from human research.

Criterion 2: assessments must predict behaviours and real-world outcomes

For personality traits to be of any use, ultimately they must predict behaviours and the real-world outcomes. Few animal studies have tested the reality of personality measures (Gosling 2001), but the handful of studies which have been done provide strong evidence for concurrent and predictive validity. Personality traits have been shown to predict specific behaviours (e.g., Pederson, King and Landau 2005), occupational success (e.g., Maejima Inoue-Murayama, Tonosaki *et al.* 2006), and health outcomes. For example, Capitanio, Mendoza and Baroncelli (1999) found that sociable rhesus monkeys showed a stronger immune response to experimental inoculation with the simian immunodeficiency virus than did less sociable individuals.

Criterion 3: ratings must reflect attributes of targets, not observers' implicit personality theories

Several studies of personality structure in animals have identified a number of broad dimensions, which often resemble dimensions found in studies of humans

(Gosling and John 1999). These findings could be taken as evidence that animals have personality. However, it is possible that observers are not detecting the true structure of personality traits in animals, but are instead simply 'filling in the blanks' using their knowledge of human personality structure. Although most animal studies of personality structure are based on personality ratings (e.g., 'curiosity'), a small number of studies are based on behavioural tests (e.g., response to a novel object) and carefully recorded ethological observations (e.g., time spent exploring environment). For example, Van Hooff (1973) meticulously observed the naturally occurring expressive behaviour of chimpanzees. A Social Play factor was marked by such behaviour patterns as 'grasp and poke', 'pull limb', and 'gymnastics' (exuberant locomotory play, such as swinging, dangling, rolling over, turning somersaults), and an Affinity factor was marked by behaviour patterns indicating social closeness, such as 'touching', 'grooming' and 'embrace'. Unlike the ratings-based factors, such behaviour-based factors cannot be explained solely in terms of observers "filling in the blanks' on the basis of the semantic similarity of the traits. Moreover, in cases where cross-study comparisons can be made, the factors obtained from behavioural codings resemble factors obtained from observer ratings, suggesting that both methods assess the same underlying constructs (Gosling and John 1999). Overall, the findings suggest that the structure of personality ratings is based, at least in part, on real attributes of the individuals being rated.

Why study animal personality?

Weinstein, Capitanio and Gosling (2008) recently outlined three primary domains in which animal personality could be useful: behavioural ecology, animal-model research and practical applications.

Behavioural ecology

The concept of animal personality is tightly tied to the existence of individual differences; that is, a personality trait can be identified only if individuals vary on that trait. Thus, for boldness to be identified in a species it is necessary for variation to exist, with different individuals expressing different levels of boldness; if all individuals in a species had exactly the same levels of boldness then that trait would be said to be characteristic of the species and would not be considered a personality trait.

The necessity for individual variation raises some theoretical issues within the context of evolutionary processes because selection tends to reduce or eliminate differences. Thus, researchers in Behavioural Ecology and Ethology are primarily interested in learning about the ecological and evolutionary implications of consistent individual differences in behaviour (e.g., Carere and Eens 2005; Dall, Houston and McNamara 2004; Dingemanse and Reale 2005; McElreath and

Strimling 2006; Nettle 2006). Research has focused on documenting the existence of individual differences across a broad range of species, identifying the adaptive function of various traits, and generating evolutionarily plausible accounts of how individual differences could be maintained within populations.

In the field of Behavioural Ecology, behaviours that are correlated within a given context (e.g., correlations between activity and exploratory behaviours in a foraging context) or across different contexts (e.g., correlations among foraging, anti-predator and mating behaviours) are often referred to as behavioural syndromes (Sih, Bell, Johnson and Ziemba et al. 2004). These suites of behaviours are presumably linked by genetic or physiological mechanisms. Such behavioural syndromes are sometimes used to explain the existence of apparently maladaptive behaviours. For example, it may be maladaptive to be overly aggressive in a mating situation but the costs of aggression in this context may be offset by the benefits of being aggressive in other contexts (e.g., foraging, defence of territory). It is possible that the cost-benefit trade-offs vary from year to year or from niche to niche such that different suites (e.g., high aggression vs. low aggression) are adaptive at different times or locales. In a series of long-term studies of personality in a natural population of a passerine bird species (*Parus major*) one research group has generated compelling evidence for the idea that different personalities are adaptive under different conditions (Dingemanse, Both, Drent and Tinbergen 2004; Drent, van Oers and van Noordwijk 2003; Groothuis and Carere 2005).

Animal model research

Researchers in psychology tend to use animal models to understand the biological and environmental bases of personality (e.g., Ray, Hansen and Waters 2006; Willis-Owen and Flint 2007) and the implications of various personality traits (e.g., Capitanio, Mendoza and Baroncelli 1999; Pederson, King and Landau 2005). Compared with human studies, animal studies afford greater experimental control of both environmental and genetic factors, as well as greater ability to manipulate independent variables and assess dependent variables (Gosling 2001; Mehta and Gosling 2006; Vazire and Gosling 2003).

Animal studies afford four major benefits over human research. First, animal studies allow greater experimental control and facilitate more extensive experimental manipulations than is possible in studies of humans. Secondly, observations of animals can be made in far greater detail and for more extensive periods than is possible for humans. Thirdly, the accelerated life history of many species means that longitudinal studies can be conducted in substantially shorter periods than possible with humans. Fourthly, for many species it is possible to obtain detailed quantitative and molecular genetic information and to conduct transgenic, knock-out and cloning studies (Gosling and Mollaghan 2006).

Ultimately animal studies can be used to test specific hypotheses that, with humans, must often rely on sub-optimal designs. To illustrate, consider John Capitanio's research programme, which for over a decade has been accruing personality data on over 175 rhesus monkeys (see Weinstein, Capitanio and Gosling 2008, for description of this research programme). He assessed their personalities at five–ten years of age, identifying a four-factor structure, which was later confirmed with confirmatory factor analysis in a separate sub-sample. Animals were tested in a variety of social and non-social situations and behavioural and physiological measures were obtained in these situations for up to several years following the initial personality assessments; personality was found to predict various measures of social behaviour and emotionality, plasma cortisol concentrations, tetanus- and herpesvirus-specific antibody responses, heart rate and central nervous system functioning. For example, Sociability scores predicted patterns of neural innervation of lymph nodes, moderated the response to a social stressor, and influenced expression of genes associated with innate immune responses.

Practical applications of animal research

Animal personality research has numerous practical applications, including improving the welfare of animals used in scientific experiments, helping the selection of animals as pets, and directing conservation of endangered species. Researchers in various applied fields, like Applied Ethology, focus on practical issues such as predicting working dog performance (e.g., Maejima, Inoue-Murayama, Tonosaki *et al.* 2006; Svartberg 2005) and applications in animal welfare and management (e.g., McDougall, Reale, Sol and Reader 2006; Watters and Meehan 2007).

In the case of working animals, the principles of human personnel selection can be applied to the animal domain. For example, dogs that are temperamentally predisposed to fearful behaviour are more likely to become anxious in the presence of loud noises, impeding their ability to work effectively as explosive or narcotic detection dogs in a wide range of real-world contexts (e.g., shipyards, combat). In one study of drug-detection dogs, personality trait scores obtained after two weeks of training substantially predicted the dogs' detection success assessed after four months of training (Maejima, Inoue-Murayama, Tonosaki *et al.* 2006).

Research methods, traits and species

The field of animal personality is very diverse. In addition to the variability in research aims described in the previous section, studies differ in terms of methods used, traits examined and species studied.

Methods

The research methods used to examine personality are quite diverse (Gosling 2001; Jones and Gosling 2005). Broadly speaking, the two main methods for obtaining information about individual animals are codings of an animal's behaviours, and subjective ratings of traits. These two methods reflect different resolutions to the supposed trade-off between quantifying personality in terms of objective behaviours and using humans to record and collate information more subjectively. Behavioural coding methods are used to gather data from test situations in which animals are put in situations designed to elicit personality-relevant responses (e.g., exposure to a novel stimulus), or from observations of naturalistic behaviour (Freeman, Gosling and Schapiro in press). Ratings are used to gather data from either of the above contexts (test situations and naturalistic behaviour) as well as drawing on the accumulated experience of humans who know the animals well (rather like informant reports in human personality research).

Direct comparisons of the two methods suggest that rating methods are superior to coding methods for capturing personality traits because rating methods are more reliable, are not as subjective as is sometimes assumed, and are generally much more practical (Vazire, Gosling, Dickey and Shapiro 2007). Vazire *et al.*'s analyses of ratings and codings of chimpanzees demonstrated that trait ratings are well-suited for detecting consistencies in animals' behaviours, the very foundation of personality. Behaviour codings, in contrast, are notoriously difficult to measure reliably, particularly when observations are made across different times of day or under varying conditions. Even when behaviours are measured at the same time of day or under the same conditions, they may reflect other characteristics of the environment (e.g., situational influences) and not personality. It is important to note that behaviour codings are not poor measures of *behaviour*, but that they are poor measures of *personality*. Behaviour-coding methods may be better suited for experimental manipulations, where researchers are concerned with detecting the effects of situational variables on behaviour.

Traits

Empirical research on animal personality is essentially comprised of studies of traits – behavioural regularities that are relatively consistent across time and contexts. Commonly studied personality traits include: exploration, boldness, fearfulness, aggression, general activity, emotionality, confidence and timidity.

To get a better idea of which traits emerge in structural analyses of personality Gosling and John (1999) reviewed nineteen factor analytic studies across twelve non-human species. They used the Five-Factor Model (FFM) plus Dominance and Activity as an organizing framework for the findings. The FFM dimensions of Extraversion, Neuroticism and Agreeableness showed considerable generality across the twelve species included in their review. For example, of the nineteen studies reviewed, seventeen identified a factor closely related to Extraversion, capturing dimensions ranging from Surgency in chimpanzees, Sociability in pigs, dogs and rhesus monkeys, Energy in cats and dogs, Vivacity in donkeys, to a dimension contrasting Bold approach vs. Avoidance in octopuses. Of course, the way these personality dimensions are manifested depends on the species; whereas the human scoring low on Extraversion stays at home on Saturday night, or tries to blend into a corner at a large party, the octopus scoring low on Boldness stays in its protective den during feedings and attempts to hide itself.

However, some dimensions showed less cross-species generality. Chimpanzees were the only non-human species with a separate Conscientiousness factor, which was defined more narrowly than in humans but included the lack of attention and goal-directedness and erratic, unpredictable and disorganized behaviour typical of the low pole. The existence of a separate Conscientiousness factor in only humans and their closest relative suggests that the trait evolved relatively recently in the evolution of *Homininae* (Gosling and Graybeal 2007). The finding is consistent with the fact that both humans and chimpanzees have relatively developed frontal cortices, the area of the brain associated with higher executive function like making plans and controlling impulses (Beer, Shimamura and Knight 2004).

Species

The most comprehensive review to date of the animal personality literature identified personality studies in sixty-four different non-human species (Gosling 2001). The species studied were far from representative of the species in existence: 84 per cent of the studies in Gosling's review focused on mammals (29 per cent primates, 55 per cent non-primates), 8 per cent focused on fish, 4 per cent focused on birds, and the remaining 4 per cent were divided among reptiles, amphibians, arthropods and molluscs. Since that review, studies of personality in numerous other species have emerged, ranging from water striders (Sih and Watters 2005), lizards (Cote and Clobert 2007), and squid (Sinn, Gosling and Moltschaniwskyj 2008), to tropical fish (Brown, Jones and Braithwaite 2005), geese (Kralj-Fiser, Scheiber, Blejec *et al.* 2007), and orangutans (Weiss, King and Perkins 2006). It should be noted, however, that researchers do not always explicitly use the term 'personality'. For example, researchers may use terms like 'behavioural syndromes', 'behavioural types', or 'temperament', often not for theoretical reasons but in an effort to avoid the anthropomorphic connotations of a word with 'person' in it.

Cross-species comparisons

Establishing cross-species equivalence of personality traits

One challenge facing any comparative researcher is determining the degree to which apparently similar traits really are tapping the same underlying trait. How can it be determined that what appears to be boldness in squid or trout or chimpanzees is in any way similar to boldness in humans? After all, there are very few literal similarities in how the same trait could be expressed across species.

It is easy to make errors of interpretation; for example, the chimpanzee facial display in which the lips are retracted so that clenched teeth are exposed reflects fear, not happiness, as might be assumed by the expression's apparent similarity to a human smile.

To solve this challenge, cross-species researchers can draw on the lessons learned by cross-cultural researchers. In a sense, a comparative researcher asking whether the apparently sociable behaviour of a rhesus monkey reflects the sociability that we know in humans is analogous to the cross-cultural emotions researcher asking whether the apparently angry expression of a hitherto isolated group of humans reflects the anger that we know in our own culture. The solution to determining cross-cultural equivalence of anger expressions is examining what comes before and after the expressions, and where possible, looking for commonalities in underlying physiology. Thus, if this expression that resembles anger comes after an event that might reasonably elicit anger, and results in actions that might reasonably follow anger, and displays the physiological signature of anger, then the researcher can be reasonably confident that the facial expression does indeed reflect anger as we know it. Likewise, an animal researcher can examine the apparently sociable behaviour in the context of what comes before and after the behaviour and, where possible, if it shares physiological, biological and genetic commonalities with human sociability. In essence, this procedure is what many animal researchers already do implicitly and explains why researchers with experience of a species do not make mistakes about behaviour (e.g., mistaking a chimpanzee's fear grin for a smile). Nonetheless, this procedure offers a set of steps that researchers can take when they encounter unfamiliar species or when they want to establish cross-species equivalences empirically.

Framework for cross-species comparisons

When generalizing across species, scientists must consider several dimensions of similarity and difference (Gosling 2001). As a rule, researchers making cross-species comparisons should consider the species' environmental and social ecologies, their biology, and their phylogenetic relationships with other species, and the importance of these criteria should be weighed according to what phenomenon is being examined. For example, Sapolsky (1990) has used Serengeti baboons to examine the links between stress and personality in humans; he notes that unlike many animals whose experience of stress is typically sudden and severe (e.g., escaping from an attacking predator), Serengeti baboons are relatively free from predation and have a plentiful supply of food so their main stressors are social in nature and are relatively chronic. This chronic form of stress is similar to the kinds of stressors to which humans are exposed, making baboons a good species to model the relations between stress and personality in humans.

Likewise, to investigate some social phenomena associated with group living in humans, scientists may find it more useful to focus on a social species such as lions or hyenas rather than a less social species such as orangutans, despite the fact that orangutans are more closely related to humans and are more similar to humans in terms of biology.

Researchers interested in the origin and function of traits should consider the phylogenetic relationships among the species compared. By examining the existence of traits against a backdrop of known phylogenetic relationships among species, researchers can pinpoint the likely period during which that trait emerged and can use this information to infer the original function of that trait (Fraley, Brumbaugh and Marks 2005; Gosling and Graybeal 2007). For example, as noted earlier, it was the discovery of a separate Conscientiousness dimension in humans and chimpanzees (but not in orangutans or gorillas) that permits phylogenetically oriented researchers to date the emergence of Conscientiousness to the period after the common ancestor to chimpanzees and humans diverged from the other apes (i.e., 7–10 million years ago).

In short, the choice of species studied should be driven by the question being addressed, with consideration paid to the species' environmental and social ecologies, their biology and their phylogenetic relationships. Fortunately, the biological, phylogenetic and social similarities of species are often correlated. Thus, chimpanzees may be the best choice to investigate group-based social phenomena because they are more similar to humans in social terms than lions, and more similar to humans than orangutans in phylogenetic and biological terms. Of course, other considerations such as cost and availability will almost certainly also feature heavily in decisions about which species to study.

Conclusions

Over the past five years or so, research on animal personality has emerged as a thriving topic in fields as diverse as Psychology, Primatology, Veterinary Medicine, Genetics, Applied Ethology and Behavioural Ecology. Personality researchers are now drawing on the benefits of animal models to address questions that are difficult or impossible to address by relying on human research alone (Mehta and Gosling 2006). We anticipate that the next decade will witness the growth of new cross-disciplinary collaborations that contribute to theory and practice in several areas of personality and beyond.

References

Beer, J. S., Shimamura, A. P. and Knight, R. T. 2004. Frontal lobe contributions to executive control of cognitive and social behaviour, in M. S. Gazzaniga (ed.) *The cognitive neurosciences III*, pp. 1091–04. Cambridge, MA: MIT Press

Brown, C., Jones, F. and Braithwaite, V. 2005. In situ examination of boldness-shyness traits in the tropical *poeciliid, Brachyraphis episcopi, Animal Behaviour* 70: 1003–9

Capitanio, J. P., Mendoza, S. P. and Baroncelli, S. 1999. The relationship of personality dimensions in adult male rhesus macaques to progression of Simian Immunodeficiency Virus disease, *Brain, Behaviour, and Immunity* 13: 138–54

Carere, C. and Eens, M. 2005. Unravelling animal personalities: how and why individuals consistently differ, *Behaviour* 142: 1149–57

Cote, J. and Clobert, J. 2007. Social personalities influence natal dispersal in a lizard, *Proceedings of the Royal Society B* 274: 383–90

Dall, S. R. X., Houston, A. I. and McNamara, J. M. 2004. The behavioural ecology of personality: consistent individual differences from an adaptive perspective, *Ecology Letters* 7: 734–9

Dingemanse, N. J., Both, C., Drent, P. J. and Tinbergen, J. M. 2004. Fitness consequences of avian personalities in a fluctuating environment, *Proceedings of the Royal Society of London Series B – Biological Sciences* 271: 847–52

Dingemanse, N. J. and Reale, D. 2005. Natural selection and animal personality, *Behaviour* 142: 1159–84

Drent, P. J., Van Oers, K. and Van Noordwijk, A. J. 2003. Realized heritability of personalities in the great tit (*Parus major*), *Proceedings of the Royal Society Biological Sciences Series B* 270: 45–51

Edwards, A. C., Rollmann, S. M., Morgan, T. J. and Mackay, T. F. C. 2006. Quantitative genomics of aggressive behaviour in *Drosophila melanogaster*, *PLoS Genetics* 2: e154. DOI: 10.1371/journal.pgen.0020154

Fraley, R. C., Brumbaugh, C. C. and Marks, M. J. 2005. The evolution and function of adult attachment: a comparative and phylogenetic analysis, *Journal of Personality and Social Psychology* 89: 808–22

Freeman, H., Gosling. S. D. and Schapiro, S. J. in press. Methods for assessing personality in non-human primates, in A. Weiss, J. King and L. Murray (eds.), *Personality and behavioral syndromes in nonhuman primates*. New York: Springer

Funder, D. C. Kolar, D. C. and Blackman, M. C. 1995. Agreement among judges of personality: interpersonal relations, similarity, and acquaintance, *Journal of Personality and Social Psychology* 69: 656–72

Gosling, S. D. 1998. Personality dimensions in spotted hyenas (*Crocuta crocuta*), *Journal of Comparative Psychology* 112: 107–18
  2001. From mice to men: what can we learn about personality from animal research?, *Psychological Bulletin* 127: 45–86

Gosling, S. D. and Graybeal, A. 2007. Tree thinking: a new paradigm for integrating comparative data in psychology, *Journal of General Psychology* 134: 259–77

Gosling, S. D. and John, O. P. 1999. Personality dimensions in non-human animals: a cross-species review, *Current Directions in Psychological Science* 8: 69–75

Gosling, S. D., Kwan, V. S. Y. and John, O. P. 2003. A dog's got personality: a cross-species comparative approach to evaluating personality judgments, *Journal of Personality and Social Psychology* 85: 1161–9

Gosling, S. D., Lilienfeld, S. O. and Marino, L. 2003. Personality, in D. Maestripieri (ed.), *Primate psychology: the mind and behaviour of human and nonhuman primates*, pp. 254–88. Cambridge, MA: Harvard University Press

Gosling, S. D. and Mollaghan, D. M. 2006. Animal research in social psychology: a bridge to functional genomics and other unique research opportunities, in P. A. M. van

Lange (ed.), *Bridging social psychology: benefits of transdisciplinary approaches*, pp. 123–8. Mahweh NJ: Erlbaum

Gosling, S. D. and Vazire, S. 2002. Are we barking up the right tree? Evaluating a comparative approach to personality, *Journal of Research in Personality* 36: 607–14

Groothuis, T. G. G. and Carere, C. 2005. Avian personalities: characterization and epigenesis, *Neuroscience and Biobehavioral Reviews* 29: 137–50

Jones, A. C. and Gosling, S. D. 2005. Temperament and personality in dogs (*Canis familiaris*): a review and evaluation of past research, *Applied Animal Behaviour Science* 95: 1–53

Kenrick, D. T. and Funder, D. C. 1988. Profiting from controversy: lessons from the person-situation debate, *American Psychologist* 43: 23–34

Kralj-Fiser, S. Scheiber, I. B. R., Blejec, A., Moestl, E. and Kotrschal, K. 2007. Individualities in a flock of free-roaming greylag geese: behavioural and physiological consistency over time and across situations, *Hormones and Behaviour* 51: 239–48

Maejima, M., Inoue-Murayama, M., Tonosaki, K., Matsuura, N., Kato, S., Saito, Y., Weiss, A., Murayama, Y. and Ito, S. 2006. Traits and genotypes may predict the successful training of drug detection dogs, *Applied Animal Behaviour Science* 0168-1591

McDougall, P. T., Reale, D., Sol, D. and Reader, S. M. 2006. Wildlife conservation and animal temperament: causes and consequences of evolutionary change for captive, reintroduced, and wild populations, *Animal Conservation* 9: 39–48

McElreath, R. and Strimling, P. 2006. How noisy information and individual asymmetries can make 'personality' an adaptation: a simple model, *Animal Behaviour* 72: 1135–9

Mehta, P. H. and Gosling, S. D. 2006. How can animal studies contribute to research on the biological bases of personality?, in T. Canli (ed.), *Biology of personality and individual differences*, pp. 427–48. New York: Guilford

Nettle, D. 2006. The evolution of personality variation in humans and other animals, *American Psychologist* 61: 622–31

Pederson, A. K., King, J. E. and Landau, V. I. 2005. Chimpanzee (*Pan troglodytes*) personality predicts behaviour, *Journal of Research in Personality* 39: 534–49

Ray, J., Hansen, S. and Waters, N. 2006. Links between temperamental dimensions and brain monoamines in the rat, *Behavioural Neuroscience* 120: 85–92

Sapolsky, R. M. 1990. Adrenocortical functions, social rank, and personality among wild baboons, *Biological Psychiatry* 28: 862–78

Sih, A., Bell, A. M., Johnson, J. C. and Ziemba, R. E. 2004. Behavioural syndromes: an integrative overview, *Quarterly Review of Biology* 79: 241–77

Sih, A. and Watters, J. V. 2005. The mix matters: behavioural types and group dynamics in water striders, *Behaviour* 142: 1417–31

Sinn, D. L., Gosling, S. D. and Moltschaniwskyj, N. A. 2008. Development of shy/bold behaviour in squid: context-specific phenotypes associated with developmental plasticity, *Animal Behaviour* 75: 433–42

Svartberg, K. 2005. A comparison of behaviour in test and in everyday life: evidence of three consistent boldness-related personality traits in dogs, *Applied Animal Behaviour Science* 91: 103–28

Van Hooff, J. A. R. A. M. 1973. A structural analysis of the social behaviour of a semi-captive group of chimpanzees, in M. Von Cranach and I. Vine (eds.), *Social communication and movement: studies of interaction and expression in man and chimpanzee*, pp. 75–162. London: Academic Press

Vazire, S. and Gosling, S. D. 2003. Bridging psychology and biology with animal research, *American Psychologist* 5: 407–8

Vazire, S., Gosling, S. D., Dickey, A. S. and Schapiro, S. J. 2007. Measuring personality in nonhuman animals, in R. W. Robins, R. C. Fraley and R. F. Krueger (eds.), *Handbook of research methods in personality psychology*, pp. 190–206. New York: Guilford Press

Watters, J. V. and Meehan, C. L. 2007. Different strokes: can managing behavioural types increase post-release success?, *Applied Animal Behaviour Science* 102: 364–79

Weinstein, T. A. R., Capitanio, J. P. and Gosling, S. D. 2008. Personality in animals, in O. P. John, R. W. Robins and L. A. Pervin (eds.), *Handbook of personality theory and research*, pp. 328–48. New York: Guilford Press

Weiss, A., King, J. E. and Perkins, L. 2006. Personality and subjective well-being in orangutans (*Pongo pygmaeus* and *Pongo abelii*), *Journal of Personality and Social Psychology* 90: 501–11

Willis-Owen, S. A. G. and Flint, J. 2007. Identifying the genetic determinants of emotionality in humans: insights from rodents, *Neuroscience and Biobehavioural Reviews* 31: 115–24

Wilson, A. D. M. and Stevens, E. D. 2005. Consistency in context-specific measures of shyness and boldness in Rainbow Trout, *Oncorhynchus mykiss, Ethology* 111: 849–62

Wilson, D. S. 1998. Adaptive individual differences within single populations, *Philosophical Transactions of the Royal Society of London, Series B* 353: 199–205

18 Behavioural genetics: from variance to DNA

Marcus R. Munafò

Introduction

Investigation of the association between DNA variants and psychological phenotypes has the potential to determine which genes influence heritable psychological traits, such as personality (Ebstein, Benjamin and Belmaker 2000; Eysenck 1977). Such research has a long history, beginning with the observation that behavioural phenotypes (including personality) tend to show greater similarity between pairs of individuals as genetic similarity increases. There is now a considerable corpus of research literature, comprising twin, adoption and family studies, as well as more recent molecular genetic studies, which attempt to quantify and characterize the role of genetic variation in human personality. Twin, adoption and family studies have consistently indicated that genetic variation contributes to variability in human personality traits. However, molecular genetic studies have so far been characterized more by the inconsistency of their results than by the provision of novel biological information. Given the large number of candidate genes that can be hypothesized to influence psychological traits, the extent of DNA sequence variation and the numerous, often conflicting, methods of measuring phenotypic variation in psychological and behavioural science, the task of evaluating competing statistical hypotheses is likely to be onerous.

Most trait psychologists argue that a small number of factors can be used to account for individual differences in personality. For example, there is strong agreement that the dimensions of Extraversion-Introversion and Neuroticism-Stability are fundamental parts of any personality taxonomy. Causal theorists of personality have attempted to go further and associate known neurobiological mechanisms with personality dimensions, measured using a range of instruments. These are discussed in more detail elsewhere in this book (see Ian J. Deary, Chapter 6) and reviewed only briefly here. Recent behaviour genetic, and in particular molecular genetic research, relies heavily on the assumption that these measures of personality traits reflect underlying biological mechanisms which can be related to a number of relevant candidate genes which influence inter-individual variation in the neurobiology of these mechanisms.

Following Revelle's typology (Revelle 1995), three fundamental behavioural dimensions have been proposed to correspond to differential activity in neurotransmitter systems (Ebstein, Benjamin and Belmaker 2000; Munafò, Clark,

Moore *et al.* 2003): dopamine for approach behaviours, serotonin and noradrenaline for avoidance behaviours, and serotonin, noradrenaline and GABA for aggressive or fight-flight behaviours. There is considerable consensus over the construct validity of the first two of these dimensions, but there remains equally considerable debate over the third. These issues are also discussed elsewhere (see Chapter 6), but can indicate potential molecular targets for genetic dissection. Since the majority of behaviour genetic studies to date have focused on what may be broadly characterized as approach-related traits and avoidance-related traits, this chapter will focus predominantly on these. Nevertheless, it should be borne in mind that there remains considerable debate regarding the exact structure and basis of human personality.

Avoidance-related (or negative emotionality) traits comprise facets of anxiety, negative affect (i.e., depression) and anger. Neuroticism, as measured using the class of questionnaires derived from Costa and McCrae's (1997) NEO-PI, NEO-PI-R, NEO FFI and Eysenck and Eysenck's (1975) EPI, EPQ, EPQ-R models of personality, reflects anxiety and negative affect. Harm avoidance, as measured using the class of questionnaires derived from Cloninger's (1986) tridimensional theory of personality and temperament (TCI, TPQ), reflects sensitivity to signals of punishment. These measures are commonly assumed to reflect a common underlying mechanism, although this is debated (Schinka, Busch and Robichaux-Keene 2004; Sen, Burmeister and Ghosh 2004).

A second major dimension of current theories of human personality reflects approach-related (or positive emotionality) traits which, broadly defined, encompasses novelty-seeking, sensation-seeking, extraversion and impulsivity traits. Extraversion, as measured using the NEO family of instruments (Costa and McCrae 1997) or those derived from Eysenck's personality taxonomy (Eysenck and Eysenck 1975), reflects gregariousness, sensation-seeking and high levels of activity. Novelty-seeking, as in questionnaires derived from Cloninger's theory of personality and temperament (Cloninger 1986), reflects sensitivity to novelty and signals of reward. As with Neuroticism and harm avoidance, while Extraversion and novelty-seeking are not identical constructs, they are thought to be intercorrelated (Doyle, Faraone, Seidman *et al.* 2005), and may both reflect individual differences in different facets of a common underlying neurobiological motivational mechanism.

Behaviour genetics refers to the study of the role of genetic influences on variation in behavioural traits such as these. By quantifying the genetic influence on these traits we also, indirectly, quantify the environmental influence, so behaviour genetic research can afford as much information about environmental influences as it can genetic influences. Until relatively recently the only means by which the relative contribution of genetic and environmental variability to this variability in behavioural traits could be studied was by means of twin, family and adoption studies. New advances in molecular genetics, however, have meant that behaviour genetics now encompasses molecular genetic studies as well as traditional twin, family and adoption studies.

Twin and adoption studies

Modern behaviour genetics still depends heavily on the use of twin, family and adoption studies, with the cornerstone being the 'natural experiment' of twinning. Approximately one in eighty-five live births are twin births, and of these approximately two-thirds will be identical (monozygotic or MZ) twins and the remaining one-third non-identical or fraternal (dizygotic or DZ) twins. Since MZ twins have identical genotypes, whereas DZ twins share only 50 per cent of their variegated genotype, and yet in both cases twins will be raised in (what are assumed to be) identical environments, the logic of twin studies is that if a behavioural trait is more similar in pairs of MZ twins than it is in pairs of DZ twins, then that trait must presumably be under a degree of genetic influence. Family and adoption studies provide other means by which naturally occurring variation in genotypic similarity and environmental similarity can be associated with phenotypic variability to calculate the proportion of variation in the phenotype that can be accounted for by variation in the genotype.

The proportion of variation in phenotype that is due to variation in genotype is expressed as the *heritability* of a trait (h^2) – a heritability coefficient of 0.50 means that 50 per cent of the variation in that trait is due to genotypic variation. When we talk about the relative influence of genotype and environment on phenotype we are talking about the relative influence of *variability* in the former on *variability* in the latter. Accurate estimates of h^2 can be arrived at using structural equation modelling, which assumes that there are three distinct influences on phenotypic variation, comprising additive genetic effects (A), common or shared environmental effects (C), and unique or non-shared environmental effects (E). Such models are often referred to as ACE models.

The calculation of the heritability coefficient rests on several assumptions, such as that genes influence phenotypes in an additive (rather than multiplicative, or interactive) way, and that genotype is not correlated with, and does not interact with, environment. In fact, it is likely that these assumptions do not always hold, and that gene × gene interactions (also known as epistatic genetic influences), gene × environment interactions, and gene – environment correlations do in fact occur. More complex statistical and methodological techniques exist for investigating these effects.

Twin studies

Twin studies consistently report a higher degree of similarity on measures of personality between MZ twins than between DZ twins, suggesting substantial heritability of these traits. For example, data from Canada and Germany (Jang, Livesley and Vernon 2002) on twins who completed the NEO-PI-R indicated correlation coefficients of approximately 0.45 for MZ twins, and 0.20 for DZ twins. This reflects a likely heritability of approximately 50 per cent for these traits. Moreover, these correlation coefficients were extremely similar in both

Table 18.1 *Heritability coefficients for personality traits.*

	Loehlin (1992) (Review)	Jang *et al.* (1996) (Canada)	Waller (1999) (United States)	Loehlin *et al.* (1998) (United States)	Riemann *et al.* (1997) (Germany)
Extraversion	0.49	0.53	0.49	0.57	0.56
Agreeableness	0.35	0.41	0.33	0.51	0.42
Conscientiousness	0.38	0.44	0.48	0.52	0.53
Neuroticism	0.41	0.41	0.42	0.58	0.52
Openness	0.45	0.61	0.58	0.56	0.53

Data from a review of the literature (Loehlin 1992), selected primary studies (Jang, Livesley and Vernon 1996; Riemann, Angleitner and Strelau 1997; Waller 1999) and an analysis (Loehlin 1998) of previously collected data (Loehlin and Nichols 1976), all of which indicate relatively consistent and substantial heritability coefficients for all major personality traits. *Source:* Bouchard and Loehlin 2001.

countries, suggesting similar heritability in both populations. A number of reviews and meta-analyses of the twin study literature on personality traits have been published in recent years, and all consistently demonstrate heritability coefficients of approximately 50 per cent, with a range typically between 40–60 per cent. These results are summarized in Table 18.1.

It is striking that these findings appear to be relatively independent of the measurement instruments used, and hold for traits drawn from Eysenck's tripartite theory of personality and those drawn from Costa and McCrae's 'Big Five' model (Bouchard and Loehlin 2001). In particular, there appears to be little or no effect of shared family environment; residual variance is typically labelled as non-shared environment, but it should be noted that this term also includes gene × environment effects and measurement error. The majority of genetic influence appears to be additive, although there is some evidence of non-additive genetic effects (i.e., gene × gene interactions).

Adoption studies

Analyses of the heritability of personality traits based on twin samples alone have consistently indicated higher heritability coefficients than those based on twin, adoption and family samples, with sibling-sibling correlations of 0.17 and parent-offspring correlations of 0.14 (Bouchard and Loehlin 2001). These values suggest heritability coefficients of the order of approximately 30 per cent, compared to those of 50 per cent suggested by twin studies. One possible explanation for this is the presence of non-additive genetic effects (i.e., gene × gene interactions) which would result in higher levels of similarity between MZ twins than DZ twins, but would not contribute to the similarity of offspring to parents (Bouchard and McGue 2003). Studies which have explicitly investigated the contribution of non-additive genetic effects have indicated that these effects are indeed present in the context of human personality, although they make up a relatively small proportion (c. 10–20 per cent) of the overall contribution of genetic variation (Bouchard and Loehlin 2001).

Conclusions

It is clear that twin, family and adoption studies all consistently demonstrate a strong contribution of genetic variation to variation in personality. The majority of this appears to be additive genetic influence, although there is also evidence for a non-additive genetic component to this variation, indicating gene × gene inter-action effects. Nevertheless, the heritability statistic has limitations, not least that it reflects only the heritability within the population from which the sample used to calculate it was drawn, at the time when these data were collected. It also rests on several assumptions which may or may not hold; for example, it assumes little or no assortative mating (where mating occurs between individuals who are more similar than could be expected by chance on the trait of interest), and there is evidence that assortative mating on the basis of personality does indeed occur (Redden and Allison 2006). It also does not readily allow an estimation of gene × environment interaction effects, and these are typically included in the non-shared environment term, which also includes measurement error and other unmeasured effects such as developmental accidents due to chance. For these reasons, as genotyping of specific loci has become more cost-effective, research has moved towards the molecular genetic investigation of the biological basis of personality.

Molecular genetic studies

While twin studies consistently indicate that human personality traits are under a substantial degree of genetic influence (Heath, Cloninger and Martin 1994; Plomin, Owen and McGuffin 1994), in the ten years since the first pub-lication of studies reporting an association between specific genetic variants and human personality traits (Ebstein, Novick, Umansky et al. 1996; Lesch, Bengel, Heils et al. 1996) a substantial literature has developed reporting data on the role of a variety of genetic variants, although only modest progress has been made in identifying molecular loci which robustly demonstrate association (Munafò, Clark, Moore et al. 2003). One possible reason for this is the small magnitude of effect sizes which are likely to be typical of single gene effects on complex behavioural phenotypes such as personality (Munafò and Flint 2004), so that the majority of studies conducted to date may be underpowered. While large-scale primary studies offer the best means of achieving sufficient power to detect genetic effects of small magnitude, these may not be achievable in practice.

In common with genetic association studies in other disciplines, reports of highly significant associations between candidate genes and personality traits have typically not been followed by convincing replications. For instance, the report by Lesch's group in 1996 (Lesch, Bengel, Heils *et al.* 1996) of an association between variation in the promoter region of the serotonin transporter gene and emotional stability (or Neuroticism) generated much interest, but subsequent work has delivered inconsistent conclusions (Munafò, Clark and Flint 2005; Munafò, Clark, Moore *et al.* 2003; Schinka, Busch and Robichaux-Keene 2004; Sen, Burmeister and Ghosh 2004). Similar reservations surround the claims for an effect of the dopamine D4 receptor gene on Extraversion (Munafò, Yalcin, Willis-Owen and Flint 2008; Schinka, Letsch and Crawford 2002). Nevertheless, a great deal of research activity in recent years, comprising both animal and human studies, has begun to offer promise that the genetic basis for human personality traits may eventually be understood.

Animal studies

Some encouraging progress has been made in studies of animal models of temperament, which offer several attributes useful in genetic research, including short gestation, early puberty and large litters, as well as a greater degree of experimental control, by means of directed mating and environmental control, all of which are valuable when attempting to map the genetic architecture of these traits (Willis-Owen and Flint 2007).

Defining an animal's temperament, which should reflect an analogue of human personality traits, is not easy, and operational definitions typically require the animal to show a consistent pattern of response to a behavioural task or series of tasks. For example, an animal model of personality might be operationally defined as the length of time it takes an animal to emerge into an aversive or threatening environment, which might be considered to be an analogue of the human personality trait of Extraversion or novelty seeking. This obviously requires relatively strong assumptions regarding the extent to which this operational definition is an accurate analogue of the same construct in humans. The majority of animal studies of emotionality have employed rodent models (i.e., mouse or rat). A number of tests of temperament in animals exist, which can be divided into measures that depend on unconditioned (ethological) or conditioned responses, and the relationship between these and human personality is discussed elsewhere (see Samuel D. Gosling and B. Austin Harley, Chapter 17). Conditioned responses have the advantage of offering much more experimental control. These measures are founded on principles of avoidance, autonomic activation and behavioural inhibition (i.e., the discontinuation of species-typical behaviours such as exploration).

The mouse genome is well-characterized, comprising around 22,000 predicted genes, of which approximately 80 per cent have an identifiable human orthologue. Inbred rodent strains exhibit substantial variability in temperament, and these differences can be exploited for the purposes of quantitative trait mapping. Crosses between inbred strains of rodents are frequently used to map quantitative trait loci (QTL) that give rise to the genetic component of variation in behavioural traits such as temperament. The basic experimental design is the analysis of association between genotypic and phenotypic variation in a cross between two inbred strains of rodents (usually, but not necessarily, with contrasting temperament phenotypes). Several strategies exist, but in the most widely-used either the offspring of the cross (the F1 generation) are mated to produce an F2 intercross, or the offspring are backcrossed to either of the parental strains. Molecular genetic markers are then used to determine which chromosomal segments segregate with the trait (that is, which chromosomal regions are shared by animals that are phenotypically similar for the trait of interest). Over the past ten years, QTL putatively related to temperament have been identified on a number of chromosomes, although the molecular nature of these remains unclear.

One problem is that genetic mapping identifies a potential functional variant, rather than a gene, and functionally-important variants that affect gene expression may lie some distance away from a gene, or even in the location of an unrelated gene. Another problem is that this experimental design offers only a limited number of recombinants in a single generation (typically, between one and two), so that the resolution to map a specific locus is limited, and may identify regions which can still contain hundreds or perhaps thousands of genes. Finally, one potential difficulty in animal studies lies in whether genes identified in animal studies have an orthologue in man (i.e., are functionally related to a human gene, with extensive sequence similarity), although the conservation of much of the genome in rodents and man is one reason for the extensive use of rodents as an animal model of human traits.

It is possible to remedy the problem of limited mapping resolution by mapping loci in genetically heterogeneous stocks of rodents which are generated from multiple (usually eight) inbred strains which have been successively intercrossed for maximal diversity and maintained over multiple generations through a programme of pseudo-random mating. Since these animals are several generations removed from the original progenitor strains, this offers the potential of mapping a QTL to a limited number of genes, although this requires a substantial increase in marker density, and the analysis is considerably more complex in this case. At present, this is most economical once broad chromosomal regions have been identified, thereby limiting the number of markers required for QTL localization.

There also exists a potential solution to the problem of ensuring that the identification of loci related to temperament in rodent models are specific to this trait, described above. This is to attempt to identify chromosomal regions that influence multiple measures of temperament but *not* control measures, on the assumption that a single underlying trait should influence performance on multiple measures of temperament to a comparable degree, and should not influence performance on control measures.

Human studies

The majority of genetic association studies of human personality traits have focused on anxiety-related traits, due in part to the relationship between these traits and major depressive disorder, and evidence that this relationship is due to shared genetic factors (Fanous and Kendler 2004). The serotonin (5-HT) system has received considerable attention in attempts to understand the determinants of avoidance- or anxiety-related traits, and serotonergic genes represent good candidates for the study of these phenotypes. One such candidate is the serotonin transporter gene (*SLC6A4*), which encodes a transmembrane transporter responsible for reuptake of serotonin at the synapse. A functional polymorphism in the promoter region of the serotonin transporter gene (*5-HTTLPR*) has been identified, comprising a 44bp deletion (short) or insertion (long), and is known to be associated with altered serotonin activity, with the short (S) form of this polymorphism being associated with reduced transcriptional efficiency compared to the long (L) form, thereby decreasing serotonin transporter expression and serotonin uptake (Heils, Teufel, Petri *et al.* 1996). The short allele has also been reported to be associated with elevated anxiety-related traits (Munafò, Clark and Flint 2005; Munafò, Clark, Moore *et al.* 2003; Schinka, Busch and Robichaux-Keene 2004; Sen, Burmeister and Ghosh 2004), although there remains disagreement over the strength of this relationship, and the extent to which it is captured by various measures of personality. In particular, it has been suggested that the genetic signal captured by measures of Neuroticism is stronger than that captured by measures of harm avoidance (Schinka, Busch and Robichaux-Keene 2004; Sen, Burmeister and Ghosh 2004). In addition, recent evidence suggests that a single nucleotide polymorphism in the *5-HTTLPR*, comprising a G>A substitution, may modulate the effect of the 44bp variant (Parsey, Hastings, Oquendo *et al.* 2006). Including this variant in addition to the more commonly investigated 44bp variant may capture a greater proportion of genetic variance, and thereby increase the likelihood of detecting association with behavioural traits. To date, no studies have done this with respect to human personality traits.

The dopaminergic system is involved in appetitive and motivational behaviours (Comings and Blum 2000), and pharmacological challenge studies indicate a relationship between dopaminergic hyperactivity and reward-seeking, as well as motivational factors associated with both Extraversion and novelty-seeking (Netter 2006), suggesting that these traits may share a common neurobiological basis. Dopaminergic genes may therefore be considered plausible candidates for certain human personality traits, in particular those related to motivational behaviours, such as novelty-seeking or Extraversion. The dopamine D4 receptor (*DRD4*) gene is highly polymorphic, although research evaluating behavioural and psychiatric phenotypes has focused largely on a variable number of tandem repeats (VNTR) polymorphism in exon III, and in particular the presence or absence of the seven-repeat ('long') allele. This variant has been reported to be associated with decreased ligand binding (Asghari, Schoots, Van Kats *et al.* 1994), decreased gene expression *in vitro*, and attenuation of cyclic AMP formation when dopamine is bound to the receptor (Asghari, Sanyal, Buchwaldt *et al.* 1995), compared to six-repeat or fewer ('short') alleles, although there is some disagreement regarding the optimal grouping of variants. The *DRD4* gene also includes a single nucleotide polymorphism in the promoter region (C-521T), which has been reported to be in linkage disequilibrium with the exon III polymorphism (Ekelund, Suhonen, Jarvelin *et al.* 2001; Strobel *et al.* 2002), and is associated with variation in expression of the D4 receptor, with the T allele associated with a reduction in transcription levels of up to 40 per cent compared to the C allele (Okuyama, Ishiguro, Toru and Arinami 1999; Ronai, Barta, Guttman *et al.* 2001).

A recent meta-analysis (Munafò, Yalcin, Willis-Owen and Flint 2008) of the association of the *DRD4* gene and approach-related traits, which included new data on the role of the *DRD4* C-521T polymorphism in Extraversion, failed to support the association of either the C-521T or VNTR polymorphisms with approach-related traits. Although the results of the initial meta-analysis indicated possible association with the C-521T polymorphism, this association was not detected in a replication sample comprising individuals at the extremes of the trait distribution with sufficient power to detect an association equivalent to less than 1 per cent of phenotypic variance. When these data were incorporated into the meta-analysis, the overall evidence for association of the C-521T polymorphism with approach-related traits was non-significant (Munafò *et al.* 2008).

These variants are by no means the only ones to have been investigated in relation to their association with human personality, and phenotypes beyond simply those which may be characterized as avoidance- or approach-related have been employed. Studies of the *5-HTTLPR* and *DRD4* VNTR dominate, however, and among the other studies which exist there is a similar lack of consistency. One possible explanation for these discrepancies between studies is that there remain unpublished data that relate to these putative associations, and that the true effect sizes are considerably smaller than those indicated by early studies. There is evidence for this phenomenon in other areas of psychiatric genetics, where individual study effect size estimates have been reported to be significantly correlated with year of publication (Munafò, Matheson and Flint 2007; Munafò, Thiselton, Clark and Flint 2006). Evidence from a number of meta-analyses indicates that true effect sizes, if genuine, may account for only 0.01 per cent of phenotypic variance, although there has been some debate that specific measurement instruments may be more sensitive to genetic variation.

Conclusions

A reasonable interim conclusion after over ten years of personality genetics research is that main effects of single genetic variants are likely to be of small magnitude, and unlikely to account for more than 1 per cent of phenotypic variance (and possibly much less). In addition, publication of non-significant results is important to avoid disorting the corpus of publicly-available data (Munafò, Clark and Flint 2004). While no formal evidence of publication bias in the field of personality genetics currently exists, there is evidence that this phenomenon exists in other fields of psychiatric genetics (Munafò, Matheson and

Flint 2007). Given that formal tests of publication are weak, it is possible (arguably, likely) that these biases exist in the field of personality genetics as well but remain undetected to date.

It is also likely that a proportion of the variance in human personality which may ultimately be traced to genetic (or partially genetic) causes is due to gene × gene and gene × environment interactions. Evidence for the latter is reviewed later, but the study of interaction effects is complicated by the requirement for extremely large sample sizes in order to achieve sufficient power to detect such interactions, in particular in the case of gene × gene interaction effects involving genes with low minor allele frequencies. It is accepted that genetic influences on personality will be polygenic (i.e., comprise effects of multiple genes, each of small effect, as well as numerous gene × gene interactions) and will be modified by environmental effects (i.e., gene × environment interactions). It is therefore perhaps not surprising that the evidence to date has not strongly implicated any single genetic variant in the etiology of human personality.

Future directions

Given the limited success of studies to date, along with the clear evidence that genetic variation plays a role in contributing to individual differences in personality, what opportunities exist for making better progress? Two broad areas of research have indicated substantial early promise. The first relates to the integration of molecular genetic with more traditional epidemiological methods, which investigate the role of environmental influences on behaviour, to better characterize the interplay of molecular and environmental influences. The second relates to the use of more sophisticated measures of individual differences in behaviour than the traditional psychometric instruments employed in the vast majority of molecular genetic studies of human personality to date.

Gene × environment interactions

Main effects of genotype on personality phenotypes appear to be modest (Munafò, Clark, Moore *et al.* 2003), as discussed above. One likely reason which may partially account for this is that genes interact with environmental influences to determine risk of any particular outcome, including personality. A gene × environment interaction occurs when the effect of exposure to an environmental risk factor is conditional upon an individual's genotype, or vice versa (Caspi, Sugden, Moffitt *et al.* 2003). Several studies of emotional disorders have tested for possible gene × environment interactions, which themselves may operate via personality traits given the known associations between personality and risk of psychiatric illness (e.g., Neuroticism and major depression).

In one of the first studies to attempt to combine molecular genetic approaches with the study of environmental effects on personality, a gene × environment interaction effect on the likelihood of aggressive behaviour in adolescence was observed (Caspi, McClay, Moffitt *et al.* 2002). Specifically, variation in the monoamine oxidase A (*MAO-A*) gene moderated the relationship between early childhood maltreatment and subsequent aggressive behaviour in adolescence. Those individuals with the low activity variant of the *MAO-A* gene demonstrated a stronger relationship between early childhood maltreatment and aggressive behaviour in adolescence compared with those individuals with the high activity variant. This evidence supports the central premise of gene × environment interactions, which is that individuals of differing genotypes may respond differently to specific environmental influences.

Most studies of gene × environment interactions to date have focused on the serotonin transporter gene and stressful life events, with contrasting results. In the original study (Caspi, Sugden, Moffitt *et al.* 2003), the *5-HTTLPR* variant moderated the effect of stressful life events on the onset of depression among youngsters. The presence of life events was associated with an increased risk of depression in heterozygous subjects, or those homozygous for the S allele, but not in LL homozygotes (Caspi, Sugden, Moffitt *et al.* 2003). These results are presented in Figure 18.1.

Other studies testing similar interactions have found positive results in adults of both sexes (Kendler, Kuhn, Vittum *et al.* 2005; Wilhelm, Mitchell, Niven *et al.*

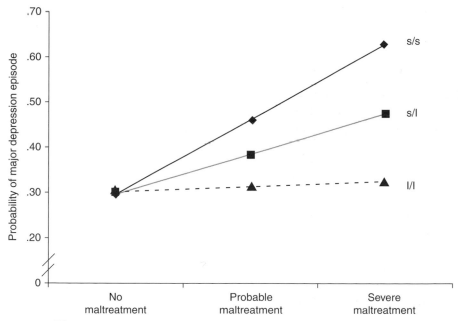

Figure 18.1. *Incidence of major depression as a function of* 5-HTTLPR *genotype and number of life events. Results of regression analysis estimating the association between severity of childhood maltreatment (between the ages of 3 and 11 years) and subsequent adult depression (between the ages of 18 and 26 years), as function of* 5-HTTLPR *genotype.*

2006), in females only (Grabe, Lange, Wolff *et al.* 2005), and have failed to detect these interactions (or even observed some in the opposite direction) (Gillespie, Whitfield, Williams *et al.* 2005; Surtees, Wainwright, Willis-Owen *et al.* 2006). Reaching more definitive conclusions is made difficult because of the different methodologies used in these studies. In addition, the phenotype studied is typically the incidence of major depression, as opposed to personality per se, although it is possible (indeed likely) that any observed effects on depression may be mediated via individual differences in negative emotionality traits such as Neuroticism.

One particular difficulty in such studies lies in the accurate specification of environmental effects. While genotype can be ascertained with a high degree of accuracy (subject to appropriate quality control measures), environmental effects are typically ascertained using either self- or parent-report measures. Moreover, the underlying constructs which are so measured (e.g., 'stressful life events') may be somewhat vague, and in fact represent a constellation of underlying constructs. This is not always the case; for example, exposure to specific drugs such as cannabis or nicotine may be biochemically-verified, and represent a more unitary environmental effect. Nevertheless, it is difficult to determine whether the inconsistency in results to date is due to differences in the characteristics of the samples employed, in the outcome measures used, in the measures of life events used, and so on. For a recent critical review of gene × environment interactions, see Munafò, Durrant, Lewis and Flint (2009).

Endophenotype studies

The concept of the endophenotype was introduced to psychiatry over thirty years ago by Gottesman and Shields (1973), but its popularity is more recent: there are eight PubMed entries before the year 2000 compared to 150 in the current century. Gottesman and Shields (1973) adapted the term from a 1966 paper that attributed the geographical distribution of grasshoppers to the insects' 'endophenotype' (John and Lewis 1966), a neologism alluding to a phenotype that was microscopic and internal, and therefore obscure to casual observation. Endophenotypes in behavioural science retain the notion of an internal process, but one that can be objectively measured, ideally in a robust and reliable fashion, a characteristic often lacking in the diseases with which they are associated.

Gottesman's definition of an endophenotype is that it should be heritable, co-segregate with a psychiatric illness, yet be present even when the disease is not (i.e., state independent), and be found in non-affected family members at a higher rate than in the population (Gottesman and Gould 2003). The criterion of state independence was modified to take into account the importance of epigenetic and developmental factors so that the endophenotype can be manifest only at a certain age and/or after a challenge (in the same way that a glucose challenge is used for a glucose tolerance test) (Hasler, Drevets, Gould *et al.* 2006). Others have added criteria that require endophenotypes to be part of the causal process by which disease arises (Lavori, Krause-Steinrauf, Brophy *et al.* 2002), or at least be involved in a biologically plausible mechanism of pathogenesis (Castellanos and Tannock 2002; Tsuang, Faraone and Lyons 1993), or, following Almasy and Blangero (2001), require that an endophenotype 'should be continuously quantifiable, should predict disorder probabilistically and should be closer to the site of primary causative agent (whether genetic or environmental) than to diagnostic categories'. It has also been suggested that 'priority should be given to endophenotypes that are based or anchored in neuroscience' (Doyle, Faraone, Seidman *et al.* 2005).

A number of recent endophenotype studies suggest possible research directions which may allow the more detailed dissection of the neurobiological mechanisms which mediate the relationships between genetic variation at specific loci and variation in personality traits. Hariri and colleagues reported that variation in the *5-HTTLPR* was associated with the response of the amygdala to fearful stimuli (Hariri, Mattay, Tessitore *et al.* 2002). In a comparison of two groups of fourteen individuals, carriers of the S allele at the *5-HTTLPR* were found to exhibit an increased amygdala fearful response compared with those homozygous for the L allele (Hariri *et al.* 2002). In comparison with the main effects of genotype on psychometrically-assessed personality described above, the effect size reported in this study was enormous (equivalent to approximately 40 per cent of phenotypic variance), and could be detected at a significance threshold of 0.05 with less than twenty participants. These results are presented in Figure 18.2.

These reports are particularly compelling as they build on the emerging (albeit inconsistent) evidence for a role of variation at the *5-HTTLPR* in relation to anxiety-related traits and, thereby, major depression. In particular, they suggest a specific neurobiological mechanism which may subserve this association. Of course, this finding could be due to chance statistical fluctuation. Indeed, a subsequent larger study carried out by the same group again showed a significant effect, but with a reduction in the effect size (Hariri, Drabant, Munoz *et al.* 2005), equivalent to an effect size of just over 10 per cent of the phenotypic variance, and additional studies are needed to confirm whether the effect is indeed this large. We have recently argued (Flint and Munafò 2007) that the assumption that endophenotype measures will necessarily afford a stronger genetic signal than phenotypes assessed using traditional psychometric instruments has not yet been unequivocally supported, although there is some early promise.

One difficulty lies in the inherent complexity of genetic effects; for example, analyses of gene expression variation in yeast, rodents and humans concur in finding that the genetic architecture of gene expression is polygenic and that the genetic effects on even these extremely proximal phenotypes are relatively small (Flint and Munafò 2007). Therefore, even when we consider a phenotype that is directly linked to the genetic constitution of the organism, genetic architecture is not radically different from complex phenotypes (Flint and Munafò 2007). While endophenotype studies, such as the imaging genetic studies described above,

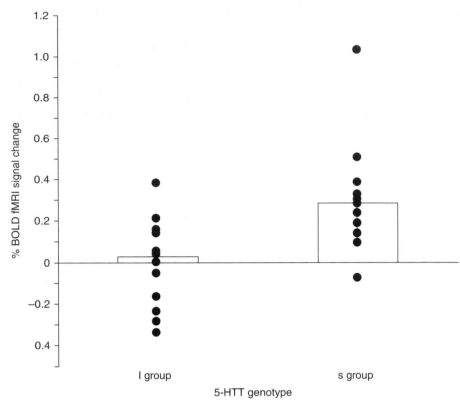

Figure 18.2. *Amygdala activation to fearful faces compared to neutral stimuli as a function of* 5-HTTLPR *genotype. Effect of* 5-HTTLPR *genotype on amygdala activity, representing activity in a region of interest comprising the entire right amygdala in the S and L groups. Individual circles represent activity for each participant. Note that there remains substantial inter-individual variability.*

offer a potentially exciting means by which the pathways between genotype and personality may be dissected and better understood, caution is necessary given the history of failure to replicate in more traditional genetic association studies, despite initial excitement and early promise.

Conclusions

Both the study of gene × environment interaction effects, and the use of endophenotype measures (in particular involving neuroimaging techniques) have generated considerable excitement that genuine progress may be possible in our understanding of the genetic and neurobiological basis of personality and related phenotypes. However, the number of studies remains small, and the history of psychiatric genetics suggests that caution is necessary. In particular, given the large number of loci which it is possible (and, increasingly, cost-effective) to investigate, there is a risk that at least some of the promising findings published to date will represent false positives. Nevertheless, the rationale behind the employment of these methods is sound: genetic effects will certainly operate via the modification of environmental pressures, while measures of the neurobiological correlates of personality will allow the closer mapping of the pathways that lead from genetic variation to individual differences in personality. As evidence grows we will be in an increasingly strong position to integrate these findings into a comprehensive model of the neurobiology of personality.

References

Almasy, L. and Blangero, J. 2001. Endophenotypes as quantitative risk factors for psychiatric disease: rationale and study design, *American Journal of Medical Genetics* 105: 42–44

Asghari, V., Sanyal, S., Buchwaldt, S., Paterson, A., Jovanovic, V. and Van Tol, H. H. 1995. Modulation of intracellular cyclic AMP levels by different human dopamine D4 receptor variants, *Journal of Neurochemistry* 65: 1157–65

Asghari, V., Schoots, O., Van Kats, S., Ohara, K., Jovanovic, V., Guan, H. C. *et al.* 1994. Dopamine D4 receptor repeat: analysis of different native and mutant forms of the human and rat genes, *Molecular Pharmacology* 46: 364–73

Bouchard, T. J., Jr and Loehlin, J. C. 2001. Genes, evolution, and personality, *Behavioural Genetics* 31: 243–73

Bouchard, T. J., Jr and McGue, M. 2003. Genetic and environmental influences on human psychological differences, *Journal of Neurobiology* 54: 4–45

Caspi, A., McClay, J., Moffitt, T. E., Mill, J., Martin, J., Craig, I. W. *et al.* 2002. Role of genotype in the cycle of violence in maltreated children, *Science* 297: 851–4

Caspi, A., Sugden, K., Moffitt, T. E., Taylor, A., Craig, I. W., Harrington, H., *et al.* 2003. Influence of life stress on depression: moderation by a polymorphism in the 5-HTT gene, *Science* 301: 386–9

Castellanos, F. X. and Tannock, R. 2002. Neuroscience of attention-deficit/hyperactivity disorder: the search for endophenotypes, *Nature Neuroscience* 3: 617–28

Cloninger, C. R. 1986. A unified biosocial theory of personality and its role in the development of anxiety states, *Psychiatric Developments* 4: 167–226

Comings, D. E. and Blum, K. 2000. Reward deficiency syndrome: genetic aspects of behavioural disorders, *Progress in Brain Research* 126: 325–41

Costa, P. T., Jr and McCrae, R. R. 1997: Stability and change in personality assessment: the revised NEO Personality Inventory in the year 2000, *Journal of Personality Assessment* 68: 86–94

Doyle, A. E., Faraone, S. V., Seidman, L. J., Willcutt, E. G., Nigg, J. T., Waldman, I. D. *et al.* 2005: Are endophenotypes based on measures of executive functions useful for molecular genetic studies of ADHD?, *Journal of Child Psychology and Psychiatry* 46: 774–803

Ebstein, R. P., Benjamin, J., Belmaker, R. H. 2000. Personality and polymorphisms of genes involved in aminergic neurotransmission, *European Journal of Pharmacology* 410: 205–14

Ebstein, R. P., Novick, O., Umansky, R., Priel, B., Osher, Y., Blaine, D., *et al.* 1996. Dopamine D4 receptor (D4DR) exon III polymorphism associated with the human personality trait of Novelty Seeking, *Nature Genetics* 12: 78–80

Ekelund, J., Suhonen, J., Jarvelin, M. R., Peltonen, L., Lichtermann, D. 2001. No association of the -521 C/T polymorphism in the promoter of DRD4 with novelty seeking, *Molecular Psychiatry* 6: 618–19

Eysenck, H. J. 1977. National differences in personality as related to ABO blood group polymorphism, *Psychology Reports* 41: 1257–8

Eysenck, H. J. and Eysenck, S. B. G. 1975. *Manual of the Eysenck Personality Questionnaire*. London: Hodder and Stoughton

Fanous, A. H. and Kendler, K. S. 2004. The genetic relationship of personality to major depression and schizophrenia, *Neurotoxicology Results* 6: 43–50

Flint, J. and Munafò, M. R. 2007. The endophenotype concept in psychiatric genetics, *Psychological Medicine* 37: 163–80

Gillespie, N. A., Whitfield, J. B., Williams, B., Heath, A. C. and Martin, N. G. 2005. The relationship between stressful life events, the serotonin transporter (5-HTTLPR) genotype and major depression, *Psychological Medicine* 35: 101–11

Gottesman, I. I. and Gould, T. D. 2003. The endophenotype concept in psychiatry: etymology and strategic intentions, *American Journal of Psychiatry* 160: 636–45

Gottesman, I. I. and Shields, J. 1973. Genetic theorizing and schizophrenia, *British Journal of Psychiatry* 122: 15–30

Grabe, H. J., Lange, M., Wolff, B., Volzke, H., Lucht, M., Freyberger, H. J., *et al.* 2005. Mental and physical distress is modulated by a polymorphism in the 5-HT transporter gene interacting with social stressors and chronic disease burden, *Molecular Psychiatry* 10: 220–4

Hariri, A. R., Drabant, E. M., Munoz, K. E., Kolachana, B. S., Mattay, V. S., Egan, M. F., Weinberger, D. R. 2005. A susceptibility gene for affective disorders and the response of the human amygdala, *Archives of General Psychiatry* 62: 146–52

Hariri, A. R., Mattay, V. S., Tessitore, A., Kolachana, B., Fera, F., Goldman, D., *et al.* 2002. Serotonin transporter genetic variation and the response of the human amygdala, *Science* 297: 400–3

Hasler, G., Drevets, W. C., Gould, T. D., Gottesman, I. I. and Manji, H. K. 2006. Toward constructing an endophenotype strategy for bipolar disorders, *Biological Psychiatry* 60: 93–105

Heath, A. C., Cloninger, C. R. and Martin, N. G. 1994. Testing a model for the genetic structure of personality: a comparison of the personality systems of Cloninger and Eysenck, *Journal of Personality and Social Psychology* 66: 762–75

Heils, A., Teufel, A., Petri, S., Stober, G., Riederer, P., Bengel, D. and Lesch, K. P. 1996. Allelic variation of human serotonin transporter gene expression, *Journal of Neurochemistry* 66: 2621–4

Jang, K. L., Livesley, W. J. and Vernon, P. A. 1996. Heritability of the big five personality dimensions and their facets, *Journal of Personality* 64: 577–91

2002. The etiology of personality function: the University of British Columbia Twin Project, *Twin Results* 5: 342–6

John, B. and Lewis, K. R. 1966. Chromosome variability and geographic distribution in insects, *Science* 152: 711–21

Kendler, K. S., Kuhn, J. W., Vittum, J., Prescott, C. A. and Riley, B. 2005. The interaction of stressful life events and a serotonin transporter polymorphism in the prediction of episodes of major depression: a replication, *Archives of General Psychiatry* 62: 529–35

Lavori, P. W., Krause-Steinrauf, H., Brophy, M., Buxbaum, J., Cockroft, J., Cox, D. R., *et al.* 2002. Principles, organization, and operation of a DNA bank for clinical trials: a Department of Veterans Affairs cooperative study, *Controlled Clinical Trials* 23: 222–39

Lesch, K. P., Bengel, D., Heils, A., Sabol, S. Z., Greenberg, B. D., Petri, S. *et al.* 1996. Association of anxiety-related traits with a polymorphism in the serotonin transporter gene regulatory region, *Science* 274: 1527–31

Loehlin, J. C. 1992. *Genes and environment in personality development*. Newbury Park, CA: Sage

1998. *Latent variable models: an introduction to factor, path, and structural analysis*, 3rd edn. Mahwah, NJ: Erlbaum

Loehlin, J. C. and Nichols, R. C. 1976. *Heredity, environment and personality: a study of 850 sets of twins*, Austin, TX: University of Texas

Munafò, M. R., Clark, T. G. and Flint, J. 2004. Assessing publication bias in genetic association studies: evidence from a recent meta-analysis, *Psychiatry Results* 129: 39–44

2005. Does measurement instrument moderate the association between the serotonin transporter gene and anxiety-related personality traits? A meta-analysis, *Molecular Psychiatry* 10: 415–19

Munafò, M. R., Clark, T. G., Moore, L. R., Payne, E., Walton, R. and Flint, J. 2003. Genetic polymorphisms and personality in healthy adults: a systematic review and meta-analysis, *Molecular Psychiatry* 8: 471–84

Munafò, M. R., Durrant, C., Lewis, G. and Flint, J. 2009. Gene × environment interactions at the serotonin transporter locus, *Biological Psychiatry* 65: 211–19

Munafò, M. R. and Flint, J. 2004. Meta-analysis of genetic association studies, *Trends in Genetics* 20: 439–44

Munafò, M. R., Matheson, I. J. and Flint, J. 2007. Association of the DRD2 Taq1 polymorphism and alcoholism: a meta-analysis of case-control studies and evidence of publication bias, *Molecular Psychiatry* 12: 454–61

Munafò, M. R., Thiselton, D. L., Clark, T. G. and Flint, J. 2006. Association of the NRG1 gene and schizophrenia: a meta-analysis, *Molecular Psychiatry* 11: 539–46

Munafò, M. R., Yalcin, B., Willis-Owen, S. A. G. and Flint, J. 2008. Association of the dopamine D4 receptor (DRD4) gene and approach-related personality traits: a meta-analysis and new data, *Biological Psychiatry* 63: 197–206

Netter, P. 2006. Dopamine challenge tests as an indicator of psychological traits, *Human Psychopharmacology* 21: 91–9

Okuyama, Y., Ishiguro, H., Toru, M. and Arinami, T. 1999. A genetic polymorphism in the promoter region of DRD4 associated with expression and schizophrenia, *Biochemical and Biophysical Research Communications* 258: 292–5

Parsey, R. V., Hastings, R. S., Oquendo, M. A., Hu, X., Goldman, D., Huang, Y. Y. *et al.* 2006. Effect of a triallelic functional polymorphism of the serotonin-transporter-linked promoter region on expression of serotonin transporter in the human brain, *American Journal of Psychiatry* 163: 48–51

Plomin, R., Owen, M. J. and McGuffin, P. 1994. The genetic basis of complex human behaviours, *Science* 264: 1733–9

Redden, D. T. and Allison, D. B. 2006. The effect of assortative mating upon genetic association studies: spurious associations and population substructure in the absence of admixture, *Behavioural Genetics* 36: 678–86

Revelle, W. 1995. Personality processes, *Annual Review of Psychology* 46: 295–328

Riemann, R., Angleitner, A. and Strelau, J. 1997. Genetic and environmental influences on personality: a study of twins reared together using the self- and peer report NEO-FFI scales, *Journal of Personality* 65: 449–75

Ronai, Z., Barta, C., Guttman, A., Lakatos, K., Gervai, J., Staub, M. and Sasvari-Szekely, M. 2001. Genotyping the -521C/T functional polymorphism in the promoter region of dopamine D4 receptor (DRD4) gene, *Electrophoresis* 22: 1102–5

Schinka, J. A., Busch, R. M. and Robichaux-Keene, N. 2004. A meta-analysis of the association between the serotonin transporter gene polymorphism (5-HTTLPR) and trait anxiety, *Molecular Psychiatry* 9: 197–202

Schinka, J. A., Letsch, E. A. and Crawford, F. C. 2002. DRD4 and novelty seeking: results of meta-analyses, *American Journal of Medical Genetics* 114: 643–8

Sen, S., Burmeister, M. and Ghosh, D. 2004. Meta-analysis of the association between a serotonin transporter promoter polymorphism (5-HTTLPR) and anxiety-related personality traits, *American Journal of Medical Genetics B Neuropsychiatric Genetics* 127: 85–9

Strobel, A., Lesch, K. P., Hohenberger, K., Jatzke, S., Gutzeit, H. O., Anacker, K., Brocke, B. 2002. No association between dopamine D4 receptor gene exon III and -521C/T polymorphism and novelty seeking, *Molecular Psychiatry* 7: 537–8

Surtees, P. G., Wainwright, N. W., Willis-Owen, S. A., Luben, R., Day, N. E. and Flint, J. 2006. Social adversity, the serotonin transporter (5-HTTLPR) polymorphism and major depressive disorder, *Biological Psychiatry* 59: 224–9

Tsuang, M. T., Faraone, S. V. and Lyons, M. J. 1993. Identification of the phenotype in psychiatric genetics, *European Archichives of Psychiatry and Clinical Neuroscience* 243: 131–42

Waller, N. G. 1999. Evaluating the structure of personality, in C. R. Cloninger (ed.), *Personality and psychopathology*, pp. 155–97. Washington, DC: American Psychiatric Association

Wilhelm, K., Mitchell, P. B., Niven, H., Finch, A., Wedgwood, L., Scimone, A., *et al.* 2006. Life events, first depression onset and the serotonin transporter gene, *British Journal of Psychiatry* 188: 210–15

Willis-Owen, S. A. and Flint, J. 2007. Identifying the genetic determinants of emotionality in humans; insights from rodents, *Neuroscience and Biobehavioral Reviews* 31: 115–24

19 Neuroimaging of personality

Turhan Canli

The topic of emotion in human behaviour has made a major comeback in Psychology. In the early days of the field, emotion was an integral part in the thinking of William James and others. With the emergence of behaviourism and later cognitive approaches to the study of human behaviour, emotion took a back-seat. Emotion became again a research topic of interest in the 1980s and 1990s, which can be attributed to the development of non-invasive brain imaging techniques, and the successes achieved in animal studies of emotional behaviour, particularly the elegant studies of emotion-based learning and memory (Aggleton 1992; LeDoux 1992; McGaugh, Cahill and Roozendaal 1996; Davis 2000; Davis, Walker and Myers 2003; McGaugh 2004).

The literature on human imaging studies of emotion has by now become large enough to support several critical systematic reviews and meta-analyses (Phan, Wager, Taylor *et al.* 2002; Phillips, Drevets, Rauch *et al.* 2003a; Phillips, Drevets, Rauch *et al.* 2003b; Wager, Phan, Liberzon *et al.* 2003; Baas, Aleman and Kahn 2004; Phan, Wager, Taylor *et al.* 2004). In addition, clinical neuroscience has devoted significant attention to emotion and personality-related disorders (Brendel, Stern and Silbersweig 2005; Chamberlain and Sahakian 2006; Meyer-Lindenberg and Zink 2007; Pearlson and Calhoun 2007). Because both of these aspects of neuroimaging of emotion and personality have been covered elsewhere, I will instead focus on individual differences in brain emotional processing and their relation to personality in healthy individuals. Specifically, I will discuss our work investigating the affective traits of Extraversion and Neuroticism, and most recently, Agreeableness. These traits are of importance to personality psychologists because they comprise three of the 'Big Five' personality traits (Conscientiousness and Openness to Experience being the remaining two), and they are also of interest to affective and social neuroscientists because they map onto negative affect (Neuroticism), or positive affect and social interactions (Extraversion and Agreeableness). I will close with an outlook on future directions, which will involve investigations of the molecular genetic mechanisms, and their interactions with an individual's life experience, that may underlie individual differences in personality traits and their neural correlates.

The work discussed in this review was supported by grants from the General Clinical Research Center (5-MO1-RR-10710), and the National Science Foundation (BCS-0224221).

Individual differences in brain emotional responses

The 'Big Five' personality traits of Extraversion, Neuroticism, Agreeableness, Openness to Experience and Conscientiousness (John and Srivastava 1999; McCrae and Costa 1999) represent an influential model of human personality. Of these, Extraversion and Neuroticism are particularly prominent, because they also played a role in other theorists' thinking (Eysenck 1994; Depue and Collins 1999), and because they map onto individual differences in positive and negative affect, respectively (Costa and McCrae 1980). Indeed, in our own line of research, we exploited the fact that we can use affective stimuli to draw out individual differences in traits such as Extraversion and Neuroticism (Canli 2004). Most recently, we have added work on Agreeableness, which can be construed as a personality trait that spans both social behaviour and positive affect.

Our first foray into this subject matter (Canli, Zhao, Desmond *et al.* 2001) was an imaging study using a passive viewing task, in which participants were presented with alternating blocks of positive and negative pictures selected from the International Affective Picture Series, IAPS (Lang, Bradley and Cuthbert 2001). In this study, we avoided the use of neutral stimuli, because we were concerned that affect generated during the emotional blocks would be sustained into the presumed neutral blocks, and instead opted for sharp contrasts in affective valence between highly positive and negative stimuli sets. However, this design came at a cost, in that we did not have a non-emotional baseline condition. We found that Extraversion and Neuroticism were indeed associated with individual differences in brain activation to positive and negative emotional stimuli, respectively (Canli, Zhao, Desmond *et al.* 2001). There were numerous subcortical and cortical activation foci, including brain regions involved in affective and cognitive processing, such as the amygdala, caudate nucleus, ACC and DLPFC. Amygdala activation, for example, was found to vary in response to positive (relative to negative) pictures as a function of Extraversion. This discovery was very intriguing, given that prior work had mostly (but not exclusively, see e.g. Canli, Zhao, Desmond *et al.* 1999; Hamann, Ely, Grafton *et al.* 1999) focused on the amygdala's response to negative stimuli. Our data suggested that it may also respond to positive stimuli, but that the degree of responding may vary across individuals as a function of personality. However, the lack of task constraints and the post-hoc nature of the discovery cautioned against an over-interpretation of this finding.

Individual differences in the amygdala

In our next set of studies we took an *a priori* approach, using tasks designed to activate specific regions of interest. Of particular interest were the amygdala and anterior cingulate cortex, which both have been implicated in cognitive and affective processes. We began this strategy with a study that focused on the role of the amygdala in facial affect processing (Canli, Sivers, Whitfield *et al.* 2002). Prior work had consistently shown that the amygdala exhibits greater activation to fearful

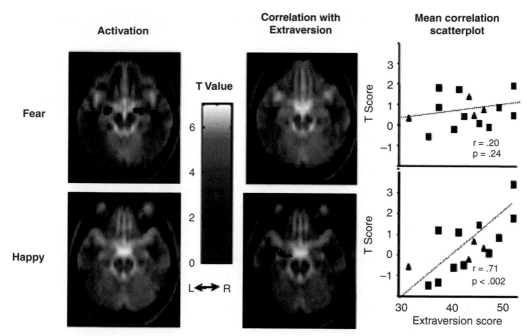

Figure 19.1. *Amygdala response to emotional faces. Left: significant amygdala activation to fearful, but not happy, faces (left: -23, -6, -18; right: +24, -7, -17). Middle: Extraversion correlated with left amygdala activation (-22, -9, -20) to happy, but not fearful, faces. Right: participants' mean activations (in T scores) as a function of Extraversion, from voxels surviving small volume correction. For fearful-neutral, no voxels survived at p < .05 threshold, which was therefore reduced to p < .25. Black squares represent females, black triangles represent males.*

than to neutral faces, but evidence for the amygdala's response to happy faces had been mixed. We hypothesized that some of these inconsistencies may be attributable to sample differences in Extraversion (most imaging studies until then had used small samples, so that the presence or absence of a few extraverted subjects could possibly affect the mean level of Extraversion of the sample), and that amygdala response to happy (but not fearful) facial expressions, when compared to neutral faces, would vary as a function of Extraversion. This prediction was confirmed (Figure 19.1). Furthermore, the observed associations were specific to Extraversion (and not any of the other Big Five traits) and happy facial expressions.

Since then, other groups have investigated the association of Extraversion and amygdala activation. Deckersbach and colleagues (Deckersbach, Miller, Klibanski *et al.* 2006) correlated participants' Extraversion scores with resting regional cerebral glucose metabolism (rCMRglu), using (18F)FDG (18F-fluorodeoxyglucose) positron emission tomography (PET). Although there were significant correlations with resting activation in the orbitofrontal cortex, these investigators failed to find a correlation between Extraversion and resting amygdala activation. On the other hand, Vaidya and colleagues (Vaidya, Paradiso, Andreasen *et al.* 2007) measured regional cerebral blood flow (rCBF) using [(15)O] water PET when they presented pleasant and unpleasant olfactory stimuli, and reported a significant correlation between amygdala response to pleasant scents and individual differences in Extraversion. These studies therefore suggest that amygdala response to positively valenced stimuli varies as a function of Extraversion, but that Extraversion may not affect resting amygdala activation in the absence of an emotionally valenced stimulus.

In addition to functional considerations, amygdala structure may also be associated with individual differences in self-reported personality traits, although the data so far are difficult to interpret. For example, using high-resolution structural MRI, one can measure the gray matter density or the gray matter volume of a given brain structure. We used a non-biased automated analysis approach (voxel-based morphometry) to evaluate high-resolution structural images of the amygdala, to calculate gray matter density and volume as a function of Extraversion and Neuroticism (Omura, Constable and Canli 2005). We found that extraversion correlated positively with gray matter density in the *left* amygdala, whereas neuroticism correlated negatively with gray matter density in the *right* amygdala. While the laterality pattern is consistent with models of brain laterality and affect (Davidson 1995), it is not clear why or how Extraversion and Neuroticism should correlate with amygdala gray matter density in the observed manner. Furthermore, these data have not yet been replicated by other groups, so the significance of this association remains to be determined. Using measures of gray matter volume (as opposed to gray matter density), data from three groups provide an inconsistent picture. We and another group (Wright, Williams, Feczko *et al.* 2006; Wright, Feczko, Dickerson *et al.* 2007) failed to find any significant association between amygdala volume and Extraversion or Neuroticism. On the other hand, another group (Iidaka, Matsumoto, Ozaki *et al.* 2006), reported a significant correlation between left amygdala volume and harm avoidance, a construct related to Neuroticism but derived from Cloninger's model of personality (Cloninger, Svrakic and Przybeck 1993), which was only seen in women. Given the small number of studies and inconsistent findings, the existing data are very preliminary but suggest that individual differences in personality traits may affect brain structure. Such variation may explain why prior structural imaging studies in mood-disordered patients produced conflicting findings and suggest that future clinical studies should control for personality traits.

Individual differences in the anterior cingulate cortex

Another *a priori* region of interest in our laboratory has been the anterior cingulate cortex (ACC). This region of the brain is of particular interest because it is engaged in both cognitive and affective processes that can be spatially dissociated within the ACC (Devinsky, Morrell and Vogt 1995; Bush, Luu and Posner 2000; Botvinick, Cohen and Carter 2004), and because it is sensitive to individual differences in affect (Lane, Fink, Chau *et al.* 1997; Lane 2000). Our first study (Canli, Zhao, Desmond *et al.* 2001) identified the ACC as a region in which individual activation differences to positive (relative to negative) pictures varied as a function of Extraversion. Because of the unconstrained nature of the task and the post-hoc nature of the result, subsequent studies used well-characterized cognitive tasks specifically designed to activate the ACC. In two follow-up studies, we used the emotional word Stroop task, which had been shown to activate the ACC (Whalen, Bush, McNally *et al.* 1998). Based on self-reported mood and personality data, we found that Extraversion was correlated with ACC activation to positive (relative to neutral) word stimuli, and confirmed that this association was moderated by personality trait, and not by positive mood state (Canli, Amin, Haas *et al.* 2004). We also found that activation to positive stimuli within the ACC and its functional connectivity with other structures varies as a function of specific Extraversion facets (Haas, Omura *et al.* 2006a).

ACC activation to negative stimuli also varies as a function of personality, specifically Neuroticism, as well as negative mood state. During the emotional word Stroop task, for example, we found that ACC response to negative (relative to neutral) words correlated with Neuroticism, but that this association was moderated by negative mood state, and not personality trait per se (Canli, Amin, Haas *et al.* 2004). This contrasts with the ACC's response to positive stimuli (see above), which was independent of participants' mood state. The intriguing hypothesis to emerge from these data is that the ACC may be endowed with a mechanism for intra-individual 'tuning' in response to negative stimuli (i.e., the ACC is less responsive to negative stimuli when the individual is in a neutral mood, and more responsive to negative stimuli when the individual is in a negative mood). This would give the ACC a much wider 'dynamic range' in the processing of negative information, which may be computationally advantageous. On the other hand, the ACC's response to positive stimuli may not change within subjects as a function of mood state, and is therefore more stable within individuals.

Although the emotional Stroop task is quite popular in neuroimaging studies, it is conceptually messy, because it confounds affect and attentional conflict. That is, emotional word stimuli may elicit brain activation due to their valence or due to the fact that participants are instructed to pay attention to non-affective characteristics of the stimulus (such as its colour or the number of times it appears on the screen) that are competing with (in conflict with) attentional characteristics. To better dissociate affect and conflict, we developed the emotional word-face Stroop task for neuroimaging studies (Haas, Omura *et al.* 2006b). In this paradigm, valenced or neutral words are superimposed on valenced or neutral faces. Participants are instructed to press one button if the word and face stimuli are congruent in valence, and a different button if they are incongruent. Thus, there are three trial types: neutral, emotionally congruent (EC), and emotionally incongruent (EI).

Consistent with the traditional Stroop interference paradigm, we showed that reaction times to EI trials are longer than to EC trials (Haas, Omura *et al.* 2006b), which replicated an earlier behavioural study (Stenberg, Wiking and Dahl 1998). With respect to ACC activation, we were primarily interested in the dissociation between cognitive and affective regions. We predicted that EI, relative to EC, trials should activate the caudal region of the ACC, which has been hypothesized to be engaged in conflict monitoring (Botvinick, Braver, Barch *et al.* 2001; Botvinick, Cohen and Carter 2004). Indeed, emotionally incongruent trials (which presumably generate more response conflict) were associated with greater caudal ACC activation then emotionally congruent trials (note that both trial types contain the same set of emotional stimuli, and are therefore equivalent with respect to emotional salience; they differ in how the emotional stimuli relate to one another).

Somewhat surprisingly, we did not find that rostral regions of the ACC, previously associated with affective processing (Whalen, Bush, McNally *et al.* 1998; Canli, Amin, Haas *et al.* 2004), exhibited greater activation to emotionally congruent trials, relative to neutral trials. It is possible that the word-face Stroop task is sufficiently different from the standard emotional Stroop task to explain this inconsistency. For example, differences exist with respect to task instructions. Subjects render a colour judgement in the emotional Stroop task, but a valence judgement in the word-face Stroop task. Within the word-face Stroop task, the emotional and neutral conditions differ in response selection criteria: during the EC condition, two correct responses (positive and negative) are available, whereas in the N condition, there is only one (neutral). Although we failed to detect rostral ACC activation during the EC-neutral contrast, we did observe activation in the border between the caudal ACC and the supplemental motor area, which is similar to another study in which trials with greater response selection were compared to trials with less response selection (Lau, Rogers and Passingham 2006).

In a follow-up study (Haas, Omura *et al.* 2007a) using this task, we showed that Neuroticism correlated positively with amygdala and subgenual ACC activation during trials of high emotional conflict, compared to trials of low emotional conflict. Moreover, we further dissected Neuroticism into two sub-facets, depressive and anxious, and found that the anxious form of Neuroticism explained a greater proportion of variance within the observed clusters than the sub-scale of Neuroticism that reflected the depressive form of Neuroticism. Thus, brain response in an emotional conflict paradigm was associated with anxious (but not depressive) Neuroticism.

Beyond single loci: an expansion of the methodological toolkit

The previous two sections may reinforce the impression that some sceptics may have that much neuroimaging is concerned with a phrenology-like, point-to-point, correspondence between single traits and single brain regions. However, this is not a viewpoint shared by neuroimagers. Indeed, several approaches have been developed to look beyond single activation regions.

One approach is to report the results of whole-brain analyses, in addition to analyses from *a priori* regions of interest. Usually, the statistical thresholds for inclusion are set more stringently for whole-brain analyses than for *a priori* regions, reflecting the post-hoc nature of the effort. Meta-analyses of imaging studies of emotion have identified a wide network of brain regions involved in emotional processing (Phan, Wager, Taylor *et al.* 2002; Phillips, Drevets,

Rauch *et al.* 2003a; Phillips, Drevets, Rauch *et al.* 2003b; Wager, Phan, Liberzon *et al.* 2003; Baas, Aleman and Khan *et al.* 2004; Phan, Wager, Taylor *et al.* 2004). In our own work, we have implicated a number of brain regions other than amygdala and anterior cingulate associated with Extraversion and Neuroticism, although the exact role of these regions remains to be worked out.

Another approach is to conduct functional connectivity analyses, to investigate how activation across spatially distinct regions is correlated. For example, in our study of state-trait associations of Extraversion and Neuroticism with ACC activation (Canli, Amin, Haas *et al.* 2004), we found that processing of negative stimuli activated a network that included the ACC, left middle frontal gyrus and left inferior parietal lobule, and that the functional connectivity between the nodes of this network varied across individuals as a function of negative mood state. Surprisingly, we found no corresponding modulation as a function of Neuroticism, or for the processing of positive stimuli as a function of either positive mood state or Extraversion. We suggested that greater functional connectivity as a function of negative mood could reflect a biological mechanism to account for state-dependent learning (Bower 1981). It could also explain why negative stimuli tend to be better processed when participants are in dysphoric states (MacLeod, Mathews and Tata 1986; Gotlib, McLachlan and Katz 1988; Bradley, Mogg, Galbraith *et al.* 1993). It is unclear whether the absence of similar mechanisms for the traits of Extraversion and Neuroticism, or for positive mood states, reflects a true absence of similar mechanisms, or simply a lack of sensitivity to detect this effect, given the study design and sample size.

We have developed a third approach (Omura, Aron and Canli 2005), which represents an alternative to the traditional regions of interest (ROI) approach, which we termed the 'regions of variance' (ROV) approach. The ROI approach focuses on regions that have been shown to be consistently activated across prior studies that employed a similar task paradigm. This approach, as illustrated in the previous two sections, certainly has its utility: it constrains the number of voxels that comprise the brain search space and generates hypothesis-driven research. However, these ROIs also represent those brain regions that are *least likely* to exhibit much variability across individuals. On the other hand, brain regions that exhibit a great deal of variance from one study participant to another may never show sufficient group-level activation to pass statistical thresholds in traditional imaging studies, and therefore not ever be reported. We therefore developed an alternative methodology that identifies *regions of variance* (ROVs), i.e., areas that display the most variability across subjects for a given within-subject contrast. We then treat these ROVs as regions of interest to assess whether particular variables of interest can explain the variance exhibited in these regions. The conceptual difference between the ROV and ROI approaches is considerable: ROVs are empirically derived and therefore devoid of any theoretical assumptions or biases about the neural substrate and its relation to the cognitive process under study. In contrast, ROIs typically represent considerable assumptions about the cognitive functions they are believed to play a role in.

We compared the analysis outcomes obtained with both approaches using a previously published dataset (Canli, Amin, Haas *et al.* 2004). To some extent, the two approaches converged. For example, both approaches confirmed a positive correlation between Extraversion and ACC activation to positive stimuli. But whereas the ROI approach is usually limited to one, or only very few, *a priori* regions, the ROV approach will include any region that shows significant variance across the dataset. For example, the ROV approach revealed that activation in the cerebellum varies as a function of positive mood in response to positive words, and as a function of negative mood in response to negative words. This region was not an *a priori* region, nor did a whole-brain analysis (which used a very stringent statistical threshold, see above) detect the cerebellum's association with mood state. Yet, others have recognized a potentially important role for the cerebellum in affective processing (Schmahmann and Sherman 1998), so the result of the ROV analysis is not without some credibility, and deserves future follow-up. On the other hand, we also discovered that the ROV approach does, on occasion, miss interesting brain-behaviour correlations. For example, the ROV approach missed the association between Extraversion and ACC response to positive stimuli in the left hemisphere. It turned out that, although the correlation between Extraversion and ACC activation was highly significant, the actual range of values that contributed to this correlation was relatively narrow, producing a low degree of between-subject variance. We concluded that a combination of both approaches would probably be best to maximize the opportunity to discover trait-brain associations, or other types of individual differences in the brain.

Imaging brain temporal dynamics related to personality

We recently began to investigate how personality traits such as Neuroticism affect temporal dynamics of brain affective processes. Although the brain is a highly dynamic system in which much information is represented in the temporal dynamics of brain activity, next to nothing is known about how such temporal dynamics are related to individual differences in personality. However, work by Siegle and colleagues suggests that individual differences in affective states or traits affect the temporal dynamics of physiological responses. For example, depressed patients exhibit more sustained autonomic arousal (as measured by pupil dilation) in response to negative words then healthy controls do (Siegle, Steinhauer *et al.* 2003), and also show more sustained amygdala activation (Siegle, Steinhauer *et al.* 2002). Indeed, whereas healthy controls' amygdala response returned to baseline within ten seconds of stimulus presentation, depressed individuals' amygdala response remained active and even lasted through the next (non-emotional) trial twenty-five seconds later. It is unknown whether this sustained activation represents a consequence of depression, or possibly an antecedent vulnerability marker. If it were the latter, and given that Neuroticism is a risk factor for depression (Martin 1985; Boyce, Parker, Barnett *et al.* 1991; Kendler, Neale, Kessler *et al.* 1993; Duggan, Shan, Lee *et al.* 1995), then we would expect that Neuroticism would correlate positively with sustained amygdala reactivity to negative emotional stimuli.

Another *a priori* region of interest where Neuroticism might be associated with sustained activation is the medial prefrontal cortex (MedPFC), which is involved, among other things, in self-referential emotional processing (Fossati, Hevenor, Graham *et al.* 2003; Ochsner, Knierim, Ludlow *et al.* 2004). Because Neuroticism is associated with increased automatic negative self-evaluation and appraisal (Stöber 2003; Robinson and Meier 2005), we predicted that higher scores of Neuroticism would be associated with more sustained MedPFC activity when processing negative stimuli.

We investigated the temporal dynamics of brain activation in these two *a priori* regions of interest in response to fearful, happy, sad and neutral emotional facial expressions (Haas, Constable and Canli 2008). We found a positive correlation between Neuroticism and sustained activation during presentation of sad facial expressions in the MedPFC, but not the amygdala. This association was very specific: there were no other brain regions that displayed this relationship in response to sad facial expressions. Additionally, we verified that this effect was specific to the MedPFC by identifying that no voxels within this cluster were localized in a neighbouring structure, the anterior cingulate cortex. Furthermore, we confirmed that the observed sustained activation was specific to sad facial expressions: no other clusters were identified that displayed greater sustained responses to any of the other emotional conditions (happy or fear). A more fine-grained analysis of the time course confirmed that Neuroticism correlated pos-itively with sustained activation (Figure 19.2).

The data suggest that sustained activation in response to negative stimuli may serve as a neural substrate of neuroticism in a brain region that is engaged in self-referential processing. It is important to point out, however, that the fMRI task we used (gender discrimination) did not instruct subjects to make self-referential judgements. Activation in this region may therefore either reflect an automatic unconscious self-referential process, or reflect another aspect of face processing that is independent of self-refencing. Nonetheless, sustained activation to sad faces in the MedPFC as a function of Neuroticism is consistent with other work that links Neuroticism with greater sensitivity to negative stimuli (Derryberry 1994), and with greater sustained processing of negative information in patients diag-nosed with depression and/or scoring higher on trait rumination (Deldin, Deveney, Kim *et al.* 2001; Siegle, Granholm 2001; Siegle, Steinhauer *et al.* 2002; Siegle, Steinhauer *et al.* 2003). Our observation of sustained response to sad stimuli was unique to the MedPFC. The location of sustained activation is consistent with a previous study that reported a significant correlation between MedPFC activation and rumination (Ray, Ochsner, Cooper *et al.* 2005). One intriguing hypothesis to emerge from this data is that sustained MedPFC activation to sad stimuli may represent a vulnerability biomarker for later mood disorders. Future longitudinal

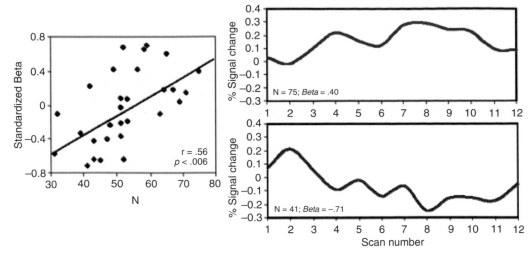

Figure 19.2. *Relationship between Neuroticism (N) and change of slopes of MedPFC activity within blocks of sad facial expressions. Data were extracted and converted to per cent signal change (relative to neutral) from the cluster identified in the MedPFC. Slope (Standardized Beta) values were calculated for each subject during average blocks of sad facial expressions and entered into a regression analysis with higher scores of Neuroticism predicting more positive (sustained) slope values (left). Right side: extracted average time-course of per cent signal change and Beta values are presented for an individual scoring high on Neuroticism (N = 75; blue) and low on Neuroticism (N = 41; red).*

studies with much larger samples (our study was based on a sample of twenty-nine individuals) will be able to assess this hypothesis empirically.

Unlike the MedPFC, there was no sustained amygdala activation as function of Neuroticism (even when we reduced the significance threshold to a very lenient $p < .05$). It is possible that the sustained activation observed in Siegle *et al.*'s patients represents a consequence of depression, rather than an antecedent. However, there are also many methodological differences between the two studies that will need to be teased apart in future work.

Summing up our current state of knowledge on temporal dynamics related to personality, we find that individuals who score high in Neuroticism display greater sustained activation in response to sad facial expressions than less neurotic individuals do in a region associated with self-evaluation. Whether this association is causally significant as a biological marker for susceptibility to mood disorders among highly neurotic individuals is currently unknown (a longitudinal follow-up study would be necessary). Nor does this association demonstrate that sustained activation in the MedPFC promotes high levels of rumination or negative self-evaluation (we did not measure these variables). Nonetheless, the data show that future work should consider both spatial and temporal parameters when studying neural correlates of personality traits. Well-designed, longitudinal studies may then be able to develop more sophisticated biological models of human personality.

Beyond Extraversion and Neuroticism: a first look at Agreeableness

Recently, we have expanded our investigations to other traits such as Impulsivity and Agreeableness. Here, I will only focus on Agreeableness, which represents one-third of the 'Big Five' traits, and can also be viewed as a trait associated with affective processing (readers interested in Impulsivity are referred to Congdon and Canli (2005)). For example, Agreeableness is associated with greater effort to regulate negative affect (Tobin, Graziano, Vanman *et al.* 2000). This tendency to minimize negative affect is even on display in implicit processing paradigms, suggesting that the regulation of negative affect can be automatic (Meier, Robinson and Wilkowski 2006).

The elegant work of Ochsner and colleagues (Ochsner and Gross 2005) has begun to identify neural circuits involved in emotion regulation. One key region appears to be the right lateral prefrontal cortex (LPFC) in the conscious regulation of negative affect (Ochsner, Knierim, Ludlow *et al.* 2004). However, it was unknown whether this region also activates during implicit emotion regulation, and whether it does so as a function of Agreeableness. We tested this hypothesis using the standard gender discrimination emotional face processing task (Haas, Omura *et al.* 2007b).

We found that activation in the right LPFC in response to fearful faces correlated significantly with Agreeableness (Figure 19.3). The correlation with agreeableness

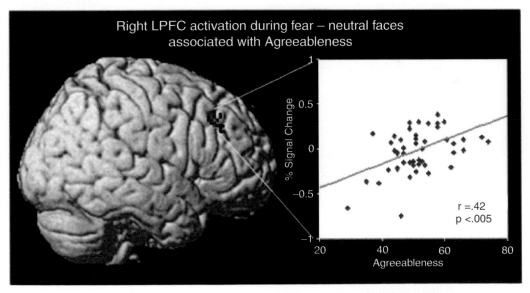

Figure 19.3. *Lateral prefrontal cortex (LPFC) activation to fearful, relative to neutral, faces correlated with Agreeableness. Figure shows a significant cluster located within the right LPFC, projected onto a template brain. Scatterplot shows individual data with the x-axis representing Agreeableness and the y-axis representing the mean percent signal change across the cluster based on activation during the fearful, relative to neutral, face presentations.*

was specific to fearful, and not happy or sad, facial expressions. Furthermore, the correlation was specific to the right LPFC, because there was no significant correlation in the left LPFC.

This data is consistent with the interpretation that highly agreeable individuals automatically engage neural mechanisms of affect regulation when facing negative stimuli. However, it is possible that other cognitive processes unrelated to emotion regulation were engaged, and therefore follow-up work using an explicit emotion-regulation task needs to be conducted to assess this alternative interpretation. It is also somewhat surprising that the observed correlation is specific to fearful, but not sad, facial expressions. It is possible that the element of social conflict, which is present in the fearful faces but not in the sad faces, is a driving contributor to the observed LPFC activation. If this is so, then a future study comparing fearful and angry facial expressions would be very informative, because both emotions signal social conflict, but differ in their motivational approach and withdrawal dimensions for highly agreeable individuals. One would predict, based on the work of Harmon-Jones and colleagues on laterality differences as a function of approach versus withdrawal (Harmon-Jones, Lueck, Fearn *et al.* 2006), that Agreeableness would correlate with activation in the left LPFC for approach-related social conflict (fear) and the right LPFC for withdrawal-related social conflict (anger).

Future directions

Much of the work discussed in the preceding section represents a starting point for neuroimaging of personality traits. Where appropriate, I have sketched out limitations of the current knowledge, and the need to evaluate alternative interpretations. Methodological advances in the design and analysis of fMRI studies will further elucidate networks of neural circuits, as well as the temporal dynamics that regulate their activation.

Beyond the affective traits I discussed here, there is a great deal of interest in the neurobiology of social behaviour (of course, traits such as Extraversion and Agreeableness have an inherent social component, as well). For example, recent reviews have been published on a number of social behaviours, including aggression (Blair 2001), attachment (Insel and Young 2001), empathy (Singer 2006), love (Fisher, Aron and Brown 2006), moral cognition (Casebeer 2003), and trust (Zak, Kurzban and Matzner 2004). Most of the work to date has not investigated individual differences in these social traits, and we can expect much exciting work in this topic area.

Perhaps the most transformative element for future biological studies of personality will come from molecular biology. Personality traits have a high degree of heritability (Defries, McClearn, McGuffin *et al.* 2000) and studies have begun to identify specific gene variations that are associated with individual differences within these traits (Reif and Lesch 2003). The most intensively studied of these gene variations is the serotonin transporter gene linked polymorphic region (*5-HTTLPR*), which is associated with neuroticism (Lesch, Bengel, Heils *et al.* 1996) and amygdala reactivity to negative (relative to neutral) stimuli (Hariri, Mattay, Tessitore *et al.* 2002). Our work has begun to elucidate the underlying mechanism, which we suggest involves modulation of tonic amygdala activation, which is further amplified by life stress experiences (Canli, Omura, Haas *et al.* 2005; Canli, Qiu, Omura *et al.* 2006; Canli and Lesch 2007). Indeed, elegant work on the molecular epigenetic processes that underlie such gene × environment interactions is already being conducted in animals (Weaver, Cervoni, Champagne *et al.* 2004; Meaney and Szyf 2005a; Meaney and Szyf 2005b; Weaver, Meaney and Szyf 2006). Applications to epigenetic programming of the human genome in relation to personality are not far off. Other gene variants have been identified that are associated with individual differences in cognition or emotion, and are therefore likely candidates for future imaging studies of personality traits. Beyond individual genes, the development of gene arrays that can probe simultaneously for hundreds of thousands, and soon a million, different gene variations will revolutionize the field. Whole-genome scans, if conducted with the proper statistical safeguards, hold the promise of a kind of *genomic* psychology (Canli 2007), in which the effects of dozens, if not hundreds, of gene variations on neural correlates of personality traits can be evaluated. The challenge for personality psychologists will be to incorporate this deluge of biological data in the development of the next generation of personality models, and provide theoretically-based guidance for neuroscientists and molecular geneticists.

References

Aggleton, J. P. (ed.) 1992. *The amygdala: neurobiological aspects of emotion, memory, and mental dysfunction*. New York, Wiley-Liss

Baas, D., Aleman, A. and Kahn, R. S. 2004. Lateralization of amygdala activation: a systematic review of functional neuroimaging studies, *Brain Research Reviews* 45: 96–103

Blair, R. J. 2001. Neurocognitive models of aggression, the antisocial personality disorders, and psychopathy, *Journal of Neurology Neurosurgery and Psychiatry* 71: 727–31

Botvinick, M. M., Braver, T. S., Barch, D. M. *et al.* 2001. Conflict monitoring and cognitive control, *Psychological Review* 108: 624–52

Botvinick, M. M., Cohen, J. D. and Carter, C. S. 2004. Conflict monitoring and anterior cingulate cortex: an update, *Trends in Cognitive Sciences* 8: 539–46

Bower, G. H. 1981. Mood and memory, *American Psychologist* 36: 129–48

Boyce, P., Parker, G., Barnett, B. *et al.* 1991. Personality as a vulnerability factor to depression, *British Journal of Psychiatry* 159: 106–14

Bradley, B., Mogg, K., Galbraith, M. *et al.* 1993. Negative recall bias and neuroticism: state vs trait effects, *Behaviour Research and Therapy* 31: 125–7

Brendel, G. R., Stern, E. and Silbersweig, D. A. 2005. Defining the neurocircuitry of borderline personality disorder: functional neuroimaging approaches, *Development and Psychopathology* 17: 1197–206

Bush, G., Luu, P. and Posner, M. I. 2000. Cognitive and emotional influences in anterior cingulate cortex, *Trends in Cognitive Science* 4: 215–22

Canli, T. 2004. Functional brain mapping of extraversion and neuroticism: learning from individual differences in emotion processing, *Journal of Personality* 72: 1105–32

2007. Genomic psychology: an emerging paradigm. *EMBO Reports* 8 (Special Edition on Science and Society (S1)): S30–4

Canli, T., Amin, Z., Haas, W. *et al.* 2004. A double dissociation between mood states and personality traits in the anterior cingulate. *Behavioral Neuroscience* 118: 897–904

Canli, T. and Lesch, K. P. 2007. Long story short: the serotonin transporter in emotion regulation and social cognition. *Nature Neuroscience* 10: 1103–9

Canli, T., Omura, K., Haas, W. *et al.* 2005. Beyond affect: a role for genetic variation of the serotonin transporter in neural activation during a cognitive attention task. *Proceedings of National Academy of Sciences USA* 102: 12224–9

Canli, T., Qiu, M., Omura, K. *et al.* 2006. Neural correlates of epigenesis. *Proceedings of National Academy of Sciences USA* 103: 16033–8

Canli, T., Sivers, H., Whitfield, S. L. *et al.* 2002. Amygdala response to happy faces as a function of extraversion, *Science* 296: 2191

Canli, T., Zhao, Z., Desmond, J. E. *et al.* 1999. fMRI identifies a network of structures correlated with retention of positive and negative emotional memory, *Psychobiology* 27: 441–52

2001. An fMRI study of personality influences on brain reactivity to emotional stimuli. *Behavioral Neuroscience* 115: 33–42

Casebeer, W. D. 2003. Moral cognition and its neural constituents, *Nature Reviews Neuroscience* 4: 840–6

Chamberlain, S. R. and Sahakian, B. J. 2006. The neuropsychology of mood disorders, *Current Psychiatry Reports* 8: 458–63

Cloninger, C. R., Svrakic, D. M. and Przybeck, T. R. 1993. A psychobiological model of temperament and character, *Archives of General Psychiatry* 50: 975–90

Congdon, E. and Canli, T. 2005. The endophenotype of impulsivity: reaching consilience through behavioural, genetic, and neuroimaging approaches. *Behavioural and Cognitive Neuroscience Review* 4: 262–81

Costa, P. T., Jr and McCrae, R. R. 1980. Influence of extraversion and neuroticism on subjective well-being: happy and unhappy people, *Journal of Personality and Social Psychology* 38: 668–78

Davidson, R. J. 1995. Cerebral asymmetry, emotion, and affective style, in R. J. Davidson and K. Hugdahl, *Brain asymmetry.* Cambridge, MA: MIT Press

Davis, M. 2000. The role of the amygdala in conditioned and unconditioned fear and anxiety, in J. P. Aggleton, *The amygdala: a functional analysis*, pp. 213–88. New York: Wiley-Liss

Davis, M., Walker, D. L. and Myers, K. M. 2003. Role of the amygdala in fear extinction measured with potentiated startle. *Annals of New York Academy of Sciences* 985: 218–32

Deckersbach, T., Miller, K. K., Klibanski, A. *et al.* 2006. Regional cerebral brain metabolism correlates of neuroticism and extraversion, *Depression and Anxiety* 23: 133–8

Defries, J. C., McClearn, G. E., McGuffin, P. *et al.* (eds.) 2000. *Behavioural Genetics.* New York: Worth Publishers

Deldin, P. J., Deveney, C. M., Kim, A. S. *et al.* 2001. A slow wave investigation of working memory biases in mood disorders, *Journal of Abnormal Psychology* 110: 267–81

Depue, R. A. and Collins, P. F. 1999. Neurobiology of the structure of personality: dopamine, facilitation of incentive, motivation and extraversion, *Behavioural and Brain Sciences* 22: 491–517

Derryberry, D. 1994. Temperament and attention: orienting towards and away from positive and negative signals, *Journal of Personality and Social Psychology* 66: 1128–39

Devinsky, O., Morrell, M. J. and Vogt, B. A. 1995. Contributions of anterior cingulate cortex to behaviour, *Brain* 118(Pt 1): 279–306

Duggan, C., Sham, P., Lee, A. *et al.* 1995. Neuroticism: a vulnerability marker for depression: evidence from a family study, *Journal of Affective Disorders* 35: 139–43

Eysenck, H. J. (ed.) 1994. *Personality: biological foundations*, The Neuropsychology of Individual Differences Series. San Diego, CA: Academic Press

Fisher, H. E., Aron, A. and Brown, L. L. 2006. Romantic love: a mammalian brain system for mate choice, *Philosophical Transactions of the Royal Society of London B-Biological Sciences* 361: 2173–86

Fossati, P., Hevenor, S. J., Graham, S. J. *et al.* 2003. In search of the emotional self: an fMRI study using positive and negative emotional words, *American Journal of Psychiatry* 160: 1938–45

Gotlib, I. H., McLachlan, A. L. and Katz, A. N. 1988. Biases in visual attention in depressed and nondepressed individuals, *Cognition and Emotion* 2: 185–200

Haas, B. W., Constable, R. T. and Canli, T. 2008. Stop the sadness: Neuroticism is associated with sustained medial prefrontal cortex response to emotional facial expressions, *Neuroimage* 42: 385–92

Haas, B. W., Omura, K. *et al.* 2006a. Functional connectivity with the anterior cingulate is associated with extraversion during the emotional stroop task, *Social Neuroscience* 1: 16–24

2006b. Interference produced by emotional conflict associated with anterior cingulate activation, *Cognitive Affect and Behavioural Neuroscience* 6: 152–6

2007a. Emotional conflict and neuroticism: personality-dependent activation in the amygdala and subgenual anterior cingulate, *Behavioural Neuroscience* 121: 249–56

2007b. Is automatic emotion regulation associated with agreeableness? A perspective using a social neuroscience approach, *Psychological Science* 18: 130–2

Hamann, S. B., Ely, T. D., Grafton, S. T. *et al.* 1999. Amygdala activity related to enhanced memory for pleasant and aversive stimuli. *Nature Neuroscience* 2: 289–93

Hariri, A. R., Mattay, V. S., Tessitore, A. *et al.* 2002. Serotonin transporter genetic variation and the response of the human amygdala, *Science* 297: 400–3

Harmon-Jones, E., Lueck, L., Fearn, M. *et al.* 2006. The effect of personal relevance and approach – related action expectation on relative left frontal cortical activity, *Psychological Science* 17: 434–40

Iidaka, T., Matsumoto, A., Ozaki, N. *et al.* 2006. Volume of left amygdala subregion predicted temperamental trait of harm avoidance in female young subjects. A voxel-based morphometry study, *Brain Research* 1125: 85–93

Insel, T. R. and Young, L. J. 2001. The neurobiology of attachment, *Nature Review of Neuroscience* 2: 129–36

John, O. P. and Srivastava, S. 1999. The Big Five trait taxonomy: history, measurement, and theoretical perspectives, in L. A. Pervin and O. P. John (eds.), *Handbook of personality: theory and research*, pp. 102–38. New York: Guilford Press

Kendler, K. S., Neale, M. C. Kessler, R. C. *et al.* 1993. A longitudinal twin study of personality and major depression in women. *Archives of General Psychiatry* 50: 853–62

Lane, R. D. 2000. Neural correlates of conscious emotional experience, in R. D. Lane, *Cognitive neuroscience of emotion*, pp. 345–70. New York: Oxford University Press

Lane, R. D., Fink, G. R., Chau, P. M. *et al.* 1997. Neural activation during selective attention to subjective emotional responses, *Neuroreport* 8: 3969–72

Lang, P. J., Bradley, M. M. and Cuthbert, B. N. 2001. International affective picture system (IAPS): instruction manual and affective ratings, Technical Report A-5. Gainesville, FL: Center for Research in Psychophysiology, University of Florida

Lau, H., Rogers R. D. and Passingham, P. E. 2006. Dissociating response selection and conflict in the medial frontal surface, *Neuroimage* 29: 446–51

LeDoux, J. E. 1992. Emotion and the amygdala, in J. P. Aggleton, *The amygdala: neurobiological aspects of emotion, memory, and mental dysfunction*, pp. 339–52. New York: Wiley-Liss

Lesch, K. P., Bengel, D., Heils, A. *et al.* 1996. Association of anxiety-related traits with a polymorphism in the serotonin transporter gene regulatory region, *Science* 274: 1527–31

MacLeod, C., Mathews, A. and Tata, P. 1986. Attentional bias in emotional disorders, *Journal of Abnormal Psychology* 95: 15–20

Martin, M. 1985. Neuroticism as predisposition toward depression: a cognitive mechanism, *Personality and Individual Differences* 6: 353–65

McCrae, R. R. and Costa, P. T. Jr 1999. A five-factor theory of personality, in L. A. Pervin and O. P. John (eds.), *Handbook of personality: theory and research*, pp. 139–53. New York: Guilford Press

McGaugh, J. L. 2004. The amygdala modulates the consolidation of memories of emotionally arousing experiences, *Annual Review of Neuroscience* 27: 1–28

McGaugh, J. L., Cahill, L. and Roozendaal, B. 1996. Involvement of the amygdala in memory storage: interaction with other brain systems, *Proceedings of the National Academy of Sciences USA* 93: 13508–14

Meaney, M. J. and Szyf, M. 2005a. Environmental programming of stress responses through DNA methylation: life at the interface between a dynamic environment and a fixed genome, *Dialogues in Clinical Neuroscience* 7: 103–23

　　2005b. Maternal care as a model for experience-dependent chromatin plasticity?, *Trends in Neuroscience* 28: 456–63

Meier, B. P., Robinson, M. D. and Wilkowski, B. M. 2006. Turning the other cheek: Agreeableness and the regulation of aggression-related primes, *Psychological Science* 17: 136–42

Meyer-Lindenberg, A. and Zink, C. F. 2007. Imaging genetics for neuropsychiatric disorders, *Child and Adolescent Psychiatric Clinics of North America* 16: 581–97

Ochsner, K. N. and Gross, J. J. 2005. The cognitive control of emotion, *Trends in Cognitive Sciences* 9: 242–9

Ochsner, K. N., Knierim, K., Ludlow, D. H. *et al.* 2004. Reflecting upon feelings: an fMRI study of neural systems supporting the attribution of emotion to self and other, *Journal of Cognitive Neuroscience* 16: 1746–72

Omura, K., Aron, A. and Canli, T. 2005. Variance maps as a novel tool for localizing regions of interest in imaging studies of individual differences, *Cognitive Affect and Behavioural Neuroscience* 5: 252–61

Omura, K., Constable, R. T. and Canli, T. 2005. Amygdala gray matter concentration is associated with extraversion and neuroticism, *Neuroreport* 16: 1905–8

Pearlson, G. D. and Calhoun, V. 2007. Structural and functional magnetic resonance imaging in psychiatric disorders, *Canadian Journal of Psychiatry* 52: 158–66

Phan, K. L., Wager, T., Taylor, S. F. *et al.* 2002. Functional neuroanatomy of emotion: a meta-analysis of emotion activation studies in PET and fMRI, *Neuroimage* 16: 331–48

2004. Functional neuroimaging studies of human emotions, *CNS Spectrums* 9: 258–66

Phillips, M. L., Drevets, W. C., Rauch, S. L. *et al.* 2003a. Neurobiology of emotion perception I: The neural basis of normal emotion perception, *Biological Psychiatry* 54: 504–14

2003b. Neurobiology of emotion perception II: Implications for major psychiatric disorders. *Biological Psychiatry* 54: 515–28

Ray, R. D., Ochsner, K. N., Cooper, J. C. *et al.* 2005. Individual differences in trait rumination and the neural systems supporting cognitive reappraisal, *Cognitive Affect and Behavioural Neuroscience* 5: 156–68

Reif, A. and Lesch K. P. 2003. Toward a molecular architecture of personality, *Behavioural Brain Research* 139: 1–20

Robinson, M. D. and Meier, B. P. 2005. Rotten to the core: neuroticism and implicit evaluations of the self, *Self and Identity* 4: 361–72

Schmahmann, J. D. and Sherman, J. C. 1998. The cerebellar cognitive affective syndrome, *Brain* 121: 561–79

Siegle, G. J., Granholm, E., Ingram, R. E. *et al.* 2001. Pupillary and reaction time measures of sustained processing of negative information in depression, *Biological Psychiatry* 49: 624–36

Siegle, G. J., Steinhauer, S. R. *et al.* 2002. Can't shake that feeling: event-related fMRI assessment of sustained amygdala activity in response to emotional information in depressed individuals, *Biological Psychiatry* 51: 693–707

2003. Do the seconds turn into hours? Relationships between sustained pupil dilation in response to emotional information and self-reported rumination, *Cognitive Therapy and Research* 27: 365–82

Singer, T. 2006. The neuronal basis and ontogeny of empathy and mind reading: review of literature and implications for future research, *Neuroscience and Biobehavioural Reviews* 30: 855–63

Stenberg, G., Wiking, S. and Dahl, M. 1998. Judging words at face value: interference in a word processing task reveals automatic processing of affective facial expressions, *Journal of Cognition and Emotion* 12: 755–82

Stöber, J. 2003. Self-pity: exploring the links to personality, control beliefs, and anger, *Journal of Personality* 71: 183–220

Tobin, R. M., Graziano, G., Vanman, E. J. *et al.* 2000. Personality, emotional experience, and efforts to control emotions, *Journal of Personal and Social Psychology* 79: 656–69

Vaidya, J. G., Paradiso, S., Andreasen, N. C. *et al.* 2007. Correlation between extraversion and regional cerebral blood flow in response to olfactory stimuli, *American Journal of Psychiatry* 164: 339–41

Wager, T. D., Phan, K. L., Liberzon, I. *et al.* 2003. Valence, gender, and lateralization of functional brain anatomy in emotion: a meta-analysis of findings from neuroimaging, *Neuroimage* 19: 513–31

Weaver, I. C., Cervoni, N., Champagne, F. A. *et al.* 2004. Epigenetic programming by maternal behaviour, *Nature Neuroscience* 7: 847–54

Weaver, I. C., Meaney, M. J. and Szyf, M. 2006. Maternal care effects on the hippocampal transcriptome and anxiety-mediated behaviours in the offspring that are reversible in adulthood, *Proceedings of the National Academy of Sciences USA* 103: 3480–5

Whalen, P. J., Bush, G., McNally, R. J. *et al.* 1998. The emotional counting Stroop paradigm: a functional magnetic resonance imaging probe of the anterior cingulate affective division, *Biological Psychiatry* 44: 1219–28

Wright, C. I., Feczko, E., Dickerson, B. *et al.* 2007. Neuroanatomical correlates of personality in the elderly, *Neuroimage* 35: 263–72

Wright, C. I., Williams, D., Feczko, E. *et al.* 2006. Neuroanatomical correlates of extraversion and neuroticism, *Cerebral Cortex* 16: 1809–19

Zak, P. J., Kurzban, R. and Matzner, W. T. 2004. The neurobiology of trust, *Annals of the New York Academy of Science* 1032: 224–7

20 Personality neuroscience: explaining individual differences in affect, behaviour and cognition

Colin G. DeYoung and Jeremy R. Gray

Human behaviours and experiences are generated by biological processes, primarily within the brain. On this basis, we may assume that the regularities in these behaviours and experiences that constitute personality are associated with regularities in the biological functions of the brain, making personality neuroscience possible. It is increasingly easy to study psychologically relevant individual differences using neuroscientific methods. Personality neuroscience endeavours to understand the proximal sources of personality in the brain and to trace those brain processes back to their distal sources in complex interactions between genes and environment. Heritability estimates for personality traits are typically around 50 per cent or higher, indicating that the distal sources of personality lie in both the genome and the environment (Bouchard 1994; Loehlin 1992; Riemann, Angleitner and Strelau 1997). Both genes and environment must make their mark on the brain, however, if they are to have a lasting influence on personality.

Personality psychology attempts to answer some of the most fundamental questions about people: Why are individuals the way they are? How and why do people differ from each other? For much of the past century, personality psychology has been concerned more with describing personality than with explaining it – that is, with *how* people differ from each other rather than with *why* they differ from each other. One reason for this emphasis on description rather than explanation was the immaturity of human neuroscience. Tools for investigating the neurobiological underpinnings of individual differences have greatly increased in power with the rise of neuroimaging and molecular genetics.

Another reason that personality psychology tended to focus on description rather than explanation was the necessity of developing an adequate categorization system for personality traits. Traits are relatively stable patterns of affect, behaviour and cognition (Fleeson 2001; Pytlik Zillig, Hemenover and Dienstbier 2002). The existence of a multitude of such patterns raises the question of whether some relatively small number of broad trait categories can be used to classify and organize the majority of traits. Over the past twenty-five years, this question has been largely resolved by the emergence of the Five-Factor Model or Big Five, which postulates that almost all trait descriptors can be categorized within five broad domains (or as blends of two or more of those domains): Extraversion, Neuroticism, Agreeableness, Conscientiousness and Openness/Intellect (Costa and McCrae 1992; Digman 1990; Hofstee, de Raad and Goldberg 1992; John and Srivastava 1999; Robert R. McCrae, Chapter 9). Our emphasis on the Big Five should not be misconstrued as a suggestion that the trait level of analysis alone can capture everything about personality – it cannot. Characteristic adaptations to particular situations and self-defining life narratives constitute two additional major levels of analysis that are more specific and better able to capture the rich detail and uniqueness of individual personalities (McAdams and Pals 2006; Mischel and Shoda 1998; Wood and Roberts 2006). Incorporating these levels can complement and enrich the trait approach. At this early stage in personality neuroscience, however, linking traits to neurobiological substrates is a promising start.

The Big Five model offers a useful categorization scheme for personality neuroscience and can effectively organize a review of this young field. Despite some debate in lexical research on personality about whether a six- or seven-factor model might be more robust across languages (Ashton, Lee, Perugini *et al.* 2004; Saucier and Goldberg 2001), the Big Five is the most widely used taxonomy of personality and provides a useful common language for personality research, helping to ensure that results are comparable across different studies. Behaviour genetic research shows that the Big Five are substantially heritable, with estimates ranging from 40 or 50 per cent up to 80 per cent, depending on trait and method (Reimann, Angleitner and Strelau 1997). Recently, the genetic factor structure of the Big Five, as measured by the Revised NEO Personality Inventory, was shown to be invariant across European, North American and East Asian samples, suggesting the biological universality of these traits (Yamagata, Suzuki, Ando *et al.* 2006). When measures of abnormal and normal personality traits are factor analysed together, the standard Big Five solution appears (Markon, Krueger and Watson 2005), suggesting the utility of the Big Five for studying psychopathology. Finally, the Big Five appears to be an effective taxonomy of descriptors of individual differences in other species (Gosling and John 1999), and cross-species comparisons are often important in neuroscience. All of these considerations suggest the potential utility of the Big Five for personality neuroscience, *as long as models can be developed that identify possible biological substrates of the Big Five and lead to testable hypotheses*. Fortunately, the field has now developed to the point where a synthesis of the literature may contribute to this sort of model.

Our aims in this chapter are, first, to review the methods and history of personality neuroscience, and then to attempt a synthesis of findings across the range of personality traits, as represented primarily by the Big Five. The goal here is not to summarize every result for any particular method, but to determine how the array of findings to date contributes to a larger picture of the relation between variation in the brain and variation in personality. This strategy will highlight a point that we consider to be of major conceptual importance, namely that theories of personality must not be limited to a particular domain of information-processing, but must consider individual differences in affect, behaviour and cognition, as well as how these different domains are integrated and interact (Gray 2004; Gray, Braver and Raichle 2002). Only by taking a broad view will the field be able to fulfil the promise of personality psychology to understand the individual as he or she actually functions as a whole.

Methods in personality neuroscience

Personality neuroscience reflects the conjunction of personality psychology with methods for discovering the biological sources of individual differences. The measurement of personality is typically accomplished by questionnaire, through self-report and/or through ratings by peers or other knowledgable informants. 'Personality' is sometimes taken to mean the set of variables that result from questionnaire measures, but this confuses the instruments with the constructs. Questionnaires are simply a convenient and reliable method for assessing a broad range of stable individual differences, drawing on subjects' experiences over a far greater span of time than is available in the laboratory. Other methods can be used to measure personality, if they can be validated psychometrically (i.e., as measuring stable patterns of affect, behaviour and cognition). Measures of intelligence and of the ability to delay gratification (Ohmura, Takahashi, Kitamura and Wehr 2006) are a good example. The challenge with such behavioural measures, because models of personality structure like the Big Five are typically operationalized with questionnaires, is to relate them back to those models so that they may be incorporated into the larger nomological network of personality psychology.

The general categories of neuroscientific methods that we see as currently most relevant to personality are (1) neuroimaging (e.g., magnetic resonance imaging (MRI) or proton emission tomography (PET)); (2) molecular genetics (a.k.a. genomics); (3) electrophysiological techniques (e.g., electroencephalography (EEG) or measurement of electrodermal activity (EDA)); (4) assays of endogenous psychoactive substances or their by-products (e.g., hormone levels in saliva or neurotransmitter metabolites in cerebrospinal fluid); and (5) psychopharmocological manipulation (e.g., tryptophan depletion or augmentation to alter levels of serotonin).

Studies of personality using structural and functional MRI and PET are appearing at a rapid rate; over fifty have been published since 2003, almost tripling the existing number (see Turhan Canli, Chapter 19). Molecular genetics has seen a similar explosion of personality research since the first studies of the effects of genetic variation on normal personality traits appeared in 1996 (Marcus R. Munafò, Chapter 18, this volume). Electrophysiological research was the primary tool for investigating the biology of personality, prior to the advent of neuro-imaging and molecular genetics; with a few exceptions, however, associations of electrophysiological variables with personality have been inconsistent (Zuckerman 2005). Excellent reviews of research on the influence of neurotransmitters and hormones on personality have been written by Netter (2004), Hennig (2004) and Zuckerman (2005). Many inferences about personality can be drawn from the study of non-human animals (see Samuel D. Gosling and B. Austin Healey,

Chapter 17), and consistency with non-human analogs is a hallmark of good theory in personality neuroscience, but we limit our review to human methods.

Influential theories in personality neuroscience

We briefly describe the influential models of Eysenck, Gray, Zuckerman, Cloninger, Depue and Panksepp and relate each model to the Big Five, with the aim of translating results from different systems into a single common language. This approach is readily justified by the fact that these models have been demonstrated to fall within the same factor structure as the Big Five (e.g., Markon, Krueger and Watson 2005; Angleitner, Riemann and Spinath 2004). Most of the theorists have revised their models substantially over time; in the interest of space we discuss only the latest version of each.

Eysenck assigned traits to three 'superfactors', Extraversion, Neuroticism and Psychoticism (Eysenck and Eysenck 1985). Extraversion and Neuroticism are nearly identical in Eysenck's system and the Big Five, whereas the unfortunately-labelled Psychoticism reflects a roughly equal blend of low Conscientiousness and low Agreeableness (Goldberg and Rosolack 1994). In his biological theorizing, Eysenck (1967; Eysenck and Eysenck 1985) relied heavily on the functions of the brain's ascending reticular activating system, associating Extraversion with the reticulo-cortical circuit and Neuroticism with the reticulo-limbic circuit. Eysenck hypothesized that extraverts have a higher threshold for cortical arousal than introverts and therefore choose more stimulating activities and experiences in order to achieve their preferred level of arousal. He hypothesized that neurotics are more easily aroused by emotion-inducing stimuli than are emotionally stable people. Eysenck did not develop as well-specified a biological model of Psychoticism, but at different times he hypothesized that Psychoticism was negatively associated with serotonergic function (Eysenck 1992) and positively associated with dopaminergic function (Eysenck 1997).

Jeffrey Gray, who was Eysenck's student, focused more heavily on neurobiology than on personality, with an emphasis on the development of a 'conceptual nervous system' describing functional systems that could be mapped onto brain systems. The main components of this conceptual nervous system are the behavioural approach system (BAS), which responds to cues for reward, and the fight-flight-freeze system (FFFS) and behavioural inhibition system (BIS), which respond to two distinct classes of threatening stimuli (Gray and McNaughton 2000; Pickering and Gray 1999). Immediately threatening, punishing or frustrating stimuli activate the FFFS, which produces active avoidance (panic and flight) or attempted elimination (anger and attack). Stimuli that one needs or desires to approach but that also contain potential threat (thus creating an approach-avoidance conflict) activate the BIS, which produces vigilance, rumination and passive avoidance, as well as anxiety and even potentially depression (Gray and McNaughton 2000). (Approach-approach or avoidance-avoidance conflicts are less common but can also activate the BIS, which responds specifically to any conflict between goals.) Biologically, Gray linked the BAS to the dopaminergic system, the BIS primarily to the septo-hippocampal system but also to the amygdala, and the FFFS to the amygdala, hypothalamus and periaqueductal gray.

Gray's model of personality, Reinforcement Sensitivity Theory (RST; see Philip J. Corr, Chapter 21, this volume), describes personality traits as a function of individual differences in the sensitivities of BIS, BAS and FFFS. Gray (1982) originally described two dimensions of personality associated with BIS sensitivity and BAS sensitivity, which he labelled Anxiety and Impulsivity respectively. Gray viewed Anxiety and Impulsivity as 30° rotations from Neuroticism and Extraversion, respectively. Gray and McNaughton (2000) noted, however, that questionnaire measures of Anxiety or BIS sensitivity are, in practice, difficult to distinguish from Neuroticism. Further, they described Neuroticism as a general sensitivity to threat produced jointly by FFFS and BIS. Additionally, several of Gray's colleagues have recently suggested that measures of Extraversion (not Impulsivity) may be the best measures of BAS sensitivity (Pickering 2004; Smillie, Pickering and Jackson 2006). These parallels are consistent with research showing that measures of BIS and BAS sensitivity tap the same latent constructs as measures of Neuroticism and Extraversion (Elliot and Thrash 2002; Zelenski and Larsen 1999).

Zuckerman (2005) has provided the most extensive review of personality neuroscience to date, in the second edition of his book, *Psychobiology of personality*. This book is organized around a hybrid of the Big Five and Zuckerman's own model of personality, the Alternative Five, which are Sociability, Neuroticism-Anxiety, Aggression-Hostility, Impulsive Sensation-Seeking and Activity. Zuckerman identified the first four of these with Extraversion, Neuroticism, Agreeableness (reversed) and Conscientiousness (reversed), respectively, in the Big Five. Factor analyses largely bear out these associations (Aluja, Garcia and Garcia 2002, 2004; Angleitner, Riemann and Spinath 2004; Zuckermana, Kuhlman, Joireman *et al.* 1993), though the situation is somewhat complicated for Impulsive Sensation-Seeking, which is sometimes as strongly associated with Extraversion and Openness/Intellect as with Conscientiousness and also tends to show a moderate negative association with Agreeableness. Aditionally, these factor analyses show that Zuckerman's Activity scale serves as a marker of Extraversion, Conscientiousness, or both.

We cannot hope to summarize all of the biological research relevant to the Alternative Five that is synthesized in Zuckerman's (2005) *Psychobiology of personality* (some of it will be discussed below). In brief, Zuckerman linked personality traits to underlying behavioural mechanisms, which he in turn linked to the brain functions of various neurotransmitters, hormones and enzymes. One notable feature of his theorizing is that he described behavioural mechanisms (including approach, inhibition and arousal) as determined by multiple biological systems and as contributing to multiple traits. In his model, for example, approach is influenced by both dopamine and testosterone and contributes to both Sociability and Impulsive Sensation-Seeking.

In contrast, Cloninger (1987) developed a model of personality traits based on the premise that individual neurotransmitter systems might be related uniquely to specific traits. Cloninger hypothesized that the dopaminergic system was linked to a trait of Novelty-Seeking, the serotonergic system to Harm Avoidance, and the norepinephrine system to Reward Dependence. Cloninger's latest model includes these three traits plus four others: Persistence, Self-Directedness, Cooperativeness and Self-Transcendence (Cloninger, Svrakic and Przybeck 1993). He hypothesized that the original three traits and Persistence reflect dimensions of *temperament*, meaning that they should be evident early in ontogeny and strongly genetically determined. In contrast, he hypothesized that Self-Directedness, Cooperativeness and Self-Transcendence reflect dimensions of *character*, meaning that they should develop later, being determined by experience during development rather than primarily by genes.

Research has demonstrated several problems with Cloninger's model. First, a simple distinction between temperament and character appears untenable. The character traits show much the same levels of heritability as the temperament traits (Ando, Suzuki, Yamagata *et al.* 2004; Gillespie, Cloninger, Heath and Martin 2003). Secondly, evidence has accumulated to contradict the idea that single neurotransmitter systems are responsible for Novelty-Seeking, Harm Avoidance and Reward Dependence (Paris 2005). Finally, Cloninger's seven-factor structure has not proven consistently replicable. Factor analyses have demonstrated (a) that the scales Cloninger developed do not group together in the manner that he assigned them to his seven traits (Ando, Suzuki, Yamagata *et al.* 2004; Ball, Tennen and Kranzler 1999; Herbst, Zonderman, McCrae and Costa 2000), and (b) that his instrument is best described by the five factor structure of the Big Five (Markon, Krueger and Watson 2005; Ramanaiah, Rielage and Cheng 2002). Harm Avoidance and Self- Determination (reversed) are both markers of Neuroticism. Cooperativeness, Persistence and Self-Transcendence are markers of Agreeableness, Conscientiousness and Openness/Intellect, respectively. Reward Dependence combines Agreeableness and Extraversion. Finally, Novelty-Seeking shows a pattern similar to Zuckerman's Impulsive Sensation-Seeking: it is most strongly associated with Conscientiousness (reversed), but also consistently loads positively on Extraversion as well as sometimes negatively on Agreeableness and positively on Openness.

Depue describes five trait dimensions: Agentic Extraversion, Affiliation, Anxiety, Fear and Nonaffective Constraint (Depue and Lenzenweger 2005). Depue and Collins (1999) proposed a theory of Extraversion linking it to the network of brain systems controlling sensitivity to cues of reward and generating approach behaviour in response. They focused primarily on what they called 'Agentic Extraversion', encompassing assertiveness, dominance and ambition, and distinguished this from 'Affiliative Extraversion', which is related to sociability and affiliative social bonding. 'Extraversion' was eventually dropped from the label for the latter trait, and Depue and Morrone-Strupinsky (2005) proposed a theory of Affiliation, linking it to the brain systems controlling sensitivity to affiliative bonding and consummatory reward, focusing particularly on the endogenous opioids and sociosexual peptides like oxytocin. White and Depue (1999) distinguished Anxiety, which they associated with Neuroticism, from Fear, citing evidence that the amygdala responds to specific localized threat (producing fear), whereas the bed nucleus of the stria terminalis (BNST), which is often considered part of the 'extended amygdala', responds to indications of non-localized or potential threat (producing anxiety). Finally, Depue and Lenzenweger (2005) associated Nonaffective Constraint with Conscientiousness and with the broad inhibitory functions of the serotonergic system.

Depue has typically operationalized his constructs with the Multidimensional Personality Questionnaire (MPQ) (Tellegen 1982). The MPQ scales of Social Potency and and Social Closeness, used to represent Agentic Extraversion and Affiliation respectively, both load primarily on Extraversion (Markon, Krueger and Watson 2005). Depue associates Anxiety most strongly with the MPQ Stress Reaction scale, which is a clear marker of Neuroticism. Fear he associates with MPQ Harm Avoidance, which, unlike Cloninger's Harm Avoidance, specifically assesses aversion to physical danger and is not well described by the Big Five (Markon *et al.* 2005) (potentially because many of its items are forced choices between danger and boredom). MPQ Control vs. Impulsivity, which Depue identifies as the best marker of Nonaffective Constraint, loads strongly on Conscientiousness (Markon *et al.* 2005).

Panksepp has focused primarily on animal research, but his name should be mentioned here because of his importance in the development of affective neuroscience and his advocacy of the idea that research in other mammals is strongly relevant to theories of human emotional functioning (Panksepp 1998). He has recently developed a personality model for human research, hypothesizing the existence of six traits reflecting distinct emotional systems: Playfulness, Seeking, Caring, Fear, Anger and Sadness. Playfulness correlates most strongly with Extraversion, Seeking with Openness/Intellect, and Caring with Agreeableness; Fear, Anger and Sadness all correlate strongly with Neuroticism (Davis, Panksepp and Normansell 2003).

Neurobiological substrates of the personality hierarchy

Personality traits are arranged hierarchically, with correlated groups of more specific traits categorized together in broader traits. For example, the lower-level traits of talkativeness, assertiveness, enthusiasm and sociability are all grouped within the trait of Extraversion. A key premise of the factor-analytic approach is that specific traits fall within the same larger factor because of some shared underlying cause (Haig 2005). Though this cause need not be exclusively biological, the correlational structure of traits provides a useful clue for personality neuroscience. The Big Five were originally conceived as independent traits at the highest level of the personality hierarchy, but research has shown that they are regularly intercorrelated and possess a higher-order factor structure (DeYoung 2006; DeYoung, Peterson and Higgins 2002; Digman 1997;

Jang, Livesley, Ando *et al.* 2006; Markon, Krueger and Watson 2005). Neuroticism (reversed), Agreeableness and Conscientiousness form one higher-order factor or metatrait, labelled α or *Stability*, and Extraversion and Openness/Intellect form another, labelled β or *Plasticity*. Behaviour genetic analysis has shown that the two meta-traits have genetic origins (Jang *et al.* 2006), and evidence is accumulating that Stability is related to serotonin, whereas Plasticity may be related to dopamine (DeYoung 2006; DeYoung, Peterson and Higgins 2002; Yamagata, Suzuki, Ando *et al.* 2006). Serotonin and dopamine act as diffuse neuromodulators affecting a wide array of brain systems, and their broad influence is consistent with a role in the broadest level of personality structure.

The history of research on serotonin's role in psychopathology provides good reason to expect that increased serotonergic function should be associated positively with Agreeableness and Conscientiousness and negatively with Neuroticism. Low levels of serotonin are associated with aggression, poor impulse control, depression and anxiety, and drugs that boost serotonergic function are used successfully to treat all of these problems (Spoont 1992). More direct evidence exists as well. A combined behaviour genetic and genomic study demonstrated that the correlation between Neuroticism and Agreeableness has a genetic basis and that variation in the serotonin transporter gene accounted for 10 per cent of that correlation (Jang, Hu, Livesley *et al.* 2001). A pharmacological manipulation that promotes serotonin release and inhibits reuptake has demonstrated that both low Neuroticism and high Conscientiousness are associated with increased serotonergic responsiveness (Manuck, Flory, McCaffery *et al.* 1998). And variation in the monoamine oxidase-A gene, which affects levels of serotonin, is associated with differences in Agreeableness and Concsientiousness (Rosenberg, Templeton, Feigin *et al.* 2006). The discovery of Stability as a meta-trait encompassing the shared variance of Neuroticism, Agreeableness and Conscientiousness may allow a parsimonious description of the broad effects of serotonin on personality, which largely reconciles the various hypotheses regarding serotonin proposed by the theorists described above.

Plasticity appears to reflect a general exploratory tendency, with Extraversion representing a more behavioural mode of exploration and Openness/Intellect a more cognitive mode. The role of dopamine in exploratory behaviour and cognitive flexibility is well-established, making it a plausible biological substrate for Plasticity (Ashby, Isen and Turken 1999; Braver and Barch 2002; Depue and Collins 1999; Panksepp 1998). A growing body of evidence indicates that Extraversion is partly a function of dopaminergic activity (Depue and Collins 1999; Wacker, Chavanon and Stemmler 2006; Wacker and Stemmler 2006). Some evidence suggests that Openness/Intellect might also be modulated by dopamine. Both Openness/Intellect and Extraversion are associated with decreased latent inhibition, a low-level cognitive phenomenon that is known to be mediated by dopamine, and Plasticity predicts low latent inhibition better than either Extraversion or Openness/Intellect alone (Peterson and Carson 2000; Peterson, Smith and Carson 2002). Additionally, variation in the catechol-*O*-methyltransferase gene (*COMT*), which regulates levels of dopamine in the prefrontal cortex, has been associated with Openness/Intellect in a sample of older adults (Harris, Wright, Hayward *et al.* 2005).

Identifying serotonin and dopamine as likely biological substrates for the meta-traits begins to develop a psychobiological model of the personality hierarchy based on the Big Five. However, the correlations among the Big Five that reveal the meta-traits are not very strong, and each Big Five trait describes a clearly distinct domain of personality. Biological substrates must exist that are unique to each trait, in addition to the shared substrates that produce the meta-traits. The following literature review allows the generation of hypotheses about what these unique substrates might be. We begin with Extraversion and Neuroticism, which appear to represent the primary manifestations in personality of sensitivity to reward and sensitivity to threat and punishment.

Extraversion

Depue's model of Extraversion is the most thorough and promising to date, linking it to the brain systems that govern sensitivity to reward and related positive emotions (Depue and Collins 1999; Depue and Lenzenweger 2005; Depue and Morrone-Strupinsky 2005). This model is largely congruent with Gray's theory of the BAS, which has been increasingly linked to Extraversion (Smillie, Pickering and Jackson 2006). The dopaminergic component of this reward circuitry may be particularly influential on the 'agentic' aspect of Extraversion associated with drive and assertiveness (Depue and Collins 1999), whereas the affiliative aspect of Extraversion may be associated more strongly with the endogenous opioid systems involved in the positive emotions that follow attainment or consumption of reward and that are particularly important in social bonding (Depue and Morrone-Strupinsky 2005).

Multiple neuroimaging studies have found that brain activity at rest or in response to positive or rewarding stimuli is positively associated with Extraversion (or questionnaire measures of BAS sensitivity; Beaver, Lawrence, van Ditzhuijzen et al. 2006) in the brain regions that both Depue and Gray identify as particularly important in the circuitry of reward and approach behaviour. These include the medial orbito-frontal cortex, nucleus accumbens, amygdala and striatum (Canli, Zhao, Desmond et al. 2001; Canli, Sivers, Whitfield et al. 2002; Cohen, Young, Baek et al. 2005; Deckersbach, Miller, Klibanski et al. 2006; Mobbs, Hagan, Azim et al. 2005). Additionally, genetic studies have found associations between Extraversion and several genes involved in the dopaminergic system (Benjamin, Li, Patterson et al. 1996; Bookman, Taylor, Adams-Campbell and Kittles 2002; Eichhammer, Sand, Stoertebecker et al. 2005; Ozkaragoz and Noble 2000; Reuter and Hennig 2005; Reuter, Schmitz, Corr and Hennig 2005; Tochigi, Otowa, Hibino et al. 2006), though these associations are not yet well established (see Marcus R. Munafò, Chapter 18).

Some aspects of Eysenck's theory that Extraversion is associated with cortical arousal may be compatible with the reward sensitivity model. Evidence for the cortical arousal theory is complicated by the fact that EEG and fMRI studies have found that the association between Extraversion and arousal is sometimes positive and sometimes negative (Matthews and Gilliland 1999; Zuckerman 2005). These seemingly contradictory effects may be moderated by the type of situation in which arousal is measured and by the pattern of cortical arousal in question (Matthews and Gilliland 1999; Wacker, Chavanon and Stemmler 2006). The effect of a given situation on cortical arousal may depend in part on the situation's reward properties and may be mediated by dopamine. For example, pharmaco-logical manipulation of dopamine D2 receptors has been shown to modulate frontal (relative to parietal) brain activity in EEG, but in opposite directions for groups high versus low in Extraversion (Wacker and Stemmler 2006).

Several brain imaging studies have demonstrated that Extraversion is predictive of brain activity in cortical areas influenced by dopamine (such as the anterior cingulate), during working memory tasks that have no apparent affective content (Gray and Braver 2002; Gray, Burgess, Schaefer *et al.* 2005; Kumari, ffytche, Williams and Gray 2004). Interestingly, however, Extraversion is not typically predictive of work-ing memory performance. These findings suggest the degree to which affective and cognitive processes are interrelated. Extraversion may be related to the ways in which individuals are motivated to perform difficult cognitive tasks and even to the manner in which those tasks are processed in the brain, whereas other traits, like Openness/Intellect (see below), may be more directly related to performance of those tasks.

Finally, testosterone levels have been positively associated with Extraversion, especially with assertiveness and dominance, in a number of studies (Netter 2004; Zuckerman 2005). Zuckerman (2005) has suggested that the effects of testoster-one on Extraversion may be due to interaction between testosterone and reward circuitry, particularly in the nucleus accumbens.

Neuroticism

Neuroticism appears to reflect sensitivity to threat and the whole range of negative emotions and cognitions that accompany experiences of threat and punishment, including anxiety, depression, anger, irritation, self-consciousness and vulnerability. Because Neuroticism and sensitivity to threat are so strongly implicated in psychopathology, research on their likely biological substrates has been extensive. Gray and McNaughton's (2000) model of the BIS and FFFS, which jointly determine Neuroticism, is very thoroughly elaborated. This model is reasonably compatible with Depue's model of Anxiety and Fear, although Depue believes that Fear is not well represented within Neuroticism.[1] (Depue's use of the term 'Fear' is complicated by the fact that colloquial usage often treats 'fear' and 'anxiety' as nearly equivalent, with the result that, in the Big Five, both fall within Neuroticism.) Gray and McNaughton associated the FFFS not only with fear but also with panic and anger, and these emotions are also associated with

---

[1] Depue and Lenzenweger (2005) criticized Gray's theory of the BIS because they consider 'behavioural inhibition' to be a marker of fear rather than anxiety; however, Gray and McNaughton (2000) clearly differentiated the general behavioural inhibition associated with anxiety and passive avoidance from the more immediate and stereotyped behavioural inhibition (which they labelled 'freezing') associated with fear.

Neuroticism (Costa and McCrae 1992; DeYoung, Quilty and Peterson 2007; Saucier and Goldberg 2001).

Various brain systems associated with reactions to threat and punishment have been linked to Neuroticism. Neuroimaging studies have found that Neuroticism is associated with brain activity at rest or in response to aversive or novel stimuli, in brain regions associated with negative affect, including the amygdala, insula and anterior cingulate (Deckersbach, Miller, Klibanski *et al.* 2006; Eisenberger, Lieberman and Satpute 2005; Etkin, Klemenhagan, Dudman *et al.* 2004; Cools, Calder, Lawernce *et al.* 2005; Haas, Omura, Constable and Canli 2007; Keightley, Seminowicz, Bagby *et al.* 2003; Reuter, Stark, Henning *et al.* 2004). Gray and McNaughton (2000) describe both serotonin and norepinephrine as modulators of the BIS and FFFS. Neuroticism has been associated with lower levels of serotonergic function through various methods, including genomics, PET, psychopharmacological manipulation, and assays of cerebrospinal fluid (Cools, Calder, Lawrence *et al.* 2005; Hennig 2004; Lesch, Bengel, Heils *et al.* 1996; Manuck *et al.* 1998; Schinka, Busch and Robichaux-Keene 2004; Sen, Burmeister and Ghosh 2004; Tauscher, Bagby, Javanmard *et al.* 2001). A smaller body of evidence links Neuroticism to higher levels of norepinephrine (White and Depue 1999; Hennig 2004; Zuckerman 2005). Neuroticism has been associated also with higher baseline levels of the stress hormone cortisol, but with lower levels of cortisol in response to specific stressors (Netter 2004). The association of Neuroticism with cortisol function is consistent with the importance of the hypothalamic-pituitary-adrenal (HPA) axis in responding to threat and other stressors (McEwen 1998).

Finally, a number of EEG studies have demonstrated that Neuroticism (including various trait measures of negative emotionality) is associated with greater activation of the right frontal lobe relative to the left (Davidson 2002; Zuckerman 2005). Davidson (2002) has argued that the right hemisphere is preferentially involved in emotions and motivational states associated with withdrawal, whereas the left hemisphere is preferentially involved in approach. The one complication in linking the right hemisphere to Neuroticism is that anger is associated with approach motivation, and EEG studies have shown anger to be associated with greater relative left frontal lobe activation (Harmon-Jones 2004; Harmon-Jones and Allen 1998). Perhaps, therefore, hemispheric asymmetries may aid in differentiating the sources of two classes of negative emotions that have been identified within Neuroticism: those associated with withdrawal and those associated with volatility and anger (DeYoung, Quilty and Peterson 2007).

Agreeableness

Because of the relation of Extraversion and Neuroticism to emotion and to reward and punishment, and because of the long history of biological theorizing about them, there is more evidence regarding their biological substrates than there is for Agreeableness, Conscientiousness and Openness/Intellect. Additionally, few theories have been put forth to explain the nature of the latter three trait domains from biological or evolutionary perspectives (but see MacDonald 1998;

Nettle 2006). Consideration of their grouping within the meta-traits of Stability and Plasticity presents a useful starting point in this endeavour. Agreeableness, for example, appears to reflect a tendency toward the maintenance of social stability, encompassing traits reflecting prosociality vs. antisociality: compassion, empathy, cooperation, politeness – a general tendency to be interested in and considerate of others' needs, desires and feelings and to refrain from aggressing or imposing one's will on others. Such altruistic tendencies are of particular importance for social species, and traits resembling Agreeableness are found consistently in social mammals (Gosling and John 1999).

Agreeableness seems likely to be supported by brain systems that are involved in social information-processing. The growing body of neuroscience research on empathy, theory of mind and perception of biological motion and intention is thus likely to be relevant to understanding the neurobiological substrates of Agreeableness. Brain regions associated with these forms of social information-processing include the medial prefrontal cortex (Seitz, Nickel and Azari 2006), superior temporal sulcus (Allison, Puce and McCarthy 2000), temporal-parietal junction (Saxe and Powell 2006), and the mirror neuron system that includes inferior frontal gyrus and rostral posterior parietal cortex (Iacoboni 2007; Rizzolatti and Craighero 2004). (Mirror neurons respond similarly when watching another agent perform a task and when performing it oneself.)

Several fMRI studies using trait measures of empathy have reported findings that are directly relevant to the link between Agreeableness and social information-processing. In these studies, empathy was positively associated with activity in the mirror neuron system, medial prefrontal cortex, and/or superior temporal sulcus during observation and imitation of others' actions (Gazzola, Aziz-Zadeh and Keysers 2006; Kaplan and Iacoboni 2006) or during perception of others' emotional expressions (Chakrabarti, Bullmore and Baron-Cohen 2007; Schulte-Rüther, Markowitsch, Fink et al. 2007). Another study (Tankersley, Stowe and Huettel 2007) found that a self-report measure of altruism was positively associated with individual differences in activity in posterior superior temporal sulcus, while observing another agent perform a task, in contrast to performing the task oneself.

Other brain regions, beyond those typically identified as involved in social information-processing, have also been associated with trait measures of empathy. One study (Chakrabarti, Bullmore and Baron-Cohen 2007) demonstrated that viewing different emotional expressions led to correlations of empathy with activity in brain regions functionally relevant to the specific emotion in question (e.g., observing happiness activated the ventral striatal reward system more strongly for participants high in empathy). Another study (Singer, Seymour, O'Doherty et al. 2004) found that empathy was associated with brain activity in the insula and anterior cingulate (regions involved in the affective component of pain), while watching a loved one experience pain. These findings suggest the degree to which empathy may involve recruiting brain regions involved in relevant emotions while observing others, a process potentially coordinated by the brain regions described above as subserving social information-processing.

Agreeableness, like Neuroticism, has been associated with variation of the serotonin transporter gene (Canli and Lesch 2007; Jang, Hu, Livesley *et al.* 2001; Wand, McCaul, Yang *et al.* 2002), but there are other endogenous psycho-active substances in addition to serotonin that may contribute to Agreeableness, including the socio-sexual neuropeptides oxytocin and vasopressin and the sex hormones testosterone and estrogen. Oxytocin is involved in social bonding (Depue and Morrone-Strupinsky 2005), and acute administration of oxytocin in human males has been found to improve their ability to identify others' emotional states from facial expressions (Domes, Heinrichs, Michel *et al.* 2007). Testosterone is linked to aggression, and evidence exists to suggest that higher exposure to testosterone is linked to reduced Agreeableness. The ratio of the length of the fourth finger to the second (4D:2D) is an index of prenatal exposure to testosterone (Manning 2002; McIntyre 2006). Not only has 4D:2D been linked to aggression (McIntyre, Barrett, McDermott *et al.* 2007), it has also been shown to correlate negatively with Agreeableness (Luxen and Buunk 2005).

Conscientiousness

Whereas Agreeableness is associated with the maintenance of social stability between individuals, Conscientiousness appears to reflect the tendency to maintain motivational stability within the individual, to make plans and carry them out in an organized and industrious manner. Such top-down control of motivation should be necessary only in species capable of formulating long-term goals that might conflict with more immediate urges. In personality studies of other species, only the chimpanzee, our nearest evolutionary neighbour, has yet been found to possess a trait directly analogous to Conscientiousness (Gosling and John 1999).

Conscientiousness may represent the purest manifestation in personality of the ability and tendency to constrain immediate impulses in favour of longer-term goals. Many traits that are theoretically and statistically related to Conscientiousness, such as Cloninger's Novelty-Seeking or Zuckerman's Impulsive Sensation-Seeking, appear to be less specific than Conscientiousness, in that they load heavily on other Big Five factors in addition to Conscientiousness. This non-specificity may reflect the fact that problems of impulse control could be exacerbated both by weakness of whatever systems override impulses (the presumed substrate of Conscientiousness) or by potentiation of the impulses themselves. A factor analysis of many questionnaire measures of impulsivity (Whiteside and Lynam 2001) found four factors, only two of which (labelled *lack of perseverance* and *lack of premeditation*) mapped onto Conscientiousness. The other two, labelled *urgency* and *sensation-seeking*, mapped onto Neuroticism and Extraversion, respectively, and appeared to describe strong impulses related to punishment and reward. In a similar vein, Depue and Collins (1999) argued that, although theorists have often associated impulsivity with Extraversion, impulsivity might be better conceived as a compound trait emerging from the combination of high Extraversion and low Constraint or Conscientiousness.

High Neuroticism may also play a role in this compound (Whiteside and Lynam 2001).

When considering research on the biological basis of the various impulsivity-related traits, one must bear in mind that most are related to multiple Big Five dimensions. Zuckerman (2005) noted that many studies have found Impulsive Sensation-Seeking and similar traits to be associated with high levels of dopaminergic function and low levels of serotonergic function. However, he argued that dopamine is associated with the approach tendencies reflected in these traits, whereas low serotonin is related to the absence of control or restraint. Involvement of serotonin in control and restraint is consistent with findings that serotonin is associated with Conscientiousness (Manuck, Flory, McCaffery *et al.* 1998, Rosenberg, Templeton, Feigin *et al.* 2006).

Another biological factor that may be related to Conscientiousness is glucose metabolism. Glucose represents the basic energy source for the brain, and a number of studies indicate that blood-glucose is depleted by acts of self-control and that the extent of this depletion predicts failures of self-control (Gailliot, Baumeister, DeWall *et al.* 2007; Gailliot and Baumeister 2007). Further, a self-report measure of trait self-control, which correlates highly with Conscientiousness, similarly predicts failures of self-control (Gailliot, Schmeichel and Baumeister 2006; Tangney, Baumeister and Boone 2004). Perhaps individuals whose metabolism provides their brains with an ample and steady supply of glucose are likely to be higher in Conscientiousness. If individual differences in glucose metabolism prove to be involved in Conscientiousness, one will also want to know what brain systems are consuming glucose to fuel acts of self-control. The prefrontal cortex seems likely to be involved, given its central role in planning and voluntary control of behaviour, and given that its consumption of glucose appears relatively high (Gailliot and Baumeister 2007). An fMRI study (Brown, Manuck, Flory and Hariri 2006) showed that brain activity in ventral prefrontal cortex during a response inhibition task was negatively associated with a questionnaire measure of impulsivity that is strongly negatively correlated with Conscientiousness (Whiteside and Lynam 2001).

Openness/Intellect

Openness/Intellect is perhaps the least studied of the Big Five from a psychobiological perspective. However, Openness/Intellect is the only Big Five trait consistently positively associated with intelligence, and one study found it to be the only Big Five trait associated with performance on a battery of working memory and cognitive control tests (DeYoung, Peterson and Higgins 2005), all of which had been validated through neuroimaging and brain lesion studies as indices of dorsolateral prefrontal cortical function. The attentional network in which the dorsolateral prefrontal cortex plays a key role has been consistently linked to fluid intelligence, the ability to solve novel problems (Gray and Thompson 2004). Work on the neurobiology of intelligence, working memory and attention may, therefore, aid in identifying the neural substrates of Openness/Intellect. As mentioned above, dopamine may be involved in Openness/Intellect (DeYoung, Peterson and Higgins 2005; Harris, Wright, Hayward *et al.* 2005); dopamine strongly modulates the function of lateral prefrontal cortex (Arnsten and Robbins 2002) and has been linked to individual differences in fluid intelligence and working memory through genomics, pharmacological manipulation and neuroimaging (e.g., Volkow 1998; Mattay, Goldberg, Fera *et al.* 2003).

Though some have argued that intelligence and personality are categorically distinct (e.g., Eysenck 1994), such an approach is not consistent with the rationale behind the development of the Big Five personality model as a comprehensive classification of trait descriptors – as such, it cannot arbitrarily exclude descriptors related to intelligence. Some of the debate on this subject has stemmed from the fact that the label 'Openness to Experience' is not very similar to 'intelligence', conceptually (McCrae 1994; McCrae and Costa 1997). However, other researchers have used the label 'Intellect' for this trait, and use of the compound label Openness/Intellect reflects the conclusion that Openness and Intellect simply reflect different aspects of one larger domain of personality (DeYoung, Peterson and Higgins 2005; Johnson 1994; Saucier 1992). These two aspects are related but separable and appear to have partially distinct genetic bases (DeYoung, Quilty and Peterson 2007). Fluid intelligence and working memory seem to be related primarily to the aspect of Openness/Intellect that can be described as Intellect, whereas crystallized or verbal intelligence is associated not only with Intellect but also with the artistic and contemplative traits that characterize the Openness aspect of the domain (DeYoung, Peterson and Higgins 2005; DeYoung, Quilty and Peterson 2007). Together Openness and Intellect appear to describe a range of traits related to cognitive and perceptual flexibility and exploration and to the various brain processes that support these cognitive functions (DeYoung, Peterson and Higgins 2005).

Conclusion

A neuroscience approach to personality research has the potential to provide personality psychology with explanatory models. The Big Five appears to be a promising broad framework for conceptualizing individual differences in phenotypic traits in terms of basic psychobiological functions. The Five-Factor Theory of McCrae and Costa (1999) makes a similar claim but does not go on to elaborate specific hypotheses about the biological sources of individual traits. As the above review demonstrates, however, neuroscientific research on personality has advanced to the point where some hypotheses can be made.

The youth of the field of personality neuroscience necessitates that many of these hypotheses currently exist at a fairly low level of resolution. Both traits and the brain systems that underlie them will need to be more specifically defined as the field progresses. Each of the Big Five covers a broad domain of psychological functioning. Although the biological mechanisms discussed above may be at least partially responsible for the coherence of these domains (i.e., the co-variance of the lower-level traits within them), specific biological mechanisms must also differentiate their lower-level traits. For example, each of the Big Five appears to be divisible into two distinct phenotypic aspects with partially distinct genetic bases (DeYoung, Quilty and Peterson 2007; Jang, Hu, Livesley *et al.* 2002). At an even lower level of the hierarchy, the many facet-level traits within each domain similarly show unique genetic contributions (Jang, Hu, Livesley *et al.* 2002; Jang, McCrae, Angleitner *et al.* 1998). Eventually, personality neuroscience may explain the co-variation of traits at many levels of the personality hierarchy.

Traits are probabilistic constructs representing the frequencies and intensities of particular classes of affect, behaviour and cognition across situations (Fleeson 2001; Mischel and Shoda 1998). Standard personality measures provide little information about the situations that elicit these processes for any given individual, but methods exist to make such assessments (Fleeson 2007; Roberts 2007; Wood and Roberts 2006). Exploring the neural mechanisms involved in linking basic tendencies to specific eliciting stimuli may become the ultimate in fine-grained analysis, as the field of personality neuroscience progresses. Such investigations, however, must be integrated with knowledge of how personality is organized at the broadest levels, where large neural networks and broadly acting neuromodulators are likely to be important across situations that share only some broad features. Psychobiological models of the Big Five and their meta-traits are a promising place to begin.

References

Allison, T., Puce, A. and McCarthy, G. 2000. Social perception from visual cues: role of the STS region, *Trends in Cognitive Sciences* 4: 267–78

Aluja, A., García, O. and García, L. F. 2002. A comparative study of Zuckerman's three structural models for personality through the NEO-PI-R, ZKPQ-III-R, EPQ-RS and Goldberg's 50-bipolar adjectives, *Personality and Individual Differences* 33: 713–25

  2004. Replicability of the three, four and five Zuckerman's personality super-factors: exploratory and confirmatory factor analysis of the EPQ-RS, ZKPQ and NEO-PI-R, *Personality and Individual Differences* 36: 1093–108

Ando, J., Suzuki, A., Yamagata, S., Kijima, N., Maekawa, H., Ono, Y. and Jang, K. L. 2004. Genetic and environmental structure of Cloninger's temperament and character dimensions, *Journal of Personality Disorders* 18: 379–93

Angleitner, A., Riemann, R. and Spinath, F. M. 2004. Investigating the ZKPQ-III-R: psychometric properties, relations to the Five-Factor Model and genetic and environmental influences on its scales and facets, in R. M. Stelmack (ed.), *On the psychobiology of personality: essays in honor of Marvin Zuckerman*, pp. 89–105. New York: Elsevier

Arnsten, A. F. T. and Robbins, T. W. 2002. Neurochemical modulation of prefrontal cortical function, in D. T. Stuss and R. T. Knight (eds.), *Principles of frontal lobe function*, pp. 51–84. New York: Oxford University Press

Ashby, F. G., Isen, A. M. and Turken, A. U. 1999. A neuropsychological theory of positive affect and its influence on cognition, *Psychological Review* 106: 529–50

Ashton, M. C., Lee, K., Perugini, M., Szarota, P., de Vries, R. E., Blas, L. D., Boies, K. and De Raad, B. 2004. A six-factor structure of personality descriptive adjectives:

solutions from psycholexical studies in seven languages, *Journal of Personality and Social Psychology* 86: 356–66

Ball, S. A., Tennen, H. and Kranzler, H. R. 1999. Factor replicability and validity of the Temperament and Character Inventory in substance-dependent patients, *Psychological Assessment* 11: 514–24

Beaver, J. D., Lawrence, A. D., van Ditzhuijzen, J., Davis, M. H., Woods, A. and Calder, A. J. 2006. Individual differences in reward drive predict neural responses to images of food, *Journal of Neuroscience* 26: 5160–6

Benjamin, J., Li, L., Patterson, C., Greenberg, B. D., Murphy, D. L. and Hamer, D. H. 1996. Population and familial association between the D4 dopamine receptor gene and measures of novelty seeking, *Nature Genetics* 12: 81–4

Bookman, E. B., Taylor, R. E., Adams-Campbell, L. and Kittles, R. A. 2002. DRD4 promoter SNPs and gender effects on Extraversion in African Americans, *Molecular Psychiatry* 7: 786–9

Bouchard, T. J. 1994. Genes, environment, and personality, *Science* 264: 1700–1

Braver, T. S. and Barch, D. M. 2002. A theory of cognitive control, aging cognition, and neuromodulation, *Neuroscience and Biobehavioural Review* 26: 809–17

Brown, S. M., Manuck, S. B., Flory, J. D. and Hariri, A. R. 2006. Neural basis of individual differences in impulsivity: contributions of corticolimbic circuits for behavioural arousal and control, *Emotion* 6: 239–45

Canli, T. and Lesch, K.-P. 2007. Long story short: the serotonin transporter in emotion regulation and social cognition, *Nature Neuroscience* 10: 1103–9

Canli, T., Sivers, I., Whitfield, S. L., Gotlib, I. H. and Gabrieli, J. D. E. 2002. Amygdala response to happy faces as a function of Extraversion, *Science* 296: 2191

Canli, T., Zhao, Z., Desmond, J. E., Kang, E., Gross, J. and Gabrieli, J. D. E. 2001. An fMRI study of personality influences on brain reactivity to emotional stimuli, *Behavioural Neuroscience* 115: 33–42

Chakrabarti, B., Bullmore, E. and Baron-Cohen, S. 2007. Empathizing with basic emotions: common and discrete neural substrates, *Social Neuroscience* 1: 364–84

Cloninger, C. R. 1987. A systematic method for clinical description and classification of personality variants, *Archives of General Psychiatry* 44: 573–88

Cloninger, C. R., Svrakic, D. M. and Przybeck, T. R. 1993. A psychobiological model of temperament and character, *Archives of General Psychiatry* 50: 975–90

Cohen, M. X., Young, J., Baek, J.-M., Kessler, C. and Ranganath, C. 2005. Individual differences in extraversion and dopamine genetics predict neural reward responses, *Cognitive Brain Research* 25: 851–61

Cools, R., Calder, A. J., Lawrence, A. D., Clark, L., Bullmore, E. and Robbins, T. W. 2005. Individual differences in threat sensitivity predict serotonergic modulation of amygdala response to fearful faces, *Psychopharmacology* 180: 670–9

Costa, P. T., Jr. and McCrae, R. R. 1992. Four ways five factors are basic, *Personality and Individual Differences* 13: 653–65

Davidson, R. J. 2002. Anxiety and affective style: role of prefrontal cortex and amygdala, *Biological Psychiatry* 51: 68–80

Davis, K. L., Panksepp, J. and Normansell, L. 2003. The Affective Neuroscience Personality Scales: normative data and implications, *Neuro-Psychoanalysis* 5: 57–69

Deckersbach, T., Miller, K. K., Klibanski, A., Fischman, A., Dougherty, D. D., Blais, M. A., Herzog, D. B. and Rauch, S. L. 2006. Regional cerebral brain metabolism correlates of Neuroticism and Extraversion, *Depression and Anxiety* 23: 133–8

Depue, R. A. and Collins, P. F. 1999. Neurobiology of the structure of personality: dopamine, facilitation of incentive motivation, and extraversion, *Behavioural and Brain Sciences* 22: 491–569

Depue, R. A. and Lenzenweger, M. F. 2005. A neurobehavioural dimensional model of personality disturbance, in M Lenzenweger and J Clarkin (eds.), *Theories of personality disorders*, 2nd edn, pp. 391–454. New York: Guilford Press

Depue, R. A. and Morrone-Strupinsky, J. V. 2005. A neurobehavioural model of affiliative bonding: implications for conceptualizing a human trait of affiliation, *Behavioural and Brain Sciences* 28: 313–50

DeYoung, C. G. 2006. Higher-order factors of the Big Five in a multi-informant sample, *Journal of Personality and Social Psychology* 91: 1138–51

DeYoung, C. G., Peterson, J. B. and Higgins, D. M. 2002. Higher-order factors of the Big Five predict conformity: are there neuroses of health? *Personality and Individual Differences* 33: 533–52

   2005. Sources of Openness/Intellect: cognitive and neuropsychological correlates of the fifth factor of personality, *Journal of Personality* 73: 825–58

DeYoung, C. G., Quilty, L. C. and Peterson, J. B. 2007. Between facets and domains: ten aspects of the Big Five, *Journal of Personality and Social Psychology* 93: 880–96

Digman, J. M. 1990. Personality structure: emergence of the five-factor model, *Annual Review of Psychology* 41: 417–40

   1997. Higher-order factors of the Big Five, *Journal of Personality and Social Psychology* 73: 1246–56

Domes, G., Heinrichs, M., Michel, A., Berger, C. and Herpertz, S. C. 2007. Oxytocin improves 'mind-reading' in humans, *Biological Psychiatry* 61: 731–3

Eichhammer, P., Sand, P. G., Stoertebecker, P., Langguth, B., Zowe, M. and Hajak, G. 2005. Variation at the DRD4 promoter modulates extraversion in Caucasians, *Molecular Psychiatry* 10: 520–2

Eisenberger, N. I., Lieberman, M. D. and Satpute, A. B. 2005. Personality from a controlled processing perspective: an fMRI study of neuroticism, extraversion, and self-consciousness, *Cognitive Affective Behavioural Neuroscience* 5: 169–81

Elliot, A. J. and Thrash, T. M. 2002. Approach-avoidance motivation in personality: approach and avoidance temperaments and goals, *Journal of Personality and Social Psychology* 82: 804–18

Etkin, A., Klemenhagen, K. C., Dudman, J. T., Rogan, M. T., Hen, R., Kandel, E. R. and Hirsch, J. 2004. Individual differences in trait anxiety predict the response of the basolateral amygdala to unconsciously processed fearful faces, *Neuron* 44: 1043–55

Eysenck, H. J. 1967. *The biological basis of personality.* Springfield, IL: Thomas

   1992. The definition and measurement of Psychoticism, *Personality and Individual Differences* 13: 757–85

   1994. Personality and intelligence: psychometric and experimental approaches, in R. J. Sternberg and P. Ruzgis (eds.), *Personality and intelligence*, pp. 3–31. New York: Cambridge University Press

   1997. Personality and experimental psychology: the unification of psychology and the possibility of a paradigm, *Journal of Personality and Social Psychology* 73: 1224–37

Eysenck, H. J. and Eysenck, M. W. 1985. *Personality and individual differences.* New York: Plenum

Fleeson, W. 2001. Towards a structure- and process-integrated view of personality: traits as density distributions of states, *Journal of Personality and Social Psychology* 80: 1011–27

2007. Situation-based contingencies underlying trait-content manifestation in behaviour, *Journal of Personality* 75: 825–62

Gailliot, M. T. and Baumeister, R. F. 2007. The physiology of willpower: linking blood glucose to self-control, *Personality and Social Psychology Review* 11: 303–27

Gailliot, M. T., Baumeister, R. F., DeWall, C. N., Maner, J. K., Plant, E. A., Tice, D. M., Brewer, L. E. and Schmeichel, B. J. 2007. Self-control relies on glucose as a limited energy source: willpower is more than a metaphor, *Journal of Personality and Social Psychology* 92: 325–36

Gailliot, M. T., Schmeichel, B. J. and Baumeister, R. F. 2006. Self-regulatory processes defend against the threat of death: effects of self-control depletion and trait self-control on thoughts and fears of dying, *Journal of Personality and Social Psychology* 91: 49–62

Gazzola, V., Aziz-Zadeh, L. and Keysers, C. 2006. Empathy and the somatotopic auditory mirror system in humans, *Current Biology* 16: 1824–9

Gillespie, N. A., Cloninger, C. R., Heath, A. C. and Martin, N. G. 2003. The genetic and environmental relationship between Cloninger's dimensions of temperament and character, *Personality and Individual Differences* 35: 1931–46

Goldberg, L. R. and Rosolack, T. K. 1994. The big five factor structure as an integrative framework: an empirical comparison with Eysenck's P-E-N model, in C. F. Halverson, Jr, G. A. Kohnstamm and R. P. Martin (eds.), *The developing structure of temperament and personality from infancy to adulthood*, pp. 7–35. Hillsdale, NJ: Lawrence Erlbaum Associates

Gosling, S. D. and John, O. P. 1999. Personality dimensions in nonhuman animals: a cross-species review, *Current Directions in Psychological Science* 8: 69–75

Gray, J. A. 1982. *The neuropsychology of anxiety: an enquiry into the functions of the septo-hippocampal system*. New York: Oxford University Press

Gray, J. A. and McNaughton, N. 2000. *The neuropsychology of anxiety: an enquiry into the functions of the septo-hippocampal system*, 2nd edn. New York: Oxford University Press

Gray, J. R. 2004. Integration of emotion and cognitive control, *Current Directions in Psychological Science* 13: 46–8

Gray, J. R. and Braver, T. S. 2002. Personality predicts working memory related activation in the caudal anterior cingulate cortex, *Cognitive, Affective, and Behavioural Neuroscience* 2: 64–75

Gray, J. R., Braver, T. S. and Raichle, M. E. 2002. Integration of emotion and cognition in the lateral prefrontal cortex, *Proceedings of the National Academy of Sciences USA* 99: 4115–20

Gray, J. R., Burgess, G. C., Schaefer, A., Yarkoni, T., Larsen, R. J. and Braver, T. S. 2005. Affective personality differences in neural processing efficiency confirmed using fMRI, *Cognitive, Affective and Behavioural Neuroscience* 5: 182–90

Gray, J. R. and Thompson, P. M. 2004. Neurobiology of intelligence: science and ethics, *Nature Reviews Neuroscience* 5: 471–82

Haas, B. W., Omura, K., Constable, T. and Canli, T. 2007. Emotional conflict and Neuroticism: personality-dependent activation in the amygdala and subgenual anterior cingulate, *Behavioural Neuroscience* 121: 249–56

Haig, B. D. 2005. Exploratory factor analysis, theory generation, and scientific method, *Multivariate Behavioural Research* 40: 303–29

Harmon-Jones, E. 2004. Contributions from research on anger and cognitive dissonance to understanding the motivational functions of asymmetrical frontal brain activity, *Biological Psychology* 67: 51–76

Harmon-Jones, E. and Allen, J. J. B. 1998. Anger and frontal brain activity: EEG asymmetry consistent with approach motivation despite negative affective valence, *Journal of Personality and Social Psychology* 74: 1310–16

Harris, S. E., Wright, A. F., Hayward, C., Starr, J. M., Whalley, L. J. and Deary, I. J. 2005. The functional COMT polymorphism, Val158Met, is associated with logical memory and the personality trait intellect/imagination in a cohort of healthy 79 year olds, *Neuroscience Letters* 385: 1–6

Hennig, J. 2004. Personality, serotonin, and noradrenaline, in R. M. Stelmack (ed.), *On the psychobiology of personality: essays in honor of Marvin Zuckerman*, pp. 379–95. New York: Elsevier

Herbst, J. H., Zonderman, A. B., McCrae, R. R. and Costa, P. T. 2000. Do the dimensions of the Temperament and Character Inventory map a simple genetic architecture? Evidence from molecular genetics and factor analysis, *American Journal of Psychiatry* 157: 1285–90

Hofstee, W. K., de Raad, B. and Goldberg, L. R. 1992. Integration of the Big Five and circumplex approaches to trait structure, *Journal of Personality and Social Psychology* 63: 146–63

Iacoboni, M. 2007. Face to face: the neural basis of social mirroring and empathy, *Psychiatric Annals* 37: 236–41

Jang, K. L., Hu, S., Livesley, W. J., Angleitner, A., Riemann, R., Ando, J., Ono, Y., Vernon, P. A. and Hamer, D. J. 2001. Covariance structure of Neuroticism and Agreeableness: a twin and molecular genetic analysis of the role of the serotonin transporter gene, *Journal of Personality and Social Psychology* 81: 295–304

Jang, K. L., Hu, S., Livesley, W. J., Angleitner, A., Riemann and Vernon, P. A. 2002. Genetic and environmental influences on the covariance of facets defining the domains of the Five-Factor Model of personality, *Personality and Individual Differences* 33: 83–101

Jang, K. L., Livesley, W. J., Ando, J., Yamagata, S., Suzuki, A., Angleitner, A., Ostendorf, F., Riemann, R. and Spinath, F. 2006. Behavioural genetics of the higher-order factors of the Big Five, *Personality and Individual Differences* 41: 261–72

Jang, K. L., McCrae, R. R., Angleitner, A., Riemann, R. and Livesley, W. J. 1998. Heritability of facet-level traits in a cross-cultural twin sample: support for a hierarchical model of personality, *Journal of Personality and Social Psychology* 74: 1556–65

John, O. P. and Srivastava, S. 1999. The Big Five trait taxonomy: history, measurement, and theoretical perspectives, in L. A. Pervin and O. P. John (eds.), *Handbook of personality: theory and research*, 2nd edn, pp. 102–38. New York: Guilford Press

Johnson, J. A. 1994. Clarification of factor five with the help of the AB5C model, *European Journal of Personality* 8: 311–34

Kaplan, J. T. and Iacoboni, M. 2006. Getting a grip on other minds: mirror neurons, intention understanding and cognitive empathy, *Social Neuroscience* 1: 175–83

Keightley, M. L., Seminowicz, D. A., Bagby, R. M., Costa, P. T., Fossati, P. and Mayberg, H. S. 2003. Personality influences limbic-cortical interactions during sad mood, *NeuroImage* 20: 2031–9

Kumari, V., Ffytche, D. H., Williams, S. C. R. and Gray, J. A. 2004. Personality predicts brain responses to cognitive demands, *Journal of Neuroscience* 24: 10636–41

Lesch, K. P., Bengel, D., Heils, A., Sabol, S. Z., Greenberg, B. D., Petri, S., Benjamin, J., Muller, C. R., Hamer, D. H. and Murphy, D. L. 1996. Association of anxiety-related traits with a polymorphism in the serotonin transporter gene regulatory region, *Science* 274: 1527–31

Loehlin, J. C. 1992. *Genes and environment in personality development*. Newbury Park, CA: Sage

Luxen, M. F. and Buunk, B. P. 2005. Second-to-fourth digit ratio related to verbal and numerical intelligence and the Big Five, *Personality and Individual Differences* 39: 959–66

MacDonald, K. 1998. Evolution, culture, and the Five-Factor Model, *Journal of Cross-Cultural Psychology* 29: 119–49

Manning, J. T. 2002. *Digit ratio: a pointer to fertility, behaviour, and health*. New Brunswick, NJ: Rutgers University Press

Manuck, S. B., Flory, J. D., McCaffery, J. M., Matthews, K. A., Mann, J. J. and Muldoon, M. F. 1998. Aggression, impulsivity, and central nervous system serotonergic responsivity in a nonpatient sample, *Neuropsychopharmacology* 19: 287–99

Markon, K. E., Krueger, R. F. and Watson, D. 2005. Delineating the structure of normal and abnormal personality: an integrative hierarchical approach, *Journal of Personality and Social Psychology* 88: 139–57

Mattay, V. S., Goldberg, T. E., Fera, F., Hariri, A. R., Tessitore, A., Egan, M. F., Kolachana, B., Callicott, J. H. and Weinberger, D. R. 2003. Catechol O-methyltransferase val158-met genotype and individual variation in the brain response to amphetamine, *Proceedings of the National Academy of Science USA* 100: 6186–91

Matthews, G. and Gilliland, K. 1999. The personality theories of H. J. Eysenck and J. A. Gray: a comparative review, *Personality and Individual Differences* 26: 583–626

McAdams, D. P. and Pals, J. L. 2006. A new Big Five: fundamental principles for an integrative science of personality, *American Psychologist* 61: 204–17

McCrae, R. R. 1994. Openness to experience: expanding the boundaries of Factor V, *European Journal of Personality* 8: 251–72

McCrae, R. R. and Costa, P. T., Jr 1997. Conceptions and correlates of Openness to Experience, in R. Hogan, J. Johnson and S. Briggs (eds.), *Handbook of personality psychology*, pp. 825–47. Boston: Academic Press

1999. A five factor theory of personality, in L. A. Pervin and O. P. John (eds). *Handbook of personality: theory and research*, pp. 102–38. New York: Guilford Press

McEwen, B. S. 1998. Stress, adaptation, and disease: allostasis and allostatic load, *Annals of the New York Academy of Science* 840: 33–44

McIntyre, M. H. 2006. The use of digit ratios as markers for perinatal androgen action, *Reproductive Biology and Endocrinology* 2: 10

McIntyre, M. H., Barrett, E. S., McDermott, R., Johnson, D. D. P., Cowden, J. and Rosen, S. P. 2007. Finger length ratio (2D:4D) and sex differences in aggression during a simulated war game, *Personality and Individual Differences* 42: 755–64

Mischel, W. and Shoda, Y. 1998. Reconciling processing dynamics and personality dispositions, *Annual Review of Psychology* 49: 229–58

Mobbs, D., Hagan, C. C., Azim, E., Menon, V. and Reiss, A. L. 2005. Personality predicts activity in reward and emotional regions associated with humor, *Proceedings of the National Academy of Science USA* 102: 16502–6

Netter, P. 2004. Personality and hormones, in R. M. Stelmack (ed.), *On the psychobiology of personality: essays in honor of Marvin Zuckerman*, pp. 353–77. New York: Elsevier

Nettle, D. 2006. The evolution of personality variation in humans and other animals, *American Psychologist* 61: 622–31

Ohmura, Y., Takahashi, T., Kitamura, N. and Wehr, P. 2006. Three-month stability of delay and probability discounting measures, *Experimental and Clinical Psychopharmacology* 14: 318–28

Ozkaragoz, T. and Noble, E. P. 2000. Extraversion: interaction between D2 dopamine receptor polymorphisms and parental alcoholism, *Alcohol* 22: 139–46

Panksepp, J. 1998. *Affective neuroscience: the foundations of human and animal emotion.* New York: Oxford University Press

Paris, J. 2005. Neurobiological dimensional models of personality: a review of the models of Cloninger, Depue, and Siever, *Journal of Personality Disorders* 19: 156–70

Peterson, J. B. and Carson, S. 2000. Latent inhibition and openness to experience in a high-achieving student population, *Personality and Individual Differences* 28: 323–32

Peterson, J. B., Smith, K. W. and Carson, S. 2002. Openness and Extraversion are associated with reduced latent inhibition: replication and commentary, *Personality and Individual Differences* 33: 1137–47

Pickering, A. D. 2004. The neuropsychology of impulsive antisocial sensation seeking personality traits: from dopamine to hippocampal function?, in R. M. Stelmack (ed.), *On the psychobiology of personality: essays in honor of Marvin Zuckerman*, pp. 453–77. New York: Elsevier

Pickering, A. D. and Gray, J. A. 1999. The neuroscience of personality, in L. A. Pervin and O. P. John (eds.), *Handbook of personality: theory and research*, 2nd edn, pp. 277–99. New York: Guilford Press

Pytlik Zillig, L. M., Hemenover, S. H. and Dienstbier, R. A. 2002. What do we assess when we assess a Big 5 trait? A content analysis of the affective, behavioural and cognitive processes represented in the Big 5 personality inventories, *Personality and Social Psychology Bulletin* 28: 847–58

Ramanaiah, N. V., Rielage, J. K. and Cheng, Y. 2002. Cloninger's temperament and character inventory and the NEO Five–Factor Inventory, *Psychological Reports* 90: 59–63

Reuter M. and Hennig, J. 2005. Association of the functional catechol-O-methyltransferase VAL158MET polymorphism with the personality trait of Extraversion, *NeuroReport* 16: 1135–8

Reuter, M., Schmitz, A., Corr, P. and Henning, J. 2005. Molecular genetics support Gray's personality theory: the interaction of *COMT* and *DRD2* polymorphisms predicts the behavioural approach system, *International Journal of Neuropsychopharmacology* 8: 1–12

Reuter, M., Stark, R., Henning, J., Walter, B., Kirsch, P., Schienle, A. and Vaitl, D. 2004. Personality and emotion: test of Gray's personality theory by means of an fMRI study, *Behavioural Neuroscience* 118: 462–9

Riemann, R., Angleitner, A. and Strelau, J. 1997. Genetic and environmental influences on personality: a study of twins reared together using the self- and peer report NEO-FFI scales, *Journal of Personality* 65: 449–76

Rizzolatti, G. and Craighero, L. 2004. The mirror-neuron system, *Annual Review of Neuroscience* 27: 169–92

Roberts, B. W. 2007. Contextualizing personality psychology, *Journal of Personality* 75: 1071–81

Rosenberg, S., Templeton, A. R., Feigin, P. D., Lancet, D., Beckmann, J. S., Selig, S., Hamer, D. H. and Skorecki, K. 2006. The association of DNA sequence variation at the MAOA genetic locus with quantitative behavioural traits in normal males, *Human Genetics* 120: 447–59

Saucier, G. 1992. Openness versus intellect: much ado about nothing?, *European Journal of Personality* 6: 381–6

Saucier, G. and Goldberg, L. R. 2001. Lexical studies of indigenous personality factors: premises, products, and prospects, *Journal of Personality* 69: 847–79

Saxe, R. and Powell, L. J. 2006. It's the thought that counts: specific brain regions for one component of theory of mind, *Psychological Science* 17: 692–9

Schinka, J. A., Busch, R. M. and Robichaux-Keene, N. 2004. A meta-analysis of the association between the serotonin transporter gene polymorphism (5-HTTLPR) and trait anxiety, *Molecular Psychiatry* 9: 197–202

Schulte-Rüther, M., Markowitsch, H. J., Fink, G. R. and Piefke, M. 2007. Mirror neuron and theory of mind mechanisms involved in face-to-face interactions: a functional magnetic resonance imaging approach to empathy, *Journal of Cognitive Neuroscience* 19: 1354–72

Seitz, R. J., Nickel, J. and Azari, N. P. 2006. Functional modularity of the medial prefrontal cortex: involvement in human empathy, *Neuropsychology* 20: 743–51

Sen, S., Burmeister, M. and Ghosh, D. 2004. Meta-analysis of the association between a serotonin transporter promoter polymorphism (5-HTTLPR) and anxiety-related personality traits, *American Journal of Medical Genetics Part B (Neuropsychiatric Genetics)* 127B: 85–9

Singer, T., Seymour, B., O'Doherty, J., Kaube, H., Dolan, R. J. and Frith, C. D. 2004. Empathy for pain involves the affective but not sensory components of pain, *Science* 303: 1157–62

Smillie, L. D., Pickering, A. D. and Jackson, C. J. 2006. The new Reinforcement Sensitivity Theory: implications for personality measurement, *Personality and Social Psychology Review* 10: 320–35

Spoont, M. R. 1992. Modulatory role of serotonin in neural information processing: implications for human psychopathology, *Psychological Bulletin* 112: 330–50

Tangney, J. P., Baumeister, R. F. and Boone, A. L. 2004. High self-control predicts good adjustment, less pathology, better grades, and interpersonal success, *Journal of Personality* 72: 271–322

Tankersley, D., Stowe, C. J. and Huettel, S. A. 2007. Altruism is associated with an increased neural response to agency, *Nature Neuroscience* 10: 150–1

Tauscher, J., Bagby, M. R., Javanmard, M., Christensen, B. K., Kasper, S. and Kapur, S. 2001. Inverse relationship between serotonin 5-HT1a receptor binding and anxiety: a [^{11}C]WAY-100635 PET investigation in healthy volunteers, *American Journal of Psychiatry* 158: 1326–8

Tellegen, A. 1982. *Brief manual for the Multidimensional Personality Questionnaire.* Unpublished manuscript. Minneapolis, MN: University of Minnesota

Tochigi, M., Otowa, T., Hibino, H., Kato, C., Otani, T., Umekage, T., Utsumi, T., Kato, N. and Sasaki, T. 2006. Combined analysis of association between personality traits and three functional polymorphisms in the tyrosine hydroxylase, monoamine oxidase A, and catechol-O-methyltransferase genes, *Neuroscience Research* 54: 180–5

Volkow, N. D., Gur, R. C., Wang, G.-J., Fowler, J. S., Moberg, P. J., Ding, Y.-S., Hitzemann, R., Smith, G. and Logan, J. 1998. Association between decline in brain dopamine activity with age and cognitive and motor impairment in healthy individuals, *American Journal of Psychiatry* 155: 344–9

Wacker, J., Chavanon, M.-L. and Stemmler, G. 2006. Investigating the dopaminergic basis of Extraversion in humans: a multilevel approach, *Journal of Personality and Social Psychology* 91: 71–87

Wacker, J. and Stemmler, G. 2006. Agentic extraversion modulates the cardiovascular effects of the dopamine D2 agonist bromocriptine, *Psychophysiology* 43: 372–81

Wand, G. S., McCaul, M., Yang, X., Reynolds, J., Gotjen, D., Lee, S. and Ali, A. 2002. The mu-opioid receptor gene polymorphism (A118G) alters HPA axis activation induced by opioid receptor blockade, *Neuropsychopharmacology* 26: 106–14

White, T. L. and Depue, R. A. 1999. Differential association of traits of fear and anxiety with norepinephrine- and dark-induced pupil reactivity, *Journal of Personality and Social Psychology* 77: 863–77

Whiteside, S. P. and Lynam, R. W. 2001. The Five Factor Model and impulsivity: using a structural model of personality to understand impulsivity, *Personality and Individual Differences* 30: 669–89

Wood, D. and Roberts, B. W. 2006. Cross-sectional and longitudinal tests of the personality and role identity structural model (PRISM), *Journal of Personality* 74: 779–809

Yamagata, S., Suzuki, A., Ando, J., Ono, Y., Kijima, N., Yoshimura, K., Ostendorf, F., Angleitner, A., Riemann, R., Spinath, F. M., Livesley, W. J. and Jang, K. L. 2006. Is the genetic structure of human personality universal? A cross-cultural twin study from North America, Europe, and Asia, *Journal of Personality and Social Psychology* 90: 987–98

Zelenski, J. M. and Larsen, R. J. 1999. Susceptibility to affect: a comparison of three personality taxonomies, *Journal of Personality* 67: 761–91

Zuckerman, M. 2005. *Psychobiology of personality*, 2nd edn rev. and updated. New York: Cambridge University Press

Zuckerman, M., Kuhlman, D. M., Joireman, J., Teta, P. and Kraft, M. 1993. A comparison of three structural models of personality: the Big Three, the Big Five, and the Alternative Five, *Journal of Personality and Social Psychology* 65: 757–68

21 The Reinforcement Sensitivity Theory of Personality

Philip J. Corr

> Nature has placed mankind under the governance of two sovereign masters, pain and pleasure. It is for them alone to point out what we ought to do as well as to determine what we shall do. On the other hand, the standard of right and wrong, on the other chain of causes and effects, are fastened to their throne. They govern us in all we do, in all we say, in all we think; every effort we can make to throw off our subjection, will serve but to demonstrate and confirm it. In words a man may pretend to abjure their empire: but in reality he will remain subject to it all the while.
>
> (Jeremy Bentham, *Introduction to the Principles of Morals and Legislation* (1781))

In one form or another, Bentham's 'masters' of pain and pleasure remain the sovereign of behaviour, and underpin the moral and judicial framework of all societies. We have yet to document a society where behaviour is governed by the dominant pursuit of pain and the avoidance of pleasure – for sure, there are organizations (e.g., the Roman Catholic *Opus Dei*) where mortification, entailing physical pain, is sanctioned (indeed, in this example, sanctified); but, typically, these relatively mild forms of suffering are in the service of a greater pleasure (e.g., eternity in Heaven). Moving from the spiritual to the temporal plane, day-to-day life is regulated by striving for the good things (e.g., safety, food, drink and fulfilling social, personal and occupational pursuits), as well as the avoidance of bad things (e.g., dangerous animals, rotting food and criticism from other people) – that is, 'goods' and 'bads' in the nomenclature of rational economics. In our personal life, the power and ubiquity of these 'sovereign masters' is such that we rarely have the need to reflect upon them: they are accepted 'givens' of everyday life, even though they populate much of our conscious awareness, and in psycho-pathological conditions (e.g., Obsessional-Compulsive Disorder) dominate it. Their importance was recognized by twentieth century academic psychology, which was dominated by Behaviourism, with its focus on the role of reinforcement (positive and negative) and punishment in shaping behaviour (and the mind more generally), as well as the early philosophers of Ancient Greece (e.g., Epicures of Samos 341–270 BC, and Aristotle 384–322 BC). In other realms of life, such as the penal-justice system, considerations of 'right' and 'wrong' often reduce to questions of how best to design behavioural control instruments that, it is hoped, deter transgression of legal codes.

We may, therefore, sensibly enquire after a scientific theory that helps us to understand the psychology of the control of behaviour based on these sovereign masters; and we may also wonder why these sovereign masters are so often implicated in aberrations of normally-regulated behaviour, expressed in the variety of forms of psychopathology (e.g., the affective disorders and various addictions). Moreover, we may wonder as to the evolutionary foundations of these regulatory forces, and how they give rise to individual differences in the underlying neuropsychological systems that comprise 'personality' (Corr 2007). Indeed, we may go further to enquire as to the role they play in consciousness, where these sovereign masters are often found to exert their influence. This chapter discusses these issues in the context of one major neuropsychological theory that attempts to account for the influence of pain and pleasure on the variety of factors that compose human behavioural choreography.

Foundations of Reinforcement Sensitivity Theory

The Reinforcement Sensitivity Theory (RST)[1] of personality represents a bold attempt to account for the neuropsychological regulation of behaviour, and how individual differences in neuropsychological systems give rise to what we commonly label 'personality'. RST is based upon notions of central states of emotion and motivation that mediate the relations between stimulus input and behavioural response: here 'stimulus' and 'response' can be internal processes, and only inferred from ingenious behavioural experiments (e.g., sensory preconditioning; see McNaughton and Corr 2008).

In this section, I summarize the development of Jeffrey Gray's (1970, 1975, 1976, 1982) neuropsychological theory of emotion, motivation, learning and personality, which is now widely known as RST. Although it will be seen that much of the analysis of behaviour follows standard procedures used in behavioural psychology, as well as many of the experimental tools of the behaviourist, the explanatory framework is very different to that of the strict behaviourist, most famously B. F. Skinner who considered central states of emotion, etc. as wrong-headed causal 'fictions' (Skinner 1953). Stimuli per se do not affect behaviour (at least, in any simple sense); they merely have the potential to activate neuropsychological systems (i.e., internal processes) that control behavioural reactions: the mind is not a series of black boxes.[2] For a fully-satisfying scientific

---

[1] As noted by one of the originators of the name, 'Reinforcement Sensitivity Theory' (Pickering, Diaz and Gray 1995), Pickering (2008) considered alternative names: 'Reinforcement Reactivity Theory' and 'Motivational Input Sensitivity Theory'. Reinforcement 'sensitivity' is arguably the best choice as it does not require that activation of the systems will always be evident in overt, and directly measurable, behavioural reactions.

[2] The power of behavioural techniques, when stripped of related explanatory framework, provide the best behavioural evidence for the existence of central states of emotion and motivation; we see examples of this in the case of 'frustrative non-reward' and 'relief of non-punishment', which are, in strict behaviourist terms, non-events. Their effects only make sense if we infer central states of expectation, suggesting an internal comparator that compares expected and actual motivationally-significant inputs. For example, frustrative non-reward effects are seen in the partial reinforcement

explanation of behaviour control and regulation, it is to these neuropsychological systems that we must turn our attention.

RST evolved over the past forty years, from its inception in 1970, and it has gone through several refinements, most notably by Gray and McNaughton (2000). As we shall see throughout this chapter, RST can appear, at first blush, complex, indeed confusing, because it encompasses a number of approaches that move at different paces. This point is well made by Smillie, Pickering and Jackson (2006, p. 320), who note that, although RST is often seen as a theory of personality, it is 'more accurately identified as a neuropsychology of emotion, motivation and learning. In fact, RST was born of basic animal learning research, initially not at all concerned with personality'. The fact that RST is an evolving theory is a strength (i.e., it is 'progressive' theory; see Lakatos 1970); however, this state of flux makes it something of a moving target for personality researchers, 'as if it were frozen in time, Gray's "personality model" is a relatively discrete slice of an otherwise continuous and ongoing field of knowledge' (Smillie, Pickering and Jackson 2006, p. 321). As we shall see below, this problem can be much reduced by separating RST into its *state* and *traits* components.

Another important aspect of RST is the distinction between those parts that belong to the *conceptual nervous system* (cns) and those parts that belong to the *central nervous system* (CNS) (a distinction advanced by Hebb 1955). The cns component of RST provides the behavioural scaffolding, formalized within some theoretical framework (e.g., learning theory; see Gray 1975; or, ethoexperimental analysis; see Gray and McNaughton 2000); the CNS component specifies the brain systems involved, couched in terms of the latest knowledge of the neuro-endocrine system (see McNaughton and Corr 2008). As noted by Gray (1972a), these two levels of explanation *must* be compatible. Thus, we can talk of a *neuropsychology* of behaviour, as well as the effects of individual differences in the operating parameters of these systems that give rise to 'personality'. Gray used the language of cybernetics (cf. Weiner 1948) – the science of communication and control, comprising end-goals and feedback processes containing control of values within the system that guide the organism towards its final goal – in the form of a cns-CNS bridge, to show how the flow of information and control of outputs is achieved (see also, Gray 2004).

Identification and clarification of emotion and motivation systems

Before delving into the details of RST, it is important to appreciate the logic that underlies Gray's approach to science. In common with other theorists, Gray faced two major problems: first, how to identify brain systems responsible for behaviour; and, secondly, how to characterize these systems once identified.

---

extinction effect (PREE), the effects of which do not find cogent explanation in terms of non-emotional learning (see Fowles 2006).

The individual differences perspective is one major way of identifying major sources of variation in behaviour; by inference, there must be causal systems (i.e., sources) giving rise to observed variations in behaviour. Hans Eysenck's (1947, 1957, 1967) approach was to use multivariate statistical analysis to identify these major sources of variation in the form of personality dimensions. Gray accepted that this 'top-down' approach can identify the minimum *number* of sources of variation (i.e., the 'extraction problem' in factor analysis), but he argued that such statistical approaches can never resolve the correct *orientation* of these observed dimensions (i.e., the 'rotation problem' in factor analysis). Gray's alternative 'bottom-up' approach to identifying major systems of causal influence rested on other forms of evidence, including the effects of brain lesions, experimental brain research (e.g., intracranial self-stimulation studies), and, of most importance, the effects on behaviour of classes of drugs known to be effective in the treatment of psychiatric disorders: this was Gray's 'philosopher's stone' – transforming base pharmacological findings into a valuable neuropsychological theory. This was a subtle and clever way to expose the nature of fundamental emotion and motivation systems, especially those implicated in major forms of psychopathology.

Gray argued the following: if we want to know what is the brain-behavioural nature of 'anxiety' (the scary quotes here reflect the fact that the phenomenon to be explained has received only a partial and rather superficial description), then we can pursue the following course of action: (a) take drugs that are effective against human anxiety (i.e., those psychological disorders recognized as falling under the rubric of 'anxiety'); then (b) analyse their behavioural profile in non-human animals to understand their more fundamental nature; and then (c) compare these behavioural profiles with other drugs (e.g., psychostimulates). Thus, by a careful analysis of the behavioural effects of different *classes* of drugs (e.g., anxiety vs. psychostimulates), a detailed description may be formed of the underlying systems – the assumption that these different behavioural effects reflect different underlying systems follows standard neuroscientific reasoning (see Corr 2006).

Gray reasoned that anxiolytic (i.e., anti-anxiety) drugs provided a criterion for what constitutes anxiety. Gray (1977) provided an exhaustive review of the behavioural effects of minor tranquilizers (i.e., barbiturates, alcohol and benzodiazepines, which at that time were the dominant class of anxiolytic drugs) on the following behavioural paradigms: rewarded behaviour, passive avoidance, classical conditioning of fear, escape behaviour, one-way active avoidance, two-way active avoidance, responses elicited by aversive stimuli, and frustrative non-reward (as seen in resistance to extinction), discrimination learning, intermittent reinforcement schedules in the Skinner box, reduction of reward and the after-effects of reward. The reasoning proceeds that once a behavioural dissection has been achieved, based on behavioural reactions to classes of drugs, then it is much easier to identify actual neuropsychological systems that these drugs act upon. Following the emphasis of behavioural psychology on overt behaviour, Gray did not favour a research strategy based on a purely human and verbal source of information (e.g., self-reports of patients), but one that could be tested, via rigorous experimentation, in non-human animals: the goal of identifying the neural substrate for anxiety was, and largely still is, only possible with the use of experimental animals. Gray's whole theoretical approach rests and falls on these major assumptions.

The major findings from Gray's (1977) exhaustive review of the behavioural effects of anxiolytic drugs were: they anatagonize or reduce the behavioural effects (i.e., suppression of behaviour) associated with conditioned stimuli for punishment (Pun-CSs) and frustative non-reward (nonRew-CSs; i.e., the non-delivery of expected reward), as well as, but less strongly, novel stimuli. Noteworthy, was the relative absence of effects on behaviour controlled by *unconditioned* punishing or rewarding stimuli (i.e., innate stimuli). As discussed below, this evidence suggested that anxiolytic drugs acted on a system that was responsible for *behavioural inhibition* in reaction to conditioned signals of punishment, non-reward (frustration) and novelty.

States and traits

RST is built upon a description of the immediate/short-term *state* of neural systems: how animals, including the human form, respond to motivationally significant (i.e., 'reinforcing') stimuli, and which neuropsychological systems mediate these responses. Built upon this state infrastructure are longer-term *trait* dispositions of emotion, motivation and behaviour. As we move to psychopathology, we see the role played by both factors. Figure 21.1 shows a conceptual framework that illustrates these different processes.

RST assumes that personality factors revealed by multivariate statistical analysis (e.g., factor analysis) reflect sources of variation in neuropsychological systems that are stable over time – that is, they are properties of the individual. Personality traits account for behavioural *differences* between individuals presented with identical environments, and, also, the consistency of behaviour seen in any one individual over time. According to this position, the ultimate goal of personality research is to identify the relatively stable biological (i.e., genes and neuroendocrine systems) variables that determine the factor structure that is 'recovered' from statistical analysis of behaviour (including verbal output and checking boxes on personality questionnaires; Corr 2004; Corr and McNaughton 2008; McNaughton and Corr 2004). This theoretical position is not to deny the importance of the environment in controlling behaviour (for example, the environment seems to determine whether depression or anxiety is expressed in individuals with the same genes for internalizing disorders; e.g., Kendler, Prescott, Myers and Neale 2003; see below). However, to produce consistent long-term effects, environmental influences must be instantiated in biological systems: environmental influences do not have any substance unless there is a biological system to mediate them.

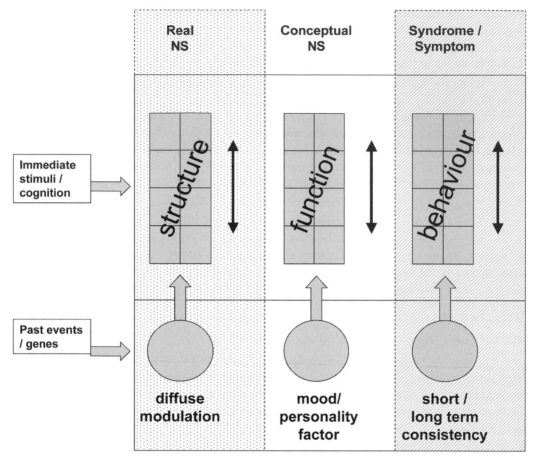

Figure 21.1. *The relationship between (a) the real nervous system (Real NS), (b) the conceptual nervous system (Conceptual NS), (c) syndromes/behaviours related to (d) immediate stimuli/cognitions, and (e) past events/genes, providing descriptions in terms of structure, function and behaviour.*

Development of Reinforcement Sensitivity Theory

RST has gone through several phases of development. In the sections to follow, I concentrate on the theory as it exists in 2009. However, a brief 'Cook's Tour' of the milestones in RST's development is necessary in order to appreciate how the current theory developed (for a fuller discussion, see Corr 2008a).

The 'necessity' handmaiden to the mother of the invention of RST was the need to resolve the gross cracks that appeared in the major biological personality theory of that time, namely, Hans Eysenck's (1967) arousal/activation theory of Introversion-Extraversion (E) and Neuroticism (N). Eysenck's 'top-down' approach consisted in first 'discovering' the major dimensions of personality, and, secondly, providing a theoretical (biological) account for their existence. But, as discussed elsewhere (Corr and McNaughton 2008), multivariate statistical analysis is unable to 'recover' the separate causal influences that get conflated in immediate/short-term behaviour responses, as well as in the longer-term development of personality: what is measured in behaviour is the net products of, possibly separate, causal influences and the operation of their underlying systems. What Eysenck seemed to have found were major *descriptive* dimensions of personality (principally, E and N), that reflect the causal influences of separate, and interacting, underlying systems, and which, as such, could only ever be tied to very general biological processes that cut across these underlying systems, specifically neuropsychological arousal and activation, of the ascending reticular activating system (ARAS) and visceral system, respectively (for a summary, see Corr 2004). Given the fundamental limitation of multivariate statistical techniques of extraction (e.g., factor analysis; see Lykken 1971), arguably Eysenck's approach never stood a decent chance of unravelling the complexity of underlying biological systems. This fact alone may well account for the multiple cracks that rapidly appeared in his theoretical edifice (see Gray 1981). As Gray's RST is usually seen as a development and refinement of Eysenck's *general* approach, we now need to turn to the specific details of Eysenck's theory to see the problems that Gray attempted to solve.

Hans Eysenck's personality theory

Eysenck's (1967) personality theory states that individuals differ with respect to the sensitivity of their ARAS, which serves to dampen or amplify incoming sensory stimulation. Those of us with an active ARAS easily generate cortical arousal, whereas those of us with a less active ARAS generate cortical arousal much more slowly. It was assumed (but no theoretical rationale was given for this) that there exists an optimal level of arousal: too little or too much leads to poor hedonic tone, which motivates us to alter this sub-optimal arousal state. According to this view, those of us with an overactive ARAS are, generally, more cortically aroused and closer to our optimal point of arousal; therefore, we do not seek out more stimulation, and we shy away from stimulation that we encounter: we are introverts. In contrast, those of us with an underactive ARAS are, generally, less cortically aroused and are not close to this optimal point of arousal; therefore, we seek out more stimulation, and we benefit from stimulation that we encounter: we are extraverts. Most people are in the middle range of these extreme values (i.e., ambiverts). What we measure in personality questionnaires are these preferences and behaviours.

Inspired by Pavlov's theory of excitatory and inhibitory brain processes being associated with conditioning (a theory capitalized upon in Eysenck's 1957 theory), Eysenck stated that introverted individuals (i.e., high arousal, or excitable process, type) are relatively easy to condition; whereas, extraverts (i.e., low arousal, or inhibitory process, type) are relatively less easy to condition. The observation that clinical neurotics are indeed introverts (they are also high on neurosis, which adds negative emotional fuel to the high-arousal fire) fitted the theory well, as did the clinical observation that behaviour therapy, which was based upon conditioning principles, was effective in the treatment of a number of neurotic conditions. Such was the elegance and wide-range explanatory power of Eysenck's theory, it became highly influential and widely accepted – it was seen as a *tour de force* in personality-psychopathology research. Alas, ugly data – including Eysenck's very own – was to ruin this beautiful theory.

The first problem was that, at high levels of stimulation, introverts were actually *worse* than extraverts at conditioning (Eysenck and Levey 1972). Although this supported the Pavlovian notion of transmarginal inhibition (TMI) of response (i.e., a breakdown of the orderly stimuli-response relationship at too-high levels of stimulation), it simultaneously corroded the very foundations of the theory, for it led to the conclusion that extraverts should condition best to high arousing stimuli (including the panoply of aversive stimuli found in neurosis) and, therefore, should be overrepresented in the psychiatric clinic, which they are not for typical neurotic conditions.

Secondly, compounded with this first problem was the finding, again from Eysenck's own work (Eysenck and Levey 1972) but also from other researchers (Revelle 1997), that it is impulsivity, not sociability, that carried the causal burden of the arousal-conditioning link. As impulsivity is orthogonal, and thus independent of sociability (the main trait of Eysenck's Extraversion scale), this destroyed not only the arousal-conditioning-Extraversion link, but also the relevance of Extraversion at all in conditioning effects, including those supposedly so crucial in the development of neurotic conditions.

If these two problems were not enough to destroy finally Eysenck's already tarnished theory, thirdly, the relations observed between arousal and conditioning were observed to vary as a function of time of day: Eysenck-like sociability/impulsivity x arousal effects that are found with morning testing (e.g., introverts showing superior performance under placebo and TMI-related performance deficits under arousal, relative to extraverts) are reversed with evening testing. As ruefully noted by Gray (1981), one is not a neurotic in the morning and a psychopath in the evening!

While these findings pointed to the power of general arousal theory, at the same moment they undermined the particulars of Eysenck's personality theory.[3]

However, worse still was to follow. *Even if we assume* that Eysenck's theory were correct, classical conditioning cannot account for the known phenomena

---

[3] It is not too fanciful to propose the following in defence of Eysenck's theory. First, most aversive conditioning of children is during the earlier part of the day (i.e., during school hours); secondly, much aversive stimulation is relatively mild; and thirdly, and perhaps of most importance, conditioning entails an incubation period (Eysenck 1979) consisting of rehearsal in memory of the aversive experience, over extensive periods of time, during states of lower arousal. As shown below, the Extraversion-arousal link may still be a viable part of personality theory, including RST (e.g., how initially neutral stimuli get conditioned in the first place).

of neurosis. As discussed by Corr (2008a), the classical conditioning theory of neurosis assumes that, as a result of the conditioned stimulus (CS) (e.g., hairy animal) and unconditioned stimulus (UCS) (e.g., pain of dog bite) getting paired, the CS comes to take on the eliciting properties of the UCS, such that, after conditioning and when presented alone, the CS produces a response (i.e., the conditioned response (CR), e.g., fear, and its associated behaviours) that resembles the unconditioned response (UCR) (e.g., pain, and its associated behaviours) elicited by the UCS. All well and good thus far (assuming that 'fear' is equivalent to 'pain', which itself is something of a leap of faith). But, there is a major problem with this theory. The CR (e.g., fear) *does not* substitute for the UCR (e.g., pain). In some crucial respects, the CR does not even resemble the UCR. For example, a pain UCS will elicit a wide variety of reactions (e.g., vocalization and behavioural excitement – recall the last time an object hit you hard!); but these reactions are quite different – in fact, opposite to – a CS *signalling* pain, which consists of a different range of behaviours (e.g., quietness and behavioural inhibition). A lingering problem here concerns emotion: where does fear come from? More technically, where is fear generated in the brain, and how is this fear-system related to conditioning? Eysenck seemed just to assume that emotion arose spontaneously; but this simply will not do. In addition, if there is a fear generating system, then maybe that is where we should look for the genesis of clinical neurosis.

Another clue to the potential importance of an innate fear system was the debate between Eysenck's and Spence's laboratories where, in the latter, it was found that conditioning was related to anxiety not (low) Extraversion. This debate was finally resolved by the realization that it is anxiety related to conditioning in laboratories that is more threatening (as in the case of Spence's; Spence 1964). This realization was accepted by Eysenck as a satisfactory resolution to this empirical difference; however, it could have occurred to him, as it did to Gray later, that the very resolution was bought at the cost of an even greater problem: what led to the greater threat-related conditioning in Spence's laboratory? Emotion was never satisfactorily explained in Eysenck's theory: it was seen, at varying times, as a cause (e.g., in Spence's conditioning studies), as an outcome (e.g., in neurosis), and as a regulatory set point mechanism (e.g., in arousal and hedonic tone relations). In Eysenck's theory, it remained something of an unruly, even delinquent, construct.

Jeffrey Gray's reward and punishment systems

As a former doctoral student of Eysenck's, and much later as the successor to his Departmental Chair at the Institute of Psychiatry in London, Gray was well aware of his former mentor's theory, as well as the deep roots it had in Pavlovian psychology and in the relatively newer Hullian learning theory and neurophysiology (e.g., Gray 1964). This knowledge allowed Gray not just to criticize Eysenck's personality theory, but to dismantle its theoretical foundations, especially the focus on one system of drive/arousal that was fundamentally Hullian in

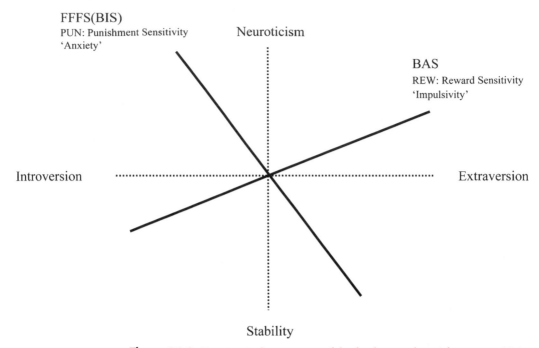

Figure 21.2. *Position in factor space of the fundamental punishment sensitivity and reward sensitivity (unbroken lines) and the emergent surface expressions of these sensitivities, i.e., Extraversion (E) and Neuroticism (N) (broken lines). In the revised theory (see text), a clear distinction exists between fear (FFFS) and anxiety (BIS), and separate personality factors may relate to these systems; however, for the present exposition, these two systems are considered to reflect a common dimension of punishment sensitivity.*

nature (see Corr 2008a; Corr, Pickering and Gray 1995). In its place came a two-process theory of learning, entailing separate dimensions of reward and punishment, a focus on the fundamental role of internal states of emotion, and a much more sophisticated neuropsychology.

In brief, Gray (1970, 1972b, 1981) proposed a modification of Eysenck's theory thus: (a) to the position of Extraversion (E) and Neuroticism (N) in multivariate statistical factor space; and (b) to their neuropsychological bases. According to Gray, E and N should be rotated, approximately, 30° to form the more causally efficient axes of 'punishment sensitivity', reflecting Anxiety (Anx), and 'reward sensitivity', reflecting Impulsivity (Imp) (Figure 21.2).

Gray's modification stated that highly impulsive individuals (Imp+) are most sensitive to *signals* of reward, relative to their low impulsive (Imp−) counterparts;[4] and highly anxious individuals (Anx+) are most sensitive to *signals* of punishment, relative to low anxiety (Anx−) counterparts. It was assumed that Imp

---

[4] The notion that impulsivity, which has its high pole in the neurotic-extravert quadrant of E/N space, was related to reward came from several sources of evidence: (a) two-factor learning theory

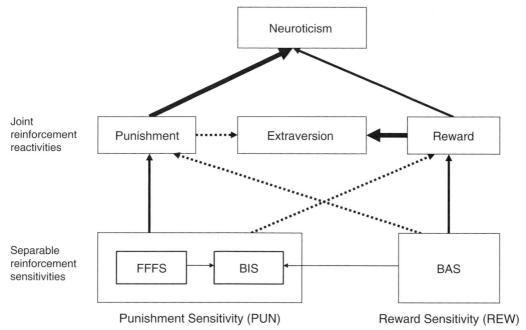

Figure 21.3. *A schematic representation of the hypothesized relationship between (a) FFFS/BIS (punishment sensitivity; PUN) and BAS (reward sensitivity; REW); (b) their joint effects on reactions to punishment and reward; and (c) their relations to Extraversion (E) and Neuroticism (N). E is shown as the balance of punishment (PUN) and reward (REW) reactivities; N reflects their combined strengths. Inputs from the FFFS/BIS and BAS are excitatory (unbroken line) and inhibitory (broken line) – their respective influences are dependent on experimental factors (see text). The strength of inputs to E and N reflects the 30° rotation of PUN/REW and E/N (see Figure 21.2): relatively strong (thick line) and weak (thin line) relations. The input from punishment reactivity to E is inhibitory (i.e., it reduces E), the input from reward reactivity is excitatory (i.e., it increases E). The BIS is activated by simultaneous activation of the FFFS and the BAS, and its activation increases punishment sensitivity. It is hypothesized that the joint effects of PUN and REW gives rise to the surface expression of E and N: PUN and REW represent the underlying biology; E and N represent their joint influences at the level of integrated behaviour.*

and Anx, and their processes, were independent – this position is now known as 'separable subsystems hypothesis' (Corr 2001, 2002a; see Corr and McNaughton 2008). According to this new view, Eysenck's E and N dimensions are secondary (conflated) factors of these more fundamental traits/processes (see Figure 21.3).

(Mowrer 1960; Konorski 1967), that showed that behavioural reactions to aversive stimuli are controlled by a different system to that controlling behavioural reactions to appetitive stimuli; (b) the *relative* insensitivity of anxiolytic drugs to affect behavioural reactions to appetitive stimuli; and (c) the psychological data showing that highly impulsive people are more prone to engage in a variety of 'sociopsychiatric' behaviours (e.g., gambling, and other 'externalizing disorders' of an extraverted and sociable nature).

Gray's (1970) theory deftly side-stepped the problems accompanying Eysenck's, and it also explained *why* introverts were, generally, more cortically aroused: they are more punishment sensitive (punishment is more arousing than reward); and, as extraverts are more sensitive to reward, not punishment, they are, accordingly, less aroused. In addition, Gray (1970) argued that drugs that reduce clinical anxiety lower N and raise E scores, as does psychosurgery to the frontal cortex (whether caused by accident or surgical design) – both sets of findings suggest that a single anxiety dimension is a better account than two, separate, dimensions.

Two factor learning theory

Lurking behind these theoretical developments were advances being made in learning theory. As already noted, Eysenck's theory followed in the tradition of Hullian (1952) learning theory, which reduced all forms of motivationally-salient reinforcement to a single process of 'drive-reduction'; as noted by Gray (1975, p. 25), the 'Hullian concept of general drive, to the extent that it is viable, does not differ in any important respects from that of arousal'. However, at this time, there was a strong movement away from Hull's grand theory of behaviour – which has now fallen by the wayside of science – towards a two factor theory of learning based upon reward and punishment systems. It was Mowrer's (1960) seminal work that contributed to this development: he argued that the effects of reward and punishment had different behavioural effects, as well as different underlying bases, and he specifically introduced the notion that central states of emotion (e.g., 'hope') mediate stimuli and responses. For a mediation to occur, there must be a mediating system. These general ideas entered mainstream psychology through the writings of such people as Konorski (1967) and Mackintosh (1983). Gray's (1975) *Elements of a two-process theory of learning* fully embodied this tradition in personality psychology.[5] On the real nervous system side of the coin, the conceptual nervous system work was strengthened by neurophysiological findings pointing to specific emotion centres in the brain (e.g., the 'pleasure centres'; Olds and Milner 1954; see Corr 2006).

From these converging lines of evidence, Gray (1970) advanced the claim that the 'emotions' are elicited by motivationally-significant ('reinforcing') stimuli (of any kind) that activate innate systems in the brain. Now seen as rather innocuous, this claim has important and widespread implications for personality psychology: if emotion, and its related motivation, were fundamental to personality (as suggested by Eysenck's own work in linking personality to psychopathology) then we may better understand personality by understanding emotion systems in the brain.

In critiquing Eysenck's approach, Gray noted that classical conditioning does not, indeed cannot, create emotion, normal or pathological; all it can do is to

---

[5] For a rebuttal of the claim (widely held, if not so frequently articulated) that non-human behaviour/cognition is irrelevant to our understanding of human emotion, motivation and personality, see McNaughton and Corr (2008b).

transform initially neutral stimuli into conditioned (reinforcing) stimuli that, via Pavlovian classical conditioning, acquire the power to activate innate systems of emotion which, themselves, are responsible for generating emotion. Thus, according to this position, reduction of pathological emotions can be achieved in one of two ways: (a) deconditioning aversive reinforcing stimuli, which weakens the strength of stimulus inputs into the innate emotion systems; or (b) by dampening down the activity in the systems themselves (e.g., by the use of drugs that target key molecules in parts of the innate system). We may see the effectiveness of cognitive-behavioural therapy (CBT) as another way to 'decondition' the power of hitherto aversive stimuli to activate the emotion systems (e.g., by restructuring 'irrational' cognitions that serve as inputs into these systems).

Two broad affective dimensions

We have now covered the main conceptual and developmental parts of the evolution of Gray's RST, which we can summarize in the words of Fowles (2006, p. 8):

> In this view, organisms are seen as maximizing exposure to rewarding ('appetitive') events and minimizing exposure to punishing ('aversive') events. Rewarding or appetitive events consist of the presentation of a reward (Rew), termination of a punishment (Pun!), or omission of an expected punishment (nonPun), while punishing or aversive events consist of the punishment (Pun), termination of reward (Rew!), and omission of an expected reward (nonRew). Through a process of classical conditioning, conditioned stimuli (CSs) paired with events come to acquire some of their emotional and motivational properties.

An important point to note here is the fact that reward (Rew) itself and the termination of a punishment (Pun!) or omission of an expected punishment (nonPun; relief of non-punishment), share much in common in terms of their functions and pharmacology; and in a complementary way, punishment (Pun) itself and the termination of reward (Rew!), and omission of an expected reward (nonRew; 'frustrative non-reward'), are similarly common. Somewhat unique to RST, this analysis draws attention not to observed behaviour but to the internal, central states that underlie them. It is at this deeper level of analysis that we see the operation of core psychological processes (McNaughton and Corr 2008).

Summary of Pre-2000 RST

We now know that the anxiety system was characterized on the basis of a detailed analysis of the pattern of behavioural effects of classes of drugs known to affect anxiety in human beings (mainly barbiturates and the benzodiazepines (Gray 1977), later to be extended to novel anxiety reducing drugs, i.e., novel anxiolytics; see below). This detailed analysis (summarized in Gray 1982) led to the formal definition of the BIS.

(1) The behavioural inhibition system (BIS) was postulated to be sensitive to *conditioned* aversive stimuli, omission/termination of expected reward, and conditioned frustration (i.e., conditioning to stimuli that signalled expected reward, non-reward), as well as an assortment of other inputs, including extreme novelty, high intensity stimuli and innate fear stimuli (e.g., snakes, blood). This system was charged with suppressing ongoing operant behaviour in the face of threat, which allowed for enhanced information-processing and vigilance. The BIS was related to the personality factor of Anxiety (Anx). The neural instantiation of the BIS was postulated to be in the septo-hippocampal system of the brain.

According to Gray, anxiolytic drugs work by impairing the activity of the BIS and thus its outputs, making behaviour less risk averse and, colloquially speaking, less concerned (worried) with potential sources of danger. Although anxiety was associated with BIS activity, its phenomenological nature was not considered, and it is still unclear how and where this subjective state is generated (this problem is not restricted to Gray's theory, but to all subjective experiences; see below).

(2) The fight-flight system (FFS) was postulated to be sensitive to *unconditioned* aversive stimuli (i.e., innately painful stimuli), mediating the emotions of rage and panic. This system was related to the state of negative affect (NA) (associated with pain) and speculatively associated by Gray with Eysenck's personality factor of Psychoticism (P) (Eysenck and Eysenck 1976). The neural instantiation of the FFS was postulated to be in the periaqueductal grey and (various nuclei of) the hypothalamus.

(3) The behavioural approach system (BAS) was postulated to be sensitive to *conditioned* appetitive stimuli, forming a positive feedback loop, activated by the presentation of stimuli associated with reward and the termination/omission of signals of punishment. This system was related to state positive affect (PA) and the personality dimension of Impulsivity (Imp). The neural instantiation of the BAS was postulated to be in the mesolimbic dopamine circuit.

The experimental evidence testing the pre-2000 theory was summarized by a review paper, (Corr 2004) and an edited book (Corr 2008b) that surveyed all the main areas of RST.

Post-2000 RST

Gray and NcNaughton (2000) substantially revised BIS theory and RST more generally. This revision updates and elaborates the older theory and, crucially in some important respects, makes different predictions (for more detailed discussion of these matters, see Corr 2004, 2008a; Corr and McNaughton 2008; McNaughton and Corr 2004, 2008a).

Revised RST, once again, postulates three systems.

(1) The fight–flight–freeze system (FFFS) is now responsible for mediating reactions to *all* aversive stimuli, conditioned and unconditioned. It updates the FFS to include 'freezing' (see below). In addition, the theory proposes a

hierarchical array of neural modules, each responsible for a specific defensive behaviour (e.g., avoidance and freezing). The FFFS mediates the emotion of fear, not anxiety. The associated personality factor consists of fear-proneness and avoidance, which clinically may be mapped onto such disorders as phobia and panic. This is the 'Get me out of here!' system.

(2) The behavioural approach system (BAS) mediates reactions to *all* appetitive stimuli, conditioned and unconditioned, and is the least changed of the three systems. It interfaces with dedicated consummatory systems (e.g., eating and drinking) which are responsible for the final consumption of unconditioned stimuli (e.g., food); the BAS is involved in the incentive processes moving the animals up the temporo-spatial gradient to the final biological reinforcer. It is responsible for generating the emotion of 'anticipatory pleasure', and hope itself. The associated personality factor consists of optimism, reward-orientation and (especially in very high BAS-active individuals) impulsiveness (but see below), which clinically may be mapped onto addictive behaviours (e.g., pathological gambling) and various varieties of high-risk, impulsive behaviour. This is the 'Let's go for it!' system.

(3) The Behavioural Inhibition System (BIS) is the most changed system in revised RST. It is responsible, not, as in the 1982 version, for mediating reactions to conditioned aversive stimuli and the special class of innate fear stimuli, but rather for the resolution of *goal conflict* in general (e.g., between BAS-approach and FFFS-avoidance, as in foraging situations, but it is also involved in BAS-BAS and FFFS-FFFS conflicts; see Corr 2008a). In typical animal learning situations, BIS outputs have evolved to permit an animal to enter a dangerous situation (i.e., leading to cautious 'risk assessment' behaviour) or to withhold entrance (i.e., passive avoidance).

The BIS is involved in the processes that finally generate the emotion of anxiety, and entails the inhibition of prepotent conflicting behaviours, the engagement of risk assessment processes, and the scanning of memory and the environment to help resolve concurrent goal conflict, which is experienced subjectively as worry, apprehension and the feeling that actions may lead to a bad outcome; there is also an exaggerated startle reaction (Caseras, Fullana, Riba *et al.* 2006). The revised BIS resolves goal conflicts by increasing, through recursive loops, the negative valence of stimuli, via activation of the FFFS, until resolution occurs either in favour of approach or avoidance. In this important sense, there is a close relationship between the BIS and FFFS (see McNaughton and Corr 2008a).

The associated personality factor consists of worry-proneness and anxious rumination, leading to being constantly on the look-out for possible signs of danger, which map clinically onto such conditions as generalized anxiety and Obsessional-Compulsive Disorder (OCD). This is the 'Watch out, be very careful!' system. When activated by conflict stimuli, it is said to be in 'control mode', and when not activated, in 'just checking' mode (see Gray 1981). In support of this claim, using fMRI in a conflict paradigm, Haas, Omura, Constable and Canli (2007) found that the anxiety component of general Neuroticism was related to activation in the amygdala (see below).

Neural systems of FFFS-fear and BIS-anxiety

One major alteration in revised RST is the inclusion of a hierarchical arrangement of *distributed* brain systems that mediate specific defensive behaviours associated with level of threat experienced, ranging from the prefrontal cortex, at the highest level, to the periaqueductal grey, at the lowest level. To each structure is assigned a specific class of mental disorder (McNaughton and Corr 2008a). The evolution of these separate systems that form a whole system most probably evolved by a 'rule of thumb' (ROT) approach (McNaughton and Corr in press). According to this perspective, separate emotions (e.g., fear, panic, etc.) may be seen as reflecting the evolution of specific neural modules to deal with specific environmental demands (e.g., flee in the face of a predator) and, as these separate systems evolved and started to work together, some form of regulatory process (e.g., when one module is active, others are inactivated) evolved. The resulting hierarchical nature of this defence system reflects the fact that simpler systems must have evolved before more complex ones, which provides a solution to the problem of conflicting action systems: the later systems evolved to have inhibitory control on lower-level systems. The result of this process of evolution is the existence of hierarchically ordered series of defensive reactions, each appropriate for a given defensive distance (i.e., level of threat perceived; see below).

This hierarchical arrangement may seem at first to be complex; however, it can be conveniently summarized in terms of a two-dimensional scheme, consisting of 'defensive distance' and 'defensive direction' – the prize we win from tolerating some modicum of complexity is synthesis of a vast literature of research findings into a coherent whole, showing, for example, why psychological disorders have specific elements while at the same time showing co-morbidity with other disorders. The two-dimensional neural (CNS) theory translates this two-dimensional (cns) psychological schema, reflecting two broad affective dimensions (Figure 21.4).

We now turn to the two dimensions of this hierarchical neural arrangement: *defensive direction* and *defensive distance*.

Defensive direction: fear versus anxiety

The avoidance of, or approach to, a dangerous stimulus is reflected in the categorical dimension of 'defensive direction', which further reflects a functional distinction between behaviours (a) that remove an animal from a source of danger (FFFS-mediated, fear), and (b) that allow it cautiously to approach a source of potential danger (BIS-mediated, anxiety). These functions are ethologically and pharmacologically distinct and, on each of these separate grounds, can be identified with fear and anxiety, respectively. To better understand this distinction, a few words must be spent on the influential work of Robert and Caroline Blanchard (Blanchard and Blanchard 1988, 1990; Blanchard, Griebel, Henrie and Blanchard 1997), who were most responsible for moving Gray away from a formal analysis

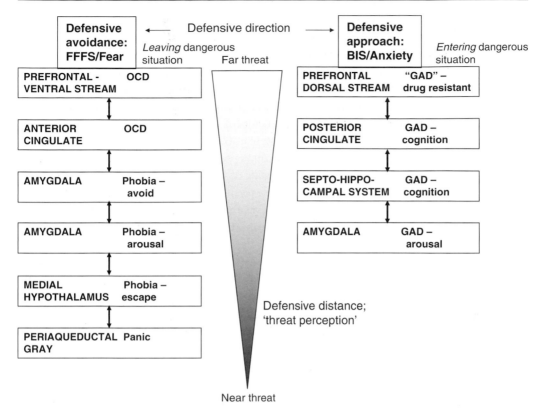

Figure 21.4. *The two dimensional defence system. On either side are defensive avoidance and defensive approach, respectively (this is a categorical dimension of 'defensive direction'). Each is divided, down the page, into a number of hierarchical levels, both with respect to neural level (and cytoarchitectonic complexity) and to functional level (this is a qualitative dimension of 'defensive distance', or more generally 'threat perception'). Each level is associated with specific classes of behaviour and so symptom and syndrome (as shown).*

of behaviour based on learning theory (Gray 1975, 1982) to one based on functional classes of behaviour (e.g., freezing vs. cautious approach) (Gray and McNaughton 2000).

Over an extensive period of research, the Blanchards examined the behavioural effects of classes of psychiatric drugs on defensive behaviours of rodents in realistic experimental situations, known as 'ethoexperimental analysis': 'etho' to reflect the natural behaviours shown by rodents in real-like environments (e.g., freezing in the face of threat), and 'experimental' to reflect the control over the features of this reality-like environment (e.g., smell vs. presence of cat in the reality-like visual burrow designed by the Blanchards): to the rodents, this world is real enough, the threat stimuli are highly salient, and the behaviours observed and measured are not predefined by the experimenter (as would be the case with the use of a Skinner box). Careful analysis of the behavioural effects on rodents of clinically effective psychiatric drugs (e.g., anxiolytics) revealed a set of findings that pointed to the existence of two broad classes of defensive behaviour (avoidance of threat and cautious approach to threat) – or, in the Blanchards' view, immediate vs. potential threat. In passing, we should note that the Blanchards' research approach very much parallelled Gray's own (see above), therefore it is not surprising that their results were to prove of such value to Gray, along with colleague Neil McNaughton, in revising RST.

The Blanchards' findings may be summarized as follows. First, one class of behaviours was elicited by the immediate presence of a predator (e.g., a cat) – this class could clearly be attributed to a state of fear. The behaviours were observed to be highly sensitive to panicolytic (i.e., panic-reducing) drugs, but not so much to drugs that are specifically anxiolytic (i.e., anxiety-reducing). Secondly, a quite distinct class of behaviours (including 'risk assessment') was elicited by the potential presence of a predator – this class of behaviours was highly sensitive to anxiolytic drugs. Both functionally and pharmacologically, this class was distinct from the behaviours attributed to fear and could be attributed to a state of anxiety. As this distinction shows, in some important functional respects, fear and anxiety can reflect opposing motivations (avoiding vs. entering dangerous situations).

Defensive distance: fear and anxiety

The type of behavioural reaction to a threat is reflected in the second dimension of 'defensive distance', which reflects further the actual, or perceived, distance from threat. This dimension applies equally to fear and anxiety but operates differently in each case: anxiolytic drugs change it in the case of the BIS-anxiety, but not in the case of FFFS-fear. The main point is that defensive distance (i.e., how far you think you are from the threat, which closes with increasing magnitude of threat) corresponds to activation of specific neural modules (e.g., at very close defensive distance, PAG activation and panic): the common expletive 'Oh shit!' is more than being merely figurative, because one of the most reliable signs of intense fear in rodents and man (e.g., soldiers in battle) is defecation (Stouffer *et al.* 1950).

Although we can equate defensive distance with real distance, it is more accurately seen as a *perception*; that is, an internal quantity that defines defensive reactions to a fixed unit of threat (i.e., magnitude x distance). This rather humble statement provides an immediate explanation for 'neurosis'; that is, individual differences in the susceptibility to neurotic disorder. As shown in Table 21.1, a more defensive person (for simplicity here, defined so as to cut across both fear and anxiety) will *perceive* a threat of a fixed objective value as being more threatening (i.e., closer) than a less defensive person. Indeed, this hypothesis helps to explain the actions of drugs: they do not affect the *intensity* of a particular behaviour (e.g., avoidance); rather they affect 'perceived distance' (i.e., the magnitude of perceived threat), and thus they lead to *different* behaviours being shown (e.g., from avoidance to cautious approach).

Table 21.1 *Relationship between personality trait of 'defensiveness' (FFFS/ BIS), difference between actual and perceived defensive distance, and the real defensive difference required to elicit defensive behaviour.*

Personality trait	Defensive distance	Real defensive distance required for elicitation of defensive behaviour
High defensive individual	Perceived distance < actual distance	Long
Normal defensive individual	Perceived distance = actual distance	Medium
Low defensive individual	Perceived distance > actual distance	Short

This form of analysis counsels us not to focus on behaviour per se, but rather to view behaviour as a reflection of central states of emotion and motivation: as an overt, and measurable, indicator of internal states. Much of behavioural pharmacology results would simply not make sense if we only looked at the intensity of a particular behaviour. This point deserves emphasizing. Take a foraging (conflict) situation in which the perceived intensity of threat is high (i.e., small defensive distance). An animal that is not drugged is likely to remain behaviourally still and anxiolytic drugs serve to *increase* risk assessment (i.e., lead to behavioural exploration). However, if the perceived threat is only medium, now the undrugged animal is likely to engage in exploratory, risk-assessment behaviour and anxiolytic drugs will serve to *decrease* risk-assessment behaviour (because the animal is now experiencing the threat as more distant and is no longer anxious and, thus, returns to normal appetitive behaviour). The important point is that the drug does not alter a specific risk assessment in any simple fashion, but leads to changes in behaviour that depend on the animal's internal state (Blanchard and Blanchard 1990).

BIS-mediated conflict

As noted above, the BIS has been substantially revised and updated: it is now defined in terms of defensive *approach* (i.e., behavioural caution in a rewarding environment, e.g., foraging). However, revised RST argues that this behaviour, along with the previously emphasized conditioned aversive stimuli that were said to activate the BIS, are only examples of a more fundamental aspect of the BIS, namely that it is sensitive to goal *conflict* (e.g., approach-avoidance; e.g., an animal will approach a threat only if there is some possibility of a rewarding outcome, such as food). However, threats (as opposed to primary punishment itself) are only one source of aversion. Revised RST argues that, in principle, approach-approach and avoidance-avoidance conflicts also involve activation of the same system and have essentially the same effects as the classic approach-avoidance. An example of an approach-approach conflict is: which equally appealing job should you take? The aversive element resides in the possibility of making a mistake, thus we typically spend time weighing up all the possibilities, and searching for potential downsides to each decision. We may speculate – and it can only be that – that much of modern-day angst comes from the conflicting choices available in our successful economic system. Novelty is another type of stimuli that may activate the BIS (although, if sufficiently intense it is likely to activate the FFFS) as it entails a conflict between what is expected and what is perceived. Little research attention work has been devoted to this aspect of BIS theory, however one study has provided evidence for a preference for familiarity (as opposed to novelty) in high BIS individuals (Quilty, Oakman and Farolden 2007).

Before ending this section, an important asymmetry must be noted: fear can be generated without a significant degree of anxiety (i.e., in the absence of goal-conflict), but BIS activation always leads to FFFS activation via the increase in negative valence. For this reason FFFS and BIS will often be co-activated – and, as we will see below, this is a good reason for lumping them together into a single 'Punishment Sensitivity' factor of personality.

This revised view of the BIS is starting to explain previous anomalies in the literature and is pointing to new research questions. For example, Wallace and Newman (2008) discussed the relationship between an impaired BIS and psychopathy, which was in the old version of the theory associated with an absence of anxiety (and fear more broadly). However, these authors note that the evidence in favour of an impairment of anxiety/fear in psychopaths is weak; indeed, under certain conditions, psychopaths display normal reactions when anxiety/fear is present. Wallace and Newman (2008) point to the response modulation deficit seen in psychopathy, which impairs responses to aversive stimuli when a dominant response set to reward has been established. The revised conception of the BIS explains this finding: an impaired BIS does not signal prepotent (BAS-related) response conflict when environmental contingencies change to favour aversive motivation and avoidance, and in consequence the psychopath does not respond in an adaptive manner to the presence of aversive stimuli. BIS underactivity seems to be especially marked in primary (low fear) psychopathy (Ross, Mottó, Poy et al. 2007).

Behavioural approach system

There is little new to add on the BAS in terms of the Gray and McNaughton (2000) revision. However, work by the author, as well other RST researchers (e.g., Pickering 2008), have highlighted a number of issues that require attention. One such issue concerns the complexity of the BAS and the implications of this complexity for personality measurement. Elsewhere (Corr 2008a), I have pointed out that, on evolutionary grounds, it may be assumed that the BAS is more complex than conventionally thought – and, indeed, may be more complex than either the FFFS or the BIS.[6] I (Corr 2008a) developed the concept of *sub-goal scaffolding*, which reflects the separate, though overlapping, stages of BAS behaviour, consisting in a series of appetitively-motivated sub-goals. Sub-goal scaffolding reflects the fact that, in order to move along the temporo-spatial gradient to the final primary biological reinforcer, it is necessary to engage a number of distinct processes. Complex approach behaviour entails a series of behavioural processes, some of which oppose each other. Such behaviour often demands *restraint* and *planning*, but, especially at the final point of *capture* of the biological reinforcer, impulsivity is more appropriate. Therefore, simply being a highly impulsive person (i.e., not planning and acting fast without thinking) would be detrimental to effective BAS behaviour. For these reasons, 'impulsivity' may not be the most appropriate name for the personality dimension that reflects BAS processes (Franken and Muris 2006; Smillie, Jackson and Dalgleish 2006)

There is evidence that, at the psychometric level, the BAS is multidimensional. For example, the Carver and White (1994) BIS/BAS scales measure three aspects of BAS: Reward Responsiveness, Drive and Fun-Seeking – these scales have good psychometric properties in both adolescents and adults (e.g., Caci, Deschaux and Baylé 2007; Cooper, Gomez and Aucute 2007). In accordance with the concept of sub-goal scaffolding, we may see that Drive is concerned with actively pursuing desired goals, Reward-Responsiveness is concerned with excitement at doing things well and winning, and Fun-Seeking is concerned with the impulsivity aspect of the BAS.

There is also the issue of the involvement of the BAS in negative emotional states. On the basis of an analysis of the BAS and frustrative non-reward, it has been hypothesized that reward sensitive individuals would be the first to detect a lower than expected level of reward and, thus, experience frustration (Corr 2002b; see also Carver 2004, and Harmon-Jones 2003). Important in this regard is the system that mediates these negative states: must it be either the FFFS or the BIS, or might only the BAS be involved, and if the latter, how?

Personality factors

So far we have equated 'personality' with individual variations in the major brain-behavioural systems that underlie the FFFS, BAS and BIS. Existing RST

---

[6] The 'life-dinner principle' (Dawkins and Krebs 1979) suggests that the evolutionary selective pressures on prey are much stronger than on predators: if a predator fails to kill its prey then it has lost its dinner, but if the prey fails to avoid/escape being the predator's dinner then it has lost its life. Although defensive behaviours (e.g., freezing, fleeing and defensive attack) are relatively complex (Eilam 2005), it is nonetheless true that the behaviour of prey is intrinsically simpler than that of predator: all it has to do is avoid/escape – it really is life-or-death behaviour. In contrast, the predator has to develop counter-strategies to meet its BAS aims, which entail a higher degree of organization and planning. In addition, the heterogeneity of appetitive goals (e.g., securing food and finding/keeping a sexual mate) demands a heterogeneity of BAS-related strategies: no one set of behaviours would be sufficient to achieve these very different BAS goals.

questionnaire measures were developed on the basis of the pre-2000 theory. For example, in addition to the three sub-scales of the Carver and White (1994) BAS scale, it provides an apparently unitary measure of BIS. Importantly, however, fear and anxiety are not differentiated. To some extent, within the BIS scale it is possible to separate fear from anxiety (Corr and McNaughton 2008; putative FFFS-Fear and BIS-Anxiety in square brackets), although for some items this differentiation is blurred.

(1) Even if something bad is about to happen to me, I rarely experience fear or nervousness. [FFFS]
(2) Criticism or scolding hurts me a lot. [FFFS/BIS]
(3) I feel pretty worried or upset when I think or know somebody is angry at me. [FFFS/BIS]
(4) If I think something unpleasant is going to happen I usually get pretty 'worked up'. [FFFS/BIS]
(5) I feel worried when I think I have done poorly at something. [BIS]
(6) I have few fears compared to my friends. [FFFS]
(7) I worry about making mistakes. [BIS]

Poythress, Skeem, Weir *et al.* (2008) reported that, in an offender sample, the BIS scale does, indeed, break down into two sub-scales, as indicated above (see also, Johnson, Turner and Iwata 2004), suggesting that closer attention should be paid to differentiating fear and anxiety even in existing questionnaires. However, if we are interested in measuring non-specific punishment sensitivity then a conflation of FFFS-fear and BIS-anxiety may work quite well, and this possibility may account for the popularity of the BIS scale of the Carver and White scales. In terms of revised RST, Corr and McNaughton (2008) inclined to the view that the old 'Anxiety' axis (i.e., Neurotism-Introversion) reflects 'Punishment Sensitivity', or 'Threat Perception', or simply 'Defensive Distance', with lower-order factors of this orthogonal 'dimension' breaking down into specific oblique FFFS-fear and BIS-anxiety factors. There remains much work needed to develop revised RST scales that display theoretical fidelity and psychometrical rigour. That the differentiation of fear and anxiety is needed in terms of personality scales is shown by the following studies. Recent structural equation modelling has confirmed the fear-anxiety differentiation hypothesis (Cooper, Perkins and Corr 2007), as have predictive validity studies (Perkins, Kemp and Corr 2007).

Cutting across the BAS, FFFS and BIS is physiological arousal – here we return to the main concern of Eysenck's theory. Concurrent activation of the FFFS, BIS and BAS sums in the production of general arousal; this summation of 'intensity' function, as distinct from the 'direction of behaviour', has a long history in behavioural psychology (e.g., Duffy 1962). This common summation of input from all the systems provides a source for a very general factor of 'arousability' that reflects changes in the responsiveness of the autonomic nervous system. We only now have to assume that Eysenck's Extraversion factor reflects the balance of reward and punishment systems (a central assumption in RST) for a viable explanation as to why Extraversion and arousal are so often associated in experimental studies of personality. So too, we might infer a general factor of emotional activation, reflecting the summed activity of reward and punishment systems, to derive a general dimension of Neuroticism.

We, thus, have a choice of personality levels of description. On the one hand, if we want to measure separable causally-efficient systems in the brain (i.e., FFFS, BIS and BAS), then we should opt for specific personality questionnaires that faithfully measure the activity of these systems. On the other hand, if we want to measure the net product of the interplay of these systems, then we should opt for Eysenckian-type personality questionnaires that measure broad dimensions of personality (e.g., Extraversion and Neuroticism) relating to broad neurophysiological factors (e.g., arousal). We may further want to measure, in addition to these factors, those relating to styles of personality (e.g., Agreeableness in the Five-Factor Model). Each of these levels of analysis are complementary.

Personality and psychopathology

The two constructs of 'defensive direction' and 'defensive distance', and their mapping onto the series of neural modules that comprise the FFFS and BIS which, in turn, are attributed particular functions, can be related to common symptomatology (see Figure 21.5).

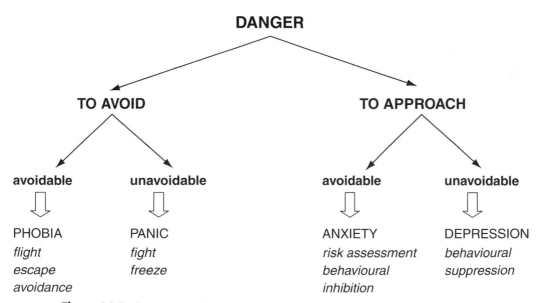

Figure 21.5. *Categories of emotion and defensive responses derived from 'defensive direction' (i.e., motivation to avoid or approach the source of danger) and avoidability of the threat (given constraints of the environment). Emotions in capitalization are psychiatric-based, and defensive behaviours in italics are derived from animal learning paradigms.*

In addition to hypersensitivity in a particular neural module giving rise to a specific set of symptoms (e.g., periaqueductual grey and panic), there are interactions of the FFFS and BIS that have important implications for explicating the underlying basis of a specific disorder. For example, pathologically excessive (BIS) anxiety could generate (FFFS) panic with the latter being entirely appropriate to the level of apprehension experienced. Also, pathological panic could, with repeated experience, condition anxiety with the level of the latter being appropriate to the panic experienced. This state of affairs means that symptoms alone may offer a misleading picture of the basic neural dysfunction. Specifically, hypersensitivity and activity in one neural module may well activate other modules as a secondary consequence and, furthermore, over time sensitize the whole defensive system to ease of activation. This may well explain the considerable co-morbidity seen in neurotic conditions.

In a quite separate part of the psychopathology literature, the distinction between fear and anxiety has been identified. A behavioural genetic study of ten major psychiatric disorders, in a sample of 5,600 twins (Kendler, Prescott, Myers and Neale 2003) revealed the following findings: (a) two major dimensions emerged, one relating to *internalizing* disorders (i.e., major depression, generalized anxiety disorder and phobia), the other to *externalizing* disorders (i.e., alcohol dependence, drug abuse/dependence, adult antisocial behaviour and conduct disorder); (b) no differences in genetic and environmental influences for males and females, despite the large difference in prevalence rates; (c) unique (i.e., non-shared family) environment effects for internalizing disorders; (d) and, of most relevance to RST, the structure of genetic risk for internalizing disorders broken down into an 'anxious-misery' factor (i.e., depression, generalized disorder and panic) and a specific 'fear' factor (i.e., animal and situational phobia).

Earlier, Prescott and Kendler (1998) noted that mild depression and generalized anxiety do not appear to have distinct genetic etiologies, but rather a common genetic basis, perhaps a disposition to dysphoric mood which is shaped by individual experiences into symptoms of depression, anxiety, or both. (See also, Kendler *et al.* (1992.) As Kender *et al.* (2003, p. 935) themselves speculated, 'It is tempting to speculate that these genetic factors on risk might be mediated through personality.'

Indeed, this genetic risk structure for internalizing disorders – with one major factor breaking down into fear and anxiety sub-factors – is the same as that proposed in Figure 21.3 (here fear and anxiety factors are collapsed together to give a general punishment factor). Behavioural studies of rodent defensive behaviour are also starting to differentiate fear and anxiety (e.g., Tsetsenis, Ma, Iacono *et al.* 2007); this study also suggests that the hippocampus is important in the response to ambiguous aversive stimuli.

Important in this regard are quantitative genetic analysis of both change and continuity in BIS/BAS sensitivity over a period of two to three years. One study showed the following: genetic factors accounted for approximately one-third of variance in BIS and BAS; genetic factors contributed to continuity, but not change, whereas environmental factors accounted for both continuity and change in both traits. In this study, the degree of genetic influence did not differ across time (Takashasi, Ma, Iacono *et al.* 2007). On the basis of the relative magnitude of effects, these authors concluded that, at least in this age group (mean age early to mid-twenties), temporal stability of individual differences in these RST traits 'owes more to genetic than to environmental factors'. Given that the Carver and White BIS/BAS scales were used in this study, it would have been interesting if FFFS-fear and BIS-anxiety item clusters had been analysed separately.

Conclusions

Over a forty-year period, RST has developed into a sophisticated model of emotion, motivation, personality and psychopathology, and to this achievement we owe a debt of gratitude to the fundamental work of Jeffrey Gray. Although in a continual state of development, the general model of RST synthesizes vast literatures (e.g., behavioural pharmacology of emotion, motivation and learning) and forges bridges between hitherto unrelated areas (e.g., ethoexperimental studies and personality). Of importance is the translational nature of this research: we can now go from basic non-human animal studies to human ones, armed with a rigorous theory to guide the difficult process of understanding the neuropsychology of human personality. As an example of such translational research, Perkins and Corr (2006) confirmed that the basic defensive reactions of rodents to cats in ethologically-valid situations are found in human defensive reactions to a range of threatening situations.

There are many problems still to be addressed in RST, including the following (non-exhaustive) list: (a) how best to characterize BAS processes and how to measure them by questionnaire (Corr 2008a; Pickering and Smillie 2008); (b) what is the relationship between conscious awareness, its functions and emotion/motivation (Gray 2004; Corr 2006, 2008a); (c) how best to operationalize reward and punishment variables in the laboratory and what predictions we should make about their possible interaction (Corr 2002a, 2008a); (d) what is the most appropriate way to measure FFFS, BIS and BAS in human beings, and how such measures can be validated; and (e) are the principles of frustrative non-reward and relief of non-punishment useful in explaining counter-productive and paradoxical behaviour (McNaughton and Corr in press). RST may also have gone some way to help explain the phenomological nature of fear, anxiety and hope: why they 'feel' the way they do; however, it will be some time before we have a consensual model of why emotions are conscious in the first place – although, arguably, Gray (2004) himself has gone a long way to elucidating the functions of consciousness (Corr 2006, 2008a). On top of these problems are wider ones, ranging from the role of 'free will' in behaviour, and how individual behaviour is regulated by society (e.g., effective penal systems).

RST has come a long way, but it still has a long way to go before it can be said to provide a comprehensive model of emotion, motivation, personality and psychopathology. As shown in this chapter, it is a *general* theory that aspires to encapsulate most of the biologically-relevant findings, as well as having the capacity to incorporate new developments. Inevitably, the *specific* form of the theory, at any one 'flash-bulb' moment, will appear in certain respects ill-specified and incomplete.

This chapter has covered a lot of ground and encountered some of the difficulties and unresolved issues that remain; and it has revealed that we must continue to tolerate considerable uncertainty as to the best way to relate fundamental systems of emotion and motivation to personality factors and psychopathology – this is not unique to the RST but to the field in general. Although much work lies ahead, arguably, large areas of hitherto wild growth have been cleared away to reveal the fundamental terrain of the neuropsychology of personality.

References

Blanchard, D. C. and Blanchard, R. J. 1988. Ethoexperimental approaches to the biology of emotion, *Annual Review of Psychology* 39: 43–68

Blanchard, R. J. and Blanchard, D. C. 1990. An ethoexperimental analysis of defense, fear and anxiety, in N. McNaughton and G. Andrews (eds.), *Anxiety*, pp. 12–133. Dunedin: Otago University Press

Blanchard, R. J., Griebel, G., Henrie, J. A. and Blanchard, D. C. 1997. Differentiation of anxiolytic and panicolytic drugs by effects on rat and mouse defense test batteries, *Neuroscience and Biobehavioral Reviews* 21: 783–9

Caci, H., Deschaux, O. and Baylé, F. J. 2007. Psychometric properties of the French versions of the BIS/BAS and the SPSRQ, *Personality and Individual Differences* 42: 987–98

Carver, C. S. 2004. Negative affects deriving from the Behavioral Approach System, *Emotion* 41: 3–22

Carver, C. S. and White, T. L. 1994. Behavioral inhibition, behavioral activation, and affective responses to impending reward and punishment: the BIS/BAS scales, *Journal of Personality and Social Psychology* 67: 319–33

Caseras, F. X., Fullana, M. A., Riba, J., Barbanoj, M. J., Aluja A. and Torrubia, R. 2006. Influence of individual differences in the Behavioural Inhibition System and stimulus content (fear versus blood-disgust) on affective startle reflect modulation, *Biological Psychology* 72: 251–6

Cooper, A., Gomez, R. and Aucute, H. 2007. The Behavioural Inhibition System and Behavioural Approach System (BIS/BAS) scales: measurement and structural invariance across adults and adolescents, *Personality and Individual Differences* 43: 295–305

Cooper, A. J., Perkins, A. and Corr, P. J. 2007. A confirmatory factor analytic study of anxiety, fear and Behavioural Inhibition System measures, *Journal of Individual Differences* 28: 179–87

Corr, P. J. 2001. Testing problems in J. A. Gray's personality theory: a commentary on Matthews and Gilliland (1999), *Personal Individual Differences* 30: 333–52

2002a. J. A. Gray's reinforcement sensitivity theory: tests of the joint subsystem hypothesis of anxiety and impulsivity, *Personality and Individual Differences* 33: 511–32

2002b. J. A. Gray's reinforcement sensitivity theory and frustrative nonreward: a theoretical note on expectancies in reactions to rewarding stimuli, *Personality and Individual Differences* 32: 1247–53

2004. Reinforcement sensitivity theory and personality, *Neuroscience and Biobehavioral Reviews* 28: 317–32

2006. *Understanding biological psychology.* Oxford: Blackwell

2007. Personality and psychology: Hans Eysenck's unifying themes, *The Psychologist* 20: 666–9

2008a. Reinforcement sensitivity theory (RST): Introduction, in P. J. Corr (ed). *The reinforcement sensitivity theory of personality*, pp. 1–43. Cambridge University Press

2008b. *The Reinforcement Sensitivity Theory of Personality*, Cambridge University Press

Corr, P. J. and McNaughton, N. 2008. Reinforcement sensitivity theory and personality, in P. J. Corr (ed). *The reinforcement sensitivity theory of personality*, pp. 155–87. Cambridge University Press

Corr, P. J., Pickering, A. D. and Gray, J. A. 1995. Gray, Personality and reinforcement in associative and instrumental learning, *Personal Individual Differences* 19: 47–71

Dawkins, R. and Krebs, J. R. 1979. Arms races between and within species, *Proceeding of the Royal Society of London Series B* 205: 489–511

Duffy, E. 1962. *Activation and behaviour.* London: Wiley

Eilam, D. 2005. Die hard: a blend of freezing and fleeing as a dynamic defense – implications for the control of defensive behavior, *Neuroscience and Biobehavioral Reviews* 29: 1181–91

Eysenck, H. J. 1947. *Dimensions of personality.* London: K. Paul/Trench Trubner

1957. *The dynamics of anxiety and hysteria.* New York: Preger

1967. *The biological basis of personality.* Springfield, IL: Thomas

1979. The conditioning model of neurosis, *Behavioural and Brain Sciences* 2: 155–99

Eysenck, H. J. and Eysenck, S. G. B. 1976. *Psychoticism as a dimension of personality.* London: Hodder and Stoughton

Eysenck, H. J. and Levey, A. 1972. Conditioning, Introversion–Extraversion and the strength of the nervous system, in V. D. Nebylitsyn and J. A. Gray (eds), *The biological bases of individual behaviour*, pp. 206–20. London: Academic Press

Fowles, D. C. 2006. Jeffrey Gray's contributions to theories of anxiety, personality, and psychopathology, in T. Canli (ed.), *Biology of personality and individual differences*, pp. 7–34. New York: Guilford Press

Franken, I. H. A. and Muris, P. 2006. Gray's impulsivity dimension: a distinction between Reward Sensitivity versus Rash Impulsiveness, *Personality and Individual Differences* 40: 1337–47

Gray, J. A. 1964. *Pavlov's typology.* Oxford: Pergamon Press

1970. The psychophysiological basis of Introversion–Extraversion, *Behaivour Research and Therapy* 8: 249–66

1972a. Learning theory, the conceptual nervous system and personality, in V. D. Nebylitsyn and J. A. Gray (eds.), *The biological bases of individual behaviour*, pp. 372–99. New York: Academic Press

1972b. The psychophysiological nature of Introversion-Extraversion: a modification of Eysenck's theory, in V. D. Nebylitsyn and J. A. Gray (eds.), *The biological bases of individual behaviour*, pp. 182–205. New York: Academic Press

1975. *Elements of a two-process theory of learning*. London: Academic Press

1976. The behavioural inhibition system: a possible substrate for anxiety, in M. P. Feldman and A. M. Broadhurst (eds.), *Theoretical and experimental bases of behaviour modification*, pp. 3–41. London: Wiley

1977. Drug effects on fear and frustration: possible limbic site of action of minor tranquillizers, in L. L. Iversen, S. D. Iversen and S. H. Snyder (eds), *Handbook of psychopharmacology*, vol. VIII, *Drugs, neurotransmitters, and behavior*, pp. 433–529. New York: Plenum Press

1981. A critique of Eysenck's theory of personality, in H. J. Eysenck (ed.), *A model for personality*, pp. 246–76. Berlin: Springer

1982. *The neuropsychology of anxiety: an enquiry into the functions of the septo-hippocampal system*. Oxford University Press

2004. *Consciousness: creeping up on the Hard Problem*. Oxford University Press

Gray, J. A. and McNaughton, N. 2000. *The neuropsychology of anxiety: an enquiry into the functions of the septo-hippocampal system*. Oxford University Press

Haas, B. W., Omura, K., Constable, R. T. and Canli, T. 2007. Emotional conflict and neuroticism: personality-dependent activation in the amygdala and subgenual anterior cingulated, *Behavioural Neuroscience* 121: 249–56

Harmon-Jones, E. 2003. Anger and the behavioral approach system, *Personality and Individual Differences* 35: 995–1005

Hebb, D. O. 1955. Drives and the C. N. S. (Conceptual Nervous System), *Psychological Review* 62: 243–54

Hull, C. L. 1952. *A behaviour system*. New Haven: Yale University Press

Johnson, S. L., Turner, R. J and Iwata, N. 2004. BIS/BAS levels and psychiatric disorder: an epidemiological study, *Journal of Psychopathology and Behavioral Assessment* 25: 25–36

Kendler, K. S., Neale, M. C., Kessler, R. C., Heath, A. C. and Eaves, L. J. 1992. Major depression and generalized anxiety disorder: same genes, (partly) different environments?, *Archives of General Psychiatry* 49: 716–22

Kendler, K. S., Prescott, C. A., Myers, J. and Neale, M. C. 2003. The structure of genetic and environmental risk factors for common psychiatric and substance use disorders in men and women, *Archives of General Psychiatry* 60: 929–37

Konorski, J. 1967. *Integrative activity of the brain*. Chicago University Press

Lakatos, I. 1970. Falsification and the methodology of scientific research programmes, in I. Lakatos and A. Musgrave (eds.), *Criticism and the growth of knowledge*, pp. 91–196. Cambridge University Press

Lykken, D. T. 1971. Multiple factor analysis and personality research, *Journal of Research in Personality* 5: 161–70

Mackintosh, N. J. 1983. *Conditioning and Associative Learning*. Oxford: Clarendon Press

McNaughton, N. and Corr, P. J. 2004. A two-dimensional neuropsychology of defense: fear/anxiety and defensive distance, *Neuroscience and Biobehavioral Reviews* 28: 285–305

2008a. The neuropsychology of fear and anxiety: a foundation for reinforcement sensitivity theory, in P. J. Corr (ed). *The reinforcement sensitivity theory of personality*, pp. 44–94. Cambridge University Press

2008b. Animal cognition and human personality, in P. J. Corr (ed.), *The Reinforcement Sensitivity Theory of Personality*, pp. 95–119. Cambridge University Press

in press. Central theories of motivation and emotion, in G. G. Berntson and J. T. Cacioppo (eds), *Handbook of neuroscience for the behavioural sciences*. London: Wiley

Mowrer, H. O. 1960. *Learning theory and behavior*. New York: Wiley

Olds, J. and Milner, P. 1954. Positive reinforcement produced by electrical stimulation of septal area and other regions of rat brain, *Journal of Comparative and Physiological Psychology* 47: 419–27

Perkins, A. M. and Corr, P. J. 2006. Reactions to threat and personality: psychometric differentiation of intensity and direction dimensions of human defensive behaviour, *Behavioural Brain Research* 169: 21–8

Perkins, A. M., Kemp, S. E. and Corr, P. J. 2007. Fear and anxiety as separable emotions: an investigation of the revised reinforcement sensitivity theory of personality, *Emotion* 7: 252–61

Pickering, A. D. 2008. Format and computational models of Reinforcement Sensitivity Theory, in P. J. Corr (ed.), *The Reinforcement Sensitivity Theory of Personality*, pp. 453–81. Cambridge University Press

Pickering, A. D., Díaz, A. and Gray, J. A. 1995. Personality and reinforcement: an exploration using a maze-learning task, *Personality and Individual Differences* 18: 541–58

Pickering, A. D. and Smillie, L. D. 2008. The behavioural activation system: challenges and opportunities, in P. J. Corr (ed). *The reinforcement sensitivity theory of personality*, pp. 120–54. Cambridge University Press

Poythress, N. G., Skeem, J. L., Weir, J., Lilienfeld, S. O., Douglas, K. D., Edens, J. F. P. and Kennealy, J. 2008. Psychometric properties of Carver and White's (1994) BIS/BAS scales in a large sample of offenders, *Personality and Individual Differences* 45: 732–7

Prescott. C. A. and Kendler, K. S. 1998. Do anxious and depressive states share common genetic factors?, *European Neuropsychopharmacology* 8 Suppl. 2: S76–S77

Quilty, L. C., Oakman, J. M. and Farolden, P. 2007. Behavioural inhibition, behavioural activation, and the preference for familiarity, *Personality and Individual Differences* 42: 291–303

Revelle, W. 1997. Extraversion and impulsivity: the lost dimension, in H. Nyborg (ed.), *The scientific study of human nature: tribute to Hans J. Eysenck at eighty*, pp. 189–212. Oxford: Elsevier Science Press

Ross, S. R., Mottó, J., Poy, R., Seganra, P., Pastor, M. C. and Montañés, S. 2007. Gray's model and psychopathy: BIS but not BAS differentiates primary from secondary psychopathy in noninstitutionalized young adults, *Personality and Individual Differences* 43: 1644–55

Skinner, B. F. 1953. *Science and human behaviour*. New York: Macmillan

Smillie, L. D., Jackson, C. J. and Dalgleish, L. I. 2006. Conceptual distinctions among Carver and White's (1994) BAS scales: a reward-reactivity versus trait impulsivity perspective, *Personality and Individual Differences* 40: 1039–50

Smillie, L. D., Pickering, A. D. and Jackson, C. J. 2006. The new reinforcement sensitivity theory: implications for personality measurement, *Personality and Social Psychology Review* 10: 320–35

Spence, K. W. 1964. Anxiety (drive) level and performance in eyelid conditioning, *Psychological Bulletin* 61: 129–39

Stouffer, S. A., Guttman, L., Suchman, E. A., Lazarsfeld, P. F., Star, S. A. and Clausen, J. A. 1950. *Studies in social psychology in World War II, Vol. IV, Measurement and prediction.* Princeton University Press

Takashasi, Y., Yamagata, S., Kijima, N., Shigemasu, K., Ono, Y. and Ando, J. 2007. Continuity and change in behavioural inhibition and activation systems: a longitudinal behavioural genetic analysis, *Personality and Individual Differences* 43: 1616–23

Tsetsenis, T., Ma, X.-H., Iacono, L. L., Beck, S. G. and Gross, C. 2007. Suppression of conditioning to ambiguous cues by pharmacogenetic inhibition of the dentate gyrus, *Nature Neuroscience* 10: 896–902

Wallace, J. F. and Newman, J. P. 2008. Reinforcement Sensitivity Theory and psychopathy: associations between psychopathy and the behavioral activation and inhibition systems, in P. J. Corr (ed). *The reinforcement sensitivity theory of personality*, pp. 398–414. Cambridge University Press

Weiner, N. 1948. *Cybernetics, or control and communication in the animal and machine.* Cambridge: MIT Press

PART V

Cognitive Perspectives

22 Semantic and linguistic aspects of personality

Gerard Saucier

Distinctions that refer to personality are embedded within languages, and form an important component of the semantic content of a lexicon. The science of personality builds on these distinctions that are represented in language. This chapter focuses on several crucial semantic and linguistic issues with regard to personality: (a) the scientific semantics of personality, especially in relation to aspectual types in language; (b) what kinds of content are included within the concept of personality; (c) effects of content (or variable) selection on findings; (d) possibly ubiquitous dimensions in the language of personality description; and (e) relations between individual and aggregated levels in personality, language and culture.

Defining personality

Definitions give clarity, making one's assumptions explicit. How one defines personality importantly affects how one selects variables when studying the phenomena of personality and how one determines what is to be tested for on a personality test. A source of difficulty is that scientists (a) define the concept in varying ways, and (b) are prone to define the concept more broadly than they operationalize it. Investigators tend to give personality a rather grand and inclusive definition (which serves to underscore its importance) while measuring it with instruments that capture only a segment of this grand, inclusive range.

Personality can be defined in either of two strongly contrasting ways, either as (a) a set of attributes that characterize an individual, or as (b) the underlying system that generates such attributes. Funder (1997, pp. 1–2) provided a definition that takes in both (a) and (b): personality is 'an individual's characteristic patterns of thought, emotion, and behaviour, together with the psychological mechanisms – hidden or not – behind those patterns'.

Funder's definition focuses on 'characteristic patterns' without specifying whether the patterns primarily inhere within the individual or exist at the interface between the individual and his/her interpersonal environment. Nor does it specify whether the 'mechanisms' are within the person or between persons. This ambiguity helps this definition to be comprehensive with respect to other definitions. For example, fifty distinct meanings of 'personality' were reviewed by Allport (1937) in a classic early textbook. These diverse meanings can be arrayed in a continuum ranging from one's externally observable manner to one's internal self, and the entire continuum might fit within Funder's definition.

Allport, in contrast, focused on one end of this continuum and derogated the other. Critical of inclusive omnibus definitions of personality (e.g., Prince 1924), Allport attempted a more specific one: 'personality is the dynamic organization within the individual of those psychophysical systems that determine his unique adjustments to his environment' (1937, p. 48). Allport called this a 'biophysical' conception. It focused on 'what an individual *is* regardless of the manner in which other people perceive his qualities or evaluate them' (p. 40). Phrasings like 'within the individual' and 'systems that determine' reveal an emphasis on the underlying mechanisms behind behaviour.

Before discussing other mechanism-focused definitions of personality, I begin with those focused on a person's attributes. Attributes are labelled variously as traits, or characteristics, or qualities – whether of personality, of character, or of temperament. In English usage the term 'personality' is the broader concept; character attributes tend to be those associated with volition and morality, whereas temperament attributes tend to be associated with emotional, attentional and motor activity and reactivity (Rothbart and Bates 1998).

Personality consists of which kinds of attributes?

One approach to defining personality focuses on attributes. In this approach, personality is a particular set of predications, that is, statements about a subject or entity. Person-description is predication where the entity is a person, and both trait descriptors and situation descriptors are predicates. Consider the following phrases: Robin is diligent, Robin is tired, Robin is at work, and Robin is alone. All these phrases include predicates that state (predicate) something about Robin (the subject or entity).

Lehmann (1994) summarized the major aspectual types – varieties of predicates – conceived in linguistics. The summary reveals a continuum of predicate types ranging from the most static to the most dynamic.

At one end of this continuum is an entity's class or *category membership* (e.g., Robin is a male), which tends to imply not only time-stability, but also something about the essence of an entity. Category membership suggests substantive rather than accidental features of the entity, and functions to name the entity. Another type of time-stable predicate is the *property* (e.g., Robert is small), which is an aspect of an entity that is relatively stable, but can change while a category membership is left intact (e.g., Robert becomes tall, but remains a male).

Neither class membership nor property specifies any contingency with respect to time; both are distinguished from other predicate types by their atemporality – relative stability across time. A *state* differs from a property in being more transitory (e.g., Robert feels small) or contingent (e.g., Robert looks tall in those shoes), characterizing the entity in the moment. A *process* is even more dynamic and less static than a state; it requires a continuous input of energy in order for the aspect to be present or persist (e.g., Robert is being peppered with difficult questions). And whereas a state (or a property or category membership) is just the case, a process can be said to happen at some point in time. How is a process usually distinguished from an *action*? The process (like a state, property or category membership) is uncontrolled or high in affectedness (e.g., Robert is falling; Robert has been billed), whereas an action is controlled or high in agentivity (e.g., Robert is jumping; Robert is paying bills). Processes and actions typically involve verbs.

Personality attributes are *properties* ascribed to persons. Some might appear to be category memberships (as in type-nouns like cynic, genius, or jerk) but these would be categories distinguished by having a single common property. Situation descriptors, in contrast, don't involve properties, but rather the dynamic, more transitory aspects toward the other end of the predicate continuum. Situations include the contexts set by uncontrolled processes (e.g., being challenged or threatened) and intentional actions (e.g., driving, doing homework), as well as states. States might include physical-environmental states (e.g., at work, at home), consensually defined social states (e.g., with friends, with family), as well as the person's subjective states (Saucier, Bel-Bahar and Fernandez 2007).

As properties, personality attributes are qualities of a human entity, more mutable than category memberships, yet less transitory and dynamic than states, processes and actions. Personality attributes are usefully compared to the physical properties of colour. Colours likewise denote attributes without indicating the essential category-defining nature of an entity. Both colour and personality are organized better by dimensions than by categories, and in both cases there are multiple dimensions (for colours: hue, saturation and brightness/luminance).

Understood as attributes, personality is a set of predications made of persons. Dynamic situational aspects that are transitory, existing in the moment only, would be excluded, unless they linger and become recurrent or chronic. Only predicates with atemporality – relative stability across time – can be considered personality.

Can we then say that personality is all of the relatively time-stable attributes of persons? Some definitions do come close to this view, for example Roback's: 'an integrative combination of all our cognitive (knowledge), affective (feeling), conative (volitional) and even physical qualities' (1931, pp. 31–2). Menninger (1930, p. 21) provided a playful but similar definition: 'the individual as a whole, his height and weight and loves and hates and blood pressure and reflexes; his smiles and hopes and bowed legs and enlarged tonsils'.

However, attributes common to all persons (e.g., that you are a human being or that you live on planet Earth) hardly seem to describe your personality. Excluding such attributes, one arrives at a reduced but still broad definition: all of the relatively time-stable attributes on which there are individual differences.

What is a personality descriptor? Twelve disputed categories

There are at least twelve categories of person-descriptors that are subject to controversy – whether they should or should not be considered personality attributes.

(1) *Situational predicates that are recurrently applicable to a particular person, that is, have high atemporality.* In psychology, situations are typically contrasted with dispositional concepts like personality, and the typical situation descriptor is no personality attribute. However, even dynamic situation descriptors, put into a static and consistent aspect, might become personality descriptors. A person could be 'always at home' or 'constantly with friends' or 'always cleaning'. Accordingly, one might identify personality tendencies by looking for extremes in the frequency distribution of situations for a person. Of course, this may be unnecessary to the extent that the most important of these chronic situational tendencies become sedimented in more trait-like descriptors, such as 'homebody' or 'gregarious' or 'obsessive-compulsive'.

(2) *Indicators of geographical or ethnic origin.* Does being 'Estonian' or 'Mexican-American' or 'from Paris' indicate personality? Such characterizations do not directly indicate a behavioural, affective, motivational or cognitive tendency. There may be an indirect reference to a psychological pattern, by way of stereotypes associated with geographical or ethnic origin. Some such origin-indicators eventually become disconnected from the original referent groups, and come to refer to attributes, as in terms like gypsy, provincial and byzantine. So this is a class of descriptors with occasional features of personality reference, although the features may not be very reliable, because they are based on often misleading stereotypes.

(3) *Social and occupational role categories.* Socially-defined roles are often predicated of a person, and such roles do have some stability. For example, you may be a podiatrist, or a mechanical engineer, or a nurse, or a student. As with geographical and ethnicity indicators, prototypical or stereotypical attributes may become associated with the role-category, though perhaps more so for some categories (e.g., politician, criminal, schoolmarm, professor, fraternity member, cowboy, mother, child) and less for others (e.g., office manager, photographer, waitress, bus driver). And for any role-category, one's degree of interest in the role suggests psychological (behavioural, affective, motivational, cognitive) tendencies. Thus, having an interest in a role, or being described as typical for those in the role, would be more personality-relevant than would be merely occupying the role at a particular point in time. Indeed, contemporary occupational interest inventories tend to blur the distinction between interest and typicality: if you respond to items in the way typical for those in a given occupational role, you are scored high for 'interest' in (implying fit with) the role. It is noteworthy that career-interest measures show even higher stability than do personality measures

(Low, Yoon, Roberts and Rounds 2005), and that there are dimensions of variation in career-interest items that are relatively independent of currently popular trait dimensions (Ackerman and Heggestad 1997).

(4) *Physical attributes.* Those physical attributes that are not perceptible to others and therefore have no role in impression formation, reputation and social interactions (such as the size of one's spleen or whether one has a fracture in one's tibia) lack psychological reference. But many physical attributes represented in language (e.g., clumsy, graceful, stylish, sexy) are suggestive of behavioural tendencies. Yet other physical attributes (e.g., tall, fat, attractive) are psychologically significant because of their importance in impression formation. Of course, objective measurements of physical characteristics should be distinguished from ascribed attributes: judgements of how tall or fat a person seems (to self or others) are likely to be imperfectly correlated with actual measured height or weight.

(5) *Attributes denoting social status.* Are terms like famous, prosperous, wealthy, successful and popular personality attributes? Indicants of power and privilege of social position are very important in self-presentation, in reputation, and in human transactions more generally; one of the axes of personality psychology's well-known Interpersonal Circle can be interpreted as power (Leary 1957). Fame, success and popularity can more easily be seen as the *outcome* of characteristic patterns of behaviour, emotion and thought, than as being such patterns themselves. However, these status attributes have psychologically significant effects on the behaviour, affect, motivation and thought of others. So their acceptance as personality attributes may depend on our decision regarding 'social effects', described next.

(6) *Attributes indicating the effect one has on others (i.e., social effects).* Do characterizations of a person as charming, intimidating, or lovable constitute personality? Are such attributes, which involve the effect one has on others, personality attributes? Allport, for whom personality resided 'within' the individual, regarded such attributes as indicators of a person's 'social stimulus value' (Allport 1937, p. 41; based on May 1932), not personality. Indeed, some definitions of personality stress that it consists of 'internal' factors (Child 1968; Hampson 1988), at least those that are not strictly observable. However, social effects provide an ecological angle on personality. They describe the pattern of impacts a person creates around him/her, rather like a social footprint. Social effects fall within Funder's broad definition: they do describe characteristic patterns associated with an individual. Some apparently physical attributes (denoted by terms such as attractive and sexy) may function largely as social effects. Because the criterion is effect on others, the prime data source for social effects might well be informant data rather than self-report.

(7) *Attributes that involve global evaluations.* Personality descriptors in general contain a mixture of descriptive and evaluative components (Peabody 1967). Some terms (e.g., good and bad) used to describe people have a particularly heavy dose of global evaluation, but do still refer to properties of human entities. A study of the most evaluative personality descriptors isolated multiple, clear

content dimensions among them (Benet-Martínez and Waller 2002), tending to refute the objection that there are pure evaluation terms without any personality-related content. Another objection is that highly evaluative items and scales may be especially susceptible to social desirability responding (in self-report) and halo bias (in informant report). More research is needed on this, on the extent to which self and informant ratings converge for highly evaluative attributes, and on the stability of such attributes.

(8) *Attributes indicating eccentricity, deviance, normality or conformity to convention*. Some attributes primarily indicate the degree to which the person fits in with social norms, rather than any specific characteristic of behaviour or thought. In some instances such non-normativity is viewed pejoratively, as in characterizations like weird, strange, or deviant (as opposed to normal). In other instances (probably more common in societies where a degree of deviation from social norms is tolerated or even celebrated) non-normativity is seen in a partially more positive light, as in terms like unique and non-conforming (as opposed to conventional and traditional).

(9) *Attributes indicative of psychopathology*. Because of substantial correlations between variables in the two domains (Krueger and Tackett 2003), one can indeed say that 'the field of personality abuts abnormal psychology' (Buss 1995, p. 3). In the field of abnormal psychology, one finds disorder-attributes are relatively stable patterns of behaviour, affect, motivation and/or cognition that show individual differences – and thus fit the definition of personality. And these disorders are not only the so-called personality disorders: tendencies toward the Axis I disorders also show a good deal of cross-time stability (Shea and Yen 2003) and relations to personality (Krueger and Tackett 2003; Trull and Sher 1994). Psychopathology attributes tend to indicate deviance and be more evaluative than many prototypical personality attributes. The language of psychopathological attributes is primarily an expert language (cf. Block 1995), but this expert language does filter down into lay language, so that terms originally of a professional/technical nature (e.g., depressed, anxious, neurotic, obsessive and compulsive) freely enter the everyday vocabulary. One might object that psychopathology requires expert diagnosis, whereas personality attributes are conventionally measured using self and informant ratings. However, self and informant reports are widely used in the measurement of psychopathology (e.g., in screening measures; Meyer, Finn, Eyde *et al.* 2001), and expert observations can also be useful in the assessment of personality (Block 1995; Tanaka and Taylor 1991).

(10) *Generalized attitudes, values and belief dispositions*. Beliefs, values and social attitudes may seem to be of a very different character than personality traits. They involve valuations of, and expectations with regard to, specific objects (e.g., ideas, governments, groups of people, supernatural entities). Allport (1937) regarded attitudes as behavioural dispositions of a specific and external sort, being 'bound to an object or value' (p. 294), aroused in the presence of a specifiable class of stimuli. If, however, an attitude is 'chronic and "temperamental", expressed in almost any sphere of the person's behaviour' (p. 294)

then for Allport it differed little from a trait, and he gave radicalism and conservatism as examples. Such *generalized* attitudes – those for which it is difficult to specify the exact object – can be considered personality traits. Although single items referencing attitudes, values and beliefs about specific topics cannot indicate traits, factors based on a large number and range of such items can. An example of factors based on such wide-ranging content are the four dimensions found among 'isms' terms from the natural language (Saucier 2000; Krauss 2006): Tradition-oriented Religiousness, Subjective Spirituality, Unmitigated Self-interest, and another factor referencing the civic belief system. These dimensions are roughly as stable across time as personality attributes (Saucier 2008), and appear to be relatively independent of them.

(11) *'Temporary state' attributes*. Stability across time is a part of most definitions of personality. Based on this, investigators might exclude any variables that seem to refer to attributes of temporary duration. However, as with situations (category 1 above), an attribute that usually refers to something temporary (e.g., angry, surprised) might also be a stable 'property of a human entity'. For example, a chronic tendency toward a particular emotion (as in easily or often angry, easily or often surprised) fits well with the classic conception of temperament.

(12) *Attributes that indicate abilities*. We might say that ability tests reference the maximum-performance capabilities of the individual, whereas personality tests reference the individual's typical performance. Based on this, attributes indicating abilities might not be considered personality, but rather part of some other domain (e.g., Eysenck 1993). However, we must distinguish between perceived virtues of intellect (e.g., wise, insightful, astute, knowledgeable, creative, brilliant, talented, smart, clever) and scores on tests of general mental ability. These terms do not commonly denote that a person does well on tests, but rather that the person typically and in naturalistic situations demonstrates reactions, understanding and decision-making processes that seem adaptive and intelligent. The modest (r roughly .30*)* level of association between lexically derived Intellect factors and IQ tests (Goldberg and Rosolack 1994; McCrae and Costa 1985) indicates as much. The terms may refer to social, practical or emotional intelligence as much as to academic intelligence.

Comparing narrow and inclusive variable-selection strategies

Operational definitions of personality are embodied in variable-selection strategies. The most narrow operational definition of personality would exclude all of the twelve categories of attributes above and accept only what remains. In contrast, the most inclusive operational definition would include all or most of the twelve categories, only specifying that there must be chronicity or temporal stability and that there must be some psychological aspect to the attribute (whether in the perceiver or the perceived).

The narrow and inclusive variable-selection approaches have differing strengths. The narrow approach concentrates only on the lowest common denominator: those descriptors everyone would agree are attributes of personality. The inclusive approach, on the other hand, still includes the lowest common denominator (which one can always access simply by selecting a sub-set of variables for analysis) but enables the investigator to find useful additional sources of variance.

Likewise, the narrow and inclusive approaches each have their own hazards. Use of the narrow approach risks throwing out the baby with the bathwater – losing important information that is referenced in the excluded attributes. Moreover, since predictors that are inclusive in nature should be predictive of a wider range of criteria, one might expect lower average validity for measurement models based on the narrow operational approach. As for the inclusive approach, it might yield factors that would (a) turn out eventually not to meet many criteria for personality attributes, or (b) be a difficult-to-interpret mixture of heterogeneous categories.

How does variable selection (and thus the definition of personality) affect structure?

Differences in structure between personality inventories are rooted to some degree in the differing variable-selection strategies used to construct them. But the effect of differing strategies – of differing operational definitions of personality – is most clear when we examine the results of lexical studies.

What are lexical studies? As has long been recognized (e.g., Allport and Odbert 1936; Cattell 1943; Goldberg 1981; Norman 1963), basic personality dimensions might be discovered by studying conceptions implicit in use of the natural language. If a distinction is highly represented in the lexicon, it can be presumed to have practical importance. This leads us to a key premise of the lexical approach: *the degree of representation of an attribute in language has some correspondence with the general importance of the attribute in real-world transactions*. This premise links semantic representation directly with a social-importance criterion.

Two other considerations make lexical studies of crucial importance. First, lexicalized concepts can be found in *standard sources* created by disinterested parties (e.g., linguists and lexicographers), and basing variable selection on such a source reduces the likelihood of investigator bias in deciding what is or is not an important variable. Secondly, because lexicalized concepts constitute a finite domain, one can sample them representatively to establish *content-validity* benchmarks for personality variables.

The lexical-study paradigm gives special importance to *cross-cultural generalizability*. Structural models derived within one limited population are prone to reflect the unique patterns found within that population. Models that transfer well across populations, across languages and socio-cultural settings satisfy better the scientific ideals of replicability and generalizability.

The lexical approach involves an indigenous research strategy. Analyses are carried out separately within each language, using a representative set of native-language descriptors, rather than merely importing selections of variables from other languages (e.g., English). An indigenous structure is discovered, and then compared to previously derived structures.

The majority of lexical studies of personality descriptors have attempted to test the most widely influential structural model of the last two decades, the Big Five factor structure (Goldberg 1990; John 1990). The Big Five factors are customarily labelled Extraversion, Agreeableness, Conscientiousness, Emotional Stability (versus Neuroticism), and Intellect (or, in one inventory representation, Openness to Experience). Although there were signs of the Big Five structure in some studies from an earlier era (as detailed by Digman 1990; John 1990), its identification in studies of English descriptors (e.g., Goldberg 1990) was decisive.

If we value cross-cultural generalizability, however, applicability to one language is not enough. Lexical studies have yielded structures resembling the Big Five most consistently in languages from the Germanic and Slavic language families of northern Europe, but more inconsistently elsewhere. The subsequent review therefore focuses not only on the five-factor level, but on other numbers of factors as well.

As will be seen, variable selection matters, especially if one extracts three or more factors. Lexical studies have had imperfect agreement regarding *exactly* how inclusive or narrow the variable selection should be. This is true even for studies with a narrower selection, which have differed with respect to their inclusion of descriptors from categories 11 and 12 in particular.

The 'Big One' factor

Several lexical studies have reported evidence about factor solutions containing only one factor (Boies, Lee, Ashton *et al.* 2001; Di Blas and Forzi 1999; Goldberg and Somer 2000; Saucier 1997, 2003b; Saucier, Georgiades, Tsaousis and Goldberg 2005; Saucier, Ole-Kotikash and Payne 2006; Zhou, Saucier, Gao and Liu in press), with consistent findings. The single factor contrasts a heterogeneous mix of desirable attributes at one pole with a mix of undesirable attributes at the other pole. This unrotated factor can be labelled Evaluation (following Osgood 1962), or as Socially Desirable versus Undesirable Qualities. If psychopathology variables are constrained to only one dimension, it represents general maladjustment, likely strongly related to the evaluation factor in personality attributes. Overall, there is as yet no evidence that variable selection – how inclusively versus narrowly personality is conceived – affects structure at the one-factor level.

The Big Two

Lexical-study two-factor solutions also suggest a consistent pattern: one factor includes attributes associated with positively valued dynamic qualities and individual ascendancy, whereas the other factor includes attributes associated with socialization, morality, social propriety, solidarity and community cohesion (Caprara, Barbanelli and Zimbardo 1997; Di Blas and Forzi 1999; Goldberg and Somer 2000; Hřebíčková, Ostendorf, Osecká and Čermák 1999; Saucier 1997, 2003b; Saucier, Georgiades, Tsaousis and Goldberg 2005; Saucier, Ole-Kotikash and Payne 2006; Zhou, Saucier, Gao and Liu in press). These two factors may be aligned with some of the sets of dual personological constructs reviewed by Digman (1997) and by Paulhus and John (1998), including Hogan's (1983) distinction between 'getting ahead' (Dynamism) and 'getting along' (Social Propriety). They seem to resemble also higher-order factors of the Big Five (DeYoung 2006; Digman 1997).

Like the one-factor structure, this two-factor structure appears to be as ubiquitous across languages and cultures and appears to be relatively impervious to variable-selection effects. That is, these two factors seem to appear whether there is a relatively restricted or inclusive selection of variables (Saucier 1997), and whether one studies adjectives or type-nouns (Saucier 2003b) or even more diverse combinations of variable types (Saucier, Ole-Kotikash and Payne 2006). And there may be strong homology with the structure of the domain of psychopathology at the two-factor level. The best replicated two-dimensional model for psychopathology distinguishes externalizing and internalizing disorders (e.g., Krueger and Markon 2006). A reasonable hypothesis is that externalizing disorders represent low Social Propriety (Morality) whereas internalizing disorders have a stronger relation to low Dynamism.

Three-dimensional space

In three-factor solutions, studies of most languages of European origin (plus those in Turkish, Korean and Chinese) have produced factors corresponding to Extraversion, Agreeableness and Conscientiousness. Although this structure was not observed in Filipino, French, Greek or Maasai studies, it appears readily in a sub-set of languages that is larger than the sub-set that yields the Big Five. Its generalizability across variable selections is unclear. Among English adjectives, this structure was as robust across variable selections as were one- and two-factor structures (Saucier 1997). But studies of English type-nouns (Saucier 2003b) and of other inclusive selections of variables (Saucier, Georgiades, Tsaousis and Goldberg 2005; Saucier, Ole-Kotikash and Payne 2006) failed to find it.

Five lexical factors

Lexical studies in Slavic and Germanic languages (including English) have been quite supportive of the Big Five, and so has a study in Turkish. But other studies (e.g., Di Blas and Forzi 1998; Saucier, Georgiades, Tsaousis and Goldberg 2005; Szirmák and De Raad 1994) have found no clear counterpart to the Intellect factor in five-factor solutions.

Several lexical studies have had a relatively inclusive selection of variables, each including many terms that could be classified as referring to emotions and moods or as highly evaluative. Some of these studies (Goldberg and Somer 2000; Saucier 1997) included terms referring to physical appearance. None of these analyses has found the Big Five in a five-factor solution. The appearance of the Big Five is clearly contingent upon the variable-selection procedure, and thus on the operational definition of personality.

Lexical six factor models

Ashton, Lee, Perugini *et al.* (2004) have presented evidence that many of the lexical studies conducted to date yield a consistent pattern in six factor solutions: six factors that can be labelled as Extraversion, Emotionality, Agreeableness, Honesty/Humility, Conscientiousness and Openness. Although the structural pattern was first detected in studies of Korean (Hahn, Lee and Ashton 1999) and French (Boies, Lee, Ashton *et al.* 2001), it has appeared to a recognizable degree also in Dutch, German, Hungarian, Italian and Polish. The six factor structure appears in a wide variety of languages, well beyond Germanic and Slavic groups, and its replicability appears to exceed that for the Big Five. Another advantage: six independent factors can provide more information than the Big Five. In the first reported 'horse races' between the models, (Saucier, Georgiades, Tsaousis and Goldberg 2005; Saucier, Ole-Kotikash and Payne 2006), the six factor model seemed about equally as replicable as the Big Five, although not nearly as well replicated as were one and two factor models.

This six factor model may be found, however, only in the adjective domain. Saucier (2003b) found that type-nouns in English yielded six factors very similar to those found in earlier studies of Dutch and German. But these six factors as a set do not correspond closely to the Cross-Language Six.

Seven factors found with a wider inclusion of lexical variables

Consistent with early practice in the field (Allport and Odbert 1936; Norman 1963), analyses leading to the five or six factor structures have involved, in each study, removal of all terms from the great majority of the twelve controversial categories reviewed earlier. When investigators have used wider variable selections (i.e., those including many or all of these excluded types of variables), studies in English and Turkish did find Big-Five-like factors within a seven-factor solution (Goldberg and Somer 2000; Saucier 1997; Tellegen and Waller 1987). Of the two additional factors in these studies, one was found in all three: 'Negative Valence' (NV) is a factor emphasizing attributes with extremely low desirability and endorsement rates and with descriptive content involving morality/depravity, dangerousness, worthlessness, peculiarity and stupidity (cf., Benet-Martínez and Waller 2002). A core content theme seems to be Noxious Violativeness – attributes reflecting a tendency to harmfully violate the rights of others, corresponding in many ways to contemporary definitions of antisocial personality disorder (Saucier 2007).

Is there convergence at the seven-factor level? Studies with inclusive variable-selection criteria in some languages do converge on a seven-factor structural pattern, in spite of many differences in study methodology. Lexical studies in Filipino (Church, Reyes, Katigbak *et al.* 1997) and Hebrew (Almagor, Tellegen and Waller 1995) – languages from unrelated language-families and cultures – tend to exhibit this structural pattern, even if divergent labelling of the factors obscures it (Saucier 2003a). Moreover, a lexical study of the language with the largest number of native speakers (Chinese) generated seven emic factors with some resemblance to this structure (Zhou, Saucier, Gao and Liu in press). The seven factors include Negative Valence (or Noxious Violativeness), Conscientiousness, Intellect, Gregariousness, Self-Assurance, Even Temper and Concern for Others (versus Egotism). A comparison of seven-factor solutions from numerous studies indicates that the first six of these are particularly recurrent across studies. These six resemble the Cross-Language Six, except for one apparent effect of variable selection: with an inclusive selection, the (Dis)Honesty factor tends to morph into the slightly more evaluatively extreme Noxious Violativeness factor (Saucier in press).

Epilogue: effects of variable selection and of operational definitions

The foregoing review underscores the important downstream effects of variable selection (cf., Saucier 1997), of how personality is operationally defined. These effects of variable selection should come as no surprise, as they are pervasive across the sciences. If astronomers focused entirely on the zone of the ecliptic – that narrow band of the firmament in which the sun, moon and planets appear to rotate and where the zodiac is found – astronomy's conclusions about the nature of the universe would no doubt be altered. It would be prudent for psychologists to couple a focus on the most prototypical attributes of personality with a simultaneous 'bigger picture' examination of all psychological attributes on which there are stable individual differences. The same dual focus is advisable in lexical studies (as in Goldberg and Somer 2000; Saucier 1997; Saucier, Ole-KotiKash and Payne 2006).

Personality as a system

A very different approach to defining personality focuses on the underlying system that drives or generates the set of personality attributes. Good examples are definitions by Cloninger (2000, p. 3): 'the underlying causes within the person of individual behaviour and experience'; by Pervin (1996, p. 414): 'the complex organization of cognitions, affects, and behaviours that gives direction and pattern (coherence) to the person's life'; and by Mayer (2007, p. 14; cf., Wundt 1896/1969, p. 26): 'the organized, developing system within the individual that represents the collective action of that individual's major psychological subsystems.' On this view, personality is not a set of predications (i.e., attributes) that are clearly represented in language, but instead a set of mechanisms that may operate differently from one individual to another.

The history of psychology has seen rich theoretical developments using 'personality as system' conceptions. I will briefly review some prominent examples. Then I will review in more detail another, less well-known, conception that is relevant to a semantic and linguistic standpoint, and offers novel insights regarding integration of the personality and culture levels of analysis.

Conceptions of the personality system developed within psychology

Psychodynamic theories (of Freud, Jung, Adler, and others) posit a distinction between unconscious (or automatic) and conscious (or controlled) processing, and identifying certain energetically powerful motivational forces operating from the unconscious (automatic) side. They posit multiple internal forces or tendencies that may conflict (and thus need harmonizing) with one another, which may give rise to mechanisms (e.g., ego, defences, an individuation process) that in effect respond to the conflicts and the anxiety they generate. Of course, psychodynamic theories are ideationally rich but have proven difficult to empirically confirm (or falsify).

Rooted in contemporary neuroscience are promising theories that posit distinct brain systems or circuits, and then link individual differences in the functioning of these systems/circuits, via psychobiological endophenotypes, to overt personality characteristics. A prime example is the set of theories (e.g., Carver and White 1994; Torrubia, Avila, Molto and Caseras 2001), emanating originally from Gray (1983) that set out distinct brain systems for approach (or reward-sensitivity, or behavioural activation) and avoidance (or withdrawal, or threat- or punishment-sensitivity, or behavioural inhibition), sometimes adding a third 'constraint' or self-regulation system (Carver 2005; cf. Rothbart and Bates 1998).

Mischel and colleagues have proposed a cognitive-affective personality system that includes prominently (a) the encoding or appraisal of particular types of situations; (b) expectancies and values that may become activated if relevant in a situation; (c) competencies; and (d) self-regulatory strategies. These components interact in relation to the particular type of situation the individual encounters, generating the overt behavioural pattern (Mischel 1999). A distinct feature of this approach is that overt attributes – personality dispositions – are seen contextually and conditionally, appearing based on the type of situation present. A partially related description of the personality system is provided by Cervone and Pervin (2008), who see the operation of the system in terms of four principal types of variables: beliefs and expectancies, evaluative standards, goals and skills/competencies.

However, none of the approaches just reviewed compellingly integrates the personality system with the 'culture' level of analysis. For an approach that does so, I turn to a sister field.

Personality system as conceived in psychological anthropology

To explore how personality and culture might be integrated, we must begin by defining culture. A mainstream definition in cultural psychology is this: culture is 'the set of attitudes, values, beliefs, and behaviours shared by a group of people, communicated from one generation to the next via language or some other means of communication' (Matsumoto 1997, pp. 4–5). Thus, culture is *shared* patterns. But shared by whom? How much has to be shared for two persons to be considered as from the same culture? The definition is fuzzy and hard to operationalize: 'there are necessarily no hard and fast rules of how to determine what a culture is or who belongs to that culture' (Matsumoto 1997, p. 5).

A problem with this definition is that it prompts one to look for *the* (one) pattern shared by a whole distinct group, relying on the common but unexamined assumption that cultures are homogeneous. A set of persons is postulated to all be members in a culture in an equivalent way. One goes to Italy and finds there 'Italian culture' – the same thing theoretically in every region of Italy and in every Italian. Then one crosses into France, and now finds 'French culture.' Cultures might be assumed to correspond to nations, but on other occasions to ethnic groupings (e.g., Hispanic-American) or even racial constructs (e.g., Caucasians). But in reality, culture does not regularly correspond to nations, ethnicities or so-called 'races'. Some individuals are 'bicultural', able to operate in two different cultures. One can learn a new culture without necessarily giving up an old one. Nor is culture homogeneous: within any nation one typically finds numerous sub-cultures, which might be organized along what are seen as ethnic or racial lines, or alternatively by language, lifestyle or ideology. And there is plenty of variation from one individual to another within one apparent culture.

Psychological anthropology has developed a way of taking account of culture's heterogeneity, through a 'distributive model of culture'. The first explicit versions of a distributive model were put forward by Devereux (1945), Spiro (1951) and Wallace (1961). Schwartz (1978) and Goodenough (1981) provided the fullest versions.

For Schwartz, to define culture one must define its representation in individuals. This he calls the 'idioverse'. It is the individual's portion of his/her culture, an open system, subject to change . It can be more clearly defined as the total set of cognitive, evaluative and affective constructs – the schemas, or construals of (and rules and standards about) events, objects and persons (both self and others) – held by the individual. Included are an individual's scripts, norms, goals, values, beliefs, expectancies and knowledge structures. One could use 'mindset' as a more colloquial synonym for idioverse, although idioverse does nicely convey the notion of 'an individual's *idio*syncratic view of the uni*verse*'. The idioverse (mindset) is an organizing system that generates regularities in thought, emotion and behaviour. It is a personality system.

Culture, according to Schwartz, is a population of personalities, that is, of idioverses or mindsets. Personality is culture at the individual level, and culture is personality at an aggregated level. For Schwartz, culture includes all of the content of all of the idioverses of all individuals who participate in the culture. This may seem overly inclusive, but such a wide conception is necessary in order to account for cultural innovation. A single individual may develop a new 'construct' (e.g., self-esteem, non-violent resistance, a Super Bowl party) that eventually becomes more widely shared. If one does not include all of the contents of all of the idioverses (what Goodenough (1981) calls the 'cultural pool') as somehow part of culture, these innovations seem to appear out of nowhere.

Goodenough's (1981) approach emphasizes the similarities of how *culture* is represented in individuals with how *language* is represented in individuals. Speakers of one language (one might call them a language-community) are not one homogeneous group. There are individual differences in knowledge as well as usage of both grammar and vocabulary. One person may know slang or technical or other vocabulary that another person does not; the individual's unique version of the language might be called an 'idiolect'. The analogue of a sub-culture would be a dialect. One can learn to speak more than one language, and even so, to participate in more than one culture. Like a culture, a language embodies a set of standards (for how to communicate).

The standards attributed to a group can come to be seen as operating apart from the individuals in the group – a common illusion. But logically, it is as nonsensical to speak of 'belonging to a culture' (or being a member of it) as it is to speak of 'belonging to a language'. As Goodenough puts it, you 'cannot be a member of a set of standards or of a body of knowledge of customs' (1981, p. 103). You utilize a culture, just as you utilize a language.

Goodenough itemizes the contents of culture in systematic relation to one another, beginning with the most basic units, moving from (a) forms (categories, concepts, ideas), up to (b) propositions, up to (c) beliefs. Personal values (d) are those personal beliefs associated with inner feeling states, wants, felt needs, interests, and with maximizing gratification and minimizing frustration. The next most abstract units seem less overtly psychological and more overtly cultural. There are (e) rules and public values – systems that set out rules, codes, duties, obligations, rights, privileges and standards of fairness; (f) recipes (known procedural requirements for accomplishing a purpose, as in how-to and etiquette guides); (g) routines and customs; and finally (h) institutions that organize and systematize units (e) through (g).

These are proposed to be the contents of culture, and also the key components of personality, but only if we think of personality in the sense of mindset or personality system: the guidance system for behaviour rather than attributes (observable patterns of behaviour). The personality system may appear to give way to the cultural system when we go from personal values (d) to public values (e), but features of cultural systems are internalized in individuals, and features of personality systems continually impact the cultural systems.

Integrating personality-attribute and personality-system approaches

In some ways the two approaches to defining personality embody different perspectives on the person. Seeing personality as *attributes*, we take an external perspective that averages across behavioural instances in conceiving generalized qualities and tendencies. This is fundamentally how others see us, and is the basis for reputations. Although we may commonly use this attribute-oriented perspective also in viewing ourselves, the informant perspective is ultimately more reliable with respect to defining a real basis for attributes: when many informants tend to agree about a target person, this yields a degree of objectivity that is not possible from a single self-report (Hofstee 1994). Whether a person objectively has an attribute is a matter distinct from whether the person believes he or she does, or even whether any other single person has that belief.

When we conceive of personality as a behaviour-generating *system*, we focus instead on the standards, expectancies, beliefs, values, goals and other schemas held 'within' the individual. Such contents can certainly be inferred from behavioural observations, task performance and implicit attitudes (observing how the presentation of the concept affects judgements), but self-report is often the most direct way to elicit such contents.

As different as these two approaches are, there are important intersections between them.

(1) The character of one's personality system (or mindset) affects the character of one's behaviour, and thus the attributes one is perceived to have.

(2) Some attributes (those that refer to an individual's cognitive and motivational tendencies, including many generalized attitudes) reference primarily mindset and simultaneously suggest how an individual's personality system is organized. Examples are Radical, Conservative, Perfectionistic, Machiavellian and Sensation-Seeking.

(3) Beliefs about self play an important role under either conception. For example, the belief that I am honest or extraverted is part of my mindset, as is a representation about how much honesty and extraversion are valued. Self-report directly reflects such beliefs and values. Even if a self-report is not validated by informant reports, it can still be taken as evidence of personal beliefs and values.

(4) The NV (Negative Valence or Noxious Violativeness) factor seems to index tendencies to gross and wide-ranging violations of the rights of others, and of normative standards for behaviour. But this probably also reflects a central tendency in mindset: monitoring for individuals who cannot be 'counted on' for the behaviour expected in the cultural context. Highly evaluative attribute-concepts (e.g., Good, Holy, Impressive, Evil) reference perceived competence with respect to consensual standards for proper behaviour. We tend to have contempt for those who disappoint us by showing deficits

in such competence, who run askew of the standards of public culture. Allport and Odbert (1936) argued that the science of personality would do well to ignore highly evaluative concepts, but they may be a vital part of the operation of mindset.

(5) Attributes so important as to anchor major personality dimensions may reveal key features of the personality system, and of its preoccupations. For example, the Big Two Dynamism and Morality/Social Propriety dimensions may arise out of the relative independence of tendencies for others to be rewarding (those you would approach) or threatening (those you would avoid). And the single evaluative factor may be a simple combination of these two: attributes of people you would approach contrasted with attributes of people you would avoid.

Conclusions

As this chapter demonstrates, attending to semantic and linguistic aspects of personality is no idle exercise, but leads to crucial insights. Personality has no single consensual definition. If one defines it as attributes (i.e., properties of persons) that show individual differences, one must deal with controversy regarding which categories of attributes should be included in the domain of personality. Many categories that appear to fall easily within definitions of personality tend to be operationally excluded from personality research. The dimensions one finds from studying lexicons demonstrate the effects of how one operationally defines personality and thus selects variables. Nonetheless, some dimensions (the Big One and those in the Big Two) seem to arise across variations in operational definition. If one defines personality as a system, as mechanisms that affect behaviour, one confronts many alternative conceptions of what this system contains. However, it is possible to see the personality system as integrally related to the meaning of 'culture', and language itself, existing in individual- and group-level variants, has some analogies to personality and culture. Central semantic themes in personality may reveal not just the character of human variation in the real world, but also the evolved preoccupations of human mindsets. More work is needed to create a truly integrative view of personality that incorporates both attribute and system perspectives.

References

Ackerman, P. L. and Heggestad, E. D. 1997. Intelligence, personality, and interests: evidence for overlapping traits, *Psychological Bulletin* 121: 218–45
Allport, G. W. 1937. *Personality: a psychological interpretation*. New York: Holt
Allport, G. W. and Odbert, H. S. 1936. Trait names: a psycho-lexical study, *Psychological Monographs* 47: Whole No. 211

Almagor, M., Tellegen, A. and Waller, N. 1995. The Big Seven model: a cross-cultural replication and further exploration of the basic dimensions of natural language of trait descriptions, *Journal of Personality and Social Psychology* 69: 300–7

Ashton, M. C., Lee, K., Perugini, M., Szarota, P. De Vries, R. E., Di Blas, L., Boies, K. and De Raad, B. 2004. A six-factor structure of personality-descriptive adjectives: solutions from psycholexical studies in seven languages, *Journal of Personality and Social Psychology* 86: 356–66

Ashton, M. C., Lee, K., Vernon, P. A. and Jang, K. L. 2000. Fluid intelligence, crystallized intelligence, and the openness/intellect factor, *Journal of Research in Personality* 34: 198–207

Benet-Martínez, V. and Waller, N. G. 2002. From adorable to worthless: implicit and self-report structure of highly evaluative personality descriptors, *European Journal of Personality* 16: 1–41

Block, J. 1995. A contrarian view of the five-factor approach to personality description, *Psychological Bulletin* 117: 187–215

Boies, K., Lee, K., Ashton, M. C., Pascal, S. and Nicol, A. A. M. 2001. The structure of the French personality lexicon, *European Journal of Personality* 15: 277–95

Buss, A. H. 1995. *Personality: temperament, social behaviour, and the self.* Boston: Allyn and Bacon

Caprara, G. V., Barbanelli, C. and Zimbardo, P. G. 1997. Politicians' uniquely simple personalities, *Nature* 385: 493

Carver, C. S. 2005. Impulse and constraint: perspectives from personality psychology, convergence with theory in other areas, and potential for integration, *Personality and Social Psychology Review* 9: 312–33

Carver, C. S. and White, T. 1994. Behavioural inhibition, behavioural activation, and affective responses to impending reward and punishment: the BIS/BAS scales, *Journal of Personality and Social Psychology* 67: 319–33

Cattell, R. B. 1943. The description of personality: basic traits resolved into clusters, *Journal of Abnormal and Social Psychology* 38: 476–506

Cervone, D. and Pervin, L. A. 2008. *Personality: theory and research*, 10th edn. New York: Wiley

Child, I. L. 1968. Personality in culture, in E. F. Borgatta and W. W. Lambert (eds.), *Handbook of personality theory and research*. Chicago: Rand McNally

Church, A. T., Reyes, J. A. S., Katigbak, M. S. and Grimm, S. D. 1997. Filipino personality structure and the Big Five model: a lexical approach, *Journal of Personality* 65: 477–528

Cloninger, S. C. 2000. *Theories of personality: understanding persons*, 3rd edn. Upper Saddle River, NJ: Prentice-Hall

Devereux, G. 1945. The logical foundations of culture and personality studies, *Transactions of the New York Academy of Sciences* Series 2, 7: 110–30

DeYoung, C. G. 2006. Higher-order factors of the Big Five in a multi-informant sample, *Journal of Personality and Social Psychology* 91: 1138–51

Di Blas, L. and Forzi, M. 1998. An alternative taxonomic study of personality descriptors in the Italian language, *European Journal of Personality* 12: 75–101

1999. Refining a descriptive structure of personality attributes in the Italian language: the abridged Big Three circumplex structure, *Journal of Personality and Social Psychology* 76: 451–81

Digman, J. M. 1990. Personality structure: emergence of the Five-Factor Model, in M. R. Rosenzweig and L. W. Porter (eds.), *Annual review of psychology*, vol. 41, pp. 417–40. Palo Alto, CA: Annual Reviews

1997. Higher order factors of the Big Five, *Journal of Personality and Social Psychology* 73: 1246–56

Eysenck, H. J. 1993. The relationship between IQ and personality, in G. L. Van Heck, P. Bonaiuto, I. J. Deary and W. Nowack (eds.), *Personality psychology in Europe*, vol. IV, pp. 159–81. Tilburg University Press

Funder, D. C. 1997. *The personality puzzle*. New York: Norton

Goldberg, L. R. 1981. Language and individual differences: the search for universals in personality lexicons, in L. W. Wheeler (ed.), *Review of personality and social psychology*, vol. II, pp. 141–65. Beverly Hills, CA: Sage

1990. An alternative 'description of personality': the Big-Five factor structure, *Journal of Personality and Social Psychology* 59: 1216–29

Goldberg, L. R. and Rosolack, T. K. 1994. The Big Five factor structure as an integrative framework: an empirical comparison with Eysenck's P-E-N model, in C. F. Halverson, G. A. Kohnstamm, A. Geldolph and R. P. Martin (eds.), *The developing structure of temperament and personality from infancy to adulthood*, pp. 7–35. Hillsdale, NJ: Erlbaum

Goldberg, L. R. and Somer, O. 2000. The hierarchical structure of common Turkish person-descriptive adjectives, *European Journal of Personality* 14: 497–531

Goodenough, W. H. 1981. *Culture, language, and society*. Menlo Park, CA: Benjamin/ Cummings

Gray, J. A. 1983. Where should we search for biologically based dimensions of personality?, *Zeitschrift für Differentielle und Diagnostische Psychologie* 42: 163–74

Hahn, D. W., Lee, K. and Ashton, M. C. 1999. A factor analysis of the most frequently used Korean personality trait adjectives, *European Journal of Personality* 13: 261–82

Hampson, S. E. 1988. *The construction of personality: an introduction*, 2nd edn. London: Routledge

Hofstee, W. K. B. 1994. Who should own the definition of personality?, *European Journal of Personality* 8: 149–62

Hogan, R. 1983. A socioanalytic theory of personality, in M. M. Page (ed.), *Nebraska symposium on motivation*, pp. 336–55. Lincoln, NE: University of Nebraska Press

Hřebíčková, M., Ostendorf, F., Osecká, L. and Čermák, I. 1999. Taxonomy and structure of Czech personality-relevant verbs, in I. Mervielde, I. J. Deary, F. De Fruyt and F. Ostendorf (eds.), *Personality psychology in Europe*, vol. VII, pp. 51–65. Tilburg University Press

John, O. P. 1990. The 'Big Five' factor taxonomy: dimensions of personality in the natural language and in questionnaires, in L. A. Pervin (ed.), *Handbook of personality: theory and research*, pp. 66–100. New York: Guilford

Krauss, S. 2006. Does ideology transcend culture? A preliminary examination in Romania, *Journal of Personality* 74: 1219–56

Krueger, R. F. and Markon, K. E. 2006. Reinterpreting comorbidity: a model-based approach to understanding and classifying psychopathology, *Annual Review of Clinical Psychology* 2: 111–33

Krueger, R. F. and Tackett, J. L. 2003. Personality and psychopathology: working toward the bigger picture, *Journal of Personality Disorders* 17: 109–28

Leary, T. 1957. *Interpersonal diagnosis of personality*. New York: Ronald

Lehmann, C. 1994. Predicates: aspectual types, in R. E. Asher (ed.), *The encyclopedia of language and linguistics*, vol. I, pp. 3297–302. Oxford: Pergamon

Low, K. S. D., Yoon, M., Roberts, B. W. and Rounds, J. 2005. Stability of vocational interests from early adolescence to middle adulthood: a quantitative review of longitudinal studies, *Psychological Bulletin* 131: 713–37

Matsumoto, D. 1997. *Culture and modern life*. Pacific Grove, CA: Brooks/Cole

May, M. A. 1932. The foundations of personality, in P. S. Achilles (ed.), *Psychology at work*. New York: McGraw-Hill

Mayer, J. D. 2007. *Personality: a systems approach*. Boston: Pearson

McCrae, R. R. and Costa, P. T. 1985. Updating Norman's 'adequate taxonomy': intelligence and personality dimensions in natural language and in questionnaires, *Journal of Personality and Social Psychology* 49: 710–21

Menninger, K. A. 1930. *The human mind*. New York: Literary Guild of America

Meyer, G. J., Finn, S. E., Eyde, L. D., Kay, G. G., Moreland, K. L., Dies, R. R., Eisman, E. J., Kubiszyn, T. W. and Read, G. M. 2001. Psychological testing and psychological assessment: A review of evidence and issues, *American Psychologist* 56: 128–165.

Mischel, W. 1999. Personality coherence and dispositions in a Cognitive-Affective Personality System (CAPS) approach, in D. Cervone and Y. Shoda (eds.), *The coherence of personality: social-cognitive bases of consistency, variability, and organization*, pp. 37–60. New York: Guilford

Norman, W. T. 1963. Toward an adequate taxonomy of personality attributes: replicated factor structure in peer nomination personality ratings, *Journal of Abnormal and Social Psychology* 66: 574–83

Osgood, C. E. 1962. Studies on the generality of affective meaning systems, *American Psychologist* 17: 10–28

Paulhus, D. L. and John, O. P. 1998. Egoistic and moralistic biases in self-perception: the interplay of self-descriptive styles with basic traits and motives, *Journal of Personality* 66: 1025–60

Peabody, D. 1967. Trait inferences: evaluative and descriptive aspects, *Journal of Personality and Social Psychology* 7 Whole Pt. 2, 1–18

Pervin, L. A. 1996. *The science of personality*. New York: Wiley

Prince, M. 1924. *The unconscious*, 2nd edn. New York: MacMillan

Roback, A. A. 1931. *Personality: the crux of social intercourse*. Cambridge, MA: Sci-Art

Rothbart, M. K. and Bates, J. E. 1998. Temperament, in W. Damon (Series ed.) and N. Eisenberg (Vol. ed.), *Handbook of child psychology*, vol. III, *Social, emotional and personality development*, 5th edn, pp. 105–76. New York: Wiley

Saucier, G. 1997. Effects of variable selection on the factor structure of person descriptors, *Journal of Personality and Social Psychology* 73: 1296–1312

  2000. Isms and the structure of social attitudes, *Journal of Personality and Social Psychology* 78: 366–85

  2003a. An alternative multi-language structure of personality attributes, *European Journal of Personality* 17: 179–205

2003b. Factor structure of English-language personality type-nouns, *Journal of Personality and Social Psychology* 85: 695–708

2008. Measures of the personality factors found recurrently in human lexicons, in G. J. Boyle, G. Matthews and D. Saklofske (eds.), *Handbook of personality theory and testing*, vol. II, *Personality measurement and assessment*, pp. 29–54. London: Sage

in press. Recurrent personality dimensions in inclusive lexical studies: indications for a Big Six structure, *Journal of Personality*

Saucier, G., Bel-Bahar, T. and Fernandez, C. 2007. What modifies the expression of personality tendencies? Defining basic domains of situation variables, *Journal of Personality* 75: 479–504

Saucier, G., Georgiades, S., Tsaousis, I. and Goldberg, L. R. 2005. The factor structure of Greek personality adjectives, *Journal of Personality and Social Psychology* 88: 856–75

Saucier, G., Ole-Kotikash, L. and Payne, D. L. 2006. *The structure of personality and character attributes in the language of the Maasai.* Unpublished report. University of Oregon

Schwartz, T. 1978. Where is the culture? Personality as the distributive locus of culture, in G. D. Spindler (ed.), *The making of psychological anthropology*, pp. 419–41. Berkeley, CA: University of California Press

Shea, M. T. and Yen, S. 2003. Stability as a distinction between Axis I and Axis II disorders, *Journal of Personality Disorders* 17: 373–86

Spiro, M. E. 1951. Culture and personality: the natural history of a false dichotomy, *Psychiatry* 14: 19–46

Szirmák, Z. and De Raad, B. 1994. Taxonomy and structure of Hungarian personality traits, *European Journal of Personality* 8: 95–118

Tanaka, J. W. and Taylor, M. 1991. Object categories and expertise: is the basic level in the eye of the beholder?, *Cognitive Psychology* 23: 457–82

Tellegen, A. and Waller, N. G. 1987. *Re-examining basic dimensions of natural language trait descriptors.* Paper presented at the 95th annual convention of the American Psychological Association, August 1987

Torrubia, R., Avila, C., Molto, J. and Caseras, X. 2001. The Sensitivity to Punishment and Sensitivity to Reward Questionnaire (SPSRQ) as a measure of Gray's anxiety and impulsivity dimensions, *Personality and Individual Differences* 31: 837–62

Trull, T. J. and Sher, K. J. 1994. Relationship between the Five-Factor Model of personality and Axis I disorders in a nonclinical sample, *Journal of Abnormal Psychology* 103: 350–60

Wallace, A. F. C. 1961. *Culture and personality.* New York: Random House

Wundt, W. M. 1896/1969. *Outlines of psychology* (C. H. Judd (trans.)). New York: G. E. Stechert. Originally published in German in 1896

Zhou, X., Saucier, G., Gao, D. and Liu, J. in press. The factor structure of Chinese personality descriptors, *Journal of Personality*. Unpublished manuscript. Sun Yat-Sen University

23 Personality and performance: cognitive processes and models

Gerald Matthews

Introduction

This chapter provides an introductory review of research that has addressed personality correlates of performance through application of cognitive psychological models. Early experimental studies (e.g., Eysenck 1957, 1967) showed that basic traits such as Extraversion (E) and Neuroticism (N) relate to performance on a variety of standard laboratory tasks requiring cognitive functions such as perception, attention, memory and speeded response. Eysenck (1967) attempted to explain these findings in terms of traditional arousal theory. However, failings of arousal theory (Matthews and Gilliland 1999) imply that we must look more closely at the different information-processing components that may be sensitive to personality.

First, I will discuss the background to the field provided by psychobiological models of traits, and the theoretical and methodological issues that cognitive science brings into focus. Secondly, I will review some of the major cognitive systems, such as those controlling attention and memory, to which personality traits relate. The ultimate goals of this research are to specify in detail how traits may bias specific parameters within a computational model of cognition. I will conclude by revisiting theoretical issues, including the key question of how studies of performance may contribute to an integrated, coherent theory of traits.

The chapter aims to introduce the idea that understanding linkages between personality and performance can be treated as a problem in cognitive science. Hence, it does not attempt to review the various traits relevant to performance systematically. Elsewhere, I have provided more detailed reviews of Extraversion (Matthews 1997) and Neuroticism (Matthews 2004a), as well as theoretical syntheses (Matthews 2008a; Matthews, Derryberry and Siegle 2000a).

A brief history

Studies that link traits to performance in experimentally-controlled settings have a number of inspirations. The pioneering psychobiological theories of personality (notably, Eysenck 1957, 1967) hypothesized that variations in basic attributes of the brain such as inhibition and arousal should influence performance of simple tasks such as choice reaction time and paired-associate learning. The E and N traits predicted performance on tasks requiring attention, memory and rapid execution of motor response. In effect, performance measures functioned as another psychophysiological index akin to EEG or EDA.

The impact of the 'cognitive revolution' on personality arrived first via clinical psychology, and the insight that emotional pathology reflected distortions and impairments in cognition (Beck 1967). Such ideas generated a wave of research on the cognitive deficits associated with trait anxiety (Spielberger 1972). Some years later, clinical research also inspired studies showing that anxiety relates to bias in selective attention and other cognitive functions (Williams, Watts, MacLeod and Matthews 1997). In the 1970s and 1980s, researchers also turned to a wider variety of traits, exploring the full range of processing functions differentiated by cognitive psychology (Eysenck 1981).

Recent research has continued efforts to build information-processing models of the major traits on the basis of performance data (Matthews 2008a). Performance studies have become increasingly integrated with cognitive neuroscience. In part, such research is an extension of the traditional psychophysiology central to Eysenck's (1967) arousal theory; for example, through relating traits to evoked potentials that signal information-processing components (e.g., De Pascalis 2004; Stelmack and Rammsayer 2008). Other research has picked up on newer trends in the field, including attempts to map traits directly onto fundamental brain systems, for different attentional functions, for example (Derryberry and Reed 1997), and use of neuroimaging and other cognitive neuroscience techniques (Turhan Canli, Chapter 19; Colin G. DeYoung and Jeremy R. Gray, Chapter 20).

These multifarious approaches have generated a large but poorly integrated literature demonstrating various performance correlates of various traits. The majority of work relates to Eysenck's E and N traits, and to related dimensions such as trait anxiety. Although largely beyond the scope of this chapter, there are also growing literatures on the additional broad traits of Agreeableness, Conscientiousness and Openness, as well as more narrowly defined traits including Impulsivity, Sensation-Seeking, Optimism-Pessimism and many others. This chapter will try to identify some broad trends and themes among the labyrinth of data.

Methods for performance research

Studies of personality and performance offer some unique methodological challenges (Robinson 2007). The simplest designs simply correlate a given trait with a given performance index, as we might, for example, test whether Extraversion correlates with simple reaction time. Such studies have a place, but cognitive psychology derives much of its power as an investigative approach through systematically manipulating task factors to uncover fundamental processing mechanisms. Thus, demonstrations that associations between personality and performance are moderated by task parameters are more informative than simple correlational data. For example, studies that show that the detrimental effects of anxiety on performance increase with the memory load of the task (cf., Eysenck 1992) link anxiety specifically to the cognitive processes supporting working memory. Personality psychologists must also address a basic difficulty inherent in cognitive research: that different models may explain the data equally well (the 'identifiability problem'). A simple example is that a given effect may equally reflect basic parameters of the cognitive architecture (e.g., speed of execution of a given component) or voluntary strategy choice (e.g., whether to run a check on the output of a given component). Performance data on response time and accuracy are often open to differing interpretations of this kind. Thus, to link traits to specific processing mechanisms, it is essential both to have a good theory of the process of interest and to choose carefully task manipulations that will expose individual differences in the process of interest.

Another methodological issue is the frequent dependence of personality effects on contextual factors such as level of stimulation, motivational factors or even time of day (Revelle, Humphreys, Simon and Gilliland 1980). Extraversion, in particular, may have either facilitative or detrimental effects on performance depending on factors of this kind. Detrimental effects of Neuroticism may be more evident in stressful environments (Cox-Fuenzalida, Swickert and Hittner 2004). As discussed below, interactive effects of personality and contextual factors have often been taken as evidence for arousal theory, although such explanations have been challenged (Matthews 1992). The more general implication is that researchers must take great care in controlling and assessing the levels of arousal, stress and motivation afforded by the test environment.

A final methodological issue refers to the choice of traits for study. As already indicated, much research focuses on broad 'superfactors' such as E and N, but other research strategies may also be productive. For example, there has been important work on impulsivity and other traits linked to abnormal personality (e.g., Stanford and Barratt 1996). Recent work has sometimes employed the BAS and BIS dimensions of Jeffrey Gray's Reinforcement Sensitivity Theory (RST: see Philip J. Corr 2004, Chapter 21), although it may be difficult to differentiate these traits from E and N in research practice (Gray, Burgess, Schaefer *et al.* 2005). In addition, especially in more applied studies, researchers work with 'contextualized traits', such as scales for test anxiety (Zeidner 1998; Zeidner and Matthews 2005) rather than general anxiety in relating anxiety to academic performance. Similarly, scales for driver stress vulnerability appear to be more predictive of criteria for driver safety than general traits (Matthews 2002).

Associations between personality, performance and individual differences in cognition are often rather unstable and sensitive to various moderator factors. Furthermore, effect sizes are often modest (e.g., Koelega 1992). Thus, demonstrating robust, theoretically meaningful results in this field requires considerable care in experimental design.

Theoretical perspectives

There are different theoretical purposes to which data on personality traits and performance may be put. First, studies of performance may be used to test predictions from theory. As noted previously, systematic performance research was first featured in psychobiological studies of E and N (Eysenck 1957, 1967). That is, performance indices provide behavioural criteria against which predictions from theory may be validated, providing data that complement studies of psychophysiological criteria. Cognitive theories of personality that link traits to constructs such as attentional resources and working memory may be similarly tested (e.g., Eysenck 1992; Humphreys and Revelle 1984). A second purpose is more exploratory in nature. Performance data may be used to relate personality to individual differences in the multiple processing modules that contribute to the cognitive architecture. Broad constructs like arousal or resources may fail to account for the full range of findings on personality and performance (e.g., Matthews and Gilliland 1999). When general theories fail, it is important to go back to data, and conduct a fine-grained investigation of exactly how personality relates to information-processing in order to improve future efforts at theory. A third purpose (reversing the normal causal assumption) is to investigate how individual differences in cognition may influence personality. For example, negative biases in attention, in interpretation of events, and in self-beliefs may contribute to development of an anxiety-prone personality (Wells and Matthews 2006; Wilson, MacLeod, Mathews and Rutherford 2006).

Whatever the theoretical purpose, the detailed specification of the underlying processes that control behaviour is central to cognitive psychology. It assumes a 'virtual' cognitive architecture that can be specified separately from the underlying neural architecture (e.g., Ortony, Norman and Revelle 2005). Individual differences in attention, memory and other cognitive functions are of interest in their own right as attributes of personality traits. The cognitive correlates of traits are more than just expressions of neural functioning; biases in symbolic information-processing may be intrinsic to personality.

Cognitive psychology also offers a number of levels at which performance data may be understood. Most broadly, it divides mental functioning into a number of broad areas such as attention, memory, language and so forth. Each may be subdivided and sub-divided again until we have identified basic component processes. For example, attention is conventionally divided into several aspects or branches (Matthews, Davies, Westerman and Stammers 2000). Selective attention refers to focusing on a source of stimuli (while ignoring distractors), divided attention to processing multiple input channels, and sustained attention to maintaining an attentional focus over extended time periods. Each one of these broad attentional functions appears to be supported by a number of separate processing components and brain systems. For example, focusing on a particular location in space requires separate processes of disengaging attention from its current location, shifting to the new location, and engaging attention with stimuli at that location (Posner and DiGirolamo 1998). Personality traits may influence all these different varieties of attention, and their various component processes. Traits may relate both to overall efficiency of processing (e.g., Eysenck 1992) and to qualitative biases in attention. Anxiety appears to prioritize selection of threatening stimuli in preference to those that are benign (Bar-Haim, Lamy, Pergamin et al. 2007).

Uncovering the component processes that mediate personality effects requires careful and theoretically-informed experimental design. I will describe one example only, a study of anxiety effects on selective attention. A well-regarded theory of the cognitive neuroscience of attention developed by Michael Posner (e.g., Posner and DiGirolamo 1998) states that different cues are processed by different brain attentional systems. Sensory cues presented at the periphery engage a 'posterior' system concerned with visual orienting. Symbolic cues (an arrow pointing left or right) presented at the centre of the visual field activate an 'anterior' system that implements executive control of the system. In addition, manipulating the time interval between onsets of the cue and the target may differentiate unconscious priming effects from conscious attention. Poy, del Carmen Eixarch and Avila (2004) employed a 'covert visual orienting' task, in which subjects were required to respond to a target stimulus (a white asterisk) that might appear on either the left or the right side of the visual field. Subjects were also presented with cues that indicated the side on which the target was more likely to appear. Results showed that anxiety related to slow disengagement of attention from invalid peripheral cues over short time intervals, implicating a specific sub-component of Posner's anterior orienting system. Poy *et al.* (2004) suggest that sensitivity to peripheral cues affords earlier threat detection in anxious individuals. This example shows how, by using an informed choice of tasks and performance measures, traits may be linked to specific information-processing mechanisms. Because Posner also specifies the corresponding neural circuitry we might also use methods such as brain imaging to explore the neurological underpinnings of the behavioural effect.

The example study described represents a 'molecular' approach to cognition that seeks to identify ever more fine-grained component processes. At a more molar level, we may also seek to relate personality to higher-level cognitive structures such as the 'schemas' that are said to maintain a stable sense of self (Beck 1967). This approach converges with social-cognitive theories of personality (e.g., Cervone 2008). Suppose anxiety relates to vulnerability to overload, to selective attention to threat, and negative biases in higher-level thinking. Individuals high and low in anxiety may then differ fundamentally in how they cognize the world around them and their own place in it; they inhabit different subjective worlds.

Researchers may then have different motives for running studies of personality and performance: to test psychobiological theories, to relate traits to information-processing, and to link traits to high level cognitive functions that shape the person's sense of self. Later in this chapter I will argue that these different research goals correspond to different explanations within cognitive science (Pylyshyn 1999). Somewhat separate theories may be developed that variously account for personality in terms of individual differences in (1) key neural functions, (2) parameters of the virtual cognitive architecture that supports information-processing, and (3) self-knowledge and personal goals.

Personality and performance: an overview of research

In this section, I will aim to summarize the main fields of research into personality and cognitive performance. Much of this work is concerned with attention. It seems reasonable that traits may influence how readily individuals are able to establish and maintain an attentional focus. Personality may influence whether the person can concentrate effectively, as opposed to being easily distracted. First, I will illustrate work on *attentional capacity* or *resources*. The idea here is that people may differ in their capabilities for concentration and managing high levels of demand for attention. Next, I will survey studies of the selective rather than the intensive aspect of attention. Individuals may differ in how easily they can establish and shift the focus of attention. Thirdly, I will briefly highlight some additional cognitive functions to which research has been directed, including speed response, memory and verbal processing.

Attentional capacity

The idea that attention is limited in capacity is intuitively appealing. So too is the notion that personality influences attention in some general sense; anxious people often seem distractible and unfocused. A major development was the formal exposition of theories of 'attentional resources' (see Matthews, Davies, Westerman and Stammers 2000, for a review). A resource is a metaphorical reservoir of energy for processing whose availability may limit speed and accuracy of performance, especially on demanding tasks. There may be multiple resources supporting different processing functions, such as verbal and visuospatial processing. The theory has proved contentious, in that resources are hard to define and differentiate from more specific attentional processes. However, resource theories have been quite successful in predicting how performance varies with overall task demands or workload. The essence of resource theories is that pools of 'energy' for processing shrink or replenish themselves as the person's state of arousal or affect varies. If we can predict how personality influences state change, we can predict personality effects on performance.

Resource theory approaches have also been strengthened by convergence with accounts of working memory that specify the underlying cognitive and neural architecture with more precision than traditional resource theory. Working memory theory posits a capacity-limited supervisory executive system that directs both short-term storage and voluntary attention. It is localized in the prefrontal cortex, the anterior part of the frontal lobes of the brain (Kane and Engle 2002). As further discussed below, advances in understanding executive functioning may help to clarify some of the ambiguities of resource theory (Eysenck, Derakshan, Santos and Calvo 2007).

There are several types of experimental paradigm that link personality traits to attentional capacity (or to more specific components of attention). Variation of personality effects with overall workload may imply a capacity-based mechanism. Studies of dual-task performance are also important; traits may relate to the amount of dual-task interference seen when attention is overloaded. Most recently, studies of sustained attention showing loss of perceptual sensitivity over time have been attributed to resource depletion (Warm, Matthews and Finomore 2008).

Resource theory was applied to personality research initially to explain detrimental effects of trait anxiety. Early research (e.g., Spielberger 1966) established that state anxiety disrupted information-processing on demanding tasks, but theory was vague about the nature of the interference. The greater sensitivity of performance to worry, rather than anxious emotion and autonomic arousal (Zeidner 1998), encouraged a cognitive rather than an arousal theory perspective. Irwin Sarason's (e.g., Sarason, Sarason and Pierce 1995) influential theory of test anxiety suggested that the effects of worry are mediated by diversion of resources onto 'off-task' processing of personal concerns. The anxious student is essentially in a dual-task situation, in combining task performance with attending to thoughts about personal failure and other worries, a process termed 'cognitive interference'. As the theory predicts, attentionally demanding tasks appear to be especially sensitive to detrimental effects of worry (Zeidner 1998). In line with the role of the supervisory executive in working memory (Kane and Engle 2002), anxiety also impairs tasks of this kind (Eysenck 1992). Another line of evidence concerns variability in performance, which may provide an index of executive dysfunction. Across three tasks, Robinson and Tamir (2005) found that Neuroticism correlated positively with the trial-to-trial variability of response time across trials of reaction time tasks.

The Humphreys and Revelle (1984) theory. Resource theory also inspired a landmark theory in research on personality and cognition, proposed by Humphreys and Revelle (1984). The theory is an ambitious attempt to integrate various lines of research on personality, motivation and emotion, and only a simplified account can be offered here. It attempts to integrate resources with earlier conceptions of arousal as a pivotal mediator of personality effects (Eysenck 1967), so that the causal chain is as shown in Figure 23.1.

Humphreys and Revelle (1984) described separate resource pools for sustained information transfer (SIT; similar to attention) and for short-term memory (STM). Arousal, in their model, leads to increased availability of SIT resources, but loss of STM resources. Directing effort to the task is distinct from arousal, and influences SIT resources only. Traits that influence arousal and effort will then have differing effects on qualitatively different tasks, overcoming a major weakness of traditional arousal theory. The parts of the causal chain most proximal to performance

Figure 23.1. *Humphreys and Revelle theory: causal chain.*

are quite well supported by empirical evidence. Detrimental effects of anxiety states are attributed primarily to loss of on-task effort as the person becomes preoccupied with their own problems and worries, consistent with much anxiety research (e.g., Zeidner 1998). There is also growing evidence that subjective energetic arousal relates to superior performance on demanding sustained and selective attention tasks just as the theory predicts (Matthews, Davies and Lees 1990; Warm, Mathews and Finomore 2008).

Evaluation of the hypothesized role of personality is more difficult because both Extraversion and trait anxiety operate in concert with other variables: arousal factors in the case of Extraversion, and motivational factors in the case of anxiety. High impulsives (similar to extraverts) are hypothesized to be lower in arousal in the early part of the day (the theory aims to accommodate time of day effects). It follows that Extraversion should be negatively correlated with attentionally demanding tasks, such as vigilance, but positively correlated with short-term memory.

There is indeed considerable evidence that Extraversion relates to poorer vigilance (Beauducel, Brocke and Leue 2006; Koelega 1992), and to superior recall on traditional, verbal short-term memory tasks (e.g., Eysenck 1981; Matthews 1992). Studies using working memory paradigms, requiring processing as well as storage of material, have also found extravert superiority in some instances (Lieberman 2000). A study using functional magnetic resonance imaging (fMRI) confirmed that, during task performance, Extraversion correlates with activity in brain areas believed to be implicated in working memory and executive control (Gray, Burgess, Schaefer *et al.* 2005). Humphreys and Revelle (1984) also derived the traditional inverted-U function linking arousal to performance as a special case applying to complex tasks such as intelligence tests only.

Challenges to resource theory. The Humphreys and Revelle (1984) theory successfully predicts the trend towards Extraversion enhancing short-term memory but impairing attention (subject to arousal and time of day factors). The theory also states that the key mediating factors are resource availability and arousal, but substantiating these mediating mechanisms has proved more difficult. One problem is that arousal is likely multidimensional, with different arousal dimensions impacting performance in different ways. Although Extraversion may correlate negatively with some psychophysiological indices of arousal (De Pascalis 2004), the trait also tends to correlate positively with subjective energetic arousal. This state tends, if anything, to enhance working memory performance (Matthews and Campbell in press), contrary to prediction from the resource theory.

The Humphreys and Revelle (1984) theory is compatible with the superior performance of introverts on vigilance tasks (Koelega 1992), but two difficulties should be pointed out. First, we would expect introvert superiority to be especially marked on the most demanding vigilance tasks that, presumably, require the maximal allocation of resources (cf., Warm, Matthews and Finomore 2008). However, this prediction is not confirmed; studies using high-workload tasks failed to find any general advantage for introverts (Matthews, Davies and Lees

1990; Matthews, Davies and Holley 1990). Instead, personality differences may reflect other task attributes and processes other than resource allocation. Matthews, Davies and Holley (1990) noticed an advantage for extraverts on symbolic tasks, but an advantage for introverts on tasks requiring demanding visual discriminations. Secondly, tests for mediation have failed to confirm that Extraversion differences are a consequence of variation in arousal, whether measured subjectively (Matthews, Davies and Lees 1990) or using the EEG (Matthews and Amelang 1993). Extraversion and arousal often appear to have separable effects in these studies.

On some tasks, Extraversion interacts with arousal. Extraverts tend to perform better when higher in arousal, but introverts benefit from low arousal. The Humphreys and Revelle (1984) theory attributes Extraversion x arousal interactions to variations in resource availability. Hence, these interactive effects should be found primarily with those more demanding tasks that are highly resource-limited, rather than simple tasks requiring little attentional capacity. A review of the evidence (Matthews 1997) failed to confirm this prediction. In fact, interactive effects of Extraversion and arousal on performance were most reliable with rather simple, routine encoding tasks, as opposed to demanding, resource-limited tasks (Matthews 1997; Matthews and Harley 1993). Alternative mechanisms such as automatic activation processes may provide a better explanation, as explored in a study that modelled the effect using neural nets (Matthews and Harley 1993).

Another challenge to resource theory comes from studies of dual-task performance. Assuming that dual-task interference reflects an insufficiency of attentional resources, extraverts should be more vulnerable to interference (subject to the usual caveats concerning time of day and arousal). In fact, broadly, extraverts tend to out-perform introverts in dual-task performance studies (Matthews, Deary and Whiteman 2003), but studies also show that finding the effect is dependent on careful control of task stimuli (e.g, Szymura and Necka 1998).The discrepancy between Extraversion tending to impair performance on traditional vigilance tasks, but to facilitate dual-task performance in especially demanding conditions is striking, and difficult to explain on the basis of resource theory.

Attentional control theory. As already noted, the resource metaphor may apply best to the specific neural and cognitive operations of the frontal supervisory executive system. Like other attentional systems, executive operations may be fractionated into more specific processes, including inhibition of strong but inappropriate responses, shifting between different processing operations, and updating the contents of working memory. Attentional control theory (Eysenck, Derakshan, Santos and Calvo 2007) seeks to relate anxiety not to the potentially nebulous resource construct but to these specific operations. Anxiety relates to weaker executive inhibition, evidenced in part by vulnerability to distraction, and also to difficulties in shifting between alternate task sets (although few studies have addressed this issue). The third function, updating, contributes to a number of prototypical working memory tasks, but tends to rely more on short-term storage processes than on direct attentional control. It appears to be less sensitive to anxiety than the other two executive processes. Eysenck *et al.*'s attentional control theory shows how differentiating executive processes may support a more detailed account of anxiety effects on attention than afforded by traditional resource theories.

Two other features of the theory are also of note. In addition to effects of anxiety on executive control of attention, Eysenck *et al.* (2007) also propose that anxiety increases the influence of stimulus-driven processes, such as involuntary attention to threat. This effect of anxiety is relevant to effects on selective attention, discussed below. Also, Eysenck *et al.* (2007) point out that anxiety effects on performance are moderated by strategy use. For example, anxious individuals may attempt to compensate for attentional deficits by increasing task-directed effort, maintaining processing effectiveness at the cost of lower processing efficiency.

Selective attention

Selective attention refers to focusing attention on one of several stimulus sources. Personality may influence the efficiency of selective attention. Some people may be faster to direct attention towards a designated stimulus source, or they may be better at resisting distraction from irrelevant stimuli. Also of interest is bias in selective attention; people may differ, for example, in their tendencies to direct attention towards potentially threatening stimuli.

Personality and distractibility. A simple demonstration that selective attention (to neutral, non-emotive stimuli) varies with personality comes from studies of performance under distraction. Furnham and Strbac (2002) found that extraverts were more resistant to background noise than introverts across a range of tasks; extraverts may indeed prefer to study with music or other noise in the background. Anxiety and Neuroticism are also commonly found to be associated with selective attention deficits, a result that may reflect a more general attentional impairment related to these traits. Newton, Slade, Butler and Murphy (1992) found that both Extraversion and low Neuroticism were associated with faster speed of visual search, when subjects were required to find a single letter target in a random display of letters.

Another line of research in this area concerns the abnormal personality trait of schizotypy, which broadly relates to oddities in perception and cognition that may indicate vulnerability to schizophrenia. Difficulties in inhibiting aberrant thoughts and images may contribute to the 'positive symptoms' of schizophrenia including hallucinations and delusions (Lubow and Gewirtz 1995). A 'latent inhibition' process is implicated; in experimental studies, stimuli that are ignored on one trial are attended more slowly on later trials, implying that unattended stimuli are actively inhibited. Schizotypal individuals may be deficient in inhibition of irrelevant stimuli. Studies using attentional tasks that provide measures of latent inhibition have confirmed this hypothesis (e.g., Tsakanikos 2004). Abnormal personality traits may relate to specific information-processing deficits that increase vulnerability to mental disorder.

Anxiety, threat and bias in selective attention. Turning from general attentional deficits to cognitive bias, an important line of research is concerned with selective attention bias in trait anxiety. A variety of paradigms have been used to demonstrate that anxiety relates to preferential selection of threat stimuli (see Bar-Haim,

Lamy, Pergamin *et al.* 2007; Williams, Watts, MacLeod and Mathews 1997 for reviews). The emotional Stroop test requires the subject to name the ink colour of a series of printed words. Anxious individuals are slow in colour-naming threat words such as TORTURE or FAILURE, relative to neutral control words. Bias to some degree matches the individual's concerns; individuals who fear spiders may be especially slow in their response to words such as COBWEB or TARANTULA. A second common paradigm is the 'dot-probe' technique. Stimuli are presented at two locations on a screen, one of which is a threat and the other is neutral. After the subject has identified the stimulus at one of the locations, a simple probe stimulus, such as a dot, is presented at either the attended or the unattended locations. Analysis of response time to the probe indicates how attentive the person is to each screen position. Typically, anxious individuals attend preferentially to locations in which the threat word is presented, as evidenced by a relatively faster response when the probe is presented in the location of the threat. As with general attentional deficits, such observations are open to a variety of theoretical interpretations.

Much of the debate has centred on whether bias is unconscious, perhaps driven by early pre-attentive processes, or whether it reflects a voluntary strategy of active search for potential threats (Matthews and Wells 2000). It is plausible that both types of process may be involved. Mathews and Mackintosh (1998) proposed a dual-process approach, within which bias is produced initially by an automatic threat evaluation system, but may be compensated by voluntary effort. Evidence for an automatic process comes from studies showing that anxiety-related bias in attention may be demonstrated even when stimuli are presented subliminally so that they cannot be consciously perceived (Fox 1996). On the other hand, bias appears to be sensitive to conscious expectancies and operates over a longer time period than a simple automatic bias would predict (Matthews and Wells 2000; Phaf and Kan 2007). A recent meta-analysis of seventy studies of anxiety effects on the emotional Stroop studies failed to find any significant effect size in studies using subliminal stimuli (Phaf and Kan 2007). Phaf and Kan (2007, p. 184) concluded that 'the emotional Stroop effect seems to rely more on a slow disengagement process than on a fast, automatic, bias'.

Progress has also been made in identifying specific component processes that support bias. It seems that anxiety relates to difficulties in disengaging from threat stimuli, following attentional focusing, rather than more rapid initial detection of threat. I have already described one of several studies that demonstrate this process (Poy, del Carman Eixarch and Avila). Other studies have confirmed that anxious persons tend to 'lock onto' potential sources of threat and are slow to disengage attention (Derryberry and Reed 1997, 2002). Anxiety effects are not restricted to slower disengagement, and various other specific attentional mechanisms are implicated (Calvo and Avero 2005; Matthews, Derryberry and Siegle 2000). Thus, attentional bias may be a product of several interacting processes, and careful computational modelling may be needed to understand this anxiety effect (Hudlicka 2004).

Cognitive patterning of performance effects

The research reviewed thus far has been concerned with fairly general mechanisms and processes, such as resource availability. Researchers have hoped that a variety of performance correlates of traits might be reduced to a small number of underlying processes. However, I have argued elsewhere (e.g., Matthews 2000, 2008a) that traits typically relate to a multiplicity of biases in information-processing, which cannot be reduced to any general attentional (or arousal) mechanism. Personality research may usefully learn from stress research. Reviews of stressor effects (e.g., Hockey 1984; Matthews, Davies, Westerman and Stammers 2000) have concluded that stressors such as noise and heat typically influence multiple processes. Hockey (1984) advocates exploring the *cognitive patterning* of each individual stressor, i.e., evaluating in detail which processing functions are facilitated, impaired or unaffected by the stressful agent. Typically, cognitive patternings are complex, reflecting multiple mechanisms of different types. Effects may be structural, in affecting basic parameters of component processes, or strategic, referring to the person's choice of goals and sub-goals in dealing with the task (Hockey 1984). Similarly, personality traits too are associated with cognitive patternings composed of multiple, independent effects (Matthews 2008a). The research on attention reviewed previously isolates a part of the patternings for E, N/anxiety and other traits.

Next, I will briefly survey some additional cognitive functions at which research has been directed: (1) speeded response, as investigated using reaction time-tasks; (2) efficiency and bias in memory; and (3) language processes contributing to speed production and interpretation of events. I will make no attempt to review research on these topics in detail; the aim is to illustrate how personality may be linked to a variety of different aspects of cognition and information-processing through experimental studies of performance tasks.

Speeded response. Speed of response selection and execution seems like a basic behavioural attribute that should be sensitive to personality. However, like other cognitive functions, variation in reaction time depends on a variety of factors. Stage models of RT discriminate a variety of separate processes ranging from encoding to motor response; moreover, RT is strategically regulated, as evidenced by the well-known speed-accuracy trade-off function (see Matthews, Davies, Westerman and Stammers 2000).

Although it is often assumed that traits including Extraversion should be associated with a general pattern of fast, inaccurate performance, no such relationship is supported by the literature. Instead, a careful focus on different component processes is needed to demonstrate personality effects. Doucet and Stelmack (2000) used reaction time paradigms that provided separate measures of decision time (analysing the stimulus and selecting the response), and movement time (executing the motor response of pressing the correct response key). Extraversion was found to relate only to faster movement time, linking this trait to a peripheral motor function. Further research on Extraversion and motor processes (reviewed by De Pascalis 2004) has shown that these individual differences in motor response may relate to motoneuronal sensitivity, so that a purely neurological account of the finding may be advanced. De Pascalis (2004) also discusses evidence relating to shorter-latency lateralized readiness potentials that index speed of response organization (i.e., a central rather than a peripheral process), demonstrating how multiple component processes may contribute to observed personality effects.

Memory. Work done from an arousal theory perspective suggested that extraverts tend to have better short-term recall but also poorer long-term memory (Eysenck 1967). More cognitively oriented research has explored relationships with specific cognitive processes supporting memory such as encoding, retrieval and organization (see Eysenck 1981; Zeidner 1998). An application of cognitive research on memory is to understand the math anxiety that may impair the person's ability to perform arithmetic in educational and every-day life contexts. Math anxiety can be seen as a stable trait that is distinct from general anxiety, and relates to impairments in performance and working memory. Studies based on an understanding of mathematical cognition have helped to elucidate the impairment. As discussed in a recent review (Ashcraft and Krause 2007), solving math problems depends both on retrieval of arithmetic knowledge held in long-term memory, and on use of strategies for solving unfamiliar problems that require working memory. Experiments show that anxiety affects working memory rather than retrieval, and manipulations that increase working memory load, such as adding a dual-task component, produce increasingly large performance deficits in math-anxious individuals. Ashcraft and Krause (2007) also point out that math-anxious persons tend to sacrifice accuracy for speed, especially on difficult problems, in an effort to conclude the aversive experience (i.e., a form of avoidance coping).

Work on attentional bias has also been extended to the investigation of memory bias. Would a trait-anxious individual encode threat-related stimuli more readily than someone low in anxiety? Would trait anxiety influence the ease with which threatening information could be retrieved from storage? Early studies of personality and cognitive bias suggested that depression related to memory bias (perhaps because depressives tend to ruminate and elaborate on negative events) but anxiety related only to selective attention bias (Williams, Watts, MacLeod and Mathews 1997).

More recent work provides a more nuanced picture. As in other research areas, careful attention to underlying processes is the key to obtaining reliable results. One of the paradigms frequently used is incidental learning. Participants process word stimuli in the context of some task that does not require subsequent recall, such as a selective attention task. After the task is concluded, they are given an unexpected memory test requiring them to recognize the words previously presented. If trait-anxious individuals are vulnerable to memory bias, they should show enhanced recognition of threatening words, but, typically, no such bias effect has been found (Williams *et al.* 1997). However, Russo, Whittuck, Roberson *et al.* (2006) argued that the recognition test lacks sufficient sensitivity to pick up what may be modest biases in memory. Furthermore, if task conditions promote deep semantic analysis (attention to word meaning), then both anxious and non-anxious persons will encode the stimuli efficiently, leaving little scope for individual variation. Russo *et al.* predicted that anxiety would affect memory bias on a free recall test, following incidental learning using a 'shallow' encoding; i.e., an attentional task (the Stroop task) in which subjects aimed to ignore word meaning. The prediction was confirmed; anxious subjects recalled more threat-related words than did those individuals low in anxiety. There was no effect of anxiety on recall of neutral words. As Russo *et al.* (2006) suggest, heightened attention to threatening material may in some cases lead to subsequent memory bias.

Language. Given that our impressions of an individual's personality are powerfully influenced by their speech, it is surprising that the psycholinguistics of personality has been neglected. Talkativeness is a central feature of Extraversion, and, indeed, extraverts appear to talk more than introverts in social situations (Dewaele and Furnham 1999). However, Extraversion does not relate to linguistic processing in any general sense; often, no extravert-introvert differences on verbal tasks (including verbal ability tasks) are found. Dewaele and Furnham (1999) provide some insights into Extraversion effects on language use. Studies of learning a second language show no effect of Extraversion on formal proficiency tests. However, when speakers' verbal utterances are recorded and analysed in detail, extraverts are found to be more fluent (and perhaps more colloquial) in speech production, in both first and second language use. Dewaele and Furnham suggest several possible explanations for personality differences in speech production. In terms of information-processing, introverts may be hindered by limits on verbal working memory, and slower retrieval processes. Extraverts may also be more motivated to engage in conversation, they may have acquired greater proceduralization of speech, and they may be less vulnerable to social anxiety that may disrupt fluent speech. Extraverts may also be more willing to risk making errors during conversation in order to maintain fluency (i.e., speed-accuracy trade-off).

Some similar issues surface in studies of verbal problem-solving. Extraversion relates to deficits in solving problems requiring protracted reflection, because they tend to accept false solutions prematurely (Weinman 1987). By contrast, fluency and a focus on speed of response may be beneficial for creative problem-solving and generation of original ideas (Martindale 2007). Interestingly, as Martindale (2007) also discusses, the trait of psychoticism is also linked to creativity; creative genius does indeed seem to be associated with 'psychotic' traits, though not actual psychosis (Eysenck 1995).

An entirely different approach to personality and linguistic processing is provided by studies of interpretative bias. Early studies of anxiety and cognitive bias (see Williams, Watts, MacLeod and Mathews 1997) showed that anxious persons tend to attach threatening meanings to ambiguous spoken words (homophones) that might be interpreted as having either a threatening or neutral meaning (e.g., DIE vs. DYE). Such bias may impact the person's understanding of events. Calvo and Castillo (2001) used a predictive inferencing task that probed the expectancies people formed from reading a partial sentence that suggested either a threatening or non-threatening event. Trait anxious individuals were especially likely to infer a negative outcome to a potentially threatening event. Careful analysis of the time-course of reading suggested that the bias depended on voluntary rather than involuntary processes.

In real life, interpretation biases may be especially important in social anxiety. The person anxious about being negatively evaluated by others may be prone to interpret ambiguous statements as being critical or hostile. Huppert, Pasupuleti, Foa and Mathews (2007) suggest several processes that may contribute to bias in resolving ambiguous sentences, including negative bias in both generating and selecting responses, and negative self-appraisals. Lack of positive bias may also be a factor. Interestingly, interpretation bias may be a causal factor in anxiety. A variety of cognitive biases have been cited as risk factors for clinical anxiety, on the basis of evidence from longitudinal but correlational studies (Wells and Matthews 2006). However, recent work also shows that experimental induction of a negative interpretive bias through a training procedure also elevates vulnerability to anxiety (Wilson, MacLeod, Mathews and Rutherford 2006). It can plausibly be suggested

Table 23.1 *Outline cognitive patterning for Extraversion-Introversion.*

Cognitive function	Sample task	Result
Extravert superiority		
Divided attention	Memory search for single or multiple targets	Extraverts faster in dual-task version conditions
Short-term memory	Free recall of video sequences	Extraverts better at immediate recall
Resisting distraction	Performing verbal tasks with background music	Extraverts less distracted by extraneous noise
Retrieval from semantic memory	Retrieval of semantic category instances	Extraverts faster at retrieving low dominance ('unusual') instances
Speed of movement	Choice reaction time?	Extraverts show faster response execution
Speech production	Conversation in a second language	Extraverts more fluent in speech production
Introvert superiority		
Visual vigilance	Detecting line signal	Introverts show higher detection rate
Long-term memory	Paired-associate learning	Introverts better at long-term recall
Problem-solving	Problem-solving tasks requiring insight	Introverts faster and more accurate: extraverts finish impulsively
Qualitative performance differences		
Vigilance	Detection of brighter target stimulus	Extraverts adopt a lower response criterion
Response to stress and arousal	Serial choice reaction time	Extraverts are faster when high in arousal; introverts are faster when low in arousal (also depends on time of day)

Note. References for studies may be found in Matthews, Deary and Whiteman 2003.

Table 23.2 *Outline cognitive patterning for anxiety/Neuroticism.*

Cognitive function	Sample task	Result
Processing efficiency effects		
Divided attention	Concurrent math and verbal memory	Anxiety leads to impairment in dual-task performance (especially on secondary tasks)
Working memory	Mental transformation of letter sequences	Anxiety-related impairment increases with memory load
Resisting distraction	Comprehending text with background speech	Anxiety relates to distraction by irrelevant speech
Verbal reasoning	Verifying accuracy of sentences	Anxiety relates to slower response time
Visual vigilance	Detecting line signal	Anxiety relates to lower detection rate
Cognitive bias effects		
Selective attention (single channel)	Emotional Stroop	Anxiety subjects are slow to name ink colours of threat words
Selective attention (multiple channel)	'Dot-probe' visual attention task	Anxious subjects respond more quickly to probe presented at location of threat
Disengagement from threat	Spatial orienting to cued and uncued locations	Anxious subjects are slow to disengage attention from a threatening cue
Semantic processing	Interpreting spoken homophones: e.g. 'die' vs. 'dye'	Anxious subjects biased towards selecting threatening interpretation
Predictive inference	Naming a word presented in a threatening or non-threatening context	Anxiety facilitates naming of threat words in threatening context
Qualitative performance differences		
Response to evaluative stress	Performance with evaluative instructions	Anxiety relates to performance impairment when evaluated
Memory strategies	Free recall of word lists	Anxiety relates to reduced strategic reorganization of words

Note. References for studies may be found in Matthews, Deary and Whiteman 2003.

that individual differences in interpretative processes shape the subjective worlds we inhabit.

Personality effects are multifaceted. Although space constraints prevent a detailed review of these different research directions, it should be apparent that personality traits relate to a diversity of distinct processes, some strategic (e.g., impulsive problem exit), some relating to basic component parameters of the cognitive architecture (e.g., short-term memory capacity), and some to non-symbolic neural processes (e.g., motoneuronal excitability). As in the case of external stressors (Hockey 1984), traits relate to a set of typically small biases in multiple, independent processes. Tables 23.1 and 23.2 illustrate cognitive patternings for E and N (although note that the details are provisional, given the patchy nature of the evidence).

Contrary to the assumptions of many traditional theories of personality, we cannot find any single master-process that controls the impact on performance of any given trait. The diffusion of traits across the cognitive (and neural) architecture provides a theoretical conundrum, which I will address in the next section.

Cognitive science of personaltiy

The varied nature of personality effects on performance poses a considerable challenge for theory. The hope of the early psychobiologists (e.g., Eysenck 1967) that a small number of arousal mechanisms might explain personality effects in all their diversity has not been fulfilled. It appears that personality is *distributed* across an extensive set of mechanisms. I have proposed previously (e.g., Matthews 2000, 2008a) that the various types of effect may be differentiated within a cognitive science framework that allows for three qualitatively different levels of explanation (Pylyshyn 1999), illustrated in Figure 23.2. Some effects may be directly attributed to neural processes (biological level), some to basic parameters of the cognitive architecture (symbol-processing or syntactic level) and some to higher-level self-regulation guided by personal meaning (knowledge or semantic level). Next, I will briefly review the strengths and limitations of these different perspectives.

Biological perspectives

The traditional paradigm for biological explanations of personality effects on performance is Eysenck's (1967) arousal theory. According to the Yerkes-Dodson

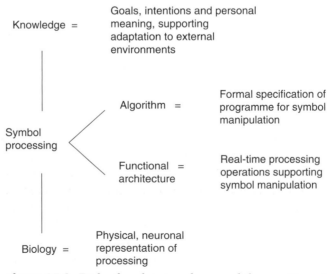

Figure 23.2. *Tri-level explanatory framework for cognitive science.*

Law, cortical arousal is linked to processing efficiency and performance by an inverted-U function. Moderate levels of arousal are optimal for performance; extremes of both low arousal (e.g., fatigue) and high arousal (e.g., anxiety) are damaging. The theory specifies that a cortico-reticular circuit controlling alertness and arousal is more easily activated in introverts than in extraverts. Hence, introverts are prone to performance deficits due to over-arousal, whereas extraverts are vulnerable to under-arousal. The theory makes a simple prediction that introverts should perform better than extraverts in understimulating conditions, whereas extraverts should outperform introverts in arousing settings. The prediction has been confirmed in a number of studies; for example, time pressure and caffeine enhance performance of extraverts but impair performance in introverts (Revelle, Amaral and Turriff 1976).

Unfortunately, on closer scrutiny, the Yerkes-Dodson Law fails to provide a satisfactory explanation for Extraversion-Introversion effects. Psychophysiological findings suggest that Extraversion is only weakly linked to indices of arousal (Matthews and Amelang 1993; Matthews and Gilliland 1999). Indeed, at the subjective level, Extraversion tends to be positively correlated with energetic arousal, as measured by arousal checklists. As previously discussed, there is little evidence that Extraversion effects on performance are directly mediated by arousal. The Yerkes-Dodson Law is also discredited as a principle for stress research (Matthews, Davies, Westerman and Stammers 2000). It claims that higher levels of arousal are optimal for easier tasks, but Matthews, Davies and Lees (1990) provided a direct disconfirmation. Energetic arousal related to better performance on difficult vigilance tasks, but not easy ones.

Other biologically-based theories may do a better job of explanation. For example, Reinforcement Sensitivity Theory (RST) (Philip J. Corr 2004, Chapter 21) links the impulsivity and anxiety traits to the sensitivity of brain systems for reward and punishment. Hence, these traits should interact with motivational factors to influence outcomes, including learning and performance. There is indeed some evidence for interactions of this kind, within various task paradigms (Corr 2004; Chapter 21). However, as with arousal theory, it is questionable whether the theory's predictions are supported in detail (see Matthews 2008b, for a critique).

The recent surge of interest in brain imaging studies of personality is likely to boost neuroscience accounts of individual differences in performance. Studies using fMRI have shown meaningful personality effects on regional brain activations in several of the paradigms discussed in this chapter, including Extraversion and working memory (Gray, Burgess, Schaefer *et al.* 2005) and anxiety and attentional bias (Bishop, Duncan, Brett and Lawrence 2004). Although beyond the scope of this chapter (see Turhan Canli, Chapter 19, and Colin G. DeYoung and Jeremy R. Gray, Chapter 20, for reviews), research of this kind is likely to be increasingly important for the cognitive neuroscience of personality.

Despite grounds for optimism, biological theories are vulnerable to two types of difficulty. First, although they identify important moderator factors including arousal and motivation, predictions of the theories have often been disconfirmed (Matthews and Gilliland 1999). Secondly, it is questionable whether, in principle, biological theories are even capable of explaining the variation of personality effects with information-processing demands – the cognitive patternings described above. (The issue, of course, is the extent to which the cognitive can be reduced to the physical.) Personality effects that are not mediated by symbolic processes including language may be most readily described in terms of neurological functioning. Examples are individual differences in conditioning and in the startle reflex (Corr 2002). Connectionist models may also contribute to integration of biological and cognitive explanations (Matthews and Harley 1993; Matthews, Derryberry and Siegle 2000). Future progress requires a clear demarcation of which personality effects are open to direct biological explanation, and which effects are cognitively (symbolically) mediated.

Information-processing theory

The cognitive patternings of traits (i.e., biases in multiple, independent, processing components) support theories that link traits to individual differences in information-processing. We have seen already how specific effects may be interpreted in relation to standard constructs of cognitive psychology. In fact, the more productive research areas show a progression in three steps. The first step is simply to show that a broadly-defined effect exists, such as an impairment in working memory, or a selective attention bias. The second step is to outline a broad theory that makes some general predictions. For example, the theory that bias in anxiety operates pre-attentively leads to the prediction that it should be evident even when stimuli are subliminally presented. The third step is to develop a detailed computational model, such as building a connectionist network that simulates the phenomenon in detail (Matthews and Harley 1996; Mathews and Mackintosh 1998).

Most research areas have yet to progress much beyond the second step, but the outcome of the research progression is clear. Application of the normal methods of cognitive psychology should yield detailed computational models for numerous specific effects of traits on parameters of individual processing components. Parameters might include the speed with which a process is activated, or its likelihood of generating an error (see Matthews and Harley 1993). At least a sub-set of models might be integrated with neuroscience via connectionism.

Supposing we have such a detailed specification of trait effects, what then? The enterprise has both advantages and limitations (Matthews 2004b). On the positive side, accurate description of phenomena is necessary for personality science, and cognitive psychology provides a conceptual language that supports precision of description. We can also hope to predict how personality effects are moderated by tasks and task parameters, e.g., how we should configure a selective attention task so as to observe bias related to anxiety.

On the negative side, information-processing accounts are incomplete. Sometimes, personality effects are strategic in nature; that is, there may be no personality effect on the parameters of information-processing, but different individuals use the functionality provided by the cognitive architecture to pursue different task goals, e.g., in terms of valuing speed over accuracy. To understand how personality impacts voluntary choice of strategy, we must look at high-level self-regulation and the self-knowledge that supports it. More generally, the information-processing approach risks losing sight of the forest for the trees. Describing a multitude of small biases in attention, memory and speeded response does not in itself tell us why extraverts are sociable and introverts are reserved. A different perspective is needed to understand the unity and coherence of traits, as I will next discuss.

Personality and self-regulation

A part of the cognitive patternings for the major traits reflects individual differences in strategy choice. For example, studies of problem-solving show that extraverts are prone to choose a solution impulsively, without due reflection (Weinman 1987). Often, it is difficult to tell whether a given effect derives from basic parameters of processing or from strategy use. Effects of anxiety on attentional bias are a case in point. As previously discussed, both automatic biases and voluntary search for threat may contribute to bias. Careful experimentation is required to test which type of mechanism is operative in any given instance. We can build processing models for strategic bias. For example, Matthews and Harley (1996) found support for a connectionist model of the emotional Stroop effect in which strategic threat monitoring was modelled as activation of a 'task demand' unit which modulates the sensitivity of the network to threat stimuli. However, while such models are useful descriptively, they cannot explain *why* personality influences top-down regulation of processing. To do so, we need a 'knowledge-level' analysis (Newell 1982); that is, we need to understand how personality affects the personal meaning that people attribute to tasks, and the goals they set for themselves.

Such issues are commonly addressed by self-regulative theories of personality (e.g., Carver and Scheier 2005; Michael D. Robinson and Constantine Sedikides, Chapter 26; Wells and Matthews 1994). Such theories suppose that behaviour is driven by self-representations that activate goals such as reducing a perceived discrepancy between actual and ideal status. In the performance context, the person is typically motivated to maintain some personally acceptable level of performance, to maintain self-esteem and a sense of control and to appear competent to others. Traits may influence the meanings that shape these motivations. For example, anxious or neurotic individuals tend to underestimate their performance and competence (Matthews, Deary and Whiteman 2003). Wells and Matthews (1994) suggest that anxious persons' tendencies to appraise task environments as threatening lead to increased monitoring for threat as a coping strategy. Thus, information-processing biases should be understood within the context of the different meanings that individuals 'read into' performance environments.

Cognitive-adaptive theory of traits

Thus far, I have made the case that understanding personality effects on performance requires multiple levels of explanation, referring to neuroscience, information-processing and self-understanding. No single level is adequate by itself. We still have the problem of finding coherence among these different types of personality expression. This issue is addressed by cognitive-adaptive theory (Matthews 1999, 2000, 2008a; Matthews and Zeidner 2004). In brief, the theory proposes that traits have functional coherence, not structural coherence; that is, there is no single 'master-process' that mediates behavioural expressions of traits, including performance effects. Traits relate to multiple, structurally independent biases in a variety of neural, computational and self-regulative processes. However, these processing biases are related in that they support common adaptive goals that are central to the trait concerned. Traits represent different modes of adaptation to the major challenges of human life.

Anxiety/Neuroticism represents the individual's (partly unconscious) choice of strategy for handling social threats. The anxious individual adapts to threat through anticipating and avoiding threats, whereas the emotionally stable person has a preference for more direct, task-focused coping. The various processing attributes of anxiety support the overall adaptation. Sensitivity of neural systems for threat detection, biases in symbolic computation of threat and beliefs that one is vulnerable to danger all contribute to the adaptive stance of seeking to detect and pre-empt threats before they become imminent. Other traits that influence performance can be similarly characterized. Extraversion may be seen as an adaptation to socially demanding environments. Cognitive features of Extraversion such as efficient multitasking, verbal skills and rapid response work together to facilitate adaptation. Conversely, the various characteristics of Introversion support adaptation to solitary environments requiring self-direction.

Cognitive-adaptive theory emphasizes the role of personality in adapting to real-life challenges (see Figure 23.3). Often, successful adaptation requires acquisition of skills for managing the demands of specific contexts; e.g., taking tests or driving a car. Thus, the cognitive correlates of personality traits observed in performance studies may be precursors of these contextualized skills (Matthews 1999). For example, the attentional characteristics of Extraversion may help to build specific social skills for dealing with strangers and other social challenges. The information-processing attributes of a given trait represent a platform on which the individual builds the skills that support their adaptive specialization. The execution of skills is supported (or sometimes hindered) by self-regulative processes; e.g., extraverts are encouraged to practice their social skills by confidence in the outcome. Adaptation represents a complex interplay between basic

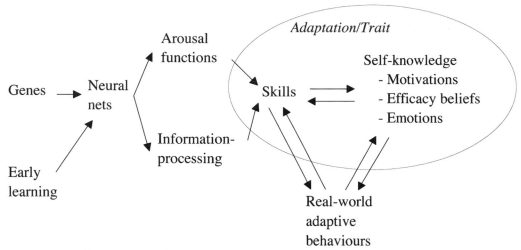

Figure 23.3. *Cognitive-adaptive processes supporting personality traits.*

information-processing, learned skills and self-beliefs and coping strategies. Research on personality and performance may contribute to understanding individual differences in the adaptive process.

Conclusions

Studies of personality and performance have come a long way from their origins in psychobiological research on personality. The introduction of the research methods of cognitive psychology has allowed researchers to link personality traits to a multitude of specific information-processing routines, such that each trait has its own distinct 'cognitive patterning'. Research has typically progressed from identifying broad cognitive functions sensitive to personality towards more fine-grained computational models of specific effects. The cognitive science perspective advanced here indicates that the interaction between the person and the task environment is complex and multilayered. Understanding relationships between personality and cognition needs the additional perspectives provided by neuroscience and by theories of self-regulation. Specification of the information-processing characteristics of traits may be increasingly supplemented with cognitive neuroscience models. Relationships between traits and strategy use may be understood from a self-regulative perspective; performance reflects the individual's understanding of the task and its personal significance. The cognitive science approach provides a new understanding of the integrity and coherence of personality traits. Rather than linking traits to any neural or cognitive 'master-process', the cognitive-adaptive theory suggests that traits represent adaptive specialization supported by multiple biases in neural, cognitive and self-regulative functioning. The two traits emphasized in this chapter, E and N, may relate to adaptations to social challenge and to threat, respectively. The cognitive-adaptive perspective may help us to understand their rich and complex associations with performance.

References

Ashcraft, M. H. and Krause, A. 2007. Working memory, math performance, and math anxiety, *Psychonomic Bulletin and Review* 14: 243–8

Bar-Haim, Y., Lamy, D., Pergamin, L., Bakermans-Kranenburg, M. J. and van IJzendoorn, M. H. 2007. Threat-related attentional bias in anxious and non-anxious individuals: a meta-analytic study, *Psychological Bulletin* 133: 1–24

Beauducel, A., Brocke, B. and Leue, A. 2006. Energetical bases of Extraversion: effort, arousal, EEG, and performance, *International Journal of Psychophysiology* 62: 212–23

Beck, A. T. 1967. *Depression: causes and treatment.* Philadelphia: University of Pennsylvania Press

Bishop, S., Duncan, J., Brett, M. and Lawrence, A. D. 2004. Prefrontal cortical function and anxiety: controlling attention to threat-related stimuli, *Nature Neuroscience* 7: 184–8

Calvo, M. G. and Avero, P. 2005. Time course of attentional bias to emotional scenes in anxiety: gaze direction and duration, *Cognition and Emotion* 19: 433–51

Calvo, M. G. and Castillo, M. D. 2001. Bias in predictive inferences during reading, *Discourse Processes* 32: 43–71

Carver, C. S. and Scheier, M. F. 2005. Engagement, disengagement, coping, and catastrophe, in A. J. Elliot and C. S. Dweck (eds.), *Handbook of competence and motivation*, pp. 527–47. New York: Guilford Press

Cervone, D. 2008. Explanatory models of personality: social-cognitive approaches, in G. J. Boyle, G. Matthews and D. H. Saklofske (eds.), *Handbook of personality theory and testing, vol.I, Personality theories and models*, pp. 80–100. Thousand Oaks, CA: Sage

Corr, P. J. 2002. J. A. Gray's Reinforcement Sensitivity Theory: tests of the joint subsystems hypothesis of anxiety and impulsivity, *Personality and Individual Differences* 33: 511–32

2004. Reinforcement Sensitivity Theory and personality, *Neuroscience and Biobehavioural Reviews* 28: 317–32

Cox-Fuenzalida, L., Swickert, R. and Hittner, J. B. 2004. Effects of Neuroticism and workload history on performance, *Personality and Individual Differences* 36, 447–56

De Pascalis, V. 2004. On the psychophysiology of Extraversion, in R. Stelmack (ed.), *On the psychobiology of personality: essays in honor of Marvin Zuckerman*, pp. 295–327. Amsterdam: Elsevier Science

Derryberry, D. and Reed, M. A. 1997. Motivational and attentional components of personality, in G. Matthews (ed.), *Cognitive science perspectives on personality and emotion*, pp. 443–73. Amsterdam: Elsevier

2002. Anxiety-related attentional biases and their regulation by attentional control, *Journal of Abnormal Psychology* 111: 225–36

Dewaele, J. and Furnham, A. 1999. Extraversion: the unloved variable in applied linguistic research, *Language Learning* 49: 509–44

Doucet, C. and Stelmack, R. M. 2000. An event-related potential analysis of Extraversion and individual differences in cognitive processing speed and response execution, *Journal of Personality and Social Psychology* 78: 956–64

Eysenck, H. J. 1957. *The dynamics of anxiety and hysteria*. London: Routledge and Kegan Paul

  1967. *The biological basis of personality*. Springfield, IL: Thomas

  1995. Creativity as a product of intelligence and personality, in D. H. Saklofske and M. Zeidner (eds.), *International handbook of personality and intelligence*. New York: Plenum

Eysenck, M. W. 1981. Learning, memory and personality, in H. J. Eysenck (ed.), *A model for personality*. Berlin: Springer

  1992. Anxiety: the cognitive perspective. Hillside, NJ: Erlbaum

Eysenck, M. W., Derakshan, N., Santos, R. and Calvo, M. G. 2007. Anxiety and cognitive performance: attentional control theory, *Emotion* 7: 336–53

Fox, E. 1996. Selective processing of threatening words in anxiety: the role of awareness, *Cognition and Emotion* 10: 449–80

Furnham, A. and Strbac, L. 2002. Music is as distracting as noise: the differential distraction of background music and noise on the cognitive test performance of introverts and extraverts, *Ergonomics* 45: 203–17

Gray, J. R., Burgess, G. C., Schaefer, A., Yarkoni, T., Larsen, R. J. and Braver, T. S. 2005. Affective personality differences in neural processing efficiency confirmed using fMRI, *Cognitive, Affective and Behavioural Neuroscience* 5: 182–90

Hockey, G. R. J. 1984. Varieties of attentional state: the effects of environment, in R. Parasuraman and D. R. Davies (eds.), *Varieties of attention*, pp. 449–83. London: Academic Press

Hudlicka, E. 2004. Beyond cognition: modeling emotion in cognitive architectures, in M. Lovett, C. Schunn, C. Lebiere and P. Munro (eds.), *Proceedings of the sixth international conference on cognitive modeling, ICCCM 2004, Integrating models*, pp. 118–23. Mahwah, NJ: Lawrence Erlbaum

Humphreys, M. S. and Revelle, W. 1984. Personality, motivation and performance: a theory of the relationship between individual differences and information processing, *Psychological Review* 91: 153–84

Huppert, J. D., Pasupuleti, R. V., Foa, E. B. and Mathews, A. 2007. Interpretation biases in social anxiety: response generation, response selection, and self-appraisals, *Behaviour Research and Therapy* 45: 1505–15

Kane, M. J. and Engle, R. W. 2002. The role of prefrontal cortex in working-memory capacity, executive attention, and general fluid intelligence: an individual-differences perspective, *Psychonomic Bulletin and Review* 9: 637–71

Koelega, H. S. 1992. Extraversion and vigilance performance: 30 years of inconsistencies, *Psychological Bulletin* 112: 239–58

Lieberman, M. D. 2000. Introversion and working memory: central executive differences, *Personality and Individual Differences* 28: 479–86

Lubow, R. E. and Gewirtz, C. 1995. Latent inhibition in humans: data, theory, and implications for schizophrenia, *Psychological Bulletin* 117: 87–103

Martindale, C. 2007. Creativity, primordial cognition, and personality, *Personality and Individual Differences* 43: 1777–85

Mathews, A. and Mackintosh, B. 1998. A cognitive model of selective processing in anxiety, *Cognitive Therapy and Research* 22: 539–60

Matthews, G. 1992. Extraversion, in A. P. Smith and D. M. Jones (eds.), *Handbook of human performance,* vol. III, *State and trait*, pp. 95–126. London: Academic Press

　　1997. Extraversion, emotion and performance: a cognitive-adaptive model, in G. Matthews (ed.), *Cognitive science perspectives on personality and emotion*, pp. 339–442. Amsterdam: Elsevier

　　1999. Personality and skill: a cognitive-adaptive framework, in P. L. Ackerman, P. C. Kyllonen and R. D. Roberts (eds.), *The future of learning and individual differences research: processes, traits, and content*, pp. 251–70. Washington, DC: APA

　　2000. A cognitive science critique of biological theories of personality traits, *History and Philosophy of Psychology* 2: 1–17

　　2002. Towards a transactional ergonomics for driver stress and fatigue, *Theoretical Issues in Ergonomics Science* 3: 195–211

　　2004a. Neuroticism from the top down: psychophysiology and negative emotionality, in R. Stelmack (ed.), *On the psychobiology of personality: essays in honor of Marvin Zuckerman*, pp. 249–66. Amsterdam: Elsevier Science

　　2004b. Designing personality: cognitive architectures and beyond, in *Proceedings of the American Artificial Intelligence Society Symposium on architectures for modeling emotion: cross-disciplinary foundations*, pp. 83–91. Menlo Park, CA: AAIS

　　2008a. Personality and information processing: a cognitive-adaptive theory, in G. J. Boyle, G. Matthews and D. H. Saklofske (eds.), *Handbook of personality theory and testing, vol. I, Personality theories and models*, pp. 56–79. Thousand Oaks, CA: Sage

　　2008b. Reinforcement Sensitivity Theory: a critique from cognitive science, in P. L. Corr (ed.), *The Reinforcement Sensitivity Theory of personality*, pp. 482–507 Cambridge University Press

Matthews, G. and Amelang, M. 1993. Extraversion, arousal theory and performance: a study of individual differences in the EEG, *Personality and Individual Differences* 14: 347–64

Matthews, G. and Campbell, S. E. in press. Sustained performance under overload: personality and individual differences in stress and coping, *Theoretical Issues in Ergonomics Science*

Matthews, G., Davies, D. R. and Holley, P. J. 1990. Extraversion, arousal and visual sustained attention: the role of resource availability, *Personality and Individual Differences* 11: 1159–73

Matthews, G., Davies, D. R. and Lees, J. L. 1990. Arousal, Extraversion, and individual differences in resource availability, *Journal of Personality and Social Psychology* 59: 150–68

Matthews, G., Davies, D. R., Westerman, S. J. and Stammers, R. B. 2000. *Human performance: cognition, stress and individual differences*. London: Psychology Press

Matthews, G., Deary, I. J. and Whiteman, M. C. 2003. *Personality traits*, 2nd edn. Cambridge University Press

Matthews, G., Derryberry, D. and Siegle, G. J. 2000. Personality and emotion: cognitive science perspectives, in S. E. Hampson (ed.), *Advances in personality psychology*, vol. I, pp. 199–237. London: Routledge

Matthews, G. and Gilliland, K. 1999. The personality theories of H. J. Eysenck and J. A. Gray: a comparative review, *Personality and Individual Differences* 26: 583–626

Matthews, G. and Harley, T. A. 1993. Effects of Extraversion and self-report arousal on semantic priming: a connectionist approach, *Journal of Personality and Social Psychology* 65: 735–56

1996. Connectionist models of emotional distress and attentional bias, *Cognition and Emotion* 10: 561–600

Matthews, G. and Wells, A. 2000. Attention, automaticity and affective disorder, *Behaviour Modification* 24: 69–93

Matthews, G. and Zeidner, M. 2004. Traits, states and the trilogy of mind: an adaptive perspective on intellectual functioning, in D. Dai and R. J. Sternberg (eds.), *Motivation, emotion, and cognition: integrative perspectives on intellectual functioning and development*, pp. 143–74. Mahwah, NJ: Lawrence Erlbaum

Newell, A. 1982. The knowledge level, *Artificial Intelligence* 18: 87–127

Newton, T., Slade, P., Butler, N. M. and Murphy, P. 1992. Personality and performance on a simple visual search task, *Personality and Individual Differences* 13: 381–2

Ortony, A., Norman, D. A. and Revelle, W. 2005. Affect and proto-affect in effective functioning, in J-M. Fellous and M. A. Arbib (eds.), *Who needs emotions? The brain meets the robot*, pp. 173–202. New York: Oxford University Press

Phaf, R. H. and Kan, K. 2007. The automaticity of emotional Stroop: a meta-analysis, *Journal of Behaviour Therapy and Experimental Psychiatry* 38: 184–99

Posner, M. I. and DiGirolamo, G. J. 1998. Executive attention: conflict, target detection and cognitive control, in R. Parasuraman (ed.), *The attentive brain*, pp. 401–23. Cambridge, MA: MIT Press

Poy, R., del Carmen Eixarch, M. and Avila, C. 2004. On the relationship between attention and personality: covert visual orienting of attention in anxiety and impulsivity, *Personality and Individual Differences* 36: 1471–81

Pylyshyn, Z. W. 1999. What's in your mind?, in E. Lepore and Z. W. Pylyshyn (eds.), *What is cognitive science?*, pp. 1–25. Oxford: Blackwell

Revelle, W., Amaral, P. and Turriff, S. 1976. Introversion/Extraversion, time stress, and caffeine: effect on verbal performance, *Science* 192: 149–50

Revelle, W., Humphreys, M. S., Simon, L. and Gilliland, K. 1980. The interactive effect of personality, time of day and caffeine: a test of the arousal model, *Journal of Experimental Psychology: General* 109: 1–31

Robinson, M. D. 2007. Lives lived in milliseconds: using cognitive methods in personality research, in R. W. Robins, R. C. Fraley and R. F. Krueger (eds.), *Handbook of research methods in personality psychology*, pp. 345–59. New York: Guilford Press

Robinson, M. D. and Tamir, M. 2005. Neuroticism as mental noise: a relation between neuroticism and reaction time standard deviations, *Journal of Personality and Social Psychology* 89: 107–14

Russo, R., Whittuck, D., Roberson, D., Dutton, K., Georgiou, G. and Fox, E. 2006. Mood-congruent free recall bias in anxious individuals is not a consequence of response bias, *Memory* 14: 393–9

Sarason, I. G., Sarason, B. R. and Pierce, G. R. 1995. Cognitive interference: at the intelligence-personality crossroads, in D. H. Saklofske and M. Zeidner (eds.), *International handbook of personality and intelligence*, pp. 285–319. New York: Plenum

Spielberger, C. D. 1966. The effects of anxiety on complex learning and academic achievement, in C. D. Spielberger (ed.), *Anxiety and behaviour*, pp. 3–20. London: Academic Press

1972. Anxiety as an emotional state, in C. D. Spielberger (ed.), *Anxiety: current trends in theory and research*, vol. I, pp. 481–93. London: Academic Press

Stanford, M. S. and Barratt, S. 1996. Verbal skills, finger tapping, and cognitive tempo define a second-order factor of temporal information processing, *Brain and Cognition* 31: 35–45

Stelmack, R. M. and Rammsayer, T. H. 2008. Psychophysiological and biochemical perspectives on personality, in G. J. Boyle, G. Matthews and D. H. Saklofske (eds.), *Handbook of personality theory and testing, vol. I, Personality theories and models*, pp. 33–55. Thousand Oaks, CA: Sage

Szymura, B. and Necka, E. 1998. Visual selective attention and personality: an experimental verification of three models of Extraversion, *Personality and Individual Differences* 24: 713–29

Tsakanikos, E. 2004. Latent inhibition, visual pop-out and schizotypy: is disruption of latent inhibition due to enhanced stimulus salience?, *Personality and Individual Differences* 37: 1347–58

Warm, J. S., Matthews, G. and Finomore, V. S. 2008. Workload and stress in sustained attention, in P. A. Hancock and J. L. Szalma (eds.), *Performance under stress*, pp. 115–41. Aldershot: Ashgate Publishing

Weinman, J. 1987. Non-cognitive determinants of perceptual problem-solving strategies, *Personality and Individual Differences* 8: 53–8

Wells, A. and Matthews, G. 1994. *Attention and emotion: a clinical perspective*. Hove: Erlbaum

Wells, A. and Matthews, G. 2006. Cognitive vulnerability to anxiety disorders: an integration, in L. B. Alloy and J. H. Riskind (eds.), *Cognitive vulnerability to emotional disorders*, pp. 303–25. Hillsdale, NJ: Lawrence Erlbaum

Williams, J. M. G., Watts, F. N., MacLeod, C. and Mathews, A. 1997. *Cognitive psychology and emotional disorders*, 2nd edn. Chichester: Wiley

Wilson, E. J., MacLeod, C., Mathews, A. and Rutherford, E. M. 2006. The causal role of interpretive bias in anxiety reactivity, *Journal of Abnormal Psychology* 115: 103–11

Zeidner, M. 1998. *Test anxiety: the state of the art*. New York: Plenum

Zeidner, M. and Matthews, G. 2005. Evaluation anxiety, in A. J. Elliot and C. S. Dweck (eds.), *Handbook of competence and motivation*, pp. 141–63. New York: Guilford Press

Zuckerman, M. 1991. *Psychobiology of personality*. Cambridge University Press

24 Self-regulation and control in personality functioning

Charles S. Carver and Michael F. Scheier

Personality has been viewed in many ways (Carver and Scheier 2008). This chapter outlines a view in which personality is viewed through the lens of feedback control processes. We address two layers of control processes, managing two different aspects of behaviour. The layers function to permit people to handle multiple tasks across time. More specifically, they help transform simultaneous motives into a stream of actions that shifts repeatedly from one goal to another.

The view described here has long been identified with the term *self-regulation* (Carver and Scheier 1981, 1998). That term has different connotations in different contexts. When we use it, we intend to convey the sense of purposive processes, involving self-corrective adjustments as needed, and that the adjustments originate within the person.

This view is not an approach to personality but a way of talking about how personality becomes expressed in behaviour. It focuses on general principles concerning how people negotiate life. Although it certainly is possible to examine individual differences within this framework, we focus here on broad functions we believe are part of everyone's personality.

Behaviour as goal directed and feedback controlled

A basic concept here is the feedback loop. An easy way to approach it is to start with the more intuitive concept of a goal. Everyone knows what a goal is: a mental representation of a state the person is trying to attain. People have many goals, at varying levels of abstraction and importance. Most can be reached in many ways, and a given action can create movement toward very different goals.

Feedback processes

Approaching a goal illustrates the principle of feedback control. A feedback loop involves four sub-functions (Miller, Galanter and Pribram 1960; MacKay 1966; Powers 1973; Wiener 1948): an input, a reference value, a comparison, and an output (Figure 24.1). Think of the input as perception; input is information about

Preparation of this chapter was facilitated by grants CA64710, BCS0544617, HL65111, HL65112, HL076852, and HL076858.

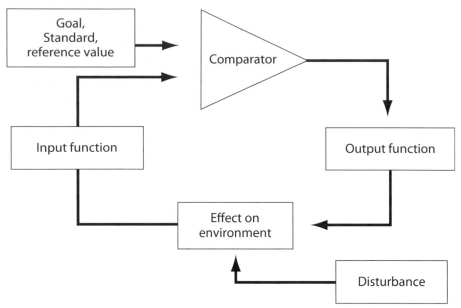

Figure 24.1. *Schematic depiction of a feedback loop, the basic unit of cybernetic control. In a discrepancy reducing loop, a sensed value is compared to a reference value or standard, and adjustments occur in an output function (if necessary) that shift the sensed value in the direction of the standard. In a discrepancy enlarging loop, the output function moves the sensed value away from the standard.*

present circumstances. A reference value is a goal. The input is compared to the reference value. Any discrepancy detected is called an 'error signal'. We treat the output here as behaviour, but sometimes the behaviour is internal.

If the comparison detects no discrepancy, the output remains as it was. How detection of a discrepancy affects output depends on what kind of loop it is. In a discrepancy reducing loop, the output acts to reduce the discrepancy. Such an effect is seen in attempts to reach a valued goal, maintain a desired condition, or conform to a standard. There also are discrepancy-enlarging loops, which avoid the reference value rather than approach it. The value in this case is a threat or an 'anti-goal', for example, a feared or disliked possible self (Carver, Lawrence and Scheier 1999; Ogilvie 1987). A discrepancy enlarging loop senses existing conditions, compares them to the anti-goal, and enlarges the discrepancy.

The effects of discrepancy enlarging processes in living systems are typically constrained by discrepancy reducing processes. Put differently, acts of avoidance often lead into acts of approach. Imagine a person escaping a threat. There may be a goal to approach that keeps the person distant from the threat. Thus, the tendency to avoid the threat is joined by the tendency to approach that goal. This pattern of dual influence defines active avoidance: an organism facing a feared stimulus picks a safer location to escape to, and approaches that location.

Feedback loops are ubiquitous in living systems. The feedback concept is most often applied to physiological systems, such as the homeostatic systems that maintain blood pressure and body temperature. We have argued, however, that the same structural elements underlie the behaviours that are of interest to personality psychologists. Remember, personality emerges from a body that stays alive through feedback processes. Nature is a miser. If the same structure that ensures continued life can also yield more complex phenomena, there is no need for a new kind of structure – the existing one will be used.

A few more points: it is easy to portray the elements of a feedback loop conceptually. In some cases (e.g., in electronic systems), it is also easy to point to each element. In other cases, this is harder. In particular, some feedback processes have no explicit representation of a reference value. The system regulates around a value, but no value is represented as a goal (Berridge 2004; Carver and Scheier 2002).

Another point concerns using homeostasis as an illustration of feedback processes. Some infer from this that feedback loops act only to create and maintain steady states. Not so. Some goals *are* static end states. But others are dynamic and evolving (e.g., the goal of taking a week's vacation, the goal of raising a child to become a good citizen). In such cases, the 'goal' is the process of traversing the changing trajectory of the activity, not just to be at the endpoint. Feedback processes apply perfectly well to moving targets (Beer 1995).

Finally, goals vary in abstractness. You may have the goal of being a good citizen, but you can also have the goal of recycling refuse, a narrower goal that contributes to being a good citizen. To recycle entails concrete goals: placing newspapers into containers and moving them to a pick-up location. Thus, it is often said that goals form a hierarchy (Carver and Scheier 1998; Powers 1973; Toates 2006; Vallacher and Wegner 1987). Abstract goals are attained by the attaining of the concrete goals that help define them.

Feedback and affect

Personality is manifest partly in behaviour – how people spend their time and energy. Personality is also manifest in affects, feelings, emotions. What is affect? Where does it come from? Affect pertains to one's desires and whether they are being met (Clore 1994; Frijda 1988; Ortony, Clore and Collins 1988). But what is the internal mechanism by which feelings arise?

Answers range from neurobiological (e.g., Davidson 1992) to cognitive (Ortony, Clore and Collins 1988). We posed an answer that focuses on what appear to be some of the functional properties of affect (Carver and Scheier 1990, 1998). We used feedback control once more as an organizing principle, but now focusing on a different quality than before.

We suggest that feelings arise as a consequence of another feedback process that operates simultaneously with the behaviour-guiding process and in parallel to it. It operates automatically and without supervision. The easiest characterization of what this second process is doing is that it is checking on how well the first process is doing. The input for this second loop, thus, is the *rate of progress in the action system over time*.

Consider a physical analogy. Action implies change between states. Thus, behaviour is analogous to distance. If the action loop controls distance, and if the affect loop assesses the action loop's progress, then the affect loop is controlling the psychological analog of velocity, the first derivative of distance over time. If this analogy is meaningful, the perceptual input to the affect loop would be the first derivative over time of the input used by the action loop.

Input alone does not create affect; a given rate of progress has different affective effects in different contexts. We think this input is compared to a reference value (cf. Frijda 1988), as in other feedback systems. In this case, the reference is an acceptable or expected rate of behavioural discrepancy reduction. As in other feedback loops, the comparison checks for deviation from the standard. If there is a discrepancy, the output function changes.

We believe the error signal in this loop is manifest as affect, a positive or negative valence. A rate of progress below the criterion creates negative affect. A rate exceeding the criterion creates positive affect. In essence, feelings with a positive valence mean you are doing better at something than you need to, and feelings with a negative valence mean you are doing worse than you need to (for detail see Carver and Scheier 1998, chs. 8 and 9).

What determines the criterion value for the velocity loop? There surely are many influences. Framing the action to oneself in different ways may change the criterion (Brendl and Higgins 1996). If the activity is unfamiliar, what is used as a criterion probably is quite flexible. If the activity is familiar, however, the criterion is likely to reflect accumulated experience, an expected rate. Whether 'expected' or 'desired' or 'needed' rate is more accurate as a depiction may depend greatly on the context.

The criterion can also change. We think that change in rate criterion in a relatively familiar behaviour domain occurs relatively slowly. Repeated overshoots result automatically in an upward drift, repeated undershoots result in a downward drift (see Carver and Scheier 2000, for greater detail). A somewhat ironic consequence of such a recalibration would be to keep the balance of a person's emotional experience (positive to negative, aggregated across a span of time) relatively similar, even when the rate criterion changes considerably.

Two kinds of behavioural loops, two dimensions of affect

So far we have focused on approach loops, but the same logic applies to avoidance loops. We just said that positive feeling exists when a behavioural system is making rapid progress *doing what it is organized to do*. Some systems are organized to approach. Others are organized to avoid. If such a system is making rapid progress attaining its ends, there should be positive affect. If it is doing poorly, there should be negative affect. Thus, we believe that both approach and avoidance have the potential to induce positive feelings (by doing well), and that both have the potential to induce negative feelings (by doing poorly).

But doing well at approaching an incentive is not quite the same as doing well at moving away from a threat, and there may be differences between the two positives, and between the two negatives. As have Higgins (e.g., 1987, 1996) and his collaborators, we argue for two dimensions of affect, one concerning approach, the other concerning avoidance (Carver 2001; Carver and Scheier 1998). Approach yields such positive affects as elation, eagerness and excitement, and such negative affects as frustration, anger and sadness (Carver 2004). Avoidance yields such positive affects as relief, serenity and contentment and such negative affects as fear, guilt and anxiety.

Merging affect and action

This description implies a natural connection between affect and action; that is, if the input of the affect loop is a rate of progress in action, the output function of the affect loop must be a change in rate of that action. Thus, the affect loop has a direct influence on what occurs in the action loop.

Some changes in rate are straightforward. If you are lagging behind, you try harder. Some changes are less straightforward. The rates of many 'behaviours' reflect not the pace of physical action but choices among potential actions. For example, increasing your rate of progress on a project at work may mean choosing to spend a weekend working rather than playing with family and friends. Increasing your rate of being kind means choosing to do an act that reflects kindness, when an opportunity arises. Thus, change in rate must often be translated into other terms, such as concentration, or allocation of time and effort.

The idea of two layers of feedback systems functioning together turns out to be quite common in control engineering (e.g., Clark 1996). Engineers have long recognized that having two systems – one controlling position, one controlling velocity – permits the device they control to respond in a way that is both quick and stable, without overshoots and oscillations.

The combination of quickness and stability in responding is desirable in the kinds of devices engineers deal with, but it is also desirable in living beings. A person with very reactive emotions overreacts, and oscillates behaviourally. A person who is emotionally unreactive is slow to respond even to urgent events. A person whose reactions are between those extremes responds quickly but without overreaction and oscillation.

For biological entities, being able to respond quickly yet accurately confers a clear adaptive advantage. We believe this combination of quick and stable responding is a consequence of having both behaviour-managing and affect-managing control systems. Affect makes people's responses quicker (because this system is time sensitive); as long as the affective system is not overresponsive, the responses are also stable.

Unexpected implications

This model differs in several ways from other views of the meaning and consequences of affect. The argument that affect reflects the error signal from a comparison in a feedback loop has a very counter-intuitive implication concerning positive affect (Carver 2003).

As noted, if affect reflects the error signal in a feedback loop, affect is a signal to adjust rate of progress. This would be true whether the rate is above the mark or below it, that is, whether affect is positive or negative. For negative feelings, this notion is not at all controversial: indeed, it is quite intuitive. The first response to negative feelings is usually to try harder. (For now we disregard the possibility of quitting; we return to it later.) If the person tries harder, and assuming more effort (or better effort) increases the rate of intended movement, the negative affect diminishes or ceases.

What about positive feelings? Here prediction is less intuitive. In this model, positive feelings arise when things are going better than they need to. But the feelings still reflect a discrepancy, and discrepancy reducing loops minimize discrepancies. Thus, such a system 'wants' to see neither negative nor positive affect. Either quality (deviation from the standard in either direction) would lead to changes in output that would eventually reduce it.

This view argues that people who exceed the criterion rate of progress (and thus have positive feelings) will automatically tend to reduce subsequent effort in this domain. They will 'coast' a little (cf. Frijda 1994, p. 113); not necessarily stop, but ease back, such that subsequent rate of progress returns to the criterion. The impact on subjective affect would be that the positive feeling itself is not sustained for very long. It begins to fade.

Expending greater effort to catch up when behind, and coasting when ahead, are both presumed to be specific to the goal domain to which the affect is attached. Usually this is the goal from which the affect arises in the first place (for exceptions see Schwarz and Clore 1983). We are not arguing that positive affect creates a tendency to coast *in general*, but rather that it creates a tendency to coast with respect to the specific activity producing the positive feelings.

This is a kind of 'cruise control' model of affect; that is, a system of this sort would operate in the same way as a car's cruise control. Coming to a hill slows you down; the cruise control responds by giving the engine more fuel, speeding back up. If you come across the crest of a hill and roll downward too fast, the system cuts back the fuel and the speed drags back down.

Both in a car and in behaviour, doing something about going too slow requires adding resources. Doing something about going too fast requires only reducing resources. The cruise control does not engage the brakes, it just reduces fuel. The car coasts back to the velocity set point. Thus, the effect of the cruise control on a high rate of speed depends in part on external circumstances. If the hill is steep, the car may exceed the cruise control's set point all the way to the valley below.

In the same way, people usually do not react to positive affect by actively trying to make themselves feel less good (though there are exceptions). They just ease back a little on resources devoted to the domain in which the affect has arisen. The positive feelings may be sustained for a long time (depending on circumstances), as the person coasts down the subjective analog of the hill. Eventually, though, the reduced resources cause the positive affect to diminish. Generally, then, the system acts to prevent great amounts of pleasure as well as great amounts of pain (Carver 2003; Carver and Scheier 1998).

To test the idea that positive affect leads to coasting, a study must assess coasting with respect to the same goal as underlies the affect. Many studies have created positive affect in one context and assessed its influence on another task. However, that does not test this question. Suggestive evidence has been reported by Mizruchi (1991) and Louro, Pieters and Zeelenberg (2007), but the question remains relatively untested at present.

Coasting and multiple goals

Why would a process be built in that limits positive feelings – indeed, dampens them? After all, people seek pleasure and avoid pain. We believe the adaptive value of a tendency to coast derives from the fact that people have multiple simultaneous goals (Carver 2003; Carver and Scheier 1998; Frijda 1994). Given multiple goals, people generally do not optimize on any one goal, but rather 'satisfice' (Simon 1953): do a good enough job on each to deal with it satisfactorily.

A tendency to coast would virtually define satisficing regarding that particular goal; that is, reduction in effort prevents you from attaining the best possible outcome on that goal. A tendency to coast would also foster satisficing on a broader set of goals; that is, if progress in one domain yields a tendency to coast in that domain, it would be easy to shift to another domain, at little or no cost. This would help ensure satisfactory goal attainment in the other domain and ultimately across multiple domains.

Continued pursuit of one goal without let-up, in contrast, can have adverse effects. Continuing a rapid pace in one arena may sustain positive affect in that arena, but by diverting resources from other goals it also increases the potential for problems elsewhere. Indeed, a single-minded pursuit of yet-more-positive feelings in one domain can even be lethal, if it causes the person to disregard threats looming elsewhere.

Priority management as a core issue in self-regulation

This line of argument begins to implicate positive feelings in a broad function within the organism that deserves further consideration: shifting from one goal to another as focal in behaviour (Dreisbach and Goschke 2004; Shallice

1978). This critical phenomenon is often overlooked. Many goals are under pursuit simultaneously, but only one can have top priority at a given moment. People need to shift flexibly among goals.

The problem of priority management was addressed many years ago by Simon (1967), who pointed out that any entity with many goals needs a way to rank them for pursuit and a mechanism to change rankings as necessary. He argued as follows: most of people's goals are largely out of awareness at any given moment. Only the one with the highest priority has full access to consciousness. Sometimes events occur during the pursuit of that top-priority goal that create problems for another goal that currently has a lower priority. Indeed, the mere passing of time sometimes creates a problem for the second goal, by making its attainment less likely. If the second goal is also important, an emerging problem for its attainment needs to be registered and taken into account. If the situation evolves enough to seriously threaten the second goal, some mechanism is needed for changing priorities, so that the second goal replaces the first one as focal.

Negative feelings and shifting prioritization

Simon (1967) proposed that emotions are calls for reprioritization. He suggested that emotion arising with respect to a goal that is out of awareness eventually causes people to interrupt their behaviour and give that goal a higher priority than it had. The stronger the emotion, the stronger is the claim being made that the unattended goal should have higher priority than the presently focal goal. The affect is what pulls the out-of-awareness into awareness.

Simon's analysis applies readily to negative feelings such as anxiety and frustration. If you promised your spouse you would go to the post office this afternoon and you've been too busy to go, the creeping of the clock toward closing time can cause an increase in frustration or anxiety (or both). Neither affect would pertain to the work you are doing, however. They would pertain to a potentially unmet obligation and a potentially angry spouse. The stronger the affect, the more likely it is that the goal it relates to will rise in priority until it comes fully to awareness and becomes the focal reference point for behaviour.

Positive feelings and reprioritization

Simon's discussion focused on cases in which a non-focal goal demands a higher priority than it now has and *intrudes* on awareness. By strong implication, his discussion dealt only with negative affect. However, there is another way in which priority ordering can shift: the currently focal goal can *relinquish its place*. Simon addressed this possibility obliquely, by noting that goal completion terminates pursuit of that goal. However, he did not address the possibility that an as-yet-unattained goal might yield its place in line.

Positive feelings may represent a reprioritization cue, but a cue to *reduce* the priority of the goal to which the feeling pertains; that is, the function Simon asserted for affect may pertain to affects of both valences. Positive affect regarding an avoidance effort (relief or tranquility) indicates that a threat has dissipated, no longer requires as much attention as it did, and can now assume a lower priority. Positive feelings regarding approach (happiness, joy) indicate that an incentive is being attained. If it is fully attained, effort can cease, as Simon noted; if it is not yet attained, the affect is a signal that you could temporarily put this goal aside, because you are doing so well (Carver 2003).

If a focal goal diminishes in priority, what follows? It depends partly on what is waiting in line. It also depends partly on whether the context has changed in any important way while you were busy with the focal goal. That is, opportunities to attain incentives sometimes appear unexpectedly, and people put aside their plans to take advantage of them (Hayes-Roth and Hayes-Roth 1979; Payton 1990). It seems reasonable that people with positive affect should be more prone to shift goals at this point if something else needs fixing or doing (regarding a next-in-line goal or a newly emergent goal) or if an unanticipated opportunity for gain has appeared.

Sometimes the next item in line is of fairly high priority in its own right. Sometimes the situation has changed and a new goal has emerged for consideration. On the other hand, sometimes neither of these conditions exists. In that case, no change would occur, because the downgrade in priority of the focal goal does not make it lower than the priorities of the alternatives. Positive affect does not *require* a change in direction. It simply sets the stage for such a change to be more likely. Indirect support for this general line of reasoning is reviewed elsewhere (Carver 2003).

We should be clear that we are not claiming that affect is the only source of shifts in goal prioritization. Changes in context can also produce shifts, because different contexts have been linked in the past to different goals. The resulting associations in memory mean that a change in context can prompt the emergence of a different goal via those associations. Our position is simply that affect is part of the prioritization process.

Effortfully evading automatic functions of affect

We have been describing what we see as a set of automatic effects of emotions in priority management. However, it may also be useful to note briefly that people learn to intervene in these effects by regulating their emotions. For example, suppose you are an athlete trying to perform in a timed event. Suppose you get ahead quickly. By our reasoning, if you therefore feel happy, you may relax a little. But relaxing – becoming vulnerable to distraction – is undesirable in this situation. How can you prevent that from happening?

A common strategy for athletes is to try to prevent feelings of pleasure from arising. One stra tegy is maintaining an extremely high level of aspiration, so that it could hardly ever be exceeded (thus no positive affect). Another strategy is to artificially generate anger, taking the place of any pleasure that exists in being ahead. Yet another strategy is to remind yourself that your lead is small and you are still vulnerable, or even to pretend that you are not really ahead at all.

The point more generally is that there often are ways to trick the automatic system of affective response by reframing the situation in various ways. If the affective reaction itself can be changed, the resulting impact on priority management should also change.

Priority management and depressed affect

One more aspect of priority management concerns the idea that goals sometimes are not attainable and are better abandoned. We argue that sufficient doubt about goal attainment results in disengagement from efforts to reach the goal, and even from the goal itself (Carver and Scheier 1981, 1998). This is a kind of priority adjustment, in that the abandoned goal is now receiving an even lower priority than it had before; that is, no behaviour is being directed to its attainment at all.

How does this sort of reprioritization fit into the picture sketched up to here? At first glance, the idea that doubt about goal attainment (and the negative feelings associated with that doubt) cause reduction in effort seems to contradict Simon's (1967) position that negative affect is a call for higher priority. However, two very different negative affects relate to approach (Carver 2003, 2004; a parallel line of reasoning applies to avoidance, but we limit ourselves here to approach). Some approach-related negative affects coalesce around frustration and anger. Others coalesce around sadness, depression and dejection. The former relate to an increase in priority, the latter to a decrease.

We believe that approach-related affects form a dimension, but not a simple straight line. We think that falling behind creates negative affect as the incentive slips away: frustration, irritation and anger. These feelings (or the mechanism that underlies them) engage more effort, to overcome obstacles and reverse the inadequacy of current progress. If more effort (or better effort) can improve progress, it allows the person to move toward the incentive at an adequate rate, and attaining the incentive seems likely. This case fits the priority management model of Simon (1967).

Sometimes, however, continued efforts do not produce adequate movement forward. Indeed, if the situation involves loss, movement forward is precluded, because the incentive is gone. In a situation where failure seems (or is) assured, the feelings are sadness, depression, despondency, dejection, grief and hopelessness (cf. Finlay-Jones and Brown 1981). Accompanying behaviours reflect disengagement from – giving up on – effort toward the incentive (Klinger 1975; Wortman and Brehm 1975).

Two published studies reported patterns of emotions consistent with this portrayal (Mikulincer 1994; Pittman and Pittman 1980). In each, participants received varying amounts of failure, and their emotional responses were assessed.

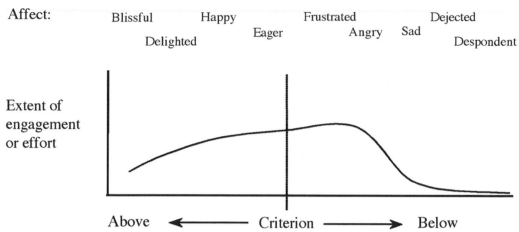

Figure 24.2. *Hypothesized approach-related affects as a function of doing well versus doing poorly compared to a criterion velocity. A second (vertical) dimension indicates the degree of behavioural engagement posited to be associated with affects at different degrees of departure from neutral.*

In both cases, anger was most intense after small amounts of failure and lower after larger amounts of failure. Depression was low after small amounts of failure and intense after larger amounts of failure.

Both kinds of reactions have adaptive properties. In the first situation – falling behind, but the goal not lost – frustration and anger accompany an increase in effort, a struggle to gain the incentive despite setbacks. As Frijda (1986, p. 429) argued, anger implies having the hope that things can be set right. This struggle is adaptive because it fosters goal attainment. In the second situation – when effort appears futile – feelings of sadness and depression accompany reduction of effort. In this case, things cannot be set right; further effort is pointless. Reduction of effort here is adaptive (Carver and Scheier 2003; Wrosch, Scheier, Carver and Schulz 2003; Wrosch, Scheier, Miller, Schulz and Carver 2003). It conserves energy rather than wastes it in futile pursuit of the unattainable (Nesse 2000), and it eventually readies the person to take up pursuit of alternative incentives (Klinger 1975).

The variations in effort described in the preceding paragraphs are portrayed in Figure 24.2. The left side portrays the hypothesized reduction in effort when velocity exceeds the criterion, discussed earlier. The right side portrays both the strong engagement that is implied by frustration and anger and the disengagement of sadness and dejection. This part of the figure has much in common with several other depictions of variations in effort when difficulty in moving toward a goal gives way to loss of the goal (for detail see Carver and Scheier 1998, Ch. 11). Best known is Wortman and Brehm's (1975) integration of reactance and helplessness, which portrays a region of threat to control (where there is enhanced effort to regain control) and a region of loss of control (where efforts diminish).

Concluding comment

This chapter described basic principles of a control-process view of behavioural self-regulation. We have necessarily left aside a number of issues that pertain to self-regulation. For example, we have not addressed self-control and the processes that are involved in overriding impulses, which clearly are important to the understanding of self-regulation (Baumeister and Vohs 2004). We have also omitted many more issues that pertain to personality. For example, we have not discussed how self-regulatory functions map onto dimensions of individual differences that have been identified by other approaches to personality. Nor have we considered the relations of this viewpoint to others that it complements (though see Carver and Scheier 2008, ch. 18 for discussion of that issue). Nonetheless, we hope the picture we have sketched will be seen as a useful complement to principles discussed in other chapters in this volume.

References

Baumeister, R. F. and Vohs, K. D. (eds.) 2004. *Handbook of self-regulation: research, theory and applications*. New York: Guilford Press

Beer, R. D. 1995. A dynamical systems perspective on agent-environment interaction, *Artificial Intelligence* 72: 173–215

Berridge, K. C. 2004. Motivation concepts in behavioural neuroscience, *Physiology and Behaviour* 81: 179–209

Brendl, C. M. and Higgins, E. T. 1996. Principles of judging valence: what makes events positive or negative?, *Advances in experimental social psychology* 28: 95–160

Carver, C. S. 2001. Affect and the functional bases of behaviour: on the dimensional structure of affective experience, *Personality and Social Psychology Review* 5: 345–56

2003. Pleasure as a sign you can attend to something else: placing positive feelings within a general model of affect, *Cognition and Emotion* 17: 241–61

2004. Negative affects deriving from the behavioural approach system, *Emotion* 4: 3–22

Carver, C. S., Lawrence, J. W. and Scheier, M. F. 1999. Self-discrepancies and affect: incorporating the role of feared selves, *Personality and Social Psychology Bulletin* 25: 783–92

Carver, C. S. and Scheier, M. F. 1981. *Attention and self-regulation: a control-theory approach to human behaviour*. New York: Springer Verlag

1990. Origins and functions of positive and negative affect: a control-process view, *Psychological Review* 97: 19–35

1998. *On the self-regulation of behaviour*. New York: Cambridge University Press

2000. Scaling back goals and recalibration of the affect system are processes in normal adaptive self-regulation: understanding 'response shift' phenomena, *Social Science and Medicine* 50: 1715–22

2002. Control processes and self-organization as complementary principles underlying behaviour, *Personality and Social Psychology Review* 6: 304–15

2003. Three human strengths, in L. G. Aspinwall and U. M. Staudinger (eds.), *A psychology of human strengths: fundamental questions and future directions for a positive psychology*, pp. 87–102. Washington, DC: American Psychological Association

2008. *Perspectives on personality*, 6th edn. Boston, MA: Allyn and Bacon

Clark, R. N. 1996. *Control system dynamics*. New York: Cambridge University Press

Clore, G. C. 1994. Why emotions are felt, in P. Ekman and R. J. Davidson (eds.), *The nature of emotion: fundamental questions*, pp. 103–111. New York: Oxford University Press.

Davidson, R. J. 1992. Anterior cerebral asymmetry and the nature of emotion, *Brain and Cognition* 20: 125–51

Dreisbach, G. and Goschke, T. 2004. How positive affect modulates cognitive control: reduced perseveration at the cost of increased distractibility, *Journal of Experimental Psychology: Learning, Memory, and Cognition* 30: 343–53

Finlay-Jones, R. and Brown, G. W. 1981. Types of stressful life event and the onset of anxiety and depressive disorders,. *Psychological Medicine* 11: 803–15

Frijda, N. H. 1986. *The emotions*. Cambridge University Press

1988. The laws of emotion, *American Psychologist* 43: 349–58

1994. Emotions are functional, most of the time, in P. Ekman and R. J. Davidson (eds.), *The nature of emotion: fundamental questions*, pp. 112–26. New York: Oxford University Press

Hayes-Roth, B. and Hayes-Roth, F. 1979. A cognitive model of planning, *Cognitive Science* 3: 275–310

Higgins, E. T. 1987. Self-discrepancy: a theory relating self and affect, *Psychological Review* 94: 319–40

1996. Ideals, oughts, and regulatory focus: affect and motivation from distinct pains and pleasures, in P. M. Gollwitzer and J. A. Bargh (eds.), *The psychology of action: linking cognition and motivation to behaviour*, pp. 91–114. New York: Guilford Press

Klinger, E. 1975. Consequences of commitment to and disengagement from incentives, *Psychological Review* 82: 1–25

Levenson, R. W. 1994. Human emotion: a functional view, in P. Ekman and R. Davidson (eds.), *The nature of emotions: fundamental questions*, pp. 123–6. New York: Oxford University Press

Louro, M. J., Pieters, R. and Zeelenberg, M. 2007. Dynamics of multiple-goal pursuit, *Journal of Personality and Social Psychology* 93: 174–93

MacKay, D. M. 1966. Cerebral organization and the conscious control of action, in J. C. Eccles (ed.), *Brain and conscious experience*, pp. 422–45. Berlin: Springer-Verlag

Mikulincer, M. 1994. *Human learned helplessness: a coping perspective*. New York: Plenum

Miller, G. A., Galanter, E. and Pribram, K. H. 1960. *Plans and the structure of behaviour*. New York: Holt, Rinehart and Winston

Mizruchi, M. S. 1991. Urgency, motivation, and group performance: the effect of prior success on current success among professional basketball teams, *Social Psychology Quarterly* 54: 181–9

Nesse, R. M. 2000. Is depression an adaptation?, *Archives of General Psychiatry* 57: 14–20

Ogilvie, D. M. 1987. The undesired self: a neglected variable in personality research, *Journal of Personality and Social Psychology* 52: 379–85

Ortony, A., Clore, G. L. and Collins, A. 1988. *The cognitive structure of emotions*. New York: Cambridge University Press

Payton, D. W. 1990. Internalized plans: a representation for action resources, in P. Maes (ed.), *Designing autonomous agents: theory and practice from biology to engineering and back*, pp. 89–103. Cambridge, MA: MIT Press

Pittman, T. S. and Pittman, N. L. 1980. Deprivation of control and the attribution process, *Journal of Personality and Social Psychology* 39: 377–89

Powers, W. T. 1973. *Behaviour: the control of perception*. Chicago, IL: Aldine

Schwarz, N. and Clore, G. L. 1983. Mood, misattribution, and judgments of well-being: informative and directive functions of affective states, *Journal of Personality and Social Psychology* 45: 513–23

Shallice, T. 1978. The dominant action system: an information-processing approach to consciousness, in K. S. Pope and J. L. Singer (eds.), *The stream of consciousness: scientific investigations into the flow of human experience*, pp. 117–57. New York: Wiley

Simon, H. A. 1953. *Models of man*. New York: Wiley

  1967. Motivational and emotional controls of cognition, *Psychological Review* 74: 29–39

Toates, F. 2006. A model of the hierarchy of behaviour, cognition, and consciousness, *Consciousness and Cognition: An International Journal* 15: 75–118

Vallacher, R. R. and Wegner, D. M. 1987. What do people think they're doing? Action identification and human behaviour, *Psychological Review* 94: 3–15

Wiener, N. 1948. *Cybernetics: control and communication in the animal and the machine*. Cambridge, MA: MIT Press

Wortman, C. B. and Brehm, J. W. 1975. Responses to uncontrollable outcomes: an integration of reactance theory and the learned helplessness model, in L. Berkowitz (ed.), *Advances in experimental social psychology*, vol. VIII, pp. 277–336. New York: Academic Press

Wrosch, C., Scheier, M. F., Carver, C. S. and Schulz, R. 2003. The importance of goal disengagement in adaptive self-regulation: when giving up is beneficial, *Self and Identity* 2: 1–20

Wrosch, C., Scheier, M. F., Miller, G. E., Schulz, R. and Carver, C. S. 2003. Adaptive self-regulation of unattainable goals: goal disengagement, goal re-engagement, and subjective well-being, *Personality and Social Psychology Bulletin* 29: 1494–1508

25 Self-determination theory: a consideration of human motivational universals

Edward L. Deci and Richard M. Ryan

Psychologists have long agreed that human beings have basic physiological needs such as hunger, thirst and sex. These needs specify nutriments that are essential for people in order to develop optimally and to be physically healthy. These needs have played a role in general theories of behaviour (e.g., Hull 1943) as well as in more specific theories related to behavioural domains more directly linked to the needs. There has been far less agreement, however, about whether people also have basic psychological needs – that is, needs of the psyche that are essential for psychological wellbeing and thriving.

Most motivational psychologists do not acknowledge psychological needs as a fundamental aspect of human motivation, instead arguing that the cognitive concept of goals is more useful in explaining motivated behaviour. Furthermore, those who do use the concept of psychological needs have tended to treat them as individual differences in the degree to which people desire such things as achievement (e.g., McClelland 1985) or cognition (Cacioppo and Petty 1982) rather than as psychological universals. From the individual-difference perspective, 'needs' are viewed as being learned through socialization rather than being an inherent aspect of people's nature.

Gradually, however, over the past fifty years, the view that all people have basic psychological needs that must be satisfied for optimal psychological development and wellbeing has been receiving wider acceptance and has been an important basis for an increasing number of theories. For example, White (1959) argued for the concept of effectance as a basic need; De Charms (1968) proposed that the experience of personal causation is a psychological need; Baumeister and Leary (1995) suggested that belongingness is a need fundamental to all humans; and Deci and Ryan (1985, 2000) have postulated that human beings have three basic and universal psychological needs: the needs for competence, autonomy and relatedness. Being basic and universal means that, just as certain physiological nutriment such as water, are necessary for the wellbeing of all people, these three psychological nutriments are also necessary for the wellbeing and flourishing of all people. Thus, when people's needs for competence, autonomy and relatedness are thwarted, there will be detriments in their psychological health, and to some extent in their physical health (e.g., Ryan 1995).

Self-determination theory (SDT) has been formulated in relation to the concept of these three basic psychological needs. Simply stated, the theory proposes that aspects of people's interpersonal environments and their own individual differences will affect the degree to which they are able to satisfy their basic psychological needs and sustain their growth-oriented nature. The outcome of this ongoing interaction of people's inherent proactivity with the social environment that is either supportive or thwarting of their basic psychological needs has a profound impact on their motivation, cognition, affect and wellbeing.

SDT has many components that deal with the interactions of people's needs, personalities and social contexts. Among them are ones that: address types of motivation, specifically intrinsic motivation and four types of extrinsic motivation; consider developmental processes through which these types of motivation change; examine how aspects of the social context enhance versus deplete the different types of motivation; relate types of motivation to a range of outcomes including learning, performance, cognitive functioning and wellbeing; relate various aspirations or life-goals to basic psychological need satisfaction and both performance and wellbeing outcomes; explore the importance of autonomy across cultures; and apply these components of SDT to such life-domains as parenting, education, work and healthcare.

Intrinsic and extrinsic motivation

The first important distinction in types of motivation is between intrinsic and extrinsic motivation. Intrinsic motivation refers to doing an activity because the activity itself is interesting and spontaneously satisfying (Ryan and Deci 2000). Intrinsic motivation is said to be invariantly autonomous or self-determined because it is a reflection of people's inner interests. In other words, when intrinsically motivated, people experience volition and a sense of choice as they fully endorse the activities in which they are engaged. Csikszentmihalyi (1990) referred to intrinsically motivated activities as *autotelic*. In contrast, extrinsic motivation refers to doing an activity because it is instrumental to some operationally separable consequence. The classic instance of extrinsic motivation is doing an activity because it is expected to lead to a reward or the avoidance of a punishment.

Internalization of extrinsic motivation

SDT has moved beyond the simple dichotomy between intrinsic and extrinsic motivation to suggest that extrinsic motivation can be internalized and, thus, like intrinsic motivation, can become the basis for autonomous actions. More specifically, internalization is a developmental process through which external values and regulations can, to varying degrees, be taken in and integrated with one's sense of self. SDT proposes that there is a natural developmental tendency for people to take in the values, behaviours and opinions they encounter in their lives and to move toward accepting them as their own. However, this process will function more or less effectively depending on the degree to which the person experiences basic psychological need satisfaction while that process is operating.

The theory outlines four types of extrinsic motivation that differ in the degree to which the motivation has been internalized and assimilated with the self. The behaviours that follow from these four types of extrinsic motivation differ in their degree of autonomy. Those that have been more fully internalized will be the basis for more autonomous or self-determined actions. Thus, the degree of internalization and the type of regulation that follows from these degrees of internalization are ordered along a relative autonomy continuum.

External regulation, which is the least autonomous type of extrinsic motivation, is the classic type mentioned above, which depends on rewards and punishments. It is the type of extrinsic motivation that occurs when no internalization has taken place. When externally regulated, people act because of the external contingencies impinging upon them. External regulation can be powerfully motivating, but it is not a reflection of people's interests and values and it is controlled by contingencies rather than emanating from themselves.

Next along the relative autonomy continuum is *introjected regulation*. This type of extrinsic motivation involves behaviour being controlled by partially internalized, rather than strictly external, contingencies. With introjection, people have taken in a regulation or contingency but have not fully endorsed it as their own. Thus, introjected regulation involves people controlling their own behaviours in order to maintain or affirm their self-worth, avoid guilt, or feel the approval of others. Introjected regulation is a type of motivation that is more controlled than autonomous, but it is a type of regulation that is within the person and is thus more autonomous than external regulation.

Identified regulation, which is the third type of extrinsic motivation, is a more autonomous type of motivation. It results from people identifying with the personal importance of an activity for their own self-selected goals and values. When people have accepted a behavioural regulation as their own, the regulation will have been transformed and will likely be experienced as volitional and self-endorsed. The final type of extrinsic motivation, which results when the internalization process has functioned most effectively, is *integrated regulation*. It results from people assimilating an identification with other aspects of their core self. All identifications are important to people, but if they have not been well integrated with the people's sense of self the identifications will not be unified and consonant with other values, goals and regulations. Integrated extrinsic motivation shares many qualities with intrinsic motivation, for both are autonomous and are associated with flexible, rather than rigid, thinking and behaving. These two types of autonomous motivation differ, however, in that intrinsic motivation is the inherent motivation based in *interest and enjoyment*, whereas the integrated form of extrinsic motivation is based in *values* that have been well internalized.

Relative autonomy continuum

As can be seen in Figure 25.1, the relative autonomy continuum thus includes these four types of extrinsic motivation that differ in their degree of internalization and autonomy. Further, the continuum includes amotivation and intrinsic motivation. Amotivation represents a lack of motivation, and thus is at the left of external regulation indicating that it indexes the least autonomy or self-determination. Intrinsic motivation exists on the other end of the continuum, reflecting a highly autonomous form of regulation. Thus, the relative autonomy continuum extends from amotivation to intrinsic motivation, with the four types of extrinsic motivation falling in between (external and introjection being relatively controlled, and identified and integrated being relatively autonomous). Considerable work in SDT has used these six motivational concepts to predict a wide range of outcomes, as we will see later in the chapter.

Social environments and motivation

Much work has examined the effects of various aspects of the social environment on autonomous versus controlled types of motivation. The general hypothesis guiding this work is that social environments that facilitate satisfaction of the basic psychological needs for competence, autonomy and relatedness will lead to more autonomous types of motivation – namely, identified, integrated and intrinsic – whereas social environments that are thwarting of the basic needs will lead to either controlled motivation or amotivation.

Effects of the social environment on intrinsic motivation

Initial work on the motivational effects of social environments was a set of laboratory experiments that examined how various factors such as rewards, feedback and deadlines affect intrinsic motivation. In the first studies, Deci (1971) found that when participants received monetary rewards for solving an interesting spatial-relations puzzle, they were subsequently less intrinsically motivated for the activity than were participants who had done the same activity without receiving the rewards. The extrinsic rewards seemed to undermine the participants' intrinsic motivations. This finding has been replicated dozens of times, and a meta-analysis (Deci, Koestner and Ryan 1999) confirmed this effect across more than 100 experiments.

Studies (e.g., Vallerand and Reid 1984) further showed that positive feedback enhanced the intrinsic motivation of participants relative to those who did not get the feedback. This finding, too, has been replicated many times with children and adults. Thus, it appears that feedback that affirms competence when accompanied by a sense of autonomy typically enhances intrinsic motivation (Ryan 1982). In contrast, research has indicated that negative performance feedback tends to

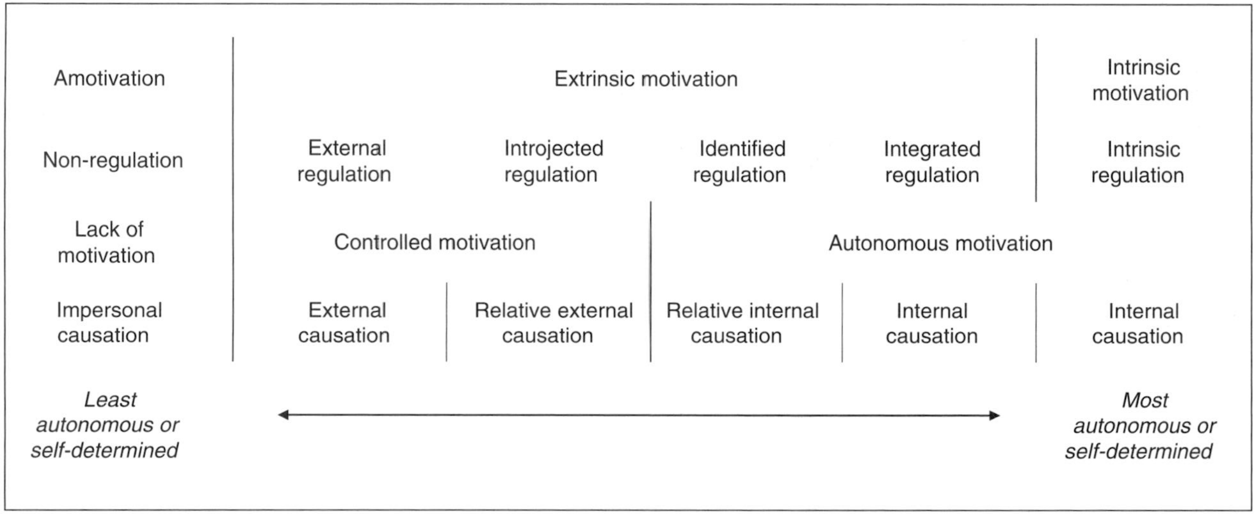

Figure 25.1. *Representation of the SDT continuum of relative autonomy, showing types of motivation, types of regulation, the nature of perceived causation, and the degree of autonomy or self-determination for each type of motivation. Moving left to right involves movement toward greater autonomy or self-determination.*

decrease intrinsic motivation because it signifies incompetence (e.g., Deci and Cascio 1972). In fact, negative feedback will often also decrease extrinsic motivation by conveying that people cannot attain desired outcomes, thus leaving the people amotivated.

Within SDT, these different effects are interpreted in terms of their relation to the basic psychological needs. Specifically, the theory proposes that when people do activities to get tangible rewards, their behaviour tends to become dependent on the rewards, so they perceive the locus of causality (De Charms 1968; Heider 1958) to shift from internal to external, they feel more controlled, their need for autonomy is thus thwarted, and their intrinsic motivation is undermined. The theory states that the *controlling* aspect of this external event is salient to the people, and that is what initiates the change in perceived locus of causality and decrease in intrinsic motivation. In contrast, when people receive positive feedback, they are less likely to be doing the activity explicitly to get the feedback, so they are less likely to have their need for autonomy thwarted; instead, they tend to feel satisfaction of their need for competence and this enhances intrinsic motivation. In such cases, it is the *informational* aspect of the event that is salient to people. When the feedback is negative, however, it tends to thwart people's need for competence and leaves them amotivated.

Many early studies examined the effects of other external events on intrinsic motivation. The studies have indicated, for example, that intrinsic motivation was also undermined by imposed goals (Mossholder 1980), surveillance (Lepper and Greene 1975; Plant and Ryan 1985), deadlines (Amabile, DeJong and Lepper 1976), competition (Deci, Betley, Kahle *et al.* 1981), and evaluations, even if they led to positive feedback (Smith 1975). All of these external events are ones frequently used as 'motivators' to get people to do things they might otherwise not do, and thus people come to experience them as controls. As such, it is to be expected that the events would have a negative effect on intrinsic motivation by diminishing people's sense of autonomy. In contrast, taking others' internal frame of reference, for example by acknowledging their feelings about a situation (Koestner, Ryan, Bernieri and Holt 1984) and offering them choice about what activities to do or how to do them (Moller, Deci and Ryan 2006; Zuckerman, Porac, Lathin *et al.* 1978), has been found to enhance intrinsic motivation and vitality, because it tends to promote a more internal perceived locus of causality for the behaviour and satisfy people's need for autonomy.

Other research has tested the proposition that the way in which external events such as rewards or feedback are administered significantly influences their effects. For example, experiments have shown that positive feedback, which typically has a positive effect on intrinsic motivation, instead has a negative effect if given with controlling language (e.g., 'Good, you did just as you should') because people will not feel personally responsible for the performance that is being affirmed in this way (Ryan 1982). Similarly, if limits are set in a controlling way they tend to diminish intrinsic motivation, but if they are presented in a way that supports people's sense of autonomy and choice they are not detrimental (Koestner, Ryan, Bernieri and Holt 1984). As well, tangible rewards, which tend to undermine intrinsic motivation, tend not to be detrimental if the rewards are given in a way that acknowledges competent performance without being pressuring (Deci, Koestner and Ryan 1999).

Effects of the social environment on internalization

SDT is built on the assumption that people are naturally inclined to internalize values and behaviours that are exhibited by important others in their socializing environment. The theory proposes, however, that internalization will work effectively to promote integration only to the extent that people experience satisfaction of the basic needs as they are acquiring the values and behaviours. That is, environments that support need satisfaction will lead people to accept the structures that are endorsed by the social world, but those that are rejecting or controlling will impair internalization, leaving the people controlled either by external or introjected regulatory processes.

Many studies, primarily field studies, have supported the hypothesis that need supportive social contexts lead to fuller internalization of values and behavioural regulations (e.g., Niemiec, Lynch, Vansteenkiste *et al.* 2006; Williams and Deci 1996). In one laboratory experiment (Deci, Eghrari, Patrick and Leone 1994) found that three facilitating factors – namely, providing a rationale for a requested behaviour, acknowledging people's feelings about the behaviour, and highlighting choice rather than control – all contributed to facilitating internalization of extrinsic motivation. By understanding why they were being asked to do something, having their perspective acknowledged, and feeling a sense of choice, people were more open to accepting the values and behaviours that were being endorsed in their social environments. In the presence of these facilitating factors, there was not only more internalization, but the internalization was more integrated rather than just introjected. When the facilitating factors were not present, there was less internalization and it took the form of introjection rather than integration.

Motivation and outcomes

Thus far our discussion has focused on types of motivation, the processes through which these different types of motivation develop or change, and the social contextual factors that affect motivation by either supporting or thwarting satisfaction of the basic psychological needs. We have focused on how to promote different types of motivation in part because they are associated with different qualities of outcomes. We now turn to a discussion of the outcomes of different motivations.

Simply stated, studies have shown that autonomous motivation, which comprises intrinsic motivation and the more fully internalized forms of extrinsic motivation (i.e., identified and integrated), has consistently been associated with more positive relational, performance and wellbeing outcomes.

For example, an experiment by McGraw and McCullers (1979) examined the relation of motivation to cognitive flexibility. In it, they gave participants a problem-solving task in which the participants tended to develop a mental set for solving the problems. Half of the participants were rewarded for solving the puzzles and half were not. Then, participants were given a problem that required breaking their mental set and thinking in a fresher way, and the results showed that those who had been rewarded for solving the earlier problems had a harder time breaking set and thus did less well on the new problem. In motivational terms, this suggests that rewarded participants had become more controlled in their motivation and this was associated with a more rigid, less flexible mode of thinking and information-processing.

Experiments by Amabile (1979, 1982) showed that participants who were told their artistic work would be evaluated and those who competed to win a reward for their artistic endeavours made products that were judged to be less creative than did participants who were not being evaluated or competing for a reward. Here too, we see that external events that have been found to control participants and undermine their intrinsic motivation also have negative effects on the quality of their performance.

Other studies have examined students' learning under conditions that are either controlling or supportive of their need satisfaction (see Reeve, Ryan, Deci and Jang 2007). For example, Benware and Deci (1984) did an experiment in which college students read a detailed article on neurophysiology under one of two learning sets. One condition was made controlling by telling students they would have a graded exam, whereas the other encouraged the students' active involvement by offering them the opportunity to have a subsequent impact on their environment; that is, they would teach the material to others. A subsequent exam administered to all participants revealed that the two groups of students were about equal in terms of how well they memorized the facts, but the students who learned in order to put the material to active use gained a much fuller understanding of the concepts that tied together those facts than did the students who learned in order to be tested. Further, students in the active-learning condition also reported finding the material more intrinsically interesting. In short, learning in order to put the material to use led students to be more intrinsically motivated and in turn to evidence a deeper, more conceptual learning.

Finally, many studies have shown that more autonomous types of motivation are associated with greater psychological wellbeing. For example, a study of close friends indicated that when people experienced need satisfaction in a close friendship, they also evidenced greater psychological health and wellbeing (Deci, La Guardia, Moller *et al.* 2006). In a study of participants' daily activities, researchers found that on days the participants experienced more satisfaction of the basic psychological needs they also experienced greater positive affect and wellbeing (Reis, Sheldon, Gable *et al.* 2000).

Goals, motives, needs and outcomes

Another component of SDT concerns the types of goals or aspirations people pursue in their lives. Kasser and Ryan (1993, 1996) examined two sets of goals: those for wealth, fame and image, which they referred to as extrinsic goals, and those for growth, affiliation and community, which they referred to as intrinsic goals. The researchers hypothesized that the intrinsic goals would be associated with greater wellbeing than would the extrinsic goals because intrinsic goals are more closely linked to satisfaction of the basic psychological needs. Kasser and Ryan found that the relative importance people place on extrinsic goals was negatively related to indicators of wellbeing, whereas the relative importance they placed on intrinsic goals was positively related to the same indicators of wellbeing. Simply stated, the content of people's life-goals makes a difference in terms of the people's wellbeing.

Subsequent work by Sheldon, Ryan, Deci and Kasser (2004) showed that both the goal contents (extrinsic versus intrinsic) people pursue and the motives they have for pursuing the goals (controlled versus autonomous) are associated with their wellbeing. When both goals and motives were entered simultaneously into regression analyses, the researchers found that each variable contributed significant independent variance. In other words, the relative importance of extrinsic goals was positively related to psychological illbeing even after the variance in illbeing explained by controlled regulation had been removed.

Whereas the studies of goal contents thus far reviewed all considered the value or importance of these goals to people, another set of studies has examined the results of attaining extrinsic versus intrinsic outcomes that people value or consider important. The research addressed the question of whether the attainment of all valued goals would yield positive wellbeing outcomes, a question that many psychologists would answer yes. A longitudinal study by Niemiec, Ryan and Deci (in press) examined change in wellbeing as a function of change in intrinsic and extrinsic goal attainment, and the results showed that attainment of intrinsic goals led to increased wellbeing and decreased illbeing; however, attainment of extrinsic goals had no effect on wellbeing but led to greater illbeing. Further, the positive effect of intrinsic aspirations on wellbeing was mediated by satisfaction of the three basic psychological needs. In sum, the pursuit and attainment of intrinsic goals has been found to relate positively to psychological health and wellbeing, whereas the pursuit and attainment of extrinsic goals has been found to relate negatively to these outcomes.

Finally, research by Vansteenkiste and his colleagues has examined whether introducing people to a task in terms of whether it is instrumental to intrinsic or extrinsic goals affects their performance on the task. In all the studies mentioned above, intrinsic versus extrinsic goal pursuit was examined in terms of individual differences, but these studies manipulated type of goals experimentally. As an example, consider two experiments by Vansteenkiste, Simons, Lens *et al.* (2004)

in which education students learned about pro-environmental behaviours either to help save the world (an intrinsic goal) or to save money (an extrinsic goal), or business students learned about communication approaches either for personal development (intrinsic) or to earn more money at work (extrinsic). The results indicated that students given intrinsic goal framing indicated subsequently that they had learned the material more deeply, took additional opportunities to find out about the topics, and performed better when tested on what they had learned compared with students given extrinsic goal framing.

To summarize, studies of intrinsic versus extrinsic goals done both with individual differences in the importance of the goals and with the framing of an activity in terms of intrinsic versus extrinsic goals, have indicated that holding intrinsic goals is associated with more positive learning, performance and wellbeing outcomes than is the case for holding extrinsic goals.

Need satisfaction across cultures

Because SDT argues that satisfaction of the basic needs is essential for all people, several cross-cultural studies have been done to confirm that need satisfaction is essential in cultures that are vastly different. This is an important point because cultural relativists (e.g., Markus, Kitayama and Heiman 1996) have claimed that the need for autonomy is not relevant for Eastern, collectivist cultures.

Chirkov, Ryan, Kim and Kaplan (2003) investigated the internalization of the values of individualism (a strongly endorsed Western value) and collectivism (a strongly endorsed Eastern value) within four disparate cultures (Turkey, Korea, Russia and the United States). Their reasoning was that the more fully any value was internalized the more the individuals would be satisfying their need for autonomy, so the degree of internalization should be predictive of psychological health and wellbeing regardless of culture.

Chirkov et al. (2003) found that the higher people's relative autonomy for both individualist and collectivist practices, the higher their level of psychological wellbeing in each of the four cultures. That is, to the degree that people in any culture can enact a value autonomously, even if it does not match the dominant value of their culture, those individuals will display higher levels of wellbeing. In short, satisfaction of the autonomy need does indeed appear to be essential for wellbeing regardless of culture, although, of course, the values and practices through which people express their autonomy may vary as a function of cultural socialization.

Motivation in life's domains

SDT has been applied to several life-domains, and many of the studies of outcomes associated with different types of motivation have been field studies in these various domains. We turn now to a consideration of the domains of education and parenting, work and healthcare as examples of the type of research that has been done to apply the theory to real-life situations.

Motivation in education and parenting

Several studies in the educational domain have explored whether social contexts tend to be autonomy supportive and need satisfying or, alternatively, controlling and need thwarting. For example, in a study of late elementary-school students, Deci, Schwartz, Sheinman and Ryan (1981) found that in classrooms where teachers were more autonomy supportive, students displayed increased intrinsic motivation and wellbeing. Ryan and Grolnick (1986) obtained comparable results.

Ryan and Connell (1989) examined the relations of introjected regulation (i.e., more controlled motivation) and identified regulation (i.e., more autonomous motivation) to school engagement and wellbeing. They found that both types of motivation were correlated with children's self-reports of trying hard in school and with the parents' reports of the children being motivated. However, introjection was positively correlated with anxiety in school and maladaptive coping with failures, whereas identification was positively correlated with interest and enjoyment of school and proactive coping with failures. These findings suggest that being more autonomous is associated not only with greater engagement in school but also with enhanced wellbeing. In short, students who are relatively controlled may look as motivated as students who are more autonomous, but they are likely to be paying a psychological cost for their controlled motivation.

Grolnick and Ryan (1989) interviewed parents to assess the degree to which they were autonomy supportive versus controlling in dealing with their children around schoolwork. The researchers found that when parents were more autonomy supportive, their children were more intrinsically motivated and had more fully internalized extrinsic motivation for school. Further, parental autonomy support was positively related to children being viewed by their teachers as more capable and better adjusted, and to the children's school achievement.

A study in medical schools (Williams and Deci 1996) confirmed that students' internalization of the values espoused in a medical interviewing course was fuller and more effective when the instructors were more autonomy supportive. This showed up in the students' interviewing behaviour six months after the class ended and also in their beliefs about medical interviewing assessed eighteen months later.

Motivation in work organizations

A study of a major corporation by Deci, Connell and Ryan (1989) found that managerial autonomy support, defined as managers acknowledging their subordinates' perspectives, providing relevant information, offering choice and encouraging self-initiation rather than pressuring subordinates to behave in specified ways, was associated with employees' being more satisfied with their jobs, having a higher level of trust in the top management of the corporation, and displaying other positive work-related attitudes. The researchers then conducted an intervention in some sites, training managers to be more autonomy supportive, and the results indicated that trained managers did become more autonomy supportive and that, in turn, led their subordinates to report greater perceptions of the quality of supervision, trust in the organization, and job-related satisfactions.

Two articles report studies in which employees' need satisfaction was examined as a function of managers' autonomy support. In one, conducted in Bulgaria and the United States, Deci, Ryan, Gagné et al. (2001) assessed satisfaction of employees' needs for competence, autonomy and relatedness at work, and they found both that managers' autonomy support predicted need satisfaction and that need satisfaction predicted work engagement and wellbeing on the job in both countries. Baard, Deci and Ryan (2004) found in a study of US bankers that managers' autonomy support predicted need satisfaction, which in turn predicted the employees' work performance.

Motivation in healthcare

In numerous studies, researchers have focused on the change of health-compromising behaviours, such as stopping smoking, improving diet, exercising regularly, and adhering better to medication prescriptions. The studies have tended to focus on the degree to which the physicians or other healthcare providers were autonomy supportive, relating that to the patients' autonomous motivation, perceived competence, maintained behaviour change, and improved physiological indicators. Williams, Grow, Freedman et al. (1996) found that morbidly obese patients who perceived their providers as more autonomy supportive were more autonomously motivated and perceived themselves as more competent in losing weight, and further that these motivation variables predicted maintained weight loss. Parallel results were found for patients with diabetes controlling their glucose levels (Williams, Freedman and Deci 1998), adult outpatients adhering to medical regimens (Williams et al. 1998), and patients who smoked tobacco stopping doing so (Williams, Gagné, Ryan and Deci 2002).

Summary

SDT is a macro-theory of personality in the tradition of the grand theories that characterized personality during the first half of the twentieth century, although it is built on an empirical foundation whereas most of the earlier theories were built with information derived from careful examination of clinical encounters. SDT posits a set of three fundamental, universal psychological needs – the needs for autonomy, competence and relatedness – and uses these needs to organize research into types of motivation, types of goals, the relation of the social context to motivation and goals both developmentally and in particular situations, and the effects of the different types of goals and motives on outcomes such as the quality of performance and psychological wellbeing in a variety of domains.

References

Amabile, T. M. 1979. Effects of external evaluations on artistic creativity, *Journal of Personality and Social Psychology* 37: 221–33

1982. Children's artistic creativity: detrimental effects of competition in a field setting, *Personality and Social Psychology Bulletin* 8: 573–8

Amabile, T. M., DeJong, W. and Lepper, M. 1976. Effects of externally imposed deadlines on subsequent intrinsic motivation, *Journal of Personality and Social Psychology* 34: 92–8

Baard, P. P., Deci, E. L. and Ryan, R. M. 2004. Intrinsic need satisfaction: a motivational basis of performance and well-being in two work settings, *Journal of Applied Social Psychology* 34: 2045–68

Baumeister, R. and Leary, M. R. 1995. The Need to belong: desire for interpersonal attachments as a fundamental human motivation, *Psychological Bulletin* 117: 497–529

Benware, C. and Deci, E. L. 1984. Quality of learning with an active versus passive motivational set, *American Educational Research Journal* 21: 755–65

Cacioppo, J. R. and Petty, R. E. 1982. The need for cognition, *Journal of Personality and Social Psychology* 42: 116–31

Chirkov, V. Ryan, R. M., Kim, Y. and Kaplan, U. 2003. Differentiating autonomy from individualism and independence: a self-determination theory perspective on internalization of cultural orientations and well-being, *Journal of Personality and Social Psychology* 84: 97–110

Csikszentmihalyi, M. 1990. *Flow.* New York: Harper and Row

De Charms, R. 1968. *Personal causation: the internal affective determinants of behaviour.* New York: Academic Press

Deci, E. L. 1971. Effects of externally mediated rewards on intrinsic motivation, *Journal of Personality and Social Psychology* 18: 105–15

Deci, E. L., Betley, G., Kahle, J., Abrams, L. and Porac, J. 1981. When trying to win: competition and intrinsic motivation, *Personality and Social Psychology Bulletin* 7: 79–83

Deci, E. L. and Cascio, W. F. 1972. *Changes in intrinsic motivation as a function of negative feedback and threats.* Paper presented at the Eastern Psychological Association, Boston, April 1972

Deci, E. L., Connell, J. P. and Ryan, R. M. 1989. Self-determination in a work organization, *Journal of Applied Psychology* 74: 580–90

Deci, E. L., Eghrari, H., Patrick, B. C. and Leone, D. R. 1994. Facilitating internalization: the self-determination theory perspective, *Journal of Personality* 62: 119–42

Deci, E. L., Koestner, R. and Ryan, R. M. 1999. A meta-analytic review of experiments examining the effects of extrinsic rewards on intrinsic motivation, *Psychological Bulletin* 125: 627–68

Deci, E. L., La Guardia, J. G., Moller, A. C., Scheiner, M. J. and Ryan, R. M. 2006. On the benefits of giving as well as receiving autonomy support: mutuality in close friendships, *Personality and Social Psychology Bulletin* 32: 313–27

Deci, E. L. and Ryan, R. M. 1985. *Intrinsic motivation and self-determination in human behaviour*. New York: Plenum
  2000. The 'what' and the 'why' of goal pursuits: human needs and the self-determination of behaviour, *Psychological Inquiry* 11: 227–68

Deci, E. L., Ryan, R. M., Gagné, M., Leone, D. R., Usunov, J. and Kornazheva, B. P. 2001. Need satisfaction, motivation, and well-being in the work organizations of a former Eastern Bloc country, *Personality and Social Psychology Bulletin* 27: 930–42

Deci, E. L., Schwartz, A. J., Sheinman, L. and Ryan, R. M. 1981. An instrument to assess adults' orientations toward control versus autonomy with children: reflections on intrinsic motivation and perceived competence, *Journal of Educational Psychology* 73: 642–50

Grolnick, W. S. and Ryan, R. M. 1989. Parent styles associated with children's self-regulation and competence in school, *Journal of Educational Psychology* 81: 143–54

Heider, F. 1958. *The psychology of interpersonal relations*. New York: Wiley

Hull, C. L. 1943. *Principles of behaviour: an Introduction to behaviour theory*. New York: Appleton-Century-Crofts

Kasser, T. and Ryan, R. M. 1993. A dark side of the American dream: correlates of financial success as a central life aspiration, *Journal of Personality and Social Psychology* 65: 410–22
  1996. Further examining the American dream: differential correlates of intrinsic and extrinsic goals, *Personality and Social Psychology Bulletin* 22: 80–7

Koestner, R., Ryan, R. M., Bernieri, F. and Holt, K. 1984. Setting limits on children's behaviour: the differential effects of controlling versus informational styles on intrinsic motivation and creativity, *Journal of Personality* 52: 233–48

Lepper, M. R. and Greene, D. 1975. Turning play into work: effects of adult surveillance and extrinsic rewards on children's intrinsic motivation, *Journal of Personality and Social Psychology* 31: 479–86

Markus, H. R., Kitayama, S. and Heiman, R. J. 1996. Culture and basic psychological principles, in E. T. Higgins and A. W. Kruglanski (eds.), *Social psychology: Handbook of basic principles*, pp. 857–913. New York: Guilford Press

McClelland, D. C. 1985. *Human motivation*. Glenview, IL: Scott, Foresman

McGraw, K. O. and McCullers, J. C. 1979. Evidence of a detrimental effect of extrinsic incentives on breaking a mental set, *Journal of Experimental Social Psychology* 15: 285–94

Moller, A. C., Deci, E. L. and Ryan, R. M. 2006. Choice and ego-depletion: the moderating role of autonomy, *Personality and Social Psychology Bulletin* 32: 1024–36

Mossholder, K. W. 1980. Effects of externally mediated goal setting on intrinsic motivation: a laboratory experiment, *Journal of Applied Psychology* 65: 202–10

Niemiec, C. P., Lynch, M. F., Vansteenkiste, M., Bernstein, J., Deci, E. L. and Ryan, R. M. 2006. The antecedents and consequences of autonomous self-regulation for college: a self-determination theory perspective on socialization, *Journal of Adolescence* 29: 761–75

Niemiec, C. P., Ryan, R. M. and Deci, E. L. in press. The path taken: consequences of attaining intrinsic and extrinsic aspirations in post-college life, *Journal of Research in Personality*

Plant, R. and Ryan, R. M. 1985. Intrinsic motivation and the effects of self-consciousness, self-awareness, and ego-involvement: an investigation of internally controlling styles, *Journal of Personality* 53: 435–49

Reeve, J., Ryan, R. M., Deci, E. L. and Jang, H. (2007). Understanding and promoting autonomous self-regulation: a self-determination theory perspective, in D. Schunk and B. Zimmerman (eds.), *Motivation and self-regulated learning: theory, research, and applications*, pp. 221–42 Mahwah, NJ: Erlbaum

Reis, H. T., Sheldon, K. M., Gable, S. L., Roscoe, J. and Ryan, R. M. 2000. Daily well-being: the role of autonomy, competence, and relatedness, *Personality and Social Psychology Bulletin* 26: 419–35

Ryan, R. M. 1982. Control and information in the intrapersonal sphere: an extension of cognitive evaluation theory, *Journal of Personality and Social Psychology* 43: 450–61

  1995. Psychological needs and the facilitation of integrative processes, *Journal of Personality* 63: 397–427

Ryan, R. M. and Connell, J. P. 1989. Perceived locus of causality and internalization: examining reasons for acting in two domains, *Journal of Personality and Social Psychology* 57: 749–61

Ryan, R. M. and Deci, E. L. 2000. Intrinsic and extrinsic motivation: classic definitions and new directions, *Contemporary Educational Psychology* 25: 54–67

Ryan, R. M. and Grolnick, W. S. 1986. Origins and pawns in the classroom: self-report and projective assessments of individual differences in children's perceptions, *Journal of Personality and Social Psychology* 50: 550–8

Sheldon, K. M., Ryan, R. M., Deci, E. L. and Kasser, T. 2004. The independent effects of goal contents and motives on well-being: it's both what you pursue and why you pursue it, *Personality and Social Psychology Bulletin* 30: 475–86

Smith, W. E. 1975. *The effect of anticipated vs. unanticipated social reward on subsequent intrinsic motivation*. Unpublished doctoral dissertation. Cornell University

Vallerand, R. J. and Reid, G. 1984. On the causal effects of perceived competence on intrinsic motivation: a test of cognitive evaluation theory, *Journal of Sport Psychology* 6: 94–102

Vansteenkiste, M., Simons, J., Lens, W., Sheldon, K. M. and Deci, E. L. 2004. Motivating learning, performance, and persistence: the synergistic effects of intrinsic goal contents and autonomy-supportive contexts, *Journal of Personality and Social Psychology* 87: 246–60

White, R. W. 1959. Motivation reconsidered: the concept of competence, *Psychological Review* 66: 297–333

Williams, G. C. and Deci, E. L. 1996. Internalization of biopsychosocial values by medical students: a test of self-determination theory, *Journal of Personality and Social Psychology* 70: 767–79

Williams, G. C., Freedman, Z. and Deci, E. L. 1998. Supporting autonomy to motivate patients with diabetes for glucose control, *Diabetes Care* 21: 1644–51

Williams, G. C., Gagné, M., Ryan, R. M. and Deci, E. L. 2002. Supporting autonomy to motivate smoking cessation: a test of self-determination theory, *Health Psychology* 21: 40–50

Williams, G. C., Grow, V. M., Freedman, Z., Ryan, R. M. and Deci, E. L. 1996. Motivational predictors of weight loss and weight-loss maintenance, *Journal of Personality and Social Psychology* 70: 115–26

Williams, G. C., Rodin, G. C., Ryan, R. M., Grolnick, W. S. and Deci, E. L. 1998. Autonomous regulation and long-term medication adherence in adult outpatients, *Health Psychology* 17: 269–76

Zuckerman, M., Porac, J., Lathin, D., Smith, R. and Deci, E. L. 1978. On the importance of self-determination for intrinsically motivated behaviour, *Personality and Social Psychology Bulletin* 4: 443–6

26 Traits and the self: toward an integration

Michael D. Robinson and Constantine Sedikides

In his influential text, William James (1890) devoted separate chapters to the self and to its habits. His chapter on the self highlighted the multifaceted nature of the self-concept, including in material, social and spiritual domains. By contrast, his chapter on habits highlighted their role in understanding dispositional differences. Whether functional or dysfunctional, habits are likely to persist over time. Such considerations led James to suggest that personality, understood in terms of dispositional habits, is relatively fixed by the age of thirty.

James' (1890) separate treatments of the self and its habits may have contributed to divergent streams of research in empirical psychology. Self researchers (who are primarily social psychologists) often operate under the assumption that the self is multifaceted, malleable, and low in cross-situational consistency (McGuire and McGuire 1988). By contrast, trait researchers (who are primarily personality psychologists) have converged on the idea that there are a few basic dimensions of personality that are quite stable and consistent across situations (Benet-Martínez and John 1998). This tension between malleable and stable views was brought to a sharp focus with Mischel's (1968) critique of the trait construct. Although much of the dust from the person-situation debate has settled (Kenrick and Funder 1988; Mischel 2004), there continue to be separate social and trait traditions on the self.

The objective of this chapter is to examine the potential interface between trait and social cognitive views of the self. In some cases, links have already been forged. In other cases, links are tenuous and would benefit from further research. Regardless, the potential for cross-fertilization is high.

Using the trait perspective to understand the self

Overview

Trait psychologists have made important advances in the last thirty years (John and Srivastava 1999). Researchers now know a good deal more about traits than they did prior to Mischel's (1968) critique, and this knowledge can inform our understanding of the self. We highlight several recent advances, and point to new research directions.

Trait stability

When trait scales are administered twice, even if separated by five to ten years, test-retest correlations are remarkably strong – typically in the .6–.8 range (McCrae and Costa 1994). Such stability coefficients suggest that at least certain aspects of the self, such as global self-esteem, are likely to be quite stable as well. Research by Trzesniewski, Donnellan and Robins (2003) supports this conjecture. In a secondary analysis of four national archival datasets, they examined the test-retest stability of self-esteem from ages six to eighty-three. Self-esteem had considerable continuity over time, comparable to trait stability. This finding contradicts the notion that the global self-concept is highly malleable.

Trait-based predictions

Traits are relatively poor predictors of momentary experiences or behaviours (Kenrick and Funder 1988). Rather, traits capture average tendencies and are therefore best suited to predicting outcomes that have been aggregated across situations or over time (Epstein 1983). Thus, the social cognitive critique of traits, perhaps most strongly expressed by Ross and Nisbett (1991), now seems mis-guided to a certain extent. Indeed, it is notable that modern social cognitive researchers often use individual difference measures in their research and do so to a far greater extent than in the 1970s and 1980s (Baumeister 1997; Sedikides, Gregg and Hart 2007).

Structural considerations

Self-reported traits can be integrated into a common structural model, often referred to as the Big Five (John and Srivastava 1999). One of the assumptions of this model is that seemingly diverse individual difference variables, including those linked to the self, are likely to overlap considerably with one or more traits of the Big Five. Increasingly, this appears to be so. For example, Watson, Suls and Haig (2002) found that global self-esteem could be conceptualized largely in terms of low Neuroticism and high Extraversion. Other recent investigations have forged links between the Big Five structural model and other self-constructs such as self-discrepancies (i.e. actual, ideal, ought selves: Hafdahl, Panter, Gramzow *et al*. 2000) and self-regulation (i.e., ego-control and ego-resilience: Gramzow, Sedikides, Panter *et al*. 2004). Clearly, these lines of research suggest an important integrative role for the Big Five in understanding the self-concept.

Genetic basis of traits

Behavioural genetic studies have shown that 40–50 per cent of the variance in trait self-reports has a heritable component (Loehlin, McCrae and Costa 1998). Similarly, global evaluations of the self, along with other self-aspects, have a genetic basis (Neiss, Sedikides and Stevenson 2006; Neiss, Stevenson, Sedikides *et al.* 2005). These latter findings challenge views of the self as merely the product of social-situational feedback (Mead 1934; see also Leary, Tambor, Terdal and Downs 1995). It will be interesting to explore how social cognitive models of the self could be modified to incorporate its genetic heritability.

Approach and avoidance

Theoretical perspectives and empirical findings link Extraversion and Neuroticism to approach and avoidance motivation, respectively (Carver, Sutton and Scheier 2000; Elliot and Thrash 2002). Given that global self-esteem is related to Extraversion and Neuroticism (Watson, Suls and Haig 2002), the approach/ avoidance perspective should have theoretical implications for understanding global self-esteem as well (Baumeister, Tice and Hutton 1989). This focus on approach/avoidance motives seems likely to contribute to new knowledge in understanding how global self-esteem functions.

Summary

Traits are stable, predictive of aggregated outcomes, and have a genetic basis. These insights have already made inroads into research on global self-esteem. Still, however, new research directions beckon. For example, approach/avoidance frameworks, as applied to Extraversion and Neuroticism (Carver, Sutton and Scheier 2000) as well as anxiety and impulsivity (Gray 1987), have interesting implications for self-esteem and self-perception. Likewise, malleability and stability perspectives on the self will need to be reconciled, a topic that is gaining increased attention (Caspi, Roberts and Shiner 2005).

Using the self perspective to understand traits

Overview

The trait literature has been successful in understanding the structural and genetic basis of traits, but less successful in elucidating their processing-basis (Matthews and Gilliland 1999). Given that social cognitive views of the self are often centrally concerned with issues of process (Sedikides and Gregg 2003), applying the social cognitive perspective to traits is likely to be generative. Here, we highlight several potential insights along these lines.

Self-verification motive

Why are traits so stable over time? Swann's (e.g., Swann and Schroeder 1995) influential research on self-verification processes may provide an answer to this question. Swann contends that people are motivated to confirm rather than dis-confirm strongly held views of the self (see also Sedikides 1995). Thus, a given self-view (e.g., that the self is high in Neuroticism) is likely to create its own reality through trait-consistent processes related to self-verification (Swann, Rentfrow and Guinn 2002). In a review article on the surprising stability of traits, McCrae and Costa (1994) cited Swann's research favourably, yet very little extant research has applied the self-verification perspective to traits of the Big Five (for an exception, see Tamir 2005).

Self-enhancement motive

Self-enhancement reflects a motive to view the self as positively as possible (Sedikides and Gregg 2008; Sedikides and Strube 1997). On the basis of this motive, one can explain why individuals (a) view their own traits as more socially desirable than the average person (Alicke and Govorun 2005); (b) interpret ambiguous trait terms in a way that reflects best on the self (Dunning, Meyerowitz and Holzberg 1989); (c) choose questions likely to confirm their positive (versus negative) traits (Sedikides 1993); and (d) manifest superior memory for feedback related to their positive (versus negative) traits (Sedikides and Green 2000).

Individual differences in trait self-reports, too, can be understood in terms of socially desirable responding (Edwards 1953; Paulhus and John 1998). Although accounts differ on whether such responding compromises the validity of trait-based judgements, this is clearly a concern (Robins and John 1997). Rather than reflecting objective reality, that is, trait self-reports may often reflect individual differences in the strength of the self-enhancement motive.

The heterogeneous self

When describing themselves, individuals mention a variety of self-aspects, only some of which would qualify as traits (Gordon 1968). Also mentioned are important relationships, social roles, goals and motives, preferences and values, as well as rules and strategies for self-regulation (Markus 1983; McConnell and Strain 2007). When individuals rate their traits in relation to different role-contexts (e.g., in school versus at home), their traits differ in ways that are particular to a given role-context (Donahue and Harary 1998). There has been an attempt to incorporate role-specific tendencies into more general models of traits (Wood and Roberts 2006), but additional integration efforts are needed.

The hierarchical self

The self is hierarchically organized. Its most abstract features are captured when individuals characterize themselves in general, irrespective of context or social role (Schell, Klein and Babey 1996). Note that this abstract level is consistent with the manner in which personality traits are typically assessed. At a lower level of abstraction, social roles encompass aspects of personality that, although generalized, are specific to the role under consideration (Donahue and Harary 1998). At the lowest level of abstraction, self-views are particular to a given day (Kernis, Grannemann and Barclay 1989) or moment in time (Heatherton and Polivy 1991). Such levels of the self function differently. For example, momentary self-esteem varies substantially from day to day, whereas this is not true of global self-esteem (Heatherton and Polivy 1991).

An implication of the preceding points is that personality self-reports will be both stable and malleable, depending on the level of analysis. If the focus is on the self in general terms, then state-related variables should be relatively inconsequential (Schell, Klein and Babey 1996). On the other hand, if the focus is on self-views that are specific to a social role, then personality traits will exhibit a greater degree of context sensitivity (Wood and Roberts 2006). Finally, when individuals are asked to rate their momentary emotions or self-views, such variables exhibit a great deal of flux across situation and over time (Diener and Larsen 1984). Thus, it is crucial to distinguish generalized self-views from those that are more contextual in nature.

Central versus peripheral aspects of the self

People can describe themselves in terms of both central and peripheral self-aspects (Sedikides 1993). People view central self-aspects as more important and hold them with greater certainty (Rosenberg 1979). Furthermore, central self-aspects are endorsed more quickly (Markus 1977), are less influenced by current mood (Sedikides 1995), and are associated with a greater degree of motivated processing (Sedikides 1993). These findings parallel the attitude strength literature, in which stronger attitudes are associated with faster processing, less context-dependence, and a greater degree of motivated processing (Petty and Krosnick 1995).

Applying the attitude strength perspective to the trait literature, it is likely that central (versus peripheral) aspects of the self will be more stable over time, more predictive of trait-relevant outcomes, and more resistant to trait-inconsistent feedback or contextual influences. Relevant findings have been reported in the self literature (Markus 1977; Sedikides 1995; Sedikides and Green 2000), but the promise of this perspective remains largely unfulfilled in the trait literature (Fuhrman and Funder 1995). For example, do individual differences in strength/ centrality moderate relations between a given trait (e.g., Neuroticism) and a trait-relevant outcome (e.g., negative affect)? We simply do not know at the present time.

Self-certainty

Individuals higher in self-esteem are more certain about themselves, and this contributes to higher levels of self-esteem stability (Campbell 1990), higher levels of internal consistency among different self-aspects (Campbell and Fehr 1990), and reduced susceptibility to social feedback (Campbell, Chew and Scratchley 1991). Although self-esteem and self-certainty overlap, they can be distinguished by the use of a recently developed dispositional measure of self-certainty (Campbell, Trapnell, Heine *et al*. 1996). Based on the idea that higher levels of self-certainty are associated with a greater degree of consistency across time and context (Campbell *et al*. 1996), it seems likely that traits might be better predictive of trait-relevant outcomes at higher levels of self-certainty. Thus, the dispositional analysis of self-certainty has promising implications for the trait-prediction literature.

The self as a memory structure

Generalized self-knowledge has properties of association consistent with semantic memory networks (Kihlstrom, Beer and Klein 2003; Robinson and Clore 2002a). These associative links should, in turn, have systematic implications for understanding how traits function. For example, a greater interconnectivity of positive affective knowledge should render it more likely that one positive thought would trigger another one in daily life (Robinson and Compton 2008). In support of this sort of analysis, a series of studies have shown that higher levels of life satisfaction are associated with stronger positive affective priming effects (Robinson and Kirkeby 2005; Robinson and von Hippel 2006), whereas higher levels of Neuroticism are associated with stronger negative affective priming effects (Robinson, Ode, Moeller and Goetz 2007). In short, traits may be profitably viewed as associative memory structures, as assessed within semantic and affective priming paradigms.

Other memory structure paradigms have focused on individual differences in the manner in which different self-aspects are organized (Linville 1985; Showers 1992). Individuals first list their important, yet distinct, self-aspects. They then assign traits to each self-aspect. Individuals differ in the extent to which their self-concept is simple – defined by fewer roles and more trait-overlap between roles – or complex. Those with relatively simple self-concepts evaluate the self in a manner that is more strongly influenced by success or failure feedback (McConnell and Strain 2007) or current mood states (Showers and Kling 1996). Such findings are understood in terms of a greater degree of spreading activation among different self-aspects at lower levels of self-complexity (Linville 1985; Showers 1992).

The memory structure paradigms discussed here would be useful in examining other important questions in the area of trait psychology. For example, associations among the Big Five traits appear to differ across individuals in a manner consistent with self-enhancement motives (Paulhus and John 1998). That is, some individuals may view the self in more global evaluative terms (Saucier 1994), in turn resulting in systematic relations among the Big Five traits (e.g., stronger inverse correlations between Extraversion and Neuroticism). In the spirit of understanding such differences, we suggest that memory structure paradigms may complement factor analytic techniques in understanding why it is that evaluative considerations play a larger role in trait self-ratings among some individuals relative to others.

Summary

Social psychologists have made significant advances in understanding the self. People are inclined to confirm strongly held self-views or select environments (e.g., occupations, neighbourhoods) that are likely to provide self-confirmation. Such considerations help to explain why it is that trait self-judgements are so stable over time. People are motivated to view the self in a positive manner, and this may help explain why trait self-judgements are polarized in a positive direction. Trait self-knowledge is general and abstract and may not capture important aspects of self-representation in everyday life. Yet, the abstractness of trait self-judgements is conducive to examining how individual differences in traits map onto, and likely follow from, individual differences in memory structure. Conceptualizing trait self-judgements as abstract beliefs concerning the self has implications for thinking about when and why traits will predict trait-relevant outcomes, a topic to which we now turn.

Trait self-knowledge as abstract beliefs about the self

Overview

Traits reflect and predict daily behaviour and experience (McCrae and Costa 1999) and traits have a genetic basis (Loehlin, McCrae and Costa 1998). Yet, research on the processing correlates of traits thought to produce trait-relevant outcomes has resulted in an inconsistent literature (Matthews and Gilliland 1999; Robinson, Vargas and Crawford 2003). Our review will not seek to document the successes and failures of this literature. Rather, our review will highlight a particular theory of trait-outcome relations and emerging support for it.

The theory

Personality traits could be assessed by aggregating across multiple observers (Funder 1991) or across momentary samples of experience and behaviour in daily life (Epstein 1983). Yet, this is not common practice. Instead, researchers typically assess traits by asking people to self-report on their broad (i.e., 'in general') tendencies to think, feel and act in particular ways. Likely, then, there is a close link between trait self-judgements and the global self-concept. This observation led Robinson and Clore (2002a) to suggest that trait self-reports assess abstract or generalized self-views rather than those more closely tied to momentary experience and behaviour. This theoretical perspective has important implications for understanding how traits are likely to function from a social-cognitive perspective.

Traits as generalized self-knowledge

When individuals rate themselves in general, they are likely to retrieve different sources of information than when they judge themselves in particular social roles or contexts. At least three sources of data attest to this point. First, generalized self-views are more consistent with self-relevant stereotypes than are ratings obtained in experience-sampling protocols (e.g., women are more emotional than men: Barrett, Robin, Pietromonaco and Eyssell 1998). Secondly, amnesic, autistic or demented patients can make reliable and valid trait judgements about the self, despite a complete inability to recall specific trait-relevant experiences or behaviours (e.g., Klein, Loftus and Kihlstrom 1996). Thirdly, reaction time paradigms converge on the point that ratings of the self 'in general' are made on a fundamentally different basis than are ratings of the self within more momentary timeframes (Robinson and Clore 2002b). In short, trait self-judgements tap generalized beliefs about the self somewhat independently of more momentary self-views (Robinson and Clore 2002a,2002b).

Priming stereotypic self-knowledge

Above, we noted that trait self-reports appear to be more stereotypic than are momentary ratings of the self (Robinson and Clore 2002a). If so, priming stereotypes, such as those related to the idea that women are more emotional than men, should differentially influence trait judgements of the self relative to state judgements of the self. This prediction was systematically confirmed in a study reported by Robinson and Clore (2002b), who primed gender stereotypes prior to asking individuals to rate their emotions both in general and in more momentary terms. As predicted, the priming manipulation led women to report that they had more intense emotions than men, but this priming effect was only observed when participants rated their emotions 'in general' or over long timeframes (e.g., the 'last few years'). Thus, there is some experimental evidence for the idea that trait self-reports are more stereotyped than are views of the self over more recent timeframes (e.g., the 'last few days').

Trait-state interactions

If trait- and state-related views of the self rely on different sources of self-knowledge, then they may often conflict with each other. Indeed, relations between Extraversion and Neuroticism on the one hand, and positive and negative mood states on the other, are often modest (Matthews and Gilliland 1999). Irrespective of mood manipulations, then, there are many moments in life in which individuals high in Neuroticism feel calm and individuals low in

Extraversion feel excited. Of interest here is what happens when trait and state sources of self-knowledge conflict with each other.

We suggest that conflicts between trait and state sources of self-knowledge are likely to be problematic. From the self-verification perspective, people desire trait-consistent mood states in part because such states are more frequent in daily life and therefore more conducive to habitual ways of interacting with the world (Swann and Schroeder 1995). Therefore, trait-inconsistent mood states may engender some degree of uncertainty and confusion, in turn disrupting established routines for appraising the significance of momentary events. In support of such a framework, trait-state mismatches, whether related to Extraversion and positive mood (Tamir, Robinson and Clore 2002) or Neuroticism and negative mood (Tamir and Robinson 2004), have been shown to undermine appraisal abilities, defined in terms of slowed reaction times in evaluating affective stimuli. Thus, individuals appear to function better when trait and state sources of self-knowledge converge rather than conflict with each other.

Trait self-knowledge as a default

The material presented above makes the case for separable sources of self-knowledge related to trait and state. Moreover, we have suggested that people generally prefer to make their emotion judgements on the basis of state-related knowledge to the extent possible (Robinson and Clore 2002b). However, when such knowledge is less accessible, we have suggested that individuals may 'default' to their more generalized beliefs concerning the self, and a large body of research at least inferentially supports this prediction (Robinson and Clore 2002a).

In recent studies, we have sought to provide more direct support for this trait-as-default perspective. If we are correct, individuals who are less capable of appraising the significance of momentary events should report emotional states that are more biased by their emotional traits. The most systematic body of research along these lines has examined relations between trait Neuroticism and state-related experiences of distress. Neuroticism/distress relations are higher among individuals: (a) less capable of making momentary distinctions between threatening and non-threatening stimuli (Tamir, Robinson and Solberg 2006); (b) higher in cognitive perseveration tendencies (Robinson, Wilkowski, Kirkeby and Meier 2006); (c) higher in dominant-response tendencies (Robinson, Goetz, Wilkowski and Hoffman 2006); (d) slower in reaction time (Robinson and Clore 2007); (e) higher in reaction time variability (Robinson, Wilkowski and Meier 2006); and (f) lower in self-regulation capacity (Robinson, Ode, Wilkowski and Amodio 2007).

Trait Neuroticism, then, appears to play an important 'fill in' role among individuals less capable of appreciating the nuances of moment-to-moment experience (Robinson and Clore 2007). Importantly, parallel findings have been reported in relation to the link between Extraversion and positive affect (Robinson and Oishi 2006; Robinson, Solberg, Vargas and Tamir 2003). The implications of this research are notable. Traits are not inevitable predictors of emotion and behaviour in daily functioning. Rather, their influence on such outcomes depends on the extent to which the individual is attuned to the nuances of daily life. Among less attuned individuals, traits are especially consequential. However, among more attuned individuals, traits are less consequential (e.g., Robinson and Clore 2007; Robinson and Oishi 2006).

Summary

We have suggested that trait self-knowledge can be conceptualized, at least in part, in terms of generalized beliefs concerning the self. This theoretical perspective has been especially generative. For example, the perspective can explain why trait self-reports are often more stereotypic than state self-reports are (Robinson and Clore 2002a). The theory also helps to explain why trait-state mismatches are problematic for making evaluations (e.g., Tamir and Robinson 2004). Finally, the theory makes the unique prediction that trait-state relations should be higher among individuals less capable of appreciating distinctions at encoding, and such predictions have received systematic support (e.g., Robinson and Clore 2007). Although we hasten to add that the theory presented here clearly has limitations, for example in explaining relations between traits and biological outcome variables, we nevertheless suggest that the theory has strengths in linking trait and social cognitive views of the self.

Future directions

A number of future directions were mentioned above; here, we focus on three such directions. Psychometric work reveals that global self-esteem is largely isomorphic with high levels of Extraversion in combination with low levels of Neuroticism (Watson, Suls and Haig 2002). Therefore, the trait literature on approach and avoidance motivation, linked to Extraversion and Neuroticism, can further inform the self-concept literature on global self-esteem. Also, the literature on global self-esteem, which highlights differences in self-certainty (Campbell 1990) and reactivity to feedback (Campbell, Chew and Scratchley 1991), should in turn contribute to our understanding of the manner in which Extraversion and Neuroticism function. For example, we would expect Extraversion to relate to higher levels of self-certainty and Neuroticism to relate to lower levels of self-certainty (see Campbell, Trapnell, Heine *et al.* 1996).

The self-concept literature highlights the manner in which various aspects of the self-concept can be either strongly or weakly held. The idea that strong self-views are more consequential has been confirmed in the social cognition literature (Markus 1977; Sedikides 1993; Sedikides and Green 2000), and it is thus surprising that there are so few applications of this strength-related perspective to the trait literature (for an exception, see Fuhrman and Funder 1995). Given the substantial role that strength-related variables play in moderating stability, attitude-behaviour relations and other attitude-related effects (Petty and Krosnick 1995), one would expect that strength-related variables, such as the speed of making trait self-judgements, would moderate trait-outcome relations.

We presented evidence for the idea that trait-state relations appear stronger among, and even exclusive to, individuals less capable of making distinctions at encoding (e.g., Robinson and Oishi 2006). This perspective can be extended in at least two ways. First, such moderating effects should extend to trait-behaviour relations in addition to trait-state relations, but we have very little evidence in support of this point (for an exception, see Robinson, Goetz, Wilkowski and Hoffman 2006). Secondly, basic features of intellect, such as general intelligence, should also moderate trait-outcome relations (e.g., Robinson and Clore 2007). Such demonstrations would not only support the theory advanced in the latter section of the review, but also better link research on personality and intelligence, hitherto examined in separate research traditions (Eysenck and Eysenck 1985). In general terms, we suggest that a concerted focus on processing-related moderators of trait-state relations seems especially important in understanding how and why traits influence state-related outcomes from a social cognitive perspective.

Conclusions

The goal of this chapter was to promote an integration of trait and social cognitive views of the self. In the first major section, we highlighted the manner in which the trait literature can inform the self-concept literature. In the second major section, we reversed such considerations by highlighting the manner in which the self-concept literature can inform the literature on personality traits. In the third major section, we presented a model proposing that trait self-judgements can be viewed in terms of generalized beliefs concerning the self. Given that multiple lines of research have demonstrated the benefits of integrating trait and social cognitive views of the self, we are optimistic that future integration efforts will be similarly successful.

References

Alicke, M. D. and Govorun, O. 2005. The better-than-average effect, in M. D. Alicke, D. A. Dunning and J. I. Krueger (eds.), *The self in social judgement*, pp. 85–106. Philadelphia, PA: Psychology Press

Barrett, L. F., Robin, L., Pietromonaco, P. R. and Eyssell, K. M. 1998. Are women the 'more emotional' sex?: evidence from emotional experiences in social context, *Cognition and Emotion* 12: 555–78

Baumeister, R. F. 1997. Identity, self-concept, and self-esteem: the self lost and found, in R. Hogan, J. A. Johnson and S. R. Briggs (eds.), *Handbook of personality psychology*, 1st edn, pp. 681–710. San Diego, CA: Academic Press

Baumeister, R. F., Tice, D. M. and Hutton, D. G. 1989. Self-presentational motivations and personality differences in self-esteem, *Journal of Personality* 57: 547–79

Benet-Martínez, V. and John, O. 1998. Los Cinco Grandes across cultures and ethnic groups: multitrait-multimethod analyses of the Big Five in Spanish and English, *Journal of Personality and Social Psychology* 75: 729–50

Campbell, J. D. 1990. Self-esteem and clarity of the self-concept, *Journal of Personality and Social Psychology* 59: 538–49

Campbell, J. D., Chew, B. and Scratchley, L. S. 1991. Cognitive and emotional reactions to daily events: the effects of self-esteem and self-complexity, *Journal of Personality* 59: 473–505

Campbell, J. D. and Fehr, B. 1990. Self-esteem and perceptions of conveyed impressions: is negative affectivity associated with greater realism?, *Journal of Personality and Social Psychology* 58: 122–33

Campbell, J. D., Trapnell, P. D., Heine, S. J., Katz, I. M., Lavallee, L. F. and Lehman, D. R. 1996. Self-concept clarity: measurement, personality correlates, and cultural boundaries, *Journal of Personality and Social Psychology* 70: 141–56

Carver, C. S., Sutton, S. K. and Scheier, M. F. 2000. Action, emotion, and personality: emerging conceptual integration, *Personality and Social Psychology Bulletin* 26: 741–51

Caspi, A., Roberts, B. W. and Shiner, R. L. 2005. Personality development: stability and change, *Annual Review of Psychology* 56: 453–84

Diener, E. and Larsen, R. J. 1984. Temporal stability and cross-situational consistency of affective, behavioural, and cognitive responses, *Journal of Personality and Social Psychology* 47: 871–83

Donahue, E. M. and Harary, K. 1998. The patterned inconsistency of traits: mapping the differential effects of social roles on self-perceptions of the Big Five, *Personality and Social Psychology Bulletin* 24: 610–19

Dunning, D., Meyerowitz, J. A. and Holzberg, A. D. 1989. Ambiguity and self-evaluation: the role of idiosyncratic trait definitions in self-serving assessments of ability, *Journal of Personality and Social Psychology* 57: 1082–90

Edwards, A. L. 1953. The relationship between the judged desirability of a trait and the probability that the trait will be endorsed, *Journal of Applied Psychology* 37: 90–3

Elliot, A. J. and Thrash, T. M. 2002. Approach-avoidance motivation in personality: approach and avoidance temperaments and goals, *Journal of Personality and Social Psychology* 82: 804–18

Epstein, S. 1983. Aggregation and beyond: some basic issues on the prediction of behaviour, *Journal of Personality* 51: 360–92

Eysenck, H. J. and Eysenck, M. W. 1985. *Personality and individual differences: a natural science approach*. New York: Plenum

Fuhrman, R. W. and Funder, D. C. 1995. Convergence between self and peer in the response-time processing of trait-relevant information, *Journal of Personality and Social Psychology* 69: 961–74

Funder, D. C. 1991. Global traits: a neo-Allportian approach to personality, *Psychological Science* 2: 31–9

Gordon, C. 1968. Self-conceptions: configurations of content, in C. Gordon and K. J. Gergen (eds.), *The self in social interaction*, pp. 115–36. New York: Wiley

Gramzow, R. H., Sedikides, C., Panter, A. T., Sathy, V., Harris, J. and Insko, C. A. 2004. Patterns of self-regulation and the Big Five, *European Journal of Personality* 18: 367–85

Gray, J. A. 1987. Perspectives on anxiety and impulsivity: a commentary, *Journal of Research in Personality* 21: 493–509

Hafdahl, A. R., Panter, A. T., Gramzow, R. H., Sedikides, C. and Insko, C. A. 2000. Free-response self-discrepancies across, among, and within FFM personality dimensions, *Journal of Personality* 68: 111–51

Heatherton, T. F. and Polivy, J. 1991. Development and validation of a scale for measuring state self-esteem, *Journal of Personality and Social Psychology* 60: 895–910

James, W. 1890. *The principles of psychology.* New York: Henry Holt and Company

John, O. P. and Srivastava, S. 1999. The Big Five trait taxonomy: history, measurement, and theoretical perspectives, in L. A. Pervin and O. P. John (eds.), *Handbook of personality: theory and research*, 2nd edn, pp. 102–38. New York: Guilford Press

Kenrick, D. T. and Funder, D. C. 1988. Profiting from the controversy: lessons from the person-situation debate, *American Psychologist* 43: 23–34

Kernis, M. H., Grannemann, B. D. and Barclay, L. C. 1989. Stability and level of self-esteem as predictors of anger arousal and hostility, *Journal of Personality and Social Psychology* 56: 1013–22

Kihlstrom, J. F., Beer, J. B. and Klein, S. B. 2003. Self and identity as memory, in M. R. Leary and J. P. Tangney (eds.), *Handbook of self and identity*, pp. 68–90. New York: Guilford Press

Klein, S. B., Loftus, J. and Kihlstrom, J. F. 1996. Self-knowledge of an amnesic patient: toward a neuropsychology of personality and social psychology, *Journal of Experimental Psychology: General* 125: 250–60

Leary, M. R., Tambor, E. S., Terdal, S. K. and Downs, D. L. 1995. Self-esteem as an interpersonal monitor: the sociometer hypothesis, *Journal of Personality and Social Psychology* 68: 518–30

Linville, P. W. 1985. Self-complexity and affective extremity: don't put all of your eggs in one cognitive basket, *Social Cognition* 3: 94–120

Loehlin, J. C., McCrae, R. R. and Costa, P. T. 1998. Heritabilities of common and measure-specific components of the Big Five personality factors, *Journal of Research in Personality* 32: 431–53

Markus, H. 1977. Self-schemata and processing information about the self, *Personality and Social Psychology Bulletin* 35: 63–78

1983. Self-knowledge: an expanded view, *Journal of Personality* 51: 543–65

Matthews, G. and Gilliland, K. 1999. The personality theories of H. J. Eysenck and J. A. Gray: a comparative review, *Personality and Individual Differences* 26: 583–626

McConnell, A. R. and Strain, L. M. 2007. Structure and content of the self, in C. Sedikides and S. Spencer (eds.), *The self in social psychology*, pp. 51–73. New York: Psychology Press

McCrae, R. R. and Costa, P. T. 1994. The stability of personality: observation and evaluations, *Current Directions in Psychological Science* 3: 173–5

1999. A Five-Factor theory of personality, in L. A. Pervin and O. P. John (eds.), *Handbook of personality: theory and research*, 2nd edn, pp. 139–53. New York: Guilford Press

McGuire, W. J. and McGuire, C. V. 1988. Content and process in the experience of the self, in L. Berkowitz (ed.), *Advances in experimental social psychology*, vol. XXI, pp. 97–144. San Diego, CA: Academic Press

Mead, G. H. 1934. *Mind, self, and society from the standpoint of a social behaviourist.* University of Chicago Press

Mischel, W. 1968. *Personality and assessment.* Hoboken, NJ: John Wiley and Sons
  2004. Toward an integrative science of the person, *Annual Review of Psychology* 55: 1–22

Neiss, M. B., Sedikides, C. and Stevenson, J. 2006. Genetic influences on level and stability of self-esteem, *Self and Identity* 5: 247–66

Neiss, M. B., Stevenson, J., Sedikides, C., Kumashiro, M., Finkel, E. J. and Rusbult, C. E. 2005. Executive self, self-esteem, and negative affectivity: relations at the phenotypic and genotypic level, *Journal of Personality and Social Psychology* 89: 593–606

Paulhus, D. L. and John, O. P. 1998. Egoistic and moralistic biases in self-perception: the interplay of self-deceptive styles with basic traits and motives, *Journal of Personality* 66: 1025–60

Petty, R. E. and Krosnick, J. 1995. *Attitude strength: antecedents and consequences.* Hillsdale, NJ: Lawrence Erlbaum Associates

Robins, R. W. and John, O. P. 1997. The quest for self-insight: theory and research on accuracy and bias in self-perception, in R. Hogan, J. A. Johnson and S. R. Briggs (eds.), *Handbook of personality psychology*, 1st edn, pp. 649–79. San Diego, CA: Academic Press

Robinson, M. D. and Clore, G. L. 2002a. Belief and feeling: an accessibility model of emotional self-report, *Psychological Bulletin* 128: 934–60
  2002b. Episodic and semantic knowledge in emotional self-report: evidence for two judgment processes, *Journal of Personality and Social Psychology* 83: 198–215
  2007. Traits, states, and encoding speed: support for a top-down view of neuroticism/stress relations, *Journal of Personality* 75: 95–120

Robinson, M. D. and Compton, R. J. 2008. The happy mind in action: the cognitive basis of subjective well-being, in M. Eid and R. J. Larsen (eds.), *The science of subjective well-being*, pp. 220–38 New York: Guilford Press

Robinson, M. D., Goetz, M. C., Wilkowski, B. M. and Hoffman, S. J. 2006. Driven to tears or to joy: response dominance and trait-based predictions, *Personality and Social Psychology Bulletin* 32: 629–40

Robinson, M. D. and Kirkeby, B. S. 2005. Happiness as a belief system: individual differences and priming in emotion judgments, *Personality and Social Psychology Bulletin* 31: 1134–44

Robinson, M. D., Ode, S., Moeller, S. K. and Goetz, P. W. 2007. Neuroticism and affective priming: evidence for a Neuroticism-linked negative schema, *Personality and Individual Differences* 42: 1221–31

Robinson, M. D., Ode, S., Wilkowski, B. M. and Amodio, D. M. 2007. Neurotic contentment: a self-regulation view of Neuroticism-linked distress, *Emotion* 7: 579–91

Robinson, M. D. and Oishi, S. 2006. Trait self-report as a 'fill in' belief system: categorization speed moderates the Extraversion/life satisfaction relation, *Self and Identity* 5: 15–34

Robinson, M. D., Solberg, E. C., Vargas, P. and Tamir, M. 2003. Trait as default: Extraversion, subjective well-being, and the distinction between neutral and positive events, *Journal of Personality and Social Psychology* 85: 517–27

Robinson, M. D., Vargas, P. T. and Crawford, E. G. 2003. Putting process into personality, appraisal, and emotion: evaluative processing as a missing link, in J. Musch and K. C. Klauer (eds.), *The psychology of evaluation: affective processes in cognition and emotion*, pp. 275–306. Mahwah, NJ: Lawrence Erlbaum Associates

Robinson, M. D. and von Hippel, W. 2006. Rose-colored priming effects: life satisfaction and affective priming, *Journal of Positive Psychology* 1: 187–97

Robinson, M. D., Wilkowski, B. M., Kirkeby, B. S. and Meier, B. P. 2006. Stuck in a rut: perseverative response tendencies and the Neuroticism/distress relationship, *Journal of Experimental Psychology: General* 135: 78–91

Robinson, M. D., Wilkowski, B. M. and Meier, B. P. 2006. Unstable in more ways than one: reaction time variability and the Neuroticism/distress relationship, *Journal of Personality* 74: 311–43

Rosenberg, M. 1979. *Conceiving the self*. New York: Basic Books

Ross, L. and Nisbett, R. E. 1991. *The person and the situation: perspectives of social psychology*. New York: McGraw-Hill

Saucier, G. 1994. Separating description and evaluation in the structure of personality attributes, *Journal of Personality and Social Psychology* 66: 141–54

Schell, T. L., Klein, S. B. and Babey, S. H. 1996. Testing a hierarchical model of self-knowledge, *Psychological Science* 7: 170–3

Sedikides, C. 1993. Assessment, enhancement, and verification as determinants of the self-evaluation process, *Journal of Personality and Social Psychology* 65: 317–38

  1995. Central and peripheral self-conceptions are differentially influenced by mood: tests of the differential sensitivity hypothesis, *Journal of Personality and Social Psychology* 69: 759–77

Sedikides, C. and Green, J. D. 2000. On the self-protective nature of inconsistency/negativity management: using the person memory paradigm to examine self-referent memory, *Journal of Personality and Social Psychology* 79: 906–22

Sedikides, C. and Gregg, A. P. 2003. Portraits of the self, in M. A. Hogg and J. Cooper (eds.), *Sage handbook of social psychology*, pp. 110–38. London: Sage Publications

  2008. Self-enhancement: food for thought, *Perspectives on Psychological Science* 3: 102–16

Sedikides, C., Gregg, A. P. and Hart, C. M. 2007. The importance of being modest, in C. Sedikides and S. Spencer (eds.), *The self: frontiers in social psychology*, pp. 285–324. New York: Psychology Press

Sedikides, C. and Strube, M. J. 1997. Self-evaluation: to thine own self be good, to thine own self be sure, to thine own self be true, and to thine own self be better, in M. P. Zanna (ed.), *Advances in experimental social psychology*, vol. XXIX, pp. 209–69. New York: Academic Press

Showers, C. 1992. Compartmentalization of positive and negative self-knowledge: keeping bad apples out of the bunch, *Journal of Personality and Social Psychology* 62: 1036–49

Showers, C. J. and Kling, K. C. 1996. Organization of self-knowledge: implications for recovery from sad mood, *Journal of Personality and Social Psychology* 70: 578–90

Swann, W. B., Rentfrow, P. J. and Guinn, J. 2002. Self-verification: the search for coherence, in M. R. Leary and J. P. Tangney (eds.), *Handbook of self and identity*, pp. 367–83. New York: Guilford Press

Swann, W. B. and Schroeder, D. G. 1995. The search for beauty and truth: a framework for understanding reactions to evaluations, *Personality and Social Psychology Bulletin* 21: 1307–18

Tamir, M. 2005. Don't worry, be happy?: Neuroticism, trait-consistent affect regulation, and performance, *Journal of Personality and Social Psychology* 89: 449–61

Tamir, M. and Robinson, M. D. 2004. Knowing good from bad: the paradox of Neuroticism, negative affect, and evaluative processing, *Journal of Personality and Social Psychology* 87: 913–25

Tamir, M., Robinson, M. D. and Clore, G. L. 2002. The epistemic benefits of trait-consistent mood states: an analysis of Extraversion and mood, *Journal of Personality and Social Psychology* 83: 663–77

Tamir, M., Robinson, M. D. and Solberg, E. C. 2006. You may worry, but can you recognize threats when you see them?: Neuroticism, threat identifications, and negative affect, *Journal of Personality* 74: 1481–1506

Trzesniewski, K. H., Donnellan, M. B. and Robins, R. W. 2003. Stability of self-esteem across the lifespan, *Journal of Personality and Social Psychology* 84: 205–20

Watson, D., Suls, J. and Haig, J. 2002. Global self-esteem in relation to structural models of personality and affectivity, *Journal of Personality and Social Psychology* 83: 185–97

Wood, D. and Roberts, B. W. 2006. Cross-sectional and longitudinal tests of the personality and role identity structural model (PRISM), *Journal of Personality* 74: 779–809

27 Personality as a cognitive-affective processing system

Ronald E. Smith and Yuichi Shoda

Because relations between cognitive and affective processes are such an important aspect of human behaviour, virtually all formal theories of personality, beginning with Freudian psychoanalysis, have addressed their interaction. Cognitive-affective models have also been highly influential in more restricted domains, such as emotion (Arnold 1960; Schachter 1966; Smith 1984), stress and coping (Lazarus and Folkman 1984), and burnout (Pines and Aronson 1981; Smith 1986). They are currently a major focus of social cognitive approaches to personality.

A key goal of social-cognitive theories is to account for two types of behavioural variability: individual differences between people and changes in behaviour as individuals interact with different life situations. In this chapter, we describe an ongoing attempt to develop a more comprehensive model – actually, a meta-model – of personality that helps to account for both inter-individual and intra-individual variability in behaviour.

The 'personality paradox'

Personality is typically defined as a construct that underlies individual differences in people's customary thoughts, feelings and behaviours. The implication is that there is stability in these aspects of personal functioning, and that consistencies in behaviour should result. By the late 1920s, however, research on the stability of particular behaviours across situations was providing challenges to the assumption of cross-situational consistency (Hartshorne and May 1928; Newcomb 1929). Comprehensive reviews of the literature on situational consistency by Mischel (1968) and Peterson (1968) indicated that cross-situational inconsistency in behaviour is the rule rather than the exception, and that global trait measures typically correlated weakly with relevant behaviours. Aggregating behavioural responses across varying situations to produce an 'average' behavioural measure produced more favourable correlational results (Epstein 1983), but attempts to demonstrate cross-situational consistency in specific behaviours across different contexts continued to yield disappointing findings (e.g., Mischel and Peake 1982).

Although there existed clear individual differences in people's 'average' levels of particular behaviours when aggregated across situations (i.e., inter-individual variability), the consistent failure to find evidence for behavioural stability across situations (intra-individual variability) caused some to question the tenability of the basic concept of personality as a causal agent in behaviour (e.g., Shweder 1975). Clearly, the consistency results were at odds with a long tradition of Western thought, dating to the ancient Greeks, that assumed a stable personality structure that underlies the 'customary' behaviour of people. This puzzling state of affairs – presumption of a stable dispositional structure, combined with little evidence for behavioural consistency – was dubbed the 'personality paradox' by Bem and Allen (1974). Attempts to reconcile this paradox have fuelled debate in the field of personality for more than three decades. Needed to resolve it was a reconceptualization of personality that would allow one to predict and understand stable and unique patterns of intra-individual (transituational) variability. As Mischel (1973) noted, this might require a new approach to the nature of situations and of personality stability that could reconcile the variability of behaviour, on the one hand, with the stability of the personality structure, on the other (Mischel and Shoda 1995).

Discovery of behaviour-situation 'signatures'

Some personality psychologists portrayed Mischel, Peterson and others who challenged the consistency assumption as 'attacking' the field of personality. Instead, Mischel (1968, 1973) defended the concept of personality, but called for a re-examination of the consistency assumption. Perhaps, he suggested, a view of personality dispositions as less global and more situation-specific than commonly believed could be a starting point for a reconceptualization of personality. One focus of such an approach would be the study of individual differences in *patterns* of cross-situational variability that might reveal the coherence and stability in behaviour typically ascribed to personality.

Resolving the personality paradox thus called for a conceptual model that could account not only for individual differences in the mean or 'average' levels of behaviour across situations that are the focus of trait conceptions, but also for the distinctive and unique ways that a person's behaviour can change across situations. Such a model would necessarily incorporate both situational and dispositional factors, but in a manner that built upon the concept of triadic reciprocal causation that specifies bidirectional causal relations between person, environment and behaviour (Bandura 1986). Because of its cognitive emphasis, it would move beyond *nominal* situational factors (i.e., physical or social features) to their *psychological* ingredients as encoded or construed by the person. Likewise, dispositional variables would go beyond static trait concepts to specify cognitive-affective personality processes that become activated by situational elements, interact with and influence one another in a systemic and stable manner, and generate output behaviours. In other words, if individuals are responding to specific aspects of situations that activate the internal processing system, then

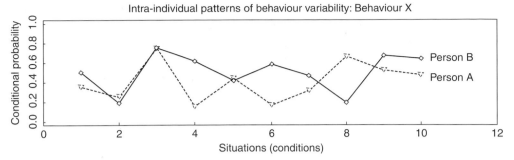

Figure 27.1. *Illustrative intra-individual, situation-behaviour profiles for verbal aggression in relation to five situations in two time samples (*solid *and* dotted lines*). Data are shown in standardized scores (Z) relative to the normative levels of verbal aggression in each situation.*

we might expect their behaviour to show distinctive and idiosyncratic patterning across situations.

Such patterning has been empirically demonstrated through fine-grained analysis of behaviour in specific situations. In a study by Shoda, Mischel and Wright (1994), for example, children were intensively observed within a residential summer camp over a six-week period, and a variety of specific behaviours were coded, including verbal aggression. Indiographic analyses of the children's responses provided evidence for stable and consistent situation-behaviour profiles across five different and well-defined classes of situations (e.g., teased by another child, praised by an adult, warned by an adult). The children differed not only in the total number of aggressive responses they made, but also in the situations in which the behaviours occurred, and their situation-behaviour profiles across different time periods were often highly consistent. Most significantly, as shown in Figure 27.1, children who on average were virtually identical in their aggressive behaviour output showed sharp and stable variations in their situation-behaviour patterns, a fact that would not have been revealed by the aggregation of aggressive responses across the five situations.

Behavioural signatures are not restricted to aggressive children. A recent analysis of more than 33,000 observed behaviours of 28 youth baseball coaches during 139 complete games revealed stable individual patterns of coaching behaviour in specifically defined situations, such as when the team was winning, tied or losing. Clearly evident were distinctive *if ... then ...* situation-behaviour relations, or 'coaching behavioural signatures' that were not evident from the coaches' overall percentages of supportive, instructive and punitive behaviours across all observations. Moreover, situation-behaviour patterns had differential relations with other measures, such as children's liking for the coach and desire to play for him in the future (Smith, Shoda, Cumming and Smoll in press). Stable behavioural signatures have also been observed in business (Ilies, Scott and Judge 2006) and laboratory task situations (Borkenau, Riemann, Spinath and Angleitner

2006). We should note, however, that the stability of behavioural signature patterns are not universal, as some individuals fail to exhibit profile stability across repeated assessments in similar situations. As Fleeson (2004) has noted, individuals' level of situation-behaviour consistency could itself be an individual difference factor having currently unknown antecedents and consequences.

Previous versions of social learning theory have sometimes been criticized for emphasizing the role of situational factors and basic learning mechanisms of behaviour acquisition and change while failing to specify internal 'person' variables that (a) mediate the effects of situational variables on behaviour, and (b) account for the individual differences that are so clearly evident to even the casual observer of human behaviour (Kenrick and Funder 1988). Building on a theoretical article by Mischel (1973) that specified a set of 'person variables' consistent with the social learning theory approach of that time, a more recent formulation has yielded a new model that specifies internal mediating factors in a way that helps account for both personality coherence and cross-situational variability in a way that helps resolve the personality paradox.

Cognitive-affective processing system (CAPS)

Social cognitive theory's concept of reciprocal determinism (Bandura 1986) provides a useful framework for analysing bidirectional causal interactions involving person, environment and behaviour. Mischel and Shoda's (1995) cognitive-affective processing system (CAPS) fleshed out the 'person' portion of the triadic framework by specifying important person variables and the processing dynamics that create a stable personality structure capable of producing situation-behaviour regularities. The CAPS model was inspired in part by recent information-processing, connectionist and neural network models in areas such as perception, social cognition and cognitive neuroscience (Read and Miller 1998; Rumelhart and McClelland 1986). Such models focus on organized networks of cognitive-affective processing units whose interconnections form a unique network. This network functions as an organized whole and its units are activated by the specific features of the situation that are being processed and interpreted by the individual. Individuals differ in the *chronic accessibility* of network elements, that is, the ease with which the particular cognitive-affective units become activated (Higgins 1990). They also differ in the levels of activation that occur in response to (a) elements of the 'psychological situation' that is being processed, and (b) the activity of other associated units, which can stimulate, inhibit or exert no influence on the unit.

Mischel and Shoda's person variables, or 'cognitive-affective units' include the person's encoding (i.e., 'construal' or interpretation) of the self and of situations, expectancies (including stimulus-stimulus, response-outcome and self-efficacy expectancies), enduring goals and values, affective states and dispositions, and competencies and self-regulation capabilities. The dynamic interactions among the units mediate relations between situations and behaviours in a manner that can be quite distinctive for different individuals, and stability in activation patterns among individuals underlies the coherence of personality. In this model, therefore, invariance resides not at the situation-behavioural level, but at the level of internal processing dynamics. We now consider the CAPS components in greater detail.

Encodings

We respond to the world as perceived. Therefore, what constitutes a psychological situation depends on the acquired meanings of the stimulus elements for the person, as well as the specific aspects of the situation that are selectively focused upon. One important set of CAPS units are the mental categories, or personal constructs, used to encode, or mentally represent, the self, other people and events. People differ in how they customarily encode both internal and external stimuli (Higgins 1990). For example, performers differ in how they construe physiological arousal during performance situations (Jones and Swain 1992). Some interpret the arousal cues as something that will aid their performance, whereas for others, arousal is an indication that they are 'choking'.

In the course of their social learning history, people also develop relational schemas (Baldwin 1999), cognitive representations of how social relationships are expected to play out, or 'work'. These schemas influence how they encode and respond to social interactions. Consider three workers who receive corrective feedback from a supervisor. One worker who is 'rejection sensitive' (Downey and Feldman 1996) construes the feedback as a signal that she is being rejected by the supervisor and becomes depressed. A second worker views the correction as an indication of the supervisor's desire to insult him and responds with anger and defiance. The third worker views the instruction as constructive feedback and responds with receptiveness and appreciation. Attention and perception are by their very nature selective, and the elements of a particular situation that are encoded and how they are construed has important consequences for the rest of the CAPS processing system.

Among the most significant encodings are the personal constructs used to represent one's own characteristics (i.e., the self-schema). For example, research has shown that athletes differ in the extent to which their personal identity revolves around the role of 'athlete'. Differences in degree of athletic identity influence how athletes encode events in their lives, which goals they consider most important, and how they react to events such as athletic success and failure or retirement from sport (Brewer, Van Raalte and Linder 1993).

Expectancies and beliefs

Beliefs about the self, the world, and 'how things are' play a key role in behaviour. People's belief systems help confer meaning on events and are involved in selecting goals, planning behavioural strategies and understanding oneself and others. Among the individual's beliefs are situationally-specific and more global expectations of 'what leads to what'. Expectancies have always occupied a central role in cognitive conceptions of learning and behaviour (e.g., Bolles 1972; Tolman 1932), and they are well represented in contemporary social-cognitive theories (Bandura 1997). Encodings frequently evoke expectancies, as when a student with facilitative anxiety anticipates that his arousal will enhance test performance, or when the rejection-sensitive worker views the supervisor's well-intentioned corrective feedback as a sign of future rejection.

Expectancies take a variety of forms. Stimulus-outcome expectancies represent a predictive relation between a stimulus and a later outcome. They are the basis for classical conditioning (i.e., the CS-UCS relation), as illustrated in the ability of situational cues to evoke automatic emotional reactions in many individuals. In operant conditioning, discriminative stimuli allow people to predict what is going to happen, given particular stimulus conditions. Response-outcome expectancies represent *if ... then ...* relations between behaviour and its anticipated outcomes, and are the cognitive basis for operant conditioning. The perceived relation between situational demands and personal resources is the basis for self-efficacy expectancies (Bandura 1997). A more generalized expectancy, locus of control, relates to individual differences in the tendency to see one's outcomes as under the control of personal or situational influences (Rotter 1966).

Affects

Early information-processing models developed within cognitive psychology focused on 'cool cognitions', such as facts and propositions processed in a logical fashion. These models changed as it became clear that affects, or emotions, profoundly influence many aspects of behaviour, including how stimuli are encoded and the expectancies that are evoked by situational cues (Forgas 1995). Cognitions about the self and one's future are inherently affect laden, or 'hot' (Shoda and Mischel 1998). Moreover, affective responses can influence a wide range of behaviours, including evaluative responses and social behaviour, in a pre-conscious fashion that occurs automatically and outside of awareness (Gollwitzer and Bargh 1996).

People exhibit stable individual differences in emotionality. Some have a tendency to experience negative *affect*, or emotion, in an intense fashion, a factor that influences many of their perceptions and behaviours, whereas others seem predisposed to experience mainly positive affect in their lives (Watson and Clark 1984). Affective responses can have diverse effects on interpersonal behaviour and task performance, depending on the nature of the situation, other characteristics of the individual, and cognitive or physiological components of the emotion. Emotions also affect other CAPS components. Anxiety, for example, can significantly lower outcome expectancies in performance situations (Smith 2006).

Goals and values

Motivation and emotion are intimately connected. According to Lazarus (1991), emotions are aroused when personally significant goals are attained, threatened or frustrated. Each emotion thus has an underlying 'relational theme'. Joy resides in the attainment of an important goal. A perceived threat to some important aspect of wellbeing evokes anxiety. In depression, the theme involves the actual or impending loss of something of value.

Within the CAPS model, motives and values play a central role, guiding the short- and long-term goals that people seek, the ways they encode certain events, the situations and outcomes they approach or avoid, and their emotional reactions to such situations. Individual differences in the meaning ascribed to an athletic situation depend in part on the goals and subjective values that people bring to it. As noted above, expectancies and values also interact in important ways (Brehm and Self 1989). Even if a person has a strong behaviour-outcome expectancy for the attainment of a potential outcome, he or she may not pursue the outcome if it has low hedonic value or significance. Some people have the potential for great success if they would only apply themselves, yet they may underachieve if that outcome is not sufficiently important to them. In contrast, frustration or depression are likely to be experienced if a desired or avoided outcome has high valence but the person has a low expectancy of goal attainment.

Some goals involve the attainment of desired outcomes, whereas others involve the avoidance of undesired consequences. In the domain of achievement, achievement motivation is regarded as the positive motive, whereas fear of failure is its negative counterpart (Atkinson 1964). Anxiety is a response to a potential negative consequence, and the specific type of anxiety depends on the nature of the consequence, which may involve threats of disapproval, rejection, failure, embarrassment or exposure to some phobic object. Because people differ widely in the kinds of consequences that have personal significance, personality plays an important role in the kinds of affective reactions that they experience and the conditions under which they experience them.

Competencies and self-regulation skills

People's cognitive, affective and behavioural capabilities are key factors in how they are influenced by, respond to, and influence their environments. The final CAPS component – competencies and self-regulatory systems – receive strong emphasis in current social-cognitive theories (e.g., Bandura 1997; Mischel and Shoda 1995). They include self-monitoring capabilities, self-reinforcement processes and the personal standards that underlie them, task-relevant attentional skills, cognitive restructuring and self-instructional skills, the ability to set goals and develop effective action plans for goal attainment, behavioural self-control strategies directed at modifying antecedents and consequences, delay-of-gratification capability, affect-control skills, and relapse prevention strategies.

Consciously-applied self-regulatory competencies are a particular focus of applied sport psychologists who do psychological skills training.

Self-regulatory functions interact reciprocally with all of the other CAPS components in ways that differ from person to person in a coherent fashion. Self-regulation units influence how situations are encoded, which expectancies (particularly behaviour-outcome and self-efficacy expectancies) are evoked, how effectively the person generates plans and executes goal-directed behaviour, and the affects that the person experiences in particular situations. As Mischel (1973) has noted, well-developed self-regulation skills help liberate people from external stimulus control of their behaviour.

CAPS as a dynamic system

A schematic representation of the CAPS model is shown in Figure 27.2. The cognitive-affective components are represented by the interconnections shown within the larger circle. The encoding units respond to specific aspects of the situation (producing the psychological situation) and the encodings both influence and are affected by other units (expectancies, goals, affects). Some links (shown by the dotted lines) are inhibitory in nature. The total pattern of activations and inhibitions results in certain behaviours, which may themselves alter the situation (as represented by the arrow leading back from behaviours to the situation). These behaviours may also affect ongoing CAPS dynamics. For example, self-perceptions of successful performance may trigger increasing confidence, efficacy beliefs and positive affect. Such relations illustrate the influence of behaviours on person and environment, as posited by the reciprocal determinism model (Bandura 1986).

In the CAPS model, the focus is not just on 'how much' of a particular unit (e.g., self-efficacy belief, performance anxiety, mastery goal orientation) a person has, but in how these cognitive-affective units are organized with one another within the person, forming a network of interconnections that can operate, in a parallel rather than serial manner, at multiple levels of accessibility, awareness and automaticity. Individuals differ stably and uniquely in this network of interconnections or associations, and such differences constitute a major aspect of personality (Mischel and Shoda 1995; Shoda and Mischel 1998). For a given individual the likelihood that a particular feature of a situation triggers thought A, which leads to thought B, emotion C, and behaviour D may be relatively stable and predictable, reflecting a network of chronically accessible associations among cognitions and affects available to that individual. Thus, the CAPS model posits an internal set of *if ... then ...* relations as well the external situation-behaviour *if ... then ...* relations discussed earlier, and the cognitions and affects that are activated at a given time depend on situations, either internal or external to an individual. But *how* they depend, and the relations between features present in a situation encountered and the cognitions and affects that are activated in response to

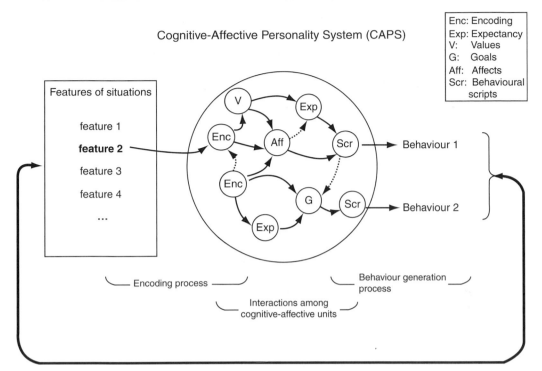

Figure 27.2. *The cognitive-affective personality system (CAPS). Situational features activate a given mediating unit which activates specific sub-sets of other mediating units through a stable network of relations that characterize an individual, generating a characteristic pattern of behaviour in response to different situations. The relation may be positive (solid line), which increases the activation, or negative (dashed line), which decreases the activation.*

them, are assumed to reflect the stable personality structure of the individual (Mischel and Shoda 1995; Shoda and Mischel 1998).

The system that underlies an individual's cognitive-affective and behavioural dynamics typically contains extensive internal feedback loops, meaning that 'downstream' units can activate 'upstream' units, generating a flow of thoughts, feelings and even behaviours without necessarily requiring an outside stimulus. Thus, when an individual is in an angry affective state, he or she may be more likely to selectively encode negative aspects of situations, attribute malevolent intent to others' actions, and generate aggressive behavioural scripts. Moreover, the elements in an individual's CAPS network are likely to form a system of mutually supporting components. For example, the many beliefs we maintain are not independent of each other, but support one another in a way that helps us 'make sense' of the world and constitutes a personal philosophy of life. Further, components of a belief system are related to affective reactions, goals and values, and behaviours in a way that forms a coherent organic whole.

Dynamic network systems like the CAPS have important implications for the development of regularities in psychological functioning (Shoda and Smith

2004). One notable property of dynamic networks is the emergence of distinctive sets of activation patterns into which the network settles over time (Hopfield 1982). Called *attractor states*, these stable patterns are analogous to the shapes that straw hats can snap into. These shapes represent 'stable' states because the hat takes on, and remains in, one of these shapes when it is let go after being distorted. Because component parts of the straw hat mutually support each other, the hat tends to remain in that shape (Shoda and Smith 2004). Analogously, networks often have multiple attractor states that produce distinctive reaction patterns.

To illustrate how a cognitive-affective network may be said to have attractor states, consider a mutually supporting constellation of elements. They might be considered an attractor state if, once activated, these cognitions and affects remain salient. For example, prior to an athletic event, an athlete may enter a facilitative state by thinking about a recent outstanding performance, which may in turn reactivate elements of the psychological state she was in at the time. This may in turn help her encode the current situation as a welcome challenge likely to lead to another positive outcome, rather than a threat that can lead to potential disaster. To the extent that related cognitions and affects as well as the adaptive behaviours that they help evoke mutually activate each other, this state is likely to be sustained during the contest. Even when the athlete experiences an occasional setback, the mutually supporting cognitions and affects may help the network remain in the positive and performance-facilitating attractor state.

One other principle from neural network models deserves mention. As originally proposed by Hebb (1949), a basic neural network mechanism of learning is that the simultaneous activation of two units in a network strengthens the association between them. This principle has been used in a variety of neural network models, playing an important role in cognitive neuroscience (e.g., Rumelhart and McClelland 1986). Applied to the CAPS system, it suggests that CAPS elements that become activated simultaneously may begin to form stronger associations with one other, eventually becoming a nodal cluster of mutually activating thoughts. Once any component of this cluster of thoughts becomes activated, it may in turn activate others in such a way that it becomes very difficult to break out of the cycle of mutual activation among the component cognitions that make up the attractor state. In this manner, chronic accessibility of the network connections may increase over time. Berkowitz (1990) has applied such a model in his description of the development and functioning of chronically aggressive individuals.

Despite the chronic accessibility of specific cognitive-affective units, they are not always activated, however. Rather, their activation levels change from one time to another and from one situation to another, depending on the cues that impinge upon the person (Shoda and LeeTiernan 2002). The key to individuality (and to understanding a person) therefore lies in understanding the organization of relations among the units and in specifying how they mutually influence one another and are activated by particular aspects of the situation in which the person is behaving. The processing dynamics of the CAPS, operating in concert with the environment, produce the stable patterns of situation-behaviour relations, or behavioural signatures, illustrated earlier in Figure 27.1. The CAPS formulation thus accounts not only for stability in behaviour, but also for the variability in behaviour across situations.

Recent developments and future directions

Researchers have been replicating the existence of meaningful behavioural signatures in diverse domains, measured in a variety of ways (e.g., Andersen and Chen 2002; English and Chen in press; Cervone and Shoda 1999; Fournier, Moskowitz and Zuroff 2008; Shoda and LeeTiernan 2002; Vansteelandt and Van Mechelen 1998). Borkenau, Riemann, Spinath and Angleitner (2006) studied the role of genes and environments on person-by-situation interaction patterns. The behaviours of 168 identical and 132 fraternal twins were carefully observed and coded as each person reacted to 15 different situations, some involving social encounters and others requiring problem solving. By comparing the degree of similarity in person-by-situational behavioural profiles across the fifteen situations in the two types of twin pairs, the researchers established that about 25 per cent of the variation in behavioural profiles could be attributed to genetic factors. As in previous studies, shared environment effects were negligible. This study shows that genetic factors not only influence what people say about their personality, but how they adjust their behaviour to different situations.

Recent research has also demonstrated the feasibility and value of directly studying the CAPS network of cognitive, affective and behavioural reactions. For example, characteristic associations between situation features and cognitive and emotional reactions underlie the phenomenon of 'transference' (Andersen and Chen 2002; English and Chen in press). Implicit measures, such as the Implicit Association Test (Greenwald, McGhee and Schwartz 1998), made it possible to assess the strength of automatic associations between the concept of their mother or current romantic partner and positive reactions (Zayas and Shoda 2005). This led to a discovery that when secure individuals think about their mother, for example, the result is an automatic activation of positive reactions. Positive automatic reactions also result when insecure individuals think about their mother, but the magnitude of such reactions are significantly weaker.

New methods are also being developed for the analysis of psychological features of situations, and identifying individuals' behavioural signatures with regard to such features. In a 'top-down' approach, past research and theory are used to identify candidate features of situations that are likely to influence a given behaviour. For example, in a study examining the commonly held belief that women who have been the victim of psychological abuse in the past are more likely to prefer an abusive dating partner in the future, situation features were identified *a priori* using existing research on the characteristics associated with victimized women and abusive men (Zayas and Shoda 2007).

Even in well developed research areas, however, it is possible that not all the relevant psychological features affecting behaviour have been identified. Thus, for some research questions, it may be useful to utilize bottom-up approaches in which psychologically active features of situations are identified based on responses provided from participants rather than from existing theory and research. For example, Whitsett (described in Zayas, Whitsett, Lee *et al.* in press) asked: what are the features of situations that influence the perception that a given person needs help? Past research has shown that it is not simply a matter of hearing the person say 'I need help'. It turns out that subtle non-verbal behaviours such as eye gaze or vocal intonation play a key role. These features were identified by first querying potential support providers to develop a large pool of potentially important features, mentioned by at least some individuals. The effect of these features on willingness to provide help to a stranger were then systematically tested by analysing the responses of a new group of participants to these features, using a multilevel modelling approach. In future research, methods like this will be needed to determine the 'active ingredients' of the psychological situation and to thereby assess how situational, cognitive, affective and behavioural factors interact with one another in producing both the behavioural consistency *and* variability that reside in personality.

References

Andersen, S. M. and Chen, S. 2002. The relational self: an interpersonal social-cognitive theory, *Psychological Review* 109: 619–45

Arnold, M. B. 1960. *Emotion and personality*. New York: Columbia University Press

Atkinson, J. W. 1964. *An introduction to motivation*. Princeton, NJ: Van Nostrand

Baldwin, M. W. 1999. Relational schemas: research into social-cognitive aspects of interpersonal experience, in D. Cervone and Y. Shoda (eds.), *The choherence of personality: social-cognitive bases of consistency, variability, and organization*, pp. 127–54. New York: Guilford Press

Bandura, A. 1986. *Social foundations of thought and action: a social cognitive theory*. Englewood Cliffs, NJ: Prentice-Hall

    1997. *Self-efficacy: the exercise of control*. New York: Freeman

Bem, D. J. and Allen, A. 1974. On predicting some of the people some of the time: the search for cross-situational consistencies in behaviour, *Psychological Review* 81: 506–20

Berkowitz, L. 1990. On the formation and regulation of anger and aggression, *American Psychologist* 45: 494–503

Bolles, R. C. 1972. Reinforcement, expectancy, and learning, *Psychological Review* 79: 394–409

Borkenau, P., Riemann, R., Spinath, F. M. and Angleitner, A. 2006. Genetic and environmental influences on person x situation profiles, *Journal of Personality* 74: 1451–80

Brehm, J. W. and Self, E. A. 1989. The intensity of motivation, *Annual Review of Psychology* 40: 109–31

Brewer, B. W, Van Raalte, J. L and Linder, D. E. 1993. Athletic identity: Hercules' muscles or Achilles heel?, *International Journal of Sport Psychology* 24: 237–54

Cervone, D. and Shoda, Y. 1999. Social cognitive theories and the coherence of personality, in D. Cervone and Y. Shoba (eds.), *The coherence of personality: social-cognitive bases of consistency, variability, and organization*, pp. 3–33. New York: Guilford Press

Downey, G. and Feldman, S. I. 1996. Implications of rejection sensitivity for intimate relationships, *Journal of Personality and Social Psychology* 70: 1327–43

English, T. and Chen, S. 2007. Culture and self-concept stability: consistency across and within contexts among Asian- and European-Americans, *Journal of Personality and Social Psychology* 93: 478–90

Epstein, S. 1983. Aggregation and beyond: some basic issues on the prediction of behaviour, *Journal of Personality* 51: 360–92

Fleeson, W. 2004. Moving personality beyond the person-situation debate: the challenge and the opportunity of within-person variation, *Current Directions in Psychological Science* 13: 83–7

Forgas, J. P. 1995. Mood and judgment: the affect-infusion model (AIM), *Psychological Bulletin* 117: 39–66

Fournier, M. A., Moskowitz, D. S. and Zuroff, D. C. 2008. Integrating dispositions, signatures, and the interpersonal domain, *Journal of Personality and Social Psychology* 94: 531–45

Gollwitzer, P. M. and Bargh, J. A. (eds.) 1996. *The psychology of action: linking motivation and cognition to behaviour.* New York: Guilford Press

Greenwald, A. G., McGhee, D. E. and Schwartz, J. L. K. 1998. Measuring individual differences in implicit cognition, *Journal of Personality and Social Psychology* 7: 1464–80

Hartshorne, H. and May, A. 1928. *Studies in the nature of character, vol. 1, Studies in deceit.* New York: Macmillan

Hebb, D. O. 1949. *The organization of behavior.* New York: Wiley

Higgins, E. T. 1990. Personality, social psychology, and person-situation relations: standards and knowledge activation as a common language, in L. A. Pervin (ed.), *Handbook of personality: theory and research*, pp. 301–38. New York: Guilford Press

Hopfield, J. J. 1982. Neural networks and physical systems with emergent collective computational abilities, *Proceedings of the National Academy of Sciences* 79: 2554–8

Ilies, R., Scott, B. A. and Judge, T. A. 2006. The interactive effects of personal traits and experienced states on intraindividual patterns of citizenship behaviour, *Academy of Management Journal* 49: 561–75

Jones, G. and Swain, A. B. J. 1992. Intensity and direction dimensions of competitive state anxiety and relationships with competitiveness, *Perceptual and Motor Skills* 74: 467–72

Kenrick, D. T. and Funder, D. C. 1988. Profiting from controversy: lessons from the person-situation debate, *American Psychologist* 43: 23–34

Lazarus, R. S. 1991. *Emotion and adaptation.* New York: Oxford University Press

Lazarus, R. S. and Folkman, S. 1984. *Stress, appraisal, and coping.* New York: Springer

Meichenbaum, D. 1985. *Stress inoculation training.* New York: Pergamon

Mischel, W. 1968. *Personality and assessment*. New York: Wiley

    1973. Toward a cognitive social learning reconceptualization of personality, *Psychological Review* 80: 252–83

Mischel, W. and Peake, P. K. 1982. Beyond déjà vu in the search for cross-situational consistency, *Psychological Review* 89: 730–55

Mischel, W. and Shoda, Y. 1995. A cognitive-affective system theory of personality: reconceptualizing situations, dispositions, dynamics, and invariance in personality structure, *Psychological Review* 102: 246–68

Newcomb, T. M. 1929. *Consistency of certain extrovert-introvert behaviour patterns in 51 problem boys*. New York: Columbia University, Teachers College, Bureau of Publications

Peterson, D. R. 1968. *The clinical study of social behaviour*. New York: Appleton

Pines, A. M. and Aronson, E. 1981. *Burnout: from tedium to personal growth*. New York: Free Press

Read, S. J. and Miller, L. C. (eds.) 1998. *Connectionist and PDP models of social reasoning and social behaviour*. Hillsdale, NJ: Erlbaum

Rotter, J. B. 1966. Generalized expectancies for internal versus external locus of control of reinforcement, *Psychological Monographs: General and Applied* 80: 1–28

Rumelhart, D.E. and McClelland, J.L. 1986. *Parallel distributed processing: explorations in the microstructure of cognition*, vols. I and II. Cambridge, MA: MIT Press

Schachter, S. 1966. The interaction of cognitive and physiological determinants of emotional state, in C. D. Spielberger (ed.), *Anxiety and behaviour*, pp. 193–224. New York: Academic Press

Shoda, Y. and LeeTiernan, S. 2002. What remains invariant?: finding order within a person's thoughts, feelings, and behaviours across situations, in D. Cervone and W. Mischel, *Advances in personality science*, pp. 241–70. New York: Guilford Press

Shoda, Y. and Mischel, W. 1998. Personality as a stable cognitive-affective activation network: characteristic patterns of behaviour variation emerge from a stable personality structure, in S. J. Read and L. C. Miller (eds.), *Connectionist and PDP models of social reasoning and social behaviour*, pp. 175–208. Hillsdale, NJ: Erlbaum

Shoda, Y., Mischel, W. and Wright, J. C. 1994. Intra-individual stability in the organization and patterning of behaviour: incorporating psychological situations into the idiographic analysis of personality, *Journal of Personality and Social Psychology* 67: 674–87

Shoda, Y. and Smith, R. E. 2004. Conceptualizing personality as a cognitive-affective processing system: a framework for models of maladaptive behaviour patterns and change, *Behaviour Therapy* 35: 147–65

Shweder, R. A. 1975. How relevant is an individual difference theory of personality?, *Journal of Personality* 43: 455–85

Smith, R. E. 1984. Theoretical and treatment approaches to anxiety reduction, in J. M. Silva and R. S. Weinberg (eds.), *Psychological foundations of sport*. Champaign, IL: Human Kinetics

    1986. Toward a cognitive-affective model of athletic burnout, *Journal of Sport Psychology* 8: 36–50

2006. Understanding sport behavior: a cognitive-affective processing systems approach, *Journal of Applied Sport Psychology* 18: 1–27

Smith, R. E., Shoda, Y. Cumming, S. P. and Smoll, F. L. in press. Behavioral signatures at the ballpark: intraindividual consistency of adults' situation-behavior patterns and their interpersonal consequences, *Journal of Research in Personality*

Steptoe, A. 2001. Negative emotions in music making: the problem of performance anxiety, in P. N. Juslin and J. A. Sloboda (eds.), *Music and emotion: theory and research*, pp. 291–307. New York: Oxford University Press

Tolman, E. C. 1932. *Purposive behaviour in animals and men.* New York: Century

Vansteelandt, K. and Van Mechelen, I. 1998. Individual differences in situation-behavior profiles: a triple typology model, *Journal of Personality and Social Psychology* 75: 751–65

Zayas, V. and Shoda, Y. 2005. Do automatic reactions elicited by thoughts of romantic partner, mother, and self relate to adult romantic attachment?, *Personality and Social Psychology Bulletin* 31: 1011–25

2007. Predicting preferences for dating partners from past experiences of psychological abuse: identifying the psychological ingredients' of situations?, *Personality and Social Psychology Bulletin* 33: 123–38

Zayas, V., Whitsett, D., Lee, J., Wilson, N. and Shoda, Y. 2008. From situation assessment to personality: building a social-cognitive model of a person, in G. Boyle, G. Matthews and D. Saklofske (eds.), *Handbook of personality theory and testing: personality theories and models*, pp. 377–401. London: Sage

PART VI

Social and Cultural Processes

28 The storied construction of personality

Avril Thorne and Vickie Nam

In the last twenty years, the notion that people tell stories to manage and make sense of their lives has permeated much of psychology. The basic premise of narrative psychology is that human beings are natural story-tellers, and that stories transmit and create an evolving sense of self within local and larger cultural systems of meaning (Bruner 1990; McAdams 1985). This chapter reviews narrative work that informs understanding of how a distinctive sense of self, or personality, develops through storying everyday and momentous life experiences.

To narrative psychologists, stories are something that people make, rather than something that people have (McAdams 1995). Just as stories are psychosocial constructions, so, too, is personality, which is a joint production of individuals and their communities. People primarily story their lives not in pursuit of objective truth, but to make subjective and intersubjective sense of who they are, where they have been, and where they are going. Throughout this storying process, which begins in early childhood and lasts a lifetime, personal narratives are shared with family members and friends, who may affirm or contest the contours of the story and its meaning (Bamberg and Andrews 2004; Pasupathi 2001; Thorne 2000).

Current work in narrative psychology addresses many kinds of stories, moving from the early memories favoured by Adler (1927), to richly elaborated and momentous high points, low points and turning points, extended life stories that connect memorable episodes across the lifespan, and stories about everyday troubles and transgressions. Stories and the story-telling process have been captured with interviews, open-ended questionnaires, and naturalistic and quasi-experimental observations. The commonality across these methods is that informants story their experience in their own words, with personal narratives. A number of nuanced coding systems have been developed to capture the content and structure of stories, as well as patterns of participation in story-telling. Unless otherwise indicated, participants in the studies cited in this chapter primarily have been of European-American descent; notable exceptions include studies by Peggy Miller (e.g., Miller 1994) and Qi Wang (e.g., Wang and Fivush 2005), which involve cross-cultural comparisons, and Dan McAdams' studies of Americans' life stories, which are ethnically diverse (McAdams 2006).

Previous drafts of this chapter benefited from feedback from the Narrative Research and Identity Group at the University of California, Santa Cruz, and from Margarita Azmitia, Phillip Hammack, Dan McAdams, Kate McLean, Peggy Miller and Monisha Pasupathi.

Narrative research that informs understanding of personality development has either focused on story-telling episodes in particular social contexts, or on the content and structure of stories per se. This review begins with literature on *story-telling*, which centres on when, why and how story-telling occurs in everyday settings. Much of this work reveals how mothers in particular cultural communities use stories to teach children how to manage negative emotional experiences, to develop a sense of self that extends across time, and to develop a culturally appropriate sense of self-regard. The second corpus of research, studies of stories per se, or *the story told*, centres on the content and structure of stories apart from the discursive context in which the stories emerge. This latter body of work, which is much more visible in current personality psychology, has focused on how adolescents and adults represent, make meaning of, and draw connections across momentous life experiences. In reviewing each strand of narrative research, we summarize major theories, methods and findings, and suggest directions for future research. We then consider the problem of how to conceptualize the relationship between personal story-telling and personality traits. The chapter concludes with a discussion of how narrative research can bring greater coherence to the larger field of personality psychology.

Storytelling

Theoretical frameworks

Most studies of the story-telling process have focused on how stories are used to socialize a child's sense of self. This work draws from a number of disciplines in the social sciences, including symbolic interactionism in sociology, the pragmatic movement in linguistics, and social practice theories in developmental and cultural psychology. Early symbolic interactionists emphasized that the self is socially constructed through the appraisals of others, and that self-knowledge develops from social interactions, as children initially imitate and gradually learn to take the perspective of others (Mead 1934). Everyday conversation became a focal point with the emergence of the pragmatic movement in linguistics; socio-linguists emphasize that words have an illocutionary force that can make people do things, and that conversations are partly regulated by social norms that dictate, for example, who gets to talk (Austin 1962; Hymes 1974).

Current studies of story-telling also incorporate social practice theories, which have increasingly been used to explain the social and cultural origins of a sense of self and are thereby more pertinent to personality development (e.g., Miller 1994; Shweder, Goodnow, Hatano *et al*. 1998). These theories emphasize that certain kinds of personhood come to be emphasized through participation in everyday practices such as story-telling, which convey local and larger systems of meaning. The concept of a multiplicity of cultural narratives on which individuals draw to affirm or contest the meaning of memorable experiences provides a dynamic and complex field for narrative psychology (Bruner 1990; Rosenwald and Ochberg 1992). In short, current work in this approach emphasizes that the opinions of others not only are incorporated, in concert with early symbolic interactionists, but also are potentially resisted or transformed in the process of sharing stories.

Methods

Observational studies, sometimes natural, sometimes quasi-experimental, have been the most common method for studying the story-telling process (e.g., Miller 1994; Fivush, Haden and Reese 2006; Pasupathi and Rich 2005; Thorne, Korobov and Morgan 2007). Episodes of telling memories to others can also be memorable, as shown in the facility with which individuals can provide retrospective accounts of such episodes (Thorne and McLean 2003; McLean 2005). In addition, experience sampling, or beeper studies, have been used to capture the topography of everyday engagement in social reminiscence (McLean and Pasupathi 2006). In many of these studies, story-telling has been elicited by the researchers. Observations of naturally occurring story-telling have relied on the classic work of Labov and Waletzky (1967) to identify what counts as a story, and the work of Ochs and Capps (2001) has been useful in capturing co-participation in storytelling. Coding systems have focused on how speakers jointly contribute to elaborating the emotional quality and meaning of shared or non-shared, often emotionally negative or transgressive, past experiences. For example, Fivush, Haden and Reese (2006) asked mothers to help their children narrate a recent sad experience, and Miller, Wiley, Fung and Liang (1997) observed how mothers narratively managed young children's misconduct, such as scribbling on the wall. Of particular interest is how listeners help to elicit and make meaning of salient experiences, including how the experience is emotionally labelled, and elaborated with regard to causes and consequences.

Major findings

Ubiquity of natural story-telling

Observations of spontaneous story-telling in home and laboratory settings have found that story-telling is ubiquitous. For example, stories told around children in South Baltimore, Maryland, were found to occur at an average rate of 8.5 stories per hour (Miller 1994). Observations of family dinner table conversations and of conversations between college-age friends have found that stories about the past were told at an average rate of at least once every five minutes (Bohanek, Marin, Fivush and Duke 2006; Thorne, Korobov and Morgan 2007).

Socializing the child's sense of self

Story-telling has not only been found to be ubiquitous, but to be critical for the development of an understanding of self and others (e.g., Fivush and Nelson

2006). Stories first emerge once a child begins to talk, and early story-telling is usually guided by parents or other cultural experts who informally teach the child what kind of events are worth storying, and the emotions that are appropriate to label the experience. The parent's label does not always match the child's label, particularly for negative emotional events (e.g., Levine, Stein and Liwag 1999), a difference that contributes to understanding that self and others can have unique perspectives about past events (Fivush and Nelson 2006).

A number of studies have found that parent-child talk about the meaning of *negative* past events is particularly important for the child's developing sense of self. Young children have been found to be more likely than their mothers to remember and to want to share negative emotional experiences (Burger and Miller 1999). Maternal talk about negative emotional experiences is particularly likely to reference causes and consequences (Lagattuta and Wellman 2002), thereby scaffolding a temporally extended sense of self (Fivush, Berlin, Sales *et al.* 2003). Furthermore, talking with five-year-old children about the causes and resolution of their sadness has been found to be associated with greater consistency in children's self-concepts. Such findings suggest that explaining and resolving negative emotional experience helps the child to establish the personal meaning of the events and to incorporate the events into a coherent autobiography (Bird and Reese 2006). A somewhat similar finding emerged in a longitudinal study of nine- to eleven-year-old children, except that explanatory talk about negative emotions was associated with higher self-esteem (Bohanek, Marin, Fivush and Duke 2006).

Parental story-telling style and the child's attachment and temperament

A highly elaborative parental style, which involves active questioning, evaluations and support for the child's perspective, has been found to be more prevalent with children who are securely attached (see Fivush, Haden and Reese 2006). The child's temperament has also been implicated in elaborative reminiscing, which is more prevalent when mothers perceive their children as 'intensely emotional, sociable, moderately active, and focused;' these attributes perhaps signal to the parent that the child is interested in reminiscing (Fivush, Berlin, Sales *et al.* 2006, p. 1573). Studies of European-American families have found that as parents become more narratively elaborative, so do their children, a finding that has been obtained in natural observations of families across time, and in experimental studies of maternal interventions (cf. McLean, Pasupathi and Pals 2007).

Cultural differences in story-telling with children

Cross-cultural studies have found that parent-child reminiscence tends to be occasioned differently depending on the cultural community, and to serve different purposes in the socialization of young children. Miller, Fung, and colleagues found that Taiwanese families were much more likely than their Euro-American counterparts to tell stories in which they cast young children as trangressors in past events, using stories of the child's misdeeds didactically, to teach proper conduct (e.g., Miller, Fung and Mintz 1996; Miller, Wiley, Fung and Liang 1997; see also Wang and Fivush 2005). The Euro-American families, in contrast, enacted a self-favourability bias when co-narrating stories with young children, using stories as a medium for entertaining and affirming the child's self-esteem. These differences tend to reflect Confucian and Western values, respectively.

Social class and gender differences in story-telling

Story-telling practices in the United States have been found to vary by social class and gender. Working class mothers have been found to challenge their children's stories more so than middle class mothers, a finding that appears to reflect differential strategies for fostering a child's autonomy (Heath 1983). Stories about negative emotional experiences have been found to be key sites for the socialization of gender differences. Whereas mothers have been found to encourage little girls to emotionally elaborate experiences of sadness, little boys were encouraged to solve the problem and move on (e.g., Fivush, Brotman, Buckner and Goodman 2000). Similar gender differences were found in how college students narrated self-defining memories about distressing life experiences (Thorne and McLean 2003), suggesting that early gender socialization experiences may be carried into later life.

Implications of mother-child co-reminiscence for child personality

To summarize, many studies of story-telling have focused on how mothers use stories to teach young children how to manage negative emotional experiences. Co-reminiscing with children about negative emotional experiences can scaffold a unique and temporally extended sense of self. The degree to which mothers help children elaborate their emotional experience has been found to be associated with the temperament of the child, the security of the child's attachment, and the child's self-esteem. Notable gaps in this literature are that the contributions of the mother's personality have not been studied, and that fathers are nearly absent in this research.

Story-telling and personality development in adolescence and adulthood

To date, very few studies have addressed how the story-telling process informs and is informed by personality in adolescence and early adulthood (Pasupathi 2001; Thorne 2000), the era in which who one is and where one belongs becomes a salient concern (Erikson 1963). During this era, youth increasingly encounter new reference groups, and seek to establish intimate relationships with peers (e.g., Youniss and Smollar 1985). Although contextualized studies of personal story-telling during adolescence and early adulthood are sparse, peers clearly play an increasingly large role in this process (McLean 2005). Early and mid-adolescents tend to be particularly concerned with the opinions of peers, a concern that can create a feeling of harbouring multiple selves or a 'false self' (Harter 1999). For example, young adolescent girls sometimes mask their intelligence with boys so that they will feel attractive. A feeling of false self has been found to be especially salient for adolescents who experience low social support, suggesting the importance of providing opportunities for adolescents to voice their 'true self' in a secure and accepting environment (Harter 1999). Although story-telling has not been a focus of personality research with early and mid-adolescents, stories told by this age group may be especially likely to 'play' to the audience.

A study of retrospective accounts of memorable episodes of self-defining memory telling suggests that adolescents actively shop for listeners who will be sympathetic to their stories, sometimes repeatedly telling a traumatic life experience until a satisfactory peer response is found (Thorne and McLean 2003). The personal meaning of dating and romantic relationships has also been found to be contoured by story-telling between friends. A study of spontaneous stories in conversations between male college-age friends found that story-tellers, with appreciable help from the friend, oscillated between positioning themselves as wanting to be in love, and not wanting to surrender a sovereign sense of self (Korobov and Thorne 2006). Alternately positioning oneself toward and away from romantic relationships may help young adults to decide what they do and do not want in a love relationship.

Recent studies of youth whose communities are rife with socio-cultural conflict are beginning to reveal diverse patterns of managing ideological discord (e.g., Hammack 2006; Schachter 2004). For example, life story interviews with Jewish modern Orthodox youth found that personal identity conflicts arose from the friction between modern sexual values and Orthodox religious values (Schachter 2004). Young men's narratives about how they managed this conflict revealed that some youth suppressed the ideological conflict between their worlds, whereas others synthesized it, compartmentalized it, or experienced a 'thrill of dissonance' between their worlds. Although this conflict management was primarily studied as a psychological process, it would also be interesting to explore how this conflict was socially managed, for example, by suppressing or amending particular stories with particular reference groups (Thorne 2004).

Challenge for research on story-telling

To date, studies of story-telling in context primarily have focused on how mothers in particular cultural communities socialize the child's sense of self. Given the greater cognitive capacities and life experience of adolescents and adults, an important challenge for this literature is to incorporate how particular past experiences become psychologically connected. This phenomenon has been a central focus of studies of the life story, or the story told.

The life story, or the story told

Theoretical framework

Tomkins' script theory (1979) arguably marks the point at which the metaphor of the person as playwright entered modern-day personality psychology. In this approach, storying personal experience is a life-long individual project, akin to perpetually working on an autobiography in an effort to synthesize and make meaning of one's life. This integrative function is the focus of McAdams' theory of the life story (1985, 1995, 2001). Notably, McAdams introduced the life story in 1985, the historical era in which the Big Five personality traits were on the ascendance in personality psychology (e.g., Costa and McCrae 1985). McAdams construed the life story as a special domain of personality, conceptually separable from that of impersonal, biogenetic traits, and instilling individual lives with a sense of personal integration and meaning. Such meaning making draws heavily from cultural repertoires (McAdams and Pals 2006), but the ultimate interest is in the individual person, who creates an internalized, evolving story to fit the unique configuration of his or her life. McAdams posited that individuals begin to story their lives in earnest in late adolescence and emerging adulthood, and that this personal project optimally imbues individual lives with an increasing sense of unity and purpose. Historically, the life story approach returns personality psychology to its original calling, in which individual lives rather than traits were regarded as the basic unit of personality (Allport 1937; Murray 1938).

Studies of life stories uniquely appreciate the complexity of an individual life, and the importance of understanding how individuals account for life's contradictions and challenges. Although meaning is partially in the eye of the beholder, meaning is also assumed to draw from dominant cultural narratives, which dictate what counts as a good story. In reviewing the broad outlines of this large body of work, which focuses on stories apart from the immediate discursive contexts in which they are told, we suggest how key research findings could be embedded in everyday life by incorporating the contributions of listeners. In this way, we hope to contribute to the convergence of the two major strands of narrative personality research, studies of story-telling, and the story told.

Methods

Distinguishing most studies of the story told is a focus on momentous events, which are usually older than the recent events that tend to be the stuff of everyday conversations (Thorne, Koborov and Morgan 2007). Life stories have usually been elicited with semi-structured interviews or open-ended questionnaires, and samples have usually ranged in age from late adolescence to middle age. Because the extended life story is bulky, researchers have tended to elicit particular kinds of personal memories, such as earliest memories, high points, low points, turning points, and, more generally, self-defining memories (e.g., McAdams, Bauer, Sakeda 2006; Singer and Salovey 1993). These momentous memories are assumed to be important building blocks for the extended life story.

Personal memory narratives can be very complex and nuanced representations, rich with ideological settings, characters, intentions, plots, emotional tones and meanings. To capture this variation, narrative researchers have developed and validated a number of elaborate coding systems. These coding systems articulate particular kinds of motivational themes (e.g., needs for agency, communion or generativity), emotional tone (positive or negative), structural complexity (e.g., evidence of multiple or contradictory points of view), and references to meaning (e.g., having gained insight or personal growth) (e.g., Josselson and Lieblich 1993; King 2003; McAdams, Bauer, Sakeda *et al.* 2006; McLean 2005; Singer and Salovey 1993; Thorne and Michaelieu 1996; Woike, Gersekovich, Piorkowski and Polo 1999).

Major findings

Continuity in the life story

Evidence of continuity in the life story has been found in several longitudinal studies of late adolescents and young adults (McAdams, Bauer, Sakeda *et al.* 2006; Thorne, Cutting and Skaw 1998). These studies used interviews or open-ended questionnaires to elicit collections of self-salient memories across periods ranging from three months to three years. Two sources of continuity were examined, which we will refer to as 'event specific' and 'schematic'. *Event specific continuity* accrues from the repeated telling of the same event at different points in time. In both longitudinal studies, relatively few events were found to be repeatedly told, perhaps reflecting the large store of autobiographical memories that have been found for adolescents and young adults (Rubin, Rahhal and Poon 1998). Future research might explore how the social sharing of the same memory across time is implicated in personality development. For example, particular stories may tend to be repeated to particular audiences, such as a father who has told the same hell-raising story so many times that his children know the story by heart. Repeated telling of the same event may enhance the personality continuity of the father, and such boastful rebellion may be emulated or repudiated by his children.

Studies of *schematic continuity* concern stability across time in particular narrative features that are apparent across a collection of memories. Schematic continuity is not carried by a particular event, but is a more general continuity, such as a consistent emotional tone. In McAdams' three-year study, the narrative feature that showed the most impressive continuity was structural complexity, e.g., the incorporation of multiple or contradictory points of view. The magnitude of continuities for two other narrative features, emotional tone and need for agency, was not far behind (McAdams, Bauer, Sakeda *et al.* 2006). Future research might examine how schematic continuity is received by family members and friends, who may remark upon chronic story tones, such as ambivalent or negative themes. Schematic continuity that burdens listeners, such as perpetually depressing story-lines, has been found to drive the audience away and to thereby enhance the isolation of the story-teller (Coyne 1976).

Growth in connections across the events of one's life

Although individuals tend to story memorable life experiences in somewhat idiosyncratic ways, such as by emphasizing positive or negative emotions, the ultimate purpose of the life story is to integrate the jumble of experiences that constitute a life. This synthesis entails drawing connections across events, for example, by attributing one's becoming a hospice worker to repudiating the stoicism that one's father showed in the face of death. The capacity to draw connections across episodes of one's past and to draw meaning from difficult life experiences has been found to develop notably from early adolescence to middle age (e.g., Bauer, McAdams and Sakaeda 2005; Bluck and Glueck 2004; Habermas and Bluck 2000; Pasupathi and Mansour 2006), suggesting that the construction of an integrative life story is a long-term project. Future research could attend to how valued listeners participate in helping the teller to connect, and/or perhaps disconnect, particular life experiences.

Negative life events, meaning making and personality

Across all ages, difficult life events have been found to be particularly fertile ground for explicit efforts at meaning-making (e.g., King 2001; McLean and Thorne 2003; McLean and Pratt 2006; Pals 2006; Singer 2004). The robustness of this finding suggests that negative life experiences are particularly important for personality development, and that the meanings that are made of difficult life experiences have important repercussions for one's sense of self. To find benefit in adversity requires acknowledging the adversity and shifting one's goals (e.g., Pals 2006). Personal growth, or positive meaning making, refers to stepping back from a difficult life event, such as divorce, to explicitly reflect on how the event improved one's sense of self or relationships with others.

How adults make meaning of negative life experiences has been found to have important implications for personality more generally. A number of studies have found that adults who story difficult life experiences in positive ways, finding benefit in adversity, tend to show higher levels of wellbeing, generativity and ego-development (e.g., Bauer, McAdams and Sakaeda 2005; King and Raspin 2004; McAdams, Reynolds, Lewis, Patten and Bowman 2001; Pals 2006). Because much of this work is correlational, it is important to determine the nature of the relationship between particular kinds of story-telling and such indices as maturity and wellbeing.

Cultural context

The role of larger cultural meaning systems in dictating what counts as a good or healthy life story has been increasingly studied in narrative research. For example, redemption stories, which emphasize such themes as atonement, going from rags to riches, and recovery, are highly valued in American culture (McAdams 2006), as are stories that promote self-esteem (Miller, Wiley, Fung and Liang 1997). Japanese stories, on the other hand, have been found to show a more self-critical focus (Heine, Lehman, Markus and Kitayama 1999). Recent work has also found that cultural narratives are not frozen in time, but change with historical era. For example, in the United States, the cultural meanings of homosexuality and divorce have changed across generations, and these historically situated master narratives have been found to inform how individuals craft their extended life stories (Cohler and Hammack 2007; Young, Stewart and Miner-Rubino 2001).

Challenge for research on the story told

Most studies of life stories have focused on momentous memories apart from the discursive context in which the stories emerge. Although momentous stories primarily have been construed as internalized, many such stories presumably do have a social presence or force, since the large majority of emotional life experiences are told soon after their occurrence, and on multiple occasions thereafter (Rimé, Mesquita, Philippot and Boca 1991). Of particular interest for future research is how listeners contribute to constructing or reconstructing connections across particular life experiences to endow a life with meaning and purpose. We now turn to the problem of how stories, both everyday and momentous, connect to another major domain of personality, dispositions or traits.

Connecting personal stories and personality traits

For some personality psychologists, stories are primarily of interest to the extent that they inform understanding of the development of personality traits. An increasing number of studies have reported correlations between features of personal memory narratives and self-report scores on personality tests (see McLean, Pasupathi and Pals 2007). Some of the most consistent findings are that Neuroticism is moderately associated with negative affect in memory narratives, and that Openness to Experience is associated with structurally complex memory narratives (e.g., McAdams, Anyidoho, Brown *et al.* 2004; Raggatt 2006). However, in much of this work, the conceptual connections between life stories and personality traits have not been well elaborated. An important obstacle is that personality traits are conceived as biogenetic essences, while personal stories are conceived as psychosocial in origin, more embedded in culture and life experience, and more dynamically evolving across the lifespan (McAdams and Pals 2006).

The idea that human beings live in a story-shaped world is not antithetical to the notion that story-telling is constrained by biological givens. For example, extraverts and introverts have been found to differ with regard to the frequency and length of their stories, the breadth of their story-telling audience, and how they participate in co-constructing each other's stories (McLean and Pasupathi 2006; Thorne, Koborov and Morgan 2007). However, for narrative psychologists, personality dispositions are of special interest when they are invoked in a personal story in an effort to explain who one is, was, and wants to become. To date, little is known about how chronic personality attributes are invoked ('I am shy'), affirmed ('Indeed, you are') or contested ('No, you are not') in the process of storying lived experience. If traits such as sociability and reserve cry out to be named (e.g., Goldberg 1981), then stories should reference such attributes, place them in context and, perhaps, account for their personal and interpersonal meanings. Future work could profitably attend to whether and how personal stories reference and make meaning of dispositions. Much more needs to be known about the import of personality dispositions from the viewpoint of the person who owns the disposition and the people who value that person.

Conclusions and implications

Although the study of personal stories is relatively new to personality psychology, narrative research has already begun to expand the explanatory scope of the field. In the past twenty years, a number of studies have demonstrated that particular features of stories show meaningful overlap with more customary domains of personality, such as traits and motives. Stories, however, are by definition inclusive of these other domains of personality, since stories organize behaviours, needs and intentions within and across time and place. This scope suggests that life stories are uniquely equipped to bring greater coherence to the larger field of personality psychology. Personality development is not fully captured by stories, but stories are a hospitable host for organizing and negotiating the array of developments – dispositions, fears, goals, ideologies, attachments – that make us ourselves.

The purpose of combining the study of personality traits and personal stories is not to reduce lives to traits, but to understand how such relatively enduring individual differences are incorporated, managed and, possibly, transformed in the course of making meaning of one's life. Personality traits are not personal, but are nonetheless properties that particular individuals live with, and that reference groups have to deal with. In short, the development of personality is an individual and social achievement, for which story-telling is an important tool.

Overall, a convergence of the story-telling and story told approaches holds promise for illuminating how valued listeners contribute to and contest the development of an individual's life story. Negative emotional experiences are likely to be particularly fertile ground for this convergence, since difficult life experiences burden both individuals and their communities. Understanding how individuals incorporate and resist the voices of others as they progressively make meaning of their lives is an exciting challenge for personality research.

References

Adler, A. 1927. *The practice and theory of individual psychology.* New York: Harcourt Brace World

Allport, G. W. 1937. *Personality: a psychological interpretation.* New York: Holt, Rinehart and Winston

Austin, J. L. 1962. *How to do things with words.* Cambridge, MA: Harvard University Press

Bamberg, M. and Andrews, M. (eds.) 2004. *Considering counter-narratives: narrating, resisting, making sense*. Amsterdam: John Benjamins

Bauer, J. J., McAdams, D. P. and Sakaeda, A. 2005. Interpreting the good life: growth memories in the lives of mature, happy people, *Journal of Personality and Social Psychology* 88: 203–17

Bird, A. and Reese, E. 2006. Emotional reminiscing and the development of an autobiographical self, *Developmental Psychology* 42: 613–26

Bluck, S. and Glueck, J. 2004. Making things better and learning a lesson: experiencing wisdom across the lifespan, *Journal of Personality* 72: 543–72

Bohanek, J., Marin, K., Fivush, R. and Duke, M. 2006. *Family narratives and adolescent identity*. Paper presented at the Society for Research on Adolescence, San Francisco, CA, 25 March 2006

Bruner, J. S. 1990. *Acts of meaning*. Cambridge, MA: Harvard University Press

Burger, L. K. and Miller, P. J. 1999. Early talk about the past revisited: affect in working-class and middle-class children's co-narrations, *Journal of Child Language* 26: 133–62

Cohler, B. J. and Hammack, P. L. 2007. The psychological world of the gay teenager: social change, narrative, and 'normality', *Journal of Youth and Adolescence* 36: 47–59

Costa, P. T., Jr. and McCrae, R. R. 1985. *The NEO Personality Inventory*. Odessa, FL: Psychological Assessment Resources

Coyne, J. C. 1976. Toward an interactional description of depression, *Psychiatry* 39: 28–39

Erikson, E. H. 1963. *Childhood and society*, 2nd edn. New York: Norton

Fivush, R., Berlin, L., Sales, J. M., Mennuti-Washburn, J. and Cassidy, J. 2003. Functions of parent-child reminiscing across negative events, *Memory* 11: 179–92

Fivush, R., Brotman, M., Buckner, J. P. and Goodman, S. H. 2000. Gender differences in parent-child emotional narratives, *Sex Roles* 20: 675–91

Fivush, R., Haden, C. A. and Reese, E. 2006. Elaborating on elaborations: role of maternal reminiscing style in cognitive and socioemotional development, *Child Development* 77: 1568–88

Fivush, R. and Nelson, K. 2006. Parent-child reminiscing locates the self in the past, *British Journal of Developmental Psychology* 24: 235–51

Goldberg, L. R. 1981. Language and individual differences: the search for universals in personality lexicons, in L. Wheeler (ed.), *Review of personality and social psychology*, Vol. II, pp. 141–66. Beverly Hills, CA: Sage

Habermas, T. and Bluck, S. 2000. Getting a life: the emergence of the life story in adolescence, *Psychological Bulletin* 126: 248–69

Hammack, P. L. 2006. Identity, conflict, and coexistence: life stories of Israeli and Palestinian adolescents, *Journal of Adolescent Research* 21: 323–69

Harter, S. 1999. Symbolic interactionism revisited: potential liabilities for the self constructed in the crucible of interpersonal relationships, *Merrill-Palmer Quarterly* 45: 677–703

Heath, S. B. 1983. *Ways with words: language, life and work in communities and classrooms*. Cambridge University Press

Heine, S. J., Lehman, D. R., Markus, H. R. and Kitayama, S. 1999. Is there a universal need for positive self-regard?, *Psychological Review* 106: 766–94

Hymes, D. 1974. *Foundations in sociolinguistics: an ethnographic approach.* Philadelphia, PA: University of Pennsylvania Press

Josselson, R. and Lieblich, A. (eds.) 1993. *The narrative study of lives.* Thousand Oaks, CA: Sage

King, L. A. 2001. The hard road to the good life: the happy, mature person, *Journal of Humanistic Psychology* 41: 51–72

2003. Measures and meanings: the use of qualitative data in social and personality psychology, in C. Sansone, C. Morf and A. Panter (eds.), *Handbook of methods in social psychology,* pp. 173–94. New York: Sage

King, L. A. and Raspin, C. 2004. Lost and found possible selves, subjective well-being, and ego development in divorced women, *Journal of Personality* 72: 602–32

Korobov, N. and Thorne, A. 2006. Intimacy and distancing: young men's conversations about romantic relationships, *Journal of Adolescent Research* 21: 27–55

Labov, W. and Waletzky, J. 1967. Narrative analysis, in J. Helm (ed.), *Essays on the verbal and visual arts,* pp. 12–44. Seattle, WA: University of Washington Press

Lagattuta, K. H. and Wellman, H. M. 2002. Differences in early parent-child conversations about negative versus positive emotions: implications for the development of psychological understanding, *Developmental Psychology* 38: 546–80

Levine, L. J., Stein, N. L. and Liwag, M. D. 1999. Remembering children's emotions: source of concordant and discordant accounts between parents and children, *Developmental Psychology* 15: 790–801

McAdams, D. P. 1985. *Power, intimacy, and the life story: personological inquiries into identity.* New York: Guilford Press

1995. What do we know when we know a person?, *Journal of Personality* 63: 365–96

2001. The psychology of life stories, *Review of General Psychology* 5: 100–22

2006. *The redemptive self: stories Americans live by.* New York: Oxford University Press

(in press). Personal narratives and the life story, in O. John, R. Robins and L. Pervin (eds.), *Handbook of personality,* 3rd edn. NewYork: Guilford Press

McAdams, D. P., Anyidoho, N. A., Brown, C., Huang, Y. T., Kaplan, B. and Machado, M. A. 2004. Traits and stories: links between dispositional and narrative features of personality, *Journal of Personality* 72: 761–84

McAdams, D. P., Bauer, J. J., Sakeda, A. R., Anyidoho, N. A., Machado, M. A., Magrino-Failla, White, K. W. and Pals, J. L. 2006. Continuity and change in the life story: a longitudinal study of autobiographical memories in emerging adulthood, *Journal of Personality* 74: 1371–1400

McAdams, D. P. and Pals, J. 2006. A new Big Five: fundamental principles for an integrative science of personality, *American Psychologist* 61: 204–17

McAdams, D. P., Reynolds, J., Lewis, M., Patten, A. H. and Bowman, P. J. 2001. When bad things turn good and good things turn bad: sequences of redemption and contamination in life narrative and their relation to psychosocial adaptation in midlife adults and in students, *Personality and Social Psychology Bulletin* 27: 474–85

McLean, K. C. 2005. Late adolescent identity development: narratives, meaning making and memory telling, *Developmental Psychology* 41: 683–91

McLean, K. C. and Pasupathi, M. 2006. Collaborative narration of the past and Extraversion, *Journal of Research in Personality* 40: 1219–31

McLean, K. C., Pasupathi, M. and Pals, J. L. 2007. Selves creating stories creating selves: a process model of narrative self-development in adolescence and adulthood, *Personality and Social Psychology Review* 11: 262–78

McLean, K. C. and Pratt, M. W. 2006. Life's little (and big) lessons: identity statuses and meaning-making in the turning point narratives of emerging adults, *Developmental Psychology* 42: 714–22

McLean, K. C. and Thorne, A. 2003. Adolescents' self-defining memories about relationships, *Developmental Psychology* 39: 635–45

Mead, G. H. 1934. *Mind, self, and society from the standpoint of a social behaviourist.* University of Chicago Press

Miller, P. J. 1994. Narrative practices: their role in socialization and self-construction, in U. Neisser and R. Fivush (eds.), *The remembering self: construction and accuracy in the self-narrative*, pp. 158–79. Cambridge University Press

Miller, P. J., Fung, H. and Mintz, J. 1996. Self-construction through narrative practices: a Chinese and American comparison of early socialization, *Ethos* 24: 1–44

Miller, P. J., Wiley, A., Fung, H. and Liang, C. H. 1997. Personal storytelling as a medium of socialization in Chinese and American families, *Child Development* 68: 557–68

Murray, H. A. 1938. *Explorations in personality.* New York: Oxford University Press

Ochs, E. and Capps, L. 2001. *Living narrative: creating lives in everyday storytelling.* Cambridge, MA: Harvard University Press

Pals, J. L. 2006. The narrative identity processing of difficult life experiences: pathways of personality development and positive self-transformation in adulthood, *Journal of Personality* 74: 2–31

Pasupathi, M. 2001. The social construction of the personal past and its implications for adult development, *Psychological Bulletin* 127: 651–72

Pasupathi, M. and Mansour, E. 2006. Adult age differences in autobiographical narratives: integrating experiences with the self, *Developmental Psychology* 42: 798–808

Pasupathi, M. and Rich, B. 2005. Inattentive listening undermines self-verification in personal storytelling, *Journal of Personality* 73: 1051–85

Raggatt, P. 2006. Putting the five-factor model in context: evidence linking Big Five traits to narrative identity, *Journal of Personality* 74: 1321–47

Rimé, B., Mesquita, B., Philippot, P. and Boca, S. 1991. Beyond the emotional event: six studies on the social sharing of emotion, *Cognition and Emotion* 5: 435–65

Rosenwald, G. C. and Ochberg, R. L., (eds.) 1992. *Storied lives: the cultural politics of self-understanding.* New Haven, CT: Yale University Press

Rubin, D. C., Rahhal, T. A. and Poon, L. W. 1998. Things learned in early adulthood are remembered best, *Memory and Cognition* 26: 3–19

Schachter, E. P. 2004. Identity configurations: a new perspective on identity formation in contemporary society, *Journal of Personality* 72: 167–200

Shweder, R. A., Goodnow, J., Hatano, G., LeVine, R., Markus, H. and Miller, P. J. 1998. The cultural psychology of development: one mind, many mentalities, in W. Damon (ed.), *The handbook of child psychology*, pp. 865–937. New York: Wiley

Singer, J. A. 2004. Narrative identity and meaning making across the adult lifespan: an introduction, *Journal of Personality* 72: 437–59

Singer, J. A. and Salovey, P. 1993. *The remembered self.* New York: Free Press

Thorne, A. 2000. Personal memory telling and personality development, *Personality and Social Psychology Review* 4: 45–56

2004. Putting the person into social identity, *Human Development* 47: 1–5

Thorne, A., Cutting, L. and Skaw, D. 1998. Young adults' relationship memories and the life story: examples or essential landmarks?, *Narrative Inquiry* 8: 237–68

Thorne, A., Korobov, N. and Morgan, E. M. 2007. Channeling identity: a study of story-telling in conversations of introverted and extraverted friends, *Journal of Research in Personality* 41: 1008–31

Thorne, A. and McLean, K. C. 2003. Telling traumatic events in adolescence: a study of master narrative positioning, in R. Fivush and C. Haden (eds.), *Connecting culture and memory: the development of an autobiographical self*, pp. 169–85. Mahwah, NJ: Erlbaum

Thorne, A. and Michaelieu, Q. 1996. Situating adolescent gender and self-esteem with personal memories, *Child Development* 67: 1362–78

Tomkins, S. S. 1979. Script theory, in H. E. Howe and R. A. Dienstbier (eds.), *Nebraska symposium on motivation*, vol. XXXI, pp. 201–36. Lincoln, NE: University of Nebraska Press

Wang, Q. and Fivush, R. 2005. Mother-child conversations of emotionally salient events: exploring the functions of emotional reminiscing in European-American and Chinese families, *Social Development* 14: 473–95

Woike, B. A., Gersekovich, I., Piorkowski, R. and Polo, M. 1999. The role of motives in the content and structure of autobiographical memory, *Journal of Personality and Social Psychology* 76: 600–12

Young, A. M., Stewart, A. J. and Miner-Rubino, K. 2001. Women's understandings of their own divorces: a developmental perspective, in D. P. McAdams, R. Josselson and A. Lieblich (eds.), *Turns in the road: narrative studies of lives in transition*, pp. 203–26. Washington, DC: American Psychological Association Press

Youniss, J. and Smollar, J. 1985. *Adolescent relations with mothers, fathers, and friends.* University of Chicago Press

29 Personality and social relations

Lauri A. Jensen-Campbell, Jennifer M. Knack
and Madeline Rex-Lear

The traditional study of personality focuses on the structure of personality and its origins (Allport 1937; McAdams 2001; Murphy 1932, p. 386). Possibly one of the most important reasons to examine personality, however, is to understand how it influences people's daily lives in meaningful and predictable ways. Personality can influence to whom individuals are attracted and how often they interact in social situations. Personality even influences how successful people are at getting along with other people. Indeed, social behaviour is often shaped by the dispositions of the individuals involved in the interactions (Ozer and Benet-Martínez 2006). Conversely, social relationships can also have a profound effect on personality (e.g., Robins, Caspi and Moffitt 2002).

This chapter will examine personality's influence on social relations. First, we will begin by examining the direct effect of personality on social relations across a range of interpersonal relationships that occur during the lifespan. Secondly, we will focus on how personality not only influences social relations, but how social relations also can shape personality. Thirdly, we will discuss how personality and social relations may be influenced by the broader cultural context within which these relations occur. We will conclude by discussing newer methodologies that allow researchers to study both personality and social relationship effects simultaneously.

The personality dimensions presented in this chapter are not meant to be exhaustive but instead are offered as examples when considering the association between personality and social relations across the lifetime. We should also note that we will use the terms *temperament* and *personality* somewhat interchangeably. Temperament is often defined as constitutionally based individual differences in both reactivity and self-control that are early-appearing; temperament is also believed to be the biological core of personality (e.g., Rothbart and Bates 2006). Personality, on the other hand, has been defined as 'an individual's characteristic pattern of thought, emotion, and behaviour' (Funder 1997, p. 1). Given that both definitions focus on characteristic patterns of responding, there is considerable overlap in these two constructs when attempting to understand how these differences influence social relations across the lifespan.

Personality's influence on social relations across the lifespan

Establishing and maintaining social relationships with others are some of the most important tasks an individual faces (Baumeister and Leary 1995). Although the interpersonal dynamics of a relationship are important in understanding how it is formed and maintained (e.g., Gottman 1998), the characteristics an individual brings to that relationship may be equally as important (Robins, Caspi and Moffitt 2002). For example, personality characteristics associated with socio-emotional competence (e.g., Extraversion, effortful control, empathic accuracy, Neuroticism) have been found to predict both the duration and quality of relationships across the lifespan (e.g., Asendorpf and van Aken 2003; Gleason, Jensen-Campbell and Ickes in press; Liew, Eisenberg and Reiser 2004; Shiner 2000; Spinrad, Eisenberg and Cumberland 2006).

Personality and socialization

The role of personality on social relations can be seen as early as infancy in the relationship between an infant and care-giver. For example, attachment researchers believe that a warm, receptive parenting style is crucial for developing secure attachments with an infant (De Wolff and Van Ijzendoorn 1997). The personality of the parent, however, appears to play a critical role in his/her ability to provide this warm, nurturing care-giving. A mother's Neuroticism has been associated with less positive affective ambience, her empathy is positively associated with responsive parenting, and her conscientiousness is related to consistent care-giving (Kochanska, Friesenborg, Lange and Martel 2004). The parents' personalities are only part of the story; the child's temperament also predicts the shared positive ambience with parents. Children who are higher on joy and lower on anger have higher shared positive ambience with both their mothers and their fathers (Kochanska *et al.* 2004).

Parenting involves finding ways to get children not only to be compliant with parental demands, but also to internalize societal and parental rules and beliefs as their own (e.g., Maccoby and Martin 1983). Recent models of socialization posit that the personality of both the child and parent can influence the socialization process (Belsky and Barends 2002; Lytton 1990; Putnam, Sanson and Rothbart 2002). In other words, there are multiple pathways to successful socialization that are influenced by the personality of the individuals involved (Kochanska, Aksan and Carlson 2005; Kochanska, Aksan and Joy 2007). For example, both the parent's and child's personality can influence the child's responsiveness to parental authority. Having a responsive mother is particularly important for anger-prone infants; when a mother is highly responsive, an anger-prone infant is likely to become highly cooperative over time. This is not the case for anger-prone infants who have non-responsive mothers (Kochanska, Aksan and Carlson 2005).

In addition to anger-proneness, the child's fearfulness is also an important moderator of successful internalization of parental beliefs. Hoffman (1983) proposed that when disciplining children, there is an optimal level of anxiety that promotes effective internalization. Fearful children who are harshly disciplined often experience an arousal level that far exceeds the optimal level. Such a high level of anxiety does not allow the child to process the parents' message effectively (Kochanska 1993, 1995). On the other hand, it is rare for fearless children to be aroused adequately by gentle discipline (Kochanska 1993). Increasing pressure to conform, however, often leads to anger in the fearless child which undermines effective internalization of the parental message (Hoffman 1983; Lytton 2000). Indeed, fearful children respond best to gentle discipline while fearless children respond best to alternate parenting methods that capitalize on a positive parent-child relationship (Kochanska, Aksan and Joy 2007).

Personality and childhood peer relations

Personality continues to play an important role in social relations during childhood and adolescence. As children grow older, peers and friends become increasingly important. Peers provide contexts for learning social skills, are resources of emotional and cognitive support, and can be used as practice for later relationships (Asher and Parker 1989; Hartup 1992). Personality can influence the formation and maintenance of peer relationships as well. Both Agreeableness and Extraversion have been linked to social competence in children (Asendorpf and Van Aken 2003). For example, agreeable children are more likely to employ more constructive resolution tactics (e.g., negotiation) in peer conflicts than less agreeable children are (e.g., Graziano, Jensen-Campbell and Hair 1996; Jensen-Campbell and Graziano 2001; Jensen-Campbell, Gleason, Adams and Malcolm 2003). On the other hand, low agreeable children are more likely to use power assertion (e.g., threats), which can ultimately harm or end a relationship. Disagreeable children are not only more likely to use power assertion, they are also more likely to be involved in more serious bullying behaviours (Bollmer, Harris and Milich 2006; Gleason, Jensen-Campbell and Richardson 2004). Indeed, low Agreeableness is associated with peer rejection and victimization (Newcomb, Bukowski and Pattee 1993; Jensen-Campbell, Adams, Perry *et al.* 2002).

The personality of a friend can also influence the child's social relations. For example, having an agreeable friend buffers against the negative influence of being low on Agreeableness oneself (Knack, Jacquot, Jensen-Campbell and Malcolm 2007); that is, there is no association between Agreeableness and peer acceptance when the child has a best friend who is high on Agreeableness. However, when the friend is average or low on Agreeableness, there is a significant relationship between the child's Agreeableness and peer acceptance. The lower the child is on Agreeableness, the more likely he or she is to be rejected by the larger peer group (Knack, Jacquot, Jensen-Cambell and Malcolm 2007).

These findings are not surprising given that Agreeableness is often characterized by traits such as being cooperative, friendly, considerate and helpful; and appears to be related to skills and motives that are necessary to build positive social relations with others. It may be that the best friend is able to smooth over the 'ruffled feathers' of peers when he/she is high on Agreeableness, which gives the disagreeable child a sort of buffer against being rejected by peers.

Other personality traits besides Agreeableness are equally important to interpersonal relations during childhood. As stated previously, Extraversion has been linked to social competence in children. Extraversion involves a person's general level of sociability (Elphick, Halverson and Marszal-Wisniewska 1998). Extraverted individuals are more likely to experience positive affect, which may in turn lead to smoother interpersonal relationships (Ashton, Lee and Paunonen 2002; Fleeson, Malanos and Achille 2002). Indeed, Extraversion has been associated with general peer acceptance (Jensen-Campbell, Adams, Perry *et al.* 2002; Lubbers, Van Der Werf, Kuyper and Offringa 2006).

Conscientiousness has also been found to be important for childhood peer relationships (Jensen-Campbell and Malcolm 2007). Conscientious children are less likely to be victimized and rejected than children lower in Conscientiousness. Moreover, Conscientiousness is positively related to friendship quality. Finally, the link between anger and aggression is strongest for individuals who are lower on Conscientiousness (Jensen-Campbell, Knack, Waldrip and Campbell 2007). Again, this is not surprising given that Conscientiousness reflects a person's self-control processes and enables them to maintain appropriate social behaviour that, in turn, allows for higher quality peer relationships (Jensen-Campbell and Malcolm 2007; Lamb, Chuang, Wessels *et al.* 2002; Shiner 2000).

Neuroticism, on the other hand, is associated with many social difficulties in childhood (Asendorpf and van Aken 2003; Eisenberg, Fabes, Guthrie and Reiser 2000; Eisenberg, Pidada and Liew 2001). Neurotic individuals tend to have a negative view of others which may be translated as feelings of dislike by others (Erez and Judge 2001; Watson and Clark 1984). Neurotic individuals also tend to be hypersensitive to negative events, and this hypersensitivity may lead to poorer peer relations and increased victimization (e.g., Suls, Martin and David 1998). For example, because neurotic children are more likely to experience negative emotions, they are angrier during peer conflict, are less forgiving of others, and are more likely to blame others, which increases the likelihood of being victimized by peers (Bollmer, Harris and Milich 2006).

The Neuroticism of a child's friends also appears to influence the child's peer relationships; that is, neurotic children who have an emotionally stable best friend do not differ from a low neurotic child on skills such as initiating relationships, resolving conflict and self-disclosing. However, there are significant differences between low and high neurotic children when they have a best friend who is also neurotic; that is, a neurotic child with a neurotic best friend has the lowest levels of interpersonal functioning (Knack, Rex-Lear, Bryant, Gomez and Jensen-Campbell 2007).

Personality and adult relationships

A large body of work has also established the link between personality and social relationships in adulthood, especially through the exploration of romantic relationships. Extraversion, Neuroticism, Conscientiousness and Agreeableness all appear to have major influences on adult relationship outcomes (Berry, Willingham and Thayer 2000; Karney and Bradbury 1995; Lehnart and Neyer 2006; White, Hendrick and Hendrick 2004). For example, among adults, Conscientiousness has been associated with mate desirability, relationship quality and marriage stability (Botwin, Buss and Shackelford 1997; Gattis, Berns, Simpson and Christensen 2004; Kelly and Conley 1987; Roberts and Bogg 2004; Robins, Caspi and Moffitt 2000). Extraversion has been linked to social status (Anderson, John, Keltner and Kring 2001). In addition, both Agreeableness and Conscientiousness are negatively related to a friend's annoyance with the individual; Conscientiousness and Extraversion are negatively associated with the number of conflicts in the adult friendships (Berry, Willingham and Thayer 2000).

Marital satisfaction has also been linked to Agreeableness (Donnellan, Conger and Bryan 2004) and Extraversion (Watson, Hubbard and Wiese 2000). Conversely, marital dissatisfaction is associated with Neuroticism (Donnellan, Conger and Bryan 2004; Karney and Bradbury 1995). More recently, Rehmatullah (2006) found that other relationship-relevant traits predicted marital satisfaction in a large community sample. For example, adults who are higher on social absorption or who have a partner high on social absorption have greater marital satisfaction. This result should not be surprising since social absorption involves being amenable to highly interdependent relationships, such as marriage (Ickes, Hutchison and Mashek 2004). Perhaps even more interestingly, Rehmatullah (2006) found that marriage partners tend to exhibit similar personality traits in terms of Openness to Experience, Neuroticism, sensation-seeking, psychological femininity, social absorption, social individuation, anxious attachment and socio-sexuality (see also, Houts, Robins and Huston 1996). However, there is conflicting evidence as to whether personality similarity leads to marital satisfaction (Gattis, Berns, Simpson and Christensen 2004; Luo and Klohnen 2005).

One limitation with many of the studies presented here is that they are concurrent designs, which do not allow the researchers to fully examine whether personality biases individuals toward certain types of relationships. One exception is a longitudinal study by Robins, Caspi and Moffitt (2002). They found that a personality profile of low negative emotionality, high positive emotionality and high constraint can predispose a person to become involved in relatively happy, non-abusive relationships. More specifically, negative emotionality at the age of eighteen predicted higher levels of conflict and abuse and lower levels of quality in romantic relationships three and eight years later. In addition, they found that the influence of negative emotionality on romantic relationships was quite stable.

Transactional models of personality development

To date, personality research has focused primarily on how personality influences relationship experiences. An equally important issue involves whether relationship experiences can cause changes in personality. Undeniably, personality development is a complex process integrating the individual and the social environment; we cannot ignore how social relations may influence an individual's personality. However, prior to 1990 most research focused on adult personality, ignoring the link between infant/childhood development and later adult personality and its association to social relations (Halverson 2005; Helson, Kwan, John and Jones 2002).

Dynamic interactionism

The notion that there is a co-development of personality and relationships was perpetuated by the *dynamic interactionist paradigm* (Caspi 1998; Magnusson 1990; Sameroff 1983). It is suggested that personality and the environment are relatively stable over short periods of time, such as a few weeks. However, both personality and the environment are subject to change over longer periods, such as months or years (Asendorpf and Wilpers 1998). With this in mind we can assume that these changes are influenced by both the individual's own personality and the social relations in which they are involved. For example, a dyadic relationship between spouses can be seen as a transactional or dynamic interactional relationship. The personality of the wife may influence and be influenced by the personality of the husband over time. In addition, the quality of the marital relationship can influence and be influenced by the personalities of both spouses.

Recent empirical consideration has been given to transactional models of personality and social relations (Asendorpf and Van Aken 2003; Endler and Magnusson 1976; Halverson and Wampler 1997; Neyer and Asendorpf 2001). For example, Robins, Caspi and Moffitt (2002) found that not only did antecedent personality characteristics predict social relations, but social relations also predicted changes in personality over time. When individuals were involved in romantic relationships that were maladaptive, their negative emotionality increased over time.

Sheese (2005) also studied the transactional influence of personality and social relations among college students during a fourteen-week interval. He found that there were individual changes in personality over time. In addition, increases in social support were associated with increases in each of the Big Five dimensions during the fourteen-week period. Contrary to the Sheese findings, Asendorpf and Wilpers (1998) determined in an eighteen-month longitudinal study of college age participants that overall personality affected relationships, but not vice versa. Asendorpdf and Wilpers, however, warn against generalizing beyond their data and making the automatic assumption that environmental effects do not influence an individual's personality.

A more stringent test of the transactional model may be to look at how social relations can influence personality change in middle adulthood. As late as the 1990s, it was assumed that personality was essentially fixed and unchanging by age thirty (e.g., plaster hypothesis; Costa and McCrae 1994). Recent empirical evidence suggests that personality does reliably change in middle adulthood; moreover, midlife concerns associated with social relations (e.g., work stress, social support) influence personality change (Van Aken, Denissen, Branje *et al*. 2006). For example, marital tensions and divorce predict changes in dominance and masculinity/femininity in women during early and middle adulthood (Roberts, Helson and Klohnen 2002). Although there appear to be personality-relationship transactions, Asendorpf and Van Aken (2003) found that surface characteristics (e.g., loneliness, self-concept) are more likely to be influenced by social relations than are more core personality characteristics (e.g., Extraversion, Agreeableness, Conscientiousness).

Another approach to understanding how social relations may influence personality change in adulthood is the Social Investment Theory, which attempts to understand *why* there are not only individual-level changes in personality (via interpersonal transactions), but also consistent mean-level changes in personality during adulthood. For example, adults as a group (i.e., mean level changes) become more agreeable, emotionally stable and conscientious over time (Wood and Roberts 2006). Experiences that are linked to social roles are believed to influence these mean-level changes in personality (Helson, Kwan, John and Jones 2002; Wood and Roberts 2006). For example, although there are increases in Conscientiousness and Emotional Stability in adulthood, only persons experiencing satisfying relationships show these predicted increases (Roberts, Wood and Smith 2005).

Is the link between personality and social relations influenced by the broader cultural context?

Surprisingly, few studies have examined whether the link between personality and social relations is influenced by the broader cultural context. The most important individual differences in interpersonal relationships become encoded into language across many cultures (Goldberg 1981; Hogan 1983; Wiggins 1991). However, different cultures may value different personality qualities in social relationships. From a psychological perspective, culture influences the ways people see the world and interpret it. As such, the function and significance of certain personality traits may differ by culture, which may have serious implications for how personality is associated with social relations (Chen, French and Schneider 2006). For example, the personality characteristic of responsibility appears to be influenced by the cultural climate that the person is part of; responsibility is lowest when individualism in the larger culture is at its highest (Helson, Jones and Kwan 2002).

Shyness-inhibition is also more a social liability in individualistic cultures that promote social initiative and independence. Behaviours associated with shyness-inhibition (e.g., being reserved), on the other hand, are more valued in collectivistic cultures that emphasize interpersonal harmony and interdependence among individuals (Chen, Wang and DeSouza 2006). Indeed, shy American children are more likely to be neglected by the peer group; shy American men are less likely to initiate relationships (Caspi, Elder and Bem 1988; Kerr, Lambert and Bem 1996). In China, a more collectivistic culture, shyness is associated with being more socially mature in children (Chen, Rubin and Li 1995). Shy Chinese children are also more likely to have a higher social status among peers (Chen, Li, Li, Li and Liu 2002); extraverted Chinese children, on the other hand, are often seen as having more externalizing problems by teachers (e.g., being less respectful and more aggressive; Chen, Rubin and Li 1995).

A dimension like Agreeableness may also be especially important in communal cultures (Graziano 1994). For example, Latin Americans have been found to value a disposition toward 'simpatía' in both adults and children (Marin and Marin 1991). Simpatía is assumed to be derived from an allocentric, communal sense, which emphasizes the need for smooth, pleasant relationships (Marin and Marin 1991; Triandis, Bontempo, Villareal *et al.* 1988). Some preliminary data support this notion; for individuals higher on collectivism, Agreeableness was negatively related to the advocacy of destructive conflict resolution tactics (e.g., manipulation, physical force, third party intervention and guilt). For individuals low on collectivism, there was no evidence that Agreeableness was related to the endorsement of destructive conflict tactics. A similar pattern emerged for Conscientiousness (Jensen-Campbell, Borja and Knack 2007). Future research must better examine culture's influence on the association between personality and social relationships.

Using interactional models to study the interplay between personality and social relations

Most researchers would agree that individuals do not live in a vacuum. Not only does one's personality influence social relations, but the vast array of interaction partners (e.g., romantic partners, friends, strangers, co-workers) a person comes into contact with influence the way a person thinks, feels and acts. This reciprocal or mutual influence is often termed interdependence. While interdependence is a central part of personality and social theories, it is only recently that statistical models have allowed researchers to account for instances of non-independence (e.g., Magnusson and Endler 1977; Snyder and Ickes 1985; Kenny 1988; Kelley and Thibaut 1978; Kenny, Mohr and Levesque 2001). The ability to statistically account for interdependence of scores allows researchers to more adequately account for the variance in outcome measures by considering more than the effect of the individual being studied (i.e., the actor effect). Below, we discuss two statistical models that account for interdependence, namely the social relations model and the actor-partner interdependence model. Other statistical models and research methodologies (e.g., hierarchical linear modelling, longitudinal designs and cross-lag designs) are equally important in studying the influence of personality to social relations (and vice versa), but are beyond the scope of this chapter.

Social relations model

The social relations model (SRM) is a two-way random effects statistical model which examines the interaction between personality characteristics and social relations (Kenny, Kashy and Cook 2006; Lashley and Kenny 1998). While SRM is an appropriate statistical analysis for studies with dyadic interaction partners (Kenny 1988), it is more commonly used in studies pairing a target individual with multiple individuals (Kenny, Kashy and Cook 2006). SRM treats each individual in an interaction as both a subject and an object (Malloy and Kenny 1986) with each dyadic score a function of four components: constant, actor, partner and the relationship (Kenny, Kashy and Cook 2006; Kenny 1988). The constant represents the group mean (i.e., the average group level of an outcome score) and accounts for the variation of an outcome measure as it differs between interactions.

To help illustrate, imagine a study in which the outcome measure is Agreeableness. The constant component accounts for differing levels of Agreeableness across dyadic interactions. The actor and partner components account for the individual responses of the dyadic members. For example, individuals may consistently rate people high or low on Agreeableness. The actor component accounts for the target member's outcome scores (i.e., how agreeable the target member consistently views his/her partners). It is important to note that the actor effect does not have predictive ability in the SRM. Instead, this effect estimates the amount of variability in how consistently the target member rates various interaction partners on a particular outcome (i.e., in this case, Agreeableness).

The partner component, on the other hand, accounts for whether the interaction partner is consistently rated on the outcome behaviour regardless of the dyadic partner. For example, the partner component would account for the degree that all interaction members view the partner as agreeable. The relationship effect reflects the variance in the outcome score above and beyond the individual contributions of each dyadic member (i.e., accounting for the variability in Agreeableness after parsing out the effects of the actor and the partner). The relationship component allows researchers to draw conclusions about social interactions above and beyond the typical responses, actions and personality of the two dyadic members. In sum, variability is accounted for at multiple levels including the group level (i.e., the constant components), the individual level (i.e., the actor and partner components), and the dyadic level (i.e., the relationship component).

A noted strength of the SRM is that analysis is not limited to dyadic partners (e.g., best friends, romantic partners) and can be utilized when examining groups (Kenny, Kashy and Cook 2006). A second strength of SRM is that the variance of the effects is estimated rather than estimating the actual effects (Kenny 1998; Kenny, Kashy and Cook 2006). Estimating the variance allows interpretation at the population level rather than at the individual level and/or specific interaction level. For instance, the actor effect allows researchers to examine how much of the variability in data is accounted for by the consistency of the target member's responses and/or behaviours. This ability to partial out actor effects has the potential to enhance the field's understanding of personality's role in social behaviour and relationships. SRM provides the unique ability to tease apart the variance of the effects and thus account for the unique influence of personality in social environments.

Although the SRM has many advantages, there are also important limitations that should be noted. First, the variance components are indirectly measured (Marcus and Kashy 1995). In addition, it is quite difficult to estimate effect size and power (Lashley and Kenny 1998). This difficulty lends itself to questions regarding sample size and the ideal size of the groups. Lashley and Kenny ran Monte Carlo simulations and repeatedly found that large-sized groups, rather than a large number of groups, had the highest power. Researchers are encouraged to carefully consider these important methodological components.

Marcus and Kashy (1995) point out that the SRM is not simply a new statistical method but is also a new methodological technique. As such, there are several important considerations to make. First, due to the necessity of each participant rating each relationship partner, it is possible that carry-over effects may be seen (Kenny, Mohr and Levesque 2001). Secondly, to date there is no way to account for missing data points (Marcus and Kashy 1995). Therefore if one relationship partner is lacking a complete set of data points, the entire group is in jeopardy of being thrown out. Thus, it is important for researchers to think about the feasibility of data collection and how best to answer the theoretical question at hand. While such considerations are necessary, the reader should bear in mind the theoretical advancements possible with the development of the SRM.

Actor-partner interdependence model

The actor-partner interdependence model (APIM) is an interactional model which assumes a causal direction in that the actor and partner components cause the outcome measure (Kenny, Kashy and Cook 2006; Cook and Kenny 2005). APIM treats the individual predictor scores as being nested within the dyadic unit (Cook and Kenny 2005). As such, both individual scores and dyadic level scores are estimated. Similar to SRM, APIM makes use of actor, partner and interaction components. However, these effects have a very different meaning in an APIM than in the SRM. Again consider the above example with Agreeableness (Kenny, Kashy and Cook 2006). In APIM, the actor effect assesses the degree to which a target dyadic member's agreeableness influences his/her own outcome score. The partner effect assesses the degree to which the partner's agreeableness influences the target dyadic member's outcome score. The actor effect is computed while holding any partner influence constant; the partner effect is computed while controlling for any actor effects. The reader can easily see the predictive nature of the APIM. Indeed, the model assumes a causal direction in that predictor variables cause or influence the outcome variable. A third component of APIM is the actor X partner interaction in which the joint influence of each dyadic partner on a particular measure affects the outcome measure (i.e., the effect of the target member's agreeableness X partner's agreeableness on adjustment).

The ability to estimate the partner effect is a key strength of APIM (Cook and Kenny 2005). Estimating the partner effect allows researchers to truly examine interpersonal effects by accounting for the variance of the partner's influence. Most social and personality theories acknowledge effects of interaction partners. APIM presents a statistical method to account for such interdependence. APIM can be used with both categorical and continuous data (Kenny, Kashy and Cook 2006) and can examine both the individual effects of each dyadic partner as well as the joint influence of the dyadic partners. In addition, APIM can be analysed with one of three underlying statistical methods, namely pooled regression, multilevel modelling or structural equation modelling. The reader is referred to Kenny, Kashy and Cook (2006) for details relating to each of the three statistical methods.

In summary, the SRM and APIM are both statistical methodologies that enable researchers to more fully and adequately account for the association between personality and social relations. Each model accounts for the non-independence of scores in a slightly different manner. SRM accounts for the overall variance of effects whereas APIM accounts for the predictive effect of each of the dyadic members on an outcome measure. The increased use of these two models will likely advance the depth and richness of our understanding of how personality influences social relations (and vice versa).

Concluding remarks

The findings presented in this chapter concerning the links between personality and social relations support several general conclusions. (1) Personality influences interpersonal relationships across the lifespan. (2) The influence of personality and social relations is bidirectional; that is, not only does personality influence social relations, but social relations also influence personality development. (3) The larger cultural context can influence the association between personality and social relations. Certain personality traits may be more valued in some cultures. Thus, culture may influence the display of certain personality traits and how they contribute to social relationships. (4) New methodologies are needed to better tease apart the unique contributions of personality in social relations. Both the Social Relations Model and the Actor-Partner Interdependence Model are steps in this direction.

Future research is still needed that assesses changes in personality as well as changes in social relations to better understand the causal relationships between the constructs and to better understand their stability versus mutability. In addition, research that better considers how culture and sub-cultural contexts influence the personality-social relations link is necessary. Nonetheless, the findings in this chapter provide a strong case that personality and social relationships share a symbiotic, dynamic relationship.

References

Allport, G. W. 1937. *Personality: a psychological interpretation*. New York: Henry Holt

Anderson, C., John, O. P., Keltner, D. and Kring, A. M. 2001. Who attains social status? Effects of personality and physical attractiveness in social groups, *Journal of Personality and Social Psychology* 81: 116–32

Asendorpf, J. B. and Van Aken, M. A. G. 2003. Personality-relationship transaction in adolescence: core versus surface personality characteristics, *Journal of Personality* 71: 629–66

Asendorpf, J. B. and Wilpers, S. 1998. Personality effects on social relationships, *Journal of Personality and Social Relationships* 74: 1531–44

Asher, S. R. and Parker, J. G. 1989. The significance of peer relationship problems in childhood, in B. H. Schneider, G. Attili, J. Nadel and R. P. Weissberg (eds.), *Social competence in developmental perspective*, pp. 5–23. Amsterdam: Kluwer

Ashton, M. C., Lee, K. and Paunonen, S. V. 2002. What is the central feature of extraversion? Social attention versus reward sensitivity, *Journal of Personality and Social Psychology* 83: 245–51

Baumeister, R. F. and Leary, M. R. 1995. The need to belong: desire for interpersonal attachments as a fundamental human motivation, *Psychological Bulletin* 117: 497–529

Belsky, J. and Barends, N. 2002. Personality and parenting, in M. H. Bornstein (ed.), *Handbook of parenting, vol. III, Being and becoming a parent*, 2nd edn, pp. 415–38. Mahwah, NJ: Erlbaum

Berry, D. S., Willingham, J. K. and Thayer, C. A. 2000. Affect and personality as predictors of conflict and closeness in young adults' friendships, *Journal of Research in Personality* 34: 84–107

Bollmer, J. M., Harris, M. J. and Milich, R. 2006. Reactions to bullying and peer victimization: narratives, physiological arousal, and personality, *Journal of Research in Personality* 40: 803–28

Botwin, M. D., Buss, D. M. and Shackelford, T. K. 1997. Personality and mate preferences: five factors in mate selection and marital satisfaction, *Journal of Personality* 35: 107–36

Caspi, A. 1998. Personality development across the life course, in W. Damon (Series ed.) and N. Eisenberg (Vol. ed.), *Handbook of child psychology, vol. III, Social, emotional, and personality development*, 5th edn, pp. 311–88. New York: Wiley

Caspi, A., Elder, G. H., Jr. and Bem, D. 1988. Moving away from the world: life-course patterns of shy children, *Developmental Psychology* 24: 824–31

Chen, X., French, D. C. and Schneider, B. H. 2006. *Peer relationships in cultural context*. New York: Cambridge University Press

Chen, X., Li, D., Li, Z., Li, B. and Lui, M. 2002. Sociable and prosocial dimensions of social competence in Chinese children: common and unique contributions to social, academic, and psychological adjustment, *Developmental Psychology* 36: 302–14

Chen, X., Rubin, K. and Li, B. 1995. Social and school adjustment of shy and aggressive children in China, *Developmental and Psychopathology* 7: 337–49

Chen, X., Wang, L. and DeSouza, A. 2006. Temperament, socioemotional functioning, and peer relationships in Chinese and North American Children, in X. Chen, D. C. French and B. H. Schneider (eds.), *Peer relationships in cultural context*, pp. 123–47. New York: Cambridge University Press

Cook, W. L. and Kenny, D. A. 2005. The actor-partner interdependence model: a model of bidirectional effects in development studies, *International Journal of Behavioural Development* 29: 101–9

Costa, P. T., Jr. and McCrae, R. R. 1994. Set like plaster: evidence for the stability of adult personality, in T. F. Heatherton and J. L. Weinberger (eds.), *Can personality change?*, pp. 21–40. Washington, DC: American Psychological Association

De Wolff, M. S. and Van Ijzendoorn, M. H. 1997. Sensitivity and attachment: a meta-analysis of parental antecedents of infant attachment, *Child Development* 68: 571–91

Donnellan, M. B., Conger, R. D. and Bryant, C. M. 2004. The Big Five and enduring marriages, *Journal of Research in Personality* 38: 481–504

Eisenberg, N., Fabes, R. A., Guthrie, I. K. and Reiser, M. 2000. Dispositional emotionality and regulation: their role in predicting quality of social functioning, *Journal of Personality and Social Psychology* 78: 136–57

Eisenberg, N., Pidada, S. and Liew, J. 2001. The relations of regulation and negative emotionality to Indonesian children's social functioning, *Child Development* 72: 1747–63

Elphick, E., Halverson, C. F. Jr. and Marszal-Wisniewska, M. 1998. Extraversion: toward a unifying description from infancy to adulthood, in C. F. Halverson, Jr. and G. A. Kohnstamm (eds.), *Parental descriptions of child personality: developmental antecedents of the Big Five*, pp. 21–48. Mahwah, NJ: Erlbaum

Endler, N. S. and Magnusson, D. 1976. Toward an interactional psychology of personality, *Psychological Bulletin* 83: 956–74

Erez, A. and Judge, T. A. 2001. Relationship of core self-evaluation to goal setting motivation, and performance, *Journal of Applied Psychology* 86: 1270–79

Fleeson, W., Malanos, A. B. and Achille, N. M. 2002. An intra-individual process approach to the relationship between Extraversion and positive affect: is acting extraverted as 'good' as being extraverted?, *Journal of Personality and Social Psychology* 83: 1409–22

Funder, D. C. 1997. *The personality puzzle*. New York: Norton

Gattis, K. S., Berns, S., Simpson, L. E. and Christensen, A. 2004. Birds of a feather or strange birds? Ties among personality dimensions, similarity, and marital quality, *Journal of Family Psychology* 18: 564–74

Gleason, K. A., Jensen-Campbell, L. A. and Ickes, W. in press. The role of empathic accuracy in adolescents' peer relations and adjustment, *Personality and Social Psychology Bulletin*

Gleason, K. A., Jensen-Campbell, L. A. and Richardson, D. 2004. Agreeableness and aggression in adolescence, *Aggressive Behaviour* 30: 43–61

Goldberg, L. R. 1981. Language and individual differences: the search for universals in personality lexicons, in L. Wheeler (ed.), *Review of personality and social psychology*, vol. II, pp. 141–65. Beverly Hills, CA: Sage

Gottman, J. M. 1998. Psychology and the study of the marital processes, *Annual Review of Psychology* 49: 169–97

Graziano, W. G. 1994. The development of Agreeableness as a dimension of personality, in C. F. Halverson, Jr. and G. A. Kohnstamm (eds.), *The developing structure of temperament and personality from infancy to adulthood*, pp. 339–54. Hillsdale, NJ: Erlbaum

Graziano, W. G., Jensen-Campbell, L. A. and Hair, E. C. 1996. Perceiving interpersonal conflict and reacting to it: the case for Agreeableness, *Journal of Personality and Social Psychology* 70: 820–35

Halverson, C. F. 2005. Personality in children, *Merrill-Palmer Quarterly* 51: 253–7

Halverson, C. F. Jr. and Wampler, K. S. 1997. Family influences on personality development, in R. Hogan, J. Johnson and S. Briggs (eds.), *Handbook of personality psychology*, pp. 241–67. San Diego, CA: Academic Press

Hartup, W. W. 1992. Peer relations in early and middle childhood, in V. B. Van Hasselt and M. Hersen (eds.), *Handbook of social development: a lifespan perspective*. New York: Plenum

Helson, R., Jones, C. and Kwan, V. S. Y. 2002. Personality change over 40 years of adulthood: hierarhical linear modeling analyses of two longitudinal samples, *Journal of Personality and Social Psychology* 83: 752–66

Helson, R., Kwan, V. S. Y., John, O. P. and Jones, C. 2002. The growing evidence for personality change in adulthood: findings from research with personality inventories, *Journal of Research in Personality* 36: 287–306

Hoffman, M. L. 1983. Affective and cognitive processes in moral internalization, in E. T. Higgins, D. Ruble and W. Hartup (eds.), *Social cognition and social development: a sociocultural perspective*, pp. 236–74. New York: Cambridge University Press

Hogan, R. T. 1983. A socioanalytic theory of personality, in M. Page (ed.), *Nebraska symposium on Motivation: personality – current theory and research*, pp. 58–89. Lincoln, NE: University of Nebraska Press

Houts, R. M., Robins, E. and Huston, T. 1996. Compatibility and the development of premarital relationships, *Journal of Marriage and the Family* 58: 7–20

Ickes, W., Hutchison, J. and Mashek, D. 2004. Closeness as intersubjectivity: social absorption and social individuation, in D. Mashek and A. Aron (eds.), *The handbook of closeness and intimacy*, pp. 357–73. Mahwah, NJ: Erlbaum

Jensen-Campbell, L. A., Adams, R., Perry, D., Furdella, J. Q., Workman, K. A. and Egan, S. 2002. Agreeableness, Extraversion, and peer relations in early adolescence: winning friends and deflecting aggression, *Journal of Research in Personality* 36: 224–51

Jensen-Campbell, L. A., Borja, T. and Knack, J. 2007. Culture as a moderator between personality and social behaviour. Unpublished manuscript

Jensen-Campbell, L. A., Gleason, K. A., Adams, R. and Malcolm, K. T. 2003. Interpersonal conflict, Agreeableness, and personality development, *Journal of Personality* 71: 1059–85

Jensen-Campbell, L. A. and Graziano, W. G. 2001. Agreeableness as a moderator of interpersonal conflict, *Journal of Personality* 69: 323–62

Jensen-Campbell, L. A., Knack, J. M., Waldrip, A. M. and Campbell, S. D. 2007. Do personality traits associated with self-control influence the regulation of anger and aggression?, *Journal of Research in Personality* 41: 403–24

Jensen-Campbell, L. A. and Malcolm, K. T. 2007. The importance of Conscientiousness in adolescent interpersonal relationships, *Personality and Social Psychology Bulletin* 33: 368–83

Karney, B. R. and Bradbury, T. N. 1995. The longitudinal course of marital quality and stability: a review of theory, methods and research, *Psychological Bulletin* 118: 3–34

Kelly, E. and Conley, J. 1987. Personality and compatibility: a prospective analysis of marital stability and marital satisfaction, *Journal of Personality and Social Psychology* 52: 27–40

Kelley, H. H. and Thibaut, J. W. 1978. *Interpersonal Relations*. New York: Wiley

Kenny, D. A. 1988. Interpersonal perception: a social relations analysis, *Journal of Social and Personal Relationships* 5: 247–61

1998. Social relations modeling information. http://davidakenny.net/srm/soremo. htm#Actor

Kenny, D. A., Kashy, D. A. and Cook, W. L. 2006. *Dyadic data analysis*. New York: Guilford Press

Kenny, D. A., Mohr, C. D. and Leveseque, M. J. 2001. A social relations variance partitioning of dyadic behaviour, *Psychological Bulletin* 127: 128–41

Kerr, M., Lambert, W. W. and Bem, D. J. 1996. Life course sequelae of childhood shyness in Sweden: comparison with the United States, *Developmental Psychology* 32: 1100–5

Knack, J. M., Jacquot, C., Jensen-Campbell, L. A. and Malcolm, K. T. 2007 The importance of having agreeable friends (especially when you are not). Unpublished manuscript

Knack, J. M., Rex-Lear, M., Bryant, N., Gomez. M. and Jensen-Campbell., L. A. 2007. Personality and social competence in close friendships during childhood. Paper presented at the biannual meeting of the Society of Research in Child Development, Boston, MA, March 2007

Kochanska, G. 1993. Toward a synthesis of parental socialization and child temperament in early development of conscience, *Child Development* 62: 1379–92

1995. Children's temperament, mothers' discipline, and the security of attachment: multiple pathways to emerging internalization, *Child Development* 64: 325–47

Kochanska, G. Aksan, N. and Carlson, J. J. 2005. Temperament, relationships, and young children's receptive cooperation with their parents, *Developmental Psychology* 41: 648–60

Kochanska, G., Aksan, N. and Joy, M. E. 2007. Children's fearfulness as a moderator of parenting in early socialization: two longitudinal studies, *Developmental Psychology* 43: 222–37

Kochanska, G., Friesenberg, A. E., Lange, L. A. and Martel, M. M. 2004. Parents' person-ality and infants' temperament as contributors to their emerging relationship, *Journal of Personality and Social Psychology* 86: 744–59

Lamb, M. E., Chuang, S. S., Wessels, H., Broberg, A. G. and Hwang, C. P. 2002. Emergence and construct validation of the Big Five factors in early childhood: a longitudinal analysis of their ontogeny in Sweden, *Child Development* 73: 1517–24

Lashley, B. R. and Kenny, D. A. 1998. Power estimation in social relations analyses, *Psychological Methods* 3: 328–38

Lehnart, J. and Neyer, F. J. 2006. Should I stay or should I go? Attachment and personality in stable and instable romantic relationships, *European Journal of Personality* 20: 475–95

Liew, J., Eisenberg, N. and Reiser, M. 2004. Preschoolers' effortful control and negative emotionality, immediate reactions to disappointment, and quality of social func-tioning, *Journal of Experimental Child Psychology* 89: 298–319

Lubbers, M. J., Van Der Werf, M. P. C., Kuyper, H. and Offringa, G. J. 2006. Predicting peer acceptance in Dutch youth: a multilevel analysis, *Journal of Early Adolescence* 26: 4–35

Luo, S. and Klohnen, E. C. 2005. Assortative mating and marital quality in newlyweds: a couple-centered approach, *Journal of Personality and Social Psychology* 88: 304–26

Lytton, H. 1990. Child and parent effects in boys' conduct disorder: a reinterpretation, *Developmental Psychology* 26: 683–97

    2000. Toward a model of family-environment and child-biological influences on development, *Developmental Review* 20: 150–79

Maccoby, E. E. and Martin, J. A. 1983. Socialization in the context of the family: parent-child interaction, in P. H. Mussen (Series ed.) and E. M. Hetherington (Vol. ed.), *Handbook of children psychology: socialization, personality, and social devel-opment*, 4th edn, pp. 1–102. New York: Wiley

Magnusson, D. 1990. Personality development from an interactional perspective, in L. A Pervin (ed). *Handbook of personality: theory and measurements*, pp. 193–222. New York, Guilford Press

Magnusson, D. and Endler, N. S. (eds.) 1977. *Personality at the crossroads: current issues in interactional psychology*. Hillsdale, NJ. Erlbaum

Malloy, T. E. and Kenny, D. A. 1986. The social relations model: an integrative method for personality research, *Journal of Personality* 54: 199–225

Marcus, D. and Kashy, D. 1995. The social relations model: a tool for group psychotherapy research, *Journal of Counseling Psychology* 42: 383–9

Marin, G. and Marin, B. V. 1991. *Research with Hispanic populations*. Newbury Park, CA: S

McAdams, D. P. 2001. *The person: an integrated introduction to personality psychology*. Fort Worth, TX: Harcourt College Publishers

Murphy, G. 1932. *An historical introduction to modern psychology*, 4th rev. edn. New York: Harcourt Brace

Newcomb, A. F., Bukowski, W. P. and Pattee, L. 1993. Children's peer relations: a meta-analytic review of popular, rejected, neglected, controversial, and average socio-metric status, *Psychological Bulletin* 113: 99–128

Neyer, F. J. and Asendorf, J. B. 2001. Personality-relationship transaction in young adulthood, *Journal of Personality and Social Psychology* 81: 1190–1204

Ozer, D. J. and Benet-Martínez, V. 2006. Personality and the prediction of consequential outcomes, *Annual Review of Psychology* 57: 401–21

Putnam, S. P., Sanson, A. V. and Rothbart, M. K. 2002. Child temperament and parenting, in M. H. Bornstein (ed.), *Handbook of parenting vol. I, Children and parenting*, pp. 255–77. Mahwah, NJ: Erlbaum

Rehmatullah, M. 2006. *Personality influences on marital satisfaction: an examination of actor, partner, and interaction effects.* Unpublished doctoral dissertation. University of Texas at Arlington

Roberts, B. W., Helson, R. and Klohnen, E. G. 2002. Personality development and growth in women across 30 years: three perspectives, *Journal of Personality* 70: 79–102

Roberts, B. W., Wood, D. and Smith, J. L. 2005. Evaluating five factor theory and social investment perspectives on personality trait development, *Journal of Research in Personality* 39: 166–84

Roberts, W. R. and Bogg, T. 2004. A longitudinal study of the relationships between conscientiousness and the social-environmental factors and substance-use behaviours that influence health, *Journal of Personality* 72: 325–53

Robins, R. W., Caspi, A. and Moffitt, T. E. 2000. Two personalities, one relationship: both partners' personality traits shape the quality of their relationships, *Journal of Personality and Social Psychology* 79: 251–9

2002. It's not just who you're with, it's who you are: personality and relationship experiences across multiple relationships, *Journal of Personality* 70: 925–64

Rothbart, M. K. and Bates, J. E. 2006. Temperament, in W. Damon and R. M. Lerner (Series eds.) and N. Eisenberg (Vol. ed.), *Handbook of child psychology*, vol. III, *Social, emotional and personality development*, 6th edn, pp. 99–166. Hoboken, NJ: Wiley

Sameroff, A. J. 1983. Development systems: contexts and evolution, in W. Kessen (ed.) *Handbook of child psychology*, vol. I, History, theory and methods, pp. 237–294. New York: Wiley

Sheese, B. E. 2005. *Social relations and personality in young adulthood: stability and change over a 14-week interval.* Unpublished doctoral dissertation. Purdue University

Shiner, R. L. 2000. Linking childhood personality with adaptation: evidence for continuity and change across time into late adolescence, *Journal of Personality and Social Psychology* 78: 310–25

Snyder, M. and Ickes, W. 1985. Personality and social behaviour, in G. Lindzey and E. Aronson (eds.), *Handbook of social psychology*, 3rd edn, pp. 883–948. Reading, MA: Addison-Wesley

Spinrad, T. L., Eisenberg, N. and Cumberland, A. 2006. Relation of emotion-related regulation to children's social competence: a longitudinal study, *Emotion* 6: 498–510

Suls, J., Martin, R. and David, J. P. 1998. Person-environment fit and its limits: Agreeableness, Neuroticism, and emotional reactivity to interpersonal conflict, *Personality and Social Psychology Bulletin* 24: 88–98

Triandis, H. C., Bontempo, R., Villareal, M. J., Asai, M. and Lucca, N. 1988. Individualism and collectivism: cross-cultural perspectives on self-ingroup relationships, *Journal of Personality and Social Psychology* 54: 323–38

Van Aken, M. A. G., Denissen, J. J. A., Branje, S. J. T., Dubas, J. S. and Goossens, L. 2006. Midlife concerns and short-term personality change in middle adulthood, *European Journal of Personality* 20: 497–513

Watson, D. and Clark, L. A. 1984. Negative affectivity: the disposition to experience aversive emotional states, *Psychological Bulletin* 96: 465–90

Watson, D., Hubbard, B. and Wiese, D. 2000. Self-other agreement in personality and affectivity: the role of acquaintanceship, trait visibility, and assumed similarity, *Journal of Personality and Social Psychology* 78: 546–58

White, J. K., Hendrick, S. S. and Hendrick, C. 2004. Big Five personality variables and relationship constructs, *Personality and Individual Differences* 37: 1519–30

Wiggins, J. S. 1991. Agency and communion as conceptual coordinates for understanding and measurement of interpersonal behaviour, in W. Grove and D. Cicchetti (eds.), *Thinking clearly about psychology: Essays in honor of Paul E. Meehl*, pp. 89–113 Minneapolis: University of Minnesota Press

Wood, D. and Roberts, B. W. 2006. The effect of age and role information on expectations for Big Five personality traits, *Personality and Social Psychology Bulletin* 32: 1482–96

30 Personality and social support processes

Rhonda Swickert

Overview of social support

Brian Clark, an executive vice president of a brokerage firm that was housed on the eighty-fourth floor of the South Trade Center Tower, was one the few people located above the point of impact to escape the terrorist attacks on September 11, 2001. When the first plane hit the North Tower he saw flames projecting from the ninety-fifth floor directly across from him. As a fire marshal, he started evacuating the floor of his building as a precaution, but within minutes, an announcement over the building's intercom system indicated that the South Tower was secure and that everyone could return to their offices. Following the announcement, Brian called his wife to tell her about what had happened and to let her know that he was safe. Shortly after 9:00 a.m., the South Tower was hit right below Brian's floor. During his escape from the building, he called his family again to let them know that he was trying to get out of the building. His family got a third call from Brian around 11:15 a.m., telling them that he was safe and as he was speaking to his wife he could hear the cheer of the crowd that had gathered at the family home when his wife told them that he had made it safely out of the building (Brian Clark, personal interview, Nova Online).

Brian Clark's story is unique, in that he survived the attack on the World Trade Center Towers. However, his seeking of contact with those important to him during the terrorist attacks of September 11, was repeated by millions of other Americans as events unfolded on this fateful day. Seeking of support from others during times of stress is a common and important coping response (Lazarus and Folkman 1987). Indeed, research conducted following the terrorist attacks of September 11, 2001, found that seeking support from others was the coping response most frequently used by individuals when responding to this event (Stein, Elliott, Jaycox *et al.* 2004). Additionally, research has shown that those with lower levels of social support seemed to be more negatively impacted by the traumatic events of September 11 (Galea, Ahern, Resnick *et al.* 2002).

The construct of social support generally refers to the perception by the individual that he or she is cared for, loved and valued by others (Cobb 1976). It is believed that this sense of support and community helps the individual to manage the uncertainty of life events by enhancing feelings of personal control (Albrecht and Adelman 1987). In conceptualizing social support, this construct has been viewed as a second-order factor that is made up of two distinct first order factors (Hittner and Swickert 2001; Russell, Booth, Reed and Laughlin 1997; Vaux and Harrison

1985). These two factors are generally labelled as functional support and structural support. Functional support is defined as an individual's perception of support available from others, as well as the support that is actually received from others (Cohen and Hoberman 1983). Within this general social support category a variety of supportive functions have been identified by researchers, including enhancement of self-esteem, feelings of belonging, guidance from others, and provision of tangible assistance (Cohen and Hoberman 1983). Regarding the assessment of functional support, various questionnaires have been developed to measure the different forms of functional support that have been identified in the literature.

The other major form of social support, structural support, refers to the degree of embeddedness of the individual within a social network of significant others (Lin and Peek 1999). This type of support is often reflected by the number of people in the individual's social network (termed network size) and is assessed by asking the individual to record the names of all people they could turn to if support were needed. Based on this listing of individuals, the respondent is then typically asked to indicate their level of satisfaction with the support provided by each network member, the level of contact they have with network members, and the density of their social support network. This last characteristic refers to the extent to which members of an individual's social network know one another (Albrecht and Goldsmith 2003).

In considering these two general social support factors (i.e., functional and structural support), it should be noted that they are not perceived equally by the individual. Indeed, work by myself and my colleague James Hittner, has shown that individuals, when making judgements regarding their sense of support from others, weigh more heavily their perception of availability of support (functional support) over the specific characteristics that define their social network (structural support) (Hittner and Swickert 2001).

Functional support, in particular, perceived availability of support, is not only weighted heavily when individuals consider their level of social support, it has been found to play an important stress-buffering role when people are under a high degree of stress (Cohen and Wills 1985; Cohen 2003; Thoits 1985). In particular, it is believed to provide a protective role as individuals experience stress, in that it might foster a less negative interpretation of the stressor which then, in turn, can help to reduce the individual's experience of stress and anxiety (Cohen 2003). In fact, research investigating the stress-buffering role of functional support has shown its effectiveness in predicting reduced mortality and physical health outcomes (Cohen 2003; Uchino, Cacioppo and Kiecolt-Glaser 1996), as well as lower levels of psychological distress (Krause, Liang and Gu 1998; Okun, Melichar and Hill 1990; Ystgaard, Tambs and Dalgard 1999). Perceived availability of social support is most effective when there is a match between what is required to successfully cope with the situation and the type of social support the individual perceives to be available. However, individuals who perceive having others they can talk to and share experiences with (belonging support), as well as individuals who make them feel good about themselves (self-esteem support), may benefit despite the coping requirements of a situation as these types of support are deemed to be helpful regardless of the nature of the stressor (Cohen 2003).

In addition to the stress-buffering model of social support, another view of social support, termed the main-effect model, suggests that social support can have a beneficial effect regardless of whether the individual is under stress. The main-effect model of social support has been associated most frequently with structural social support as this type of social support seems to be helpful regardless of the level of stress that the individual experiences (Cohen and Wills 1985). Research has shown that social network size is associated with reduced mortality rates (Berkman and Syme 1979; House, Robbins and Metzner 1982), and greater resistance to particular disease processes (Cohen, Doyle, Skoner *et al.* 1997). It also has been associated with reduced levels of anxiety, depression and psychological distress (Cohen and Wills 1985). Indeed, theorists have suggested that structural support may exert its positive effects on health indirectly, by reducing the individual's general experience of anxiety and stress (Cohen, Doyle, Skoner *et al.* 1997).

Although many positive effects of social support have been documented in the literature, it should be noted that social interactions with others are not always supportive in nature. Interacting with others who are interfering, manipulative or even hostile has been shown to have a negative impact on psychological wellbeing (Harber, Schneider, Everard and Fisher 2005; Rook 1984). Furthermore, the impact of negative interactions on the individual is often greater, compared with positive interactions (Rook 1984; Schuster, Kessler and Aseltine 1990). Fortunately, most people tend to report substantially more positive social connections than negative (Schuster *et al.* 1990), and positive social interactions have been shown to attenuate the negative effects of problematic social ties (Schuster *et al.* 1990).

Relationship between personality and social support

Much of the early work investigating the construct of social support was based on epidemiological studies which showed that having supportive contacts with others was beneficial to health and wellbeing (Caplan 1974; Cobb 1976; Dean and Lin 1977). Findings from this work led to the implicit assumption that the agent of influence regarding levels of social support was the social environment of the individual (i.e., the individual's social network size) (Pierce, Lakey, Sarason *et al.* 1997), rather than dispositional factors of the person. Additionally, with the introduction of Lazarus and Folkman's influential transactional model of coping (1987), personality's influence on coping processes was once again left unexamined. In their model, individual differences, along with other factors, such as environmental characteristics, are subsumed under the general construct of cognitive appraisal, and as such, are typically not directly studied. However, by the mid-1980s, researchers were beginning to recognize the importance of personality in predicting coping responses in general (Parkes 1986), and the use of social support, in particular (Sarason and Sarason 1982). Much work has been done in the area since this time and hundreds of studies have documented the association between social support and various personality traits.

In addressing why it is that personality might be an important predictor of social support, researchers have identified three mechanisms whereby personality could impact upon social support processes (Pierce, Lakey, Sarason *et al.* 1997). Drawing from Scarr and McCartney's (1983) model of person-environment interaction, Pierce and his colleagues suggested that, first, personality might influence how supportive behaviour is perceived and responded to (reactive interaction). Essentially, individuals who experience similar levels of support may perceive this support quite differently. To illustrate, research has shown individuals who report greater emotionality (Neuroticism) are less likely to perceive individuals in their social network as being supportive, as compared with individuals who are more emotionally stable (Russell, Booth, Reed and Laughlin 1997). Researchers also have found that individuals are more likely to perceive others as being supportive if they are similar to themselves on various personality dimensions (Lutz and Lakey 2001).

A second mechanism that appears to help account for the relationship between personality and social support, termed an evocative interaction, suggests that individuals differ in the manner in which they evoke supportive responses from others (Pierce, Lakey, Sarason *et al.* 1997). While one individual's behaviour might signal a preference for support, another person's manner might convey the need for interpersonal distance (Cutrona, Hessling and Suhr 1997). Research has shown, for example, that supportive marital interactions are influenced by the recipient's personality; that is, husbands who are more emotional and/or less conscientious in their behaviour are more likely to receive esteem support from their wives (Dehle and Landers 2005).

A final mechanism suggested by Pierce *et al.* to address the nature of the relationship between personality and social support highlights the tendency of individuals to actively structure their social environments (termed proactive interaction). Individuals are active participants in selecting and creating their social world and, as such, play an important role in influencing the level of social support available to them. For instance, individuals who are more outgoing and social (extraverted) tend to report greater numbers of people in their social network (Swickert, Rosentreter, Hittner and Mushrush 2002), probably because they are more inclined to seek out interactions with others, as compared to more introverted individuals. Similarly, research has indicated that individuals who are more extraverted and agreeable are more likely to receive support from others because, in part, they provide support to those in their social network (Bowling, Beehr and Swader 2005).

Personality traits and social support

Since the 1980s, much work has been conducted examining the relationship between personality traits and social support. Although a variety of different personality traits have been studied (e.g., locus of control, optimism), much of the work on this topic has centred on the Five-Factor Model of personality. In particular, the traits of Extraversion and Neuroticism have received the most attention in the literature, so my discussion of the relationship between specific personality traits and social support will begin with these two dimensions. After discussing these two traits, I will examine the association between social support and the remaining traits of the Five-Factor Model (Agreeableness, Conscientiousness and Openness).

Extraversion

The trait of Extraversion is associated with descriptors such as sociability, activity and excitement seeking. Individuals low in Extraversion (introverts) tend to be more socially reserved, serious and less spontaneous in their behaviour. In contrast, individuals high in Extraversion (extraverts) tend to be more gregarious, high-spirited and outspoken (Costa and McCrae 1987). Given the strong sociability component of Extraversion, it is not surprising that this dimension is an important predictor of social support. Individuals who are more extraverted enjoy interacting with others and, as such, might have more opportunities to seek out and receive social support from others than do introverts. Furthermore, during times of stress, coping responses of extraverts differ from introverts in regards to the use of social support. That is, research has shown that when compared to introverts, extraverts are more likely to report seeking out support from others when responding to a problem or stressor (Amirkhan, Risinger and Swickert 1995; Fickova 2001; Hooker, Frazier and Monahan 1994; McCrae and Costa 1986). Although most of this work is based on self-report measures of coping strategies, a few studies have behaviourally documented a stronger social support seeking tendency for extraverts. As one such example, work that I conducted with James Amirkhan and Rhonda Risinger in 1995 showed that extraverts, as compared to introverts, were more likely to ask for help when confronted by a problem. In this study, participants were given an unsolvable task to perform and were told that if they needed help with the task an assistant would be stationed outside of the room. They were also informed that they would not be penalized for seeking out assistance. Results from this study showed that extraverts sought help from the assistant much more quickly than did introverts. In short, an extravert's pattern of responding to problems or stressors is oriented much more toward seeking support from others than is that of the introvert.

Perhaps one explanation as to why Extraversion is closely associated with the coping strategy of seeking social support is that it also shares a strong relationship with perceived availability of social support. When participants are asked to report their perception of the social support available to them, extraverts, as compared with introverts, are more likely to perceive greater levels of social support. However, it should be noted that the strength of the relationship between these two constructs tends to vary depending upon the methodology of the study.

Cross-sectional studies where both personality (Extraversion) and perceived availability of social support are assessed at the same time have reported correlations between these two variables in the .4 to .5 range, suggesting that there is a considerable amount of shared variance between these two factors (Chay 1993; Finch and Graziano 2001; Halamandaris and Power 1997; Swickert, Rosentreter, Hittner and Mushrush 2002; Swickert, Hittner, Kitos and Cox-Fuenzalida 2004). However, longitudinal or prospective studies that have been conducted to examine the relationship between Extraversion and perceived availability of social support show a more modest association. Von Dras and Siegler (1997) examined the association between Extraversion, measured at college entry and again at mid-life, and perceived availability of social support. Correlational analysis showed a small, but significant relationship between Extraversion assessed during college and perception of social support during midlife ($r = .10$, $p < .0001$). The manner in which Extraversion was assessed (items drawn from the MMPI) and the relatively lengthy time span between the assessment of personality and social support, may help to explain this low, albeit significant, correlation. Examining the relationship between Extraversion and perceived social support over a shorter interval of time has shown a more robust relationship between these factors. Lakey and Dickinson (1994) followed 118 entering college freshman over the course of a fall semester. Extraversion was assessed at the beginning of the semester and perceived social support at college was assessed at the end of the students' first semester. Results showed a significant relationship between these two variables ($r = .38$, $p < .01$), such that higher levels of Extraversion were associated with greater levels of perceived social support from college peers.

Perceived availability of social support is one major form of functional support that has been shown to have a clear association with Extraversion. The other major form of functional support, received support, also has been found to be related to Extraversion. However, results from studies examining the association between these two factors are somewhat inconsistent. Of the limited number of studies that have examined this issue, most have found a small to moderate relationship between Extraversion and received support (r's range from .2 to .3) (Fyrand, Wichstrøm, Moum, Glennas and Kvien 1997; Lu 1997; Lu, Shih, Lin and Ju 1997; Suurmeijer, Van Sonderen, Krol et al. 2005; Swickert, Rosentreter, Hittner and Mushrush 2002). But some studies have shown no relationship between these factors (Krause, Liang and Keith 1990; Lakey, Adams, Neely et al. 2002; Lu and Arglye 1992). In sum, of the two major types of functional support, perceived availability of support shows a more robust and consistent relationship with Extraversion than does received social support.

In addition to the relationship between Extraversion and functional support, there have been several studies that also support the association between Extraversion and at least some forms of structural support. Although Extraversion does not appear to be strongly related to satisfaction with one's social support network, it does appear to influence the size of one's network (Henderson 1981; Russell, Booth, Reed and Laughlin 1997; Swickert, Rosentreter, Hittner and Mushrush 2002), as well as the frequency of contact one has with network members (Bolger and Eckenrode 1991; Krause, Liang and Keith 1990; Swickert *et al.* 2002). Individuals higher in Extraversion tend to report larger social networks and greater contact with network members. In addition, a study conducted by Russell and his colleagues (1997) showed that Extraversion was positively correlated with the number of people the individual believed that he or she could safely confide in.

In sum, current findings in the literature show important associations between Extraversion and various forms of social support. Researchers also have examined how Extraversion and social support together may influence important behavioural outcomes. In particular, social support has been shown to play both a mediational and moderational role in the relationship between Extraversion and factors such as depression and psychological distress. Finch and Graziano (2001) assessed Extraversion and perceived availability of social support as part of a larger study examining temperament and personality, patterns of social relations and ratings of depression. Using structural equation modelling, they found that Extraversion exerted an indirect effect on depression through the mediating influence of perceived availability of social support, such that individuals who reported higher levels of Extraversion were more likely to have greater levels of perceived support, and greater levels of perceived support were associated with lowered levels of depression. I, along with my colleagues, also reported a significant mediating effect of perceived social support when modelling the association between Extraversion and self-esteem (Swickert, Hittner, Kitos and Cox-Fuenzalida 2004). In this study, four potential mediators were considered (negative affect, optimism, perceived availability of social support, and positive affect). Results indicated that only perceived availability of social support and positive affect served as significant mediators in the association between Extraversion and self-esteem. Regarding the mediating role of perceived support, individuals higher in Extraversion reported greater levels of perceived support which, in turn, was associated with greater levels of self-esteem.

Interestingly, while this mediational work shows that social support plays a positive role between Extraversion and various outcome measures (lowered depression, greater self-esteem), the moderational work illustrates a more complex relationship between Extraversion and social support. To illustrate, Eastburg, Williamson, Gorsuch and Ridley (1994) found that individuals who were more extraverted required more work-related peer support to avoid emotional exhaustion than did introverts. Similarly, Duckitt (1984) reported that extraverts who had lower levels of perceived social support reported higher levels of psychological distress than did more introverted individuals. Considering both the mediational and moderational work, it appears that most extraverts, as compared to introverts, report greater levels of social support and that they, in turn, benefit from this enhanced social support as evidenced by lowered levels of depression and higher levels of self-esteem. However, if extraverts do not receive an appropriate level of social support, then they appear to be more negatively affected by this reduced provision of social support, as compared to introverts.

Neuroticism

The trait of Neuroticism can be characterized with descriptors such as emotional lability, impulsiveness and self-consciousness. Individuals high in Neuroticism are prone to more negative mood states (e.g., anxiety, depression), and depending on the situation, they may react defensively or become overly self-conscious. Individuals low in Neuroticism are characterized by an emotionally stable disposition. They tend to be confident and less excitable in their behaviour. Although Neuroticism is most predictive of avoidance coping, this trait also has been negatively associated with seeking of social support. Indeed, individuals who are higher in Neuroticism, compared to those lower in this dimension, may actually withdraw from others during times of stress (Lee-Baggley, Preece and DeLongis 2005; McCrae and Costa 1986; O'Brien and DeLongis 1996). Research also has shown that individuals who are high in Neuroticism, compared to those who are low, report less positive, and more negative, social interactions (Lincoln, Taylor and Chatters 2003; Russell, Booth, Reed and Laughlin 1997; Shurgot and Knight 2005).

Given the fact that neurotics report problematic social ties, it perhaps is not surprising that the trait of Neuroticism is negatively related to perceived satisfaction with one's social support network (a type of structural support). That is, individuals who are higher in Neuroticism report less satisfaction with their support network than those who are lower on this dimension (Dehle and Landers 2005; De Jong, Van Sonderen and Emmelkamp 1999; Suurmeijer, Sonderen, Krol *et al.* 2005; Tong, Bishop, Diong *et al.* 2004). Furthermore, when examining Neuroticism's relationship with different forms of social support (both structural and functional), perceived satisfaction seems to be most consistently related to Neuroticism. Indeed, no other type of structural support (e.g., network size, contact with network members) has been shown to be related to Neuroticism (Lincoln, Taylor and Chatters 2003; Russell, Booth, Reed and Laughlin 1997; Shurgot and Knight 2005), although the number of studies that have looked at the relationship between Neuroticism and these variables are relatively few.

Although perceived satisfaction with support has been most consistently related to Neuroticism, the strength of the relationship between these two variables is moderate at best (r's between -.2 and -.3). Neuroticism seems to have a stronger relationship with perceived availability of social support (a form of functional support), with correlations ranging from -.3 to -.5. However, findings from studies that have examined the association between these two variables are mixed. Of the studies published on this topic, results in about one-third of them are non-significant. It is unclear what is accounting for this inconsistency, however, circumstantial evidence suggests that the variable of gender may be influencing the results of these studies. That is, in the two studies where the effect of gender was examined (out of the twenty or so studies that examined the relationship between Neuroticism and social support), both reported significant effects between Neuroticism and perceived availability of social support for females only (Dehle and Landers 2005; Katainen, Räikkönen and Keltikangas-Järvinen

1999). While this gender difference is interesting, more studies need to be conducted before any firm conclusions can be drawn concerning the influence of gender on the association between Neuroticism and perceived availability of support.

In addition to examining the relationship between perceived availability of support and Neuroticism, researchers also have looked at the relationship between Neuroticism and the other major type of functional social support: received social support. The literature is very inconsistent concerning the relationship between these two variables, with about half of these studies documenting a small to moderate relationship (-.20 to -.35) (Dehle and Landers 2005; Fyrand, Wichstrøm, Moum *et al.* 1997) and the other half reporting no significant association between Neuroticism and received support (Bowling, Beehr and Swader 2005; Lu, Shih, Lin and Ju 1997; Shurgot and Knight 2005). In this case, sample characteristics, including gender, do not seem to differentiate the significant studies from the non-significant. Therefore, it is hard to say with any assurance whether these variables are, or are not, related.

In addition to the bivariate relationships that have been found between Neuroticism and social support, researchers have examined how social support might both mediate and moderate the relationship between Neuroticism and variables such as depression and daily hassles. Research in this area suggests that social support plays a modest role in mediating the relationship between Neuroticism and negative mood states such as depression. For example, using structural equation modelling, Finch and Graziano (2001) found that both negative social interactions and support satisfaction partially mediated the relationship between Neuroticism and depression. However, the relationship between Neuroticism and depression remained significant even after accounting for these mediators. Suurmeijer et al. documented this same partial mediation effect when they examined the relationship between Neuroticism, support satisfaction and depression. Partial mediation of social support also has been found when examining the relationship between Neuroticism and daily hassles (De Jong, Van Sonderen and Emmelkamp 1999), quality of life (Burgess, Carretero, Elkington *et al.* 2000), and care-giving stressfulness (Shurgot and Knight 2005). Regarding the moderational effects of social support on Neuroticism, only one study was found that examined this issue. Emery, Huppert and Schein (1996) examined the moderational role of social support, when considering the relationship between Neuroticism and psychological distress. Although Neuroticism was significantly related to psychological distress, social support was not found to moderate this relationship.

Agreeableness

The trait of Agreeableness is associated with descriptive terms such as trusting, altruistic and tender-minded. Individuals who are high in agreeableness are considered warm, generous and kind. Individuals scoring low in this dimension tend to be more selfish, demanding and outspoken. Regarding this dimension's relationship with social support, individuals who are high in agreeableness, compared to those who are low, are motivated to maintain positive relationships with others (Jensen-Campbell and Graziano 2001) and they tend to engage in social behaviours that facilitate intimacy (Branje, Van Lieshout and Van Aken 2005). As such, individuals who are high in agreeableness are more likely to turn to others when coping with stressors (Fickova 2001; Hooker, Frazier and Monahan 1994; Jung 1995) and they are more likely to provide support to others as well (Bowling et al. 2005).

Most of the work conducted on the topic of Agreeableness and social support has focused on how this personality trait is related to the perception of availability of social support. Research shows a moderate relationship between these two variables, with correlations ranging from .2 to .55. Individuals who are more agreeable, compared to those lower on the dimension, tend to perceive greater levels of support available to them (Finch and Graziano 2001; Branje, Van Lieshout and Van Aken 2005; Asendorpf and Van Aken 2003). Although most of this work is cross-sectional in nature, there was a study conducted by Lakey and Dickinson (1994) that followed 118 entering college freshman over the course of a fall semester. Agreeableness was assessed at the beginning of the semester and perceived social support of college friends was assessed at the end of the students' first semester. Results showed a significant relationship between these two variables ($r = .44$, $p < .01$), such that higher levels of Agreeableness were associated with greater levels of perceived social support.

Less is know about Agreeableness' relationship with received support or various types of structural support. Only two studies were found that examined the relationship between this personality trait and received support. One study found significant effects between Agreeableness and job-related and non-job-related support (Bowling, Beehr and Swader 2005), however, another study that looked at the relationship between Agreeableness and received support reported a non-significant relationship. Additionally, a study conducted by Tong, Bishop, Diong et al. (2004) examined the relationship between Agreeableness and the number of people in one's social support network as well as satisfaction with one's social network providers. Results from the study showed significant, but small correlations between Agreeableness and these network characteristics.

In addition to the associations reported above, research has also shown that perceived availability of social support moderates the effect of Agreeableness when predicting depressive symptoms (Hoth, Christensen, Ehlers et al. 2007). Patients with chronic kidney disease were recruited for this seventeen-month long prospective study. After researchers controlled for initial depressive symptoms, Agreeableness was found to predict depressive symptoms and social support was shown to moderate this relationship. That is, patients who reported higher levels of Agreeableness and higher levels of social support also reported a reduction of depressive symptoms over the time period of study. In contrast, those patients who were low in Agreeableness showed no real benefit of higher levels of social support.

To summarize, Agreeableness has been related to social support, in particular perceived availability of social support. But more work is needed to determine its relationship with other forms of social support as well as how Agreeableness might work together with social support (via mediation or moderation) to influence complex forms of behaviour.

Conscientiousness

Conscientiousness is associated with terms such as ambitious, resourceful and persistent. Individuals high in Conscientiousness are efficient, organized and industrious. Individuals who are low in this dimension tend to be careless, impatient and lazy. Only a small number of studies have examined the relationship between Conscientiousness and social support ($N = 5$). These studies allow for some general, albeit still speculative, conclusions. First, individuals higher in Conscientiousness perceive more support available to them (Asendorpf and Van Aken 2003; Lakey, Adams, Neely *et al.* 2002), but at the same time they report receiving lower levels of support from others (Dehle and Landers 2005; Lu and Arglye 1992). It appears then from these findings that although support is available to those high in Conscientiousness, given their competence and resourcefulness, they may simply not require as much support from others. An additional finding regarding the relationship between Conscientiousness and social support indicates that individuals who are high in Conscientiousness report greater levels of satisfaction with support providers (Asendorpf and Van Aken 2003; Dehle and Landers 2005; Tong, Bishop, Diong *et al.* 2004). So, as regards to the support that high Conscientiousness individuals do receive from others, they appear to be satisfied with it.

Openness

The trait of Openness can be characterized by descriptors such as imaginative, spontaneous and adventurous. Individuals who are high on this trait tend to be curious, imaginative and unconventional. People scoring lower in this dimension tend to be cautious and more conservative in their thinking. Few studies have looked at the relationship between Openness and social support, and those that have tend to be inconsistent. Regarding seeking of social support, one study reported that individuals high in Openness are more likely to withdraw from others when coping with problems, although a second study reported in the same paper did not support this finding (McCrae and Costa 1986). Additionally, in a study by Fickova (2001), a positive relationship between Openness and seeking of support from others was found for boys who participated in the study, but not for girls. Finally, in a study of personality and social network support, Openness was positively associated with network size, although the correlation was modest ($r = .23$). Clearly, more work needs to be done in examining the relationship between Openness and social support before any definitive conclusions can be drawn.

Summary and suggestions for future research

Much work has been conducted that has looked at the relationship between personality and social support. Of the Big Five traits that have been reviewed in this chapter, Extraversion has received the most attention and has shown the most pervasive and consistent associations with social support. Extraversion is associated with support seeking as a coping strategy, and shows relationships with both functional and structural forms of social support. Extraversion has been related to both forms of functional support, but of the two, it is most consistently related to perceived availability of support. It also has been linked to structural measures of support, including network size and contact with network members. Neuroticism has been associated with the stress coping response of social withdrawal, as well as more negative social interactions in general. This dimension has been shown to be negatively related to perceived satisfaction with support providers and perceived availability of support, although in the case of perceived availability of support, this effect might be stronger for females than males. The trait of Agreeableness has been associated with social support seeking as a coping strategy and provision of support to others. It appears to be most strongly related to perception of availability of social support. The traits of Conscientiousness and Openness have received less attention in the literature. However, findings from the studies that have examined Conscientiousness and social support suggest that Conscientiousness is negatively associated with received support, but it is positively associated with perceived availability of support and support satisfaction. Regarding the trait of Openness, more work is needed before any definitive conclusions can be drawn about whether this trait is significantly associated with social support.

Clearly, of the work that has been conducted to investigate the relationship between 'Big Five' personality traits and social support, most of it has focused on determining the bivariate relationships that exist between various personality traits and social support. While this initial approach was necessary (and needs to continue for most of these Big Five traits), work in this area could now evolve to examine more complex questions. As an example, researchers should test the predictions made by Pierce and his colleagues (1997) concerning the three mechanisms whereby personality is believed to impact upon social support processes (i.e., reactive, evocative and proactive interaction). In fact, work on this issue has already started. For example, Russell, Booth, Reed and Laughlin (1997) demonstrated the proactive influence of Extraversion on social support processes. They showed that for the trait of Extraversion, perception of support availability is mediated by the individual's social network size. This finding indicates that one reason why extraverts perceive more available support, compared to introverts, is because they construct a bigger social network for themselves.

An additional issue that should also be addressed in the literature concerns the directionality of influence when considering the relationship between personality and social support. Much of the work that has examined the association between personality and social support processes is cross-sectional in nature and as such, cannot allow for causal conclusions. Therefore, researchers should utilize other methods of study (i.e., longitudinal designs) which can provide a direct test of the influence of personality on social support. As an example, work by Lakey and Dickinson (1994) followed college freshman over the course of a fall semester. They assessed personality at the beginning of the students' first semester and then measured students' perceived social support of college friends at the end of the semester. In doing so, they were able to examine the influence of personality on the construction of a new social support network.

Another interesting issue that should be addressed by researchers is determining whether there are important interactions between two or more of the five factor traits in predicting social support. For instance, Extraversion and Agreeableness both show significant associations with social support. So what happens when their effects are combined? Does an individual who is high in both traits now show enhanced support seeking tendencies compared to the individual who is high in only one of the two traits? Or, is there a ceiling effect of sorts, such that being high on both traits does not lead to any greater levels of support seeking?

As a final recommendation, researchers should include gender as a variable in their studies of personality and social support. It has been known for some time that there are important gender differences concerning both functional and structural social support (Shumaker and Hill 1991). However, very few of the studies reviewed in this chapter took into consideration the role of gender and how it might serve as a moderator of the association between personality and social support. By examining the moderational role of gender, greater precision can be gained in understanding the relationship between personality and social support.

References

Albrecht, T. and Adelman, M. 1987. *Communicating social support*. Newbury Park, CA: Sage

Albrecht, T. and Goldsmith, D. 2003. Social support, social networks, and health, in T. L. Thompson, A. M. Dorsey, K. I. Miller and R. Parrott (eds.), *Handbook of health communication*, pp. 263–84. Mahwah, NJ: Lawrence Erlbaum Associates Publishers

Amirkhan, J., Risinger, R. and Swickert, R. 1995. Extraversion: a 'hidden' personality factor in coping?, *Journal of Personality* 63: 189–212

Asendorpf, J. and Van Aken, M. 2003. Personality-relationship transaction in adolescence: core versus surface personality characteristics, *Journal of Personality* 71: 629–66

Berkman, L. F. and Syme, S. L. 1979. Social networks, host resistance, and mortality: a nine-year follow-up study of Alameda county residents, *American Journal of Epidemiology* 109: 186–204

Bolger, N. and Eckenrode, J. 1991. Social relationships, personality, and anxiety during a major stressful event, *Journal of Personality and Social Psychology* 61: 440–9

Bowling, N., Beehr, T. and Swader, W. 2005. Giving and receiving social support at work: the roles of personality and reciprocity, *Journal of Vocational Behaviour* 67: 476–89

Branje, S., Van Lieshout, C. and Van Aken, M. 2005. Relations between Agreeableness and perceived support in family relationships: why nice people are not always supportive, *International Journal of Behavioural Development* 29: 120–8

Burgess, A., Carretero, M., Elkington, A., Pasqual-Marsettin, E., Lobaccaro, C. and Catalan, J. 2000. The role of personality, coping style and social support in health-related quality of life in HIV infection, *Quality of life Research* 9: 423–37

Caplan, G. 1974. Support systems and community mental health: lectures on concept development, *Behavioural Publications* 17: 267

Chay, Y. 1993. Social support, individual differences and well-being: a study of small business entrepreneurs and employees, *Journal of Occupational and Organizational Psychology* 66: 285–302

Cobb, S. 1976. Social support as a moderator of life stress, *Psychosomatic Medicine* 38: 300–14

Cohen, S. 2003. Psychosocial models of the role of social support in the etiology of physical disease, in P. Salovey and A. J. Rothman (eds.), *Social psychology of health*, pp. 227–44. New York: Psychology Press

Cohen, S., Doyle, W., Skoner, D., Rabin, B. and Gwaltney, J. 1997. Social ties and susceptibility to the common cold, *Journal of the American Medical Association* 277: 1940–4

Cohen, S. and Hoberman, H. 1983. Positive events and social supports as buffers of life change stress, *Journal of Applied Social Psychology* 13: 99–125

Cohen, S. and Wills, T. 1985. Stress, social support, and the buffering hypothesis, *Psychological Bulletin* 98: 310–57

Costa, P. and McCrae, R. 1987. *The NEO Personality Inventory manual*. Odessa, FL: Psychological Assessment Resources

Cutrona, C., Hessling, R. and Suhr, J. 1997. The influence of husband and wife personality on marital social support interactions, *Personal Relationships* 4: 379–93

De Jong, G., Van Sonderen, E. and Emmelkamp, P. 1999. A comprehensive model of stress: the roles of experience stress and Neuroticism in explaining the stress-distress relationship, *Psychotherapy and Psychosomatics* 68: 290–8

Dean A. and Lin, N. 1977. The stress-buffering role of social support, *Journal of Nervous and Mental Disease* 165: 403–17

Dehle, C. and Landers, J. 2005. You can't always get what you want, but can you get what you need? Personality traits and social support in marriage, *Journal of Social and Clinical Psychology* 24: 1051–76

Duckitt, J. 1984. Social support, personality and the prediction of psychological distress: an interactionist approach, *Journal of Clinical Psychology* 40: 1199–205

Eastburg, M., Williamson, M., Gorsuch, R. and Ridley, C. 1994. Social support, personality, and burnout in nurses, *Journal of Applied Social Psychology* 24: 1233–50

Emery, C., Huppert, F. and Schein, R. 1996. Health and personality predictors of psychological functioning in a 7-year longitudinal study, *Personality and Individual Differences* 20: 567–73

Fickova, E. 2001. Personality regulators of coping behaviour in adolescents, *Studia Psychologica* 43: 321–9

Finch, J. and Graziano, W. 2001. Predicting depression from temperament, personality and patterns of social relations, *Journal of Personality* 69: 27–55

Fyrand, L., Wichstrøm, L., Moum, T., Glennas, A. and Kvien, T. 1997. The impact of personality and social support on mental health for female patients with rheumatoid arthritis, *Social Indicators Research* 40: 285–98

Galea, S., Ahern, J., Resnick, H., Kilpatrick, D., Bucuvalas, M., Gold, J. and Vlahov, D. 2002. Psychological sequelae of the September 11 terrorist attacks in New York City, *New England Journal of Medicine* 346: 982–7

Halamandaris, K. and Power, K. 1997. Individual differences, dysfunctional attitudes, and social support: a study of the psychosocial adjustment to university life of home students, *Personality and Individual Differences* 22: 93–104

Harber, K., Schneider, J., Everard, K. and Fisher, E. 2005. Directive support, nondirective support, and morale, *Journal of Social and Clinical Psychology* 24: 691–722

Henderson, S. 1981. *Neurosis and the social environment*. New York: Academic Press

Hittner, J. and Swickert, R. 2001. Modeling functional and structural social support via confirmatory factor analysis: evidence for a second-order global support construct, *Journal of Social Behaviour and Personality* 16: 69–80

Hooker, K., Frazier, L. and Monahan, D. 1994. Personality and coping among caregivers of spouses with dementia, *Gerontologist* 34: 386–92

Hoth, K., Christensen, A., Ehlers, S., Raichle, K. and Lawton, W. 2007. A longitudinal examination of social support, agreeableness and depressive symptoms in chronic kidney disease, *Journal of Behavioural Medicine* 30: 69–76

House, J. S., Robbins, C. and Metzner, H. A. (1982). The association of social relationships and activities with mortality: prospective evidence from the Tecumseh Community Health Study, *American Journal of Epidemiology* 116: 123–40

Jensen-Campbell, L. and Graziano, W. 2001. Agreeableness as a moderator of interpersonal conflict, *Journal of Personality* 69: 323–62

Jung, J. 1995. Ethnic group and gender differences in the relationship between personality and coping, *Anxiety, Stress and Coping* 8: 113–26

Katainen, S., Räikkönen, K. and Keltikangas-Järvinen, L. 1999. Adolescent temperament, perceived social support, and depressive tendencies as predictors of depressive tendencies in young adulthood, *European Journal of Personality* 13: 183–207

Krause, N., Liang, J. and Gu, S. 1998. Financial strain, received support, anticipated support, and depressive symptoms in the People's Republic of China, *Psychology and Aging* 13: 58–68

Krause, N., Liang, J. and Keith, V. 1990. Personality, social support, and psychological distress in later life, *Psychology and Aging* 5: 315–26

Lakey, B., Adams, K., Neely, L., Rhodes, G., Lutz, C. and Sielky, K. 2002. Perceived support and low emotional distress: the role of enacted support, dyad similarity, and provider personality, *Personality and Social Psychology Bulletin* 11: 1546–55

Lakey, B. and Dickinson, L. 1994. Antecedents of perceived support: is perceived family environment generalized to new social relationships?, *Cognitive Therapy and Research* 18: 39–53

Lazarus, R. and Folkman, S. 1987. Transactional theory and research on emotions and coping, *European Journal of Personality* 1: 141–69

Lee-Baggley, D., Preece, M. and DeLongis, A. 2005. Coping with interpersonal stress: role of Big Five traits, *Journal of Personality* 73: 1141–80

Lin, N. and Peek, K. 1999. Social networks and mental health, in A. Horiwitz and T. Scheid (eds.), *A handbook for the study of mental health: social contexts, theories, and systems*, pp. 241–58. New York: Cambridge University Press

Lincoln, K., Taylor, R. and Chatters, L. 2003. Correlates of emotional support and negative interaction among older Black Americans, *Journal of Gerontology* 58: S225–S233

Lu, L. 1997. Social support, reciprocity, and well-being, *Journal of Social Psychology* 137: 618–28

Lu, L. and Argyle, M. 1992. Receiving and giving support: effects on relationships and well-being, *Counseling Psychology Quarterly* 5: 123–33

Lu, L., Shih, J., Lin, Y. and Ju, L. 1997. Personal and environmental correlates of happiness, *Personality and Individual Differences* 23: 453–62

Lutz, C. and Lakey, B. 2001. How people make support judgments: individual differences in the traits used to infer supportiveness in others, *Journal of Personality and Social Psychology* 81: 1070–9

McCrae, R. and Costa, P. 1986. Personality, coping, and coping effectiveness in an adult sample, *Journal of Personality* 54: 385–405

Nova Online n.d.. *Building on ground zero: a survivor's story*, www.pbs.org/wgbh/nova/wtc/above.html

O'Brien, T. B. and DeLongis, A. 1996. The interactional context of problem-, emotion-, and relationship-focused coping: the role of the Big Five personality factors, *Journal of Personality* 64: 775–813

Okun, M., Melichar, J. and Hill, M. 1990. Negative daily events, positive and negative social ties, and psychological distress among older adults, *Gerontologist* 30: 193–9

Parkes, K. 1986. Coping in stressful episodes: the role of individual differences, environmental factors, and situational characteristics, *Journal of Personality and Social Psychology* 6: 1277–92

Pierce, G., Lakey, B., Sarason, I., Sarason, B. and Joseph, H. 1997. Personality and social support processes: a conceptual overview, in G. Pierce, B. Lakey, I. Sarason and B. Sarason (eds.), *Sourcebook of social support and personality*, pp. 3–18. New York: Plenum Press

Rook, K. 1984. The negative side of social interaction: impact on psychological well-being, *Journal of Personality and Social Psychology* 46: 1097–1108

Russell, D., Booth, B., Reed, D. and Laughlin, P. 1997. Personality, social networks, and perceived social support among alcoholics: a structural equation analysis, *Journal of Personality* 65: 649–92

Sarason, I. and Sarason, B. 1982. Concomitants of social support: attitudes, personality characteristics, and life experiences, *Journal of Personality* 50: 331–44

Scarr, S. and McCartney, K. 1983. How people make their own environments: a theory of genotype → environment effects, *Child Development* 54: 424–35

Schuster, T., Kessler, R. and Aseltine, R. 1990. Supportive interactions, negative interactions, and depressed mood, *American Journal of Community Psychology* 18: 423–38

Shumaker, S. and Hill, D. 1991. Gender differences in social support and physical health, *Health Psychology* 10: 102–11

Shurgot, G. and Knight, B. 2005. Influence of Neuroticism, ethnicity, familism, and social support on perceived burden in dementia caregivers: pilot test of the transactional stress and social support model, *Journal of Gerontology* 60: P331–P334

Stein, B., Elliott, M., Jaycox, L., Collins, R., Berry, S., Klein, D. and Schuster, M. 2004. A national longitudinal study of the psychological consequences of the September 11, 2001 terrorist attacks: reactions, impairment, and help-seeking, *Psychiatry: Interpersonal and Biological Processes* 67: 105–17

Suurmeijer, Th., Van Sonderen, F., Krol, B., Doeglas, D., Van Den Heuvel, W. and Sanderman, R. 2005. The relationship between personality, supportive trans-actions and support satisfaction, and mental health of patients with early rheu-matoid arthritis. Results from the Dutch part of the EURIDISS study, *Social Indicators Research* 73: 179–97

Swickert, R., Hittner, J., Kitos, N. and Cox-Fuenzalida, E. 2004. Direct or indirect, that is the question: a re-evaluation of Extraversion's influence on self-esteem, *Personality and Individual Differences* 36: 207–17

Swickert, R., Rosentreter, C., Hittner, J. and Mushrush, J. 2002. Extraversion, social support processes, and stress, *Personality and Individual Differences* 32: 877–91

Thoits, P. 1985. Social support processes and psychological well-being: theoretical possi-bilities, in I. G. Sarason and B. Sarason (eds.), *Social support: theory, research and applications*, pp. 51–72. The Hague: Martinus Nijhoff

Tong, E., Bishop, G., Diong, S., Enkelmann, H., Why, Y., Ang, J. and Khader, M. 2004. Social support and personality among male police officers in Singapore, *Personality and Individual Differences* 36: 109–23

Uchino, B., Cacioppo, J. and Kiecolt-Glaser, J. 1996. The relationship between social support and physiological processes: a review with emphasis on underlying mechanisms and implications for health, *Psychological Bulletin* 119: 488–531

Vaux, A. and Harrison, D. 1985. Support network characteristics associated with support satisfaction and perceived support, *American Journal of Community Psychology* 13: 245–64

Von Dras, D. and Siegler, I. 1997. Stability in Extraversion and aspects of social support at midlife, *Journal of Personality and Social Psychology* 72: 233–41

Ystgaard, M., Tambs, K. and Dalgard, O. 1999. Life stress, social support and psycho-logical distress in late adolescence: a longitudinal study, *Society of Psychiatric Epidemiology* 34: 12–19

31 Social pain and hurt feelings

Geoff MacDonald

Physical injury may not be the only cause of pain. In a striking case study, Danziger and Willer (2005) describe a thirty-two-year-old woman diagnosed with congenital insensitivity to pain (a disruption of pain sensation capacity) who had never experienced physical pain despite a life that included fractures, burns, appendicitis and two anaesthetic-free births. However, not long after her younger brother died in a tragic automobile accident, this woman suffered an intense, days-long headache – her first and only experience of pain. Although an extreme example, this case is consistent with recent research suggesting that threats to social connection may stimulate painful feelings, or social pain, via some of the same physiological mechanisms activated by physical injury.

In this chapter, my goal is to examine whether a better understanding of the experience of hurt feelings can be achieved by conceptualizing this emotion as another form of such social pain. I will begin by providing the basis for construing hurt feelings as genuinely painful, including definitions of relevant terms, evidence for functional overlap between social and physical pain, and arguments for considering hurt feelings as a discrete emotional state. Next, I will examine research on the causes of hurt feelings, concluding that *social injury*, or damage to beliefs about the availability of social support, leads to such hurt. I will then explore documented reactions to hurt feelings including surprise and confusion, relational distancing, conflict de-escalation tactics, and the pursuit of social connection. This constellation of reactions suggests an inherent approach/avoidance conflict motivated by hurt that becomes apparent in research on individual differences in sensitivity to hurt feelings. Finally, I will briefly note some implications for future research of framing reactions to hurt feelings in approach/avoidance terms.

Hurt feelings as a form of emotional pain

Pain affect and emotional pain

Emotional pain can be as excruciating as physical pain. For example, individuals who were asked to relive the pain from a past instance of betrayal rated that pain

Thanks to Nathan DeWall, Marc Fournier, Tara Marshall and Terry Borsook for their helpful suggestions. This work was supported by a Social Sciences and Humanities Research Council of Canada grant. I am grateful to the Canadian government for their support of research in the social sciences.

(using the McGill Pain Index) at levels equivalent to cancer patient norms (Chen, Williams, Fitness and Newton 2008). The experience of physical pain involves two distinguishable physiological systems (e.g., Craig 1999; Price 2000). The *pain sensation* system involves receptors at the site of physical injury that collect information about the nature of the damage (e.g., cutting or burning) and communicate this information to the brain for further processing. The *pain affect* system is associated with the emotional and motivational component of pain, and has been argued to underlie the experience of emotional pain (Eisenberger and Lieberman 2004; MacDonald and Leary 2005a; Panksepp 1998). Pain affect is the experience of discomfort and urgent desire to escape a harmful stimulus that frequently accompanies pain sensation. Because pain affect is separable from pain sensation, any number of inputs could theoretically stimulate painful feelings via connection to pain affect mechanisms. Shortly, I will review evidence that social exclusion is one such input.

Emotional pain, social pain and hurt feelings

Before reviewing the evidence, it is important to be clear on some key terms. As used in this chapter, *emotional pain* refers to the activation of pain affect by any stimulus other than physical injury. *Social pain* refers to the activation of pain affect in response to threats to, or losses of, social connection. *Hurt feelings* are a sub-type of social pain that are experienced specifically in response to perceptions of *social injury*, or threats to beliefs about one's potential for recruiting social support. I will expand on the concept of social injury later, but for now, the distinction between social pain and hurt feelings can be highlighted through an example provided by Leary and Springer (2001). They note that the death of a loved one may cause tremendous social pain, but is unlikely to cause hurt feelings.

Evidence for overlap between social and physical pain

Recently, Mark Leary and I (2005a) reviewed evidence supporting the overlap between social and physical pain. We found that injury-related terms such as hurt and heartbreak are used to describe responses to social exclusion across multiple languages and cultures. We also found that a number of individual differences including Extraversion, anxiety, depression, aggressiveness, and perceived social support are related similarly to social and physical pain (e.g., Gatchel and Weisberg 2000). Examination of non-human animal research provided evidence that opioid and oxytocin neuroendocrine systems as well as the periaqueductal gray brain structure are involved in response to both social separation and physical injury (e.g., Panksepp 1998). We also noted Eisenberger, Lieberman and Williams' (2003) research with human participants demonstrating activation of the dorsal anterior cingulate cortex (ACC) and right ventral prefrontal cortex (PFC) in response to social exclusion. These brain areas have been shown to be specifically involved in the processing of pain affect (e.g., Rainville, Duncan, Price *et al.* 1997).

Since our review, more evidence has appeared supporting the link between social and physical pain. DeWall, MacDonald, Webster *et al.* (2008) reasoned that if emotional pain is processed using physical pain mechanisms, then analgesic drugs may diminish hurt feelings. Participants were randomly assigned to take acetaminophen or a placebo daily for three weeks and report each day on the extent to which they experienced hurt feelings. By day 15, those taking the pain-killer reported significantly lower daily hurt feelings than those taking placebo, an effect that grew stronger each day to the end of the study.

Although pain often results from physical injury, more severe injury can lead to decreased pain sensitivity, or analgesia. Analgesia is functional in cases of severe injury as the distraction caused by severe pain could impair effective escape from a threatening situation (Eccleston and Crombez 1999). MacDonald and Leary (2005a) reviewed evidence from non-human animal research that social separation also leads to analgesia (e.g., Konecka and Sroczynska 1990). This research has now been extended to humans. DeWall and Baumeister (2006) demonstrated that participants told they would have a lonely future experienced decreased sensitivity to physical pain.

Finally, Eisenberger, Jarcho, Lieberman and Naliboff (2006) demonstrated a correlation between social distress and perceptions of physical pain among participants who were not included in an online ball toss game (due to ostensible technical difficulties). This correlation was not found among those who were included in the game, nor, surprisingly, among those who could participate but were ignored by the other two players. The authors suggest this latter finding may have resulted from the activation of affect regulation mechanisms triggered by such blatant social exclusion. Nevertheless, it is clear that substantial evidence supporting the link between social and physical pain is mounting.

Hurt feelings as a discrete emotion

Given the demonstrated link between social and physical pain, it appears reasonable to suggest that hurt feelings may result from the activation of pain affect (MacDonald and Leary 2005b). As a form of emotional pain, hurt feelings should be discrete from other emotions, although this point is not universally accepted. For example, Vangelisti (2001) describes hurt as a blend of fear and sadness. Certainly, hurtful episodes do more than just hurt: reports of hurt feelings are usually accompanied by reports of other emotions including fear, sadness, anger, anxiety and shame (Feeney 2005; Leary and Springer 2001; Sanford and Rowatt 2004).

Although hurtful events may trigger a range of emotional states, Leary and Springer (2001) have provided evidence that the experience of hurt feelings is not reducible to other emotions. In one approach, Leary, Springer, Negel *et al.* (1998) simultaneously regressed a number of emotional states reported to result from hurtful episodes on reports of hurt feelings. This analysis showed that hurt feelings were associated with higher levels of general distress and lower levels of generic positive affect, but were not associated with more specific emotions including anxiety, hostility and guilt. In another approach, when controlling for a comprehensive set of negative emotions, a significant association between two separate measures of hurt feelings remained (Leary and Springer 2001). These results suggest that measures of hurt feelings cannot be reduced to measures of other emotional states.

These findings are consistent with the notion that there is a unique emotional aspect to hurt feelings that may be explainable in terms of pain affect, although further research is needed to more strongly support this conclusion. Should emotional pain ultimately gain recognition as a discrete emotion, research will be needed to understand the antecedents, consequences and functional value of what could be one of our most evolutionarily primitive feeling states. The following sections begin an exploration of these issues by examining the causes and consequences of hurt feelings.

Social injury: exploring the causes of hurt feelings

Feelings of rejection as a cause of hurt feelings

MacDonald and Leary (2005a) argue that pain affect evolved to become associated with social exclusion because belonging is crucial for survival and reproduction among social animals. Hurt feelings are clearly associated with feelings of rejection (Leary, Springer, Negel et al. 1998). For example, Buckley, Winkel and Leary (2004) demonstrated experimentally that rejecting messages are more hurtful than accepting or neutral messages. When asked to describe hurtful episodes, participants in another study most commonly listed incidents of criticism, betrayal and explicit rejection (Leary et al. 1998). Messages perceived as most hurtful are those delivered by close others (Leary et al. 1998; Vangelisti, Young, Carpenter-Theune and Alexander 2005), perceived to be intentionally hurtful (Feeney 2004), or perceived as more humiliating and denigrating to a relationship (Vangelisti et al. 2005). Such messages appear to provide the clearest signs of rejection in the most important relationships, and thus may be perceived as especially threatening.

Loss of social reward as a cause of hurt feelings

There are a number of reasons why social exclusion may be perceived as threatening, perhaps none more important than the concern that a rejection may reflect one's generally low social standing. However, exclusion from a particular relationship involves not just the presence of threat but also the loss of important rewards. For example, feelings of intimacy and validation can be considered some of the primary rewards of romantic relationships. These rewards are lost if the relationship dissolves, potentially leading to immense distress. Further, the frustration caused by a failure to obtain strongly desired relationship rewards, such as in unrequited love, can also be highly distressing (Baumeister, Wotman and Stillwell 1993). Apart from the threatening aspects of social exclusion, evidence suggests that such frustration or lost reward may be a painful aspect of rejection.

Gray (1987) argued for a neurological overlap between fear and frustration. This formulation suggests that the unexpected loss of or failure to obtain a desired reward may promote similar emotional experiences as the presence of a threatening stimulus, including pain. For example, athletes may describe defeat in a championship match as painful despite the absence of any obvious threat to their wellbeing. Work with non-human animals has suggested that reward loss promotes responses similar to those associated with painful stimuli. For example, an unexpected downshift in the degree of sucrose in a sucrose solution facilitates escape and startle responses in rats (Papini, Wood, Daniel and Norris 2006). Also, similar to the analgesic response to physical injury and social isolation, rats show decreased pain sensitivity following reward loss (Mustaca and Papini 2005). Papini *et al.* (2006) argue that these effects of reward loss are mediated by pain affect mechanisms. This claim has been supported in research with humans showing that reward loss is associated with activation in brain regions associated with pain affect (i.e., ACC and PFC; Abler, Walter and Erk 2005).

Research suggests that the failure to receive positive behaviour from others (i.e., *non-inclusion*) may be painful in a fashion similar to the threats caused by negative behaviour from others (i.e., *rejection*). For example, being ignored or ostracized (where no threats are made but social rewards are withheld) is associated with hurt feelings (Leary and Springer 2001; Williams 2001). Further, if rejection and non-inclusion have independent influences on hurt feelings, events that combine both social threat and loss of social reward should be most hurtful. Buckley, Winkel and Leary (2004) randomly assigned participants to receive a constantly negative evaluation from another 'participant' (actually a computer program) or an evaluation that changed from positive to negative over time. Participants in the acceptance-to-rejection condition reported higher levels of hurt feelings than those in the constant rejection condition. Although feelings of rejection did not differ between the two conditions, those in the acceptance-to-rejection condition did report a higher desire to be accepted by the other participant. These data suggest that a loss of social reward in addition to the presence of rejection threat led to especially high levels of hurt feelings.

An interesting potential application of the notion that hurt feelings arise from loss of social reward involves infidelity. Feeney (2004) found the most hurtful episodes in romantic relationships involved infidelity. When asked which would hurt more, sexual or emotional infidelity (i.e., a partner having sex vs. falling in love with a rival), people are more likely to choose emotional infidelity (Green and Sabini 2006; Sabini and Green 2004). Sabini and Green (2004) suggest that emotional infidelity provides a stronger signal that the cheating partner devalues the relationship, but do not clarify why emotional infidelity signals greater devaluation. One possibility is that love is seen as a more limited resource than sex, such that emotional infidelity has the potential to lead to a stronger sense of loss. Whereas falling in love with a rival necessarily means sharing emotional intimacy, sexual infidelity need not involve these deeper feelings. To the extent that romantic love is seen as a shared bond between only two people, intimacy becomes a zero-sum game; that is, a partner's emotional infidelity necessarily reduces intimacy in the original relationship in a fashion that sexual infidelity may not. As a result, even if emotional and sexual infidelity feel equally threatening, emotional infidelity appears to involve a stronger and more irrevocable sense of lost reward, possibly explaining why it may be more hurtful.

Integrating the causes of hurt feelings

How can the root cause of hurt feelings be described most succinctly? Leary and Springer (2001) argue that the primary cognitive appraisal underlying hurt feelings is relational devaluation, or a sense that the transgressor does not view her or his relationship with the victim to be as valuable, close or important as the victim desires. In Leary, Springer, Negel et al.'s (1998) research, 99 per cent of hurtful events were evaluated as involving instances of relational devaluation. Certainly, then, relational devaluation can contribute to hurt feelings.

Vangelisti, Young, Carpenter-Theune and Alexander (2005) argue that hurt feelings may not always be caused by relational factors. These authors argue that participants in their research who were asked to describe the causes of past hurtful events frequently listed non-relational issues. They specifically note threats to the self-concept as an exemplar of a common non-relational cause. However, self-esteem, or the summary evaluation of one's self-concept, is closely tied to feelings of acceptability to others (Leary and MacDonald 2003) and may have evolved specifically to provide an internal metric of social value (Leary, Tambor, Terdal and Downs 1995). In Leary, Springer, Negel et al.'s (1998) research, intensity of hurt feelings correlated strongly with internalizing the hurtful episode, suggesting that hurt feelings can reflect accepting negative social feedback as an accurate portrayal of the self-concept.

However, trait self-esteem provides information about acceptability to others across many relationships rather than in one specific relationship (MacDonald 2007). Thus, Vangelisti et al.'s (2005) argument highlights the idea that hurt feelings may be especially strong when the event is interpreted as having implications across many relationships. The most hurtful messages may be those that connote threats to multiple sources of connection (e.g., 'Nobody loves you'). In fact, most of the hurtful incidents in Leary et al.'s (1998) study were rated as having direct ramifications for the individuals' social desirability and such incidents were rated as the most hurtful. Those incidents that were not directly related to social desirability involved attributes that have important implications for social acceptance (e.g., intelligence, attitudes).

Feeney (2005) provides a different challenge to the relational devaluation perspective. In examining descriptions of hurtful events in romantic relationships,

Feeney found a substantial portion of events that involved jealousy and distrust on the part of the transgressor (e.g., checking on a partner's whereabouts) or acts of concealment intended to protect the victim (e.g., holding back gossip about a partner). Although provoking hurt, these incidents could not be explained in terms of relational devaluation because they signalled that the transgressor did indeed care deeply about the victim. Feeney (2005) frames these results in attachment terms, suggesting that hurt feelings can result from threats to the belief that one is worthy of love (as in instances of relational devaluation) and/or from threats to the belief that others are dependable sources of support (as in distrusting behaviour). Hurt feelings arising from a partner's jealousy are an interesting case in that they may provide both a threat of rejection (by providing a signal that one is not trustworthy) and a loss of reward (by portraying one's partner as not as trusting as hoped). Feeney (2005) thus describes hurt feelings as arising from a sense of *personal injury*, or damaged cognitive models of self as lovable and/or others as dependable.

Overall, Feeney's (2005) analysis appears to capture the widest range of hurtful events, accounts for both social threat and loss of social reward as causes of hurt feelings, and can accommodate the influence of transgressions that have implications across relationships (via influence on general cognitive models). One way to frame Feeney's conclusions is that hurt feelings arise when one's perceived ability to find comfort through relationships is diminished. Both threats to the belief that one is worthy of love and to the belief that relational partners can be counted on create disruptions to one's certainty that support can be found when needed. Perhaps, then, it is violence done to expectations of support, now and in the future, that is the injury that leads to hurt feelings.

One advantage of this explanation is that it can answer the question of why losing someone to death hurts but does not create hurt feelings (Leary and Springer 2001). Death may cause lost access to a particular relational partner, but if it is not a volitional act it cannot speak to one's potential to find future support. Hurt feelings may only arise when events carry messages relevant to one's future social prospects. For this reason, I prefer the term *social injury* rather than personal injury, as I believe this term highlights the relational nature of hurt feelings.

Reactions associated with hurt feelings

Surprise and confusion

Eisenberger and Lieberman (2004) describe pain as a system that signals the detection of harmful stimuli, recruiting attention and coping resources to minimize exposure to threat. They argue that the role of the ACC in pain is as a mechanism that detects discrepancies, such as those between desired and actual conditions, using feelings of pain as an alarm or warning signal. This pain signal disrupts attention, freeing it to focus on the source of threat (Eccleston and Crombez 1999).

If the social pain of hurt feelings functions to alert individuals to sources of social injury, then hurt feelings should trigger an attention-orienting response.

One marker of attention disruption could be a sense of surprise, which is often conceptualized as an orienting response but not an emotion (Feeney 2005). In open-ended descriptions of responses to hurtful events, terms connoting surprise (e.g., confused) were frequently mentioned (Feeney 2005). The association between hurt feelings and the orienting response of surprise suggests that hurt may be the initial reaction to cognitive appraisals of social injury. Hurt may draw attention to the source of injury, motivating further processing to delineate the meaning of the hurtful event. For example, one participant in Leary, Springer, Negel et al.'s (1998) study wrote, 'At first I was surprised. Then I wanted to cry ... A few minutes later I was furious at him' (p. 1235). Another participant wrote, 'Eventually I became angry, but initially it was just plain painful' (Leary et al. 1998, p. 1235).

The role of confusion in hurt feelings may help explain why social pain often lingers. For example, 90% of the hurtful events described by participants in Leary et al.'s (1998) study still hurt even though the majority occurred a year or more past. Chen, Williams, Fitness and Newton (2008) showed that reliving memories of betrayal led to considerably more experienced pain than reliving memories of physical injury, despite the fact that participants rated the original social and physical injuries as equally painful. Strongly hurtful events like the breakdown of a marriage are complicated and multifaceted, touching on core aspects of the self that are extremely sensitive and possibly resistant to change. Such events can take months or years to process and fully integrate with one's views of the self as lovable and of others as dependable. As a result, social pain may remain as a signal that beliefs about the accessibility of support are in need of repair. In this sense, although distressing, lingering social pain may be functional in promoting cognitive reorganization to make sense of social exclusion and its implications for future support. This analysis also suggests that deeply hurtful events such as divorce may leave a lasting sense of loss that may cause lingering pain until an alternate means for satisfying belongingness needs is found.

Distancing from the source of threat

Vangelisti (2001) argues that the core feature distinguishing hurt from other emotional states is vulnerability. Much of the research on hurt feelings has focused on how this sense of vulnerability heightens perceptions of risk for further harm and thus motivates emotional distancing from the perpetrator. Experimental research has shown that excluded individuals respond with higher levels of aggression (e.g., Buckley, Winkel and Leary 2004) and lower levels of prosocial behaviour (Twenge, Baumeister, DeWall et al. 2007). In Leary, Springer, Negel et al.'s (1998) research, higher levels of hurt feelings were associated with higher levels of expressed anger and verbal attacks. Such aggressive and antisocial responses appear to represent a devaluation of the relationship that facilitates emotional distance and reduced vulnerability to further pain. Indeed, 67 per cent of victims reported that their relationship with the perpetrator was weakened temporarily by the hurtful event and 42 per cent reported the relationship was damaged permanently. Further, features of a hurtful event perceived to signal an increased risk of continued or increased harm are especially likely to lead to distancing (Vangelisti 2001; Vangelisti, Young, Carpenter-Theune and Alexander 2005). Hurtful messages perceived to communicate relational denigration or the perception of an intrinsic flaw in the victim, to be intentionally hurtful, or to be a result of the transgressor's self-centred motives or stable personality traits led to especially strong distancing tendencies.

Threat de-escalation

Hurt feelings may also help increase protection from social injury by motivating responses that reduce threat at its source. Sanford and Rowatt (2004) describe hurt, as well as other feeling states such as sadness, as *soft emotions* that motivate the pursuit of comfort, support and assistance from others. These authors suggest that soft emotions can facilitate relationship functioning by eliciting empathy and understanding, especially from close others. The expression of hurt can de-escalate tense relationship situations by signalling vulnerability, need or weakness (Sanford and Rowatt 2004). For example, in Leary *et al.*'s (1998) research, more intense hurt feelings were associated with more crying by victims of hurtful episodes. Seeing a partner's or friend's tears may well lead an individual to restrain attacks, thus sparing further social injury.

Pursuing social connection

Hurt feelings may also induce an approach-oriented strategy of seeking social connection. Maner, DeWall, Baumeister and Schaller (2007) argue that the hurt caused by social injury should lead to a desire for new avenues of social connection. In general, they argue that when a goal is blocked, efforts to find a new path to that goal should be energized. In fact, experiencing and expressing hurt may facilitate unique opportunities for pursuing intimacy (Sanford and Rowatt 2004). Intimacy in close relationships is built on self-disclosure, particularly when that disclosure is met by one's relational partner with responsiveness (Reis and Patrick 1996). Exposing core vulnerabilities through the expression of hurt creates the opportunity to share important aspects of the self that may then be validated. For example, L'Abate (1977) argued that the most intimate level of relationship conflict involves sharing the hurt that underlies anger. Frey, Holley and L'Abate (1979) found that couples evaluated conflict resolution involving the expression of hurt to be especially intimate.

Research supports the notion that hurt individuals pursue social connection in response to a hurtful episode. Many participants in Leary *et al.*'s (1998) study described seeking out new relationships in response to a hurtful event (Leary and Springer 2001). Ostracism has been shown to lead to increased conformity (Williams, Cheung and Choi 2000) and cooperation (for women only; Williams and Sommer 1997), suggesting increased desire for social connection. Social exclusion has also been shown to lead to increased interest in a friend introduction service and more positive evaluations of potential interaction partners (Maner, DeWall, Baumeister and Schaller 2007). Importantly, however, the prosocial behaviour demonstrated by Maner and colleagues was neither directed at the excluder nor toward those with whom no future interaction was possible. In addition, individuals chronically fearful of rejection did not appear strongly motivated to seek connection following exclusion. These findings suggest that hurt individuals seek support only from safe and available sources.

Approach/avoidance conflict

Conflicting motives

Overall, this review of the reactions associated with hurt feelings suggests that hurt promotes potentially conflicting approach and avoidance action tendencies. Maner *et al.* (2007, p. 52) suggest that socially excluded individuals may be 'vulnerable but needy and those two feelings may push in opposite directions'. Those whose feelings are hurt appear motivated to avoid closeness, especially with the hurtful individual. At the same time, hurt individuals may be motivated to reveal vulnerabilities and pursue social connection to soothe their sense of injury. Although Maner *et al.*'s (2007) work in the lab suggests that hurt individuals may attempt to forge connections with new relational partners, real-world dynamics may constrain this tendency. When the hurtful individual is also one's primary source of social support (e.g., a romantic partner) an especially strong approach/ avoid conflict focused on the source of hurt may be experienced. Given that such approach/avoid conflicts are the primary source of anxiety (Gray and McNaughton 2000), this dynamic may help explain the relation of hurt feelings with anxiety (see also Corr 2005).

A more direct source of evidence for the simultaneous motivations of desire for relational distance (avoidance) and desire for connection (approach) comes from Gardner and colleagues' research on the Social Monitoring System (Gardner, Pickett and Brewer 2000; Gardner, Pickett, Jefferis and Knowles 2005). Heightened desire to avoid social threats should lead to greater sensitivity to negative social information (e.g., scowls) whereas heightened desire to approach social rewards should lead to greater sensitivity to positive social information (e.g., smiles). Both social exclusion (Gardner, Pickett and Brewer 2000) and loneliness (Gardner, Pickett, Jefferis and Knowles 2005) are associated with improved memory for both positive and negative social information but unrelated to memory for non-social information.

Individual differences in hurt feelings proneness

Individual difference research provides more nuanced evidence for the conflicting approach and avoidance motivations associated with hurt feelings. Leary and

Springer's (2001) measure of hurt feelings proneness (HFP) assesses the ease with which people experience hurt feelings. This scale is associated with the frequency with which people's feelings are hurt but not the intensity of specific hurtful episodes (Leary and Springer 2001). In this sense, HFP may be thought of as a measure of threshold for social pain, but not a predictor of degree of experienced hurt.

In a study investigating sensitivity to social threat and reward, participants expected to engage in a social interaction after completing a number of questionnaires including HFP (MacDonald 2008). The key scale in this package was a measure of perceived social threat (e.g., 'I'm worried what my interaction partner will think of me') and perceived social reward (e.g., 'This interaction is a fun opportunity'). Higher HFP was associated with both higher perceptions of potential threat and higher perceptions of potential reward. Again, hurt feelings appear to be associated with simultaneous approach and avoidance motivations.

HFP is related to other individual difference measures that reflect both sensitivity to social threat and sensitivity to social reward. HFP correlates strongly and positively with Neuroticism, anxious attachment, fear of negative evaluation, and self-reported behavioural inhibition system activity (Leary and Springer 2001; MacDonald 2008). These findings reflect an association between sensitivity to both hurt feelings and threat. However, HFP is also related positively to the need to belong (Leary and Springer 2001; MacDonald 2008), a variable reflecting one's appetite for social connection. Those higher in HFP have also been shown to place more value on true friendship and mature love (Leary and Springer 2001). Thus, those more prone to hurt feelings appear to have stronger motivation to engage with social rewards.

The relations of the attachment dimensions of anxiety and avoidance with HFP are of particular interest. Anxiously attached individuals tend to be hypervigilant for rejection cues and seek closeness to soothe emotional distress, whereas avoidantly attached individuals are uncomfortable with intimacy and avoid acknowledging distress (Shaver and Mikulincer 2002). Anxious attachment is associated with higher levels of both perceived social threat and perceived social reward (MacDonald 2008). Whereas the relation between anxious attachment and perceived social threat is mediated by fear of negative evaluation, the relation between anxious attachment and perceived social reward is mediated by HFP. Sensitivity to hurt feelings may play an important role in anxiously attached individuals' belief that they can find relief from emotional distress through social connection.

Higher levels of avoidant attachment are associated significantly with lower levels of perceived social reward and marginally with higher levels of perceived social threat (MacDonald 2008). The negative relation between avoidant attachment and perceived social reward is partially mediated by HFP. In addition, HFP acts as a suppressor variable in the positive relation between avoidant attachment and perceived social threat. That is, were it not for their tendency to be less sensitive to hurt feelings, avoidantly attached individuals would perceive higher levels of social threat. This pattern of findings suggests that avoidantly attached individuals distance themselves from social pain in order to avoid engaging with social threat. However, the cost of down-regulating sensitivity to hurt feelings appears to be a decreased sensitivity to potentially rewarding social opportunities.

Conclusion

This review has suggested that hurt feelings are the experience of pain affect triggered by perceptions of threat to cognitive models of support availability. Hurt feelings appear to promote both increased defence against social threat and increased drive for social connection. Thus, hurt feelings have the potential to create intense approach/avoidance conflict. This social reward/threat framework suggests that the traditional construal of belongingness as a unidimensional construct ranging from inclusion to exclusion may not be correct. Instead, perceptions of social connection may involve independent assessments of the degree of rejection (i.e., social threat) and the degree of inclusion (i.e., social reward). Upon reflection, such a distinction appears easily recognizable in daily life. For example, a wordless interaction with a store clerk may not lead to warm feelings of intimacy but neither should it lead to feelings of rejection. Conversely, a potential romantic partner who 'just wants to be friends', conveys simultaneous messages of inclusion and rejection.

One of many remaining questions is the relative extent to which the presence of social threat and the loss of social reward each contribute to feelings of hurt. In addition to such quantitative comparisons, researchers are beginning to be mindful of qualitative differences in reactions to rejection and non-inclusion. Molden *et al.* (in press) argue that being actively rejected (which provides a clear signal of social threat) should be associated with motivation to prevent further social losses, whereas being ignored (which provides a signal of lack of social reward) should be associated with motivation to promote social gains. Consistent with these hypotheses, these researchers showed that experiences of rejection led to higher levels of social withdrawal, whereas experiences of being ignored led to higher levels of social engagement.

As noted, the potentially conflicting approach and avoidance tendencies described in this review are manifest in trait sensitivity to hurt feelings. This suggests that individuals prone to hurt feelings may experience chronic sensitivity to social threat and social reward. Potential implications of such heightened awareness of positive and negative social cues may include chronic relationship ambivalence and anxiety, susceptibility to influence by situationally salient social cues, and relatively unstable evaluations of relational partners. More generally, this review suggests that the approach/avoidance framework provided by Gray and McNaughton's (2000) threat defence system model may be helpful in framing research on the regulation of social behaviour. It appears increasingly clear that one of the most important proximal motivators of such social approach and avoidance tendencies is the genuine feeling of pain that helps protect our connections to others.

References

Abler, B., Walter, H. and Erk, S. 2005. Neural correlates of frustration, *Neuroreport: For Rapid Communication of Neuroscience Research* 16: 669–72

Baumeister, R. F., Wotman, S. R. and Stillwell, A. M. 1993. Unrequited love: on heartbreak, anger, guilt, scriptlessness, and humiliation, *Journal of Personality and Social Psychology* 64: 377–94

Buckley, K. E., Winkel, R. E. and Leary, M. R. 2004. Reactions to acceptance and rejection: effects of level and sequence of relational evaluation, *Journal of Experimental Social Psychology* 40: 14–28

Chen, Z., Williams, K. D., Fitness, J. and Newton, N. C. 2008. When hurt will not heal: exploring the capacity to relive social and physical pain, *Psychological Science* 19: 789–95

Corr, P. J. 2005. Social exclusion and the hierarchical defense system: comment on MacDonald and Leary (2005), *Psychological Bulletin* 131: 231–6

Craig, K. D. 1999. Emotions and Psychobiology, in P. Wall and R. Melzack (eds.), *Textbook of pain*, pp. 331–43. New York: Churchill Livingstone

Danziger, N. and Willer, J. C. 2005. Tension-type headache as the unique pain experience of a patient with congenital insensitivity to pain, *Pain* 117: 478–83

DeWall, C. N. and Baumeister, R. F. 2006. Alone but feeling no pain: effects of social exclusion on physical pain tolerance and pain threshold, affective forecasting, and interpersonal empathy, *Journal of Personality and Social Psychology* 91: 1–15

DeWall, C. N., MacDonald, G., Webster, G. D., Tice, D. M. and Baumeister, R. F. 2008. Acetaminophen reduces psychological hurt feelings over time. Manuscript under review

Eccleston, C. and Crombez, G. 1999. Pain demands attention: a cognitive-affective model of the interruptive function of pain, *Psychological Bulletin* 125: 356–66

Eisenberger, N. I., Jarcho, J. M., Lieberman, M. D. and Naliboff, B. D. 2006. An experimental study of shared sensitivity to physical pain and social rejection, *Pain* 126: 132–8

Eisenberger, N. I. and Lieberman, M. D. 2004. Why rejection hurts: a common neural alarm system for physical and social pain, *Trends in Cognitive Sciences* 8: 294–300

Eisenberger, N. I., Lieberman, M. D. and Williams, K. D. 2003. Does rejection hurt? An fMRI study of social exclusion, *Science* 302: 290–2

Feeney, J. 2004. Hurt feelings in couple relationships: towards integrative models of the negative effects of hurtful events, *Journal of Social and Personal Relationships* 21: 487–508

2005. Hurt feelings in couple relationships: exploring the role of attachment and perceptions of personal injury, *Personal Relationships* 12: 253–72

Frey, J., Holley, J. and L'Abate, L. 1979. Intimacy is sharing hurt feelings: a comparison of three conflict resolution models, *Journal of Marital and Family Therapy* 5: 35–41

Gardner, W., Pickett, C. L. and Brewer, M. B. 2000. Social exclusion and selective memory: how the need to belong influences memory for social events, *Personality and Social Psychology Bulletin* 26: 486–96

Gardner, W. L., Pickett, C. L., Jefferis, V. and Knowles, M. 2005. On the outside looking in: loneliness and social monitoring, *Personality and Social Psychology Bulletin* 31: 1549–60

Gatchel, R. J. and Weisberg, J. N. (eds.) 2000. *Personality characteristics of patients with pain*. Washington, DC: American Psychological Association

Gray, J. A. 1987. *The psychology of fear and stress*. Cambridge University Press

Gray, J. A. and McNaughton, N. 2000. *The neuropsychology of anxiety*. New York: Oxford University Press

Green, M. C. and Sabini, J. 2006. Gender, socioeconomic status, age, and jealousy: emotional responses to infidelity in a national sample, *Emotion* 6: 330–4

Konecka, A. M. and Sroczynska, I. 1990. Stressors and pain sensitivity in CFW mice: role of opioid peptides, *Archives Internationales de Physiologie et de Biochimie* 98: 245–52

L'Abate, L. 1977. Intimacy is sharing hurt feelings: a reply to David Mace, *Journal of Marriage and Family Counseling* 3: 13–16

Leary, M. R. and MacDonald, G. 2003. Individual differences in self-esteem: a review and theoretical integration, in M. R. Leary and J. P. Price (eds.), *Handbook of self and identity*, pp. 401–18. New York: Guilford Press

Leary, M. R. and Springer, C. 2001. Hurt feelings: the neglected emotion, in R. M. Kowalski (ed.), *Behaving badly: aversive behaviours in interpersonal relationships*, pp. 151–75. Washington, DC: American Psychological Association

Leary, M. R., Springer, C., Negel, L., Ansell, E. and Evans, K. 1998. The causes, phenomenology, and consequences of hurt feelings, *Journal of Personality and Social Psychology* 74: 1225–37

Leary, M. R., Tambor, E. S., Terdal, S. K. and Downs, D. L. 1995. Self-esteem as an interpersonal monitor: the sociometer hypothesis, *Journal of Personality and Social Psychology* 68: 518–30

MacDonald, G. 2007. Self-esteem: a human elaboration of prehuman belongingness motivation, in C. Sedikides and S. Spencer (eds.) *The self in social psychology*, pp. 412–56. New York: Psychology Press

2008. The social threat and reward scale. Unpublished data.

MacDonald, G. and Leary, M. R. 2005a. Why does social exclusion hurt? The relationship between social and physical pain, *Psychological Bulletin* 131: 202–23

2005b. Roles of social pain and defense mechanisms in response to social exclusion: reply to Panksepp (2005) and Corr (2005), *Psychological Bulletin* 131: 237–40

Maner, J. K., DeWall, C. N., Baumeister, R. F. and Schaller, M. 2007. Does social exclusion motivate interpersonal reconnection? Resolving the 'porcupine problem.', *Journal of Personality and Social Psychology* 92: 42–55

Molden, D. C., Lucas, G. M., Gardner, W. L., Dean, K. and Knowles, M. L. in press. Motivations for prevention or promotion following social exclusion: being rejected versus being ignored, *Journal of Personality and Social Psychology*

Mustaca, A. E. and Papini, M. R. 2005. Consummatory successive negative contrast induces hypoalgesia, *International Journal of Comparative Psychology* 18: 255–62

Panksepp, J. 1998. *Affective neuroscience: the foundations of human and animal emotions*. London: Oxford University Press

Papini, M. R., Wood, M., Daniel, A. M. and Norris, J. N. 2006. Reward loss as psychological pain, *International Journal of Psychology and Psychological Therapy* 6: 189–213

Price, D. 2000. Psychological and neural mechanisms of the affective dimension of pain, *Science* 288: 1769–72

Rainville, P. D., Duncan, G. H., Price, D. D., Carrier, B. and Bushnell, M. C. 1997. Pain affect encoded in human anterior cingulate but not somatosensory cortex, *Science* 277: 968–71

Reis, H. T. and Patrick, B. 1996. Attachment and intimacy: component processes, in E. T. Higgins and A. Kruglanski (eds.), *Handbook of basic processes in social psychology*. New York: Guilford Press

Sabini, J. and Green, M. C. 2004. Emotional responses to sexual and emotional infidelity: constants and differences across genders, samples, and methods, *Personality and Social Psychology Bulletin* 30: 1375–88

Sanford, K. and Rowatt, W. C. 2004. When is negative emotion positive for relationships? An investigation of married couples and roommates, *Personal Relationships* 11: 329–54

Shaver, P. R. and Mikulincer, M. 2002. Attachment-related psychodynamics, *Attachment and Human Development* 4: 133–61

Twenge, J. M., Baumeister, R. F., DeWall, C. N., Ciarocco, N. J. and Bartels, J. M. 2007. Social exclusion decreases prosocial behaviour, *Journal of Personality and Social Psychology* 92: 56–66

Vangelisti, A. L. 2001. Making sense of hurtful interactions in close relationships: when hurt feelings create distance, in V. Manusov and J. H. Harvey (eds.), *Attribution, communication behaviour, and close relationships: advances in personal relations*, pp. 38–58. New York: Cambridge University Press

Vangelisti, A. L., Young, S. L., Carpenter-Theune, K. and Alexander, A. L. 2005. Why does it hurt? The perceived causes of hurt feelings, *Communication Research* 32: 443–77

Williams, K. D. 2001. *Ostracism: the power of silence*. New York: Guilford Publications

Williams, K. D., Cheung, C. K. and Choi, W. 2000. Cyberostracism: effects of being ignored over the internet, *Journal of Personality and Social Psychology* 79: 748–62

Williams, K. D. and Sommer, K. L. 1997. Social ostracism by one's coworkers: does rejection lead to loafing or compensation, *Personality and Social Psychology Bulletin* 23: 693–706

32 Personality in cross-cultural perspective

Juris G. Draguns

Introduction

All human beings are products of concurrent and lifelong processes of enculturation and individuation. Thus, they absorb the accumulated experience of their culture and develop their unique personality. The relationship between culture and personality is not only given, it is inextricable. Yet relatively little is known about the way in which culture and personality interact. This chapter will attempt to provide an introductory account about research approaches and results pertaining to the links between culture and personality.

Culture and personality: conceptions and definitions

Personality: its differential and defining features

At this point in the Handbook there is no need to define personality. Suffice it to say that research on personality is focused upon two major topics: individual differences in the distribution of various traits and dispositions across persons and the organization of these characteristics within the person (Draguns 1979). According to Kluckhohn and Murray (1950, p. 190), 'every man is in certain respects: (a) like all other men, (b) like some other men, and (c) like no other man'. Personality theorists and researchers concede the study of laws and principles of behaviour to general psychology. They concentrate their effort upon traits, wherein an individual is like some other persons, and aspire to investigate the selves of unique persons that are in some respects different from those of all other persons.

Culture: its defining properties and features

Herskovits (1949) elegantly characterized culture as the part of the environment that was created by human beings. Culture encompasses both artifacts and mental products. It enables human beings to build on the achievements of their predecessors and makes it unnecessary for each generation to start anew. In particular, culture includes shared learned behaviour as well as beliefs, values, attitudes, knowledge and skills (Marsella 1988). Hofstede and Hofstede (2005, p. 3) equated culture with the 'software of the mind', a set of programs or templates for guiding behaviour and structuring experience.

From the past to the present: the search for a comprehensive relationship

Culture and personality as a movement: promise and achievement

Empirical investigation of culture and personality was initiated by cultural anthroplogists early in the twentieth century. Franz Boas (1910) envisaged, and Ruth Benedict (1934) and Margaret Mead (1935) implemented, a systematic programme of investigations of psychological phenomena in their respective cultural contexts. In this manner, hypotheses, principally derived from psychoanalytic theory, were tested in very different cultural milieu. In particular, parent-child interactions, especially in relation to weaning, toilet training and the development of gender roles, were investigated as plausible antecedents of adult personality traits.

Ralph Linton (1945) and Abram Kardiner (1939) proposed a model of integrative culture and personality research. Psychoanalysis would serve as the source of theoretical formulations, to be tested in the course of anthropological fieldwork. In this manner, features of the modal personality within a culture were expected to emerge. Thus, Dubois (1944) collected copious ethnographic data in Alor, in an island in what is now Indonesia, which suggested a strong relationship between early socialization experiences and adult personality patterns. Other studies yielded less conclusive findings, and the extension of the culture and personality approach to national cultures, such as Japan (Benedict 1946) and Russia (Gorer and Rickman 1950), brought intractable conceptual, methodological and empirical problems to the fore. Even in small-scale cultures such as that of Tuscarora Indians, personality traits were found to be distributed multimodally rather than unimodally (Wallace 1952).

Thus, establishing a simple and direct relationship between personality and culture proved to be an elusive goal. Disillusionment set in, and Bruner (1974, p. 395) dismissed the entire culture and personality enterprise as a 'magnificent failure'. Bock (2000) pinpointed five questionable assumptions on which the culture and personality investigation rested: (1) childhood experience as the principal determinant of adult personality characteristics and of the corresponding cultural patterns; (2) one specific personality pattern as characteristic or prevalent within a culture; (3) cultural and personality characteristics being inferred from the same data; (4) projective tests such as Rorschach and TAT being appropriate instruments for assessing personalities across cultures; and (5) anthropologists being objective observers of other cultures, free of misconceptions and biases.

In defence of culture and personality studies, LeVine (2001) has maintained that the role of psychoanalytic conceptualization was not exclusive or monopolistic.

Inputs from Gestalt psychology, psychodynamic revisionists and stimulus-response theory were influential in both data gathering and conceptualization. The construct of modal personality was not universally accepted, and its blanket extension to all cultures was not advocated. Thus, the decline of the culture and personality school was more attributable to a shifting zeitgeist than to conceptual impasse or empirical disconfirmation.

Psychological anthropology

On a less ambitious scale, psychological anthropology has continued to employ traditional naturalistic methods in investigating manifestations of higher mental processes and structures, including personality, within their respective contexts (Piker 1998). Sweeping generalization is avoided, and such concepts as modal personality are rarely invoked. However, the study of infancy and early childhood and of their reverberations throughout the lifespan has not been abandoned (Spiro 1982). LeVine and LeVine (1988) and LeVine, Dixon, LeVine et al. (1994) have investigated the impact of multiple care-takers in East Africa. Consistent with the results obtained by a variety of other methods (Okeke, Draguns, Sheku and Allen 1999), sociocentric orientation was found to prevail throughout the lifespan, with security, harmony and social sensitivity in one's accustomed milieu, and help-lessness and disorientation outside of it. Other examples of topics investigated by psychological anthropologists include the complexities of developing male gen-der identity of the Sambia of Papua New Guinea (Herdt 1981) and the regulation and control of aggression among the Inuit in the Arctic (Briggs 1970).

Compatibly with the thrust of psychological anthropology, Parin, Morgenthaler and Parin-Mathey (1963, 1980) combined ethnographic fieldwork with concur-rent psychoanalytic exploration, including the use of free associations, among the Dogon of Mali and the Agni of Côte d'Ivoire, thereby following in the footsteps of Devereux (1969) who was the first to apply psychoanalytic procedures in the field.

From a unique culture to a multiplicity of cultures: toward intercultural comparison human research area files

Culture has traditionally been regarded as a descriptive and qualitative concept. As such, it may possess a considerable explanatory value, yet is not amenable to direct quantitative comparisons that are necessary for establishing functional relationships between cultural and psychological variables. To meet this need, Murdock (1967) established a world sample of ethnographies or culture descrip-tions that evolved into the Human Research Area Files (HRAF), a unique repository of ethnographic data from all regions of the world. Each of the ethnographies is rigorously and uniformly coded for all cultural features included in the description. For purposes of worldwide or hologeistic compar-ison, each culture in the HRAF sample is considered a unit, and correlation coefficients between cultural attributes can be computed for the total set of cultures or for specially designed sub-sets. As Naroll, Michik and Naroll (1980) emphasized, HRAF makes it possible to test theories on the basis of worldwide information. Relevant to personality, Rohner (1986) prominently used HRAF in examining the validity of his Parental Acceptance-Rejection Theory. An ambitious objective, not yet implemented (Draguns 2007), would be to score the traditional cultures in HRAF for Hofstede's (2001) cultural dimensions, which will be described in the next section.

Dimensions of national cultures: Geert Hofstede's contribution

In an international project of unparalleled magnitude, Geert Hofstede (1980) collected survey data on attitudes of employees of IBM, a major multinational corporation. Close to 117,000 protocols were so gathered in seventy-one countries, and were then subjected to multistage multivariate analyses. As a result of these procedures, four relatively independent dimensions were identified that Hofstede labelled power distance, individualism-collectivism, uncertainty avoidance and masculinity-femininity. Extensive definitions of these four dimensions are provided by Hofstede (1980, 2001). In brief, power distance refers to acceptance of economic and social inequality; individualism–collectivism pertains to the degree to which a person is integrated into groups; uncertainty avoidance taps the discomfort experienced in ambiguous or unstructured situations; and masculinity-femininity describes the distribution of emotional roles. Subsequently, a fifth dimension was added. It was first called Confucian dynamism and was more recently renamed long-term versus short-term orientation. Long-term orientation is expressed through persistence, thrift, modesty and respect for tradition.

It is important to emphasize that these five dimensions describe cultures and not individuals. Hofstede (2001) was adamant in warning that the two levels of analysis never be confounded. Correlates of a cultural dimension across countries in no way imply the existence of an identical relationship within a country. At most, such a relationship can be hypothesized and empirically tested.

Culture dimensions and personality

Over more than two decades, a wealth of information has accrued on the correlates of Hofstede's dimensions across cultures, in family, school and work settings (Hofstede 2001; Hofstede and Hofstede 2005) some of which are germane to personality. Results converge in demonstrating that high power distance is associated with conformity, obedience and emphasis on vertical, authoritarian-submissive over horizontal, egalitarian relationships. Uncertainty avoidance has been found to go together with high anxiety levels, experience of stress and a generally reduced sense of wellbeing. High scorers in uncertainty avoidance are less likely to attribute their achievements to ability and more to effort or circumstance. However, uncertainty avoiders also described themselves as sincere, serious, independent and peace loving, though dissatisfied with their finances and state of health. Feminine cultures place emphasis on the individual's personal characteristics; masculine cultures value a person's achievements and performance. Tender-mindedness prevails in feminine cultures, and tough-mindedness in masculine ones. Masculine cultures feature a clear-cut delineation of gender roles; in feminine cultures, overlap prevails. Feminine cultures are characterized by higher scores in subjective wellbeing and quality of life indicators (Arrindell and Veenhoven 2001). Long-term orientation promotes modest self-presentation, self-control and subordination of personal impulses, aspirations and preferences to group goals (Peabody 1999).

Individualism-collectivism within Hofstede's framework and outside of it

Individualism-collectivism has been studied more intensively and systematically, both within and outside of Hofstede's multidimensional framework, than any of the other four cultural dimensions. Triandis (1995, 2001) has pursued a programme of investigations that has yielded a pattern of consistent results. In collectivist cultures, people have been found to describe themselves as group members rather than as individuals, to emphasize collective goals, to pay more attention to external than internal determinants of social behaviour, and to be self-effacing. Individualists tend to be dominant, self-enhancing and optimistic. Hofstede (2001) and Hofstede and Hofstede (2005) reported that individualists express their happy feelings openly and keep unhappiness to themselves, with the opposite pattern observed among collectivists. Substantial correlations across countries between individualism and subjective wellbeing have been reported in several studies, even when income disparities were controlled (Diener and Diener 1995; Diener, Diener and Diener 1995). Recent research points to a more complex relationship. In samples from two individualistic and three collectivistic cultures, Schimmack, Radhakrishnan, Oishi *et al.* (2002) demonstrated that Extraversion was positively and Neuroticism negatively correlated with affective expressions of subjective wellbeing (SWB). The relationship of these two personality variables with cognitive aspects of SWB in the form of life histories was moderated by culture and was more pronounced in individualistic than collectivistic nations.

Over several decades, individualism-collectivism has emerged as one of the most prominent variables to be cross-culturally investigated. Kağitçibaşi (1997) considers the continued research on the basic psychological processes of individualism-collectivism and of its behavioural correlates crucial for the clarification of this multifaceted concept and for the determination of its explanatory value and range of convenience.

Moreover, investigators and theorists have come to realize that individualism-collectivism constitutes a complex cluster of interrelated yet distinct traits, which Triandis (1995) has termed cultural syndromes. Realo (1999) introduced the distinction between the manifestations of collectivism in familial and in institutional, state or national, contexts. A similar differentiation of relational and collective or group variants of collectivism has been proposed by Brewer and Chen (2007). The former is centred on a quest for harmony and avoidance of conflict within the ingroup; the latter is experienced through a sense of belonging and bond to a supra-individual social entity. The meta-analysis of collectivism measures by Oyserman, Coon and Kemmelmeier (2002) demonstrated that the various components of collectivism stand in a different relationship to individualism. In particular, high scores in group collectivism are quite compatible with high scores in individualism. Independently, similar expectations have been voiced by Cross and Cross (2008): a pronounced group identification can coexist with crystallized individualism. Schimmack, Oishi and Diener (2005), however, have found that individualism is an important and valid unipolar cultural dimension, in contrast to collectivism that breaks down into a number of quasi-independent components.

Toward fundamental and stable personality traits: NEO-PI-R – the search for universals

Concurrently with the search for cultural dimensions, the quest for basic and interculturally constant units of personality has been vigorously pursued, notably within the Five Factor Theory (Allik and McCrea 2002; McCrea and Costa 1997). In the process, the Revised NEO Personality Inventory (NEO-PI -R) was developed and validated and its basic dimensions were identified and confirmed on the basis of factor analysis. A novel feature of the development of NEO-PI-R has been the international scope of the ongoing research effort. The Big Five factors thus derived were labelled Neuroticism (N), Extraversion (E), Openness to Experience (O), Agreeableness (A) and Conscientiousness (C), characterized by emotional instability, assertive sociability, imaginativeness and curiosity, kindness and generosity, and reliability and honesty, respectively (Rolland 2002). On the basis of research accumulated throughout the world, Poortinga, Van de Vijver and Van Hemert (2002) concluded that the evidence for the cross-cultural invariance of the Big Five factors was substantial. Moreover, McCrea and Costa (1997, 2003) advanced the daring and controversial tenet that the five fundamental personality traits have fundamentally biological bases and that culture only shapes the expression of traits and not their level. This conclusion is based on the remarkable robustness of the Five-Factor scores across age levels and lifespans, languages, cultures, socialization experiences, and economic and political transformations (Allik and McCrea 2002; McCrea and Allik 2002; Rolland 2002). Moreover, comparisons of monozygotic and dizygotic twins in the Big Five factors have yielded heritability estimates ranging from 0.42 to 0.58 (Amelang, Bartussek, Stemmler and Hagemann 2006; Riemann, Angleitner and Strelau 1997).

Comparisons of lexicons of trait descriptive terms across languages (Allik and McCrea 2002; Rolland 2002; Saucier and Goldberg 2001) have revealed all of the five factors in English, German, and a number of other related languages of Northern Europe. With increasing linguistic and cultural dissimilarity, E, A and C continued to emerge in virtually all languages (Saucier and Goldberg 2001), while O and N proved to be less constant, and six factor (De Raad 2008) and seven factor (Saucier and Goldberg 2001) solutions have been proposed for the worldwide composite of psycholexical findings.

There is, moreover, no compelling reason to expect a complete correspondence between the natural vocabularies of personality trait descriptors and personality structure (Church and Lonner 1998; McCrea and Costa 1997).

What is then the role of culture and the scope of its influence in the outspokenly biological Five Factor Model? Allik and McCrea (2002) explicitly provide for characteristic modes of adaptation, biographical experiences, external influences and self-concepts, all of which continuously and bilaterally interact with a person's genetics. Meaningful findings that have been obtained at intercultural, and intracultural levels include elevated scores on several facets of N and O and lower scores within several facets of E by comparison with international norms in a representative sample of Portuguese (Lima 2002); differences between Czech, Polish and Slovak samples in O and N (Hřebickova, Urbanek, Cermak *et al.* 2002) and between ethnic Russians and Estonians (Konstabel, Realo and Kallasmaa 2002), and even reflection of acculturation in Vietnamese immigrants in the United States in O (Leininger 2002).

Hofstede and McCrea (2004) proceeded to link Hofstede's four original culture dimensions with the Big Five personality traits in thirty-three cultures for which both sets of scores were available. A total of nine significant correlation coefficients emerged. Positive relationships were found, in descending order, between individualism and E; uncertainty avoidance and N; masculinity and N; power distance and C; and masculinity and O. The highest negative relationships were between uncertainty avoidance and A and between power distance and E, followed by correlation coefficients between power distance and O, masculinity and A, and uncertainty avoidance and A. Thus, there were one or more Big Five correlates for each of the four cultural dimensions. These correlations, though substantial, provided no support for the notion that culture is personality writ large or that it is automatically reflected within the personality. The co-authors, however, disagreed in their interpretations, with Hofstede regarding these findings as evidence for culture's impact on personality and McCrea reaffirming the biogenesis of personality and maintaining that personalities shape culture rather than are shaped by it (Hofstede and McCrea 2004). In an overlapping sample of thirty-six cultures, Allik and McCrea (2004) were able to show that geographic distance from the equator was related to personality traits, and that proximate cultures were similar in personality dimensions but different from distant cultures, with A higher and E and O lower in Africa and Asia than in America and Europe. Complementary findings were contributed by Realo, Allik and Vadi (1997) in

Estonia, who reported positive correlations between A and C with a locally developed measure of collectivism and negative correlations with O.

Beyond the Big Five: exploring and accommodating differences

Beyond worldwide constants and global trends, the Big Five factor framework has been vigorously pursued across and within a variety of cultures. A complex picture has emerged on the basis of research that combined locally prevalidated versions of NEO-PI-R, other measures developed within the Big Five framework, and several multidimensional instruments entirely devised within their cultures. Cheung, Leung, Fan *et al.* (1996) constructed the Chinese Personality Assessment Inventory (CPAI) and subjected it to factor analysis together with the Chinese version of NEO-PI-R. Six personality factors emerged, including the Big Five traits except O. An additional factor, principally based on CPAI, was labelled Chinese Tradition, and Bond (2000) found that this emic factor enhanced predictions related to such variables as filial piety. In the Philippines, Church and Katigbak (2000) concluded on the basis of using emic psychometric and psycholexical approaches that the Big Five dimensions are applicable for describing the Philippine personality structure. Criterion validities and interjudge agreements on these measures were, however, somewhat lower than the corresponding values in North America. Similar findings were reported for Malay students studying in Australia, with only O showing a culturally distinctive composition of facets. In Spain, Benet-Martínez and John (2000) supplemented the Big Five Inventory with local and culturally relevant personality descriptors. The Spanish terms grouped into all of the Big Five factors, with additional features: amusement and humour fitted into E, unconventionality and sophistication into O, and good nature and unpretentiousness into A. The five factor solution was also upheld in a multiethnic sample in South Africa by Heuchert, Parker, Stumpf *et al.* (2000), but intergroup differences were found, with higher E and O in Whites as compared with Africans and Indians. Heuchert *et al.* (2000) noted a striking parallel with the findings by Draguns, Krylova, Oryol *et al.* (2000), who reported higher E and O among ethnic Russians as compared to the Nentsy, a small ethnic group in the Russian Arctic. Could low self-assertion and security, possibly characteristic of disadvantaged or stressed ethnic groups, depress scores in these two traits? This possibility deserves to be further investigated. Shifting from test scores to self-ratings and those of others, Zhang, Lee, Liu and McCawley (1999) reported that Chinese students in the United States rated Americans as higher in A and lower in O and E than the Chinese.

These results highlight the complexity of relationships between personality traits and cultures. To unravel it, Marsella (2000) proposed that cultural factors influence patterns in which such traits are displayed, situations in which they tend to be elicited, their value in behavioural description, interpersonal responses to them, and meanings attributed to them.

From observable traits to experienced selves: reflection of culture in the self

Beginning with William James (1891/1952), Western psychologists have tended to view the self as a pivotal concept of psychology and as a core of personality. The notion of the self as a clearly delineated, highly differentiated, and unique entity stands in contrast to several non-Western conceptions (Gaines 1982; Ho 1998; Landrine 1992; Chang 1988; Kimura 1995; Markus and Kitayama 1991, 1998; Roland 1996; Triandis 1989) all of which posit an interdependent self that is more responsive to situational and social influences. Chang (1988) likened the Western self to a wall that separates the person from other people and the Asian self to a bridge that connects human beings. Hofstede (2001) and Triandis (1995) have extended this contrast to individualistic and collectivistic cultures. The individualistic self is conceived as a bundle of personal attributes; the collectivistic self constitutes a composite of social ties and relationships. Proceeding from the distinctions between relational and group collectivism, Brewer and Chen (2007) have proposed trichotomizing the self into individual, relational and group segments.

Draguns (2004) has formulated predictions pertaining to self-experience in the other four Hofstede's dimensions, specifically by positing relationships between high power distance and an encapsulated and crystallized self, and low power distance and a more permeable self, less concerned with power and more with people; between high uncertainty avoidance and consistency and explicitness within the self and reduced tolerance for ambiguity; between masculinity and a performance-oriented, pragmatic and practical self, and femininity and a caring and feeling-oriented self, and between long-term orientation and self-restraint, modesty and humility, and short-range orientation and self-expression and self-assertion.

As yet, comprehensive measures that would be useful for a comparison of self-experience across cultures have not been developed. A host of specific predictions derived from the conceptions of individual versus interdependent self in North America and East Asia have been tested. Heine (2001) has reviewed these findings. He has concluded that, compared with North Americans, East Asians exhibit less of a striving for consistency across situations, are less likely to assign trait names to themselves, regard their selves as more malleable and the external world to be less changeable. They value perseverance and effort, strive for approval from others, and are more critical of themselves and of their performance.

Impact of parental acceptance-rejection: a theory tested on a worldwide basis

For close to four decades, Rohner (1975, 1986, 2004) has been engaged in a programme of studies concerned with the consequences of parental acceptance-rejection throughout the lifespan. To this end, he has consistently relied on a three-pronged approach consisting of holocultural research based on HRAF samples, community studies in various parts of the world, and conventional psychological experimental and quasi-experimental studies with explicit research designs and significance tests. Behavioural observations, interviews and questionnaires were utilized. Parental Acceptance-Rejection Interview Schedule (PARIS) and Parental Acceptance Questionnaire (PAQ) have been the principal research instruments developed, validated and translated for use at a variety of sites and in numerous languages.

Rohner (1975, 1986, 2004) systematically traced the effects of four classes of parental behaviour: perceived warmth or coldness; hostility-aggression; indifference-neglect; and undifferentiated rejection. Seven consequences of rejection were investigated: dependence, emotional unresponsiveness, hostility, aggression, low self-esteem, a negative worldview, and emotional instability. As anticipated, hostility and a pessimistic conception of the world were prominent consequences of rejection, both in the HRAF sample and in studies within communities in North America and elsewhere. Fortunately, in most of the societies studied, acceptance has predominated over rejection in frequency and prominence. The cultural context of rejection has so far not been systematically or definitively investigated. Hunter-forager societies have been found to be virtually free of parental rejection and, in general, rejection appears to be less prevalent in societies low in complexity (Rohner 1975). Single parenting increases the risk of rejection, and both parents' participation in childcare reduces it. Certain combinations of gender and class characteristics affect acceptance/rejection. For example, in Bengal children's perceived acceptance has been found to vary inversely with the caste status. In Mexico, middle-class children perceived their parents to be less warm than did their working-class counterparts, but this relationship was reversed in a sample of Korean Americans. A rich and complex pattern of findings has been brought to the fore, demonstrating the usefulness of cultural and hologeistic data in testing the worldwide applicability of personality-related theories. This research programme deserves to be emulated in investigating other personality-related constructs and variables.

Beyond traits and dimensions: toward an integrative ethnopsychology

Psychology of personality originated at a point in time and space. Personality concepts have radiated from Western Europe and North America. Numerous objections have been voiced to the hidden assumptions on which these notions rest. Cross-cultural psychology has in part been envisaged as a corrective for such distortions, but has also been accused of succumbing to them. As a response, indigenous psychologies have come into being, organized around concepts of local origin. Proceeding from folk experience, pioneers of indigenous psychology have endeavoured to construct scientifically based bodies of information that would be relevant to the needs and outlooks of the culture. Such attempts have been undertaken in India (Sinha 1993), Korea (Choi, Kim and Choi 1993) and the Philippines (Enriquez 1993). Church and Katigbak (2000) drew upon the rich and differentiated vocabulary of trait names in order to test the relevance of the Big Five model to the Filipino culture.

In Mexico, notions of indigenous psychology have been incorporated into a more inclusive ethnopsychology that endeavours to integrate all information pertinent to the description and explanation of the behaviour of an ethnocultural group (Díaz-Guerrero 1994; Díaz-Loving and Draguns 1999). Prominent Mexican adaptive characteristics include a sociocentric emphasis upon lifelong relationships with family and friends, predominance of compliance over self-assertion, endurance and passivity in coping with stress, and clear-cut differences between the gender roles, especially within the family. *Simpatía*, translated as geniality or likeability, is a key concept, highlighting the value placed upon expressive sociability and affectionate social interaction. These concepts describe themes in Mexican culture and do not preclude situational fluctuations or individual differences. Substantial ethnopsychological information is also available on the personalities of the Chinese (Yang 1997), Africans South of the Sahara (Okeke, Draguns, Sheku and Allen 1999), Japanese (Sera 1963; Sofue 1976), Russians (Stefanenko 1999) and Swedes (Daun 1989). Laungani (1999) has identified four major normative expectations in India that stand in contrast to those in Great Britain and elsewhere in the West: collectivism, emotionalism, determinism or fatalism, and spiritualism.

Ho, Peng, Cheng Lai and Chan (2001) have gone even further and have proposed that the indigenous East Asian Confucian point of view be used as a point of departure in defining personality and constructing personality theory on the basis of interrelatedness rather than of individuality.

On a more modest scale, the culture-specific concepts of *amae* and *ki* shed light on the subjective aspects of personality in Japan. *Amae*, described by Doi (1973), involves a frequently frustrated and persistent striving to presume upon another person's benevolence in order to have an often unreasonable and excessive request fulfilled. The underlying wish is for a close and asymmetrical relationship (Kim and Park 2006). Doi (1973) surmised that *amae* is a state for which the Japanese have a word, but which other people are capable of experiencing. Kim and Park (2006) have shown that *amae* is even more frequently reported in the United States and Taiwan than it is in Japan. Kimura (1995) has explored the personal meaning of *ki*, roughly translated as 'co-humanity'. In Japan, the disruption of *ki*, akin to loneliness and alienation, is experienced as an aversive state that motivates the person's efforts toward its reduction or elimination.

National character: a once and future concept?

The concept of national character, dormant for several decades, has shown tentative signs of a potential revival. As conceived by Inkeles and Levinson (1969), national character is primarily manifested in a culturally characteristic response to three issues: relations to authority, conceptions of self, and the nature of primary conflicts and dilemmas, as well as the preferred modes for their resolution. Lynn (1971) and Lynn and Martin (1995) have concentrated on characteristic responses to stress, mainly based on social and medical statistics exemplified by caffeine and alcohol consumption, rates of incarceration and vehicular accidents. At first eighteen, and then thirty-six economically developed countries in Europe were included in these comparisons. Findings coalesced into two factors, Extraversion and Neuroticism, derived from Eysenck's (1982) personality theory and closely related to E and N within the Big Five.

Peabody's (1985) approach was very different. His interest was focused on attributions of evaluative and descriptive adjectives assigned to six major nations, Britain, Germany, France, Italy, Russia and the United States. Raters were from all of the target nations and they rated their own as well as the other five nations. Surprisingly, neutral or descriptive ratings were much more in agreement than the evaluative ones, which were equated with stereotypes. Indirect evidence indicated that these ratings were reasonably realistic and suggested that personality characteristics prevalent throughout one's own and other nations are based more on observation than preconception. Terraciano *et al.* (2005), however, found no correlation between mean profiles of reported personality traits in forty-nine cultures and the levels of the same traits as rated by outsiders to the culture. Terraciano *et al.* (2005) concluded that cross-cultural perceptions of national character are illusory.

This conclusion was challenged by Heine, Buchtel and Norenzayan (in press) who attributed the results of Terraciano *et al.* (2005) to the reference group effect, defined as the tendency for persons to respond to subjective self-report tasks by comparing themselves with the implicit standards for their own culture. Because such standards differ across cultures, they selectively distort cross-cultural, but not intracultural, comparisons. On the basis of prior multinational research on Conscientiousness (Heine, Lehman, Peng and Greenholtz 2002), Heine *et al.* (in press) concluded that behavioural and demographic indicators of Conscientiousness tend to be correlated with perceptions of national character, but not with the aggregate self-report and peer-report measures, similar to the distinction between the across-country and within-country levels of analysis emphasized by Hofstede (2001).

Perhaps the largest-scale research project on national character has been completed by Allik, Realo, Mottus *et al.* (in press). A total of 7,065 respondents rated a person they knew well on the observer rating version of the Russian Revised NEO-PI-R (Martin, Costa, Oryol *et al.* 2002). The resulting profile of domains and facets exhibited little divergence from the international norms for fifty countries (McCrea, Terraciano *et al.* 2005). Although Allik *et al.* (in press) made a special effort to capture emic, distinctively Russian, personality traits gleaned from the writings of philosophers, historians and novelists, hypotheses derived from these sources received no support. Thus, the Russian soul has eluded psychometric investigation.

Perhaps the proposals by Stefanenko (1999) and Vexliard (1970) to shift the focus in studying national character from statistical indicators and behavioural manifestations to the themes and structures that underlie observable responses are worth pursuing. Within these formulations, national character is construed as a nucleus of meaning. Traditionally amenable to qualitative study by historical and biographical methods, this nucleus can now be explored by the quantitative and objective approaches developed for investigating subjective culture (Triandis 1972) and by constructing lifelike situations in which personally relevant dilemmas must be resolved (Volovikova, Grenkova and Morskova 1996).

Current state, future directions

Within the last ten years, the field of culture and personality has made remarkable advances. Fundamental dimensions of both culture and personality have been identified and initial steps have been taken to explore their relationship. Networks of interrelated international studies have been expanded and new areas of research have been opened up. Concurrently, traditional avenues of research have continued to be pursued and have demonstrated a new vitality in the process. Several integrative volumes and special issues have appeared in the last decade (Church 2001b; Church and Lonner 1998; Lee, McCauley and Draguns 1999; McCrea 2000; McCrea and Allik 2002). The revitalization of the culture and personality enterprise has brought with it challenges, among them those posed by fragmentation, isolation and overspecialization. To counteract them, it is essential to transcend disciplinary, methodological and conceptual barriers. Church (2000) has proposed an elaborate scheme for bridging the gap between the investigators of personality traits across cultures and the explorers of the complex and unique cultural contexts within which personality is expressed. In general, etic and worldwide investigation of personality should now be complemented by equally vigorous study of culturally unique, emic phenomena relevant to personality in culture and culture in personality. Complex quantitative research should be parallelled and followed by the intensive application of sophisticated qualitative methods of inquiry. Dimensions should be studied in contexts, and contexts should be dimensionalized.

On the basis of an analysis of the methods and results in this field, Poortinga and Van Hemert (2001) concluded that the pioneers of the culture and personality investigation had substantially overestimated the impact of culture upon personality. In the short run, trait-oriented research holds the greatest degree of promise. Moreover, attention should be paid to the interaction between the person and his or her environment and situational influences, hitherto neglected or underestimated, should be accorded their due importance. Poortinga and Van Hemert (2001) are moderately sceptical of the explanations that posit internalized socio-cultural values as a major avenue of culture's influence on personality. Nonetheless, they encourage the pursuit of relativistic cultural traditions of inquiry and concede that 'an important part of the variance in behaviour of interest to psychologists can probably never be explained satisfactorily with experimental and psychometric methods' (p. 1054).

The following additional recommendations are offered to help advance this, once again vibrant, area of inquiry.

(1) Findings obtained so far have documented the case for the stability of both cultural dimensions and personality traits. However, what if anything about personality changes in response to culture change and under what conditions and to what degree? This question is not idle in view of ongoing globalization and in light of the cataclysmic socio-political and economic transformations experienced in many regions of the world during the last two decades.

(2) Social transformations, gradual or sudden, should be considered independent variables in natural experiments in order to study their effects upon personality in cultures in which such changes occur, as Oettingen and Maier (1999) have done in East Germany, Russia, Poland and Czech Republic. So far, such changes have resulted in specific shifts, but have not appreciably affected fundamental personality traits (cf., Allik and McCrea 2002).

(3) Cultural characteristics should continue to be investigated around the world, but culturally oriented personality research should be extended and expanded within the culturally pluralistic nations of the Old and New World (as exemplified by Konstabel, Realo and Kallasmaa 2002; Leininger 2002; McCrea, Yik, Trapnell *et al.* 1998).

(4) It is not enough to study personality as a function of culture from the perspective of outside researchers; interactions and mutual perceptions of persons across cultures are a challenging and important object of investigation (cf. Lee, McCauley and Draguns 1999).

(5) The time has come to extend cross-cultural research on personality to applied settings in organizations, schools, clinics, hospitals and communities and to monitor such applications (cf. McCauley, Ottati and Lee 1999; Miller 1999).

(6) An important arena of application of findings on culture and personality is preparing migrants, sojourners and visitors for encounters with their host culture. As Brislin (1999) has demonstrated, information on personality characteristics is relevant in designing and implementing such programmes.

(7) An ecological and evolutionary orientation, such as Buss (2001) has proposed, holds the promise of providing direction for further efforts to integrate the interplay of culture and personality into a comprehensive interdisciplinary framework.

(8) Generally, the field of culture and personality will be advanced by the simultaneous and flexible pursuit of multiple research strategies designed to investigate how culture affects personality, how personalities change culture, and how culture and personality interact.

References

Allik, J. and McCrea, R. R. 2002. A five-factor theory perspective, in R. R. McCrea and J. Allik (eds.) *The Five-Factor Model of personality across cultures*, pp. 301–22. New York: Kluwer Academic/Plenum Publishers

2004. Toward a geography of personality traits: patterns of profiles from 36 cultures, *Journal of Cross-Cultural Psychology* 35: 13–28

Allik, J., Realo, A., Mottus, R., Pullmann, H., Trifonova, A., McCrea, R. R. and 55 members of the Russian Character and Personality Survey in press. Personality profiles and the 'Russian soul': literary and scholarly views evaluated, *Journal of Cross-Cultural Psychology*

Amelang, M., Bartussek, D., Stemmler, G. and Hagemann, D. 2006. *Differentielle Psychologie und Persönlichkeitsforschung [Differential psychology and personality research]*, 6th edn. Stuttgart: Kohlhammer

Arrindell, W. A. and Veenhoven, R. 2001. Feminine values and happy life expectancy in nations, *Personality and Individual Differences* 33: 803–13

Benedict, R. 1934. *Patterns of culture*. New York: Mentor
1946. *The chrysanthemum and the sword*. Boston: Houghton Mifflin

Benet-Martínez, V. and John, O. P. 2000. Toward the development of quasi-indigenous personality constructs, *American Behavioural Scientist* 44: 141–57

Boas, F. 1910. Psychological problems in anthropology, *American Journal of Psychology* 21: 371–84

Bock, P. K. 2000. Culture and personality revisited, *American Behavioural Scientist* 44: 32–40

Bond, M. H. 2000. Localizing the imperial outreach: the Big Five and more in Chinese culture, *American Behavioural Scientist* 44: 63–72

Brewer, M. B. and Chen, Y.-R. 2007. Where (who) are collectives in collectivism? Toward conceptual clarification of individualism and collectivism, *Psychological Review* 114: 133–57

Briggs, J. L. 1970. *Never in anger: portrait of an Eskimo family*. Cambridge, MA: Harvard University Press

Brislin, R. 1999. Communicating information on culture and personality in formal cross-cultural training programs, in Y. T. Lee, C. R. McCauley and J. G. Draguns (eds.), *Personality and person perception across cultures*, pp. 255–78. Mahwah, NJ: Erlbaum

Bruner, J. S. 1974. Concluding comments and summary of conference, in J. M. L. Dawson and W. J. Lonner (eds.), *Readings in cross-cultural psychology*, pp. 389–94. University of Hong Kong Press

Buss, D. M. 2001. Human nature and culture: an evolutionary psychological perspective, *Journal of Personality* 69: 955–78

Chang, S. C. 1988. The nature of self: a transcultural view, Part 1, Theoretical aspects, *Transcultural Psychiatric Research Review* 25: 169–204

Cheung, F. M., Leung, K., Fan, R. M., Song, W. Z., Zhang, J. X. and Zhang, J. P. 1996. Development of the Chinese Personality Assessment Inventory, *Journal of Cross-Cultural Psychology* 27: 181–99

Choi, S.-C., Kim, U. and Choi, S.-H. 1993. Indigenous analysis of collective representations: a Korean perspective, in U. Kim and J. W. Berry (eds.), *Indigenous psychologies: research and experience in cultural context*, pp. 193–210. Newbury Park, CA: Sage Publications

Church, A. T. 2000. Culture and personality: toward an integrated cultural trait psychology, *Journal of Personality* 68: 651–703
2001a. Cross-cultural personality measurement, *Journal of Personality* 69: 980–1003

2001b. Special issue: culture and personality research, *Journal of Personality* 69

Church, A. T. and Katigbak, M. S. 2000. Trait psychology in the Philippines, *American Behavioural Scientist* 44: 73–94

Church, A. T. and Lonner, W. J (eds.) 1998. The cross-cultural perspective on the study of personality: rationale and current research, *Journal of Cross-Cultural Psychology* 29: 32–62

Cross, W. T. and Cross, B. T. 2008. The big picture: theorizing self structure and construal, in P. B. Pedersen, J. G. Draguns, W. J. Lonner and J. E. Trimble (eds.) *Counseling across cultures*, 6th edn, pp. 73–88. Thousand Oaks, CA: Sage

Daun, A. 1989. *Svensk mentalitet (Swedish mentality)*. Simrishamn, Sweden: Raben and Sjogren (cited in Stefanenko 1999)

De Raad, B. 2008. The architecture of personality traits. Presidential address, Fourteenth European Conference on Personality, Tartu, Estonia

Devereux, G. 1969. *Reality and the dream: psychotherapy of a Plains Indian*. Garden City, NY: Doubleday

Díaz-Guerrero, R. 1994. *Psicología del mexicano: descubrimiento de la etnopsicología* [*Psychology of the Mexican: the discovery of ethnopsychology*], 6th edn. Mexico City: Trillas

Díaz-Loving, R. and Draguns, J. G. 1999. Culture, meaning, and personality in Mexico and in the United States, in Y. T. Lee, C. R. McCauley and J. G. Draguns (eds.), *Personality and person perception across cultures*, pp. 103–26. Mahwah, NJ: Erlbaum

Diener, E. and Diener. M. 1995. Cross-cultural correlates of life-satisfaction and self-esteem, *Journal of Personality and Social Psychology* 68: 653–63

Diener, E., Diener, M. and Diener, C. 1995. Factors predicting the subjective well-being of nations, *Journal of Personality and Social Psychology* 69: 851–64

Doi, T. L. 1973. *Amae: anatomy of dependence*. Tokyo: Kodansha

Draguns, J. G. 1979. Culture and personality, in A. J. Marsella, R. Tharp and T. J. Ciborowski (eds.), *Perspectives on cross-cultural psychology*, pp. 179–207. New York: Academic Press

2004. From speculation through description toward investigation: a prospective glimpse at cultural research in psychotherapy, in U. P. Gielen, J. F. Fish and J. G. Draguns (eds.), *Handbook of culture, therapy, and healing*, pp. 369–88. Mahwah, NJ: Erlbaum

2007. Culture's impact at the workplace and beyond, *Reviews in Anthropology* 36: 43–58

Draguns, J. G., Krylova, A. V., Oryol, V. E., Rukavishnikov, A. A. and Martin, T. A. 2000. Personality characteristics of the Nentsy in the Russian Arctic: a comparison by means of Neo-PI-R and POI, *American Behavioural Scientist* 44: 112–25

Dubois, C. 1944. *The people of Alor*. Minneapolis: University of Minnesota Press

Enriquez, G. V. 1993. Developing a Filipino psychology, in U. Kim and J. W. Berry (eds.), *Indigenous psychologies: research and experience in cultural contexts*, pp. 152–69. Thousand Oaks, CA: Sage

Eysenck, H. J. 1982. *Personality genetics and behaviour*. New York: Praeger

Gaines, A. 1982. Cultural definitions, behaviour, and the person in American psychiatry, in A. J. Marsella and E. J. White (eds.), *Cultural conceptions of mental health and therapy*, pp. 167–92. London: Reidel

Gorer, J. and Rickman, J. 1950. *The people of Great Russia*. New York: Norton

Heine, S. J. 2001. Self as cultural product: an examination of East Asian and North American selves, *Journal of Personality* 69: 880–902

Heine, S. J., Buchtel, E. E. and Norenzayan, A. in press. What do cross-cultural comparisons of personality tell us? The case of Conscientiousness, *Psychological Science*

Heine, S. J., Lehman, D. R., Peng, K. and Greenholtz, J. 2002. What's wrong with cross-cultural comparisons of subjective Likert scales? The reference group effect, *Journal of Personality and Social Psychology* 82: 903–16

Herdt, G. 1981. *Guardians of the flutes*. New York: McGraw-Hill

Herskovits, M. 1949. *Man and his works*. New York: Knopf

Heuchert, J. W. P., Parker, W. D., Stumpf, H. and Myburgh, C. P. H. 2000. The Five Factor model of personality in South African college students, *American Behavioural Scientist* 44: 112–25

Ho, D. Y. F. 1998. Indigenous psychologies: Asian perspectives, *Journal of Cross-Cultural Psychology* 29: 88–103

Ho, D. Y. F., Peng. S., Cheng Lai, A. and Chan, S. F. 2001. Indigenization and beyond: methodological relationalism in the study of personality across cultural traditions, *Journal of Personality* 69: 925–54

Hofstede, G. 1980. *Culture's consequences: international differences in work-related values*. Beverly Hills, CA: Sage Publications

    2001. *Culture's consequences: comparing values, behaviours, institutions, and organizations across nations*, 2nd edn. Thousand Oaks, CA: Sage Publications

Hofstede, G. and Hofstede, G. J. 2005. *Cultures and organizations: software of the mind*, 2nd edn. New York: Mc Graw-Hill

Hofstede, G. and McCrea, R. R. 2004. Personality and culture revisited: linking traits and dimensions of culture, *Cross-Cultural Research* 38: 52–88

Hřebickova, M., Urbanek, T., Cermak, I., Szarota, P., Fickova, E. and Orlicka, L. 2002. The NEO Five-Factor Inventory in Czech, Polish, and Slovak contexts, in R. R. McCrea and J. Allik (eds.), *The Five-Factor Model of personality across cultures*, pp. 53–78. New York: Kluwer Academic/Plenum Publishers

Inkeles, A. and Levinson, D. J. 1969. The study of modal personality and sociocultural systems, in G. Lindzey and E. Aronson (eds.), *Handbook of social psychology*, vol. IV, 2nd edn, pp. 418–99. Cambridge, MA: Addison-Wesley

James, W. 1891/1952. *Principles of psychology*. Chicago: Encyclopedia Britannica

Kağitçibaşi, C. 1997. Individualism and collectivism, in J. W. Berry, M. H. Segall and C. Kagitcibasi (eds.), *Handbook of cross-cultural psychology*, pp. 1–50. Boston, MA: Allyn and Bacon

Kardiner, A. 1939. *The individual and his society*. New York: Columbia University Press

Kim, U. and Park, Y.-S. 2006. Development of indigenous psychologies: understanding people in a global context, in M. J. Stevens and U. P. Gielen (eds.), *Toward a global psychology: theory. research, intervention, and pedagogy*, pp. 147–72. Mahwah, NJ: Erlbaum

Kimura. B. 1995. *Zwischen Mensch und Mensch [Between one human being and another]*, H. Weinhendl (trans.). Darmstadt: Akademische Verlagsanstalt

Kluckhohn, C. and Murray, H. A. (eds.) 1950. *Personality in nature, society, and culture*. New York: Knopf.

Konstabel, K., Realo, A. and Kallasmaa, T. 2002. Exploring the sources of variation in the structure of personality traits across cultures, in R. R. McCrea and J. Allik (eds.), *The Five-Factor Model of personality across cultures*, pp. 29–52. New York: Kluwer Academic/Plenum Press.

Landrine, H. 1992. Clinical implications of cultural differences: the referential versus the indexical self, *Clinical Psychology Review* 12: 401–15

Laungani, H. 1999. Cultural influences on identity and behaviour: India and Britain, in Lee, Y.-T., McCauley, C. R. and Draguns, J. G. (eds.), *Personality and person perception across cultures*, pp. 191–212. Mahwah, NJ: Erlbaum

Lee, Y.-T., McCauley, C. R. and Draguns, J. G. (eds.) 1999. *Personality and person perception across cultures*. Mahwah, NJ: Erlbaum

Leininger, A. 2002. Vietnamese-American personality and acculturation: an exploration of relation between personality traits and cultural goals, in R. R McCrea and J. Allik (eds.), *The Five-Factor Model of personality across cultures*, pp. 197–226. New York: Kluwer Academic/Plenum Press

LeVine, R. A. 2001. Culture and personality studies 1918–1960: myth and history, *Journal of Personality* 69: 603–17

LeVine, R. A., Dixon, S., LeVine, S., Richman, A., Liederman, P. H. Keefer, C. H. and Brazerton, T. B. 1994. *Children and culture: lessons from Africa*. New York: Cambridge University Press

LeVine, R. A. and LeVine, S. E., 1988. Parental strategies among the Gusii in Kenya, in R. A. LeVine, P. M. Miller and M. M. West (eds.), *Parental behaviour in diverse societies*, pp. 27–36. San Francisco, CA: Jossey Bass

Lima, M. P. 2002. Personality and culture: the Portuguese case, in R. R. McCrea and J. Allik (eds.), *The Five-Factor Model of personality across cultures*, pp. 249–60. New York: Kluwer Academic/Plenum Press

Linton, R. 1945. *The cultural background of personality*. New York: Appleton Century Crofts

Lynn, R. 1971. *Personality and national character*. Oxford: Pergamon

Lynn, R. and Martin, T. 1995. National differences in 37 nations in Extraversion, Neuroticism, psychoticism, and economic, demographic, and other correlates, *Personality and Individual Differences* 19: 403–6

Martin, T. A., Costa, P. T., Jr, Oryol, V. E., Rukavishnikov, A. A. and Senin, I. G. 2002. Applications of the Russian NEO-PI-R, in R. R. McCrea and J. Allik (eds.), *The Five-Factor Model of personality across cultures*, pp. 261–77. New York: Kluwer Academic/Plenum Press

Markus, H. R. and Kitayama. S. 1991. Culture and the self: implications for cognition, emotion, and motivation, *Psychological Review* 98: 224–53

Markus, H. R. and Kitayama, S. 1998. The cultural psychology of personality, *Journal of Cross-Cultural Psychology* 29: 63–87

Marsella, A. J. 1988. Cross-cultural research on severe mental disorders: issues and findings, *Acta Psychiatrica Scandinavica* Suppl. 344, 7–22

    2000. The measurement of personality across cultures: historical, conceptual, and methodological features and considerations, *American Behavioural Scientist* 44: 41–62

McCauley, C. R., Draguns, J. G. and Lee, Y.-T 1999. Person perception across cultures, in Y.-T. Lee, C. R. McCawley and J. G. Draguns (eds.), *Personality and person perception across cultures*, pp. 279–96. Mahwah, NJ: Erlbaum

McCauley, C. R., Ottati, V. and Lee, Y.-T. 1999. National differences in economic growth: the role of personality and culture, in Y.-T. Lee, C. R. McCawley and J. D. Draguns (eds.), *Personality and person perception across cultures*, pp. 85–103. Mahwah, NJ: Erlbaum

McCrea, R. R (ed.) 2000. Personality traits and culture: new perspectives on some classic issues, *American Behavioural Scientist* 44: 3–151

McCrea, R. R. and Allik, J. (eds.) 2002. *The Five-Factor Model of personality across cultures*. New York: Kluwer Academic/Plenum Publishers

McCrea, R. R. and Costa, P. T., Jr 1997. Personality trait structure as a human universal, *American Psychologist* 52: 509–16

2003. *Personality in adulthood: a Five-Factor Theory perspective*. New York: Guilford Press

McCrea, R. R., Terraciano, A. and 78 members of the Personality Profiles of Cultures Project 2005. Universal features of personality traits from the observer's perspective: data from 50 cultures, *Journal of Personality and Social Psychology* 88: 547–61

McCrea, R. R., Yik, M. S. M., Trapnell, P. D., Bond, M. H. and Paulhus, D. L. 1998. Interpreting personality profiles across cultures: bilingual, acculturation, and peer rating studies of Chinese undergraduates, *Journal of Personality and Social Psychology* 74: 1041–55

Mead, M. 1935. *Sex and temperament in three primitive societies*. New York: Mentor

Miller, L. 1999. Stereotype legacy: culture and person in Japanese/American business interactions, in Y.-T. Lee, R. C. McCauley and J. G. Draguns (eds.), *Personality and person perception across cultures*, pp. 213–34. Mahwah. NJ: Erlbaum

Murdock, G. P. 1967. *Ethnographic atlas*. Pittsburgh University Press

Naroll, R., Michik, G. I. and Naroll, F. 1980. Holocultural research methods, in H. C. Triandis and J. W. Berry (eds.), *Handbook of cross-cultural psychology*, vol. II, pp. 479–522. Boston, MA: Allyn and Bacon

Oettingen, G. and Maier, H. 1999. When political system meets culture: effect on efficiency appraisal, in Y.-T. Lee. C. R. McCauley and J. G. Draguns (eds.), *Personality and person perception across cultures*, pp. 153–90. Mahwah, NJ: Erlbaum

Okeke, B. I., Draguns, J. G., Sheku, B. and Allen, W. 1999. Culture, self, and personality in Africa, in Y.- T. Lee, C. R. Mc Cauley and J. G. Draguns (eds.), *Personality and person perception across cultures*, pp. 139–63. Mahwah, NJ: Erlbaum

Oyserman, D., Coon, H. M. and Kemmelmeier, M. 2002. Rethinking individualism and collectivism: evaluation of theoretical assumptions and meta-analyses, *Psychological Bulletin* 128: 3–72

Parin, P., Morgenthaler, F. and Parin-Mathey, G. 1963. *Die Weissen denken zu viel: Psychoanalytische Untersuchungen bei den Dogon in Westafrika [The whites think too much: psychoanalytic investigations among the Dogon of West Africa]*. Zurich: Atlantis Verlag

1980. *Fear thy neighbor as thyself*, P. Klameth (trans.). University of Chicago Press

Peabody, D. 1985. *National characteristics*. Cambridge University Press

1999. Nationality characteristics: dimensions for comparison, in Y. T Lee, C. R, McCawley and J. G. Draguns (eds.), *Personality and person perception across culture*, pp. 65–85. Mahwah, NJ: Erlbaum

Piker, S. 1998. Contributions of psychological anthropology, *Journal of Cross-Cultural Psychology* 29: 9–31

Poortinga, Y. P., Van de Vijver, F. J. R. and Van Hemert, D. A. 2002. Cross-cultural equivalence of the Big Five: a tentative interpretation of the evidence, in R. R. McCrea and J. Allik (eds.), *The Five-Factor Model of personality across cultures*, pp. 261–78. New York: Kluwer Academic/Plenum Press

Poortinga, Y. P. and Van Hemert, D. A. 2001. Personality and culture: demarcating between the common and the unique, *Journal of Personality* 69: 1032–58

Realo, A. 1999. *Individualism and collectivism: an exploration of individual and cultural differences*. Tartu University Press

Realo. A., Allik, J. and Vadi, M. 1997. The hierarchical structure of collectivism, *Journal of Research in Personality* 31: 93–116

Riemann, R., Angleitner, A. and Strelau, J. 1997. Genetic and environmental influences on personality: a study of twins reared together using the self- and peer report NEO-FFI scales, *Journal of Personality* 65: 449–75

Rohner, R. P. 1975. *They love me, they love me not*. New Haven, CT: HRAF Press
    1986. *The warmth dimension: foundations of Parental Acceptance-Rejection Theory*. Thousand Oaks, CA: Sage
    2004. The parental acceptance-rejection syndrome, *American Psychologist* 59: 830–9

Roland, A. 1988. *In search of self in India and Japan*. Princeton University Press
    1996. *Cultural pluralism and psychoanalysis: the Asian and North American experience*. New York: Routledge

Rolland, J. P. 2002. The cross-cultural generalizability of the Five-Factor Model of personality, in R. R. McCrea J. Allik (eds.), *The Five-Factor Model of personality across cultures*, pp. 7–28. New York: Kluwer Academic/ Plenum Press

Saucier, G. and Goldberg, L. R. 2001. Lexical studies of indigenous personality factors: premises, products, and prospects, *Journal of personality* 69: 847–80

Schimmack, U., Oishi, S. and Diener, E. 2005. Individualism: a valid and important dimension of cultural differences between nations, *Personality and Social Psychology Review* 9: 63–87

Schimmack, U., Radhakrishnan, P., Oishi, S., Dzokoto, V. and Ahadi, S. 2002. Culture, personality, and subjective well-being: integrative process models of life satisfaction, *Journal of Personality and Social Psychology* 82: 582–93

Sera, M. 1963. *The Japanese personality*. Tokyo: Kinokuya Publishers

Sinha, D. 1993. Indigenization of psychology in India and its relevance, in U. Kim and J. W. Berry (eds.), *Indigenous psychologies*, pp. 30–44. Newbury Park, CA: Sage

Sofue, T. 1976. *Culture and personality*. Tokyo: Kobundo

Spiro, M. E. 1982. *Oedipus in the Trobriands*. University of Chicago Press

Stefanenko, T. 1999. *Etnopsikhologiya [Ethnopsychology]*. Moscow: Akademicheskiy Proyekt

Terraciano, A. and 79 members of Personality Profiles of Cultures Project 2005. National character does not reflect mean personality trait levels in 49 cultures, *Science* 310: 96–100

Triandis, H. C. 1972. *Subjective culture*. New York: Wiley
    1989. The self and social behaviour in differing cultural contexts, *Psychological Review* 96: 506–20
    1995. *Individualism and collectivism*. Boulder, CO: Westview

2001. Individualism-collectivism and personality, *Journal of Personality* 69: 910–28

Vexliard, A. 1970. *Le caractère national: une structure en profondeur [National character: a structure in depth]*. Istanbul Universitesi Edebiyat Fakultesi

Volovikova, M. I., Grenkova, L. L. and Morskova, A. A. 1996. Utverzhdeniye cherez otritsaniye [Affirmation through negation], in K. A. Abulkhanova – Slavskaya (ed.), *Rossiyskiy mentalitet: Psikhologiya lichnosti, soznaniye, sotsial'nye predstavleniyal*, pp. 86–98. Moscow: RAS Psychological Institute

Wallace, A. F. C. 1952. The modal personality of Tuscarora Indians as revealed by the Rorschach test, *Smithsonian Institution Bureau of American Ethnology* 150

Yang, K.-S. 1997. Theories and research in Chinese personality: an indigenous approach, in H. S. B. Kao and D. Sinha (eds.), *Asian perspectives on psychology*, pp. 236–64. Thousand Oaks, CA: Sage Publications

Zhang, K., Lee, Y.-T., Liu, Y. and McCawley, C. R. 1999. Chinese-American differences: a Chinese view, in Y.-T. Lee, C. R. McCawley and J. G. Draguns (eds.), *Personality and person perception across cultures*, pp. 127–38. Mahwah, NJ: Erlbaum

33 Culture and personality

Robert Hogan and Michael Harris Bond

In some cultures, I would be considered normal.

Bumper sticker, Tulsa, Oklahoma, 2006

On 13 April 1769, Captain James Cook anchored his ship, H. M. Bark Endeavour, in a Tahitian harbour. His assignment was to build a small fort and an observatory in order to measure the transit of the moon, which would occur on 3 June. Within minutes of anchoring, the ship was swarming with local Tahitians, none of whom had ever seen a European, none of whom spoke English, and all of whom wanted to trade with the visitors. The trade was brisk and mutually beneficial. After a while, the British caught some Tahitians stealing. Cook reported them to their own authorities, and they were duly punished, much as Cook expected.

This historical anecdote presents grave problems for naïve cultural relativity. Specifically, the Cook anecdote shows that people from vastly different cultures are able to interact effectively with little difficulty. This speaks to the existence of an underlying human communality, an important starting point for any discussion of culture and personality. Not only are people all alike beneath the cultural trappings, but all cultures are alike, because they rest upon a shared human nature – see Carneiro (1970) for a discussion of the universal features of cultural evolution based on human nature.

The literature on culture and personality starts in the late nineteenth century with the beginnings of cultural anthropology. A trip through this literature resembles a visit to a museum of natural history. There are lots of interesting exhibits (e.g., DuBois 1960; Turnbull 1963) that appeal to our taste for the exotic, the arcane and the surprising, but they do not add up to a coherent story. The literature linking culture and personality is fragmentary and inconclusive, for at least two reasons.

First, it is based on the natural science model which assumes that virtually any phenomenon can be studied for its own sake, with no concern about practical applications; that is, the research on culture and personality was not intended to solve a well-defined question. Smith, Bond and Kagitcibasi (2006, p. 127) suggest that the central question in cross-cultural personality psychology concerns … 'the extent to which personality differences may account for the evident differences in behaviour around the world'; they remind us that, 'it was the kaleidoscopic

Both authors wish to thank Lew Goldberg, Robert R. McCrae and Peter B. Smith for their acute comments on earlier versions of this chapter.

diversity in observable behaviours that led to our seeking explanations for cultural differences in the first place' (*ibid.*). The second reason the culture and personality literature is so fragmentary is that, until very recently, there was no agreement among personality psychologists on the agenda for, or definition of, their subject matter (Hogan 2005). In this chapter, we deal with both issues.

We believe that three concepts are necessary to understand human behaviour: (1) personality, which concerns basic human needs; (2) social interaction, which functions to satisfy these basic needs; and (3) culture, which provides group-anchored rules for these social interactions. The rest of this chapter is organized in five sections based on these three concepts. In the first section, we define personality. In the second, we define culture. In the third section, we describe the structure of social interactions, through which personality becomes linked with culture. In the fourth section, we describe some personality-based, cultural universals. In the last section, we offer an agenda for future research in culture and personality.

Defining personality

> In my beginning is my end.   T. S. Eliot, *Four quartets*

Personality psychology concerns the nature of human nature. It answers two big questions: (1) in what ways are people all alike; and (2) in what ways is each person different? Biology and evolutionary theory provide the necessary framework for conceptualizing human nature, and the study of human origins leads to three useful generalizations. The first is that we evolved as group-living and culture-using animals, meaning that we are inherently social; our need for culture is built into our DNA through the processes of natural selection. The second generalization is that every human group has a status hierarchy. In some groups, e.g., Cistercian monks as opposed to the Masai, the hierarchies may be based on different criteria, e.g., knowledge, money, family background, athletic ability, etc. and may be hard to discern, but they are always there. Moreover, the hierarchies begin developing very early and they are quite powerful, although many people socialized into relatively egalitarian cultural systems try to ignore them, downplaying their existence and importance for orchestrating social life.

The third generalization is that every human group has a religion of some sort. By religion we mean a theory regarding a people's relation to the physical and supernatural world, with an associated set of beliefs and practices involving fellow believers. Not only is religion a cultural universal, but religious observances also seem to be an ancient feature of human groups. Anthropologists report systematic burial practices 100,000 years ago. Such practices are probably older, but hard data are difficult to obtain. Nested within each group's religious practices are prescribed and proscribed behaviours; e.g., husbands should not covet their mothers-in-law, wives should prepare foods in certain ways, the genders should be separated during religious ceremonies, believers should avoid contact with non-believers, etc., which we moderns deem superstitions, while treasuring our own equally distinctive practices, such as separating religion from politics.

These three generalizations allow us to draw some inferences about the nature of human motivation, i.e., about how people are alike beneath the apparent surface variation. The fact that we evolved as group-living animals suggests that, at a deep and also perhaps unconscious level, we need ongoing social contact and acceptance; we find the prospects of being rejected aversive.

The fact that every human group is organized in terms of a status hierarchy suggests that, at a deep and again perhaps unconscious level, we need a ranking system to organize ourselves and distribute resources. So, we reflect on our place in the various hierarchies of our daily rounds and try to advance our positions when we can. It also suggests that we will find the loss of status threatening, if not traumatic.

The fact that every human culture has a religion and a network of rules designed to regulate conduct suggests that, at a deep and yet again perhaps unconscious level, we need structure, predictability and meaning in our lives. We create myths, religious systems and moralities to provide ourselves with those reassuring structures and regularities. We then legitimize and justify the belief system that provides us with that order and meaning (Berger 1967; Jost and Hunyady 2005), and become poised to reject others who disagree with our 'way of life'.

We end this discussion of motivation with four observations: first, there are numerous motives at play in life; for example, we share with reptiles the needs for food, water, territory, sex and the desire to protect our young, and we share with chimpanzees the needs for social contact, status and the social ordering it provides. The motivational model we have described here is, with the religious dimension however, distinctly human. Secondly, the needs for social contact, status and belief structure are biologically mandated; those who can successfully negotiate more respect and status in their community are better able to provide for themselves and their offspring. Thirdly, we use as shorthand terms for these three motive patterns the phrases 'getting along', 'getting ahead' and 'finding meaning'. Our needs for social contact lead to behaviours designed to survive and get along; our needs for status result in behaviours designed to acquire more resources and get ahead; and our needs for predictability and order lead to efforts to regulate our life with others and find meaning and purpose in our daily activities. Finally, there will be individual differences in peoples' desire and ability to get along, to get ahead and to find meaning, and these differences lead to differences in life outcomes, both intrapsychically and socially. These differences arise from genetic differences in temperament (Thomas and Chess 1977) and intelligence (Eysenck 1998) which confer from birth differential advantages for playing the game of life and flourishing.

In everyday language the word personality has two meanings. These meanings serve very different purposes and it is important to keep them distinct. On the one hand, there is 'the actor's view' of personality and it concerns 'the you that *you* know': your hopes, beliefs, values, fears and theories about how to get along, get ahead and find meaning. On the other hand, there is 'the observer's view' of personality and it concerns 'the you that *others* know': the person others think you are, based on their judgements of your overt behaviours.

There are several points to be noted about these two aspects of personality: first, the actor's view of personality is your *identity*, whereas the observer's view of personality is your *reputation*. Your identity is the story you tell yourself and others about your self in diary entries, during conversations and on self-report measures of personality. Your reputation is the summary evaluation of your past performances as shared by the members of your proximal social communities.

Secondly, the concepts of identity and reputation serve very different functions for psychologists: we, and people who interact with you, use your reputation to describe your past performance or to predict your future performance; we use your identity to explain your behaviour. Reputation concerns what you do; identity concerns why you do it.

A third point concerns the relative verifiability of these concepts. Identity concerns your self view, and Sigmund Freud would say that it is largely a fantasy created out of the interplay of unconscious needs and defensive processes. Identity is hard to study because it is so subject to self-deception and strategies of impression management. Implicit measures of personality are often used to evade these biases, though they, too, present challenges in capturing your 'true' identity (Hofer and Bond 2008). In contrast, reputation is easy to study: we simply ask your peers to describe you using a standardized reporting format. Such descriptions typically show high agreement across observers, and the descriptions tend to be stable over long periods of time (Roberts and DelVecchio 2000). Moreover, because the best predictor of future behaviour is past behaviour, and because reputations reflect past behaviour, a person's reputation is the best single predictor of his/her future behaviour (Dunnette 1966).

Finally, research over the past 100 years shows that reputation, on however many dimensions it is assessed, has a stable (e.g., Funder, Kolar and Blackman 1995) and universal structure (e.g., McCrae, Terracciano *et al.* 2005). Regardless of the culture in which a person lives or the language that the community speaks, reputations can be characterized in terms of at least five broad themes: (1) Adjustment (fearfulness versus courage; Neuroticism); (2) Ascendance (shyness versus social boldness; Extraversion); (3) Agreeableness (rudeness versus tact); (4) Conscientiousness (recklessness versus prudence); and (5) Intellect/Openness (narrow-mindedness versus open-mindedness). Despite the various labels given to these factors, personality psychologists refer to this as the Five Factor Model (FFM) (Wiggins 1996) whose development has transformed personality research since about 1990.

The FFM argues that individual differences in social behaviour, as reflected in their reputations and the structure of personality assessment, can be adequately described in terms of these five dimensions. Adjustment is important because the low end of the dimension concerns maladaptive thought and self-defeating behaviour, e.g., anxiety, hostility and depression. Ascendance is related to status seeking, e.g., achieving power by accumulating resources and building coalitions, i.e, by using intimidation and the various self-enhancement tactics (Jones and Pittman 1982). Agreeableness concerns seeking social acceptance by the conscious or unconscious use of ingratiation and relationship-building tactics. Prudence concerns achieving social acceptance by following the rules and obeying established authority, i.e., by using exemplification tactics. Intellect/Openness concerns exploration, creativity and imagination. The FFM provides an agreed-upon taxonomy of the major dimensions of personality, although there is some recent debate about whether additional dimensions are needed for cross-cultural comprehensiveness (Cheung, Leung, Zhang *et al.* 2001). Moreover, an overwhelming body of research shows that all (thousands of them) current measures of personality assess these same five dimensions with varying degrees of adequacy and efficiency. In addition, the FFM has been replicated in languages and cultures all over the world (McCrae, Costa, Pilar *et al.* 1998). The evidence also suggests that scores on measures of the FFM are (a) heritable, and (b) stable over time (Costa and McCrae 1994). Finally, the FFM provides a common and generally agreed-upon and apparently universal vocabulary for talking about personality – defined as reputation and as rated by other people.

Culture

> Culture is simply how one lives and is connected to history by habit.
>
> Le Roi Jones, *The legacy of Malcolm X*

Culture is defined by the patterns of thought and behaviour shared by a group of people. Bond (2004, p. 63) provided a psychological definition of culture consistent with this description:

> A shared system of beliefs (what is true), values (what is important), expectations, especially about scripted behavioural sequences, and behaviour meanings (what is implied by engaging in a given action) developed by a group over time to provide the requirements of living (food and water, protection against the elements, security, social belonging, appreciation and respect from others, and the exercise of one's skills in realizing one's life purpose) in a particular geographical niche.

There are five points about culture that should be remembered. First, it is learned, and must be learned anew by each generation. The process of inculcating the rules of culture is called socialization, and the dynamics of socialization are a human universal, because people evolved as group-living and culture-using animals (cf. Keller 2007).

Secondly, the specific contents of any culture are somewhat accidental. They result from the interplay of historical events in an ecological niche that afforded differing survival possibilities (cf., Diamond 1998). The socialization process insures that members of each culture can survive in their specific ecology (rain forest, savannah, coast-line, etc.) and adapt to a changing world.

The third point is that cultures vary independently of race or ethnicity. Members of all races acquire the cultural patterns that are inculcated by their socializing agents. Children are first taught by their families, then by the social institutions – schools, religious groups and political agencies – of their wider society. They in their turn become the culture-teachers of their own and others' children.

Fourthly, cultures exist in two forms, objective and subjective. They exist 'out there' in society in the form of architecture, modes of transportation and eating utensils, as well as written rules and informal customs. But, they also exist inside peoples' heads in the form of judgements regarding what is important, what is true and what counts as correct social behaviour. Each member of a culture will internalize his/her external culture in varying degrees, a socialization process that Berger (1967, p. 17) described as, …'the reabsorption into consciousness of the objectivated world in such a way that the structures of this world come to determine the subjective structures of consciousness itself'.

Finally, our definition of personality stipulates that people are inherently social and meet their primary needs during social interaction. Culture provides the rules for those interactions: 'This shared system enhances communication of meaning and coordination of actions among a culture's members by reducing uncertainty and anxiety through making its members' behaviour predictable, understand-able, and valued' (Bond 2004, p. 63). Thus, culture provides the rules for social interaction and the methods for enforcing those rules, legitimizing both.

Social interaction

> The mutual and universal dependence of individuals who remain indifferent to one another constitutes the social network that binds them together.
>
> Karl Marx, *Das Kapital*

Much human behaviour takes place during social interaction. Even in private, we spend time reviewing past interactions and planning future encounters that will advance our personal agendas. It is useful to reflect on what is needed for an interaction. Every interaction has three essential components. The first is an agenda, a reason or pretext for the interaction. Agendas range from the casual and informal ('Let's get together sometime and have a beer') to the consequential and formal (members of the Security Council at the United Nations debate sending a peace-keeping force to Rwanda). Persons with position power and/or social skills are better able to control the agenda for interactions, and are often required to do so by the roles they occupy in the interaction.

The second major component of an interaction is roles being played; we can only interact with others in the context of roles which provide the essential goal orientation, structure and predictability for the interaction. Consider the game of jump rope: the game can only take place if there is some desire to play physically, agreement about how to play (the rules), and if children are available to fill the required roles of rope turner or rope jumper. Roles range from informal and loosely scripted (guest at a cocktail party) to formal and tightly scripted (bride in a wedding ceremony). As Sarbin and Allen (1968) point out, people differ in their ability to learn and play roles so that some people are more successful in more types of social interaction than others.

The final ingredient needed for an interaction is the rules for the game, ritual or ceremony in which a person is involved. These rules are usually understood by the participants prior to the interaction, although they can be negotiated and some interactions allow for greater negotiability on the rules governing their interpersonal exchanges. The socialization process, which begins in infancy and continues thereafter, is largely about teaching people the requirements for playing various roles, including the rules that apply for instantiating such an interaction in that cultural setting. People who ignore the rules, or will not honour the requirements of their roles, risk ruining the game and may be forced to leave the interaction. Their reputation as bad players will quickly spread, and in more extreme cases they may be denied access to normal social life by being imprisoned.

As an example, consider the interaction that is called a college lecture. The major agenda concerns students learning something from a teacher in a conducive setting. Persons playing the role of the lecturer are supposed to act in an organized, knowledgeable and wise manner; persons playing the role of student are supposed to act interested in the lecture. Even small deviations from the norms (a male instructor wearing a red evening gown, a student talking on a cell phone) will threaten to disrupt the proceedings, requiring its renegotiation. This example shows how we require and invent rituals and roles to regulate our interactions so that we can meet our needs for social contact, status and meaning or purpose.

Finally, every interaction may be considered a competitive game, and as Wiggins (1996) notes, after every interaction, people gain or lose a certain amount of status and acceptance. A person's reputation, as defined by the FFM, reflects the current outcome of the ongoing accounting process that occurs among the people who form the actor's social network. There is high consensus among these people regarding the character of the actor, i.e., his or her reputation (see e.g., Funder and West 1993), which may not agree with the actor's own view of himself or herself. In these cases, the actor is said 'not to know his (or her) place', and pressure may be applied so that the actor accepts the social consensus.

Cultural universals

> Every man is in certain respects (a) like all other men, (b) like some other men, (c) like no other man.
> Kluckholn and Murray, *Personality in nature, society and culture*

Peoples' public behaviour changes substantially from culture to culture. Anthropologists have traditionally argued that culture determines behaviour and explains the differences that occur across cultures. In this chapter, we argue that: (1) there is a universal core to human nature defined by the needs for social acceptance, status and meaning; (2) these needs are met during interaction;

(3) culture provides the rules for interaction; and (4) the contents of culture reflect the imprint of local ecologies and history. We believe that peoples' behaviour differs from culture to culture, not because the people are differently endowed by nature, but because the rules for social interaction are different in their proximal social environments. Although the rules may vary, people's need for culture is universal.

Although people's behaviour varies from culture to culture, there are, nonetheless, some important cultural universals to be noted. These universals exist because ultimately culture reflects human nature. We will mention six such universals, although it is possible to identify more (cf., Eibl-Eibesfeldt 1989).

First, every culture is organized around the family, and family bonds are a defining feature of every culture. If food supplies are sufficient, families will aggregate into larger human groups, tribes and even societies. Under pressure, societies will devolve back into tribes, and tribes will devolve into family units. When families fall apart, human groups have failed utterly, and 'mere anarchy is loosed upon the world', as Yeats observed. Every society understands the concept of the family and its importance. Confucian philosophy explicitly defines family harmony as the foundation of a viable social system.

Secondly, in every culture, human development proceeds through the same stages (Erikson 1963). The first stage concerns forming secure attachment bonds with a child's primary care-takers. A failure here leads to major dysfunction in adulthood (Bowlby 1982; Rohner 1975). The second stage concerns adjusting to adult authority, and internalizing the rules of the culture, a process that Freud identified with resolving the Oedipus complex. Learning language, for example, depends on being exposed to and accepting adult instruction. The third stage involves learning to interact in the peer group, a process facilitated by the development of role-taking ability (Mead 1934) or imaginative empathy (Sarbin and Allen 1968). Finally, at the end of adolescence, every young person must learn to become a productive member of his/her society within the limits imposed by his/her intelligence, skills and temperamental dispositions (Erikson 1963). Cultures will vary in terms of their timing and methods for easing children through these transitions, but every culture must deal with these same universals of human development.

Thirdly, every culture will devise rituals and design settings to encourage social interaction: harvest feasts; birth ceremonies; seasonal festivals, like Christmas; rites of transition, like confirmation ceremonies in religious groups. People need to socialize and every society will meet this need by establishing recognized gathering places: pubs in rural Ireland, community centres in Western China, trade shows in Chicago, the island church in Tristan da Cunha, and so forth.

Fourthly, every culture will be characterized by the status-striving of individuals and their families. There are substantial cultural differences in achievement motivation (McClelland 1967), with some people (the gypsies of Eastern Europe, the untouchables of India) making little or no effort to advance, probably due to discriminatory practices in their host societies, and other people striving mightily to gain and/or maintain status (the oligarchs of modern Russia). The principal dynamic in every society is the individual search for power. What varies are the acceptable means for doing so. Even so, as Balzac noted, behind every great fortune is a great crime, usually perpetrated against one's fellow citizens.

Fifthly, as noted earlier, every culture will have a religious system. Although academic psychologists have tended to avoid the subject (but note Argyle 1958), religion is the most powerful force in human affairs. Ironically, religion and the quest for power often go hand in hand; powerful people everywhere have used religion to justify their privileged positions and extend it to their families and descendants, e.g., 'the divine right of kings'. Religious beliefs constitute part of the personality domain called 'worldviews' (Koltko-Rivera 2004) and are often used to legitimate 'the ideologies of antagonism' (Staub 1989) that fuel collective violence against outgroups (Bond 2007).

Finally, every culture will be characterized by periodic warfare. Sometimes cultures attack neighbouring cultures because the resources of their own land are exhausted or have been depleted by natural disaster (Ember and Ember 1992); an example would be the Viking excursions into Western and Central Europe in the ninth century A. D. But, many times cultural groups invade neighbouring territories in order to enrich themselves, and they justify their actions, often on religious grounds (the Christian Crusades of the Middle Ages). The methods of warfare will vary by culture, but the motivation to protect or enhance one's cultural group will always be the same. Growing awareness across cultural groups about the costs of engaging in collective violence may modify this calculus in the twenty-first century, however (Bond 2007).

This is only a partial list of the cultural universals that are driven by human nature. Every culture will contain these six themes; although they will be expressed in differing ways, they will always be apparent by examining the rules for individual and group interaction devised by each cultural group to meet these universal human needs.

A research agenda for culture and personality

> Time present and time past
> Are both perhaps present in time future,
> And time future in time past.
>
> T. S. Eliot, *Four quartets*

The foregoing discussion suggests two over-arching research agendas for the field of culture and personality, agendas that have generally been neglected in the past. The first is a basic agenda; the second, an applied agenda. With regard to the basic agenda, the model outlined in this chapter can be easily tested by seeing if high status people in different cultures have the same personality profiles (as defined by some universal personality structure, like the FFM) relative to persons of lower status. Our hypothesis is that, controlling for such variables as age and gender, higher status people across cultures will be characterized by high scores on all five dimensions of the FFM; that is, relative to their peers, higher status people will be more confident, ascendant, charming, conscientious and visionary or imaginative. Conversely, lower status people will be characterized by low scores on all five dimensions. The more that status is assigned by achievement rather than ascription due to family background, caste, ethnicity, religion or the like, the greater these differences will be.

A second basic agenda for culture and personality research involves comparing the way social rules are used across cultural groups. People are rule-following animals (Peters, 1960), but what rules does each person perceive to be important in what social situations, and is the person able and willing to observe them? This analysis depends on having an available taxonomy for situations, and some work has already been done on this topic within and across cultures (Marwell and Hage 1970; McAuley, Bond and Kashima 2002). For example, recent cross-cultural research on the rules for emotional expression suggests that the distinction between public and private situations is quite important in shaping the expression of one's feelings (Matsumoto, Nezlek and Koopmann 2007).

This applied agenda is driven by the fact of globalization. The 24 June 2006 issue of *The Economist* makes the following two points: first, multinational firms hire and deploy people all over the world; for example, HSBC has 284,000 employees worldwide, including 800 senior managers as expatriates with 1,600 backups; other multinationals face the same problem of workforce integration across cultures. How are their people going to work together across the cultural divide created by different methods of socialization (see e.g., Friedman, Chi and Liu 2006 on resolving interpersonal conflict)? Secondly, the methods used to select people for expatriate jobs are arbitrary; there is little or no science involved in these selection decisions. Measures of social competence are essential, especially measures of intercultural adaptability and resourcefulness. Work on this topic has begun (e.g., Thomas and Inkson 2004), but more needs to be done within a framework that links cultural processes to personality development and socially appropriate ways to meet fundamental human concerns. Perhaps the enraged Captain Cook need not have been murdered by 'thieving' Hawaiians some ten years after the first episode of 'theft' in Tahiti, had he come to understood the Polynesian worldview regarding relationship obligations in the interim.

> The individual does not exist apart from cultural influence, but is born into – and can only develop within – particular worlds that come culturally configured.   Adams and Markus 2004, p. 346

References

Adams, G. and Markus, H. R. 2004. Toward a conception of culture suitable for a social psychology of culture, in C. S. Crandall and M. Schaller (eds.), *The psychological foundations of culture*, pp. 335–60. Mahwah, NJ: Erlbaum

Argyle, M. 1958. *Religious behaviour*. Glencoe, IL: Free Press

Berger, P. L. 1967. *The sacred canopy: elements of a sociological theory of religion*. New York: Anchor

Bond, M. H. 2004. Culture and aggression: from context to coercion, *Personality and Social Psychology Review* 8: 62–78

　　2007. Culture and collective violence: how good people, usually men, do bad things, in B. Drozdek and J. P. Wilson (eds.), *Voices of trauma: treating survivors across cultures*, pp. 27–57. New York: Springer

Bowlby, J. 1982. *Attachment and loss*. New York: Basic Books

Carneiro, R. L. 1970. A theory of the origin of the state, *Science* 169: 733–8

Cheung, F. M., Leung, K., Zhang, J. X., Sun, H. F., Gan, Y. Q., Song, W. Z. and Xie, D. 2001. Indigenous Chinese personality constructs: is the five-factor model complete?, *Journal of Cross-Cultural Psychology* 32: 407–33

Costa, P. T., Jr and McCrae, R. R. 1994. Set like plaster? Evidence for the stability of adult personality, in T. F. Heatherton and J. L. Weinberger (eds.), *Can personality change?*, pp. 21–40. Washington, DC: American Psychological Association

Diamond, J. 1998. *Guns, germs and steel: the fates of human societies*. New York: Norton

DuBois, C. A. 1960. *The people of Alor: a social psychological study of an East Indian island*. Cambridge, MA: Harvard University Press

Dunnette, M. D. 1966. *Personnel selection and placement*. Belmont, CA: Wadsworth

Eibl-Eibesfeldt, I. 1989. *Human ethology*. New York: Aldine

Ember, C. R. and Ember, M. 1992. Resource unpredictability, mistrust and war: a cross-cultural study, *Journal of Conflict Resolution* 36: 242–62

Erikson, E. 1963. *Childhood and society*, 2nd edn. New York: Norton

Eysenck, H. J. 1998. *Intelligence: a new look*. New Brunswick, NJ: Transaction Publishers

Friedman, R., Chi, S. and Liu, L. A. 2006. An expectancy model of Chinese-American differences in conflict avoiding, *Journal of International Business Studies* 37: 76–91

Funder, D. C., Kolar, D. W. and Blackman, M. C. 1995. Agreement among judges of personality: interpersonal relations, similarity, and acquaintanceship, *Journal of Personality and Social Psychology* 69: 656–72

Funder, D. C. and West, S. G. (Eds.) 1993. Special issue: viewpoints on personality: consensus, self-other agreement, and accuracy in personality judgment, *Journal of Personality* 64: 43–58

Hofer, J. and Bond, M. H. 2008. Do implicit motives add to our understanding of psychological and behavioural outcomes within and across cultures?, in R. Sorrentino and S. Yamaguchi (eds.), *Handbook of motivation and cognition across cultures*, pp. 95–118. Amsterdam: Elsevier

Hogan, R. 2005. In defense of personality measurement: new wine for old whiners, *Human Performance* 18: 331–41

Jones, E. E. and Pittman, T. S. 1982. Toward a general theory of strategic self-presentation, in J. Suls (ed.), *Psychological perspectives on the self*, vol. I. Hillsdale, NJ: Erlbaum

Jost, J. T. and Hunyady, O. 2005. Antecedents and consequents of system-justifying ideologies, *Current Directions in Psychological Science* 14: 260–5

Keller, H. 2007. *Cultures of infancy*. Mahwah, NJ: Erlbaum

Koltko-Rivera, M. E. 2004. The psychology of worldviews, *Review of General Psychology* 8: 3–58

Marwell, G. and Hage, J. 1970. The organization of role-relationships: a systematic description, *American Sociological Review* 35: 884–900

Matsumoto, D., Nezlek, J. and Koopmann, B. 2007. Evidence for universality in phenomenological emotion response system coherence, *Emotion* 7: 57–67

McAuley, P., Bond, M. H. and Kashima, E. 2002. Towards defining situations objectively: a culture-level analysis of role dyads in Hong Kong and Australia, *Journal of Cross-Cultural Psychology* 33: 363–80

McClelland, D. C. 1967. *The achieving society*. New York: Free Press

McCrae, R. R., Costa, P. T., Jr, Pilar, G. H., Rolland, J.-P. and Parker, W. D. 1998. Cross-cultural assessment of the five-factor model: the Revised NEO Personality Inventory, *Journal of Cross-Cultural Psychology* 29: 171–88

McCrae, R. R., Terracciano, A. *et al.* 2005. Universal features of personality traits from the observer's perspective: data from 50 cultures, *Journal of Personality and Social Psychology* 88: 547–61

Mead, G. H. 1934. *Mind, self, and society*. University of Chicago Press

Peters, R. S. 1960. *The concept of motivation*, 2nd edn. London: Routledge and Kegan Paul

Roberts, B. W. and DelVecchio, W. F. 2000. The rank-order consistency of personality from childhood to old age: a quantitative review of longitudinal studies, *Psychological Bulletin* 132: 1–25

Rohner, R. P. 1975. *They love me, they love me not: a worldwide study of the effects of parental acceptance and rejection*. New Haven, CN: HRAF

Sarbin, T. R. and Allen, V. L. 1968. Role theory, in G. Lindzey and E. Aronson (eds.), *Handbook of social psychology*, 2nd edn, vol. 1, pp. 488–567. Reading, MA: Addison-Wesley

Smith, P. B., Bond, M. H. and Kagitcibasi, C. 2006. *Understanding social psychology across cultures*. London: Sage

Staub, E. 1989. *The roots of evil*. Cambridge University Press

Thomas, A. and Chess, S. 1977. *Temperament and development*. New York: Brunner/Mazel

Thomas, D. C. and Inkson, K. 2004. *Cultural intelligence: people skills for global business*. San Francisco, CA: Berrett-Koehler

Turnbull, C. M. 1963. *The forest people*. London: Reprint Society

Wiggins, J. S. 1996. *The five-factor model of personality: theoretical perspectives*. New York: Guilford Press

34 Personality and politics

Gianvittorio Caprara and Michele Vecchione

Personality assumes an increasingly central role in the analysis of political behaviour as traits and values are found to be more influential than traditional socio-demographic characteristics such as gender, age, educational level, occupation and income in explaining ideological orientation and political preferences. Ultimately, personality seems to play a crucial role with regard to both the distinctive features of democratic systems, namely, the freedom of voice allowed to citizens by voting and choosing the representatives that mostly suit their opinions and interests.

This chapter starts by pointing to two different views of personality that may help to make sense of the increasing personalization of contemporary politics. Then, a short review of the literature on personality and politics will be presented, while readers are referred to other sources for a thorough and detailed discussion of previous major contributions. Finally, the contribution that a science of personality may offer to a better understanding of ideological orientation and political preferences will be discussed.

Role of personality in the personalization of contemporary politics

Personality is a concept, as difficult and as familiar as many others in psychology. In reality, none can elude such a concept in everyday discourse as one cannot avoid a theory. In particular, the more one is concerned with the functioning of democracy, namely, the free expression of citizens' ideas and dissent and the legitimate exercise of power, the more one cannot avoid the conceptual network that organizes knowledge, impressions and conjectures that, in turn, make sense of leaders' and followers' political choices and behaviours.

Yet, personality is complex as it includes behavioural tendencies and involves internal systems and processes that guide people towards the attainment of individual and collective goals, account for coherence and behavioural continuity across contexts, and ultimately, explains one's personal identity. Contemporary scholars have addressed personality under two distinct perspectives. One may view personality as a self-regulatory agentic system that is capable of reflecting on its own experiences and that interacts with the environment in conformity with personal criteria and goals. Others may view personality as an architecture of habitual behaviours and behavioural tendencies that allow us both to distinguish

589

one person from another and to make conjectures and predictions regarding individuals' conduct and goals.

These two perspectives produce diverse questions and pave the way to distinct research programmes. Some programmes focus on the organization of affect and cognitions conducive to beliefs and goals that guide individuals' behaviour from within. Other research programmes focus on the individual features that help to recognize, group and distinguish individuals from one another and that are most likely to influence others' impressions. Both perspectives may complement each other in making sense of political choices and preferences given that modern politics of Western democracies attest to an increasing personalization as the individual characteristics of voters and candidates assume greater importance in political rhetoric and choices.

By personalization of politics, one generally refers to the personality characteristics of political candidates and to the substantial investments made by political campaigns aimed at crafting and delivering personal images that are most attractive to voters. In reality, the personalization of politics does not only concern the significant impact of politicians' personality characteristics on voters' preferences, but it also relates to the role of both voters' and politicians' personality with respect to their own ideological orientation and decision-making. Thus, the same concept encompasses diverse phenomena that reflects two distinct groups of related factors: voters' and politicians' personality as operating and politicians' personality as perceived. It is likely that the former has primacy over the latter, as the personality of voters *and of politicians* mostly accounts for what of politicians' personality is perceived *by voters*. Viewing citizens as reasoning agents who pursue the best match between their beliefs and values and political offerings (Himmelweit, Humphreys, Jaeger and Katz 1981; Popkin 1991) points to the unique organization of affect, cognitions and habits which, taken together, make sense of their political choices. Thus, political preferences appear increasingly dependent on individuals' likes and dislikes, cognitive strategies, and personal concerns, rather than on previously identified categorical variables such as gender, age, educational level, and income. While the ideological distinction between left and right or between liberal and conservative may continue to be useful for capturing the major divisions in the sphere of political ideals and movements, at least in Western democracies (Bobbio 1996; Miller and Shanks 1996), recent findings show significant co-variations of ideological self-placement with meaningful psychological differences in the domain of personality in both voters and politicians (Barbaranelli, Caprara, Vecchione and Fraley 2007; Caprara, Barbaranelli, Consiglio, Picconi and Zimbardo 2003; Caprara, Barbaranelli and Zimbardo 1999; Caprara, Francescato, Mebane *et al.* submitted; Jost 2006).

Earlier explorations on personality and politics

The study of personality within the domain of political science is longstanding. Yet, its progress has not been fully continuous. Early generations of theorists have focused on the personalities of main actors, including leaders and followers (Brewster-Smith 1968; Eysenck 1954; Knutson 1973; Greenstein 1975; McGuire 1993). As personality is complex and made up of different kinds of variables, including traits, motives and values that all interact within varied social contexts, a vast literature over the years has attested to the merits and limits of various approaches that have pointed to different personality characteristics and used different methods (Caprara and Zimbardo 2004; Simonton 1990; Winter 2003).

A focus on personality marked the first phase of political psychology by pointing to early experiences and traits as main determinants of political orientation and stability of political attitudes and choices (McGuire 1993). Psychoanalysis seemed to provide a reasonable theoretical basis for selecting and organizing empirical findings relating personality types to political orientation. Personality provided a framework for organizing phenotypic behavioural differences and dispositions, attitudes and motives, and it provided a lexicon to tap stable individual tendencies underlying recurring or habitual behavioural patterns.

Early intuitions drawn on clinical reasoning and the Authoritarian Personality exemplify most contributions prior to the Second World War and during the following decade (Adorno, Frenkel-Brunswik, Levinson and Sanford 1950; Lasswell 1930, 1948). These clinical studies turned into psychobiographical studies and continued to develop over the ensuing decades, primarily focusing on the personalities of leaders. Eventually, interest in psychoanalytical exploration declined and most scholars turned toward sophisticated, in-depth case studies and historiographical analyses (see Barber 1965; Cocks 1986; Erikson 1969; George and George 1956; Glad 1973; Hermann 1977).

Criticism of psychodynamic approaches promoted a new wave of research using individual differences which, although more limited in scope, aimed at enhancing our understanding of stable behavioural patterns related to political behaviour. Championing the nomothetical approach versus more qualitative inquiry were researchers from a host of theoretical perspectives that proposed connections between political behaviour and various individual-difference constructs in personality and social psychology, such as dispositions, social attitudes, motives or values. From this foundation, emerged research on tender-mindedness vs. tough-mindedness (Eysenck 1954), conservatism (McClosky 1958), alienation (Seeman 1959), dogmatism (Rokeach 1960), and power (Browning and Jacob 1964; Winter 1973).While most of this research examined potential voters and only speculated on the personality of leaders, the research of Di Renzo (1963) was a major contribution to the study of a relevant personality variable, dogmatism, among a large number of active politicians (congressmen and senators in the Italian Parliament). It was subsequently replicated in the United States (Di Renzo 1977) and later in Japan (Feldman 1996).

Yet, the lack of a general theory of personality functioning represented a major limitation of earlier approaches to individual differences in politics. This limitation was further aggravated by the lack of consensus on any standardized assessment of personality. Since the study of multiple constructs was not guided by an integrated conceptual vision (Brewster-Smith 1968; Knutson 1973), findings regarding individual psychological differences taken in isolation and in disregard of situational variables were difficult to compare and could hardly lead to the development of cumulative knowledge in this domain (Greenstein 1975).

Recent and current research on personality of politicians and voters

Following the cognitive revolution of the late 1960s, studies of political reasoning pointed to a variety of strategies that people use to select and organize political information, to manage complexity, and to make reasonable choices (Lau 2003; Lau and Sears 1986; Lodge and McGraw 1995; Simon 1985, 1995). One branch of research investigated the path people take to deal with political issues, and the interrelated patterns of affect and cognition that result in stable individual characteristics such as *integrative complexity*. This research received considerable attention for examining personalities of members of political elites and of the general public, pointing to two different dimensions that combine in political reasoning, those of differentiation and integration. *Differentiation* refers to the variety of aspects of an issue or decision that an individual takes into account in making judgements; *integration* refers to the connections that are perceived and formed among various ideas and elements of judgement (Tetlock 1983, 1984). Current studies continue to point to individual differences in complexity and sophistication as critical in political reasoning and choice (Knight 1985; Krosnick 1990; Luskin 1987, 1990; Pierce 1993; Suedfeld and Tetlock 2001).

At the intersection of personality and social psychology, the study of right-wing authoritarianism and political conservativism has cast a bridge between the study of social attitudes and a variety of individual differences in personality, such as self-esteem, openness to experience, need for order and structure, cognitive closure, uncertainty tolerance, integrative complexity and fear of threat or loss (Altemeyer 1996, 1998; Pratto, Sidanius, Stallworth and Malle 1994; Gruenfeld 1995; Jost and Thompson 2000; Lavine, Burgess, Snyder *et al.* 1999). The recent meta-analysis of this extensive literature by Jost, Glaser, Kruglanski and Sulloway (2003a) makes a strong case for political conservatism as motivated social cognition. While the core ideology of conservativism stresses justification for social-economic inequality and resistance to change, its motivational dynamism centres around the need to manage uncertainty and threat (see also the challenge by Greenberg and Jonas 2003, and rebuttal by Jost, Glaser, Kruglanski and Sulloway 2003b).

In general, studies of politicians have focused mostly on leaders' decisions, interpersonal styles, motives and worldviews, and have primarily relied on indirect means for assessing personality at a distance, such as content analysis of narratives or archival material, as well as on biographies or expert evaluation of politicians' personalities (Barber 1985; Etheredge 1978; George and George

1998; Prost 2003; Rubenzer, Faschingbauer and Ones 2000; Simonton 1986; Winter 1987, 1992). In comparison, studies of voters' personality have mostly focused on traits, values, social attitudes and cognitive styles' co-variation with ideological self-placement or voting and have primarily relied on self-report methods (Altemeyer 1996; Barbaranelli, Caprara, Vecchione and Fraley 2007; Barnea and Schwartz 1998; Caprara, Barbaranelli and Zimbardo 1999; Carney, Jost, Gosling and Potter 2008; Jost, Glaser, Kruglanski and Sulloway 2003a; McCrae 1996; Rentfrow, Jost, Gosling and Potter 2006).

Only few individual differences in attitudes like dogmatism, right-wing authoritarianism (Altemeyer 1996, 1998), motives (Winter 1987, 1992), and information-processing (Suedfeld and Tetlock 2001; Tetlock 1983, 1984) have been assessed in both voters and politicians and very few studies have pursued a comprehensive assessment of personality traits which enable comparisons among politicians and voters within and between opposite parties or coalitions (Caprara, Barbaranelli, Consiglio *et al.* 2003; Costantini and Craik 1980).

In reality, nomothetic studies focusing on multiple aspects of psychological functioning and relying on direct methods of assessment such as self-reports from a large sample of voters and politicians are crucial for uncovering new insights into the relationship between personality and ideological orientation. Likewise it is crucial, while focusing on multiple constructs, to be guided by an integrated conceptual vision and to rely upon consensual and standardized methods of personality assessment. In this regard, the real novelty of current studies with respect to the past draws upon the broad consensus on the appropriateness of two taxonomies to assess traits and values, namely, the Big Five or Five-Factor Model (Digman 1990) and Shwartz's ten basic values (Schwartz 1992, 1996).

These taxonomies, in particular, served to convey a more comprehensive view of personality and contributed to achieve unexpected findings regarding the role of personality in posing the foundations of ideological orientations.

Traits, values and ideological orientation

Traits and values are rooted in different intellectual traditions and tell us different things about personality functioning. Traits are 'dimensions of individual differences in tendencies to show consistent patterns of thought, feelings, and actions' (McCrae and Costa 1990, p. 23). Values are cognitive representations of desirable, abstract, trans-situational goals that serve as guiding principles in people's lives (Schwartz 1992). Traits are enduring dispositions; values are enduring goals. Traits describe what people are like; values refer to what people consider important. Traits vary in the frequency and intensity of their occurrence; values vary in their priority as standards for judging behaviour, events and people. People may explain behaviour by referring to traits or to values, but they refer to values when they wish to justify choices or actions as legitimate or worthy.

It is likely that values and traits operate in concert, as several mechanisms link traits and values (Roccas, Sagiv, Schwartz and Knafo 2002). Inborn temperament (e.g., high need for arousal) may give rise to parallel traits (e.g., excitement-seeking) and values (stimulation). Values and traits may also influence one another reciprocally. Values may affect traits because, other things being equal, people try to behave consistently with their values (Rokeach 1973; Schwartz 1996). Traits may affect values because people who consistently exhibit a behavioural trait are likely to increase the degree to which they value the goals that trait serves.

Both earlier and contemporary scholars have pointed to the influence that traits may exert on political orientation (Block and Block 2006; Eysenck 1954; Jost 2006; McCrae 1996; Tomkins 1963) and to the central role of values in politics as major organizers of political evaluations (Feldman 2003; Knutsen 1995; Mitchell, Tetlock, Mellers and Ordonez 1993; Rokeach 1973). Yet, as stated above, only recently can one rely upon consensual taxonomies of traits and values to examine their effect on ideological orientation and political preferences.

First, McCrae (1996) among the most convinced advocates of the Five-Factor Model, pointed to Openness to Experience as the personality trait that mostly distinguishes between liberal and conservative in the political realm. In his conceptualization, this trait is characterized mainly by fantasy, love for aesthetics, openness to feelings and to actions, tolerance for ideas and values. As noted by the author, 'within Western societies, open individuals have an affinity for liberal, progressive, left-wing political views, whereas closed individuals prefer conservative, traditional, right-wing views' (McCrae 1996, p. 325, see also Trapnell 1994). In his review on the social consequences of Openness, McCrae reports the results of several studies that attest to 'ample evidence that political conservatism is in fact related to psychological conservatism' (McCrae 1996, p. 325), with low sensation-seeking, behavioural rigidity, social conformity and conventionality in moral reasoning as major psychological correlates of socio-political conservatism. While Openness is likely to predispose individuals toward liberal political views, Closeness, the negative pole of Openness, may be closely related to authoritarianism as suggested by Trapnell (1994) who reports a very low correlation among NEO-PI-R Openness to Experience Scale and Altemeyer's (1981) Right Wing Authoritarianism Scale. Similarly, McCrae (1996) reports a high negative correlation of NEO-PI-R Openness with an Authoritarianism scale derived from the California Psychological Inventory.

Support on the relation between Openness and ideological orientation comes from the recent meta-analysis of Jost, Glaser, Kruglanski and Sulloway (2003a), as well as from studies conducted in Italy by Caprara, Barbaranelli and Zimbardo (1999, 2002), attesting to higher scores in Openness among voters and politicians of the centre-left than among voters and politicians of the centre-right. Studies in the United States and in Belgium confirm the early results of McCrae as well as the results of Italian studies. Both Gosling, Rentfrow and Swann (2003) and Carney, Jost, Gosling and Potter (2008) in the United States found that the politically conservative are less open than the politically liberal. In Belgium, Van Hiel, Mervielde and De Fruyt (2004) found significant negative correlations among Openness and right-wing authoritarianism, left/right self-placement, and political party preference.

However, there is no accord as far as the other Big Five dimensions are concerned, namely: Extraversion or Energy, Agreeableness, Conscientiousness and Emotional Stability versus Neuroticism. According to McCrae (1996, pp. 328–9), one cannot 'find systematic differences in Neuroticism, Extraversion, or Conscientiousness among political groups. The case is more complex with regard to Agreeableness that … does affect political sentiments forming a factor … called *Tender-mindedness*' in combination with Openness. In reality, while the Italian studies as well as the Belgian study of Van Hiel, Mervielde and De Fruyt 2004 seem to support the idea that centre-right voters are less agreeable than centre-left voters, the US data from Carney and colleagues are in the opposite direction, showing a 'very weak overall tendency for Agreeableness to be positively associated with conservativism' (Carney, Jost, Gosling and Potter 2008, p. 14).

Regarding Extraversion, while there is some evidence of a negative association among sensation-seeking, one specific component of Extraversion, and political conservativism (Jost, Glaser, Kruglanski and Sulloway 2003a), the Italian results evidence an effect that goes in the opposite direction, with centre-right voters showing higher scores in a global measure of Energy/Extraversion than centre-left voters.

Gosling, Rentfrow and Swann (2003) found that Conscientiousness was negatively associated with liberalism, and positively associated with conservatism, although both correlations were small. The same pattern was obtained by Carney in the United States and by Caprara in Italy, where centre-right voters showed higher scores than centre-left voters.

Finally, results regarding emotional stability seem to be rather inconsistent. Only Gosling and colleagues found that the politically conservative are more emotionally stable than the politically liberal. Jost *et al.* (2003a) noted that to the extent that conservatives are more generally fearful than others, one might expect that they would also exhibit higher levels of Neuroticism. However, they did not find evidence of this in their meta-analysis, nor did a similar tendency emerge in the studies conducted in Italy. In the end, Emotional Stability seems to be a personality dimension largely independent from the political domain.

Schwartz's theory includes ten basic values derived from universal requirements of human condition: power, achievement, hedonism, stimulation, self-direction, universalism, benevolence, tradition, conformity and security. Each value expresses a distinct motivational goal. Table 34.1 presents the definitions of each of the ten values in terms of its central goal, that is, the endstate to which it is directed.

The theory specifies the structure of dynamic relations among the values. Openness to change values (self-direction, stimulation) encourage independence of thought, feeling and action, and receptiveness to change. They conflict with conservation values (conformity, tradition, security) that call for submissive self-restriction, preserving traditional practices and protecting stability. Self-transcendence values (universalism, benevolence) emphasize accepting others as equals and concern for their welfare. They conflict with self-enhancement values (power, achievement) that encourage pursuing one's own relative success and

Table 34.1 *Definitions of ten value constructs and sample PVQ items.*

Value and motivational goal	Sample items[a]
Power: social status and prestige, control or dominance over people and resources	'He likes to be in charge and tell others what to do. He wants people to do what he says'
Achievement: personal success through demonstrating competence according to social standards	'Being very successful is important to him. He likes to stand out and to impress other people'
Hedonism: pleasure and sensuous gratification for oneself	'He really wants to enjoy life. Having a good time is very important to him'
Stimulation: excitement, novelty and challenge in life	'He looks for adventures and likes to take risks. He wants to have an exciting life'
Self-direction: independent thought and action –choosing, creating, exploring	'He thinks it's important to be interested in things. He is curious and tries to understand everything'
Universalism: understanding, appreciation, tolerance and protection for the welfare of all people and for nature	'He wants everyone to be treated justly, even people he doesn't know. It is important to him to protect the weak in society'
Benevolence: preservation and enhancement of the welfare of people with whom one is in frequent personal contact	'He always wants to help the people who are close to him. It's very important to him to care for the people he knows and likes'
Tradition: respect, commitment and acceptance of the customs and ideas that traditional culture or religion provide the self	'He thinks it is important to do things the way he learned from his family. He wants to follow their customs and traditions'
Conformity: restraint of actions, inclinations, and impulses likely to upset or harm others and violate social expectations or norms	'He believes that people should do what they're told. He thinks people should follow rules at all times, even when no-one is watching'
Security: safety, harmony and stability of society, of relationships and of self	'It is important to him to live in secure surroundings. He avoids anything that might endanger his safety'

[a] The PVQ forms were gender appropriate, varying only in the pronouns.

dominance over others. Hedonism values share elements of both openness and self-enhancement.

The ten values form a motivational continuum based on their pattern of compatibility and conflict. Figure 34.1 depicts this continuum in the form of a motivational circle. The order of the values in Table 34.1 follows this circle. Tests of the theory in more than 200 samples from 67 countries largely support both the content of the ten values and the structure of relations among them (Schwartz 1992, 1994, 2005).

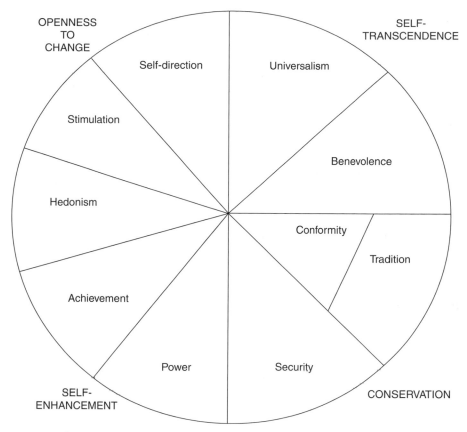

Figure 34.1. *The motivational continuum of basic values.*

Values have been used as predictors of voting behaviour in fourteen democratic countries chosen to represent culturally distinct world regions (Barnea 2003; Barnea and Schwartz 1998). In every country, value priorities discriminated significantly among supporters of the different political parties. The specific values that predicted voting varied across countries. Which values were crucial depended on the nature of the political conflict or discourse in each nation. Every one of the ten values was a significant discriminator in at least several countries. People tended to vote for parties whose platform or image suggested that electing them would promote attainment or preservation of their own cherished, personal values. They did not vote for parties whose election they perceived as threatening these values. For example, voters who gave high priority to self-direction and universalism but low priority to power and security tended to vote for parties that emphasized individual freedom and programmes to help the poor but not for parties that were more concerned with nationalism and maintaining law and order.

Caprara *et al.* (2006) have examined the co-variation between traits, values and political orientation among voters and politicians in a number of studies. In these studies, political orientation co-varied with both traits and values and both traits and values accounted for a substantial portion of variance, more than any socio-demographic variable. Centre-left voters and politicians assigned higher importance to universalism and lower importance to security, conformity, tradition and power than centre-right voters and politicians. Congruency between traits and values and political orientation suggested that people adopt ideological belief systems and endorse political programmes that are more likely to match their own traits and values.

Yet, values were found to be superior to traits in accounting for both ideological orientation and voting, with centre-left partisans assigning higher importance to self-transcendence values than centre-right voters, who in turn assigned higher importance to self-enhancement and conservation values than centre-left partisans. These results accord well with a view of personality in which personal goals and standards usually drive voluntary behaviour (Bandura 2001; Caprara and Cervone 2000). These findings further attest to the reflexiveness and purposefulness of individuals whose habits and choices often match the moral principles that guide their lives.

The centre-left coalition in Italy includes traditional left parties either of Catholic or Marxist inspirations and advocates social welfare, concern for social justice, equality, pluralism and tolerance of diverse groups. Such policies match traits like Openness and are most expressive of universalism values. The centre-right coalition, instead, is the heir to diverse ideological traditions that meshed together under the pressure of contingent and pragmatic convenience: on the one hand, it advocates the virtues of a market economy while encouraging individual freedom and achievements; on the other hand, it advocates the merits of tradition, community and family ties while promoting order, stability and security.

Both these claims are congruent with traits like Conscientiousness and with values like power, security and tradition. Ultimately, these findings attest to the role that personality may play in making sense of ideological orientation, much beyond traditional variables like gender, age, education and income, not only in voters but also in politicians with high education, expertise and political sophistication.

Personality at the origin of ideological divide in contemporary democracies

Findings we have collected over the years have led to the belief that personality, including traits, needs, motives, values and self-beliefs, not only co-vary with ideological orientation, but set the foundation for *the major ideological division in Western democracies*. We came to this belief for two reasons: (a) the knowledge that has cumulated over the years regarding personality functioning, and (b) the major changes that have occurred in most democratic countries regarding political participation and voting.

The first reason draws upon our recent knowledge of personality functioning as a self-regulatory agentic system. There is a substantial amount of evidence that people are purposive agents who behave in accordance with the goals and standards that guide their life and that a certain degree of stability in their habits and values is critical to keep their identity and to attest to their agency. People derive their identity from what they do and pursue. People derive their sense of agency from the control they exert over their behaviour and over the environment in pursuing their goals. When people vote in modern democracies, despite knowing that it is very improbable that their single vote will influence the results of an election, they express their individual autonomy, assert the equal dignity of their views, affirm their belongingness to groups and communities, and attest to their trust in concerted action (Nozick 1989). While it is likely that people vote mostly in accordance with their own values, the extent to which values that are decisive in political choices are rooted in individuals' predispositions, as well as the nature of these predispositions, remains to be clarified.

Evidence for the long-term persistence of political preferences has led a number of scholars to point to political predispositions as resulting from acquired attitudes infused through early socialization practices and then crystallized over the course of life (Sears and Funk 1999). Other scholars have argued that basic traits are at the root of any behavioural tendency as well as of social attitudes and values and point to the Five-Factors as the genotype of personality (McCrae and Costa 1999). Whereas both views point to the high stability of ideological orientation and political preferences, advocates of traditional predispositional models have mostly drawn their reasoning from learning theory, while advocates of the Five-Factor theory instead point to heredity.

In reality, recent findings suggest that genetics may play an important role in shaping political ideologies as it does in shaping other social attitudes and personality features (Alford, Funk and Hibbing 2005; Bouchard and Lohelin 2001; Hastemi, Medland, Morley *et al.* 2007). However, current progress in molecular genetics while emphasizing the pervasive influence of 'gene x environment' interactions points to a kind of genetic probabilism rather than genetic determinism. Genes in fact do not work in isolation and influence the extent to which organisms are responsive to particular environments. Thus, one may guess that genes account for a certain sensitivity towards conservative or liberal ideologies, but environmental affordances are crucial to turn sensitivities into stable preferences and behavioural tendencies.

Other scholars have argued that self-beliefs, personal standards and goals guide behaviour and point mostly to the properties of human mind that emerge from the encountering of the organism with the environment (Caprara and Cervone 2000).

The above findings are compatible with all of these views since one may guess that basic traits and socialization experiences set the stage for ideological orientation, whereas values mediate the influence of both on political choice and careers.

Yet, a number of issues remain to be clarified. First, one should clarify through 'which gene x environment' interactions mere sensitivities to particular features of the environment turn into stable attitudes and political preferences. Then, one needs to identify the extent to which traits' influence on political preferences is mediated by values, and whether other genetic factors operating in concert with environmental factors shape both traits and values conducive to ideological place-ment. Finally, the extent to which congruency among traits, values and ideologies reflect not only individuals' needs but also social roles that shape personal identities in accordance with the principles that govern social systems at different times and in different cultural contexts, remains to be seen.

As values remain at the core of both personal and social identities (Hiltin 2003), they can attest both to individuals' degrees of freedom in choosing the kind of person to become as well as to the pervasive influence of socialization practices on individual development. Social theories focusing on the special properties of human agency view individuals as agents, entitled with broad degrees of autonomy in selecting environments, activities and people, in pursuing goals that accord with their own values, and in advocating a unique sense of one's own self (Bandura 2001). Yet, other social theories focusing on the influence that membership to families, group, class and communities exert on individuals' development and functioning remind us that self-beliefs, attitudes and values are largely dictated by shared social conventions as well as by the place people occupy in society (Emler 2002).

In reality, personal and social identities are inextricably linked together and as such, contribute to political preference. Previous findings are not incompatible with these views as one may guess that the values that guide political choices reflect both socialization influences and individuals' autonomous appropriation of social values. However, we believe that viewing oneself as a unique individual versus viewing oneself as a member of a family, group or community, plays a major role in ideological self-placement today, more so than in the past, due to major changes in mature and recent democracies.

This leads to our second reason for believing that personality sets the founda-tion for ideological divide. Whereas differences in prioritizing self-enhancement or self-transcendence values further attests to the left-right polarity as a reasonable representation of ideological differences in the political domain, these differences draw upon categorical memberships like gender, generation, religion and class much less than in the past in most Western democracies.

In addition, the power of a traditional source of stability in political preferences like party identification (Campbell, Converse, Miller and Stokes 1960; Miller and Shanks 1996), has been substantially challenged by the turnover of parties. This might be particularly true in countries like Italy, where none of the parties that have dominated politics from the end of the Second World War to the fall of the Berlin Wall are still present in the Italian Parliament. Likewise, most European countries that turned to democratic elections after the fall of the Berlin Wall, as most other countries that only recently conquered democracy, demonstrate a political climate that can claim very little party identification.

In Western democracies, voting has traditionally attested to the power of ideologies, party identification and class solidarity. Yet, the extent to which the same factors account for voting in both well-established and recent democracies around the world remains debatable. We are inclined to believe that the broader the latitude of political offerings, the less polarized the ideological debate, the higher individuals' liberty to express preferences in the various domains of life, and the more personal views about the world dictate individuals' political choices. Thus, one should clarify the extent to which parties continue to shape citizens' political choices no less than the extent to which citizens' values contribute to shape parties' changing identities.

Conclusions

Recent findings on voters and politicians contribute to fill a long-standing gap in the personality underpinnings of ideological orientation and political choices and attest to the importance of studying politics from a psychological position. Yet, the same findings may not replicate to the same extent in political systems where political rights have different status and notions like human agency and personal and social identity have different meanings and latitudes. Thus, further studies in other cultural contexts and political systems are needed to corroborate these findings. One should not underestimate the fact that self-reported traits may be differently desirable and that the priority of values (universalism vs. security; equality vs. freedom) can shift from one setting to another, or across time, political systems and culture. It is an empirical task to examine the extent to which traits and values match political preferences, as well as the contribution of both traits and values to the ideological divide in different political contexts.

While believing that personality sets the foundation for ideological divide, we are convinced that one should specify not only the distinct contribution of traits and values, but also examine the contribution of other features of personality such as needs, motives, self-beliefs and social attitudes. Likewise, we are convinced that one should not underestimate, in addition to and in combination with personality features, the contribution of a variety of environmental factors in actualizing individuals' potentials and in channelling and crystallizing individuals' proclivities into a system of political beliefs, preferences and decisions. Nor should one underestimate the diversities of political systems and the different role and expressions of ideology in different contexts. Although attitudes toward social change and equality still signal the ideological line of division in most political systems (Jost 2006), ideologies may differently correspond to belief systems and cognitive schemes that serve to organize or to distort political information.

Conservative and liberal ideologies may correspond to different priorities, emphases and expectations and can operate though different mechanisms in different political systems that may draw upon more or less solid democratic traditions. Whereas left-right cleavages may be very subtle in countries where opposite coalitions share similar concerns for freedom, equity and tolerance, left and right ideologies can still be very divisive in countries where opposite factions pursue the exclusion of each other.

Party identification may exert a different influence on citizens' political choices in countries with parties like the UK Conservatives and Labour or the US Republicans and Democrats, which have ruled the political scene for centuries. In contrast, party identification may mean little for citizens that have not been accustomed to voicing their opinions in free elections until very recently.

Voting may serve instrumental and expressive functions, reflect the degree of political participation and attest to the functioning of democracy in different ways across different political systems. In reality, the number of people who have never voted and cannot vote in free elections is still largely superior to the number of people who enjoy the liberty of voting around the world. As a consequence, the contribution of personality to ideology and political participation and choices, while substantial, may significantly change across political contexts.

Ultimately, we agree with Jost (2006) both in believing that the end of ideology has been prematurely declared and in arguing that much of ideology, whatever its expression in different cultural and political latitudes, reflects human nature, namely, individuals' needs and their diversities in pursuing their fulfilments. Thus, further studies able to focus on the manifold facets of personality functioning in multiple cultural contexts and across different political systems are needed to supply the empirical support that may enable further development of our reasoning.

References

Adorno, T., Frenkel-Brunswik, E., Levinson, D. and Sanford, R. 1950. *The authoritarian personality*. New York: Harper

Alford, J. R., Funk, C. L. and Hibbing, J. R. 2005. Are political orientations genetically transmitted?, *American Political Science Review* 99: 153–67

Altemeyer, R. A. 1981. *Right-wing authoritarianism*. Winnipeg: University of Manitoba Press

1996. *The authoritarian specter*. Cambridge, MA: Harvard University Press

1998. The other 'authoritarian personality', in M. P. Zanna (ed.), *Advances in experimental social psychology*, vol. XXX, pp. 47–91. New York: Academic Press

Bandura, A. 2001. Social cognitive theory: an agentic perspective, *Annual Review of Psychology* 52: 1–26

Barbaranelli, C., Caprara, G. V., Vecchione, M. and Fraley, R. C. 2007. Voters' personality traits in presidential elections, *Personality and Individual Differences* 42: 1199–1208

Barber, J. D. 1965. *The lawmakers*. New Haven: Yale University Press

1985. *The presidential character: predicting performance in the White House*, 3rd edn. Englewood Cliffs, NJ: Prentice Hall

Barnea, M. 2003. *Personal values and party orientations in different cultures*. Unpublished doctoral dissertation. Hebrew University of Jerusalem

Barnea, M. and Schwartz, S. H. 1998. Values and voting, *Political psychology* 19: 17–40

Block, J. and Block, J. H. 2006. Nursery school personality and political orientation two decades later, *Journal of Research in Personality*, 40: 734–49

Bobbio, N. 1996. *Left and right*. Cambridge: Polity Press

Bouchard, T. J., Jr and Lohelin, J. C. 2001. Genes, personality, and evolution, *Behaviour Genetics* 31: 23–73

Brewster-Smith, M. 1968. A map for the analysis of personality and politics, *Journal of Social Issues* 24: 15–28

Browning, R. and Jacob, H. 1964. Power motivation and the political personality, *Public Opinion Quarterly* 28: 75–90

Campbell, A., Converse, P. E., Miller, W. E. and Stokes, D. E. 1960. *The American voter*. New York: Wiley

Caprara, G. V. and Barbaranelli, C. 2000. *Capi di governo, telefonini e bagni di schiuma*. [*Chiefs of government, cellular phones and bath foam*]. Milan: Raffaello Cortina

Caprara, G. V., Barbaranelli, C., Consiglio, C., Picconi, L. and Zimbardo, P. G. 2003. Personalities of politicians and voters: unique and synergistic relationships, *Journal of Personality and Social Psychology* 84: 849–56

Caprara, G. V., Barbaranelli, C. and Zimbardo, P. G. 1999. Personality profiles and political parties, *Political Psychology* 20: 175–97

   2002. When parsimony subdues distinctiveness: simplified public perception of politicians' personality, *Political Psychology* 23: 77–96

Caprara, G. V. and Cervone, D. 2000. *Personality: determinants, dynamics and potentials*. Cambridge University Press

Caprara, G. V., Francescato, D., Mebane, M., Sorace, R. and Vecchione, M. submitted. *Personality foundation of ideological divide*. Manuscript submitted for publication

Caprara, G. V., Schwartz, S., Capanna, C., Vecchione, M. and Barbaranelli, C. 2006. Values, traits, and political choice, *Political Psychology* 27: 1–28

Caprara, G. V. and Zimbardo, P. 2004. Personalizing politics, *American Psychologist* 59: 581–94

Carney, D., Jost, J. T., Gosling, S. D. and Potter, J. 2008. *The secret lives of liberals and conservatives: personality profiles, interaction styles, and the things they leave behind*, *Political Psychology* 29: 807–40

Cocks, G. 1986. Contribution of psychohistory to understanding politics, in M. G. Hermann (ed.), *Political Psychology*, pp. 139–66. San Francisco, CA: Jossey-Bass

Costantini, E. and Craik, K. H. 1980. Personality and politicians: California party leaders, 1960–1976, *Journal of Personality and Social Psychology* 38: 641–61

Di Renzo, G. 1963. *Personalità e potere politico*. [*Personality and political leadership*]. Bologna: Il Mulino

   1977. Politicians and personality. A cross cultural perspective. In M. G. Hermann (ed.), *A psychological examination of political leaders,* pp. 147–204. New York: Free Press

Digman, J. M. 1990. Personality structure: emergence of the Five Factor Model, *Annual Review of Psychology* 41: 417–40

Emler, N. 2002. Morality and political orientation: an analysis of their relationship, *European Review of Social Psychology* 13: 259–91

Erikson, E. H. 1969. *Gandhi's truth*. New York: Norton

Etheredge, L. S. 1978. Personality effects on American foreign policy, 1898–1968: a test of interpersonal generalization theory, *American Political Science Review* 72: 434–51

Eysenck, H. 1954. *The psychology of politics*. London: Routledge and Kegan Paul

Feldman, O. 1996. The political personality of Japan: an inquiry into the belief systems of Diet Members, *Political Psychology* 17: 657–82

Feldman, S. 2003. Values, ideology, and structure of political attitudes, in D. O. Sears, L. Huddy and R. Jervis (eds.), *Oxford handbook of political psychology*, pp. 477–508. New York: Oxford University Press

George, A. L. and George, J. L. 1956. *Woodrow Wilson and Colonel House: a personality study*. New York: John Day
    1998. *Presidential personality*. Boulder, CO: Westview Press

Glad, B. 1973. Contributions of psychobiography, in J. N. Knutson (ed.), *Handbook of political psychology*, pp. 296–321. San Francisco, CA: Jossey-Bass

Gosling, S. D., Rentfrow, P. J. and Swann, W. B., Jr 2003. A very brief measure of the Big Five personality domains, *Journal of Research in Personality* 37: 504–28

Greenberg, J. and Jonas, E. 2003. Psychological motives and political orientation – the left, the right, and the rigid: comment on Jost *et al.* (2003), *Psychological Bulletin* 129: 376–82

Greenstein, F. I. 1975. Personality and politics, in F. I. Greenstein and N. W. Polsby (eds.), *The handbook of political science*, vol. II, pp. 1–92. Reading, MA: Addison Wesley

Gruenfeld, D. H. 1995. Status, ideology, and integrative ideology on the U.S. Supreme Court: rethinking the politics of political decision making, *Journal of Personality and Social Psychology* 68: 5–20

Hastemi, P. K., Medland, S. E., Morley, K. I., Heath, A. and Martin, N. C. 2007. *The genetics of voting: an Australian twin study*, Behavior Genetics 37: 435–48

Hermann, M. G. (ed.) 1977. *A psychological examination of political leaders*. New York: Free Press

Hiltin, S. 2003. Values as the core of personal identity: drawing links between two theories of the self, *Social Psychology Quarterly* 66: 118–37

Himmelweit, H., Humphreys, P., Jaeger, M. and Katz, M. 1981. *How voters decide: a longitudinal study of political attitudes and voting extending over fifteen years*. London: Academic Press

Jost, J. T. 2006. The end of the end of ideology, *American Psychologist* 61: 651–70

Jost, J. T., Glaser, J., Kruglanski, A. W. and Sulloway, F. J. 2003a. Political conservatism as motivated social cognition, *Psychological Bulletin* 129: 339–75
    2003b. Exceptions that prove the rule – using a theory of motivated social cognition to account for ideological incongruities and political anomalies: reply to Greenberg and Jonas (2003), *Psychological Bulletin* 129: 383–93

Jost, J. T. and Thompson, E. P. 2000. Group-based dominance and opposition to equality as independent predictors of self esteem, ethnocentrism, and social policy attitudes among African Americans and European Americans, *Journal of Experimental Social Psychology* 36: 209–33

Knight, K. 1985. Ideology in the 1980 election: ideological sophistication does matter, *Journal of Politics* 47: 828–53

Knutsen, O. 1995. Party choice, in J. W. van Deth and E. Scarbrough (eds.), *The impact of values*, pp. 460–91. New York: Oxford University Press

Knutson, J. 1973. *Handbook of political psychology*. San Francisco, CA: Jossey-Bass

Krosnick, J. A. 1990. Expertise and political psychology, *Social Cognition* 8: 1–8

Lasswell, H. D. 1930. *Psychopathology and politics*. New York: Viking

1948. *Power and personality*. New York: Norton

Lau, R. R. 2003. Models of decision-making, in D. O. Sears, L. Huddy and R. Jervis (eds.), *Oxford handbook of political psychology*, pp. 19–59. New York: Oxford University Press

Lau, R. R. and Sears, D. O. (eds.). *Political cognition*. Hillsdale, NJ: Erlbaum

Lavine, H., Burgess, D., Snyder, M., Transue, J., Sullivan, J., Haney, B. and Wagner, S. H. 1999. Threat, authoritarianism, and voting: an investigation of personality and persuasion, *Personality and Social Psychology Bulletin* 25: 337–47

Lodge, M. and McGraw, K. M. (eds.) 1995. *Political judgment: structure and processes*. Ann Arbor, MI: University of Michigan Press

Luskin, R. 1987. Measuring political sophistication, *American Journal of Political Science* 31: 856–99

1990. Explaining political sophistication, *Political Behaviour* 12: 331–62

McClosky, H. 1958. Conservativism and personality, *American Political Science Review* 52: 27–45

McCrae, R. R. 1996. Social consequences of experiential Openness, *Psychological Bulletin* 120: 323–37

McCrae, R. R. and Costa, P. T. 1990. *Personality in adulthood*. New York: Guilford Press

1999. A five-factor theory of personality, in L. A. Pervin and O. P. John (eds.), *Handbook of personality: theory and research*, pp. 139–53. New York: Guilford Press

McGuire, W. J. 1993. The poli-psy relationship: three phases of a long affair, in S. Yengar and W. J. McGuire (eds.), *Explorations in political psychology*, pp. 9–35. Durham: Duke University Press

Miller, W. E. and Shanks, J. M. 1996. *The new American voter*. Cambridge, MA: Harvard University Press

Mitchell, P. G., Tetlock, P. E., Mellers, B. A. and Ordonez, L. 1993. Judgments of social justice: compromises between equality and efficiency, *Journal of Personality and Social Psychology* 65: 629–39

Nozick, R. 1989. *The examined life: philosophical meditations*. New York: Simon and Shuster

Pierce, P. 1993. Political sophistication and the use of candidate traits in candidate evaluation, *Political psychology* 14: 21–35

Popkin, S. 1991. *The reasoning voter*. Chicago University Press

Pratto, F., Sidanius, J., Stallworth, L. M. and Malle, B. F. 1994. Social dominance orientation: a personal variable predicting social and political attitudes, *Journal of Personality and Social Psychology* 67: 741–63

Prost, J. M. (ed). 2003. *The psychological assessment of political leaders*. Ann Arbor, MI: University of Michigan Press

Rentfrow, P. J., Jost, J. T., Gosling, S. D. and Potter, J. 2006. *Regional differences in personality predict voting patterns in 1996–2004 U.S. presidential elections*. Manuscript submitted for publication

Roccas, S., Sagiv, L., Schwartz, S. H. and Knafo, A. 2002. The Big Five personality factors and personal values, *Personality and Social Psychology Bulletin* 28: 789–801

Rokeach, M. 1960. *The open and closed mind*. New York: Basic Books
   1973. *The nature of human values*. New York: Free Press

Rubenzer, S. J., Faschingbauer, T. R. and Ones, D. S. 2000. Assessing the U.S. Presidents using the revised NEO Personality Inventory, *Assessment* 7: 403–20

Schwartz, S. H. 1992. Universals in the content and structure of values: theoretical advances and empirical tests in 20 countries, in M. Zanna (ed.), *Advances in experimental social psychology*, vol. XXV, pp. 1–65. Orlando, FL: Academic Press
   1994. Are there universal aspects in the structure and contents of human values?, *Journal of Social Issues* 50: 19–45
   1996. Value priorities and behaviour: applying a theory of integrated value systems, in C. Seligman, J. M. Olson and M. P. Zanna (eds.), *The psychology of values: the Ontario Symposium*, vol. XIII, pp. 1–24. Hillsdale, NJ: Erlbaum
   2005. Basic human values: their content and structure across cultures, in A. Tamayo and J. Porto (eds.), *Valores e trabalho* [*Values and work*]. Brasilia: Editora Vozes

Sears, D. O. and Funk, C. L. 1999. Evidence of long-term persistence of adult's political predispositions, *Journal of Politics* 61: 1–28

Seeman, M. 1959. On the meaning of alienation, *American Sociological Review* 24: 783–91

Simon, H. A. 1985. Human nature in politics: the dialogue of psychology with political science, *American Political Science Review* 79: 293–304
   1995. Rationality in political behaviour, *Political Psychology* 16: 45–61

Simonton, D. K. 1986. Presidential personality: biographical use of the Gough Adjective Check List, *Journal of Personality and Social Psychology* 51: 149–60
   1990. Personality and politics, in L. Pervin (ed.), *Handbook of personality*, pp. 670–92. New York: Guilford Press

Suedfeld, P. and Tetlock, P. E. 2001. Individual differences in information processing, in A. Tesser and N. Schwartz, *Blackwell international handbook of social psychology: intra-individual processes*, vol. I, pp. 284–304. London: Blackwell Publishers

Tetlock, P. E. 1983. Cognitive style and political ideology, *Journal of Personality and Social Psychology* 45: 118–26
   1984. Cognitive style and political belief system in the British House of Commons, *Journal of Personality and Social Psychology* 46: 365–75

Tomkins, S. S. 1963. Left and right: a basic dimension of ideology and personality, in R. W. White (ed.), *The study of lives*, pp. 388–411. Chicago, IL: Atherton

Trapnell, P. D. 1994. Openness versus intellect: a lexical left turn, *European Journal of Personality* 8: 273–90

Van Hiel, A., Mervielde, I. and De Fruyt, F. 2004. The relationship between maladaptive personality and right wing ideology, *Personality and Individual Differences* 36: 405–17

Winter, D. G. 1973. *The power motive*. New York: Free Press
   1987. Leader appeal, leader performance, and the motive profiles of leaders and followers: a study of American presidents and elections, *Journal of Personality and Social Psychology* 52: 196–202

1992. Content analysis of archival data, personal documents and everyday verbal productions, in C. P. Smith (ed.), *Motivation and personality: Handbook of thematic content analysis*, pp. 110–25. New York: Cambridge University Press

2003. Personality and political behaviour, in D. O. Sears, L. Huddy and R. Jervis (eds.), *Oxford handbook of political psychology*, pp. 110–45. New York: Oxford University Press

PART VII

Psychopathology

35 Mood and anxiety disorders: the hierarchical structure of personality and psychopathology

David D. Vachon and R. Michael Bagby

The doctrine of the four humours, commonly associated with Hippocrates (460–370 BC) and later with the Roman physician Galen (131–200), may represent the first model to view personality and psychopathology as related domains (Maher and Maher 1994). According to this doctrine, an imbalance in the four humours – phlegm, blood (*sanguis*), bile (*choler*) and black bile (*melancholer*) – caused one's temperament to become phlegmatic, sanguine, choleric or melancholic, respectively. Personality and psychopathology were connected through their common dependence on humoural balance; from this perspective, the restoration of humoural balance – and thus healthy temperament – was achieved through such techniques as bleeding, vomiting and purging. Nearly two millennia later, these techniques were deposed by new practices associated with the late nineteenth century advent of modern science and the rise of the degeneracy concept.

With the emergence of the Darwinian revolution, the relationship between personality and psychopathology became linked to natural selection and the basic theme that all types of mental illness reflect a general deficiency in character (Maher and Maher 1994). Proponents of this degeneracy theory held that disease, mental illness, poverty, alcoholism, gambling, mental retardation and low life expectancy were symptomatic of a fundamental genetic inferiority; those afflicted were by definition lower on the evolutionary scale than those who flourished. Personality correlates of this general character deficiency were thought to include laziness, disagreeableness, impulsivity, aggressiveness and a lack of self-control. In contrast to bleeding, vomiting and purging, the proper treatment for degeneracy was sterilization, institutionalization and elimination of free medical treatment for the poor.

Interestingly, the ancient humoural model was rejuvenated by mid-twentieth century Pavlovians, although these conditioning theorists substituted variation in neuronal responses for balance in the four humours (Maher and Maher 1994). Eysenck (1947) also related his personality model to these Pavlovian concepts and noted that the two broad dimensions derived using factor analysis – Neuroticism (N), the tendency to experience negative emotions, and Extraversion (E), the tendency to experience positive emotions – could be combined to produce each of the four humoural imbalances: high N and E (choleric type), high N and low E (melancholic type), low N and high E (sanguine type), low N and E (phlegmatic type). Subsequent factor analyses by Eysenck (Eysenck and Eysenck 1976) also yielded a third factor – Psychoticism, a heterogeneous concept related to low Five-Factor Model (Costa and McCrae 1992) Agreeableness (A) and Conscientiousness (C). Psychoticism, as it relates to low A and C, represents a proclivity for disagreeable and unconscientious disinhibition, traits that have been associated with a number of so-called degeneracy characteristics, including impulsivity, laziness, disagreeableness, aggressiveness and a lack of self-control. Thus, while the theories and treatments associated with Hippocratic humoural imbalance and Darwinian character deficiency were clearly erroneous, consequent empirically-based analyses have yielded a set of three personality factors clearly related to both movements.

After the 1965 split of the *Journal of Abnormal and Social Psychology* into the *Journal of Abnormal Psychology* and the *Journal of Personality and Social Psychology*, the fields of personality and psychopathology became increasingly independent (Watson and Clark 1995). This trend continued for a number of years, and personality and psychopathology became relatively discrete areas of inquiry. With the 1990s emergence of temperament-based models of personality, however, came a renaissance of interest in how these areas intersect; traits began to transcend their role as behavioural descriptions, instead becoming reasonable causal agents of this behaviour (Watson, Kotov and Gamez 2006). Several significant programs of research and theorizing have emerged at the intersection of personality and psychopathology, helping to clarify excessive psychiatric co-occurrence and explicate the etiological bases of psychiatric disorders. Furthermore, evidence of continuity between personality and psychopathology suggests an inherent interconnectedness between these domains such that one cannot be understood independent of the other (Watson, Gamez and Simms 2005).

Although a detailed review describing the relationships between extant personality models and each of the twenty mood and anxiety disorders would be informative, such an endeavour is beyond the scope of this chapter. Rather, the primary goal of this chapter is to provide an overview of the relationship between personality and psychopathology in general, and between personality traits and mood and anxiety disorders in particular, using the hierarchical structural relationships within and between these domains as an organizing framework. Moreover, because investigations of the bipolar disorders typically suffer from low base rates in the general population (Krueger 1999; Vollebergh, Iedema, Bijil *et al.* 2001) and include analyses convoluted by hierarchical exclusion rules that prohibit the concurrent diagnosis of most unipolar and bipolar mood disorders (Watson 2005), discussion will be limited to unipolar mood disorders.

Models of personality

Personality disorders

In 1980, the American Psychiatric Association (APA) released its third edition of the *Diagnostic and statistical manual of mental disorders* (DSM-III). Unlike the first two editions (DSM-I, DSM-II; American Psychiatric Association 1952 1968), personality pathology was not considered alongside other disorders; instead, personality disorders (PDs) were coded categorically and placed on a new 'Axis II'. Although DSM-III explicitly declared its atheoretical intent, the advent of this multiaxial system clearly invited a systematic study of the inter-relation between axes and suggested that PDs were a distinct type of psychopathology. This system, though slightly modified, continues to be used in DSM-IV (APA 1994).

General diagnostic criteria for a PD include an enduring and pervasive pattern of inner experience and behaviour that deviates markedly from cultural norms in at least two of four areas (cognition, affectivity, interpersonal functioning, impulse control), leads to clinically significant distress or impairment, has an early onset, and is not better accounted for as a consequence of another mental disorder or due to the direct physiological effects of a substance or general medical condition (APA 2000). In addition to these general criteria, each of the ten PDs is defined by a set of symptom criteria, a number of which must be met for the conferral of a diagnosis. The PDs themselves group into three clusters based on descriptive similarities: Cluster A ('odd/eccentric' cluster) includes Paranoid, Schizoid and Schizotypal PDs; Cluster B ('dramatic/erratic' cluster) includes Antisocial, Borderline, Histrionic and Narcissistic PDs; and Cluster C ('anxious/fearful' cluster) includes Avoidant, Dependent and Obsessive-Compulsive PDs (APA 2000).

Although the DSM presents a taxonomy in which, ideally, diagnoses are distinct entities, Axis I clinical disorders and Axis II PDs often co-occur (Clark 2005). Despite its near universal usage, 'co-morbidity' often blurs the distinction between latent constructs and manifest indicators (Lilienfeld, Waldman and Israel 1994); as such, and given that current causal models of personality and psycho-pathology are at best tentative, the simultaneous presence of more than one mental disorder in an individual will herein be referred to as co-occurrence. With respect to cross-Axis co-occurrence, Widiger and Shea (1991) note three different relationships between pairs of co-occurring disorders: (1) *spectrum* (e.g., avoidant PD as a more extreme version of social phobia); (2) *cross-over* (e.g., borderline PD has features of both an Axis I mood disorder and an Axis II personality disorder); and (3) *overlapping* (e.g., antisocial PD and pathological gambling share criteria). Given that Axis II personality disorders may represent more severe versions of Axis I disorders, be characterized by a mixture of Axis I and Axis II symptoms, or lack distinct criteria, cross-Axis differentiation is often problematic and perhaps even illusory.

Detailed assessments of the full range of Axis II PDs suggest that approximately one-half of those who meet criteria for a mood disorder have a co-occurring PD (Brieger, Ehrt and Marneros 2003), one-quarter of those with an anxiety disorder have a co-occurring PD (Dyck, Phillips, Warshaw *et al.* 2001), and one-half of those with a PD receive more than one PD diagnosis (Skodol 2005). Several researchers have argued that these rates are unacceptable, that PDs are deeply flawed, and that the same problems repeat themselves across the individual disorders; these problems include excessive co-occurrence, inadequate coverage, arbitrary and unstable boundaries with normal psychological functioning, heterogeneity among persons with the same diagnosis, low inter-rater reliability, inadequate scientific base, and questionable clinical utility (Clark, Livesley and Morey 1997; Livesley 1985a 1985b 1998; Ryder, Bagby and Schuller 2002; Widiger 1993; Widiger and Trull 2007).

In response to these enduring criticisms, several authors have suggested that PDs are best conceptualized as extreme variants of general personality traits (Clark and Watson 1999; Costa and Widiger 2002; Harkness and McNulty 1994; Krueger and Markon 2006; Livesley 1998; Markon, Krueger and Watson 2005; Widiger 2000; Widiger, Costa and McCrae 2002). From this perspective, the recurring problem of co-occurrence is to be expected: PDs will co-vary to the extent that they represent overlapping constellations of personality traits. Longitudinal evidence also suggests that PDs are stable by virtue of underlying maladaptive personality traits and that change in relevant personality traits leads to subsequent change in PDs (Warner, Morey, Finch *et al.* 2004). Given the wide range of potential trait combinations associated with clinically significant distress or dysfunction, it is not surprising that 21–49 per cent of diagnosed PDs are classified as Personality Disorder Not Otherwise Specified (Verheul and Widiger 2004). Taken together, research suggests that many of the problems associated with PDs are a result of imposing a categorical system on dimensional phenomena, and that a dimensional model of personality is more compatible with extant phenomenological, biological and genetic evidence.

Personality traits

Prominent trait models feature nomothetic descriptions of continuous characteristics. These dimensional models frequently adhere to a hierarchical structure, composed of broad, higher-order domain traits (e.g., Extraversion, Agreeableness) and narrow, lower-order facet traits (e.g., assertiveness, modesty). Models of universal, 'normal-range' personality traits are developed independently from a diagnostic system and assume a variety of theoretical perspectives and methodological approaches. The Five-Factor Model (Costa and McCrae 1992), for example, was derived using factor analyses of trait descriptors found within language, while the Seven-Factor Psychobiological Model of Temperament and Character (Cloninger, Svrakic and Przybeck 1993) was shaped by neuroanatomical and psychopharmacological evidence (Bagby, Quilty and Ryder 2007). Although traits from such universal models are not specifically intended to evaluate pathological personality, research suggests that 'normal-range' trait extremity is often associated with clinically significant distress and/or impairment, that measures of normal personality discriminate well between different PDs and other forms of psychopathology, and that abnormal personality can be modelled as extremes of normal personality variation (Clark and Watson 1999; Costa and Widiger 2002; Harkness and McNulty 1994; Krueger and Markon 2006; Livesley 1998; Markon, Krueger and Watson 2005; O'Connor and Dyce 2001; Widiger 2000; Widiger, Costa and McCrae 2002).

In contrast, models of pathological personality are typically developed by factor analysing PD criteria and associated features; this process identifies dimensional personality traits underlying the PDs (Bagby, Quitty and Ryder 2007). As with models of normal personality, the rationale of this approach is to collect a representative sample of traits used to describe individuals (with personality disorder, in this case), factor analyse these traits to delineate a set of lower-order traits, then factor analyse these lower-order traits to delineate a set of higher-order traits. Segments of several popular models have been developed using this strategy, including the Schedule for Nonadaptive and Adaptive Personality (SNAP) (Clark 1993) and the Dimensional Assessment of Personality Pathology (DAPP) (Livesley, Jackson and Schroeder 1991).

Despite a general consensus that normal and abnormal personality can be modelled by a single structural model, attempts to unify these structures have been inconclusive (O'Connor 2002). Traits relevant to abnormal personality often constitute a sub-set of those pertinent to normal personality (Livesley, Jang and Vernon 1998); meta-analytic investigations of personality disorder, for example, suggest a 'Big Four' abnormal personality structure, with four orthogonal factors reasonably isomorphic with the 'Big Five' model of normal personality but lacking an equivalent of Openness (O'Connor and Dyce 1998). Conversely, some traits relevant to abnormal personality (e.g., psychoticism, disconstraint, dependency, submissiveness, etc.) are not well represented by 'normal-range' personality models. Moreover, while considerable evidence suggests that the dimensionality of personality inventories is generally similar in clinical and non-clinical samples, and despite general support for the notion of structural continuity between normal and abnormal personality, the dimensionality of any given inventory varies (O'Connor 2002) and the nature of the continuity between structures is unclear (Markon, Krueger and Watson 2005).

A hierarchical model of normal and abnormal personality traits

Some researchers have stressed the significance of a hierarchical understanding of personality variation, suggesting that various levels of a common hierarchical structure are of differential consequence in understanding normal versus abnormal personality structure (Harkness 1992; Markon, Krueger and Watson 2005). Factors that occupy superordinate hierarchical positions in the abnormal range (e.g., Psychoticism) may become less important in the normal range and occupy subordinate positions; conversely, factors that occupy superordinate hierarchical positions in the normal range (e.g., Openness) may become less important in the abnormal range and occupy subordinate positions. This account, then, supposes factors of personality change in prominence, rather than in any absolute sense, as one traverses between normal and abnormal ranges (Harkness 1992; Markon, Krueger and Watson 2005).

Recently, Markon *et al.* (2005) applied a constructive replication approach to identify a single integrated structure of normal and abnormal personality. In an attempt to delineate the joint structure of normal and abnormal personality, Markon *et al.* (2005) examined the factor structure of personality measures in a meta-analysis and an empirical study, and used a variety of major personality models to generalize their findings to a broad set of theoretical and descriptive perspectives in the normal and abnormal ranges. Using meta-analytic correlation estimates and sample-based maximum-likelihood methods (exploratory factor analyses), and replicating across samples and measures, Markon *et al.* (2005) identified a trait hierarchy of normal and abnormal personality that integrates Big Two, Big Three, Big Four and Big Five models of personality (see Figure 35.1).

Big Two. At the superordinate position of this hierarchy are two factors, which Markon and colleagues referred to as Alpha (α) and Beta (β) after the super-ordinate two-factor solution reported by Digman (1997). Here, α and β represent general negative and positive emotionality/affectivity factors, respectively.

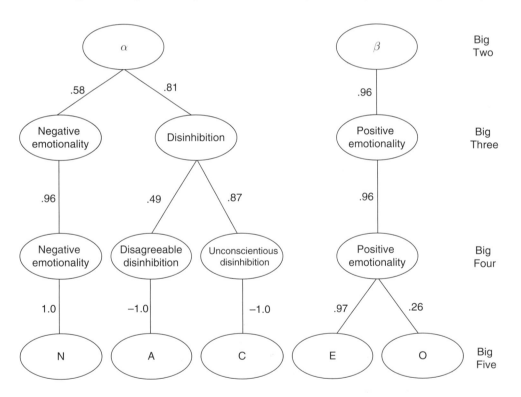

N = Neuroticism, A = Agreeableness, C = Conscientiousness, E = Extraversion, O = Openness.

Figure 35.1. *Correlations between subordinate and superordinate factors from an integrated hierarchical account of the structure of normal and abnormal personality.*

Big Three. Subordinate to α and β is a three-factor solution that strongly resembles standard three-factor models presented in the literature on temperament (e.g., Clark 2005). At this level of resolution, α splits into two factors: the first factor strongly resembles a Negative Emotionality factor positively related to measures of anxiety, neuroticism and stress reaction, while the second factor resembles a general Disinhibition factor positively related to measures of stimulus seeking, conduct problems, aggression and novelty seeking, and negatively related to measures of control, agreeableness, conscientiousness and cooperativeness. The third factor, represented by β in the superordinate two-factor solution, strongly resembles a Positive Emotionality factor positively related to measures of extraversion, wellbeing and reward dependence, and negatively related to measures of restricted expression, intimacy problems and social avoidance.

Big Four. Subordinate to the three-factor solution is a four-factor model consistent with four-factor models frequently reported in the literature on abnormal personality. At this level of resolution, the four-factor model differs from the three-factor model only in its bifurcation of Disinhibition into a Disagreeable Disinhibition factor and an Unconscientious Disinhibition factor. Here, Disagreeable Disinhibition is positively related to measures of callousness, rejection, conduct problems and aggression, and negatively related to measures of agreeableness and cooperativeness. In contrast, Unconscientious Disinhibition is negatively related to measures of compulsivity, achievement, control, conscientiousness and persistence.

Big Five. Subordinate to the four-factor solution is a five-factor model that strongly resembles the Big Five model of 'normal-range' personality. At this level of resolution, Big Five Neuroticism, Agreeableness and Conscientiousness are similar to the Negative Emotionality, Disagreeable Disinhibition (reversed), and Unconscientious Disinhibition (reversed) factors of the four-factor model, respectively; Positive Emotionality, however, finally splits into Big Five Extraversion and Openness. Here, Extraversion is positively related to measures of social closeness and negatively related to measures of restricted expression and intimacy problems, while Openness is positively related to measures of absorption and transcendence (Markon, Krueger and Watson 2005).

It is important to note that Markon and colleagues' integrative hierarchy of normal and abnormal personality is unbalanced; that is, objects at a given level of the hierarchy differ in their level of abstraction. In a balanced personality hierarchy, traits must exist at only one level of abstraction, but in an unbalanced personality hierarchy, some traits can continue through multiple levels of the hierarchy while others coalesce and separate (Markon *et al.* 2005). As traits (e.g., Negative Emotionality) continue through multiple levels of an unbalanced hierarchy, however, they may shift in their degree of abstraction relative to other traits in the same level of the hierarchy. Thus, the extent to which variance in any given subordinate trait is accounted for by a superordinate trait (even a manifestation of the same trait at a higher level in the hierarchy) may be affected by the shifting degree of abstraction associated with an unbalanced hierarchy. Worded differently, a portion of the unique variance associated with a particular trait located on multiple levels of a hierarchy may be linked to its relative level of abstraction. If various levels of a common hierarchical structure are of differential consequence in understanding normal versus abnormal personality structure, future research investigating the relationship between psychopathology and trait resolution must consider issues associated with unbalanced trait hierarchies (e.g., novel methods for delineating trait hierarchy might be preferable to commonly used methods for latent variable analysis, such as exploratory factor analysis, which often assume that observed variables can be accounted for by discrete levels of abstraction and tend to distort latent structure when traits are highly correlated; Bacon 2001; Gerbing and Hamilton 1996; Markon, Krueger and Watson 2005).

Personality markers and the hierarchical structure of Axis I disorders

Co-occurrence is a pervasive problem throughout the DSM (Widiger and Clark 2000), including the mood and anxiety disorders (Mineka, Watson and Clark 1998). Much of the structural work in the area of personality and psychopathology was stimulated by accumulating evidence that anxiety disorders often co-occur with mood disorders, and vice versa (Mineka, Watson and Clark 1998); that the various anxiety disorders typically co-occur with one another (Brown and Barlow 1992; Brown, Campbell, Lehman *et al.* 2001); and that the mood and anxiety disorders both show extensive co-occurrence with other forms of psychopathology, such as Axis I eating disorders, substance use disorder, somatoform disorders and Axis II PDs (Mineka, Watson and Clark 1998; Watson 2005; Widiger and Clark 2000).

Two factor model of affectivity

The high degree of co-occurrence between mood and anxiety disorders has prompted several investigators to develop explanatory models that draw on key findings from the basic mood, personality and temperament literatures. Watson, Clark and Carey (1988), for example, developed a two-factor model of affectivity based on extensive evidence that there are two primary dimensions of emotional experience: (1) Negative Affectivity (NA), a general dimension of subjective distress that subsumes a broad range of negative emotional states, such as sadness, fear, guilt, disgust and anger (comparable to Big Three Negative Emotionality), and (2) Positive Affectivity (PA), a general dimension of subjective wellbeing that includes a variety of positive emotional states, such as happiness, confidence, excitement, interest and alertness (comparable to Big Three Positive Emotionality) (Watson and Tellegen 1985). Based on such evidence, Watson and colleagues argued that NA represents a non-specific factor common to depression and anxiety, whereas low PA (anhedonia) represents a specific factor relatively unique to depression.

Tripartite model

Several years later, Clark and Watson (1991) expanded their two factor model of affectivity to include physiological hyperarousal (PHY), a specific factor relatively unique to anxiety. In this 'tripartite model', NA represents a non-specific factor common to depression and anxiety and shared symptoms (anxious and depressed mood, poor concentration, sleep disturbance), low PA/anhedonia represents a specific factor unique to depression and related symptoms (e.g., loss of interest, feeling that nothing is enjoyable), and PHY represents a specific factor unique to anxiety and related symptoms (e.g., sweating, dizziness, shortness of breath). Although elements of the tripartite model have received support in several studies (see Mineka, Watson and Clark 1998), significant evidence suggests that this model fails to account for the substantial heterogeneity among the anxiety disorders; more specifically, the PHY component is not generally characteristic of the anxiety disorders, but instead represents the unique, specific component of panic disorder (Brown, Chorpita and Barlow 1998) and the hyperarousal sub-factor of post-traumatic stress disorder (Brown, Campbell, Lehman *et al.* 2001). Moreover, several studies show a consistent negative association between PA and social phobia, thus demonstrating that PA is not uniquely linked to depression (Brown, Chorpita and Barlow 1998; Watson, Clark and Carey 1988; Watson 2005; Watson, Gamez and Simms 2005).

Barlow's hierarchical model of the anxiety disorders

In addition to this evidence, research on the heterogeneity of anxiety disorders suggested that individual anxiety disorders are differentially related to depression (Clark 1989), individual anxiety disorders are differentially related to one another (Brown, Chorpita and Barlow 1998), and a single specific factor (e.g., PHY component of the tripartite model) is insufficient to account for the diversity of symptoms across anxiety disorders (Brown, Chorpita and Barlow 1998). In response to these findings, Barlow and colleagues (Barlow 1991; Brown and Barlow 1992; Zinbarg and Barlow 1996) developed a hierarchical model of the anxiety disorders. In this model, anxiety disorders represent a two-level hierarchy, each of which contains (1) a higher-order shared component (tripartite NA) common to other anxiety disorders and depression, and (2) a specific component unique to each anxiety disorder that distinguishes it from all other disorders. Barlow's hierarchical model of anxiety disorders has received strong support from several structural analyses that used both self-report and interview-based data (Brown, Chorpita and Barlow 1998; Spence 1997; Zinbarg and Barlow 1996).

Integrative hierarchical model

More recently, Mineka, Watson and Clark (1998) developed a comprehensive integrative hierarchical model that is consistent with both genotypic and phenotypic data and incorporates key elements of Clark and Watson's (1991) tripartite model and Barlow's (1991; Zinbarg and Barlow 1996) hierarchical organization of the anxiety disorders. In this integrative, hierarchical scheme, each individual disorder can be viewed as containing both a common and unique component. Consistent with Barlow's model, the shared component represents broad individual differences in general distress or NA, a pervasive higher-order factor common to mood and anxiety disorders and primarily responsible for the co-occurrence of these disorders. In addition, each individual disorder includes unique features that differentiate it from all others; low PA, for example, comprises the specific component of depression, while PHY represents the unique component of panic disorder. Mineka and colleagues (1998) also discussed three additional points worth noting. First, the size of the general and specific components clearly differs across the individual anxiety disorders (e.g., the NA component is much more modest in obsessive-compulsive disorder, social phobia and specific phobia than in depression or generalized anxiety disorder). Secondly, the general distress or NA component is not restricted to the mood and anxiety disorders, but also characterizes many other types of psychopathology; that 'neuroticism is an almost ubiquitously elevated trait within clinical populations' (Widiger and Costa 1994, p. 81) helps explain the extensive co-occurrence between mood/anxiety disorders and other forms of psychopathology, such as Axis I eating disorders, substance use disorders, somatoform disorders and Axis II PDs (Mineka, Watson and Clark 1998; Watson 2005; Widiger and Clark 2000). Thirdly, Mineka and colleagues stress that specificity must be viewed in relative terms; low PA, for example, is not only unique to depression, but also characterizes social phobia, schizophrenia, and other disorders (Brown, Chorpita and Barlow 1998; Watson and Clark 1995; Watson, Clark and Carey 1988), while PHY is common to both panic disorder and the hyperarousal sub-factor of post-traumatic stress disorder (Brown, Campbell, Lehman *et al.* 2001).

Quantitative hierarchical model for DSM-V

Although the integrative hierarchical model represents an improvement over earlier structural models of personality and psychopathology, it fails to account fully for psychiatric co-occurrence (Watson, Gamez and Simms 2005). This model posits that observed patterns of co-occurrence are largely attributable to variance in a single, general NA factor; more specifically, it predicts (1) that two disorders with strong components of NA will have high rates of co-occurrence, and (2) that two disorders with weak components of NA will have low rates of co-occurrence. While the former prediction has garnered substantial empirical support (e.g., major depressive disorder and generalized anxiety disorder are saturated with NA factor variance and have high rates of co-occurrence; Krueger 1999; Vollebergh, Iedema, Bijil *et al.* 2001), the latter proposition has proven much more problematic (e.g., specific phobia and social phobia contain relatively little NA factor variance but have high rates of co-occurrence; Krueger 1999; Vollegergh *et al.* 2001). Thus, more than one non-specific factor is required to effectively model psychiatric co-occurrence (Watson, Gamez and Simms 2005).

Although charting specific and non-specific temperament and personality factors for each disorder is an important area for future research, the benefit of this procedure is a direct function of current DSM diagnostic validity; that is, mapping empirically-derived and genetically-based temperament factors onto a rationally organized nosology (a set of categorical disorders that often suffer from heterogeneity among persons with the same diagnosis, arbitrary and unstable boundaries with normal psychological functioning, low inter-rater reliability, and inadequate scientific base) seems of limited and questionable utility. Similarly, the value of mapping temperament and personality variables on a hierarchical structural model of psychopathology is dependent on the legitimacy of that hierarchy. Evidence put forth by Krueger and colleagues (Krueger 1999; Krueger, Caspi, Moffit and Silva 1998; Krueger and Markon 2006), for example, strongly suggests an alternative hierarchical structure of common mental disorders in which psychiatric disorders load onto two higher-order factors – *internalizing disorders* (e.g., unipolar mood disorders, anxiety disorders) and *externalizing disorders* (e.g., antisocial personality disorder, substance-related disorders). Using data from the National Co-morbidity Survey, Krueger (1999) suggested that the internalizing dimension further bifurcates into two lower-order factors; interestingly, these factors are not equivalent to the traditional mood and anxiety disorders (see Figure 35.2); rather, internalizing disorders split into the subordinate factors *anxious-misery* (major depressive disorder, dysthymic disorder, generalized anxiety disorder) and *fear* (social phobia, simple/specific phobia, agoraphobia, panic disorder). This factor structure has subsequently been replicated in large-scale phenotypic (Vollebergh, Iedema, Bijil *et al.* 2001) and genotypic (Kendler, Prescott, Myers and Neale 2003) analyses (see Figure 35.3).

Recently, Watson (2005) proposed a quantitative hierarchical model that integrates the hierarchy of common mental disorders with research on post-traumatic stress disorder, obsessive-compulsive disorder and the bipolar disorders. Watson's taxonomy extends the work of Krueger (1999), Vollebergh, Iedema, Bijil *et al.* (2001), and Kendler, Prescott, Myers and Neale (2003) by including post-traumatic stress disorder as one of the anxious-misery disorders (which he dubbed *distress disorders*) and, on the basis of structural analyses, creating a third diagnostic sub-class for bipolar disorders within the broader category of internalizing disorders. Although Watson (2005) intentionally left obsessive-compulsive disorder out of his quantitative hierarchical model (because of ambiguous correlational and structural evidence) and described the placement of post-traumatic stress disorder in his proposed hierarchy as tentative, subsequent evidence from a large-scale community epidemiological survey of mental disorders suggests that obsessive-compulsive disorder is a subordinate factor to the fear disorders, and that post-traumatic stress disorder fits well within the distress disorders (Slade and Watson 2006).

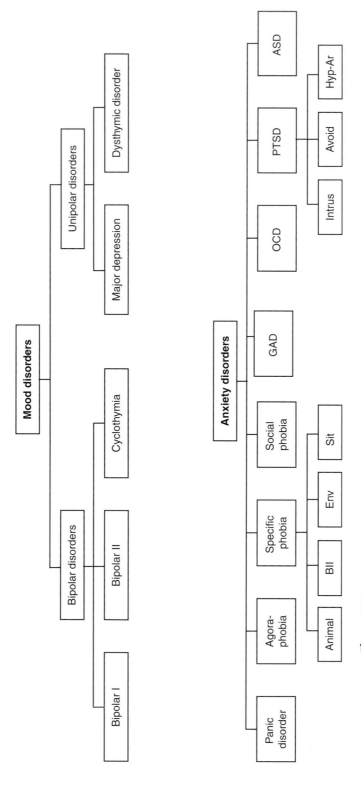

Figure 35.2. *A schematic structural model of the DSM-IV mood and anxiety disorders*

GAD = generalized anxiety disorder; OCD = obsessive-compulsive disorder; PTSD = post-traumatic stress disorder; ASD = acute stress disorder; BII = blood-injection-injury; Env = natural environment, Sit = situational, Intrus = intrusions, Avoid = avoidance/numbing, Hyp-Ar = hyper-arousal.

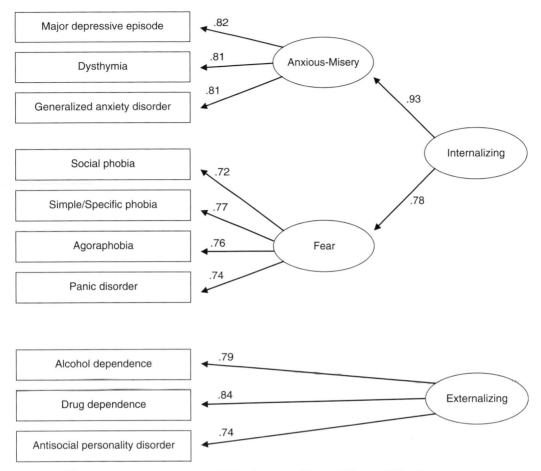

Figure 35.3. *Best-fitting model for the entire National Co-morbidity Survey, a three-factor variant of the two-factor internalizing/externalizing model. All parameter estimates are standardized and significant at p < .05.*

Relating personality markers and hierarchical models of psychopathology

As described above, data clearly suggests that both NA and PA have important links to psychopathology in general, and to the distress and fear disorders in particular. While NA is an almost ubiquitously elevated trait within clinical populations, research also suggests that NA is differentially related to the heterogeneous symptom clusters comprising post-traumatic stress disorder (Dysphoria sub-factor, based on factor analyses of the Military Version of the PTSD Checklist, Simms, Watson and Doebbelling 2002); obsessive-compulsive disorder (Checking sub-factor, based on factor analyses of the Obsessive-Compulsive Inventory, Wu and Watson 2003); specific phobia (Social sub-factor,

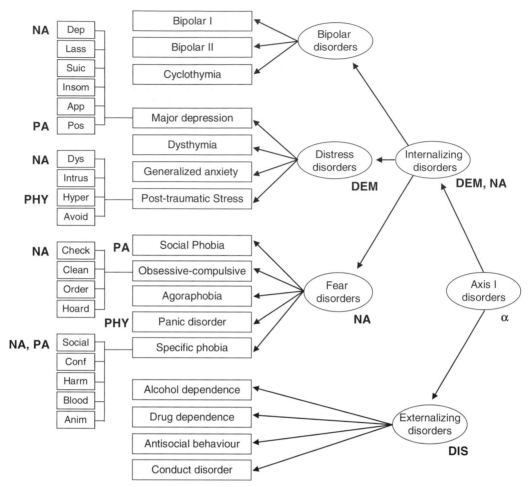

Figure 35.4. *An integrated representation of major personality markers of psychopathology, Watson's (2005) quantitative hierarchical model for DSM-V and Krueger's (1999) structure of common mental disorders*
α = Digman's (1997) Alpha, NA = Negative Affectivity, PA = low Positive Affectivity, DIS = Disinhibition, DEM = Demoralization, PHY = Physiological Hyperarousal; Dep = Depressed Affect, Lass = Lassitude, Suic = Suicidal Ideation, Insom = Insomnia, App = Loss of Appetite, Pos = Positive Mood (reversed); Dys = Dysphoria, Intrus = Intrusions, Hyper = Hyperarousal, Avoid = Avoidance; Check = Checking, Clean = Cleaning, Order = Ordering, Hoard = Hoarding; Conf = Physical Confinement, Harm = Bodily Harm, Blood = Blood-injection, Anim = Animals.

based on factor analyses of the Phobic Stimuli Response Scales, Cutshall and Watson 2004); and depression (Depressed Affect sub-factor, based on factor analyses of the Iowa Depression and Anxiety Scales, Watson, Gamez and Simms 2005). In contrast, low PA shows relatively specific associations with the Depressed Affect sub-factor of major depressive disorder (Watson, Gamez and

Simms 2005), social phobia and schizophrenia (Brown, Chorpita and Barlow 1998; Watson and Clark 1995; Watson, Clark and Carey 1988). In addition to NA and PA, several non-specific factors are closely linked to certain psychiatric disorders, including PHY (common to both panic disorder and the hyperarousal sub-factor of post-traumatic stress disorder; Brown, Campbell, Lehman *et al.* 2001), and an unidentified factor (common to both social phobia and specific phobia, which have very high rates of co-occurrence but contain relatively little NA factor variance; Krueger 1999; Vollegergh, Iedema, Bijil *et al.* 2001).

Superordinate factors of Watson's quantitative hierarchical model for DSM-V are also differentially related to hierarchical personality markers. Externalizing disorders, for example, are closely linked to Big Three Disinhibition, Big Four Disagreeable Disinhibition and Unconscientious Disinhibition, and Big Five Agreeableness (reversed) and Conscientiousness (reversed). In contrast, internalizing disorders are typically characterized by NA (comparable to Big Three and Four Negative Emotionality and Big Five Neuroticism). Although the majority of research also relates NA to the fear and distress disorders, a recent study by Sellbom, Ben-Porath and Bagby (2007) suggests that Tellegen, Watson and Clarks' (1999) higher-order Demoralization (DEM) dimension, representing the shared and inversely related hedonic features of NA and PA, differentiates between the fear and distress disorders. Under this conceptualization, distress disorders are distinguished by DEM and fear disorders by NA. Finally, the bifurcation of Markon, Krueger and Watson's (2005) superordinate α factor into Negative Emotionality and Disinhibition factors appears analogous to the bifurcation of Axis I disorders into internalizing disorders (characterized by NA and DEM) and externalizing disorders (characterized by Disinhibition). Figure 35.4 summarizes these relationships and integrates them with a hierarchical structural model of Axis I disorders based on Watson's (2005) quantitative hierarchical model, Krueger's (1999) structural modelling of common mental disorders, and related phenotypic (Vollebergh, Iedema, Bijil *et al.* 2001) and genotypic evidence (Kendler, Prescott, Myers and Neale 2003).

Concluding remarks

Collectively, these findings raise the fundamental issue of etiology: what causal parameters describe the observed set of relations between temperament-personality and psychopathology? As described by Watson, Gamez and Simms (2005), three possibilities have received at least some support in the literature, each of which can be decomposed into more specific deviations (for an extensive review of this issue, see Bagby, Quitty and Ryder 2007; Watson and Clark 1995; Widiger and Trull 1992). First, temperament-personality features may exert a causal influence on psychopathology, either by increasing the probability that a person will develop a disorder (Vulnerability Model) or by affecting the severity or course of a disorder, including response to treatment (Pathoplasty Model). Secondly, psychopathology may exert a causal influence on personality, either temporarily (Complication Model) or permanently (Scar Model). Thirdly, personality and psychopathology may both reflect similar core processes, such that neither can be viewed as a clear causal agent. A shared etiological factor (e.g., genetic diathesis), for example, may exert a causal influence on both temperament-personality and psychopathology (Common Cause Model). Alternatively, an underlying dimension or continuum that extends from normal to pathological processes may exist, such that psychopathology essentially represents an extreme manifestation of individual differences in temperament-personality (Spectrum Model).

Three related issues merit further discussion. First, these models are not mutually exclusive; for example, the Vulnerability and Scar Models together would predict that personality affects the probability that a person will develop a disorder that, in turn, permanently changes that person's personality. Secondly, the precise relationship between innate temperament dimensions and the adult personality traits that emerge through differentiation of these dimensions is unclear; as such, the associations between psychopathology and innate temperament elements versus temperament-like, higher-order personality features versus differentiated, lower-order personality dimensions remain blurred. Thirdly, it may be useful to differentiate between variable (state) and stable (trait) components of personality when examining personality-psychopathology relationships. Research suggests, for example, that although both state and trait components are correlated with concurrent depression severity level, only the trait portion predicts future levels (Clark, Vittengl, Kraft and Jarrett 2003).

Mounting evidence suggests a strong, systematic and continuous link between personality and psychopathology, such that one domain cannot be fully appreciated independent of the other. Future work is needed to determine how psychiatric disorders are differentially related to personality dimensions as they develop from innate biobehavioural dimensions, are characterized at various levels of abstraction in an unbalanced trait hierarchy, and represent mixtures of state/trait components. The current renaissance of interest in this topic will benefit from future work using innovative structural modelling techniques, novel genetic data, unique experimental designs and integrative theoretical approaches.

References

American Psychiatric Association 1952. *Diagnostic and statistical manual of mental disorders*, 1st edn. Washington, DC: APA

   1968. *Diagnostic and statistical manual of mental disorders*, 2nd edn. Washington, DC: APA

   1980. *Diagnostic and statistical manual of mental disorders*, 3rd edn. Washington, DC: APA

   1994. *Diagnostic and statistical manual of mental disorders*, 4th edn. Washington, DC: APA

2000. *Diagnostic and statistical manual of mental disorders*, 4th edn, Text Revision. Washington, DC: APA

Bacon, D. R. 2001. Evaluation of cluster analytic approaches to initial model specification, *Structural Equation Modeling* 8: 397–429

Bagby, R. M, Quilty, L. C. and Ryder, A. G. 2007. Personality and depression. Manuscript under review

Barlow, D. H. 1991. The nature of anxiety: anxiety, depression and emotional disorders, in R. M. Rapee and D. H. Barlow (eds.), *Chronic anxiety: generalized anxiety disorder and mixed anxiety-depression*, pp. 1–28. New York: Guilford Press

Brieger, P., Ehrt, U. and Marneros, A. 2003. Frequency of comorbid personality disorders in bipolar and unipolar affective disorders, *Comprehensive Psychiatry* 34: 28–34

Brown, T. A. and Barlow, D. H. 1992. Comorbidity among anxiety disorders: implications for treatment and DSM-IV, *Journal of Consulting and Clinical Psychology* 60: 835–44

Brown, T. A., Campbell, L. A., Lehman, C. L., Grisham, J. R. and Mancill, R. B. 2001. Current and lifetime comorbidity of the DSM-IV anxiety and mood disorders in a large clinical sample, *Journal of Abnormal Psychology* 110: 585–99

Brown, T. A., Chorpita, B. F. and Barlow, D. H. 1998. Structural relationships among dimensions of the DSM-IV anxiety and mood disorders and dimensions of negative affect, positive affect, and autonomic arousal, *Journal of Abnormal Psychology* 107: 179–92

Clark, L. A. 1989. The anxiety and depressive disorders: descriptive psychopathology and differential diagnosis, in P. C. Kendall and D. Watson (eds.), *Anxiety and depression: distinctive and overlapping features*, pp. 83–129. San Diego, CA: Academic Press

1993. *Schedule for Nonadaptive and Adaptive Personality (SNAP). Manual for administration, scoring and interpretation*. Minneapolis, MN: University of Minnesota Press

2005. Temperament as a unifying basis for personality and psychopathology, *Journal of Abnormal Psychology* 114: 505–21

Clark, L. A., Livesley, W. J. and Morey, L. 1997. Personality disorder assessment: the challenge of construct validity, *Journal of Personality Disorders* 11: 205–31

Clark, L. A., Vittengl, J., Kraft, D. and Jarrett, R. B. 2003. Separate personality traits from states to predict depression, *Journal of Personality Disorders* 17: 152–72

Clark, L. A. and Watson, D. 1991. Tripartite model of anxiety and depression: psychometric evidence and taxonomic implications, *Journal of Abnormal Psychology, Special Issue: diagnoses, dimensions, and DSM-IV: -n the science of classification* 100: 316–36

1999. *Temperament: a new paradigm for trait psychology.* New York: Guilford Press

Cloninger, C. R., Svrakic, D. M. and Przybeck, T. R. 1993. A psychobiological model of temperament and character, *Archives of General Psychiatry* 50: 975–90

Costa, P. T. and McCrae, R. R 1992. *Revised NEO Personality Inventory. Professional manual*. Odessa, FL: Psychological Assessment Resources

Costa, P. T. J. and Widiger, T. A. (eds.) 2002. *Personality disorders and the five-factor model of personality*, 2nd edn. Washington, DC: American Psychological Association

Cutshall, C. and Watson, D. 2004. The phobic stimuli response scales: a new self-report measure of fear, *Behaviour Research and Therapy* 42: 1193–201

Digman, J. M. 1997. Higher-order factors of the Big Five, *Journal of Personality and Social Psychology* 73: 1246–256

Dyck, I. R., Phillips, K. A., Warshaw, M. G., Dolan, R. T., Shea, M. T. and Stout, R. L. *et al.* 2001. Patterns of personality pathology in patients with generalized anxiety disorder, panic disorder with and without agoraphobia, and social phobia, *Journal of Personality Disorders* 15: 60–71

Eysenck, H. J. 1947. *The dimensions of personality.* London: Routledge and Kegan Paul

Eysenck, H. J. and Eysenck, S. B. G. 1976. *Psychoticism as a dimension of personality.* London: Hodder and Stoughton

Gerbing, D. W. and Hamilton, J. G. 1996. Viability of exploratory factor analysis as a precursor to confirmatory factor analysis, *Structural Equation Modeling* 3: 62–72

Harkness, A. R. 1992. Fundamental topics in the personality disorders: candidate trait dimensions from lower regions of the hierarchy, *Psychological Assessment* 4: 251–9

Harkness, A. R. and McNulty, J. L. 1994. The personality psychopathology five (PSY-5): issues from the pages of a diagnostic manual instead of a dictionary, in S. Strack, and M. Lorr (eds.), *Differentiating normal and abnormal personality*, pp. 291–315. New York: Springer Publishing Co

Kendler, K. S., Prescott, C. A., Myers, J. and Neale, M. C. 2003. The structure of genetic and environmental risk factors for common psychiatric and substance use disorders in men and women, *Archives of General Psychiatry* 60: 929–37

Krueger, R. F. 1999. The structure of common mental disorders, *Archives of General Psychiatry* 56: 921–26

Krueger, R. F., Caspi, A., Moffitt, T. E. and Silva, P. A. 1998. The structure and stability of common mental disorders (DSM-III-R): a longitudinal-epidemiological study, *Journal of Abnormal Psychology* 107: 216–27

Krueger, R. F. and Markon, K. E. 2006. Understanding psychopathology: melding behaviour genetics, personality, and quantitative psychology to develop an empirically based model, *Current Directions in Psychological Science* 15: 113–17

Lilienfeld, S. O., Waldman, I. D. and Israel, A. C. 1994. A critical examination of the use of the term and concept of comorbidity in psychopathology research, *Clinical Psychology: Science and Practice* 1: 71–83

Livesley, W. J. 1985a. The classification of personality disorder: I. The choice of category concept, *Canadian Journal of Psychiatry* 30: 353–8

Livesley, W. J. 1985b. The classification of personality disorder: II. The problem of diagnostic criteria, *Canadian Journal of Psychiatry* 30: 359–62

Livesley, W. J. 1998. Suggestions for a framework for an empirically based classification of personality disorder, *Canadian Journal of Psychiatry* 43: 137–47

Livesley, W. J., Jackson, D. W. and Schroeder, M. L. 1991. Dimensions of personality pathology, *Canadian Journal of Psychiatry* 36: 557–62

Livesley, W. J., Jang, K. L. and Vernon, P. A. 1998. Phenotypic and genetic structure of traits delineating personality disorder, *Archives of General Psychiatry* 55: 941–8

Maher, B. A. and Maher, W. B. 1994. Personality and psychopathology: a historical perspective, *Journal of Abnormal Psychology, Special Issue: Personality and Psychopathology* 103: 72–7

Markon, K. E., Krueger, R. F. and Watson, D. 2005. Delineating the structure of normal and abnormal personality: an integrative hierarchical approach, *Journal of Personality and Social Psychology* 88: 139–57

Mineka, S., Watson, D. and Clark, L. A. 1998. Comorbidity of anxiety and unipolar mood disorders, *Annual Review of Psychology* 49: 377–412

O'Connor, B. P. 2002. The search for dimensional structure differences between normality and abnormality: a statistical review of published data on personality and psychopathology, *Journal of Personality and Social Psychology* 83: 962–82

O'Connor, B. P. and Dyce, J. A. 1998. A test of models of personality disorder configuration, *Journal of Abnormal Personality* 107: 3–16

　　2001. Rigid and extreme: a geometric representation of personality disorders in five-factor model space, *Journal of Personality and Social Psychology* 81: 1119–30

Ryder, A. G., Bagby, R. M. and Schuller, D. R. 2002. The overlap of depressive personality disorder and dysthymia: a categorical problem with a dimensional solution, *Harvard Review of Psychiatry* 10: 337–52

Sellbom, M., Ben-Porath, Y. S. and Bagby, R. M. 2007. On the hierarchical structure of mood and anxiety disorders: confirmatory evidence and elaboration of a model of temperament markers. Manuscript under review

Simms, L. J., Watson, D. and Doebbelling, B. N. 2002. Confirmatory factor analyses of posttraumatic stress symptoms in deployed and nondeployed veterans of the gulf war, *Journal of Abnormal Psychology* 111: 637–47

Skodol, A. E. 2005. Manifestation, clinical diagnosis, and comorbidity, in J. M. Oldham, A. E. Skodol, and D. S. Bender (eds.), *Textbook of personality disorders*. Washington, DC: American Psychiatric Publishing

Slade, T. and Watson, D. 2006. The structure of common DSM-IV and ICD-10 mental disorders in the Australian general population, *Psychological Medicine* 36: 1593–1600

Spence, S. H. 1997. Structure of anxiety symptoms among children: a confirmatory factor-analytic study, *Journal of Abnormal Psychology* 106: 280–97

Tellegen, A., Watson, D. and Clark, L. A. 1999. On the dimensional and hierarchical structure of affect, *Psychological Science* 10: 297–303

Verheul, R. and Widiger, T. A. 2004. A meta-analysis of the prevalence and usage of the personality disorder not otherwise specified (PDNOS) diagnosis, *Journal of Personality Disorders* 18: 309–19

Vollebergh, W. A. M., Iedema, J., Bijil, R. V., de Graff, R., Smit, F. and Ormel, J. 2001. The structure and stability of common mental disorders: the NEMISIS Study, *Archives of General Psychiatry* 58: 597–603

Warner, M. B., Morey, L. C., Finch, J. F., Gunderson, J. G., Skodol, A. E. and Sanislow, C. A. *et al.* 2004. The longitudinal relationship of personality traits and disorders, *Journal of Abnormal Psychology* 113: 217–27

Watson, D. 2005. Rethinking the mood and anxiety disorders: a quantitative hierarchical model for DSM-V, *Journal of Abnormal Psychology, Special Issue: toward a dimensionally based taxonomy of psychopathology* 114: 522–36

Watson, D. and Clark, L. A. 1995. Depression and the melancholic temperament, *European Journal of Personality, Special Issue: personality and depression* 9: 351–66

Watson, D., Clark, L. A. and Carey, G. 1988. Positive and negative affectivity and their relation to anxiety and depressive disorders, *Journal of Abnormal Psychology* 97: 346–53

Watson, D., Gamez, W. and Simms, L. J. 2005. Basic dimensions of temperament and their relation to anxiety and depression: a symptom-based perspective, *Journal of Research in Personality* 39: 46–66

Watson, D., Kotov, R. and Gamez 2006. Basic dimensions of temperament in relation to personality and psychopathology, in R. F. Krueger and J. L. Tackett (eds.), *Personality and psychopathology*, pp. 7–38. New York: Guilford Press

Watson, D. and Tellegen, A. 1985. Toward a consensual structure of mood, *Psychological Bulletin* 98: 219–35

Widiger, T. A. 1993. The DSM-III–R categorical personality disorder diagnoses: a critique and an alternative, *Psychological Inquiry* 4: 75–90

    2000. Personality disorders in the 21st century, *Journal of Personality Disorders* 14: 3–16

Widiger, T. A. and Clark, L. A. 2000. Toward DSM–V and the classification of psychopathology, *Psychological Bulletin, Special Issue: psychology in the 21st century* 126: 946–63

Widiger, T. A. and Costa, P. T. 1994. Personality and personality disorders, *Journal of Abnormal Psychology, Special Issue: Personality and Psychopathology* 103: 78–91

Widiger, T. A., Costa, P. T. J. and McCrae, R. R. 2002. A proposal for Axis II: diagnosing personality disorders using the Five-Factor Model, in P. T. J. Costa, Jr and T. A. Widiger (eds.), *Personality disorders and the Five-Factor Model of personality*, 2nd edn, pp. 431–56. Washington, DC: American Psychological Association

Widiger, T. A., and Shea, T. 1991. Differentiation of axis I and axis II disorders, *Journal of Abnormal Psychology, Special Issue: Diagnoses, Dimensions and DSM-IV – the Science of Classification* 100: 399–406

Widiger, T. A. and Trull, T. J. 1992. Personality and psychopathology: an application of the Five-Factor Model, *Journal of Personality, Special Issue: the Five-Factor Model, issues and applications* 60: 363–93

    2007. Plate tectonics in the classification of personality disorder: shifting to a dimensional model, *American Psychologist* 62: 71–83

Wu, K. D. and Watson, D. 2003. Further investigation of the obsessive-compulsive inventory: psychometric analysis in two non-clinical samples, *Journal of Anxiety Disorders* 17: 305–19

Zinbury, R. E. and Barlow, D. H. 1996. Structure of anxiety and the anxiety disorders: a hierarchical model, *Journal of Abnormal Psychology* 105: 181–93

36 Personality and psychosis

Gordon Claridge

Constructs and terminology

The inclusion of this chapter in a book primarily devoted to normal individual differences might look surprising: the serious mental illnesses do not, on the face of it, seem the most obvious illustration of where personality and pathology meet or where study of one can help elucidate the other. Yet it is precisely there that an interesting dialogue exists about how personality and psychological disorders relate, with important implications for general, abnormal and clinical psychology, and for psychiatry. In this chapter I shall try to draw out the main issues in that debate. The natural starting-point is to outline some terminology and theoretical constructs that inform the topic.

The term 'psychosis' has traditionally been accepted as the professional's generic descriptor for states of madness: these include, on the one hand, the various types of schizophrenia and, on the other, manic-depression, also known as bipolar affective disorder. Interest in the connection of such illnesses to personality is predicated on the notion that features recognizable as 'psychotic' can be observed in many people who do not, and never will, meet the clinical criteria for either form of madness. This dimensional idea about psychosis is by no means new and historically grew out of several lines of thought in psychology and psychiatry. These were often intertwined but two relatively distinct research traditions can be discerned, each with its own language, terms of reference and theoretical underpinning.

One angle on the topic originated in, and has tended to remain close to, the schizophrenia concept. The descriptor 'schizophrenia' – or more strictly 'the schizophrenias' – was introduced at the beginning of the twentieth century by the Swiss psychiatrist, Eugen Bleuler, to denote the group of mental illnesses still bearing that name and characterized by symptoms which variously include hallucinations, delusional ideas, disordered associative thought and inappropriate, flat or otherwise disturbed affect (Bleuler 1911). Almost from the beginning Bleuler recognized a degree of continuity in the illness, as seen in some people who did not show the full-blown symptoms but who appeared odd, strange or eccentric in a way reminiscent of schizophrenia itself. Manfred Bleuler (1978), Eugen's son and himself a psychiatrist, records in his own writings about schizophrenia how his father and colleagues coined the label 'schizoid' to describe such individuals.

'Schizoid' and 'schizoid personality' (as well as derivatives like 'schizoidia' and 'schizoidness') enjoyed some earlier usage in personality psychology as ways of describing individuals who are cold, aloof and indifferent to social relationships. Nowadays the schizoid construct is more often encountered in a manifestly clinical context to denote extreme deviation on such traits; for example, as Schizoid Personality Disorder, used as a diagnostic label in the DSM (American Psychiatric Association 2000) and ICD (World Health Organisation 1992) psychiatric manuals. As will become clear later, despite falling out of favour in the psychological literature, schizoidness – or something like it – remains an important element in attempts to dimensionalize psychosis. Looked at from a purely historical viewpoint, however, its significance has been overshadowed by another more popular construct: schizotypy.

The term 'schizotype' was originally coined by an American psychoanalyst, Rado (1953), and then elaborated – as 'schizotypy' – by the late Paul Meehl who used the construct to articulate a theory about the etiology of schizophrenia (Meehl 1962, 1990). Meehl's writings were extremely influential in stimulating a major research effort under the schizotypy label: this has been concerned with the psychometric measurement of schizotypal traits, investigating their experimental correlates in laboratory based paradigms, and examining the validity of schizotypy as a framework for understanding schizophrenia (see Raine, Lencz and Mednick 1995).

Schizotypy will figure greatly in this chapter; though not always in the sense in which it has been construed by Meehl and his followers. Indeed, to anticipate slightly, it is precisely that issue – how to interpret what is meant by 'schizotypy' – that fuels much of the current debate about the nature of psychosis and its dimensionality. The Meehl view sits firmly in the tradition of a medical model of schizophrenia. But there is an alternative perspective, which forms a second strand in the history of the topic. This belongs more in theories of healthy individual differences and their application to abnormal behaviour. The exemplar is the dimensional theory of personality developed over many years by Eysenck (Eysenck 1947; Eysenck and Eysenck 1985).

Theories such as Eysenck's partly originated in early attempts to create typologies or descriptively based dimensional schemes of personality. Most relevant here is the continuum model of psychosis proposed by Ernst Kretschmer (1925). This included the notion of 'schizothymia' as a dimension of normal temperament, defined at its far end first by schizoid personality, and then by schizophrenia. Kretschmer was actually a psychiatrist working (as his use of the term schizoid indicates) in the Swiss/German tradition; but his writings had more impact in psychology. This included Eysenck who used Kretschmer's model as a template for developing his own statistically derived dimensional analysis of psychosis (Eysenck 1952).

We also need to note a further difference between Eysenck's formulation and the narrowly defined schizotypy construct developed in the Meehl school. Those familiar with Eysenck's work will know that his statistical alternative to

Kretschmer's model was a broad dimension of 'psychoticism', meant to capture personality connections to *all* forms of psychosis, both schizophrenia and manic-depression. This was in keeping with Eysenck's ideas about personality structure, as being reducible to a few dimensions of great generality. In linking normal to abnormal, Psychoticism was therefore a logical parallel to his already established dimension of Neuroticism. Although the precise manner in which Eysenck originally arrived at the new dimension does not concern us here, two related points are worth noting for future reference. First, Eysenck's thinking about serious mental illness was influenced by the *Einheitpsychose* (or unitary) theory: the idea that the schizophrenias and manic-depression are not distinct diseases but are variable expressions of a common psychotic process. (Although the theory was unfashionable at the time – and Eysenck ridiculed for his use of it – the unitary model is now being revived in the light of new clinical and biological evidence (Kendell 1991; Maier, Rietschel, Lichtermann and Wildenauer 1999; Berettini 2003.)) Secondly, some form of unitary view of psychosis was implicit in Kretschmer's own model which visualized schizophrenia as occupying one end of a single continuum, with manic-depression at the opposite pole. Eysenck merely rejigged this scheme statistically by collapsing the two ends of Kretschmer's dimensions together to form Psychoticism, leaving Introversion-Extraversion to account for schizophrenic and manic-depressive variations, respectively.

There are, then, two points at issue about dimensionality in psychosis. One is its generality: how useful it might be to abandon the traditional classification of the psychoses in favour of a unitary view; and, correspondingly, in the personality sphere to talk of 'psychoticism', rather than separate dimensions relating to schizophrenia and bipolar affective disorder. The other question is how dimensionality itself is to be conceptualized. Elsewhere (Claridge 1997) I have distinguished two different perspectives on that, labelled *quasi-dimensional* and *fully dimensional*. The former, mostly North American, view assumes that psychotic features, when seen in the general population in the absence of overt illness, nevertheless represent attenuated forms of clinical symptomatology. 'Dimensionality' in that model therefore refers to continuity only in the sense of *forme fruste* of disease; and because quasi-dimensionalists tend not to favour the unitary model of psychosis this usually refers to a *schizophrenia* spectrum. In contrast, fully dimensional theory – more favoured in Europe – assumes that, as with other traits (e.g. anxiety), psychotic characteristics merely form part of normal personality structure, though similarly doubling up as predispositions to mental illness. This theory accommodates the *forme fruste* element from the quasi-dimensional model by making the distinction between traits and symptoms and recognizing that the shift into illness does involve varying degrees of discontinuity implied by the notion of a psychosis spectrum (Claridge and Davis 2003). On unitary psychosis, fully dimensional theorists either accept the idea, or are prepared to leave the matter open. Even they, however, have tended to focus more on schizophrenic forms of psychosis and therefore to publish mostly under the schizotypy umbrella. This, together with growing ambiguity in the meaning and interpretation of 'psychoticism', has led to some confusion in terminology that needs explaining.

Although 'psychoticism' was originally envisaged as a broad dimension encompassing all of the personality correlates of psychotic illness, Eysenck's eventual use of it turned the construct into something quite different, and much narrower (Eysenck and Eysenck 1991). As demonstrated in the items of his P-scale, it now represents traits more specifically associated with antisocial behaviour, lack of conformity, aggressiveness and impulsivity. This does not mean that psychoticism as P has nothing to do with psychosis – I believe it does – but that its significance conceptually is much more limited than the word 'psychoticism' implies. The reader should be aware of these differing usages of the term (see Rawlings and Dawe (2007) for a recent detailed discussion of the matter).

Measuring psychotic traits

Self-report questionnaires – and their psychometric analysis – have formed a pivotal feature of research on schizotypy/psychoticism.[1] This work has proceeded in two, roughly chronologically distinct, phases. The first, going back more than three decades, has involved developing individual scales for assessing psychotic traits in various ways (for listings and reviews see Mason, Claridge and Williams 1997; Chapman, Chapman and Kwapil 1995). The instruments have different labels and vary in their generality or specificity; i.e., whether they purport to measure a global dimension of, say, schizotypy, schizoidia or psychoticism, or some particular aspect of these. Of the latter type the most prominent is a large suite of questionnaires developed by the Chapmans at the University of Wisconsin. Their scales include some that are widely regarded as essentially 'schizotypal': either cognitive (Perceptual Aberration, Chapman, Chapman and Raulin 1978; Magical Ideation, Eckblad and Chapman 1983) or concerned with anhedonic affect (Chapman, Chapman and Raulin 1976). Several, however, are meant to tap other aspects of psychosis: i.e., Hypomanic Personality (Eckblad and Chapman 1986) and Impulsive Non-conformity (Chapman, Chapman, Numbers *et al.* 1984). It is presumably for this reason that the Chapmans describe their questionnaires as measures of what they refer to as '*psychosis* proneness', in a manner reminiscent of the original meaning of psychoticism. Whether judged as a contribution to measurement in that broader domain or more narrowly on the schizophrenia spectrum, the Chapmans' work is significant in implicitly recognizing the heterogeneity of psychotic traits. This was later formally established in what amounted to a second phase of research,

---

[1] Awkward though it is, I shall often use this phrase to avoid foreclosing on the unitary psychosis issue introduced here. It will be obvious from the context when 'psychoticism' is being used to denote what the P-scale measures.

where multivariate techniques were used to identify components of schizotypy/psychoticism. These studies have mostly involved factor analysing varying selections of the scales available in the area, almost always including some of the Chapman measures.

The first such analysis can be credited to Muntaner and his colleagues (Muntaner, Garcia, Fernandez and Torrubia 1988), and since then a steady stream of further reports has appeared in the literature (for early reviews see Mason, Claridge and Williams 1997; Vollema and van den Bosch 1995; for some more recent analyses see Vollema and Hoijtink 2000; Venables and Rector 2000; Reynolds, Raine, Mellingen *et al.* 2000). The conclusion that most investigators have reached from these analyses is that schizotypy consists of three major components. These concern, respectively, aberrant perception, cognitive disorganization and interpersonal, schizoid or anhedonic features. Authors have often differed in the way they have labelled these, but the conceptual similarities are quite evident. And, usefully, the three factors have been said to line up well with a similar three-dimensional structure for schizophrenic symptoms (e.g., Liddle 1987).

Somewhat at variance with the above conclusion is the claim by some workers that they can identify *four* factors in their analyses (Bentall, Claridge and Slade 1989; Claridge, McCreery, Mason *et al.* 1996; Hay, Martin, Foley *et al.* 2001). This fourth factor has the trait qualities of impulsiveness, mood-related disinhibition and asocial behaviour: it has often been labelled 'impulsive non-conformity'. The latter has also been found in some analyses where only *three* factors were extracted overall (Muntaner, Garcia, Fernandez and Torrubia 1988; Kendler and Hewitt 1992); in those cases the third factor substituted for one of the components in the more orthodox three-factor schizotypy solutions referred to earlier.

How do we judge these findings alongside the three-dimensional model that most schizotypy researchers usually consider definitive? As a first point it is worth drawing attention to the 'smoke and mirrors' nature of multivariate analysis and the old adage that you get out of factor analysis what you put in! Thus, it should be noted that all of the 'rogue' studies described have differed from other analyses of 'schizotypy' in one important respect: they have employed a wider than usual range of scales. These have included, in varying combinations, the Chapmans' Impulsive Non-conformity and Hypomanic Personality scales, the Claridge and Rawlings Borderline Personality scale (Claridge and Broks 1984), and the Eysenck P-scale. So one possibility is that 'impulsive non-conformity' emerged as a factor in its own right merely because it was entered in the first place into the analyses in question – but that it really has nothing to do with psychosis. However, there is good reason to believe that that is *not* the case; that what is actually being demonstrated in these studies is evidence – at the personality trait level – for the *Einheitpsychose* theory.

Take, for example, the pattern of cross-loadings found in some of the analyses in question. In the Bentall, Claridge and Slade (1989) and Claridge, McCreery, Mason *et al.* (1996) studies what was called there an 'asocial behaviour' factor was defined by the borderline and hypomania personality scales, as well as the

P-scale. Yet these also loaded (very significantly in the case of hypomanic personality) on the main positive symptoms component usually reserved as one of the primary defining features of schizotypy/schizophrenia. In other words, 'positive symptoms' could not be considered uniquely schizotypal in the narrow sense in which it has usually been interpreted; it also correlated with affective traits normally associated with bipolar disorder.

'Borderline personality' is also of particular interest here, both in relation to a so-called bipolar spectrum and in its association to schizotypy. The suggestion that some borderline characteristics are a risk factor for bipolar disorder is a live issue in psychiatry (Perugi and Akiskal 2002). Convergent with this is evidence that individuals high in hypomanic personality, as assessed by the Chapman scale, are more prone to develop symptoms of both affective disorder and borderline personality disorder (Kwapil, Miller, Zinser *et al.* 2000). Furthermore, strong positive correlations have been found between borderline and schizotypy, both as personality traits (Claridge and Broks 1984) and as overlap between the personality disorders they define (Spitzer, Endicott and Gibbon 1979; George and Soloff 1986). Add to this some evidence that bipolar patients score highly on scales specifically designed to measure schizotypy (Heron, Jones, Williams *et al.* (2003) and it is difficult to escape the conclusion that there is considerable co-mingling of the schizophrenic, the borderline, the affective and the schizotypal. On the purely factor analytic front, it is scarcely surprising that a fourth, genuinely psychotic, component will emerge when scales are included that allow that to happen.

The other measurement issue in this field – confined for the moment to narrow schizotypy – concerns the dimensionality of the construct. Does schizotypy define a dichotomous all-or-none characteristic or is it a truly continuous complex of traits? The answer has mostly been sought in questionnaire data, a playing out in the psychometric arena of the quasi versus fully dimensional debate referred to earlier. By definition, the fully dimensional view is that schizotypy, like all psychotic traits, is continuously variable; though its expression will become increasingly discontinuous in clinical states (Claridge and Davis 2003). The alternative theory is that, even when observed in non-clinical populations, schizotypy defines a discrete category or taxon. Individuals either belong in the taxon or not, any appearance of dimensionality resulting from the influence of many small effects that mask the defining feature of the taxon. The advocates of this model argue that what matters is the *latent structure* of the measuring scale and that special statistical techniques are required to determine this: such procedures were developed by Meehl and his colleagues as part of the search for a schizotypy taxon (Meehl and Golden 1982; Meehl 1995; see also Cole 2004). Taxonometric analysis has now been applied to a variety of data from the normal and abnormal domains (Haslam and Williams 2006); but schizotypy continues to be its main focus. There the most prominent contemporary exponent of the taxonic model is Lenzenburger (Lenzenburger and Korfine 1992; Korfine and Lenzenburger 1995); though other workers have also published data in support of the theory (Blanchard, Gangestad, Brown and Horan 2000; Meyer and Keller 2001).

The majority of findings demonstrating taxonicity in schizotypy have been based on the Chapman scales: Perceptual Aberration, Magical Ideation, Physical and Social Anhedonia. Therein, perhaps, lies one of the frailties of the taxonic case for schizotypy. The scores on such measures depart markedly from a normal distribution, due to the rather 'strong' symptom-like quality of the items. This skewness was deliberately built into their construction to make them more discriminating at the extreme (Chapman, Chapman and Kwapil 1995). However, it would tend to favour finding taxonicity in data, a conclusion confirmed by the results of a recent study by Rawlings, Haslam, Williams and Claridge (2008a). They showed that, after correcting for skew, there was no evidence that the Chapman scales were taxonic. They concluded that, contrary to the claims of the Meehl school, schizotypy is in all probability genuinely dimensional. The authors also make two other observations: first, that previous claims for taxonicity were based on samples of less than optimum size (their own sample consisted of 1000+ subjects); secondly, that taxonicity has been more often found in special groups of already identifiably distinct individuals, selected as at high risk for schizophrenia (Erlenmeyer-Kimling, Golden and Cornblatt 1989; Tyrka, Haslam and Cannon 1995). Such samples (almost by default) are more likely to form taxa; and the results are fully in keeping with the distinction made here between trait and symptom expressions of schizotypy/ psychoticism. (See Beauchaine, Lenzenburger and Waller 2008 and Rawlings, Haslam, Williams and Claridge 2008b for a lively debate on this issue that ensued with publication of the Rawlings, Haslam, Williams and Claridge 2008b study.)

As discussed shortly, there is much interest in using questionnaires in clinical risk research. Here, because of their psychometric properties, the most popular instruments continue to be the Chapman scales, at least the four scales measuring perceptual aberration, magical ideation and anhedonia (physical and social). This despite the slight limitation that the scales do not cover the full range of schizotypal characteristics revealed in factor analytic studies; the items actually factor down to just two – positive and negative – components (Kwapil, Barrentes-Vidal and Silvia 2008).

Another currently popular and more comprehensive instrument is the Schizotypal Personality Questionnaire (SPQ), devised by Raine (1991). This was modelled on DSM-III-R criteria for Schizotypal Personality Disorder and gives scores on nine scales which, when factor analysed, have been shown to reduce to three familiar sounding components, labelled by the investigators Cognitive-Perceptual, Interpersonal and Disorganized (Reynolds, Raine, Mellingen et al. 2000).

Only one questionnaire attempts to measure all four of the dimensions of schizotypy/psychoticism found in some of the factor analyses described earlier. This is the Oxford-Liverpool Inventory of Feelings and Experiences (O-LIFE) (Mason, Claridge and Jackson 1995). Using the same large dataset of scales that had originally yielded four factors, the O-LIFE was constructed around four corresponding scales: Unusual Experiences, Cognitive Disorganization, Introvertive Anhedonia and Impulsive Non-conformity. In addition to being modelled on the unitary view of psychosis, the O-LIFE was also designed around a fully dimensional theory of psychotic traits, avoiding the stronger clinically worded items found in some other scales. This has encouraged its use in a variety of research domains (Mason and Claridge 2006).

Psychotic traits as risk for psychosis

Considerable research has tried to identify individuals who are vulnerable to psychoses, with the hope of using that information both for clinical prediction and for understanding the etiology of these illnesses. Attention has mostly focused on schizophrenia, using three main methods for identifying persons at risk. The first, against the background of genetic evidence, has been to study relatives of already diagnosed schizophrenics (e.g. Cannon and Mednick 1993). The second selects individuals with one of the DSM Cluster A personality disorders, usually Schizotypal Personality Disorder, on the grounds that they are strongly located on the schizophrenia spectrum (e.g Siever, Koenigsberg, Harvey *et al.* 2002). Thirdly there is the screening of general population samples using the questionnaires described in the previous section. Definitive studies there are the longitudinal follow-up investigations carried out by the Chapmans and their colleagues. The basic design of that research has been to administer their questionnaires to very large student samples and then after some years examine the clinical outcome for participants who score highly on individual scales or combinations of scales. Their results can be summarized as follows.

In a ten-year reassessment Chapman and colleagues reported that, compared with controls, extreme scorers on their 'positive symptom' scales (Perceptual Aberration and Magical Ideation) more frequently experienced psychotic-like symptoms, as well as actual psychosis (both schizophrenia and mood disorder) (Chapman, Chapman, Kwapil, Eckblad and Zinser 1994). Rates were increased when Social (though *not* Physical) Anhedonia was added to the equation, a result mostly replicated in independent studies by Kwapil (1998) and Kwapil, Miller, Zinser, Chapman and Chapman (1997). These findings have been further elaborated and clarified in a further, cross-sectional, study recently reported by Kwapil, Barrantes-Vidal and Silvia (2008). They first factor analysed the Chapman scales, demonstrating (as mentioned in the previous section) two predicted – positive and negative – components of schizotypy. Kwapil and his colleagues then used factor scores in a series of regression analyses to explore associations with measures from a large battery of other personality and clinical test procedures they had administered. They showed that negative symptom traits alone certainly predicted some psychopathology; this was mostly in the form of blunted affect, diminished sensation-seeking and schizoidness. The positive symptoms component, however, predicted a wider range of impairments, including more psychotic-like experiences, paranoid symptoms, increased substance use and abuse, and cyclical mood episodes. As the authors themselves point out, there seemed here to be yet further evidence for a unitary psychosis interpretation of schizotypy/psychoticism, despite the use of scales formally restricted to the measurement of 'schizotypy'.

Another finding from the above study is worth noting. As part of their test battery the authors also administered the NEO Five-Factor personality question-naire (Costa and McCrae 1992). They report that, in terms of the NEO factors, the difference between negative and positive expressions of schizotypy was best captured by opposite correlations with Openness to Experience: negative symp-tom traits were associated with a low degree of Openness, whereas positive symptoms were associated with high Openness.

A corollary of questionnaire risk research is seeing how the scales relate to laboratory-based measures. Part of the aim here is to try to discover so-called 'endophenotypes' (Gottesman 1991). The term refers to what can be very nar-rowly defined indices of function which, on the face of it, look distant from the clinical state or its overt predisposing features, but which there is reason to believe map onto these. Endophenotypes can be drawn from any domain – behavioural, cognitive, psychophysiological, neurophysiological or biochemical – and typi-cally serve a dual purpose One is as simple indicators of risk, complementing clinical, questionnaire and other descriptive data. The second is as a vehicle for exploring some aspect of the nature or etiology of the psychotic process (the measure will usually have been chosen according to some theory, hypothesis or speculation about that). The work complements and is complemented by parallel studies of the same experimental variables in clinical samples and in other high risk groups, such as schizophrenics' relatives. The number of measures on offer as promising endophenotypes or clues to the nature of psychosis, even just for schizophrenia, is bewildering, and here it would be impossible to review such a complex network of research in any detail. I shall try instead to offer a necessarily personalized view of themes in the topic, illustrated with occasional examples.

The first thing to note is how greatly the various types of experimental research in the area differ in focus, theoretical assumption, specificity of measurement, possible application, and clinical and etiological relevance. At one extreme are proposed measures that can almost be construed as 'markers' in the near-genetics sense. An example is the claim that psychometrically assessed schizotypy is associated with dermatoglyphic anomalies that might be construed as a sign of developmental disturbance in the prenatal environment of individuals at later risk for schizophrenia (Chok, Kwapil and Scheuermann 2005). Conceptually distant from this kind of observation is evidence based on experimental paradigms of a more psychological nature, such as executive function (Avons, Nunn, Chan and Armstrong 2003). The latter are unlikely to address embryological questions about etiology and clearly relate more directly to the mechanisms of schizotypal and schizophrenic cognition. In between these two extremes are paradigms drawn from and tested out in psychophysiology and it is here that one major theme in the literature can be discerned.

Psychosis poses unique questions about the interplay between the psycholog-ical and the biological and psychophysiology is well-placed to bridge that gap.

Furthermore, if 'survival' is a test of a good idea, then the work and writings of Peter Venables easily meet that criterion. Nearly half a century ago he proposed that schizophrenia was essentially a problem in 'input dysfunction', i.e., the modulation and control of stimuli into the nervous system (Venables 1964). It is a tribute to Venables that as recently as 2002 the importance of his simple but telling insight was celebrated in a whole issue of the journal *Schizophrenia Research* (Raine and Green 2002)). As the papers and references cited there attest, over the years Venables' theory has spawned a great deal of research attempting to identify psychophysiological measures that can act both as markers of risk and as indicators of the schizophrenic process (Cadenhead and Braff 2002).

A key feature of 'input dysfunction' is the notion that it involves some deviation in inhibitory mechanisms in the brain. This is explicitly stated in what has emerged as one of the most popular endophenotypes under investigation in schizophrenia/schizotypy research, i.e., pre-pulse inhibition (Braff, Stone, Callaway *et al.* 1978; Braff, Swerdlow and Geyer 1999). Here a preceding stimulus is tested for its ability to suppress the response to a strong startle stimulus: typically this inhibition is reduced in individuals on the schizophrenia spectrum.[2] The general idea of 'inhibition' as a mediating process in psychosis has also infiltrated other, more psychological, paradigms; for example negative priming (Williams and Beech 1997), latent inhibition (Tsakanikos, Sverdrup-Thygenson and Reed 2003), and subliminal priming (Evans 1997). All of these have been extensively studied as examples of how cognitive functioning – at all levels – in psychosis might be subject to weakened inhibitory controls, resulting in the perceptual and attentional 'flooding' and cognitive 'overinclusion' that typifies the clinical state. The idea fits well with Venables' suggestion that input dysfunction can lead to excessive openness to the environment, though it actually goes back well beyond that: to Bleuler's original proposal that associative loosening is what is wrong in schizophrenic thinking, and to Carl Jung's suggestion that in psychosis the threshold of consciousness is lowered, 'allowing normally inhibited contents of the unconsciousness to enter consciousness' (Jung 1939).

An important feature of Venables' theorizing about input dysfunction was his observation about heterogeneity: that some individuals actually have extreme 'closedness' to the environment, corresponding in current terminology to the negative side of schizophrenia/schizotypy. Even so, much of the experimental research to date has concentrated on trying to explain the positive symptom aspects. The few exceptions in the schizotypy literature have included studies of variations in electrodermal activity, a focus for much early work on input dysfunction in schizophrenia. (Bernstein and Riedel 1987; Mason, Claridge and Clark 1997).

Another approach to the explanation of psychosis/psychoticism that (so far) has stood the test of time is the idea that variations have to do with differences in

---

[2] Notably this is also true of bipolar affective disorder (Perry, Minassian, Feifel and Braff 2001).

cerebral lateralization. In the schizotypy literature this has been pursued on diverse fronts, including olfaction (Mohr, Röhrenbach, Laska and Brugger 2001), language task performance (Nunn and Peters 2001), face processing (Mason and Claridge 1999), and handedness (Shaw, Claridge and Clark 2001). Again, most attention has been paid to the positive aspects, though one writer who has deliberately departed from this is Gruzelier (1991). With colleagues he has tried to distinguish variations in the expression of schizotypy on the basis of lateralized differences in visual processing (Richardson and Gruzelier 1994) and electrodermal activity (Gruzelier and Raine 1994).

The healthy face of psychosis

The major point of contention between personality based and illness-based views of schizotypy/psychoticism is whether psychotic traits can ever serve a healthy function. In other words, whether the analogy drawn earlier between anxiety and anxiety disorder is accurate; or whether psychosis is a different sort of disorder, an organic disease of the 'broken brain' variety (Andreasen 1984). Depending on one's stance on this issue, the notion of 'healthy schizotypy' is either a given fact or a logically impossible idea. Adherents of the latter view would quote several kinds of evidence in support of their case: the claimed taxonic nature of schizotypy, the sheer severity and peculiarity of psychotic illness, and its intuitive feel as a thoroughly biological state of neurological proportion. Those of the opposite opinion point to many instances where the so-called 'psychotic' process appears to form part of, or is inextricably linked, to healthy experiences and activities. Included here are the universality of hallucinations (Posey and Losch 1983), the well-established connection to creativity (Sass and Schuldberg 2000; Benolken and Martindale 2000), and the arbitrary distinction between spiritual and psychotic experience (Clarke 2001). Yet there *is* a dilemma here. How *does* one reconcile the devastating quality of psychotic illness – which, however far one tries to push the analogy to anxiety, is clearly in a class apart – with notions of health and adaptiveness? In the short space remaining I shall try to draw out some themes that might help to resolve that problem, or at least provide a framework for thinking about it.

The first point to make concerns the role of biology. As discussed elsewhere (Claridge 2006), debates about psychosis have usually been cast as a false dichotomy between the psychological and the biological (meaning the neurological). Yet a wealth of evidence and theorizing about the biology of normal individual differences clearly shows that naturally occurring individual variations in brain function (so-called 'nervous types', in the Pavlovian sense) help to underpin observed dimensions of temperament and personality. There is every reason to include schizotypy/psychoticism on that list. Acknowledging the contribution of biology to psychotic traits does not therefore mean buying into a neurological explanation of psychosis.

A second point flows from an understanding of how traits are transformed into symptoms along the illness spectrum and how the same mechanisms that promote healthy functioning can sometimes bring about its opposite. This is best illustrated from the creativity literature. As Brod (1997) among others has emphasized, the evidence for the madness/creativity argument lies not in an association to psychosis itself – the insane are rarely able to function creatively – but rather with connections to the cognitive style found in schizotypy/psychoticism.

The third, and perhaps most fascinating, part of the topic is that we need a way of explaining how and why in some individuals psychotic traits remain adaptive while in others they are translated into illness. Quasi-dimensionalists would argue that such people are merely compensating for a hidden neurological defect. But if they are wrong then the task becomes exactly the same as that faced by research on other functional psychiatric disorders: teasing out the interaction between biological predispositions, associated personality traits, long-term social influences and immediate environmental triggers. In the case of schizophrenia there are already some signs of progress, even though different lines of research have yet to be joined up. On the one hand, there is a growing interest in the contribution of early abuse to etiology (Morrison, Frame and Larkin 2003). Then, more concerned with personality disposition, there is a convergent opinion that some clues might lie in the profile of schizotypal traits themselves. Thus, it is probably significant that the more positive features of schizotypy (unusual experiences, and so on) are not necessarily the best predictors of schizophrenic illness: they may only be necessary, but not sufficient, conditions. The evidence for this comes from several sources: the questionnaire high risk studies referred to earlier; genetic investigations (e.g. Cardno, Thomas and McGuffin 2002); and the observation that healthy individuals subject to psychotic-like phenomena, such as out-of-the-body experiences, score highly on the positive, but not on the negative, features of schizotypy (McCreery and Claridge 1995). As several very disparate kinds of literature discussed here have indicated, on the personality front, understanding the multifactorial nature of schizotypy/psychoticism is likely to prove crucial and a much needed focus for future research.

The last word on the subject and indeed in this chapter properly belongs with Peter Chadwick: psychologist, self-confessed sufferer from psychotic illness, and prolific writer on his own experiences, on creativity, and on both the healthy and the unhealthy sides of madness (Chadwick 2001, 2009). Chadwick's story can be summed up as that of someone whose personality he admits was 'schizoid … in the sense that I had very little capacity to integrate thoughts and feelings – something that one sees so beautifully in writers such as Tennyson'; whose transvestism led to much abuse and social isolation and eventually to a vicious cycle of self-confirming paranoid delusion; and who on medication recovered to continue a fulfilling professional career. His conclusions are a sharp corrective to those who doubt the mutual benefits to be had from studies of clinical psychosis and healthy personality (Chadwick 2007):

The abuse directed toward stigmatized minority group members can clearly eventuate psychosis in those who have biochemical, physiological, and intrapsychic susceptibilities. These susceptibilities can have positive connotations. The vulnerability to psychosis is eased however by changes at every level from the biochemical ambience of the brain to cognitive and psychodynamic rearrangements within to modifications in one's social situation and attitude to existence … The present author would suggest that a multifactorial conceptualising of psychosis, from a perspective which blends science, art, and spirituality, will produce greater understanding of this predicament in life and better ameliorative efforts toward it than those which obtain at present.

References

American Psychiatric Association 2000. *Diagnostic and statistical manual of mental disorders*, 4th edn, Text Revision. Washington, DC: American Psychiatric Association

Andreasen, N. 1984. *The broken brain: the biological revolution in psychiatry*. New York: Harper and Row

Avons, S. E., Nunn, J. A., Chan, L. and Armstrong, H. 2003. Executive function assessed by memory updating and random generation in schizotypal individuals, *Psychiatry Research* 120: 145–54

Beauchaine, T. P., Lenzenburger, M. F. and Waller, N. G. 2008. Schizotypy, taxometrics, and disconfirming theories in soft science: comment on Rawlings, Williams, Haslam and Claridge, *Personality and Individual Differences* 44: 1652–62

Benolken, S. and Martindale, C. (eds.) 2000. Creativity and psychopathology, *Bulletin of Psychology and the Arts* 1:(2) (Special Issue)

Bentall, R. P., Claridge, G. and Slade, P. 1989. The multidimensional nature of schizotypal traits: a factor analytic study with normal subjects, *British Journal of Clinical Psychology* 28: 363–75

Bernstein, A. S. and Riedel, J. A. 1987. Psychophysiological response patterns in college students with high physical anhedonia: scores appear to reflect schizotypy rather than depression, *Biological Psychiatry* 22: 829–47

Berettini, W. 2003. Evidence for shared susceptibility in bipolar disorder and schizophrenia, *American Journal of Medical Genetics* 123C: 59–64

Blanchard, J. J., Gangestad, S. W., Brown, S. A. and Horan, W. P. 2000. Hedonic capacity and schizotypy revisited: a taxometric analysis of social anhedonia, *Journal of Abnormal Psychology* 85: 374–82

Bleuler, E. 1911. *Dementia praecox or the group of schizophrenias*, J. Zinkin (trans.) 1950. New York: International Universities Press

Bleuler, M. 1978. *The schizophrenic disorders*, S. M. Clemens (trans). New Haven, CT: Yale University Press

Braff, D., Stone, C., Callaway, E., Geyer, M., Glick, L. and Bali, L. 1978. Prestimulus effects on human startle reflex in normals and schizophrenics, *Psychophysiology* 15: 339–43

Braff, D. L., Swerdlow, N. R. and Geyer, M. A. 1999. Symptom correlates of prepulse inhibition deficits in male schizophrenic patients, *American Journal of Psychiatry* 156: 596–602

Brod, J. H. 1997. Creativity and schizotypy, in G. Claridge (ed.), *Schizotypy: implications for illness and health*, pp 274–98. Oxford University Press

Cadenhead, K. S. and Braff, D. L. 2002. Endophenotyping schizotypy: a prelude to genetic studies within the schizophrenia spectrum, *Schizophrenia Research* 54: 47–57

Cannon, T. D. and Mednick, S. A. 1993. The schizophrenia high-risk project in Copenhagen: three decades of progress, *Acta Psychiatrica Scandinavica* 87: 33–47

Cardno, A. G., Thomas, K. and McGuffin, P. 2002. Clinical variables and genetic loading for schizophrenia: analysis of published Danish adoption study data, *Schizophrenia Bulletin* 28: 393–99

Chadwick, P. 2001. *Personality as art: artistic approaches in psychology*. Ross-on-Wye: PCCS Books

2007. Peer-professional first-person account: schizophrenia from the inside – phenomenology and the integration of causes and meanings, *Schizophrenia Bulletin* 33: 166–73

2009. *Schizophrenia: the positive perspective*, 2nd edn. London: Routledge

Chapman, J. P., Chapman, L. J. and Kwapil, T. R. 1995. Scales for the measurement of schizotypy, in A. Raine, T. Lencz and S. A. Mednick (eds), *Schizotypal personality*, pp 79–106. Cambridge University Press

Chapman, L. J., Chapman, J. P., Kwapil, T. R., Eckblad, M. and Zinser, M. C. 1994. Putatively psychosis-prone subjects 10 years later, *Journal of Abnormal Psychology* 103: 171–83

Chapman, L. J., Chapman, J. P., Numbers, J. S., Edell, W. S., Carpenter, B. N. and Beckfield, D. 1984. Impulsive nonconformity as a trait contributing to the prediction of psychotic-like and schizotypal symptoms, *Journal of Nervous and Mental Disease* 172: 681–91

Chapman, L. J., Chapman, J. P. and Raulin, M. L. 1976. Scales for physical and social anhedonia, *Journal of Abnormal Psychology* 85: 374–82

1978. Body image aberration in schizophrenia, *Journal of Abnormal Psychology* 87: 399–407

Chok, J. I., Kwapil, T. R. and Scheuermann, A. 2005. Dermatoglyphic anomalies in psychometrically identified schizotypic young adults, *Schizophrenia Research* 72: 205–14

Claridge, G. 1997. Theoretical background and issues, in G. Claridge (ed.), *Schizotypy: implications for illness and health*, pp. 3–18. Oxford University Press

2006. Divided selves as nervous types, *The Psychologist* 19: 656–8

Claridge, G. and Broks, P. 1984. Schizotypy and hemisphere function: I. Theoretical considerations and the measurement of schizotypy, *Personality and Individual Differences* 8: 303–12

Claridge, G. and Davis, C. 2003. *Personality and psychological disorders*. London: Arnold

Claridge, G., McCreery, C., Mason, O., Bentall, R., Boyle, G., Slade, P. and Popplewell, D. 1996. The factor structure of 'schizotypal' traits: a large replication study, *British Journal of Clinical Psychology* 35: 103–15

Clarke, I. (ed.) 2001. *Psychosis and spirituality*. London: Whurr

Cole, D. A. 2004. Taxometrics in psychopathology research: an introduction to some of the procedures and related methodological issues, *Journal of Abnormal Psychology* 113: 3–9

Costa, P. T., Jr and McCrae, R. R. 1992. *NEO-PI-R professional manual*. Odessa, FL: Psychological Assessment Resources

Eckblad, M. L. and Chapman, L. J. 1983. Magical ideation as an indicator of schizotypy, *Journal of Consulting and Clinical Psychology* 51: 215–25

1986. Development and validation of a scale for hypomanic personality, *Journal of Abnormal Psychology* 95: 214–22

Erlenmeyer-Kimling, L., Golden, R. R. and Cornblatt, B. A. 1989. A taxonometric analysis of cognitive and neuromotor variables in children at risk for schizophrenia, *Journal of Abnormal Psychology* 98: 203–8

Evans, J. L. 1997. Semantic activation and preconscious processing in schizophrenia and schizotypy, in G. Claridge (ed.), *Schizotypy: implications for illness and health*, pp 80–97. Oxford University Press

Eysenck, H. J. 1947. *Dimensions of personality*. London: Routledge and Kegan Paul

1952. Schizothymia-cyclothymia as a dimension of personality. II. Experimental, *Journal of Personality* 20: 345–84

Eysenck, H. J. and Eysenck, M. W. 1985. *Personality and individual differences*. New York: Plenum Press

Eysenck, H. J. and Eysenck, S. B. G. 1991. *Manual of the Eysenck Personality Scales*. London: Hodder and Stoughton

George, A. and Soloff, P. H. 1986. Schizotypal symptoms in patients with borderline personality disorders, *American Journal of Psychiatry* 143: 212–15

Gottesman, I. I. 1991. *Schizophrenia genesis: the epigenetic puzzle*. Cambridge University Press

Gruzelier, J. H. 1991. Hemispheric imbalance: syndromes of schizophrenia, premorbid personality, and neurodevelopmental influences, in S. R. Steinhauer, J. H. Gruzelier and J. Zubin (eds.), *Handbook of schizophrenia, vol V, Neuropsychology, psychophysiology, and information processing*. Oxford: Elsevier

Gruzelier, J. H. and Raine, A. 1994. Bilateral electrodermal activity and cerebral mechanisms in syndromes of schizophrenia and schizoid personality, *International Journal of Psychophysiology* 16: 1–16

Haslam, N. and Williams, B. 2006. Taxometrics, in S. Strack (ed), *Differentiating normal and abnormal personality*, pp 283–308. New York: Springer

Hay, D. A., Martin, N. G., Foley, D., Treloar, S. A., Kirk, K. M. and Heath, A. C. 2001. Phenotypic and genetic analyses of a short measure of psychosis-proneness in a large-scale Australian twin study, *Twin Research* 4: 30–40

Heron, J., Jones, I., Williams, J., Owen, M. J., Craddock, N. and Jones, L. A. 2003. Self-reported schizotypy and bipolar disorder: demonstration of a lack of specificity of the Kings Schizotypy Questionnaire, *Schizophrenia Research* 65: 153–8

Jung, C. G. 1939. On the psychogenesis of schizophrenia, *Journal of Mental Science* 85: 999–1011

Kendell, R. E. 1991. The major functional psychoses: are they independent entities or part of a continuum? Philosophical and conceptual issues underlying the debate, in: A. Kerr and H. McClelland (eds.), *Concepts of mental disorder: a continuing debate*, pp. 1–16. London: Gaskell

Kendler, K. S. and Hewitt, J. 1992. The structure of self-report schizotypy in twins, *Journal of Personality Disorders* 6: 1–17

Korfine, L. and Lenzenburger, M. F. 1995. The taxonicity of schizotypy: a replication, *Journal of Abnormal Psychology* 104: 26–31

Kretschmer, E. 1925. *Physique and character*, W. J. H. Sprott (trans.). London: Kegan, Trench, and Trubner

Kwapil, T. R. 1998. Social anhedonia as a predictor of the development of schizophrenia-spectrum disorders, *Journal of Abnormal Psychology* 107: 558–65

Kwapil, T. R., Barrantes-Vidal, N. and Silvia, P. J. 2008. The dimensional structure of the Wisconsin Schizotypy Scales: factor identification and construct validity, *Schizophrenia Bulletin* 34: 444–57

Kwapil, T. R., Miller, M. B., Zinser, M. C., Chapman, J. P. and Chapman, L. J. 1997. Magical ideation and social anhedonia as predictors of psychosis-proneness: a partial replication, *Journal of Abnormal Psychology* 106: 491–5

Kwapil, T. R., Miller, M. B., Zinser, M. C., Chapman, L. J., Chapman, J., and Eckblad, M. 2000. A longitudinal study of high scorers on the Hypomanic Personality Scale, *Journal of Abnormal Psychology* 109: 222–6

Lenzenburger, M. F. and Korfine, L. 1992. Confirming the latent structure and base rate of schizotypy: a taxometric analysis, *Journal of Abnormal Psychology* 101: 567–71

Liddle, P. F. 1987. The symptoms of chronic schizophrenia: a re-examination of the positive-negative dichotomy, *British Journal of Psychiatry* 151: 145–51

Maier, W., Rietschel, M., Lichtermann, D. and Wildenauer, D. B. 1999. Family and genetic studies on the relationship of schizophrenia to affective disorders, *European Archives of Psychiatry and Clinical Neuroscience* 249: Suppl. 4, 57–61

Mason, O. and Claridge, G. 1999. Individual differences in schizotypy and reduced asymmetry using the chimeric faces task, *Cognitive Neuropsychiatry* 4: 289–301

2006. The Oxford-Liverpool Inventory of Feelings and Experiences (O-LIFE): further description and extended norms, *Schizophrenia Research* 82: 203–11

Mason, O., Claridge, G. and Clark, K. 1997. Electrodermal relationships with personality measures of psychosis-proneness in psychotic and normal subjects, *International Journal of Psychophysiology* 27: 137–46

Mason, O., Claridge, G. and Jackson, M. 1995. New scales for the assessment of schizotypy, *Personality and Individual Differences* 18: 7–13

Mason, O., Claridge, G. and Williams, L. 1997. Questionnaire measurement, in G. Claridge (ed). *Schizotypy: implications for illness and health*, pp. 19–37. Oxford University Press

McCreery, C. and Claridge, G. 1995. Out-of-the-body experiences and personality, *Journal of the Society for Psychical Research* 60: 129–48

Meehl, P. E. 1962. Schizotaxia, schizotypy, schizophrenia, *American Psychologist* 17: 827–38

1990. Toward an integrated theory of schizotaxia, schizotypy, and schizophrenia, *Journal of Personality Disorders* 4: 1–99

1995. Bootstrap taxometrics: solving the classification problem in psychopathology, *American Psychologist* 50: 266–75

Meehl, P. E. and Golden, R. 1982. Taxometric methods, in P. Kendall and J. Butcher (eds.). *Handbook of research methods in clinical psychology*, pp. 127–81. New York: Wiley

Meyer, T. and Keller, F. 2001. Exploring the latent structure of the Perceptual Aberration, Magical Ideation and Physical Anhedonia Scales in a German sample: a partial replication, *Journal of Personality Disorders* 15: 521–35

Mohr, C., Röhrenbach, C. M., Laska, M. and Brugger, P. 2001. Unilateral olfactory perception and magical ideation, *Schizophrenia Research* 47: 255–64

Morrison, A., Frame, L. and Larkin, W. 2003. Relationships between trauma and psychosis: a review and integration, *British Journal of Clinical Psychology* 200: 331–53

Muntaner, C., Garcia, S. L., Fernandez. A. and Torrubia, R. 1988. Personality dimensions, schizotypal and borderline personality traits and psychosis proneness, *Personality and Individual Differences* 9: 257–68

Nunn, J. and Peters, E. 2001. Schizotypy and patterns of lateral asymmetry on hemisphere-specific language tasks, *Psychiatry Research* 103: 179–92

Perry, W., Minassian, A., Feifel, D. and Braff, D. L. 2001. Sensorimotor gating deficits in bipolar disorder patients with acute psychotic mania, *Biological Psychiatry* 50: 418–24

Perugi, G. and Akiskal, H. S. 2002. The soft bipolar spectrum redefined: focus on the cyclothymic, anxious-sensitive, impulse-dyscontrol, and binge-eating connection in bipolar II and related conditions, *Psychiatric Clinics of North America* 25: 713–37

Posey, T. B. and Losch, M. E. 1983. Auditory hallucinations of hearing voices in 375 normal subjects, *Imagination, Cognition and Personality* 3: 99–113

Rado, S. 1953. Dynamics and classification of disordered behaviour, *American Journal of Psychiatry* 110: 406–16

Raine, A. 1991. The SPQ: a scale for the assessment of schizotypal personality based on DSM-III-R criteria, *Schizophrenia Bulletin* 17: 555–64

Raine, A. and Green, M. F. 2002. Schizophrenia and schizotypal personality: a tribute to Peter H. Venables, *Schizophrenia Research* 54: 1–5

Raine, A., Lencz, T. and Mednick (eds.) 1995. *Schizotypal personality.* Cambridge University Press

Rawlings, D. and Dawe, S. 2007. Psychoticism and impulsivity, in G. J. Boyle, G. Matthews and D. H. Saklofske, *Handbook of personality theory and testing*, vol. 1, *Personality theories and models*, pp. 357–78. London: Sage

Rawlings, D., Haslam, N., Williams, B. and Claridge, G. (2008a). Taxometric analysis supports a dimensional latent structure for schizotypy, *Personality and Individual Differences* 44: 1640–51

2008b. Is schizotypy taxonic? Response to Beauchaine, Lenzenburger and Waller, *Personality and Individual Differences* 44: 1663–72

Reynolds, C. A., Raine, A., Mellingen, K., Venables, P. H. and Mednick, S. A. 2000. Three-factor model of schizotypal personality: invariance across culture, gender, religious affiliation, family adversity, and psychopathology, *Schizophrenia Bulletin* 26: 603–18

Richardson, A. J. and Gruzelier, J. 1994. Visual processing, lateralization and syndromes of schizotypy, *International Journal of Psychophysiology* 18: 227–39

Sass, L. A. and Schuldberg, D. (eds.) 2000. Creativity and the schizophrenia spectrum, *Creativity Research Journal* 13 (Special Issue)

Shaw, J., Claridge, G. and Clark, K. 2001. Schizotypy and the shift from dextrality: a study of handedness in a large non-clinical population, *Schizophrenia Research* 50: 181–9

Siever, L. J., Koenigsberg, H. W., Harvey, P., Mitropoulou, V., Laruelle, M., Abi-Dargham, A., Goodman, M. and Buchsbaum, M. 2002. Cognitive and brain function in schizotypal personality disorder, *Schizophrenia Research* 54: 157–67

Spitzer, R. L., Endicott, J. and Gibbon, M. 1979. Crossing the border into borderline personality and borderline schizophrenia: the development of criteria, *Archives of General Psychiatry* 36: 17–24

Tsakanikos, E., Sverdrup-Thygenson, L. and Reed, P. 2003. Latent inhibition and psychosis-proneness: visual search as a function of pre-exposure to the target and schizotypy level, *Personality and Individual Differences* 34: 575–89

Tyrka, A., Haslam, N. and Cannon, T. D. 1995. Detection of a longitudinally- stable taxon of individuals at risk for schizophrenia spectrum disorders, in A. Raine, T. Lencz and S. A. Mednick (eds.), *Schizotypal personality*, pp. 168–91. Cambridge University Press

Venables, P. H. 1964. Input dysfunction in schizophrenia, in B. A. Maher (ed.), *Progress in experimental personality research*, pp. 1–41. New York: Academic Press

Venables, P. H. and Rector, N. A. 2000. The content and structure of schizotypy, *Schizophrenia Bulletin* 26: 587–602

Vollema, M. G. and Hoijtink, H. 2000. The multidimensionality of self-report schizotypy in a psychiatric population, *Schizophrenia Bulletin* 26: 565–75

Vollema, M. G. and van den Bosch, R. J. 1995. The multidimensionality of schizotypy, *Schizophrenia Bulletin* 21: 19–31

Williams, L. and Beech, A. 1997. Investigations of cognitive inhibitory processes in schizotypy and schizophrenia, in G. Claridge (ed.), *Schizotypy: implications for illness and health*, pp 63–79. Oxford University Press

World Health Organisation 1992. *ICD: the ICD-10 Classification of Mental and Behavioural Disorders – clinical description and diagnostic guidelines*. Geneva: World Health Organisation

37 Diagnosis and assessment of disorders of personality

Stephanie N. Mullins-Sweatt and Thomas A. Widiger

The American Psychiatric Association's (APA) Diagnostic and statistical manual of mental disorders – Text Revision (DSM-IV-TR) (APA 2000) conceptualizes personality disorders as sets of traits that are inflexible and maladaptive, deviate markedly from cultural expectations, and cause either functional impairment or subjective distress. Accurate diagnosis of personality disorders can be difficult due to problems in assessment and conceptualization. We begin this chapter with a brief description of the diagnosis of maladaptive personality patterns. We will then discuss the conceptual and methodological issues of an alternative framework for classifying these maladaptive personality patterns, specifically focusing on the Five-Factor Model (FFM) of general personality structure.

DSM-IV-TR personality disorder diagnoses

Generally, maladaptive personality traits are documented by providing one of the ten officially recognized individual personality disorder diagnoses (e.g., schizoid, borderline, antisocial, dependent). For example, the narcissistic personality disorder is diagnosed by determining whether five of nine diagnostic criteria are present. However, identifying the presence of a narcissistic personality disorder does not rule out the presence of additional personality disorder diagnoses. There is a great deal of overlap among the personality disorder diagnoses of DSM-IV-TR, and more importantly, most patients rarely have features of just one personality disorder. Each person appears to have a relatively unique constellation of maladaptive (and adaptive) personality traits. 'When (as is often the case) an individual's pattern of behaviour meets criteria for more than one Personality Disorder, the clinician should list all relevant Personality Disorder diagnoses in order of importance' (APA 2000, p. 686). Research has indicated that when a systematic and comprehensive assessment is conducted, most patients do meet diagnostic criteria for more than one personality disorder (Bornstein 1998; Livesley 2003; Widiger and Trull 1998).

DSM-IV-TR provides relatively specific diagnostic criteria and thresholds for each of the ten officially recognized personality disorders. The provision of these specific guidelines has been tremendously helpful in increasing inter-rater reliability, as clinicians will disagree substantially regarding what features they will consider, how they will weigh them, and what threshold they will use for a personality disorder diagnosis (Mellsop, Varghese, Joshua and Hicks 1982). However, the bases for the DSM-IV-TR diagnostic thresholds have been largely unexplained (Samuel and Widiger 2006). In the absence of any data or rationale to guide the decision of where to set the thresholds, it is hardly surprising to find substantial variation in prevalence rates across each edition of the diagnostic manual (Frances 1998).

Clinicians also have the option of providing the diagnosis of Personality Disorder Not Otherwise Specified (PDNOS). PDNOS is perhaps the most common diagnosis in clinical practice and the most frequent diagnosis when it is considered in empirical studies (Verheul and Widiger 2004). The PDNOS diagnosis can be used to diagnose individuals with several features from more than one personality disorder that 'together cause clinically significant distress or impairment in one or more important areas of functioning (e.g., social or occupational)' (APA 2000, p. 729). For example, it is likely that an individual with only three obsessive-compulsive criteria, but also three avoidant and three dependent criteria, would have as much clinically significant impairment or distress as a person who is above the threshold for an obsessive-compulsive personality disorder diagnosis. The specific title for this PDNOS diagnosis is often given as 'mixed', followed by a specification of the particular features that were present (e.g., 301.9, PDNOS, mixed, with obsessive-compulsive, avoidant and dependent features).

Clinicians may also diagnose a client with PDNOS when they judge 'that a specific Personality Disorder that is not included in the classification is appropriate' (APA 2000, p. 729). This could include diagnoses that had previously received official or unofficial recognition (e.g., sadistic or self-defeating), that currently receive unofficial recognition by being placed within the appendix to DSM-IV-TR for diagnoses needing further research (i.e., depressive or passive-aggressive), or even those that have never received any official or unofficial recognition (e.g., alexithymic, delusional dominating, abusive or aggressive). The availability of this option is in recognition of the fact that DSM-IV-TR fails to cover all of the possible ways in which one might have a personality disorder (Westen and Arkowitz-Westen 1998). If one has a diagnostic term that adequately describes the particular constellation of personality traits, then this term could be provided (e.g., 301.9, PDNOS, sadistic). However, if there is no specific term available for that particular constellation of maladaptive personality traits, then a generic, nondescript term is typically provided (e.g., 301.9, PDNOS, atypical).

Beyond the officially recognized personality disorder diagnoses and the PDNOS category, clinicians can also indicate the presence of specific maladaptive personality traits that together are below the threshold for an officially recognized, mixed, or atypical diagnosis. 'Specific maladaptive personality traits that do not meet the threshold for a Personality Disorder may also be listed on Axis II' (APA 2000, p. 687). In such instances, the code number for the absence of a personality disorder should be provided because the judgement is that there are maladaptive personality traits but no personality disorder is present. One instance in which this occurs is when a person has features of one or more personality disorders that are below the threshold for any one of them and are also below the threshold for a mixed personality disorder. In this instance, the clinician might record, for example V71.09, no diagnosis on Axis II, histrionic and dependent personality traits. A second possibility is when the clinician observes the presence of personality traits that are not included within the ten officially recognized diagnoses. One might record in such an instance V71.09, no diagnosis on Axis II, introverted and overcontrolled personality traits.

DSM-IV-TR also provides general diagnostic criteria for the presence of a personality disorder, included specifically with the intention that they be used by clinicians when providing the PDNOS diagnoses and for distinguishing between maladaptive personality traits and a personality disorder (Frances, First and Pincus 1995). The general diagnostic criteria include the determination of whether there is an enduring pattern of inner experience and behaviour that deviates markedly from the expectations of the individual's culture, and whether this enduring pattern is manifested in two or more of the following ways: (a) cognitively; (b) affectively; (c) interpersonally; and/or (d) through impulse dyscontrol. One must also determine whether the enduring pattern is inflexible and pervasive across a broad range of personal and social situations; whether the enduring pattern leads to clinically significant distress or impairment in social, occupational or other important areas of functioning; whether the enduring pattern is indeed stable, of long duration, and can be traced back at least to adolescence or early adulthood; whether the enduring pattern is not better accounted for as a manifestation or consequence of another mental disorder; and, finally, whether the enduring pattern is due to the direct physiological effects of a substance or a medical condition, such as head trauma. If all of these criteria are met, then a personality disorder diagnosis can be provided.

Personality disorder assessment

Despite the presence of diagnostic criterion sets, much research has suggested that clinicians are not providing reliable diagnoses. Studies have consistently suggested that clinicians fail to consider all of the necessary or important diagnostic criteria, tend to diagnose personality disorders hierarchically (failing to assess additional symptoms once they reach a conclusion that a particular personality disorder is present), and even that clinicians may identify personality disorders based on idiosyncratic preferences (Widiger and Samuel 2005).

However, there are a number of instruments that can be used to obtain reliable and valid personality disorder diagnoses. Most commonly utilized are the semi-structured interviews and self-report inventories. Semi-structured interviews ensure and document that a systematic and comprehensive assessment of each personality disorder diagnostic criterion has been made. Semi-structured interviews also increase the likelihood that a reliable and replicable assessment will occur (Farmer 2000; Rogers 2001, 2003; Segal and Coolidge 2003; Wood, Garb, Lilienfeld and Nezworski 2002) by providing specific, carefully selected questions for the assessment of each diagnostic criterion. In addition, the manuals that accompany a semi-structured interview often provide a considerable amount of helpful information for understanding the rationale of each diagnostic criterion, for interpreting vague or inconsistent symptoms, and for resolving diagnostic ambiguities (e.g., Loranger 1999; Widiger, Mangini, Corbitt, Ellis and Thomas 1995). Some semi-structured interviews cover all of the DSM-IV-TR personality disorders (e.g., Loranger 1999; Widiger, Mangine, Corbitt *et al*. 1995). Others focus on individual personality disorders, such as the Revised Diagnostic Interview for Borderlines (DIB-R) (Zanarini, Gunderson, Frankenburg and Chauncey 1989). None of them are particularly effective at addressing PDNOS cases (Verheul and Widiger 2004).

Clinicians are understandably reluctant to administer an entire semi-structured interview due to the amount of time that is generally required. The complete administration of a semi-structured personality disorder interview generally requires one to two hours, with some as long as four hours (e.g., Loranger 1999). Self-report inventories may be utilized to save time by identifying which sub-set of personality disorders should be emphasized during a subsequent interview. Self-report inventories have the additional advantage of including validity scales that can alert the clinician to response sets, biases and distortions that might compromise the validity of the clinical assessments. Self-report inventories are also useful in alerting clinicians to maladaptive personality functioning that might have otherwise been missed due to false expectations or assumptions (e.g., failing to notice antisocial personality traits in female patients). A further advantage of a well-validated self-report inventory is the presence of normative data to facilitate interpretation. A substantial amount of normative data have been obtained and reported for some of the self-report inventories (e.g., Colligan, Morey and Offord 1992; Costa and McCrae 1994; Millon, Millon and Davis 1997).

Categorical and dimensional classification

The conceptualization of personality disorders in DSM-IV-TR 'represents the categorical perspective that personality disorders are qualitatively distinct clinical syndromes' (APA 2000, p. 689). The categorical perspective implies that there are clear boundaries between normal and abnormal personality, and among the individual diagnoses (Livesley 2003). Such an approach is advantageous to clinicians because categories tend to simplify groups, allowing stereotypic cases to form among the similarities of those in a group. Unfortunately, it is rare that personality disorders are that clear-cut.

Researchers have raised compelling arguments regarding the validity of the categorical model (Trull and Durrett 2005; Widiger and Mullins-Sweatt 2005) and many of the difficulties discussed above (e.g., PDNOS cases) are a result of the categorical method of diagnosis (Widiger and Trull 2007). The APA's DSM-V Research Planning Nomenclature Work Group, charged with addressing the fundamental components of the diagnostic system, reached the conclusion that it is 'important that consideration be given to advantages and disadvantages of basing part or all of DSM-V on dimensions rather than categories' (Rounsaville, Alarcon, Andrews *et al.* 2002, p. 12). They emphasized in particular the development of a dimensional model of personality disorder. 'If a dimensional system of personality performs well and is acceptable to clinicians, it might then be appropriate to explore dimensional approaches in other domains' (Rounsaville *et al.* 2002, p. 13). Toward this end, the APA sponsored an international conference devoted to the development of the research that would optimally direct the field toward a dimensional classification of personality disorder (Widiger and Simonsen 2005).

Existing research has indicated that there are maladaptive personality traits of interest to clinicians that are not included within the diagnostic manual (Verheul and Widiger 2004; Westen and Arkowitz-Westen 1998). Many (if not all) of these additional traits can perhaps be found within instruments that assess general personality structure (Widiger and Simonsen 2005). In addition, clinicians who are concerned with the boundary between normal and abnormal personality functioning might find it useful to include instruments that assess the primary traits of general personality structure.

Alternative dimensional models of personality disorder are being developed because the existing diagnostic constructs lack adequate construct validity (Blashfield and Intoccia 2000; Livesley 2001; Widiger and Mullins-Sweatt 2005). The ultimate goal of a dimensional model of personality disorder would not then be simply to reproduce the diagnostic categories of DSM-IV-TR. Some of the alternative dimensional models of personality disorder have developed proposals for how the diagnosis of a personality disorder could be made from the perspective of that particular model (Clark 2007; Trull 2005).

Five-Factor Model and personality disorders

The Five-Factor Model (FFM) is the predominant model of personality in a number of applied fields, including health psychology, aging and developmental research (McCrae and Costa 2003). The FFM was derived originally from studies of the English language to identify those traits that are most significant in describing oneself and other persons (Digman 1990). Studies of English and many other languages have generally supported the identification of five broad domains of personality: Extraversion (surgency or positive affectivity) vs. Introversion, Agreeableness vs. antagonism, Conscientiousness vs. undependability, Neuroticism (emotional instability or negative affectivity) vs. emotional stability, and Openness (intellect or unconventionality) vs. closedness to experience (Ashton and Lee 2001). Each of these five broad domains has been differentiated into six more specific facets by Costa and McCrae (1995).

Empirical support for the FFM has been extensive, including convergent-discriminant validity across self-, peer-, and spouse-ratings, temporal stability, generalizability across age, gender and culture, and heritability (Mullins-Sweatt and Widiger 2006). The FFM has also been shown to be useful in predicting important life outcomes such as happiness, physical and psychological health, longevity and occupational satisfaction (Ozer and Benet-Martínez 2006). In sum, there is a scientific foundation for construct validity that is well beyond what is evident for the personality disorder diagnostic constructs (Blashfield and Intoccia 2000; Widiger and Trull 2007).

Research studies examining relations between DSM personality disorders and measures of normal-range personality, including the FFM, have revealed that the domains of normal and abnormal personality are largely overlapping (O'Connor 2002). Well over fifty studies have supported an understanding of DSM-IV-TR personality disorders from the FFM perspective (Clark 2007; O'Connor 2005; Ostendorf 2000; Saulsman and Page 2004; Widiger and Costa 2002). In a meta-analysis examining fifteen independent samples, Saulsman and Page (2004, p. 1075) concluded that 'each of the personality disorders shows associations with the five-factor model that are meaningful and predictable given their diagnostic criteria'. On the basis of his review of the research Livesley (2001, p. 24) concluded, 'multiple studies provide convincing evidence that the DSM personality disorders diagnoses show a systematic relationship to the five-factors and that all categorical diagnoses of DSM can be accommodated within the five-factor framework'.

Widiger, Costa and McCrae (2002) have proposed a four-step procedure for the diagnosis of a personality disorder from the perspective of the FFM. The first step is to provide a comprehensive assessment of personality functioning with an existing measure of the FFM. There are quite a few alternative FFM instruments (De Raad and Perugini 2002) but the NEO PI-R is the most commonly used in clinical practice (Costa and McCrae 1992). The NEO PI-R can be used to provide a reasonably comprehensive description of normal personality traits and to alert clinicians to the potential presence of particular maladaptive personality traits. Many of the NEO PI-R scales refer explicitly to maladaptive personality functioning (e.g., vulnerability, anxiousness and impulsiveness). However, the NEO PI-R might provide somewhat less representation of maladaptive variants of high Agreeableness, high Conscientiousness and high Openness, relative to its representation of the maladaptive variants of low Agreeableness, low Conscientiousness and low Openness (Haigler and Widiger 2001). There is also a semi-structured interview for the assessment of the FFM that is coordinated explicitly with the NEO PI-R (Trull and Widiger 2002). This interview attempts to provide somewhat more representation of maladaptive variants of each of the five domains.

The second step is to identify the social and occupational impairments and distress that might be associated with the individual's characteristic personality traits (Widiger, Trull, Clarkin et al. 2002). A misconception of the FFM is that low Neuroticism, high Extraversion, high Openness, high Agreeableness and high Conscientiousness always imply adaptive personality functioning (Coker, Samuel and Widiger 2002). Widiger *et al.* (2002) and McCrae, Lockenhoff and Costa (2005) identify common impairments associated with each of the sixty poles of the thirty facets of the FFM.

The third step of the FFM diagnosis is to determine whether the dysfunction and distress reach a clinically significant level of impairment. Among the general diagnostic criteria for a DSM-IV-TR personality disorder is the requirement that 'the enduring pattern leads to clinically significant distress or impairment in social, occupational, or other important areas of functioning' (APA 2000, p. 689). Axis V of DSM-IV-TR can be used to provide a quantitative rating scale for this judgement where the clinician is instructed to 'consider psychological, social, and occupational functioning on a hypothetical continuum of mental health-illness' (APA 2000, p. 34). The FFM procedure for determining when a personality disorder diagnosis should be provided is that point at which the social and occupational impairments or personal distress would achieve a score of 60 or below on this axis. This point of demarcation is arbitrary in that it does not carve nature at a discrete joint but it is a reasonable threshold for a clinically significant level of impairment that can be consistently applied across patients and disorders (Hilsenroth, Ackerman, Blagys *et al.* 2000).

The fourth step is a quantitative matching of the individual's personality profile to prototypic profiles of theoretically, socially or clinically important diagnostic constructs. This step is provided for clinicians and researchers who would like to continue to provide or study single diagnostic labels that describe prototypic cases to characterize personality profiles. One of the perceived advantages of a categorical model is the ability to summarize a particular constellation of maladaptive personality traits with a single diagnostic label. 'There is an economy of communication and vividness of description in a categorical name that may be lost in a dimensional profile' (Frances 1993, p. 110), and there can be constellations of personality traits that may have particular theoretical significance, clinical interest or social implications, such as the borderline FFM profile (Trull, Widiger, Lynam and Costa 2003) or the psychopathic (Lynam 2002). The extent to which an individual's FFM profile matches the FFM profile for a prototypic case can be used as a quantitative indication of the likelihood that a person fits the profile for that construct, as illustrated for borderline personality disorder by Trull *et al.* (2003) and for psychopathy by Miller and Lynam (2003).

An additional advantage of the FFM method of diagnosis is that clinicians and researchers can develop FFM profiles for constructs that are not currently included within the diagnostic manual. Idiosyncratic constellations of personality traits are addressed well by a dimensional profile of the individual in terms of the thirty facets of the FFM (Costa and McCrae 1992). Clinicians and researchers interested in studying diagnostic constructs that are outside the existing nomenclature (e.g., the successful psychopath; Lynam 2002) can use the FFM to provide a reasonably specific description of a new clinical construct and use the prototypal matching methodology to empirically study it.

The purpose of the FFM of personality disorder, though, is not simply to provide another means with which to return to a single diagnostic label (Clark 2007), such as borderline (Trull, Goodwin, Schopp *et al.* 1993), psychopath (Miller and Lynam 2003), or successful psychopath (Lynam 2002). In most cases the quantitative matching will serve primarily to indicate the extent to which any single construct (e.g., borderline) is inadequately descriptive of the individual person. We expect that in the vast majority of cases, the optimal description will be provided by the actual FFM profile of the person rather than a profile of a hypothetical prototype or the extent to which the person's FFM profile resembles this prototype.

References

American Psychiatric Association 2000. *Diagnostic and statistical manual of mental disorders – Text Revision*, 4th edn. Washington, DC: APA

Ashton, M. C. and Lee, K. 2001. A theoretical basis for the major dimensions of personality, *European Journal of Personality* 15: 327–53

Blashfield, R. K. and Intoccia, V. 2000. Growth of the literature on the topic of personality disorders, *American Journal of Psychiatry* 157: 472–3

Bornstein, R. F. 1998. Reconceptualizing personality disorder diagnosis in the DSM-V: the discriminant validity challenge, *Clinical Psychology: Science and Practice* 5: 333–43

Clark, L. A. 2007. Assessment and diagnosis of personality disorder: perennial issues and an emerging reconceptualization, *Annual Review of Psychology* 58: 227–57

Coker, L. A., Samuel, D. B. and Widiger, T. A. 2002. Maladaptive personality functioning within the Big Five and the Five-Factor Model, *Journal of Personality Disorders* 16: 385–401

Colligan, R. C., Morey, L. C. and Offord, K. P. 1994. MMPI/MMPI-2 personality disorder scales: contemporary norms for adults and adolescents, *Journal of Clinical Psychology* 50: 168–200

Costa, P. T., Jr and McCrae, R. R. 1992. *The NEO PI-R professional manual*. Odessa, FL: Psychological Assessment Resources

1995. Domains and facets: hierarchical personality assessment using the Revised NEO Personality Inventory, *Journal of Personality Assessment* 64: 21–50

De Raad, B. and Perugini, M. 2002. *Big Five Assessment*. Ashland, OH: Hogrefe and Huber Publishers

Digman, J. M. 1990. Personality structure: emergence of the Five-Factor Model, *Annual Review of Psychology* 41: 417–70

Farmer, R. F. 2000. Issues in the assessment and conceptualization of personality disorders, *Clinical Psychology Review* 20: 823–51

Frances, A. J. 1993. Dimensional diagnosis of personality: not whether, but when and which, *Psychological Inquiry* 4: 110–11

1998. Problems in defining clinical significance in epidemiological studies, *Archives of General Psychiatry* 55: 119

Frances, A. J., First, M. B. and Pincus, H. A. 1995. *DSM-IV Guidebook*. Washington, DC: American Psychiatric Press

Haigler, E. D. and Widiger, T. A. 2001. Experimental manipulation of NEO PI-R items, *Journal of Personality Assessment* 77: 339–58

Hilsenroth, M. J., Ackerman, S. J., Blagys, M. D., Baumann, B. D., Baity, M. R., Smith, S. R., Price, J. L., Smith, C. L., Heindselman, T. L., Mount, M. K. and Holdwick, D. 2000. Reliability and validity of DSM-IV axis V, *American Journal of Psychiatry* 157: 1858–63

Livesley, W. J. 2001. Conceptual and taxonomic issues, in W. J. Livesley (ed.), *Handbook of personality disorders: theory, research, and treatment*, pp. 3–38. New York: Guilford Press

    2003. Diagnostic dilemmas in classifying personality disorder, in K. A. Phillips, M. B. First and H. A. Pincus (eds.), *Advancing DSM: dilemmas in psychiatric diagnosis*, pp. 153–90. Washington, DC: American Psychiatric Association

Loranger, A. W. 1999. *International personality disorder examination (IPDE)*. Odessa, FL: Psychological Assessment Resources

Lynam, D. R. 2002. Fledgling psychopathy: a view from personality theory, *Law and Human Behavior* 26: 255–9

McCrae, R. R. and Costa, P. T. 2003. *Personality in adulthood: a five-factor theory perspective*, 2nd edn. New York: Guilford Press

McCrae, R. R., Lockenhoff, C. E. and Costa, P. T., Jr 2005. A step toward DSM-V: cataloguing personality-related problems in living, *European Journal of Personality* 19: 269–86

Mellsop, G., Varghese, F. T. N., Joshua, S. and Hicks, A. 1982. The reliability of Axis II of DSM-III, *American Journal of Psychiatry* 139: 1360–1

Miller, J. D. and Lynam, D. R. 2003. Psychopathy and the Five-Factor Model of personality: a replication and extension, *Journal of Personality Assessment* 81: 168–78

Millon, T., Millon, C. and Davis, R. 1997. *MCMI-III manual*, 2nd edn. Minneapolis, MN: National Computer Systems

Morey, L. C. 1988. Personality disorders under DSM-III and DSM-III-R: an examination of convergence, coverage, and internal consistency, *American Journal of Psychiatry* 145: 573–7

Mullins-Sweatt, S. N. and Widiger, T. A. 2006. The Five-Factor Model of personality disorder: a translation across science and practice, in R. F. Krueger and J. L. Tackett (eds), *Personality and psychopathology: building bridges*, pp. 39–70. New York: Guilford Publications

O'Connor, B. P. 2002. A quantitative review of the comprehensiveness of the Five-Factor Model in relation to popular personality inventories, *Assessment* 9: 188–203

    2005. A search for consensus on the dimensional structure of personality disorders, *Journal of Clinical Psychology* 61: 323–45

Ostendorf, F. 2000. Personality disorders and the Five-Factor Model of personality: a meta-analysis, *European Psychiatry* 15: 226S–227S

Ozer, D. J. and Benet-Martínez, V. 2006. Personality and the prediction of consequential outcomes, *Annual Review of Psychology* 57: 401–21

Rogers, R. 2001. *Diagnostic and structured interviewing: a handbook for psychologists*. New York: Guilford Publications

    2003. Standardizing DSM-IV diagnoses: the clinical applications of structured interviews, *Journal of Personality Assessment* 81: 220–5

Rounsaville, B. J., Alarcon, R. D., Andrews, G., Jackson, J. S., Kendell, R. E. and Kendler, K. 2002. Basic nomenclature issues for DSM-V, in D. J. Kupfer, M. B. First and D. E. Regier (eds.), *A research agenda for DSM-V*, pp. 1–29. Washington, DC: American Psychiatric Press

Samuel, D. B. and Widiger, T. A. 2006. Clinicians' judgments of clinical utility: a comparison of the DSM-IV and Five Factor Models, *Journal of Abnormal Psychology* 115: 298–308

Saulsman, L. M. and Page, A. C. 2004. The Five-Factor Model and personality disorder empirical literature: a meta-analytic review, *Clinical Psychology Review* 23: 1055–85

Segal, D. L. and Coolidge, F. L. 2003. Structured interviewing and DSM classification, in M. Hersen and S. Turner (eds.), *Adult psychopathology and diagnosis*, 4th edn, pp. 72–103. New York: John Wiley and Sons

Trull, T. J. 2005. Dimensional models of personality disorder: coverage and cutoffs, *Journal of Personality Disorders* 19: 262–82

Trull, T. J., Goodwin, A. H., Schopp, L. H., Hillenbrand, T. L. and Schuster, T. 1993. Psychometric properties of a cognitive measure of personality disorders, *Journal of Personality Assessment* 61: 536–46

Trull, T. J. and Durrett, C. A. 2005. Categorical and dimensional models of personality disorder, *Annual Review of Clinical Psychology* 1: 355–80

Trull, T. J. and Widiger, T. A. 2002. The structured interview for the Five Factor Model of personality, in B. De Raad and M. Perugini (eds.), *Big Five assessment*, pp. 147–70. Bern: Hogrefe and Huber

Trull, T. J., Widiger, T. A., Lynam, D. R. and Costa, P. T. 2003. Borderline personality disorder from the perspective of general personality functioning, *Journal of Abnormal Psychology* 112: 193–202

Verheul, R. and Widiger, T. A. 2004. A meta-analysis of the prevalence and usage of the personality disorder not otherwise specified (PDNOS) diagnosis, *Journal of Personality Disorders* 18: 309–19

Westen, D. and Arkowitz-Westen, L. 1998. Limitations of Axis II in diagnosing personality pathology in clinical practice, *American Journal of Psychiatry* 155: 1767–71

Widiger, T. A. and Costa, P. T. 2002. Five-Factor Model personality disorder research, in T. A. Widiger and P. T. Costa (eds.) *Personality disorders and the Five-Factor Model of personality*, 2nd edn, pp. 59–87. Washington, DC: American Psychological Association

Widiger, T. A., Costa, P. T. and McCrae, R. R. 2002. A proposal for Axis II: diagnosing personality disorders using the Five-Factor Model, in T. A. Widiger and P. T. Costa (eds.), *Personality disorders and the Five-Factor Model of personality*, 2nd edn, pp. 431–56. Washington, DC: American Psychological Association

Widiger, T. A., Mangine, S., Corbitt, E. M., Ellis, C. G. and Thomas, G. V. 1995. *Personality disorder interview-IV: a semistructured interview for the assessment of personality disorders*. Odessa, FL: Psychological Assessment Resources

Widiger, T. A. and Mullins-Sweatt, S. N. 2005. Categorical and dimensional models of personality disorder, in J. M. Oldham, A. E. Skodol and D. S. Bender (eds.), *The American Psychiatric Publishing textbook of personality disorder*, pp. 35–53. Arlington, VA: American Psychiatric Publishing

Widiger, T. A. and Samuel, D. B. 2005. Evidence based assessment of personality disorders, *Psychological Assessment* 17: 278–87

Widiger, T. A. and Simonsen, E. 2005. Alternative dimensional models of personality disorder: finding a common ground, *Journal of Personal Disorder* 19: 110–30

Widiger, T. A. and Trull, T. J. 1998. Performance characteristics of the DSM-III-R personality disorder criteria sets, in T. A. Widiger, A. J. Frances, H. A. Pincus, R. Ross, M. B. First, W. W. Davis and M. Klein (eds.), *DSM-IV sourcebook*, vol. IV, pp. 357–73. Washington, DC: American Psychiatric Association

 2007. Plate tectonics in the classification of personality disorder: shifting to a dimensional model, *American Psychologist* 62: 71–83

Widiger, T. A., Trull, T. J., Clarkin, J. F., Sanderson, C. and Costa, P. T. 2002. A description of the DSM-IV personality disorders with the Five-Factor Model of personality, in P. T. Costa and T. A. Widiger (eds.), *Personality disorders and the Five-Factor Model of personality*, 2nd edn, pp. 89–99. Washington, DC: American Psychological Association

Wood, J. M., Garb, H. N., Lilienfeld, S. O. and Nezworski, M. T. 2002. Clinical assessment, *Annual Review of Psychology* 53: 519–43

Zanarini, M. C., Gunderson, J. G., Frankerburg, F. R. and Chauncey, D. 1989. The revised diagnostic interview for borderlines: discriminating BPD from other Axis II disorders, *Journal of Personality Disorders* 3: 10–18

38 Psychopathy and its measurement

Robert D. Hare and Craig S. Neumann

The modern conception of psychopathy is the result of several hundred years of clinical investigation by European and North American psychiatrists and psychologists (Berrios 1996; Cleckley 1941/1976; Coid 1993; Hare and Schalling 1978; Hervé 2007; Millon, Simonsen, Birket-Smith and Davis 1998). In North America the writings of Arieti (1967), Karpman (1961) and McCord and McCord (1964), among others, and the case studies of Cleckley (1941/1976) were particularly important for providing detailed clinical descriptions of psychopathy as well as speculations and theories concerning the nature of the disorder. These early-to-mid-twentieth century clinical accounts typically had a psychodynamic orientation and were little concerned with measurement issues. Researchers had a variety of personality scales that purported to measure psychopathy, but most were unrelated to one another and all lacked evidence of validity (see Hare 1985). The need for psychometrically-sound tools for assessing psychopathy became painfully evident at a 1975 NATO Advanced Study Institute (ASI) in Les Arcs, France, directed by the senior author (Hare and Schalling 1978). Ten days of heated and unproductive debate about potential operational definitions of psychopathy no doubt played an important role in the subsequent development of the Psychopathy Checklist (PCL) (Hare 1980) and the DSM-III (American Psychiatric Association 1980) criteria for antisocial personality disorder (see Hare and Neumann 2006 for details). The PCL combined personality traits and antisocial behaviours whereas the emphasis in antisocial personality disorder was, and continues to be, antisocial behaviour (see Hare 2003; Ogloff 2006; Widiger, Cadoret, Hare *et al.* 1996).

The PCL represented early attempts by the senior author to devise a reliable, valid and generally accepted tool for the assessment of psychopathy. It was adopted by many researchers and clinicians, resulting in a substantial body of replicated, theoretically-meaningful, empirical findings. Its successor, the Psychopathy Checklist-Revised (PCL-R) (Hare 1991/2003), rapidly gained widespread acceptance as the standard for reliable and valid assessments of psychopathy in research and applied contexts (e.g., Acheson 2005; Fulero 1995). The result has been the accumulation of a very large body of theoretical and empirical work, both basic and applied (e.g., Book, Clarke, Forth and Hare 2006; Felthous and Saß 2007; Hare 2003, 2007; Hare and Neumann 2006; Hervé and Yuille 2007; Patrick 2006). The

This chapter is adapted or reprinted, with permission, from material presented by Hare (2007) and Hare and Neumann (2005, 2008, 2009). We thank Kylie Neufeld for her help in preparing the manuscript.

popularity and importance of the PCL-R and its derivatives (see below) for basic and applied research have led to many reviews, unusually intensive conceptual and statistical scrutiny, and occasional concerns that the 'measure has become the construct'. These and related issues, including the transition from clinical to empirical conceptions of psychopathy and the overreliance of some researchers and clinicians on early conceptualizations of psychopathy, are discussed in detail elsewhere (Hare and Neumann 2008).

In this chapter, we discuss some of the recent theory and research on the measurement and structure of psychopathy, with emphasis on the PCL-R and its direct derivatives: the Psychopathy Checklist: Screening Version (PCL: SV) (Hart, Cox and Hare 1995) and the Psychopathy Checklist: Youth Version (PCL: YV) (Forth, Kosson and Hare 2003). For convenience, we refer to these three instruments as the 'PCL scales', each of which conceptualizes psychopathy in terms of four interrelated dimensions, labelled Interpersonal, Affective, Lifestyle and Antisocial. We only briefly describe several other instruments: the Antisocial Process Screening Device (APSD) (Frick and Hare 2001), used in recent research on genetic and longitudinal factors related to psychopathy; several self-report measures of psychopathy; and two related constructs, one described in the American Psychiatric Association's *Diagnostic and statistical manual of mental disorders* (DSM-IV) (American Psychiatric Association 1994), and the other in the tenth edition of the *International classification of diseases and related disorders* (ICD-10) (World Health Organization 1990).

PCL-R

Recent reviews of the development of the PCL-R and its psychometric and structural properties are available elsewhere, and provide the basis for much of the discussion in this article (e.g., Hare 2003; Hare and Neumann 2005, 2006, 2008, 2009). Briefly, the PCL-R is a twenty-item clinical construct rating scale that uses a semi-structured interview, case history information, and specific scoring criteria to rate each item on a three-point scale (0, 1, 2) according to the extent to which it applies to a given individual. In some cases, this 'standard' procedure (interview plus file information) is replaced by a 'non-standard' procedure, in which only file information is used to score the items. The items and the factors they comprise (see below) are listed in Table 38.1. Total scores can range from zero to 40 and reflect the degree to which the individual matches the prototypical psychopathic individual. Internal consistency and inter-rater reliability generally are high. Although the PCL-R yields dimensional scores (see below), it is also used to 'classify' individuals for research and clinical purposes. In North America a PCL-R cut score of 30 for psychopathy has proven useful for research and applied purposes. For convenience, we refer to individuals with scores this high as *psychopaths*. Other cut scores may be used by other investigators and authors, depending on the purpose of the assessments and the context in which

Table 38.1 *Items and factors in the Hare PCL-R.*

Interpersonal	**Affective**
1. Glibness/superficial charm	6. Lack of remorse
2. Grandiose self-worth	7. Shallow affect
4. Pathological lying	8. Lack of empathy
5. Conning/manipulative	16. Will not accept responsibility
Lifestyle	**Antisocial**
3. Need for stimulation	10. Poor behavioural controls
9. Parasitic lifestyle	12. Early behavioural problems
13. Lack of goals	18. Juvenile delinquency
14. Impulsivity	19. Revocation conditional release
15. Irresponsibility	20. Criminal versatility

Note: The items are from Hare (1991, 2003). Note that the item titles cannot be scored without reference to the formal criteria contained in the PCL-R Manual. Item 11, Promiscuous sexual behaviour, and Item 17, Many short-term marital relationships, contribute to the Total PCL-R score but do not load on any factors. The Interpersonal and Affective factors underpin a broad factor identical with the original Factor 1 described in the 1991 Manual. The Lifestyle and Antisocial factors underpin a broad factor identical with the original Factor 2 described in the 1991 Manual, but with the addition of item 20.

they are used. In each case, however, the term psychopath implies a heavy concentration of psychopathic features.

PCL: SV

The PCL: SV consists of twelve items derived from the PCL-R, each scored on a three-point scale (0, 1, 2) on the basis of interview and collateral information that is less extensive than that required for scoring the PCL-R. Total scores can vary from 0 to 24. It is conceptually and empirically related to the PCL-R (Cooke, Michie, Hart and Hare 1999; Guy and Douglas 2006), and can be used as an effective screen for psychopathy in forensic populations (Guy and Douglas 2006) or as a stand-alone instrument for research with non-criminals, including civil psychiatric patients (De Oliveira-Souza, Ignácio, Moll and Hare 2008; Steadman, Silver, Monahan *et al.* 2000). Its psychometric properties and four-factor structure (see Table 38.2) are virtually the same as those of the PCL-R (Hill, Neumann and Rogers 2004; Vitacco, Neumann and Jackson 2005). There is rapidly accumulating evidence for the construct validity of the PCL: SV, including its ability to predict aggression and violence in offenders and in both forensic and civil psychiatric patients (see below). In this respect, the correlates of the PCL: SV are much the same as those of the PCL-R. A cut score of 18 is approximately equivalent to a PCL-R score of 30.

Table 38.2 *Items and factors in the Hare PCL: SV.*

Interpersonal	Affective
1. Superficial	4. Lacks remorse
2. Grandiose	5. Lacks empathy
3. Deceitful	6. Doesn't accept responsibility
Lifestyle	**Antisocial**
7. Impulsive	8. Poor behavioural controls
9. Lacks goals	11. Adolescent antisocial behaviour
10. Irresponsibility	12. Adult antisocial behaviour

Note: The items are from Hart, Cox and Hare (1995). Note that the item titles cannot be scored without reference to the formal criteria contained in the PCL:SV Manual.

PCL: YV

The PCL: YV (Forth, Kosson and Hare 2003) is an age-appropriate modification of the PCL-R intended for use with adolescents. Like the PCL-R, it consists of twenty items and four factors (Jones, Cauffman, Miller and Mulvey 2006; Neumann, Kosson, Forth and Hare 2006). The items and factors are presented in Table 38.3. It appears to have much the same psychometric properties and much the same correlates as its adult counterpart (see Book, Clark, Forth and Hare 2006; Salekin, Neumann, Leistico *et al.* 2004; Vitacco, Neumann, Caldwell *et al.* 2006). Like the PCL-R, it appears to generalize well across ethnic groups and countries (e.g., Book *et al.* 2006; Dolan and Rennie 2006; McCoy and Edens 2006; Schrum and Salekin 2006). Although there is little doubt about the reliability and validity of the PCL: YV, concerns arise with respect to its use in the criminal justice system. The main issues have to do with: (1) the dangers of labelling an adolescent as a psychopath; (2) the implications of the PCL: YV for classification, sentencing and treatment; (3) the possibility that some features measured by the PCL: YV are found in normally developing youth; and (4) the degree of stability of psychopathy-related traits from late childhood to early adulthood. Extensive discussions of these issues are available elsewhere (e.g., Book *et al.* 2006; Forth and Book 2007; Frick 2007; Frick and Marsee 2006; Lynam and Gudonis 2005; Salekin 2006; Vitacco and Vincent 2006). Briefly, although psychopathy and its features do not suddenly emerge in early adulthood, it nonetheless should not be used to diagnose someone as psychopathic. Although some adolescents may exhibit some features of psychopathy in certain contexts or for a limited time, a high score on the PCL: YV requires evidence that the traits and behaviours are extreme and that they are manifested across social contexts and over substantial time periods. Lynam and Gudonis (2005, pp. 401–2), following their review of the literature, commented that:

> psychopathy in juveniles looks much like psychopathy in adults. The same traits characterize these individuals at different developmental time points. Additionally, juvenile psychopathy acts like adult psychopathy. Like their adult

Table 38.3 *Items and factors in the Hare PCL: YV.*

Interpersonal	Affective
1. Impression management	6. Lack of remorse
2. Grandiose sense of self-worth	7. Shallow affect
4. Pathological lying	8. Callous/lack of empathy
5. Manipulation for personal gain	16. Will not accept responsibility
Behavioural	**Antisocial**
3. Need for stimulation	10. Poor anger control
9. Parasitic orientation	12. Early behavioural problems
13. Lack of goals	18. Serious criminal behaviour
14. Impulsivity	19. Serious violations of release
15. Irresponsibility	20. Criminal versatility

Note: The items are from Forth, Kosson and Hare (2003). Note that the item titles cannot be scored without reference to the formal criteria contained in the PCL: YV Manual. Item 11, Impersonal sexual behaviour, and Item 17, Unstable interpersonal relationships, contribute to the total PCL: YV score but do not load on any factors.

counterparts, psychopathic juveniles are serious and stable offenders. They are prone to externalizing disorders ... as far as has been observed, juvenile psychopathy appears quite stable across adolescence. All of these findings replicate those observed in studies using psychopathic adults.

Antisocial Process Screening Device

The Antisocial Process Screening Device (APSD) (Frick and Hare 2001) is a teacher/parent rating scale for use with children from six to thirteen years of age. It consists of twenty scaled items that measure three dimensions of behaviour thought to be precursors to psychopathic traits: Callous/Unemotional (CU), Narcissism and Impulsivity. Research with the APSD is increasing rapidly, with considerable evidence that CU traits in particular are related to a variety of disruptive behaviours, and are relatively stable over three or four year periods (Dadds, Fraser, Frost and Hawes 2005; Frick and Marsee 2006). An expanded version of the CU traits measured by the APSD is now available as *The Inventory of Callous-Unemotional Traits* (Essau, Sasagawa and Frick 2006).

Self-report measures

Self-report psychopathy scales are beginning to broaden the repertoire of available assessment tools, and show promise of helping us to understand better the construct they purport to measure. These include the Psychopathy Personality Inventory (PPI) (Lilienfeld and Andrews 1996); the Youth Psychopathic Traits

Inventory (YPI) (Andershed, Kerr, Stattin and Levander 2002); the Child Psychopathy Scale (CPS) (Lynam 1998; Lynam and Gudonis 2005); and the experimental four-factor version of the Self-Report Psychopathy (SRP) scale (Williams, Paulhus and Hare 2007). These scales are moderately correlated with the PCL instruments. Omnibus personality inventories, including the Multidimensional Personality Questionnaire (MPQ) (Tellegen in press) and the various instruments used in the Five-Factor Model (FFM) of personality (Costa and McCrae 1992; Costa and Widiger 2002; Lynam 2002), are also proving useful in the application of general personality theory in the study of psychopathy. Recent empirical research indicates that self-report psychopathy scales have moderate predictive validity with respect to recidivism (e.g., Boccaccini, Epstein, Poythress *et al.* 2007; Lilienfeld and Fowler 2006). The SRP-III scale is a significant predictor of a variety of unethical and antisocial behaviours in college students (Nathanson, Paulhus and Williams 2006; Williams, Paulhus and Hare 2007).

There are several advantages and disadvantages to using specialized and general scales of this sort for the study of psychopathy (Lilienfeld and Fowler 2006; Westen and Weinberger 2004). They make it possible to use very large samples, in both forensic and other populations, and to extend to the general population some of the research paradigms found useful in experimental/laboratory research with forensic populations. Further, by viewing psychopathy from different perspectives, including that of the individual under study (self-reports), these scales may lead to a more complete and accurate conceptualization of the construct when combined with other measures. And, of course, they also make the researcher's task much easier, because most of the assessment work is done by the study participants, who provide their own managed view of themselves.

However, we should recognize that psychopathic individuals are particularly prone to impression management (Cooper and Yuille 2007). We also should take pains to ensure that the putative construct under investigation really is what we think it is. As Rutter (2005, p. 500) put it in his commentary on a special journal issue on adolescent psychopathy, some of the core features of psychopathy 'may not be best represented by scores on personality dimensions that are designed to pick up rather different features'.

ICD-10 and DSM-IV

The attributes measured by the PCL-R are similar in many respects to the diagnostic criteria for dissocial personality disorder listed in ICD-10 (Huchzenmeir, Geiger, Bruß *et al.* 2007; Ullrich and Marneros 2004; Widiger, Cadoret, Hare *et al.* 1996). However, they differ in important ways from the criteria for antisocial personality disorder (APD) contained in DSM-IV (American Psychiatric Association 1994) and the DSM-IV Text Revision (APA 2000). The diagnostic criteria for APD reflect the assumptions that it is difficult for clinicians to assess personality traits reliably, and that early-onset delinquency is a cardinal symptom of the disorder (Robins 1978).

These assumptions account for the heavy emphasis on delinquent and antisocial behaviour in the criteria for APD (Hare 2003; Hare and Neumann 2006; Rogers, Salekin, Sewell and Cruise 2000; Widiger *et al*. 1996). In forensic populations the prevalence of APD is much higher than the prevalence of psychopathy, resulting in an asymmetric association between the PCL-R and APD. In this respect, it is noteworthy that APD is more strongly associated with the PCL-R lifestyle and antisocial factors than with the PCL-R interpersonal and affective factors. Most psychopaths meet the criteria for APD, but most of the offenders with APD are not psychopaths. Yet, DSM-IV says that APD 'has also been referred to as psychopathy' (2000, p. 655), effectively equating the two constructs. The Associated Features and Disorders section for APD (both in DSM-IV and in the DSM-IV Text Revision; APA 2000) compounds the problem by suggesting that in forensic populations the diagnosis of APD may be facilitated by assessing traits and behaviours imported (without attribution or scoring instructions) from the ten-item Psychopathy Criteria Set that my colleagues and I had derived from the PCL-R and PCL: SV for use in the DSM-IV Field Trial for APD (Widiger *et al*. 1996). Had these imported traits been *required* for a diagnosis of APD, rather than being made optional in forensic contexts, the relation between psychopathy and APD would have been strengthened. Rogers *et al*. (2000, pp. 236–7) had this to say about the situation: 'As noted by Hare (1998), DSM-IV does considerable disservice to diagnostic clarity in its equating of APD to psychopathy'; or, as Lykken (2006, p. 4) put it, 'Identifying someone as "having" APD is about as nonspecific and scientifically unhelpful as diagnosing a sick patient as having a fever or an infectious or a neurological disorder'.

Far from being identical with APD, the construct of psychopathy seems to emerge from the confluence of multiple domains from personality pathology. For example, two large-scale empirical studies (Livesley, Jang and Vernon 1998, Ullrich and Marneros 2007) and a comprehensive review of personality disorder research (Trull and Durrett 2005) suggest that a superordinate factor reflecting dissociality/psychopathy emerges when symptoms of all personality disorders are factor analysed. A study by Livesley *et al*. (1998) is noteworthy in that use of a dimensional measure of personality disorder symptoms resulted in the same factor solution across large twin, clinical and general population samples. The psychopathy factor was composed of the following personality disorder items: callousness, conduct problems, narcissism, rejection and stimulus seeking. In an ICD-10 study by Ullrich and Marneros (2007), dimensionalized personality disorder symptoms resulted in a factor made up of the dissocial, paranoid, histrionic and impulsive traits, and was the only ICD-10 PD factor (out of three) that was strongly correlated ($r = .77$) with the PCL: SV. Based on other ICD-10 research, Ullrich and Marneros (2004, pp. 211–12) had this to say:

> Although suggestions to replace [APD] in DSM-IV with the construct of psychopathy were previously rejected, its importance within forensic contexts is established. Against the background of our findings, we conclude that specific dimensions of personality disorders are strongly interrelated and show remarkable similarities to the personality features constituting psychopathy.

A similar conclusion was drawn by Livesley and Schroeder (1991). The PCL-R and its derivatives do *not* measure the same construct as does APD, either in males or in females (Warren and South 2006).

This matter is of more than academic interest. In the criminal justice system the role of the PCL-R and its derivatives in conducting risk assessments and recommending treatment options is well known. Indeed, the literature on risk assessment is now so large that the findings are commonly summarized with meta-analyses (e.g., Leistico, Salekin, DeCoster and Rogers 2008). It would be unfortunate if a forensic clinician equates APD with psychopathy and then uses the PCL-R literature to draw conclusions about the individual's treatability and risk for reoffending.

Structural models of the PCL-R

The study of any psychological construct relies on a clear delineation of its underlying dimensionality. Understanding its dimensionality helps to interpret scores on a measure of the construct and the pattern of correlations between the dimensions and relevant external variables. Structural equation modelling (SEM) provides a powerful multivariate statistical approach for testing hypotheses about the underlying dimensionality of latent psychological constructs (Barnes, Murray, Patton *et al.* 2000; Bollen 2002; Borsboom, Mellenbergh and van Heerden 2003). A special case of SEM is confirmatory factor analysis (CFA).

Prior to the development of rigorous statistical approaches such as SEM, early exploratory factor analysis (EFA) indicated that two correlated dimensions underpinned both the twenty-two-item PCL scale that preceded the PCL-R (Harpur, Hare and Hakstian 1989) and the twenty-item PCL-R (Hare, Harpur, Hakstian *et al.* 1990; see Hare 2003). Factor 1 of the PCL-R consisted of eight 'interpersonal and affective' items (1, 2, 4, 5, 6, 7, 8 and 16), and Factor 2 consisted of nine 'socially deviant' items (3, 9, 10, 12, 13, 14, 15, 18 and 19). Three items (11, 17 and 20) did not load on either factor. Although this factor structure has been replicated several times, a review of the EFA studies (Neumann, Kosson and Salekin 2007) suggested that a more fine-grained parsing of the two-factor PCL model is possible, and investigators have recently opted to use confirmatory factor analysis and other multivariate statistical tools to provide rigorous tests of new structural models of psychopathy. Using a combination of cluster analysis, item response theory (see below), CFA, and subjective decisions, Cooke and Michie (2001) developed what they referred to as a three factor model of psychopathy consisting of thirteen selected PCL-R items. However, the model actually contains six first-order factors (testlets), three second-order factors, and a single third-order factor. Thus, this hierarchical model requires ten factors to model thirteen items. According to Cooke and Michie the retained items lie within the realm of personality and form the core of psychopathy, whereas the excluded items reflect antisociality. It is difficult to understand how the items they retained (e.g., pathological lying, irresponsibility) are any less antisocial than items excluded (e.g., early behaviour problems, poor behavioural controls). In-depth critiques of the conceptual, empirical and statistical problems are available elsewhere (Hare and Neumann 2006; Neumann and Hare 2007; Neumann 2007; Neumann, Kosson, Forth and Hare 2006; Neumann, Kosson and Sarekin 2007; Vitacco, Neumann and Jackson 2005; also see the *British Journal of Psychiatry* website, http://bjp.rcpsych.org/cgi/eletters/190/49/s39).

Paradoxically, Cooke and colleagues (Cooke, Michie, Hart and Clark 2004) attempted to propose a 'causal' model of psychopathy, i.e., that certain traits (e.g., callousness) caused other psychopathic traits (e.g., impulsive, undercontrolled tendencies), based on use of cross-sectional data. As we have pointed out (Neumann, Vitacco, Hare and Wupperman 2005), such a model is untenable. More importantly, current behaviour genetic and longitudinal research reveals that there are fundamental empirical relations among psychopathic features reflecting, for example, affective and antisocial tendencies. For instance, there is an increasing number of studies indicating that broad genetic factors account for a substantial portion of the variance and co-variance of diverse sets of psychopathy traits. Independent studies have reported bivariate analyses which suggest that there are genetic influences on the co-variance of psychopathy scales reflecting emotional detachment and antisocial tendencies (Taylor, Loney, Bobadilla *et al.* 2003; Viding, Blair, Moffitt and Plomin 2005). Similarly, based on a large sample of nine to ten-year-old twins, Baker, Jacobson, Raine *et al.* (2007) found that a common antisocial behaviour factor (composed of child psychopathy traits, aggression and delinquency) across informants was strongly heritable. Recently, Viding, Frick and Plomin (2007) reported that a common genetic component accounted for the co-variation between callous-unemotional traits and antisocial tendencies in children. Finally, based on a large adolescent twin sample, Larsson, Tuvblad, Rijsdijk *et al.* (2007) reported that interpersonal, affective, impulsive behavioural, and antisocial features of psychopathy all loaded onto a single genetic factor for both males and females. In terms of longitudinal research, there is clear evidence that earlier antisocial tendencies co-vary with (Larsson *et al.* 2007) and predict the stability of (Frick, Kimonis, Dandreaux and Farell 2003) other psychopathy traits.

The behaviour genetic and longitudinal studies in particular, as well as the structural finding presented below, indicate that in personality theory and psychopathology it is problematic to make simple distinctions between so-called basic traits and characteristic adaptations. The problem is exacerbated by the likelihood that traits and their behavioural components are linked to some of the same underlying psychobiological processes, with the pathways to the latter being more complex than those to the former. Indeed, the different features of psychopathic personality appear to reflect a functional system. As suggested by Livesley, Jang and Vernon (1998, p. 944), 'Since the components of personality are parts of an integrated system, disturbance in one system is likely to affect the whole system'. In this sense, antisocial tendencies are fundamentally tied to other psychopathy dimensions.

Even if we had clear indications of what the core psychopathic traits are, it is unclear how we could measure them directly, without reference to behavioural manifestations, except perhaps in some abstract, philosophical manner. Additionally, there are cogent arguments that, like other personality disorders, an integral part of psychopathy is the emergence of an early and persistent pattern of problematic behaviours, and that these behaviours are important in defining the condition (Frick and Marsee 2006; Harris and Rice 2006; Robins 1966). From an evolutionary psychology perspective, for example (Harris and Rice 2006; Mealey 1995), psychopathy is a heritable adaptive life strategy in which a central feature is the early emergence of antisocial behaviour, including aggressive sexuality. Clearly, the view that major dimensions of personality reflect trait dispositions *and* characteristic adaptations to the environment (Zuckerman 1991) is consistent with twin studies on the heritability of antisocial behaviour (Slutske 2001) and on the trait and action features of psychopathy in children, adolescents and adults (Blonigen, Hicks, Krueger *et al.* 2005; Larsson, Tuvblad, Rijsdijk *et al.* 2007; Viding, Frick and Plomin 2007).

A four-factor model

Consistent with the empirical findings discussed previously, Hare (2003) proposed that at least four latent variable dimensions are needed to represent the PCL-R construct of psychopathy: Interpersonal (items 1, 2, 4, 5); Affective (items 6, 7, 8, 16); Lifestyle (items 3, 9, 13, 14, 15); and Antisocial (items 10, 12, 18, 19, 20). Two items (11 and 17) did not load on any factor. The three-factor model, without use of testlets, is subsumed by the four-factor model.

A number of recent studies, based on latent variable analyses of the PCL instruments, provide considerable support for a four-factor model of psychopathy across diverse and primarily very large samples of male and female offenders (Hare and Neumann 2006; Neumann, Kosson and Salekin 2007), forensic and civil psychiatric patients (Hill, Neumann and Rogers 2004; Jackson, Neumann and Vitacco 2007; Neumann, Hare and Newman 2007; Vitacco, Neumann and Jackson 2005), youth offenders (Jones, Cauffman, Miller and Mulvey 2006; Neumann, Kosson, Forth and Hare 2006; Salekin, Brannen, Zalot *et al.* 2006, Vitacco, Neumann, Caldwell *et al.* 2006), as well as individuals from the general community (Hare and Neumann 2006; Neumann and Hare, 2008). Figure 38.1 illustrates the form and content of the model, as well as standardized item-discrimination parameters, based on a mega-sample of 6,929 male and female adult offenders and male forensic psychiatric patients. We used a relative fit index, the Tucker Lewis Index (TLI), to test how well the hypothesized four-factor model fit relative to a null (unstructured) model. We also used an absolute index, the standardized root mean square (SRMR), to determine how well the four factor model reproduced the observed data. The fit of the four factor model was excellent (TLI = 0.93, SRMR = 0.05).

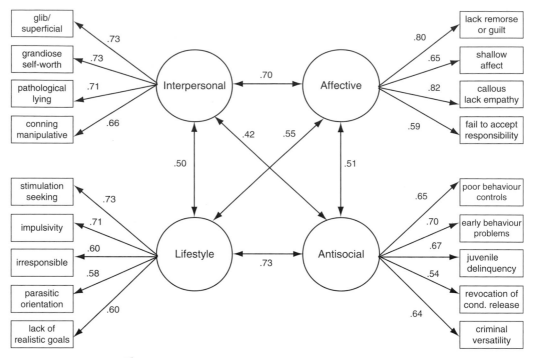

Figure 38.1 *Four factor PCL-R item-based model of psychopathy (N = 6929).*

In this model the four strongly correlated psychopathy dimensions represent interpersonal (e.g., pathological lying, conning), affective (e.g., shallow affect, remorseless), impulsive behavioural lifestyle (e.g., irresponsible, stimulus seeking, impulsivity) and diverse externalizing, antisocial tendencies (e.g., poor behavioural controls, versatile antisociality). In addition, these four correlated factors are comprehensively explained by a cohesive superordinate factor (Neumann and Hare 2008; Neumann, Hare and Newman 2007; Neumann et al 2006).

The model has also shown structural invariance across North American and United Kingdom samples of adolescent offenders (Neumann, Kosson, Forth and Hare 2006), and adult male African-American and Caucasian civil psychiatric patients (Jackson, Neumann and Vitacco 2007; see also Bolt, Hare, Vitale and Newman 2004; Bolt, Hare and Neumann 2007). Although the PCL-R and its derivatives cannot be equated with the construct of psychopathy (Neumann, Vitacco, Hare and Wupperman 2005), the robustness of the four-factor model across such a diverse set of samples suggests that the measure is highly compatible with both traditional-clinical and modern-empirical conceptualizations of psychopathy. The results show that the PCL-based psychopathic personality dimensions reflect a broadly antisocial and undercontrolled personality disposition, involving deceptiveness, pathological lying, absence of remorse and guilt, as well as irresponsible, impulsive and versatile antisocial tendencies.

These studies indicate clearly that in offender populations antisocial behaviour is an important component of psychopathy, as measured by the PCL Scales. Based on a CFA of PCL: SV data from the MacArthur Risk Assessment Study, Vitacco,

Neumann and Jackson (2005) found that the four factor model also applies to civil psychiatric patients. To determine if the model applies to the general population, Neumann and Hare 2008 conducted a CFA on the PCL: SV scores from the community sample in the MacArthur Risk Assessment Study. Fit for the four-factor model was excellent (TLI = 0.98, RMSEA = 0.04, SRMR = 0.05). The items on the Antisocial factor had substantial factor loadings and correlated significantly with the other three psychopathy factors, highlighting the critical nature of anti-social behaviour in the psychopathy construct. Moreover, it is arguable that the other psychopathy dimensions reflecting deceptive, callous and impulsive features take on the necessary flavour of dissociality, given their strong co-variation with the fourth antisocial tendencies factor (Neumann, Hare and Newman 2007).

Hill, Neumann and Rogers (2004) found that the four-factor model, relative to the three-factor model, accounts for greater variance in maximum security patients' aggression at six-month follow-up. Similar results were obtained by Vitacco, Neumann and Jackson (2005) for psychiatric patients' community violence at ten-week follow-up. Each study found that, in addition to the antisocial factor, other psychopathy factors were also critical predictors. Interestingly, Vitacco, Neumann, Caldwell et al. (2006) found that the interpersonal and anti-social factors differentially predicted instrumental violence in a sample of severe youth offenders. Lastly, Walsh, Swogger and Kosson (2003) found that the antisocial factor of the PCL-R contributed uniquely to postdicting blind ratings of instrumentality of violence. In sum, the current findings provide strong evidence that the four-factor model has incremental validity over the three-factor in predicting important external correlates of psychopathy.

A significant strength of the four-factor model is that it can be used in longi-tudinal research to study the relations between the emergence of early antisocial tendencies and development of other psychopathic personality features. For instance, psychopathic traits (callousness, impulsivity) are predictors of future antisocial behaviour (Frick, Kimonis, Dandreaux and Farell 2003; Vitacco, Neumann, Robertson and Durrant 2002). At the same time, prior antisocial behaviour is associated with higher levels of callousness and other psychopathic traits (Dowson, Sussams, Grounds and Taylor 2001; Lynam 1998). Also, early antisocial tendencies are an important predictor of stability of other psychopathic traits (Frick et al. 2003), and antecedent antisocial behaviours co-vary signifi-cantly with subsequent interpersonal and affective psychopathy traits (Larsson, Tuvblad, Rijsdijk et al. 2007). Similarly, Knight and Sims-Knight (2003) found good fit for an SEM that hypothesized that physical and/or verbal abuse produced callousness and/or lack of emotionality. Such findings are consistent with the fact that repeated exposure to antisocial acts desensitizes individuals' negative emo-tional responses to such behaviour (Anderson, Berkowitz, Donnerstein et al. 2003), suggesting that exposure to – or engagement in – antisocial behaviour can precede development of callousness or other psychopathy traits.

Of particular note, the pattern of correlations among the four factors in the PCL-R and the PCL: SV (but not in the PCL: YV) is consistent with the presence of two broad factors, one consisting of the eight items that comprise the

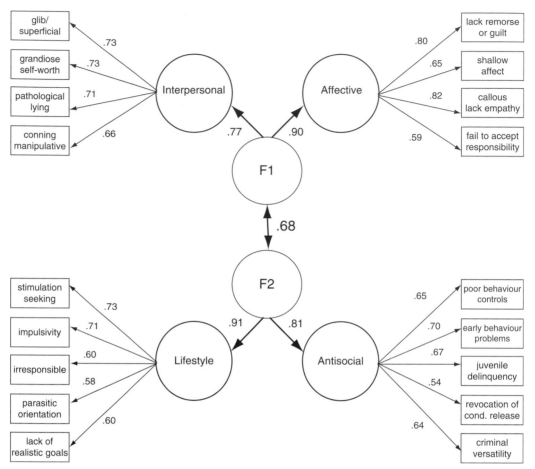

Figure 38.2. *Two-factor PCL-R higher-order representation of the four correlated factors model (N= 6929).*

Interpersonal and Affective factors, and the other consisting of the ten items that comprise the Lifestyle and Antisocial factors (Figure 38.2). These broad factors are the same as those in the original two-factor model of the PCL-R but with the addition of Item 20 to the second factor (see Hare and Neumann 2008).

Item response theory

Because of its demonstrated importance in basic and applied research, the PCL-R has been subjected to intense critical analysis, conceptual and statistical. Although it has fared well on both fronts, like all psychological instruments, its generalizability requires continual evaluation. One goal has been to determine the extent to which the PCL-R score metric has scalar equivalence, a condition that holds when test scores represent the same level of a construct (psychopathy) across diverse populations.

The application of item response theory (IRT) to psychopathy as measured by the PCL-R and the PCL: SV is described in detail elsewhere (Bolt, Hare, Vitale and Newman 2004; Cooke, Kosson and Michie 2001; Cooke and Michie 1997; Cooke, Michie, Hart and Hare 1999). Briefly, IRT models provide a mathematic expression of the relationship between a score on an individual item and the underlying construct or latent trait, theta (θ). For PCL-R items a graded response model characterizes each item according to parameters that indicate the discriminating value of the item and the threshold at which it discriminates, with respect to θ. IRT also provides estimates of the amount of information provided by a test and its items, and the precision of estimates at various levels of the trait. When comparing groups for scalar equivalence, IRT provides information on group differences in the trait-item score relationship. When a difference occurs the item is said to exhibit differential item functioning (DIF). IRT also provides information about the scalar equivalence of total test scores, depicted by test characteristic curves (TCCs).

Bolt, Hare, Vitale and Newman (2004) recently conducted a multigroup IRT analysis of the PCL-R, using large samples of male and female offenders, and male forensic psychiatric patients, assessed from interview and file information. Various indices indicated that the assumption of unidimensionality typically required for IRT analyses was met for each sample, consistent with the super-ordinate finding discussed above. Separate DIF analyses indicated that for each comparison group the items that showed DIF with respect to the reference group tended to come from the Lifestyle and Antisocial factors. For each group, the Interpersonal and Affective items had higher discrimination and threshold param-eters than did the Lifestyle and Antisocial items. However, in each sample there was considerable variation in the discriminating value of the items and in thresh-olds, suggesting that there may be cultural and ethnic variations in the way some PCL-R items function. We concluded, as have others (Cooke and Michie 1997; Cooke, Michie, Hart and Hare 1999), that the PCL–R is a good measure of psychopathy because all items contribute to the estimate of θ and because different items function efficiently at different levels of the trait.

Item response theory can be used to estimate the amount of information provided by a test and its items, and to determine the precision of estimates at various levels of the trait. Bolt et al. (2004) computed information functions for PCL-R Total and Factor scores for each of the four groups described previously, based on a common latent trait metric. The information functions for Total scores seemed similar to one another, although slightly more information was provided by the PCL-R for male offenders than for the other groups. This is shown specifically in Figure 4 of Bolt et al. (2004). The maximum amount of information was near the middle of the trait ($\theta = 0$). The Interpersonal and Affective factors provided more information than did the Lifestyle and Antisocial factors, espe-cially at higher levels of the trait. Similar results have been obtained with the PCL: YV scored for adolescent female offenders (Schrum and Salekin 2006).

Although in these samples the Interpersonal and Affective items showed less DIF than the other items, suggesting they should function well as anchors for cross-cultural research (Bolt *et al.* 2004), it does not follow that these other items are unimportant in such research. For example, an IRT analysis of a large sample of English male offenders (Bolt, Hare and Neumann 2007) indicated that the discriminating value, thresholds, and information functions of the Lifestyle and Antisocial factors were approximately as great as they were for the Interpersonal and Affective factors. It seems that the presence of impulsive lifestyle and anti-social features is more informative of psychopathy in English male offenders than in North American offenders. Additionally, recent research with adolescents and individuals from the general community indicates that the antisocial item thresholds are substantially larger than those seen in male offender samples (Hare and Neumann 2006), suggesting that antisocial behaviour may be a more salient indicator of psychopathy in adolescent or general community samples than in adult forensic samples.

A TCC plots the expected PCL–R score as a function of the latent trait. In multigroup analyses TCCs from different groups can be compared to determine if a given score on the PCL-R has the same meaning for each group, with respect to the underlying trait of psychopathy. With male offenders as the reference group, and using a common latent trait metric, Bolt *et al.* (2004) compared TCCs for each of the three datasets described previously. The TCCs were very similar for all groups, particularly in the mid-range of the trait, with only small differences at the lower and upper levels of the trait. This suggests that in mid-range a given PCL-R score represents much the same level of psychopathy in male and female offenders and male forensic psychiatric patients. Exceptions occurred at relatively low PCL-R scores, where the level of psychopathy (relative to male offenders) appeared to be slightly overestimated in the other groups, and at higher PCL-R scores the level of psychopathy appeared to be slightly underestimated, in each case by only one or two points. A similar analysis by Cooke, Kosson and Michie (2001) indicated that the TCCs for samples of African-American and white male offenders were virtually identical, indicating that a given PCL-R score had much the same meaning for each sample. Similar results were obtained in the study of English offenders described previously (Bolt, Hare and Neumann 2007). That is, the TCCs were similar for North American and English male offenders, particularly at higher levels, suggesting that in each group a given PCL-R score has much the same meaning, with respect to psychopathy. However, more research is needed on the role of ethnic and other factors in the use of the PCL instruments.

Multidimensional scaling

Although CFA and IRT help to delineate the structural properties of a test, the former assumes linearity and thus provides a limited means of understanding latent structures, whereas the latter usually requires items to reflect a single underlying dimension. An important and potentially very informative new direction in research on psychopathy makes use of multidimensional scaling (MDS) techniques (Shye and Elizur 1994). MDS can be considered as a non-parametric alternative to factor analysis that does not assume that a linear structure exists. Instead, structures are interpreted as emergent properties of the data. MDS allows statistical structures to be unfolded within a geometric space so that distances between points in space represent the strength of association. These scalograms are interpreted with respect to underlying theoretical facets. The researcher then can identify a theoretical correspondence to the structure of the data.

Interpreting a multidimensional analysis depends on a theoretical mapping of the underlying concepts that the researcher is aiming to explore within the data. These facets, if distinct, can be identified as clusters of items within the MDS space. In addition to having good face validity, the clusters should show correspondence to previous work examining the same constructs, as in all scientific methods. One study has applied MDS to the PCL: SV scores of 573 Swedish offenders and forensic patients (Campbell, Belfrage, Douglas and Strand 2004). The results indicated some correspondence to the two- and four-factor solutions for the PCL: SV.

A recent MDS study of 4,630 male offenders rated on the PCL-R was conducted by Bishopp and Hare (2008). The measure of fit in an MDS model is assessed from the amount of 'stress' present within the solution. The lower the stress the better the fit, determined by Young's stress index (Shye and Elizur 1994). Some authors are very strict about stress within an MDS analysis, whereas others argue that interpretability is more important, suggesting a more relaxed approach (Shye and Elizur 1994). A two-dimensional solution using all twenty items was associated with high stress (poor fit), primarily because of the presence of item 11 (promiscuous sexual behaviour) and item 17 (many short-term marital relationships). When these items were excluded, as they are in the two- and four-factor PCL-R models, stress was low (good fit), and the multidimensional scalograms revealed a set of facets consistent with the PCL-R four-factor solution. The MDS solutions deconstructed psychopathy into dimensions that were not all identified in the linear models, suggesting that additional dimensions may be needed for the description of psychopathy . For example, promiscuous sexual behaviour (item 11) and many marital relationships (item 17) do not load on any PCL-R factor, but the MDS analysis suggested that the former is related to the exploitative interpersonal features of psychopathy whereas the latter is related to its impulsive, irresponsible features. It is possible that there is a dimension reflecting sexual behaviour and relationships, consistent with the evolutionary psychology model (Harris and Rice 2006). In any case, the structure is readily interpreted in terms of general personality theory in which traits and actions represent the dynamic patterns of psychopathic personality.

Latent growth models

A relatively new longitudinal approach in research on psychopathy involves latent growth models (LGMs). This approach has the advantage of separating the level of some phenomenon (violence) at any given time from the rate of change or growth of the phenomenon over time (Muthen and Muthen 2001). Neumann and Vitacco (2004) recently used LGM to examine how the four psychopathy factors and a psychotic symptom factor predicted growth in violence in psychiatric outpatients. They found excellent support for the four factor model (TLI = 0.96, RMSEA = 0.05), as well as for an LGM where the four psychopathy factors and the psychotic symptom factor predicted a violence intercept factor and a slope factor (TLI = 0.97, RMSEA = 0.05). The findings indicated that the absolute level of violence at any given follow-up time was primarily explained by the antisocial psychopathy factor and the psychotic symptom factor. In terms of growth in violent behaviour, the Interpersonal psychopathy factor predicted an increased slope or rate of change in violent acts with time. This model accounted for 65 per cent and 18 per cent of the variance, respectively, in the level of and growth in violent acts during a thirty-week follow-up. Psychopathy is well-known as a potent risk factor for violence (Leistico, Salekin, DeCoster and Rogers 2008), but most research has been concerned with predicting a single event, usually the first violent act after release from custody. But the variables that predict an event at time 1 may not be the same variables that predict events at later times. Clearly, additional research using LGMs for understanding the development and consequences of psychopathy and other critical variables during multiple periods is warranted.

Psychopathy: categorical or dimensional?

Do psychopathic individuals differ from the rest of us in degree or in kind? There has been considerable debate, but little empirical research, on the topic. Many theorists and researchers prefer dimensional conceptualizations of personality disorders, whereas others adopt a categorical view (that an individual either does or does not have antisocial personality disorder/psychopathy). Harris, Rice and Quinsey (1994) used archival file information to obtain PCL–R scores for a large sample of male forensic patients. Using four different methods, they obtained results consistent with the hypothesis that psychopathy is a discrete category, or taxon, defined by antisocial behaviours and early behavioural problems. However, their taxon may have been more reflective of persistent antisociality or criminality than of psychopathy.

There now is evidence that the structure of psychopathy (and its factors) is dimensional, whether measured by the PCL-R (Edens, Marcus, Lilienfeld and Poythress 2006; Guay, Ruscio, Knight and Hare 2007; Walters, Duncan and Mitchell-Perez 2007); the PCL: YV (Murrie, Marcus, Douglas *et al.* 2007); the PCL: SV (Walters, Gray, Jackson *et al.* 2007); the ASPD (Murrie, Marcus, Douglas *et al.* 2007); or by self-report (Guay and Knight 2003; Marcus, John and Edens 2004). One interpretation of these findings, consistent with the MDS data described previously, as well as with FFM research (Lynam 2002; Lynam and Widiger 2007), is that psychopathy reflects, or emerges from, a combination of extreme variants of normal-range personality processes, many of which are antisocial in nature (Lynam and Widiger 2007).

Interestingly, such a combination of extreme traits may be taxonic. Hare (1970, p. 12) raised the possibility that psychopathy could be viewed as both a typology and as a dimensional concept. Recently, Ruscio (2007, p. 1589) noted that the structure of psychopathy may contain:

> ... both taxonic and dimensional features: within a nonpsychopathic group, a set of dimensions may capture individual differences on psychopathy-relevant traits, but hardcore psychopaths deviate substantially on multiple dimensions and form their own group.

Certainly, it is not unusual for researchers and clinicians to describe those with very high PCL-R scores as 'different' from other individuals.

Measure as construct

The PCL-R and its derivatives have become the dominant instruments for the assessment of psychopathy, and their use has resulted in the accumulation of a large body of replicable findings, both basic and applied. Not surprisingly, some commentators have expressed concern that the PCL-R has become the construct. The first two meetings (2005, 2007) of the new Society for the Scientific Study of Psychopathy (SSSP) made it clear that while the PCL-R may be the dominant measure of psychopathy, it clearly has not impeded attempts by researchers to devise and validate other measurement tools, a healthy development for the field. Indeed, efforts over the past decade have expanded the assessment repertoire to include a variety of behavioural rating scales, specialized self-report scales, and omnibus personality inventories (see Frick and Hare 2001; Lilienfeld and Fowler 2006; Livesley 2007; Lynam and Gudonis 2005; Lynam and Widiger 2007; Williams, Paulhus and Hare 2007). While many of these measures are conceptually related to the PCL-R, others have their origins in empirical research on psychopathology and general personality. All benefit from the large body of theory and research that resulted from widespread adoption of the PCL-R family of instruments. Rather than being concerned about its popularity, the PCL-R might better be viewed as an 'anchor for the burgeoning nomological network of psychopathy' (Benning, Patrick, Salekin and Leistico 2005, p. 271). This network not only includes diverse measurement tools but input from behavioural genetics, developmental psychopathology, personality theory, cognitive neuroscience and community studies.

Implications of structural models

The structural properties of the PCL Scales are of more than academic interest. Among other things, they help to delineate the latent variables that more fully articulate the nature of the psychopathy construct. The four-factor model indicates that, contrary to some arguments, the presence of early and persistent antisocial behaviour is an important feature of the construct. In line with the structural findings are those from behaviour genetic (e.g., Larsson, Tuvblad, Rijsdijk *et al.* 2007; Viding, Frick and Plomin 2007) and longitudinal (Frick, Kimonis, Dandreaux and Farell 2003; Loney, Taylor, Butler and Iacono 2007; Lynam, Caspi, Moffitt *et al.* 2007) studies. The PCL four-factor latent variable model also becomes important in accounting for the associations between the components of psychopathy and a variety of external correlates, including risk for violence, treatment options and psychobiological processes. Although factor analysis identifies four dimensions underpinning assessments of psychopathy made with the PCL scales, multidimensional scaling suggests that more dimensions may be required to fully account for the construct.

The nature of the causal relationship between early antisocial tendencies and other psychopathic traits is of considerable importance, but largely unexplored. It strikes us as too simplistic (Neumann, Vitacco, Hare and Wupperman 2005) to assume that antisocial tendencies are merely consequences of other psychopathic features (Cooke, Michie, Hart and Hare 2004). An equally plausible model is that antisocial features influence the nature and development of other psychopathic features (Frick and Marsee 2006; Neumann *et al.* 2005). For example, basic longitudinal research indicates that the imitative behaviour of toddlers plays an important role in their development of moral conscience (Forman, Aksan and Kochanska 2004). Similarly, negative parenting appears to play an important role in decreasing the level of a child's prosocial behaviour (Knafo and Plomin 2006). Thus, exposure to, and engagement in, antisocial acts may play a role in the development of callous, manipulative and impulsive psychopathic traits, which may then lead to further antisocial behaviour. Given that the modelling results described above indicate a moderate to strong co-variation of four dimensions of psychopathy (Interpersonal, Affective, Lifestyle and Antisocial), it would be prudent to assume that the longitudinal relations among these dimensions are interactive and reciprocal, and that the 'real' core of psychopathy has yet to be uncovered.

References

Acheson, S. K. 2005. Review of the Hare Psychopathy Checklist-Revised, 2nd edn, in R. A. Spies and B. S. Plake (eds.), *The sixteenth mental measurements yearbook*, pp. 429–31. Lincoln, NE: Buros Institute of Mental Measurements

American Psychiatric Association 1980. *Diagnostic and statistical manual of mental disorders*, 3rd edn. Washington, DC: APA

   1994. *Diagnostic and statistical manual of mental disorders*, 4th edn. Washington, DC: APA

   2000. *Diagnostic and statistical manual of mental disorders*, 4th edn, Text Revision. Washington, DC: APA

Andershed, H., Kerr, M., Stattin, H. and Levander, S. 2002. Psychopathic traits in non-referred youths: a new assessment tool, in E. Blauw and L. Sheridan (eds.), *Psychopaths: current international perspectives*, pp. 131–58. The Hague: Elsevier

Anderson, C. A., Berkowitz, L., Donnerstein, E., Huesmann, L. R., Johnson, J. D., Linz, D., Malamuth, N. M. and Wartella, E. 2003. The influence of media violence on youth, *Psychological Science in the Public Interest* 4: 81–110

Arieti, S. 1967. *The intrapsychic self.* New York: Basic Books

Baker, L. A., Jacobson, K. C., Raine, A., Lozano, D. I. and Bezdjian, S. 2007. Genetic and environmental bases of childhood antisocial behavior: a multi-informant twin study, *Journal of Abnormal Psychology* 116: 219–35

Barnes, G. E., Murray, R. P., Patton, D., Bentler, P. M. and Anderson, R. E. 2000. *The addiction prone personality: longitudinal research in the social sciences.* New York: Plenum Publishers

Benning, S. B., Patrick, C. J., Salekin, R. T. and Leistico, A. M. R. 2005. Convergent and discriminant validity of psychopathy factors assessed via self-report: a comparison of three instruments, *Assessment* 12: 270–89

Berrios, G. E. 1996. *The history of mental symptoms: descriptive psychopathology since the nineteenth century.* Cambridge University Press

Bishopp, D. and Hare, R. D. 2008. A multidimensional scaling analysis of the Hare PCL-R: unfolding the structure of psychopathy, *Psychology, Crime, and Law* 14: 117–32

Blonigen, D. M., Hicks, B. M., Krueger, R. F., Patrick, C. J. and Iacono, W. G. 2005. Psychopathic personality traits: heritability and genetic overlap with internalizing and externalizing psychopathology, *Psychological Medicine* 35: 637–48

Boccaccini, M. T., Epstein, M., Poythress, N., Douglas, K. S., Campbell, J., Gardner, G. and Falkenbach, D. 2007. Self-report measures of child and adolescent psychopathy as predictors of offending in four samples of justice-involved youth, *Assessment* 14: 361–74

Bollen, K. A. 2002. Latent variables in psychology and the social sciences, *Annual Review of Psychology* 53: 605–34

Bolt, D. M., Hare, R. D. and Neumann, C. S. 2007. Score metric equivalence of the Psychopathy Checklist-Revised PCL-R across criminal offenders in North America and the United Kingdom, *Assessment* 14: 44–56

Bolt, D. M., Hare, R. D., Vitale, J. E. and Newman, J. P. 2004. A multigroup item response theory analysis of the Psychopathy Checklist-Revised, *Psychological. Assessment* 16: 155–68

Book, A. S., Clark, H. J., Forth, A. E. and Hare, R. D. 2006. The PCL-R and PCL: YV: forensic applications and limitations, in R. P. Archer (ed.), *Forensic uses of clinical assessment instruments*, pp. 147–79. Mahwah, NJ: Erlbaum

Borsboom, D., Mellenbergh, G. J. and van Heerden, J. 2003. The theoretical status of latent variables, *Psychological Review* 110: 203–19

Campbell, J. S., Belfrage, H., Douglas, K. and Strand, S. 2004. *Multidimensional scaling of the PCL:SV in Swedish and North American Samples.* Paper presented at the IAFMHS Conference, Stockholm, 6–9 June 2004

Cleckley, H. 1941. *The mask of sanity.* St Louis, MO: Mosby
  1976. *The mask of sanity*, 5th edn. St Louis, MO: Mosby

Coid, J. W. 1993. Current concepts and classifications of psychopathic disorder, in P. Tyrer and G. Stein (eds.), *Personality disorder reviewed*, pp. 113–64. London: Gaskell Press

Cooke, D. J., Kosson, D. S. and Michie, C. 2001. Psychopathy and ethnicity: structural, item, and test generalizability of the Psychopathy Checklist-Revised (PCL-R) in Caucasian and African American participants, *Psychological Assessment* 13: 531–42

Cooke, D. J. and Michie, C. 1997. An item response theory analysis of the Hare Psychopathy Checklist, *Psychological Assessment* 9: 3–13
   2001. Refining the construct of psychopathy: towards a hierarchical model, *Psychological Assessment* 13: 171–88

Cooke, D. J., Michie, C., Hart, S. D. and Clark, D. A. 2004. Reconstructing psychopathy: clarifying the significance of antisocial and socially deviant behaviour in the diagnosis of psychopathic personality disorder, *Journal of Personality Disorders* 18: 337–56

Cooke, D. J., Michie, C., Hart, S. D. and Hare, R. D. 1999. Evaluating the Screening Version of the Hare Psychopathy Checklist–Revised (PCL:SV): an item response theory analysis, *Psychological Assessment* 11: 3–13

Cooper, B. S. and Yuille, J. C. 2007. Psychopathy and deception, in H. Hervé and J. C. Yuille (eds.), *The psychopath: theory, research, and practice*, pp. 487–503. Mahwah, NJ: Lawrence Erlbaum and Associates

Costa, P. T. and McCrae, R. R. 1992. The five-factor model of personality and its relevance to personality disorders, *Journal of Personality Disorders* 6: 343–59

Costa, P. T., Jr and Widiger, T. A. (eds.) 2002. *Personality disorders and the five-factor model of personality*, 2nd edn. Washington, DC: American Psychological Association

Dadds, M. R., Fraser, J., Frost, A. and Hawes, D. J. 2005. Disentangling the underlying dimensions of psychopathy and conduct problems in childhood: a community study, *Journal of Consulting and Clinical Psychology* 73: 400–10

De Oliveira-Souza, R., Ignácio, F. A., Moll, J. and Hare, R. D. 2008. Psychopathy in a civil psychiatric out patient sample, *Criminal Justice and Behavior* 35: 427–37

Dolan, M. and Rennie, C. E. 2006. Reliability and validity of the Psychopathy Checklist: Youth Version in a UK sample of conduct disordered boys, *Personality and Individual Differences* 40: 65–75

Dowson, J. H., Sussams, P., Grounds, A. T. and Taylor, J. C. 2001. Associations of past conduct disorder with personality disorders in 'nonpsychotic' psychiatric patients, *European Journal of Psychiatry* 16: 49–56

Edens, J. F., Marcus, D. K., Lilienfeld, S. O. and Poythress, N. G. 2006. Psychopathic, not psychopath: taxometric evidence for the dimensional structure of psychopathy, *Journal of Abnormal Psychology* 115: 131–44

Essau, C. A., Sasagawa, S. and Frick, P. J. 2006. Callous-Unemotional traits in a community sample of adolescents, *Assessment* 23: 454–69

Felthous, A. R. and Saß, H. (eds.) 2007. *International handbook on psychopathic disorders and the law*. New York: Wiley

Forman, D. R., Aksan, N. and Kochanska, G. 2004. Toddlers' responsive imitation predicts preschool-age conscience, *Psychological Science* 15: 699–704

Forth, A. E. and Book, A. S. 2007. Psychopathy in youth: a valid construct, in H. Hervé and J. C. Yuille (eds.), *The psychopath: theory, research, and practice*, pp. 369–87. Mahwah, NJ: Lawrence Erlbaum and Associates

Forth, A. E., Kosson, D. and Hare, R. D. 2003. *The Hare PCL: Youth Version*. Toronto, ON: Multi-Health Systems

Frick, P. J. 2007. Using the construct of psychopathy to understand antisocial and violent youth, in H. Hervé and J. C. Yuille (eds.), *The psychopath: theory, research, and practice*, pp. 343–67. Mahwah, NJ: Erlbaum

Frick, P. J. and Hare, R. D. 2001. *The antisocial process screening device*. Toronto, ON: Multi-Health Systems

Frick, P. J., Kimonis, E. R., Dandreaux, D. M. and Farell, J. M. 2003. The 4 years stability of psychopathic traits in non-referred youth, *Behavioural Sciences and the Law* 21: 1–24

Frick, P. J. and Marsee, M. A. 2006. Psychopathy and developmental pathways to anti-social behaviour in youth, in C. J. Patrick (ed.), *Handbook of psychopathy*, pp. 353–74. New York: Guilford Press

Fulero, S. 1995. Review of the Hare Psychopathy Checklist-Revised, in J. C. Conoley and J. C. Impara (eds.), *Twelfth mental measurements yearbook*, pp. 453–4. Lincoln, NE: Buros Institute of Mental Measurements

Guay, J. P. and Knight, R. A. 2003. *Assessing the underlying structure of psychopathy factors using taxometrics*. Paper presented at the Developmental and Neuroscience Perspectives on Psychopathy conference, Madison, Wisconsin, July 2003

Guay, J. P., Ruscio, J., Knight, R. and Hare, R. D. 2007. A taxometric analysis of the latent structure of psychopathy: evidence for dimensionality, *Journal of Abnormal Psychology* 116: 701–16

Guy, L. S. and Douglas, K. S. 2006. Examining the utility of the PCL:SV as a screening measure using competing factor models of psychopathy, *Psychological Assessment* 18: 225–30

Hare, R. D. 1970. *Psychopathy: theory and research*. New York: John Wiley and Sons
  1980. A research scale for the assessment of psychopathy in criminal populations, *Personality and Individual Differences* 1: 111–19
  1985. A comparison of procedures for the assessment of psychopathy, *Journal of Consulting and Clinical Psychology* 53: 7–16
  1991. *The Hare Psychopathy Checklist-Revised*. Toronto, ON: Multi-Health Systems
  1998. Psychopaths and their nature: implications for the mental health and criminal justice systems, in T. Millon, E. Simonsen, M. Birket-Smith and R. D. Davis (eds.), *Psychopathy: antisocial, criminal and violent behaviors*, pp. 188–212. New York: Guilford Press
  2003. *The Hare Psychopathy Checklist-Revised*, 2nd edn. Toronto, ON: Multi-Health Systems
  2007. Psychological instruments in the assessment of psychopathy, in A. R. Felthous and H. Saß (eds.), *International handbook on psychopathic disorders and the law*, pp. 41–67. New York: Wiley

Hare, R. D., Harpur, T. J., Hakstian, A. R., Forth, A. E., Hart, S. D. and Newman, J. P. 1990. The Revised Psychopathy Checklist: descriptive statistics, reliability, and factor structure, *Psychological Assessment* 2: 338–41

Hare, R. D. and Neumann, C. S. 2005. Structural models of psychopathy, *Current Psychiatry Reports* 7: 57–64
  2006. The PCL-R assessment of psychopathy: development, structural properties, and new directions, in C. J. Patrick (ed.), *Handbook of psychopathy*, pp. 58–88. New York: Guilford Press
  2008. Psychopathy as a clinical and empirical construct, *Annual Review of Clinical Psychology* 4: 217–46

2009. Psychopathy, in P. Blaney and T. Millon (eds.), *Oxford textbook of psychopathology*, pp. 622–50. New York: Oxford University Press

Hare, R. D. and Schalling, D. (eds.) 1978. *Psychopathic behaviour: approaches to research*. Chichester: Wiley

Harpur, T. J., Hare, R. D. and Hakstian, A. R. 1989. Two-factor conceptualization of psychopathy: construct validity and assessment implications, *Psychological Assessment* 1: 6–17

Harris, G. T. and Rice, M. E. 2006. Treatment of psychopathy: a review of empirical findings, in C. J. Patrick (ed.), *Handbook of psychopathy*, pp. 555–72. New York: Guilford Press

Harris, G. T., Rice, M. E. and Quinsey, V. L. 1994. Psychopathy as a taxon: evidence that psychopaths are a discrete class, *Journal of Consulting and Clinical Psychology* 62: 387–97

Hart, S. D., Cox, D. N. and Hare, R. D. 1995. *Manual for the Psychopathy Checklist: Screening Version (PCL: SV)*. Toronto, ON: Multi-Health Systems

Hervé, H. 2007. Psychopathy across the ages: a history of the Hare psychopath, in H. Hervé and J. C. Yuille (eds.), *The psychopath: theory, research, and practice*, pp. 31–55. Mahwah, NJ: Erlbaum

Hervé, H. and Yuille, J. C. (eds.) 2007. *The psychopath: theory, research, and practice*. Mahwah, NJ: Erlbaum

Hill, C., Neumann, C. S. and Rogers, R. 2004. Confirmatory factor analysis of the Psychopathy Checklist: Screening Version PCL:SV in offenders with Axis I disorders, *Psychological Assessment* 16: 90–5

Huchzenmeir, C., Geiger, F., Bruß, E., Godt, N., Köhler, D., Hinrichs, G. and Aldenhoff, J. B. 2007. The relationship between DSM-IV Cluster B personality disorders and psychopathy according to Hare's criteria: clarification and resolution of previous contradictions, *Behavioural Sciences and the Law* 25: 901–11

Jackson, R. L., Neumann, C. S. and Vitacco, M. J. 2007. Impulsivity, anger, and psychopathy: the moderating effect of ethnicity, *Journal of Personality Disorders* 21: 289–304

Jones, S., Cauffman, E., Miller, J. D. and Mulvey, E. 2006. Investigating different factor structures of the Psychopathy Checklist: Youth Version PCL: YV: confirmatory factor analytic findings, *Psychological Assessment* 18: 33–48

Karpman, B. 1961. The structure of neurosis: with special differentials between neurosis, psychosis, homosexuality, alcoholism, psychopathy, and criminality, *Archives of Criminal Psychodynamics* 4: 599–646

Knafo, A. and Plomin, R. 2006. Parental discipline and affection and children's prosocial behaviour: genetic and environmental links, *Journal of Personality and Social Psychology* 90: 147–64

Knight, R. A. and Sims-Knight, J. E. 2003. The developmental antecedents of sexual coercion against women: testing alternative hypotheses with structural equation modeling, *Annals of the New York Academy of Sciences* 989: 72–85

Larsson, H., Tuvblad, C., Rijsdijk, F. V., Andershed, H., Grann, M. and Lichtenstein, P. 2007. A common genetic factor explains the association between psychopathic personality and antisocial behaviour, *Psychological Medicine* 37: 15–26

Leistico, A. M., Salekin, R. T., DeCoster, J. and Rogers, R. 2008. A large-scale meta-analysis relating the Hare measures of psychopathy to antisocial conduct, *Law and Human Behavior* 32: 28–45

Lilienfeld, S. O. and Andrews, B. P. 1996. Development and preliminary validation of a self-report measure of psychopathic personality traits in noncriminal populations, *Journal of Personality Assessment* 66: 488–524

Lilienfeld, S. O. and Fowler, K. A. 2006. The self-report assessment of psychopathy: problems, pitfalls, and promises, in C. J. Patrick (ed.), *Handbook of psychopathy*, pp. 107–32. New York: Guilford Press

Livesley, W. J. 2007. A framework for integrating dimensional and categorical classifications of personality disorder, *Journal of Personality Disorders* 21: 199–224

Livesley, W. J., Jang, K. L. and Vernon, P. A. 1998. Phenotypic and genetic structure of traits delineating personality disorder, *Archives of General Psychiatry* 55: 941–8

Livesley, W. J. and Schroeder, M. L. 1991. Dimensions of personality disorder: the DSM-III-R cluster B diagnoses, *Journal of Nervous and Mental Disease* 179: 320–8

Loney, B. R., Taylor, J., Butler, M. A. and Iacono, W. G. 2007. Adolescent psychopathy features: 6-year temporal stability and the prediction of externalizing symptoms during the transition to adulthood, *Aggressive Behavior* 33: 242–52

Lykken, D. T. 2006. Psychopathic personality: the scope of the problem, in C. Patrick (ed.), *Handbook of psychopathy*, pp. 3–13. New York: Guilford Press

Lynam, D. R. 1998. Early identification of the fledgling psychopath: locating the psychopathic child in the current nomenclature, *Journal of Abnormal Psychology* 107: 566–75

  2002. Psychopathy from the perspective of the five-factor model of personality, in P. T. Costa and T. A. Widiger (eds.), *Personality disorders and the Five-Factor Model of personality*, pp. 325–34. Washington, DC: American Psychological Association

Lynam, D. R., Caspi, A., Moffitt, T. E., Loeber, R. and Stouthamer-Loeber, M. 2007. Longitudinal evidence that psychopathy scores in early adolescence predict adult psychopathy, *Journal of Abnormal Psychology* 116: 155–65

Lynam, D. R. and Gudonis, L. 2005. The development of psychopathy, *Annual Review of Clinical Psychology* 1: 381–407

Lynam, D. R. and Widiger, T. A. 2007. Using a general model of personality to identify the basic elements of psychopathy, *Journal of Personality Disorders* 21: 160–78

Marcus, D. K., John, S. L. and Edens, J. F. 2004. A taxometric analysis of psychopathic personality, *Journal of Abnormal Psychology* 113: 626–35

McCord, W. and McCord, J. 1964. *The psychopath: an essay on the criminal mind*. Princeton, NJ: Van Nostrand

McCoy, W. K. and Edens, J. F. 2006. Do Black and White youths differ in level of psychopathic traits: a meta-analysis of the Psychopathy Checklist measures, *Journal of Consulting and Clinical Psychology* 74: 386–92

Mealey, L. 1995. The sociobiology of sociopathy: an integrated evolutionary model, *Behavioural and Brain Sciences* 18: 523–99. Reprinted in 1997 in S. Baron-Cohen, *The maladapted mind*. Philadelphia, PN: Erlbaum/Taylor-Francis

Millon, T., Simonsen, E., Birket-Smith, M. and Davis, R. D. (eds.) 1998. *Psychopathy: antisocial, criminal, and violent behaviour*. New York: Guilford Press

Murrie, D. C., Marcus, D. K., Douglas, K. S., Lee, Z., Salekin, R. T. and Vincent, G. 2007. Youth with psychopathy features are not a discrete class: a taxometric analysis, *Journal of Child Psychology and Psychiatry* 48: 714–23

Muthen, L. K. and Muthen, B. O. 2001. *Mplus user's guide*, 2nd edn. Los Angeles, CA: Muthen and Muthen

Nathanson, C., Paulhus, D. L. and Williams, K. M. 2006. Personality and misconduct correlates of body modification and other cultural deviance markers, *Journal of Research in Personality* 40: 779–802

Neumann, C. S. 2007. Psychopathy, *British Journal of Psychiatry* 191: 357–8

Neumann, C. S. and Hare, R. D. 2007. Erroneous conclusions about the PCL-R based on faulty modeling. Post on *British Journal of Psychiatry* website, http://bjp.rcpsych.org/cgi/eletters/190/49/s39

  2008. Psychopathic traits in a large community sample: links to violence, alcohol use, and intelligence, *Journal of Consulting and Clinical Psychology* 76: 893–9

Neumann, C. S., Hare, R. D. and Newman, J. P. 2007. The super-ordinate nature of the Psychopathy Checklist-Revised, *Journal of Personality Disorders* 21: 102–7

Neumann, C. S., Kosson, D. S., Forth, A. E. and Hare, R. D. 2006. Factor structure of the Hare Psychopathy Checklist: Youth Version in incarcerated adolescents, *Psychological Assessment* 18: 142–54

Neumann, C. S., Kosson, D. S. and Salekin, R. T. 2007. Exploratory and confirmatory factor analysis of the psychopathy construct: methodological and conceptual issues, in H. Hervé and J. C. Yuille (eds.), *The psychopath: theory, research, and practice*, pp. 79–104. Mahwah, NJ: Erlbaum

Neumann, C. S. and Vitacco, M. J. 2004. *Psychopathy and symptoms of psychopathology in the prediction of latent variable growth in violence.* Paper presented at the annual meeting of the Society for Research in Psychopathology, St Louis, MO, 7–10 October 2004

Neumann, C. S., Vitacco, M. J., Hare, R. D. and Wupperman, P. 2005. Reconstruing the 'reconstruction' of psychopathy: a comment on Cooke, Michie, Hart, and Clark, *Journal of Personality Disorders* 19: 624–40

Ogloff, J. R. P. 2006. Psychopathy/antisocial personality disorder conundrum, *Australian and New Zealand Journal of Psychiatry* 40: 519–28

Patrick, C. J. (ed.). 2006. *Handbook of psychopathy.* New York: Guilford Press

Robins, L. N. 1966. *Deviant children grown up.* Baltimore: Williams and Wilkins

  1978. Aetiological implications in studies of childhood histories relating to antisocial personality, in R. D. Hare and D. Schalling (eds.), *Psychopathic behaviour: approaches to research*, pp. 255–71. Chichester: John Wiley

Rogers, R., Salekin, R. T., Sewell, K. W. and Cruise, K. R. 2000. Prototypical analysis of antisocial personality disorder: a study of inmate samples, *Criminal Justice and Behaviour* 27: 234–55

Ruscio, J. 2007. Taxometric analysis: an empirically grounded approach to implementing the method, *Criminal Justice and Behaviour* 34: 1588–1622

Rutter, M. 2005. Commentary: what is the meaning and utility of the psychopathy concept?, *Journal of Abnormal Child Psychology* 33: 499–503

Salekin, R. T. 2006. Psychopathy in children and adolescents, in C. J. Patrick (ed.), *Handbook of psychopathy*, pp. 389–414. New York: Guilford Press

Salekin, R. T., Brannen, D. N., Zalot, A. A., Leistico, A. R. and Neumann, C. S. 2006. Factor structure of psychopathy in youth: testing the applicability of the new four-factor model, *Criminal Justice and Behaviour* 33: 135–57

Salekin, R. T., Neumann, C. S., Leistico, A. M., DiCiccio, T. M. and Duros, R. L. 2004. Psychopathy and comorbidity in a young offender sample: taking a closer look at psychopathy's potential importance over disruptive behaviour disorders, *Journal of Abnormal Psychology* 113: 416–27

Schrum, C. L. and Salekin, R. T. 2006. Psychopathy in adolescent female offenders: an item response theory analysis of the Psychopathy Checklist: Youth Version, *Behavioural Sciences and the Law* 24: 39–63

Shye, S. and Elizur, D. 1994. *Introduction to facet theory: content design and intrinsic data analysis in behavioural research*. Newbury Park, CA: Sage

Slutske, W. S. 2001. The genetics of antisocial behaviour, *Current Psychiatry Reports* 3: 158–62

Steadman, H. J., Silver, E., Monahan, J., Appelbaum, P. S., Clark Robbins, P., Mulvey, E. P., Grisso, T., Roth, L. H. and Banks, S. 2000. A classification tree approach to the development of actuarial violence risk assessment tools, *Law and Human Behaviour* 24: 83–100

Taylor, J., Loney, B. R., Bobadilla, L., Iacono, W. G. and McGue, M. 2003. Genetic and environmental influences on psychopathy trait dimensions in a community sample of male twins, *Journal of Abnormal Child Psychology* 31: 633–45

Tellegen, A. in press. *MPQ (Multi-Dimensional Personality Questionnaire): Manual for administration, scoring, and interpretation*. Minneapolis, MN: University of Minnesota Press

Trull, T. J. and Durrett, C. A. 2005. Categorical and dimensional models of personality disorder, *Annual Review of Clinical Psychology* 1: 355–80

Ullrich, S. and Marneros, A. 2004. Dimensions of personality disorders in offenders, *Criminal Behaviour and Mental Health* 14: 202–13

   2007. Underlying dimensions of ICD-10 personality disorders: risk factors, childhood antecedents, and adverse outcomes in adulthood, *Journal of Forensic Psychiatry and Psychology* 18: 44–58

Viding, E., Blair, R. J. R., Moffitt, T. E. and Plomin, R. 2005. Evidence for substantial genetic risk for psychopathy in 7-year-olds, *Journal of Child Psychology and Psychiatry* 46: 592–7

Viding, E., Frick, P. J. and Plomin, R. 2007. Aetiology of the relationship between Callous-Unemotional traits and conduct problems in childhood, *British Journal of Psychiatry* 190 (Suppl. 49): S33–S38

Vitacco, M. J., Neumann, C. S., Caldwell, M. F., Leistico, A. M. and Van Rybroek, G. J. 2006. Testing factor models of the Psychopathy Checklist: Youth Version and their association with instrumental aggression, *Journal of Personality Assessment* 87: 74–83

Vitacco, M. J., Neumann, C. S. and Jackson, R. 2005. Testing a four-factor model of psychopathy and its association with ethnicity, gender, intelligence, and violence, *Journal of Consulting and Clinical Psychology* 73: 466–76

Vitacco, M. J., Neumann, C. S., Robertson, A. A. and Durrant, S. L. 2002. Contributions of impulsivity and callousness in the assessment of adjudicated male adolescents: a prospective study, *Journal of Personality Assessment* 78: 87–103

Vitacco, M. J. and Vincent, G. M. 2006. Understanding the downward extension of psychopathy to youth: implications for risk assessment and juvenile justice, *International Journal of Forensic Mental Health* 5: 29–38

Walsh, Z. T., Swogger, M. T. and Kosson, D. S. 2003. *The nature of violence in psychopathic and nonpsychopathic offenders: instrumentality and related constructs.* Paper presented at the annual meeting of the Society for Research in Psychopathology, Toronto, October, 2003

Walters, G. D., Duncan, S. A. and Mitchell-Perez, K. 2007. The latent structure of psychopathy: a taxometric investigation of the Psychopathy Checklist-Revised in a heterogeneous sample of male prison inmates, *Assessment* 14: 270–8

Walters, G. D., Gray, N. S. Jackson, R. L., Sewell, K. W., Rogers, R., Taylor, J. and Snowden, R. J. 2007. A taxometric analysis of the Psychopathy Checklist: Screening Version (PCL:SV): further evidence of dimensionality, *Psychological Assessment* 19: 330–9

Warren. J. I. and South, S. C. 2006. Comparing the constructs of antisocial personality disorder and psychopathy in a sample of incarcerated women, *Behavioural Sciences and the Law* 24: 1–20

Westen, D. and Weinberger, J. 2004. When clinical description becomes statistical prediction, *American Psychologist* 59: 595–613

Widiger, T. A., Cadoret, R., Hare, R. D., Robins, L., Rutherford, M., Zanarini, M., Alterman, A., Apple, M., Corbitt, E., Forth, A. E., Hart, S. D., Kultermann, J., Woody, G. and Frances, A. 1996. DSM-IV antisocial personality disorder field trial, *Journal of Abnormal Psychology* 105: 3–16

Widiger, T. A. and Lynam, D. R. 1998. Psychopathy and the five-factor model of personality, in T. Millon, E. Simonson, M. Birket-Smith and R. D. Davis (eds.), *Psychopathy: antisocial, criminal, and violent behaviour*, pp. 171–87. New York: Guilford Press

Williams, K. M., Paulhus, D. L. and Hare, R. D. 2007. Capturing the four-factor structure of psychopathy in college students via self-report, *Journal of Personality Assessment* 88: 205–19

World Health Organization 1990. *International classification of diseases and related health problems*, 10th edn. Geneva: WHO

Zuckerman, M. 1991. *Psychobiology of personality.* Cambridge University Press

39 Personality and eating disorders

Natalie J. Loxton and Sharon Dawe

It is paradoxical that while indices of health and wellbeing indicate that many in the Western world are living longer and healthier lives, there are a significant number of young women who engage in eating behaviours that are highly detrimental to health and can, in the extreme, result in starvation and death. The phenomenon of disordered eating, in particular highly restrictive eating, has been documented since the late nineteenth century (Gull 1888; Laseque 1873). However, in recent years we have seen a marked increase in the numbers of young women engaging in a range of disordered eating patterns (Machado, Machado, Gonçalves and Hoek 2007). One factor that has been proposed as playing a causal role in the exponential rise in disordered eating in modern society is the emergence of an ideal body shape characterized by low fat and ultra slenderness; a body shape that few women can reasonably achieve. However, despite being inundated with images of the ideal body shape across all forms of popular media, there are many women who do not develop either subclinical eating problems or a diagnozable eating disorder. Indeed, many seem to accept that they do not meet cultural ideals of beauty, and while expressing dissatisfaction with some aspects of their body, do not find themselves in a pattern of increasingly dysfunctional eating behaviour. Thus, it would appear that while socio-cultural factors clearly play a role in body dissatisfaction, there are other factors that increase the risk of developing disordered eating.

Recent reviews in this area have made the observation that while socio-cultural factors may 'set the scene' for body-dissatisfaction generally, individual-based factors may drive specific eating disorder symptoms (Striegel-Moore and Bulik 2007). One promising avenue of enquiry has concentrated on personality (Cassin and von Ranson 2005; Lilenfeld, Wonderlich, Riso *et al.* 2006). Claridge and Davis (2003, p. 3) have gone so far as to state that personality and psychopathology are so intrinsically linked that 'it is impossible to understand the nature of psychological disorders, including the form in which they take in particular individuals, without knowing something about the personality characteristics from which they spring'.

With this statement in mind, the aim of this chapter is to review personality traits that have consistently been found to be associated with disordered eating. In doing so, we focus on those traits associated with women who manage to maintain low body weight (anoretic behaviour) and traits more associated with those who binge and purge (bulimic behaviour). We highlight recent studies that examine the heterogeneity among women with disordered eating that raise questions about the current nosological approach to classifying eating disorder sub-types. We also review the literature on the multidimensional status of personality traits associated with the eating disorders. We conclude with a discussion of how a renewed focus on personality and disordered eating may shine more light on these complex behaviours.

Personality and disordered eating

There is growing agreement that two broad classes of biologically-based, motivated behaviour underlie personality: the tendency to approach appetitive stimuli and to avoid aversive stimuli (Carver, Sutton and Scheier 2000; Depue and Collins 1999). The tendency to avoid aversive situations and events is variously referred to as Neuroticism, trait anxiety, harm avoidance or behavioural inhibition. Used interchangeably, individuals who score highly on measures of these traits are (i) overly sensitive to and easily aroused by threat; (ii) experience considerable negative affect in potentially aversive situations; and (iii) when in doubt, inhibit ongoing behaviour. On the other hand, the tendency to approach appetitive stimuli typically maps onto such traits as impulsivity, Extraversion and sensation-seeking. Individuals who score highly on measures of these traits tend to (i) seek out novelty; (ii) are highly sensitive to potential reward; and (iii) respond with positive affect to appetitive stimuli.

Approach and avoidance tendencies have particularly intuitive appeal when studying disordered eating. Women who restrict their eating and maintain a low body weight are typically characterized by a high avoidance of food/weight gain, whilst women who over-eat and engage in compensatory behaviours tend to be characterized by both approach tendencies (e.g., binge-eating) and avoidance behaviour (e.g., restrictive dieting between binge episodes). Indeed, early clinical reports of eating disorders typically described girls with anorexia nervosa as overly-constrained, anxious and perfectionistic (Bruch 1973), whereas women with bulimia nervosa were described as antisocial, promiscuous and impulsive (Russell 1979). Such dichotomous portrayals of women who primarily restrict their eating versus those who binge eat is supported in part by contemporary personality research. However, as will be evident, such a dichotomy is not as clear-cut as once thought.

Personality disorders, personality traits and disordered eating

Current estimates suggest as many as 60 per cent of women with an eating disorder also meet criteria for a personality disorder (PD) (Rosenvinge, Martinussen and Østensen 2000). Of particular interest are the Cluster B and Cluster C PDs, which typically reflect general tendencies to engage in dysfunctional approach behaviour (Cluster B) and dysfunctional avoidance behaviour (Cluster C). Cluster C PDs and avoidance traits are common to all forms of disordered eating, regardless of specific eating behaviour. Cluster B PDs and approach traits are more specific to binge-purge behaviour.

Avoidance tendencies

Cluster C PDs, characterized by fearfulness and inhibition, are frequently co-morbid with anorexia nervosa (45 per cent). Of these, obsessive compulsive PD (15–20 per cent) and avoidant PD (14–19 per cent) are the most frequent. Cluster C PDs also co-exist in women who binge/purge, with approximately 44 per cent of women with bulimia nervosa and 26 per cent of women with binge eating disorder (BED) also meeting criteria for a Cluster C PD (Rosenvinge, Martinussen and Østensen 2000; Sansone, Levitt and Sansone 2004). As a comparison, the prevalence of Cluster C PDs in general psychiatric samples range from 5–7 per cent (Wilfley, Friedman, Dounchis *et al.* 2000).

The frequently observed co-morbidity between Cluster C PDs across eating disorder sub-types is reflected by studies using measures of continuously distributed personality traits. Women with dysfunctional eating patterns consistently score higher than controls on measures of trait anxiety, behavioural inhibition, negative emotionality and perfectionism (e.g., Bardone-Cone, Wonderlich, Frost *et al.* 2007; Díaz Marsa, Carrasco and Saiz 2000; Fassino, Abbate Daga, Amianto *et al.* 2002; Loxton and Dawe 2007). Heightened avoidance traits are consistent with the inhibited, restrictive eating behaviour of many women with disordered eating. Such traits also reflect the high prevalence of frank anxiety disorders and depression found in disordered eating populations (Pallister and Waller 2008).

Although many studies have demonstrated an association between anxiety-related traits and dysfunctional eating, there is some question as to whether certain personality traits represent predisposing vulnerability factors (e.g., perfectionism leads to restrictive dieting), pathology-related symptoms (e.g., increased obsessiveness due to chronic starvation) or are a consequence of the disorder (e.g., down-regulation of neurotransmitter receptors compensating for chronic consumption of sweet and fatty foods). Although costly and labour-intensive, longitudinal studies are the best method of teasing apart putative causal relationships between personality traits and disordered behaviour (Jacobi, Hayward, de Zwaan *et al.* 2004; Lilenfeld, Wonderlich, Riso *et al.* 2006). To date, longitudinal research supports the role of obsessiveness, Neuroticism and negative affect in the predisposition to the development of anorexia nervosa, bulimia nervosa and dysfunctional eating in general (Cervera, Lahortiga, Martínez-González *et al.* 2003; Leon, Fulkerson, Perry *et al.* 1999; Rastam, Gillberg and Wentz 2003). Perfectionism in adolescence is predictive of anorexia nervosa, and in combination with being overweight and low self-esteem, is predictive of bulimic symptoms in adulthood (Bardone, Vohs, Abramson *et al.* 2000; Tyrka, Waldron, Graber and Brooks-Gunn 2002). However, it is still unknown whether an anxious/perfectionist temperament is a specific risk factor for developing disordered eating or increases the risk of a psychiatric condition more generally. Nevertheless, it appears that avoidance traits are common to the spectrum of women with disordered eating.

Approach tendencies

Although high levels of inhibition and the tendency to be overly self-controlled makes intuitive sense for women who strive to maintain a socially-sanctioned low body weight, women who binge eat and purge also have character traits that suggest a *lack* of self-control (Claes, Vandereycken and Vertommen 2002; Fassino, Abbate Daga, Amianto *et al.* 2002). Lack of self-control in many women who binge eat is reflected in the high co-morbidity of Cluster B PDs with binge-purge eating disorders. Cluster B PDs, which are characterized by impulsive features such as self-harm, suicide attempts and substance abuse, co-occur in approximately 44 per cent of women with bulimia nervosa, 25 per cent of women with the binge-purge sub-type of anorexia nervosa and 12 per cent of women with BED. This compares with the 6–11 per cent prevalence rate found in general psychiatric samples (Wilfley, Friedman, Dounchis *et al.* 2000). Borderline PD, in particular, is estimated to be present in up to one-third of women who binge-purge. Relatively few women (3–10 per cent) with restricting anorexia nervosa meet diagnosis of Borderline PD, suggesting approach tendencies may be more specific to those women who binge/purge.

Women with dysfunctional eating patterns and those who binge eat also score higher on measures of impulsivity and novelty-seeking than those women who successfully restrict their eating, and control women (e.g., Díaz Marsa, Carrasco and Saiz 2000; Fassino, Abbate Daga, Amianto *et al.* 2002; Loxton and Dawe 2006). However, support for impulsivity as a causal risk factor for eating disorders has been mixed. Some studies find little support for measures of impulsivity as predictors of eating disorder onset (Tyrka, Waldron, Graber and Brooks-Gunn 2002). Others have found specific types of impulsiveness to predict eating disorder onset, but not others. For instance, Wonderlich, Connolly and Stice (2004) found impulsive behaviour (e.g., substance use, delinquency) but not self-reported impulsivity to predict onset of bulimic symptoms in adolescent girls. Unfortunately, few longitudinal studies have investigated impulsivity as a causal risk factor limiting definitive conclusions.

In general, there is strong support for avoidance tendencies such as anxiety, obsessiveness and negative affectivity to exist prior to the development of eating disorders. There is currently far less support for approach tendencies such as impulsivity as predisposing factors. However, as we discuss below, the mixed findings may be related to prior research using broadly defined notions of 'impulsiveness' that may overlook more key impulsivity facets associated with disordered eating.

Current challenges in disordered eating and personality research

The *Diagnostic and statistical manual of mental disorders*, 4th edn (DSM-IV) (American Psychiatric Association 1994) provides criteria for two primary eating disorder diagnoses, anorexia nervosa and bulimia nervosa, in addition to a third catch-all category, Eating Disorders Not Otherwise Specified (EDNOS). Reflecting the atheoretical approach used within the DSM-IV, diagnoses are based on symptom presentation. The prototypical woman with an eating disorder is one who has lost such an extreme amount of weight as to be diagnosed with anorexia nervosa. Here, weight loss is the defining criteria. However, the DSM-IV allows for two distinct sub-types of anorexia nervosa; one for those women who only restrict their food intake (restricting anorexia nervosa) and those of very low body weight but who also binge and/or purge (binge-purge anorexia nervosa). Bulimia nervosa, on the other hand, is characterized by typically normal weight women who engage in recurrent binge eating episodes. A diagnosis of bulimia nervosa also requires that the person engage in compensatory behaviour such as purging, excessive exercise or fasting. Again, sub-types occur with some women compensating for their binges by self-induced purging (bulimia nervosa, purging sub-type) while others compensate via other means such as restrictive dieting (bulimia nervosa, non-purging sub-type). The EDNOS category encompasses individuals with atypical variations of clinically significant disordered eating, such as Binge Eating Disorder. BED involves the binge eating component of bulimia nervosa, but excludes the criteria of compensatory behaviours.

This current diagnostic demarcation of the eating disorders based solely on symptom presentation has recently been questioned as being the best model of classifying eating disorder sub-types (Striegel-Moore and Wonderlich 2007). For example, while restricting anorexia nervosa and binge-purge anorexia are grouped together on the shared basis of low body weight, binge-purge anorexia nervosa shares binge eating with bulimia nervosa and BED. Furthermore, many women who present for treatment do not fit one distinct sub-type, with as many as 60 per cent of eating disorder diagnoses falling under the EDNOS category (Chavez and Insel 2007). Those who binge-purge tend to be particularly variable in symptom expression, illness course and prognosis. For example, some engage in periods of highly restrictive eating prior to binge episodes, whilst others binge eat without having ever dieted. Furthermore, women with an eating disorder frequently change sub-type category over the course of their illness, with a number of women initially diagnosed with anorexia nervosa subsequently meeting diagnostic criteria for bulimia nervosa (a reverse pattern has also been found with a small proportion of women who initially develop bulimia nervosa subsequently meeting diagnosis for anorexia nervosa, Bulik, Sullivan, Fear and Pickering 1997; Fichter, Quadflieg and Hedlund 2006; Herzog and Delinsky 2001; Tozzi, Thornton, Klump *et al.* 2005). Complicating matters further is the finding that anorexia nervosa and bulimia nervosa regularly co-occur in families, suggesting some common, likely biological, connection between the various eating disorder sub-types (Strober, Freeman, Lampert *et al.* 2000).

Personality profiles

The overlap in symptoms, the fluidity in movement across eating disorder diagnoses and the aggregation of different eating disorder sub-types in families demonstrates considerable heterogeneity within women with eating disorders (Striegel-Moore and Bulik 2007). It has been suggested that sub-grouping based on personality tendencies and the functional goal of excessive dieting, binge eating and other symptoms may prove more enlightening in understanding the etiology of disordered eating than current diagnostic categorization (Steiger and Bruce 2004; Wonderlich, Crosby, Mitchell and Engel 2007). As shown in Table 39.1, a number of researchers using a range of personality measures and data analytic approaches have derived three distinct personality profiles of women with eating disorders (Claes, Vandereycken, Luyten *et al.* 2006; Espelage, Mazzeo, Sherman and Thompson 2002; Goldner, Srikameswaran, Schroeder *et al.* 1999; Thompson-Brenner and Westen 2005; Wagner, Barbarich-Marsteller, Frank *et al.* 2006; Westen and Harnden-Fischer 2001; Wonderlich, Crosby, Joiner *et al.* 2005). In general, there appears to be (1) a high functioning/perfectionist group, (2) an overcontrolling/avoidant group, and (3) an impulsive/dysregulated group.

The 'high functioning/perfectionist' group have few co-morbid PDs, show less severe levels of disordered eating symptoms, and generally have better psychosocial functioning than the other two groups. 'Impulsive/dysregulated' women are more aggressive, antisocial and more likely to abuse alcohol and other drugs than overcontrolled women (Claes, Vandereycken, Luyten *et al.* 2006; Wonderlich, Crosby, Joiner *et al.* 2005). 'Overcontrolled/avoidant women', on the other hand, show greater interpersonal difficulties and ineffectiveness than the other groups (Espelage *et al.* 2002; Goldner *et al.* 1999). Women who are classified as either 'overcontrolled/avoidant' or 'impulsive/dysregulated' tend to remain in treatment longer and to have a poorer prognosis than 'high functioning women' (Thompson-Brenner and Westen 2005).

In line with personality studies discussed earlier, women with anorexia nervosa (restricting sub-type) tend to belong to either the 'high-functioning' or 'overcontrolled' groups, whilst women who binge eat (bulimia nervosa, binge-purge anorexia nervosa, BED) are fairly evenly spread across the three groups. What is particularly striking is the unusually high replication of the three personality profiles across studies; such consistency is virtually unheard of in psychiatric research (Claes *et al.* 2006). Moreover, using these personality profiles, Thompson-Brenner and Westen (2005) found personality profile classification contributed additional prediction to whether therapy was successful beyond traditional treatment outcome predictors such as binge/purge severity or the presence/absence of co-morbid disorders.

Given the above clustering by personality and the distribution of binge-eating women across the three personality groups, it has been suggested that future research into the etiology and treatment of eating disorders may prove more productive if there was a greater focus on these underlying personality traits rather than clinical symptoms such as body weight and body dissatisfaction. For instance, personality differences may shed light on the functional motivation of specific eating disorder symptoms. For example, those women who are impulsive may binge on food to help self-regulate heightened arousal or find palatable foods particularly rewarding, whilst women who are overcontrolled binge eat in

Table 39.1 *Summary of studies investigating sub-groups of eating disorders using personality-related measures.*

Study/Data Analysis	Participants	Personality measure/s	Clusters (% of sample)	Sub-group prevalence/Additional information
Goldner *et al.* 1999 CA	136 women with eating disorders 68 controls	DAPP (measures pathological personality)	1. 'Rigid' (50%) 2. 'Severe/dysregulated' (20%) 3. 'Mild' (30%)	AN primarily in 'Rigid' BN evenly distributed across groups
Westen and Harnden-Fischer 2001 CA	Ratings of eating disorder patients by 103 psychiatrists/psychologists	Q-Sort of personality traits and personality disorders	1. 'High functioning/ perfectionistic' (45%) 2. 'Constricted/overcontrolled' (38%) 3. 'Emotionally dysregulated' (16%)	AN primarily in 'constricted/overcontrolled' and 'high functioning' BN and AN-BN distributed across groups
Espelage *et al.* 2002 CA	183 eating disorder outpatients Archival data	MCMI-II	1. High functioning (17%) 2. Undercontrolled/dysregulated (50%) 3. Overcontrolled/avoidant (34%)	AN primarily in overcontrolled and high functioning groups BN and EDNOS spread across groups
Thompson-Brenner and Westen 2005	Ratings of most recent eating disorder patient (90% BN) by 145 psychiatrists/psychologists	Scenarios of three clusters derived in Westen and Harnden-Fischer 2001	1. 'High functioning/ perfectionistic' (42%) 2. 'Constricted/overcontrolled' (31%) 3. 'Emotionally dysregulated' (27%)	Dysregulated and Constricted associated with lengthier treatment and poorer outcome Personality cluster contributed additional variance to outcome beyond binge, purge and Axis I co-morbidity
Wonderlich *et al.* 2005 LPA	178 women with BN	Perfectionism scale, impulsivity scale, depressive symptom scale, STAI, MOCI	1. 'Affective- perfectionistic' (30%) 2. 'Impulsive' (20%) 3. 'Low co-morbidity' (50%)	'Affective-perfectionistic' greatest eating pathology 'Low co-morbidity' minimal eating or personality pathology

Table 39.1 (*cont.*)

Study/Data Analysis	Participants	Personality measure/s	Clusters (% of sample)	Sub-group prevalence/Additional information
Wagner *et al.* 2006 LPA	60 recovered (>12 months) from eating disorder 47 Never ill controls	YBOCS, STAI, BDI, TCI, BIS-11	1. 'Impulsive' (53%) 2. 'Anxious' (47%)	No difference between clusters on sub-type of former ED
Claes *et al.* 2006 CA	335 women with eating disorders	NEO-FFI	1. Resilient/high functioning (27%) 2. Undercontrolled/emotionally dysregulated (31%) 3. Overcontrolled/constricted (45%)	AN primarily in overcontrolled and resilient BN across the three groups

Note. CA = cluster analysis, LPA = Latent Profile Analysis, AN = anorexia nervosa, BN = bulimia nervosa, DAPP = Dimensional Assessment of Personality Pathology, MCMI-II = Millon Clinical Multiaxial Inventory-II, STAI = state-trait anxiety inventory, MOCI = Maudsley Obsessive-Compulsive Inventory, YBOCS = Yale-Brown Obsessive Compulsive Scale, BDI = Beck Depression Inventory, TCI = Temperament and Character Inventory, BIS-11 = Barrett Impulsivity Scale, NEO-FFI = Neuroticism, Extraversion, Openness to New Experience – Five Factor Inventory.

response to caloric deprivation due to highly restrictive eating. There is some support for this proposal. Steiger, Lehoux and Gauvin (1999) monitored a sample of women who frequently binge ate over an average of two weeks. For the majority of the women the urge to binge typically increased following periods of restricted eating. However, for the highly impulsive women in the study, restricted eating had little influence on binge urges. Dietary restraint clearly played a greater role in precipitating binge episodes for less impulsive women, but other factors appeared to precipitate binge episodes in the more impulsive women. Thus, refocusing on underlying personality structure rather than overt symptoms may enhance the efficacy of current eating disorder treatment and prevention programmes (Westen and Harnden-Fischer 2001). However, in order to further understand how personality traits may drive specific eating behaviour we need to first understand the nature of personality traits involved in the eating disorder risk profile. In this chapter we have chosen to focus on the trait of impulsivity.

Facets of impulsivity

Just as researchers are now focusing on within sub-type heterogeneity we (and researchers in the addictions field) have noted considerable heterogeneity within the expression and measurement of impulsivity (Dawe and Loxton 2004; De Wit and Richards 2004; Verheul, Van den Brink and Geerlings 1999).

Reward drive

Many aspects of addictive behaviour are goal-driven and purposeful in function. Based on J. A. Gray's (1970) biological model of personality we have labelled this impulsivity facet 'Reward Drive'. Reward drive reflects individual differences in sensitivity to, and reinforcement derived from, rewarding stimuli, including drugs of abuse and palatable foods. The mesolimbic dopaminergic pathways, which are heavily involved in the reinforcing effects of drugs of abuse, palatable food, sex and other naturally rewarding activities, are proposed as the primary neural pathways involved in reward drive (Dawe, Gullo and Loxton 2004; Fowles 2001).

In particular, we have differentiated reward drive from a conceptualization of 'impulsiveness' that accords more closely with conventional definitions of the term, namely the tendency to act spontaneously and without regard to the consequences. We refer to this facet as rash impulsivity, although other researchers also use the terms disinhibition and lack of planning (e.g., De Wit and Richards 2004; Verheul, Van den Brink and Geerlings 1999; Whiteside and Lynam 2001). Rash impulsivity is proposed as reflecting the functioning of prefrontal cortex, an area of the brain involved in impulse-control and decision-making (Dawe, Gullo and Loxton 2004). The neurotransmitter serotonin may also be involved in both rash-impulsive behaviour and disinhibited eating (Steiger, Koerner, Engelberg *et al.* 2001; Steiger, Young, Ng Ying Kin *et al.* 2001).

Although attention to multifaceted definitions of impulsivity has been embraced by researchers in the drug and alcohol field (see Dawe, Loxton, Gullo *et al.* 2007 for a review of facets of impulsivity and addictive behaviour), the distinction between different aspects of impulsivity may be even more salient in the eating disorders field. As noted earlier, women who binge eat/purge typically score higher on measures of rash impulsivity such as Eysenck's impulsivity scale, novelty-seeking scales, and sensation-seeking scales, than women who restrict their eating only, or women without disturbed eating patterns (Fassino, Abbate Daga, Amianto *et al.* 2002; Kane, Loxton, Staiger and Dawe 2004; Rossier, Bolognini, Plancherel and Halfon 2000). More recent research similarly finds women who binge eat/purge to be more reward-driven than women without dysfunctional eating patterns (Davis and Woodside 2002; Hasking 2006; Kane, *et al.* 2004). Reward drive has also been found to be associated with emotional over-eating, eating in response to external food cues, a preference for foods high in fats and sugar, and food craving (Davis, Patte, Levitan *et al.* 2007; Davis, Strachan and Berkson 2004; Franken and Muris 2005). Using fMRI technology, Beaver, Lawrence, Van Ditzhuijzen *et al.* (2006) recently found activation of the reward regions of the brain in response to images of appetizing foods to be associated with self-reported reward drive.

The findings that women who binge eat score higher on measures of reward drive and engage in motivated approach behaviour in light of palatable foods and other rewarding stimuli has been likened to the compulsive use of drugs (Grigson 2002). It has also been proposed that reward drive may function as a potential common factor underlying the co-morbidity between dysfunctional eating and substance misuse (Dawe and Loxton 2004; Loxton and Dawe 2001). However, to date, no prospective studies have investigated whether reward drive plays a causal role in the predisposition to disordered eating. Nevertheless, when considering phenomenological features, binge eating is characterized by compulsive approach behaviour and an accompanied sense of loss of control, suggesting a strong approach response in light of food cues; a response that is likely to be partially biologically-based.

Urgency

While researchers in Australia, Canada and Europe were focusing on Gray's biologically-based dimension of reward drive, researchers in the United States were also investigating facets of impulsivity associated with addictive behaviour (Fischer, Smith, Spillane and Cyders 2005). Using the Five-Factor Model (FFM) of personality as a basis, Whiteside and Lynam (2001) factor analysed the NEO-PI-R (a measure of FFM) and a range of impulsivity measures (measures of Gray's reward drive, though, were a notable exception). Four impulsivity factors were derived: (1) Urgency (the tendency to act rashly to alleviate negative affect); (2) (lack of) Perseverance (also referred to as lack of self-discipline; the inability to remain focused on the task at hand); (3) (lack of) Planning (also referred to as lack of premeditation/deliberation; the failure to think ahead and consider consequences); and (4) Sensation-seeking (the tendency to seek out and enjoy new experiences). This model is referred to as the UPPS model of impulsivity.

The UPPS model has been tested across a range of addictive behaviours, including alcohol abuse, disordered eating, antisocial behaviour and gambling (Miller, Flory, Lynam and Leukefeld 2003; Smith, Fischer, Cyders *et al.* 2007). Women in treatment for bulimia nervosa score higher on all four impulsivity factors than women with anorexia nervosa (restrictive sub-type); with women with binge-purge anorexia nervosa scoring in between. Both urgency and lack of planning (similar to rash impulsivity) were associated with severity of bulimic symptoms in this sample and in a sample of university undergraduate women (Claes, Vandereycken and Vertommen 2005; Smith *et al.* 2007). Other studies using university women, though, have found only the urgency facet of the UPPS to correlate with binge-eating symptoms (Fischer, Smith and Anderson 2003; Fischer, Smith, Annus and Hendricks 2007). This has led to the suggestion that the tendency to act impulsively whilst experiencing negative mood may be a key impulsivity trait involved in the predisposition/maintenance of bulimic behaviour. Recently, Cyders and colleagues (Cyders and Smith 2007; Cyders, Smith, Spillane *et al.* 2007) expanded the concept to include positive urgency. Whereas (negative) urgency refers to acting rashly in order to alleviate negative affect, positive urgency is the tendency to act rashly in response to positive affect. Studies to date, though, have failed to find an association with dysfunctional eating. Thus, at this stage, it appears negative rather than positive urgency is more specifically related to disordered eating.

Although studies investigating the relationship between the UPPS and disordered eating find (negative) urgency to correlate with binge-eating symptoms and, with less consistency, lack of planning (i.e., rash impulsiveness), no study has concurrently included reward drive. Therefore, before definitive statements can be made regarding which specific impulsivity trait endows one with greater liability to disordered eating, further studies incorporating a more complete range of impulsivity measures (e.g., lack of planning/rash impulsivity, reward drive) are required. Further, the two traits may both assist in understanding possible pathways to disordered eating.

Implications for future research and treatment

Researchers investigating risk-taking behaviour, such as drug abuse in adolescents have proposed multiple pathways to 'impulsive behaviour'. For example, Cooper, Flanagan, Talley and Micheas (2006) propose a dual pathway in which impulsive behaviour is an outcome of (i) attempts to seek out arousal and reward, and/or (ii) attempts to alleviate negative affect. In this model, trait impulsivity is seen as a general underlying predisposition to risky behaviours (such as disordered eating, substance abuse) that serves to regulate emotions. Extrapolating from this hypothesis to bulimic behaviour, for some women (and perhaps men) binge episodes and over-eating may reflect heightened reward drive in the pursuit of enhanced positive affect. In others, the same behaviour may reflect an attempt to use food to alleviate negative affect. The same observed behaviour (binge eating), therefore, may represent an endpoint of functionally distinct emotionally-driven motives. The first pathway merges well with the notion of heightened reward drive while the second pathway merges well with the notion of trait (negative) urgency. Further research is required to test such hypotheses.

Outcome studies show that while psychological treatments are effective in reducing binge eating and purging in many clients, between 22–51 per cent of clients who do improve initially relapse post treatment (Keel, Dorer, Franko *et al.* 2005). Factors found to predict relapse include substance abuse and difficulties with impulse control (Keel and Mitchell 1997). Again, a focus on personality traits may help identify triggers to relapse that may be targeted in treatment. For example, reward drive may be involved in the tendency to break dietary rules following exposure to cues associated with food (e.g., the sight and smell of food) while urgency may be associated with an inability to tolerate negative mood states. Indeed, it has been suggested that impulsive clients would likely benefit from treatment programmes that are tailored to addressing problems with impulse control. Even the designers of the 'gold standard' treatment programme for bulimia nervosa note that traits related to an intolerance of negative mood confer additional obstacles to treatment '*in certain patients*' (Fairburn, Cooper and Shafran 2003 p. 515, original emphasis). Such programmes now incorporate modules to target this, arguably, individual difference factor. Other interventions similarly include components targeting mood intolerance and impulsive behaviour (Safer, Telch and Agras 2001). While such interventions look promising, it is not yet known whether treatments that target individual differences in impulsivity add to the efficacy of current treatments.

Concluding remarks

Corr (2004, p. 318) recently stated that the field of personality research has frequently been relegated to the status of the 'Cinderella of psychology'. Due in part to the focus on cognitions and the dominance of social psychology, there was a move against personality-based explanations of behaviour in the 1970s and 1980s. A case in point comes from the addictions field in which the failure to identify an all encompassing 'addictive personality' led to the subsequent dismissal of personality as a contributor to the vulnerability to substance misuse (Verheul and Van den Brink 2000). However, Claridge and Davis (2003, p. 142) have noted that with the emergence of neuroscience and a renewed focus on biological causes of behaviour 'the tide has turned again, and personality pathology has now regained its prominence in the addiction risk profile'. Likewise, whilst the focus of the eating disorder research lens has swung from characterological features to socio-cultural factors over the past thirty years, there is again a return to personality factors (e.g., Cassin and von Ranson 2005; Lilenfeld,

Wonderlich, Riso *et al.* 2006). Such renewed focus on personality appears warranted in light of the above literature with consistent 'personality profiles' in women with disordered eating.

In sum, although disordered eating patterns are clearly couched within historical and cultural contexts, there is growing evidence that personality matters. Indeed, in studying the eating disorders one is uniquely placed to observe the delicate interplay between broad social factors that increase the risk of developing disordered eating and personality traits that may offer insight into underlying mechanisms.

References

American Psychiatric Association 1994. *Diagnostic and statistical manual of mental disorders*, 4th edn. Washington, DC: APA

Bardone-Cone, A., Wonderlich, S. A., Frost, R. O., Bulik, C. M., Mitchell, J. E., Uppala, S. *et al.* 2007. Perfectionism and eating disorders: current status and future directions, *Clinical Psychology Review* 27: 384–405

Bardone, A. M., Vohs, K. D., Abramson, L. Y., Heatherton, T. F. and Joiner, J. T. E. 2000. The confluence of perfectionism, body dissatisfaction, and low self-esteem predicts bulimic symptoms: clinical implications, *Behaviour Therapy* 31: 265–80

Beaver, J. D., Lawrence, A. D., Van Ditzhuijzen, J., Davis, M. H., Woods, A. and Calder, A. J. 2006. Individual differences in reward drive predict neural responses to images of food, *Journal of Neuroscience* 26: 5160–6

Bruch, H. 1973. *Eating disorders: obesity, anorexia, and the person within*. New York: Basic Books

Bulik, C. M., Sullivan, P. F., Fear, J. L. and Pickering, A. 1997. Predictors of the development of bulimia nervosa in women with anorexia nervosa, *Journal of Nervous and Mental Disease* 185: 704–7

Carver, C. S., Sutton, S. K. and Scheier, M. F. 2000. Action, emotion, and personality: emerging conceptual integration, *Personality and Social Psychology Bulletin* 26: 741–51

Cassin, S. E. and von Ranson, K. M. 2005. Personality and eating disorders: a decade in review, *Clinical Psychology Review* 25: 895–916

Cervera, S., Lahortiga, F., Martínez-González, M. A., Gual, P., de Irala-Estévez, J. and Alonso, Y. 2003. Neuroticism and low self-esteem as risk factors for incident eating disorders in a prospective cohort study, *International Journal of Eating Disorders* 33: 271–80

Chávez, M. and Insel, T. R. 2007. Special issue on diagnosis and classification, *International Journal of Eating Disorders* 40: S2

Claes, L., Vandereycken, W., Luyten, P., Soenens, B., Pieters, G. and Vertommen, H. 2006. Personality prototypes in eating disorders based on the Big Five model, *Journal of Personality Disorders* 20: 401–16

Claes, L., Vandereycken, W. and Vertommen, H. 2002. Impulsive and compulsive traits in eating disordered patients compared with controls, *Personality and Individual Differences* 32: 707–14

2005. Impulsivity-related traits in eating disorder patients, *Personality and Individual Differences* 39: 739–49

Claridge, G. and Davis, C. 2003. *Personality and psychological disorders*. London: Arnold

Cooper, M. L., Flanagan, M. E., Talley, A. E. and Micheas, L. 2006. Individual differences in emotion regulation and their relation to risk taking during adolescence, in D. K. Snyder, J. A. Simpson and J. N. Hughes (eds.), *Emotion regulation in couples and families: pathways to dysfunction and health*, pp. 183–203. Washington, DC: APA

Corr, P. J. 2004. Reinforcement sensitivity theory and personality, *Neuroscience and Biobehavioural Reviews* 28: 317–32

Cyders, M. A. and Smith, G. T. 2007. Mood-based rash action and its components: positive and negative urgency, *Personality and Individual Differences* 43: 839–50

Cyders, M. A., Smith, G. T., Spillane, N. S., Fischer, S., Annus, A. M. and Peterson, C. 2007. Integration of impulsivity and positive mood to predict risky behaviour: development and validation of a measure of positive urgency, *Psychological Assessment* 19: 107–18

Davis, C., Patte, K., Levitan, R., Reid, C., Tweed, S. and Curtis, C. 2007. From motivation to behaviour: a model of reward sensitivity, overeating, and food preferences in the risk profile for obesity, *Appetite* 48: 12–19

Davis, C., Strachan, S. and Berkson, M. 2004. Sensitivity to reward: implications for overeating and overweight, *Appetite* 42: 131–8

Davis, C. and Woodside, D. B. 2002. Sensitivity to rewarding effects of food and exercise in the eating disorders, *Comprehensive Psychiatry* 43: 189–94

Dawe, S., Gullo, M. J. and Loxton, N. J. 2004. Reward drive and rash impulsiveness as dimensions of impulsivity: implications for substance misuse, *Addictive Behaviours* 29: 1389–1409

Dawe, S. and Loxton, N. J. 2004. The role of impulsivity in the development of substance use and eating disorders, *Neuroscience and Biobehavioural Reviews* 28: 343–51

Dawe, S., Loxton, N. J., Gullo, M. J., Staiger, P. K., Kambouropoulos, N., Perdon, L. *et al.* 2007. The role of impulsive personality traits in the initiation, development and treatment of substance misuse problems, in P. M. Miller and D. J. Kavanagh (eds.), *Translation of addictions science into practice*, pp. 319–37. Amsterdam: Pergamon

De Wit, H. and Richards, J. B. 2004. Dual determinants of drug use in humans: reward and impulsivity, in R. A. Bevins and M. T. Bardo (eds.), *Motivational factors in the etiology of drug abuse*, pp. 19–55. Lincoln, NE: University of Nebraska Press

Depue, R. A. and Collins, P. F. 1999. Neurobiology of the structure of personality: dopamine, facilitation of incentive motivation, and Extraversion, *Behavioural and Brain Sciences* 22: 491–569

Díaz Marsa, M., Carrasco, J. L. and Saiz, J. 2000. A study of temperament and personality in anorexia and bulimia nervosa, *Journal of Personality Disorders* 14: 352–9

Espelage, D. L., Mazzeo, S. E., Sherman, R. and Thompson, R. 2002. MCMI-II profiles of women with eating disorders: a cluster analytic investigation, *Journal of Personality Disorders* 16: 453–63

Fairburn, C. G., Cooper, Z. and Shafran, R. 2003. Cognitive behaviour therapy for eating disorders: a 'transdiagnostic' theory and treatment, *Behaviour Research and Therapy* 41: 509–28

Fassino, S., Abbate Daga, G., Amianto, F., Leombruni, P., Boggio, S. and Rovera, G. G. 2002. Temperament and character profile of eating disorders: a controlled study with the Temperament and Character Inventory, *International Journal of Eating Disorders* 32: 412–25

Fichter, M. M., Quadflieg, N. and Hedlund, S. 2006. Twelve-year course and outcome predictors of anorexia nervosa, *International Journal of Eating Disorders* 39: 87–100

Fischer, S., Smith, G. T. and Anderson, K. G. 2003. Clarifying the role of impulsivity in bulimia nervosa, *International Journal of Eating Disorders* 33: 406–11

Fischer, S., Smith, G. T., Annus, A. M. and Hendricks, M. 2007. The relationship of Neuroticism and urgency to negative consequences of alcohol use in women with bulimic symptoms, *Personality and Individual Differences* 43: 1199–1209

Fischer, S., Smith, G. T., Spillane, N. S. and Cyders, M. A. 2005. Urgency: individual differences in reaction to mood and implications for addictive behaviours, in A. V. Clark (ed.), *Psychology of moods*, pp. 85–107. New York: Nova Science Publishers

Fowles, D. C. 2001. *Biological variables in psychopathology: a psychobiological perspective*, 3rd edn. New York: Kluwer Academic/Plenum Publishers

Franken, I. H. A. and Muris, P. 2005. Individual differences in reward sensitivity are related to food craving and relative body weight in healthy women, *Appetite* 45: 198–201

Goldner, E. M., Srikameswaran, S., Schroeder, M., L., Livesley, W. J. and Birmingham, C. L. 1999. Dimensional assessment of personality pathology in patients with eating disorders, *Psychiatry Research* 85: 151–9

Gray, J. A. 1970. The psychophysiological basis of Introversion-Extraversion, *Behaviour Research and Therapy* 8: 249–66

Grigson, P. 2002. Like drugs for chocolate: separate rewards modulated by common mechanisms?, *Physiology and Behaviour* 76: 389–95

Gull, W. W. 1888. Anorexia nervosa, *Lancet* 1: 515–16

Hasking, P. A. 2006. Reinforcement sensitivity, coping, disordered eating and drinking behaviour in adolescents, *Personality and Individual Differences* 40: 677–88

Herzog, D. B. and Delinsky, S. S. 2001. Classification of eating disorders, in R. Striegel-Moore and L. Smolak (eds.), *Eating disorders: innovative directions for research and practice*, pp. 31–50. Washington, DC: American Psychological Association

Jacobi, C., Hayward, C., de Zwaan, M., Kraemer, H. C. and Agras, W. S. 2004. Coming to terms with risk factors for eating disorders: application of risk terminology and suggestions for a general taxonomy, *Psychological Bulletin* 130: 19–65

Kane, T. A., Loxton, N. J., Staiger, P. K. and Dawe, S. 2004. Does the tendency to act impulsively underlie binge eating and alcohol use problems? An empirical investigation, *Personality and Individual Differences* 36: 83–94

Keel, P. K., Dorer, D. J., Franko, D. L., Jackson, S. C. and Herzog, D. B. 2005. Postremission predictors of relapse in women with eating disorders, *American Journal of Psychiatry* 162: 2263

Keel, P. K. and Mitchell, J. E. 1997. Outcome in bulimia nervosa, *American Journal of Psychiatry* 154: 313–21

Laseque, E. C. 1873. On hysterical anorexia, *Medical Times and Gazette* 2: 265–66, 367–9

Leon, G. R., Fulkerson, J. A., Perry, C. L., Keel, P. K. and Klump, K. L. 1999. Three to four year prospective evaluation of personality and behavioural risk factors for later disordered eating in adolescent girls and boys, *Journal of Youth and Adolescence* 28: 181–96

Lilenfeld, L. R. R., Wonderlich, S., Riso, L. P., Crosby, R. and Mitchell, J. 2006. Eating disorders and personality: a methodological and empirical review, *Clinical Psychology Review* 26: 299–320

Loxton, N. J. and Dawe, S. 2001. Alcohol abuse and dysfunctional eating in adolescent girls: the influence of individual differences in sensitivity to reward and punishment, *International Journal of Eating Disorders* 29: 455–62

2006. Reward and punishment sensitivity in dysfunctional eating and hazardous drinking women: associations with family risk, *Appetite* 47: 361–71

2007. How do dysfunctional eating and hazardous drinking women perform on behavioural measures of reward and punishment sensitivity?, *Personality and Individual Differences* 42: 1163–72

Machado, P. P. P., Machado, B. C., Gonçalves, S. and Hoek, H. W. 2007. The prevalence of eating disorders not otherwise specified, *International Journal of Eating Disorders* 40: 212–17

Miller, J., Flory, K., Lynam, D. and Leukefeld, C. 2003. A test of the four-factor model of impulsivity-related traits, *Personality and Individual Differences* 34: 1403–18

Pallister, E. and Waller, G. 2008. Anxiety in the eating disorders: understanding the overlap, *Clinical Psychology Review* 28: 366–86

Rastam, M., Gillberg, C. and Wentz, E. 2003. Outcome of teenage-onset anorexia nervosa in a Swedish community-based sample, *European Child and Adolescent Psychiatry* 12: I78–I90

Rosenvinge, J. H., Martinussen, M. and Østensen, E. 2000. The comorbidity of eating disorders and personality disorders: a meta-analytic review of studies published between 1983 and 1998, *Weight and Eating Disorders* 5: 52–61

Rossier, V., Bolognini, M., Plancherel, B. and Halfon, O. 2000. Sensation seeking: a personality trait characteristic of adolescent girls and young women with eating disorders, *European Eating Disorders Review* 8: 245–52

Russell, G. 1979. Bulimia nervosa: an ominous variant of anorexia nervosa, *Psychological Medicine* 9: 429–48

Safer, D. L., Telch, C. F. and Agras, W. S. 2001. Dialectical behaviour therapy for bulimia nervosa, *American Journal of Psychiatry* 158: 632–4

Sansone, R. A., Levitt, J. L. and Sansone, L. A. 2004. The prevalence of personality disorders among those with eating disorders, *Eating Disorders* 13: 7–21

Smith, G. T., Fischer, S., Cyders, M. A., Annus, A. M., Spillane, N. S. and McCarthy, D. M. 2007. On the validity and utility of discriminating among impulsivity-like traits, *Assessment* 14: 155–70

Steiger, H. and Bruce, K. R. 2004. Personality traits and disorders associated with anorexia nervosa, bulimia nervosa, and binge eating disorder, in T. D. Brewerton (ed.), *Clinical handbook of eating disorders*, pp. 209–30. New York: Marcel Dekker

Steiger, H., Koerner, N., Engelberg, M. J., Israel, M., Ying Kin, N. M. K. and Young, S. N. 2001. Self-destructiveness and serotonin function in bulimia nervosa, *Psychiatry Research* 103: 15–26

Steiger, H., Lehoux, P. and Gauvin, L. 1999. Impulsivity, dietary control and the urge to binge in bulimic syndromes, *International Journal of Eating Disorders* 26: 261–74

Steiger, H., Young, S. N., Ng Ying Kin, N. M. K., Koerner, N., Israel, M., Lageix, P. *et al.* 2001. Implications of impulsive and affective symptoms for serotonin function in bulimia nervosa, *Psychological Medicine* 31: 85–95

Striegel-Moore, R. H. and Bulik, C. M. 2007. Risk factor for eating disorders, *American Psychologist* 62: 181–98

Striegel-Moore, R. H. and Wonderlich, S. 2007. Diagnosis and classification of eating disorders: finding the way forward, *International Journal of Eating Disorders* 40: S1

Strober, M., Freeman, R., Lampert, C., Diamond, J. and Kaye, W. 2000. Controlled family study of anorexia nervosa and bulimia nervosa: evidence of shared liability and transmission of partial syndromes, *American Journal of Psychiatry* 157: 393–401

Thompson-Brenner, H. and Westen, D. 2005. Personality subtypes in eating disorders: validation of a classification in a naturalistic sample, *British Journal of Psychiatry* 186: 516–24

Tozzi, F., Thornton, L., Klump, K. L., Fichter, M. M., Halmi, K., Kaplan, A. S. *et al.* 2005. Symptom fluctuations in eating disorders: correlates of diagnostic crossover, *American Journal of Psychiatry* 162: 732–40

Tyrka, A. R., Waldron, I., Graber, J. A. and Brooks-Gunn, J. 2002. Prospective predictors of the onset of anorexic and bulimic syndromes, *International Journal of Eating Disorders* 32: 282–90

Verheul, R. and Van den Brink, W. 2000. The role of personality pathology in the aetiology and treatment of substance use disorders, *Current Opinion in Psychiatry* 13: 163–9

Verheul, R., Van den Brink, W. and Geerlings, P. 1999. A three-pathway psychobiological model of craving for alcohol, *Alcohol and Alcoholism* 34: 197–222

Wagner, A., Barbarich-Marsteller, N. C., Frank, G. K., Bailer, U. F., Wonderlich, S. A., Crosby, R. D. *et al.* 2006. Personality traits after recovery from eating disorders: do subtypes differ?, *International Journal of Eating Disorders* 39: 276–84

Westen, D. and Harnden-Fischer, J. 2001. Personality profiles in eating disorders: rethinking the distinction between Axis I and Axis II, *American Journal of Psychiatry* 158: 547–62

Whiteside, S. P. and Lynam, D. R. 2001. The Five Factor Model and impulsivity: using a structural model of personality to understand impulsivity, *Personality and Individual Differences* 30: 669–89

Wilfley, D. E., Friedman, M. A., Dounchis, J. Z., Stein, R. I., Welch, R. R. and Ball, S. A. 2000. Comorbid psychopathology in binge eating disorder: relation to eating disorder severity at baseline and following treatment, *Journal of Consulting and Clinical Psychology* 68: 641–9

Wonderlich, S. A., Connolly, K. M. and Stice, E. 2004. Impulsivity as a risk factor for eating disorder behaviour: assessment implications with adolescents, *International Journal of Eating Disorders* 36: 172–82

Wonderlich, S. A., Crosby, R. D., Joiner, T., Peterson, C. B., Mitchell, J. E., Le Grange, D. *et al.* 2005. Personality subtyping and bulimia nervosa: psychopathological and genetic correlates, *Psychological Medicine* 35: 649–57

Wonderlich, S. A., Crosby, R. D., Mitchell, J. E. and Engel, S. G. 2007. Testing the validity of eating disorder diagnoses, *International Journal of Eating Disorders* 40: S40–S45

40 Personality and attention deficit hyperactivity disorder

Rapson Gomez

Some recent studies have examined the relationships between major temperament and personality models and attention deficit hyperactivity disorder (ADHD) (*Diagnostic and statistical manual of mental disorders*) (DSM-IV) (American Psychiatric Association (APA) 1994; see also DSM-IV TR, APA 2000). These have generally shown that ADHD is systematically related to some of the major temperament and personality dimensions. This chapter will provide a review of these studies. To better comprehend this review, I begin with a very brief overview of ADHD, germane to the present review.

Attention deficit hyperactivity disorder

According to DSM-IV, ADHD is one of the most common childhood disorders. For its diagnosis, DSM-IV has a list of eighteen symptoms under two separate symptom groups, namely inattention (IA) and hyperactivity/impulsivity (HI), with nine symptoms for each group. The IA symptom group includes behaviours such as distractibility and difficulty focusing on tasks for a sustained period, and the HI symptom group includes behaviours such as fidgeting, excessive talking and restlessness. DSM-IV indicates that there are three types of ADHD, these being ADHD inattentive type (presence of only the IA symptom group), ADHD hyperactive/impulsivity type (presence of only the HI symptom group), and ADHD combined type (presence of both IA and HI symptom groups). Presence of a symptom group is based on at least six symptoms in the group being present. Also of relevance to this review are the diagnosis criteria for ADHD in DSM-III-R (APA 1987). Although DSM-III-R also considered inattention, hyperactivity and impulsivity as core symptoms, they are grouped together in a single group. The diagnosis is based on the presence of at least eight out of fourteen symptoms. A common feature of ADHD in both children and adults is the high co-morbidity with other externalizing and internalizing disorders (Biederman, Faranone, Spencer *et al.* 1993; Spencer, Biederman and Wilens 1999). Follow up studies show that ADHD is fairly stable from childhood to adulthood.

Barkley (1997) has argued that a deficit in response inhibition leading to problems in higher order cognitive processes is the central deficit of ADHD. Others have implicated a state regulation deficit or difficulties in allocating the effort necessary for task performance (Van der Meere 2002). Based on Gray's (1981) personality theory, Quay (1988) has suggested that ADHD is due to an underactive behavioural inhibition system (BIS). Gray's theory suggests two underlying neurobiological systems, namely the BIS and the behavioural approach system (BAS). The BIS and BAS are linked to different types of reinforcements. The BIS is thought to be sensitive to signals of punishment, frustrative non-reward and novelty, and its activation is thought to decrease behaviours toward such stimuli. The BAS is believed to be sensitive to signals of reward and non-punishment, and its activation is thought to increase approach behaviours toward these stimuli. Accordingly, dysinhibition can result from either an overactive BIS, or an underactive BIS, or a BAS that is more active than the BIS. Douglas has suggested that ADHD is associated with increased arousal, distraction and sensitivity to rewards (especially immediate rewards) (Douglas and Parry 1994). Sonuga-Barke (2003) has proposed that deficits in executive functioning underlie the IA symptoms, while deficits in reward response underlie the HI symptoms. Martel and Nigg (2006) have linked problems with cognitive control processes to the IA symptoms, and problems with motivational control processes to HI symptoms. In terms of neurobiology and genetics, ADHD has been linked to imbalances in the dopaminergic and noradrenergic systems (Zametkin and Rapoport 1987). Family, twin and adoption studies have shown that ADHD is highly influenced by genetic factors (Faraone and Doyle 2001), with mean heritability of .77 (Biederman 2005), and involving the 7-repeat allele of the dopamine receptor D4 gene (Faraone, Doyle, Mick and Biederman 2001).

Links for temperament and personality models with ADHD

Among the personality models that have examined the relationships with ADHD are those expounded by Gray (1970), Eysenck and Eysenck (1975), Tellegen (2000), Cloninger (1987), and the Five-Factor Model (FFM) (Costa and McCrae 1985; Goldberg 1993; John, Angleitner and Ostendorf 1988). The temperament models examined are those proposed or derived from Rothbart's model (Eisenberg, Fabes, Guthrie *et al.* 1996; Eisenberg, Sadovsky, Spinrad *et al.* 2005; Rothbart, Ahadi and Hershey 1994). These models are covered elsewhere in this Handbook. Not surprisingly, overlaps exist between the dimensions of the temperament and personality models (Costa and McCrae 1985, 1992a; Derryberry and Rothbart 1997; Goldberg and Rosolack 1994; Nigg 2000; Saggino 2000; Scholte and De Bruyn 2004; Watson, Clark and Harkness 1994; Weyers, Krebs and Janke 1995).

Viewed from a perspective of a three-factor model of personality, there is both conceptual and empirical support for convergence of Rothbart's approach, Esyneck's extraversion, Grays' behavioural approach system (BAS) (and to a lesser degree BIS), Tellegen's positive emotionality (and to a lesser degree negative emotionality), Cloninger's novelty seeking and persistence, and the FFM Extraversion (and to a lesser degree Agreeableness and Openness). There is also support for convergence of Rothbart's reactivity, Eisenberg's negative emotionality and resiliency, Eysenck's neuroticism, Gray's BIS (and to a lesser degree BAS), Tellegen's negative emotionality (and to a lesser degree positive emotionality), Cloninger's harm avoidance and high reward dependency, and the FFM Neuroticism (and to a lesser degree Agreeableness). There is also some degree of convergence for Rothbart's effortful control, Eisenberg's reactive and effortful controls, Esyneck's psychoticism, Tellegen's constraint, and the FFM Conscientiousness and Agreeableness.

To date, two studies have examined the relevance of Rothbart's temperament model for ADHD (Goldsmith, Lemery and Essex 2004; Lemery, Essex and Smider 2002). Taken together, in terms of Rothbart's model, both studies suggest that effortful control is associated negatively with ADHD, while reactivity is associated positively with ADHD. These findings are consistent with other studies that used a different model of temperament (Bussing, Gary, Mason *et al.* 2003; Martel and Nigg 2006; McIntosh and Cole-Love 1996). For instance, Martel and Nigg (2006) found that for parent ratings, resiliency and effortful control correlated negatively with IA, while reactive control correlated negatively with HI.

Braaten and Rosén (1997) conducted a study that was relevant to Eysenck's and Gray's theories. The findings indicated lower scores for a measure of expectancy for punishment, and also higher Extraversion and Neuroticism in the ADHD group. The finding for punishment expectancy can be interpreted as ADHD individuals having low BIS.

To date only one study has examined the relevance of Tellegen's model for ADHD (Cukrowicz, Taylor, Schatschneider and Iacono 2006). It compared the personality *profile* of 'pure' ADHD (i.e., without conduct disorder (CD)), ADHD + CD, CD, and normative control groups of adolescents and children. For both age cohorts, both self- and mother ratings indicated no group difference for positive emotionality. All three clinical groups had high scores for negative emotionality and lower scores for constraint, compared to the normative mean. The ADHD + CD group had more extreme scores compared to the other two clinical groups (i.e., dose effect). The 'pure' ADHD and CD groups did not differ from each other in terms of their profiles. The findings were consistent across gender, and between eleven and seventeen-year-olds.

In relation to Cloninger's model, two studies with adults (Anckarsäter, Stahlberg, Larson *et al.* 2006; Downey, Stelson, Pomerleau and Giordani 1997) and three studies with children and adolescents (Rettew, Copeland, Stanger and Hudziak 2004; Tillman, Gellar and Craney 2003; Yoo, Kim, Ha *et al.* 2006) have been published. With reference to the temperament dimensions, and with the exception of the Downey *et al.* (1997) study, all the other studies found no difference for harm avoidance. Downey *et al.* (1997) found higher harm avoidance in the

ADHD group. Taken together, the findings in these studies suggest that ADHD individuals, including those screened for internalizing and externalizing disorders, have high novelty seeking and low persistence. There is also some evidence that novelty seeking is even higher among ADHD combined type, compared to ADHD inattentive type (Rettew *et al.* 2004). The failure to find an association between ADHD and harm avoidance would seem surprising since it is generally viewed as comparable to Neuroticism, negative affectivity and BIS. Zelenski and Larsen (1999) found that unlike Neuroticism, negative affectivity and BIS, which all loaded on a single BIS factor, harm avoidance had loadings on this and also on an impulsivity-thrill seeking factor and a BAS factor. Thus, Cloninger's harm avoidance may be confounded with impulsivity and BAS items, and this could explain why studies have not found an association between this dimension and ADHD.

In relation to character dimensions, the only study reporting such data for adults found a difference for only self-directedness, with ADHD individuals having lower scores than controls (Anckarsäter, Stahlberg, Larson *et al.* 2006). The studies on children and adolescents have also reported the same finding (Rettew *et al.* 2004; Yoo, Kim, Ha *et al.* 2006.). Tillman, Geller and Craney (2003) found differences for parent-ratings and for self-ratings. The findings for cooperativeness appear mixed, with studies reporting no difference (Rettew *et al.* 2004 for two different groups; Tillman, Geller and Craney 2003 for self-ratings) or lower scores (Tillman, Geller and Craney 2003 for parent-ratings; Yoo, Kim, Ha *et al.* 2006 for both self- and parent-ratings) for ADHD groups, compared to control groups. Since Rettew *et al.* screened their ADHD participants for co-existing externalizing and internalizing disorders, it is highly probable that low cooperativeness is a feature of ADHD + CD individuals, and not 'pure' ADHD. In terms of self-transcendence, fantasy and spirituality, virtually all studies found no difference between ADHD and control groups.

At least five studies have examined the relevance of the FFM for understanding ADHD (Nigg, Oliver, Blaskey *et al.* 2002; Parker, Majeski and Collin 2004; Ranseen, Campbell and Baer 1998; Retz, Retz-Junginger, Hengesch *et al.* 2004; Weinstein, Apfel and Weinstein 1998). It is noteworthy that the study by Nigg *et al.* (2002) involved six different samples. Overall, these studies have generally shown that when ADHD individuals, who are not screened for co-existing externalizing disorders, are compared to non-ADHD controls, the ADHD group will have higher levels of Neuroticism, and lower levels of Conscientiousness and Agreeableness. Lower Conscientiousness is likely to be more characteristic of ADHD groups with high levels of the IA symptoms, while lower Agreeableness is more likely to be characteristic of ADHD groups with high levels of the HI symptoms. The findings for Extraversion appear to vary in terms of whether group comparisons or correlations were used. While ADHD groups have generally not differed from non-ADHD groups, correlation data show that ADHD, especially IA, is negatively associated with Extraversion. Existing data are not supportive of an association between Openness and ADHD. When the findings are taken together it would appear that 'pure' ADHD (i.e., without CD) will be associated with an FFM profile of high Neuroticism and low Conscientiousness. Extraversion may also be associated negatively with IA.

Implications in relation to ADHD

Personality profile of ADHD and personality-ADHD models

Overall, based on the conceptual and empirical overlaps across the dimensions in the different temperament and personality models, the findings of past studies suggest that ADHD is positively associated with temperament reactivity, BIS, negative emotionality, Neuroticism, impulsivity and novelty seeking, and negatively associated with constraint, temperament reactive control and temperament effortful control. There is some, albeit low, support for a negative association with Extraversion, especially for IA symptoms. Overall, these findings indicate that ADHD is associated with high levels of personality and temperament dimensions reflecting reactivity and impulsivity. Recently, Miller, Flory, Lynam and Leukefeld (2003) examined the relationships between ADHD symptoms (counts) and four different impulsivity traits from the NEO-PI-R (Costa and McCrae 1992b). These were the sub-scales for impulsivity (in the Neuroticism scale, reflecting urgency), excitement seeking (in the Extraversion scale, reflecting sensation-seeking), self-discipline (in the Conscientiousness scale, reflecting perseverance), and deliberation (also in the Conscientiousness scale, reflecting premediation). They found that IA correlated positively with sensation-seeking, lack of perseverance and lack of premediation, while HI correlated positively with urgency, sensation seeking, lack of perseverance and lack of premediation. Regression analyses involving all four impulsivity scales indicated that IA was predicted by only the lack of perseverance, while HI was predicted by only the lack of premediation. This study highlights the importance of examining lower order factors within the broader dimensions. To date, such studies have not been conducted.

According to Tackett (2006) four models have gained acceptance that help explain the relationships between personality/temperament and Axis I disorders. These are the complication (or scar) model; the pathoplasty (or exacerbation) model; the vulnerability (or predisposition) model; and the spectrum model. The complication model suggests that a disorder changes a person's premorbid personality or temperament. The pathoplasty model suggests that a person's pre-existing personality or temperament influences the course, severity, presentation and prognosis of a disorder. The vulnerability model suggests that certain personality or temperament traits increase the risk for the development of a disorder. The spectrum model suggests that personality or temperament traits and the disorder lie on a continuum and they are a different manifestation of the same system. Also, the neurobiological factors underlying the personality and temperament traits that have been associated with ADHD are the same. Despite this possibility, it needs to be stressed that methodological limitations in past studies limit a clear understanding of whether the other models are also applicable.

Features, developmental course and treatment implications for ADHD

The review indicates that the association of ADHD with high levels of reactivity and impulsivity is consistent across DSM-III and DSM-IV diagnostic criteria, gender and age groups (from pre-school to adulthood). This also implies support for ADHD as an adult disorder. The review indicated that for pre-school children, the temperament dimensions of low effortful control and high reactivity are related to ADHD. For older children, low effort control is related to IA symptoms, while the HI symptoms are related to low reactive control. However, both these associations may be increased when high negative emotionality is also present. This implies an interaction between the reactivity and impulsivity dimensions. For adolescents and adults, the critical personality dimensions are those related to reactivity and impulsivity. High levels on both the reactivity and impulsivity dimensions are positively associated with ADHD. This review also suggested that such associations are also relevant to other externalizing disorders, in particular CD. Thus it could be argued that high reactivity and high impulsivity are features of externalizing disorders in general, and not specifically for ADHD.

Since social learning shapes personality it is prudent to ask what insights personality studies offer here. As noted earlier, Cloninger's psychobiological model includes three character dimensions (self-directedness, cooperation and self-transcendence), which are assumed to be influenced by social learning (Cloninger, Svrakic and Przybeck 1993). The FFM dimensions of Agreeableness and Conscientiousness can also be assumed to be influenced by social learning. For these dimensions, the review indicated that ADHD is associated with low self-directedness and Conscientiousness, while CD is associated with low Agreeableness and low cooperation. Thus it could appear that although both reactivity and impulsivity traits may be associated with both ADHD and CD, character dimensions may distinguish these disorders. More specifically, low self-directedness and low Conscientiousness are more likely to be associated with ADHD, while low Agreeableness and low cooperation are more likely to be associated with CD. As low levels of self-directedness and Conscientiousness reflect poor organization, efficiency, diligence, attention to task and responsibility, it can be argued that younger individuals with a predisposition for externalizing disorders are at greater risk for developing ADHD when they are exposed to a social environment that has limited opportunities to acquire skills that reduce or limit these behaviours. In contrast, when such children are exposed to a social environment that has limited opportunities to acquire compliance and cooperation skills, they are likely to develop CD (and by extension oppositional defiant disorder (ODD)). These possibilities mean that treatment of ADHD would benefit from social learning to improve organization, efficiency, diligence, attention to task and responsibility, while treatment of CD/ODD would benefit from social learning to improve compliance and cooperation skills. Inclusion of treatment components for learning both sets of skills may be needed when ADHD is co-morbid with CD/ODD.

Theories of ADHD

The conclusions made in this review support the response inhibition deficit theory of ADHD (Barkley 1997; Quay 1988). However, since this review concluded that ADHD is associated with high levels of the personality dimensions that are associated with the BIS (e.g., Neuroticism and negative affectivity), it follows that personality studies do not support Quay's (1988) view linking the response inhibition of ADHD to a weak BIS. As the BIS is related to sensitivity to punishment, the high scores for the BIS dimensions suggest that ADHD individuals are sensitive to such cues. The weaker support linking the personality dimensions of approach with ADHD suggests that ADHD individuals will have low sensitivity to reward. A low sensitivity implies a lower threshold for rewards. This has been proposed for ADHD (Haelein and Caul 1987). Sagvolden, Aase, Zeiner and Berger (1998) have proposed an abnormal delay-reward gradient model that suggests that for ADHD individuals, the duration of the effects of reward on the behaviours that precede and proceed the reward is reduced, compared to non-ADHD individuals. Consequently, behaviours occurring much earlier and later in this sequence fail to come under the control of the reward. This can be interpreted in terms of ADHD individuals being less controlled by rewards that are delayed in time. Such a view is also implied in the delay aversion model of ADHD proposed by Sonuga-Barke and Taylor (1992). Such models suggest that under some conditions ADHD individuals may be undersensitive to rewards. The personality studies reviewed can be taken as implicating aberrant sensitivity to reinforcements.

The current review also has implications for the state regulation deficit theory. As noted previously, the state regulation model implicated problems in effort allocation, and effort allocation is linked to arousal and activation (Sanders 1983; Van der Meere 2002). According to Strelau (1995) low Extraversion, high Neuroticism, high negative emotionality, high reactivity and high anxiety are associated with high arousability, while sensation-seeking and high impulsivity are associated with low arousability. Given that it is concluded here that ADHD is associated positively with temperament reactivity, BIS, negative emotionality, Neuroticism, impulsivity and novelty seeking, and low Extraversion, it can be argued that ADHD is associated with temperament and personality dimensions reflecting both high and low arousability. This implies an aberrant arousal state for ADHD. It is also to be noted that the effort allocation that is involved in state regulation is influenced by reinforcement contingencies. Thus the link made here for ADHD with both reward and punishment is consistent with predictions from the state regulation deficit theory. Implications of reinforcements can be taken as deficiencies in motivational processes. There is, however, some data from personality studies that executive processes mediate the effect of response inhibition when IA symptoms are concerned.

Summary

This chapter reviewed studies that have examined temperament/ personality-ADHD links. It concluded that past studies have generally linked ADHD positively to reactivity, BIS and negative emotionality, FFM Neuroticism and novelty seeking, and negatively with reactive control, effortful controls and constraint. Based on these findings it was argued that temperament and personality studies are largely supportive of the view that ADHD reflects an inhibition deficit, coupled with high reactivity. Within the FFM, these reflect associations with low Conscientiousness and high Neuroticism, respectively. In Eysenck's models, these are high neuroticism and high psychoticism, respectively. In Tellegen's model, there are high negative affectivity and low constraint, respectively. In relation to Cloninger's model, the associations found for ADHD were for high novelty seeking and low persistence, which are consistent with an inhibitory deficit view. No association was found for the reactivity dimension of harm avoidance, and this may have arisen because in Cloninger's questionnaire the harm avoidance may be confounded with the impulsivity and BAS items. It is worth noting that the association between ADHD and novelty seeking found in this review supports linking both ADHD and novelty seeking to the same gene, which has been proposed to be the dopamine receptor DRD4 gene (Barr, Xu, Kroft *et al.* 2001). Currently, although studies have not really tested the applicability of the complication, pathoplasty, vulnerability and spectrum models to explain these personality-ADHD relationships, there is suggestive support for the spectrum model.

The review raised the possibility that low inhibition and high reactivity may not be specific to ADHD, but may be general to externalizing disorders. There is some evidence, however, that character dimensions can distinguish between ADHD and CD/ODD. While ADHD is associated with low self-directedness (in Cloninger's model) and low Conscientiousness (in FFM), CD is associated with low cooperation (in Cloninger's model) and low Agreeableness (in FFM). The negative associations noted for ADHD with the character dimensions of self-directedness and Conscientiousness suggest that treatment for ADHD would benefit from social learning to improve organization, efficiency, diligence, attention to task and responsibility.

In concluding, it needs noting that virtually all ADHD-personality/temperament studies reviewed in the chapter were cross-sectional, and they have examined the higher order personality/temperament dimensions. Thus, the conclusions made here do not imply causal relationships, and do not indicate relationships involving the lower order traits. Studies that allow examination of causal relationships and lower order traits are needed in the future.

References

American Psychiatric Association 1987. *Diagnostic and statistical manual of mental disorders – Revised*, 3rd edn. Washington, DC: APA

1994. *Diagnostic and statistical manual of mental disorders*, 4th edn. Washington, DC: APA

2000. *Diagnostic and statistical manual of mental disorders* (DSM-IV TR) *Text Revision*. Washington, DC: APA

Anckarsäter, H., Stahlberg, O., Larson, T., Hakansson, C., Jutblad, S-B., Niklasson, L. *et al.* 2006. The impact of ADHD and autism spectrum disorders on temperament, character, and personality development, *American Journal of Psychiatry* 163: 1239–44

Barkley, R. A. 1997. Behavioural inhibition, sustained attention, and executive functions: constructing a unifying theory of ADHD, *Psychological Bulletin* 121: 65–94

Barr, C. L., Xu, C., Kroft, J., Feng, Y., Wigg, K. J., Zai, G. *et al.* 2001. Haplotype study of four polymorphisms at the dopamine transporter locus confirm linkage to attention deficit hyperactivity disorder, *Biological Psychiatry* 49: 333–9

Biederman, J. 2005. Attention-Deficit/Hyperactivity Disorder: a selective overview, *Biological Psychiatry* 57: 1215–20

Biederman, J., Faranone, S. V., Spencer, T., Wilens, T. E., Norman, D., Lapey, K. A. *et al.* 1993. Patterns of psychiatric comorbidity cognition and psychosocial functioning in adults with attention deficit hyperactivity disorder, *American Journal of Psychiatry* 150: 1992–8

Braaten, E. B. and Rosén, L. A. 1997. Emotional reactions in adults with symptoms of attention deficit hyperactivity disorder, *Personality and Individual Differences* 22: 355–61

Bussing, R., Gary, F. A., Mason, D. M., Leon, C. E., Sinha, K. and Wilson Garvan, C. 2003. Child temperament, ADHD, and caregiver strain: exploring relationships in an epidemiological sample, *Journal of the American Academy of Child and Adolescent Psychiatry* 42: 184–92

Cloninger, C. R. 1987. A systematic method for clinical description and classification of personality variants: a proposal, *Archives of General Psychiatry* 44: 573–88

Cloninger, C. R., Svrakic, D. M. and Przybeck, T. R. 1993. A psychobiological model of temperament and character, *Archives of General Psychology* 50: 975–90

Costa, P. T. and McCrae, R. R. 1985. *The NEO Personality Inventory manual.* Odessa, FL: Psychological Assessment Resources

1992a. Four ways five factors are basic, *Personality and Individual Differences* 12: 887–98

1992b. *Revised NEO Personality Inventory (NEO PI-R) and NEO Five Factor Inventory (NEO-FFI).* Odessa, FL: Psychological Assessment Resources

Cukrowicz, K. C., Taylor, J., Schatschneider, C. and Iacono, W. G. 2006. Personality differences in children and adolescents with Attention-Deficit/Hyperactivity Disorder, conduct disorder, and controls, *Journal of Child Psychology and Psychiatry* 47: 151–9

Derryberry, D. and Rothbart, M. K. 1997. Reactive and effortful processes in the organization of temperament, *Development and Psychopathology* 9: 633–52

Douglas, V. I. and Parry, P. A. 1994. Effects of reward and non reward on frustration and attention in Attention Deficit Disorder, *Journal of Abnormal Child Psychology* 22: 281–302

Downey, K. K., Stelson, F. W., Pomerleau, O. F. and Giordani, B. 1997. Adult Attention Deficit Hyperactivity Disorder: psychological test profiles in a clinical population, *Journal of Nervous and Mental Disease* 185: 32–8

Eisenberg, N., Fabes, R. A., Guthrie, I. K., Murphy, B. C., Maszk, P., Holmgren, R. *et al.* 1996. The relations of regulation and emotionality to problem behaviour in elementary school children, *Development and Psychopathology* 8: 141–62

Eisenberg, N., Sadovsky, A., Spinrad, T. L., Fabes, R. A, Losoya, S. H., Valiente, C. *et al.* 2005. *Developmental Psychology* 41: 193–211

Eysenck, H. J. 1967. *The biological basis of personality.* Springfield, IL: Thomas

Eysenck, H. J. and Eysenck, S. B. G. 1975. *Manual of the Eysenck Personality Questionnaire (adult).* London: Hodder and Stoughton

Faraone, A. V. and Doyle, A. E. 2001. The nature and heritability of Attention-Deficit/ Hyperactivity Disorder, *Child and Adolescent Psychiatric Clinics of North America* 10: 299–316

Faraone, A. V., Doyle, A. E., Mick, E. and Biederman, J. 2001. Meta-analysis of the association between the 7-repeat allele of the dopamine d(4) receptor gene and attention deficit hyperactivity disorder, *American Journal of Psychiatry* 158: 1052–7

Goldberg, L. R. 1993. The structure of phenotypic traits, *American Psychologist* 48: 26–34

Goldberg, L. R. and Rosolack, T. K. 1994. The Big Five factor structure as an integrative framework: an empirical comparison with Eysenck's P-E-N model, in C. F. Halverson, Jr, G. A. Kohnstamm and R. P. Martin (eds.), *The developing structure of temperament and personality from infancy to childhood*, pp. 7–35. Hillsdale, NJ: Lawrence Erlbaum Associates

Goldsmith, H., Lemery, K. S. and Essex, M. J. 2004. Temperament as a liability factor for behavioural disorders of childhood, in L. Fisher DiLalla (ed.), *Behaviour genetics principles: perspectives in development, personality, and psychopathology*, pp. 19–39. Washington, DC: American Psychological Association

Gray, J. A. 1970. The psychophysiological basis of Introversion-Extraversion, *Behaviour Research and Therapy* 8: 249–66

1981. A critique of Eysenck's theory of personality, in H. J. Eysenck (ed.), *A model of personality*, pp. 246–76. New York: Springer

Haelein, M. and Caul, W. F. 1987. Attention deficit disorder with hyperactivity: a specific hypothesis of reward dysfunction, *Journal of the American Academy of Child and Adolescent Psychiatry* 26: 356–62

John, O. P., Angleitner, A. and Ostendorf, F. 1988. The lexical approach to personality: a historical review of trait taxonomic research, *European Journal of Personality* 2: 171–203

Lemery, K. S., Essex, M. J. and Smider, N. A. 2002. Revealing the relation between temperament and behaviour problem symptoms by eliminating measurement confounding: expert ratings and factor analyses, *Child Development* 73: 867–82

Martel, M. M. and Nigg, J. T. 2006. Child ADHD and personality/temperament traits of reactive and effortful control, resiliency, and emotionality, *Journal of Child Psychology and Psychiatry* 47: 1175–83

McIntosh, D. E. and Cole-Love, A. S. 1996. Profile comparisons between ADHD and non-ADHD children on the temperament assessment battery for children, *Journal of Psychoeducational Assessment* 14: 362–72

Miller, J., Flory, K., Lynam, D. and Leukefeld, C. 2003. A test of the four-factor model of impulsivity-related traits, *Personality and Individual Differences* 34: 1403–18

Nigg, J. T. 2000. On inhibition/disinhibition in developmental psychopathology: views from cognitive and personality psychology and a working inhibition taxonomy, *Psychology Bulletin* 126: 220–46

Nigg, J. T., Oliver, J. P., Blaskey, L. G., Huang-Pollock, C. L., Willcutt, E. G., Hinshaw, S. P. and Pennington, B. 2002. Big Five dimensions and ADHD symptoms: links between personality traits and clinical symptoms, *Journal of Personality and Social Psychology* 83: 451–69

Parker, J. D. A., Majeski, S. A. and Collin, V. T. 2004. ADHD symptoms and personality: relationships with the Five-Factor Model, *Personality and Individual Differences* 36: 977–87

Quay, H. C. 1988. The behavioural reward and inhibition systems in childhood behaviour disorders, in L. M. Bloomingdale (ed.), *Attention deficit disorder*, vol. III, pp. 176–86. Oxford: Pergamon

Ranseen, J. D., Campbell, D. A. and Baer, R. A. 1998. NEO PI-R profiles of adults with attention deficit disorder, *Assessment* 5: 19–24

Rettew, D. C., Copeland, W., Stanger, C. and Hudziak, J. J. 2004. Associations between temperament and DSM-IV externalizing disorders in children and adolescents, *Journal of Developmental and Behavioural Pediatrics* 25: 383–91

Retz, W., Retz-Junginger, P., Hengesch, G., Schneider, M., Thome, J., Pajonk, F. G. *et al.* 2004. Psychometric and psychopathological characterization of young male prison inmates with and without Attention Deficit/Hyperactivity Disorder, *European Archives of Psychiatry and Clinical Neuroscience* 254: 201–8

Rothbart, M. K., Ahadi, S. A. and Hershey, K. 1994. Temperament and social behaviour in childhood, *Merrill-Palmer Quarterly* 40: 21–39

Saggino, A. 2000. The Big Three of the Big Five: a replication study, *Personality and Individual Differences* 28: 879–86

Sagvolden, T., Aase, H., Zeiner, P. and Berger, D. F. 1998. Altered reinforcement mechanisms in Attention Deficit/Hyperactivity Disorder, *Behavioural Brain Research* 94: 61–71

Sanders, A. F. 1983. Towards a model of stress and human performance, *Acta Psychologica* 53: 61–97

Scholte, R. H. J. and De Bruyn, E. E. J. 2004. Comparison of the Giant Three and Big Five in early adolescents, *Personality and Individual Differences* 36: 1353–71

Sonuga-Barke, E. J. S. 2003. The dual pathway model of AD/HD: an elaboration of neuro-developmental characteristics, *Neuroscience and Biobehavioural Reviews* 27: 593–604

Sonuga-Barke, E. J. S. and Taylor, E. 1992. The effect of delay on hyperactive and non-hyperactive children's response times: a research note, *Journal of Child Psychology and Psychiatry* 33: 1091–6

Spencer, T., Biederman, J. and Wilens, T. 1999. Attention-Deficit/Hyperactivity Disorder and comorbidity, *Pediatric Clinics of North America* 46: 915–27

Strelau, J. 1998. *Temperament: a psychological perspective*. New York: Plenum

Tackett, J. L. 2006. Evaluating models of the personality-psychopathology relationship in children and adolescents, *Clinical Psychology Review* 26: 584–99

Tellegen, A. 2000. *Manual for the Multidimensional Personality Questionnaire*. Minneapolis, MN: University of Minnesota Press

Tillman, R., Geller, B. and Craney, J. L. 2003. Temperament and character factors in a prepubertal and early adolescent bipolar disorder phenotype compared to Attention Deficit Hyperactive and normal controls, *Journal of Child and Adolescent Psychopharmacology* 13: 531–43

Van der Meere, J. J. 2002. The role of attention, in S. T. Sandberg (ed.). *Monographs in child and adolescent psychiatry: hyperactivity disorders of childhood*, pp. 109–46. Cambridge University Press

Watson, D., Clark, L. A. and Harkness, A. R. 1994. Structures of personality and their relevance to psychopathology, *Journal of Abnormal Psychology* 103: 18–31

Weinstein, C. S., Apfel, R. J. and Weinstein, S. R. 1998. Description of mothers with ADHD with children with ADHD, *Psychiatry: Interpersonal and Biological Processes* 61: 12–19

Weyers, P., Krebs, H. and Janke, W. 1995. Reliability and construct validity of the German version of Cloninger's Tridimensional Personality Questionnaire, *Personality and Individual Differences* 19: 853–61

Yoo, H. J., Kim, M., Ha, H. J., Chung, A., Sim, M. E., Kim., S. J. and Lyoo, I. K. 2006. Biogenetic temperament and character and attention deficit hyperactivity disorder in Korean children, *Psychopathology* 35: 25–31

Zametkin, A. J. and Rapoport, J. L. 1987. Noradrenergic hypothesis of Attention Deficit Disorder with hyperactivity: a clinical review, in H. Y. Meltzer (ed.). *Psychopharmacology: the third generation of progress*, pp. 837–42. New York: Raven Press

Zelenski, J. M. and Larsen, R. J. 1999. Susceptibility to affect: a comparison of three personality taxonomies, *Journal of Personality* 67: 761–91

PART VIII

Applied Personality Psychology

41 Personality in school psychology

Moshe Zeidner

Overview

Broadly speaking, contemporary school psychology aims at servicing the educational community by applying psychological principles to help foster students' emotional and intellectual adjustment. In contrast to educational psychologists, who focus largely on problems of student learning and achievement, school psychologists are often, although not exclusively, interested in identifying and diagnosing abnormality (e.g., personality disorders, exceptional student groups) and in applying psychological research and sound interventions to schools in order to remedy difficulties in school adjustment.

The emotional health needs of students, in both the United States and across the globe, have received increasing attention over the past years. It is estimated that about one-fifth of America's children and adolescents have diagnosable disorders that require some form of mental health treatment (Nastasi, Moore and Varjas 2004). Internationally, it is predicted that mental illness will become one of the five most common causes of childhood disability, morbidity or mortality within the next two decades. Personality factors have been shown to influence vulnerability (or resilience) to a host of psychological problems and disorders, including anxiety, depression, aggression and cognate personality dysfunctions (Livesely 2001).

School psychologists are frequently charged with the responsibility of designing interventions to help ameliorate or remedy abnormal emotional states and conditions. Recent efforts have focused on the prevention of later personal and social maladjustment by providing primary prevention programmes in the school system. Indeed, schools provide an especially suitable site for the provision and delivery of psychological services, including early diagnosis of difficulties, primary and secondary prevention programmes, social skills training, mental health promotion and various risk reduction programmes (drugs, violence, unwanted pregnancy, etc.).

Goals and structure. This chapter discusses the pivotal role of personality in relation to a number of key concerns of modern school psychology – diagnosing and treating personality disorders and school-based interventions. This chapter is divided into two main sections. In the first section I examine how personality disorders contribute to adjustment difficulties in school settings. In the second section I briefly discuss a number of exemplary psychoeducational intervention programmes. I conclude with some general remarks on the role of personality in school psychology.

Personality disorders and school adjustment

In the following passages I briefly examine how personality traits and trait models may inform the intersecting concerns of school and clinical psychologists working with school-aged populations in diagnosing, understanding and treating children with behavioural and/or emotional problems (for a fuller treatment see Matthews, Zeidner and Roberts 2006). The following brief review is organized around the distinction between: (a) *internalizing* problems (e.g., inhibition, negative affect), and (b) *externalizing* problems (e.g., aggression, conduct problems and poor behavioural control).

Internalizing problems

The major emotional disorders of adults, including depression, generalized anxiety, phobias, post-traumatic stress disorder and obsessive-compulsive disorder, are also seen in children and adolescents, with broadly similar symptoms (Kendall 2000). The prevalence of internalizing disorders has proved difficult to estimate, but they may approach up to 5 per cent for depression and 9 per cent for anxiety disorders, tending to increase in adolescence and adulthood (Kamphaus and Frick 2002). In around 75 per cent of cases, school avoidance or refusal appears as a symptom (House 2002). However, anxiety disorders may be difficult to diagnose in younger children, because of their limited capacity to verbalize their mental states.

Disordered self-regulation in children, much like in adults, is expressed through biases and deficits in multiple cognitive processes, though limited by cognitive development. For example, meta-cognitions, such as excessive concerns about internal thoughts and images, play an important role in adult pathology (Wells and Matthews 1994), but younger children do not have the facility to reflect on their own thought processes.

Temperamental factors linked to negative affect, including behavioural inhibition, act as general risk factors for the spectrum of emotional disorders (Kagan and Snidman 1999; Rothbart and Bates 1998). Internalized behaviours have been associated with neurological 'soft signs' (Shafer, Schonfeld, O'Conner *et al.* 1985), including dysfunction of the left hemisphere and overreactivity of the right hemisphere. Environmental factors including life events, deprivation and family interaction patterns are also critical (Kendall 2000). Southam-Gerow and Kendall (2002) highlight the importance of dysfunctional emotion regulation in childhood pathology. Inhibition of emotional expression, poor control of expression and unusual expression may all occur.

Shiner and Masten (2002) reported results for a longitudinal study of 205 children who were assessed around ages ten, twenty, and thirty. Negative emotionality at age twenty was correlated with poor adaptation concurrently and ten years previously. House (2002), however, draws attention to the high levels of co-morbidity for the different anxiety disorders, which call into question their distinctiveness. In general, it seems that temperamental factors linked to negative effect, including behavioural inhibition, act as general risk factors for the spectrum of emotional disorders (Kagan and Snidman 1999; Rothbart and Bates 1998). Low positive affectivity may also contribute to risk of depression, but not anxiety – especially in adolescents (Johnston and Murray 2003).

Externalizing problems and disorders of impulse control

Externalizing antisocial behaviours are one of the most frequent bases for which school psychologists refer children for treatment. These dysfunctional behaviours have serious immediate consequences both for the children who perform them (e.g., punishment, detention, school expulsion) and for those with whom they interact (e.g., victims). Apart from the immediate effects of the acts themselves, the long-term consequences are unfortunate in that antisocial behaviours in children and adolescents often continue into adulthood. About 6 per cent of all boys appear to follow a 'life course persistent' developmental pathway for conduct problems characterized by violence and serious antisocial behaviour in adolescence (Moffitt, Caspi, Dickson *et al.* 1996). These externalizing youth are at risk for criminal behaviour, alcoholism, psychiatric problems and a variety of social and personal problems such as poor work and marital adjustment. Thus, as pointed out by Kazdin (1985), the fact that youths often do not grow out of antisocial behaviours augments the clinical and social significance of dysfunction during the school years.

Undercontrolled students share several characteristics, such as being impulsive, self-centred, manipulative, confrontational, and also show both poor classroom conduct and poor school attainment. In a study of 1,978 adolescents Cooper, Wood, Orcutt and Albino (2003) confirmed the existence of a general factor of problem behaviour, related to impulsive personality. However, they also found more fine-grained associations between specific aspects of personality and behaviour: for example, thrill seeking was significantly related to alcohol use, tobacco use and violent acts.

As is the case for internalizing behaviour, multiple factors are implicated in the development of externalizing behaviours. Early predictors of problem behaviour include temperament difficulties, aggression and non-compliance (Stormont 2002). Situational factors such as parenting style and deprivation also play major roles as influences on antisocial behaviour; these factors may moderate the impact of temperamental factors. In specific, family factors that are associated with problem behaviours include harsh parenting, parental psychopathology, stressful family life events, broken homes and marital discord (Hemmeter, Ostrosky and Fox 2006). Parental discipline, in fact, may be more effective in building conscience in fearful, as opposed to non-fearful, children (Shiner and Caspi 2003).

Temperament influences problem behaviours in interaction with important situational factors, including the family environment, teachers' behaviour management skills and demographic factors (Stormont 2002).

Research on younger children identifies behaviourally disinhibited temperament as a precursor to a variety of disruptive behavioural conditions, including aggression and oppositional defiant disorder (Hirshfeld-Becker, Biederman, Faraone *et al.* 2002). Disinhibition also relates to indices of school problems and academic dysfunction, such as being placed in special classes and repeating grades (Hirshfeld-Becker *et al.* 2002). Various longitudinal studies in the United States and Europe have confirmed that childhood temperament measures related to aggressiveness and misconduct are predictive of criminal behaviours later in life. The Dunedin study in New Zealand (Roberts, Caspi and Moffitt 2001) has tracked personality and antisocial behaviours in a representative community sample from birth through to age twenty-one. At age three, children were classified as being undercontrolled, inhibited or well-adjusted. Undercontrolled children tended, at age twenty-one, to score as aggressive in personality, and they were more likely to report antisocial behaviours, to have a criminal conviction, and to be diagnosed with antisocial personality disorder. However, effect sizes associated with personality were quite modest, suggesting that temperament at age three is not destiny.

Furthermore, many cross-sectional studies show that personality traits including impulsivity, hostility and low self-esteem are associated with various indices of aggression, delinquency and illegal acts, in both children and adults (Furnham and Heaven 1999). A meta-analysis has shown that the traits associated with antisocial behaviour typically relate to a number of broad factors comprising the Five-Factor ('Big Five') Model of personality. Thus, antisocial behaviour relates to low Agreeableness or to low Conscientiousness, with traits associated with Neuroticism showing a smaller but significant relation also (Miller, Lynam, Widiger and Leukefeld 2001). Comparable findings are obtained in school settings, using criteria such as violence, vandalism and theft (e.g., Heaven 1996). It may also be important to distinguish personality facets beyond the FFM. Thus, Miller, Lynam and Leukefeld (2003) found that angry hostility and impulsiveness, measured as facets of Neuroticism, correlated with antisocial behaviour, but other facets, such as anxiety and stress vulnerability, did not.

Aggression is often divided into cold-blooded proactive aggression, employed as a means to an end, and reactive aggression, involving angry outbursts to perceived provocation (Coie and Dodge 1998). Although aggressive children often display both forms of behaviour, measures of the two traits show discriminant validity. Compared with proactive aggressors, reactively aggressive children show more difficulties in interpersonal interaction, more internalizing problems, less self-efficacy but less delinquency (Vitaro, Gendreau, Tremblay and Oligny 1998). Bullying children tend to be high on both aspects of aggression, but their victims are marked by reactive aggression only (Camodeca, Goossens, Terwogt and Schuengel 2002).

Furthermore, effortful control may also be implicated in externalization, in that fearfulness in young children relates positively to this aspect of temperament (Kochanska and Knaack 2003). Frick and Morris (2004) see lack of fearful inhibition as directly influencing risk-taking behaviours, including aggressive acts. Self-regulative processes, including coping, may be implicated in disorders of conduct (Kendall 2000). Cooper, Wood, Orcutt and Albino (2003) suggest that avoidance coping (in the forms of denial of problems or engagement in risk-taking behaviour as a form of mood-elevation) may play a key role. Effortful control may facilitate the development of coping strategies that allow the child to resist immediate impulses according to his or her moral values and beliefs about personal control.

A consistent finding is that antisocial children, who are disproportionately boys, suffer from academic deficiencies as reflected in achievement level, grades and special skill areas, particularly reading. According to Block (1995) impulsive students are predisposed to distraction, lack of attention and concentration, conduct disorder, disobedience and absence from school These undercontrolled children may cumulatively register loss of information and reasoning skills, failing to develop cognitive processes important both for school achievement and success on ability test exams. Consequently, these children are more likely to be left behind in grades, to show lower achievement levels and stop their schooling sooner than controls (Kazdin 1985). Furthermore, academic failure constitutes a risk factor for antisocial behaviour in school.

While some children with conduct problems are overemotional, a sub-group possessing callous-unemotional traits may be identified (Loney, Frick, Clements *et al.* 2003). These junior psychopaths show little concern for others, impaired moral understanding and empathy, and tend to be more predatory in their violent activities than other children with conduct problems. At a psychobiological level, there is evidence that antisocial personality disorder relates to low arousability, as measured by indices of the autonomic nervous system (Zuckerman 2005). Such individuals may be deficient in their emotional responses, and they may also need to commit extreme, exciting acts in order to counter the boredom that results (Raine 2002). However, probably, multiple mechanisms contribute to aggressive behaviours, with different mechanisms more prominent in different impulsive-aggressive disorders.

In sum: On one hand, both externalized and internalized problems represent quite heterogeneous categories, possibly subsuming numerous different sub-types (Hale and Fiorello 2004). On the other hand, the distinction is not rigid: externalizing and internalizing problems are frequently co-morbid and strongly correlated (Dickey and Blumberg 2004). Negative emotions (anxiety, depression, hostility) may be a driver of problems in social behaviours, and the social disapprobation that attaches to conduct problems may be a source of unhappiness for the child. In addition, both groups may have associated neuropsychological deficits, possibly executive frontal dysfunctions.

School-based psychological interventions

School psychologists are often charged with the responsibility of promoting students' positive psychological health by designing school-based psychological health education programmes. These programmes are targeted at the general school population and aim at fostering culture-valued competencies (cognitive, social, emotional), developmentally appropriate behaviours, socially valued relationship skills (e.g., negotiation, peaceful conflict resolution), and culturally relevant coping strategies (e.g., personal and interpersonal problem-solving skills). Although school psychologists have had to devote most of their time and energies to remediation of current problems, with prevention a secondary goal, there have also been serious efforts to provide primary prevention programmes in the school system which stress early identification and treatments of individuals at risk and promotion of wellness or health as a means of reducing later life difficulties (Braden and Hightower 1998). Primary prevention psychoeducational programmes complement secondary and tertiary interventions targeted at high-risk and impacted students, respectively.

With the aim of presenting the reader with the flavour of contemporary psychoeducational school-based programmes, I briefly present three school-based programmes targeting the following three foci: social and emotional skills, test anxiety and traumatic reactions following disaster experiences.

Cultivating social and emotional competencies in schools

The rising popularity of the emotional intelligence construct in educational circles, coupled with the purported significance of social and emotional competencies for promoting student achievement and social adjustment, has spurred on efforts to address students' emotional and social problems through school-based intervention programmes.

Programmes designed to foster emotional intelligence (EI) in the classrooms fall under the general rubric of social and emotional learning programmes (SEL) – an umbrella term that provides a common framework for programmes with a wide array of specified outcomes. SEL refers to the process through which students enhance their ability to integrate thinking, feelings and behaving to achieve life tasks, such as school attainment and success (Zins, Weissberg, Wang *et al*. 2004). A broad spectrum of EI intervention programmes designed to teach emotional competencies in the school is now available, including social skills training, cognitive-behavioural modification, self-management and multimodal programmes. The Collaborative for Academic, Social, and Emotional Learning at the University of Illinois reports that more than 150 different emotional literacy programmes are being used today by thousands of American schools. Programmes seeking to inculcate emotional and social competencies go under a variety of names, such as 'life skills training', 'self-science', 'education for care', 'social awareness', 'social problem solving', 'social competency' and 'resolving conflicts creatively'.

Zins, Weissberg and O'Brien (2007) propose that SEL interventions may be enhanced through explicit focus on five key emotional competencies. These are:

A. *self-awareness*: knowing what one is feeling, accurately assessing self strengths and weakness, enhanced sense of confidence, etc.;
B. *self-management*: setting goals and monitoring progress toward achievement of personal and academic goals, regulating emotions for stress management, impulse control, motivating oneself to overcome obstacles, etc.;
C. *social awareness*: recognizing individual and group similarities and differences, empathizing with others, taking the perspectives of others in a conflictual relationship, etc.;
D. *relationship skills*: demonstrating cooperation with others, resisting inappropriate social pressure, negotiating skills, managing conflict constructively, etc.;
E. *responsible decision-making*: learning to consider all relevant factors, including the feelings of self and others, generating alternative solutions and anticipating the consequences of each, selecting the best solution and monitoring implementation, evaluating results, etc.

A sensible evaluation of current SEL programmes by Zins, Weissberg, Wang *et al*. (2004, p. 5) is 'a number of analyses of school-based prevention programmes conducted in recent years provide general agreement that some of these programmes are effective in reducing maladaptive behaviours'. Thus, students who participate in high quality SEL programmes show a higher sense of self-efficacy, a better sense of community, and greater trust and respect for their teachers. They were also found to have positive school behaviours, such as more prosocial behaviour, more classroom participation and involvement in positive activities (e.g., sports), fewer absences and suspensions, and less classroom disruptions and incidences of interpersonal violence.

A major problem in the evaluation of EI programmes is that many programmes have not been systematically constructed according to a conceptual EI programme planning model, nor have most of these programmes been adequately evaluated. In addition, we really do not know *how* they work. Even staunch advocates agree that we will only be able to speak to the optimistic claims about EI programmes (e.g., reducing drug use, student drop out or violence) after they have been subjected to rigorous, controlled evaluation. Because recent standards adopted by educators to assess the efficacy of interventions are exceedingly rigorous, certainly in the United States, this is no trivial undertaking.

Enhancing student coping with evaluative situations

A wise Chinese proverb states: 'You cannot prevent the birds of worry and care from flying over your head. But, you can stop them from building a nest in your head'. In order to prevent the birds of worry from nesting in students' heads in the face of social evaluation encounters, a wide array of test anxiety treatment programmes have been developed and evaluated over the past three decades (Zeidner 1998). Test anxiety intervention programmes have flowered largely due to the salience of test anxiety in modern society and the general concern for the debilitating effects of test anxiety on the emotional wellbeing and cognitive performance of many.

Treatment fashions and orientations in the area of test anxiety intervention have swayed sharply from the clinical to the behavioural, and more recently to the cognitive perspective, essentially mirroring the evolution of the behaviour therapies (Spielberger and Vagg 1987). For illustrative purposes, we now briefly describe a popular psychoeducational intervention programme implemented in elementary schools in Northern Israel (Zeidner, Klingman and Papko 1988). Following is a brief description of the five major phases of the cognitive-behavioural modification programme.

(1) *Educational presentation*. The major aim of the first session was to provide the student with a conceptual framework for understanding the nature of test anxiety by illuminating the nature, origins and antecedents of test anxiety. Detailed information was given about the behavioural and emotional dynamics of test anxiety, and about a number of strategies for coping with it. Through discussion and guided imagery, students were encouraged to reveal how they generally felt under test conditions and how they had typically handled evaluative stress and anxiety reactions in the past.

(2) *Training in relaxation techniques and in the fundamentals of rational thinking*. This session was mainly devoted to training students in the use of deep-breathing relaxation exercises as a major tension-reduction technique and as a means of controlling emotional reactions during exams. In addition, students were introduced to the topic of rational thinking and self-analysis. Particular emphasis was placed on 'A-B-C' analysis (activating event, belief system and emotional consequences) as a tool for countering irrational thoughts and beliefs.

(3) *Coping imagery and attentional focusing skills*. The third session introduced students to coping imagery. With the aid of guided imagery techniques, students reported their emotional reactions and thoughts under a variety of imagined anxiety-evoking situations (e.g., preparing for an exam, taking an exam, discussing examination results with classmates). Irrational thoughts underlying students' reported emotional reactions were identified and analysed. In addition, students practised the use of positive self-statements under imagined stressful test-taking conditions ('You're doing fine; just have to keep calm').

(4) *Time management and work schemes*. This session instructed students on how to carefully plan and space their exam study sessions and how to prepare for exams. Students were also introduced to various test-taking strategies (e.g., quick overview of exam items, careful reading of questions and options; tackling easy problems first and leaving more difficult problems for the end; helpful cues in identifying the correct answer).

(5) *Rehearsal and strengthening of coping skills*. The fifth and final session was aimed at rehearsing and fortifying the coping skills taught in previous sessions,

primarily with the aid of guided coping imagery. Students were given instruction in using the coping techniques in future test situations. In conclusion, students summarized what they thought they had learned during the course of the training programme.

Evaluation of the effects of this programme points to its effectiveness in meaningfully enhancing students' cognitive performance in test situations, with student performance meaningfully improving on three cognitive measures. Apparently, while not meaningfully reducing test anxiety per se, the programme taught students some important test-taking skills that may have improved performance (Zeidner, Klingman and Papko 1988).

Primary prevention for coping with trauma

School-based interventions for community disasters and mass trauma have recently been the focus of considerable attention in the literature, particularly in light of the alarming escalation of mass trauma in children and youth toward the beginning of the third millennium. Current research shows that children who are exposed to stressful and traumatic events are at risk for a variety of future emotional, behavioural and physical difficulties (van der Kolk, McFarlane and Weiseth 1996). These traumatic experiences, especially when repeated over time, affect children's cognitive, social, emotional and somatic functioning, deplete children's coping resources, and lead to a downward spiral of events and reactions that are difficult to reverse (Green 2003). Schools are viewed as having the unique capacity for ongoing screening and identification of childrens' intervention needs before, during and immediately after a crisis or disaster, as well as implementing post-disaster programmes targeting those students at risk or those who have already developed chronic maladaptive symptoms.

School-based interventions can help students regain a sense of inner equilibrium and self-efficacy that has been disrupted by the traumatic events, secure emotional and instrumental support by affiliating with others in time of need, process their stressful emotions symbolically, develop problem-solving schemes, and create new narratives out of experiences, and to be inspired by their meanings (Klingman and Cohen 2004). Most children are assumed to possess a sufficiently strong sense of resilience and self-agency, coupled with psychological coping mechanisms, that enables them to recover naturally from potentially traumatic events. At the same time, teaching and mental health staff, along with significant familial attachment figures, can help promote adaptive coping with trauma by serving as natural support systems in times of disaster.

Current school-based interventions (e.g., Klingman and Cohen 2004) are based on a number of generic principles, including:

(1) *immediacy of intervention*: intervening as soon as possible after the impact of trauma, thus preventing hiatuses that deepen the sense of disruption in children. The hours and days after the traumatic event are viewed as

the key period for generic intervention, in order to minimize adjustment difficulties;

(2) *proximity of intervention*: taking preventive measures as close as possible to the child's natural setting, in order to protect the existing personal networks within which they usually function. Children should be aided in remaining in, or quickly returning to, the community and school whenever possible, rather than being separated from the school or community;

(3) *expectancy*: communicating confidence in the child's ability to recover and employ coping resources and grow from the experience;

(4) *simplicity*: employing simple, clear interventions aimed at normalization of stress reactions, including provision of rest, relaxation, information, opportunities for ventilation, attentive and sensitive listening, caring and companionship;

(5) *continuity*: assuring the preservation and restoration of functioning at the individual, familial, organizational and community levels.

A variety of different psychoeducational programmes have been developed, targeting different phases of the crisis situation. In preparation for the impending Gulf War, Kingman developed an intervention programme aimed at preparing students and staff to cope effectively with the upcoming threat of missile attacks on Israel by focusing on behavioural rehearsals (e.g., entering sealed rooms, donning gas masks) prior to the stress point (see Klingman and Cohen 2004). The programme consisted of three major phases: (a) an *educational phase*, providing reliable information about the disaster situation and legitimization of student emotional responses; (b) *a skill-training phase*, involving instruction and physical demonstration of the protective equipment against biological warfare and chemical fallout; and (c) *training and practice*, involving a few standardized training sessions, based on gradual exposure. Through simulations of donning, learning to fasten, and breathing through the gas masks, students were expected to gain a sense of control over the impending threat. Trainers conveyed the expectation that students would withstand the threat of unconventional warfare effectively should it erupt. Trainers also conveyed the expectation that students could help train siblings and older persons in the household to employ protective measures properly in real time. On a personal note: having undergone this preparatory school-based programme in 1991, my own two sons were most helpful in training their parents how to don the masks and employ them effectively during the barrage of missile attacks on Haifa during the Persian Gulf War.

Mitchell (1983) developed a widely employed structured approach to post-disaster psychological debriefing, *Critical Incident Stress Debriefing*, a group session held from two days to two weeks post-disaster. The seven-phase standardized debriefing of the traumatic event consists of the following components: (a) introduction; (b) fact finding; (c) exploration of the cognitions experienced during and following the event; (d) identification and expression of emotional reactions experienced; (e) acknowledgement of post-incident cognitive, somatic, emotional and behavioural signs of distress; (f) psychoeducation about stress and self-care; and (g) facilitation of referrals and of returning to everyday life. Despite its widespread use, its unique effectiveness in preventing post-traumatic stress disorder (PTSD) remains ambiguous, and is in need of further study. In fact, whereas some forms of formal psychological debriefing may be helpful, others may be shown to be harmful for some students (Klingman and Cohen 2004).

Concluding remarks

Although the literature on personality in educational and school psychology is too vast to be summarized in a single chapter, our selective review suggests that personality does matter when it comes to socio-emotional adjustment. Furthermore, students may benefit from psychological interventions that target such different outcomes as social skills, test anxiety and traumatic reactions. Thus, psychological research and practice could benefit considerably by incorporating student affective processes into theories of school adjustment.

From a practical point of view, personality assessment of students may be informative about a student's strengths and weaknesses at the process level (Matthews, Zeidner and Roberts 2006). For example, high N or test anxious students may need help with anxiety and stress management; high E students may need help with managing social distractions and keeping their mind focused on their learning goals instead of socializing and partying; and low C students may need help in maintaining interest and investment in their learning.

In addition, when examining the effects of broad personality dispositions on educational outcomes, it is often profitable to unpack the generalized trait into specific facets and then proceed to examine differential patterns of relationships between specific traits and educational outcomes. For example, children with internalizing problems include both anxious and depressed sub-types and children with externalizing conduct problems include both callous and unemotional children, as well as those that show emotional hyperresponsivity to provocations and frustrations (Kamphaus and Frick 2002). Each of these sub-types may be differentially related to school functioning and attainment.

It is now readily apparent that any attempt to understand the complete causal chain associated with school adjustment requires examining the effects of affective factors, such as personality, emotions and motivational processes, in concert with ability and social, cultural and economic factors at home and in the community. Personality traits and student adjustment are best modelled as being reciprocally related, acting in mutually reinforcing ways. Furthermore, effects of personality may in part be mediated by transient states such as negative affect, worry and fatigue, that influence basic parameters of processing (Matthews, Campbell, Falconer *et al.* 2002).

As a major context within the lives of children and adolescents, school is clearly a setting in which students can experience a range of affective responses, including dysfunctional emotional processes (Schutz and Pekrun 2007). It is readily apparent that future work in school psychology would benefit by focusing on student affective processes in school adjustment. To cope with learning or adjustment problems, the school psychologist may choose to implement primary prevention programmes, refer students to psychotherapeutic interventions, or suggest some form of cognitive-behavioural modification programme. A biological perspective would also suggest a role for medication in severe cases.

References

Block, J. 1995. On the relation between IQ, impulsivity, and delinquency: remarks on the Lynam, Moffitt, and Stouthamer-Loemer (1993) interpretation, *Journal of Abnormal Psychology* 104: 395–8

Braden, J. P. and Hightower, A. D. 1998. Prevention, in R. J. Morris and T. R. Kratochwill (eds), *The practice of child therapy*, 3rd edn, pp. 510–39. Needham Heights, MA: Allyn and Bacon

Camodeca, M., Goossens, F. A., Meerum Terwogt, M. and Schuengel, C. 2002. Bullying and victimization among school-age children: stability and links to proactive and reactive aggression, *Social Development* 11: 332–45

Coie, J. D. and Dodge, K. A. 1998. Aggression and antisocial behaviour, in N. Eisenberg and W. Damon (eds.), *Handbook of child psychology*, vol. III, *Social, emotional, and personality development*, 5th edn, pp. 779–862. New York: Wiley

Cooper, M. L., Wood, P. K., Orcutt, H. K. and Albino, A. 2003. Personality and the predisposition to engage in risky or problem behaviors during adolescence, *Journal of Personality and Social Psychology* 84: 390–410

Dickey, W. C. and Blumberg, S. J. 2004. Revisiting the factor structure of the Strengths and Difficulties Questionnaire: United States, 2001, *Journal of the American Academy of Child and Adolescent Psychiatry* 43: 1159–67

Frick, P. J. and Morris, A. S. 2004. Temperament and developmental pathways to conduct problems, *Journal of Clinical Child and Adolescent Psychology* 33: 54–68

Furnham, A. and Heaven, P. 1999. *Personality and social behaviour*. London: Arnold

Green, B. L. 2003. Traumatic stress and its consequences, in Green, B. L., Friedman, M. J., Solomon, S. D., Keane, T. M., Fairbank, J. A., Donelan, Frey-Wouters, E. and Danieli, Y. (eds.), *Trauma interventions in war and peace: prevention, practice, and policy*, pp. 17–33. New York: Kluwer Academic/Plenum

Hale, J. B. and Fiorello, C. A. 2004. *School neuropsychology: a practitioner's handbook*. New York: Guilford Press

Heaven, P. C. L. 1996. Personality and self-reported delinquency: a longitudinal analysis, *Journal of Child Psychology and Psychiatry and Allied Disciplines* 37: 747–51

Hemmeter, M. L., Ostrosky, M. and Fox, L. 2006. Social and emotional foundations for early learning: a conceptual model for intervention, *School Psychology Review* 35: 583–602

Hirshfeld-Becker, D. R., Biederman, J., Faraone, S. V., Vioilette, H., Wrightsman, J. and Rosenbaum, J. F. 2002. Temperamental correlates of disruptive behaviour disorders in young children: preliminary findings, *Biological Psychiatry* 51: 563–74

House, A. E. 2002. *DSM-IV diagnosis in the schools*. New York: Guilford Press

Johnston, C. and Murray, C. 2003. Incremental validity in the psychological assessment of children and adolescents, *Psychological Assessment* 15: 496–507

Kagan, J. and Snidman, N. 1999. Early childhood predictors of adult anxiety disorders, *Biological Psychiatry* 46: 1536–41

Kamphaus, R. W. and Frick, P. J. 2002. *Clinical assessment of child and adolescent personality and behaviour*, 2nd edn. Needham Heights, MA: Allyn and Bacon

Kazdin, A. E. 1985. *Treatment of antisocial behaviour in children and adolescents.* Homewood, IL: Dorsey

Kendall, P. C. 2000. *Childhood disorders*. Hove: Psychology Press

Klingman, A. and Cohen, E. 2004. *School-based multisystemic intervention for mass trauma*. New York: Kluwer Academic/Plenum

Kochanska, G. and Knaack, A. 2003. Effortful control as a personality characteristic of young children: antecedents, correlates, and consequences, *Journal of Personality* 71: 1087–112

Livesley, W. J. 2001. A framework for an integrated approach to treatment, in W. J. Livesley (ed.), *Handbook of personality disorders: theory, research, and treatment*, pp. 570–600. New York: Guilford Press

Loney, B. R., Frick, P. J., Clements, C. B., Ellis, M. L. and Kerlin, K. 2003. Callous unemotional traits, impulsivity, and emotional processing in adolescents with antisocial behaviour problems, *Journal of Clinical Child and Adolescent Psychology* 32: 66–80

Matthews, G., Campbell, S. E., Falconer, S., Joyner, L. A., Huggins, J. G. K., Grier, R. and Warm, J. S. 2002. Fundamental dimensions of subjective state in performance settings: task engagement, distress, and worry, *Emotion* 2: 315–40

Matthews, G., Zeidner, M. and Roberts, R. 2006. Models of personality and affect for education: a review and synthesis, in P. A. Alexander and P. H. Winne (eds.), *Handbook of educational psychology*, pp. 163–86. Mahwah, NJ: Lawrence Erlbaum

Miller, J. D. and Lynam, D. 2001. Structural models of personality and their relation to antisocial behaviour: a meta-analytical review, *Criminology* 39: 765–98

Miller, J. D., Lynam, D. and Leukefeld, C. 2003. Examining antisocial behaviour through the lens of the Five Factor Model of personality, *Aggressive Behaviour* 29: 497–514

Miller, J. D., Lynam, D., Widiger, T. A. and Leukefeld, C. 2001. Personality disorders as extreme variants of common personality dimensions: can the Five-Factor Model adequately represent psychopathy?, *Journal of Personality* 69: 253–76

Mitchell, J. T. 1983. When disaster strikes: the critical incident stress debriefing process, *Journal of the Emergency Medical Services* 8: 38–43

Moffitt, T. E., Caspi, A., Dickson, N., Silva, P. and Stanton, W. 1996. Childhood-onset versus adolescent-onset antisocial conduct problems in males: natural history from ages 3 to 18 years, *Development and Psychopathology* 8: 399–424

Nastasi B. K., Moore, R. B. and Varjas, K. M. 2004. *School-based mental health services: creating comprehensive and culturally specific programs*. Washington, DC: APA

Raine, A. 2002. The role of prefrontal deficits, low autonomic arousal and early health factors in the development of antisocial and aggressive behaviour in children, *Journal of Child Psychology and Psychiatry* 43: 417–34

Roberts, B. W., Caspi, A. and Moffitt, T. 2001. The kids are alright: growth and stability in personality development from adolescence to adulthood, *Journal of Personality and Social Psychology* 81: 670–83

Rothbart, M. K. and Bates, J. E. 1998. Temperament, in W. Damon and N. Eisenberg (eds.), *Handbook of child psychology*, vol. III, *Social, emotional, and personality development*, 5th edn pp. 105–76. New York: Wiley

Salovey, P., Bedell, B. T., Detweiler, J. B. and Mayer, J. D. 1999. Coping intelligently: emotional intelligence and the coping process, in C. R. Snyder (ed.), *Coping: the psychology of what works*, pp. 141–64. New York: Oxford University Press

Schutz, P. and Pekrun, R. (eds.) 2007. *Emotions in education*. Beverly Hills, CA: Sage

Shafer, D., Schonfeld, L., O'Conner, P. A., Stokman, C., Trautman, P., Shafer, S. *et al.* 1985. Neurological soft signs, *Archives of General Psychology* 42: 342–51

Shiner, R. L. and Caspi, A. 2003. Personality differences in childhood and adolescence: measurement, development, and consequences, *Journal of Child Psychology and Psychiatry* 44: 2–32

Shiner, R. L. and Masten, A. S. 2002. Self-efficacy, attribution, and outcome expectancy mechanisms in reading and writing achievement: grade level and achievement level differences, *Journal of Educational Psychology* 87: 386–98

Southam-Gerow, M. A. and Kendall, P. C. 2002. Emotion regulation and understanding: implications for child psychopathology and therapy, *Clinical Psychology Review* 22: 189–222

Spielberger, C. D. and Vagg, P. R. 1987. The treatment of test anxiety: a transactional process model, in R. Schwarzer, H. M. Van der Ploeg and C. D. Spielberger (eds.), *Advances in test anxiety research*, vol. V, pp. 179–86. Berwyn, PA: Swets North America

Stormont, M. 2002. Externalizing behaviour problems in young children: contributing factors and early intervention, *Psychology in the Schools* 39: 127–38

Van der Kolk, B. A., McFarlane, A. C. and Weiseth, L. 1996. *Traumatic stress*. New York. Guilford Press

Vitaro, F., Gendreau, P. L., Tremblay, R. E. and Oligny, P. 1998. Reactive and proactive aggression differentially predict later conduct problems, *Journal of Child Psychiatry and Psychology* 39: 377–85

Wells, A. and Matthews, G. 1994. *Attention and emotion: a clinical perspective*. Hillsdale, NJ: Lawrence Erlbaum Associates

Zeidner, M. 1998. *Test anxiety: the state of the art*. New York: Plenum

Zeidner, M, Klingman, A. and Papko, O. 1988. Enhancing students' test coping skills: report of a psychological health education program, *Journal of Educational Psychology* 80: 95–101

Zins, J. E., Weissberg, R. P. and O'Brien, M. U. 2007. Building success in school and life on social and emotional learning, in G. Matthews, M. Zeidner and R. D. Roberts (eds.), *Emotional intelligence: knowns and unknowns*, pp. 376–95. New York: Oxford University Press

Zins, J. E., Weissberg, R. P., Wang, M. C., Walberg, H. J. and Goleman, D. (eds.) 2004. *Building academic success on social and emotional learning: what does the research say?*. New York: Teachers College Press

Zuckerman, M. 2005. *Psychobiology of personality* 2nd edn. New York: Cambridge University Press

42 Personality in educational psychology

Moshe Zeidner

Overview

This chapter examines the role of personality in educational psychology, with primary interest in student learning and academic attainment. Personality may play out its role in education by influencing social interactions in the classroom, teacher-student rapport, students' self-esteem, prosocial behaviour, motivation and classroom conduct, and cognitive performance. Personality traits are most likely linked to both negative and positive affect (Matthews, Zeidner and Roberts 2006), and so may colour the entire gamut of student's affective and motivational experiences at school.

Attempts to explicate the role of personality in educational settings have met with varying degrees of success over the years and are characterized by short-lived periodic spurts of interest by educational psychologists (De Raad and Schouwenburg 1996). The search for personality factors at the crossroads of student learning and achievement has generally been devoid of a coherent referential theoretical framework or sound methodological paradigm to systematically guide research. There are scores of personality variables appearing in the literature sprawling in conceptual disarray, with no overarching paradigm to integrate personality variables and achievement. The lack of coherent theory and methodology has frequently lead to periodic 'fishing expeditions' in search for potential individual difference variables that may be relevant to educational settings (dispositional factors, temperament, character, cognitive style, achievement motivation, self-related cognitions, etc.). Recently, however, there have been a number of promising attempts to develop integrative theoretical frameworks for understanding the relationship between cognitive ability and non-intellective variables, including personality traits, interests and knowledge (e.g., Goff and Ackerman 1992; cf., Zeidner and Matthews 2005). Future research based on these models may help cast light on the role of personality in the development of student knowledge and individual differences in learning and student achievement.

This chapter focuses on the interface of personality and education, two very broad and somewhat nebulous constructs. The construct of *personality*, as used in this chapter, is based on the *dimensional* paradigm, as opposed to typological descriptive schemes, psychodynamic models, or idiographic case studies. This current approach to personality conceptualization and research describes multiple continuous and relatively enduring traits. This approach assumes that personality traits or dispositions probabilistically impact on behaviours (learning, achievement, etc.). In reference to the concept of *education*, I examine personality as an independent variable impacting on student learning and scholastic achievements.

Individual differences researchers traditionally make a sharp distinction between personality *traits* discussed herein, as reflecting styles of behaviour or preferences, and *abilities* that represent individual differences in aptitude for performance. Despite the frequently claimed cognitive-conative aptitude interactions in learning, the study of personality traits in relation to academic achievement has been limited in comparison to research in the area of cognitive abilities in educational psychology. Whereas the domain of ability is largely beyond the scope of this chapter, it is acknowledged at the outset that intelligence typically dwarfs personality as a predictor of academic performance (e.g., Jensen 1998). At the same time, personality measures may nicely complement cognitive ability and other measures when included in prediction batteries.

Goals and structure

This chapter sets out to inform researchers and practitioners in the behavioural, educational and health sciences about the pivotal role of non-intellective factors in achievement. Educational practitioners (teachers, educational administrators, guidance counsellors) are often ill-informed about contemporary research on the role of personality and temperament in school settings. Thus, practitioners have much to learn about such matters as handling normal variations in temperament and personality, managing negative feelings elicited by 'difficult' children, modifying teaching or counselling styles to avoid 'personality clashes' with students, and developing professional skills for dealing with children of variable temperamental qualities.

In the first part of this chapter I review the role of broad dimensional constructs, under the rubric of the Five-Factor Model (FFM), in school learning and attainment. This is followed by a discussion of the role of a number of contextualized cognitive-social and motivational traits in school performance, as they may more directly impact on learning and achievement and mediate, in part, the effects of broader personality dimensions on academic outcomes. I note at the outset that the range and variety of educational issues raised by studies of personality and learning and achievement is taxing for the reviewer of the field, and I emphasize that my coverage here has been selective.

Five-Factor Model and achievement

Although many different personality traits have been linked to individual differences in both academic aptitude and academic performance, research is increasingly structured around the FFM (Costa and McCrae 1992). The model distinguishes five broad dimensions of personality: Openness (O), Conscientiousness (C), Extraversion (E), Agreeableness (A) and Neuroticism (N). Many of the standard questionnaires that assess primary and secondary traits are available in forms suitable for adolescents and older students. Next I examine the links of the FFM to academic achievement, pointing to some possible contextualized mediating mechanisms in the process.

Conscientiousness

C has been consistently found to predict academic achievement from childhood to adulthood (Chamorro-Premuzic and Furnham 2003), with high C identified as a significant characteristic of successful students. C has been associated with personal attributes necessary for learning and academic pursuits, including striving for success, dutifulness, exercising self-control, being organized, dependable and efficient (Chamorro-Premuzic and Furnham 2003). Emotional control and self-discipline may be particularly important early on in learning, when the task is likely to appear most daunting to the learner and when failure of emotional control can divert attentional resources away from the task (Kanfer and Ackerman 1996). Also, self-discipline, a trait closely related to C, has been shown to predict school performance more strongly than intelligence among girls (Duckworth and Seligman 2005). Recent meta-analytic data reported by Judge and Ilies (2002) shows that C is modestly related to goal setting, expectancy of outcomes, as well as self-efficacy in academic settings. It is plausible that high C students succeed because of their tendency to favour learning-oriented goals, thus contributing to their competence and success in school.

Neuroticism   → factor may predispose individuals to TA.

High N subsumes elements of trait social evaluation anxiety, low self-esteem and effectance, and difficulty in coping with environmental stress and challenges (De Raad and Schouwenburg 1996). While some earlier studies showed that high N predicts lower academic performance among school-aged children, more recent studies among both school children (Heaven, Mak, Barry and Ciarrochi 2002) and university students (Busato, Prins, Elshout and Hamaker 2000), failed to find any significant correlations between N and attainment. Furthermore, the relationship between N and achievement may be moderated by ability levels and age. For example, a positive correlation was found between N and achievement for twelve to thirteen-year-old students; no significant correlation was found for thirteen to fourteen-year-olds; and a negative correlation was found for college students (Leith and Davis 1972). These findings may be explained by the changes occurring in the educational settings which become increasingly formal and competitive, thus enhancing the evaluative atmosphere, and concomitantly, student anxiety, so that high anxious students perform worse than their low N counterparts. Such inconsistencies may reflect the role of moderator factors. The motivational effects of N may have a facilitating impact on the performance of high ability students and a debilitating impact on the performance of low ability students. In addition, emotional factors may be a more prominent cause of student attrition in college than academic factors, with anxious students being more likely to drop out and depressed students having lower grade point average (GPA) (Pritchard and Wilson 2003).

Openness

O entails perceived intellect, curiosity, originality, developed imagination, creativity, and a wide range of intellectual, artistic and aesthetic interests. All of these attributes potentially contribute to student learning and achievement. Ackerman and Heggestad's (1997) meta-analysis revealed a positive modest relation between O and standardized measures of knowledge and achievement. Furthermore, even when statistically controlling for intelligence, O has been found to be positively correlated with final grades (Farsides and Woodfield 2003).

The positive relation frequently reported between O and scholastic achievements is possibly mediated by an interest and openness to learning activities and learning strategies. O may have particularly positive effects when artistic and creative processes are engaged in college students (Chamorro-Premuzic and Furnham 2003). Furthermore, open children may seek more novel educational experiences and thus profit from education to a greater extent then their less open peers (Hair and Graziano 2003). O may also work through heightened value of academic materials, higher expectations for success, intrinsic value of learning, greater perceived utility of learning, and sensation value of encountering new materials.

Notwithstanding, a number of recent studies of college students have failed to replicate significant relations between O and academic achievement (e.g., Busato, Prins, Elshout and Hamaker 2000). Also, the creative and imaginative nature of open individuals may sometimes be a disadvantage in academic settings, particularly when students are required to reproduce curricular content in a rote fashion rather than produce novel responses or exhibit creative problem-solving behaviours.

Extraversion

The effect of E on academic success appears age-dependent, facilitating success in elementary school but debilitating academic success in high school and college. Whereas before the age of eleven to twelve years extraverted children seem superior to introverted children in school achievements (Entwistle and Entwistle 1970), introverts show higher achievement than extraverts among adolescents and adults (e.g., Chamorro-Premuzic and Furnham 2003). This change in the direction of the correlation has been attributed to the move from the sociable, less competitive, atmosphere of primary school to the rather formal and highly competitive atmospheres of secondary school and higher education, in which introverted behaviours such as avoidance of intensive socializing become advantageous. Indeed, sociability may divert resources to socializing rather than studying, with sociability found to be inversely, though modestly, related to GPA over four years of assessment (Martin, Montgomery and Saphian 2006). In addition, compared to extraverts, introverts have been claimed to possess a number of attributes conducive to academic success, such as greater ability in consolidating their learning, better study habits, and lower distractibility (Entwistle and Entwistle 1970).

Agreeableness

Although the temperamental precursors of A, such as prosocial orientation, relate to better social adjustment, and may possibly be useful in a cooperative or team learning classroom environment, relations between this trait and academic attainment are consistently of negligible importance (Shiner, Masten and Roberts 2003).

In sum

Personality traits constitute one of several non-intellective factors that may impact classroom learning and academic performance. Whereas C, low N, and O, to a lesser degree, appear to be positive predictors of learning and achievement outcomes, A and E have little or inconsistent effects on student learning and achievement. These factors often work through a number of narrow-banded mediational variables in impacting learning and performance.

As is readily apparent from the foregoing survey of the literature, the FFM has loomed large in research on personality in education. Although some would argue that the FFM is a fact of nature (McCrae and John 1992), others (e.g., Block 1995) are much less sanguine about adopting the FFM as a universal framework for personality description, organization and dynamics. The Big Five dimensions may simply be too global and fuzzy a framework to be useful for educational settings, for a number of reasons. To begin with, the five factor structure may not be inclusive enough to cover the entire universe of discourse (i.e., personality in education). Thus, any attempt to reduce the rich tapestry of student personality into five factors may be doomed to failure. The five factors are not sufficient in number so that the personalities of students (perfectionists, procrastinators, overachievers, etc.) and the dynamics of their problematic behaviours (ADHD, externalizing behaviours, internalizing problems, etc.) can be adequately represented in a differentiated and articulated manner. Also, the trait descriptors used to assess the Big Five may fail in conveying crucial features of personality and its dynamic functioning. For example, how does one use the FFM to convey the personality of the class bully, the psychologically minded student, or the social pecking order in the classroom? Thus, a number of potentially important personality qualities found in students and their dynamics may escape analysis when using the FFM.

From a practical point of view, the five factors do not seem to be uniquely positioned to provide comprehensive and penetrating descriptions of personality for educational practice, including diagnosis and intervention. For one, the FFM conflates distinct personality traits. For example, under the broad umbrella of the N factor, the FFM conflates anxiety, hostile impulsivity and depression, while failing to consider clinical distinctions among these categories (Block 1995). Whereas anxiety in students is characterized by worries and anticipations about danger looming ahead in a yet escapable future (e.g., exam failure), depression is characterized by ruminations about the sad, irretrievable still reverberating past (breaking up with a cherished girlfriend after going steady for a year). It may well be that the FFM may be fundamentally flawed as a description of the dynamics of the complex nature of personality in true-to-life settings.

Furthermore, the Big Five model does not provide sufficiently discriminating guidelines for clinical work in diagnosing and treating learning and school-adjustment problems, and the implications of FFM scores for clinical treatment of school-related problems is insufficiently articulated. For instance, what clinical guidelines does the FFM provide for treating externalizers or autistic children? Or, what clinical guidance does the FFM provide for treating failure avoiding versus failure accepting students?

Finally, the FFM model fails to sufficiently specify variables that mediate the broadband behaviours implied by the facets. In fact, lower level and contextualized facets (e.g., goal orientation, self-efficacy, self-determination, optimism, sense of autonomy) may be more easily tied to student classroom behaviours and problems in classroom learning and social adjustment. We now turn to examine some contextualized cognitive-social and motivational processes that may prove to be of higher fidelity, although of lower broadband, in shedding light on student achievement and learning.

Social-cognitive variables

In this section we look at a number of social-cognitive variables that may serve as mediating processes between broader personality variables and school learning and attainment. We begin with examining self-related cognitions and then move on to examine the pivotal role in learning of a number of salient control beliefs.

Academic self-concept

Academic self-concept refers to students' self-perceptions of their academic competencies and achievements, formed through experience with and interpretation of one's academic environment. There is now a vast literature suggesting that high self-esteem promotes learning goals, expectancies, coping mechanisms and behaviours that facilitate academic performance, as well as contributing to mental and physical health and prosocial behaviours (Marsh 2005).

Recent research supports the *reciprocal effects* model, i.e., academic effects and achievement are reciprocally related and each a cause and effect of each other. Hence, academic self-concept is both an important outcomes variable but also mediates the effects of other desirable educational outcomes. Furthermore, longitudinal causal designs provide evidence in support of the causal flow from a favourable self-concept to subsequent achievement outcomes, rather than the other way around (Marsh 2005).

Academic self-concept in a particular domain (e.g., math) is formed in relation to both external (e.g., normative performance of others) and internal comparisons (in which performance in one domain, say math, is compared with others, say verbal). Both current theory and prior research suggest that students' perceptions of the self cannot be adequately understood if the role of student frames of reference are ignored (Praekel, Zeidner, Goetz and Schleyer 2008). Thus, the same objective academic characteristics (e.g., GPA) can lead to disparate self-concepts depending on the frames of reference or standards of comparison individuals use to evaluate themselves.

Educational psychologists would do well to measure and target interventions at a level of specificity that is appropriate to the aims of their assessment. Thus, if our interest is in enhancing a child's math self-concept, the most appropriate means to intervene is by directly targeting math self-concept rather than general or reading self-concept.

Self-efficacy and self-regulated learning

In the academic setting, self-efficacy beliefs refer to students' beliefs in their capabilities to master challenging academic demands by organizing and executing the courses of action (i.e., cognitive, behavioural or social skills) necessary for successful academic performance (Bandura 1977). Although Bandura (e.g., 1997) has preferred to see self-efficacy beliefs as dynamic and context-specific, self-efficacy may also be conceptualized as a stable personality trait.

Perceived self-efficacy may impact directly on academic performance by enhancing efficient use of acquired skill, and indirectly, by heightening goal setting, management of work time, persistence and flexibility in testing problem-solving strategies. An integrative review shows that efficacy beliefs contribute meaningfully to scholastic performance in both children and adults (Multon, Brown and Lent 1991). A recent meta-analysis (Robbins, Lauver, Le-Huy *et al.* 2004) of 109 studies relating psychosocial factors to college achievement found that academic self-efficacy was among the most predictive factors of academic success, correlating around 0.5 with GPA. Furthermore, level of student achievement proved to be an important moderator variable, with students' self-efficacy beliefs more highly related to academic outcomes for low than for high achievers (Zimmerman 2000).

It is noted that self-efficacy is often viewed as being a key component in self-regulated learning (SRL). A good number of studies have documented the important contribution of SRL to learning and academic success (Pintrich and De Groot

1990; Schunk and Zimmerman 1994). Learners who believe in their capability to perform specific tasks reveal perseverance and enact a great number of meta-cognitive skills, while low efficacy learners might avoid future performance of similar tasks. Also, self-regulated learners exhibit higher levels of involvement, effort and consistency while performing academic tasks than do their low self-regulated peers (Ruban, McCoach and Reis 2002), with students' achievements related to their self-reported SRL (Corno 1986). Recent work by Zimmerman and Kitsantas (2005) shows that female high school students who held self-efficacious beliefs regarding use of learning processes (organizing materials, memory, etc.) also held richer perceptions of academic responsibility for outcomes, which in turn, predicted end of school term GPAs. Furthermore, self-regulated learning may serve as a buffer against procrastination, a prevalent phenomena among student populations (Schouwenburg 1995).

Attributional styles

Attributional styles refer to the nature of causal explanations individuals provide for outcomes, experiences or events, in an attempt to understand their environment (García and Pintrich 1994). The following four causal dimensions underlying attributions have gained wide currency: (a) *locus of causality* (whether the cause is seen as internal or external to the student); (b) *stability* (whether the cause is viewed to be transient or chronic); (c) *globality* (whether cause is specific to the situation or context or can be expected in other contexts); and (d) *controllability* (degree of control one has over the assumed cause of an outcome or event).

The attributional model proposed by Weiner and his co-workers (Weiner, Frieze, Kukla *et al.* 1987) specifies four causal factors, i.e., ability, effort, task difficulty and luck, defined jointly by the dimensions of locus of causality and stability. Ability (or aptitude) and long-term effort are viewed as internal determinants of performance, whereas task difficulty and luck are external determinants. Furthermore, luck and short-term effort are classified as unstable.

Research suggests that different types of attributions are related to different affective, cognitive and motivational effects (Weiner 1986). Thus, an attribution of lack of effort (internal/unstable) to a failure outcome is shown to be related to a less negative affective response, higher expectations and increased future levels of persistence, than an attribution to low ability (internal/stable), which is related to depressed affect, lower expectancies and future levels of persistence. Since internal attributions, such as aptitude or long-term effort, are relatively unchanging factors, failure attributed to these factors is seen as being predictive of subsequent failure. Thus, an integrative meta-analytic review by Findley and Cooper (1983) pointed to a positive relationship between internality and academic achievement, with an average correlation of about .18 across studies. The relationship is stronger for adolescents than for children and adults and more substantial among males compared to females. However, we don't really know for sure what the causal direction is: do attributions affect cognitive test performance, or do low achievers rely more on luck and accidental or external factors than their own abilities?

In the next section I examine how beliefs and attributions are translated into 'can do' cognitions and motivational processes and behaviours more directly related to achievement.

Motivational processes

Goal orientations, values and expectancies

Motivation is believed to result from both the perceived likelihood (expectancy) that an achievement outcome will be obtained (e.g., '80 per cent probability that I will get a B on the chemistry final'), as well as how much that outcome is desired or valued (e.g., 'extremely important for medical school admissions'). Early motivational models formulated by Atkinson (1964) suggested that the motivational tendency to approach a task is a multiplicative function of the need for achievement, the incentive value of the task, and the probability of task achievement. Some modern models suggest that motivation is a multiplicative function of goals, personal agency and emotions (see Pintrich and Schunk 1996).

Research has shown that achievement tasks can be predicted as a function of different forms of values: attainment value (i.e., value in achieving the task or goal); intrinsic value (i.e., the inherent importance of doing well on the task); the task's utility value (i.e., how the task relates to future goals); and cost (i.e., the negative consequences of engaging in a task). Developmental research indicates a general decline in students' valuing of achievement tasks across the elementary school years and into the middle school years (Wigfield and Eccles 1992).

Over the past two decades the achievement goal approach to achievement motivation has become a predominant conceptual framework used to study behaviour in the schools. Achievement goals refer to the purpose focus of competence related activity. Goal orientation is currently viewed as a relatively stable motivational variable that assumes two forms: *learning* outcomes or *performance* outcomes (Dweck 1986). The focus of *learning* goal orientation is to increase student competence by developing new skills and promoting mastery oriented responses to failure. Performance goals, by contrast, orient students to a concern for their ability and performance relative to others. A body of literature supports the claim that learning goals relate to various adaptive outcomes, including performance, interest and positive affect, whereas performance goals have been linked to less adaptive outcomes (Pintrich 2000). Research by Kanfer and her co-workers (Kanfer, Ackerman and Heggestad 1996) shows that changes in goal attributes (e.g., difficulty, specificity, proximity, orientation, etc.) can affect both self-regulatory processes (monitoring, self-evaluation, self-reinforcement, etc.) as well as learning and performance outcomes.

In the recently revised goal theory perspective, several researchers (e.g., Elliot and Thrash 2001) have made an important distinction between two categories of performance goals: (a) *approach performance goals*, in which students approach tasks in terms of demonstrating their ability and competence by trying to best or outperform others; and (b) *avoidance performance goals*, where students are attempting to avoid looking stupid or incompetent, which leads them to avoid the task. Elliot and McGregor (2001) demonstrated that approach performance goals are positively related to college exam performance, in contrast to avoidance performance goals, which has been reported to be a negative predictor of college exam performance. Antecedent factors underlying the low performance of students with avoidance performance goals are high fear of failure, low classroom engagement, low self-determination.

Test anxiety

Test anxiety refers to the set of phenomenological, physiological and behavioural responses that accompany concern about possible negative consequences or poor performance in evaluative situations (Zeidner 1998). Test anxiety is incontestably the most researched of all situation-specific personality traits in education and one of the personality factors most consistently related to educational achievement (Schutz and Pekrun 2007).

Zeidner's (1998) integrative review of the literature showed that test anxiety correlates negatively, though modestly, with a wide array of conventional measures of school achievement and ability at both high school and college level. Correlations are typically found to be about -.20. Cognitive measures (i.e., aptitude and achievement measures combined) correlate more strongly with the Worry than Emotionality component of test anxiety. Thus, intrusive cognitions are often more damaging to performance than negative affect itself. Higher effects sizes are reported for low than high ability students and for tasks perceived as difficult than those perceived as being easy. The anxiety-related deficits at various stages of processing suggest some general impairment in attention and/or working memory. These various performance deficits are often attributed to high levels of worry and cognitive interference.

Behavioural avoidance, generated in part by performance-avoidance goals in high test anxious students (Elliot and McGregor 2001), plays a key role in maintenance of evaluative anxiety and concomitant skill degradation. High fear of failure, low classroom engagement and low self-determination are among the possible antecedent factors underlying the low performance of college students characterized by avoidance performance goals (Cury, Elliot, Sarrazin *et al.* 2002). Furthermore, evaluative anxiety and fear of failure frequently lead to failure to complete homework assignments or to study for the test, thus resulting in a deficiency in acquiring the required knowledge to succeed in classroom assessments (Dewitte and Lens 2000). This lack of preparation leads to poor performance and anxiety in the test situation (Naveh-Benjamin 1991), increasing subsequent test anxiety and avoidance of study.

Concluding remarks

Thomas Edison once quipped that 'genius is 1 per cent inspiration and 99 per cent perspiration'. This quote suggests that there are basically two pathways that may be negotiated in attaining competency in educational settings: cognitive aptitude and expended effort. Thus, although both ability and personality states, affect and motivational processes are implicated in varying degrees in student learning and achievement, students may achieve their educational goals and attainments through various pathways, employing different combinations of intellective and non-intellective factors (schematically shown in Figure 42.1). Whereas some students (student A in Figure 42.1) may attain normative levels of achievement largely through their reliance on 'inspiration' (i.e., fluid or crystallized cognitive abilities), other students (student B in Figure 42.1) may reach acceptable achievement levels through increased reliance on 'perspiration' (hard work, perseverance, expended effort, efficient study skills, self-regulated learning, etc.).

School is clearly a major setting in the lives of children and adolescents, who report experiencing a rich array of affective responses in school contexts (Schutz and Pekrun 2007). Our selective review suggests that personality does matter when it comes to school learning and attainment. Thus, psychological research and practice could benefit considerably by incorporating student affective processes into theories of classroom learning, instruction and school adjustment.

Different component weights contributing to
academic success in two hypothetical students

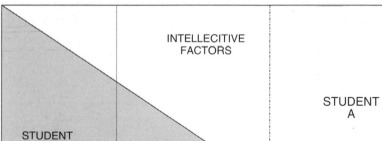

Figure 42.1 *Different component weights contributing to academic success in two hypothetical students.*

From a practical point of view, personality assessment of students may be informative about a student's strengths and weaknesses at the process level (Matthews, Zeidner and Roberts 2006). For example, students with low self-esteem may profit from teacher support, encouragement and positive feedback following success experiences, that can help them bolster their self-esteem; low achieving students with unrealistic outcome expectancies may profit from feedback helping them achieve a closer fit between their competencies and expectations; and students with global internal attributions of failure (low ability) may profit from educational presentations helping them understand the role factors such as expended effort, persistence and hard work may play in achievement-related outcomes. Also, teachers need to be cognizant of the many dynamic variables (aside from ability) that affect student performance, including goals, learning strategies and plans, which must be combined with confidence in the ability to reach the goals by developing and using a plan with effective learning strategies.

There are potentially multiple explanations, not limited to affect, for personality differences seen in the classroom. For example, in addressing excessive negative emotionality in high anxious children, the educator may need to choose between restructuring negative appraisals, training more effective coping skills, training interpersonal skills to reduce conflict with others, or teaching the child to actively seek non-stressful settings and activities. To cope with learning or adjustment problems, the psychologist may choose to implement primary prevention programmes, refer students to psychotherapeutic interventions, or suggest some form of cognitive-behavioural modification programme. A biological perspective would also suggest a role for medication in severe cases.

Furthermore, studies of anxiety-by-treatment interaction in education, although often not vindicated by empirical research, imply that educators may attempt to design personalized learning environments matched with key personality factors (Snow, Corno and Jackson III 1997). For example, students high in evaluative anxiety may benefit more from structured learning-teaching environments, whereas students low on anxiety (as well as those higher on E or O) may benefit from unstructured learning-teaching environments (Zeidner 1998).

I conclude by reiterating Corno et al.'s (2002) call, urging psychologists to work towards the development of dynamic, integrative models that include not only cognitive processes but affective and motivational processes as well. Accordingly, future research would benefit greatly by directing research at uncovering the cognitive, affective and motivational determinants of educational performance and school adjustment in a dynamic, transactional process unfolding over time.

References

Ackerman, P. L. and Heggestad, E. D. 1997. Intelligence, personality, and interests: evidence for overlapping traits, *Psychological Bulletin* 121: 219–45

Atkinson, J. W. 1964. *An introduction to motivation*. Princeton, NJ: Van Nostrand

Bandura, A. 1977. Self-efficacy: toward a unifying theory of behavioral change, *Psychological Review* 84: 191–215

1997. *Self-efficacy: the exercise of control*. New York: Freeman

Block, J. 1995. On the relation between IQ, impulsivity, and delinquency: remarks on the Lynam, Moffitt, and Stouthamer-Loemer (1993) interpretation, *Journal of Abnormal Psychology* 104: 395–8

Busato, V. V., Prins, F. J., Elshout, J. J. and Hamaker, C. 2000. Intellectual ability, learning style, personality, achievement motivation and academic success of psychology students in higher education, *Personality and Individual Differences* 29: 1057–68

Chamorro-Premuzic, T. and Furnham, A. 2003. Personality traits and academic examination performance, *European Journal of Personality* 17: 237–50

Corno, L. 1986. The metacognitive control components of self-regulated learning, *Contemporary Educational Psychology* 11: 333–46

Corno, L., Cronbach, L., Kupermintz, H., Lohman, D., Mandinach, E., Porteus, A. and Talbert, J. 2002. *Remaking the concept of aptitude: extending the legacy of Richard E. Snow*. Mahwah, NJ: LEA

Costa, P. T., Jr and McCrae, R. R. 1992. Four ways five factors are basic, *Personality and Individual Differences* 135: 653–65

Cury, F., Elliot, A., Sarrazin, P., Da Fonseca, D. and Rufo, M. 2002. The trichotomous achievement goal model and intrinsic motivation: a sequential mediational analysis, *Journal of Experimental Social Psychology* 38: 473–81

De Raad, B. and Schouwenburg, H. C. 1996. Personality in learning and education: a review, *European Journal of Personality* 10: 303–36

Dewitte, S. and Lens, W. 2000. Procrastinators lack a broad action perspective, *European Journal of Personality* 14: 121–40

Duckworth, A. L. and Seligman, M. E. P. 2005. Self-discipline outdoes IQ in predicting academic performance of adolescents, *Psychological Science* 16: 939–44

Dweck, C. S. 1986. Motivational processes affecting learning, *American Psychologist* 41: 1040–8

Elliot, A. J. and McGregor, H. A. 2001. A 2 x 2 achievement goal framework, *Journal of Personality and Social Psychology* 80: 501–19

Elliot, A. J. and Thrash, T. M. 2001. Achievement goals and the hierarchical model of achievement motivation, *Educational Psychology Review* 13: 139–56

Entwistle, N. J. and Entwistle, D. 1970. The relationship between personality, study methods and academic performance, *British Journal of Educational Psychology* 40: 132–43

Farsides, T. and Woodfield, R. 2003. Individual differences and undergraduate academic success: the roles of personality, intelligence, and application, *Personality and Individual Differences* 34: 1225–43

Findley, M. J. and Cooper, H. M. 1983. Locus of control and academic achievement: a literature review, *Journal of Personality and Social Psychology* 44: 419–27

García, T. and Pintrich, P. 1994. Regulating motivation and cognition in the classroom: the role of self-schemas and self-regulatory strategies, in D. Schunk and B. Zimmerman (eds.), *Self-regulated learning: issues and applications*, pp. 127–53. Hillsdale, NJ: Erlbaum

Goff, M. and Ackerman, Ph. L. 1992. Personality-intelligence relations: assessment of typical intellectual engagement, *Journal of Educational Psychology* 84: 537–52

Hair, E. C. and Graziano, W. G. 2003. Self-esteem, personality and achievement in high-school: a prospective longitudinal study in Texas, *Journal of Personality* 71: 971–94

Heaven, P., Mak, A., Barry, J. and Ciarrochi, J. 2002. Personality and family influences on adolescent attitudes to school and academic performance, *Personality and Individual Differences* 32: 453–62

Jensen, A. 1998. *The g factor: the science of mental ability.* Westport, CT: Praeger

Judge, T. A. and Ilies, R. 2002. Relationship of personality to performance motivation: a meta-analytic review, *Journal of Applied Psychology* 87: 797–807

Kanfer, R. and Ackerman, P. L. 1996. A self-regulatory skills perspective to reducing cognitive interference, in I. G. Sarason, G. R Pierce, and B. R. Sarason (eds), *Cognitive interference: theories, methods, and findings*, pp. 153–71. Hillsdale, NJ: Lawrence Erlbaum Associates

Kanfer, R., Ackerman, Ph. L. and Heggestad, E. D. 1996. Motivational skills and self-regulation for learning: a trait perspective, *Learning and Individual Differences* 3: 185–209

Leith, G. and Davis, T. 1972. Age changes in the relationship between Neuroticism and achievement, *Research in Education* 8: 61–9

Lens, W., Simons, J. and Dewitte, D. 2002. From duty to desire: the role of students' future time perspective and instrumentality perceptions for study motivation and self-regulation, in F. Pajares and T. Urdan (eds.), *Academic motivation of adolescents*, pp. 221–45. Greenwich, CT: Information Age Publishing

Marsh, H. W. 2005. *Self-concept theory, measurement and research into practice: the role of self-concept in educational psychology.* Twenty-sixth Vernon-Wall Lecture, British Psychological Society

Martin, J. H., Montgomery, R. L. and Saphian, D. 2006. Personality, achievement test scores, and high school percentile as predictors of academic performance across four years of coursework, *Journal of Research in Personality* 40: 424–31

Matthews, G., Zeidner, M. and Roberts, R. 2006. Models of personality and affect for education: a review and synthesis, in P. A. Alexander and P. H. Winne (eds.), *Handbook of educational psychology*, pp. 163–86. Mahwah, NJ: Lawrence Erlbaum

McCrae, R. R. and John, O. P. 1992. An introduction to the Five-Factor Model and its applications, *Journal of Personality* 60: 175–215

Multon, K. D., Brown, S. D. and Lent, R. W. 1991. Relation of self-efficacy beliefs to academic outcomes: a meta-analytic investigation, *Journal of Counseling Psychology* 38: 30–8

Naveh-Benjamin, M. 1991. A comparison of training programs intended for different types of test-anxious students: further support for an information-processing model, *Journal of Educational Psychology* 83: 134–9

Pintrich, P. R. 2000. Multiple goals, multiple pathways: the role of orientation in learning and achievement, *Journal of Educational Psychology* 92: 544–55

Pintrich, P. R. and De Groot, E. V. 1990. Motivational and self-regulated learning components of classroom academic performance, *Journal of Educational Psychology* 82: 33–40

Pintrich, P. R. and Schunk, D. 1996. *Motivation in education: theory, research, and application.* Columbus, OH: Merrill/Prentice Hall

Praekel, F., Zeidner, M., Goetz, T. and Schleyer, E. 2008. Female big fish swimming against the tide: the BFLPE and gender ratio in special gifted classes, *Contemporary Educational Psychology* 33: 78–96

Pritchard, M. E. and Wilson, G. S. 2003. Using emotional and social factors to predict student success, *Journal of College Student Development* 44: 18–28

Robbins, S. B., Lauver, K., Le-Huy, D. D., Langley, R. and Carlstrom, A. 2004. Do psychosocial and study skill factors predict college outcomes? A meta-analysis, *Psychological Bulletin* 130: 261–88

Ruban, L., McCoach, D. B. and Reis, S. M. 2002. *Gender invariance in the impact of pre-college scholastic factors and self-regulated learning variables on the academic attainment of undergraduate students*. Paper presented at the Annual Convention of the American Research Association, New Orleans, LA, April 2002

Schouwenburg, H. C. 1995. Academic procrastination: theoretical notions, measurement, and research, in J. R. Ferrari, J. L. Johnson and W. G. McCown (eds.), *Procrastination and task avoidance: theory, research, and treatment*, pp. 71–96. New York: Plenum

Schunk, D. H. and Zimmerman, B. J. (eds.) 1994. *Self-regulation of learning and performance: issues and educational implications*. New York: Guilford Press

Schutz, P. and Pekrun, R. (eds.). 2007. *Emotions in education*. Beverly Hills, CA: Sage

Shiner, R. L., Masten, A. S. and Roberts, J. M. 2003. Childhood personality foreshadows adult personality and life outcomes two decades later, *Journal of Personality* 71: 1145–70

Snow, R. E., Corno, L. and Jackson, D. N., III 1997. Individual differences in affective and conative functions, in D. C. Berliner and R. C. Calfee (eds.), *Handbook of educational psychology*, pp. 243–308. New York: Simon and Schuster

Weiner, B. 1986. *An attributional theory of motivation and emotion*. New York: Springer Verlag

Weiner, B., Frieze, I., Kukla, A., Reed, L., Rest, S. and Rosenbaum, R. M. 1987. Perceiving the causes of success and failure, in E. E. Jones, D. E. Kanouse, H. H. Kelley, R. E. Nisbett and S. Valins (eds.), *Attribution: perceiving the causes of behaviour*, pp. 95–120. Hillsdale, NJ: Lawrence Erlbaum Associates

Wigfield, A. and Eccles, J. S. 1992. The development of achievement task values: a theoretical analysis, *Developmental Review* 12: 265–310

Zeidner, M. 1998. Test anxiety: the state of the art. New York: Plenum

Zeidner, M. and Matthews, G. 2005. Evaluative anxiety, in A. Elliot and C. Dweck (eds.), *Handbook of competence and motivation*, pp. 141–66. New York: Guilford Press

Zimmerman, B. J. 1998. Test anxiety: the state of the art. New York: Plenum

Zimmerman, B. J. 2000. Self-efficacy: an essential motive to learn, *Contemporary Educational Psychology* 25: 82–91

Zimmerman, B. J. and Kitsantas, A. 2005. Homework practices and academic achievement: the mediating role of self-efficacy and perceived responsibility beliefs, *Contemporary Educational Psychology* 30: 397–417

43 Personality at work

Giles St J. Burch and Neil Anderson

Introduction

Personality has a prominent role in industrial/organizational (IO) psychology at both a theoretical and an applied level. The level of this prominence can be gauged by the number of (a) academic publications describing the relationship between personality and work performance; (b) applied IO psychologists drawing on personality theory to inform their practice; and (c) commercial test publishers developing work-related personality questionnaires. The aim of this chapter is to provide an overview of the literature pertaining to the study of personality at work. In reviewing major developments, we also highlight the issue of fraught relations between the *science* of personality research and theory on the one hand, and the *practice* of personality assessment and measurement in organizations on the other. The operationalization of personality measurement, often being done by commercial test publishers and human resource management (HRM) consultancies, has positive and negative facets which we mention at several points in this chapter to illustrate the tension (and at times distance) between psychometric research and theory into personality, and organizational practices in personality evaluation during employee selection, performance appraisal and other key HRM activities.

Personality in the workplace: current status

The study of personality at work is currently very much to the fore, having been banished in the 1960s amid conclusions that personality was a poor predictor of work performance (e.g., Guion and Gottier 1965). This was particularly the case in the United States where Ghiselli's (1973) critical review of the value of personality testing in selection led to a marked decline in its popularity. Counter to this trend in North America, personality testing and use of personality inventories for employee selection has remained far more popular in Europe and other parts of the world over recent decades, indeed with there being evidence of its use becoming increasingly frequent by organizations engaged in employee recruitment and selection (Anderson 2005).

The resurgence has been due to a number of factors, most of which are concerned with major advances in our understanding of personality and job performance constructs, and the development of taxonomies that have allowed for the effective translation of theory into practice (e.g., Hough and Ones 2001;

Salgado and De Fruyt 2005). Most notable in terms of a taxonomy of personality has been the development and general acceptance of the 'Big Five' or Five-Factor Model (FFM) as a latent model of personality and individual differences (Digman 1990), with growing evidence that inventories based on the FFM demonstrate greater criterion-related validity than do non-FFM inventories (e.g., Salgado 2003). However, despite the widespread use of the FFM in research, this appears to have had only limited influence in the design of commercially developed and published personality inventories for use in employee selection, with only a minority of those being directly based upon the FFM (Anderson 2005). It appears instead that commercially published measures use lower-order models or variants of the FFM, that are comprised of a larger number of dimensions of personality, which may or may not bear higher order resemblance to the FFM (see also, Salgado 2003).

The literature regarding personality at work is dominated by descriptions of the relationship of personality as a predictor of job performance; this will be reviewed first in this chapter. However, the field is not limited to this, and we also provide an overview of other key areas of personality research in the workplace, for example, in relation to counter-productive behaviours at work, leadership, team-working, the 'dark side' of personality at work, occupational/career choice, and finally the adverse impact of personality measures in IO psychology.

Personality as a predictor of work-related performance

One of the key questions that organizations, and thus IO psychologists, are concerned to answer is the extent to which personality can predict job performance. This is a critical question for line and human resource managers, who constantly seek to find a panacea for their recruitment dilemma, that is, 'how can we recruit the best person for the job?'. For personality psychologists this question translates into one of 'to what extent can models of personality predict job performance?'. This is not an easy question to answer, as job performance is a complex issue; however, developments in our understanding of personality, personality measurement and job performance have allowed IO psychologists to conceptualize these issues in a more systematic and coherent manner. This, coupled with advancements in meta-analytic techniques, has resulted in the publication of a number of important analyses over the last two decades, considering the relationship between personality and job performance, core self-evaluations and job performance, personality and citizenship performance, and personality and performance motivation. Each of these will be considered in turn in this section.

Personality and job performance

One of the first influential meta-analyses describing the relationship between personality and job performance was that of Barrick and Mount (1991), who classified personality scales into a five factor framework and investigated their relationship with job performance across a range of occupational groups. The most notable finding from this analysis was that Conscientiousness was the strongest predictor across all occupational groups (.22) and across all job perform-ance criteria (job proficiency (.23); training proficiency (.23); and personnel data (.20)). Additionally it was found that training proficiency was predicted by Extraversion (.26) and Openness (.25). Subsequently, there have been a growing number of meta-analyses investigating the relationship between personality and performance with generally consistent findings. These have been usefully sum-marized in Barrick, Mount and Judge's (2001) second-order meta-analysis (that is, a meta-analysis of existing meta-analyses), which showed Conscientiousness to be a valid predictor for all work performance criteria (overall work performance (non-independent analysis (.24); independent analysis (.27); supervisor ratings (.31); objective performance (.23); training performance (.27); and team-work (.27)), and occupational groups (sales performance (.25); managerial performance (.25); professionals (.24); police (.26); and skilled or semi-skilled (.23)). Additionally, Emotional Stability was shown to be a valid predictor of overall work performance across all jobs (non-independent analysis (.15); independent analysis (.13)). While Neuroticism has generally been found negatively to predict effective job perform-ance, it is interesting to note at this point the findings from a recent study which found anxiety to be *positively* related to job performance in those scoring high in cognitive ability (Perkins and Corr 2005).

Further to their study, Barrick, Mount and Judge (2001) called for a moratorium on the type of meta-analyses described in their review; and while this may have suggested an acceptance of the predictive relationships between personality and job performance, this is not the case (see e.g., Murphy and Dzieweczynski 2005; Morgeson, Campion, Dipboye *et al.* 2007). For example, Murphy and Dzieweczynski (2005) suggested that many of the concerns raised by Guion and Gotlier (1965) are still not resolved, such as low validities, poor choice in person-ality measures used in organizations, and poor understanding of the link between personality and jobs. Counter-arguments have been presented elsewhere so will not be considered further here; however, the reader is referred to Burch and Anderson 2008; Hogan 2005a, 2005b; Hogan and Roberts 2001; Ones, Dilchert, Viswesvaran and Judge 2007). It is worth mentioning at this juncture an important recent meta-analysis of studies using only the Hogan Personality Inventory (HPI) (Hogan and Hogan 1995), which revealed even stronger validities between job performance and personality Emotional Stability (.43); Extraversion (.35); Intellect-Openness to Experience (.34); Agreeableness (.34); Conscientiousness (.36); and Intellect-Oppenness to Experience (.34)), suggesting that when more rigorous criteria are applied to classifying personality variables in meta-analyses, the results may be more powerful (Hogan and Holland 2003).

While the FFM provides a useful way to categorize personality at work, as highlighted by Ones and Viswesvaran (1996), the increased use of personality measures in the workplace returns us to the 'bandwidth-fidelity dilemma'

(Cronbach and Gleser 1965). This effectively refers to the width of the constellation of personality constructs being measured versus the depth of detail or measurement fidelity achievable within each factor. According to Ones and Viswesvaran (1996) there is a trade-off between these two in that, for most commercial settings, there will be a time constraint on how long the personality inventory can take to complete. Indeed, pressures for short, fast and restricted personality inventories in employee selection are commonplace, but are likely to stand in stark contrast to measurement comprehensiveness, criterion-related validity and reliability. Ones and Viswesvaran (1996) cautioned wisely against the trend for overly quick and superficial measures, instead arguing that to achieve psychometrically robust measurement of the gamut of personality traits will require longer and thus more time-consuming inventories if this is to be done properly in selection situations.

Dudley, Orvis, Lebiecki and Cortina (2006) recently found evidence that sub-traits subsumed under Conscientiousness incrementally predict performance better than global Conscientiousness. Dudley *et al.* went on to point out that it is necessary for us to develop a clearer understanding of the predictive power of narrower traits before the argument for the use of broad traits in the prediction of job performance can be accepted. Certainly the relationship between the narrower traits of all global factors requires further investigation, and as suggested by others (e.g., Barrick, Mount and Judge 2001; Burch and Anderson 2008) should form a major part on our ongoing research agenda. Additionally, there is growing evidence of curvilinear and non-linear relationships between personality and job performance, which may account to some extent for the low (linear) correlations reported in the literature. For example, LaHuis, Martin and Avis (2005) found evidence for an asymptotic relationship between Conscientiousness and job performance – this is an area of the research that should also receive increased interest.

Core self-evaluations

While the research suggests Conscientiousness to be the strongest and most consistent predictor of job performance, Judge and Bono (2001) have suggested that three of the four core self-evaluations traits predict job performance as well as, or better than, Conscientiousness. Core self-evaluations have been defined as a higher-order trait of positive self-concept. In their meta-analysis of the relationship between core self-evaluation traits (self-esteem, generalized self-efficacy, locus of control and Emotional Stability (low Neuroticism)) with job performance, Judge and Bono (2001) found the following correlations with job performance: self-esteem (.26), generalized self-efficacy (.23), internal locus of control (.22) and Emotional Stability (.19). These findings put a new perspective on the personality and job performance literature, and suggest that these traits may have a useful role in predicting job performance, and thus in employee selection. Indeed, Judge and Bono (2001) suggest that at least one of these traits should be assessed in selection decisions.

Personality and citizenship performance

Citizenship performance is becoming widely recognized as an essential element of job performance, and is comprised of those behaviours at work that go beyond the call of duty, for example, volunteering to take on additional duties, responsibility and helping others with their workload (Borman and Penner 2001). The notion of citizenship performance is not new, and is related to a number of concepts, such as *contextual performance* (e.g., Borman and Motowidlo 1993, 1997) and *organizational citizenship behaviour* (e.g., Organ 1988). An important issue to note at this juncture is the distinction between citizenship performance and task performance, where task performance includes tasks, activities and technical proficiency associated with specific jobs (e.g., Borman and Motowidlo 1993). This distinction is important for personality psychologists as there is growing evidence that while personality is a more effective predictor of citizenship performance, cognitive ability is a more effective predictor of task performance (see Borman, Penner, Allen and Motowidlo 2001).

A number of studies have been carried out investigating the relationship between personality and citizenship performance, with the first key analysis being Organ and Ryan's (1995) review of attitudinal and dispositional predictors of organizational citizenship behaviour, using two component factors as indices of organizational citizenship behaviours: *altruism* (e.g., giving help to co-workers) and *compliance* (e.g., time-keeping, respect for property, following rules). Their meta-analysis found personality to be a weaker predictor of organizational citizenship behaviour than job satisfaction, with Conscientiousness correlating .22 with altruism and .30 with generalized compliance. However, it should be noted that these correlations reduced to .04 and .23 respectively when studies including self-ratings were excluded from the analysis. Additionally, they found Agreeableness to correlate .13 with altruism and .11 with generalized compliance, negative affectivity to correlate -.06 with altruism and -.12 with generalized compliance, and positive affectivity to correlate .15 with altruism and .07 with generalized compliance. More recently, Organ, Podsakoff and MacKenzie (2006) have suggested that personality may only be related to organizational citizenship behaviour through its relationship with job satisfaction, given the wealth of evidence that variance in job satisfaction can be explained by personality (e.g., Judge and Bono 2001). Indeed, Ilies, Scott and Judge (2006) recently found that positive affect and job satisfaction predicted organizational citizenship behaviour, and secondly that cross-level interaction between Agreeableness and positive affect predicted organizational citizenship behaviour.

Further to Organ and Ryan's (1995) review, a more recent meta-analysis provided estimated correlations of .32 between Conscientiousness and citizenship performance (.27 with self-rating data excluded), .22, .33 and .27 between positive affectivity, other orientated empathy, helpfulness (respectively) and citizenship performance (Borman, Penner, Allen and Motowidlo 2001). Findings also provided evidence confirming Conscientiousness to be more highly correlated with citizenship performance than with task performance.

To conclude, it can be seen that there is *some* evidence of meaningful relationships between personality variables and citizenship performance, although these relationships may not be particularly strong. To this end, Organ (e.g., Organ and McFall 2004; Organ, Podsakoff and MacKenzie 2006) suggested that if we accept that these relationships are weak, then it may be that personality acts indirectly on organizational citizenship behaviour through its effect on attitudes; personality may influence an individual's *motives* for engaging in such behaviours, rather than the behaviours in themselves; and that personality effects may be suppressed by the constraints of working in an organization. Clearly, further research needs to be carried out in order to investigate the nature of these possible relationships.

Personality and performance motivation

While reviewing the literature relating to personality and job performance, it is appropriate to briefly discuss the relationship between personality and performance motivation, given that motivation is an essential element in workplace performance (e.g., Campbell, McCloy, Oppler and Sager 1993). While the research into personality and motivation has been dogged with many of the same issues as the research into job performance, e.g., lack of adequate constructs or taxonomies, Judge and Ilies' (2002) recent meta-analytic review of the literature has provided some meaningful results, with the strongest predictors of performance motivation being Neuroticism (-.31) and Conscientiousness (.24).

To conclude, it can be seen from the literature described in this section on personality and work-related performance that both Emotional Stability and Conscientiousness have an important role to play in numerous dimensions of job performance.

We will now turn to the literature describing the relationship between personality and deviance/counter-productive behaviours at work.

Personality and counter-productive behaviours at work

Counter-productive and deviant behaviours at work are those which can range from the 'mildly annoying' to the 'criminal' (Schmitt and Kim 2007), and include theft, alcohol/drug use, damaging property, absence, unauthorized use of time and inappropriate actions towards others (e.g., Sackett and DeVore 2001).

While a number of meta-analyses of the relationship between personality and counter-productive behaviours at work have been reported, these have tended to focus on narrow behaviours such as theft, absenteeism, and so forth. However, a recent meta-analysis has provided more meaningful estimates by employing broader measures of *interpersonal* deviance and *organizational* deviance, with results revealing Emotional Stability to be correlated with both interpersonal deviance (-.24) and organizational deviance (-.23), Agreeableness to be correlated with both interpersonal deviance (-.46) and organizational deviance (-.32), and Conscientiousness to be correlated with both interpersonal deviance (-.23) and organizational deviance (-.42) (Berry, Ones and Sackett 2007).

It can be seen that personality appears to be a useful predictor of deviant or counter-productive behaviours at work. To this point, Salgado and De Fruyt (2005) have advocated the use of personality measurement in employee selection when the objective is to reduce such deviant behaviours. While screening for counter-productive and deviant behaviours in employee selection appears to be a worthwhile approach for organizations, it is important to note the distinction between counter-productive behaviours and organizational citizenship behaviour, that is, these are two distinct constructs, rather than two ends of a continuum (Sackett, Berry, Wiemann and Laczo 2006). Therefore, it is necessary for *separate* predictions to be made in relation to these two constructs (Schmitt and Kim 2007). Paradoxically, there may be a positive side to the more mild aspects of counter-productive behaviour, for example, as Anderson and Gasteiger (2007) have recently argued, some of these behaviours correlate with the early phases of creativity and innovation in the workplace (especially rule challenging, 'stealing' of time for unauthorized projects, and pursuing intrinsic job role objectives). Thus, it has been suggested that the very mild aspects of counter-productive behaviour may well be necessary evils to incubate creative ideas and innovative improvements at work, and thus that strict conformity to organizational regulations and authority structures may conversely inhibit innovation attempts.

Personality and leadership

The study of leadership is a key area of interest for both personality research and the more pragmatic concerns of organizations. While much of the research into leadership does not consider personality per se, there is a growing literature regarding this relationship. One would certainly expect personality to have an important influence on leadership capability and style, and such a view has been clearly expressed by 'experts' in personality psychology. For example Kaiser and Hogan (2007, p. 2) have stated that 'Personality matters – who leaders are determines how they lead, for better or worse'. However, even leaders without an 'expertise' in personality psychology have stressed the importance of personality characteristics in leadership. For example, Field-Marshal Viscount Montgomery of Alamein (Montgomery 1961, p. 17) wrote 'The first characteristic of the leader we seek must be a deep, great, and genuine sincerity'.

In respect to the relationship between the FFM and leadership, Judge, Bono, Ilies and Gerhardt (2002) in a meta-analysis of the leadership and personality research found leadership to be positively related to Extraversion (.31), Openness (.24) and Conscientiousness (.28), and negatively related to Neuroticism (-.24), while Agreeableness was only correlated with leadership (.08). In a meta-analysis of the relationship between the FFM and 'transformational leadership' (which has been described as encouraging other people to perform and develop beyond what is normally expected of them; Avolio and Bass 2004) Bono and Judge (2004) found Extraversion to be the most significant and consistent correlate with transformational leadership dimensions, and the strongest predictor of overall transformational leadership (.24).

Taking a different approach, Nicholson (1998) profiled a sample of chief executive officers (CEOs) of leading UK independent companies and compared these with NEO PI-R (Costa and McCrae 1992) norms. Results showed that leaders demonstrated significantly higher levels of Extraversion and Conscientiousness, and lower levels of Neuroticism and Agreeableness. The finding in relation to Agreeableness is interesting to note. While Nicholson's (1998) sample were CEOs of leading companies, no data was presented on leadership performance per se, therefore, the low Agreeableness scores may reflect traits that facilitate individuals' rise into leadership positions, but are not necessarily an indicator of subsequent leadership success. Such a view would be consistent with those suggested in the literature on narcissistic leaders, i.e. that while some of the traits associated with narcissistic personality may help an individual attain a leadership position, they do not predict success in those leadership positions (e.g., Rosenthal and Pittinsky 2006) – in fact, it is more likely that such traits will predict the leader's subsequent 'derailment' (Hogan and Hogan 2001).

As can be seen from the literature described, there do appear to be some consistent findings in the personality and leadership research. Indeed, Kaiser and Hogan (2007) have suggested personality to be the most important factor in explaining the individual differences between leaders, pointing out that the validity of personality as a predictor of leadership is greater than that for cognitive ability (e.g., Judge, Ilies and Colbert 2004), while Ilies, Gerhardt and Le (2004) also suggested that personality is a stronger predictor of leader emergence than intelligence.

Personality and teamworking

The relationship between personality and teamworking is an area that is gathering momentum in the IO psychology literature. One line of enquiry has been to investigate the relationship of personality with team performance. For example, Barrick, Stewart, Neubert and Mount (1998), in a study of fifty-one work teams, examined the relationships among team composition (ability and personality), team processes (social cohesion), and team outcomes (team viability and performance). Results found that teams higher in Conscientiousness, Agreeableness, Extraversion, and lower in Neuroticism, were rated higher by supervisors in terms of team performance. Meanwhile, Morgeson, Reider and Campion (2005) found that Conscientiousness, Extraversion, Agreeableness and Emotional Stability all predicted contextual performance, while Conscientiousness, Extraversion and teamwork knowledge incrementally predicted contextual performance (.48), in highly interdependent teams within a manufacturing organization.

More recently, Bennett and Burch (2007) investigated the relationship between team leader personality and team climate in a study of 63 four-person interdependent emergency service teams, with results revealing team leader Extraversion to be positively related with team climate scale scores of 'Participative Safety' and 'Support for Innovation', as measured by the Team Climate Inventory (TCI) (Anderson and West 1998). These results suggest Extraversion, not surprisingly, to be an important dimension in relation to teamworking.

'Dark side' of personality at work

In addition to the interest in 'normal' personality and work performance, there is a growing interest in the 'dark side' of personality in the workplace (that is, more negatively connotated traits and behaviours), with much of this pertaining to the leadership literature. For example, there have been numerous publications in the management literature describing disordered personalities at work, most notably related to narcissism (e.g., Rosenthal and Pittinsky 2006) and psychopathy (e.g., Babiak and Hare 2006), and even schizotypy (e.g., Burch 2006). However, these have tended to be clinically descriptive or based on case studies rather than empirical findings. This being said, from the more limited empirical literature, some interesting findings are reported. For example, Judge, LePine and Rich (2006) found that while narcissism was positively related to self-perceptions and self-reports of leadership practices, it was negatively related to others' reports of leadership. Additionally, Judge, LePine and Rich (2006) found that narcissism was associated with favourable *self-reports* of citizenship performance and deviant behaviours when contrasted with supervisor ratings. In contrast, however, Khoo and Burch (2008) recently found narcissistic personality to be a negative predictor of *self-reported* transformational leadership scores. Meanwhile, Benson and Campbell (2007) recently found evidence of a non-linear relationship between 'dark side' and supervisor and others' ratings of leadership performance.

Taking a somewhat different approach to studying the 'dark side' of leadership personality, Board and Fritzon (2005) found that CEOs and senior managers of leading UK companies demonstrated similar levels of narcissism as a sample of patients at Broadmoor Special Hospital (a secure psychiatric hospital in the United Kingdom), and significantly higher levels of histrionic personality than the 'clinical' group. Similarly, Khoo and Burch (2008) found histrionic personality to be a positive predictor of self-reported transformational leadership scores. These findings suggest that further research should be carried out to investigate the role of histrionic personality in leadership, in a literature that is preoccupied with narcissism and psychopathy.

Aside of leadership, Moscoso and Salgado (2004) investigated the relationship between 'dark side' personality styles with task, contextual and overall job performance. Their results found that paranoid, avoidant, depressive, passive-aggressive, self-defeated, schizotypal and antisocial personality scores negatively predicted task performance, contextual performance and overall performance, while narcissistic personality negatively predicted contextual performance, and dependent personality negatively predicted task performance.

Empirical research on the dark side of personality at work is gathering momentum (particularly following the development of such measures as the Hogan Development Survey (HDS) (Hogan and Hogan 1997), a questionnaire specifically designed to measure dysfunctional dispositions in the workplace), with some interesting findings revealed. Clearly, more research needs to be carried out in this area if personality psychologists are to develop a fuller (or more holistic) understanding of the impact of personality at work, in particular relating to leadership, job performance, counter-productive behaviours and creativity.

Personality, career choice and career success

Throughout this chapter we have been discussing the relationship between personality and a range of work-related behaviours and performance. It is important now to consider how personality may influence career choice and career success. In terms of career choice, Barrick, Mount and Gupta's (2003) meta-analysis of the relationship between the FFM and Holland's occupational types (e.g., Holland 1997), revealed some interesting results. Holland (1997) proposed that there are six types of vocational personality: (1) *realistic*, those who prefer practical or physical activity; (2) *investigative*, those who are analytical and curious; (3) *artistic*, those who are imaginative and introspective; (4) *social*, those who enjoy working with and helping other people; (5) *enterprising*, those who enjoy managing and leading others; and (6) *conventional*, those who enjoy organizational and administrative work. Results from the meta-analysis found the strongest relationships existed between Extraversion and enterprising (.41), Extraversion and social (.29) and Openness and artistic (.39).

In relation to career success, Boudreau, Boswell and Judge (2001) investigated the relationship of the FFM with extrinsic career success (remuneration, ascendancy, job level and employability) and intrinsic career success (job, life and career satisfaction). Results found that Extraversion was positively related to intrinsic career success, while neuroticism was negatively related to the dimensions of career success. Unexpectedly, Conscientiousness was found to be negatively related to intrinsic success, and Agreeableness negatively related to extrinsic success. In another study, Seibert and Kraimer (2001) found Extraversion to be positively related to salary levels, promotion and satisfaction with careers, and Emotional Stability to be positively related to career satisfaction, while Agreeableness was negatively related to career satisfaction, and Openness was negatively related with salary levels. Finally, in a longitudinal study, Judge, Higgins, Thoresen and Barrick (1999) found that intrinsic career success in mid-adulthood was positively predicted by childhood Conscientiousness, and that extrinsic career success in mid-adulthood was negatively predicted by childhood Neuroticism and positively predicted by childhood Conscientiousness.

Adverse impact of personality measures

Long-standing concerns that poorly constructed personality inventories might adversely affect the employment selection ratios of minority groups have led to ongoing research efforts, both independently and by commercial test publishers themselves, to minimize and mitigate such undesirable unequal opportunity differences. Ones and Anderson (2002; but see Goldberg, Lee and Ashton 2008) for instance, compared the sub-group differences (male versus female, and white versus ethnic minorities) across three popular and commercially published personality inventories in the United Kingdom (the 'Occupational Personality Questionnaire', 'Hogan Personality Inventory' and 'Business Personality Inventory'). They found only small effect size differences on all three measures between majority (male; white) and minority (female; ethnic minority) groups and concluded that these three measures showed an encouraging lack of sub-group differences across all of their scales. While research in other countries generally supports this conclusion, it is important to note the findings of a recent analysis of New Zealand occupational personality data which found samples of both Māori and Pacific Islanders scored higher than New Zealand Europeans in Neuroticism, and Māori to score lower than New Zealand Europeans in Extraversion, as measured by the 15 Factor Questionnaire Plus (Packman, Brown, Englert *et al.* 2005). Clearly, there is a demonstrable need for ongoing studies to verify a general lack of adverse impact as several authors internationally have called for in recent years (e.g., Burch and Anderson 2008; Packman, Brown, Englert *et al.* 2005; Te Nijenhuis and Van der Flier 2002). The question of equal opportunities and adverse impact is an important one, although in this area far less research appears to have been conducted and published (especially by researchers independent of the commercial test publishers) compared with the bulk of research into predictive validity.

Conclusion

In this chapter we have reviewed several of the major areas of developments in research, practical importance and applications of personality theory in the workplace. From this review it can be seen that personality has an important role to play in the workplace (at both a theoretical and applied level), with a number of meaningful relationships reported. Given the progress made over the last two decades, accompanied by the wealth of evidence that the FFM may be a useful predictor of work-related behaviours, it is apparent that the research must now become more targeted in order to further develop our understanding of personality in the workplace. To this end, Burch and Anderson (2008) have recently highlighted seven directions for future research into workplace personality: (1) the 'dark side' of personality in the prediction of work-related behaviour and performance; (2) the neurobiological basis of personality (e.g., Reinforcement Sensitivity Theory) as part of an integrated causal model of work-related behaviour and performance; (3) facet-specific outcomes and lower-level traits of the FFM; (4) non-linear and curvilinear relationships between personality and work-related behaviour and performance; (5) personality variable interactions and work-related behaviour and performance; (6) self- versus observer-ratings; and (7) expanded research into ethnic and gender differences.

In relation to the translation of this theory-base into applied practice, while there has been a growth in the transfer from theory and research in personality on the one side, there remains a clear gulf between important research findings and practice on the other. The fraught relationship between academic research and the interests of commercial test publishers may be one of the elements at play here, although in fairness there has been a notable improvement in transfer between personality research and theorizing, on the one hand, and organizational and consultancy practices on the other, comprising such activities as personality assessment, selection, appraisal and monitoring for adverse impact and equal opportunities.

In a short review chapter such as this, it has been impossible to cover all developments in this field, but rather we have attempted to highlight major research findings over job performance, counter-productive behaviours, leadership, equal opportunities, and so forth.

References

Anderson, N. 2005. Relationships between practice and research in personnel selection: does the left hand know what the right is doing?, in A. Evers, N. Anderson and O. Voskuijl (eds.), *The Blackwell handbook of personnel selection*, pp. 1–24. Oxford: Blackwell Publishing

Anderson, N. and Gasteiger, R. 2007. Helping creativity and innovation thrive in organizations: functional and dysfunctional perspectives, in J. Langan-Fox, C. L. Cooper and R. Klimoski (eds.), *Research companion to the dysfunctional workplace: management challenges and symptoms*, pp. 422–40. London: Edward Elgar Publishing

Anderson, N. and West, M. 1998. Measuring climate for work group innovation: development and validation of the team climate inventory, *Journal of Organizational Behaviour* 19: 235–58

Avolio, B. J. and Bass, B. M. 2004. *Multifactor leadership questionnaire*, 3rd edn. Redwood City, CA: Mind Garden, Inc.

Babiak, P. and Hare, R. D. 2006. *Snakes in suits: when psychopaths go to work*. New York: Harper Collins

Barrick, M. R. and Mount, M. K. 1991. The Big Five personality dimensions and job performance: a meta-analysis, *Personnel Psychology* 44: 1–26

Barrick, M. R., Mount, M. K. and Gupta, R. 2003. Meta-analysis of the relationship between the Five-Factor Model of personality and Holland's occupational types, *Personnel Psychology* 56: 45–74

Barrick, M. R., Mount, M. K. and Judge, T. A. 2001. Personality and performance at the beginning of the new millennium: what do we know and where do we go next?, *International Journal of Selection and Assessment* 9: 9–30

Barrick, M. R., Stewart, G. L., Neubert, M. J. and Mount, M. K. 1998. Relating member ability and personality to work-team processes and team effectiveness, *Journal of Applied Psychology* 85: 377–91

Bennett, J. and Burch, G. St. J. 2007. *Team leader personality, team climate and relations in the team*. Paper presented at the 2007 conference of the Association of Industrial Relations Academics of Australia and New Zealand (AIRAANZ), Auckland, February 2007

Benson, M. J. and Campbell, J. P. 2007. To be, or not to be, linear: an expanded representation of personality and its relationship to leadership performance, *International Journal of Selection and Assessment* 15: 232–49

Berry, C. M., Ones, D. M. and Sackett, P. R. 2007. Interpersonal deviance, organizational deviance, and their common correlates: a review and meta-analysis, *Journal of Applied Psychology* 92: 410–24

Board, B. J. and Fritzon, K. 2005. Disordered personalities at work, *Psychology, Crime and Law* 11: 17–32

Bono, J. E. and Judge, T. A. 2004. Personality and transformational and transactional leadership: a meta-analysis, *Journal of Applied Psychology* 89: 901–10

Borman, W. C. and Motowidlo, S. J. 1993. Expanding the criterion domain to include elements of contextual performance, in N. Schmitt and W. C. Borman (eds.), *Personnel selection in organizations*, pp. 71–89. San Francisco, CA: Jossey-Bass
    1997. Task performance and contextual performance: the meaning for personnel selection research, *Human Performance* 10: 99–109

Borman, W. C. and Penner, L. A. 2001. Citizenship performance: its nature, antecedents, and motives, in B. W. Roberts and R. Hogan (eds.), *Personality psychology in the workplace*, pp. 45–61. Washington, DC: American Psychological Association

Borman, W. C., Penner, L. A., Allen, T. D. and Motowidlo, S. J. 2001. Personality predictors of citizenship performance, *International Journal of Selection and Assessment* 9: 52–69

Boudreau, J. W., Boswell, W. R. and Judge, T. A. 2001. Effects of personality on executive career success in the United States and Europe, *Journal of Vocational Behaviour* 58: 53–81

Burch, G. St J. 2006. The 'creative-schizotype': help or hindrance to team-level innovation?, *University of Auckland Business Review* 8: 43–51

Burch, G. St J. and Anderson, N. 2008. Personality as a predictor of work-related behaviour and performance: recent advances and directions for future research, in G. P. Hodgkinson and J. K. Ford (eds.), *International review of industrial and organizational psychology*, vol. XXIII, pp. 261–305. Chichester: John Wiley and Sons Ltd

Campbell, J., McCloy, R., Oppler, S. and Sager, C. 1993. A theory of performance, in N. Schmitt and W. Borman (eds.), *Personnel selection in organizations*, pp. 35–70. San Francisco, CA: Jossey-Bass

Cronbach, L. J. and Gleser, G. C. 1965. *Psychological tests and personnel decisions.* Urbana, IL: University of Illinois

Costa, P. T. and McCrae, R. R. 1992. *Revised NEO Personality Inventory (NEO PI-R): professional manual.* Odessa, FL: Psychological Assessment Resources, Inc.

Digman, J. M. 1990. Personality structure: emergence of the Five Factor Model, *Annual Review of Psychology* 41: 417–40

Dudley, N. M., Orvis, K. A., Lebiecki, J. E. and Cortina, J. M. 2006. A meta-analytic investigation of Conscientiousness in the prediction of job performance: examining the intercorrelations and the incremental validity of narrow traits, *Journal of Applied Psychology* 91: 40–57

Ghiselli, E. E. 1973. The validity of aptitude tests in personnel selection, *Personnel Psychology* 26: 461–77

Goldberg, L. R., Lee, K. and Ashton, M. C. 2008. Comment on Anderson and Ones. *European Journal of Personality* 22: 151–56

Guion, R. M. and Gottier, R. F. 1965. Validity of personality measures in personnel selection, *Personnel Psychology* 18: 135–64

Hogan, R. 2005a. In defense of personality measurement: new wine for old whiners, *Human Performance* 18: 331–41

2005b. Comments, *Human Performance* 18: 405–7

Hogan, R. and Hogan, J. 1995. *Hogan personality inventory.* Tulsa, OK: Hogan Assessment Systems

1997. *Hogan development survey.* Tulsa, OK: Hogan Assessment Systems

2001. Assessing leadership: a view from the dark side, *International Journal of Selection and Assessment* 9: 40–51

Hogan, J. and Holland, B. 2003. Using theory to evaluate personality and job performance relations, *Journal of Applied Psycholgy* 88: 100–12

Hogan, R. and Roberts, B. W. 2001. Introduction: personality and industrial and organizational psychology, in B. W. Roberts and R. Hogan (eds.), *Personality psychology in the workplace*, pp. 3–16. Washington, DC: American Psychological Association

Holland, J. L. 1997. *Making vocational choices: a theory of vocational personalities and work environments*, 3rd edn. Englewood Cliffs, NJ: Prentice-Hall

Hough, L. M. and Ones, D. S. 2001. The structure, measurement, validity, and use of personality variables in industrial, work and organizational psychology, in N. Anderson, D. S. Ones, H. K. Sinangil and C. Viswesvaran (eds.), *Handbook of industrial, work and organizational psychology*, vol I, pp. 233–67. London: Sage Publications

Ilies, R., Gerhardt, M. W. and Le, H. 2004. Individual differences in leadership emergence: integrating meta-analytic findings and behavioural genetics estimates, *International Journal of Selection and Assessment* 12: 207–19

Ilies, R., Scott, B. A. and Judge, T. A. 2006. The interactive effects of personal traits and experienced states on intraindividual patterns of citizenship behaviour, *Academy of Management Journal* 49: 561–75

Judge, T. A. and Bono, J. E. 2001. Relationship of core self-evaluations traits – self-esteem, generalized self-efficacy, locus of control, and emotional stability – with job satisfaction and job performance: a meta-analysis, *Journal of Applied Psychology* 86: 80–92

Judge, T. A., Bono, J. E., Ilies, R. and Gerhardt, M. W. 2002. Personality and leadership: a qualitative and quantitative review, *Journal of Applied Psychology* 87: 765–80

Judge, T. A., Higgins, C. A., Thoresen, C. J. and Barrick, M. 1999. The Big Five personality traits, general mental ability, and career success across the life span, *Personnel Psychology* 52: 621–52

Judge, T. A. and Ilies, R. 2002. Relationship of personality to performance motivation: a meta-analytic review, *Journal of Applied Psychology* 87: 797–807

Judge, T. A., Ilies, R. and Colbert, A. E. 2004. Intelligence and leadership: a quantitative review and test of theoretical propositions, *Journal of Applied Psychology* 89: 452–552

Judge, T. A., LePine, J. A. and Rich, B. L. 2006. Loving yourself abundantly: relationship of the narcissistic personality to self- and other perceptions of workplace deviance, leadership, and task and contextual performance, *Journal of Applied Psychology* 91: 762–76

Kaiser, R. B. and Hogan, R. 2007. The dark side of discretion, in R. Hooijberg, J. Hunt, K. Boal, W. Macy and J. Antonakis (eds.), *Leadership in and out of organizations*, pp. 177–97. Amsterdam: Elsevier

Khoo, H. S. and Burch, G. St J. 2008. The 'dark side' of leadership personality and transformational leadership: an exploratory study, *Personality and Individual Differences* 44: 86–97

LaHuis, D. M., Martin, N. R. and Avis, J. M. 2005. Investigating nonlinear Conscientiousness-job performance relations for clerical employees, *Human Performance* 18: 199–212

Montgomery, B. 1961. *The path to leadership*. London: Collins

Morgeson, F. P., Campion, M. A., Dipboye, R. L., Hollenbeck, J. R., Murphy, K. and Schmitt, N. 2007. Reconsidering the use of personality tests in personnel selection contexts, *Personnel Psychology* 60: 683–729

Morgeson, F. P., Reider, M. H. and Campion, M. A. 2005. Selecting individuals in team settings: the importance of social skills, personality characteristics, and teamwork knowledge, *Personnel Psychology* 58: 583–611

Moscoso, S. and Salgado, J. F. 2004. 'Dark side' personality styles as predictors of task, contextual, and job performance, *International Journal of Selection and Assessment* 12: 356–62

Murphy, K. R. and Dzieweczynski, J. L. 2005. Why don't personality measures of broad dimensions of personality perform better as predictors of job performance?, *Human Performance* 18: 343–57

Nicholson, N. 1998. Personality and entrepreneurial leadership: a study of the heads of the UK's most successful independent companies, *European Management Journal* 16: 529–39

Ones, D. S. and Anderson, N. 2002. Gender and ethnic group differences on personality scales in selection: some British data, *Journal of Occupational and Organizational Psychology* 75: 255–76

Ones, D. S. and Viswesvaran, C. 1996. Bandwidth-fidelity dilemma in personality measurement for personnel selection, *Journal of Organizational Behaviour* 17: 609–26

Ones, D. S., Dilchert, S., Viswesvaran, C. and Judge, T. A. 2007. In support of personality assessment in organizational settings, *Personnel Psychology* 60: 995–1027

Organ, D. W. 1988. *Organizational citizenship behaviour: the good soldier syndrome*. San Francisco, CA: New Lexington Press

Organ, D. W. and McFall, J. B. 2004. Personality and citizenship behaviour in organizations, in B. Schneider and D. B. Smith. (eds.), *Personality and organizations*, pp. 291–314. Mahwah, NJ: Lawrence Erlbaum Associates

Organ, D. W., Podsakoff, P. M. and MacKenzie, S. B. 2006. *Organization citizenship behaviour: its nature, antecedents and consequences*. Thousand Oaks, CA: Sage Publications

Organ, D. W. and Ryan, K. 1995. A meta-analytic review of attitudinal and dispositional predictors of organizational citizenship behaviour, *Personnel Psychology* 48: 775–802

Packman, T., Brown, G. S., Englert, P., Sisarich, H. and Bauer, F. 2005. Differences in personality traits across ethnic groups within New Zealand and across an international sample, *New Zealand Journal of Psychology* 34: 77–85

Perkins, A. M. and Corr, P. J. 2005. Can worriers be winners? The association between worrying and job performance, *Personality and Individual Differences* 38: 25–31

Rosenthal, S. A. and Pittinsky, T. L. 2006. Narcissistic leadership, *Leadership Quarterly* 17: 617–33

Sackett, P. R., Berry, C. M., Wiemann, S. A. and Laczo, R. M. 2006. Citizenship and counterproductive work behaviour: clarifying relationships between the two domains, *Human Performance* 19: 441–64

Sackett, P. R. and DeVore, C. J. 2001. Counterproductive behaviours at work, in N. Anderson, D. S. Ones, H. K. Sinangil and C. Viswesvaran (eds.), *Handbook of industrial, work and organizational psychology*, vol I, pp. 145–64. London: Sage Publications

Salgado, J. F. 2003. Predicting job performance using FFM and non-FFM personality measures, *Journal of Occupational and Organizational Psychology* 76: 323–46

Salgado, J. F. and De Fruyt, F. 2005. Personality in personnel selection, in A. Evers, N. Anderson and O. Voskuijl (eds.), *The Blackwell handbook of personnel selection*, pp. 174–98. Oxford: Blackwell Publishing

Schmitt, N. and Kim, B. 2007. Selection decision making, in P. Boxall, J. Purcell and P. Wright (eds.), *The Oxford handbook of human resource management*, pp. 300–23. Oxford University Press

Seibert, S. E. and Kraimer, M. L. 2001. The Five-Factor Model of personality and career success, *Journal of Vocational Behaviour* 58: 1–21

Te Nijenhuis, J. and Van der Flier, H. 2002. Differential prediction of immigrant versus majority group training performance using cognitive ability and personality measures, *International Journal of Selection and Assessment* 8: 54–60

44 Workplace safety and personality

Alice F. Stuhlmacher, Andrea L. Briggs
and Douglas F. Cellar

The human and financial cost of accidents in the workplace is staggering. Although no reliable estimates exist on the extent of human suffering related to accidents, one assessment places accidents and work-related diseases as costing 4 per cent of the world's gross domestic product (International Labor Organization 2006). In 2005, in the United States alone, over four million non-fatal injuries and illnesses and 5,000 fatal work-related injuries were reported in the private sector (Bureau of Labor Statistics 2005).

This chapter examines the role that personality plays in safety behaviour and accidents in the workplace. We discuss traits that have been proposed to constitute an 'accident prone' personality, the strength and direction of various dispositional predictors of accidents, and how personality fits with other variables in explaining safe and unsafe behaviour. The traits of individuals with safe and unsafe behaviour are one factor in the prediction of safety and risk; personality differences need to be put in context of other issues. Although safety can also be addressed through behaviours, the physical work environment (e.g., equipment design) or interpersonal factors (e.g., supervision, work climate), the role of personality in accidents and safety has been of interest across decades of research and is worthy of review. In particular, a review at this point can direct future research and improve safety applications by clarifying the evidence for various dispositions, integrating current thinking on broad versus narrow trait definitions, and speculating what dispositions connect to safe behaviour patterns.

Traits as predictors

Tables 44.1 and 44.2 report correlations of some personality variables with safety criteria. Even though many work contexts (e.g., construction, public safety, healthcare, manufacturing, chemical handling) have safety concerns, the tables suggest that the most frequently studied work areas relate to driving or operating vehicles. Driving has been widely investigated due to the number and variety of organizations that employ drivers or require driving. Interestingly, vehicular safety has been defined and measured in a number of ways; later we will consider why job performance criteria are important in understanding the relationship between personality and safety.

Table 44.1 *Personality variables correlated with workplace safety.*

Variable	Study name	Sample	Sample size	Safety criteria	Correlation
Impulsiveness	Dahlen et al. 2005	College students	224	Aggressive driving	.23
Distractibility	Hansen 1989	Production and maintenance workers	362	Accident consistency	.31
Sensation-seeking	Burns and Wilde 1995	Male taxi drivers	51	Speeding violations	.42
				Traffic violations	.35
	Dahlen et al. 2005	College students	224	Aggressive driving	.20
				Risky driving	.33
				Loss of vehicle control	.22
				Physically aggressive driving expressions	.25
				Verbally aggressive driving expressions	.24
	Ulleberg and Rundmo 2003	Adolescent drivers	1932	Risk-taking behaviour in traffic	.34
Boredom proneness	Dahlen et al. 2005	College students	224	Aggressive driving	.18
				Risky driving	.20
				Minor loss of vehicle control	.16
				Physically aggressive driving expressions	.15
				Angry driving	.19
Global risk-taking	Westaby and Lowe 2005	Employed adolescents	2542	Work injury	.07
Risk-taking orientation at work	Westaby and Lowe 2005	Employed adolescents	2542	Work injury	.30

Table 44.2 *Five-Factor Model personality variables correlations with workplace safety.*

Variable	Study name	Sample	Sample size	Safety criteria	Correlation
Agreeableness	Arthur and Graziano 1996	Temporary employees	250	Moving violation tickets	-.14
	Cellar et al. 2000	College students	202	Combined total accidents and driving tickets	-.16
	Cellar et al. 2001	College students	202	Combined total accidents	-.13
	Cellar et al. 2004	College students	202	Workplace accidents	-.13
	Tubre et al. 2006	Drivers	308	Aggressive driving	-.42
Conscientiousness	Arthur and Doverspike 2001	Volunteers	48	Total crashes	-.40
	Arthur and Graziano 1996	College students	227	At-fault accidents	-.14
		Temporary employees	250	At-fault accidents	-.19
				Moving violation tickets	-.16
	Cellar et al. 2001	College students	202	Combined total accidents	-.16
	Cellar et al. 2004	College students	202	Workplace accidents	-.16
	Tubre et al. 2006	Drivers	308	Aggressive driving	-.32
Extraversion	Arthur and Graziano 1996	College students	227	Total driving accidents	.15
				At-fault accidents	.13
Neuroticism	Tubre et al. 2006	Drivers	308	Aggressive driving	.33
				Angry driving	.18
Openness	Arthur and Graziano 1996	College students	227	At-fault accidents	.13

Although there is considerable debate on what constitutes an accident prone personality, possible traits include impulsivity, distractibility, sensation-seeking, boredom proneness, risk-seeking, locus of control (see Table 44.1) and variables in the Five-Factor Model of personality (see Table 44.2). We offer a brief review of these traits and their research support. To organize the review, we first discuss variables that share common bases, in particular, attention control, arousal levels and internal orientation, and then discuss the Five-Factor Model. This organization is somewhat artificial given that there is substantial overlap between variables, particularly in regard to the sub-factors of the Five-Factor Model and other traits. For simplicity, we turn to the global Five-Factor Model traits after discussing individual traits.

Traits relating to attention control

A couple of traits relating to safety are associated with attention control: impulsiveness and distractibility. *Impulsiveness* deals with one's control over thoughts and behaviours. In regards to safety, impulsiveness leads to accidents because the individual lacks the control to refrain from engaging in risky behaviour (Barratt 1994; Dahlen, Martin, Ragan and Kuhlman 2005). Impulsiveness has been associated with impaired driving behaviour, accident rates, and a reduced ability to perceive traffic signs (Hansen 1988). Dahlen, Martin, Ragan and Kuhlman (2005) found impulsiveness was related to risky and aggressive driving. A workforce characterized by impulsiveness would likely have less safe work behaviours than a less impulsive workforce (Kamp and Krause 1997). Similarly, *distractibility* is a lapse of attention that stems from an individual's inability to concentrate, indecisiveness, as well as fatigue levels and anxiety (Hansen 1989). Distractibility involves task attention deficits and is correlated with accident consistency; increased distractibility has been related to an increased number of accidents per year over time (Hansen 1989).

Traits relating to arousal level

In addition to attention control variables, a set of traits are associated with arousal levels: sensation-seeking, risk-taking and boredom proneness. *Sensation-seeking* is an individual difference in optimal levels of arousal and desires for new and intense stimuli (Zuckerman 1979). Individuals higher in sensation-seeking are expected to take risks because of the pleasure that is associated with the experience (Zuckerman 1979). Sensation-seeking has been examined widely in the area of driving safety, correlating with speeding violations, traffic violations (Burns and Wilde 1995), risky driving (Dahlen, Martin, Ragan and Kuhlman 2005) and risk-taking behaviour in traffic (Ulleberg and Rundmo 2003). Sensation-seeking predicts risky behaviour; risky behaviour is likely to lead to accidents (Nicholson, Soane, Fenton-O'Creevy and Willman 2005); for example, sensation-seekers tend to drive at faster speeds and with less care (Burns and Wilde 1995). Dahlen *et al.*'s

(2005) findings suggest that sensation-seeking correlates with a variety of factors from aggressive driving, risky driving, minor losses of vehicular control, and physically and verbally aggressive driving anger expressions. In an extensive qualitative review, Jonah (1997) found correlations of .30 to .40 between sensation-seeking and risky driving across thirty-six of forty studies. The strongest relations were for men, compared to women, and for facets of Zuckerman's Sensation Seeking Scale compared to other measures. Additionally, sensation-seeking was a key predictor of other risk factors like alcohol use.

Also associated with arousal level is *risk-taking orientation*, or a person's motivation to engage in activities that may have certain elements of danger (Westaby and Lowe 2005). Risk-taking orientation differs from sensation-seeking by being narrower in focus. Risk-taking orientation specifically refers to an individual's urge to engage in activities that have an element of actual physical danger; sensation-seeking includes activities that merely involve novel stimuli that optimize levels of arousal (Westaby and Lowe 2005). For example, running a marathon would be a sensation-seeking activity which is low on risk-taking. Competing in a marathon has high levels of arousal for the individual participating, but is not usually considered to have elements of actual physical danger. Hansen (1988) concluded that not enough direct research exists to draw conclusions about risk-taking's effect on safety behaviour and accidents. Others disagree; Westaby and Lowe (2005) found that employees, especially young employees, with a strong risk-taking orientation reported more injuries than those with a weak risk-taking orientation.

Finally, another aspect of arousal level is *boredom proneness* (Dahlen, Martin, Ragan and Kuhlman 2005). Boredom proneness is one's tendency to experience feelings of apathy or disinterest. Boredom proneness has been found to be significantly positively related to both aggressive and risky driving, minor loss of vehicle control, physically aggressive driving and angry driving (Dahlen *et al.* 2005).

Traits relating to internal orientation

A third general category of traits relate to orientation to self versus orientation to the external world; this includes locus of control and Introversion-Extraversion. *Locus of control* (Janicak 1996; Rotter 1966) relates to beliefs that one can affect one's life. An external locus of control implies weak beliefs about influencing one's own life; an internal locus of control implies that one has the power to achieve control over one's life (Rotter 1966). Workers who feel little control over the events in their lives (i.e., an external locus of control) have a higher likelihood of accident occurrence (Hansen 1988). Hansen's findings coincide with Klonowicz and Sokolowska (1993) who conclude that locus of control influences risk analysis. Specifically, those with an internal locus of control can better analyse the possible risk for an accident, the consequences of an accident, and their own resources to deal with an accident. In other words, because individuals with an internal locus of control can better analyse all the possible outcomes of an accident, they are better able to avoid an accident and the risks associated with it (Klonowicz and Sokolowska 1993). A meta-analysis by Arthur, Barrett and Alexander (1991) found overall locus of control to have a positive mean correlation ($r = .20$) with car accidents. External locus of control would be exemplified in the case of miners or construction workers who do not wear safety helmets or follow safety procedures because they believe that when 'one's time has come' there is nothing to do to prevent injury or death.

The personality dimensions of Introversion-Extraversion, originally defined by Eysenck (1947), have been investigated in relation to risk and safety more than any other personality trait (Hansen 1988). Introversion has been defined as a 'person's preference for attending to this inner world of experience, with an emphasis on reflective, introspective thinking' (Morris 1979, p. 6). Extraversion has been defined as the 'preference for attending to the outer world of objective events with an emphasis upon active involvement in the environment' (Morris 1979, p. 6). Research finds extraverts having higher accident rates than introverts (Hansen 1988). Introverts value being in control of their experiences and tend to be more careful when doing things than extraverts (Hansen 1988). Introversion-Extraversion has also been investigated as part of the Five-Factor Model of personality, which we discuss next.

Five-Factor Model

Another approach to explain accident prone personalities is through broader personality models. The most common model has been the personality traits in the Five-Factor Model involving Agreeableness, Conscientiousness, Extraversion, Neuroticism and Openness to Experience (Costa and McCrae 1992; Costa and McCrae 1995; Digman 1990). The Five-Factor Model provides an organized and comprehensive approach to the study of personality and accident involvement beyond single traits (Arthur and Graziano 1996).

Despite enthusiasm for the Five-Factor Model, researchers have found a variety of results in predicting workplace accidents (see Table 44.2). Arthur and Graziano (1996) investigated the five factors and driving accidents in college students and with participants from a temporary employment agency. For the college sample, Extraversion had a significant relationship with total accidents. Extraversion, Conscientiousness and Openness were also related to at-fault accidents. In the temporary employment sample, Conscientiousness was negatively correlated with at-fault total accidents and moving violations. Cellar, Nelson, Yorke and Bauer (2001) found Conscientiousness and Agreeableness negatively correlated with total accidents (both at-fault and not-at-fault). In a similar study, Cellar, Yorke, Nelson and Carroll (2004) found Conscientiousness and Agreeableness negatively correlated with total work accidents; this suggests that individuals low on Agreeableness and Conscientiousness are more likely to be involved in workplace accidents than their agreeable and conscientious counterparts. Additionally, Arthur and Doverskpike (2001) found a negative correlation with Conscientiousness and total crashes.

Agreeableness has been related to the number of moving violation tickets (Arthur and Graziano 1996). Interestingly, a study (Cellar, Nelson and Yorke 2000) found Agreeableness to be the only factor significantly correlated with both the number of driving tickets and the combined sum of reported total driving accidents and tickets. Likewise, Tubre, Edwards, Zyphur and Warren (2006) found positive relationships between Neuroticism and both aggressive driving and driving angry. Furthermore, negative relationships were found between aggressive driving and Agreeableness and Conscientiousness. However, they found no significant relationships between aggressive driving and Extraversion or Openness to Experience. Garrity and Demick (2001) looked at the relations among personality traits, mood states and driving behaviours; contrary to their prediction, none of the personality traits of the Five-Factor Model significantly related to driving behaviour.

Clarke and Robertson (2005) meta-analytically reviewed the Five-Factor Model and accident involvement in both occupational and non-occupational settings. Individuals low in Agreeableness and low in Conscientiousness were more likely to be involved in accidents. Furthermore, in occupational settings, low Agreeableness and Neuroticism were also significant predictors of accidents. In non-occupational settings (i.e., non-work related traffic accidents), Extraversion, low Conscientiousness and low Agreeableness were significant predictors of accidents. These results are similar to previously mentioned studies (i.e., Arthur and Graziano 1996; Cellar, Nelson and Yorke 2000; Cellar, Yorke, Nelson and Carroll 2004; Tubre, Edwards, Zyphur and Warren 2006). Because Agreeableness was a consistent predictor for both occupation and non-occupational accidents, Clarke and Robertson (2005) suggest that accidents are triggered because low Agreeableness individuals are less able to manage interpersonal relations with others. Specifically, in the case of road-related accidents, those low on Agreeableness may be less likely to interact well with other drivers and choose behaviours that do not reduce risk or hazards.

In summary, across personality variables, Tables 44.1 and 44.2 suggest that the most frequently studied personality variables in safety research are sensation-seeking, Agreeableness and Conscientiousness. These traits also show some of the strongest correlations with safety in Tables 44.1 and 44.2 (maximum $rs = .42, -.42, -.40$ respectively for sensation-seeking, Agreeableness and Conscientiousness). Substantial variability exists, however. Correlations with safety criteria ranged from .20 to .42 for sensation-seeking, from $-.13$ to $-.42$ for Agreeableness, and from $-.14$ to $-.40$ for Conscientiousness. Other variables, such as impulsiveness and risk-taking orientation, have limited research available for drawing conclusions.

Current research and new directions

The data presented here has led to some mixed interpretations and concern. Of concern are the relatively low correlations and small amount of common variance accounted for in the studies of personality and safety. Despite some consistent findings, critics note that personality accounts for only a small percentage of the variance in predicting safety. In Tables 44.1 and 44.2, the maximum variance accounted for (r^2) ranges from 5 to 16 per cent. Current attempts to make sense of findings involve looking at a combination of factors rather than a trait in isolation. For example, overall risk-taking is positively correlated with Extraversion, Openness and low Neuroticism, and is negatively correlated with Agreeableness and Conscientiousness (Nicholson, Soane, Fenton-O'Creevy and Willman 2005). The researchers interpreted this pattern as 'high extraversion and openness supply the motivational force for risk taking; low neuroticism and agreeableness supply the insulation against guilt or anxiety about negative consequences; and low conscientiousness makes it easier to cross the cognitive barriers of need for control, deliberation, and conformity' (Nicholson *et al.* 2005, p. 170). This profile approach holds promise to better understand the complexity of dispositional patterns in safety.

Other concerns regarding personality and work performance have centred on the use of the Five-Factor Model. While the Five-Factor Model offers an organizing framework for personality, some question the usefulness of broad rather than narrow factors (e.g., Murphy and Dzieweczynski 2005). Support is growing for using narrow sub-traits instead of broad predictors (Paunonen, Rothstein and Jackson 1999) to predict a range of work behaviours, particularly for predicting specific behaviours. Increasingly, multidimensional predictors within and beyond the Five-Factor Model are being suggested. Ashton, Jackson, Paynonen *et al.* (1995) found facet scales correlating more strongly with work behaviour criteria than the global dimensions. Others maintain that facets offer more opportunity for understanding the construct being predicted (Tett, Guterman, Bleier and Murphy 2000) and are theoretically more precise than broad factors. In correlating both broad and narrow traits with job performance, Stewart (1999) found validity differences across Conscientiousness and its sub-traits over time based on employee tenure.

The potential for narrow versus broad factors has been supported in some safety research (e.g., Ashton 1998; Dorn and Matthews 1995; Westaby and Lowe 2005). Narrow measures of responsibility and risk-taking had higher relations with workplace delinquency than the five factor dimensions (Ashton 1998). In particular, unsafe behaviour had stronger correlations with the facets of self-esteem ($r = .22$), risk-taking ($r = .24$) and responsibility ($r = -.20$) than any of the five factor dimensions (r's $= -.17$ to .12). Similarly, Westaby and Lowe (2005) reported that a specific measure (risk-taking at work, $r = .30$) was a better predictor of work injury than global risk-taking ($r = .07$). Ulleberg and Rundmo (2003) measured facets of the Five-Factor Model and found moderately strong relationships of risk-taking behaviour in traffic with the facets of sensation-seeking ($r = .34$), aggression ($r = .21$), anxiety ($r = -.25$) and altruism ($r = -.31$). These facet correlations are much higher than the average correlations for global five factor variables in Table 44.2.

Although not explicitly involving safety, a recent meta-analysis (Dudley, Orvis, Lebiecki and Cortina 2006) found narrow traits contributed beyond global measures of Conscientiousness in predicting performance criteria of task performance, job dedication, interpersonal and counter-productive work behaviours. The strength of these relationships varies by the criterion and occupational type. Similarly, within the Five-Factor Model, Mount and Barrick (1995) found that when narrower facets have explained additional variance in performance beyond the broad five factor dimensions, it occurred when there were strong conceptual links between the narrow trait and the criterion. Thus, it seems that the level of specificity in the criterion behaviour as well as the conceptual linkage between the trait and criterion of interest are important determinants of the predictive efficacy of specific traits beyond broad personality dimensions.

Researchers have also considered the context in which criterion performance occurs; personality measures designed for a particular context such as work or academic domains should lead to greater prediction in those contexts compared to more abstract measures of personality (e.g., VandeWalle 1997). For example, research has shown that more context-oriented scales may have greater predictive efficacy than more abstract scales (e.g., Cellar, Miller, Doverspike and Klawsky 1996) and that five factor items revised to reflect a work domain increased the prediction of work performance compared to more general measures (Mount, Barrick and Strauss 1994; Schmit, Ryan, Stierwalt and Powell 1995).

It is important to distinguish trait specificity from context specificity. Generally, trait specificity has been defined as the bandwidth or narrowness of more abstract traits (e.g., Cronbach and Gleser 1965; Ones and Viswesvaran 1996) while context specificity is the domain or context in which the trait is affecting behaviour (e.g, Schmit *et al.* 1995). It is recommended that this distinction be considered and more clearly articulated in future research on personality and safety.

In short, the safety research to date appears encouraging regarding the relative predictive efficacy of specific traits compared to more general ones, but studies in the safety literature have not made clear comparisons between specific and general traits from the same model and using the same criterion measures. Therefore, it is difficult to address the issue of incremental prediction because of differences across studies in personality models and criteria used.

It is recommended that future research directly evaluates the predictive efficacy of relatively narrow traits such as sensation-seeking (e.g., Dahlen, Martin, Ragan and Kuhlman 2005) in comparison to broader traits like Extraversion (e.g., Arthur and Graziano 1996), as well as comparing facets and broad dimensions within the Five-Factor Model. The fact that Westaby and Lowe's study found greater predictive efficacy for a context specific measure of risk-taking compared to a more global measure is encouraging and parallels the research that has examined this issue in the work performance literature. More research of this nature would serve to further clarify the utility of contextually based personality measures.

Criteria issues: defining and measuring safety and accidents

As more attention is paid to sub-traits or narrow factors in the predictor, it is helpful to consider specificity in the criterion of interest. As mentioned, narrow sub-traits are thought to be a better predictor of specific or narrow criteria, while broad factors have been suggested to be better predictors of more global criteria (Schneider, Hough and Dunnette 1996). Thus, some attention to the criteria and measures of safety is warranted to understand the role of personality in predicting safe and unsafe behaviour. Criteria can be classified in different ways but it is helpful to distinguish between objective and subjective measures as well as the source of the data (e.g., observer, self-report, archival). Objective measures involve a countable or relatively factual set of observations or data while subjective measures involve a judgement, rating or interpretation of the performance criterion. Driving safety offers a useful illustration of the variety of measures and some of the difficulties operationalizing the criterion. Common objective measures in vehicle safety research include the number of driving tickets or accident reports. Somewhat less objective, but still quantifiable, are observations by trained observers of predetermined behaviours or consequences. For example, taxi speed and lane changes were observed unobtrusively by passengers (Burns and Wilde 1995); stopping and turn signal use were observed of pizza delivery drivers (Ludwig, Biggs, Wagner and Geller 2001; Ludwig and Geller 1997); and trained observers recorded unsafe bakery worker behaviour such as oil spills or climbing over conveyor belts (Komaki, Barwick and Scott 1978). Likewise, observations regarding specific industry accidents (cracking of chips, misdirected flow, explosions) have also been operationalized as safety measures (Klonowicz and Sokolowska 1993). These types of observational and objective measures require countable and visible actions and must be carefully defined in order for reliable measurement. Objective measures avoid self-report biases, but require substantial time and resources for sampling and monitoring. Observational studies of safety are criticized for the possibility that awareness of being monitored temporarily changes behaviour and thwarts accurate measurement. Objective measures from archival or personnel data from records also have been criticized as having potential contamination from intentional or unintentional variability in documenting behaviours or consequences. Archival data rarely capture all relevant data. Systematic or unsystematic errors in recording are assumed to underestimate the extent of accidents and safety behaviour.

Other research has turned to more subjective criteria such as self-reports. Rather than relying on archival evidence or observation, participants may be asked to recall at-fault, not-at-fault or driving tickets (e.g., Cellar, Nelson and Yorke 2000), minor accidents, major accidents, close call, lost concentration, or moving tickets (e.g. Dahlen, Martin, Ragan and Kuhlman 2005) or unreported events (e.g., Smith, Silverman, Heckert *et al.* 2001). Given that personality scales are often self-report, self-reports of safety may have potential contamination from common method bias. It is plausible that any self-presentation effect operating in personality measures would also be present in reporting safety events. Others suggest that self-reports offer important information (Smith *et al.* 2001) and should be included as measures of safety and accidents. In support of this, Smith *et al.* (2001) report that objective and self-report measures differentially predicted recorded injury events, unreported injury events and near injury events across both a plastics plant and a glass plant. Smith *et al.* suggest that self-report constructs are separate constructs from recorded events and both self-report and records are needed to understand workplace injuries.

It is clear that each assessment has its own limitations. While self-report potentially suffers from social desirability and memory effects, organizational records are subject to reporting biases or are poorly tracked. Multiple data sources on safety are desirable. A meta-analysis found an average correlation of .39 between objective measures of job performance and subjective measure of job performance (Bommer, Johnson, Rich *et al.* 1995). This effect is likely similar for safety criteria; while there should be a relationship, objective and subjective measures should not be considered equivalent. In brief, it remains important to attend to how safety is defined and measured.

Personality in context

While our discussion has centred on the association of particular traits and safety outcomes, the context also remains a major factor relating to the impact of personality. Thus, to understand the role of personality, we need also to examine the situational context of work environment. Figure 44.1 presents a model, based

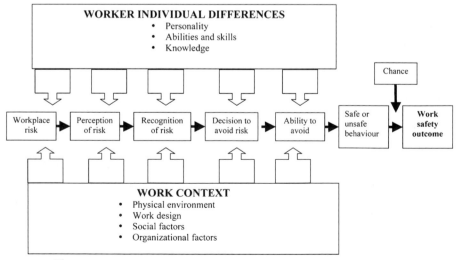

Figure 44.1. *Model of the safety process.*

on McCormick and Sanders (1982), of the safety process. The model acknowledges that individual differences and work context affect the safety process. The first variable in the model is the existence of workplace risk. Given workplace risk, future events depend on recognition of this risk, followed by decisions about avoiding the risk. After decisions are made (or not made) about avoiding risk, ability influences the behaviour displayed. The behaviour that follows may or may not lead to a negative work safety outcome, depending to some degree on chance. From the figure, we see multiple points where worker individual differences and work context influence the safety process.

Relevant here is that personality, as well as other variables, plays a role at several points in the process of explaining safety behaviour. Specific personality characteristics may be more influential at certain points. Traits relating to attention control (e.g., distractibility and impulsiveness of workers or co-workers) may be most influential in creating risky situations and perceiving if a risk or hazard is present. Likewise, Conscientiousness may be related to the recognition of risk and decisions to avoid risks. Agreeableness may reflect how a specific behaviour is performed, that is, if the behaviour is appropriate to resolve the hazard or not. Traits relating to arousal level (e.g., boredom proneness, sensation-seeking) may relate to tendencies to perceive a risk or seek out a risk. Locus of control may be tied to decisions to act to avoid risk. In looking at a process model of safety such as Figure 44.1, we see many opportunities in how theory could be more precise in detailing when specific traits contribute to workplace safety outcomes. Given the number of intervening factors in the safety process, it is not surprising that personality has some small effects. The model suggests that traits will be more effective in predicting specific aspects or precursors of work safety than the actual work safety outcome.

Personality does not exist in a vacuum. In addition to using personality measures as selection tools, accident reduction has focused on training, feedback, incentives for safe behaviours, or modification of the environment. The model shows that these would influence the safety process in several ways. Modification of the environment (e.g., equipment design, warning signs, noise reduction, lighting, safety guards) may reduce workplace risk or increase the likelihood of perceiving a risk. Training would increase recognition of risk or abilities to avoid risk. The sequence of actions in the safety process would be affected by social factors (e.g., safety norms, communication practices, worker interaction) as well as organization factors like policies, training, incentives, feedback and safety climate.

Safety research has moved into areas beyond the individual by considering the role of the organization and supervisors in creating a climate for safety. Workplace climates are the perceptions shared across individuals on the practices, procedures and rewards. Indeed, safety climate is seen as an important mediator in predicting accidents (Wallace, Popp and Mondore 2006). While the research on climate and safety is valuable, personality remains a factor in shaping the climate and individual behaviours.

Implications for research and application

In general, research that has examined relationships between personality characteristics and safety criteria has been fruitful. Consistent relationships have been found for both specific traits and broad personality factors such as those articulated by the Five-Factor Model. Furthermore, the direction of obtained relationships has generally been consistent with theoretical expectations and predictions. And finally, the magnitude of these relationships has been consistent with personality research that has studied the prediction of other behaviour-based criteria, such as performance, explaining moderate to small amounts of criterion variance.

It is suggested that future research should focus on further clarifying if, and under what conditions, specific traits better predict safety criteria compared to more general traits. In addition, it is recommended that more research is warranted to investigate the predictive efficacy of more contextualized measures of personality in predicting safe behaviour. Safety research in this area has been promising but more definitive research is justifiable. More data may be one means of increasing relationships between personality variables and safety indices in organizations. In addition, more research should be done that examines the use of personality variables in combination with other cognitive and perceptual variables to better understand the nature of the criterion space and the extent to which personality explains unique variance in safety criteria.

An additional suggestion for future research is to study the relationships of personality variables to the perception of climate for safety. Such research could provide insights into the role of personality traits in the formation and maintenance of climate for safety. Research linking climate to safety has been promising and we believe that considering the role of personality in the creation of safety climates would be useful.

Regarding application to the workplace, this review found the general traits of both Conscientiousness and Agreeableness as viable predictors of safety criteria; this also seems to be the case in the work performance literature. To the extent that an organization is hiring based on direct or indirect measures of these constructs, safety should be enhanced as well. However in situations where a trait, such as Extraversion, might well have positive correlations with certain aspects of performance but a negative relationship with safety, there could be a potential conflict of interest. In such a situation one might well consider additional training to ensure safety is not compromised.

References

Arthur, W., Jr, Barrett, G. V. and Alexander, R. A. 1991. Prediction of vehicular accident involvement: a meta-analysis, *Human Performance* 4: 89–105

Arthur, W. A., Jr and Doverspike, D. 2001. Predicting motor vehicle crash involvement from a personality measure and a driving knowledge test, in A. F. Stuhlmacher and D. F. Cellar (eds.), *Workplace safety: individual differences in behaviour*, pp. 35–42. Binghamtom, NY: Hawthorne Press

Arthur, W. and Graziano, W. G. 1996. The Five Factor Model, Conscientiousness, and driving accident involvement, *Journal of Personality* 64: 593–618

Ashton, M. C. 1998. Personality and job performance: the importance of narrow traits, *Journal of Organizational Behaviour* 19: 289–303

Ashton, M. C., Jackson, D. N., Paunonen, S. V., Helmes, E. and Rothstein, M. G. 1995. The criterion validity of broad factor scales versus specific facet scales, *Journal of Research in Personality* 29: 432–42

Barratt, E. S. 1994. Impulsiveness and aggression, in J. Monahan and H. J. Steadman (eds.), *Violence and mental disorder: developments in risk assessment*, pp. 61–79. University of Chicago Press

Bommer, W. H., Johnson, J., Rich, G. A., Podsakoff, P. M. and MacKenzie, S. B. 1995. On the interchangeability of objective and subjective measures of employee performance: a meta-analysis, *Personnel Psychology* 48: 587–605

Bureau of Labor Statistics 2005. *Latest numbers*, www.bls.gov/iif/home.htm

Burns, P. C. and Wilde, G. J. S. 1995. Risk taking in male taxi drivers: relationships among personality, observational data and driver records, *Personality Individual Differences* 18: 267–78

Cellar, D. F., Miller, M. L., Doverspike, D. D. and Klawsky, J. D. 1996. Comparison of factor structures and criterion-related validity of coefficients for two measures of personality based on the Five Factor Model, *Journal of Applied Psychology* 81: 694–704

Cellar, D. F., Nelson, Z. C. and Yorke, C. M. 2000. The Five Factor Model and driving behaviour: personality and involvement in vehicular accidents, *Psychological Reports* 86: 454–6

Cellar, D. F., Nelson, Z. C., Yorke, C. M. and Bauer, C. 2001. The Five Factor Model and safety in the workplace: investigating the relationship between personality and accident involvement, in A. F. Stuhlmacher and D. F. Cellar (eds.), *Workplace safety: individual differences in behaviour*, pp. 43–52, Binghamtom, NY: Hawthorne Press

Cellar, D. F., Yorke, C. M., Nelson, Z. C. and Carroll, K. A. 2004. Relationships between five factor personality variables, workplace accidents, and self-efficacy, *Psychological Reports* 94: 1437–41

Clarke, S. and Robertson, I. T. 2005. A meta-analytic review of the Big Five personality factors and accident involvement in occupational and non-occupational settings, *Journal of Occupational and Organizational Psychology* 78: 355–76

Costa, P. T., Jr and McCrae, R. R. 1992. Four ways five factors are basic, *Personality and Individual Differences* 13: 653–65

1995. Domains and facets: hierarchical personality assessment using the revised NEO personality inventory, *Journal of Personality Assessment* 64: 21–50

Cronbach, L. J. and Gleser, G. C. 1965. *Psychological tests and personnel decisions*. Urbana, IL: University of Illinois

Dahlen, E. R., Martin, R. C., Ragan, K. and Kuhlman, M. M. 2005. Driving anger, sensation seeking, impulsiveness, and boredom proneness in the prediction of unsafe driving, *Accident Analysis and Prevention* 37: 341–8

Digman, J. M. 1990. Personality structure: emergence of the Five Factor Model, *Annual Review of Psychology* 41: 417–40

Dorn, L. and Matthews, G. 1995. Prediction of mood and risk appraisals from trait measures: two studies of stimulated driving, *European Journal of Personality* 9: 25–42

Dudley, N. M., Orvis, K. A., Lebiecki, J. E. and Cortina, J. M. 2006. A meta-analytic investigation of Conscientiousness in the prediction of job performance: examining the intercorrelations and the incremental validity of narrow traits, *Journal of Applied Psychology* 91: 40–57

Eysenck, H. J. 1947. *Dimensions of personality.* London: Routledge and Kegan Paul

Garrity, R. D. and Demick, J. 2001. Relations among personality traits, mood states, and driving behaviours, *Journal of Adult Development* 8: 109–18

Hansen, C. P. 1988. Personality characteristics of the accident involved employee, *Journal of Business and Psychology* 2: 346–65

1989. A causal model of the relationship among accidents, biodata, personality, and cognitive factors, *Journal of Applied Psychology* 74: 81–90

International Labor Organization 2006. *Occupational injuries,* www.ilo.org/public/english/bureau/stat/portal/topics.htm#occinj

Janicak, C. A. 1996. Predicting accidents at work with measures of locus of control and job hazards, *Psychological Reports* 78: 115–21

Jonah, B. A. 1997. Sensation seeking and risky driving: a review and synthesis of the literature, *Accident Analysis and Prevention* 29: 651–65

Kamp, J. and Krause, T. R. 1997. Selecting safe employees: a behavioural science perspective, *Professional Safety* 42: 24–8

Klonowicz, T. and Sokolowska, J. 1993. Everyday danger: individual differences, accident perception, and safety behaviour, *Polish Psychological Bulletin* 24: 51–61

Komaki, J., Barwick, K. D. and Scott, L. 1978. A behavioural approach to occupational safety: pinpointing and reinforcing safe performance in a food processing plant, *Journal of Applied Psychology* 61: 229–33

Ludwig, T. D., Biggs, J., Wagner, S. and Geller, E. S. 2001. Using public feedback and competitive rewards to increase the safe driving of pizza deliverers, *Journal of Organizational Behaviour Management* 21: 75–104

Ludwig, T. D. and Geller, E. S. 1997. Assigned versus participative goal setting and response generalization: managing injury control among professional pizza deliverers, *Journal of Applied Psychology* 82: 253–61

McCormick, E. J. and Sanders, M. S. 1982. *Human factors in engineering and design,* 5th edn. New York: McGraw-Hill

Morris, L. W. 1979. *Extroversion and introversion: an interactional perspective.* New York: Halstead Press

Mount, M. K. and Barrick, M. R. 1995. The Big Five personality dimensions: implications for research and practice in human resource management, *Research in Personnel and Human Resources Management* 13: 153–200

Mount, M. K., Barrick, M. R. and Strauss, J. P. 1994. Validity of observer ratings of the Big Five personality factors, *Journal of Applied Psychology* 79: 272–80

Murphy, K. R. and Dzieweczynski, J. L. 2005. Why don't measures of broad dimensions of personality perform better as predictors of job performance?, *Human Performance* 18: 343–57

Nicholson, N., Soane, E., Fenton-O'Creevy, M. and Willman, P. 2005. Personality and domain-specific risk taking, *Journal of Risk Research* 8: 157–76

Ones, D. S. and Viswesvaran, C. 1996. Bandwidth-fidelity dilemma in personality measurement for personnel selection, *Journal of Organizational Behaviour* 17: 609–26

Paunonen, S. V., Rothstein, M. G. and Jackson, D. N. 1999. Narrow reasoning about the use of broad personality measures for personnel selection, *Journal of Organizational Behaviour* 20: 389–405

Rotter, J. B. 1966. Generalized expectancies for internal versus external control of reinforcement, *Psychological Monographs: General and Applied* 80: No. 1 (Whole No. 609)

Schmit, M. J., Ryan, A. M., Stierwalt, S. L. and Powell, A. B. 1995. Frame-of-reference effects on personality scale scores and criterion-related validity, *Journal of Applied Psychology* 80: 607–20

Schneider, R. J., Hough, L. M. and Dunnette, M. D. 1996. Broadsided by broad traits: how to sink science in five dimensions or less, *Journal of Organizational Behaviour* 17: 639–55

Smith, C. S., Silverman, G. S., Heckert, T. M., Brodke, M. H., Hayes, B. E., Silverman, M. K. and Mattimore, L. K. 2001. A comprehensive method for the assessment of industrial injury events, in A. F. Stuhlmacher and D. F. Cellar (eds.), *Workplace safety: individual differences in behaviour*, pp 5–20. Binghamtom, NY: Hawthorne Press

Stewart, G. L. 1999. Trait bandwidth and stages of job performance: assessing differential effects for Conscientiousness and its subtraits, *Journal of Applied Psychology* 84: 959–68

Tett, R. P., Guterman, H. A., Bleier, A. and Murphy, P. J. 2000. Development and content validation of a 'hyperdimensional' taxonomy of managerial competence, *Human Performance* 13: 205–51

Tubre, T., Edwards, B. D., Zyphur, M. and Warren, C. 2006. *Predicting aggressive driving using the Five-Factor Model personality variables*. Paper presented at the annual meeting of the Society for Industrial/Organizational Psychology, Dallas, TX, April 2006

Ulleberg, P. and Rundmo, T. 2003. Personality, attitudes and risk perception as predictors of risky driving behaviour among young drivers, *Safety Science* 41: 427–43

VandeWalle, D. 1997. Development and validation of a work domain goal orientation instrument, *Educational and Psychological Measurement* 57: 995–1015

Wallace, J. C., Popp, E. and Mondore, S. 2006. Safety climate as a mediator between foundation climates and occupational accidents: a group-level investigation, *Journal of Applied Psychology* 91: 681–8

Westaby, J. D. and Lowe, J. K. 2005. Risk-taking orientation and injury among youth workers: examining the social influence of supervisors, coworkers, and parents, *Journal of Applied Psychology* 5: 1027–35

Zuckerman, M. 1979. *Sensation seeking: beyond the optimal level of arousal*. Hillsdale, NJ: Lawrence Erlbaum

45 Personality and crime

David Canter and Donna Youngs

The relationship between personality and crime is complex. Because most criminals are to some degree versatile there has been a tendency to focus on the general characteristics that distinguish criminals from non-criminals. The general trends from these studies are rather weak, but add up to the prospect that criminals tend to act impulsively with disregard for others or the norms of society, i.e. they are criminal. The attempt to link violent crime, in particular, to mental disorder has also proved problematic except at the extremes of the personality disorder continuum.

In recent years, studies have demonstrated that there are some differences in the sorts of offences that any given criminal prefers to commit. The major distinction here relates to the interpersonal characteristics of the crime and thus opens up the possibility that it is the characteristic way of dealing with others that may be an important personality dimension for distinguishing between criminals. A further aspect that is emerging is based on the exploration of what the emotional benefits to the offender are in carrying out the crime and how they are embedded in their personal narratives.

These issues are relevant to many areas of application including the popularly misconceived aspects of 'offender profiling', which is often misunderstood as a process by which, through analysis of a crime, an offender's personality can be described.

Why should personality relate to crime?

In popular understanding criminals are assumed to be distinct from the rest of law-abiding society. The question often follows from this premise of how a person may come to be part of that separate sub-group of humanity? The simple and often favoured answer is that there is something distinct about the sort of people who commit crimes which sets them apart. In other words, it is assumed that criminals have a different personality and that, in effect, it is this personality that *causes* them to become criminal.

The assumption that there is a criminal personality underlies all claims that criminals are 'born not made', i.e. that there is some significant genetic factor that creates the conditions for criminality. But it is also implicit in arguments about the social processes that may give rise to criminality, the so called 'nurture' of criminals, because the social process is seen as creating a particular type of person, prone to carry out criminal acts. The more subtle and generally accepted argument that some form of interaction between psychophysiological make-up and environment gives rise to offending still assigns considerable weight to an assumption that there are some enduring characteristics of people that are the basis of their offending; their 'personality'.

There is a very important consequence of looking for the causes of criminality within aspects of a person's make-up, whether it derives from nature or nurture. This is the consequent implication that criminals are not really responsible for their actions, but it is whatever created their personality that is to blame. Such a view is at variance with the legal perspective on criminality, which holds a mentally competent person to be fully responsible for his or her actions. If it is not the person as such who intentionally committed the criminal act, but something about their 'personality' that made them do it, then this undermines the whole basis for conviction and punishment. If psychology is not to be dismissed by the law as being irrelevant to legal decision-making, a way needs to be found that will accommodate personal accountability with aspects of personality.

In other words, if psychologists are to have some 'professional humility' (as discussed by Canter 2007) they must recognize that the legal notion of *mens rea*, whereby the criminal has a clear and conscious intent to commit the act, assigns the active role to the person. This role involves more than just a manifestation of their enduring characteristics as captured by the psychological conceptualization of personality. An understanding of the role invites a careful consideration of the nature of crime and criminality, together with a full exploration of what aspects of personality are likely to be relevant. If psychological perspectives on crime and personality can be connected to the ancient and well-established legal perspective on offenders' *mens rea* then the benefits to both psychology and the law could be very great indeed.

Problem of specifying what is criminal

The starting point for understanding how the legal perspective on offending can be made compatible with psychological theories is to recognize that the view that offenders have personalities that can be distinguished from the rest of the population does not survive as a simple explanation of criminality after even moderately close scrutiny. The major challenges to this view come from an understanding of crime rather than of personality.

The first problem comes from the fact that crime is not one objectively defined, universal set of actions. It is the interpretations of actions that make them criminal. These interpretations come from the legal and cultural context within which actions occur. Even the most obviously offensive action of killing another person may not be criminal, for example when perpetrated by a soldier in a war or, in some jurisdictions, in defence of one's own life. More complex and subtle issues surround crimes such as rape, where consent is a central factor, and theft, where intention to steal is crucial. When it comes to fraud and other crimes typically associated with bureaucracies and professional work, then the laws of the land may vary so considerably from one country to another that what is illegal in one place may be common practice in another.

The variability on what a criminal act is leads to the awareness that any link between personality and crime cannot be a simple function of the nature of the act. It does not make sense to look for a relationship between criminal violence, say, and aspects of personality, if those acts of violence may be condoned or even encouraged in some contexts and totally outlawed in others. Unless a rather indefensible and implicitly racist argument is put forward that, for example, especially violent societies are made up of people with different personalities from more peaceful societies, then the variations in the prevalence of different types of crime show that it is not the acts themselves that have psychological roots but the meaning of those actions within their socio-cultural context.

This contextualization of the meaning of offending opens the possibility that the personality characteristics of relevance are those that are more to do with law-breaking and the refusal, or inability, to follow the norms of society than any particular predilection for specific sorts of criminal acts. Taken at face value this would lead to the assumption that criminals just have some lower level of moral reasoning than non-criminals. They are just more primitive in their acceptance of what is moral. However, a number of studies discussed by Stephenson (1992) which attempted to employ Kohlberg's (1981) idea of moral development to test whether it was the basis of criminality, found that there was no simple link between criminal actions and scores on a Kohlberg test (Emler, Heather and Winton 1978; Jurokovic 1980).

What the studies of moral development in delinquents and others do reveal is that actions are not a simple function of moral perspective but relate to the nature of the context. As Denton and Krebs (1990), for example, show, people bring their particular level of morality to bear on the situation as they see it. In other words, when considering criminal activity it is simple-minded to regard all law-breaking as psychologically equivalent, or even that the same action would have the same criminal meaning in two different situations.

In every culture crime covers a great variety of very different sorts of activities, from fraud to serial killing of strangers. Even within a sub-group of crimes there are big variations. Burglary can include stealing a purse through an open window or breaking into a fortified warehouse to steal carefully selected works of art. Fraud can be signing a cheque from someone else's account or a complex abuse of pension funds. Murder can be a violent emotional outburst or a studied and prepared killing for profit. It seems unlikely that the same personality issues are relevant for all these different forms of law-breaking. Indeed, one would expect individuals who choose to act in rather different ways in pursuance of the same overt aim (e.g., obtaining funds) may be more distinct from each other than people who seek different objects by the same means.

The problem of the variety of activities that can be criminal is compounded by the lack of any strong psychological basis to legal definitions of crimes. An arson attack carried out to hide the evidence of a crime would be classed as the same sort of crime as one which was an act of revenge. This is a problem of particular significance when reviewing published accounts of psychological research on crime. When studies are carried out of the characteristics of offenders, they typically use the legal definition of the crime for which the offender was convicted, not some subtler exploration of what sort of actions were involved.

These considerations indicate that a distinction needs to be made in relation to the level in the hierarchy of criminal behaviour at which the criminality is defined. Canter and Youngs (2003) make a distinction between three broad aspects of criminality. The most general is between those who commit crimes and those who do not. In practice, this tends to mean those who have been convicted of crimes and those who have not. Such a distinction is, of course, fraught with the difficulty that many people do something illegal for which they are not caught. There is no easy way of determining if those who are caught are different from those who are not, although recent research by Youngs, Canter and Cooper (2004) does indicate that there are important differences in what people are convicted of and what they will admit to anonymously. These differences understandably vary with the seriousness of the crime. The less serious, the more likely are the official criminal records to under-record the amount of criminal activity. But such concerns do mean that studies of criminals that assign them to categories based on their official records have to be treated with caution.

There is the further problem that people who are convicted of crimes will have been sentenced before they become part of a research sample. Often they will be in prison. In his extensive review, Haney (2007) has shown that prisons have wide-ranging debilitating effects on their inmates. It is therefore difficult to establish if the responses obtained in prison are a valid reflection of how the respondent would react when not incarcerated. There is also the strong possibility that the answers prisoners give to any questions are not necessarily truthful, but will serve their purposes within prison and the legal system.

Beyond the comparison of people who are criminal or not, with all the difficulties that throws up, is the more refined comparison of offenders who have committed different types of crime. There are two crucial difficulties in doing this. One is that research generally points to a broad versatility in offending. Many people who commit more than one crime commit a mix of different sorts of crimes. Thus, specifying someone as a burglar, or fraudster, or rapist, may be ignoring the fact that in whichever category he is placed, he has also carried out at some time the offences in the other categories. This understanding of how to distinguish between offenders appropriately would be crucial in identifying any personality-crime relationship. The way forward, as Canter and Youngs (2009) show in some detail, would appear to lie in the recognition that some forms of criminality are general to most offenders, while other forms of criminal action are more specialized. It is then this sub-group of specialized criminal activity that is most productive as the basis for distinguishing between offenders rather than looking for distinct and exclusive overall patterns of offending.

A second difficulty is that, like other people, criminals develop and change over time. Changes in physical abilities, knowledge or skills may lead them into different sorts of criminal actions. Thus, assigning them to a particular type of criminality may be short-lived. As Youngs (2007) discusses, this means that any attempt to specify the characteristics of an offender that are revealed by criminal actions require a careful and subtle exploration of both the context of the crime and the likely stage in the offender's criminal and psychological development.

Yet another level of refinement may be to consider what may be called the 'style' of criminality; how offenders go about carrying out their crimes. This has been the focus of a number of studies carried out within the realm of Investigative Psychology. Here, the attempt is to distinguish within crimes of a similar type, for example rape (Canter, Kaouri and Ioannou 2003), arson (Fritzon, Canter and Wilton 2001) or homicide (Salfati and Haratsis 2001). The studies look closely at exactly what went on within any given crime and assign the crime to a particular theme on the basis of a multivariate statistical analysis. Linking such variations in the thematic emphasis to variations in personality is, however, extremely problematic, for two reasons. One as Youngs (2007) has discussed in some detail, is that it cannot be expected that offenders will be precisely consistent from one crime to the next, so some estimate and compromise needs to be made if an offender is to be assigned to a particular style.

A more practical problem is that it is extremely difficult to obtain both detailed information about what went on in an offence and about the offender's personality as measured by some standardized means. For these and other practical reasons the possibility of linking offence style to personality remains to be thoroughly explored, although one intriguing study by Lobato (2000) does show the potential for this type of exploration. She found that the degree of Extraversion of offenders in Brazil did relate to the weapons they preferred to use. As might be expected, the extraverts chose large obvious weapons like machine guns, the introverts smaller discreet weapons like pistols. However, such studies relating the details of how offences are committed to personality are very unusual.

Mental disorder and crime

The complexity and variety of criminal activity has not prevented a substantial body of research being carried out to explore the forms of mental illness or, more generally, mental disorder that may be at the heart of criminality. Such studies, though, are confounded by their focus being in the main on clinical populations. This has meant that the aspect of the examination of criminals that emphasizes a clinical psychological or psychiatric perspective has tended to be biased towards rather extreme and unusual sub-sets of criminals. In essence, the people studied by clinicians have been those who have been referred to them for treatment, or people who are in an environment that has at least therapeutic aims, if not therapeutic achievements. They, therefore, are likely to be people who are obviously mentally disturbed or whose crimes have bizarre or extreme qualities to them, such as serial rape, or arson, or violent homicide.

The clinical focus has produced the rather distorted picture that much of the psychological literature on offending is devoted to violent criminals and those whose actions are extreme and rare, whereas the broader criminological literature tends to explore the actions of delinquents and those who have carried out what is often called 'volume crime', such as burglary, theft and car crime. It is perhaps therefore not surprising that there is such a difference in perspective between criminologists and clinical psychologists about the causes of crime because they are really talking about different populations.

The question thus emerges as to the role of mental illness in criminality. This is remarkably difficult to determine, but Singleton, Meltzer, Gatward *et al.* (1998) do report that mental disorder amongst prison groups ranges from 10 to 78 per cent. Thus, although this is a very wide range, showing how diverse different prison groups are, it is nonetheless rather higher than would be expected for the population at large, which Singleton, Bumpstead, O'Brien *et al.* (2001) put at not more than 19 per cent. The challenge here, though, is to disentangle cause from effect. The people assessed were in prison. As Haney (2007) has reviewed, prison can be very debilitating. Indeed, as Ly and Foster (2005) point out, a high proportion of people identified as mentally disordered find their way into hospital from prison. The issue may be clarified by a consideration of the nature of the mental disorder that relates to offending. Hodgins, Mednick, Brennan *et al.* (1996) claim that a higher proportion of people diagnosed with schizophrenia and personality disorder commit violent crimes and are involved in general criminality than people without such disorders.

The interpretation of these general results requires the sort of close analysis that is often not possible from the way the broad statistics are presented. Perhaps people unable to cope in the way that is typical of schizophrenia are more likely to be caught or to find themselves in situations that are interpreted as criminal, or they may be drawn more readily from a crimogenic environment? Certainly Ly and Foster (2005) report that only a very small proportion of people diagnosed with a psychotic illness are criminally active.

The role of personality disorder is rather more problematic. It is widely demonstrated that people who are classified as psychopathic are more likely to commit serious crimes. Hare (2003), who developed the most widely used systematic procedure for assessing psychopathy, claims it is a very good predictor of offending violence. The difficulty in taking this claim at its face value relates to the nature of the assessment process and the way in which psychopathy is defined. Cooke (2007, p. 108) described psychopathy as:

> a personality disorder, that is a chronic disturbance in an individual's relations with self, others and their environment which results in distress or failure to fulfil social roles and obligations ... that is characterised by ... an interpersonal style which is dominant, forceful, deceptive and grandiose, by ... a failure to experience remorse or guilt, and by behaviour that can be described as impulsive or reckless.

Such a definition clearly describes a chronic criminal. There can be no surprise that impulsive, reckless people who do not feel guilt and tend to deceit and dominance may commit many crimes, including especially violent crimes. What the 'diagnosis' of psychopathy adds is the proposal that this is an enduring characteristic of the individual which will be reflected in many aspects of his life, especially in his dealings with others. It draws attention to the criminal activity being an integrated part of how the person deals with the world, not some aberrant act that is 'out of character'. Psychopathy therefore is especially helpful when considering offenders whose actions are chronically violent and disruptive. At the extremes of the rating scale, assigning the person to a clinical category may be of help in focusing attention on the sorts of assistance the person needs rather than just concentrating on his criminal actions and the punishment they deserve.

In general, then, although many offenders are characterized by some form of mental disorder, a very small proportion of the mentally disordered population turn to crime. There are some extreme forms of mental illness, notably paranoid schizophrenia, that may lead some of its sufferers to be more violent than the population at large, but even those trends are slight and do not support the view that the illness causes the violence. Indeed, through the *McNaughten* rule that emerged out of the case of a mentally ill man attempting to kill the Prime Minister in 1843, and similar US guidelines such as the Brawner Rule established in 1962, most legal systems recognize that a person can be 'not guilty by reason of insanity' (O'Reilly-Fleming 1992). This accepts that there is a difference between a mentally ill offender and one who is not, thus presuming that the great majority of criminality is not shaped by mental illness. The suggestion that personality can be 'disordered' (O'Leary 1993), such as in the diagnosis of psychopathy, rather blurs the boundary between the actions of a chronic offender and the cognitive and emotional processes that may be seen as the psychological basis of those actions. This blurring can become of particular significance if legislation is introduced that would allow people to be incarcerated because of an assessment of their thoughts and emotions rather than their actions, as has been proposed by some in recent years.

Characterizing offenders

Thus, although there has been a tendency to look for mental disorder as a basis for criminality, careful study indicates that it is only at the extremes that such an aspect of a person may be considered relevant. Even within the criminal community, mental illness does not appear to be a distinguishing feature. The most fundamental distinctions between people who typically offend and those who do not derive from differences in their family and social experiences. Criminals in general come from dysfunctional families that are deprived, have lower socio-economic backgrounds and exist within a culture of crime

(Farrington, Jolliffe, Loeber *et al.* 2001). However, although growing up in a criminal environment in which offending may not only be accepted but actively encouraged provides a basis for understanding many criminal acts, it cannot be the whole explanation. The majority of people who grow up in such environments are not criminals and many criminals have their origins in quite different sorts of families and cultures. It is therefore tempting to look for aspects of criminals which make them especially vulnerable to opportunities for crime.

One feature of offenders that many researchers claim regularly distinguishes criminals from non-offenders is their intellectual ability. In contrast to the public image of the highly intelligent master criminal, Farrington in his (1995) study of 411 London boys showed that those who became persistent criminals had below average IQs at ages eight to ten. Lynam, Moffitt and Stouthamer-Loeber (1993) reported that offenders typically had IQs eight to ten points lower than non-criminals. This puts many criminals in learning disabled categories, where they would require educational support to be effective. Curiously, it is rare for people to mention failures of educational systems as a possible cause of crime, although many prison programmes do emphasize the need to educate inmates.

Lynam *et al.* (1993) show that the average lower IQ of persistent criminals survives careful analysis allowing for family backgrounds, ethnicity and socio-economic status, although subsequent studies, notably by Cullen, Gendreau, Jarjara and Wright (1997) with very careful analysis using different measures of criminality came to the conclusion that IQ has only a moderate correlation with offending. Even this weaker claim for the role of intellectual ability in criminality is open to question, not least because IQ itself is only a moderate indicator of a later effectiveness in life that would protect against becoming involved in criminality. As Richardson (1999) has discussed in detail, IQ is mainly an assessment of ability to cope with the educational environment. It says nothing about how an individual who can hardly read or write is still able to avoid detection for considerable time, being wise to ways of the street. Indeed as Roazzi showed many years ago (1990, personal communication), street children in Brazil may not pass maths tests but can calculate currency exchange and other financial dealings at the high level they need to survive on the fringes of society.

The general intellectual weakness of prolific offenders may be more readily understood as part of their lack of commitment or focus on ways of behaving that accord with social norms. This is reflected in some studies by an emphasis on criminals' impulsivity and sensation-seeking (e.g. Horvath and Zuckerman 1992) and in others by low social skills (Dishion, Loeber, Stouthame-Loeber and Skinner 1984). Indeed, Gottfredson and Hirschi (1990) developed the earlier perspective of Hirschi (1969) to argue that the fundamental explanation of criminality is a lack of control over antisocial behaviour. This view draws together a number of the perspectives that emphasize characteristics of persistently criminal individuals; they do not have the intelligence or social skills to deal appropriately with others, and they have a higher propensity to seek out gratifying sensations than non-criminals. It has even been suggested, especially by Gatzke-Kopp, Raine, Loeber *et al.* (2002), that the sensation-seeking is a product of persistent offenders' low levels of arousal as indicated by their reduced resting skin conductance.

The view that there is a physiological basis to criminality inherent in the impulsivity and lack of control over desires for gratification accords well with the most widely quoted claims of the link between personality and criminality derived from Eysenck and Gudjonsson's (1989) studies that showed that, in general, criminals tended to be more extravert and neurotic than the population at large. They explained that these higher personality scores were related to lower levels of autonomic arousal which in turn gave rise to a limited ability to learn. It was this lack of responsiveness to reinforcement that meant offenders did not internalize the rules of society and thus were more likely to perpetrate antisocial acts.

Distinguishing between offenders

Given the complexity of defining what is criminal and the range of criminal acts, any simple explanations of criminality relating directly to some key aspect of personality, whether 'disordered' or not, have to be treated with some scepticism. Certainly, many offenders do learn to be very skilled as criminals, and can be patient in planning their crimes and ensuring they can escape. There are also wide variations between offenders in their impulsivity, arousal-seeking and Extraversion, as well as there being a notable proportion who do not have low IQ or poor social skills. It may therefore be more appropriate to consider the other side of the coin. Perhaps intelligence, Introversion, social skill and self-control are protective factors that enable people to avoid the temptations of crime that may be present in their social environment? But such protective factors are likely to interact in a variety of complex ways with the different opportunities for crime that are available in any given context.

Of even greater significance may be the types of positive reinforcement for actions from which offenders may have a propensity to learn. In other words, rather than considering the generality of criminality it may be more appropriate to consider the different patterns of learning that may be typical of different emphases in offending. This is more clearly expressed by Bandura (1986) as differentiation in the incentives that dominate any person's actions. Youngs (2004) argues that Bandura's social cognitive theory of behaviour implies that the social context of criminality gives shape to the forms of incentive that may characterize any individual offender. Thus, rather than a limited capacity to learn, offenders learn that criminal behaviours are rewarding and different offenders learn that different particular criminal reinforcements are satisfying. They may be distinguished then by the particular incentives that dominate and differentiate their criminal actions.

Youngs proposes that because social cognitive theory posits that the performance of behaviour is first acquired (or learned) vicariously through exposure to social models, it is dependent on, and shaped by, positive reinforcement relating to different combinations of fundamental human incentives. Grounded in the core biological and cognitive processes of human beings, the incentives motivate by providing particular sets of outcome expectations for a given behaviour. To the extent that different criminal behaviours carry different sets of outcome expectations she proposes that these incentives will provide the basis for the differentiation of criminal styles. For the full range of human action, Bandura (1986) puts forward seven different fundamental incentives: Primary incentives, Sensory incentives, Social incentives, Monetary incentives, Activity incentives, Power/Status incentives and Self-Evaluative incentives. In Youngs' framework, criminal and deviant behaviours form a distinct sub-set of this general set of human actions, distinguished from other behaviour by the contravention of the legal and/or moral code involved. It may be then that a sub-set of the incentives is sufficient to account for variation in criminal involvement.

Youngs argues that three of Bandura's incentives are highly pertinent to the range of acts covered by mainstream criminality: Monetary, Power/Status and Sensory incentives. The Monetary incentive is about acquiring the ability to obtain whatever one desires. Where this means taking from others in some way, the behaviour will typically fall within the realms of criminality. Behaviours as diverse as forging a cheque, carrying out a bank robbery, or stealing cash from a wallet, can be readily understood as normal attempts to acquire monetary gain but through means which society deems criminal. The incentive underlying all these behaviours is best conceptualized as a Material incentive, rather than a Monetary incentive, since the gain is actually derived from the possession of the goods in a material sense. Moreover, goods are not desired simply for their monetary value alone. The possession of goods may be rewarding in a variety of other ways, such as in a symbolic sense or an emotional or physical sense.

Power and Status incentives provide a further form of motivation. The principal goal here is obtaining control over others. As Bandura points out, most societies and groups are structured as a status or power-based hierarchy. People's behaviours are shaped by the desire to increase their rank in these hierarchies. Bandura argues that the Power and Status incentives motivate independently of the material benefits increased power affords. There is a range of behaviours that people may use to acquire this type of control. The Power and Status incentive is highly relevant to crime since in many cases the behaviours used to acquire control will be criminal. In particular, where violence or certain coercive tactics are used, almost invariably the activity would fall within the realms of criminality.

Sensory incentives motivate human behaviour through the desire for novel, pleasurable, stimulating experiences and the avoidance of aversive experiences, including boredom. Katz (1988, p. 3) highlights the role of sensory reward in criminal behaviour, discussing at length 'the seductive qualities of crimes: those aspects in the foreground of criminality that makes its various forms sensible, even sensually compelling, ways of being'. Where individuals attempt to achieve this type of gain through destruction these behaviours will tend to fall within the scope of criminal activity. Other types of activity may carry sensory gain *because* of their deviant or criminal status. As such, the sensory gain would be derived from the internal stimulation of the emotional effects associated with committing a pro-scribed behaviour, rather than the direct stimulation of the senses.

This framework incorporates the possibilities of Extraversion and low self-control as well as sensation-seeking, but it suggests that these will be reflected in different ways by different criminals because of the different mix of incentives that they have learned will help satisfy them. This implies that style of offending may be considered a direct aspect of personality in its own right, rather than some by-product of a more general enduring characteristic of the person.

Youngs finds support for this perspective in the co-occurrence of self-reported criminal actions. She demonstrated this by analysing the patterns of co-occurrence of self-reported crimes of 207 offenders. This allowed her to assign offenders to one of three dominant criminal styles that she was able to show described behaviours reflecting the Material, Power and Sensory incentives respectively.

Crime as an interpersonal activity

The identification of distinct themes in criminal activity that enables them to be differentiated from each other does raise the question of whether these different criminal emphases may be linked to more generally recognized aspects of personality. However, the earlier discussion indicates that it may not be appropriate to consider broad aspects of personality because what is at the heart of criminality does not appear to be some general mental or emotional process. Rather, it is the ways of relating to others, whether it be identified as an aspect of Extraversion or psychopathy.

It can therefore be proposed that any potential relationship between crime and personality should be looked for in areas that may be most likely to reflect those particular aspects of a person that relate to their criminality. Canter (1989) argued that the central feature of being criminal was what it implied about the relationship between people. It is the breaking of social norms, rather than some objective act, and thus always implies that the offender is doing something of social significance not just of material import. In other words, crime is an interpersonal transaction. Therefore it is proposed that an index of personality that reflects styles of contact between the criminal and others may be especially relevant. This is distinct from a clinical or psychiatric view of crime that is inherently individualistic. It is also different from the criminological perspective that interprets crime entirely in terms of social and cultural processes.

The interpersonal perspective on the differences in offence themes also addresses the important point articulated in most detail by Mischel and Peake (1982) that any consistency found in a person's actions are likely to be related to the nature of the situation in which the actions occur. By focusing on crime one step is being taken towards consistency in situation, but by taking the further step of identifying the dominant incentive that characterizes that event for the person acting, the situation is defined even more precisely. The third clarification comes from addressing just the interpersonal characteristics of the interaction.

This interpersonal approach is developed from the recognition that all crimes involve a relationship, to a greater or lesser degree, between the offender and his/her victim. In some cases, such as rape or murder, this relationship will be explicit. In other crimes, such as burglary or theft, there will be an implicit relationship. In these crimes, although the offender and victim do not relate to each other directly, aspects of the victim and his/her behaviour will still have some bearing on the behaviour of the offender. Thus, whether explicit or implicit, most crimes involve some sort of relationship between offender and victim.

An approach to personality that is particularly relevant to the interpersonal perspective is Schutz's (1958) Fundamental Interpersonal Orientations (FIRO) theory of personality. FIRO theory considers both the interpersonal tendencies that the individual has in relation to others and the behaviour that the individual tends to receive from others. This holistic conception of personality, as not simply the outward dispositional tendencies of the individual, but also the habitual responses he or she tends to elicit from others, may be particularly pertinent to the criminal's transactions with others.

Schutz posits three core personality facets on which these interpersonal tendencies will vary: Control, Inclusion and Openness. Youngs (2004) hypothesized that these would relate directly to the distinctions in offending derived from the social cognitive incentive-based perspective. She therefore examined the correlations between FIRO score and the dominant themes in her sample of 207 young offenders.

The Control facet is concerned with power, authority and dominance; individuals vary in the extent to which they attempt to exert control over others (Expressed Control). Individuals high on Expressed Control feel comfortable giving orders to and competing with others. Received Control is the interpersonal desire tendency to allow oneself to be controlled by others. The Control aspect of personality was found to be related in some way to each of the three styles of offending.

The findings distinguished power gain offending, in which higher levels of offending were related to increased levels of Expressed Control, from both material and sensory high gain offending, in which higher levels of offending were related to decreased levels of Received Control. The high levels of Expressed Control, reflected in agreement with interpersonal tendencies such as 'I take charge when I am with people' can be readily understood within a social cognitive framework as a reflection of the higher levels of skill in these acts, which result in better outcomes and increases incentive to exhibit these types of behaviours.

In contrast, high levels of material and sensory styles were found to be related to lower levels of Received Control. According to Bandura, this fits with the idea that personality may impact on behaviour though self-regulatory processes, and suggests that these individuals have a general tendency to self-regulate rather than allow others to proscribe activities. Material crime can be conceptualized in this way as the taking of items that are not available only because society deems that taking them is against the law. Increased levels of sensory crime can be understood in terms of the implication that these individuals are less controllable, and are therefore expected to have a greater need for stimulation.

The dominant distinction here is between crimes that relate directly to control over others, most clearly seen in crimes of violence, and crimes that are more directly related to the instrumental benefits to the individual. The overlap in results for the sensation-seeking and material gain offenders may be because of the need for monetary gain to feed sensation-seeking habits, notably drug addiction. This all adds up to a complex mix of ways of relating to others, both in terms of the extent of how open or inclusive the interactions are and also how much the individual wants to be in control. The findings indicate that the profile across these different ways of relating to others will be characteristically different for offenders who tend to one sort of crime or another, in particular whether their crimes are typically violent or property-related.

Criminals' emotions and personal constructs

Viewing crime as an interpersonal activity in which people seek power or other forms of gratification by the way they interact with others or their property presupposes fundamental psychological benefits to criminal activity. As mentioned, Katz (1988) eloquently argued that these benefits derived from the emotions evoked from criminal activity, captured in the title of his book *The seductions of crime*. This is a different perspective from expecting there to be some emotional disturbance in the offender, although that is doubtless present in some cases. It also implies that all crimes have some of the sensation-related aspects that are so strong in the sub-set Youngs (2004) described as having a dominant incentive in this area. However, there seems to have been little empirical exploration of the emotional benefits of crime except for the initial study by Canter and Ioannou (2004). They asked a wide range of eighty-three incarcerated offenders to indicate how they felt when committing a crime they could remember well.

Using the framework for the structure of emotions proposed by Russell (1997), they were able to show that the same variety of emotions did occur across crimes but that there was a tendency for criminals' emotions to be more extremely positive or negative. In other words, offending was associated with more extreme emotions than other aspects of daily life. Furthermore, there was a tendency for crimes against property to be associated with pleasant or even exciting emotions, whilst crimes against the person were more likely to have negative emotional associations. This raises the question of what it is about the person and the criminal activities they perform which is generated by or gives rise to the emotional content of criminality. A cognitive perspective would lead to the proposal that it is the offender's interpretation of the criminal situation that generates the emotional frisson; for example, the excitement of obtaining goods illegally, or the despair and anger with a partner who has cheated the offender.

The emphasis on the way offenders make sense of their context, the people within it and their actions has been explored in particular depth by Personal Construct Psychologists as espoused by Kelly (1955). Houston (1998) has laid out this perspective in some detail. She explored offenders' construct systems, which incorporates their construing of both themselves and the others with whom they interact, as well as their criminal actions. The structure and content of this system, especially as revealed through the use of the Repertory Grid (Fransella, Bell and Bannister 2004) can indicate whether the offender is readily open to change in his actions or has such a rigid view of others and himself that modification of his behaviour will be extremely difficult. However, a strongly cognitive approach tends to undervalue the importance of the emotional benefits of crime, which must also be explored.

Criminal roles and personal narratives

At the heart of the personal construct approach is the exploration of the offender's self-concept and how that is construed in relation to others and the unfolding criminal actions. So although constructs are seen as dynamic and changeable and there is a definite emphasis on the way a person sees himself at different stages in his life, nonetheless the repertory grid and conceptualization of the construct system tend to be a rather static slice through an evolving cognitive process. Unless explored with great subtlety the construct system derived from the grid can be a rather abstract exploration of the individual independent of the social context. It thus can underplay the worldview that the offender creates for himself.

The consideration of the criminal as making choices and re-interpreting the blame for their actions is most clearly articulated by Yochelson and Samenow (Samenow 1984). This may be mistaken for a clinical diagnosis similar to the notion of psychopathy or personality disorder, as Wrightsman, Nietzel and Fortune (1998) suggest. But that is to undervalue the construct system that gives shape to the decisions to offend and the emotional benefits that derive from criminal actions.

An approach that is being explored to elaborate the dynamic nature of criminal actions is what is being called the 'narrative approach' within psychology, most clearly articulated in the writing of McAdams (1988), as developed by Canter (1994). Within this framework the individual is seen as developing an understanding of himself and his interactions as an unfolding narrative, a story we all create in which we are the dominant protagonist. This perspective has been developed for empirical study by Canter, Kaouri and Ioannou (2003) by asking offenders to indicate the role they think best describes what they were doing when committing a crime, e.g., victim, hero, professional, criminal, etc. The idea here is that the role label captures an implicit narrative within which the offender can see himself acting through a series of episodes.

Analysis of responses from 161 convicted offenders suggested that the dominant narratives that offences enshrined related to the four major myths identified by the literary critic Frye (1957). They see their actions as tragic, adventures, romances or meaningless comedies. This speculative framework has the strength of showing how a criminal's view of himself and his actions may have roots in the culture of which he is a part, but gives emphasis to his interpretation of his criminal role in a way that is compatible with a personal construct perspective. It also helps to provide a framework for what drives the emotional content of the criminal's actions. It would be hypothesized that there will be a strong relationship between the roles a person associates with his actions and the emotions that he feels. The causal direction for the association between roles and emotions requires further careful study.

The embedding of a criminal role within a personal narrative that the offender sees himself acting out must be assumed to evolve and develop during his criminal career. This framework therefore does not seek an enduring aspect of a person's personality traits as a useful aspect of his criminality. Rather, it sees the person building a criminal narrative for himself. This helps to explain offences such as terrorism, fraud or murders that are committed by people who have no obvious criminal precursors in their lives. It also connects more directly with the legal emphasis on human agency that is so different from the biosocial emphasis on causation outside of the person. The concept a person has of himself, however confused, which underlies his actions in dealing with others, given direction and life by the narrative it is part of, recognizes that actions are the product of a person and his experiences. It is thus fundamentally psychological. Yet it also puts the individual in the driving seat, giving agency a distinct part to play. Unless the person is unaware of his actions or their consequences because of mental disability, the narrative perspective holds them responsible, just as the law does.

Implications of linking personality and crime

These issues are relevant to many areas of application including the popularly misconceived aspects of 'offender profiling'. The prospect that it should be possible to identify distinct features of an offender's personality from the details of the crime he has committed seems only feasible under very special circumstances. There may be some general trends that distinguish offenders from non-offenders but beyond that, as Youngs (2007) has elaborated, the details of the criminal actions require very careful scrutiny if they are to indicate anything distinct about the offender. The task is made more demanding by the fact that it is necessary to understand what the crime means to the offender, not just what its objective characteristics are.

There is also the interesting relationship between the consideration of the personality of offenders and the ways in which juries may take note of evidence about the character of a defendant, as explored for example by Hunt and

Budesheim (2004). The research reviewed above indicates that juries should be very cautious about assuming there will be very distinct and clear aspects of a defendant's personality that will mark him out as a criminal. Consistency across a range of similar situations may be a reasonable assumption provided those situations are perceived as similar by the defendant.

Programmes for the rehabilitation of offenders generally avoid any attempt to take account of the offender's personality, but rather (as explored in some detail for example by Houston (1998)) seek to connect with his understanding of his crimes and their consequences. The narrative framework adds a further emphasis to this process by proposing that the offender should be encouraged to develop a different role for himself and try to see himself as part of a different sort of life story, as elaborated in narrative therapy (Crossley 2000). Interestingly, the emergence of restorative justice procedures, whereby the offender is confronted by his victims, can be seen as a way of enabling the offender to understand more fully the interpersonal role he is actually playing and to help him find a more productive life story to live by.

Conclusions

Focusing on aspects of the personality of offenders is not to deny the social, economic, cultural and even political foundations out of which crime grows. Nor is it an attempt to explain criminality solely in terms of genetic, hormonal or other physiological aspects of criminals and thereby deny the societal causes of crime. Rather, the purpose is to focus attention on the crucial role that the person has in carrying out a crime. This is essential if the social and behavioural sciences are to be integrated within the legal system that puts so much emphasis on the intention and conscious action of the criminal.

The study of the relationship between crime and personality also offers some real insights for the more general consideration of personality. It draws attention to the importance of building up frameworks for considering the situations in which people act. Defining personality as an enduring aspect of an individual independently of where those acts take place will doom this area of psychology to what McAdams (1994) calls 'a psychology of the stranger'. Crime is an example of a complex human process that is defined by social norms and consists of many different types of activity. The relevance of the personality of the individual who carries out criminal actions, just as for those who carry out any other naturally occurring action, has to be understood within the social and cultural context of those actions. What the individual brings to the criminal event, as to any other, is an evolving changing set of interactions. The underlying theme of these interactions will be a subtle mix of their experiences and their interpretation of those experiences. Criminals are more like the rest of us than it is often comfortable to accept.

References

Bandura, A. 1986. *Social foundations of thought and action: a social cognitive theory.* Englewood Cliffs, NJ: Prentice-Hall

Canter, D. 1989. Offender profiles, *The Psychologist* 2: 12–16

1994. *Criminal shadows.* London: HarperCollins

Canter, D., Bennell, C., Alison, L. and Reddy, S. 2003. Differentiating sex offences: a behaviourally based thematic classification of stranger rapes, *Behavioural Sciences and the Law* 21: 157–74

Canter, D. and Ioannou, M. 2004. A multivariate model of stalking behaviours, *Behaviourmetrika* 31: 1–18

Canter, D., Kaouri, C. and Ioannou, M. 2003. The facet structure of criminal narratives, in S. Levy and D. Elizur (eds.), *Facet theory: towards cumulative social science*, pp. 27–38. Ljubljana: Center for Educational Development

Canter, D. and Youngs, D. 2003. Beyond 'offender profiling': the need for an investigative psychology, in D. Carson and R. Bull (eds.), *Handbook of psychology in legal contexts*, 2nd edn, pp. 171–205. Chichester: Wiley

2009. *Investigative psychology: offender profiling and the analysis of criminal action.* Chichester: Wiley

Cooke, D. J. 2007. Psychopathy and an important construct: past, present and future, in D. Canter and R. Zukauskiene (eds.), *Psychology and law: bridging the gap*, pp. 167–90. Aldershot: Ashgate

Crossley, M. L. 2000. *Introducing narrative psychology: self, trauma and the construction of meaning.* Milton Keynes: Open University Press

Cullen, F. T., Gendreau, P., Jarjoura, G. R. and Wright, J. P. 1997. Crime and the bell curve: lessons from intelligent criminology, *Crime and Delinquency* 3: 387–411

Denton, K. and Krebs, D. 1990. From the scene to the crime: the effect of alcohol and social context on moral judgement, *Journal of Personality and Social Psychology* 59: 242–8

Dishion, T. J., Loeber, R., Stouthame-Loeber, M. and Skinner, M. L. 1984. Skills deficits and male adolescent delinquency, *Journal of Abnormal Child Psychology* 12: 37–53

Emler, N. P., Heather, N. and Winton, M. 1978. Delinquency and the development of moral reasoning, *British Journal of Social and Clinical Psychology* 17: 321–5

Eysenck, H. J. and Gudjonsson, G. H. 1989. *The causes and consequences of crime.* New York: Plenum Press

Farrington, D. P. 1995. The development of offending and anti-social behaviour from childhood: key findings from the Cambridge study on Delinquent Development, *Journal of Child Psychology and Psychiatry* 360: 929–64

Farrington, D. P., Jolliffe, D., Loeber, R., Stouthamer-Loeber, M. and Kalb, L. 2001. The concentration of offenders in families, and family criminality in the prediction of boys' delinquency, *Journal of Adolescence* 24: 579–96

Fazel, S. and Danesh, J. 2002. Serious mental disorder in 23,000 prisoners: a systematic review of 62 surveys, *The Lancet* 359: 545–50

Fransella, F., Bell, B. and Bannister, D. 2004. *A Manual for repertory grid technique*, 2nd edn. Chichester: Wiley

Fritzon, K., Canter, D. and Wilton, Z. 2001. The application of an action systems model to destructive behaviour: the examples of arson and terrorism, *Behavioural Sciences and Law* 19: 657–90

Frye, N. 1957. *Anatomy of criticism*. Princeton University Press

Gatzke-Kopp, L. M., Raine, A., Loeber, R., Stouthamer-Loeber, M. and Steinhauer, S. R. 2002. Serious delinquent behaviour, sensation seeking, and electrodermal arousal, *Journal of Abnormal Child Psychology* 30: 477–86

Gottfredson, M. R. and Hirschi, T. 1990. *A general theory of crime*. Stanford University Press

Haney, C. 2007. The consequences of prison life: notes on the new psychology of prison effects, in D. Canter and R. Zukauskiene (eds.), *Psychology and law: bridging the gap*, pp. 143–66. Aldershot: Ashgate

Hare, R. D. 2003. *Hare Psychopathy Checklist – Revised*, 2nd edn. Toronto: Multi Health Systems, Inc

Hirschi, T. 1969. *Causes of delinquency* Berkeley, CA: University of California Press

Hodgins, S., Mednick, S. A., Brennan, P. A., Schulsinger, F. and Engberg, M. 1996. Mental disorder and crime: evidence from a Danish birth cohort, *Archives of General Psychiatry* 53: 489–96

Horvath, P. and Zuckerman, M. 1992. Sensation seeking, risk appraisal, and risky behaviour, *Personality and Individual Psychology* 14: 41–52

Houston, J. 1998. *Making sense with offenders: personal constructs, therapy and change*. Chicester: Wiley

Hunt, J. S. and Budesheim, T. L 2004. How jurors use and misuse character evidence, *Journal of Applied Psychology* 89: 347–61

Jurokovic, G. J. 1980. The juvenile delinquent as a moral philosopher: a structural-developmental perspective, *Psychological Bulletin* 88: 709–27

Katz, J. 1988. *Seductions of crime: moral and sensual attractions in doing evil*. New York: Basic Books

Kelly, G. E. 1955. *The psychology of personal constructs*. New York: Norton

Kohlberg, L. 1981. *The philosophy of moral development: moral stages and the idea of justice*. San Francisco, CA: Harper and Row

Lobato, A. 2000. Criminal weapon use in Brazil: a psychological analysis, in D. Canter and L. Alison (eds.), *Profiling property crimes*, pp. 107–46. Aldershot: Ashgate

Ly, L. and Foster, S. 2005. *Statistics of mentally disordered offenders 2004: England and Wales*. London: Home Office Statistical Bulletin 22/05, www.homeoffice.gov.uk/rds

Lynam, D., Moffitt, T. and Stouthamer-Loeber, M. 1993. Explaining the relation between I.Q. and delinquency: class, race, test motivation, school-failure, and self-control, *Journal of Abnormal Psychology* 102: 187–96

McAdams, D. P. 1988. *Power, intimacy and the life story: personological inquiries into identity*. New York: Guilford Press

  1994. A psychology of the stranger, *Psychological Inquiry* 5: 145–8

Mischel, W. and Peake, P. K. 1982. Beyond déjà vu in the search for cross-situational consistency, *Psychological Review* 89: 730–55

O'Leary, K. D. 1993. Through a psychological lens: personality traits, personality disorders, and levels of violence, in R. J. Gelles and D. R. Loseke (eds.), *Current controversies on family violence*, pp. 7–30. Newbury Park, CA: Sage

O'Reilly-Fleming, T. 1992. From beasts to bedlam: Hadfield, the Regency crisis, McNaughton and the 'mad' business in Britain, 1788–1843, *Journal of Psychiatry and Law* 20: 167–90

Richardson, K. 1999. *The making of intelligence*. London: Weidenfeld and Nicolson

Russell, J. A. 1997. How shall an emotion be called?, in R. Plutchik and H. R. Conte (eds.), *Circumplex models of personality and emotions*, pp. 205–20. Washington, DC: American Psychological Association

Salfati, C. G. and Haratsis, E. 2001. Greek homicide: a behavioural examination of offender crime scene actions, *Homicide Studies* 5: 335–62

Samenow, S. E. 1984. *Inside the criminal mind*. New York: Times Books

Schutz, W. 1958. *FIRO: a three dimensional theory of interpersonal behaviour*. New York: Rinehart

Singleton, N., Bumpstead, R., O'Brien, M., Lee, A. and Meltzer, H. 2001. *Psychiatric morbidity among adults living in private households, 2000*. London: The Stationery Office, www.statistics.gov.uk

Singleton, N., Meltzer, H., Gatward, R., Coid, J. and Deasy, D. 1998. *Psychiatric morbidity among prisoners in England and Wales*. London: The Stationery Office, www.statistics.gov.uk

Stephenson, G. M 1992. *The psychology of criminal justice*. Oxford: Blackwell

Wrightsman, L. S., Nietzel, M. T. and Fortune, W. H. 1998. *Psychology and the legal system*, 4th edn. London: Brooks/Cole

Youngs, D. 2004. Personality correlates of offence style, *Journal of Investigative Psychology and Offender Profiling* 1: 99–119

    2007. Contemporary challenges in investigative psychology: revisiting the offender profiling equations, in D. Canter and R. Zukauskiene (eds.), *Psychology and law: bridging the gap*, pp. 23–30. Aldershot: Ashgate

Youngs, D., Canter, D. and Cooper, J. 2004. The facets of criminality: a cross-modal and cross-gender validation, *Behaviourmetika* 31: 1–13

46 Treatment of personality disorders

Fiona Warren

Clinical and research activity directed at understanding and treating personality disorders has increased considerably over the past two decades. However, some basic aspects, such as definition and assessment, are still unresolved. The treatment of personality disorder, in particular, is beset with problems. These problems arise from such issues as its theoretical basis, co-morbidity with other disorders, and its interpersonal nature. The design, delivery and evaluation of treatment for personality disorders have been hampered by these problems. A key tension throughout the literature is between clinical experience/practice and scientific description. This chapter provides an introduction to the major issues in this area, including a necessarily selective overview of thinking and research concerning treatment.

Recognizing personality disorder: difficulties with diagnoses

Personality disorders are defined in the two primary classification systems used for mental disorders: the *Diagnostic and statistical manual of mental disorders* (DSM), produced by the American Psychiatric Association, now in its fourth revision (DSM-IV, DSM-IV-TR) (American Psychiatric Association 1995, 2000), and the International Classification of Diseases (ICD), produced by the World Health Organization and now in its tenth revision (World Health Organization 1992). These systems were developed in the latter half of the nineteenth century to provide a common language in medicine and since the 1970s have been systematically aligned with each other (Widiger 2001); however, differences still remain between them.

There are ten sub-types of personality disorder in DSM-IV-TR, organized into three 'clusters'. Table 46.1 gives a summary of the diagnoses in the two classification systems. It can readily be seen that 'personality disorder' comprises a set of disorders with very different qualities. In addition, there is a further category of 'personality disorder not otherwise specified' which allows for situations where an individual meets the core criteria for personality disorder (see Box 46.1) but does not meet the threshold for any one of the specific sub-types (or meets criteria for a personality disorder no longer included in the classifications,

Table 46.1 *Sub-categories of personality disorders in the DSM-IV and ICD-10 classification systems.*

DSM clusters	DSM-IV	ICD-10
Cluster A Odd or eccentric	**Paranoid** – interpretation of people's actions as deliberately demeaning or threatening	**Paranoid** – excessive sensitivity, suspiciousness, preoccupation with conspiratorial explanations of events, with a persistent tendency to self-reference
	Schizoid – indifference to social relationships and restricted range of emotional experience and expression	**Schizoid** – emotional coldness, detachment, lack of interest in other people, eccentricity and introspective fantasy
	Schizotypal – deficit in interpersonal relatedness with peculiarities of ideation, appearance and behaviour	*No equivalent*
Cluster B Dramatic, erratic	**Antisocial** – evidence of repeated conduct disorder before the age of 15	**Dyssocial** – callous unconcern for others, with irresponsibility, irritability with aggression, and incapacity to maintain enduring relationships
	Borderline – pervasive instability of mood, interpersonal relationships and self-image	**Impulsive** – inability to control anger, to plan ahead or to think before acts, with unpredictable mood and quarrelsome behaviour
	Histrionic – excessive emotionality and attention-seeking	**Histrionic** – self-dramatization, shallow mood, egocentricity and craving for excitement with persistent manipulative behaviour
	Narcissistic – pervasive grandiosity, lack of empathy and hypersensitivity to the evaluation of others	*No equivalent*
Cluster C Anxious, fearful	**Avoidant** – pervasive social discomfort, fear of negative evaluation and timidity	**Anxious** – persistent tension, self-consciousness, exaggeration of risks and dangers, hypersensitivity to rejection and restricted lifestyle because of insecurity
	Dependent – persistent dependent and submissive behaviour	**Dependent** – failure to take responsibility for actions, with subordination of personal needs to those of others, excessive dependence with need for constant reassurance and feelings of helplessness when a close relationship ends
	Obsessive-compulsive – pervasive perfectionism and inflexibility	**Anankastic** – indecisiveness, doubt, excessive caution, pedantry, rigidity and need to plan in immaculate detail

---

Box 46.1   General diagnostic criteria for a personality disorder (DSM-IV)

A. An enduring pattern of inner experience and behaviour that deviates markedly from the expectations of the individual's culture. This pattern is manifested in two or more of the following areas:

    a. Cognition (i.e. ways of perceiving and interpreting self, other people and events)

    b. Affectivity (i.e. the range, intensity, lability and appropriateness of emotional response)

    c. Interpersonal functioning

    d. Impulse control

The enduring pattern:

B. is inflexible and pervasive across a broad range of personal and social situations

C. leads to clinically significant distress or impairment in social, occupational or other important areas of functioning

D. is stable and of long duration – onset can be traced back to at least adolescence or early adulthood

E. is not better accounted for as manifestation of other mental disorder

F. is not due to the physiological effects of a substance (drug of abuse, exposure to a toxin) or medical condition such as head injury

---

such as passive-aggressive personality disorder). The core criteria make it clear that the disorder is long-standing, central to the individual's way of interacting with the world around them, and causes significant impairment of functioning at work, at home and in relationships with others. In order for a diagnosis of one of the specific personality disorders to be made, the individual must meet these general criteria and a certain proportion of features. The literature on personality disorders is dominated by 'borderline personality disorder' (from Cluster B; the criteria for a diagnosis of this disorder are shown in Box 46.2). To improve the detection of underlying personality disorder in clinical practice, the third edition of the DSM separated personality disorders out from other mental disorders in a separate 'axis' (Axis II) (American Psychiatric Association 1980).

Whilst the official classification systems give apparently clear sets of criteria for making diagnoses, they are widely considered inadequate for various conceptual and practical reasons which affect both the design of treatment strategies and the evaluation of their effectiveness.

The implication of the categorical approach enshrined in these classification systems (reflecting the 'medical model' of psychopathology) is that the disorders are qualitatively distinct and either present or absent. However, there is little empirical evidence for this major assumption: research has not supported the distinctness of the diagnoses or their thresholds (Blais and Norman 1997). There is support for some clustering of personality disorders, but not the three cluster

> **Box 46.2   Criteria for borderline personality disorder (Cluster B)**
>
> A. A pervasive pattern of instability of interpersonal relationships, self-image and affects, and marked impulsivity beginning by early adulthood and present in a variety of contexts, as indicated by five (or more) of the following:
>
> a. frantic efforts to avoid real or imagined abandonment
>   Note: Do not include suicidal or self-mutilating behaviour covered in Criterion 5
> b. a pattern of unstable and intense interpersonal relationships character-ized by alternating between extremes of idealization and devaluation
> c. identity disturbance: markedly and persistently unstable self-image or sense of self
> d. impulsivity in at least two areas that are potentially self-damaging (e.g., spending, sex, substance abuse, reckless driving, binge eating)
>   Note: Do not include suicidal or self-mutilating behaviour covered in Criterion 5
> e. recurrent suicidal behaviour, gestures, or threats, or self-mutilating behaviour
> f. affective instability due to a marked reactivity of mood (e.g., intense episodic dysphoria, irritability or anxiety usually lasting a few hours and only rarely more than a few days)
> g. chronic feelings of emptiness
> h. inappropriate, intense anger or difficulty controlling anger (e.g., frequent displays of temper, constant anger, recurrent physical fights)
> i. transient, stress-related paranoid ideation or severe dissociative symptoms

structure (Parker and Barrett 2000; Widiger and Costa 1994). Dimensional conceptualizations (reflecting a dimensional model of personality and psychopathology) have been argued to be more suitable (Trull and Durret 2005).

In addition to the poor psychometric support for the diagnoses as set out in the classification systems, diagnostic criteria are also of limited use in clinical practice. Being derived using expert consensus and consequently (and deliberately) atheoretical, these criteria do not provide one single, agreed, coherent, theoretical understanding of the disorder from which a treatment approach could be derived; and, in addition, they are not useful for dictating treatment strategies for individuals (Livesley 2001a). Futhermore, as diagnoses are made on the basis of a proportion of features being present, two individuals with the same diagnostic label may have quite different symptomatic features and clinicians may not be able to relate criteria to disorders (Blashfield and Breen 1989). The identification of the disorders is also troubled by a multiplicity of poorly-agreeing assessment tools and differences in clinical and research diagnoses (Zimmerman and Mattia 1999a). In line with the poor evidence for specificity, it has also been repeatedly shown that, in practice, it is rare that individuals meet criteria for only one personality disorder: this occurs in only around 3 per cent of cases (Widiger and Rogers 1989).

Prevalence

There are relatively few data, but it is generally agreed that personality disorder is a prevalent disorder, found in between 4 and 15 per cent of the general population (Samuels, Nestadt, Romanoski *et al.* 1994; Singleton, Bumpstead, O'Brien *et al.* 2000). Its prevalence seems to increase with the level of health service input (Widiger and Weissman 1991). For example, approximately one-quarter of UK attenders at primary care, half of in-patients with depression in the United States, and 95 per cent of offenders detained in high secure psychiatric hospitals meet criteria for at least one personality disorder.

Cluster A and C personality disorders, such as paranoid and obsessive-compulsive personality disorder, are more common in the general population, but borderline personality disorder is more common in treatment samples.

Co-morbidity, co-occurrence and playing the patient role

Not only do personality disordered individuals frequently also meet criteria for other personality disorder diagnoses, but they are also very often suffering from other (Axis I) disorders such as major depression, bipolar disorder, panic disorder and other phobias, post-traumatic stress disorder, eating disorder and substance misuse (Dolan-Sewell, Krueger and Shea 2001). This fact seems to be particularly true for those with borderline personality disorder (Zimmerman and Mattia 1999b). Patients with an unaddressed co-morbid personality disorder may not benefit as much from treatment for Axis I disorders as those patients with an Axis I disorder alone (Mulder 2002); this observation has historically contributed to severe 'therapeutic pessimism' in the psychiatric and mental health community, large parts of which did not believe that personality disorders could be treated.

Given the features of the disorders, for example, the wide range of impulsive behaviours given in criterion d for borderline personality disorder (see Box 46.2), and the co-morbidity with Axis I disorders, it is unsurprising that personality disordered individuals are frequent users of a wide range of services including general practitioner, psychiatry, accident and emergency, general medical and criminal justice services (Perry, Lavori and Hoke 1987). Personality disordered individuals will often have extensive histories of previous 'failed' treatments before they are referred for specialist treatments (Chiesa, Bateman, Wilberg *et al.* 2002).

Engaging personality disordered clients in treatment is a central difficulty and 'drop-out' rates are a key concern of specialist treatments as well as of general ones (Chiesa, Drahorad and Longo 2000; Verheul, Van Den Bosch, Koeter *et al.* 2003). Those with personality disorder may not 'play the patient role' well, mistrusting figures in positions of power, and acting on their distress rather than thinking, feeling (and asking for help).

Impact on staff

These aspects of personality disorders present challenges, which are significant but often unacknowledged outside specialist centres, to staff who work with them. Staff may struggle to maintain a positive approach to the individual with important negative consequences for both the staff and the patient/client (Bowers, McFarlane, Kiyimba *et al.* 2000; Main 1957). For example, it is a frequent experience for therapists to be idealized and highly praised by their client with borderline personality disorder in one moment and then to be in receipt of strongly felt denigration from them in the next. The strong feelings evoked by working with personality disordered clients can engender disturbance in the services around them. They have been described as 'the patients psychiatrists dislike' (Lewis and Appleby 1988) and access to services has traditionally been difficult for these individuals.

What treatments are available for personality disorder?

Nonetheless, in practice, the difficulties suffered by those with personality disorder (such as self-harming and substance misuse, severe feelings of misery) require intervention and the majority of personality disordered individuals in contact with services will be receiving interventions from more than one service at any one time. Often this can involve several piecemeal interventions that are not well co-ordinated. There is general agreement that treatment needs to be specifically tailored to personality disorder and that treatments unmodified from their conventional form used in the treatment of (Axis I) disorders, such as depression and anxiety, are inadequate and even potentially harmful.

The theoretical traditions underpinning current treatment approaches can be divided into three main strands: medical model, psychoanalytic/psychodynamic theory, and (cognitive-)behavioural theory. However, the distinctions between these traditions are not absolute: many treatments actually involve an eclectic approach that borrows from different theories leading to some authors hailing a 'paradigm shift' towards more integration of previously quite distinct ways of thinking about personality disorders. Similarities between these theories have also more recently been highlighted (Bateman 1997; Livesley 2001b).

Below, examples of five treatment approaches are given with reference to the three main traditions and with the intention of drawing out a flavour of the key issues and some of the essential features of each approach, such as the goals of treatment, length of treatment and evidence of effectiveness. Box 46.3 gives key references for these and other treatment approaches not covered in this chapter.

Box 46.3   Some approaches to the treatment of personality disorders

Treatment approach	Key references
Pharmacological treatment	Markowitz 2001b; Siever and Davis 1991
Cognitive-behavioural treatment (CBT)	Beck and Freeman 1990; Beck 1996; Young 1990
Psychoanalysis and psychoanalytic psychotherapy	Gabbard 2001; Gunderson and Gabbard 2000; Kernberg 1986
Democratic therapeutic community (DTC)	Jones 1957; Kennard 1998; Main 1983; Norton 1992
Group psychotherapy	Blum 1988; Piper *et al.* 1993
Dialectical behaviour therapy (DBT)	Linehan 1993
Interpersonal treatment	Benjamin 1996; Benjamin and Pugh 2001; Benjamin 1997
Cognitive-analytic therapy (CAT)	Ryle 1997; Ryle and Marlow 1995
Mentalization-based treatment (MBT)	Allen and Fonagy 2006; Bateman and Fonagy 2004, 2006

Pharmacological treatment

Pharmacological approaches are based on a medical conceptualization of personality disorder in which symptoms are seen to arise from disorder or abnormality of brain chemistry or structure. Although now there is increasing recognition of the role of temperament (biological disposition) in the composition of personality and personality disorder (Cloninger and Przybeck 1993; Linehan 1987) and support for a neurochemical basis for behavioural traits (Markowitz 2001a; Siever and Davis 1991), the practice of prescribing medication for personality disorder did not arise from theory or from the development of medications specifically for these disorders (Tyrer 2000). The treatment of personality disorders with medication is guided by the similarity of groups of symptoms seen in both personality disorders and Axis I disorders (e.g. impulse control or depression).

However, the effectiveness of a wide range of pharmacological interventions, such as traditional antipsychotics through anti-convulsants to the gamut of antidepressants (tricyclic (TCA), monoamine oxidase inhibitors (MAOI) and serotoninergic reuptake inhibitors (SSRIs)) has been tested but the evidence consistently judged to be inadequate (Binks, Fenton, McCarthy *et al.* 2006; Warren, Preedy-Fayers, McGauley *et al.* 2003).

Psychological treatments

The dominant treatment conceptualizations of the etiology of personality disorder (PD) have attributed cause primarily to environmental factors and understood

Table 46.2 *Examples of cognitive distortions.*

Dichotomous thinking	Failing to see grey areas, e.g., believing yourself to be *either* a success *or* a failure
Labelling	Considering that one event represents a characteristic of yourself, e.g., thinking 'I'm a failure' rather than 'Oops I really messed that up'
Emotional reasoning	Thinking that the way you feel about a situation reflects the reality, e.g., thinking that because you feel despairing, there is nothing that can be done
Overgeneralization	Considering that one event represents how things always are and always will be, e.g., thinking that lack of consideration from your partner means they do not care, even when they have been considerate at other times

Source: Adapted from Pretzer and Beck 1996.

personality disorders in terms of development of distorted fundamental ideas about, and ways of relating to, the world learned from a neglectful or directly abusive childhood environment.

Cognitive-behavioural treatment

Cognitive-behavioural therapy (CBT) (Beck 1996) was originally developed for Axis I disorders, such as depression and phobias. Beck also discussed this treatment for personality disorders (Beck and Freeman 1990) and subsequent treatment approaches, such as dialectical behaviour therapy (see below), Schema-focused therapy (Young 1990) and cognitive-analytic therapy (Ryle 1997), have drawn on these original ideas. The cognitive-behavioural approach relies on the idea that when we enter new situations, 'schemas' (constellations of ideas learned through our infancy as ways of summarizing and managing all the new information and experiences we are gathering) are activated. Drawing on these embedded arrangements of ideas about people and situations, stored in our long-term memory and unconscious, we are able to recognize new situations as being similar to previous experiences (Pretzer and Beck 1996) and to activate the requisite 'interpersonal strategies' for responding to the new situation. Schemas dictate the information to which we pay attention in a situation. We may also then make some errors in our interpretation of the situation via 'cognitive distortions' (see Table 46.2 for examples of some cognitive distortions commonly employed by individuals with PD). When activated, schemas give rise to 'automatic thoughts' which are not conscious unless we focus on them (Cottraux and Blackburn 2001). Schemas, strategies and automatic thoughts develop and are maintained in a cyclical process as we progress through life (see Figure 46.1). Through selectively attending to particular aspects of scenarios,

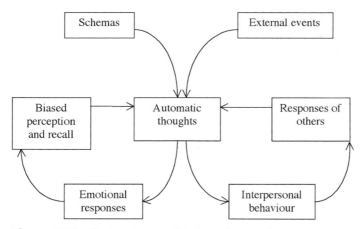

Figure 46.1. *The cognitive model of psychopathology.*

interpreting those and responding accordingly we can receive feedback from the environment that confirms our original assumptions and strengthens our core beliefs. For example, an individual with paranoid personality disorder who believes that others are generally malicious, may respond aggressively to an enquiry from her boss about how she is getting on with a particular project. Her suspicion-based aggression is likely to suggest to her boss that, indeed, she is not getting on well with the project. The boss may decide to supervise her more closely. The boss is now in the position that the worker assumed she was in at the beginning: of suspecting the employee of underperformance, though his initial enquiry had, in fact, been genuine.

The early theory and associated therapy developed by Beck has been modified variously to improve its applicability to therapeutic work with personality disorders because those who tried to apply the original approach found that clients with personality disorder differ from those with Axis I disorders alone in key ways that made it difficult to do the original therapy with them (see Box 46.4 for some examples) (McGinn and Young 1996).

In CBT for Axis I disorders, such as depression, the therapist aims to help the individual identify and change their automatic thoughts and associated behaviours. However, in the case of personality disorders, the individual has distortions and negativity in their fundamental views of themselves and others and, therefore, these are also the target for treatment. Table 46.3 gives some examples of the types of core beliefs, views of self and others that may be typical of each of the personality disorders. Traditionally, CBT has focused on the client alone. However, as stated above, it is usual for the relationship between therapists and clients with personality disorders to be difficult and emotionally demanding. Therefore, in CBT for personality disorders, the relationship between the client and therapist may also be a focus of therapy.

> **Box 46.4   Differences between Axis I and Axis II difficulties**
>
> • Diffuse presentation of problems rather than discrete single target for treatment (such as phobia or depression)
> • The interpersonal nature of the difficulties of personality disorders makes it difficult to establish the kind of collaborative client-therapist relationship used in cognitive therapy of Axis I
> • Personality disordered individuals tend to find it harder to be sufficiently flexible to practise alternative ways of thinking and behaving and to gain from these alternatives as much or as quickly as individuals with Axis I disorders alone
> • People with personality disorders frequently block or avoid their distress and it is then more difficult for them to access their cognitive and affective distortions in the context of the therapy

Dialectical behaviour therapy

Derived from the theory and principles of CBT, dialectical behaviour therapy (DBT) was developed specifically for the treatment of borderline personality disorder (BPD), and focused primarily on the suicidal and self-harming behaviour characteristic of this group (see Box 46.2) (Linehan 1987). Linehan's view was that one of the difficulties with the CBT approach to treating clients with BPD was the focus of CBT on change. She argued that this may be experienced as 'invalidating' by clients who then found it difficult to continue to engage with the treatment (Dimeff and Linehan 2001). DBT draws on Zen philosophy, and the 'dialectical' addition to CBT is the emphasis on the synthesis of polarized views such as the need for both acceptance and for change. This may be particularly useful for the dichotomous thinking (see Table 46.2) or 'splitting' (see below) characteristic of BPD.

DBT is predicated on a biosocial model of the development and maintenance of BPD (Linehan 1993). This approach emphasizes the interaction of a poor emotion-regulation system (comprised of a sensitive temperament and a lack of skill in managing emotions) with an invalidating environment (one in which expressions of emotion are trivialized, punished, mocked or dismissed) in the development of the emotional instability and impulsivity (see Figure 46.2).

Unlike traditional CBT, in which one therapist and one client work together, DBT is a 'system' treatment, with different elements designed to bring the individual with BPD from a state of 'loud desperation' to a state of 'quiet desperation' (Lynch, Chapman, Rosenthal *et al.* 2006).

In the package of DBT, an individual is expected to attend individual sessions with one therapist, focused on identifying patterns of behaviour and thinking that are maladaptive, as well as skills training in groups focused on teaching about the condition and specific strategies for managing feelings and interpersonal interactions. Unlike most other therapies, telephone contact with the therapist at any

Table 46.3 *Examples of Core beliefs, views of self and others typical of each personality disorder.*

Personality disorder	Core beliefs	View of self	View of others	Main beliefs	Main strategy
Paranoid	People are likely to be against me	Righteous	Interfering	Motives are suspect	Be wary
		Innocent, noble	Malicious	Be on guard	Look for hidden motives
		Vulnerable	Discriminatory Abusive motives	Don't trust	Accuse Counter-attack
Schizoid	I need plenty of space	Self-sufficient Loner	Intrusive	Others are unrewarding Relationships are messy, undesirable	Stay away
Schizotypal	*No typical set of idiosyncratic beliefs but beliefs will be idiosyncratic in themselves*				
Antisocial	People don't deserve anything from me	A loner	Vulnerable	Entitled to break rules	Attack, rob
		Autonomous Strong	Exploitative	Others are wimps Others are exploitative	Deceive, manipulate
Borderline	*No typical set of idiosyncratic beliefs, may have many of those exhibited by other specific personality disorders*				
Histrionic	I must impress	Glamorous	Seducible	People are there to serve or admire me	Use dramatics, charm; temper tantrums, crying; suicide gestures
		Impressive	Receptive	They have no right to deny me my just desserts	
Narcissistic	I am special	Special, unique	Admirers Inferior	I can go by my feeling Since I'm special, I deserve special rules	Use others

Table 46.3 (*cont.*)

Personality disorder	Core beliefs	View of self	View of others	Main beliefs	Main strategy
		Deserve special rules, superior Above the rules	Admirers	I'm above the rules	Transcend rules Manipulative
Avoidant	I may get hurt	Vulnerable to depression, rejection Socially inept Incompetent	Critical Demeaning Superior	I'm better than others It's terrible to be rejected, put down If people know the real me, they will reject me Can't tolerate unpleasant feelings	Avoids evaluative situations Avoids unpleasant feelings or thoughts
Dependent	I am helpless	Needy Weak Helpless Incompetent	(Idealized) Nurturant Supportive Competent	Need people to survive, be happy Need for steady flow of support, encouragement	Cultivate dependent relationships
Obsessive-compulsive	I must not make a mistake	Responsible Accountable Fastidious Competent	Irresponsible Casual Incompetent Self-indulgent	I know what's best Details are crucial People should do better, try harder	Apply rules Perfectionism Evaluate, control, 'Shoulds', criticize, punish

Source: Adapted from Beck and Freeman 1990.

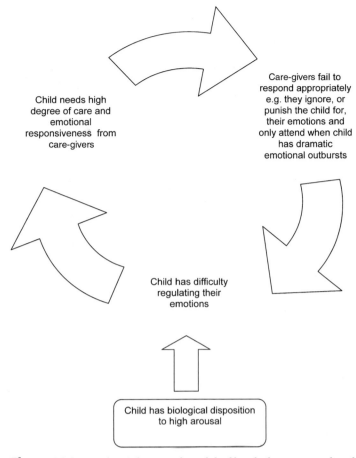

Figure 46.2. *Linehan's biosocial model of borderline personality disorder.*

time of day or night in a crisis is also part of the DBT approach. The consultation team provides DBT therapy to the therapists themselves in order to provide them with support in challenging the client, and helping them to remain committed to the work and to the DBT approach. An important feature of DBT is that the client and therapist make explicit agreements about treatment goals. For example, a pre-treatment phase involves a commitment not to self-harm. Clients may only progress to the next treatment stage by passing the previous stage.

Psychoanalysis and psychodynamic psychotherapy

Freud considered an individual's thoughts, feelings and behaviours to be the result of 'drives' or 'instincts' (sexual and aggressive) that were unconscious. He viewed the mind as comprised of three agents: the Id (i.e., the selfish unconscious), the Superego (i.e., conscience and morality), and the Ego (i.e., the public self, which manages the integration of, and conflicts between, the Id and Superego). These are the 'internalized value systems'. He contended that these three agents would conflict with each other at times and that, to manage these conflicts, the mind uses 'defence mechanisms' (such as denial). Mental processes were construed as movement of energy, analogous to physical mechanisms of movement in thermo-dynamics, hence *psycho*dynamics.

However, Freud was concerned primarily with neurosis and, as therapists working with his theories noticed, there were clients whose pathology was more evident in interpersonal relationships, affected more areas of their lives and was more 'pernicious' than that of other patients. As a result of this realization, a new branch of psychoanalysis, object-relations theory, developed (Westen 1991). Some object-relations theorists suggested that an innate drive for humans was for relationships with others (not for sex as Freud had hypothesized) (Fairbairn 1952) and that experiences of relationships with others (especially primary care-givers) in the first few years of life provided fundamental platforms from which personality developed (Winnicott 1971). Object-relations can be seen simply as internalizations of relationships with people. Object–relations can be seen as 'shorthand' for constellations of processes of thinking and feeling that inform our interpersonal activities and can be seen as similar to the concept of schemata in cognitive theory (see above). The object-relations we have under-lying our psyche may manifest themselves externally, in our relationships with others.

Object-relations theorists, such as Otto Kernberg (Kernberg 1984), see border-line personality organization as a failure in the development of well-rounded (or complex) views of the self and others. For example, in line with the dichotomous thinking style noted by the cognitive theorists (see above), people with borderline personalities see the world only in terms of 'good or bad'. They cannot reconcile the 'good' aspects of themselves and others with the 'bad', instead 'splitting' them into one or the other. The aim of this therapy is to support the 'weak ego' of the person so that they can integrate the good and bad.

In this way, traditionally, psychodynamic psychotherapy has aimed to change the personality structure of the client and is a long-term treatment, typically taking place over at least three sessions per week over four or more years. The therapist tends to take a neutral and more passive stance in traditional psychoanalysis and psychodynamic psychotherapy, offering interpretations of what the individual talks about in therapy sessions and therapy only ends when the individual and therapist agree the individual is ready. More recently, time-limited approaches have also been developed.

There is a significant difficulty applying traditional, experimental, test of effec-tiveness to psychoanalytic treatment, not least because of the length of the treatment, but there is some evidence that psychoanalytic therapy may be helpful (see below).

Mentalization-based treatment and partial hospitalization

Mentalization-based treatment (MBT) is a recently developed intervention approach that draws on the psychoanalytic tradition (Allen and Fonagy 2006). MBT is based on attachment theory (Bowlby 1988) which suggests that infants *learn* about their own and others' minds. First, they have a mind which is separate from the other's mind from their early relationships with primary care-givers. If the primary care-giver is sufficiently 'attuned' to the child, they will respond appropriately to the child's needs and emotions and the child will learn through that process about how to regulate their own emotions. They learn that others have minds that they can learn about and with which they can empathize. If the primary care-giver is poorly attuned to the child's needs and does not respond appropriately or consistently then the child does not develop this capacity (for mentalization) very well. Mentalization is the 'implicit or explicit perception or interpretation of the actions of others or oneself as intentional, that is, mediated by mental states or mental processes' (Bateman and Fonagy 2004). The disturbance in personality disorder derives from a failure in the capacity to mentalize. The therapeutic approach to borderline personality disorder in MBT entails that the relationship with the therapist needs to be a safe place (or secure-base in attachment terminology) within which the client can experiment with exploring their own mind by 'seeing' its representation in the mind of the therapist.

There is emerging evidence to support this approach to treating individuals with borderline personality disorder in the context of a day hospital setting (Bateman and Fonagy 2001).

Democratic therapeutic community

Democratic therapeutic communities (DTCs) were first set up in the 1940s to respond to the need for rehabilitation of ex-servicemen who were failing to readjust to civilian life (Campling and Haigh 1999). Their development was informed by the observation that new patients accepted therapeutic ideas more easily from their peers than from staff (Jones 1957). The involvement of each client in their own and others' treatment became and remains a cornerstone of the treatment, promoting responsibility-taking and commitment to therapy (Norton 1992).

DTCs involve a highly-structured treatment programme composed almost exclusively of group-based therapeutic and work activities. Many decisions about the day-to-day running of the community, including admission and discharge, are usually taken democratically and, as client numbers outweigh staff numbers, this ensures that responsibility for welcoming new members and for enforcing rules against transgression by current members rests with the client group. DTC treatment is usually relatively long term, six months to one or two years and, as clients are admitted at regular intervals, there is a 'hierarchy of experience'.

The rules of the DTC are applied with 'permissiveness' in order that an individual's difficulties may come to light, be examined, and new ways of interacting with others explored and practised. In addition to permissiveness and the democratic structure (democratization), there are two other pillars of the DTC: communalism (shared facilities, tasks and responsibilities which may foster a sense of belonging in individuals who feel that they do not belong in most situations); and reality confrontation (the process of continual presentation to individuals of interpretations of their behaviour as seen by others) (Rapoport

1960). This process is seen to counteract the defences of denial, distortion, withdrawal or other mechanisms that interfere with the development and maintenance of healthy relationships, working together to engender a 'culture of enquiry' by which the community itself becomes the therapeutic agent (or doctor) through the examination of interactions amongst members. Whilst DTCs are considered to have these common features, and are accredited in this way (Keenan and Paget 2006), the term has been used to refer to a variety of institutions (Kennard 1998) and DTCs are distinct from the 'concept' therapeutic community, more common in the United States as a treatment for drug addiction.

Studies suggest effectiveness in terms of reductions over comparison groups of non-treated referrals in borderline symptoms, other symptoms, and service usage and cost-effectiveness (Lees, Manning and Rawlings 1999).

Psychological treatment: overall effectiveness

Most psychological treatments have been examined for effectiveness. In their review, Perry and Bond (2000) calculated mean effect sizes for the improvement between baseline and follow-up for fifteen studies of psychological interventions for personality disorders finding an effect size of between 1.14 and 1.31.

Treatment effectiveness

Whilst the evidence base for treatment of personality disorders, both psychological and pharmacological, has been increasing and improving, there are, as yet, relatively few randomized-controlled trials (RCTs), which are the 'gold standard' of treatment studies. There are some who believe that the social complexity, particularly of group-based treatments and therapeutic communities, render the RCT inappropriate as a test of effectiveness in this field (Wolff 2001), but the primary reason for their lack is more likely a result of the long length of treatments, high drop-out rates and consequently high cost of trials, coupled with the unpopularity of this group of disorders.

The evidence base as it stands does not allow clear conclusions that one treatment approach is the best for any of the personality disorders. The personality disorders are a group of disparate disorders which have a problematic conceptual base and about the assessment of which there has been little consensus. In addition, the chronic nature of personality disorder is enshrined in its definition, implying little expectation of change, and there is no agreement about the key outcome measure on which to test effectiveness. Studies, therefore, include a wide range of symptoms and behaviours as outcome measures, rendering synthesis of results difficult. Reviews of the evidence in this area have, unsurprisingly, been mostly critical of the quality of evidence (Duggan, Adams, McCarthy et al. 2005; Warren, Preedy-Fayers, McGauley et al. 2003).

The studies of treatment effectiveness in the personality disorder field have primarily used designs which compare change in a group of individuals receiving a treatment which is being provided specifically for people with personality disorders against a group of individuals who do not receive this 'specialist' treatment but who may continue to see their psychiatrist or attend a clinic. This uncontrolled comparison condition can be seen as 'treatment as usual': people *are* continuing to receive some services but just not the specialist one of interest in the study. Most specialist treatments tested in this design appear from preliminary evidence to be more effective than treatment as usual but few treatments have been directly compared with each other, thus their relative effectiveness has not been tested directly (Duggan, Adams, McCarthy *et al.* 2005).

Conclusions and future directions

Personality disorder is not one disorder but a group of disorders with disparate characteristics and high levels of co-occurrence. There is a lack of an agreed model of etiology for the disorders and consequently considerable variation in treatment strategies. Patient/client engagement in treatment can be problematic and levels of drop-out are high. There is no single therapeutic approach to personality disorder, pharmacological or psychological, which has been proven to be the definitive treatment of choice, but there is promising evidence for several approaches and it is not yet clear 'what works for whom'. Many similarities can be seen in the treatment approaches, such as a structured and predictable format (Bateman and Fonagy 2000) and a focus on the relationship between therapist and client. Treatments are usually medium to long-term.

Continued improvement in methodological design and assessment of outcomes is needed, as is dissemination of some common lessons from specialists to the wider mental health staff community. The future of research into the effectiveness of treatment for the personality disorders will benefit from consistency in assessment of both the personality disorder and the outcome and in improvement in the design of studies that compare one treatment with another.

References

Allen, J. G. and Fonagy, P. 2006. *Handbook of mentalization-based treatment*. Chichester: John Wiley

American Psychiatric Association 1980. *Diagnostic and statistical manual of mental disorders*, 3rd edn. Washington, DC: American Psychiatric Association

1995. *Diagnostic and statistical manual of mental disorders*, 4th edn. Washington, DC: APA

2000. *Diagnostic and statistical manual of mental disorders – text revision*, 4th, edn. Washington DC: APA

Bateman, A. W. 1997. Borderline personality disorder and psychotherapeutic psychiatry: an integrative approach, *British Journal of Psychotherapy* 13: 489–99

Bateman, A. and Fonagy, P. 2000. Effectiveness of psychotherapeutic treatment of personality disorder, *British Journal of Psychiatry* 177: 138–43

2001. Treatment of borderline personality disorder with psychoanalytically oriented partial hospitalization: an 18-month follow-up, *American Journal of Psychiatry* 158: 36–42

2004. *Psychotherapy for borderline personality disorder: mentalization-based treatment*. Oxford University Press

2006. *Mentalization-based treatment for borderline personality disorder: a practical guide*. Oxford University Press

Beck, A. and Freeman, A. 1990. *Cognitive therapy of personality disorders*. New York: Guilford Press

Beck, J. 1996. Cognitive therapy of personality disorders, in P. Salkovskis (ed.), *Frontiers of cognitive therapy*, pp. 165–81. New York: Guilford Press

Benjamin, L. 1996. *Interpersonal diagnosis and treatment of personality disorders*. New York: Guilford Press

1997. Special feature: Personality disorders: models for treatment and strategies for treatment development, *Journal of Personality Disorders* 11: 307–24

Benjamin, L. and Pugh, C. 2001. Using interpersonal theory to select effective treatment interventions, in J. W. Livesley (ed.), *Handbook of personality disorders: theory, research and treatment*, pp. 414–36. New York: Guilford Press

Binks, C. A., Fenton, M., McCarthy, L., Lee, T., Adams, C. E. and Duggan, C. 2006. Pharmacological interventions for people with borderline personality disorder, *Cochrane Database of Systematic Reviews* (online) CD005653

Blais, M. and Norman, D. 1997. A Psychometric evaluation of the DSM-IV personality disorder criteria, *Journal of Personality Disorders* 11: 168–76

Blashfield, R. K. and Breen, M. J. 1989. Face validity of the DSM-III-R personality disorders, *American Journal of Psychiatry* 146: 1575–9

Blum, H. 1988. Time-limited, group psychotherapy for borderline patients, *Canadian Journal of Psychiatry* 33: 364–9

Bowers, L., McFarlane, L., Kiyimba, F., Clark, N. and Alexander, J. 2000. Factors underlying and maintaing nurses' attitudes to patients with severe personality disorder: final report to national Forensic Mental Health R and D. London: City University, Department of Mental Health Nursing National Forensic Mental Health R and D

Bowlby, J. 1988. *A secure base: clinical applications of attachment theory*. London: Routledge

Campling, P. and Haigh, R. (eds.) 1999. *Therapeutic communities: past, present and future*. London: Jessica Kingsley

Chiesa, M., Bateman, A., Wilberg, T., *et al.* 2002. Patients' characteristics, outcome and cost-benefit of hospital-based treatment for patients with personality disorder: a comparison of three different programmes, *Psychology and Psychotherapy: Theory, Research and Practice* 75: 381–92

Chiesa, M., Drahorad, C. and Longo, S. 2000. Early termination of treatment in personality disorder treated in a psychotherapy hospital: quantitative and qualitative study, *British Journal of Psychiatry* 177: 107–11

Cloninger, C. D. S. and Przybeck, T. 1993. *A psychobiological model of temperament and character, Archives of General Psychiatry* 50: 957–90

Cottraux, J. and Blackburn, I. 2001. Cognitive therapy, in J. W. Livesley (ed.), *Handbook of personality disorders: theory, research and treatment*, pp. 377–99. New York: Guilford Press

Dimeff, L. and Linehan, M. 2001. *Dialectical behaviour therapy in a nutshell*, *California Psychologist* 34: 10–13

Dolan-Sewell, R. T., Krueger, R. F. and Shea, M. T. 2001. Co-occurrence with syndrome disorders, in J. W. Livesley (ed.), *Handbook of personality disorders: theory, research and treatment*, pp. 84–106. New York: Guilford Press

Duggan, C., Adams, C., McCarthy, L., Fenton, M., Lee, T., Binks, C. and Stocker, O. 2005. *A systematic review of the effectiveness of pharmacological and psychological treatments for those with personality disorder*. London: National Programme on Forensic Mental Health

Fairbairn, W. R. D. 1952. *Psychoanalytic studies of the personality*. London: Routledge and Kegan Paul

Gabbard, G. 2001. J. W. Livesley (ed.), *Psychoanalysis and psychoanalytic psychotherapy: research and treatment*, pp. 359–76. New York: Guilford Press

Gunderson, J. and Gabbard, G. 2000. *Psychotherapy for personality disorders*. Washington, DC: American Psychiatric Press

Jones, M. 1957. The treatment of personality disorders in a therapeutic community, *Psychiatry* 20: 211–20

Keenan, S. and Paget, S. 2006. *Community of communities: a quality network of therapeutic communities*, 5th edn. London: Royal College of Psychiatrists

Kennard, D. 1998. *An introduction to therapeutic communities*. London and Philadelphia: Jessica Kingsley Publishers

Kernberg, O. 1984. *Severe personality disorders: psychotherapeutic strategies*. New Haven, CT: Yale University Press

  1986. *Severe personality disorders: psychotherapeutic strategies*. New Haven, CT: Yale University Press

Lees, J., Manning, N. and Rawlings, B. 1999. *Therapeutic effectiveness: a systematic international review of therapeutic community treatment for people with personality disorders and mentally disordered offenders*. Univeristy of York NHS Centre for Reviews and Dissemination

Lewis, G. and Appleby, L. 1988. Personality disorders: the patients psychiatrists dislike, *British Journal of Psychiatry* 153: 44–9

Linehan, M. 1987. Dialectical behaviour therapy: a cognitive-behavioural approach to parasuicide, *Journal of Personality Disorders* 1: 328–33

  1993. *Cognitive-behavioural treatment of borderline personality disorder*. New York: Guilford Press

Livesley, J. 2001a. Conceptual and taxonomic issues: research and treatment, in J. W. Livesley (ed.), *Handbook of personality disorders: theory, research and treatment*, pp. 3–38. New York: Guilford Press

  2001b. A framework for an integrated approach to treatment, in J. W. Livesley (ed.), *Handbook of personality disorders: theory, research and treatment*, pp. 570–600. New York: Guilford Press

Lynch, T. R., Chapman, A. L., Rosenthal, M. Z., Kuo, J. R. and Linehan, M. 2006. *Mechanisms of change in dialectical behaviour therapy: theoretical and empirical observations*, *Journal of Clinical Psychology* 62: 459–80

Main, T. 1983. The concept of the therapeutic community: variations and vicissitudes, in M. Pines (ed.), *The evolution of group analysis*, pp. 197–217

Main, T. F. 1957. The ailment, *British Journal of Medical Psychology* 30: 129–45

Markowitz, P. 2001a. Pharmacotherapy, in J. W. Livesley (ed.), *Handbook of personality disorders: theory, research and treatment*, pp. 475–93. New York: Guilford Press
    2001b. Pharmacotherapy: research and treatment, in J. W. Livesley (ed.), *Handbook of personality disorders: theory research and treatment*, pp. 475–93. New York: Guilford Press

McGinn, L. and Young, J. 1996. Schema-focused therapy, in P. Salkovskis (ed.), *Frontiers of cognitive therapy*, pp. 182–207. New York: Guilford Press

Mulder, R. T. 2002. Personality pathology and treatment outcome in major depression: a review, *American Journal of Psychiatry* 159: 359–71

Norton, K. 1992. A culture of enquiry: its preservation or loss, *Therapeutic Communities: International Journal for Therapeutic and Supportive Organizations* 13: 3–26

Parker, G. and Barrett, E. 2000. Personality and personality disorder: current issues and directions, *Psychological Medicine* 30: 1–9

Perry, J. and Bond, M. 2000. Empirical studies of psychotherapy for personality disorders, in J. Gunderson (eds.), *Psychotherapy for personality disorders*, pp. 1–31. Washington, DC: American Psychiatric Press

Perry, J. C., Lavori, P. W. and Hoke, L. 1987. A Markow model for predicting levels of psychiatric service use in borderline and anti-social personality disorders and bi-polar type II affective disorder, *Journal of Psychiatric Research* 21: 213–32

Piper, W. E., Rosie, J. S., Azim, H. F. A. and Joyce, A. S. 1993. A randomized trial of psychiatric day treatment for patients with affective and personality disorders, *Hospital and Community Psychiatry* 44: 757–63

Pretzer, J. and Beck, A. 1996. A cognitive theory of personality disorders, in J. F. Lenzenweger (ed.), *Major theories of personality disorder*. New York: Guilford Press

Rapoport, R. 1960. *The community as doctor*. London: Tavistock

Ryle, A. 1975. Self-to-self, self-to-other: the world's shortest account of object-relations theory, *New Psychiatry* 12–13: 53–6
    1997. *Cognitive analytic therapy and borderline personality disorder: the model and the method*. Chichester: John Wiley

Ryle, A. and Marlow, M. J. 1995. Cognitive analytic therapy of borderline personality disorder: theory, practice, and the clinical and research uses of the self states sequential diagram, *International Journal of Short Term Psychotherapy* 10: 21–34

Samuels, J. F., Nestadt, G., Romanoski, A. J., *et al.* 1994. DSM-III personality disorders in the community, *American Journal of Psychiatry* 151: 1055–62

Siever, L. and Davis, K. 1991. A psychobiological perspective on the personality disorders, *American Journal of Psychiatry* 148: 1647–58

Singleton, N., Bumpstead, R., O'Brien, M. *et al.* 2000. *Psychiatric morbidity among adults living in private households*. London: Office for National Statistics

Trull, T. J. and Durret, C. A. 2005. Categorical and dimensional models of personality disorder, *Annual Review of Clinical Psychology* 1: 355–80

Tyrer, P. 2000. Drug treatment of personality disorders, in P. Tyrer (ed.), *Personality disorders: diagnosis, management and course*, pp. 100–4. Oxford: Butterworth Heineman

Verheul, R., Van Den Bosch, L. M. C., Koeter, M. W. J., De Ridder, M., Stijnen, T. and Van den Brink, W. 2003. Dialectical behaviour therapy for women with borderline personality disorder, *British Journal of Psychiatry* 182: 135–40

Warren, F., Preedy-Fayers, K., McGauley, G. *et al*. 2003. *Review of treatments for severe personality disorder*. London: Home Office Online Publication 30/03, www. homeoffice.gov.uk/rds/onlinepubs1.html

Westen, D. 1991. Social cognition and object relations, *Psychology Bulletin* 109: 429–55

Widiger, T. A. 2001. Official classification systems, in J. W. Livesley (ed.), *Handbook of personality disorders: theory, research and treatment*, pp. 60–84. New York: Guilford Press

Widiger, T. A. and Costa, P. T. 1994. Personality and personality disorders, *Journal of Abnormal Psychology* 103: 78–91

Widiger, T. A. and Rogers, J. 1989. Prevalence and comorbidity of personality disorders, *Psychiatric Annals* 19: 132–6

Widiger, T. A. and Weissman, M. M. 1991. Epidemiology of borderline personality disorder, *Hospital and Community Psychiatry* 42: 1015–21

Winnicott, D. W. 1971. *Playing and reality*. New York: Basic Books

Wolff, N. 2001. Randomised trials of socially complex interventions: promise or peril?, *Journal of Health Services Research and Policy* 6: 123–6

World Health Organization 1992. *The ICD-10 classification of mental and behavioural disorders*. Geneva: World Health Organization

Young, J. 1990. *Cognitive therapy for personality disorders: a schema-focused approach*. Sarasota, FL: Professional Resources Exchange

Zimmerman, M. and Mattia, J. 1999a. Differences between clinical and research practices in diagnosing borderline personality disorder, *American Journal of Psychiatry* 156: 1570–4

1999b. Axis-I diagnostic comorbidity and borderline personality disorder, *Comprehensive Psychiatry* 40: 245–52

Index

Locators in **bold** refer to major content
Locators in *italic* refer to figures/tables
Locators for headings which have subheadings refer to general aspects of the topic